D0470016

Lord Byron

The Works of
Lord Byron

❦

with an Introduction and Bibliography

The Wordsworth Poetry Library

This edition published 1994 by Wordsworth Editions Ltd,
Cumberland House, Crib Street, Ware, Hertfordshire SG12 9ET.

Copyright © Wordsworth Editions 1994.

All rights reserved. This publications may not be
reproduced, stored in a retrieval system,
or transmitted, in any form or by any means, electronic,
mechanical, photocopying, recording or otherwise,
without the prior permission of the publishers.

ISBN 1-85326-406-7

Printed and bound in Denmark by Nørhaven.

The paper in this book is produced from pure wood
pulp, without the use of chlorine or any other substance
harmful to the environment. The energy used in its
production consists almost entirely of hydroelectricity
and heat generated from waste materials, thereby
conserving fossil fuels and contributing little to the
greenhouse effect.

Introduction

THE BYRONIC MYTH is so persistent and seductive that even the new reader will come to his work with preconceived notions about the man and the poet. He chafed at the view that his work was in any way autobiographical but, while the 'Byronic' heroes who feature so seductively in his longer poems and his plays are undoubtedly autonomous, part of the poems' aesthetic scheme, each, at the very least, represents an important facet of the poet's personality. The suffering wanderer of *Childe Harold*, Cantos I and II, and the embittered exile of Cantos III and IV accurately reflect Byron's own view of himself at the time, while that much-seduced erotic Candide, Don Juan, is also how the poet saw himself. (He wrote to his last love, Teresa Guiccioli, 'I should like to know *who* has been carried off – except poor dear *me*. I have been more ravished myself than any body since the Trojan war'.) But the elegantly cynical narrator of *Don Juan* is also unmistakeably Byron, the writer of gossipy, witty and clear-sighted letters to his friends.

In short, Byron was fascinatingly contradictory. If an important part of Romanticism is the poignant recognition that the real can never conform to the ideal, then Byron was a Romantic. But he detested being classified with the Romantic school, perceiving himself as heir to the Augustan and aristocratic tradition. His *English Bards and Scotch Reviewers* of 1809 was a satire avowedly – and not very successfully – in the manner of Pope. Those famous letters are written with deliberate *sprezzatura* (an aristocratic lightness and apparent ease) which conceals the anguish he often felt. He was a political radical, yet fiercely proud of his patrician lineage, a famous rake whose great love seems to have been a choirboy, a noted beauty with a club foot which marked his entire perception of himself.

These contradictions started with his very birth. His father, 'Mad Jack' Byron, had scandalised society by eloping with the wife of a peer. This marriage produced a daughter, Augusta, but her mother's death led the profligate young gambler to marry a Scottish heiress, Catherine Gordon. George Gordon Byron was born in some poverty, in 1788, and his father's death in 1791 did little to improve matters. Catherine moved back to Scotland and the little boy had a broad Scots accent when, at the age of ten, he inherited the title. Mother and son moved to the crumbling ancestral home, Newstead Abbey in Nottinghamshire and, though Byron loved the place, money troubles were to dog him until he finally managed to

sell it shortly before his early death. He attended Harrow school, where he made some intense friendships and in 1805 went to Trinity College, Cambridge. Here he established his reputation for extravagant debauchery (at one stage he kept a bear in his rooms) while falling innocently in love with John Edlestone, a choirboy. (The 'Thyrza' poems were probably addressed to him, along with the tender 'There be none of Beauty's daughters' – 'like music on the waters/Is thy sweet voice to me'.) Byron's first collection of poems, *Hours of Idleness*, was published in 1807 and he took his seat in the House of Lords, before embarking on a Grand Tour. Now he started *Childe Harold* 'amidst the scenes it attempts to describe'. The publication of Cantos I and II in 1812 brought him instant and overwhelming fame. As potently as Goethe's Young Werther it established a hero who, identified with his handsome young creator, caused a sensation and gave Byron celebrity. Lionized by London's literary and aristocratic circles, Byron was avidly pursued by women. One of these, Lady Caroline Lamb, presciently remarked that he was 'mad, bad and dangerous to know' but, sometimes dressed as his page, gave herself up to a hectic and ultimately anguished affair with him. Afterwards he wrote in bitter rage, 'Remember thee! remember thee!' ('Remorse and shame shall cling to thee,/And haunt thee like a feverish dream!'). These were the years of the long poems with exotic themes and settings – *The Giaour*, *The Corsair* and its sequel, *Lara* – all of which sold massively and enhanced his dashing reputation. By now he had become close to his half-sister, Augusta Leigh. Given the persistence of incest themes in Byron's writing, and the sense of some dark secret (the hinge of the dramatic poem, *Manfred*, is the hero's love for a woman 'like me in lineaments; her eyes/Her hair, her features, all, to the very tone/Even of her voice . . . were like to mine'; the amorous cousins in *The Bride of Abydos* were originally brother and sister, and we see in *Parisina* the fascination he felt towards forbidden love), it is natural to assume that he was in love with Augusta. Certainly his friend, Lady Melbourne, thought so, and pushed his marriage with her niece, the learned and priggish Annabella Milbanke. Byron's courtship of the 'Princess of parallelograms', as he called her, was protracted and ambiguous and the marriage itself startlingly brief. Married in early 1815, they had a daughter, Ada, the same year, but Lady Byron returned to her parents soon afterwards, and rumours of incest and unnatural practices proliferated. Byron left England in 1816, an embittered pariah. He was never to return.

By now the idealistic Claire Claremont had pursued and become pregnant by Byron, and he spent some time at Geneva, where she was living in the household of Shelley who was married to her

stepsister, Mary. Here he wrote *The Prisoner of Chillon* and started *Manfred* and the second half of *Childe Harold*. Claire's daughter, Allegra, was born early in 1817. Byron had moved to Venice, where he threw himself into all the excesses which that decaying society offered. His delight in the pragmatism Italians brought to their love lives inspired the rollicking *Beppo*, a joyously discursive Venetian story written in *ottava rima*, the form he was about to employ with such success in *Don Juan*.

But he seems to have felt increasing weariness at his life. It was about now that he wrote the beautiful lyric, 'So we'll go no more a-roving':

> For the sword outwears its sheath,
> And the soul wears out the breast,
> And the heart must pause to breathe,
> And love itself have rest.

In 1818 he met the young Countess Teresa Guiccioli and started an affair which was to ripen, though fitfully, into lasting love. He was writing incessantly: along with his vigorous correspondence, he completed *Childe Harold*, wrote the *Lament of Tasso*, *Mazeppa* and embarked on his mock-epic, *Don Juan*. The production of this lively, comic, ruefully ironic poem was interrupted by the disapproval of Teresa and his London publisher, John Murray, but during the following years he was to reach Canto XVII of this discursive, inclusive masterpiece. In it he employs outrageous rhymes ('But – Oh! ye lords of ladies intellectual,/Inform us truly, have they not hen pecked you all?') and satire both sweet-tempered and savage; gives us reflections on the Condition of England, hangover cures ('that draught of hock and soda-water') and stanza upon stanza of acute social comment and erotic picaresque.

Teresa's father and brother were involved in forbidden Italian nationalism, and drew Byron into their schemes when he joined the family at Ravenna, Her husband, hitherto compliant, applied for a separation, and the couple moved to Tuscany, where Byron started writing drama – *The Two Foscari*, *Sardanapalus*, *Cain*, and, unfinished, *Heaven and Earth* and *The Deformed Transformed*. In 1822, to his deep grief, his little daughter Allegra died. Still prodigally productive – he was constantly working on *Don Juan*, along with *The Vision of Judgment*, *Werner*, *The Age of Bronze* and *The Island* – he began yearning for a life of action. In 1823, with money from the sale of Newstead, he embarked for Greece, whose subjection to the Ottoman empire had disturbed him since that first visit in 1810-11, to give financial and practical support to the Greek revolutionaries. He had written. 'I have a presentiment I shall die in Greece': his presentiment was fulfilled at Missolonghi in April

1824, when he succumbed to a fever.

His reputation in England was so scandalous that Westminster Abbey and St Paul's refused him funeral services. And Byron's sheer 'Byronism' still excercises a powerful fascination. Certainly both *Childe Harold* and *Don Juan* – which could be said to represent the two sides of his complex nature, the romantic idealist and the hardened, amoral cynic – are masterpieces. But a different Byron can often be found in his lyrics, some of which are incorporated in his longer poems, and many of which are small miracles of tenderness and truth. It has to be said that some selectivity is required: Byron is an uneven poet, frankly confessing, 'I can never *recast* anything. I am like the Tiger: if I miss at the first spring, I go growling back to my jungle again; but if I *do hit*, it is crushing'. Even more apt is his judgement on *Don Juan*, a verdict which could stand for much of his writing: 'It may be profligate but is not *life*, is it not *the thing*?'

FURTHER READING

Leslie Marchand (ed.), *Byron's Letters and Journals* (London, 1973-6)

Leslie Marchand, *Byron: A Biography* (New York, 1957)

Leslie Marchand, *Byron's Poetry: A Critical Introduction* (London, 1966)

Andrew Rutherford, *Byron, A Critical Study* (London, 1961)

M.K. Joseph, *Byron, the Poet* (London, 1964)

Peter J. Manning, *Byron and his Fictions* (Detroit, 1978)

Iris Origo, *The Last Attachment* (London, 1947)

Contents

Contents.

Contents.

Contents.

THE
POETICAL WORKS
OF
LORD BYRON.

𝔥𝔬𝔲𝔯𝔰 𝔬𝔣 𝔍𝔡𝔩𝔢𝔫𝔢𝔰𝔰:

A SERIES OF POEMS ORIGINAL AND TRANSLATED.

[FIRST PUBLISHED IN 1807.]

"Virginibus puerisque canto."—HORACE, lib. iii, Ode 1.

"Μήτ' ἄρ με μάλ' αἴνεε, μήτε τι νείκει."—HOMER, *Iliad*, x. 249.

"He whistled as he went, for want of thought."—DRYDEN.

PREFACE TO THE FIRST EDITION.

IN submitting to the public eye the following collection, I have not only to combat the difficulties that writers of verse generally encounter, but may incur the charge of presumption for obtruding myself on the world, when, without doubt, I might be, at my age, more usefully employed.

These productions are the fruits of the lighter hours of a young man who has lately completed his nineteenth year. As they bear the internal evidence of a boyish mind, this is, perhaps, unnecessary information. Some few were written during the disadvantages of illness and depression of spirits: under the former influence, "CHILDISH RECOLLECTIONS," in particular, were composed. This consideration, though it cannot excite the voice of praise, may at least arrest the arm of censure. A considerable portion of these poems has been privately printed, at the request and for the perusal of my friends. I am sensible that the partial and frequently injudicious admiration of a social circle is not the criterion by which poetical genius is to be estimated, yet "to do greatly" we must "dare greatly;" and I have hazarded my reputation and feelings in publishing this volume. I have "passed the Rubicon," and must stand or fall by the "cast of the die." In the latter event I shall submit without a murmur; for, though not without solicitude for the fate of these effusions, my expectations are by no means sanguine. It is probable that I may have dared much and done little; for, in the words of Cowper, "it is one thing to write what may please our friends, who, because they are such,

are apt to be a little biassed in our favour, and another to write what may please everybody; because they who have no connexion, or even knowledge of the author, will be sure to find fault if they can." To the truth of this, however, I do not wholly subscribe; on the contrary, I feel convinced that these trifles will not be treated with injustice. Their merit, if they possess any, will be liberally allowed; their numerous faults, on the other hand, cannot expect that favour which has been denied to others of maturer years, decided character, and far greater ability.

I have not aimed at exclusive originality, still less have I studied any particular model for imitation; some translations are given, of which many are paraphrastic. In the original pieces there may appear a casual coincidence with authors whose works I have been accustomed to read; but I have not been guilty of intentional plagiarism. To produce anything entirely new, in an age so fertile in rhyme, would be a Herculean task, as every subject has already been treated to its utmost extent. Poetry, however, is not my primary vocation; to divert the dull moments of indisposition, or the monotony of a vacant hour, urged me "to this sin;" little can be expected from so unpromising a muse. My wreath, scanty as it must be, is all I shall derive from these productions; and I shall never attempt to replace its fading leaves, or pluck a single additional sprig from groves where I am, at best, an intruder. Though accustomed, in my younger days, to rove a careless mountaineer on the Highlands of

Scotland, I have not, of late years, had the benefit of such pure air, or so elevated a residence, as might enable me to enter the lists with genuine bards, who have enjoyed both these advantages. But they derive considerable fame, and a few not less profit, from their productions; while I shall expiate my rashness as an interloper, certainly without the latter, and in all probability with a very slight share of the former. I leave to others "virûm volitare per ora." I look to the few who will hear with patience, "dulce est desipere in loco." To the former worthies I resign, without repining, the hope of immortality, and content myself with the not very magnificent prospect of ranking amongst "the mob of gentlemen who write;"—my readers must determine whether I dare say "with ease," or the honour of a posthumous page in "The Catalogue of Royal and Noble Authors,"—a work to which the Peerage is under infinite obligations, inasmuch as many names of considerable length, sound, and antiquity, are thereby rescued from the obscurity which unluckily overshadows several voluminous productions of their illustrious bearers.

With slight hopes, and some fears, I publish this first and last attempt. To the dictates of young ambition may be ascribed many actions more criminal and equally absurd. To a few of my own age the contents may afford amusement; I trust they will, at least, be found harmless. It is highly improbable, from my situation and pursuits hereafter, that I should ever obtrude myself a second time on the public; nor even, in the very doubtful event of present indulgence, shall I be tempted to commit a future trespass of the same nature. The opinion of Dr. Johnson on the poems of a noble relation of mine *, "That when a man of rank appeared in the character of an author, he deserved to have his merit handsomely allowed," can have little weight with verbal, and still less with periodical censors; but were it otherwise, I should be loth to avail myself of the privilege, and would rather incur the bitterest censure of anonymous criticism, than triumph in honours granted solely to a title.

* The Earl of Carlisle, whose works have long received the meed of public applause, to which, by their intrinsic worth, they were well entitled.

HOURS OF IDLENESS.

TO

THE RIGHT HONOURABLE FREDERICK, EARL OF CARLISLE,

KNIGHT OF THE GARTER, ETC., ETC.,

THE SECOND EDITION OF THESE POEMS IS INSCRIBED,

BY HIS OBLIGED WARD AND AFFECTIONATE KINSMAN,

THE AUTHOR.

ON THE DEATH OF A YOUNG LADY,

Cousin to the Author, and very dear to him.

HUSH'D are the winds, and still the evening gloom,
 Not e'en a zephyr wanders through the grove,
Whilst I return, to view my Margaret's tomb,
 And scatter flowers on the dust I love.

Within this narrow cell reclines her clay,
 That clay, where once such animation beam'd;
The King of Terrors seized her as his prey,
 Not worth nor beauty have her life redeem'd.

Oh! could that King of Terrors pity feel,
 Or Heaven reverse the dread decrees of fate,
Not here the mourner would his grief reveal,
Not here the muse her virtues would relate.

But wherefore weep? Her matchless spirit soars
 Beyond where splendid shines the orb of day;
And weeping angels lead her to those bowers
 Where endless pleasures virtue's deeds repay.

And shall presumptuous mortals Heaven arraign,
 And, madly, godlike Providence accuse?
Ah! no, far fly from me attempts so vain;—
 I'll ne'er submission to my God refuse.

Yet is remembrance of those virtues dear,
 Yet fresh the memory of that beauteous face;
Still they call forth my warm affection's tear,
 Still in my heart retain their wonted place.
 1802.

TO E——.

Let Folly smile, to view the names
 Of thee and me in friendship twined;
Yet Virtue will have greater claims
 To love, than rank with vice combined.

And though unequal is thy fate,
 Since title deck'd my higher birth;
Yet envy not this gaudy state;
 Thine is the pride of modest worth.

Our souls at least congenial meet,
 Nor can thy lot my rank disgrace;
Our intercourse is not less sweet,
 Since worth of rank supplies the place.

November, 1802.

TO D——.

In thee I fondly hoped to clasp
 A friend whom death alone could sever;
Till envy, with malignant grasp,
 Detach'd thee from my breast for ever.

True, she has forced thee from my breast,
 Yet in my heart thou keep'st thy seat;
There, there thine image still must rest,
 Until that heart shall cease to beat.

And when the grave restores her dead,
 When life again to dust is given,
On thy dear breast I'll lay my head—
 Without thee where would be my heaven?

February, 1803.

EPITAPH ON A FRIEND.

Ἀστὴρ πρὶν μὲν ἔλαμπες ἐνὶ ζωοῖσιν ἑῷος.

LAERT.

Oh, Friend! for ever loved, for ever dear!
What fruitless tears have bathed thy ho-
 nour'd bier!
What sighs re-echo'd to thy parting breath,
Whilst thou wast struggling in the pangs of
 death!
Could tears retard the tyrant in his course;
Could sighs avert his dart's relentless force;
Could youth and virtue claim a short delay,
Or beauty charm the spectre from his prey;
Thou still hadst lived to bless my aching sight,
Thy comrade's honour and thy friend's delight.
If yet thy gentle spirit hover nigh
The spot where now thy mouldering ashes lie,
Here wilt thou read, recorded on my heart,
A grief too deep to trust the sculptor's art.
No marble marks thy couch of lowly sleep,
But living statues there are seen to weep;
Affliction's semblance bends not o'er thy tomb,
Affliction's self deplores thy youthful doom.

What though thy sire lament his failing line,
A father's sorrows cannot equal mine!
Though none, like thee, his dying hour will
 cheer,
Yet other offspring soothe his anguish here:
But who with me shall hold thy former place?
Thine image what new friendship can efface?
Ah, none!—a father's tears will cease to flow,
Time will assuage an infant brother's woe;
To all, save one, is consolation known,
While solitary friendship sighs alone.

1803.

A FRAGMENT.

When, to their airy hall, my fathers' voice
Shall call my spirit, joyful in their choice;
When, poised upon the gale, my form shall ride,
Or, dark in mist, descend the mountain's side;
Oh! may my shade behold no sculptured urns,
To mark the spot where earth to earth returns!
No lengthen'd scroll, no praise-encumber'd
 stone;
My epitaph shall be my name alone:
If *that* with honour fail to crown my clay,
Oh! may no other fame my deeds repay!
That, only *that,* shall single out the spot;
By that remember'd, or with that forgot.

1803.

ON LEAVING NEWSTEAD ABBEY.

"Why dost thou build the hall, son of the winged
days? Thou lookest from thy tower to-day: yet
a few years, and the blast of the desert comes, it
howls in thy empty court."—OSSIAN.

Through thy battlements, Newstead, the
 hollow winds whistle;
 Thou, the hall of my fathers, art gone to
 decay;
In thy once smiling garden, the hemlock and
 thistle
 Have choked up the rose which late bloom'd
 in the way.

Of the mail-cover'd Barons, who proudly to
 battle
 Led their vassals from Europe to Palestine's
 plain,
The escutcheon and shield, which with every
 blast rattle,
 Are the only sad vestiges now that remain.

No more doth old Robert, with harp-stringing
 numbers,
 Raise a flame in the breast for the war-
 laurell'd wreath;
Near Askalon's towers, John of Horistan
 slumbers,
 Unnerved is the hand of his minstrel by
 death.

Paul and Hubert, too, sleep in the valley of
 Cressy;
 For the safety of Edward and England they
 fell:
My fathers! the tears of your country redress
 ye;
 How you fought, how you died, still her
 annals can tell.

On Marston, with Rupert, 'gainst traitors
 contending,
 Four brothers enrich'd with their blood the
 bleak field;
For the rights of a monarch their country de-
 fending,
 Till death their attachment to royalty seal'd.

Shades of heroes, farewell! your descendant,
 departing
 From the seat of his ancestors, bids you
 adieu!
Abroad, or at home, your remembrance im-
 parting
 New courage, he'll think upon glory and you.

Though a tear dim his eye at this sad separa-
 tion,
 'Tis nature, not fear, that excites his regret;
Far distant he goes, with the same emulation,
 The fame of his fathers he ne'er can forget.

That fame, and that memory, still will he
 cherish;
 He vows that he ne'er will disgrace your
 renown:
Like you will he live, or like you will he perish;
 When decay'd, may he mingle his dust with
 your own!

 1803.

LINES

WRITTEN IN "LETTERS OF AN ITALIAN NUN AND
AN ENGLISH GENTLEMAN: BY J. J. ROUSSEAU:
FOUNDED ON FACTS."

"AWAY, away, your flattering arts
 May now betray some simpler hearts;
 And you will smile at their believing,
 And they shall weep at your deceiving."

ANSWER TO THE FOREGOING, ADDRESSED TO
 MISS ——.

Dear, simple girl, those flattering arts,
From which thou'dst guard frail female hearts,
Exist but in imagination,—
Mere phantoms of thine own creation;
For he who views that witching grace,
That perfect form, that lovely face,

With eyes admiring, oh! believe me,
He never wishes to deceive thee:
Once in thy polish'd mirror glance,
Thou'lt there descry that elegance
Which from our sex demands such praises,
But envy in the other raises:
Then he who tells thee of thy beauty,
Believe me, only does his duty:
Ah! fly not from the candid youth;
It is not flattery,—'tis truth.

 July, 1804.

ADRIAN'S ADDRESS TO HIS SOUL
WHEN DYING.

[ANIMULA! vagula, blandula,
Hospes comesque corporis,
Quæ nunc abibis in loca—
Pallidula, rigida, nudula,
Nec, ut soles, dabis jocos?]

AH! gentle, fleeting, wav'ring sprite,
Friend and associate of this clay!
 To what unknown region borne,
Wilt thou now wing thy distant flight?
No more with wonted humour gay,
 But pallid, cheerless, and forlorn.

TRANSLATION FROM CATULLUS.

AD LESBIAM.

EQUAL to Jove that youth must be—
Greater than Jove he seems to me—
Who, free from Jealousy's alarms,
Securely views thy matchless charms.
That cheek, which ever dimpling glows,
That mouth, from whence such music flows,
To him, alike, are always known,
Reserved for him, and him alone.
Ah! Lesbia! though 'tis death to me,
I cannot choose but look on thee;
But, at the sight, my senses fly;
I needs must gaze, but, gazing, die;
Whilst trembling with a thousand fears,
Parch'd to the throat my tongue adheres,
My pulse beats quick, my breath heaves
 short,
My limbs deny their slight support,
Cold dews my pallid face o'erspread,
With deadly languor droops my head,
My ears with tingling echoes ring,
And life itself is on the wing;
My eyes refuse the cheering light,
Their orbs are veil'd in starless night:
Such pangs my nature sinks beneath,
And feels a temporary death.

TRANSLATION OF THE EPITAPH ON VIRGIL AND TIBULLUS.

BY DOMITIUS MARSUS.

HE who sublime in epic numbers roll'd,
 And he who struck the softer lyre of love,
By Death's unequal hand alike controll'd,
 Fit comrades in Elysian regions move!

IMITATION OF TIBULLUS.

"Sulpicia ad Cerinthum."—*Lib.* iv.

CRUEL Cerinthus! does the fell disease
Which racks my breast your fickle bosom
 please?
Alas! I wish'd but to o'ercome the pain,
That I might live for love and you again;
But now I scarcely shall bewail my fate:
By death alone I can avoid your hate.

TRANSLATION FROM CATULLUS.

[Lugete, Veneres, Cupidinesque, &c.]

YE Cupids, droop each little head,
Nor let your wings with joy be spread;
My Lesbia's favourite bird is dead,
 Whom dearer than her eyes she loved:
For he was gentle, and so true,
Obedient to her call he flew,
No fear, no wild alarm he knew,
 But lightly o'er her bosom moved:

And softly fluttering here and there,
He never sought to cleave the air,
But chirrup'd oft, and, free from care,
 Tuned to her ear his grateful strain.
Now having pass'd the gloomy bourne
From whence he never can return,
His death and Lesbia's grief I mourn,
 Who sighs, alas! but sighs in vain.

Oh! curst be thou, devouring grave!
Whose jaws eternal victims crave,
From whom no earthly power can save,
 For thou hast ta'en the bird away:
From thee my Lesbia's eyes o'erflow,
Her swollen cheeks with weeping glow;
Thou art the cause of all her woe,
 Receptacle of life's decay.

IMITATED FROM CATULLUS.

TO ELLEN.

OH! might I kiss those eyes of fire,
A million scarce would quench desire:
Still would I steep my lips in bliss,
And dwell an age on every kiss:
Nor then my soul should sated be;
Still would I kiss and cling to thee:

Nought should my kiss from thine dissever;
Still would we kiss and kiss for ever;
E'en though the numbers did exceed
The yellow harvest's countless seed.
To part would be a vain endeavour:
Could I desist?—ah! never—never!

TRANSLATION FROM HORACE.

[Justum et tenacem propositi virum, &c.]

THE man of firm and noble soul
No factious clamours can control;
No threat'ning tyrant's darkling brow
 Can swerve him from his just intent:
Gales the warring waves which plough,
 By Auster on the billows spent,
To curb the Adriatic main,
Would awe his fix'd, determined mind in vain.

Ay, and the red right arm of Jove,
Hurtling his lightnings from above,
With all his terrors there unfurl'd,
 He would unmoved, unawed, behold.
The flames of an expiring world,
 Again in crashing chaos roll'd,
In vast promiscuous ruin hurl'd,
Might light his glorious funeral pile:
Still dauntless 'midst the wreck of earth he'd
 smile.

FROM ANACREON.

[Θέλω λέγειν 'Ατρείδας, κ. τ. λ.]

I WISH to tune my quivering lyre
To deeds of fame and notes of fire;
To echo, from its rising swell,
How heroes fought and nations fell,
When Atreus' sons advanced to war,
Or Tyrian Cadmus roved afar;
But still, to martial strains unknown,
My lyre recurs to love alone.
Fired with the hope of future fame,
I seek some nobler hero's name;
The dying chords are strung anew,
To war, to war, my harp is due:
With glowing strings, the epic strain
To Jove's great son I raise again;
Alcides and his glorious deeds,
Beneath whose arm the Hydra bleeds.
All, all in vain; my wayward lyre
Wakes silver notes of soft desire.
Adieu, ye chiefs renown'd in arms!
Adieu the clang of war's alarms!
To other deeds my soul is strung,
And sweeter notes shall now be sung;
My harp shall all its powers reveal,
To tell the tale my heart must feel;
Love, love alone, my lyre shall claim,
In songs of bliss and sighs of flame.

FROM ANACREON.

[Μεσονυκτιαις ποθ' ὡραις, κ. τ. λ.]

'Twas now the hour when Night had driven
Her car half round yon sable heaven;
Boötes, only, seem'd to roll
His arctic charge around the pole;
While mortals, lost in gentle sleep,
Forgot to smile, or ceased to weep:
At this lone hour the Paphian boy,
Descending from the realms of joy,
Quick to my gate directs his course,
And knocks with all his little force.
My visions fled, alarm'd I rose,—
"What stranger breaks my blest repose?"
"Alas!" replies the wily child,
In faltering accents sweetly mild,
"A hapless infant here I roam,
Far from my dear maternal home.
Oh! shield me from the wintry blast!
The nightly storm is pouring fast.
No prowling robber lingers here.
A wandering baby who can fear?"
I heard his seeming artless tale,
I heard his sighs upon the gale:
My breast was never pity's foe,
But felt for all the baby's woe.
I drew the bar, and by the light
Young Love, the infant, met my sight;
His bow across his shoulders flung,
And thence his fatal quiver hung
(Ah! little did I think the dart
Would rankle soon within my heart).
With care I tend my weary guest,
His little fingers chill my breast;
His glossy curls, his azure wing,
Which droop with nightly showers, I wring;
His shivering limbs the embers warm;
And now reviving from the storm,
Scarce had he felt his wonted glow,
Than swift he seized his slender bow:—
"I fain would know, my gentle host,"
He cried, "if this its strength has lost;
I fear, relax'd with midnight dews,
The strings their former aid refuse."
With poison tipt, his arrow flies,
Deep in my tortured heart it lies:
Then loud the joyous urchin laugh'd:—
"My bow can still impel the shaft:
'Tis firmly fix'd, thy sighs reveal it;
Say, courteous host, canst thou not feel it?"

FROM THE PROMETHEUS VINCTUS OF ÆSCHYLUS.

[Μηδαμ' ὁ πάντα νέμων, κ. τ. λ.]

Great Jove, to whose almighty throne
Both gods and mortals homage pay,
Ne'er may my soul thy power disown,
Thy dread behests ne'er disobey.

Oft shall the sacred victim fall
In sea-girt Ocean's mossy hall;
My voice shall raise no impious strain
'Gainst him who rules the sky and azure main.

How different now thy joyless fate,
Since first Hesione thy bride,
When placed aloft in godlike state,
The blushing beauty by thy side,
Thou sat'st, while reverend Ocean smiled,
And mirthful strains the hours beguiled;
The Nymphs and Tritons danced around,
Nor yet thy doom was fix'd, nor Jove relent-
less frown'd.

HARROW, *Dec.* 1, 1804.

TO EMMA.

Since now the hour is come at last,
When you must quit your anxious lover;
Since now our dream of bliss is past,
One pang, my girl, and all is over

Alas! that pang will be severe,
Which bids us part to meet no more;
Which tears me far from one so dear,
Departing for a distant shore.

Well! we have pass'd some happy hours,
And joy will mingle with our tears;
When thinking on these ancient towers,
The shelter of our infant years;

Where from this Gothic casement's height,
We view'd the lake, the park, the dell,
And still, though tears obstruct our sight,
We lingering look a last farewell,

O'er fields through which we used to run,
And spend the hours in childish play;
O'er shades where, when our race was done,
Reposing on my breast you lay;

Whilst I, admiring, too remiss,
Forgot to scare the hovering flies,
Yet envied every fly the kiss
It dared to give your slumbering eyes:

See still the little painted bark,
In which I row'd you o'er the lake;
See there, high waving o'er the park,
The elm I clamber'd for your sake.

These times are past—our joys are gone,
You leave me, leave this happy vale;
These scenes I must retrace alone:
Without thee what will they avail?

Who can conceive, who has not proved,
The anguish of a last embrace?
When, torn from all you fondly loved,
You bid a long adieu to peace.

This is the deepest of our woes,
 For this these tears our cheeks bedew;
This is of love the final close,
 Oh, God! the fondest, last adieu!

———+———

TO M. S. G.

WHENE'ER I view those lips of thine,
 Their hue invites my fervent kiss;
Yet I forego that bliss divine,
 Alas! it were unhallow'd bliss.

Whene'er I dream of that pure breast,
 How could I dwell upon its snows!
Yet is the daring wish represt,
 For that—would banish its repose.

A glance from thy soul-searching eye
 Can raise with hope, depress with fear;
Yet I conceal my love,—and why?
 I would not force a painful tear.

I ne'er have told my love, yet thou
 Hast seen my ardent flame too well;
And shall I plead my passion now,
 To make thy bosom's heaven a hell?

No! for thou never canst be mine,
 United by the priest's decree:
By any ties but those divine,
 Mine, my beloved, thou ne'er shalt be.

Then let the secret fire consume,
 Let it consume, thou shalt not know:
With joy I court a certain doom,
 Rather than spread its guilty glow.

I will not ease my tortured heart
 By driving dove-eyed peace from thine;
Rather than such a sting impart,
 Each thought presumptuous I resign.

Yes! yield those lips, for which I'd brave
 More than I here shall dare to tell;
Thy innocence and mine to save,—
 I bid thee now a last farewell.

Yes! yield that breast, to seek despair,
 And hope no more thy soft embrace;
Which to obtain my soul would dare
 All, all reproach, but thy disgrace.

At least from guilt shalt thou be free,
 No matron shall thy shame reprove;
Though cureless pangs may prey on me,
 No martyr shalt thou be to love.

TO CAROLINE.

THINK'ST thou I saw thy beauteous eyes,
 Suffused in tears, implore to stay;
And heard unmoved thy plenteous sighs,
 Which said far more than words can say?

Though keen the grief thy tears exprest,
 When love and hope lay both o'erthrown,
Yet still, my girl, this bleeding breast
 Throbb'd with deep sorrow as thine own.

But when our cheeks with anguish glow'd,
 When thy sweet lips were join'd to mine,
The tears that from my eyelids flow'd
 Were lost in those which fell from thine.

Thou couldst not feel my burning cheek,
 Thy gushing tears had quench'd its flame;
And as thy tongue essay'd to speak,
 In signs alone it breathed my name.

And yet, my girl, we weep in vain,
 In vain our fate in sighs deplore;
Remembrance only can remain,—
 But that will make us weep the more.

Again, thou best beloved, adieu!
 Ah! if thou canst, o'ercome regret;
Nor let thy mind past joys review,—
 Our only hope is to forget!

———+———

TO CAROLINE.

WHEN I hear you express an affection so
 warm,
 Ne'er think, my beloved, that I do not
 believe;
For your lip would the soul of suspicion
 disarm,
 And your eye beams a ray which can
 never deceive.

Yet still this fond bosom regrets, while ador-
 ing,
 That love, like the leaf, must fall into the
 sere;
That age will come on, when remembrance,
 deploring,
 Contemplates the scenes of her youth with
 a tear;

That the time must arrive, when, no longer
 retaining
 Their auburn, those locks must wave thin
 to the breeze,
When a few silver hairs of those tresses
 remaining,
 Prove nature a prey to decay and disease.

'Tis this, my beloved, which spreads gloom
 o'er my features,
 Though I ne'er shall presume to arraign
 the decree
Which God has proclaim'd as the fate of his
 creatures,
 In the death which one day will deprive
 you of me.

Mistake not, sweet sceptic, the cause of
 emotion,
 No doubt can the mind of your lover in-
 vade;
He worships each look with such faithful
 devotion,
 A smile can enchant, or a tear can dis-
 suade.

But as death, my beloved, soon or late shall
 o'ertake us,
 And our breasts, which alive with such
 sympathy glow,
Will sleep in the grave till the blast shall
 awake us,
 When calling the dead, in earth's bosom
 laid low,—

Oh! then let us drain, while we may, draughts
 of pleasure,
 Which from passion like ours may un-
 ceasingly flow;
Let us pass round the cup of love's bliss
 in full measure,
 And quaff the contents as our nectar below.
 1805.

TO CAROLINE.

Oh! when shall the grave hide for ever my
 sorrow?
 Oh! when shall my soul wing her flight
 from this clay?
The present is hell, and the coming to-
 morrow
 But brings, with new torture, the curse
 of to-day.

From my eye flows no tear, from my lips
 flow no curses,
 I blast not the fiends who have hurl'd me
 from bliss;
For poor is the soul which bewailing re-
 hearses
 Its querulous grief, when in anguish like
 this.

Was my eye, 'stead of tears, with red fury
 flakes bright'ning,
 Would my lips breathe a flame which no
 stream could assuage,
On our foes should my glance launch in
 vengeance its lightning,
 With transport my tongue give a loose to
 its rage.

But now tears and curses, alike unavailing,
 Would add to the souls of our tyrants
 delight;
Could they view us our sad separation be-
 wailing,
 Their merciless hearts would rejoice at
 the sight.

Yet still, though we bend with a feign'd
 resignation,
 Life beams not for us with one ray that
 can cheer;
Love and hope upon earth bring no more
 consolation;
 In the grave is our hope, for in life is
 our fear.

Oh! when, my adored, in the tomb will they
 place me,
 Since, in life, love and friendship for ever
 are fled?
If again in the mansion of death I embrace
 thee,
 Perhaps they will leave unmolested the
 dead.
 1805.

STANZAS TO A LADY, WITH THE POEMS OF CAMOËNS.

This votive pledge of fond esteem,
 Perhaps, dear girl! for me thou 'lt prize;
It sings of Love's enchanting dream,
 A theme we never can despise.

Who blames it but the envious fool,
 The old and disappointed maid;
Or pupil of the prudish school,
 In single sorrow doom'd to fade?

Then read, dear girl! with feeling read,
 For thou wilt ne'er be one of those;
To thee in vain I shall not plead
 In pity for the poet's woes.

He was in sooth a genuine bard;
 His was no faint, fictitious flame.
Like his, may love be thy reward,
 But not thy hapless fate the same.

THE FIRST KISS OF LOVE.

'Ά βάρβιτος δὲ χορδαῖς
'Ερωτα μοῦνον ηχεῖ.—ANACREON.

Away with your fictions of flimsy romance;
 Those tissues of falsehood which folly has
 wove!
Give me the mild beam of the soul-breathing
 glance,
 Or the rapture which dwells on the first
 kiss of love.

Ye rhymers, whose bosoms with phantasy
 glow,
 Whose pastoral passions are made for the
 grove;
From what blest inspiration your sonnets
 would flow,
 Could you ever have tasted the first kiss of
 love!

If Apollo should e'er his assistance refuse,
 Or the Nine be disposed from your service
 to rove,
Invoke them no more, bid adieu to the
 muse,
 And try the effect of the first kiss of love.

I hate you, ye cold compositions of art!
 Though prudes may condemn me, and
 bigots reprove,
I court the effusions that spring from the
 heart,
 Which throbs with delight to the first kiss
 of love.

Your shepherds, your flocks, those fantasti-
 cal themes,
 Perhaps may amuse, yet they never can
 move:
Arcadia displays but a region of dreams:
 What are visions like these to the first
 kiss of love?

Oh! cease to affirm that man, since his birth,
 From Adam till now, has with wretched-
 ness strove,
Some portion of paradise still is on earth,
 And Eden revives in the first kiss of love.

When age chills the blood, when our plea-
 sures are past—
 For years fleet away with the wings of the
 dove—
The dearest remembrance will still be the
 last,
 Our sweetest memorial the first kiss of
 love.

ON A CHANGE OF MASTERS AT A GREAT PUBLIC SCHOOL.

Where are those honours, Ida! once your
 own,
When Probus fill'd your magisterial throne?
As ancient Rome, fast falling to disgrace,
Hail'd a barbarian in her Cæsar's place,
So you, degenerate, share as hard a fate,
And seat Pomposus where your Probus sate.
Of narrow brain, yet of a narrower soul,
Pomposus holds you in his harsh control;
Pomposus, by no social virtue sway'd,
With florid jargon, and with vain parade;
With noisy nonsense, and new-fangled rules,
Such as were ne'er before enforced in
 schools.
Mistaking pedantry for learning's laws,
He governs, sanction'd but by self-applause;
With him the same dire fate attending
 Rome,
Ill-fated Ida! soon must stamp your doom;
Like her o'erthrown, for ever lost to fame,
No trace of science left you, but the name.
 July, 1805.

TO THE DUKE OF DORSET.

Dorset! whose early steps with mine have
 stray'd,
Exploring every path of Ida's glade;
Whom still affection taught me to defend,
And made me less a tyrant than a friend,
Though the harsh custom of our youthful
 band
Bade *thee* obey, and gave *me* to command;
Thee, on whose head a few short years will
 shower
The gift of riches and the pride of power;
E'en now a name illustrious is thine own,
Renown'd in rank, nor far beneath the
 throne.
Yet, Dorset, let not this seduce thy soul
To shun fair science, or evade control,
Though passive tutors, fearful to dispraise
The titled child, whose future breath may
 raise,
View ducal errors with indulgent eyes,
And wink at faults they tremble to chastise.
 When youthful parasites, who bend the
 knee
To wealth, their golden idol, not to thee,—
And even in simple boyhood's opening dawn
Some slaves are found to flatter and to
 fawn,—
When these declare, "that pomp alone should
 wait
On one by birth predestined to be great;

That books were only meant for drudging
 fools,
That gallant spirits scorn the common
 rules;"
Believe them not;—they point the path to
 shame,
And seek to blast the honours of thy name.
Turn to the few in Ida's early throng,
Whose souls disdain not to condemn the
 wrong;
Or if, amidst the comrades of thy youth,
None dare to raise the sterner voice of truth,
Ask thine own heart; 'twill bid thee, boy,
 forbear;
For *well* I know that virtue lingers there.
 Yes! I have mark'd thee many a passing
 day,
But now new scenes invite me far away;
Yes! I have mark'd within that generous
 mind
A soul, if well matured, to bless mankind.
Ah! though myself by nature haughty, wild,
Whom Indiscretion hail'd her favourite child;
Though every error stamps me for her own,
And dooms my fall, I fain would fall alone;
Though my proud heart no precept now can
 tame,
I love the virtues which I cannot claim.
'Tis not enough, with other sons of power,
To gleam the lambent meteor of an hour;
To swell some peerage page in feeble pride,
With long-drawn names that grace no page
 beside;
Then share with titled crowds the common
 lot—
In life just gazed at, in the grave forgot;
While nought divides thee from the vulgar
 dead,
Except the dull cold stone that hides thy
 head,
The mouldering 'scutcheon, or the herald's
 roll,
That well-emblazon'd but neglected scroll,
Where lords, unhonour'd, in the tomb may
 find
One spot, to leave a worthless name behind.
There sleep, unnoticed as the gloomy vaults
That veil their dust, their follies, and their
 faults,
A race, with old armorial lists o'erspread,
In records destined never to be read.
Fain would I view thee, with prophetic eyes,
Exalted more among the good and wise,
A glorious and a long career pursue,
As first in rank, the first in talent too:
Spurn every vice, each little meanness shun;
Not Fortune's minion, but her noblest son.
 Turn to the annals of a former day;
Bright are the deeds thine earlier sires dis-
 play.

One, though a courtier, lived a man of worth,
And call'd, proud boast! the British drama
 forth.
Another view, not less renown'd for wit;
Alike for courts, and camps, or senates fit;
Bold in the field, and favour'd by the Nine;
In every splendid part ordain'd to shine;
Far, far distinguish'd from the glittering
 throng,
The pride of princes, and the boast of song.
Such were thy fathers; thus preserve their
 name;
Not heir to titles only, but to fame.
The hour draws nigh, a few brief days will
 close,
To me, this little scene of joys and woes;
Each knell of Time now warns me to
 resign
Shades where Hope, Peace, and Friendship
 all were mine:
Hope, that could vary like the rainbow's hue,
And gild their pinions as the moments flew;
Peace, that reflection never frown'd away,
By dreams of ill to cloud some future day;
Friendship, whose truth let childhood only
 tell;
Alas! they love not long, who love so well.
To these adieu! nor let me linger o'er
Scenes hail'd, as exiles hail their native shore,
Receding slowly through the dark-blue deep,
Beheld by eyes that mourn, yet cannot weep.
Dorset, farewell! I will not ask one part
Of sad remembrance in so young a heart;
The coming morrow from thy youthful mind
Will sweep my name, nor leave a trace be-
 hind.
And yet, perhaps, in some maturer year,
Since chance has thrown us in the self-same
 sphere,
Since the same senate, nay, the same debate,
May one day claim our suffrage for the state,
We hence may meet, and pass each other by,
With faint regard, or cold and distant eye.
 For me, in future, neither friend nor foe,
A stranger to thyself, thy weal or woe,
With thee no more again I hope to trace
The recollection of our early race;
No more, as once, in social hours rejoice,
Or hear, unless in crowds, thy well-known
 voice:
Still, if the wishes of a heart untaught
To veil those feelings which perchance it
 ought,
If these,—but let me cease the lengthen'd
 strain,—
Oh! if these wishes are not breathed in vain,
The guardian seraph who directs thy fate
Will leave thee glorious, as he found thee
 great.

 1805.

FRAGMENT.

WRITTEN SHORTLY AFTER THE MARRIAGE OF
MISS CHAWORTH.

HILLS of Annesley, bleak and barren,
 Where my thoughtless childhood stray'd,
How the northern tempests, warring,
 Howl above thy tufted shade!

Now no more, the hours beguiling,
 Former favourite haunts I see;
Now no more my Mary smiling
 Makes ye seem a heaven to me.

 1805.

———◆———

GRANTA.

A MEDLEY.

'Αργυρέαις λόγχαισι μάχου καὶ πάντα
 κρατήσαις.

OH! could Le Sage's demon's gift
 Be realized at my desire,
This night my trembling form he'd lift
 To place it on St. Mary's spire.

Then would, unroof'd, old Granta's halls
 Pedantic inmates full display;
Fellows who dream on lawn or stalls,
 The price of venal votes to pay.

Then would I view each rival wight,
 Petty and Palmerston survey;
Who canvass there with all their might,
 Against the next elective day.

Lo! candidates and voters lie
 All lull'd in sleep, a goodly number;
A race renown'd for piety,
 Whose conscience won't disturb their slumber.

Lord H——, indeed, may not demur:
 Fellows are sage, reflecting men:
They know preferment can occur
 But very seldom,—now and then.

They know the Chancellor has got
 Some pretty livings in disposal:
Each hopes that one may be his lot,
 And therefore smiles on his proposal.

Now from the soporific scene
 I'll turn mine eye, as night grows later,
To view, unheeded and unseen,
 The studious sons of Alma Mater.

There, in apartments small and damp,
 The candidate for college prizes
Sits poring by the midnight lamp;
 Goes late to bed, yet early rises.

He surely well deserves to gain them,
 With all the honours of his college,
Who, striving hardly to obtain them,
 Thus seeks unprofitable knowledge:

Who sacrifices hours of rest
 To scan precisely metres Attic;
Or agitates his anxious breast
 In solving problems mathematic:

Who reads false quantities in Seale,
 Or puzzles o'er the deep triangle;
Deprived of many a wholesome meal;
 In barbarous Latin doom'd to wrangle:

Renouncing every pleasing page
 From authors of historic use;
Preferring to the letter'd sage
 The square of the hypothenuse.

Still, harmless are these occupations,
 That hurt none but the hapless student,
Compared with other recreations,
 Which bring together the imprudent;

Whose daring revels shock the sight,
 When vice and infamy combine,
When drunkenness and dice invite,
 As every sense is steep'd in wine.

Not so the methodistic crew,
 Who plans of reformation lay:
In humble attitude they sue,
 And for the sins of others pray:

Forgetting that their pride of spirit,
 Their exultation in their trial,
Detracts most largely from the merit
 Of all their boasted self-denial.

'Tis morn:—from these I turn my sight.
 What scene is this which meets the eye?
A numerous crowd, array'd in white,
 Across the green in numbers fly.

Loud rings in air the chapel bell;
 'Tis hush'd:—what sounds are these I hear?
The organ's soft celestial swell
 Rolls deeply on the list'ning ear.

To this is join'd the sacred song,
 The royal minstrel's hallow'd strain;
Though he who hears the music long
 Will never wish to hear again.

Our choir would scarcely be excused,
 Even as a band of raw beginners;
All mercy now must be refused
 To such a set of croaking sinners.

If David, when his toils were ended,
 Had heard these blockheads sing before him,
To us his psalms had ne'er descended,—
 In furious mood he would have tore 'em.

The luckless Israelites, when taken
 By some inhuman tyrant's order,
Were ask'd to sing, by joy forsaken,
 On Babylonian river's border.

Oh! had they sung in notes like these,
 Inspired by stratagem or fear,
They might have set their hearts at ease,
 The devil a soul had stay'd to hear.

But if I scribble longer now,
 The deuce a soul will stay to read;
My pen is blunt, my ink is low;
 'Tis almost time to stop, indeed.

Therefore, farewell, old Granta's spires!
 No more, like Cleofas, I fly;
No more thy theme my muse inspires;
 The reader's tired, and so am I.

 1806.

——◆——

ON A DISTANT VIEW OF THE VIL-
LAGE AND SCHOOL OF HARROW
ON THE HILL.

Oh! mihi præteritos referat si Jupiter annos.—
 VIRGIL.

YE scenes of my childhood, whose loved
 recollection
 Embitters the present, compared with the
 past;
Where science first dawn'd on the powers of
 reflection,
 And friendships were form'd, too romantic
 to last;

Where fancy yet joys to trace the resemblance
 Of comrades, in friendship and mischief
 allied;
How welcome to me your ne'er fading re-
 membrance,
 Which rests in the bosom, though hope is
 · denied!

Again I revisit the hills where we sported,
 The streams where we swam, and the fields
 where we fought;
The school where, loud warn'd by the bell,
 we resorted,
 To pore o'er the precepts by pedagogues
 taught.

Again I behold where for hours I have
 ponder'd,
 As reclining, at eve, on yon tombstone I lay;
Or round the steep brow of the churchyard
 I wander'd,
 To catch the last gleam of the sun's setting
 ray.

I once more view the room, with spectators
 surrounded,
 Where, as Zanga, I trod on Alonzo o'er-
 thrown;
While, to swell my young pride, such ap-
 plauses resounded,
 I fancied that Mossop himself was out-
 shone:

Or, as Lear, I pour'd forth the deep impre-
 cation,
 By my daughters of kingdom and reason
 deprived;
Till, fired by loud plaudits and self-adulation,
 I regarded myself as a Garrick revived.

Ye dreams of my boyhood, how much I regret
 you!
 Unfaded your memory dwells in my breast;
Though sad and deserted, I ne'er can forget
 you:
 Your pleasures may still be in fancy possest.

To Ida full oft may remembrance restore me,
 While fate shall the shades of the future
 unroll!
Since darkness o'ershadows the prospect
 before me,
 More dear is the beam of the past to my
 soul!

But if, through the course of the years which
 await me,
 Some new scene of pleasure should open to
 view,
I will say, while with rapture the thought
 shall elate me,
 "Oh! such were the days which my infancy
 knew."

 1806.

——◆——

TO M——.

OH! did those eyes, instead of fire,
 With bright but mild affection shine,
Though they might kindle less desire,
 Love, more than mortal, would be thine.

For thou art form'd so heavenly fair,
 Howe'er those orbs may wildly beam,
We must admire, but still despair;
 That fatal glance forbids esteem.

When Nature stamp'd thy beauteous birth,
 So much perfection in thee shone,
She fear'd that, too divine for earth,
 The skies might claim thee for their own:

Therefore, to guard her dearest work,
 Lest angels might dispute the prize,
She bade a secret lightning lurk
 Within those once celestial eyes.

These might the boldest sylph appal,
 When gleaming with meridian blaze;
Thy beauty must enrapture all;
 But who can dare thine ardent gaze?

'Tis said that Berenice's hair
 In stars adorns the vault of heaven;
But they would ne'er permit thee there,
 Thou wouldst so far outshine the seven.

For did those eyes as planets roll,
 Thy sister-lights would scarce appear:
E'en suns, which systems now control,
 Would twinkle dimly through their sphere.
 1806.

TO WOMAN.

WOMAN! experience might have told me
That all must love thee who behold thee:
Surely experience might have taught
Thy firmest promises are nought;
But, placed in all thy charms before me,
All I forget, but to adore thee.
Oh memory! thou choicest blessing
When join'd with hope, when still possessing;
But how much cursed by every lover
When hope is fled and passion's over.
Woman, that fair and fond deceiver,
How prompt are striplings to believe her!
How throbs the pulse when first we view
The eye that rolls in glossy blue,
Or sparkles black, or mildly throws
A beam from under hazel brows!
How quick we credit every oath,
And hear her plight the willing troth!
Fondly we hope 't will last for aye,
When, lo! she changes in a day.
This record will for ever stand,
"Woman, thy vows are traced in sand."

TO M. S. G.

WHEN I dream that you love me, you 'll surely
 forgive;
 Extend not your anger to sleep;
For in visions alone your affection can live,—
 I rise, and it leaves me to weep.

Then, Morpheus! envelope my faculties fast,
 Shed o'er me your languor benign;
Should the dream of to-night but resemble the
 last,
 What rapture celestial is mine!

They tell us that slumber, the sister of death,
 Mortality's emblem is given;
To fate how I long to resign my frail breath,
 If this be a foretaste of heaven!

Ah! frown not, sweet lady, unbend your soft
 brow,
 Nor deem me too happy in this;
If I sin in my dream, I atone for it now,
 Thus doom'd but to gaze upon bliss.

Though in visions, sweet lady, perhaps you
 may smile,
 Oh! think not my penance deficient!
When dreams of your presence my slumbers
 beguile,
 To awake will be torture sufficient.

TO MARY,

ON RECEIVING HER PICTURE.

THIS faint resemblance of thy charms,
 Though strong as mortal art could give,
My constant heart of fear disarms,
 Revives my hopes, and bids me live.

Here I can trace the locks of gold
 Which round thy snowy forehead wave,
The cheeks which sprung from beauty's mould,
 The lips which made me beauty's slave.

Here I can trace—ah, no! that eye,
 Whose azure floats in liquid fire,
Must all the painter's art defy,
 And bid him from the task retire.

Here I behold its beauteous hue;
 But where's the beam so sweetly straying,
Which gave a lustre to its blue,
 Like Luna o'er the ocean playing?

Sweet copy! far more dear to me,
 Lifeless, unfeeling as thou art,
Than all the living forms could be,
 Save her who placed thee next my heart.

She placed it, sad, with needless fear,
 Lest time might shake my wavering soul,
Unconscious that her image there
 Held every sense in fast control.

Through hours, through years, through time,
 't will cheer;
 My hope, in gloomy moments, raise;
In life's last conflict 't will appear,
 And meet my fond expiring gaze.

TO LESBIA.

LESBIA! since far from you I 've ranged,
 Our souls with fond affection glow not;
You say 'tis I, not you, have changed,
 I 'd tell you why,—but yet I know not.

Your polish'd brow no cares have crost;
 And, Lesbia! we are not much older
Since, trembling, first my heart I lost,
 Or told my love, with hope grown bolder.

Sixteen was then our utmost age,
 Two years have lingering pass'd away,
 love!
And now new thoughts our minds engage,
 At least I feel disposed to stray, love!

'Tis I that am alone to blame,
 I, that am guilty of love's treason;
Since your sweet breast is still the same,
 Caprice must be my only reason.

I do not, love! suspect your truth,
 With jealous doubt my bosom heaves not;
Warm was the passion of my youth,
 One trace of dark deceit it leaves not.

No, no, my flame was not pretended;
 For, oh! I loved you most sincerely;
And—though our dream at last is ended—
 My bosom still esteems you dearly.

No more we meet in yonder bowers;
 Absence has made me prone to roving;
But older, firmer hearts than ours,
 Have found monotony in loving.

Your cheek's soft bloom is unimpair'd,
 New beauties still are daily bright'ning,
Your eye for conquest beams prepared,
 The forge of love's resistless lightning.

Arm'd thus, to make their bosoms bleed,
 Many will throng to sigh like me, love!
More constant they may prove, indeed;
 Fonder, alas! they ne'er can be, love!

LINES ADDRESSED TO A YOUNG LADY.

[As the author was discharging his pistols in a garden, two ladies passing near the spot were alarmed by the sound of a bullet hissing near them; to one of whom the following stanzas were addressed the next morning.]

DOUBTLESS, sweet girl! the hissing lead,
 Wafting destruction o'er thy charms,
And hurtling o'er thy lovely head,
 Has fill'd that breast with fond alarms.

Surely some envious demon's force,
 Vex'd to behold such beauty here,
Impell'd the bullet's viewless course,
 Diverted from its first career.

Yes! in that nearly fatal hour
 The ball obey'd some hell-born guide;
But Heaven, with interposing power,
 In pity turn'd the death aside.

Yet, as perchance one trembling tear
 Upon that thrilling bosom fell;
Which I, th' unconscious cause of fear,
 Extracted from its glistening cell:

Say, what dire penance can atone
 For such an outrage done to thee?
Arraign'd before thy beauty's throne,
 What punishment wilt thou decree?

Might I perform the judge's part,
 The sentence I should scarce deplore;
It only would restore a heart
 Which but belong'd to thee before.

The least atonement I can make
 Is to become no longer free;
Henceforth I breathe but for thy sake,
 Thou shalt be all in all to me.

But thou, perhaps, may'st now reject
 Such expiation of my guilt;
Come then, some other mode elect;
 Let it be death, or what thou wilt.

Choose then, relentless! and I swear
 Nought shall thy dread decree prevent;
Yet hold—one little word forbear!
 Let it be aught but banishment.

LOVE'S LAST ADIEU.

'Αεὶ δ' ἀεί με φεύγει.—ANACREON.

THE roses of love glad the garden of life,
 Though nurtured 'mid weeds dropping pes-
 tilent dew,
Till time crops the leaves with unmerciful
 knife,
 Or prunes them for ever, in love's last adieu!

In vain with endearments we soothe the sad
 heart,
 In vain do we vow for an age to be true;
The chance of an hour may command us to
 part,
 Or death disunite us in love's last adieu!

Still Hope, breathing peace through the
 grief-swollen breast,
 Will whisper, "Our meeting we yet may
 renew:"
With this dream of deceit half our sorrow's
 represt,
 Nor taste we the poison of love's last adieu!

Oh! mark you yon pair: in the sunshine of
 youth
 Love twined round their childhood his
 flowers as they grew;
They flourish awhile in the season of truth,
 Till chill'd by the winter of love's last adieu!

Sweet lady! why thus doth a tear steal its way
 Down a cheek which outrivals thy bosom
 in hue?
Yet why do I ask?—to distraction a prey,
 Thy reason has perish'd with love's last
 adieu!

Oh! who is yon misanthrope, shunning man-
 kind?
 From cities to caves of the forest he flew:
There, raving, he howls his complaint to the
 wind;
 The mountains reverberate love's last adieu!

Now hate rules a heart which in love's easy
 chains
 Once passion's tumultuous blandishments
 knew;
Despair now inflames the dark tide of his veins;
 He ponders in frenzy on love's last adieu!

How he envies the wretch with a soul wrapt
 in steel!
 His pleasures are scarce, yet his troubles
 are few,
Who laughs at the pang which he never can
 feel,
 And dreads not the anguish of love's last
 adieu!

Youth flies, life decays, even hope is o'ercast;
 No more with love's former devotion we sue:
He spreads his young wing, he retires with
 the blast;
 The shroud of affection is love's last adieu!

In this life of probation for rapture divine,
 Astrea declares that some penance is due;
From him who has worshipp'd at love's gentle
 shrine,
 The atonement is ample in love's last adieu!

Who kneels to the god, on his altar of light
 Must myrtle and cypress alternately strew:
His myrtle, an emblem of purest delight;
 His cypress, the garland of love's last adieu!

——◆◆——

DAMÆTAS.

In law an infant, and in years a boy,
In mind a slave to every vicious joy;
From every sense of shame and virtue wean'd;
In lies an adept, in deceit a fiend;
Versed in hypocrisy, while yet a child;
Fickle as wind, of inclinations wild;
Woman his dupe, his heedless friend a tool;
Old in the world, though scarcely broke from
 school;
Damætas ran through all the maze of sin,
And found the goal when others just begin:

Even still conflicting passions shake his soul,
And bid him drain the dregs of pleasure's bowl;
But, pall'd with vice, he breaks his former
 chain,
And what was once his bliss appears his bane.

——◆◆——

TO MARION.

Marion! why that pensive brow?
What disgust to life hast thou?
Change that discontented air;
Frowns become not one so fair.
'T is not love disturbs thy rest,
Love 's a stranger to thy breast;
He in dimpling smiles appears,
Or mourns in sweetly timid tears,
Or bends the languid eyelid down,
But shuns the cold forbidding frown.
Then resume thy former fire,
Some will love, and all admire;
While that icy aspect chills us,
Nought but cool indifference thrills us.
Wouldst thou wandering hearts beguile,
Smile at least, or seem to smile.
Eyes like thine were never meant
To hide their orbs in dark restraint.
Spite of all thou fain wouldst say,
Still in truant beams they play.
Thy lips—but here my modest Muse
Her impulse chaste must needs refuse:
She blushes, curt'sies, frowns,—in short she
Dreads lest the subject should transport me;
And flying off in search of reason,
Brings prudence back in proper season.
All I shall therefore say (whate'er
I think, is neither here nor there)
Is, that such lips, of looks endearing,
Were form'd for better things than sneering:
Of soothing compliments divested,
Advice at least 's disinterested;
Such is my artless song to thee,
From all the flow of flattery free;
Counsel like mine is like a brother's,
My heart is given to some others;
That is to say, unskill'd to cozen,
It shares itself among a dozen.

Marion, adieu! oh, pr'ythee slight not
This warning, though it may delight not;
And, lest my precepts be displeasing
To those who think remonstrance teasing:
At once I 'll tell thee our opinion
Concerning woman's soft dominion:
Howe'er we gaze with admiration
On eyes of blue or lips carnation,
Howe'er the flowing locks attract us,
Howe'er those beauties may distract us,
Still fickle, we are prone to rove,
These cannot fix our souls to love;

It is not too severe a stricture
To say they form a pretty picture;
But wouldst thou see the secret chain
Which binds us in your humble train,
To hail you queens of all creation,
Know, in a word, 'tis ANIMATION.

— • • —

TO A LADY

WHO PRESENTED TO THE AUTHOR A LOCK OF
HAIR BRAIDED WITH HIS OWN, AND APPOINT-
ED A NIGHT IN DECEMBER TO MEET HIM IN
THE GARDEN.

THESE locks, which fondly thus entwine,
In firmer chains our hearts confine,
Than all th' unmeaning protestations
Which swell with nonsense love orations.
Our love is fix'd, I think we've proved it;
Nor time, nor place, nor art have moved it;
Then wherefore should we sigh and whine,
With groundless jealousy repine,
With silly whims and fancies frantic,
Merely to make our love romantic?
Why should you weep like Lydia Languish,
And fret with self-created anguish?
Or doom the lover you have chosen,
On winter nights to sigh half frozen;
In leafless shades to sue for pardon,
Only because the scene's a garden?
For gardens seem, by one consent,
Since Shakspeare set the precedent,
Since Juliet first declared her passion,
To form the place of assignation.
Oh! would some modern muse inspire,
And seat her by a sea-coal fire;
Or had the bard at Christmas written,
And laid the scene of love in Britain,
He surely, in commiseration,
Had changed the place of declaration.
In Italy I've no objection;
Warm nights are proper for reflection;
But here our climate is so rigid,
That love itself is rather frigid:
Think on our chilly situation,
And curb this rage for imitation;
Then let us meet, as oft we've done,
Beneath the influence of the sun;
Or, if at midnight I must meet you
Within your mansion let me greet you:
There we can love for hours together,
Much better, in such snowy weather,
Than placed in all th' Arcadian groves
That ever witness'd rural loves;
Then, if my passion fail to please,
Next night I'll be content to freeze;
No more I'll give a loose to laughter
But curse my fate for ever after.

OSCAR OF ALVA.
A TALE.

How sweetly shines through azure skies,
 The lamp of heaven on Lora's shore;
Where Alva's hoary turrets rise,
 And hear the din of arms no more!

But often has yon rolling moon
 On Alva's casques of silver play'd;
And view'd, at midnight's silent noon,
 Her chiefs in gleaming mail array'd:

And on the crimson'd rocks beneath,
 Which scowl o'er ocean's sullen flow,
Pale in the scatter'd ranks of death,
 She saw the gasping warrior low;

While many an eye which ne'er again
 Could mark the rising orb of day,
Turn'd feebly from the gory plain,
 Beheld in death her fading ray.

Once to those eyes the lamp of Love,
 They blest her dear propitious light;
But now she glimmer'd from above,
 A sad, funereal torch of night.

Faded is Alva's noble race,
 And gray her towers are seen afar;
No more her heroes urge the chase,
 Or roll the crimson tide of war.

But who was last of Alva's clan?
 Why grows the moss on Alva's stone?
Her towers resound no steps of man,
 They echo to the gale alone.

And when that gale is fierce and high,
 A sound is heard in yonder hall;
It rises hoarsely through the sky,
 And vibrates o'er the mould'ring wall.

Yes, when the eddying tempest sighs,
 It shakes the shield of Oscar brave;
But there no more his banners rise,
 No more his plumes of sable wave.

Fair shone the sun on Oscar's birth,
 When Angus hail'd his eldest born;
The vassals round their chieftain's hearth
 Crowd to applaud the happy morn.

They feast upon the mountain deer,
 The pibroch raised its piercing note;
To gladden more their highland cheer,
 The strains in martial numbers float:

And they who heard the war-notes wild
 Hoped that one day the pibroch's strain
Should play before the hero's child
 While he should lead the tartan train.

Another year is quickly past,
 And Angus hails another son;
His natal day is like the last,
 Nor soon the jocund feast was done.

Taught by their sire to bend the bow,
 On Alva's dusky hills of wind,
The boys in childhood chased the roe,
 And left their hounds in speed behind.

But ere their years of youth are o'er,
 They mingle in the ranks of war;
They lightly wheel the bright claymore,
 And send the whistling arrow far.

Dark was the flow of Oscar's hair,
 Wildly it stream'd along the gale;
But Allan's locks were bright and fair,
 And pensive seem'd his cheek, and pale.

But Oscar own'd a hero's soul,
 His dark eye shone through beams of truth;
Allan had early learn'd control,
 And smooth his words had been from youth.

Both, both were brave; the Saxon spear
 Was shiver'd oft beneath their steel;
And Oscar's bosom scorn'd to fear,
 But Oscar's bosom knew to feel;

While Allan's soul belied his form,
 Unworthy with such charms to dwell:
Keen as the lightning of the storm,
 On foes his deadly vengeance fell.

From high Southannon's distant tower
 Arrived a young and noble dame;
With Kenneth's lands to form her dower,
 Glenalvon's blue-eyed daughter came;

And Oscar claim'd the beauteous bride,
 And Angus on his Oscar smiled:
It soothed the father's feudal pride
 Thus to obtain Glenalvon's child.

Hark to the pibroch's pleasing note!
 Hark to the swelling nuptial song!
In joyous strains the voices float,
 And still the choral peal prolong.

See how the heroes' blood-red plumes
 Assembled wave in Alva's hall;
Each youth his varied plaid assumes,
 Attending on their chieftain's call.

It is not war their aid demands,
 The pibroch plays the song of peace;
To Oscar's nuptials throng the bands,
 Nor yet the sounds of pleasure cease.

But where is Oscar? sure 'tis late:
 Is this a bridegroom's ardent flame?
While thronging guests and ladies wait,
 Nor Oscar nor his brother came.

At length young Allan join'd the bride;
 "Why comes not Oscar," Angus said:
"Is he not here?" the youth replied;
 "With me he roved not o'er the glade:

"Perchance, forgetful of the day,
 'Tis his to chase the bounding roe;
Or ocean's waves prolong his stay;
 Yet Oscar's bark is seldom slow."

"Oh, no!" the anguish'd sire rejoin'd,
 "Nor chase, nor wave, my boy delay;
Would he to Mora seem unkind?
 Would aught to her impede his way?

"Oh, search, ye chiefs! oh, search around!
 Allan, with these through Alva fly;
Till Oscar, till my son is found,
 Haste, haste, nor dare attempt reply."

All is confusion—through the vale
 The name of Oscar hoarsely rings,
It rises on the murmuring gale,
 Till night expands her dusky wings;

It breaks the stillness of the night,
 But echoes through her shades in vain;
It sounds through morning's misty light,
 But Oscar comes not o'er the plain.

Three days, three sleepless nights, the Chief
 For Oscar search'd each mountain cave:
Then hope is lost; in boundless grief,
 His locks in gray-torn ringlets wave.

"Oscar! my son!—thou God of heaven,
 Restore the prop of sinking age!
Or if that hope no more is given,
 Yield his assassin to my rage.

"Yes, on some desert rocky shore
 My Oscar's whiten'd bones must lie;
Then grant, thou God! I ask no more,
 With him his frantic sire may die!

"Yet he may live,—away, despair!
 Be calm, my soul! he yet may live;
T' arraign my fate, my voice forbear!
 O God! my impious prayer forgive.

"What, if he live for me no more,
 I sink forgotten in the dust,
The hope of Alva's age is o'er:
 Alas! can pangs like these be just?"

Thus did the hapless parent mourn,
 Till Time, which soothes severest woe,
Had bade serenity return,
 And made the tear-drop cease to flow.

For still some latent hope survived
 That Oscar might once more appear;
His hope now droop'd and now revived,
 Till Time had told a tedious year.

Days roll'd along, the orb of light
 Again had run his destined race;
No Oscar bless'd his father's sight,
 And sorrow left a fainter trace.

For youthful Allan still remain'd,
 And now his father's only joy:
And Mora's heart was quickly gain'd,
 For beauty crown'd the fair-hair'd boy.

She thought that Oscar low was laid,
 And Allan's face was wondrous fair;
If Oscar lived, some other maid
 Had claim'd his faithless bosom's care.

And Angus said, if one year more
 In fruitless hope was pass'd away,
His fondest scruples should be o'er,
 And he would name their nuptial day.

Slow roll'd the moons, but blest at last
 Arrived the dearly destined morn:
The year of anxious trembling past,
 What smiles the lovers' cheeks adorn!

Hark to the pibroch's pleasing note!
 Hark to the swelling nuptial song!
In joyous strains the voices float,
 And still the choral peal prolong.

Again the clan, in festive crowd,
 Throng through the gate of Alva's hall;
The sounds of mirth re-echo loud,
 And all their former joy recall.

But who is he, whose darken'd brow
 Glooms in the midst of general mirth?
Before his eyes' far fiercer glow
 The blue flames curdle o'er the hearth.

Dark is the robe which wraps his form,
 And tall his plume of gory red;
His voice is like the rising storm,
 But light and trackless is his tread.

'Tis noon of night, the pledge goes round,
 The bridegroom's health is deeply quaff'd;
With shouts the vaulted roofs resound,
 And all combine to hail the draught.

Sudden the stranger-chief arose,
 And all the clamorous crowd are hush'd;
And Angus' cheek with wonder glows,
 And Mora's tender bosom blush'd.

"Old man!" he cried, "this pledge is done;
 Thou saw'st 't was duly drank by me;
It hail'd the nuptials of thy son:
 Now will I claim a pledge from thee.

"While all around is mirth and joy,
 To bless thy Allan's happy lot,
Say, hadst thou ne'er another boy?
 Say, why should Oscar be forgot?"

"Alas!" the hapless sire replied,
 The big tear starting as he spoke,
"When Oscar left my hall, or died,
 This aged heart was almost broke.

"Thrice has the earth revolved her course
 Since Oscar's form has bless'd my sight;
And Allan is my last resource,
 Since martial Oscar's death or flight."

"'Tis well," replied the stranger stern,
 And fiercely flash'd his rolling eye;
"Thy Oscar's fate I fain would learn;
 Perhaps the hero did not die.

"Perchance, if those whom most he loved
 Would call, thy Oscar might return;
Perchance the chief has only roved,
 For him thy beltane yet may burn.

"Fill high the bowl the table round,
 We will not claim the pledge by stealth;
With wine let every cup be crown'd;
 Pledge me departed Oscar's health."

"With all my soul," old Angus said,
 And fill'd his goblet to the brim:
"Here's to my boy! alive or dead,
 I ne'er shall find a son like him."

"Bravely, old man, this health has sped;
 But why does Allan trembling stand?
Come, drink remembrance of the dead,
 And raise thy cup with firmer hand."

The crimson glow of Allan's face
 Was turn'd at once to ghastly hue;
The drops of death each other chase
 Adown in agonizing dew.

Thrice did he raise the goblet high,
 And thrice his lips refused to taste;
For thrice he caught the stranger's eye
 On his with deadly fury placed.

"And is it thus a brother hails
 A brother's fond remembrance here?
If thus affection's strength prevails,
 What might we not expect from fear?"

Roused by the sneer, he raised the bowl,
 "Would Oscar now could share our mirth!"
Internal fear appall'd his soul;
 He said, and dash'd the cup to earth.

"'Tis he! I hear my murderer's voice!"
 Loud shrieks a darkly gleaming form.
"A murderer's voice!" the roof replies,
 And deeply swells the bursting storm.

The tapers wink, the chieftains shrink,
 The stranger's gone,—amidst the crew,
A form was seen in tartan green,
 And tall the shade terrific grew.

His waist was bound with a broad belt round,
 His plume of sable stream'd on high;
But his breast was bare, with the red wounds
 there,
 And fix'd was the glare of his glassy eye.

And thrice he smiled, with his eye so wild,
 On Angus bending low the knee;
And thrice he frown'd on a chief on the ground,
 Whom shivering crowds with horror see.

The bolts loud roll from pole to pole,
 The thunders through the welkin ring,
And the gleaming form, through the mist of
 the storm,
 Was borne on high by the whirlwind's wing.

Cold was the feast, the revel ceased.
 Who lies upon the stony floor?
Oblivion press'd old Angus' breast,
 At length his life-pulse throbs once more.

"Away, away! let the leech essay
 To pour the light on Allan's eyes:"
His sand is done,—his race is run,—
 Oh! never more shall Allan rise!

But Oscar's breast is cold as clay,
 His locks are lifted by the gale;
And Allan's barbed arrow lay
 With him in dark Glentanar's vale.

And whence the dreadful stranger came,
 Or who, no mortal wight can tell;
But no one doubts the form of flame,
 For Alva's sons knew Oscar well.

Ambition nerved young Allan's hand,
 Exulting demons wing'd his dart;
While Envy waved her burning brand,
 And pour'd her venom round his heart.

Swift is the shaft from Allan's bow;
 Whose streaming life-blood stains his side?
Dark Oscar's sable crest is low,
 The dart has drunk his vital tide.

And Mora's eye could Allan move,
 She bade his wounded pride rebel:
Alas! that eyes which beam'd with love
 Should urge the soul to deeds of hell.

Lo! seest thou not a lonely tomb
 Which rises o'er a warrior dead?
It glimmers through the twilight gloom;
 Oh! that is Allan's nuptial bed.

Far, distant far, the noble grave
 Which held his clan's great ashes stood;
And o'er his corse no banners wave,
 For they were stain'd with kindred blood.

What minstrel gray, what hoary bard,
 Shall Allan's deeds on harp-strings raise?
The song is glory's chief reward,
 But who can strike a murderer's praise?

Unstrung, untouch'd, the harp must stand,
 No minstrel dare the theme awake;
Guilt would benumb his palsied hand,
 His harp in shuddering chords would break.

No lyre of fame, no hallow'd verse,
 Shall sound his glories high in air:
A dying father's bitter curse,
 A brother's death-groan echoes there.

—◆◆—

THE EPISODE OF NISUS AND EURYALUS,

A PARAPHRASE FROM THE ÆNEID, LIB. IX.

NISUS, the guardian of the portal, stood,
Eager to gild his arms with hostile blood;
Well skill'd in fight the quivering lance to
 wield,
Or pour his arrows through th' embattled
 field:
From Ida torn, he left his sylvan cave,
And sought a foreign home, a distant grave.
To watch the movements of the Daunian host,
With him Euryalus sustains the post;
No lovelier mien adorn'd the ranks of Troy,
And beardless bloom yet graced the gallant
 boy;
Though few the seasons of his youthful life,
As yet a novice in the martial strife,
'Twas his, with beauty, valour's gifts to
 share—
A soul heroic, as his form was fair:
These burn with one pure flame of generous
 love;
In peace, in war, united still they move;
Friendship and glory form their joint reward;
And now combined they hold their nightly
 guard.

"What god," exclaim'd the first, "instils
 this fire?
Or, in itself a god, what great desire?
My labouring soul, with anxious thought
 oppress'd,
Abhors this station of inglorious rest;
The love of fame with this can ill accord,
Be't mine to seek for glory with my sword.
Seest thou yon camp, with torches twinkling
 dim,
Where drunken slumbers wrap each lazy
 limb?
Where confidence and ease the watch disdain,
And drowsy Silence holds her sable reign?
Then hear my thought:—In deep and sullen
 grief
Our troops and leaders mourn their absent
 chief:
Now could the gifts and promised prize be
 thine
(The deed, the danger, and the fame be mine),
Were this decreed, beneath yon rising mound,
Methinks, an easy path perchance were
 found;

Which past, I speed my way to Pallas' walls,
And lead Æneas from Evander's halls.''

With equal ardour fired, and warlike joy,
His glowing friend address'd the Dardan
 boy :—
" These deeds, my Nisus, shalt thou dare
 alone ?
Must all the fame, the peril, be thine own ?
Am I by thee despised, and left afar,
As one unfit to share the toils of war ?
Not thus his son the great Opheltes taught ;
Not thus my sire in Argive combats fought ;
Not thus, when Ilion fell by heavenly hate,
I track'd Æneas through the walks of fate :
Thou know'st my deeds, my breast devoid of
 fear,
And hostile life-drops dim my gory spear.
Here is a soul with hope immortal burns,
And life, ignoble life, for *glory* spurns.
Fame, fame is cheaply earn'd by fleeting
 breath :
The price of honour is the sleep of death."

Then Nisus:—" Calm thy bosom's fond
 alarms :
Thy heart beats fiercely to the din of arms.
More dear thy worth and valour than my own,
I swear by him who fills Olympus' throne !
So may I triumph, as I speak the truth,
And clasp again the comrade of my youth !
But should I fall,—and he who dares advance
Through hostile legions must abide by
 chance,—
If some Rutulian arm, with adverse blow,
Should lay the friend who ever loved thee
 low,
Live thou, such beauties I would fain pre-
 serve,
Thy budding years a lengthen'd term deserve.
When humbled in the dust, let some one be,
Whose gentle eyes will shed one tear for me ;
Whose manly arm may snatch me back by
 force,
Or wealth redeem from foes my captive corse :
Or, if my destiny these last deny,
If in the spoiler's power my ashes lie,
Thy pious care may raise a simple tomb,
To mark thy love, and signalize my doom.
Why should thy doting wretched mother weep
Her only boy, reclined in endless sleep ?
Who, for thy sake, the tempest's fury dared,
Who, for thy sake, war's deadly peril shared ;
Who braved what woman never braved be-
 fore,
And left her native for the Latian shore."

" In vain you damp the ardour of my soul,"
Replied Euryalus ; " it scorns control !

Hence, let us haste ! "—their brother guards
 arose,
Roused by their call, nor court again repose ;
The pair, buoy'd up on Hope's exulting wing,
Their stations leave, and speed to seek the
 king.

Now o'er the earth a solemn stillness ran,
And lull'd alike the cares of brute and man ;
Save where the Dardan leaders nightly hold
Alternate converse, and their plans unfold.
On one great point the council are agreed,
An instant message to their prince decreed ;
Each lean'd upon the lance he well could
 wield,
And poised with easy arm his ancient shield ;
When Nisus and his friend their leave request
To offer something to their high behest.
With anxious tremors, yet unawed by fear,
The faithful pair before the throne appear :
Iulus greets them ; at his kind command,
The elder first address'd the hoary band.

" With patience " (thus Hyrtacides began)
" Attend, nor judge from youth our humble
 plan.
Where yonder beacons half expiring beam,
Our slumbering foes of future conquest dream,
Nor heed that we a secret path have traced,
Between the ocean and the portal placed.
Beneath the covert of the blackening smoke,
Whose shade securely our design will cloak !
If you, ye chiefs, and fortune will allow,
We'll bend our course to yonder mountain's
 brow,
Where Pallas' walls at distance meet the
 sight,
Seen o'er the glade, when not obscured by
 night :
Then shall Æneas in his pride return,
When hostile matrons raise their offspring's
 urn ;
And Latian spoils and purpled heaps of dead
Shall mark the havoc of our hero's tread.
Such is our purpose, not unknown the way ;
Where yonder torrent's devious waters stray,
Oft have we seen, when hunting by the
 stream,
The distant spires above the valleys gleam."

Mature in years, for sober wisdom famed,
Moved by the speech, Alethes here ex-
 claim'd,—
" Ye parent gods ! who rule the fate of Troy,
Still dwells the Dardan spirit in the boy ;
When minds like these in striplings thus ye
 raise,
Yours is the godlike act, be yours the praise ;
In gallant youth, my fainting hopes revive,
And Ilion's wonted glories still survive."

Then in his warm embrace the boys he
 press'd,
And, quivering, strain'd them to his aged
 breast;
With tears the burning cheek of each be-
 dew'd,
And, sobbing, thus his first discourse renew'd:
"What gift, my countrymen, what martial
 prize,
Can we bestow, which you may not despise?
Our deities the first best boon have given—
Internal virtues are the gift of Heaven.
What poor rewards can bless your deeds on
 earth,
Doubtless await such young, exalted worth.
Æneas and Ascanius shall combine
To yield applause far, far surpassing mine."

Iulus then:—"By all the powers above!
By those Penates who my country love!
By hoary Vesta's sacred fane, I swear,
My hopes are all in you, ye generous pair!
Restore my father to my grateful sight,
And all my sorrows yield to one delight.
Nisus! two silver goblets are thine own,
Saved from Arisba's stately domes o'er-
 thrown!
My sire secured them on that fatal day,
Nor left such bowls an Argive robber's prey:
Two massy tripods, also, shall be thine;
Two talents polish'd from the glittering mine;
An ancient cup, which Tyrian Dido gave,
While yet our vessels press'd the Punic
 wave:
But when the hostile chiefs at length bow
 down,
When great Æneas wears Hesperia's crown,
The casque, the buckler, and the fiery steed
Which Turnus guides with more than mortal
 speed,
Are thine; no envious lot shall then be cast,
I pledge my word, irrevocably past:
Nay more, twelve slaves, and twice six cap-
 tive dames,
To soothe thy softer hours with amorous
 flames,
And all the realms which now the Latins
 sway,
The labours of to-night shall well repay.
But thou, my generous youth, whose tender
 years
Are near my own, whose worth my heart
 reveres,
Henceforth affection, sweetly thus begun,
Shall join our bosoms and our souls in one;
Without thy aid, no glory shall be mine;
Without thy dear advice, no great design;
Alike through life esteem'd, thou godlike
 boy,
In war my bulwark, and in peace my joy."

To him Euryalus:—"No day shall shame
The rising glories which from this I claim.
Fortune may favour, or the skies may frown,
But valour, spite of fate, obtains renown.
Yet, ere from hence our eager steps depart,
One boon I beg, the nearest to my heart:
My mother, sprung from Priam's royal line,
Like thine ennobled, hardly less divine,
Nor Troy nor king Acestes' realms restrain
Her feeble age from dangers of the main:
Alone she came, all selfish fears above,
A bright example of maternal love.
Unknown the secret enterprise I brave,
Lest grief should bend my parent to the
 grave;
From this alone no fond adieus I seek,
No fainting mother's lips have press'd my
 cheek;
By gloomy night and thy right hand I vow
Her parting tears would shake my purpose
 now:
Do thou, my prince, her failing age sustain,
In thee her much-loved child may live
 again;
Her dying hours with pious conduct bless,
Assist her wants, relieve her fond distress:
So dear a hope must all my soul inflame,
To rise in glory, or to fall in fame."
Struck with a filial care so deeply felt,
In tears at once the Trojan warriors melt;
Faster than all, Iulus' eyes o'erflow!
Such love was his, and such had been his
 woe.
"All thou hast ask'd, receive," the prince
 replied;
"Nor this alone, but many a gift beside.
To cheer thy mother's years shall be my aim,
Creusa's style but wanting to the dame.
Fortune an adverse wayward course may run,
But bless'd thy mother in so dear a son.
Now, by my life!—my sire's most sacred
 oath—
To thee I pledge my full, my firmest troth,
All the rewards which once to thee were
 vow'd,
If thou shouldst fall, on her shall be be-
 stow'd."
Thus spoke the weeping prince, then forth to
 view
A gleaming falchion from the sheath he
 drew;
Lycaon's utmost skill had graced the steel,
For friends to envy and for foes to feel:
A tawny hide, the Moorish lion's spoil,
Slain 'midst the forest, in the hunter's toil,
Mnestheus to guard the elder youth bestows,
And old Alethes' casque defends his brows.
Arm'd, thence they go, while all th' assembled
 train,
To aid their cause, implore the gods in vain.

More than a boy, in wisdom and in grace,
Iulus holds amidst the chiefs his place:
His prayer he sends; but what can prayers
 avail,
Lost in the murmurs of the sighing gale?

The trench is pass'd, and, favour'd by the
 night,
Through sleeping foes they wheel their wary
 flight.
When shall the sleep of many a foe be o'er?
Alas! some slumber who shall wake no
 more!
Chariots and bridles, mix'd with arms, are
 seen;
And flowing flasks, and scatter'd troops be-
 tween:
Bacchus and Mars to rule the camp combine;
A mingled chaos this of war and wine.
"Now," cries the first, "for deeds of blood
 prepare,
With me the conquest and the labour share:
Here lies our path; lest any hand arise,
Watch thou, while many a dreaming chief-
 tain dies:
I 'll carve our passage through the heedless
 foe,
And clear thy road with many a deadly blow."
His whispering accents then the youth re-
 press'd,
And pierced proud Rhamnes through his
 panting breast:
Stretch'd at his ease, th' incautious king
 reposed;
Debauch, and not fatigue, his eyes had closed:
To Turnus dear, a prophet and a prince,
His omens more than augur's skill evince;
But he, who thus foretold the fate of all,
Could not avert his own untimely fall.
Next Remus' armour-bearer, hapless, fell,
And three unhappy slaves the carnage swell;
The charioteer along his courser's sides
Expires, the steel his sever'd neck divides;
And, last, his lord is number'd with the dead:
Bounding convulsive, flies the gasping head;
From the swoll'n veins the blackening tor-
 rents pour;
Stain'd is the couch and earth with clotting
 gore.
Young Lamyrus and Lamus next expire,
And gay Serranus, fill'd with youthful fire;
Half the long night in childish games was
 pass'd;
Lull'd by the potent grape, he slept at last:
Ah! happier far had he the morn survey'd,
And till Aurora's dawn his skill display'd.

In slaughter'd fold, the keepers lost in
 sleep,
His hungry fangs a lion thus may steep;

'Mid the sad flock, at dead of night he prowls,
With murder glutted, and in carnage rolls:
Insatiate still, through teeming herds he
 roams;
In seas of gore the lordly tyrant foams.

Nor less the other's deadly vengeance
 came,
But falls on feeble crowds without a name;
His wound unconscious Fadus scarce can
 feel,
Yet wakeful Rhæsus sees the threatening
 steel;
His coward breast behind a jar he hides,
And vainly in the weak defence confides;
Full in his heart, the falchion search'd his
 veins,
The reeking weapon bears alternate stains;
Through wine and blood, commingling as
 they flow,
One feeble spirit seeks the shades below.
Now where Messapus dwelt they bend their
 way,
Whose fires emit a faint and trembling ray;
There, unconfined, behold each grazing steed,
Unwatch'd, unheeded, on the herbage feed:
Brave Nisus here arrests his comrade's arm,
Too flush'd with carnage, and with conquest
 warm:
"Hence let us haste, the dangerous path is
 pass'd;
Full foes enough to-night have breathed their
 last:
Soon will the day those eastern clouds adorn;
Now let us speed, nor tempt the rising morn."

What silver arms, with various art em-
 boss'd,
What bowls and mantles in confusion toss'd,
They leave regardless! yet one glittering
 prize
Attracts the younger hero's wandering eyes;
The gilded harness Rhamnes' coursers felt,
The gems which stud the monarch's golden
 belt:
This from the pallid corse was quickly torn,
Once by a line of former chieftains worn.
Th' exulting boy the studded girdle wears,
Messapus' helm his head in triumph bears;
Then from the tents their cautious steps they
 bend,
To seek the vale where safer paths extend.

Just at this hour, a band of Latian horse
To Turnus' camp pursue their destined
 course:
While the slow foot their tardy march delay,
The knights, impatient, spur along the way:
Three hundred mail-clad men, by Volscens led,
To Turnus with their master's promise sped:

Now they approach the trench, and view the
 walls,
When, on the left, a light reflection falls;
The plunder'd helmet, through the waning
 night,
Sheds forth a silver radiance, glancing bright.
Volscens with question loud the pair alarms:—
" Stand, stragglers! stand! why early thus in
 arms?
From whence? to whom?"—He meets with
 no reply;
Trusting the covert of the night, they fly:
The thicket's depth with hurried pace they
 tread,
While round the wood the hostile squadron
 spread.

With brakes entangled, scarce a path be-
 tween,
Dreary and dark appears the sylvan scene:
Euryalus his heavy spoils impede,
The boughs and winding turns his steps mis-
 lead;
But Nisus scours along the forest's maze
To where Latinus' steeds in safety graze,
Then backward o'er the plain his eyes extend,
On every side they seek his absent friend.
" O God! my boy," he cries, " of me bereft,
In what impending perils art thou left!"
Listening he runs—above the waving trees,
Tumultuous voices swell the passing breeze;
The war-cry rises, thundering hoofs around
Wake the dark echoes of the trembling ground.
Again he turns, of footsteps hears the noise;
The sound elates, the sight his hope destroys:
The hapless boy a ruffian train surround,
While lengthening shades his weary way con-
 found;
Him with loud shouts the furious knights
 pursue,
Struggling in vain, a captive to the crew.
What can his friend 'gainst thronging numbers
 dare?
Ah! must he rush his comrade's fate to
 share?
What force, what aid, what stratagem essay,
Back to redeem the Latian spoiler's prey?
His life a votive ransom nobly give,
Or die with him for whom he wish'd to live?
Poising with strength his lifted lance on high,
On Luna's orb he cast his frenzied eye:—
" Goddess serene, transcending every star!
Queen of the sky, whose beams are seen
 afar!
By night heaven owns thy sway, by day the
 grove,
When, as chaste Dian, here thou deign'st to
 rove;
If e'er myself, or sire, have sought to grace
Thine altars with the produce of the chase,

Speed, speed my dart to pierce yon vaunting
 crowd,
To free my friend, and scatter far the proud."
Thus having said, the hissing dart he flung;
Through parted shades the hurtling weapon
 sung;
The thirsty point in Sulmo's entrails lay,
Transfix'd his heart, and stretch'd him on the
 clay:
He sobs, he dies,—the troop in wild amaze,
Unconscious whence the death, with horror
 gaze.
While pale they stare, through Tagus' temples
 riven,
A second shaft with equal force is driven:
Fierce Volscens rolls around his lowering
 eyes;
Veil'd by the night, secure the Trojan lies.
Burning with wrath, he view'd his soldiers
 fall.
" Thou youth accurst, thy life shall pay for
 all!"
Quick from the sheath his flaming glaive he
 drew,
And, raging, on the boy defenceless flew.
Nisus no more the blackening shade conceals,
Forth, forth he starts, and all his love reveals;
Aghast, confused, his fears to madness rise,
And pour these accents, shrieking as he
 flies:
" Me, me,—your vengeance hurl on me alone;
Here sheathe the steel, my blood is all your
 own.
Ye starry spheres! thou conscious Heaven!
 attest!
He could not—durst not—lo! the guile con-
 fest!
All, all was mine,—his early fate suspend;
He only loved too well his hapless friend:
Spare, spare, ye chiefs! from him your rage
 remove;
His fault was friendship, all his crime was
 love."
He pray'd in vain; the dark assassin's sword
Pierced the fair side, the snowy bosom gored;
Lowly to earth inclines his plume-clad crest,
And sanguine torrents mantle o'er his breast:
As some young rose, whose blossom scents
 the air,
Languid in death, expires beneath the share;
Or crimson poppy, sinking with the shower,
Declining gently, falls a fading flower;
Thus, sweetly drooping, bends his lovely head,
And lingering beauty hovers round the dead.

But fiery Nisus stems the battle's tide,
Revenge his leader, and despair his guide;
Volscens he seeks amidst the gathering host,
Volscens must soon appease his comrade's
 ghost;

Steel, flashing, pours on steel, foe crowds on
 foe;
Rage nerves his arm, fate gleams in every
 blow;
In vain beneath unnumber'd wounds he bleeds,
Nor wounds, nor death, distracted Nisus heeds;
In viewless circles wheel'd, his falchion flies,
Nor quits the hero's grasp till Volscens dies;
Deep in his throat its end the weapon found,
The tyrant's soul fled groaning through the
 wound.
Thus Nisus all his fond affection proved—
Dying, revenged the fate of him he loved;
Then on his bosom sought his wonted place,
And death was heavenly in his friend's em-
 brace!

Celestial pair! if aught my verse can claim,
Wafted on Time's broad pinion, yours is fame!
Ages on ages shall your fate admire,
No future day shall see your names expire,
While stands the Capitol, immortal dome!
And vanquish'd millions hail their empress,
 Rome!

———— ♦ ————

TRANSLATION FROM THE MEDEA
OF EURIPIDES.

[Ἔρωτες ὑπερ μεν ἀγαν, κ. τ. λ.]

WHEN fierce conflicting passions urge
 The breast where love is wont to glow,
What mind can stem the stormy surge
 Which rolls the tide of human woe?
The hope of praise, the dread of shame,
 Can rouse the tortured breast no more;
The wild desire, the guilty flame,
 Absorbs each wish it felt before.

But if affection gently thrills
 The soul by purer dreams possest,
The pleasing balm of mortal ills
 In love can soothe the aching breast:
If thus thou comest in disguise,
 Fair Venus! from thy native heaven,
What heart unfeeling would despise
 The sweetest boon the gods have given?

But never from thy golden bow
 May I beneath the shaft expire!
Whose creeping venom, sure and slow,
 Awakes an all-consuming fire:
Ye racking doubts! ye jealous fears!
 With others wage internal war;
Repentance, source of future tears,
 From me be ever distant far!

May no distracting thoughts destroy
 The holy calm of sacred love!
May all the hours be wing'd with joy,
 Which hover faithful hearts above!

Fair Venus! on thy myrtle shrine
 May I with some fond lover sigh,
Whose heart may mingle pure with mine—
 With me to live, with me to die!

My native soil! beloved before,
 Now dearer as my peaceful home,
Ne'er may I quit thy rocky shore,
 A hapless banish'd wretch to roam!
This very day, this very hour,
 May I resign this fleeting breath!
Nor quit my silent humble bower;
 A doom to me far worse than death.

Have I not heard the exile's sigh,
 And seen the exile's silent tear,
Through distant climes condemn'd to fly,
 A pensive weary wanderer here?
Ah! hapless dame! no sire bewails,
 No friend thy wretched fate deplores,
No kindred voice with rapture hails
 Thy steps within a stranger's doors.

Perish the fiend whose iron heart,
 To fair affection's truth unknown,
Bids her he fondly loved depart,
 Unpitied, helpless, and alone;
Who ne'er unlocks with silver key
 The milder treasures of his soul,—
May such a friend be far from me,
 And ocean's storms between us roll!

———— ♦ ————

THOUGHTS SUGGESTED BY A COL-
LEGE EXAMINATION.

HIGH in the midst, surrounded by his peers,
MAGNUS his ample front sublime uprears:
Placed on his chair of state, he seems a god,
While Sophs and Freshmen tremble at his nod.
As all around sit wrapt in speechless gloom,
His voice in thunder shakes the sounding
 dome;
Denouncing dire reproach to luckless fools,
Unskill'd to plod in mathematic rules.

Happy the youth in Euclid's axioms tried,
Though little versed in any art beside;
Who, scarcely skill'd an English line to pen,
Scans Attic metres with a critic's ken.
What, though he knows not how his fathers
 bled,
When civil discord piled the fields with dead,
When Edward bade his conquering bands ad-
 vance,
Or Henry trampled on the crest of France,
Though marvelling at the name of Magna
 Charta,
Yet well he recollects the laws of Sparta;
Can tell what edicts sage Lycurgus made,
While Blackstone's on the shelf neglected laid;

Of Grecian dramas vaunts the deathless fame,
Of Avon's bard remembering scarce the name.

Such is the youth whose scientific pate
Class-honours, medals, fellowships, await;
Or even, perhaps, the declamation prize,
If to such glorious height he lifts his eyes.
But lo! no common orator can hope
The envied silver cup within his scope.
Not that our heads much eloquence require,
Th' ATHENIAN's glowing style, or Tully's fire.
A manner clear or warm is useless, since
We do not try by speaking to convince.
Be other orators of pleasing proud,—
We speak to please ourselves, not move the
 crowd:
Our gravity prefers the muttering tone,
A proper mixture of the squeak and groan:
No borrow'd grace of action must be seen;
The slightest motion would displease the
 Dean;
Whilst every staring graduate would prate
Against what he could never imitate.

The man who hopes t' obtain the promised
 cup
Must in one posture stand, and ne'er look up;
Nor stop, but rattle over every word—
No matter what, so it can *not* be heard.
Thus let him hurry on, nor think to rest:
Who speaks the fastest 's sure to speak the
 best;
Who utters most within the shortest space
May safely hope to win the wordy race.

The sons of science these, who, thus repaid,
Linger in ease in Granta's sluggish shade;
Where on Cam's sedgy banks supine they lie,
Unknown, unhonour'd live, unwept-for die:
Dull as the pictures which adorn their halls,
They think all learning fix'd within their
 walls:
In manners rude, in foolish forms precise,
All modern arts affecting to despise;
Yet prizing Bentley's, Brunck's, or Porson's
 note,
More than the verse on which the critic wrote:
Vain as their honours, heavy as their ale,
Sad as their wit, and tedious as their tale;
To friendship dead, though not untaught to
 feel
When Self and Church demand a bigot zeal.
With eager haste they court the lord of power,
Whether 'tis Pitt or Petty rules the hour;
To him, with suppliant smiles, they bend the
 head,
While distant mitres to their eyes are spread.
But should a storm o'erwhelm him with dis-
 grace,
They'd fly to seek the next who fill'd his place.

Such are the men who learning's treasures
 guard!
Such is their practice, such is their reward!
This much, at least, we may presume to say—
The premium can't exceed the price they pay.
 1806.

TO A BEAUTIFUL QUAKER.

SWEET girl! though only once we met,
That meeting I shall ne'er forget;
And though we ne'er may meet again,
Remembrance will thy form retain.
I would not say, "I love," but still
My senses struggle with my will:
In vain, to drive thee from my breast,
My thoughts are more and more represt;
In vain I check the rising sighs,
Another to the last replies:
Perhaps this is not love, but yet
Our meeting I can ne'er forget.

What though we never silence broke,
Our eyes a sweeter language spoke;
The tongue in flattering falsehood deals,
And tells a tale it never feels:
Deceit the guilty lips impart,
And hush the mandates of the heart;
But soul's interpreters, the eyes,
Spurn such restraint, and scorn disguise.
As thus our glances oft conversed,
And all our bosoms felt rehearsed,
No spirit, from within, reproved us,
Say rather, "'twas the spirit moved us."
Though what they utter'd I repress,
Yet I conceive thou'lt partly guess;
For as on thee my memory ponders,
Perchance to me thine also wanders.
This for myself, at least, I'll say,
Thy form appears through night, through
 day;
Awake, with it my fancy teems;
In sleep, it smiles in fleeting dreams;
The vision charms the hours away,
And bids me curse Aurora's ray
For breaking slumbers of delight
Which make me wish for endless night.
Since, oh! whate'er my future fate,
Shall joy or woe my steps await,
Tempted by love, by storms beset,
Thine image I can ne'er forget.

Alas! again no more we meet,
No more our former looks repeat;
Then let me breathe this parting prayer,
The dictate of my bosom's care:
"May Heaven so guard my lovely quaker,
That anguish never can o'ertake her;

That peace and virtue ne'er forsake her,
But bliss be aye her heart's partaker!
Oh! may the happy mortal, fated
To be, by dearest ties, related,
For her each hour new joys discover,
And lose the husband in the lover!
May that fair bosom never know
What 'tis to feel the restless woe
Which stings the soul, with vain regret,
Of him who never can forget!"

THE CORNELIAN.

No specious splendour of this stone
 Endears it to my memory ever;
With lustre only once it shone,
 And blushes modest as the giver.

Some, who can sneer at friendship's ties,
 Have, for my weakness, oft reproved me;
Yet still the simple gift I prize,
 For I am sure the giver loved me.

He offer'd it with downcast look,
 As fearful that I might refuse it;
I told him, when the gift I took,
 My only fear should be to lose it.

This pledge attentively I view'd,
 And sparkling as I held it near,
Methought one drop the stone bedew'd,
 And ever since I 've loved a tear.

Still, to adorn his humble youth,
 Nor wealth nor birth their treasures yield;
But he who seeks the flowers of truth
 Must quit the garden for the field.

'Tis not the plant uprear'd in sloth,
 Which beauty shows, and sheds perfume;
The flowers which yield the most of both
 In Nature's wild luxuriance bloom.

Had Fortune aided Nature's care,
 For once forgetting to be blind,
His would have been an ample share,
 If well proportion'd to his mind.

But had the goddess clearly seen,
 His form had fix'd her fickle breast;
Her countless hoards would his have been,
 And none remain'd to give the rest.

AN OCCASIONAL PROLOGUE,

DELIVERED PREVIOUS TO THE PERFORMANCE
OF "THE WHEEL OF FORTUNE" AT A
PRIVATE THEATRE.

SINCE the refinement of this polish'd age
Has swept immoral raillery from the stage;
Since taste has now expunged licentious wit,
Which stamp'd disgrace on all an author writ;

Since now to please with purer scenes we
 seek,
Nor dare to call the blush from Beauty's
 cheek;
Oh! let the modest Muse some pity claim,
And meet indulgence, though she find not
 fame.
Still, not for her alone we wish respect,
Others appear more conscious of defect
To-night no veteran Roscii you behold,
In all the arts of scenic action old;
No Cooke, no Kemble, can salute you here,
No Siddons draw the sympathetic tear;
To-night you throng to witness the *début*
Of embryo actors, to the Drama new:
Here, then, our almost unfledged wings we
 try;
Clip not our pinions ere the birds can fly:
Failing in this our first attempt to soar,
Drooping, alas! we fall to rise no more.
Not one poor trembler only fear betrays
Who hopes, yet almost dreads, to meet your
 praise,
But all our dramatis personæ wait
In fond suspense this crisis of their fate.
No venal views our progress can retard,
Your generous plaudits are our sole reward.
For these, each Hero all his power displays,
Each timid Heroine shrinks before your gaze.
Surely the last will some protection find;
None to the softer sex can prove unkind:
While Youth and Beauty form the female
 shield,
The sternest censor to the fair must yield.
Yet, should our feeble efforts nought avail,
Should, after all, our best endeavours fail,
Still let some mercy in your bosoms live,
And, if you can't applaud, at least forgive.

ON THE DEATH OF MR. FOX,

THE FOLLOWING ILLIBERAL IMPROMPTU
APPEARED IN A MORNING PAPER.

" OUR nation's foes lament on Fox's death,
But bless the hour when PITT resign'd his
 breath:
These feelings wide, let sense and truth
 unclue,
We give the palm where Justice points its
 due."

TO WHICH THE AUTHOR OF THESE PIECES
SENT THE FOLLOWING REPLY.

OH factious viper! whose envenom'd tooth
Would mangle still the dead, perverting
 truth;
What though our "nation's foes" lament the
 fate,
With generous feeling, of the good and great.

Shall dastard tongues essay to blast the name
Of him whose meed exists in endless fame?
When PITT expired in plenitude of power,
Though ill success obscured his dying hour,
Pity her dewy wings before him spread,
For noble spirits "war not with the dead:"
His friends, in tears, a last sad requiem gave,
As all his errors slumber'd in the grave;
He sunk, an Atlas bending 'neath the weight
Of cares o'erwhelming our conflicting state:
When, lo! a Hercules in Fox appear'd,
Who for a time the ruin'd fabric rear'd:
He, too, is fall'n, who Britain's loss supplied,
With him our fast reviving hopes have died;
Not one great people only raise his urn,
All Europe's far-extended regions mourn.
"These feelings wide, let sense and truth unclue,
To give the palm where Justice points its due;"
Yet let not canker'd Calumny assail,
Or round our statesman wind her gloomy veil.
Fox! o'er whose corse a mourning world must weep,
Whose dear remains in honour'd marble sleep;
For whom, at last, e'en hostile nations groan,
While friends and foes alike his talents own;
Fox shall in Britain's future annals shine,
Nor e'en to PITT the patriot's palm resign;
Which Envy, wearing Candour's sacred mask,
For PITT, and PITT alone, has dared to ask.

THE TEAR.

*O lachrymarum fons, tenero sacros
 Ducentium ortus ex animo; quater
 Felix! in imo qui scatentem
 Pectore te, pia Nympha, sensit."—GRAY.

WHEN Friendship or Love our sympathies move,
 When Truth in a glance should appear,
The lips may beguile with a dimple or smile,
 But the test of affection's a Tear.

Too oft is a smile but the hypocrite's wile,
 To mask detestation or fear;
Give me the soft sigh, whilst the soul-telling eye
 Is dimm'd for a time with a Tear.

Mild Charity's glow, to us mortals below,
 Shows the soul from barbarity clear;
Compassion will melt where this virtue is felt,
 And its dew is diffused in a Tear.

The man doom'd to sail with the blast of the gale,
 Through billows Atlantic to steer,
As he bends o'er the wave which may soon be his grave,
 The green sparkles bright with a Tear.

The soldier braves death for a fanciful wreath
 In Glory's romantic career;
But he raises the foe when in battle laid low,
 And bathes every wound with a Tear.

If with high-bounding pride he return to his bride,
 Renouncing the gore-crimson'd spear,
All his toils are repaid when, embracing the maid,
 From her eyelid he kisses the Tear.

Sweet scene of my youth! seat of Friendship and Truth,
 Where love chased each fast-fleeting year,
Loth to leave thee, I mourn'd, for a last look I turn'd,
 But thy spire was scarce seen through a Tear.

Though my vows I can pour to my Mary no more,
 My Mary to Love once so dear,
In the shade of her bower I remember the hour
 She rewarded those vows with a Tear.

By another possest, may she live ever blest
 Her name still my heart must revere:
With a sigh I resign what I once thought was mine,
 And forgive her deceit with a Tear.

Ye friends of my heart, ere from you I depart,
 This hope to my breast is most near:
If again we shall meet in this rural retreat,
 May we meet, as we part, with a Tear.

When my soul wings her flight to the regions of night,
 And my corse shall recline on its bier,
As ye pass by the tomb where my ashes consume,
 Oh! moisten their dust with a Tear.

May no marble bestow the splendour of woe
 Which the children of vanity rear;
No fiction of fame shall blazon my name,
 All I ask—all I wish—is a Tear.

October 26, 1806.

REPLY TO SOME VERSES OF J. M. B. PIGOT, ESQ., ON THE CRUELTY OF HIS MISTRESS.

WHY, Pigot, complain of this damsel's dis-
 dain,
 Why thus in despair do you fret?
For months you may try, yet, believe me, a
 sigh
 Will never obtain a coquette.

Would you teach her to love? for a time
 seem to rove;
 At first she may frown in a pet;
But leave her awhile, she shortly will smile,
 And then you may kiss your coquette.

For such are the airs of these fanciful fairs,
 They think all our homage a debt:
Yet a partial neglect soon takes an effect,
 And humbles the proudest coquette.

Dissemble your pain, and lengthen your
 chain,
 And seem her hauteur to regret;
If again you shall sigh, she no more will deny,
 That yours is the rosy coquette.

If still, from false pride, your pangs she
 deride,
 This whimsical virgin forget;
Some other admire, who will melt with your
 fire,
 And laugh at the little coquette.

For me, I adore some twenty or more,
 And love them most dearly; but yet,
Though my heart they enthral, I'd abandon
 them all,
 Did they act like your blooming coquette.

No longer repine, adopt this design,
 And break through her slight-woven net;
Away with despair, no longer forbear
 To fly from the captious coquette.

Then quit her, my friend! your bosom defend,
 Ere quite with her snares you're beset:
Lest your deep-wounded heart, when incensed
 by the smart,
 Should lead you to curse the coquette.
 October 27, 1806.

—————

TO THE SIGHING STREPHON.

YOUR pardon, my friend, if my rhymes did
 offend;
 Your pardon, a thousand times o'er:
From friendship I strove your pangs to re-
 move,
 But I swear I will do so no more.

Since your beautiful maid your flame has
 repaid,
 No more I your folly regret;
She's now most divine, and I bow at the
 shrine
 Of this quickly reformed coquette.

Yet still, I must own, I should never have
 known
 From your verses what else she deserved;
Your pain seem'd so great, I pitied your
 fate,
 As your fair was so devilish reserved.

Since the balm-breathing kiss of this magical
 miss
 Can such wonderful transports produce;
Since the "world you forget, when your lips
 once have met,"
 My counsel will get but abuse.

You say, when "I rove, I know nothing of
 love;"
 'Tis true, I am given to range;
If I rightly remember, I've loved a good
 number,
 Yet there's pleasure, at least, in a change.

I will not advance, by the rules of romance,
 To humour a whimsical fair;
Though a smile may delight, yet a frown
 won't affright,
 Or drive me to dreadful despair.

While my blood is thus warm I ne'er shall
 reform,
 To mix in the Platonists' school;
Of this I am sure, was my passion so pure,
 Thy mistress would think me a fool.

And if I should shun every woman for one,
 Whose image must fill my whole breast—
Whom I must prefer, and sigh but for her—
 What an insult 'twould be to the rest!

Now, Strephon, good bye, I cannot deny
 Your passion appears most absurd;
Such love as you plead is pure love indeed,
 For it only consists in the word.

—————

TO ELIZA.

ELIZA, what fools are the Mussulman sect,
 Who to woman deny the soul's future
 existence!
Could they see thee, Eliza, they'd own their
 defect,
 And this doctrine would meet with a general
 resistance.

Had their prophet possess'd half an atom of
 sense,
He ne'er would have women from paradise
 driven;
Instead of his houris, a flimsy pretence,
 With women alone he had peopled his
 heaven.

Yet still, to increase your calamities more,
 Not content with depriving your bodies of
 spirit,
He allots one poor husband to share amongst
 four!—
 With souls you'd dispense; but this last,
 who could bear it?

His religion to please neither party is made;
 On husbands 'tis hard, to the wives most
 uncivil;
Still I can't contradict, what so oft has been
 said,
 "Though women are angels, yet wedlock's
 the devil."

—————

LACHIN Y GAIR.

AWAY, ye gay landscapes, ye gardens of roses!
 In you let the minions of luxury rove;
Restore me the rocks, where the snow-flake
 reposes,
 Though still they are sacred to freedom
 and love:
Yet, Caledonia, beloved are thy mountains,
 Round their white summits though elements
 war;
Though cataracts foam 'stead of smooth-
 flowing fountains,
I sigh for the valley of dark Loch na Garr.

Ah! there my young footsteps in infancy
 wander'd;
 My cap was the bonnet, my cloak was the
 plaid;
On chieftains long perish'd my memory
 ponder'd,
 As daily I strode through the pine-cover'd
 glade;
I sought not my home till the day's dying glory
 Gave place to the rays of the bright polar
 star;
For fancy was cheer'd by traditional story,
 Disclosed by the natives of dark Loch na
 Garr.

"Shades of the dead! have I not heard your
 voices
 Rise on the night-rolling breath of the
 gale?"
Surely the soul of the hero rejoices,
 And rides on the wind, o'er his own High-
 land vale.

Round Loch na Garr while the stormy mist
 gathers,
 Winter presides in his cold icy car:
Clouds there encircle the forms of my fathers;
 They dwell in the tempests of dark Loch
 na Garr.

"Ill-starr'd, though brave, did no visions
 foreboding
Tell you that fate had forsaken your cause?"
Ah! were you destined to die at Culloden,
 Victory crown'd not your fall with applause:
Still were you happy in death's earthly
 slumber,
 You rest with your clan in the caves of
 Braemar;
The pibroch resounds, to the piper's loud
 number,
 Your deeds on the echoes of dark Loch na
 Garr.

Years have roll'd on, Loch na Garr, since
 I left you,
 Years must elapse ere I tread you again:
Nature of verdure and flow'rs has bereft you,
 Yet still are you dearer than Albion's plain.
England! thy beauties are tame and domestic
 To one who has roved o'er the mountains
 afar:
Oh for the crags that are wild and majestic!
 The steep frowning glories of dark Loch na
 Garr.

—————

TO ROMANCE.

PARENT of golden dreams, Romance!
 Auspicious queen of childish joys,
Who lead'st along, in airy dance,
 Thy votive train of girls and boys;
At length, in spells no longer bound,
 I break the fetters of my youth;
No more I tread thy mystic round,
 But leave thy realms for those of Truth.

And yet 'tis hard to quit the dreams
 Which haunt the unsuspicious soul,
Where every nymph a goddess seems,
 Whose eyes through rays immortal roll;
While Fancy holds her boundless reign,
 And all assume a varied hue;
When virgins seem no longer vain,
 And even woman's smiles are true.

And must we own thee but a name,
 And from thy hall of clouds descend?
Nor find a sylph in every dame,
 A Pylades in every friend?
But leave at once thy realms of air
 To mingling bands of fairy elves;
Confess that woman's false as fair,
 And friends have feeling for—themselves!

With shame I own I've felt thy sway;
 Repentant, now thy reign is o'er,
No more thy precepts I obey,
 No more on fancied pinions soar.
Fond fool! to love a sparkling eye,
 And think that eye to truth was dear;
To trust a passing wanton's sigh,
 And melt beneath a wanton's tear!

Romance! disgusted with deceit,
 Far from thy motley court I fly,
Where Affectation holds her seat,
 And sickly Sensibility;
Whose silly tears can never flow
 For any pangs excepting thine;
Who turns aside from real woe,
 To steep in dew thy gaudy shrine.

Now join with sable Sympathy,
 With cypress crown'd, array'd in weeds,
Who heaves with thee her simple sigh,
 Whose breast for every bosom bleeds;
And call thy sylvan female choir,
 To mourn a swain for ever gone,
Who once could glow with equal fire,
 But bends not now before thy throne.

Ye genial nymphs, whose ready tears
 On all occasions swiftly flow;
Whose bosoms heave with fancied fears,
 With fancied flames and phrensy glow;
Say, will you mourn my absent name,
 Apostate from your gentle train?
An infant bard at least may claim
 From you a sympathetic strain.

Adieu, fond race! a long adieu!
 The hour of fate is hovering nigh,
E'en now the gulf appears in view,
 Where unlamented you must lie:
Oblivion's blackening lake is seen,
 Convulsed by gales you cannot weather;
Where you, and eke your gentle queen,
 Alas! must perish altogether.

**ANSWER TO SOME ELEGANT VERSES
SENT BY A FRIEND TO THE AUTHOR,
COMPLAINING THAT ONE OF HIS
DESCRIPTIONS WAS RATHER TOO
WARMLY DRAWN.**

"But if any old lady, knight, priest, or physician,
Should condemn me for printing a second edition;
If good Madam Squintum my work should abuse,
May I venture to give her a smack of my muse?"
 New Bath Guide.

CANDOUR compels me, BECHER! to commend
The verse which blends the censor with the
 friend.
Your strong yet just reproof extorts applause
From me, the heedless and imprudent cause.

For this wild error which pervades my strain,
I sue for pardon,—must I sue in vain?
The wise sometimes from Wisdom's ways
 depart:
Can youth then hush the dictates of the heart?
Precepts of prudence curb, but can't control,
The fierce emotions of the flowing soul.
When Love's delirium haunts the glowing
 mind,
Limping Decorum lingers far behind:
Vainly the dotard mends her prudish pace,
Outstript and vanquish'd in the mental chase.
The young, the old, have worn the chains of
 love:
Let those they ne'er confined my lay reprove:
Let those whose souls contemn the pleasing
 power
Their censures on the hapless victim shower.
Oh! how I hate the nerveless, frigid song,
The ceaseless echo of the rhyming throng,
Whose labour'd lines in chilling numbers flow,
To paint a pang the author ne'er can know!
The artless Helicon I boast is youth;—
My lyre, the heart; my muse, the simple truth.
Far be't from me the "virgin's mind" to
 "taint:"
Seduction's dread is here no slight restraint.
The maid whose virgin breast is void of guile,
Whose wishes dimple in a modest smile,
Whose downcast eye disdains the wanton leer,
Firm in her virtue's strength, yet not severe—
She whom a conscious grace shall thus refine
Will ne'er be "tainted" by a strain of mine.
But for the nymph whose premature desires
Torment her bosom with unholy fires,
No net to snare her willing heart is spread;
She would have fallen, though she ne'er had
 read.
For me, I fain would please the chosen few,
Whose souls, to feeling and to nature true,
Will spare the childish verse, and not destroy
The light effusions of a heedless boy.
I seek not glory from the senseless crowd;
Of fancied laurels I shall ne'er be proud;
Their warmest plaudits I would scarcely prize,
Their sneers or censures I alike despise.
 November 26, 1806.

ELEGY ON NEWSTEAD ABBEY.

"It is the voice of years that are gone! they roll
before me with all their deeds."—OSSIAN.

NEWSTEAD! fast-falling, once-resplendent
 dome!
 Religion's shrine! repentant HENRY's pride!
Of warriors, monks, and dames the cloister'd
 tomb,
 Whose pensive shades around thy ruins
 glide,

Hail to thy pile! more honour'd in thy fall
　　Than modern mansions in their pillar'd state;
Proudly majestic frowns thy vaulted hall,
　　Scowling defiance on the blasts of fate.

No mail-clad serfs, obedient to their lord,
　　In grim array the crimson cross demand;
Or gay assemble round the festive board
　　Their chief's retainers, an immortal band:

Else might inspiring Fancy's magic eye
　　Retrace their progress through the lapse of
　　　　time,
Marking each ardent youth, ordain'd to die,
　　A votive pilgrim in Judea's clime.

But not from thee, dark pile! departs the
　　　　chief;
　　His feudal realm in other regions lay:
In thee the wounded conscience courts relief,
　　Retiring from the garish blaze of day.

Yes! in thy gloomy cells and shades profound
　　The monk abjured a world he ne'er could
　　　　view;
Or blood-stain'd guilt repenting solace found,
　　Or innocence from stern oppression flew.

A monarch bade thee from that wild arise,
　　Where Sherwood's outlaws once were wont
　　　　to prowl;
And Superstition's crimes, of various dyes,
　　Sought shelter in the priest's protecting cowl.

Where now the grass exhales a murky dew,
　　The humid pall of life-extinguish'd clay,
In sainted fame the sacred fathers grew,
　　Nor raised their pious voices but to pray.

Where now the bats their wavering wings
　　　　extend
　　Soon as the gloaming spreads her waning
　　　　shade,
The choir did oft their mingling vespers blend,
　　Or matin orisons to Mary paid.

Years roll on years; to ages, ages yield;
　　Abbots to abbots, in a line, succeed;
Religion's charter their protecting shield,
　　Till royal sacrilege their doom decreed.

One holy HENRY rear'd the Gothic walls,
　　And bade the pious inmates rest in peace;
Another HENRY the kind gift recalls,
　　And bids devotion's hallow'd echoes cease.

Vain is each threat or supplicating prayer;
　　He drives them exiles from their blest abode,
To roam a dreary world in deep despair—
　　No friend, no home, no refuge, but their God.

Hark how the hall, resounding to the strain,
　　Shakes with the martial music's novel din!
The heralds of a warrior's haughty reign,
　　High crested banners wave thy walls within.

Of changing sentinels the distant hum,
　　The mirth of feasts, the clang of burnish'd
　　　　arms,
The braying trumpet and the hoarser drum,
　　Unite in concert with increased alarms.

An abbey once, a regal fortress now,
　　Encircled by insulting rebel powers,
War's dread machines o'erhang thy threat'ning
　　　　brow,
　　And dart destruction in sulphureous showers.

Ah vain defence! the hostile traitor's siege,
　　Though oft repulsed, by guile o'ercomes
　　　　the brave;
His thronging foes oppress the faithful liege,
　　Rebellion's reeking standards o'er him wave.

Not unavenged the raging baron yields;
　　The blood of traitors smears the purple
　　　　plain;
Unconquer'd still, his falchion there he wields,
　　And days of glory yet for him remain.

Still in that hour the warrior wish'd to strew
　　Self-gather'd laurels on a self-sought grave;
But Charles' protecting genius hither flew,
　　The monarch's friend, the monarch's hope,
　　　　to save.

Trembling, she snatch'd him from th' unequal
　　　　strife,
　　In other fields the torrent to repel;
For nobler combats, here, reserved his life,
　　To lead the band where godlike FALKLAND
　　　　fell.

From thee, poor pile! to lawless plunder given,
　　While dying groans their painful requiem
　　　　sound,
Far different incense now ascends to heaven,
　　Such victims wallow on the gory ground.

There many a pale and ruthless robber's corse,
　　Noisome and ghast, defiles thy sacred sod;
O'er mingling man, and horse commix'd with
　　　　horse,
　　Corruption's heap, the savage spoilers trod.

Graves, long with rank and sighing weeds
　　　　o'erspread,
　　Ransack'd, resign perforce their mortal
　　　　mould:
From ruffian fangs escape not e'en the dead,
　　Raked from repose in search of buried gold.

Hush'd is the harp, unstrung the warlike lyre,
　　The minstrel's palsied hand reclines in
　　　　death;
No more he strikes the quivering chords with
　　　　fire,
　　Or sings the glories of the martial wreath.

At length the sated murderers, gorged with
 prey,
Retire : the clamour of the fight is o'er ;
Silence again resumes her awful sway,
 And sable Horror guards the massy door.

Here Desolation holds her dreary court :
 What satellites declare her dismal reign !
Shrieking their dirge, ill-omen'd birds resort,
 To flit their vigils in the hoary fane.

Soon a new morn's restoring beams dispel
 The clouds of anarchy from Britain's skies ;
The fierce usurper seeks his native hell,
 And Nature triumphs as the tyrant dies.

With storms she welcomes his expiring groans ;
 Whirlwinds, responsive, greet his labouring
 breath ;
Earth shudders as her caves receive his bones,
 Loathing the offering of so dark a death.

The legal ruler now resumes the helm,
 He guides through gentle seas the prow of
 state ;
Hope cheers, with wonted smiles, the peace-
 ful realm,
 And heals the bleeding wounds of wearied
 hate.

The gloomy tenants, Newstead ! of thy cells,
 Howling, resign their violated nest ;
Again the master on his tenure dwells,
 Enjoy'd, from absence, with enraptured zest.

Vassals, within thy hospitable pale,
 Loudly carousing, bless their lord's return ;
Culture again adorns the gladdening vale,
 And matrons, once lamenting, cease to
 mourn.

A thousand songs on tuneful echo float,
 Unwonted foliage mantles o'er the trees ;
And hark ! the horns proclaim a mellow note,
 The hunters' cry hangs lengthening on the
 breeze.

Beneath their coursers' hoofs the valleys shake :
 What fears, what anxious hopes, attend the
 chase !
The dying stag seeks refuge in the lake ;
 Exulting shouts announce the finish'd race.

Ah happy days ! too happy to endure !
 Such simple sports our plain forefathers
 knew :
No splendid vices glitter'd to allure ;
 Their joys were many, as their cares were
 few.

From these descending, sons to sires succeed ;
 Time steals along, and Death uprears his
 dart ;
Another chief impels the foaming steed,
 Another crowd pursue the panting hart.

Newstead ! what saddening change of scene
 is thine !
Thy yawning arch betokens slow decay ;
The last and youngest of a noble line
 Now holds thy mouldering turrets in his
 sway.

Deserted now, he scans thy gray worn
 towers ;
Thy vaults, where dead of feudal ages
 sleep ;
Thy cloisters, pervious to the wintry showers ;
 These, these he views, and views them but
 to weep.

Yet are his tears no emblem of regret :
 Cherish'd affection only bids them flow.
Pride, hope, and love forbid him to forget,
 But warm his bosom with impassion'd glow.

Yet he prefers thee to the gilded domes
 Or gewgaw grottos of the vainly great,
Yet lingers 'mid thy damp and mossy tombs,
 Nor breathes a murmur 'gainst the will of
 fate.

Haply thy sun, emerging, yet may shine,
 Thee to irradiate with meridian ray ;
Hours splendid as the past may still be thine,
 And bless thy future as thy former day.

CHILDISH RECOLLECTIONS.

"I cannot but remember such things were,
 And were most dear to me."

WHEN slow Disease, with all her host of pains,
Chills the warm tide which flows along the
 veins ;
When Health, affrighted, spreads her rosy
 wing,
And flies with every changing gale of spring ;
Not to the aching frame alone confined,
Unyielding pangs assail the drooping mind :
What grisly forms, the spectre-train of woe,
Bid shuddering Nature shrink beneath the
 blow,
With Resignation wage relentless strife,
While Hope retires appall'd, and clings to life !
Yet less the pang when, through the tedious
 hour,
Remembrance sheds around her genial power,
Calls back the vanish'd days to rapture given,
When love was bliss, and Beauty form'd our
 heaven ;
Or, dear to youth, portrays each childish scene,
Those fairy bowers, where all in turn have been.
As when through clouds that pour the summer
 storm
The orb of day unveils his distant form,
Gilds with faint beams the crystal dews of rain,
And dimly twinkles o'er the watery plain ;

Thus, while the future dark and cheerless gleams,
The sun of memory, glowing through my dreams,
Though sunk the radiance of his former blaze,
To scenes far distant points his paler rays;
Still rules my senses with unbounded sway,
The past confounding with the present day.

Oft does my heart indulge the rising thought,
Which still recurs, unlook'd for and unsought;
My soul to Fancy's fond suggestion yields,
And roams romantic o'er her airy fields.
Scenes of my youth, developed, crowd to view,
To which I long have bade a last adieu!
Seats of delight, inspiring youthful themes;
Friends lost to me for aye, except in dreams;
Some who in marble prematurely sleep,
Whose forms I now remember but to weep;
Some who yet urge the same scholastic course
Of early science, future fame the source;
Who, still contending in the studious race,
In quick rotation fill the senior place.
These with a thousand visions now unite,
To dazzle, though they please, my aching sight.
IDA! blest spot, where Science holds her reign,
How joyous once I join'd thy youthful train!
Bright in idea gleams thy lofty spire,
Again I mingle with thy playful quire;
Our tricks of mischief, every childish game,
Unchanged by time or distance, seem the same;
Through winding paths along the glade, I trace
The social smile of every welcome face;
My wonted haunts, my scenes of joy and woe,
Each early boyish friend, or youthful foe,
Our feuds dissolved, but not my friendship past,—
I bless the former, and forgive the last.
Hours of my youth! when, nurtured in my breast,
To love a stranger, friendship made me blest,—
Friendship, the dear peculiar bond of youth,
When every artless bosom throbs with truth;
Untaught by worldly wisdom how to feign,
And check each impulse with prudential rein;
When all we feel, our honest souls disclose—
In love to friends, in open hate to foes;
No varnish'd tales the lips of youth repeat,
No dear-bought knowledge purchased by deceit,
Hypocrisy, the gift of lengthen'd years,
Matured by age, the garb of prudence wears.
When now the boy is ripen'd into man,
His careful sire chalks forth some wary plan;
Instructs his son from candour's path to shrink,
Smoothly to speak, and cautiously to think;
Still to assent, and never to deny—
A patron's praise can well reward the lie:

And who, when Fortune's warning voice is heard,
Would lose his opening prospects for a word?
Although against that word his heart rebel,
And truth indignant all his bosom swell.

Away with themes like this! not mine the task
From flattering friends to tear the hateful mask;
Let keener bards delight in satire's sting;
My fancy soars not on Detraction's wing:
Once, and but once, she aim'd a deadly blow,
To hurl defiance on a secret foe;
But when that foe, from feeling or from shame,
The cause unknown, yet still to me the same,
Warn'd by some friendly hint, perchance, retired,
With this submission all her rage expired.
From dreaded pangs that feeble foe to save,
She hush'd her young resentment, and forgave;
Or, if my muse a pedant's portrait drew,
POMPOSUS' virtues are but known to few:
I never fear'd the young usurper's nod,
And he who wields must sometimes feel the rod.
If since on Granta's failings, known to all
Who share the converse of a college hall,
She sometimes trifled in a lighter strain,
'Tis past, and thus she will not sin again;
Soon must her early song for ever cease,
And all may rail when I shall rest in peace.

Here first remember'd be the joyous band,
Who hail'd me chief, obedient to command;
Who join'd with me in every boyish sport—
Their first adviser, and their last resort;
Nor shrunk beneath the upstart pedant's frown,
Or all the sable glories of his gown;
Who, thus transplanted from his father's school—
Unfit to govern, ignorant of rule—
Succeeded him, whom all unite to praise,
The dear preceptor of my early days!
PROBUS, the pride of science, and the boast,
To IDA now, alas! for ever lost,
With him, for years, we search'd the classic page,
And fear'd the master, though we loved the sage:
Retired at last, his small yet peaceful seat
From learning's labour is the blest retreat.
POMPOSUS fills his magisterial chair;
POMPOSUS governs,—but, my muse, forbear:
Contempt, in silence, be the pedant's lot;
His name and precepts be alike forgot;

No more his mention shall my verse de-
 grade,—
To him my tribute is already paid.

 High through those elms, with hoary
 branches crown'd,
Fair IDA'S bower adorns the landscape
 round;
There Science, from her favour'd seat,
 surveys
The vale where rural Nature claims her
 praise;
To her awhile resigns her youthful train,
Who move in joy, and dance along the plain;
In scatter'd groups each favour'd haunt
 pursue,
Repeat old pastimes, and discover new;
Flush'd with his rays, beneath the noontide
 sun,
In rival bands, between the wickets run,
Drive o'er the sward the ball with active
 force,
Or chase with nimble feet its rapid course.
But these with slower steps direct their way,
Where Brent's cool waves in limpid currents
 stray;
While yonder few search out some green
 retreat
And arbours shade them from the summer
 heat:
Others, again, a pert and lively crew,
Some rough and thoughtless stranger placed
 in view,
With frolic quaint their antic jests expose,
And tease the grumbling rustic as he goes;
Nor rest with this, but many a passing
 fray
Tradition treasures for a future day:
" 'Twas here the gather'd swains for
 vengeance fought,
And here we earn'd the conquest dearly
 bought;
Here have we fled before superior might,
And here renew'd the wild tumultuous fight."
While thus our souls with early passions
 swell,
In lingering tones resounds the distant bell,
Th' allotted hour of daily sport is o'er,
And Learning beckons from her temple's
 door.
No splendid tablets grace her simple hall,
But ruder records fill the dusky wall;
There, deeply carved, behold! each tyro's
 name
Secures its owner's academic fame;
Here mingling view the names of sire and
 son—
The one long graved, the other just begun:
These shall survive alike when son and sire
Beneath one common stroke of fate expire;

Perhaps their last memorial these alone,
Denied in death a monumental stone,
Whilst to the gale in mournful cadence wave
The sighing weeds that hide their nameless
 grave.
And here my name, and many an early
 friend's,
Along the wall in lengthen'd line extends.
Though still our deeds amuse the youthful
 race,
Who tread our steps, and fill our former
 place,
Who young obey'd their lords in silent
 awe,
Whose nod commanded, and whose voice was
 law;
And now, in turn, possess the reins of power,
To rule the little tyrants of an hour;
Though sometimes, with the tales of ancient
 day,
They pass the dreary winter's eve away—
" And thus our former rulers stemm'd the
 tide,
And thus they dealt the combat side by side;
Just in this place the mouldering walls they
 scaled,
Nor bolts nor bars against their strength
 avail'd;
Here PROBUS came, the rising fray to quell,
And here he falter'd forth his last farewell;
And here one night abroad they dared to
 roam,
While bold POMPOSUS bravely stay'd at
 home;"
While thus they speak, the hour must soon
 arrive,
When names of these, like ours, alone
 survive:
Yet a few years, one general wreck will
 whelm
The faint remembrance of our fairy realm.

 Dear honest race! though now we meet no
 more,
One last long look on what we were before—
Our first kind greetings, and our last adieu—
Drew tears from eyes unused to weep with
 you.
Through splendid circles, fashion's gaudy
 world,
Where folly's glaring standard waves un-
 furl'd,
I plunged to drown in noise my fond regret,
And all I sought or hoped was to forget.
Vain wish! if chance some well-remember'd
 face,
Some old companion of my early race,
Advanced to claim his friend with honest
 joy,
My eyes, my heart, proclaim'd me still a boy;

The glittering scene, the fluttering groups
 around,
Were quite forgotten when my friend was
 found;
The smiles of beauty — (for, alas! I've
 known
What 't is to bend before Love's mighty
 throne)—
The smiles of beauty, though those smiles
 were dear,
Could hardly charm me, when that friend
 was near;
My thoughts bewilder'd in the fond surprise,
The woods of IDA danced before my eyes;
I saw the sprightly wand'rers pour along,
I saw and join'd again the joyous throng;
Panting, again I traced her lofty grove,
And friendship's feelings triumph'd over love.

Yet why should I alone with such delight
Retrace the circuit of my former flight?
Is there no cause beyond the common claim
Endear'd to all in childhood's very name?
Ah! sure some stronger impulse vibrates
 here,
Which whispers friendship will be doubly
 dear
To one who thus for kindred hearts must
 roam,
And seek abroad the love denied at home.
Those hearts, dear IDA, have I found in
 thee—
A home, a world, a paradise to me.
Stern Death forbade my orphan youth to
 share
The tender guidance of a father's care.
Can rank, or e'en a guardian's name supply
The love which glistens in a father's eye?
For this can wealth or title's sound atone,
Made, by a parent's early loss, my own?
What brother springs a brother's love to
 seek?
What sister's gentle kiss has prest my cheek?
For me how dull the vacant moments rise,
To no fond bosom link'd by kindred ties!
Oft in the progress of some fleeting dream
Fraternal smiles collected round me seem;
While still the visions to my heart are prest,
The voice of love will murmur in my rest:
I hear—I wake—and in the sound rejoice;
I hear again,—but, ah! no brother's voice.
A hermit, 'midst of crowds, I fain must stray
Alone, though thousand pilgrims fill the way;
While these a thousand kindred wreaths
 entwine,
I cannot call one single blossom mine:
What then remains? in solitude to groan,
To mix in friendship, or to sigh alone.
Thus must I cling to some endearing hand,
And none more dear than IDA's social band.

Alonzo! best and dearest of my friends,
Thy name ennobles him who thus commends;
From this fond tribute thou canst gain no
 praise;
The praise is his who now that tribute pays.
Oh! in the promise of thy early youth,
If hope anticipate the words of truth,
Some loftier bard shall sing thy glorious
 name,
To build his own upon thy deathless fame.
Friend of my heart, and foremost of the list
Of those with whom I lived supremely blest,
Oft have we drain'd the font of ancient lore;
Though drinking deeply, thirsting still the
 more.
Yet, when confinement's lingering hour was
 done,
Our sports, our studies, and our souls were
 one:
Together we impell'd the flying ball;
Together waited in our tutor's hall;
Together join'd in cricket's manly toil,
Or shared the produce of the river's spoil;
Or, plunging from the green declining shore,
Our pliant limbs the buoyant billows bore;
In every element, unchanged, the same,
All, all that brothers should be, but the name.

Nor yet are you forgot, my jocund boy!
DAVUS, the harbinger of childish joy;
For ever foremost in the ranks of fun,
The laughing herald of the harmless pun;
Yet with a breast of such materials made—
Anxious to please, of pleasing half afraid;
Candid and liberal, with a heart of steel
In danger's path, though not untaught to
 feel.
Still I remember, in the factious strife,
The rustic's musket aim'd against my life:
High pois'd in air the massy weapon hung,
A cry of horror burst from every tongue;
Whilst I, in combat with another foe,
Fought on, unconscious of th' impending
 blow;
Your arm, brave boy, arrested his career—
Forward you sprung, insensible to fear;
Disarm'd and baffled by your conquering
 hand,
The grovelling savage roll'd upon the sand:
An act like this, can simple thanks repay?
Or all the labours of a grateful lay?
Oh no! whene'er my breast forgets the deed,
That instant, DAVUS, it deserves to bleed.

LYCUS! on me thy claims are justly great:
Thy milder virtues could my muse relate,
To thee alone, unrivall'd, would belong
The feeble efforts of my lengthen'd song.
Well canst thou boast, to lead in senates fit,
A Spartan firmness with Athenian wit:

Though yet in embryo these perfections shine,
Lycus! thy father's fame will soon be thine.
Where learning nurtures the superior mind,
What may we hope from genius thus refined!
When time at length matures thy growing
 years,
How wilt thou tower above thy fellow peers!
Prudence and sense, a spirit bold and free,
With honour's soul, united beam in thee.

Shall fair Euryalus pass by unsung?
From ancient lineage, not unworthy sprung:
What though one sad dissension bade us part?
That name is yet embalm'd within my heart;
Yet at the mention does that heart rebound,
And palpitate, responsive to the sound.
Envy dissolved our ties, and not our will:
We once were friends,—I'll think we are so
 still.
A form unmatch'd in nature's partial mould,
A heart untainted, we in thee behold:
Yet not the senate's thunder thou shalt wield,
Nor seek for glory in the tented field;
To minds of ruder texture these be given—
Thy soul shall nearer soar its native heaven.
Haply, in polish'd courts might be thy seat,
But that thy tongue could never forge deceit:
The courtier's supple bow and sneering smile,
The flow of compliment, the slippery wile,
Would make that breast with indignation burn,
And all the glittering snares to tempt thee
 spurn.
Domestic happiness will stamp thy fate;
Sacred to love, unclouded e'er by hate;
The world admire thee, and thy friends
 adore;
Ambition's slave alone would toil for more.

Now last, but nearest of the social band,
See honest, open, generous Cleon stand;
With scarce one speck to cloud the pleasing
 scene,
No vice degrades that purest soul serene.
On the same day our studious race begun,
On the same day our studious race was run;
Thus side by side we pass'd our first career,
Thus side by side we strove for many a year;
At last concluded our scholastic life,
We neither conquer'd in the classic strife:
As speakers each supports an equal name,
And crowds allow to both a partial fame:
To soothe a youthful rival's early pride,
Though Cleon's candour would the palm di-
 vide,
Yet candour's self compels me now to own
Justice awards it to my friend alone.

Oh! friends regretted, scenes for ever dear,
Remembrance hails you with her warmest
 tear!

Drooping, she bends o'er pensive Fancy's
 urn,
To trace the hours which never can return;
Yet with the retrospection loves to dwell,
And soothe the sorrows of her last farewell!
Yet greets the triumph of my boyish mind,
As infant laurels round my head were twined,
When Probus' praise repaid my lyric song,
Or placed me higher in the studious throng;
Or when my first harangue received applause,
His sage instruction the primeval cause,
What gratitude to him my soul possest,
While hope of dawning honours fill'd my
 breast!
For all my humble fame, to him alone
The praise is due, who made that fame my
 own.
Oh! could I soar above these feeble lays,
These young effusions of my early days,
To him my muse her noblest strain would
 give:
The song might perish, but the theme might
 live.
Yet why for him the needless verse essay?
His honour'd name requires no vain display:
By every son of grateful Ida blest,
It finds an echo in each youthful breast;
A fame beyond the glories of the proud,
Or all the plaudits of the venal crowd.

Ida! not yet exhausted is the theme,
Nor closed the progress of my youthful dream.
How many a friend deserves the grateful
 strain!
What scenes of childhood still unsung re-
 main!
Yet let me hush this echo of the past,
This parting song, the dearest and the last;
And brood in secret o'er those hours of joy,
To me a silent and a sweet employ,
While future hope and fear alike unknown,
I think with pleasure on the past alone;
Yes, to the past alone my heart confine,
And chase the phantom of what once was
 mine.

Ida! still o'er thy hills in joy preside,
And proudly steer through time's eventful
 tide;
Still may thy blooming sons thy name revere,
Smile in thy bower, but quit thee with a
 tear,—
That tear, perhaps, the fondest which will
 flow,
O'er their last scene of happiness below.
Tell me, ye hoary few, who glide along,
The feeble veterans of some former throng,
Whose friends, like autumn leaves by tem-
 pests whirl'd,
Are swept for ever from this busy world;

Revolve the fleeting moments of your youth,
While Care has yet withheld her venom'd
 tooth;
Say if remembrance days like these endears
Beyond the rapture of succeeding years?
Say, can ambition's fever'd dream bestow
So sweet a balm to soothe your hours of woe?
Can treasures, hoarded for some thankless
 son,
Can royal smiles, or wreaths by slaughter
 won,
Can stars or ermine, man's maturer toys
(For glittering baubles are not left to boys),
Recall one scene so much beloved to view,
As those where Youth her garland twined for
 you?
Ah, no! amidst the gloomy calm of age
You turn with faltering hand life's varied
 page;
Peruse the record of your days on earth,
Unsullied only where it marks your birth;
Still lingering pause above each chequer'd
 leaf,
And blot with tears the sable lines of grief;
Where Passion o'er the theme her mantle
 threw,
Or weeping Virtue sigh'd a faint adieu;
But bless the scroll which fairer words adorn,
Traced by the rosy finger of the morn;
When Friendship bow'd before the shrine of
 Truth,
And Love, without his pinion, smiled on
 Youth.

ANSWER TO A BEAUTIFUL POEM,

ENTITLED "THE COMMON LOT."

MONTGOMERY! true, the common lot
 Of mortals lies in Lethe's wave;
Yet some shall never be forgot,
 Some shall exist beyond the grave.

"Unknown the region of his birth,"
 The hero rolls the tide of war;
Yet not unknown his martial worth,
 Which glares a meteor from afar.

His joy or grief, his weal or woe,
 Perchance may 'scape the page of fame;
Yet nations now unborn will know
 The record of his deathless name.

The patriot's and the poet's frame
 Must share the common tomb of all;
Their glory will not sleep the same;
 That will arise, though empires fall.

The lustre of a beauty's eye
 Assumes the ghastly stare of death;
The fair, the brave, the good must die,
 And sink the yawning grave beneath.

Once more the speaking eye revives,
 Still beaming through the lover's strain;
For Petrarch's Laura still survives:
 She died, but ne'er will die again.

The rolling seasons pass away,
 And Time, untiring, waves his wing;
Whilst honour's laurels ne'er decay,
 But bloom in fresh, unfading spring.

All, all must sleep in grim repose,
 Collected in the silent tomb;
The old and young, with friends and foes,
 Fest'ring alike in shrouds, consume.

The mouldering marble lasts its day,
 Yet falls at length an useless fane;
To ruin's ruthless fangs a prey,
 The wrecks of pillar'd pride remain.

What, though the sculpture be destroy'd,
 From dark oblivion meant to guard;
A bright renown shall be enjoy'd
 By those whose virtues claim reward.

Then do not say the common lot
 Of all lies deep in Lethe's wave;
Some few who ne'er will be forgot
 Shall burst the bondage of the grave.
 1806.

TO A LADY

WHO PRESENTED THE AUTHOR WITH THE VEL-
VET BAND WHICH BOUND HER TRESSES.

THIS Band, which bound thy yellow hair,
 Is mine, sweet girl! thy pledge of love;
It claims my warmest, dearest care,
 Like relics left of saints above.

Oh! I will wear it next my heart;
 'Twill bind my soul in bonds to thee:
From me again 'twill ne'er depart,
 But mingle in the grave with me.

The dew I gather from thy lip
 Is not so dear to me as this;
That I but for a moment sip,
 And banquet on a transient bliss:

This will recall each youthful scene,
 E'en when our lives are on the wane;
The leaves of Love will still be green
 When Memory bids them bud again.

Oh! little lock of golden hue,
 In gently waving ringlet curl'd,
By the dear head on which you grew,
 I would not lose you for a world.

Not though a thousand more adorn
 The polish'd brow where once you shone,
Like rays which gild a cloudless morn,
 Beneath Columbia's fervid zone.

 1806. [First published, 1832.]

LINES

ADDRESSED TO THE REV. J. T. BECHER, ON HIS
ADVISING THE AUTHOR TO MIX MORE WITH
SOCIETY.

DEAR Becher, you tell me to mix with man-
 kind;
I cannot deny such a precept is wise;
But retirement accords with the tone of my
 mind:
I will not descend to a world I despise.

Did the senate or camp my exertions require,
 Ambition might prompt me, at once, to go
 forth;
When infancy's years of probation expire,
 Perchance I may strive to distinguish my
 birth.

The fire in the cavern of Etna conceal'd
 Still mantles unseen in its secret recess;
At length, in a volume terrific reveal'd,
 No torrent can quench it, no bounds can
 repress.

Oh! thus, the desire in my bosom for fame
 Bids me live but to hope for posterity's
 praise.
Could I soar with the phœnix on pinions of
 flame,
With him I would wish to expire in the blaze.

For the life of a Fox, of a Chatham the death,
 What censure, what danger, what woe
 would I brave!
Their lives did not end when they yielded
 their breath;
 Their glory illumines the gloom of their
 grave.

Yet why should I mingle in Fashion's full
 herd?
 Why crouch to her leaders, or cringe to
 her rules?
Why bend to the proud, or applaud the ab-
 surd?
Why search for delight in the friendship
 of fools?

I have tasted the sweets and the bitters of
 love;
In friendship I early was taught to believe;
My passion the matrons of prudence reprove;
 I have found that a friend may profess, yet
 deceive.

To me what is wealth?—it may pass in an
 hour,
 If tyrants prevail, or if Fortune should
 frown:
To me what is title?—the phantom of power;
 To me what is fashion?—I seek but re-
 nown.

Deceit is a stranger as yet to my soul:
 I still am unpractised to varnish the truth:
Then why should I live in a hateful control?
 Why waste upon folly the days of my
 youth?

 1806.

REMEMBRANCE.

'TIS done!—I saw it in my dreams;
No more with Hope the future beams;
 My days of happiness are few:
Chill'd by misfortune's wintry blast,
My dawn of life is overcast;
 Love, Hope, and Joy, alike adieu!
 Would I could add Remembrance too?

 1806. [First published, 1832.]

THE DEATH OF CALMAR AND ORLA.

AN IMITATION OF MACPHERSON'S OSSIAN.

DEAR are the days of youth! Age dwells on
their remembrance through the mist of time.
In the twilight he recalls the sunny hours of
morn. He lifts his spear with trembling hand.
"Not thus feebly did I raise the steel before
my fathers!" Past is the race of heroes. But
their fame rises on the harp; their souls ride
on the wings of the wind; they hear the
sound through the sighs of the storm, and
rejoice in their hall of clouds! Such is Calmar.
The gray stone marks his narrow house. He
looks down from eddying tempests: he rolls
his form in the whirlwind, and hovers on the
blast of the mountain.

In Morven dwelt the chief; a beam of war
to Fingal. His steps in the field were marked
in blood. Lochlin's sons had fled before his
angry spear; but mild was the eye of Calmar;
soft was the flow of his yellow locks: they
streamed like the meteor of the night. No
maid was the sigh of his soul: his thoughts
were given to friendship,—to dark-haired
Orla, destroyer of heroes! Equal were their
swords in battle; but fierce was the pride of
Orla:—gentle alone to Calmar. Together
they dwelt in the cave of Oithona.

From Lochlin, Swaran bounded o'er the
blue waves. Erin's sons fell beneath his
might. Fingal roused his chiefs to combat.
Their ships cover the ocean. Their hosts
throng on the green hills. They come to the
aid of Erin.

Night rose in clouds. Darkness veils the
armies: but the blazing oaks gleam through
the valley. The sons of Lochlin slept: their
dreams were of blood. They lift the spear
in thought, and Fingal flies. Not so the host
of Morven. To watch was the post of Orla.

Calmar stood by his side. Their spears were in their hands. Fingal called his chiefs: they stood around. The king was in the midst. Gray were his locks, but strong was the arm of the king. Age withered not his powers. "Sons of Morven," said the hero, "to-morrow we meet the foe. But where is Cuthullin, the shield of Erin? He rests in the halls of Tura; he knows not of our coming. Who will speed through Lochlin to the hero, and call the chief to arms? The path is by the swords of foes; but many are my heroes. They are thunderbolts of war. Speak, ye chiefs! Who will arise?"

"Son of Trenmor! mine be the deed," said dark-haired Orla, "and mine alone. What is death to me? I love the sleep of the mighty, but little is the danger. The sons of Lochlin dream. I will seek car-borne Cuthullin. If I fall, raise the song of bards; and lay me by the stream of Lubar."—"And shalt thou fall alone?" said fair-haired Calmar. "Wilt thou leave thy friend afar? Chief of Oithona! not feeble is my arm in fight. Could I see thee die, and not lift the spear? No, Orla! ours has been the chase of the roebuck, and the feast of shells; ours be the path of danger: ours has been the cave of Oithona; ours be the narrow dwelling on the banks of Lubar." "Calmar," said the chief of Oithona, "why should thy yellow locks be darkened in the dust of Erin? Let me fall alone. My father dwells in his hall of air: he will rejoice in his boy; but the blue-eyed Mora spreads the feast for her son in Morven. She listens to the steps of the hunter on the heath, and thinks it is the tread of Calmar. Let her not say, ' Calmar has fallen by the steel of Lochlin: he died with gloomy Orla, the chief of the dark brow.' Why should tears dim the azure eye of Mora? Why should her voice curse Orla, the destroyer of Calmar? Live, Calmar! Live to raise my stone of moss; live to revenge me in the blood of Lochlin. Join the song of bards above my grave. Sweet will be the song of death to Orla, from the voice of Calmar. My ghost shall smile on the notes of praise." "Orla," said the son of Mora, "could I raise the song of death to my friend? Could I give his fame to the winds? No, my heart would speak in sighs: faint and broken are the sounds of sorrow. Orla! our souls shall hear the song together. One cloud shall be ours on high: the bards will mingle the names of Orla and Calmar."

They quit the circle of the chiefs. Their steps are to the host of Lochlin. The dying blaze of oak dim twinkles through the night. The northern star points the path to Tura.

Swaran, the king, rests on his lonely hill. Here the troops are mixed: they frown in sleep; their shields beneath their heads. Their swords gleam at distance in heaps. The fires are faint; their embers fail in smoke. All is hushed; but the gale sighs on the rocks above. Lightly wheel the heroes through the slumbering band. Half the journey is past, when Mathon, resting on his shield, meets the eye of Orla. It rolls in flame, and glistens through the shade. His spear is raised on high. "Why dost thou bend thy brow, chief of Oithona?" said fair-haired Calmar: "we are in the midst of foes. Is this a time for delay?" "It is a time for vengeance," said Orla of the gloomy brow. "Mathon of Lochlin sleeps: seest thou his spear? Its point is dim with the gore of my father. The blood of Mathon shall reek on mine; but shall I slay him sleeping, son of Mora? No! he shall feel his wound: my fame shall not soar on the blood of slumber. Rise, Mathon, rise! The son of Conna calls; thy life is his; rise to combat." Mathon starts from sleep; but did he rise alone? No: the gathering chiefs bound on the plain. "Fly! Calmar, fly!" said dark-haired Orla. "Mathon is mine. I shall die in joy: but Lochlin crowds around. Fly through the shade of night." Orla turns. The helm of Mathon is cleft; his shield falls from his arm: he shudders in his blood. He rolls by the side of the blazing oak. Strumon sees him fall: his wrath rises: his weapon glitters on the head of Orla: but a spear pierced his eye. His brain gushes through the wound, and foams on the spear of Calmar. As roll the waves of the Ocean on two mighty barks of the north, so pour the men of Lochlin on the chiefs. As, breaking the surge in foam, proudly steer the barks of the north, so rise the chiefs of Morven on the scattered crests of Lochlin. The din of arms came to the ear of Fingal. He strikes his shield; his sons throng around; the people pour along the heath. Ryno bounds in joy. Ossian stalks in his arms. Oscar shakes the spear. The eagle wing of Fillan floats on the wind. Dreadful is the clang of death! many are the widows of Lochlin! Morven prevails in its strength.

Morn glimmers on the hills: no living foe is seen; but the sleepers are many; grim they lie on Erin. The breeze of ocean lifts their locks; yet they do not awake. The hawks scream above their prey.

Whose yellow locks wave o'er the breast of a chief? Bright as the gold of the stranger, they mingle with the dark hair of his friend. 'Tis Calmar: he lies on the bosom of Orla.

Theirs is one stream of blood. Fierce is the
look of the gloomy Orla. He breathes not;
but his eye is still a flame. It glares in death
unclosed. His hand is grasped in Calmar's;
but Calmar lives! he lives, though low.
"Rise," said the king, "rise, son of Mora:
't is mine to heal the wounds of heroes. Cal-
mar may yet bound on the hills of Morven."

"Never more shall Calmar chase the deer
of Morven with Orla," said the hero. "What
were the chase to me alone? Who should
share the spoils of battle with Calmar? Orla
is at rest! Rough was thy soul, Orla! yet
soft to me as the dew of morn. It glared on
others in lightning: to me a silver beam of
night. Bear my sword to blue-eyed Mora;
let it hang in my empty hall. It is not pure
from blood: but it could not save Orla. Lay
me with my friend. Raise the song when I am
dark!"

They are laid by the stream of Lubar.
Four gray stones mark the dwelling of Orla
and Calmar. When Swaran was bound, our
sails rose on the blue waves. The winds gave
our barks to Morven:—the bards raised the
song.

"What form rises on the roar of clouds?
Whose dark ghost gleams on the red streams
of tempests? His voice rolls on the thunder.
'T is Orla, the brown chief of Oithona. He
was unmatched in war. Peace to thy soul,
Orla! thy fame will not perish. Nor thine,
Calmar! Lovely wast thou, son of blue-eyed
Mora; but not harmless was thy sword. It
hangs in thy cave. The ghosts of Lochlin
shriek around its steel. Hear thy praise,
Calmar! It dwells on the voice of the
mighty. Thy name shakes on the echoes of
Morven. Then raise thy fair locks, son of
Mora. Spread them on the arch of the rain-
bow; and smile through the tears of the
storm."

L'AMITIÉ EST L'AMOUR SANS AILES.

Why should my anxious breast repine,
 Because my youth is fled?
Days of delight may still be mine;
 Affection is not dead.
In tracing back the years of youth,
One firm record, one lasting truth,
 Celestial consolation brings;
Bear it, ye breezes, to the seat,
Where first my heart responsive beat,—
 "Friendship is Love without his wings!"

Through few, but deeply chequer'd years,
 What moments have been mine!
Now half obscured by clouds of tears,
 Now bright in rays divine;

Howe'er my future doom be cast,
My soul, enraptured with the past,
 To one idea fondly clings;
Friendship! that thought is all thine own,
Worth worlds of bliss, that thought alone—
 "Friendship is Love without his wings!"

Where yonder yew-trees lightly wave
 Their branches on the gale,
Unheeded heaves a simple grave,
 Which tells the common tale;
Round this unconscious schoolboys stray,
Till the dull knell of childish play
 From yonder studious mansion rings;
But here whene'er my footsteps move,
My silent tears too plainly prove
 "Friendship is Love without his wings!"

Oh, Love! before thy glowing shrine
 My early vows were paid;
My hopes, my dreams, my heart was thine,
 But these are now decay'd;
For thine are pinions like the wind,
No trace of thee remains behind,
 Except, alas! thy jealous stings.
Away, away! delusive power,
Thou shalt not haunt my coming hour;
 Unless, indeed, without thy wings.

Seat of my youth! thy distant spire
 Recalls each scene of joy;
My bosom glows with former fire,—
 In mind again a boy.
Thy grove of elms, thy verdant hill,
Thy every path delights me still,
 Each flower a double fragrance flings;
Again, as once, in converse gay,
Each dear associate seems to say,
 "Friendship is Love without his wings!"

My Lycus! wherefore dost thou weep?
 Thy falling tears restrain;
Affection for a time may sleep,
 But, oh, 't will wake again.
Think, think, my friend, when next we meet,
Our long-wish'd interview, how sweet!
 From this my hope of rapture springs;
While youthful hearts thus fondly swell,
Absence, my friend, can only tell,
 "Friendship is Love without his wings!"

In one, and one alone deceived,
 Did I my error mourn?
No—from oppressive bonds relieved,
 I left the wretch to scorn.
I turn'd to those my childhood knew,
With feelings warm, with bosoms true,
 Twined with my heart's according strings;
And till those vital chords shall break,
For none but these my breast shall wake
 Friendship, the power deprived of wings!

Ye few! my soul, my life is yours,
 My memory and my hope;
Your worth a lasting love insures,
 Unfetter'd in its scope;
From smooth deceit and terror sprung
With aspect fair and honey'd tongue,
 Let Adulation wait on kings;
With joy elate, by snares beset,
We, we, my friends, can ne'er forget
 "Friendship is Love without his wings!"

Fictions and dreams inspire the bard
 Who rolls the epic song;
Friendship and truth be my reward—
 To me no bays belong;
If laurell'd Fame but dwells with lies,
Me the enchantress ever flies,
 Whose heart and not whose fancy sings;
Simple and young, I dare not feign;
Mine be the rude yet heartfelt strain,
 "Friendship is Love without his wings!"

 December, 1806.
 [First published. 1832.]

THE PRAYER OF NATURE.

FATHER of Light! great God of Heaven!
 Hear'st thou the accents of despair?
Can guilt like man's be e'er forgiven?
 Can vice atone for crimes by prayer?

Father of Light, on thee I call!
 Thou seest my soul is dark within;
Thou who canst mark the sparrow's fall,
 Avert from me the death of sin.

No shrine I seek, to sects unknown;
 Oh, point to me the path of truth!
Thy dread omnipotence I own;
 Spare, yet amend, the faults of youth.

Let bigots rear a gloomy fane,
 Let superstition hail the pile,
Let priests, to spread their sable reign,
 With tales of mystic rites beguile.

Shall man confine his Maker's sway
 To Gothic domes of mouldering stone?
Thy temple is the face of day;
 Earth, ocean, heaven, thy boundless throne.

Shall man condemn his race to hell,
 Unless they bend in pompous form?
Tell us that all, for one who fell,
 Must perish in the mingling storm?

Shall each pretend to reach the skies,
 Yet doom his brother to expire,
Whose soul a different hope supplies,
 Or doctrines less severe inspire?

Shall these, by creeds they can't expound,
 Prepare a fancied bliss or woe?
Shall reptiles, grovelling on the ground,
 Their great Creator's purpose know?

Shall those, who live for self alone,
 Whose years float on in daily crime—
Shall they by Faith for guilt atone,
 And live beyond the bounds of Time?

Father! no prophet's laws I seek,—
 Thy laws in Nature's works appear;—
I own myself corrupt and weak,
 Yet will I pray, for thou wilt hear!

Thou, who canst guide the wandering star
 Through trackless realms of æther's space;
Who calm'st the elemental war,
 Whose hand from pole to pole I trace:

Thou, who in wisdom placed me here,
 Who, when thou wilt, canst take me hence,
Ah! whilst I tread this earthly sphere,
 Extend to me thy wide defence.

To Thee, my God, to thee I call!
 Whatever weal or woe betide,
By thy command I rise or fall,
 In thy protection I confide.

If, when this dust to dust's restored,
 My soul shall float on airy wing,
How shall thy glorious name adored
 Inspire her feeble voice to sing!

But, if this fleeting spirit share
 With clay the grave's eternal bed,
While life yet throbs I raise my prayer,
 Though doom'd no more to quit the dead.

To Thee I breathe my humble strain,
 Grateful for all thy mercies past,
And hope, my God, to thee again
 This erring life may fly at last.

 December 29, 1806.
 [First published, 1830.]

TO EDWARD NOEL LONG, ESQ.

"Nil ego contulerim jocundo sanus amico."—HOR.

DEAR LONG, in this sequester'd scene,
 While all around in slumber lie,
The joyous days which ours have been
 Come rolling fresh on Fancy's eye;
Thus if amidst the gathering storm,
While clouds the darken'd noon deform,
 Yon heaven assumes a varied glow,
I hail the sky's celestial bow,
Which spreads the sign of future peace,
And bids the war of tempests cease.
 Ah! though the present brings but pain
 I think those days may come again;

Or if, in melancholy mood,
Some lurking envious fear intrude,
To check my bosom's fondest thought,
 And interrupt the golden dream,
I crush the fiend with malice fraught,
 And still indulge my wonted theme.
Although we ne'er again can trace,
 In Granta's vale, the pedant's lore;
Nor through the groves of Ida chase
 Our raptured visions as before,
Though Youth has flown on rosy pinion,
And Manhood claims his stern dominion,
Age will not every hope destroy,
But yield some hours of sober joy.

Yes, I will hope that Time's broad wing
Will shed around some dews of spring:
But if his scythe must sweep the flowers
Which bloom among the fairy bowers,
Where smiling Youth delights to dwell,
And hearts with early rapture swell;
If frowning Age, with cold control,
Confines the current of the soul,
Congeals the tear of Pity's eye,
Or checks the sympathetic sigh,
Or hears unmoved misfortune's groan,
And bids me feel for self alone;
Oh! may my bosom never learn
 To soothe its wonted heedless flow;
Still, still despise the censor stern,
 But ne'er forget another's woe.
Yes, as you knew me in the days
O'er which Remembrance yet delays,
Still may I rove, untutor'd, wild,
And even in age at heart a child.

Though now on airy visions borne,
 To you my soul is still the same.
Oft has it been my fate to mourn,
 And all my former joys are tame.
But, hence! ye hours of sable hue!
 Your frowns are gone, my sorrows o'er:
By every bliss my childhood knew,
 I'll think upon your shade no more.
Thus, when the whirlwind's rage is past,
 And caves their sullen roar enclose,
We heed no more the wintry blast,
 When lull'd by zephyr to repose.

Full often has my infant Muse
 Attuned to love her languid lyre;
But now, without a theme to choose,
 The strains in stolen sighs expire.
My youthful nymphs, alas! are flown;
 E—— is a wife, and C—— a mother,
And Carolina sighs alone,
 And Mary's given to another;
And Cora's eye, which roll'd on me,
 Can now no more my love recall:
In truth, dear Long, 't was time to flee;
 For Cora's eye will shine on all.

And though the sun, with genial rays,
His beams alike to all displays,
And every lady's eye's a *sun*,
These last should be confined to one.
The soul's meridian don't become her,
Whose sun displays a general *summer!*
Thus faint is every former flame,
And passion's self is now a name.
As, when the ebbing flames are low,
 The aid which once improved their light,
And bade them burn with fiercer glow,
 Now quenches all their sparks in night;
Thus has it been with passion's fires,
As many a boy and girl remembers,
While all the force of love expires,
 Extinguish'd with the dying embers.

But now, dear Long, 't is midnight's noon,
And clouds obscure the watery moon,
Whose beauties I shall not rehearse,
Described in every stripling's verse;
For why should I the path go o'er,
Which every bard has trod before?
Yet ere yon silver lamp of night
 Has thrice perform'd her stated round,
Has thrice retraced her path of light,
 And chased away the gloom profound,
I trust that we, my gentle friend,
Shall see her rolling orbit wend
Above the dear-loved peaceful seat,
Which once contain'd our youth's retreat;
And then with those our childhood knew
We'll mingle in the festive crew;
While many a tale of former day
Shall wing the laughing hours away;
And all the flow of souls shall pour
The sacred intellectual shower,
Nor cease till Luna's waning horn
Scarce glimmers through the mist of morn.

——+——

TO A LADY.

Oh! had my fate been join'd with thine,
 As once this pledge appear'd a token,
These follies had not then been mine,
 For then my peace had not been broken.

To thee these early faults I owe,
 To thee, the wise and old reproving:
They know my sins, but do not know
 'T was thine to break the bonds of loving.

For once my soul, like thine, was pure,
 And all its rising fires could smother;
But now thy vows no more endure,
 Bestow'd by thee upon another;

Perhaps his peace I could destroy,
 And spoil the blisses that await him;
Yet let my rival smile in joy,
 For thy dear sake I cannot hate him.

Ah! since thy angel form is gone,
 My heart no more can rest with any;
But what it sought in thee alone.
 Attempts, alas! to find in many.

Then fare thee well, deceitful maid!
 'Twere vain and fruitless to regret thee;
Nor hope nor memory yield their aid,
 But pride may teach me to forget thee.

Yet all this giddy waste of years,
 This tiresome round of palling pleasures;
These varied loves, these matron's fears,
 These thoughtless strains to passion's
 measures—

If thou wert mine, had all been hush'd:—
 This cheek, now pale from early riot,
With passion's hectic ne'er had flushed,
 But bloom'd in calm domestic quiet.

Yes, once the rural scene was sweet,
 For Nature seem'd to smile before thee;
And once my breast abhorr'd deceit,—
 For then it beat but to adore thee.

But now I seek for other joys:
 To think would drive my soul to madness;
In thoughtless throngs and empty noise
 I conquer half my bosom's sadness.

Yet, even in these a thought will steal
 In spite of every vain endeavour,—
And fiends might pity what I feel,—
 To know that thou art lost for ever.

—••—

I WOULD I WERE A CARELESS CHILD.

I WOULD I were a careless child,
 Still dwelling in my Highland cave,
Or roaming through the dusky wild,
 Or bounding o'er the dark blue wave;
The cumbrous pomp of Saxon pride
 Accords not with the freeborn soul,
Which loves the mountain's craggy side,
 And seeks the rocks where billows roll.

Fortune! take back these cultured lands,
 Take back this name of splendid sound!
I hate the touch of servile hands,
 I hate the slaves that cringe around.
Place me among the rocks I love,
 Which sound to Ocean's wildest roar;
I ask but this—again to rove
 Through scenes my youth hath known
 before.

Few are my years, and yet I feel
 The world was ne'er design'd for me:
Ah! why do dark'ning shades conceal
 The hour when man must cease to be?

Once I beheld a splendid dream,
 A visionary scene of bliss:
Truth!—wherefore did thy hated beam
 Awake me to a world like this?

I loved—but those I loved are gone;
 Had friends—my early friends are fled:
How cheerless feels the heart alone,
 When all its former hopes are dead!
Though gay companions o'er the bowl
 Dispel awhile the sense of ill;
Though pleasure stirs the maddening soul,
 The heart—the heart—is lonely still.

How dull! to hear the voice of those
 Whom rank or chance, whom wealth or
 power,
Have made, though neither friends nor
 foes,
 Associates of the festive hour.
Give me again a faithful few,
 In years and feelings still the same,
And I will fly the midnight crew,
 Where boist'rous joy is but a name.

And woman, lovely woman! thou,
 My hope, my comforter, my all!
How cold must be my bosom now,
 When e'en thy smiles begin to pall!
Without a sigh would I resign
 This busy scene of splendid woe,
To make that calm contentment mine,
 Which virtue knows, or seems to know.

Fain would I fly the haunts of men—
 I seek to shun, not hate mankind;
My breast requires the sullen glen,
 Whose gloom may suit a darken'd mind.
Oh! that to me the wings were given
 Which bear the turtle to her nest!
Then would I cleave the vault of heaven,
 To flee away, and be at rest.

—••—

WHEN I ROVED A YOUNG HIGH-
LANDER.

WHEN I roved a young Highlander o'er the
 dark heath,
 And climb'd thy steep summit, oh Morven
 of snow!
To gaze on the torrent that thunder'd beneath,
 Or the mist of the tempest that gather'd
 below,
Untutor'd by science, a stranger to fear,
 And rude as the rocks where my infancy
 grew,
No feeling, save one, to my bosom was dear;
 Need I say, my sweet Mary, 'twas centred
 in you?

Yet it could not be love, for I knew not the
 name,—
 What passion can dwell in the heart of
 a child?
But still I perceive an emotion the same
 As I felt, when a boy, on the crag-cover'd
 wild
One image alone on my bosom impress'd,
 I loved my bleak regions, nor panted for
 new;
And few were my wants, for my wishes were
 bless'd;
 And pure were my thoughts, for my soul
 was with you.

I arose with the dawn; with my dog as my
 guide,
 From mountain to mountain I bounded
 along;
I breasted the billows of Dee's rushing tide,
 And heard at a distance the Highlander's
 song:
At eve, on my heath-cover'd couch of repose,
 No dreams, save of Mary, were spread to
 my view;
And warm to the skies my devotions arose,
 For the first of my prayers was a blessing
 on you.

I left my bleak home, and my visions are
 gone;
 The mountains are vanish'd, my youth is
 no more;
As the last of my race, I must wither alone,
 And delight but in days I have witness'd
 before:
Ah! splendour has raised but embitter'd my
 lot;
 More dear were the scenes which my in-
 fancy knew:
Though my hopes may have fail'd, yet they
 are not forgot;
 Though cold is my heart, still it lingers
 with you.

When I see some dark hill point its crest to
 the sky,
 I think of the rocks that o'ershadow
 Colbleen;
When I see the soft blue of a love-speaking
 eye,
 I think of those eyes that endear'd the rude
 scene;
When, haply, some light-waving locks I be-
 hold,
 That faintly resemble my Mary's in hue,
I think on the long, flowing ringlets of
 gold,
 The locks that were sacred to beauty, and
 you.

Yet the day may arrive when the mountains
 once more
 Shall rise to my sight in their mantles of
 snow:
But while these soar above me, unchanged as
 before,
 Will Mary be there to receive me?—ah, no!
Adieu, then, ye hills, where my childhood was
 bred!
 Thou sweet flowing Dee, to thy waters
 adieu!
No home in the forest shall shelter my
 head,—
 Ah! Mary, what home could be mine but with
 you?

—— ·•· ——

TO GEORGE, EARL DELAWARR.

OH! yes, I will own we were dear to each
 other;
 The friendships of childhood, though fleet-
 ing, are true;
The love which you felt was the love of a
 brother,
 Nor less the affection I cherish'd for you.

But Friendship can vary her gentle dominion;
 The attachment of years in a moment
 expires:
Like Love, too, she moves on a swift-waving
 pinion,
 But glows not, like Love, with unquench-
 able fires.

Full oft have we wander'd through Ida to-
 gether,
 And blest were the scenes of our youth,
 I allow:
In the spring of our life, how serene is the
 weather!
 But winter's rude tempests are gathering
 now.

No more with affection shall memory blend-
 ing,
 The wonted delights of our childhood
 retrace:
When pride steels the bosom, the heart is
 unbending,
 And what would be justice appears a
 disgrace.

However, dear George, for I still must esteem
 you;
 The few whom I love I can never upbraid:
The chance which has lost may in future
 redeem you,
 Repentance will cancel the vow you have
 made.

I will not complain, and though chill'd is
affection,
 With me no corroding resentment shall
 live:
My bosom is calm'd by the simple reflection,
 That both may be wrong, and that both
 should forgive.

You knew that my soul, that my heart, my
existence,
 If danger demanded, were wholly your own;
You knew me unalter'd by years or by dis-
tance,
 Devoted to love and to friendship alone.

You knew,—but away with the vain retrospec-
tion!
 The bond of affection no longer endures;
Too late you may droop o'er the fond recollec-
tion,
 And sigh for the friend who was formerly
 yours.

For the present, we part,—I will hope not for
ever;
 For time and regret will restore you at last:
To forget our dissension we both should
endeavour,
 I ask no atonement, but days like the past.

TO THE EARL OF CLARE.

"Tu semper amoris
Sis memor, et cari comitis ne abscedat imago."
VAL FLAC.

FRIEND of my youth! when young we roved,
Like striplings, mutually beloved,
 With friendship's purest glow,
The bliss which wing'd those rosy hours
Was such as pleasure seldom showers
 On mortals here below.

The recollection seems alone
Dearer than all the joys I've known,
 When distant far from you:
Though pain, 'tis still a pleasing pain,
To trace those days and hours again,
 And sigh again, adieu!

My pensive memory lingers o'er
Those scenes to be enjoy'd no more,
 Those scenes regretted ever;
The measure of our youth is full,
Life's evening dream is dark and dull,
 And we may meet—ah! never!

As when one parent spring supplies
Two streams which from one fountain rise,
 Together join'd in vain;
How soon, diverging from their source,
Each, murmuring, seeks another course,
 Till mingled in the main!

Our vital streams of weal or woe,
Though near, alas! distinctly flow,
 Nor mingle as before:
Now swift or slow, now black or clear,
Till death's unfathom'd gulf appear,
 And both shall quit the shore.

Our souls, my friend! which once supplied
One wish, nor breathed a thought beside,
 Now flow in different channels:
Disdaining humbler rural sports,
'Tis yours to mix in polish'd courts,
 And shine in fashion's annals;

'Tis mine to waste on love my time,
Or vent my reveries in rhyme,
 Without the aid of reason;
For sense and reason (critics know it)
Have quitted every amorous poet,
 Nor left a thought to seize on.

Poor LITTLE! sweet, melodious bard!
Of late esteem'd it monstrous hard
 That he, who sang before all,—
He who the lore of love expanded,—
By dire reviewers should be branded
 As void of wit and moral.

And yet, while Beauty's praise is thine,
Harmonious favourite of the Nine!
 Repine not at thy lot.
Thy soothing lays may still be read,
When Persecution's arm is dead,
 And critics are forgot.

Still I must yield those worthies merit,
Who chasten, with unsparing spirit,
 Bad rhymes, and those who write them;
And though myself may be the next
By criticism to be vext,
 I really will not fight them.

Perhaps they would do quite as well
To break the rudely sounding shell
 Of such a young beginner:
He who offends at pert nineteen,
Ere thirty may become, I ween,
 A very harden'd sinner.

Now, Clare, I must return to you;
And, sure, apologies are due:
 Accept, then, my concession.
In truth, dear Clare, in fancy's flight
I soar along from left to right;
 My muse admires digression.

I think I said 'twould be your fate
To add one star to royal state;—
 May regal smiles attend you!
And should a noble monarch reign,
You will not seek his smiles in vain,
 If worth can recommend you.

Yet since in danger courts abound,
Where specious rivals glitter round,
 From snares may saints preserve you;
And grant your love or friendship ne'er
From any claim a kindred care,
 But those who best deserve you!

Not for a moment may you stray
From truth's secure, unerring way!
 May no delights decoy!
O'er roses may your footsteps move,
Your smiles be ever smiles of love,
 Your tears be tears of joy!

Oh! if you wish that happiness
Your coming days and years may bless,
 And virtues crown your brow;
Be still as you were wont to be,
Spotless as you've been known to me,—
 Be still as you are now.

And though some trifling share of praise,
To cheer my last declining days,
 To me were doubly dear;
Whilst blessing your beloved name
I'd waive at once a *poet's* fame,
 To prove a *prophet* here.

—◆—

LINES WRITTEN BENEATH AN ELM IN THE CHURCHYARD OF HARROW.

SPOT of my youth! whose hoary branches
 sigh,
Swept by the breeze that fans thy cloudless
 sky;
Where now alone I muse, who oft have trod,
With those I loved, thy soft and verdant sod;
With those who, scatter'd far, perchance
 deplore,
Like me, the happy scenes they knew before:
Oh! as I trace again thy winding hill,
Mine eyes admire, my heart adores thee still,

Thou drooping Elm! beneath whose boughs
 I lay,
And frequent mused the twilight hours away;
Where, as they once were wont, my limbs
 recline,
But, ah! without the thoughts which then
 were mine:
How do thy branches, moaning to the blast,
Invite the bosom to recall the past,
And seem to whisper, as they gently swell,
"Take, while thou canst, a lingering, last
 farewell!"

When fate shall chill, at length, this fever'd
 breast,
And calm its cares and passions into rest,
Oft have I thought, 'twould soothe my dying
 hour,—
If aught may soothe when life resigns her
 power,—
To know some humble grave, some narrow
 cell,
Would hide my bosom where it loved to dwell;
With this fond dream, methinks 'twere sweet
 to die—
And here it linger'd, here my heart might lie;
Here might I sleep where all my hopes arose,
Scene of my youth, and couch of my repose;
For ever stretch'd beneath this mantling
 shade,
Press'd by the turf where once my childhood
 play'd;
Wrapt by the soil that veils the spot I loved,
Mix'd with the earth o'er which my footsteps
 moved;
Blest by the tongues that charm'd my youth-
 ful ear,
Mourn'd by the few my soul acknowledged
 here;
Deplored by those in early days allied,
And unremember'd by the world beside.

 September 2, 1807.

Occasional Pieces.

1807—1824.

THE ADIEU.

WRITTEN UNDER THE IMPRESSION THAT THE
AUTHOR WOULD SOON DIE.

ADIEU, thou Hill! where early joy
 Spread roses o'er my brow;
Where Science seeks each loitering boy
 With knowledge to endow.
Adieu, my youthful friends or foes,
Partners of former bliss or woes;
 No more through Ida's paths we stray;
Soon must I share the gloomy cell,
Whose ever-slumbering inmates dwell
 Unconscious of the day.

Adieu, ye hoary Regal Fanes,
 Ye spires of Granta's vale,
Where Learning robed in sable reigns,
 And Melancholy pale.
Ye comrades of the jovial hour,
Ye tenants of the classic bower,
 On Cama's verdant margin placed,
Adieu! while memory still is mine,
For, offerings on Oblivion's shrine,
 These scenes must be effaced.

Adieu, ye mountains of the clime
 Where grew my youthful years;
Where Loch na Garr in snows sublime
 His giant summit rears.
Why did my childhood wander forth
From you, ye regions of the North,
 With sons of pride to roam?
Why did I quit my Highland cave,
Marr's dusky heath, and Dee's clear wave,
 To seek a Sotheron home!

Hall of my Sires! a long farewell—
 Yet why to thee adieu?
Thy vaults will echo back my knell,
 Thy towers my tomb will view:
The faltering tongue which sung thy fall,
And former glories of thy Hall,
 Forgets its wonted simple note—
But yet the Lyre retains the strings,
And sometimes, on Æolian wings,
 In dying strains may float.

Fields, which surround yon rustic cot,
 While yet I linger here,
Adieu! you are not now forgot,
 To retrospection dear.
Streamlet! along whose rippling surge
My youthful limbs were wont to urge,
 At noontide heat, their pliant course;
Plunging with ardour from the shore,
Thy springs will lave these limbs no more,
 Deprived of active force.

And shall I here forget the scene,
 Still nearest to my breast?
Rocks rise and rivers roll between
 The spot which passion blest;
Yet, Mary, all thy beauties seem
Fresh as in Love's bewitching dream,
 To me in smiles display'd;
Till slow disease resigns his prey
To Death, the parent of decay,
 Thine image cannot fade.

And thou, my Friend! whose gentle love
 Yet thrills my bosom's chords,
How much thy friendship was above
 Description's power of words!
Still near my breast thy gift I wear
Which sparkled once with Feeling's tear,
 Of Love the pure, the sacred gem;
Our souls were equal, and our lot
In that dear moment quite forgot;
 Let Pride alone condemn!

All, all is dark and cheerless now!
 No smile of Love's deceit
Can warm my veins with wonted glow,
 Can bid Life's pulses beat:
Not e'en the hope of future fame
Can wake my faint, exhausted frame,
 Or crown with fancied wreaths my head.
Mine is a short inglorious race,—
To humble in the dust my face,
 And mingle with the dead.

Oh Fame! thou goddess of my heart;
 On him who gains thy praise,
Pointless must fall the Spectre's dart,
 Consumed in Glory's blaze;
But me she beckons from the earth,
My name obscure, unmark'd my birth,

My life a short and vulgar dream:
Lost in the dull, ignoble crowd,
My hopes recline within a shroud,
　My fate is Lethe's stream.

When I repose beneath the sod,
　Unheeded in the clay,
Where once my playful footsteps trod,
　Where now my head must lay,
The meed of Pity will be shed
In dew-drops o'er my narrow bed,
　By nightly skies, and storms alone;
No mortal eye will deign to steep
With tears the dark sepulchral deep
　Which hides a name unknown.

Forget this world, my restless sprite,
　Turn, turn thy thoughts to Heaven:
There must thou soon direct thy flight,
　If errors are forgiven.
To bigots and to sects unknown,
Bow down beneath the Almighty's Throne;
　To Him address thy trembling prayer:
He, who is merciful and just,
Will not reject a child of dust,
　Although his meanest care.

Father of Light! to Thee I call;
　My soul is dark within:
Thou who canst mark the sparrow's fall,
　Avert the death of sin.
Thou, who canst guide the wandering star,
Who calm'st the elemental war,
Whose mantle is yon boundless sky,
My thoughts, my words, my crimes forgive:
And, since I soon must cease to live,
　Instruct me how to die.

　　　　　1807. [First published, 1832.]

TO A VAIN LADY.

Ah! heedless girl! why thus disclose
　What ne'er was meant for other ears:
Why thus destroy thine own repose
　And dig the source of future tears?

Oh, thou wilt weep, imprudent maid,
　While lurking envious foes will smile,
For all the follies thou hast said
　Of those who spoke but to beguile.

Vain girl! thy ling'ring woes are nigh,
　If thou believ'st what striplings say:
Oh, from the deep temptation fly,
　Nor fall the specious spoiler's prey.

Dost thou repeat, in childish boast,
　The words man utters to deceive?
Thy peace, thy hope, thy all is lost,
　If thou canst venture to believe.

While now amongst thy female peers
　Thou tell'st again the soothing tale,
Canst thou not mark the rising sneers
　Duplicity in vain would veil?

These tales in secret silence hush,
　Nor make thyself the public gaze:
What modest maid without a blush
　Recounts a flattering coxcomb's praise?

Will not the laughing boy despise
　Her who relates each fond conceit—
Who, thinking Heaven is in her eyes,
　Yet cannot see the slight deceit?

For she who takes a soft delight
　These amorous nothings in revealing,
Must credit all we say or write,
　While vanity prevents concealing.

Cease, if you prize your beauty's reign!
　No jealousy bids me reprove:
One, who is thus from nature vain,
　I pity, but I cannot love.

　　　　　　　　January 15, 1807.
　　　　　　　[First published, 1832.]

TO ANNE.

Oh, Anne, your offences to me have been
　　grievous:
　I thought from my wrath no atonement
　　could save you:
But woman is made to command and deceive
　　us—
　I look'd in your face, and I almost forgave you.

I vow'd I could ne'er for a moment respect you,
　　Yet thought that a day's separation was
　　long;
When we met, I determined again to suspect
　　you—
　Your smile soon convinced me suspicion
　　was wrong.

I swore, in a transport of young indignation,
　With fervent contempt evermore to disdain
　　you:
I saw you—my anger became admiration;
　And now, all my wish, all my hope's to
　　regain you.

With beauty like yours, oh, how vain the
　　contention!
　Thus lowly I sue for forgiveness before you;
At once to conclude such a fruitless dissension,
　Be false, my sweet Anne, when I cease to
　　adore you!

　　　　　　　　January 16, 1807.
　　　　　　　[First published, 1832.]

TO THE SAME.

OH, say not, sweet Anne, that the Fates have
　　decreed
　　The heart which adores you should wish to
　　　dissever;
Such Fates were to me most unkind ones
　　indeed,—
　　To bear me from love and from beauty for
　　　ever.

Your frowns, lovely girl, are the Fates which
　　alone
　　Could bid me from fond admiration re-
　　　frain;
By these, every hope, every wish were o'er-
　　thrown,
　　Till smiles should restore me to rapture
　　　again.

As the ivy and oak, in the forest entwined,
　　The rage of the tempest united must
　　　weather;
My love and my life were by nature design'd
　　To flourish alike, or to perish together.

Then say not, sweet Anne, that the Fates
　　have decreed
　　Your lover should bid you a lasting adieu;
Till Fate can ordain that his bosom shall
　　bleed,
　　His soul, his existence, are centred in you.
　　　　　　　1807.　[First published, 1832.]

TO THE AUTHOR OF A SONNET

BEGINNING " ' SAD IS MY VERSE,' YOU SAY, 'AND
YET NO TEAR.' "

THY verse is " sad " enough, no doubt:
　　A devilish deal more sad than witty!
Why we should weep I can't find out,
　　Unless for *thee* we weep in pity.

Yet there is one I pity more;
　　And much, alas! I think he needs it;
For he, I'm sure, will suffer sore,
　　Who, to his own misfortune, reads it.

Thy rhymes, without the aid of magic,
　　May *once* be read—but never after:
Yet their effect's by no means tragic,
　　Although by far too dull for laughter.

But would you make our bosoms bleed,
　　And of no common pang complain—
If you would make us weep indeed,
　　Tell us, you'll read them o'er again.
　　　　　　　　　　March 8, 1807.
　　　　　　　　[First published, 1832.]

ON FINDING A FAN.

IN one who felt as once he felt,
　　This might, perhaps, have fann'd the
　　　flame;
But now his heart no more will melt,
　　Because that heart is not the same.

As when the ebbing flames are low,
　　The aid which once improved their light,
And bade them burn with fiercer glow,
　　Now quenches all their blaze in night.

Thus has it been with passion's fires—
　　As many a boy and girl remembers—
While every hope of love expires,
　　Extinguish'd with the dying embers.

The *first*, though not a spark survive,
　　Some careful hand may teach to burn;
The *last*, alas! can ne'er survive;
　　No touch can bid its warmth return

Or, if it chance to wake again,
　　Not always doom'd its heat to smother,
It sheds (so wayward fates ordain)
　　Its former warmth around another.
　　　　　　　1807.　[First published, 1832.]

FAREWELL TO THE MUSE.

THOU Power! who hast ruled me through
　　infancy's days,
　　Young offspring of fancy, 't is time we
　　　should part;
Then rise on the gale this the last of my
　　lays,
　　The coldest effusion which springs from
　　　my heart.

This bosom, responsive to rapture no more,
　　Shall hush thy wild notes, nor implore
　　　thee to sing;
The feelings of childhood, which taught thee
　　to soar,
　　Are wafted far distant on Apathy's wing.

Though simple the themes of my rude flow-
　　ing Lyre,
　　Yet even these themes are departed for
　　　ever;
No more beam the eyes which my dream
　　could inspire,
　　My visions are flown, to return,—alas!
　　　never.

When drain'd is the nectar which gladdens
　　the bowl,
　　How vain is the effort delight to prolong!
When cold is the beauty which dwelt in my
　　soul,
　　What magic of Fancy can lengthen my
　　song?

Can the lips sing of Love in the desert alone,
 Of kisses and smiles which they now must
 resign ?
Or dwell with delight on the hours that are
 flown ?
 Ah, no ! for those hours can no longer be
 mine.

Can they speak of the friends that I lived
 but to love ?
 Ah, surely affection ennobles the strain !
But how can my numbers in sympathy move,
 When I scarcely can hope to behold them
 again ?

Can I sing of the deeds which my Fathers
 have done,
 And raise my loud harp to the fame of my
 Sires ?
For glories like theirs, oh, how faint is my
 tone !
 For Heroes' exploits how unequal my fires !

Untouch'd, then, my Lyre shall reply to the
 blast—
 'Tis hush'd ; and my feeble endeavours
 are o'er ;
And those who have heard it will pardon the
 past,
 When they know that its murmurs shall
 vibrate no more.

And soon shall its wild erring notes be
 forgot,
 Since early affection and love are o'ercast :
Oh ! blest had my fate been, and happy my
 lot,
 Had the first strain of love been the
 dearest, the last.

Farewell, my young Muse ! since we now can
 ne'er meet ;
 If our songs have been languid, they surely
 are few ;
Let us hope that the present at least will be
 sweet—
 The present—which seals our eternal
 Adieu.
 1807. [First published, 1832.]

———•♦•———

TO AN OAK AT NEWSTEAD.

YOUNG Oak ! when I planted thee deep in the
 ground,
 I hoped that thy days would be longer than
 mine ;
That thy dark-waving branches would flour-
 ish around,
 And ivy thy trunk with its mantle entwine.

Such, such was my hope, when in infancy's
 years,
 On the land of my fathers I rear'd thee
 with pride ;
They are past, and I water thy stem with my
 tears,—
 Thy decay not the weeds that surround
 thee can hide.

I left thee, my Oak, and, since that fatal hour,
 A stranger has dwelt in the hall of my sire ;
Till manhood shall crown me, not mine is the
 power,
 But his, whose neglect may have bade thee
 expire.

Oh ! hardy thou wert—even now little care
 Might revive thy young head, and thy
 wounds gently heal :
But thou wert not fated affection to share—
 For who could suppose that a stranger
 would feel !

Ah, droop not, my Oak ! lift thy head for a
 while ;
 Ere twice round yon Glory this planet
 shall run,
The hand of thy Master will teach thee to
 smile,
 When Infancy's years of probation are
 done.

Oh, live then, my Oak ! tow'r aloft from the
 weeds,
 That clog thy young growth, and assist thy
 decay,
For still in thy bosom are life s early seeds,
 And still may thy branches their beauty
 display.

Oh ! yet, if maturity's years may be thine,
 Though *I* shall lie low in the cavern of
 death,
On thy leaves yet the day-beam of ages may
 shine,
 Uninjured by time, or the rude winter's
 breath.

For centuries still may thy boughs lightly
 wave
 O'er the corse of thy lord in thy canopy
 laid ;
While the branches thus gratefully shelter
 his grave,
 The chief who survives may recline in thy
 shade.

And as he, with his boys, shall revisit this spot,
 He will tell them in whispers more softly
 to tread.
Oh ! surely, by these I shall ne'er be forgot ;
 Remembrance still hallows the dust of the
 dead.

And here, will they say, when in life's glow-
	ing prime,
	Perhaps he has pour'd forth his young
		simple lay,
And here must he sleep, till the moments of
		time
	Are lost in the hours of Eternity's day.
			1807. [First published, 1832.]

ON REVISITING HARROW.

HERE once engaged the stranger's view
	Young Friendship's record simply traced;
Few were her words,—but yet, though
		few,
	Resentment's hand the line defaced.

Deeply she cut—but not erased,
	The characters were still so plain,
That Friendship once return'd, and gazed,—
	Till Memory hail'd the words again.

Repentance placed them as before;
	Forgiveness join'd her gentle name;
So fair the inscription seem'd once more,
	That Friendship thought it still the same.

Thus might the Record now have been;
	But, ah, in spite of Hope's endeavour,
Or Friendship's tears, Pride rush'd between,
	And blotted out the line for ever.
				September, 1807.

EPITAPH ON JOHN ADAMS, OF SOUTHWELL,

A CARRIER, WHO DIED OF DRUNKENNESS.

JOHN ADAMS lies here, of the parish of South-
		well,
A *Carrier* who *carried* his can to his mouth
		well:
He *carried* so much, and he *carried* so fast,
He could *carry* no more—so was *carried* at
		last;
For, the liquor he drank, being too much for
		one,
He could not *carry* off,—so he's now *carri-on.*
				September, 1807.

TO MY SON.

THOSE flaxen locks, those eyes of blue,
	Bright as thy mother's in their hue;
Those rosy lips, whose dimples play
	And smile to steal the heart away,
Recall a scene of former joy,
	And touch thy father's heart, my Boy!

And thou canst lisp a father's name—
	Ah, William, were thine own the same,—
No self-reproach—but, let me cease—
	My care for thee shall purchase peace;
Thy mother's shade shall smile in joy,
	And pardon all the past, my Boy!

Her lowly grave the turf has prest,
	And thou hast known a stranger's breast;
Derision sneers upon thy birth,
	And yields thee scarce a name on earth;
Yet shall not these one hope destroy,—
	A Father's heart is thine, my Boy!

Why, let the world unfeeling frown,
	Must I fond Nature's claim disown?
Ah, no—though moralists reprove,
	I hail thee, dearest child of love,
Fair cherub, pledge of youth and joy—
	A Father guards thy birth, my Boy!

Oh, 'twill be sweet in thee to trace,
	Ere age has wrinkled o'er my face,
Ere half my glass of life is run,
	At once a brother and a son;
And all my wane of years employ
	In justice done to thee, my Boy!

Although so young thy heedless sire,
	Youth will not damp parental fire;
And, wert thou still less dear to me,
	While Helen's form revives in thee,
The breast, which beat to former joy,
	Will ne'er desert its pledge, my Boy!
			1807. [First published, 1830.]

FAREWELL! IF EVER FONDEST PRAYER.

FAREWELL! if ever fondest prayer
	For other's weal avail'd on high,
Mine will not all be lost in air,
	But waft thy name beyond the sky.
'Twere vain to speak, to weep, to sigh:
	Oh! more than tears of blood can tell,
When wrung from guilt's expiring eye,
	Are in that word—Farewell!—Farewell!

These lips are mute, these eyes are dry;
	But in my breast and in my brain,
Awake the pangs that pass not by,
	The thought that ne'er shall sleep again.
My soul nor deigns nor dares complain,
	Though grief and passion there rebel;
I only know we loved in vain—
	I only feel—Farewell!—Farewell!
					1808.

BRIGHT BE THE PLACE OF THY SOUL.

BRIGHT be the place of thy soul!
 No lovelier spirit than thine
E'er burst from its mortal control
 In the orbs of the blessed to shine.

On earth thou wert all but divine,
 As thy soul shall immortally be;
And our sorrow may cease to repine,
 When we know that thy God is with thee.

Light be the turf of thy tomb!
 May its verdure like emeralds be:
There should not be the shadow of gloom
 In aught that reminds us of thee.

Young flowers and an evergreen tree
 May spring from the spot of thy rest:
But nor cypress nor yew let us see;
 For why should we mourn for the blest!
 1808.

WHEN WE TWO PARTED.

WHEN we two parted
 In silence and tears,
Half broken-hearted
 To sever for years,
Pale grew thy cheek and cold,
 Colder thy kiss;
Truly that hour foretold
 Sorrow to this.

The dew of the morning
 Sunk chill on my brow—
It felt like the warning
 Of what I feel now.
Thy vows are all broken,
 And light is thy fame:
I hear thy name spoken,
 And share in its shame.

They name thee before me,
 A knell to mine ear;
A shudder comes o'er me—
 Why wert thou so dear?
They know not I knew thee,
 Who knew thee too well:—
Long, long shall I rue thee,
 Too deeply to tell.

In secret we met—
 In silence I grieve,
That thy heart could forget,
 Thy spirit deceive.
If I should meet thee
 After long years,
How should I greet thee?—
 With silence and tears.
 1808.

TO A YOUTHFUL FRIEND.

FEW years have pass'd since thou and I
 Were firmest friends, at least in name,
And childhood's gay sincerity
 Preserved our feelings long the same.

But now, like me, too well thou know'st
 What trifles oft the heart recall;
And those who once have loved the most
 Too soon forget they loved at all.

And such the change the heart displays,
 So frail is early friendship's reign,
A month's brief lapse, perhaps a day's,
 Will view thy mind estranged again.

If so, it never shall be mine
 To mourn the loss of such a heart;
The fault was Nature's fault, not thine,
 Which made thee fickle as thou art.

As rolls the ocean's changing tide,
 So human feelings ebb and flow;
And who would in a breast confide
 Where stormy passions ever glow?

It boots not that, together bred,
 Our childish days were days of joy:
My spring of life has quickly fled;
 Thou, too, hast ceased to be a boy.

And when we bid adieu to youth,
 Slaves to the specious world's control,
We sigh a long farewell to truth;
 That world corrupts the noblest soul.

Ah, joyous season! when the mind
 Dares all things boldly but to lie;
When thought ere spoke is unconfined,
 And sparkles in the placid eye.

Not so in Man's maturer years,
 When Man himself is but a tool;
When interest sways our hopes and fears,
 And all must love and hate by rule.

With fools in kindred vice the same,
 We learn at length our faults to blend;
And those, and those alone, may claim
 The prostituted name of friend.

Such is the common lot of man:
 Can we then 'scape from folly free?
Can we reverse the general plan,
 Nor be what all in turn must be?

No; for myself, so dark my fate
 Through every turn of life hath been;
Man and the world so much I hate,
 I care not when I quit the scene.

But thou, with spirit frail and light,
 Wilt shine awhile, and pass away;
As glow-worms sparkle through the night,
 But dare not stand the test of day.

Alas! whenever folly calls
 Where parasites and princes meet
(For cherish'd first in royal halls,
 The welcome vices kindly greet),

Ev'n now thou'rt nightly seen to add
 One insect to the fluttering crowd;
And still thy trifling heart is glad
 To join the vain and court the proud.

There dost thou glide from fair to fair,
 Still simpering on with eager haste,
As flies along the gay parterre,
 That taint the flowers they scarcely taste.

But say, what nymph will prize the flame
 Which seems, as marshy vapours move,
To flit along from dame to dame,
 An ignis-fatuus gleam of love?

What friend for thee, howe'er inclined,
 Will deign to own a kindred care?
Who will debase his manly mind,
 For friendship every fool may share?

In time forbear; amidst the throng
 No more so base a thing be seen;
No more so idly pass along;
 Be something, anything, but—mean.
 1808.

LINES INSCRIBED UPON A CUP FORMED FROM A SKULL.

START not—nor deem my spirit fled;
 In me behold the only skull,
From which, unlike a living head,
 Whatever flows is never dull.

I lived, I loved, I quaff'd, like thee:
 I died: let earth my bones resign;
Fill up—thou canst not injure me;
 The worm hath fouler lips than thine.

Better to hold the sparkling grape,
 Than nurse the earth-worm's slimy brood;
And circle in the goblet's shape
 The drink of gods, than reptile's food.

Where once my wit, perchance, hath shone,
 In aid of others' let me shine;
And when, alas! our brains are gone,
 What nobler substitute than wine?

Quaff while thou canst: another race,
 When thou and thine, like me, are sped,
May rescue thee from earth's embrace,
 And rhyme and revel with the dead.

Why not? since through life's little day
 Our heads such sad effects produce;
Redeem'd from worms and wasting clay,
 This chance is theirs, to be of use.
 Newstead Abbey, 1808.

WELL! THOU ART HAPPY.

WELL! thou art happy, and I feel
 That I should thus be happy too;
For still my heart regards thy weal
 Warmly, as it was wont to do.

Thy husband's blest—and 'twill impart
 Some pangs to view his happier lot:
But let them pass—Oh! how my heart
 Would hate him if he loved thee not!

When late I saw thy favourite child,
 I thought my jealous heart would break;
But when the unconscious infant smiled,
 I kiss'd it for its mother's sake.

I kiss'd it,—and repress'd my sighs
 Its father in its face to see;
But then it had its mother's eyes,
 And they were all to love and me.

Mary, adieu! I must away:
 While thou art blest I'll not repine;
But near thee I can never stay;
 My heart would soon again be thine.

I deem'd that time, I deem'd that pride,
 Had quench'd at length my boyish flame;
Nor knew, till seated by thy side,
 My heart in all,—save hope,—the same.

Yet was I calm: I knew the time
 My breast would thrill before thy look;
But now to tremble were a crime—
 We met,—and not a nerve was shook.

I saw thee gaze upon my face,
 Yet meet with no confusion there:
One only feeling could'st thou trace;
 The sullen calmness of despair.

Away! away! my early dream
 Remembrance never must awake:
Oh! where is Lethe's fabled stream?
 My foolish heart, be still, or break.
 November 2, 1808.

INSCRIPTION ON THE MONUMENT OF A NEWFOUNDLAND DOG.

WHEN some proud son of man returns to earth,
Unknown to glory, but upheld by birth,
The sculptor's art exhausts the pomp of woe,
And storied urns record who rest below:
When all is done, upon the tomb is seen,
Not what he was, but what he should have been:
But the poor dog, in life the firmest friend,
The first to welcome, foremost to defend,
Whose honest heart is still his master's own,
Who labours, fights, lives, breathes for him alone,

Unhonour'd falls, unnoticed all his worth,
Denied in heaven the soul he held on earth:
While man, vain insect! hopes to be forgiven,
And claims himself a sole exclusive heaven.
Oh man! thou feeble tenant of an hour,
Debased by slavery, or corrupt by power,
Who knows thee well must quit thee with
 disgust,
Degraded mass of animated dust!
Thy love is lust, thy friendship all a cheat,
Thy smiles hypocrisy, thy words deceit!
By nature vile, ennobled but by name,
Each kindred brute might bid thee blush for
 shame.
Ye! who perchance behold this simple urn,
Pass on—it honours none you wish to mourn:
To mark a friend's remains these stones arise;
I never knew but one,—and here he lies.

Newstead Abbey, *November* 30. 1808.

TO A LADY,

ON BEING ASKED MY REASON FOR QUITTING
ENGLAND IN THE SPRING.

When Man, expell'd from Eden's bowers,
 A moment linger'd near the gate,
Each scene recall'd the vanish'd hours,
 And bade him curse his future fate.

But, wandering on through distant climes,
 He learnt to bear his load of grief;
Just gave a sigh to other times,
 And found in busier scenes relief.

Thus, lady! will it be with me,
 And I must view thy charms no more·
For, while I linger near to thee,
 I sigh for all I knew before.

In flight I shall be surely wise,
 Escaping from temptation's snare;
I cannot view my paradise
 Without the wish of dwelling there.

December 2, 1808.

REMIND ME NOT, REMIND ME NOT.

Remind me not, remind me not,
 Of those beloved, those vanish'd hours,
 When all my soul was given to thee;
Hours that may never be forgot,
 Till time unnerves our vital powers,
 And thou and I shall cease to be.

Can I forget—canst thou forget,
 When playing with thy golden hair,
 How quick thy fluttering heart did move?
Oh! by my soul, I see thee yet,
 With eyes so languid, breast so fair,
 And lips, though silent, breathing love.

When thus reclining on my breast,
 Those eyes threw back a glance so sweet,
 As half reproach'd yet raised desire,
And still we near and nearer prest,
 And still our glowing lips would meet,
 As if in kisses to expire.

And then those pensive eyes would close,
 And bid their lids each other seek,
 Veiling the azure orbs below;
While their long lashes' darken'd gloss
 Seem'd stealing o'er thy brilliant cheek,
 Like raven's plumage smooth'd on snow.

I dreamt last night our love return'd,
 And, sooth to say, that very dream
 Was sweeter in its phantasy,
Than if for other hearts I burn'd,
 For eyes that ne'er like thine could beam
 In rapture's wild reality.

Then tell me not, remind me not,
 Of hours which, though for ever gone,
 Can still a pleasing dream restore,
Till thou and I shall be forgot,
 And senseless, as the mouldering stone
 Which tells that we shall be no more.

THERE WAS A TIME, I NEED NOT
NAME.

There was a time, I need not name,
 Since it will ne'er forgotten be,
When all our feelings were the same
 As still my soul hath been to thee.

And from that hour when first thy tongue
 Confess'd a love which equall'd mine,
Though many a grief my heart hath wrung,
 Unknown, and thus unfelt, by thine.

None, none hath sunk so deep as this—
 To think how all that love hath flown;
Transient as every faithless kiss,
 But transient in thy breast alone.

And yet my heart some solace knew,
 When late I heard thy lips declare,
In accents once imagined true,
 Remembrance of the days that were.

Yes! my adored, yet most unkind!
 Though thou wilt never love again,
To me 'tis doubly sweet to find
 Remembrance of that love remain.

Yes! 'tis a glorious thought to me,
 Nor longer shall my soul repine,
Whate'er thou art or e'er shalt be,
 Thou hast been dearly, solely mine.

AND WILT THOU WEEP WHEN I AM LOW?

AND wilt thou weep when I am low?
 Sweet lady! speak those words again
Yet if they grieve thee, say not so—
 I would not give that bosom pain.

My heart is sad, my hopes are gone,
 My blood runs coldly through my breast;
And when I perish, thou alone
 Wilt sigh above my place of rest.

And yet, methinks, a gleam of peace
 Doth through my cloud of anguish shine:
And for a while my sorrows cease,
 To know thy heart hath felt for mine.

Oh lady! blessed be that tear—
 It falls for one who cannot weep;
Such precious drops are doubly dear
 To those whose eyes no tear may steep.

Sweet lady! once my heart was warm
 With every feeling soft as thine;
But beauty's self hath ceased to charm
 A wretch created to repine.

Yet wilt thou weep when I am low?
 Sweet lady! speak those words again:
Yet if they grieve thee, say not so—
 I would not give that bosom pain.

—◦◦—

FILL THE GOBLET AGAIN.

A SONG.

FILL the goblet again! for I never before
Felt the glow which now gladdens my heart
 to its core;
Let us drink!—who would not?—since,
 through life's varied round,
In the goblet alone no deception is found.

I have tried in its turn all that life can supply;
I have bask'd in the beam of a dark rolling
 eye;
I have loved!—who has not?—but what
 heart can declare
That pleasure existed while passion was
 there?

In the days of my youth, when the heart's
 in its spring,
And dreams that affection can never take
 wing,
I had friends!—who has not?—but what
 tongue will avow,
That friends, rosy wine! are so faithful as
 thou?

The heart of a mistress some boy may
 estrange,
Friendship shifts with the sunbeam—thou
 never canst change;
Thou grow'st old—who does not?—but on
 earth what appears,
Whose virtues, like thine, still increase with
 its years?

Yet if blest to the utmost that love can
 bestow,
Should a rival bow down to our idol below,
We are jealous!—who's not?—thou hast no
 such alloy;
For the more that enjoy thee, the more we
 enjoy.

Then the season of youth and its vanities
 past,
For refuge we fly to the goblet at last;
There we find—do we not?—in the flow of
 the soul,
That truth, as of yore, is confined to the bowl.

When the box of Pandora was opened on
 earth,
And Misery's triumph commenced over Mirth,
Hope was left,—was she not?—but the goblet
 we kiss,
And care not for Hope, who are certain of
 bliss.

Long life to the grape! for when summer is
 flown,
The age of our nectar shall gladden our own:
We must die—who shall not?—May our sins
 be forgiven,
And Hebe shall never be idle in heaven.

—◦◦—

STANZAS TO A LADY, ON LEAVING ENGLAND.

'Tis done—and shivering in the gale
The bark unfurls her snowy sail;
And whistling o'er the bending mast,
Loud sings on high the fresh'ning blast;
And I must from this land be gone,
Because I cannot love but one.

But could I be what I have been,
And could I see what I have seen—
Could I repose upon the breast
Which once my warmest wishes blest—
I should not seek another zone
Because I cannot love but one.

'Tis long since I beheld that eye
Which gave me bliss or misery;
And I have striven, but in vain,
Never to think of it again:
For though I fly from Albion,
I still can only love but one.

As some lone bird, without a mate,
My weary heart is desolate;
I look around, and cannot trace
One friendly smile or welcome face,
And ev'n in crowds am still alone,
Because I cannot love but one.

And I will cross the whitening foam,
And I will seek a foreign home;
Till I forget a false fair face,
I ne'er shall find a resting-place;
My own dark thoughts I cannot shun,
But ever love, and love but one.

The poorest, veriest wretch on earth
Still finds some hospitable hearth,
Where friendship's or love's softer glow
May smile in joy or soothe in woe;
But friend or leman I have none,
Because I cannot love but one.

I go—but wheresoe'er I flee
There's not an eye will weep for me;
There's not a kind congenial heart,
Where I can claim the meanest part;
Nor thou, who hast my hopes undone,
Wilt sigh, although I love but one.

To think of every early scene,
Of what we are, and what we've been,
Would whelm some softer hearts with woe—
But mine, alas! has stood the blow;
Yet still beats on as it begun,
And never truly loves but one.

And who that dear loved one may be,
Is not for vulgar eyes to see;
And why that early love was cross'd,
Thou know'st the best, I feel the most;
But few that dwell beneath the sun
Have loved so long, and loved but one.

I've tried another's fetters too,
With charms perchance as fair to view;
And I would fain have loved as well,
But some unconquerable spell
Forbade my bleeding breast to own
A kindred care for aught but one.

'Twould soothe to take one lingering view,
And bless thee in my last adieu;
Yet wish I not those eyes to weep
For him that wanders o'er the deep;
His home, his hope, his youth are gone,
Yet still he loves, and loves but one.
 1809.

LINES TO MR. HODGSON.
WRITTEN ON BOARD THE LISBON PACKET.

Huzza! Hodgson, we are going,
 Our embargo's off at last;
Favourable breezes blowing
 Bend the canvass o'er the mast.

From aloft the signal's streaming,
 Hark! the farewell gun is fired;
Women screeching, tars blaspheming,
 Tell us that our time's expired.
 Here's a rascal
 Come to task all,
 Prying from the custom-house
 Trunks unpacking,
 Cases cracking,
 Not a corner for a mouse
'Scapes unsearch'd amid the racket,
Ere we sail on board the Packet.

Now our boatmen quit their mooring,
 And all hands must ply the oar;
Baggage from the quay is lowering,
 We're impatient, push from shore.
"Have a care! that case holds liquor—
 Stop the boat—I'm sick—oh Lord!"
"Sick, ma'am, damme, you'll be sicker
 Ere you've been an hour on board."
 Thus are screaming
 Men and women,
 Gemmen, ladies, servants, Jacks;
 Here entangling,
 All are wrangling,
 Stuck together close as wax.—
Such the general noise and racket,
Ere we reach the Lisbon Packet.

Now we've reach'd her, lo! the captain,
 Gallant Kidd, commands the crew;
Passengers their berths are clapt in,
 Some to grumble, some to spew.
"Heyday! call you that a cabin?
 Why 'tis hardly three feet square:
Not enough to stow Queen Mab in—
 Who the deuce can harbour there?"
 "Who, sir? plenty—
 Nobles twenty
 Did at once my vessel fill."—
 "Did they? Jesus,
 How you squeeze us!
 Would to God they did so still:
Then I'd scape the heat and racket
Of the good ship, Lisbon Packet."

Fletcher! Murray! Bob! where are you?
 Stretch'd along the deck like logs—
Bear a hand, you jolly tar, you!
 Here's a rope's end for the dogs.
Hobhouse muttering fearful curses,
 As the hatchway down he rolls,
Now his breakfast, now his verses,
 Vomits forth—and damns our souls.
 "Here's a stanza
 On Braganza—
 Help!"—"A couplet?"—"No, a cup
 Of warm water—"
 "What's the matter?"
 "Zounds! my liver's coming up;

I shall not survive the racket
Of this brutal Lisbon Packet."

Now at length we're off for Turkey,
　Lord knows when we shall come back!
Breezes foul and tempests murky
　May unship us in a crack.
But, since life at most a jest is,
　As philosophers allow,
Still to laugh by far the best is,
　Then laugh on—as I do now.
　　Laugh at all things,
　　Great and small things,
Sick or well, at sea or shore;
　　While we're quaffing,
　　Let's have laughing—
Who the devil cares for more?—
Some good wine! and who would lack it,
Ev'n on board the Lisbon Packet?

　　　　Falmouth Roads, *June* 30, 1809.
　　　　　　[First published, 1830.]

———————

TO FLORENCE.

Oh Lady! when I left the shore,
　The distant shore which gave me birth,
I hardly thought to grieve once more
　To quit another spot on earth:

Yet here, amidst this barren isle,
　Where panting Nature droops the head,
Where only thou art seen to smile,
　I view my parting hour with dread.

Though far from Albin's craggy shore,
　Divided by the dark-blue main;
A few, brief, rolling seasons o'er,
　Perchance I view her cliffs again:

But wheresoe'er I now may roam,
　Through scorching clime, and varied sea,
Though Time restore me to my home,
　I ne'er shall bend mine eyes on thee:

On thee, in whom at once conspire
　All charms which heedless hearts can move,
Whom but to see is to admire,
　And, oh! forgive the word—to love.

Forgive the word, in one who ne'er
　With such a word can more offend;
And since thy heart I cannot share,
　Believe me, what I am, thy friend.

And who so cold as look on thee,
　Thou lovely wand'rer, and be less?
Nor be, what man should ever be,
　The friend of Beauty in distress?

Ah! who would think that form had past
　Through Danger's most destructive path,
Had braved the death-wing'd tempest's blast,
　And 'scaped a tyrant's fiercer wrath?

Lady! when I shall view the walls
　Where free Byzantium once arose,
And Stamboul's Oriental halls
　The Turkish tyrants now enclose;

Though mightiest in the lists of fame,
　That glorious city still shall be;
On me 't will hold a dearer claim,
　As spot of thy nativity:

And though I bid thee now farewell,
　When I behold that wondrous scene,
Since where thou art I may not dwell,
　'T will soothe to be where thou hast been.

　　　　　　　　　September, 1809.

———————

LINES WRITTEN IN AN ALBUM, AT MALTA.

As o'er the cold sepulchral stone
　Some name arrests the passer-by;
Thus, when thou view'st this page alone,
　May mine attract thy pensive eye!

And when by thee that name is read,
　Perchance in some succeeding year,
Reflect on me as on the dead,
　And think my heart is buried here.

　　　　　　　　September 14, 1809.

———————

STANZAS COMPOSED DURING A THUNDER-STORM.

Chill and mirk is the nightly blast,
　Where Pindus' mountains rise,
And angry clouds are pouring fast
　The vengeance of the skies.

Our guides are gone, our hope is lost,
　And lightnings, as they play,
But show where rocks our path have crost,
　Or gild the torrent's spray.

Is yon a cot I saw, though low?
　When lightning broke the gloom—
How welcome were its shade!—ah, no!
　'Tis but a Turkish tomb.

Through sounds of foaming waterfalls,
　I hear a voice exclaim—
My way-worn countryman, who calls
　On distant England's name.

A shot is fired—by foe or friend?
　Another—'t is to tell
The mountain-peasants to descend,
　And lead us where they dwell.

Oh! who in such a night will dare
　To tempt the wilderness?
And who 'mid thunder-peals can hear
　Our signal of distress?

And who that heard our shouts would rise
 To try the dubious road?
Nor rather deem from nightly cries
 That outlaws were abroad.

Clouds burst, skies flash, oh, dreaaful hour!
 More fiercely pours the storm!
Yet here one thought has still the power
 To keep my bosom warm.

While wandering through each broken path,
 O'er brake and craggy brow;
While elements exhaust their wrath,
 Sweet Florence, where art thou?

Not on the sea, not on the sea,
 Thy bark hath long been gone:
Oh, may the storm that pours on me
 Bow down my head alone!

Full swiftly blew the swift Siroc,
 When last I press'd thy lip;
And long ere now, with foaming shock
 Impell'd thy gallant ship.

Now thou art safe; nay, long ere now
 Hast trod the shore of Spain;
'Twere hard if aught so fair as thou
 Should linger on the main.

And since I now remember thee
 In darkness and in dread,
As in those hours of revelry
 Which mirth and music sped;

Do thou, amid the fair white walls,
 If Cadiz yet be free,
At times from out her latticed halls
 Look o'er the dark blue sea;

Then think upon Calypso's isles,
 Endear'd by days gone by;
To others give a thousand smiles,
 To me a single sigh.

And when the admiring circle mark
 The paleness of thy face,
A half-form'd tear, a transient spark
 Of melancholy grace,

Again thou'lt smile, and blushing shun
 Some coxcomb's raillery;
Nor own for once thou thought'st on one,
 Who ever thinks on thee.

Though smile and sigh alike are vain,
 When sever'd hearts repine,
My spirit flies o'er mount and main,
 And mourns in search of thine.

STANZAS WRITTEN IN PASSING THE AMBRACIAN GULF.

THROUGH cloudless skies, in silvery sheen,
 Full beams the moon on Actium's coast:
And on these waves, for Egypt's queen,
 The ancient world was won and lost.

And now upon the scene I look,
 The azure grave of many a Roman;
Where stern Ambition once forsook
 His wavering crown to follow woman.

Florence! whom I will love as well
 As ever yet was said or sung
(Since Orpheus sang his spouse from hell),
 Whilst thou art fair and I am young;

Sweet Florence! those were pleasant times,
 When worlds were staked for ladies' eyes:
Had bards as many realms as rhymes,
 Thy charms might raise new Antonies.

Though Fate forbids such things to be,
 Yet, by thine eyes and ringlets curl'd!
I cannot lose a world for thee,
 But would not lose thee for a world.

 Nov. 14, 1809.

THE SPELL IS BROKE, THE CHARM IS FLOWN!

WRITTEN AT ATHENS, JANUARY 16, 1810.

THE spell is broke, the charm is flown!
 Thus is it with life's fitful fever:
We madly smile when we should groan
 Delirium is our best deceiver.

Each lucid interval of thought
 Recalls the woes of Nature's charter;
And he that acts as wise men ought,
 But lives, as saints have died, a martyr.

WRITTEN AFTER SWIMMING FROM SESTOS TO ABYDOS.

IF, in the month of dark December,
 Leander, who was nightly wont
(What maid will not the tale remember?)
 To cross thy stream, broad Hellespont!

If, when the wintry tempest roar'd,
 He sped to Hero, nothing loth,
And thus of old thy current pour'd,
 Fair Venus! how I pity both!

For me, degenerate modern wretch,
 Though in the genial month of May,
My dripping limbs I faintly stretch,
 And think I've done a feat to-day.

But since he cross'd the rapid tide,
 According to the doubtful story,
To woo,—and—Lord knows what beside,
 And swam for Love, as I for Glory;

'Twere hard to say who fared the best:
 Sad mortals! thus the gods still plague you!
He lost his labour, I my jest;
 For he was drown'd, and I've the ague.

 May 9, 1810.

LINES IN THE TRAVELLERS' BOOK AT ORCHOMENUS.

IN THIS BOOK A TRAVELLER HAD WRITTEN :—

"FAIR Albion, smiling, sees her son depart
To trace the birth and nursery of art:
Noble his object, glorious is his aim;
He comes to Athens, and he writes his name."

BENEATH WHICH LORD BYRON INSERTED THE
FOLLOWING :—

THE modest bard, like many a bard unknown,
Rhymes on our names, but wisely hides his own;
But yet, whoe'er he be, to say no worse,
His name would bring more credit than his
verse.

1810.

MAID OF ATHENS, ERE WE PART.

Ζώη μοῦ, σᾶς ἀγαπῶ.

MAID of Athens, ere we part,
Give, oh give me back my heart!
Or, since that has left my breast,
Keep it now, and take the rest!
Hear my vow before I go,
Ζώη μοῦ, σᾶς ἀγαπῶ.

By those tresses unconfined,
Woo'd by each Ægean wind;
By those lids whose jetty fringe
Kiss thy soft cheeks' blooming tinge;
By those wild eyes like the roe,
Ζώη μοῦ, σᾶς ἀγαπῶ.

By that lip I long to taste;
By that zone-encircled waist;
By all the token-flowers that tell
What words can never speak so well;
By love's alternate joy and woe,
Ζώη μοῦ, σᾶς ἀγαπῶ.

Maid of Athens! I am gone:
Think of me, sweet! when alone.
Though I fly to Istambol,
Athens holds my heart and soul:
Can I cease to love thee? No!
Ζώη μοῦ, σᾶς ἀγαπῶ.

Athens, 1810.

TRANSLATION OF THE NURSE'S DOLE IN THE MEDEA OF EURIPIDES.

OH how I wish that an embargo
Had kept in port the good ship Argo!
Who, still unlaunch'd from Grecian docks,
Had never pass'd the Azure rocks;
But now I fear her trip will be a
Damn'd business for my Miss Medea, &c. &c.

June, 1810.

MY EPITAPH.

YOUTH, Nature, and relenting Jove,
To keep my lamp *in* strongly strove;
But Romanelli was so stout,
He beat all three—and *blew* it out.

Oct. 1810.

SUBSTITUTE FOR AN EPITAPH.

KIND Reader! take your choice to cry or
laugh;
Here HAROLD lies—but where's his Epi-
taph?
If such you seek, try Westminster, and
view
Ten thousand just as fit for him as you.
Athens.

LINES WRITTEN BENEATH A PICTURE.

DEAR object of defeated care!
Though now of Love and thee bereft,
To reconcile me with despair,
Thine image and my tears are left.

'T is said with Sorrow Time can cope;
But this I feel can ne'er be true:
For by the death-blow of my Hope
My Memory immortal grew.

Athens, *January*, 1811.

TRANSLATION OF THE FAMOUS GREEK WAR SONG,

"Δεῦτε παῖδες τῶν Ἑλλήνων."

Sons of the Greeks, arise!
The glorious hour's gone forth,
And, worthy of such ties,
Display who gave us birth.

CHORUS.

Sons of Greeks! let us go
In arms against the foe,
Till their hated blood shall flow
In a river past our feet.

Then manfully despising
The Turkish tyrant's yoke,
Let your country see you rising,
And all her chains are broke.
Brave shades of chiefs and sages,
Behold the coming strife!
Hellénes of past ages,
Oh, start again to life!

At the sound of my trumpet, breaking
 Your sleep, oh, join with me!
And the seven-hill'd city seeking,
 Fight, conquer, till we 're free.
 Sons of Greeks, &c.

Sparta, Sparta, why in slumbers
 Lethargic dost thou lie?
Awake, and join thy numbers
 With Athens, old ally!
Leonidas recalling,
 That chief of ancient song,
Who saved ye once from falling,
 The terrible! the strong!
Who made that bold diversion
 In old Thermopylæ,
And warring with the Persian
 To keep his country free;
With his three hundred waging
 The battle, long he stood,
And like a lion raging,
 Expired in seas of blood.
 Sons of Greeks, &c.

TRANSLATION OF THE ROMAIC SONG,

"Μπενω μες 'το' πέριβόλι
 'Ωραιότατη Χάηδή," &c.

I ENTER thy garden of roses,
 Beloved and fair Haidée,
Each morning where Flora reposes,
 For surely I see her in thee.
Oh, Lovely! thus low I implore thee,
 Receive this fond truth from my tongue,
Which utters its song to adore thee,
 Yet trembles for what it has sung;
As the branch, at the bidding of Nature,
 Adds fragrance and fruit to the tree,
Through her eyes, through her every feature,
 Shines the soul of the young Haidée.

But the loveliest garden grows hateful
 When Love has abandon'd the bowers;
Bring me hemlock—since mine is ungrateful,
 That herb is more fragrant than flowers.
The poison, when pour'd from the chalice,
 Will deeply embitter the bowl;
But when drunk to escape from thy malice,
 The draught shall be sweet to my soul.
Too cruel! in vain I implore thee
 My heart from these horrors to save:
Will nought to my bosom restore thee?
 Then open the gates of the grave.

As the chief who to combat advances
 Secure of his conquest before,
Thus thou, with those eyes for thy lances,
 Hast pierced through my heart to its core.

Ah, tell me, my soul! must I perish
 By pangs which a smile would dispel?
Would the hope, which thou once bad'st me
 cherish,
 For torture repay me too well?
Now sad is the garden of roses,
 Beloved but false Haidée!
There Flora all wither'd reposes,
 And mourns o'er thine absence with me.
 1811.

ON PARTING.

THE kiss, dear maid! thy lip has left
 Shall never part from mine,
Till happier hours restore the gift
 Untainted back to thine.

Thy parting glance, which fondly beams,
 An equal love may see:
The tear that from thine eyelid streams
 Can weep no change in me.

I ask no pledge to make me blest
 In gazing when alone;
Nor one memorial for a breast,
 Whose thoughts are all thine own.

Nor need I write—to tell the tale
 My pen were doubly weak:
Oh! what can idle words avail,
 Unless the heart could speak?

By day or night, in weal or woe,
 That heart, no longer free,
Must bear the love it cannot show,
 And silent ache for thee.
 March, 1811.

EPITAPH FOR JOSEPH BLACKETT, LATE POET AND SHOEMAKER.

STRANGER! behold, interr'd together,
The *souls* of learning and of leather.
Poor Joe is gone, but left his *all*:
You 'll find his relics in a *stall*.
His works were neat, and often found
Well stitch'd, and with *morocco* bound.
Tread lightly—where the bard is laid
He cannot mend the shoe he made;
Yet is he happy in his hole,
With verse immortal as his *sole*.
But still to business he held fast,
And stuck to Phœbus to the last.
Then who shall say so good a fellow
Was only "leather and prunella?"
For character—he did not lack it;
And if he did, 'twere shame to "Black it."
 Malta, May 16, 1811.

FAREWELL TO MALTA.

ADIEU, ye joys of La Valette!
Adieu, sirocco, sun, and sweat!
Adieu, thou palace rarely enter'd!
Adieu, ye mansions where—I've ventured!
Adieu, ye cursed streets of stairs!
(How surely he who mounts you swears!)
Adieu, ye merchants often failing!
Adieu, thou mob for ever railing!
Adieu, ye packets—without letters!
Adieu, ye fools—who ape your betters!
Adieu, thou damned'st quarantine,
That gave me fever, and the spleen!
Adieu, that stage which makes us yawn, Sirs,
Adieu, his Excellency's dancers!
Adieu to Peter—whom no fault's in,
But could not teach a colonel waltzing;
Adieu, ye females fraught with graces!
Adieu, red coats, and redder faces!
Adieu, the supercilious air
Of all that strut " en militaire!"
I go—but God knows when, or why,
To smoky towns and cloudy sky,
To things (the honest truth to say)
As bad—but in a different way.

Farewell to these, but not adieu,
Triumphant sons of truest blue!
While either Adriatic shore,
And fallen chiefs, and fleets no more,
And nightly smiles, and daily dinners,
Proclaim you war and woman's winners.
Pardon my Muse, who apt to prate is,
And take my rhyme—because 'tis " gratis."

And now I've got to Mrs. Fraser,
Perhaps you think I mean to praise her—
And were I vain enough to think
My praise was worth this drop of ink,
A line—or two—were no hard matter,
As here, indeed, I need not flatter:
But she must be content to shine
In better praises than in mine,
With lively air, and open heart,
And fashion's ease, without its art;
Her hours can gaily glide along,
Nor ask the aid of idle song.

And now, O Malta! since thou'st got us,
Thou little military hothouse!
I'll not offend with words uncivil,
And wish thee rudely at the Devil,
But only stare from out my casement,
And ask, for what is such a place meant?
Then, in my solitary nook,
Return to scribbling, or a book,
Or take my physic while I'm able
(Two spoonfuls hourly by the label),

Prefer my nightcap to my beaver,
And bless the gods I've got a fever.

May 26, 1811.
[First published, 1832.]

TO DIVES.

A FRAGMENT.

UNHAPPY DIVES! in an evil hour
'Gainst Nature's voice seduced to deeds ac-
 curst!
Once Fortune's minion, now thou feel'st her
 power;
Wrath's vial on thy lofty head hath burst.
In Wit, in Genius, as in Wealth the first,
How wondrous bright thy blooming morn
 arose!
But thou wert smitten with th' unhallow'd
 thirst
Of crime un-named, and thy sad noon must
 close
In scorn, and solitude unsought, the worst of
 woes.

1811. [First published, 1832.]

ON MOORE'S LAST OPERATIC FARCE, OR FARCICAL OPERA.

GOOD plays are scarce,
 So Moore writes farce:
The poet's fame grows brittle—
 We knew before
 That *Little*'s Moore,
But now 'tis *Moore* that's *little*.

September 14, 1811.
[First published, 1830.]

EPISTLE TO A FRIEND,

IN ANSWER TO SOME LINES EXHORTING THE
AUTHOR TO BE CHEERFUL, AND TO " BAN-
ISH CARE."

" OH! banish care "—such ever be
The motto of *thy* revelry!
Perchance of *mine*, when wassail nights
Renew those riotous delights,
Wherewith the children of Despair
Lull the lone heart, and " banish care."
But not in morn's reflecting hour,
When present, past, and future lower,
When all I loved is changed or gone,
Mock with such taunts the woes of one,
Whose every thought—but let them pass—
Thou know'st I am not what I was.
But, above all, if thou wouldst hold
Place in a heart that ne'er was cold,

By all the powers that men revere,
By all unto thy bosom dear,
Thy joys below, thy hopes above,
Speak—speak of anything but love.

'Twere long to tell, and vain to hear,
The tale of one who scorns a tear;
And there is little in that tale
Which better bosoms would bewail.
But mine has suffer'd more than well
'Twould suit philosophy to tell.
I've seen my bride another's bride,—
Have seen her seated by his side,—
Have seen the infant, which she bore,
Wear the sweet smile the mother wore,
When she and I in youth have smiled,
As fond and faultless as her child;
Have seen her eyes, in cold disdain,
Ask if I felt no secret pain;
And *I* have acted well my part,
And made my cheek belie my heart,
Return'd the freezing glance she gave,
Yet felt the while *that* woman's slave;—
Have kiss'd, as if without design,
The babe which ought to have been mine,
And show'd, alas! in each caress
Time had not made me love the less.

But let this pass—I'll whine no more,
Nor seek again an eastern shore;
The world befits a busy brain,—
I'll hie me to its haunts again.
But if, in some succeeding year,
When Britain's "May is in the sere,"
Thou hear'st of one whose deepening crimes
Suit with the sablest of the times,
Of one, whom love nor pity sways,
Nor hope of fame, nor good men's praise;
One, who in stern ambition's pride,
Perchance not blood shall turn aside;
One rank'd in some recording page
With the worst anarchs of the age,
Him wilt thou *know*—and *knowing* pause,
Nor with the *effect* forget the cause.

<div style="text-align:right">Newstead Abbey, Oct. 11, 1811.
[First published, 1830.]</div>

—◆—

TO THYRZA.

WITHOUT a stone to mark the spot,
　And say, what Truth might well have
　　said,
By all, save one, perchance forgot,
　Ah! wherefore art thou lowly laid?

By many a shore and many a sea
　Divided, yet beloved in vain;
The past, the future fled to thee,
　To bid us meet—no—ne'er again!

Could this have been—a word, a look,
　That softly said, "We part in peace,"
Had taught my bosom how to brook,
　With fainter sighs, thy soul's release.

And didst thou not, since Death for thee
　Prepared a light and pangless dart,
Once long for him thou ne'er shalt see,
　Who held, and holds thee in his heart?

Oh! who like him had watch'd thee here?
　Or sadly mark'd thy glazing eye,
In that dread hour ere death appear,
　When silent sorrow fears to sigh,

Till all was past? But when no more
　'Twas thine to reck of human woe,
Affection's heart-drops, gushing o'er,
　Had flow'd as fast—as now they flow.

Shall they not flow, when many a day
　In these, to me, deserted towers,
Ere call'd but for a time away,
　Affection's mingling tears were ours?

Ours too the glance none saw beside;
　The smile none else might understand;
The whisper'd thought of hearts allied,
　The pressure of the thrilling hand;

The kiss, so guiltless and refined,
　That Love each warmer wish forbore;
Those eyes proclaim'd so pure a mind,
　Even Passion blush'd to plead for more.

The tone, that taught me to rejoice,
　When prone, unlike thee, to repine;
The song, celestial from thy voice,
　But sweet to me from none but thine;

The pledge we wore—I wear it still,
　But where is thine?—Ah! where art thou?
Oft have I borne the weight of ill,
　But never bent beneath till now!

Well hast thou left in life's late bloom
　The cup of woe for me to drain.
If rest alone be in the tomb,
　I would not wish thee here again.

But if in worlds more blest than this
　Thy virtues seek a fitter sphere,
Impart some portion of thy bliss,
　To wean me from mine anguish here.

Teach me—too early taught by thee!
　To bear, forgiving and forgiven:
On earth thy love was such to me;
　It fain would form my hope in heaven!

<div style="text-align:right">—◆— October 11, 1811.</div>

AWAY, AWAY, YE NOTES OF WOE!

AWAY, away, ye notes of woe!
　Be silent, thou once soothing strain,
Or I must flee from hence—for, oh!
　I dare not trust those sounds again.

To me they speak of brighter days—
　But lull the chords, for now, alas!
I must not think, I may not gaze,
　On what I am—on what I was.

The voice that made those sounds more sweet
　Is hush'd, and all their charms are fled ·
And now their softest notes repeat
　A dirge, an anthem o'er the dead!
Yes, Thyrza! yes, they breathe of thee,
　Beloved dust! since dust thou art;
And all that once was harmony
　Is worse than discord to my heart!

'Tis silent all!—but on my ear
　The well remember'd echoes thrill;
I hear a voice I would not hear,
　A voice that now might well be still:
Yet oft my doubting soul 't will shake;
　Even slumber owns its gentle tone,
Till consciousness will vainly wake
　To listen, though the dream be flown.

Sweet Thyrza! waking as in sleep,
　Thou art but now a lovely dream;
A star that trembled o'er the deep,
　Then turn'd from earth its tender beam.
But he who through life's dreary way
　Must pass, when heaven is veil'd in wrath,
Will long lament the vanish'd ray
　That scatter'd gladness o'er his path.
　　　　　　　　　December 6, 1811.

ONE STRUGGLE MORE, AND I AM FREE.

One struggle more, and I am free
　From pangs that rend my heart in twain;
One last long sigh to love and thee,
　Then back to busy life again.
It suits me well to mingle now
　With things that never pleased before!
Though every joy is fled below,
　What future grief can touch me more?

Then bring me wine, the banquet bring;
　Man was not form'd to live alone:
I'll be that light, unmeaning thing
　That smiles with all, and weeps with none.
It was not thus in days more dear,
　It never would have been, but thou
Hast fled, and left me lonely here;
　Thou 'rt nothing—all are nothing now.

In vain my lyre would lightly breathe!
　The smile that sorrow fain would wear
But mocks the woe that lurks beneath,
　Like roses o'er a sepulchre.
Though gay companions o'er the bowl
　Dispel awhile the sense of ill:
Though pleasure fires the maddening soul,
　The heart,—the heart is lonely still!

On many a lone and lovely night
　It sooth'd to gaze upon the sky;
For then I deem'd the heavenly light
　Shone sweetly on thy pensive eye:
And oft I thought at Cynthia's noon,
　When sailing o'er the Ægean wave,
"Now Thyrza gazes on that moon"—
　Alas, it gleam'd upon her grave!

When stretch'd on fever's sleepless bed,
　And sickness shrunk my throbbing veins,
"'Tis comfort still," I faintly said,
　"That Thyrza cannot know my pains:"
Like freedom to the time-worn slave,
　A boon 'tis idle then to give,
Relenting Nature vainly gave
　My life, when Thyrza ceased to live!

My Thyrza's pledge in better days,
　When love and life alike were new!
How different now thou meet'st my gaze!
　How tinged by time with sorrow's hue!
The heart that gave itself with thee
　Is silent—ah, were mine as still!
Though cold as e'en the dead can be,
　It feels, it sickens with the chill.

Thou bitter pledge! thou mournful token!
　Though painful, welcome to my breast!
Still, still preserve that love unbroken,
　Or break the heart to which thou 'rt press'd.
Time tempers love, but not removes,
　More hallow'd when its hope is fled:
Oh! what are thousand living loves
　To that which cannot quit the dead?

EUTHANASIA.

When Time, or soon or late, shall bring
　The dreamless sleep that lulls the dead,
Oblivion! may thy languid wing
　Wave gently o'er my dying bed!

No band of friends or heirs be there,
　To weep, or wish, the coming blow:
No maiden, with dishevelled hair,
　To feel, or feign, decorous woe.

But silent let me sink to earth,
　With no officious mourners near:
I would not mar one hour of mirth,
　Nor startle friendship with a tear.

Yet Love, if Love in such an hour
　Could nobly check its useless sighs,
Might then exert its latest power
　In her who lives, and him who dies.

'T were sweet, my Psyche! to the last
　Thy features still serene to see:
Forgetful of its struggles past,
　E'en Pain itself should smile on thee.

But vain the wish—for Beauty still
 Will shrink, as shrinks the ebbing breath;
And women's tears, produced at will,
 Deceive in life, unman in death.

Then lonely be my latest hour,
 Without regret, without a groan?
For thousands Death hath ceas'd to lower,
 And pain been transient or unknown.

" Ay, but to die, and go," alas!
 Where all have gone, and all must go!
To be the nothing that I was
 Ere born to life and living woe!

Count o'er the joys thine hours have seen,
 Count o'er thy days from anguish free,
And know, whatever thou hast been,
 'T is something better not to be.

AND THOU ART DEAD, AS YOUNG AND FAIR.

"Heu, quanto minus est cum reliquis versari quam
 tui meminisse!"

AND thou art dead, as young and fair
 As aught of mortal birth;
And form so soft, and charms so rare,
 Too soon return'd to Earth!
Though Earth received them in her bed
And o'er the spot the crowd may tread
 In carelessness or mirth,
There is an eye which could not brook
A moment on that grave to look.

I will not ask where thou liest low,
 Nor gaze upon the spot;
There flowers or weeds at will may grow,
 So I behold them not:
It is enough for me to prove
That what I loved, and long must love,
 Like common earth can rot;
To me there needs no stone to tell,
'Tis Nothing that I loved so well.

Yet did I love thee to the last
 As fervently as thou,
Who didst not change through all the past,
 And canst not alter now.
The love where Death has set his seal,
Nor age can chill, nor rival steal,
 Nor falsehood disavow:
And, what were worse, thou canst not see
Or wrong, or change, or fault in me.

The better days of life were ours;
 The worst can be but mine:
The sun that cheers, the storm that lowers,
 Shall never more be thine.
The silence of that dreamless sleep
I envy now too much to weep;
 Nor need I to repine,

That all those charms have pass'd away;
I might have watch'd through long decay.

The flower in ripen'd bloom unmatch'd
 Must fall the earliest prey;
Though by no hand untimely snatch'd,
 The leaves must drop away:
And yet it were a greater grief
To watch it withering, leaf by leaf,
 Than see it pluck'd to-day;
Since earthly eye but ill can bear
To trace the change to foul from fair.

I know not if I could have borne
 To see thy beauties fade;
The night that follow'd such a morn
 Had worn a deeper shade:
Thy day without a cloud hath pass'd,
And thou wert lovely to the last;
 Extinguish'd, not decay'd;
As stars that shoot along the sky
Shine brightest as they fall from high.

As once I wept, if I could weep,
 My tears might well be shed,
To think I was not near to keep
 One vigil o'er thy bed;
To gaze, how fondly! on thy face,
To fold thee in a faint embrace,
 Uphold thy drooping head;
And show that love, however vain,
Nor thou nor I can feel again.

Yet how much less it were to gain,
 Though thou hast left me free,
The loveliest things that still remain,
 Than thus remember thee!
The all of thine that cannot die
Through dark and dread Eternity
 Returns again to me,
And more thy buried love endears
Than aught except its living years.
 February, 1812.

IF SOMETIMES IN THE HAUNTS OF MEN.

IF sometimes in the haunts of men
 Thine image from my breast may fade,
The lonely hour presents again
 The semblance of thy gentle shade:
And now that sad and silent hour
 Thus much of thee can still restore,
And sorrow unobserved may pour
 The plaint she dare not speak before.

Oh, pardon that in crowds awhile
 I waste one thought I owe to thee,
And self-condemn'd, appear to smile,
 Unfaithful to thy memory:

Nor deem that memory less dear,
　That then I seem not to repine ;
I would not fools should overhear
　One sigh that should be wholly *thine*.

If not the goblet pass unquaff'd,
　It is not drain'd to banish care ;
The cup must hold a deadlier draught,
　That brings a Lethe for despair.
And could Oblivion set my soul
　From all her troubled visions free,
I'd dash to earth the sweetest bowl
　That drown'd a single thought of thee.

For wert thou vanish'd from my mind,
　Where could my vacant bosom turn ?
And who would then remain behind
　To honour thine abandon'd Urn ?
No, no—it is my sorrow's pride
　That last dear duty to fulfil :
Though all the world forget beside,
　'Tis meet that I remember still.

For well I know, that such had been
　Thy gentle care for him, who now
Unmourn'd shall quit this mortal scene,
　Where none regarded him, but thou :
And, oh ! I feel in *that* was given
　A blessing never meant for me ;
Thou wert too like a dream of Heaven
　For earthly Love to merit thee.
　　　　　　　　　March 14, 1812.

　　　　　　—◆◆—

FROM THE FRENCH.

ÆGLE, beauty and poet, has two little crimes ;
She makes her own face, and does not make
　her rhymes.

　　　　　　—◆◆—

ON A CORNELIAN HEART WHICH WAS BROKEN.

ILL-FATED Heart ! and can it be,
　That thou should'st thus be rent in twain ?
Have years of care for thine and thee
　Alike been all employ'd in vain ?

Yet precious seems each shatter'd part,
　And every fragment dearer grown,
Since he who wears thee feels thou art
　A fitter emblem of *his* own.
　　　　　　　　　March 16, 1812.

　　　　　　—◆◆—

LINES TO A LADY WEEPING.

WEEP, daughter of a royal line,
　A Sire's disgrace, a realm's decay ;
Ah ! happy if each tear of thine
　Could wash a father's fault away !

Weep—for thy tears are Virtue's tears—
　Auspicious to these suffering isles ;
And be each drop in future years
　Repaid thee by thy people's smiles !

　　　　　　—◆◆—　　　*March*, 1812.

THE CHAIN I GAVE.

FROM THE TURKISH.

THE chain I gave was fair to view,
　The lute I added sweet in sound ;
The heart that offer'd both was true,
　And ill deserved the fate it found.

These gifts were charm'd by secret spell,
　Thy truth in absence to divine ;
And they have done their duty well,—
　Alas ! they could not teach thee thine.

That chain was firm in every link,
　But not to bear a stranger's touch ;
That lute was sweet—till thou could'st think
　In other hands its notes were such.

Let him who from thy neck unbound
　The chain which shiver'd in his grasp,
Who saw that lute refuse to sound,
　Restring the chords, renew the clasp.

When thou wert changed, they alter'd too ;
　The chain is broke, the music mute.
'Tis past—to them and thee adieu—
　False heart, frail chain, and silent lute.

　　　　　　—◆◆—

LINES WRITTEN ON A BLANK LEAF OF "THE PLEASURES OF MEMORY."

ABSENT or present, still to thee,
　My friend, what magic spells belong !
As all can tell, who share, like me,
　In turn thy converse and thy song.

But when the dreaded hour shall come
　By Friendship ever deem'd too nigh,
And "MEMORY" o'er her Druid's tomb
　Shall weep that aught of thee can die,

How fondly will she then repay
　Thy homage offer'd at her shrine,
And blend, while ages roll away,
　Her name immortally with *thine !*
　　　　　　—◆◆—　　　*April* 19, 1812.

ADDRESS, SPOKEN AT THE OPENING OF DRURY-LANE THEATRE,

SATURDAY, OCTOBER 10, 1812.

IN one dread night our city saw, and sigh'd,
Bow'd to the dust, the Drama's tower of
　pride ;
In one short hour beheld the blazing fane,
Apollo sink, and Shakspeare cease to reign.

Ye who beheld, (oh! sight admired and
mourn'd,
Whose radiance mock'd the ruin it adorn'd!)
Through clouds of fire the massy fragments
riven,
Like Israel's pillar, chase the night from
heaven;
Saw the long column of revolving flames
Shake its red shadow o'er the startled
Thames,
While thousands, throng'd around the burn-
ing dome,
Shrank back appall'd, and trembled for their
home,
As glared the volumed blaze, and ghastly
shone
The skies, with lightnings awful as their own,
Till blackening ashes and the lonely wall
Usurp'd the Muse's realm, and mark'd her
fall;
Say—shall this new, nor less aspiring pile,
Rear'd where once rose the mightiest in our
isle,
Know the same favour which the former
knew,
A shrine for Shakspeare—worthy him and
you?

Yes—it shall be—the magic of that name
Defies the scythe of time, the torch of flame;
On the same spot still consecrates the scene,
And bids the Drama *be* where she hath *been:*
This fabric's birth attests the potent spell—
Indulge our honest pride, and say, *How well!*

As soars this fane to emulate the last,
Oh! might we draw our omens from the past,
Some hour propitious to our prayers may
boast
Names such as hallow still the dome we lost.
On Drury first your Siddons' thrilling art
O'erwhelm'd the gentlest, storm'd the stern-
est heart.
On Drury, Garrick's latest laurels grew;
Here your last tears retiring Roscius drew,
Sigh'd his last thanks, and wept his last
adieu:
But still for living wit the wreaths may
bloom,
That only waste their odours o'er the tomb.
Such Drury claim'd and claims—nor you
refuse
One tribute to revive his slumbering muse;
With garlands deck your own Menander's
head,
Nor hoard your honours idly for the dead.
Dear are the days which made our annals
bright,
Ere Garrick fled, or Brinsley ceased to write.
Heirs to their labours, like all high-born heirs,
Vain of *our* ancestry as they of *theirs;*

While thus Remembrance borrows Banquo's
glass
To claim the sceptred shadows as they pass,
And we the mirror hold, where imaged shine
Immortal names, emblazon'd on our line,
Pause—ere their feebler offspring you con-
demn,
Reflect how hard the task to rival them!

Friends of the stage! to whom both Players
and Plays
Must sue alike for pardon or for praise,
Whose judging voice and eye alone direct
The boundless power to cherish or reject;
If e'er frivolity has led to fame,
And made us blush that you forbore to blame;
If e'er the sinking stage could condescend
To soothe the sickly taste it dare not mend,
All past reproach may present scenes refute,
And censure, wisely loud, be justly mute!
Oh! since your fiat stamps the Drama's laws,
Forbear to mock us with misplaced applause;
So pride shall doubly nerve the actor's
powers,
And reason's voice be echo'd back by ours!

This greeting o'er, the ancient rule obey'd,
The Drama's homage by her herald paid,
Receive *our* welcome too, whose every tone
Springs from our hearts, and fain would win
your own.
The curtain rises—may our stage unfold
Scenes not unworthy Drury's days of old!
Britons our judges, Nature for our guide,
Still may *we* please—long, long may *you* pre
side.

<hr style="width:15%" />

PARENTHETICAL ADDRESS.

BY DR. PLAGIARY.

Half stolen, with acknowledgments, to be spoken
in an inarticulate voice by Master P. at the
opening of the next new theatre. Stolen parts
marked with the inverted commas of quotation—
thus "——".

"WHEN energising objects men pursue,"
Then Lord knows what is writ by Lord knows
who.
"A modest monologue you here survey,"
Hiss'd from the theatre the "other day,"
As if Sir Fretful wrote "the slumberous"
verse,
And gave his son "the rubbish" to rehearse.
"Yet at the thing you'd never be amazed,"
Knew you the rumpus which the author
raised,
"Nor even here your smiles would be represt,"
Knew you these lines—the badness of the
best,

"Flame! fire! and flame!" (words borrowed
 from Lucretius,)
"Dread metaphors which open wounds" like
 issues!
"And sleeping pangs awake—and—but away"
(Confound me if I know what next to say).
"Lo Hope reviving re-expands her wings,"
And Master G—— recites what Dr. Busby
 sings!—
"If mighty things with small we may com-
 pare,"
(Translated from the grammar for the fair!)
Dramatic "spirit drives a conquering car,"
And burn'd poor Moscow like a tub of
 "tar."
"This spirit Wellington has shown in Spain,"
To furnish melodrames for Drury Lane.
"Another Marlborough points to Blenheim's
 story,"
And George and I will dramatise it for ye.

"In arts and sciences our isle hath shone"
(This deep discovery is mine alone).
"Oh British poesy, whose powers inspire"
My verse—or I'm a fool—and Fame's a liar,
"Thee we invoke, your sister arts implore"
With "smiles," and "lyres," and "pencils,"
 and much more.
These, if we win the Graces, too, we gain
Disgraces, too! "inseparable train!"
"Three who have stolen their witching airs
 from Cupid"
(You all know what I mean, unless you're
 stupid):
"Harmonious throng" that I have kept *in
 petto*
Now to produce in a "divine *sestetto*"!!
"While Poesy," with these delightful doxies,
"Sustains her part" in all the "upper" boxes!
"Thus lifted gloriously, you'll soar along,"
Borne in the vast balloon of Busby's song;
"Shine in your farce, masque, scenery, and
 play"
(For this last line George had a holiday).
"Old Drury never, never soar'd so high,"
So says the manager, and so say I.
"But hold, you say, this self-complacent
 boast;"
Is this the poem which the public lost?
"True—true—that lowers at once our mount-
 ing pride;"
But lo:—the papers print what you deride.
"'T is ours to look on you—you hold the
 prize,"
'T is *twenty guineas,* as they advertise!
"A double blessing your rewards impart"—
I wish I had them, then, with all my
 heart.
"Our *twofold* feeling *owns* its twofold cause,"
Why son and I both beg for your applause.

"When in your fostering beams you bid us
 live,"
My next subscription list shall say how much
 you give!

<div align="right">October, 1812.</div>

VERSES FOUND IN A SUMMER-HOUSE AT HALES-OWEN.

When Dryden's fool, "unknowing what he
 sought,"
His hours in whistling spent, "for want of
 thought,"
This guiltless oaf his vacancy of sense
Supplied, and amply too, by innocence:
Did modern swains, possess'd of Cymon's
 powers,
In Cymon's manner waste their leisure hours,
Th' offended guests would not, with blushing,
 see
These fair green walks disgraced by infamy.
Severe the fate of modern fools, alas!
When vice and folly mark them as they pass.
Like noxious reptiles o'er the whiten'd wall,
The filth they leave still points out where
 they crawl.

REMEMBER THEE! REMEMBER THEE!

Remember thee! remember thee!
 Till Lethe quench life's burning stream
Remorse and shame shall cling to thee,
 And haunt thee like a feverish dream!

Remember thee! Ay, doubt it not.
 Thy husband too shall think of thee!
By neither shalt thou be forgot,
 Thou *false* to him, thou *fiend* to me!

TO TIME.

Time! on whose arbitrary wing
 The varying hours must flag or fly,
Whose tardy winter, fleeting spring,
 But drag or drive us on to die—

Hail thou! who on my birth bestow'd
 Those boons to all that know thee known;
Yet better I sustain thy load,
 For now I bear the weight alone.

I would not one fond heart should share
 The bitter moments thou hast given;
And pardon thee, since thou could'st spare
 All that I loved, to peace or heaven.

To them be joy or rest, on me
 Thy future ills shall press in vain;
I nothing owe but years to thee,
 A debt already paid in pain.

Yet even that pain was some relief,
　It felt, but still forgot thy power:
The active agony of grief
　Retards, but never counts the hour.

In joy I've sigh'd to think thy flight
　Would soon subside from swift to slow;
Thy cloud could overcast the light,
　But could not add a night to woe;

For then, however drear and dark,
　My soul was suited to thy sky;
One star alone shot forth a spark
　To prove thee—not Eternity.

That beam hath sunk, and now thou art
　A blank; a thing to count and curse,
Through each dull tedious trifling part,
　Which all regret, yet all rehearse.

One scene even thou canst not deform;
　The limit of thy sloth or speed
When future wanderers bear the storm
　Which we shall sleep too sound to heed:

And I can smile to think how weak
　Thine efforts shortly shall be shown,
When all the vengeance thou canst wreak
　Must fall upon—a nameless stone.

TRANSLATION OF A ROMAIC LOVE SONG.

Ah! Love was never yet without
　The pang, the agony, the doubt,
Which rends my heart with ceaseless sigh,
　While day and night roll darkling by.

Without one friend to hear my woe,
　I faint, I die beneath the blow.
That Love had arrows well I knew;
　Alas! I find them poison'd too.

Birds, yet in freedom, shun the net
　Which Love around your haunts hath set;
Or, circled by his fatal fire,
　Your hearts shall burn, your hopes expire.

A bird of free and careless wing
　Was I through many a smiling spring;
But caught within the subtle snare,
　I burn, and feebly flutter there.

Who ne'er have loved, and loved in vain,
　Can neither feel nor pity pain,
The cold repulse, the look askance,
　The lightning of Love's angry glance.

In flattering dreams I deem'd thee mine;
　Now hope, and he who hoped, decline;
Like melting wax, or withering flower,
　I feel my passion, and thy power.

My light of life! ah, tell me why
That pouting lip, and alter'd eye?
My bird of love! my beauteous mate!
And art thou changed, and canst thou hate?

Mine eyes like wintry streams o'erflow:
What wretch with me would barter woe?
My bird! relent: one note could give
A charm to bid thy lover live.

My curdling blood, my madd'ning brain,
In silent anguish I sustain;
And still thy heart, without partaking
One pang, exults—while mine is breaking.

Pour me the poison; fear not thou!
Thou canst not murder more than now:
I've lived to curse my natal day,
And Love, that thus can lingering slay.

My wounded soul, my bleeding breast,
Can patience preach thee into rest?
Alas! too late, I dearly know
That joy is harbinger of woe.

THOU ART NOT FALSE, BUT THOU ART FICKLE.

Thou art not false, but thou art fickle,
　To those thyself so fondly sought;
The tears that thou hast forced to trickle
　Are doubly bitter from that thought:
'Tis this which breaks the heart thou grievest,
Too well thou lov'st—too soon thou leavest.

The wholly false the heart despises,
　And spurns deceiver and deceit;
But she who not a thought disguises,
　Whose love is as sincere as sweet,—
When she can change who loved so truly,
It feels what mine has felt so newly.

To dream of joy and wake to sorrow
　Is doom'd to all who love or live;
And if, when conscious on the morrow,
　We scarce our fancy can forgive,
That cheated us in slumber only,
To leave the waking soul more lonely,

What must they feel whom no false vision,
　But truest, tenderest passion warm'd?
Sincere, but swift in sad transition;
　As if a dream alone had charm'd?
Ah! sure such grief is fancy's scheming,
And all thy change can be but dreaming!

ON BEING ASKED WHAT WAS THE "ORIGIN OF LOVE."

The "Origin of Love!"—Ah, why
　That cruel question ask of me,
When thou may'st read in many an eye
　He starts to life on seeing thee?

And should'st thou seek his *end* to know:
 My heart forebodes, my fears foresee,
He'll linger long in silent woe;
 But live—until I cease to be.

———

REMEMBER HIM WHOM PASSION'S POWER.

REMEMBER him whom passion's power
 Severely, deeply, vainly proved:
Remember thou that dangerous hour,
 When neither fell, though both were loved.

That yielding breast, that melting eye,
 Too much invited to be bless'd:
That gentle prayer, that pleading sigh,
 The wilder wish reproved, repress'd.

Oh! let me feel that all I lost
 But saved thee all that conscience fears;
And blush for every pang it cost
 To spare the vain remorse of years.

Yet think of this when many a tongue,
 Whose busy accents whisper blame,
Would do the heart that loved thee wrong,
 And brand a nearly blighted name.

Think that, whate'er to others, thou
 Hast seen each selfish thought subdued:
I bless thy purer soul even now,
 Even now, in midnight solitude.

Oh, God! that we had met in time,
 Our hearts as fond, thy hand more free;
When thou hadst loved without a crime,
 And I been less unworthy thee!

Far may thy days, as heretofore,
 From this our gaudy world be past!
And that too bitter moment o'er,
 Oh! may such trial be thy last.

This heart, alas! perverted long,
 Itself destroy'd might there destroy;
To meet thee in the glittering throng,
 Would wake Presumption's hope of joy.

Then to the things whose bliss or woe,
 Like mine, is wild and worthless all,
That world resign—such scenes forego,
 Where those who feel must surely fall.

Thy youth, thy charms, thy tenderness,
 Thy soul from long seclusion pure;
From what even here hath pass'd, may guess
 What there thy bosom must endure.

Oh! pardon that imploring tear,
 Since not by Virtue shed in vain,
My frenzy drew from eyes so dear;
 For me they shall not weep again.

Though long and mournful must it be,
 The thought that we no more may meet;
Yet I deserve the stern decree,
 And almost deem the sentence sweet.

Still, had I loved thee less, my heart
 Had then less sacrificed to thine;
It felt not half so much to part
 As if its guilt had made thee mine.

<div align="right">1813</div>

———

ON LORD THURLOW'S POEMS.

WHEN Thurlow this damn'd nonsense sent
(I hope I am not violent),
Nor men nor gods knew what he meant.

And since not even our Rogers' praise
To common sense his thoughts could raise—
Why *would* they let him print his lays?

.

To me, divine Apollo, grant—O!
Hermilda's first and second canto,
I'm fitting up a new portmanteau;

And thus to furnish decent lining,
My own and others' bays I'm twining,—
So, gentle Thurlow, throw me thine in.

———

TO LORD THURLOW.

"I lay my branch of laurel down,
 Then thus to form Apollo's crown,
Let every other bring his own."
 Lord Thurlow's lines to Mr. Rogers.

 "*I lay my branch of laurel down.*"

THOU "lay thy branch of *laurel* down!"
 Why, what thou'st stole is not enow;
And, were it lawfully thine own,
 Does Rogers want it most, or thou?
Keep to thyself thy wither'd bough,
 Or send it back to Doctor Donne:
Were justice done to both, I trow,
 He'd have but little, and thou—none.

 "*Then thus to form Apollo's crown.*"

A crown! why, twist it how you will,
 Thy chaplet must be foolscap still.
When next you visit Delphi's town,
 Inquire amongst your fellow-lodgers,
They'll tell you Phœbus gave his crown,
 Some years before your birth, to Rogers.

 "*Let every other bring his own.*"

When coals to Newcastle are carried,
 And owls sent to Athens, as wonders,
From his spouse when the Regent's un
 married,
Or Liverpool weeps o'er his blunders;

When Tories and Whigs cease to quarrel,
 When Castlereagh's wife has an heir,
Then Rogers shall ask us for laurel,
 And thou shalt have plenty to spare.

——◆——

TO THOMAS MOORE.

WRITTEN THE EVENING BEFORE HIS VISIT TO MR. LEIGH HUNT IN HORSEMONGER LANE GAOL, MAY 19, 1813.

OH you, who in all names can tickle the town,
Anacreon, Tom Little, Tom Moore, or Tom
 Brown,
For hang me if I know of which you may
 most brag,
Your Quarto two-pounds, or your Two-penny
 Post Bag;

.

But now to my letter—to *yours* 'tis an
 answer—
To-morrow be with me, as soon as you can, sir,
All ready and dress'd for proceeding to spunge
 on
(According to compact) the wit in the
 dungeon—
Pray Phœbus at length our political malice
May not get us lodgings within the same palace!
I suppose that to-night you 're engaged with
 some codgers,
And for Sotheby's Blues have deserted Sam
 Rogers;
And I, though with cold I have nearly my
 death got,
Must put on my breeches, and wait on the
 Heathcote;
But to-morrow, at four, we will both play the
 Scurra,
And you 'll be Catullus, the Regent Mamurra.
 [First published in 1830.]

——◆——

IMPROMPTU, IN REPLY TO A FRIEND.

WHEN, from the heart where Sorrow sits,
 Her dusky shadow mounts too high,
And o'er the changing aspect flits,
 And clouds the brow, or fills the eye;
Heed not that gloom, which soon shall sink:
 My thoughts their dungeon know too well;
Back to my breast the wanderers shrink,
 And droop within their silent cell.
 September, 1813.

——◆——

SONNET, TO GENEVRA.

THINE eyes' blue tenderness, thy long fair hair,
 And the wan lustre of thy features—caught
 From contemplation — where serenely
 wrought,
Seems Sorrow's softness charm'd from its
 despair—

Have thrown such speaking sadness in thine
 air,
 That—but I know thy blessed bosom
 fraught
 With mines of unalloy'd and stainless
 thought—
I should have deem'd thee doom'd to earthly
 care.
With such an aspect, by his colours blent,
 When from his beauty-breathing pencil born
(Except that *thou* hast nothing to repent),
 The Magdalen of Guido saw the morn—
Such seem'st thou—but how much more
 excellent!
 With nought Remorse can claim—nor
 Virtue scorn.
 December 17, 1813.

——◆——

SONNET, TO THE SAME.

THY cheek is pale with thought, but not from
 woe,
 And yet so lovely, that if Mirth could flush
 Its rose of whiteness with the brightest
 blush,
My heart would wish away that ruder glow:
And dazzle not thy deep-blue eyes—but, oh!
 While gazing on them sterner eyes will
 gush,
 And into mine my mother's weakness rush,
Soft as the last drops round heaven's airy bow.
For, through thy long dark lashes low depend-
 ing,
 The soul of melancholy Gentleness
Gleams like a seraph from the sky descending,
 Above all pain, yet pitying all distress;
At once such majesty with sweetness blending,
 I worship more, but cannot love thee less.
 December 17, 1813.

——◆——

FROM THE PORTUGUESE.

"TU MI CHAMAS."

IN moments to delight devoted,
 "My life!" with tenderest tone, you cry;
Dear words! on which my heart had doted,
 If youth could neither fade nor die.

To death even hours like these must roll,
 Ah! then repeat those accents never;
Or change "my life!" into "my soul!"
 Which, like my love, exists for ever.

ANOTHER VERSION.

You call me still your *life*.—Oh! change the
 word—
 Life is as transient as the inconstant sigh:
Say rather I 'm your soul; more just that
 name,
 For, like the soul, my love can never die.

THE DEVIL'S DRIVE;

AN UNFINISHED RHAPSODY.

THE Devil return'd to hell by two,
 And he stay'd at home till five;
When he dined on some homicides done in
 ragoût,
 And a rebel or so in an *Irish* stew,
And sausages made of a self-slain Jew—
 And bethought himself what next to do,
"And," quoth he, "I'll take a drive.
I walk'd in the morning, I'll ride to-night;
In darkness my children take most delight,
 And I'll see how my favourites thrive.

"And what shall I ride in?" quoth Lucifer
 then—
 "If I follow'd my taste, indeed,
I should mount in a waggon of wounded men,
 And smile to see them bleed.
But these will be furnish'd again and again,
 And at present my purpose is speed;
To see my manor as much as I may,
And watch that no souls shall be poach'd
 away.

"I have a state-coach at Carlton House,
 A chariot in Seymour Place;
But they 're lent to two friends, who make
 me amends,
 By driving my favourite pace:
And they handle their reins with such a grace,
I have something for both at the end of their
 race.

"So now for the earth to take my chance:"
 Then up to the earth sprung he;
And making a jump from Moscow to France,
 He stepp'd across the sea,
And rested his hoof on a turnpike road,
No very great way from a bishop's abode.

But first as he flew, I forgot to say
That he hover'd a moment upon his way,
 To look upon Leipsic plain;
And so sweet to his eye was its sulphury
 glare,
And so soft to his ear was the cry of despair,
 That he perch'd on a mountain of slain;
And he gazed with delight from its growing
 height,
Nor often on earth had he seen such a sight,
 Nor his work done half as well:
For the field ran so red with the blood of the
 dead,
 That it blush'd like the waves of hell!
Then loudly, and wildly, and long laugh'd he:
"Methinks they have here little need of *me!*"

But the softest note that soothed his ear
 Was the sound of a widow sighing;
And the sweetest sight was the icy tear,
Which horror froze in the blue eye clear
 Of a maid by her lover lying—
As round her fell her long fair hair;
And she look'd to heaven with that frenzied air,
 Which seem'd to ask if a God were there!
And, stretch'd by the wall of a ruin'd hut,
With its hollow cheek, and eyes half shut,
 A child of famine dying:
And the carnage begun, when resistance is
 done,
 And the fall of the vainly flying!

But the Devil has reach'd our cliffs so white,
 And what did he there, I pray?
If his eyes were good, he but saw by night
 What we see every day:
But he made a tour, and kept a journal
 Of all the wondrous sights nocturnal,
And he sold it in shares to the *Men* of the
 Row,
Who bid pretty well—but they *cheated* him,
 though!

The Devil first saw, as he thought, the *Mail*,
 Its coachman and his coat;
So instead of a pistol he cock'd his tail,
 And seized him by the throat:
"Aha!" quoth he, "what have we here?
'T is a new barouche, and an ancient peer!"

So he sat him on his box again,
 And bade him have no fear,
But be true to his club, and stanch to his
 rein,
 His brothel, and his beer;
"Next to seeing a lord at the council board,
 I would rather see him here."

The Devil gat next to Westminster,
 And he turn'd to "the room" of the Com-
 mons;
But he heard, as he purposed to enter in
 there,
 That "the Lords" had received a sum-
 mons;
And he thought, as a "*quondam* aristocrat,"
He might peep at the peers, though to *hear*
 them were flat;
And he walk'd up the house so like one of
 our own,
That they say that he stood pretty near the
 throne.

He saw the Lord Liverpool seemingly wise,
 The Lord Westmoreland certainly silly,
And Johnny of Norfolk—a man of some size—
 And Chatham, so like his friend Billy;

And he saw the tears in Lord Eldon's eyes,
 Because the Catholics would *not* rise,
 In spite of his prayers and his prophecies;
And he heard—which set Satan himself a
 staring—
A certain Chief Justice say something like
 swearing.
And the Devil was shock'd—and quoth he,
 "I must go,
For I find we have much better manners
 below:
If thus he harangues when he passes my
 border,
I shall hint to friend Moloch to call him to
 order."

WINDSOR POETICS.

Lines composed on the occasion of His Royal
Highness the Prince Regent being seen standing
between the coffins of Henry VIII. and Charles I.,
in the royal vault at Windsor.

FAMED for contemptuous breach of sacred
 ties,
By headless Charles see heartless Henry lies;
Between them stands another sceptred
 thing—
It moves, it reigns—in all but name, a king:

Charles to his people, Henry to his wife,
—In him the double tyrant starts to life:
Justice and death have mix'd their dust in
 vain,
Each royal vampire wakes to life again.
Ah, what can tombs avail!—since these dis-
 gorge
The blood and dust of both—to mould a
 George.

ODE TO NAPOLEON BUONAPARTE.

 "Expende Annibalem:—quot libras in duce summo
 Invenies?"—Juvenal, *Sat.* x.

"The Emperor Nepos was acknowledged by the
Senate, by the Italians, and by the Provincials of
Gaul; his moral virtues, and military talents, were
loudly celebrated; and those who derived any
private benefit from his government announced in
prophetic strains the restoration of public felicity.
... By this shameful abdication, he protracted his
life a few years, in a very ambiguous state, between
an Emperor and an Exile, till ——."—Gibbon's
Decline and Fall, vol. vi., p. 220.

I.

'TIS done—but yesterday a King!
 And arm'd with Kings to strive—
And now thou art a nameless thing:
 So abject—yet alive!
Is this the man of thousand thrones,
Who strew'd our earth with hostile bones,
 And can he thus survive?

Since he, miscall'd the Morning Star,
Nor man nor fiend hath fallen so far.

II.

Ill-minded man! why scourge thy kind
 Who bow'd so low the knee?
By gazing on thyself grown blind,
 Thou taught'st the rest to see.
With might unquestion'd,—power to save,—
Thine only gift hath been the grave,
 To those that worshipp'd thee;
 Nor till thy fall could mortals guess
Ambition's less than littleness!

III.

Thanks for that lesson—It will teach
 To after-warriors more,
Than high Philosophy can preach,
 And vainly preach'd before.
That spell upon the minds of men
Breaks never to unite again,
 That led them to adore
Those Pagod things of sabre sway
With fronts of brass, and feet of clay.

IV.

The triumph and the vanity,
 The rapture of the strife—
The earthquake voice of Victory,
 To thee the breath of life;
The sword, the sceptre, and that sway
Which man seem'd made but to obey,
 Wherewith renown was rife—
All quell'd!—Dark Spirit! what must be
The madness of thy memory!

V.

The Desolator desolate!
 The Victor overthrown!
The Arbiter of others' fate
 A Suppliant for his own!
Is it some yet imperial hope
That with such change can calmly cope?
 Or dread of death alone?
To die a prince—or live a slave—
Thy choice is most ignobly brave!

VI.

He who of old would rend the oak,
 Dream'd not of the rebound:
Chain'd by the trunk he vainly broke—
 Alone—how look'd he round?
Thou, in the sternness of thy strength,
An equal deed hast done at length,
 And darker fate hast found:
He fell, the forest prowlers' prey;
But thou must eat thy heart away!

VII.

The Roman, when his burning heart
　　Was slaked with blood of Rome,
Threw down the dagger—dared depart,
　　In savage grandeur, home—
He dared depart in utter scorn
Of men that such a yoke had borne,
　　Yet left him such a doom!
His only glory was that hour
Of self-upheld abandon'd power.

VIII.

The Spaniard, when the lust of sway
　　Had lost its quickening spell,
Cast crowns for rosaries away,
　　An empire for a cell;
A strict accountant of his beads,
A subtle disputant on creeds,
　　His dotage trifled well:
Yet better had he neither known
A bigot's shrine, nor despot's throne.

IX.

But thou—from thy reluctant hand
　　The thunderbolt is wrung—
Too late thou leav'st the high command
　　To which thy weakness clung;
All Evil Spirit as thou art,
It is enough to grieve the heart
　　To see thine own unstrung;
To think that God's fair world hath been
The footstool of a thing so mean;

X.

And Earth hath spilt her blood for him,
　　Who thus can hoard his own!
And Monarchs bow'd the trembling limb,
　　And thank'd him for a throne!
Fair Freedom! we may hold thee dear,
When thus thy mightiest foes their fear
　　In humblest guise have shown.
Oh! ne'er may tyrant leave behind
A brighter name to lure mankind!

XI.

Thine evil deeds are writ in gore,
　　Nor written thus in vain—
Thy triumphs tell of fame no more,
　　Or deepen every stain:
If thou hadst died as honour dies,
Some new Napoleon might arise,
　　To shame the world again—
But who would soar the solar height,
To set in such a starless night?

XII.

Weigh'd in the balance, hero dust
　　Is vile as vulgar clay;
Thy scales, Mortality! are just
　　To all that pass away:

But yet methought the living great
Some higher sparks should animate,
　　To dazzle and dismay:
Nor deem'd Contempt could thus make mirth
Of these, the Conquerors of the earth.

XIII.

And she, proud Austria's mournful flower,
　　Thy still imperial bride;
How bears her breast the torturing hour?
　　Still clings she to thy side?
Must she too bend, must she too share
Thy late repentance, long despair,
　　Thou throneless Homicide?
If still she loves thee, hoard that gem,—
'Tis worth thy vanish'd diadem!

XIV.

Then haste thee to thy sullen Isle,
　　And gaze upon the sea;
That element may meet thy smile—
　　It ne'er was ruled by thee!
Or trace with thine all idle hand
In loitering mood upon the sand
　　That Earth is now as free!
That Corinth's pedagogue hath now
Transferr'd his by-word to thy brow.

XV.

Thou Timour! in his captive's cage
　　What thoughts will there be thine,
While brooding in thy prison'd rage?
　　But one—"The world *was* mine!"
Unless, like he of Babylon,
All sense is with thy sceptre gone,
　　Life will not long confine
That spirit pour'd so widely forth—
So long obey'd—so little worth!

XVI.

Or, like the thief of fire from heaven,
　　Wilt thou withstand the shock?
And share with him, the unforgiven,
　　His vulture and his rock!
Foredoom'd by God—by man accurst,
And that last act, though not thy worst,
　　The very Fiend's arch mock;
He in his fall preserved his pride,
And, if a mortal, had as proudly died!

XVII.

There was a day—there was an hour,
　　While earth was Gaul's—Gaul thine—
When that immeasurable power
　　Unsated to resign
Had been an act of purer fame
Than gathers round Marengo's name,
　　And gilded thy decline,
Through the long twilight of all time,
Despite some passing clouds of crime.

XVIII.

But thou forsooth must be a king,
 And don the purple vest,
As if that foolish robe could wring
 Remembrance from thy breast.
Where is that faded garment? where
The gewgaws thou wert fond to wear,
 The star, the string, the crest?
Vain froward child of empire! say,
Are all thy playthings snatched away?

XIX.

Where may the wearied eye repose
 When gazing on the Great;
Where neither guilty glory glows,
 Nor despicable state?
Yes—one—the first—the last—the best—
The Cincinnatus of the West,
 Whom envy dared not hate,
Bequeath'd the name of Washington,
To make man blush there was but one!

STANZAS FOR MUSIC.

I SPEAK not, I trace not, I breathe not thy
 name,
There is grief in the sound, there is guilt in
 the fame:
But the tear which now burns on my cheek
 may impart
The deep thoughts that dwell in that silence
 of heart.

Too brief for our passion, too long for our
 peace,
Were those hours—can their joy or their
 bitterness cease?
We repent, we abjure, we will break from
 our chain,—
We will part, we will fly to—unite it again!

Oh! thine be the gladness, and mine be the
 guilt!
Forgive me, adored one!—forsake, if thou
 wilt;—
But the heart which is thine shall expire
 undebased,
And *man* shall not break it—whatever *thou*
 mayst.

And stern to the haughty, but humble to
 thee,
This soul, in its bitterest blackness, shall be;
And our days seem as swift, and our mo-
 ments more sweet,
With thee by my side, than with worlds at
 our feet,

One sigh of thy sorrow, one look of thy love,
Shall turn me or fix, shall reward or reprove;
And the heartless may wonder at all I re-
 sign—
Thy lip shall reply, not to them, but to *mine*.
 May, 1814.

ADDRESS INTENDED TO BE RECITED AT THE CALEDONIAN MEETING.

WHO hath not glow'd above the page where
 fame
Hath fix'd high Caledon's unconquer'd name;
The mountain-land which spurn'd the Roman
 chain,
And baffled back the fiery-crested Dane,
Whose bright claymore and hardihood of
 hand
No foe could tame—no tyrant could com-
 mand?
That race is gone—but still their children
 breathe,
And glory crowns them with redoubled
 wreath:
O'er Gael and Saxon mingling banners shine,
And, England! add their stubborn strength
 to thine.
The blood which flow'd with Wallace flows
 as free,
But now 'tis only shed for fame and thee!
Oh! pass not by the northern veteran's claim,
But give support—the world hath given him
 fame!

The humbler ranks, the lowly brave, who bled
While cheerly following where the mighty
 led—
Who sleep beneath the undistinguish'd sod
Where happier comrades in their triumph
 trod,
To us bequeath—'tis all their fate allows—
The sireless offspring and the lonely spouse:
She on high Albyn's dusky hills may raise
The tearful eye in melancholy gaze,
Or view, while shadowy auguries disclose
The Highland Seer's anticipated woes,
The bleeding phantom of each martial form
Dim in the cloud, or darkling in the storm;
While sad, she chants the solitary song,
The soft lament for him who tarries long—
For him, whose distant relics vainly crave
The Coronach's wild requiem to the brave!

'Tis Heaven—not man—must charm away
 the woe,
Which bursts when Nature's feelings newly
 flow;
Yet tenderness and time may rob the tear
Of half its bitterness for one so dear;

A nation's gratitude perchance may spread
A thornless pillow for the widow'd head;
May lighten well her heart's maternal care,
And wean from penury the soldier's heir.

<div align="right">

May, 1814.

</div>

FRAGMENT OF AN EPISTLE TO THOMAS MOORE.

"WHAT say *I?*"—not a syllable further in prose;
I'm your man "of all measures," dear Tom,—so here goes!
Here goes, for a swim on the stream of old Time,
On those buoyant supporters, the bladders of rhyme.
If our weight breaks them down, and we sink in the flood,
We are smother'd, at least, in respectable mud,
Where the Divers of Bathos lie drown'd in a heap,
And Southey's last Pæan has pillow'd his sleep;—
That "Felo de se," who, half drunk with his malmsey,
Walk'd out of his depth and was lost in a calm sea,
Singing "Glory to God" in a spick and span stanza,
The like (since Tom Sternhold was choked) never man saw.

The papers have told you, no doubt, of the fusses,
The fêtes, and the gapings to get at these Russes,—
Of his Majesty's suite, up from coachman to Hetman,
And what dignity decks the flat face of the great man.
I saw him, last week, at two balls and a party,—
For a prince, his demeanour was rather too hearty.
You know *we* are used to quite different graces,

.

The Czar's look, I own, was much brighter and brisker,
But then he is sadly deficient in whisker;
And wore but a starless blue coat, and in kersey-
-mere breeches whisk'd round, in a waltz with the Jersey,
Who lovely as ever, seem'd just as delighted
With Majesty's presence as those she invited.

.

<div align="right">

June, 1814.

</div>

CONDOLATORY ADDRESS TO SARAH, COUNTESS OF JERSEY,

ON THE PRINCE REGENT'S RETURNING HER PICTURE TO MRS. MEE.

WHEN the vain triumph of the imperial lord,
Whom servile Rome obey'd, and yet abhorr'd,
Gave to the vulgar gaze each glorious bust,
That left a likeness of the brave or just;
What most admired each scrutinising eye
Of all that deck'd that passing pageantry?
What spread from face to face that wondering air?
The thought of Brutus—for his was not there!
That absence proved his worth,—that absence fix'd
His memory on the longing mind, unmix'd;
And more decreed his glory to endure,
Than all a gold Colossus could secure.
 If thus, fair Jersey, our desiring gaze
Search for thy form, in vain and mute amaze,
Amidst those pictured charms, whose loveliness,
Bright though they be, thine own had render'd less:
If he, that vain old man, whom truth admits
Heir of his father's crown, and of his wits,
If his corrupted eye, and wither'd heart,
Could with thy gentle image bear depart;
That tasteless shame be *his*, and ours the grief,
To gaze on Beauty's band without its chief:
Yet comfort still one selfish thought imparts,
We lose the portrait, but preserve our hearts.
 What can his vaulted gallery now disclose?
A garden with all flowers—except the rose;—
A fount that only wants its living stream;
A night, with every star, save Dian's beam.
Lost to our eyes the present forms shall be,
That turn from tracing them to dream of thee;
And more on that recall'd resemblance pause,
Than all he *shall* not force on our applause.
 Long may thy yet meridian lustre shine,
With all that Virtue asks of Homage thine:
The symmetry of youth, the grace of mien,
The eye that gladdens, and the brow serene;
The glossy darkness of that clustering hair,
Which shades, yet shows that forehead more than fair!
Each glance that wins us, and the life that throws
A spell which will not let our looks repose,
But turn to gaze again, and find anew
Some charm that well rewards another view.
These are not lessen'd, these are still as bright,
Albeit too dazzling for a dotard's sight;

And those must wait till ev'ry charm is gone,
To please the paltry heart that pleases
 none;—
That dull cold sensualist, whose sickly eye
In envious dimness pass'd thy portrait by;
Who rack'd his little spirit to combine
Its hate of *Freedom's* loveliness, and *thine.*
<div align="right">*August,* 1814.</div>

ELEGIAC STANZAS ON THE DEATH OF SIR PETER PARKER, BART.

THERE is a tear for all that die,
 A mourner o'er the humblest grave;
But nations swell the funeral cry,
 And Triumph weeps above the brave.

For them is Sorrow's purest sigh
 O'er Ocean's heaving bosom sent:
In vain their bones unburied lie,
 All earth becomes their monument!

A tomb is theirs on every page,
 An epitaph on every tongue:
The present hours, the future age,
 For them bewail, to them belong.

For them the voice of festal mirth
 Grows hush'd, *their name* the only sound;
While deep Remembrance pours to Worth
 The goblet's tributary round.

A theme to crowds that knew them not,
 Lamented by admiring foes,
Who would not share their glorious lot?
 Who would not die the death they chose?

And, gallant Parker! thus enshrined
 Thy life, thy fall, thy fame shall be;
And early valour, glowing, find
 A model in thy memory.

But there are breasts that bleed with thee
 In woe, that glory cannot quell;
And shuddering hear of victory,
 Where one so dear, so dauntless, fell.

Where shall they turn to mourn thee less?
 When cease to hear thy cherish'd name?
Time cannot teach forgetfulness,
 While Grief's full heart is fed by Fame.

Alas! for them, though not for thee,
 They cannot choose but weep the more;
Deep for the dead the grief must be,
 Who ne'er gave cause to mourn before.
<div align="right">*October,* 1814.</div>

TO BELSHAZZAR.

BELSHAZZAR! from the banquet turn,
 Nor in thy sensual fulness fall;
Behold! while yet before thee burn
 The graven words, the glowing wall,

Many a despot men miscall
 Crown'd and anointed from on high;
But thou, the weakest, worst of all—
 Is it not written, thou must die?

Go! dash the roses from thy brow—
 Grey hairs but poorly wreathe with them;
Youth's garlands misbecome thee now,
 More than thy very diadem,
Where thou hast tarnish'd every gem:—
 Then throw the worthless bauble by,
Which, worn by thee, ev'n slaves contemn;
 And learn like better men to die!

Oh! early in the balance weigh'd,
 And ever light of word and worth,
Whose soul expired ere youth decay'd,
 And left thee but a mass of earth.
To see thee moves the scorner's mirth:
 But tears in Hope's averted eye
Lament that even thou hadst birth—
 Unfit to govern, live, or die.

HEBREW MELODIES.

ADVERTISEMENT.

THE subsequent poems were written at the request of my friend, the Hon. Douglas Kinnaird, for a Selection of Hebrew Melodies, and have been published, with the music, arranged by Mr. Braham and Mr. Nathan.

January, 1815.

SHE WALKS IN BEAUTY.

I.

SHE walks in beauty, like the night
 Of cloudless climes and starry skies;
And all that's best of dark and bright
 Meet in her aspect and her eyes:
Thus mellow'd to that tender light
 Which heaven to gaudy day denies.

II.

One shade the more, one ray the less,
 Had half impair'd the nameless grace
Which waves in every raven tress,
 Or softly lightens o'er her face;
Where thoughts serenely sweet express
 How pure, how dear their dwelling-place.

III.

And on that cheek, and o'er that brow,
 So soft, so calm, yet eloquent,
The smiles that win, the tints that glow,
 But tell of days in goodness spent,
A mind at peace with all below,
 A heart whose love is innocent!

THE HARP THE MONARCH MINSTREL SWEPT.

I.

THE harp the monarch minstrel swept,
 The King of men, the loved of Heaven,
Which Music hallow'd while she wept
 O'er tones her heart of hearts had given,
 Redoubled be her tears, its chords are riven!
It soften'd men of iron mould,
 It gave them virtues not their own;
No ear so dull, no soul so cold,
 That felt not, fired not to the tone,
 Till David's lyre grew mightier than his
 throne!

II.

It told the triumphs of our King,
 It wafted glory to our God;
It made our gladden'd valleys ring,
 The cedars bow, the mountains nod;
 Its sound aspired to heaven and there
 abode!
Since then, though heard on earth no more,
 Devotion and her daughter Love
Still bid the bursting spirit soar
 To sounds that seem as from above,
 In dreams that day's broad light can not
 remove.

IF THAT HIGH WORLD.

I.

IF that high world, which lies beyond
 Our own, surviving Love endears;
If there the cherish'd heart be fond,
 The eye the same, except in tears—
How welcome those untrodden spheres!
 How sweet this very hour to die!
To soar from earth and find all fears
 Lost in thy light—Eternity!

II.

It must be so: 'tis not for self
 That we so tremble on the brink;
And striving to o'erleap the gulf,
 Yet cling to Being's severing link.
Oh! in that future let us think
 To hold each heart the heart that shares;
With them the immortal waters drink,
 And soul in soul grow deathless theirs!

THE WILD GAZELLE.

I.

THE wild gazelle on Judah's hills
 Exulting yet may bound,
And drink from all the living rills
 That gush on holy ground:
Its airy step and glorious eye
May glance in tameless transport by:—

II.

A step as fleet, an eye more bright,
 Hath Judah witness'd there;
And o'er her scenes of lost delight
 Inhabitants more fair.
The cedars wave on Lebanon,
But Judah's statelier maids are gone!

III.

More blest each palm that shades those
 plains
 Than Israel's scatter'd race;
For, taking root, it there remains
 In solitary grace:
It cannot quit its place of birth,
It will not live in other earth.

IV.

But we must wander witheringly,
 In other lands to die;
And where our fathers' ashes be,
 Our own may never lie:
Our temple hath not left a stone,
And Mockery sits on Salem's throne.

OH! WEEP FOR THOSE.

I.

OH! weep for those that wept by Babel's
 stream,
Whose shrines are desolate, whose land a
 dream;
Weep for the harp of Judah's broken shell;
Mourn—where their God hath dwelt the god-
 less dwell!

II.

And where shall Israel lave her bleeding
 feet?
And when shall Zion's songs again seem
 sweet?
And Judah's melody once more rejoice
The hearts that leap'd before its heavenly
 voice?

III.

Tribes of the wandering foot and weary
 breast,
How shall ye flee away and be at rest!
The wild-dove hath her nest, the fox his cave,
Mankind their country—Israel but the grave!

ON JORDAN'S BANKS.

I.

ON Jordan's banks the Arab's camels stray,
On Sion's hill the False One's votaries pray,
The Baal-adorer bows on Sinai's steep—
Yet there—even there—Oh God! thy thun-
 ders sleep:

II.

There—where thy finger scorch'd the tablet
　　stone !
There—where thy shadow to thy people
　　shone !
Thy glory shrouded in its garb of fire :
Thyself—none living see and not expire !

III.

Oh ! in the lightning let thy glance appear ;
Sweep from his shiver'd hand the oppressor's
　　spear !
How long by tyrants shall thy land be trod ?
How long thy temple worshipless, Oh God ?

JEPHTHA'S DAUGHTER.

I.

Since our Country, our God—Oh, my Sire !
Demand that thy Daughter expire ;
Since thy triumph was bought by thy vow—
Strike the bosom that 's bared for thee now !

II.

And the voice of my mourning is o'er,
And the mountains behold me no more :
If the hand that I love lay me low !
There cannot be pain in the blow !

III.

And of this, oh, my Father ! be sure—
That the blood of thy child is as pure
As the blessing I beg ere it flow,
And the last thought that soothes me below.

IV.

Though the virgins of Salem lament,
Be the judge and the hero unbent !
I have won the great battle for thee,
And my Father and Country are free !

V.

When this blood of thy giving hath gush'd,
When the voice that thou lovest is hush'd,
Let my memory still be thy pride,
And forget not I smiled as I died !

OH ! SNATCH'D AWAY IN BEAUTY'S BLOOM.

I.

Oh ! snatch'd away in beauty's bloom,
On thee shall press no ponderous tomb ;
　But on thy turf shall roses rear
　　Their leaves, the earliest of the year ;
And the wild cypress wave in tender gloom :

II.

And oft by yon blue gushing stream
　　Shall Sorrow lean her drooping head,
And feed deep thought with many a dream,
　　And lingering pause and lightly tread ;
　　Fond wretch ! as if her step disturb'd the
　　　dead !

III.

Away ! we know that tears are vain,
　　That death nor heeds nor hears distress :
Will this unteach us to complain ?
　　Or make one mourner weep the less ?
And thou—who tell'st me to forget,
　　Thy looks are wan, thine eyes are wet.

MY SOUL IS DARK.

I.

My soul is dark—Oh ! quickly string
　　The harp I yet can brook to hear ;
And let thy gentle fingers fling
　　Its melting murmurs o'er mine ear.
If in this heart a hope be dear,
　　That sound shall charm it forth again :
If in these eyes there lurk a tear,
　　'Twill flow, and cease to burn my brain.

II.

But bid the strain be wild and deep,
　　Nor let thy notes of joy be first :
I tell thee, minstrel, I must weep,
　　Or else this heavy heart will burst ;
For it hath been by sorrow nursed,
　　And ach'd in sleepless silence long ;
And now 'tis doom'd to know the worst,
　　And break at once—or yield to song.

I SAW THEE WEEP.

I.

I saw thee weep—the big bright tear
　　Came o'er that eye of blue ;
And then methought it did appear
　　A violet dropping dew ;
I saw thee smile—the sapphire's blaze
　　Beside thee ceased to shine ;
It could not match the living rays
　　That fill'd that glance of thine.

II.

As clouds from yonder sun receive
　　A deep and mellow dye,
Which scarce the shade of coming eve
　　Can banish from the sky,
Those smiles unto the moodiest mind
　　Their own pure joy impart ;
Their sunshine leaves a glow behind
　　That lightens o'er the heart.

THY DAYS ARE DONE.

I.

THY days are done, thy fame begun;
 Thy country's strains record
The triumphs of her chosen Son,
 The slaughters of his sword!
The deeds he did, the fields he won,
 The freedom he restored!

II.

Though thou art fall'n, while we are free
 Thou shalt not taste of death!
The generous blood that flow'd from thee
 Disdain'd to sink beneath:
Within our veins its currents be,
 Thy spirit on our breath!

III.

Thy name, our charging hosts along,
 Shall be the battle-word!
Thy fall, the theme of choral song
 From virgin voices pour'd!
To weep would do thy glory wrong:
 Thou shalt not be deplored.

SAUL.

I.

THOU whose spell can raise the dead,
 Bid the prophet's form appear.
"Samuel, raise thy buried head!
 King, behold the phantom seer!"
Earth yawn'd; he stood the centre of a cloud:
Light changed its hue, retiring from his
 shroud.
Death stood all glassy in his fixed eye;
His hand was wither'd, and his veins were
 dry;
His foot, in bony whiteness, glitter'd there,
Shrunken and sinewless, and ghastly bare;
From lips that moved not and unbreathing
 frame,
Like cavern'd winds, the hollow accents came.
Saul saw, and fell to earth, as falls the oak,
At once, and blasted by the thunder-stroke.

II.

"Why is my sleep disquieted?
Who is he that calls the dead?
Is it thou, O King? Behold,
Bloodless are these limbs, and cold:
Such are mine; and such shall be
Thine to-morrow, when with me:
Ere the coming day is done,
Such shalt thou be, such thy son.
Fare thee well, but for a day,
Then we mix our mouldering clay.

Thou, thy race, lie pale and low,
Pierced by shafts of many a bow;
And the falchion by thy side
To thy heart thy hand shall guide:
Crownless, breathless, headless fall,
Son and sire, the house of Saul!"

SONG OF SAUL BEFORE HIS LAST BATTLE.

I.

WARRIORS and chiefs! should the shaft or the
 sword
Pierce me in leading the host of the Lord,
Heed not the corse, though a king's, in your
 path:
Bury your steel in the bosoms of Gath!

II.

Thou who art bearing my buckler and bow,
Should the soldiers of Saul look away from
 the foe,
Stretch me that moment in blood at thy feet!
Mine be the doom which they dared not to
 meet.

III.

Farewell to others, but never we part,
Heir to my royalty, son of my heart!
Bright is the diadem, boundless the sway,
Or kingly the death, which awaits us to-day!

"ALL IS VANITY, SAITH THE PREACHER."

I.

FAME, wisdom, love, and power were mine,
 And health and youth possess'd me;
My goblets blush'd from every vine,
 And lovely forms caress'd me;
I sunn'd my heart in beauty's eyes,
 And felt my soul grow tender;
All earth can give, or mortal prize,
 Was mine of regal splendour.

II.

I strive to number o'er what days
 Remembrance can discover,
Which all that life or earth displays
 Would lure me to live over.
There rose no day, there roll'd no hour
 Of pleasure unembitter'd;
And not a trapping deck'd my power
 That gall'd not while it glitter'd.

III.

The serpent of the field, by art
 And spells, is won from harming;
But that which coils around the heart,
 Oh! who hath power of charming?

It will not list to wisdom's lore,
 Nor music's voice can lure it;
But there it stings for evermore
 The soul that must endure it.

WHEN COLDNESS WRAPS THIS SUFFERING CLAY.

I.

WHEN coldness wraps this suffering clay,
 Ah! whither strays the immortal mind?
It cannot die, it cannot stay,
 But leaves its darken'd dust behind.
Then, unembodied, doth it trace
 By steps each planet's heavenly way?
Or fill at once the realms of space,
 A thing of eyes, that all survey?

II.

Eternal, boundless, undecay'd,
 A thought unseen, but seeing all,
All, all in earth or skies display'd,
 Shall it survey, shall it recall:
Each fainter trace that memory holds
 So darkly of departed years,
In one broad glance the soul beholds,
 And all, that was, at once appears.

III.

Before Creation peopled earth,
 Its eye shall roll through chaos back;
And where the furthest heaven had birth,
 The spirit trace its rising track.
And where the future mars or makes,
 Its glance dilate o'er all to be,
While sun is quench'd or system breaks,
 Fix'd in its own eternity.

IV.

Above or Love, Hope, Hate, or Fear,
 It lives all passionless and pure:
An age shall fleet like earthly year;
 Its years as moments shall endure.
Away, away, without a wing,
 O'er all, through all, its thought shall fly,
A nameless and eternal thing,
 Forgetting what it was to die.

VISION OF BELSHAZZAR.

I.

THE King was on his throne,
 The Satraps throng'd the hall:
A thousand bright lamps shone
 O'er that high festival.
A thousand cups of gold,
 In Judah deem'd divine—
Jehovah's vessels hold
 The godless Heathen's wine!

II.

In that same hour and hall,
 The fingers of a hand
Came forth against the wall,
 And wrote as if on sand:
The fingers of a man;—
 A solitary hand
Along the letters ran,
 And traced them like a wand.

III.

The monarch saw, and shook,
 And bade no more rejoice;
All bloodless wax'd his look,
 And tremulous his voice.
"Let the men of lore appear,
 The wisest of the earth,
And expound the words of fear,
 Which mar our royal mirth."

IV.

Chaldea's seers are good,
 But here they have no skill;
And the unknown letters stood
 Untold and awful still.
And Babel's men of age
 Are wise and deep in lore;
But now they were not sage,
 They saw—but knew no more.

V.

A captive in the land,
 A stranger and a youth,
He heard the king's command,
 He saw that writing's truth.
The lamps around were bright,
 The prophecy in view;
He read it on that night,—
 The morrow proved it true.

VI.

"Belshazzar's grave is made,
 His kingdom pass'd away,
He, in the balance weigh'd,
 Is light and worthless clay;
The shroud his robe of state,
 His canopy the stone;
The Mede is at his gate!
 The Persian on his throne!"

SUN OF THE SLEEPLESS!

SUN of the sleepless! melancholy star!
Whose tearful beam glows tremulously far,
That show'st the darkness thou canst not dispel,
How like art thou to joy remember'd well!
So gleams the past, the light of other days,
Which shines, but warms not with its power-
 less rays;
A night-beam Sorrow watcheth to behold,
Distinct, but distant—clear—but, oh how cold!

WERE MY BOSOM AS FALSE AS THOU DEEM'ST IT TO BE.

I.

WERE my bosom as false as thou deem'st it
 to be,
I need not have wander'd from far Galilee;
It was but abjuring my creed to efface
The curse which, thou say'st, is the crime of
 my race.

II.

If the bad never triumph, then God is with
 thee!
If the slave only sin, thou art spotless and free!
If the Exile on earth is an Outcast on high,
Live on in thy faith, but in mine I will die.

III.

I have lost for that faith more than thou
 canst bestow,
As the God who permits thee to prosper doth
 know;
In his hand is my heart and my hope—and in
 thine
The land and the life which for him I resign.

HEROD'S LAMENT FOR MARIAMNE.

I.

OH, Mariamne! now for thee
 The heart for which thou bled'st is bleeding;
Revenge is lost in agony,
 And wild remorse to rage succeeding.
Oh, Mariamne! where art thou?
 Thou canst not hear my bitter pleading:
Ah! could'st thou—thou would'st pardon now,
 Though Heaven were to my prayer unheed-
 ing.

II.

And is she dead?—and did they dare
 Obey my frenzy's jealous raving?
My wrath but doom'd my own despair:
 The sword that smote her's o'er me wav-
 ing.—
But thou art cold, my murder'd love!
 And this dark heart is vainly craving
For her who soars alone above,
 And leaves my soul unworthy saving

III.

She's gone, who shared my diadem;
 She sunk, with her my joys entombing;
I swept that flower from Judah's stem,
 Whose leaves for me alone were blooming;
And mine's the guilt, and mine the hell,
 This bosom's desolation dooming;
And I have earn'd those tortures well,
 Which unconsumed are still consuming!

ON THE DAY OF THE DESTRUCTION OF JERUSALEM BY TITUS.

I.

FROM the last hill that looks on thy once holy
 dome,
I beheld thee, oh Sion! when render'd to
 Rome:
'Twas thy last sun went down, and the
 flames of thy fall
Flash'd back on the last glance I gave to
 thy wall.

II.

I look'd for thy temple, I look'd for my
 home,
And forgot for a moment my bondage to
 come;
I beheld but the death-fire that fed on thy
 fane,
And the fast-fetter'd hands that made venge-
 ance in vain.

III.

On many an eve, the high spot whence I
 gazed
Had reflected the last beam of day as it
 blazed;
While I stood on the height, and beheld the
 decline
Of the rays from the mountain that shone
 on thy shrine.

IV.

And now on that mountain I stood on that
 day,
But I mark'd not the twilight beam melt-
 ing away;
Oh! would that the lightning had glared in
 its stead,
And the thunderbolt burst on the conqueror's
 head!

V.

But the gods of the Pagan shall never profane
The shrine where Jehovah disdain'd not to
 reign;
And scatter'd and scorn'd as thy people
 may be,
Our worship, oh Father! is only for thee.

BY THE RIVERS OF BABYLON WE SAT DOWN AND WEPT.

I.

WE sat down and wept by the waters
 Of Babel, and thought of the day
When our foe, in the hue of his slaughters,
 Made Salem's high places his prey;
And ye, oh her desolate daughters!
 Were scatter'd all weeping away.

II.

While sadly we gazed on the river
 Which roll'd on in freedom below,
They demanded the song; but, oh never
 That triumph the stranger shall know!
May this right hand be wither'd for ever,
 Ere it string our high harp for the foe!

III.

On the willow that harp is suspended,
 Oh Salem! its sound should be free;
And the hour when thy glories were ended
 But left me that token of thee:
And ne'er shall its soft tones be blended
 With the voice of the spoiler by me!

THE DESTRUCTION OF SENNACHERIB.

I.

THE Assyrian came down like the wolf on
 the fold,
And his cohorts were gleaming in purple and
 gold;
And the sheen of their spears was like stars
 on the sea,
When the blue wave rolls nightly on deep
 Galilee.

II.

Like the leaves of the forest when Summer is
 green,
That host with their banners at sunset were
 seen:
Like the leaves of the forest when Autumn
 hath blown,
That host on the morrow lay wither'd and
 strown.

III.

For the Angel of Death spread his wings on
 the blast,
And breathed in the face of the foe as he
 pass'd;
And the eyes of the sleepers wax'd deadly
 and chill,
And their hearts but once heaved, and for
 ever grew still!

IV.

And there lay the steed with his nostril all
 wide,
But through it there roll'd not the breath of
 his pride;
And the foam of his gasping lay white on
 the turf,
And cold as the spray of the rock-beating
 surf.

V.

And there lay the rider distorted and pale,
With the dew on his brow, and the rust on
 his mail:
And the tents were all silent, the banners
 alone,
The lances unlifted, the trumpet unblown.

VI.

And the widows of Ashur are loud in their
 wail,
And the idols are broke in the temple of
 Baal;
And the might of the Gentile, unsmote by
 the sword,
Hath melted like snow in the glance of the
 Lord!

A SPIRIT PASS'D BEFORE ME.

FROM JOB.

I.

A SPIRIT pass'd before me: I beheld
The face of immortality unveil'd—
Deep sleep came down on every eye save
 mine—
And there it stood,—all formless—but divine:
Along my bones the creeping flesh did quake;
And as my damp hair stiffen'd, thus it spake:

II.

"Is man more just than God? Is man more
 pure
Than he who deems even Seraphs insecure?
Creatures of clay—vain dwellers in the dust!
The moth survives you, and are ye more
 just?
Things of a day! you wither ere the night,
Heedless and blind to Wisdom's wasted
 light!"

STANZAS FOR MUSIC.

THERE be none of Beauty's daughters
 With a magic like thee;
And like music on the waters
 Is thy sweet voice to me:
When, as if its sound were causing
The charmed ocean's pausing,
The waves lie still and gleaming,
And the lull'd winds seem dreaming:

And the midnight moon is weaving
 Her bright chain o'er the deep;
Whose breast is gently heaving,
 As an infant's asleep:

So the spirit bows before thee,
To listen and adore thee;
With a full but soft emotion,
Like the swell of Summer's ocean.

———•••———

STANZAS FOR MUSIC.

"O Lachrymarum fons, tenero sacros
 Ducentium ortus ex animo: quater
Felix! in imo qui scatentem
 Pectore te, pia Nympha, sensit."
 GRAY'S *Poemata.*

THERE'S not a joy the world can give like
 that it takes away,
When the glow of early thought declines in
 feeling's dull decay;
'T is not on youth's smooth cheek the blush
 alone, which fades so fast,
But the tender bloom of heart is gone, ere
 youth itself be past.

Then the few whose spirits float above the
 wreck of happiness
Are driven o'er the shoals of guilt or ocean
 of excess:
The magnet of their course is gone, or only
 points in vain
The shore to which their shiver'd sail shall
 never stretch again.

Then the mortal coldness of the soul like
 death itself comes down;
It cannot feel for others' woes, it dare not
 dream its own;
That heavy chill has frozen o'er the fountain
 of our tears,
And though the eye may sparkle still, 't is
 where the ice appears.

Though wit may flash from fluent lips, and
 mirth distract the breast,
Through midnight hours that yield no more
 their former hope of rest;
'T is but as ivy-leaves around the ruin'd
 turret wreath,
All green and wildly fresh without, but worn
 and grey beneath.

Oh could I feel as I have felt,—or be what
 I have been,
Or weep as I could once have wept o'er
 many a vanish'd scene;
As springs in deserts found seem sweet, all
 brackish though they be,
So, midst the wither'd waste of life, those
 tears would flow to me.
 March, 1815.

ON NAPOLEON'S ESCAPE FROM ELBA.

ONCE fairly set out on his party of pleasure,
Taking towns at his liking, and crowns at his
 leisure,
From Elba to Lyons and Paris he goes,
Making *balls for* the ladies, and *bows to* his
 foes.
 March 27, 1815.

———•••———

ODE FROM THE FRENCH.

I.

WE do not curse thee, Waterloo!
Though Freedom's blood thy plain bedew;
There 't was shed, but is not sunk—
Rising from each gory trunk,
Like the water-spout from ocean,
With a strong and growing motion—
It soars, and mingles in the air,
With that of lost Labedoyère—
With that of him whose honour'd grave
Contains the "bravest of the brave."
A crimson cloud it spreads and glows,
But shall return to whence it rose;
When 't is full 't will burst asunder—
Never yet was heard such thunder
As then shall shake the world with wonder—
Never yet was seen such lightning
As o'er heaven shall then be bright'ning!
Like the Wormwood Star foretold
By the sainted Seer of old,
Show'ring down a fiery flood,
Turning rivers into blood.

II.

The Chief has fallen, but not by you,
Vanquishers of Waterloo!
When the soldier citizen
Sway'd not o'er his fellow-men—
Save in deeds that led them on
Where Glory smiled on Freedom's son—
Who, of all the despots banded,
 With that youthful chief competed?
 Who could boast o'er France defeated,
Till lone Tyranny commanded?
Till, goaded by ambition's sting,
The Hero sunk into the King?
Then he fell:—so perish all,
Who would men by man enthral!

III.

And thou, too, of the snow-white plume!
Whose realm refused thee ev'n a tomb;
Better hadst thou still been leading
France o'er hosts of hirelings bleeding,
Than sold thyself to death and shame
For a meanly royal name;

Such as he of Naples wears,
Who thy blood-bought title bears.
Little didst thou deem, when dashing
 On thy war-horse through the ranks,
 Like a stream which burst its banks,
While helmets cleft, and sabres clashing,
Shone and shiver'd fast around thee—
Of the fate at last which found thee:
Was that haughty plume laid low
By a slave's dishonest blow?
Once—as the moon sways o'er the tide,
It roll'd in air, the warrior's guide;
Through the smoke-created night
Of the black and sulphurous fight,
The soldier raised his seeking eye
To catch that crest's ascendancy,—
And, as it onward rolling rose,
So moved his heart upon our foes.
There, where death's brief pang was quickest,
And the battle's wreck lay thickest,
Strew'd beneath the advancing banner
Of the eagle's burning crest—
(There with thunder-clouds to fan her,
 Who could then her wing arrest—
 Victory beaming from her breast?)
While the broken line enlarging
 Fell, or fled along the plain;
There be sure was Murat charging!
 There he ne'er shall charge again!

IV.

O'er glories gone the invaders march,
Weeps Triumph o'er each levell'd arch—
But let Freedom rejoice,
With her heart in her voice;
But, her hand on her sword,
Doubly shall she be adored;
France hath twice too well been taught
The "moral lesson" dearly bought—
Her safety sits not on a throne,
With Capet or Napoleon!
But in equal rights and laws,
Hearts and hands in one great cause—
Freedom, such as God hath given
Unto all beneath his heaven,
With their breath, and from their birth,
Though guilt would sweep it from the earth;
With a fierce and lavish hand
Scattering nations' wealth like sand;
Pouring nations' blood like water,
In imperial seas of slaughter!

V.

But the heart and the mind,
And the voice of mankind,
Shall arise in communion—
And who shall resist that proud union?
The time is past when swords subdued—
Man may die—the soul's renew'd:

Even in this low world of care
Freedom ne'er shall want an heir;
Millions breathe but to inherit
Her for ever bounding spirit—
When once more her hosts assemble,
Tyrants shall believe and tremble—
Smile they at this idle threat?
Crimson tears will follow yet.

FROM THE FRENCH.

I.

MUST thou go, my glorious Chief,
 Sever'd from thy faithful few?
Who can tell thy warrior's grief,
 Maddening o'er that long adieu?
Woman's love, and friendship's zeal,
 Dear as both have been to me—
What are they to all I feel,
 With a soldier's faith for thee?

II.

Idol of the soldier's soul!
 First in fight, but mightiest now;
Many could a world control;
 Thee alone no doom can bow.
By thy side for years I dared
 Death; and envied those who fell,
When their dying shout was heard,
 Blessing him they served so well.

III.

Would that I were cold with those,
 Since this hour I live to see;
When the doubts of coward foes
 Scarce dare trust a man with thee,
Dreading each should set thee free!
 Oh! although in dungeons pent,
All their chains were light to me,
 Gazing on thy soul unbent.

IV.

Would the sycophants of him
 Now so deaf to duty's prayer,
Were his borrow'd glories dim,
 In his native darkness share?
Were that world this hour his own,
 All thou calmly dost resign,
Could he purchase with that throne
 Hearts like those which still are thine?

V.

My chief, my king, my friend, adieu!
 Never did I droop before;
Never to my sovereign sue,
 As his foes I now implore:
All I ask is to divide
 Every peril he must brave;
Sharing by the hero's side
 His fall, his exile, and his grave.

ON THE STAR OF "THE LEGION OF HONOUR."

[FROM THE FRENCH.]

STAR of the brave!—whose beam hath shed
Such glory o'er the quick and dead—
Thou radiant and adored deceit!
Which millions rush'd in arms to greet,—
Wild meteor of immortal birth;
Why rise in Heaven to set on Earth?

Souls of slain heroes form'd thy rays;
Eternity flash'd through thy blaze;
The music of thy martial sphere
Was fame on high and honour here;
And thy light broke on human eyes,
Like a volcano of the skies.

Like lava roll'd thy stream of blood,
And swept down empires with its flood;
Earth rock'd beneath thee to her base,
As thou didst lighten through all space;
And the shorn Sun grew dim in air,
And set while thou wert dwelling there.

Before thee rose, and with thee grew,
A rainbow of the loveliest hue
Of three bright colours, each divine,
And fit for that celestial sign;
For Freedom's hand had blended them,
Like tints in an immortal gem.

One tint was of the sunbeam's dyes;
One, the blue depth of Seraph's eyes;
One, the pure Spirit's veil of white
Had robed in radiance of its light:
The three so mingled did beseem
The texture of a heavenly dream.

Star of the brave! thy ray is pale,
And darkness must again prevail!
But, oh thou Rainbow of the free!
Our tears and blood must flow for thee.
When thy bright promise fades away,
Our life is but a load of clay.

And Freedom hallows with her tread
The silent cities of the dead;
For beautiful in death are they
Who proudly fall in her array;
And soon, oh Goddess! may we be
For evermore with them or thee!

—◆—

NAPOLEON'S FAREWELL.

[FROM THE FRENCH.]

I.

FAREWELL to the Land where the gloom of my Glory
Arose and o'ershadow'd the earth with her name—

She abandons me now—but the page of her story,
The brightest or blackest, is fill'd with my fame.
I have warr'd with a world which vanquish'd me only
When the meteor of conquest allured me too far;
I have coped with the nations which dread me thus lonely,
The last single Captive to millions in war.

II.

Farewell to thee, France! when thy diadem crown'd me,
I made thee the gem and the wonder of earth,
But thy weakness decrees I should leave as I found thee,
Decay'd in thy glory, and sunk in thy worth.
Oh! for the veteran hearts that were wasted
In strife with the storm, when their battles were won—
Then the Eagle, whose gaze in that moment was blasted,
Had still soar'd with eyes fix'd on victory's sun!

III.

Farewell to thee, France!—but when Liberty rallies
Once more in thy regions, remember me then,—
The violet still grows in the depth of thy valleys;
Though wither'd, thy tear will unfold it again—
Yet, yet, I may baffle the hosts that surround us,
And yet may thy heart leap awake to my voice—
There are links which must break in the chain that has bound us,
Then turn thee and call on the Chief of thy choice!

═══════════

DOMESTIC PIECES.

1816.

—◆—

FARE THEE WELL.

"Alas! they had been friends in youth;
 But whispering tongues can poison truth;
 And constancy lives in realms above;
 And life is thorny; and youth is vain;
 And to be wroth with one we love,
 Doth work like madness in the brain;
 "

> But never either found another
> To free the hollow heart from paining—
> They stood aloof, the scars remaining,
> Like cliffs which had been rent asunder;
> A dreary sea now flows between,
> But neither heat, nor frost, nor thunder,
> Shall wholly do away, I ween,
> The marks of that which once hath been."
> COLERIDGE'S *Christabel.*

FARE thee well! and if for ever,
 Still for ever, fare thee well:
Even though unforgiving, never
 'Gainst thee shall my heart rebel.

Would that breast were bared before thee
 Where thy head so oft hath lain,
While that placid sleep came o'er thee
 Which thou ne'er canst know again:

Would that breast, by thee glanced over,
 Every inmost thought could show!
Then thou wouldst at last discover
 'T was not well to spurn it so.

Though the world for this commend thee—
 Though it smile upon the blow,
Even its praises must offend thee,
 Founded on another's woe:

Though my many faults defaced me,
 Could no other arm be found,
Than the one which once embraced me,
 To inflict a cureless wound?

Yet, oh yet, thyself deceive not;
 Love may sink by slow decay,
But by sudden wrench, believe not
 Hearts can thus be torn away:

Still thine own its life retaineth,
 Still must mine, though bleeding, beat;
And the undying thought which paineth
 Is—that we no more may meet.

These are words of deeper sorrow
 Than the wail above the dead;
Both shall live, but every morrow
 Wake us from a widow'd bed.

And when thou wouldst solace gather,
 When our child's first accents flow,
Wilt thou teach her to say " Father ! "
 Though his care she must forego?

When her little hands shall press thee,
 When her lip to thine is press'd,
Think of him whose prayer shall bless thee,
 Think of him thy love had bless'd!

Should her lineaments resemble
 Those thou never more may'st see,
Then thy heart will softly tremble
 With a pulse yet true to me.

All my faults perchance thou knowest,
 All my madness none can know;
All my hopes, where'er thou goest,
 Wither, yet with *thee* they go.

Every feeling hath been shaken;
 Pride, which not a world could bow,
Bows to thee—by thee forsaken,
 Even my soul forsakes me now:

But 't is done—all words are idle—
 Words from me are vainer still;
But the thoughts we cannot bridle
 Force their way without the will.

Fare thee well! thus disunited,
 Torn from every nearer tie,
Sear'd in heart, and lone, and blighted,
 More than this I scarce can die.

 March 17, 1816.

———

A SKETCH.

> " Honest—honest Iago !
> If that thou be'st a devil, I cannot kill thee."
> SHAKSPEARE.

BORN in the garret, in the kitchen bred,
Promoted thence to deck her mistress' head;
Next—for some gracious service unexpress'd,
And from its wages only to be guess'd—
Raised from the toilette to the table,—where
Her wondering betters wait behind her chair.
With eye unmoved, and forehead unabash'd,
She dines from off the plate she lately wash'd.
Quick with the tale, and ready with the lie,
The genial confidante, and general spy,
Who could, ye gods! her next employment
 guess—
An only infant's earliest governess!
She taught the child to read, and taught so
 well,
That she herself, by teaching, learn'd to spell.
An adept next in penmanship she grows,
As many a nameless slander deftly shows:
What she had made the pupil of her art,
None know—but that high Soul secured the
 heart,
And panted for the truth it could not hear,
With longing breast and undeluded ear.
Foil'd was perversion by that youthful mind,
Which Flattery fool'd not, Baseness could
 not blind,
Deceit infect not, near Contagion soil,
Indulgence weaken, nor Example spoil,
Nor master'd Science tempt her to look down
On humbler talents with a pitying frown,
Nor Genius swell, nor Beauty render vain,
Nor Envy ruffle to retaliate pain,
Nor Fortune change, Pride raise, nor Passion
 bow,
Nor virtue teach austerity—till now.

Serenely purest of her sex that live,
But wanting one sweet weakness—to forgive,
Too shock'd at faults her soul can never
 know,
She deems that all could be like her below ·
Foe to all vice, yet hardly Virtue's friend,
For Virtue pardons those she would amend.

But to the theme, now laid aside too long,
The baleful burthen of this honest song,
Though all her former functions are no more,
She rules the circle which she served before.
If mothers—none know why—before her
 quake;
If daughters dread her for the mothers' sake;
If early habits—those false links, which bind
At times the loftiest to the meanest mind—
Have given her power too deeply to instil
The angry essence of her deadly will;
If like a snake she steal within your walls,
Till the black slime betray her as she crawls;
If like a viper to the heart she wind,
And leave the venom there she did not
 find;
What marvel that this hag of hatred works
Eternal evil latent as she lurks,
To make a Pandemonium where she dwells,
And reign the Hecate of domestic hells?
Skill'd by a touch to deepen scandal's tints
With all the kind mendacity of hints,
While mingling truth with falsehood, sneers
 with smiles,
A thread of candour with a web of wiles:
A plain blunt show of briefly-spoken seeming,
To hide her bloodless heart's soul-harden'd
 scheming;
A lip of lies; a face form'd to conceal,
And, without feeling, mock at all who feel:
With a vile mask the Gorgon would dis-
 own,—
A cheek of parchment, and an eye of stone.
Mark, how the channels of her yellow blood
Ooze to her skin, and stagnate there to mud,
Cased like the centipede in saffron mail,
Or darker greenness of the scorpion's scale—
(For drawn from reptiles only may we trace
Congenial colours in that soul or face)—
Look on her features! and behold her mind
As in a mirror of itself defined:
Look on the picture! deem it not o'er-
 charged—
There is no trait which might not be en-
 larged:
Yet true to "Nature's journeymen," who
 made
This monster when their mistress left off
 trade—
This female dog-star of her little sky,
Where all beneath her influence droop or
 die.

Oh! wretch without a tear—without a
 thought,
Save joy above the ruin thou hast wrought—
The time shall come, nor long remote, when
 thou
Shalt feel far more than thou inflictest now;
Feel for thy vile self-loving self in vain,
And turn thee howling in unpitied pain.
May the strong curse of crush'd affections
 light
Back on thy bosom with reflected blight!
And make thee in thy leprosy of mind
As loathsome to thyself as to mankind!
Till all thy self-thoughts curdle into hate,
Black—as thy will for others would create:
Till thy hard heart be calcined into dust,
And thy soul welter in its hideous crust.
Oh, may thy grave be sleepless as the bed,
The widow'd couch of fire, that thou hast
 spread!
Then, when thou fain wouldst weary Heaven
 with prayer,
Look on thine earthly victims—and despair!
Down to the dust!—and, as thou rott'st
 away,
Even worms shall perish on thy poisonous
 clay.
But for the love I bore, and still must bear,
To her thy malice from all ties would tear—
Thy name—thy human name—to every eye
The climax of all scorn should hang on high,
Exalted o'er thy less abhorr'd compeers—
And festering in the infamy of years.

 March 29, 1816.

ENDORSEMENT TO THE DEED OF SEPARATION.

IN THE APRIL OF 1816.

A YEAR ago, you swore, fond she!
 "To love, to honour," and so forth:
Such was the vow you pledged to me,
 And here's exactly what 'tis worth.

STANZAS TO AUGUSTA.

I.

WHEN all around grew drear and dark,
 And reason half withheld her ray—
And hope but shed a dying spark
 Which more misled my lonely way;

II.

In that deep midnight of the mind,
 And that internal strife of heart,
When dreading to be deem'd too kind,
 The weak despair—the cold depart;

III.

When fortune changed—and love fled far,
 And hatred's shafts flew thick and fast,
Thou wert the solitary star
 Which rose and set not to the last.

IV.

Oh! blest be thine unbroken light!
 That watch'd me as a seraph's eye,
And stood between me and the night,
 For ever shining sweetly nigh.

V.

And when the cloud upon us came,
 Which strove to blacken o'er thy ray—
Then purer spread its gentle flame,
 And dash'd the darkness all away.

VI.

Still may thy spirit dwell on mine,
 And teach it what to brave or brook—
There's more in one soft word of thine
 Than in the world's defied rebuke.

VII.

Thou stood'st, as stands a lovely tree,
 That still unbroke, though gently bent,
Still waves with fond fidelity
 Its boughs above a monument.

VIII.

The winds might rend—the skies might pour,
 But there thou wert—and still wouldst be
Devoted in the stormiest hour
 To shed thy weeping leaves o'er me.

IX.

But thou and thine shall know no blight,
 Whatever fate on me may fall;
For heaven in sunshine will requite
 The kind—and thee the most of all.

X.

Then let the ties of baffled love
 Be broken—thine will never break;
Thy heart can feel—but will not move;
 Thy soul, though soft, will never shake.

XI.

And these, when all was lost beside,
 Were found and still are fix'd in thee;—
And bearing still a breast so tried,
 Earth is no desert—ev'n to me.

STANZAS TO AUGUSTA.

I.

Though the day of my destiny's over,
 And the star of my fate hath declined,
Thy soft heart refused to discover
 The faults which so many could find;
Though thy soul with my grief was ac-
 quainted,
 It shrunk not to share it with me,
And the love which my spirit hath painted
 It never hath found but in *thee*.

II.

Then when nature around me is smiling,
 The last smile which answers to mine,
I do not believe it beguiling,
 Because it reminds me of thine;
And when winds are at war with the ocean,
 As the breasts I believed in with me,
If their billows excite an emotion,
 It is that they bear me from *thee*.

III.

Though the rock of my last hope is shiver'd,
 And its fragments are sunk in the wave,
Though I feel that my soul is deliver'd
 To pain—it shall not be its slave.
There is many a pang to pursue me:
 They may crush, but they shall not con-
 temn;
They may torture, but shall not subdue me;
 'Tis of *thee* that I think—not of them.

IV.

Though human, thou didst not deceive me,
 Though woman, thou didst not forsake,
Though loved, thou forborest to grieve me,
 Though slander'd, thou never couldst
 shake;
Though trusted, thou didst not disclaim me,
 Though parted, it was not to fly,
Though watchful, 'twas not to defame me,
 Nor, mute, that the world might belie.

V.

Yet I blame not the world, nor despise it,
 Nor the war of the many with one;
If my soul was not fitted to prize it,
 'Twas folly not sooner to shun:
And if dearly that error hath cost me,
 And more than I once could foresee,
I have found that, whatever it lost me,
 It could not deprive me of *thee*.

VI.

From the wreck of the past, which hath
 perish'd,
 Thus much I at least may recall,
It hath taught me that what I most cherish'd
 Deserved to be dearest of all:

In the desert a fountain is springing,
 In the wide waste there still is a tree,
And a bird in the solitude singing,
 Which speaks to my spirit of *thee*.

> *July* 24, 1816.

EPISTLE TO AUGUSTA.

I.

My sister! my sweet sister! if a name
Dearer and purer were, it should be thine;
Mountains and seas divide us, but I claim
No tears, but tenderness to answer mine:
Go where I will, to me thou art the same—
A loved regret which I would not resign.
There yet are two things in my destiny,—
A world to roam through, and a home with
 thee.

II.

The first were nothing—had I still the last,
It were the haven of my happiness;
But other claims and other ties thou hast,
And mine is not the wish to make them
 less.
A strange doom is thy father's son's, and
 past
Recalling, as it lies beyond redress;
Reversed for him our grandsire's fate of
 yore,—
He had no rest at sea, nor I on shore.

III.

If my inheritance of storms hath been
In other elements, and on the rocks
Of perils, overlook'd or unforeseen,
I have sustain'd my share of worldly shocks,
The fault was mine; nor do I seek to
 screen
My errors with defensive paradox;
I have been cunning in mine overthrow,
The careful pilot of my proper woe.

IV.

Mine were my faults, and mine be their
 reward.
My whole life was a contest, since the day
That gave me being, gave me that which
 marr'd
The gift,—a fate, or will, that walk'd
 astray;
And I at times have found the struggle
 hard,
And thought of shaking off my bonds of
 clay:
But now I fain would for a time survive,
If but to see what next can well arrive.

V.

Kingdoms and empires in my little day
I have outlived, and yet I am not old;
And when I look on this, the petty spray
Of my own years of trouble, which have
 roll'd
Like a wild bay of breakers, melts away:
Something—I know not what—does still
 uphold
A spirit of slight patience;—not in vain,
Even for its own sake, do we purchase pain.

VI.

Perhaps the workings of defiance stir
Within me—or perhaps a cold despair,
Brought on when ills habitually recur,—
Perhaps a kinder clime, or purer air,
(For even to this may change of soul refer,
And with light armour we may learn to
 bear,)
Have taught me a strange quiet, which
 was not
The chief companion of a calmer lot.

VII.

I feel almost at times as I have felt
In happy childhood; trees, and flowers,
 and brooks,
Which do remember me of where I dwelt
Ere my young mind was sacrificed to books,
Come as of yore upon me, and can melt
My heart with recognition of their looks;
And even at moments I could think I see
Some living thing to love—but none like
 thee.

VIII.

Here are the Alpine landscapes which
 create
A fund for contemplation;—to admire
Is a brief feeling of a trivial date;
But something worthier do such scenes
 inspire:
Here to be lonely is not desolate,
For much I view which I could most desire,
And, above all, a lake I can behold
Lovelier, not dearer, than our own of old.

IX.

Oh that thou wert but with me!—but I
 grow
The fool of my own wishes, and forget
The solitude which I have vaunted so
Has lost its praise in this but one regret;
There may be others which I less may
 show;—
I am not of the plaintive mood, and yet
I feel an ebb in my philosophy,
And the tide rising in my alter'd eye.

X.

I did remind thee of our own dear Lake,
By the old Hall which may be mine no more.
Leman's is fair; but think not I forsake
The sweet remembrance of a dearer shore:
Sad havoc Time must with my memory
make,
Ere *that* or *thou* can fade these eyes before;
Though, like all things which I have loved,
they are
Resign'd for ever, or divided far.

XI.

The world is all before me; I but ask
Of Nature that with which she will com-
ply—
It is but in her summer's sun to bask,
To mingle with the quiet of her sky,
To see her gentle face without a mask,
And never gaze on it with apathy.
She was my early friend, and now shall be
My sister—till I look again on thee.

XII.

I can reduce all feelings but this one;
And that I would not;—for at length I see
Such scenes as those wherein my life
begun.
The earliest—even the only paths for me—
Had I but sooner learnt the crowd to shun,
I had been better than I now can be;
The passions which have torn me would
have slept;
I had not suffer'd, and *thou* hadst not wept.

XIII.

With false Ambition what had I to do?
Little with Love, and least of all with
Fame;
And yet they came unsought, and with me
grew,
And made me all which they can make—a
name.
Yet this was not the end I did pursue;
Surely I once beheld a nobler aim.
But all is over—I am one the more
To baffled millions which have gone before.

XIV.

And for the future, this world's future may
From me demand but little of my care;
I have outlived myself by many a day;
Having survived so many things that were;
My years have been no slumber, but the
prey
Of ceaseless vigils; for I had the share
Of life which might have fill'd a century,
Before its fourth in time had pass'd me by.

XV.

And for the remnant which may be to come
I am content; and for the past I feel
Not thankless,—for within the crowded sum
Of struggles, happiness at times would
steal,
And for the present, I would not benumb
My feelings further.—Nor shall I conceal
That with all this I still can look around,
And worship Nature with a thought profound.

XVI.

For thee, my own sweet sister, in thy heart
I know myself secure, as thou in mine;
We were and are—I am, even as thou art-
Beings who ne'er each other can resign;
It is the same, together or apart,
From life's commencement to its slow de-
cline
We are entwined—let death come slow or
fast,
The tie which bound the first endures the
last!

———◦◦———

THE DREAM.

I.

OUR life is two-fold: Sleep hath its own
world,
A boundary between the things misnamed
Death and existence: Sleep hath its own
world,
And a wide realm of wild reality.
And dreams in their development have breath,
And tears, and tortures, and the touch of joy;
They leave a weight upon our waking
thoughts,
They take a weight from off our waking toils,
They do divide our being; they become
A portion of ourselves as of our time,
And look like heralds of eternity;
They pass like spirits of the past,—they speak
Like Sibyls of the future: they have power—
The tyranny of pleasure and of pain;
They make us what we were not—what they
will,
And shake us with the vision that's gone by,
The dread of vanish'd shadows—Are they so?
Is not the past all shadow?—What are they?
Creations of the mind?—The mind can make
Substance, and people planets of its own
With beings brighter than have been, and
give
A breath to forms which can outlive all flesh.
I would recall a vision which I dream'd
Perchance in sleep—for in itself a thought,
A slumbering thought, is capable of years,
And curdles a long life into one hour.

II.

I saw two beings in the hues of youth
Standing upon a hill, a gentle hill,
Green and of mild declivity, the last
As 't were the cape of a long ridge of such,
Save that there was no sea to lave its base,
But a most living landscape, and the wave
Of woods and corn-fields, and the abodes of
　　men
Scatter'd at intervals, and wreathing smoke
Arising from such rustic roofs ;—the hill
Was crown'd with a peculiar diadem
Of trees, in circular array, so fix'd,
Not by the sport of nature, but of man:
These two, a maiden and a youth, were there
Gazing—the one on all that was beneath
Fair as herself—but the boy gazed on her ;
And both were young, and one was beautiful:
And both were young—yet not alike in youth.
As the sweet moon on the horizon's verge,
The maid was on the eve of womanhood ;
The boy had fewer summers, but his heart
Had far outgrown his years, and to his eye
There was but one beloved face on earth,
And that was shining on him: he had look'd
Upon it till it could not pass away ;
He had no breath, no being, but in hers ;
She was his voice ; he did not speak to her,
But trembled on her words ; she was his
　　sight,
For his eye follow'd hers, and saw with hers,
Which colour'd all his objects :—he had ceased
To live within himself ; she was his life,
The ocean to the river of his thoughts,
Which terminated all: upon a tone,
A touch of hers, his blood would ebb and flow,
And his cheek change tempestuously—his
　　heart
Unknowing of its cause of agony.
But she in these fond feelings had no share:
Her sighs were not for him ; to her he was
Even as a brother—but no more ; 't was
　　much,
For brotherless she was, save in the name
Her infant friendship had bestow'd on him ;
Herself the solitary scion left
Of a time-honour'd race.—It was a name
Which pleased him, and yet pleased him not
　　—and why ?
Time taught him a deep answer—when she
　　loved
Another ; even *now* she loved another,
And on the summit of that hill she stood
Looking afar if yet her lover's steed
Kept pace with her expectancy, and flew.

III.

A change came o'er the spirit of my dream.
There was an ancient mansion, and before

Its walls there was a steed caparison'd :
Within an antique Oratory stood
The Boy of whom I spake ;—he was alone,
And pale, and pacing to and fro : anon
He sate him down, and seized a pen, and traced
Words which I could not guess of ; then he
　　lean'd
His bow'd head on his hands, and shook as
　　't were
With a convulsion—then arose again,
And with his teeth and quivering hands did
　　tear
What he had written, but he shed no tears,
And he did calm himself, and fix his brow
Into a kind of quiet : as he paused,
The Lady of his love re-entered there ;
She was serene and smiling then, and yet
She knew she was by him beloved,—she
　　knew,
For quickly comes such knowledge, that his
　　heart
Was darken'd with her shadow, and she saw
That he was wretched, but she saw not all.
He rose, and with a cold and gentle grasp
He took her hand ; a moment o'er his face
A tablet of unutterable thoughts
Was traced, and then it faded, as it came ;
He dropp'd the hand he held, and with slow
　　steps
Retired, but not as bidding her adieu,
For they did part with mutual smiles ; he
　　pass'd
From out the massy gate of that old Hall,
And mounting on his steed he went his way ;
And ne'er repass'd that hoary threshold more.

IV.

A change came o'er the spirit of my dream.
The Boy was sprung to manhood: in the
　　wilds
Of fiery climes he made himself a home,
And his soul drank their sunbeams : he was
　　girt
With strange and dusky aspects ; he was not
Himself like what he had been ; on the sea
And on the shore he was a wanderer :
There was a mass of many images
Crowded like waves upon me, but he was
A part of all ; and in the last he lay
Reposing from the noontide sultriness,
Couch'd among fallen columns, in the shade
Of ruin'd walls that had survived the names
Of those who rear'd them ; by his sleeping side
Stood camels grazing, and some goodly steeds
Were fasten'd near a fountain ; and a man
Clad in a flowing garb did watch the while,
While many of his tribe slumber'd around :
And they were canopied by the blue sky,
So cloudless, clear, and purely beautiful,
That God alone was to be seen in heaven.

V.

A change came o'er the spirit of my dream.
The Lady of his love was wed with One
Who did not love her better :—in her home,
A thousand leagues from his,—her native
 home,
She dwelt, begirt with growing Infancy,
Daughters and sons of Beauty,—but behold !
Upon her face there was the tint of grief,
The settled shadow of an inward strife,
And an unquiet drooping of the eye,
As if its lid were charged with unshed tears.
What could her grief be ?—she had all she
 loved,
And he who had so loved her was not there
To trouble with bad hopes, or evil wish,
Or ill-repress'd affliction, her pure thoughts.
What could her grief be ?—she had loved
 him not,
Nor given him cause to deem himself be-
 loved,
Nor could he be a part of that which prey'd
Upon her mind—a spectre of the past.

VI.

A change came o'er the spirit of my dream.
The Wanderer was return'd.—I saw him
 stand
Before an Altar—with a gentle bride ;
Her face was fair, but was not that which
 made
The Starlight of his Boyhood ;—as he stood
Even at the altar, o'er his brow there came
The self-same aspect, and the quivering
 shock
That in the antique Oratory shook
His bosom in its solitude ; and then—
As in that hour—a moment o'er his face
The tablet of unutterable thoughts
Was traced,—and then it faded as it came,
And he stood calm and quiet, and he spoke
The fitting vows, but heard not his own
 words,
And all things reel'd around him ; he could see
Not that which was, nor that which should
 have been—
But the old mansion, and the accustom'd hall,
And the remember'd chambers, and the place,
The day, the hour, the sunshine, and the
 shade,
All things pertaining to that place and hour,
And her who was his destiny,—came back
And thrust themselves between him and the
 light :
What business had they there at such a time ?

VII.

A change came o'er the spirit of my dream.
The Lady of his love :—Oh ! she was changed

As by the sickness of the soul ; her mind
Had wander'd from its dwelling, and her eyes
They had not their own lustre, but the look
Which is not of the earth ; she was become
The queen of a fantastic realm ; her thoughts
Were combinations of disjointed things ;
And forms impalpable and unperceived
Of others' sight familiar were to hers.
And this the world calls frenzy ; but the wise
Have a far deeper madness, and the glance
Of melancholy is a fearful gift ;
What is it but the telescope of truth ?
Which strips the distance of its fantasies,
And brings life near in utter nakedness,
Making the cold reality too real !

VIII.

A change came o'er the spirit of my dream.
The Wanderer was alone as heretofore,
The beings which surrounded him were gone,
Or were at war with him ; he was a mark
For blight and desolation, compass'd round
With Hatred and Contention ; Pain was mix'd
In all which was served up to him, until,
Like to the Pontic monarch of old days,
He fed on poisons, and they had no power,
But were a kind of nutriment ; he lived
Through that which had been death to many
 men,
And made him friends of mountains : with
 the stars
And the quick Spirit of the Universe
He held his dialogues ; and they did teach
To him the magic of their mysteries ;
To him the book of Night was open'd wide,
And voices from the deep abyss reveal'd
A marvel and a secret—Be it so.

IX.

My dream was past ; it had no further change.
It was of a strange order, that the doom
Of these two creatures should be thus traced
 out
Almost like a reality—the one
To end in madness—both in misery.

July, 1816.

———————

LINES ON HEARING THAT LADY BYRON WAS ILL.

AND thou wert sad—yet I was not with thee ;
 And thou wert sick, and yet I was not near ;
Methought that joy and health alone could be
 Where I was *not*—and pain and sorrow here !
And is it thus ?—it is as I foretold,
 And shall be more so ; for the mind recoils
Upon itself, and the wreck'd heart lies cold,
 While heaviness collects the shatter'd
 spoils.

It is not in the storm nor in the strife
 We feel benumb'd, and wish to be no more,
 But in the after-silence on the shore,
When all is lost, except a little life.

I am too well avenged!—but 'twas my right;
 Whate'er my sins might be, *thou* wert not
 sent
To be the Nemesis who should requite—
 Nor did Heaven choose so near an instru-
 ment.
Mercy is for the merciful!—if thou
Hast been of such, 't will be accorded now.
Thy nights are banish'd from the realms of
 sleep!—
 Yes! they may flatter thee, but thou shalt
 feel
A hollow agony which will not heal,
For thou art pillow'd on a curse too deep;
Thou hast sown in my sorrow, and must reap
 The bitter harvest in a woe as real!
I have had many foes, but none like thee;
 For 'gainst the rest myself I could defend,
 And be avenged, or turn them into friend;
But thou in safe implacability
Hadst nought to dread—in thy own weakness
 shielded,
And in my love, which hath but too much
 yielded,
 And spared, for thy sake, some I should
 not spare;
And thus upon the world—trust in thy truth,
And the wild fame of my ungovern'd youth—
 On things that were not, and on things that
 are—
Even upon such a basis hast thou built
A monument, whose cement hath been guilt!
The moral Clytemnestra of thy lord,
 And hew'd down, with an unsuspected
 sword,
Fame, peace, and hope—and all the better
 life,
 Which, but for this cold treason of thy
 heart,
Might still have risen from out the grave of
 strife,
 And found a nobler duty than to part.
But of thy virtues didst thou make a vice,
 Trafficking with them in a purpose cold,
 For present anger, and for future gold—
And buying other's grief at any price.
And thus once enter'd into crooked ways,
The early truth, which was thy proper praise,
Did not still walk beside thee—but at times,
And with a breast unknowing its own crimes,
Deceit, averments incompatible,
Equivocations, and the thoughts which dwell
 In Janus-spirits—the significant eye
Which learns to lie with silence—the pretext
Of prudence, with advantages annex'd—

The acquiescence in all things which tend,
No matter how, to the desired end—
 All found a place in thy philosophy.
The means were worthy, and the end is
 won—
I would not do by thee as thou hast done!
 September, 1816.

DARKNESS.

I HAD a dream, which was not all a dream.
The bright sun was extinguish'd, and the
 stars
Did wander darkling in the eternal space,
Rayless, and pathless, and the icy earth
Swung blind and blackening in the moonless
 air;
Morn came and went—and came, and brought
 no day,
And men forgot their passions in the dread
Of this their desolation; and all hearts
Were chill'd into a selfish prayer for light:
And they did live by watchfires—and the
 thrones,
The palaces of crowned kings—the huts,
The habitations of all things which dwell,
Were burnt for beacons; cities were con-
 sumed,
And men were gather'd round their blazing
 homes
To look once more into each other's face;
Happy were those who dwelt within the eye
Of the volcanos, and their mountain-torch:
A fearful hope was all the world contain'd;
Forests were set on fire—but hour by hour
They fell and faded—and the crackling
 trunks
Extinguish'd with a crash—and all was
 black.
The brows of men by the despairing light
Wore an unearthly aspect, as by fits
The flashes fell upon them; some lay down
And hid their eyes and wept; and some did
 rest
Their chins upon their clenched hands, and
 smiled;
And others hurried to and fro, and fed
Their funeral piles with fuel, and look'd up
With mad disquietude on the dull sky,
The pall of a past world; and then again
With curses cast them down upon the dust,
And gnash'd their teeth and howl'd: the wild
 birds shriek'd
And, terrified, did flutter on the ground,
And flap their useless wings; the wildest
 brutes
Came tame and tremulous; and vipers crawl'd
And twined themselves among the multitude,
Hissing, but stingless—they were slain for
 food

And War, which for a moment was no
 more,
Did glut himself again :—a meal was bought
With blood, and each sate sullenly apart
Gorging himself in gloom : no love was left ;
All earth was but one thought—and that was
 death
Immediate and inglorious ; and the pang
Of famine fed upon all entrails—men
Died, and their bones were tombless as their
 flesh ;
The meagre by the meagre were devour'd,
Even dogs assail'd their masters, all save
 one,
And he was faithful to a corse, and kept
The birds and beasts and famish'd men at
 bay,
Till hunger clung them, or the dropping dead
Lured their lank jaws ; himself sought out
 no food,
But with a piteous and perpetual moan,
And a quick desolate cry, licking the hand
Which answer'd not with a caress—he died.
The crowd was famish'd by degrees ; but two
Of an enormous city did survive,
And they were enemies : they met beside
The dying embers of an altar-place
Where had been heap'd a mass of holy things
For an unholy usage ; they raked up,
And shivering scraped with their cold skeleton
 hands
The feeble ashes, and their feeble breath
Blew for a little life, and made a flame
Which was a mockery ; then they lifted up
Their eyes as it grew lighter, and beheld
Each other's aspects—saw, and shriek'd, and
 died—
Even of their mutual hideousness they died,
Unknowing who he was upon whose brow
Famine had written Fiend. The world was
 void,
The populous and the powerful was a lump,
Seasonless, herbless, treeless, manless, life-
 less,
A lump of death—a chaos of hard clay.
The rivers, lakes, and ocean all stood still,
And nothing stirr'd within their silent depths ;
Ships sailorless lay rotting on the sea,
And their masts fell down piecemeal : as they
 dropp'd
They slept on the abyss without a surge—
The waves were dead ; the tides were in their
 grave,
The moon, their mistress, had expired before ;
The winds were wither'd in the stagnant
 air,
And the clouds perish'd ; Darkness had no
 need
Of aid from them—She was the Universe.
 Diodati, *July*, 1816.

MONODY ON THE DEATH

OF

THE RIGHT HON. R. B. SHERIDAN.

SPOKEN AT DRURY-LANE THEATRE.

WHEN the last sunshine of expiring day
In summer's twilight weeps itself away,
Who hath not felt the softness of the hour
Sink on the heart, as dew along the flower ?
With a pure feeling which absorbs and awes
While Nature makes that melancholy pause,
Her breathing moment on the bridge where
 Time
Of light and darkness forms an arch sublime,
Who hath not shared that calm, so still and
 deep,
The voiceless thought which would not speak
 but weep,
A holy concord, and a bright regret,
A glorious sympathy with suns that set ?
' Tis not harsh sorrow, but a tenderer woe,
Nameless, but dear to gentle hearts below,
Felt without bitterness, but full and clear,
A sweet dejection, a transparent tear,
Unmix'd with worldly grief or selfish stain,
Shed without shame, and secret without pain.

Even as the tenderness that hour instils
When Summer's day declines along the hills,
So feels the fulness of our heart and eyes
When all of Genius which can perish dies.
A mighty Spirit is eclipsed—a Power
Hath pass'd from day to darkness—to whose
 hour
Of light no likeness is bequeath'd—no name,
Focus at once of all the rays of Fame !
The flash of Wit, the bright Intelligence,
The beam of Song, the blaze of Eloquence,
Set with their Sun, but still have left behind
The enduring produce of immortal Mind ;
Fruits of a genial morn, and glorious noon,
A deathless part of him who died too soon.
But small that portion of the wondrous whole,
These sparkling segments of that circling soul,
Which all embraced, and lighten'd over all,
To cheer, to pierce, to please, or to appal.
From the charm'd council to the festive board,
Of human feelings the unbounded lord ;
In whose acclaim the loftiest voices vied,
The praised, the proud, who made his praise
 their pride.
When the loud cry of trampled Hindostan
Arose to Heaven in her appeal from man,
His was the thunder, his the avenging rod,
The wrath—the delegated voice of God !
Which shook the nations through his lips,
 and blazed
Till vanquish'd senates trembled as they
 praised.

And here, oh! here, where yet all young
 and warm,
The gay creations of his spirit charm,
The matchless dialogue, the deathless wit,
Which knew not what it was to intermit;
The glowing portraits, fresh from life, that
 bring
Home to our hearts the truth from which
 they spring;
These wondrous beings of his fancy, wrought
To fulness by the fiat of his thought,
Here in their first abode you still may meet,
Bright with the hues of his Promethean heat;
A halo of the light of other days,
Which still the splendour of its orb betrays.

But should there be to whom the fatal
 blight
Of failing Wisdom yields a base delight,
Men who exult when minds of heavenly tone
Jar in the music which was born their own,
Still let them pause—ah! little do they know
That what to them seem'd Vice might be but
 Woe.
Hard is his fate on whom the public gaze
Is fix'd for ever to detract or praise;
Repose denies her requiem to his name,
And Folly loves the martyrdom of Fame.
The secret enemy whose sleepless eye
Stands sentinel, accuser, judge, and spy,
The foe, the fool, the jealous, and the vain,
The envious who but breathe in others' pain,
Behold the host! delighting to deprave,
Who track the steps of Glory to the grave,
Watch every fault that daring Genius owes
Half to the ardour which its birth bestows,
Distort the truth, accumulate the lie,
And pile the pyramid of Calumny!
These are his portion—but if join'd to these
Gaunt Poverty should league with deep
 Disease,
If the high Spirit must forget to soar,
And stoop to strive with Misery at the door,
To soothe Indignity—and face to face
Meet sordid Rage, and wrestle with Disgrace,
To find in Hope but the renew'd caress,
The serpent-fold of further Faithlessness:—
If such may be the ills which men assail,
What marvel if at last the mightiest fail?
Breasts to whom all the strength of feeling
 given
Bear hearts electric—charged with fire from
 Heaven,
Black with the rude collision, inly torn,
By clouds surrounded, and on whirlwinds
 borne,
Driven o'er the lowering atmosphere that
 nurst
Thoughts which have turn'd to thunder-
 scorch, and burst.

But far from us and from our mimic scene
Such things should be—if such have ever
 been;
Ours be the gentler wish, the kinder task,
To give the tribute Glory need not ask,
To mourn the vanish'd beam, and add our
 mite
Of praise in payment of a long delight.
Ye Orators! whom yet our councils yield,
Mourn for the veteran Hero of your field!
The worthy rival of the wondrous *Three!*
Whose words were sparks of Immortality!
Ye Bards! to whom the Drama's muse is
 dear,
He was your Master—emulate him *here!*
Ye men of wit and social eloquence!
He was your brother—bear his ashes hence!
While Powers of mind almost of boundless
 range,
Complete in kind, as various in their change,
While Eloquence, Wit, Poesy, and Mirth,
That humbler Harmonist of care on Earth,
Survive within our souls—while lives our
 sense
Of pride in Merit's proud pre-eminence,
Long shall we seek his likeness, long in vain,
And turn to all of him which may remain,
Sighing that nature form'd but one such man,
And broke the die—in moulding Sheridan!

 Diodati. *July* 17, 1816.

———◆———

CHURCHILL'S GRAVE;

A FACT LITERALLY RENDERED.

I STOOD beside the grave of him who blazed
 The comet of a season, and I saw
The humblest of all sepulchres, and gazed
 With not the less of sorrow and of awe
On that neglected turf and quiet stone,
 With name no clearer than the names un-
 known,
Which lay unread around it; and I ask'd
 The Gardener of that ground, why it might
 be
That for this plant strangers his memory
 task'd,
 Through the thick deaths of half a century?
And thus he answer'd—"Well, I do not know
Why frequent travellers turn to pilgrims so;
He died before my day of Sextonship,
 And I had not the digging of this grave."
And is this all? I thought—and do we rip
 The veil of Immortality, and crave
I know not what of honour and of light
Through unborn ages, to endure this blight,
So soon, and so successless? As I said,
 The Architect of all on which we tread,
For Earth is but a tombstone, did essay
To extricate remembrance from the clay,

Whose minglings might confuse a Newton's
thought,
 Were it not that all life must end in one,
Of which we are but dreamers;—as he caught,
 As 'twere the twilight of a former Sun,
Thus spoke he,—" I believe the man of whom
You wot, who lies in this selected tomb,
Was a most famous writer in his day,
And therefore travellers step from out their
 way
To pay him honour,—and myself whate'er
 Your honour pleases : "—then most pleased
 I shook
 From out my pocket's avaricious nook
Some certain coins of silver, which as 'twere
Perforce I gave this man, though I could
 spare
So much but inconveniently :—Ye smile,
I see ye, ye profane ones! all the while,
Because my homely phrase the truth would
 tell.
You are the fools, not I—for I did dwell
With a deep thought, and with a soften'd eye,
On that Old Sexton's natural homily,
In which there was Obscurity and Fame—
The Glory and the Nothing of a Name.

<div align="right">Diodati, 1816.</div>

PROMETHEUS.

I.

TITAN! to whose immortal eyes
 The sufferings of mortality,
 Seen in their sad reality,
Were not as things that gods despise;
What was thy pity's recompense?
A silent suffering, and intense;
The rock, the vulture, and the chain,
All that the proud can feel of pain,
The agony they do not show,
The suffocating sense of woe,
 Which speaks but in its loneliness,
And then is jealous lest the sky
Should have a listener, nor will sigh
 Until its voice is echoless.

II.

Titan! to thee the strife was given
 Between the suffering and the will,
 Which torture where they cannot kill;
And the inexorable Heaven,
And the deaf tyranny of Fate,
The ruling principle of Hate,
Which for its pleasure doth create
The things it may annihilate,
Refused thee even the boon to die:
The wretched gift eternity
Was thine—and thou hast borne it well.
All that the Thunderer wrung from thee

Was but the menace which flung back
On him the torments of thy rack;
The fate thou didst so well foresee,
But would not to appease him tell;
And in thy Silence was his Sentence,
And in his Soul a vain repentance,
And evil dread so ill dissembled,
That in his hand the lightnings trembled.

III.

Thy Godlike crime was to be kind,
 To render with thy precepts less
 The sum of human wretchedness,
And strengthen Man with his own mind;
But baffled as thou wert from high,
Still in thy patient energy,
In the endurance, and repulse
 Of thine impenetrable Spirit,
Which Earth and Heaven could not convulse,
 A mighty lesson we inherit:
Thou art a symbol and a sign
 To Mortals of their fate and force;
Like thee, Man is in part divine,
 A troubled stream from a pure source;
And Man in portions can foresee
His own funereal destiny;
His wretchedness, and his resistance,
And his sad unallied existence:
To which his Spirit may oppose
Itself—and equal to all woes,
 And a firm will, and a deep sense,
Which even in torture can descry
 Its own concenter'd recompense,
Triumphant where it dares defy,
And making Death a Victory.

<div align="right">Diodati, *July,* 1816.</div>

A FRAGMENT.

COULD I remount the river of my years
To the first fountain of our smiles and tears,
I would not trace again the stream of hours
Between their outworn banks of wither'd
 flowers,
But bid it flow as now—until it glides
Into the number of the nameless tides.

.

What is this Death?—a quiet of the heart?
The whole of that of which we are a part?
For life is but a vision—what I see
Of all which lives alone is life to me,
And being so—the absent are the dead,
Who haunt us from tranquillity, and spread
A dreary shroud around us, and invest
With sad remembrances our hours of rest.
 The absent are the dead—for they are cold,
And ne'er can be what once we did behold;
And they are changed, and cheerless,—or if
 yet
The unforgotten do not all forget.

Since thus divided—equal must it be
If the deep barrier be of earth, or sea;
It may be both—but one day end it must
In the dark union of insensate dust.
 The under-earth inhabitants—are they
But mingled millions decomposed to clay?
The ashes of a thousand ages spread
Wherever man has trodden or shall tread?
Or do they in their silent cities dwell
Each in his incommunicative cell?
Or have they their own language? and a
 sense
Of breathless being?—darken'd and intense
As midnight in her solitude?—Oh Earth!
Where are the past?—and wherefore had they
 birth?
The dead are thy inheritors—and we
But bubbles on thy surface; and the key
Of thy profundity is in the grave,
The ebon portal of thy peopled cave,
Where I would walk in spirit, and behold
Our elements resolved to things untold,
And fathom hidden wonders, and explore
The essence of great bosoms now no more.

 Diodati, July, 1816.

SONNET TO LAKE LEMAN.

ROUSSEAU—Voltaire—our Gibbon—and De
 Staël—
 Leman! these names are worthy of thy
 shore,
 Thy shore of names like these! wert thou
 no more
Their memory thy remembrance would re-
 call:
To them thy banks were lovely as to all,
 But they have made them lovelier, for the
 lore
 Of mighty minds doth hallow in the core
Of human hearts the ruin of a wall
 Where dwelt the wise and wondrous; but
 by *thee*
How much more, Lake of Beauty! do we feel,
 In sweetly gliding o'er thy crystal sea,
The wild glow of that not ungentle zeal,
 Which of the heirs of immortality
Is proud, and makes the breath of glory real!
 Diodati, July, 1816.

STANZAS FOR MUSIC.

I.

BRIGHT be the place of thy soul!
 No lovelier spirit than thine
E'er burst from its mortal control,
 In the orbs of the blessed to shine.

On earth thou wert all but divine,
 As thy soul shall immortally be;
And our sorrow may cease to repine
 When we know that thy God is with thee.

II.

Light be the turf of thy tomb!
 May its verdure like emeralds be!
There should not be the shadow of gloom
 In aught that reminds us of thee.
Young flowers and an evergreen tree
 May spring from the spot of thy rest:
But nor cypress nor yew let us see;
 For why should we mourn for the blest?

A VERY MOURNFUL BALLAD ON THE SIEGE AND CONQUEST OF ALHAMA,

Which, in the Arabic language, is to the following purport.

I.

THE Moorish King rides up and down,
 Through Granada's royal town;
From Elvira's gate to those
 Of Bivarambla on he goes.
 Woe is me, Alhama!

II.

Letters to the monarch tell
 How Alhama's city fell:
In the fire the scroll he threw,
 And the messenger he slew.
 Woe is me, Alhama!

III.

He quits his mule, and mounts his horse,
 And through the street directs his course;
Through the street of Zacatin
 To the Alhambra spurring in.
 Woe is me, Alhama!

IV.

When the Alhambra walls he gain'd,
 On the moment he ordain'd
That the trumpet straight should sound
 With the silver clarion round.
 Woe is me, Alhama!

V.

And when the hollow drums of war
 Beat the loud alarm afar,
That the Moors of town and plain
 Might answer to the martial strain.
 Woe is me, Alhama!

VI.

Then the Moors, by this aware,
That bloody Mars recall'd them there,
One by one, and two by two,
To a mighty squadron grew.
　　　　Woe is me, Alhama!

VII.

Out then spake an aged Moor
In these words the king before,
"Wherefore call on us, oh King?
What may mean this gathering?"
　　　　Woe is me, Alhama!

VIII.

"Friends! ye have, alas! to know
Of a most disastrous blow;
That the Christians, stern and bold,
Have obtain'd Alhama's hold."
　　　　Woe is me, Alhama!

IX.

Out then spake old Alfaqui,
With his beard so white to see,
"Good King! thou art justly served,
Good King! this thou hast deserved.
　　　　Woe is me, Alhama!

X.

"By thee were slain, in evil hour,
The Abencerrage, Granada's flower;
And strangers were received by thee
Of Cordova the Chivalry.
　　　　Woe is me, Alhama!

XI.

"And for this, oh King! is sent
On thee a double chastisement:
Thee and thine, thy crown and realm,
One last wreck shall overwhelm.
　　　　Woe is me, Alhama!

XII.

"He who holds no laws in awe,
He must perish by the law;
And Granada must be won,
And thyself with her undone."
　　　　Woe is me, Alhama!

XIII.

Fire flash'd from out the old Moor's eyes,
The Monarch's wrath began to rise,
Because he answer'd, and because
He spake exceeding well of laws.
　　　　Woe is me, Alhama!

XIV.

"There is no law to say such things
As may disgust the ear of kings:"—
Thus, snorting with his choler, said
The Moorish King, and doom'd him dead.
　　　　Woe is me, Alhama!

XV.

Moor Alfaqui! Moor Alfaqui!
Though thy beard so hoary be,
The King hath sent to have thee seized,
For Alhama's loss displeased.
　　　　Woe is me, Alhama!

XVI.

And to fix thy head upon
High Alhambra's loftiest stone;
That this for thee should be the law,
And others tremble when they saw.
　　　　Woe is me, Alhama!

XVII.

"Cavalier, and man of worth!
Let these words of mine go forth!
Let the Moorish Monarch know,
That to him I nothing owe.
　　　　Woe is me, Alhama!

XVIII.

"But on my soul Alhama weighs,
And on my inmost spirit preys;
And if the King his land hath lost,
Yet others may have lost the most.
　　　　Woe is me, Alhama!

XIX.

"Sires have lost their children, wives
Their lords, and valiant men their lives!
One what best his love might claim
Hath lost, another wealth, or fame.
　　　　Woe is me, Alhama!

XX.

"I lost a damsel in that hour,
Of all the land the loveliest flower;
Doubloons a hundred I would pay,
And think her ransom cheap that day."
　　　　Woe is me, Alhama!

XXI.

And as these things the old Moor said,
They sever'd from the trunk his head;
And to the Alhambra's wall with speed
'T was carried, as the King decreed.
　　　　Woe is me, Alhama!

XXII.

And men and infants therein weep
Their loss, so heavy and so deep;
Granada's ladies, all she rears
Within her walls, burst into tears.
 Woe is me, Alhama!

XXIII.

And from the windows o'er the walls
The sable web of mourning falls;
The King weeps as a woman o'er
His loss, for it is much and sore.
 Woe is me, Alhama!

STANZAS FOR MUSIC.

I.

They say that Hope is happiness;
 But genuine Love must prize the past,
And Memory wakes the thoughts that bless:
 They rose the first—they set the last;

II.

And all that Memory loves the most
 Was once our only Hope to be,
And all that Hope adored and lost
 Hath melted into Memory.

III.

Alas! it is delusion all:
 The future cheats us from afar,
Nor can we be what we recall,
 Nor dare we think on what we are.

TRANSLATION FROM VITTORELLI.

ON A NUN.

Sonnet composed in the name of a father, whose
daughter had recently died shortly after her
marriage; and addressed to the father of her who
had lately taken the veil.

Of two fair virgins, modest, though admired,
 Heaven made us happy; and now, wretched
 sires,
 Heaven for a nobler doom their worth
 desires,
And gazing upon *either*, *both* required.
Mine, while the torch of Hymen newly fired
 Becomes extinguish'd, soon—too soon—
 expires:
But thine, within the closing grate retired,
 Eternal captive, to her God aspires.

But *thou* at least from out the jealous door,
 Which shuts between your never-meeting
 eyes,
 May'st hear her sweet and pious voice once
 more:
I to the marble, where *my* daughter lies,
 Rush,—the swoln flood of bitterness I pour,
 And knock, and knock, and knock—but
 none replies.

ON THE BUST OF HELEN BY CANOVA.

In this beloved marble view,
 Above the works and thoughts of man,
What Nature *could*, but *would not*, do,
 And Beauty and Canova *can!*
Beyond imagination's power,
 Beyond the Bard's defeated art,
With immortality her dower,
 Behold the *Helen* of the *heart!*
 November, 1816.

SONG FOR THE LUDDITES.

I.

As the Liberty lads o'er the sea
Bought their freedom, and cheaply, with
 blood,
 So we, boys, we
Will *die* fighting, or *live* free,
And down with all kings but King Ludd!

II.

When the web that we weave is complete,
And the shuttle exchanged for the sword,
 We will fling the winding sheet
 O'er the despot at our feet,
And dye it deep in the gore he has pour'd.

III.

Though black as his heart its hue,
Since his veins are corrupted to mud,
 Yet this is the dew
 Which the tree shall renew
Of Liberty, planted by Ludd!
 December, 1816.

VERSICLES.

I read the "Christabel;"
 Very well!
I read the "Missionary;"
 Pretty—very:
I tried at "Ilderim;"
 Ahem!
I read a sheet of "Marg'ret of *Anjou*;"
 Can you?

I turn'd a page of Scott's "Waterloo;"
 Pooh! pooh!
I look'd at Wordsworth's milk-white
 "Rylstone Doe;"
 Hillo!
&c. &c. &c. *March*, 1817.

SO, WE'LL GO NO MORE A ROVING.

I.

So, we'll go no more a roving
 So late into the night,
Though the heart be still as loving,
 And the moon be still as bright.

II.

For the sword outwears its sheath,
 And the soul wears out the breast,
And the heart must pause to breathe,
 And love itself have rest.

III.

Though the night was made for loving,
 And the day returns too soon,
Yet we'll go no more a roving
 By the light of the moon.
 1817.

TO THOMAS MOORE.

WHAT are you doing now,
 Oh Thomas Moore?
What are you doing now,
 Oh Thomas Moore?
Sighing or suing now,
Rhyming or wooing now,
Billing or cooing now,
 Which, Thomas Moore?

But the Carnival's coming,
 Oh Thomas Moore!
The Carnival's coming,
 Oh Thomas Moore!
Masking and humming,
Fifing and drumming,
Guitaring and strumming,
 Oh Thomas Moore!

TO MR. MURRAY.

To hook the reader, you, John Murray,
 Have publish'd "Anjou's Margaret,"
Which won't be sold off in a hurry
 (At least, it has not been as yet);
And then, still further to bewilder 'em,
Without remorse, you set up "Ilderim;"

So mind you don't get into debt,
 Because as how, if you should fail,
These books would be but baddish bail.

And mind you do *not* let escape
 These rhymes to Morning Post or Perry,
 Which would be *very* treacherous—*very*,
And get me into such a scrape!
For, firstly, I should have to sally,
 All in my little boat, against a *Galley;*
And, should I chance to slay the Assyrian
 wight,
Have next to combat with the female knight.
 March 25, 1817.

TO THOMAS MOORE.

I.

My boat is on the shore,
 And my bark is on the sea;
But, before I go, Tom Moore,
 Here's a double health to thee!

II.

Here's a sigh to those who love me,
 And a smile to those who hate;
And, whatever sky's above me,
 Here's a heart for every fate.

III.

Though the ocean roar around me,
 Yet it still shall bear me on;
Though a desert should surround me,
 It hath springs that may be won.

IV.

Were't the last drop in the well,
 As I gasp'd upon the brink,
Ere my fainting spirit fell,
 'Tis to thee that I would drink.

V.

With that water, as this wine,
 The libation I would pour
Should be—peace with thine and mine,
 And a health to thee, Tom Moore.
 July, 1817.

EPISTLE FROM MR. MURRAY TO DR. POLIDORI.

DEAR Doctor, I have read your play,
Which is a good one in its way,—
Purges the eyes and moves the bowels,
And drenches handkerchiefs like towels
With tears, that, in a flux of grief,
Afford hysterical relief
To shatter'd nerves and quicken'd pulses,
Which your catastrophe convulses.

I like your moral and machinery;
Your plot, too, has such scope for scenery;

Your dialogue is apt and smart:
The play's concoction full of art;
Your hero raves, your heroine cries,
All stab, and everybody dies.
In short, your tragedy would be
The very thing to hear and see:
And for a piece of publication,
If I decline on this occasion,
It is not that I am not sensible
To merits in themselves ostensible,
But—and I grieve to speak it—plays
Are drugs—mere drugs, sir—now-a-days.
I had a heavy loss by " Manuel,"—
Too lucky if it prove not annual,—
And Sotheby, with his " Orestes,"
(Which, by the by, the author's best is,)
Has lain so very long on hand,
That I despair of all demand.
I 've advertised, but see my books,
Or only watch my shopman's looks ;—
Still Ivan, Ina, and such lumber,
My back-shop glut, my shelves encumber.

There 's Byron too, who once did better,
Has sent me, folded in a letter,
A sort of—it 's no more a drama
Than Darnley, Ivan, or Kehama:
So alter'd since last year his pen is,
I think he 's lost his wits at Venice.
In short, sir, what with one and t'other,
I dare not venture on another.
I write in haste ; excuse each blunder;
The coaches through the street so thunder!
My room 's so full—we 've Gifford here
Reading MS., with Hookham Frere,
Pronouncing on the nouns and particles
Of some of our forthcoming Articles.

The Quarterly—Ah, sir, if you
Had but the genius to review !—
A smart critique upon St. Helena,
Or if you only would but tell in a
Short compass what——but to resume:
As I was saying, sir, the room—
The room 's so full of wits and bards,
Crabbes, Campbells, Crokers, Freres, and
 Wards,
And others, neither bards nor wits:—
My humble tenement admits
All persons in the dress of gent,
From Mr. Hammond to Dog Dent.

A party dines with me to-day,
All clever men, who make their way ;
Crabbe, Malcolm, Hamilton, and Chantrey,
Are all partakers of my pantry.
They 're at this moment in discussion
On poor De Staël's late dissolution.
Her book, they say, was in advance—
Pray Heaven, she tell the truth of France!

Thus run our time and tongues away ;—
But, to return, sir, to your play:
Sorry, sir, but I cannot deal,
Unless 't were acted by O'Neill ;
My hands so full, my head so busy,
I 'm almost dead, and always dizzy ;
And so, with endless truth and hurry,
Dear Doctor, I am yours,
 JOHN MURRAY.
 August, 1817.

—◆◆—

EPISTLE TO MR. MURRAY.

My dear Mr. Murray,
You 're in a damn'd hurry,
 To set up this ultimate Canto;
But (if they don't rob us)
You 'll see Mr. Hobhouse
 Will bring it safe in his portmanteau.

For the Journal you hint of,
As ready to print off,
 No doubt you do right to commend it;
But as yet I have writ off
The devil a bit of
 Our " Beppo:"—when copied, I 'll send it.

Then you 've's Tour,—
No great things, to be sure,—
 You could hardly begin with a less work;
For the pompous rascallion,
Who don't speak Italian
 Nor French, must have scribbled by guess
 work.

You can make any loss up
With " Spence" and his gossip,
 A work which must surely succeed;
Then Queen Mary's Epistle-craft,
With the new "Fytte" of "Whistlecraft,"
 Must make people purchase and read.

Then you 've General Gordon,
Who girded his sword on,
 To serve with a Muscovite master
And help him to polish
A nation so owlish,
 They thought shaving their beards a dis-
 aster.

For the man, "poor and shrewd,"
With whom you 'd conclude
 A compact without more delay,
Perhaps some such pen is
Still extant in Venice ;
 But please, sir, to mention *your pay*.
 Venice, *January* 8, 1818.

TO MR. MURRAY.

STRAHAN, Tonson, Lintot of the times,
Patron and publisher of rhymes,
For thee the bard up Pindus climbs,
　　　My Murray.

To thee, with hope and terror dumb,
The unfledged MS. authors come;
Thou printest all—and sellest some—
　　　My Murray.

Upon thy table's baize so green
The last new Quarterly is seen,—
But where is thy new Magazine,
　　　My Murray?

Along thy sprucest bookshelves shine
The works thou deemest most divine—
The "Art of Cookery," and mine,
　　　My Murray.

Tours, Travels, Essays, too, I wist,
And Sermons, to thy mill bring grist;
And then thou hast the "Navy List,"
　　　My Murray.

And Heaven forbid I should conclude
Without "the Board of Longitude,"
Although this narrow paper would,
　　　My Murray.

　　　　Venice, *March* 25, 1818.

ON THE BIRTH OF
JOHN WILLIAM RIZZO HOPPNER.

His father's sense, his mother's grace,
　In him, I hope, will always fit so;
With—still to keep him in good case—
　The health and appetite of Rizzo.

　　　　　February, 1818.

ODE ON VENICE.

I.

OH Venice! Venice! when thy marble walls
Are level with the waters, there shall be
A cry of nations o'er thy sunken halls,
　A loud lament along the sweeping sea!
If I, a northern wanderer, weep for thee,
What should thy sons do?—anything but
　weep:
And yet they only murmur in their sleep.
In contrast with their fathers—as the slime,
The dull green ooze of the receding deep,
Is with the dashing of the spring-tide foam
That drives the sailor shipless to his home,
Are they to those that were; and thus they
　creep,
Crouching and crab-like, through their sap-
　ping streets.
Oh! agony—that centuries should reap

No mellower harvest! Thirteen hundred
　years
Of wealth and glory turn'd to dust and tears;
And every monument the stranger meets,
Church, palace, pillar, as a mourner greets;
And even the Lion all subdued appears,
And the harsh sound of the barbarian drum,
With dull and daily dissonance, repeats
The echo of thy tyrant's voice along
The soft waves, once all musical to song,
That heaved beneath the moonlight with the
　throng
Of gondolas—and to the busy hum
Of cheerful creatures, whose most sinful
　deeds
Were but the overbeating of the heart,
And flow of too much happiness, which needs
The aid of age to turn its course apart
From the luxuriant and voluptuous flood
Of sweet sensations, battling with the blood.
But these are better than the gloomy errors,
The weeds of nations in their last decay,
When Vice walks forth with her unsoften'd
　terrors,
And Mirth is madness, and but smiles to
　slay;
And Hope is nothing but a false delay,
The sick man's lightning half an hour ere
　death,
When Faintness, the last mortal birth of
　Pain,
And apathy of limb, the dull beginning
Of the cold staggering race which Death is
　winning,
Steals vein by vein and pulse by pulse away;
Yet so relieving the o'er-tortured clay,
To him appears renewal of his breath,
And freedom the mere numbness of his chain;
And then he talks of life, and how again
He feels his spirit soaring—albeit weak,
And of the fresher air, which he would seek:
And as he whispers knows not that he gasps,
That his thin finger feels not what it clasps,
And so the film comes o'er him, and the
　dizzy
Chamber swims round and round, and
　shadows busy,
At which he vainly catches, flit and gleam,
Till the last rattle chokes the strangled
　scream,
And all is ice and blackness,—and the earth
That which it was the moment ere our birth.

II.

There is no hope for nations!—Search the
　page
Of many thousand years—the daily scene,
The flow and ebb of each recurring age,
The everlasting *to be* which *hath been*,
Hath taught us nought, or little: still we lean

On things that rot beneath our weight, and
 wear
Our strength away in wrestling with the air:
For 'tis our nature strikes us down: the
 beasts
Slaughter'd in hourly hecatombs for feasts
Are of as high an order—they must go
Even where their driver goads them, though
 to slaughter.
Ye men, who pour your blood for kings as
 water,
What have they given your children in re-
 turn?
A heritage of servitude and woes,
A blindfold bondage, where your hire is blows.
What! do not yet the red-hot plough-shares
 burn,
O'er which you stumble in a false ordeal,
And deem this proof of loyalty the *real;*
Kissing the hand that guides you to your
 scars,
And glorying as you tread the glowing bars?
All that your sires have left you, all that
 Time
Bequeaths of free, and History of sublime,
Spring from a different theme! Ye see and
 read,
Admire and sigh, and then succumb and
 bleed!
Save the few spirits who, despite of all,
And worse than all, the sudden crimes en-
 gender'd
By the down-thundering of the prison-wall,
And thirst to swallow the sweet waters ten-
 der'd,
Gushing from Freedom's fountains, when the
 crowd,
Madden'd with centuries of drought, are
 loud,
And trample on each other to obtain
The cup which brings oblivion of a chain
Heavy and sore, in which long yoked they
 plough'd
The sand,—or if there sprung the yellow
 grain,
'Twas not for them, their necks were too
 much bow'd,
And their dead palates chew'd the cud of
 pain:
Yes! the few spirits, who, despite of deeds
Which they abhor, confound not with the
 cause
Those momentary starts from Nature's laws,
Which, like the pestilence and earthquake,
 smite
But for a term, then pass, and leave the earth
With all her seasons to repair the blight
With a few summers, and again put forth
Cities and generations—fair, when free—
For, Tyranny, there blooms no bud for thee!

III.

Glory and Empire! once upon these towers
 With Freedom—godlike Triad! how ye
 sate!
The league of mightiest nations, in those
 hours
When Venice was an envy, might abate,
But did not quench her spirit; in her fate
All were enwrapp'd: the feasted monarchs
 knew
And loved their hostess, nor could learn to
 hate,
Although they humbled—with the kingly few
The many felt, for from all days and climes
She was the voyager's worship; even her
 crimes
Were of the softer order—born of Love,
She drank no blood, nor fatten'd on the dead,
But gladden'd where her harmless conquests
 spread;
For these restored the Cross, that from above
Hallow'd her sheltering banners, which in-
 cessant
Flew between earth and the unholy Crescent,
Which, if it waned and dwindled, Earth may
 thank
The city it has clothed in chains, which clank
Now, creaking in the ears of those who owe
The name of Freedom to her glorious
 struggles;
Yet she but shares with them a common woe,
And call'd the "kingdom" of a conquering
 foe,
But knows what all—and, most of all, *we*
 know—
With what set gilded terms a tyrant juggles!

IV.

The name of Commonwealth is past and gone
 O'er the three fractions of the groaning
 globe;
Venice is crush'd, and Holland deigns to own
 A sceptre, and endures the purple robe;
If the free Switzer yet bestrides alone
His chainless mountains, 'tis but for a time,
For tyranny of late is cunning grown,
And in its own good season tramples down
The sparkles of our ashes. One great clime,
Whose vigorous offspring by dividing ocean
Are kept apart and nursed in the devotion
Of Freedom, which their fathers fought for,
 and
Bequeath'd—a heritage of heart and hand,
And proud distinction from each other land,
Whose sons must bow them at a monarch's
 motion,
As if his senseless sceptre were a wand
Full of the magic of exploded science—
Still one great clime, in full and free defiance,

Yet rears her crest, unconquer'd and sub-
 lime,
Above the far Atlantic!—She has taught
Her Esau-brethren that the haughty flag,
The floating fence of Albion's feebler crag,
May strike to those whose red right hands
 have bought
Rights cheaply earn'd with blood. Still, still,
 for ever,
Better, though each man's life-blood were a
 river,
That it should flow, and overflow, than creep
Through thousand lazy channels in our veins,
Damm'd like the dull canal with locks and
 chains,
And moving, as a sick man in his sleep,
Three paces, and then faltering: better be
Where the extinguish'd Spartans still are
 free,
In their proud charnel of Thermopylæ,
Than stagnate in our marsh,—or o'er the
 deep
Fly, and one current to the ocean add,
One spirit to the souls our fathers had,
One freeman more, America, to thee!

STANZAS TO THE PO.

RIVER, that rollest by the ancient walls,
 Where dwells the lady of my love, when
 she
Walks by thy brink, and there perchance
 recalls
 A faint and fleeting memory of me;

What if thy deep and ample stream should
 be
A mirror of my heart, where she may read
The thousand thoughts I now betray to thee,
 Wild as thy wave, and headlong as thy
 speed!

What do I say—a mirror of my heart?
 Are not thy waters sweeping, dark, and
 strong?
Such as my feelings were and are, thou art;
 And such as thou art were my passions
 long.

Time may have somewhat tamed them,—not
 for ever;
 Thou overflow'st thy banks, and not for
 aye
Thy bosom overboils, congenial river!
 Thy floods subside, and mine have sunk
 away:

But left long wrecks behind, and now again,
 Borne on our old unchanged career, we
 move:
Thou tendest wildly onwards to the main,
 And I—to loving *one* I should not love.

The current I behold will sweep beneath
 Her native walls, and murmur at her feet;
Her eyes will look on thee, when she shall
 breathe
 The twilight air, unharm'd by summer's heat.

She will look on thee,—I have look'd on thee,
 Full of that thought: and, from that
 moment, ne'er
Thy waters could I dream of, name, or see
 Without the inseparable sigh for her!

Her bright eyes will be imaged in thy stream,
 Yes! they will meet the wave I gaze on
 now:
Mine cannot witness, even in a dream,
 That happy wave repass me in its flow!

The wave that bears my tears returns no
 more:
 Will she return by whom that wave shall
 sweep?—
Both tread thy banks, both wander on thy
 shore,
 I by thy source, she by the dark-blue deep.

But that which keepeth us apart is not
 Distance, nor depth of wave, nor space of
 earth,
But the distraction of a various lot,
 As various as the climates of our birth.

A stranger loves the lady of the land,
 Born far beyond the mountains, but his
 blood
Is all meridian, as if never fann'd
 By the black wind that chills the polar
 flood.

My blood is all meridian; were it not,
 I had not left my clime, nor should I be,
In spite of tortures ne'er to be forgot,
 A slave again of love,—at least of thee.

'Tis vain to struggle—let me perish young—
 Live as I lived, and love as I have loved;
To dust if I return, from dust I sprung,
 And then, at least, my heart can ne'er be
 moved. *April*, 1819.

SONNET TO GEORGE THE FOURTH,

ON THE REPEAL OF LORD EDWARD FITZ-
GERALD'S FORFEITURE.

To be the father of the fatherless,
 To stretch the hand from the throne's
 height, and raise
 His offspring, who expired in other days
To make thy sire's sway by a kingdom less,—
 This is to be a monarch, and repress
Envy into unutterable praise.
 Dismiss thy guard, and trust thee to such
 traits,

For who would lift a hand, except to bless?
 Were it not easy, sir, and is't not sweet
 To make thyself beloved? and to be
Omnipotent by mercy's means? for thus
 Thy sovereignty would grow but more
 complete:
A despot thou, and yet thy people free,
 And by the heart, not hand, enslaving us.
 Bologna, *August* 12, 1819.

EPIGRAM.

FROM THE FRENCH OF RULHIÈRES.

If, for silver or for gold,
 You could melt ten thousand pimples
 Into half a dozen dimples,
Then your face we might behold,
 Looking, doubtless, much more snugly;
 Yet even *then* 'twould be d—d ugly.
 August 12, 1819.

STANZAS.

Could Love for ever
Run like a river,
And Time's endeavour
 Be tried in vain—
No other pleasure
With this could measure;
And like a treasure
 We'd hug the chain.
But since our sighing
Ends not in dying,
And, form'd for flying,
 Love plumes his wing;
Then for this reason
Let's love a season;
But let that season be only Spring.

When lovers parted
Feel broken-hearted,
And, all hopes thwarted,
 Expect to die;
A few years older,
Ah! how much colder
They might behold her
 For whom they sigh!
When lihk'd together,
In every weather,
They pluck Love's feather
 From out his wing—
He'll stay for ever,
But sadly shiver
Without his plumage, when past the Spring.

Like chiefs of Faction,
His life is action—
A formal paction

That curbs his reign,
Obscures his glory,
Despot no more, he
Such territory
 Quits with disdain.
Still, still advancing,
With banners glancing,
His power enhancing,
 He must move on—
Repose but cloys him,
Retreat destroys him,
Love brooks not a degraded throne.

Wait not, fond lover!
Till years are over,
And then recover
 As from a dream.
While each bewailing
The other's failing,
With wrath and railing,
 All hideous seem—
While first decreasing,
Yet not quite ceasing,
Wait not till teasing
 All passion blight:
If once diminish'd,
Love's reign is finish'd—
Then part in friendship—and bid good-night

So shall Affection
To recollection
The dear connexion
 Bring back with joy:
You had not waited
Till, tired or hated,
Your passions sated
 Began to cloy.
Your last embraces
Leave no cold traces—
The same fond faces
 As through the past:
And eyes, the mirrors
Of your sweet errors,
Reflect but rapture—not least though last.

True, separations
Ask more than patience;
What desperations
 From such have risen!
But yet remaining,
What is't but chaining
Hearts which, once waning,
 Beat 'gainst their prison?
Time can but cloy love
And use destroy love:
The winged boy, Love,
 Is but for boys—
You'll find it torture,
Though sharper, shorter,
To wean, and not wear out your joys.
 1819.

ON MY WEDDING-DAY.

Here's a happy new year! but with reason
I beg you'll permit me to say—
Wish me *many* returns of the *season*,
But as *few* as you please of the day.
 January 2, 1820.

EPITAPH FOR WILLIAM PITT.

With death doom'd to grapple,
 Beneath this cold slab, he
Who lied in the Chapel
 Now lies in the Abbey.
 January, 1820.

EPIGRAM.

In digging up your bones, Tom Paine,
 Will. Cobbett has done well:
You visit him on earth again,
 He'll visit you in hell.
 January, 1820.

STANZAS.

When a man hath no freedom to fight for at
 home,
 Let him combat for that of his neighbours;
Let him think of the glories of Greece and of
 Rome,
 And get knock'd on the head for his labours.

To do good to mankind is the chivalrous plan,
 And is always as nobly requited;
Then battle for freedom wherever you can,
 And, if not shot or hang'd, you'll get
 knighted.
 November, 1820.

EPIGRAM.

The world is a bundle of hay,
 Mankind are the asses who pull;
Each tugs it a different way,
 And the greatest of all is John Bull.

THE CHARITY BALL.

What matter the pangs of a husband and
 father,
 If his sorrows in exile be great or be small,
So the Pharisee's glories around her she
 gather,
 And the saint patronizes her "charity
 ball!"

What matters—a heart which, though faulty,
 was feeling,
 Be driven to excesses which once could
 appal—
That the sinner should suffer is only fair
 dealing,
 As the saint keeps her charity back for
 "the ball!"

EPIGRAM,

ON THE BRAZIERS' COMPANY HAVING RESOLVED
TO PRESENT AN ADDRESS TO QUEEN CAROLINE.

The braziers, it seems, are preparing to pass
An address, and present it themselves all in
 brass;—
A superfluous pageant—for, by the Lord
 Harry!
They'll find where they're going much more
 than they carry.

EPIGRAM ON MY WEDDING-DAY.

TO PENELOPE.

This day, of all our days, has done
 The worst for me and you:—
'Tis just *six* years since we were *one*,
 And *five* since we were *two*.
 January 2, 1821.

ON MY THIRTY-THIRD BIRTHDAY.

JANUARY 22, 1821.

Through life's dull road, so dim and dirty,
I have dragg'd to three-and-thirty.
What have these years left to me?
Nothing—except thirty-three.

MARTIAL, LIB. I., EPIG. I.

"Hic est, quem legis, ille, quem requiris,
 Tota notus in orbe Martialis," &c.

He unto whom thou art so partial,
Oh, reader! is the well-known Martial,
The Epigrammatist: while living,
Give him the fame thou wouldst be giving;
So shall he hear, and feel, and know it—
Post obits rarely reach a poet.

BOWLES AND CAMPBELL.

To the tune of "Why, how now, saucy jade?"

Why, how now, saucy Tom?
 If you thus must ramble,
I will publish some
 Remarks on Mister Campbell.

ANSWER.

WHY, how now, Billy Bowles?
 Sure the priest is maudlin!
(*To the public*) How can you, d—n your souls!
 Listen to his twaddling?
 February 22, 1821.

EPIGRAMS.

OH, Castlereagh! thou art a patriot now;
Cato died for his country, so didst thou:
He perish'd rather than see Rome enslaved,
Thou cutt'st thy throat that Britain may be
 saved!

So Castlereagh has cut his throat!—The worst
Of this is,—that his own was not the first.

So *He* has cut his throat at last!—He! Who?
The man who cut his country's long ago.

EPITAPH.

POSTERITY will ne'er survey
 A nobler grave than this:
Here lie the bones of Castlereagh:
 Stop, traveller——

JOHN KEATS.

WHO kill'd John Keats?
 "I," says the Quarterly,
 So savage and Tartarly;
"'Twas one of my feats."

Who shot the arrow?
 "The poet-priest Milman
 (So ready to kill man),
 Or Southey, or Barrow."
 July, 1821.

THE CONQUEST.

[This fragment was found amongst Lord Byron's pa-
pers after his departure from Genoa for Greece.]

THE Son of Love and Lord of War I sing;
 Him who bade England bow to Normandy,
And left the name of conqueror more than king
 To his unconquerable dynasty.
Not fann'd alone by Victory's fleeting wing,
 He rear'd his bold and brilliant throne on
 high:
The Bastard kept, like lions, his prey fast,
And Britain's bravest victor was the last.
 March 8–9, 1823.

TO MR. MURRAY.

FOR Orford and for Waldegrave
You give much more than me you gave;
Which is not fairly to behave,
 My Murray.

Because if a live dog, 't is said,
Be worth a lion fairly sped,
A *live lord* must be worth *two* dead,
 My Murray.

And if, as the opinion goes,
Verse hath a better sale than prose,—
Certes, I should have more than those,
 My Murray.

But now this sheet is nearly cramm'd,
So, if *you will*, *I* shan't be shamm'd,
And if you *won't*, *you* may be damn'd,
 My Murray.

THE IRISH AVATAR.

"And Ireland, like a bastinadoed elephant, kneel-
ing to receive the paltry rider."—CURRAN.

ERE the daughter of Brunswick is cold in
 her grave,
 And her ashes still float to their home o'er
 the tide,
Lo! George the triumphant speeds over the
 wave,
 To the long-cherish'd isle which he loved
 like his—bride!

True, the great of her bright and brief era
 are gone,
 The rainbow-like epoch where Freedom
 could pause
For the few little years, out of centuries won,
 Which betray'd not, or crush'd not, or wept
 not her cause.

True, the chains of the Catholic clank o'er
 his rags,
 The castle still stands, and the senate's no
 more,
And the famine which dwelt on her freedom-
 less crags
 Is extending its steps to her desolate shore.

To her desolate shore—where the emigrant
 stands
 For a moment to gaze ere he flies from his
 hearth;
Tears fall on his chain, though it drops from
 his hands,
 For the dungeon he quits is the place of
 his birth.

But he comes! the Messiah of royalty comes!
 Like a goodly Leviathan roll'd from the
 waves;
Then receive him as best such an advent
 becomes,
 With a legion of cooks, and an army of
 slaves!

He comes in the promise and bloom of
　　threescore,
　　To perform in the pageant the sovereign's
　　　part—
But long live the shamrock, which shadows
　　him o'er!
　　Could the green in his *hat* be transferr'd to
　　　his *heart!*

Could that long-wither'd spot but be verdant
　　again,
　　And a new spring of noble affections
　　　arise—
Then might freedom forgive thee this dance
　　in thy chain,
　　And this shout of thy slavery which saddens
　　　the skies.

Is it madness or meanness which clings to
　　thee now?
　　Were he God—as he is but the commonest
　　　clay,
With scarce fewer wrinkles than sins on his
　　brow—
　　Such servile devotion might shame him
　　　away.

Ay, roar in his train! let thine orators lash
　　Their fanciful spirits to pamper his pride—
Not thus did thy Grattan indignantly flash
　　His soul o'er the freedom implored and
　　　denied.

Ever glorious Grattan! the best of the good!
　　So simple in heart, so sublime in the rest!
With all which Demosthenes wanted endued,
　　And his rival or victor in all he possess'd.

Ere Tully arose in the zenith of Rome,
　　Though unequall'd, preceded, the task was
　　　begun—
But Grattan sprung up like a god from the
　　tomb
　　Of ages, the first, last, the saviour, the *one!*

With the skill of an Orpheus to soften the
　　brute;
　　With the fire of Prometheus to kindle
　　　mankind;
Even Tyranny listening sate melted or mute,
　　And Corruption shrunk scorch'd from the
　　　glance of his mind.

But back to our theme! Back to despots and
　　slaves!
　　Feasts furnish'd by Famine! rejoicings by
　　　Pain!
True freedom but *welcomes,* while slavery
　　still *raves,*
　　When a week's saturnalia hath loosen'd
　　　her chain.

Let the poor squalid splendour thy wreck
　　can afford
　　(As the bankrupt's profusion his ruin would
　　　hide),
Gild over the palace, Lo! Erin, thy lord!
　　Kiss his foot with thy blessing, his bless-
　　　ings denied!

Or *if* freedom past hope be extorted at last,
　　If the idol of brass find his feet are of clay,
Must what terror or policy wring forth be
　　class'd
　　With what monarchs ne'er give, but as
　　　wolves yield their prey?

Each brute hath its nature; a king's is to
　　reign,—
　　To *reign!* in that word see, ye ages, com-
　　　prised
The cause of the curses all annals contain,
　　From Cæsar the dreaded to George the
　　　despised!

Wear, Fingal, thy trapping! O'Connell, pro-
　　claim
　　His accomplishments! *His!!!* and thy
　　　country convince
Half an age's contempt was an error of fame,
　　And that "Hal is the rascaliest, sweetest
　　　young prince!"

Will thy yard of blue riband, poor Fingal, recall
　　The fetters from millions of Catholic limbs?
Or, has it not bound thee the fastest of all
　　The slaves, who now hail their betrayer
　　　with hymns?

Ay! "Build him a dwelling!" let each give
　　his mite!
　　Till, like Babel, the new royal dome hath
　　　arisen!
Let thy beggars and helots their pittance
　　unite—
　　And a palace bestow for a poor-house and
　　　prison!

Spread—spread, for Vitellius, the royal repast,
　　Till the gluttonous despot be stuff'd to the
　　　gorge!
And the roar of his drunkards proclaim him
　　at last
　　The fourth of the fools and oppressors
　　　call'd "George!"

Let the tables be loaded with feasts till they
　　groan!
　　Till they *groan* like thy people, through
　　　ages of woe!
Let the wine flow around the old Bacchanal's
　　throne,
　　Like their blood which has flow'd, and
　　　which yet has to flow.

But let not *his* name be thine idol alone—
On his right hand behold a Sejanus appears!
Thine own Castlereagh! let him still be thine
　own!
A wretch never named but with curses and
　jeers!

Till now, when the isle which should blush
　for his birth,
Deep, deep as the gore which he shed on
　her soil,
Seems proud of the reptile which crawl'd
　from her earth,
And for murder repays him with shouts
　and a smile.

Without one single ray of her genius, without
The fancy, the manhood, the fire of her
　race—
The miscreant who well might plunge Erin
　in doubt
If *she* ever gave birth to a being so base.

If she did—let her long-boasted proverb be
　hush'd,
Which proclaims that from Erin no reptile
　can spring—
See the cold-blooded serpent, with venom full
　flush'd,
Still warming its folds in the breast of
　a king!

Shout, drink, feast, and flatter! Oh! Erin,
　how low
Wert thou sunk by misfortune and tyranny,
　till
Thy welcome of tyrants hath plunged thee
　below
The depth of thy deep in a deeper gulf still!

My voice, though but humble, was raised for
　thy right,
My vote, as a freeman's, still voted thee free,
This hand, though but feeble, would arm in
　thy fight,
And this heart, though outworn, had a
　throb still for *thee!*

Yes, I loved thee and thine, though thou art
　not my land,
I have known noble hearts and great souls
　in thy sons,
And I wept with the world, o'er the patriot band
Who are gone, but I weep them no longer
　as once.

For happy are they now reposing afar,—
Thy Grattan, thy Curran, thy Sheridan, all
Who, for years, were the chiefs in the elo-
　quent war,
And redeem'd, if they have not retarded,
　thy fall.

Yes, happy are they in their cold English
　graves!
Their shades cannot start to thy shouts of
　to-day—
Nor the steps of enslavers and chain-kissing
　slaves
Be stamp'd in the turf o'er their fetterless
　clay.

Till now I had envied thy sons and their shore,
Though their virtues were hunted, their
　liberties fled;
There was something so warm and sublime
　in the core
Of an Irishman's heart, that I envy—thy
　dead.

Or, if aught in my bosom can quench for an hour
My contempt for a nation so servile,
　though sore,
Which though trod like the worm will not
　turn upon power,
'Tis the glory of Grattan, and genius of
　Moore!　　　　　　*September,* 1821.

————

STANZAS WRITTEN ON THE ROAD BETWEEN FLORENCE AND PISA.

OH, talk not to me of a name great in story;
The days of our youth are the days of our
　glory;
And the myrtle and ivy of sweet two-and-
　twenty
Are worth all your laurels, though ever so
　plenty.

What are garlands and crowns to the brow
　that is wrinkled?
'Tis but as a dead-flower with May-dew be-
　sprinkled.
Then away with all such from the head that
　is hoary!
What care I for the wreaths that can *only*
　give glory!

Oh FAME!—if I e'er took delight in thy praises,
'Twas less for the sake of thy high-sounding
　phrases,
Than to see the bright eyes of the dear one
　discover,
She thought that I was not unworthy to love
　her.

There chiefly I sought thee, *there* only I
　found thee;
Her glance was the best of the rays that
　surround thee;
When it sparkled o'er aught that was bright
　in my story,
I knew it was love, and I felt it was glory.
　　　　　　　　　　　November, 1821.

STANZAS TO A HINDOO AIR.

Oh! my lonely—lonely—lonely—Pillow!
Where is my lover? where is my lover?
Is it his bark which my dreary dreams dis-
 cover?
 Far—far away! and alone along the billow?

Oh! my lonely—lonely—lonely—Pillow!
Why must my head ache where his gentle
 brow lay?
How the long night flags lovelessly and
 slowly,
 And my head droops over thee like the
 willow!

Oh! thou, my sad and solitary Pillow!
Send me kind dreams to keep my heart from
 breaking,
In return for the tears I shed upon thee
 waking;
 Let me not die till he comes back o'er the
 billow.

Then if thou wilt—no more my *lonely*
 Pillow,
In one embrace let these arms again enfold
 him,
And then expire of the joy—but to behold
 him!
 Oh! my lone bosom!—oh! my lonely
 Pillow!

IMPROMPTU.

Beneath Blessington's eyes
 The reclaimed Paradise
Should be free as the former from evil;
 But if the new Eve
 For an Apple should grieve,
What mortal would not play the Devil?
 1823.

TO THE COUNTESS OF BLESSINGTON.

You have ask'd for a verse:—the request
 In a rhymer 'twere strange to deny;
But my Hippocrene was but my breast,
 And my feelings (its fountain) are dry.

Were I now as I was, I had sung
 What Lawrence has painted so well;
But the strain would expire on my tongue,
 And the theme is too soft for my shell.

I am ashes where once I was fire,
 And the bard in my bosom is dead;
What I loved I now merely admire,
 And my heart is as grey as my head.

My life is not dated by years—
 There are moments which act as a plough;
And there is not a furrow appears
 But is deep in my soul as my brow.

Let the young and the brilliant aspire
 To sing what I gaze on in vain;
For sorrow has torn from my lyre
 The string which was worthy the strain.

ON THIS DAY I COMPLETE MY THIRTY-SIXTH YEAR.

Missolonghi, Jan. 22, 1824.

'Tis time this heart should be unmoved,
 Since others it hath ceased to move:
Yet, though I cannot be beloved,
 Still let me love!

My days are in the yellow leaf;
 The flowers and fruits of love are gone;
The worm, the canker, and the grief
 Are mine alone!

The fire that on my bosom preys
 Is lone as some volcanic isle;
No torch is kindled at its blaze—
 A funeral pile.

The hope, the fear, the jealous care,
 The exalted portion of the pain
And power of love, I cannot share,
 But wear the chain.

But 'tis not *thus*—and 'tis not *here*—
 Such thoughts should shake my soul, nor
 now,
Where glory decks the hero's bier,
 Or binds his brow.

The sword, the banner, and the field,
 Glory and Greece, around me see!
The Spartan, borne upon his shield,
 Was not more free.

Awake! (not Greece—she *is* awake!)
 Awake, my spirit! Think through *whom*
Thy life-blood tracks its parent lake,
 And then strike home!

Tread those reviving passions down,
 Unworthy manhood!—unto thee
Indifferent should the smile or frown
 Of beauty be.

If thou regrett'st thy youth, *why live?*
 The land of honourable death
Is here:—up to the field, and give
 Away thy breath!

Seek out—less often sought than found—
 A soldier's grave, for thee the best;
Then look around, and choose thy ground,
 And take thy rest.

SATIRES.

English Bards and Scotch Reviewers:

A SATIRE.

"I had rather be a kitten, and cry mew!
Than one of these same metre ballad-mongers."
SHAKSPEARE.
"Such shameless bards we have; and yet 't is true,
There are as mad, abandon'd critics too."—POPE.

PREFACE*.

ALL my friends, learned and unlearned, have urged me not to publish this Satire with my name. If I were to be "turned from the career of my humour by quibbles quick, and paper bullets of the brain," I should have complied with their counsel. But I am not to be terrified by abuse, or bullied by reviewers, with or without arms. I can safely say that I have attacked none personally, who did not commence on the offensive. An author's works are public property: he who purchases may judge, and publish his opinion if he pleases; and the authors I have endeavoured to commemorate may do by me as I have done by them. I dare say they will succeed better in condemning my scribblings, than in mending their own. But my object is not to prove that I can write well, but, if possible, to make others write better.

As the poem has met with far more success than I expected, I have endeavoured in this edition to make some additions and alterations, to render it more worthy of public perusal.

In the first edition of this satire, published anonymously, fourteen lines on the subject of Bowles's Pope were written by, and inserted at the request of, an ingenious friend of mine†, who has now in the press a volume of poetry. In the present edition they are erased, and some of my own substituted in their stead; my only reason for this being that which I conceive would operate with any other person in the same manner,—a determination not to publish with my name any production which was not entirely and exclusively my own composition.

With * regard to the real talents of many of the poetical persons whose performances are mentioned or alluded to in the following pages, it is presumed by the author that there can be little difference of opinion in the public at large; though, like other sectaries, each has his separate tabernacle of proselytes, by whom his abilities are over-rated, his faults overlooked, and his metrical canons received without scruple and without consideration. But the unquestionable possession of considerable genius by several of the writers here censured renders their mental prostitution more to be regretted. Imbecility may be pitied, or, at worst, laughed at and forgotten: perverted powers demand the most decided reprehension. No one can wish more than the author that some known and able writer had undertaken their exposure; but Mr. Gifford has devoted himself to Massinger, and, in the absence of the regular physician, a country practitioner may, in cases of absolute necessity, be allowed to prescribe his nostrum to prevent the extension of so deplorable an epidemic, provided there be no quackery in his treatment of the malady. A caustic is here offered; as it is to be feared nothing short of actual cautery can recover the numerous patients afflicted with the present prevalent and distressing *rabies* for rhyming.—As to the Edinburgh Reviewers, it would indeed require an Hercules to crush the Hydra; but if the author succeeds in merely "bruising one of the heads of the serpent," though his own hand should suffer in the encounter, he will be amply satisfied.

* This preface was written for the second edition, and printed with it. The noble author had left this country previous to the publication of that edition, and is not yet returned.—*Note to the fourth edition*, 1811.

† [Mr. Hobhouse.]

* [Here the preface to the first edition commenced.]

ENGLISH BARDS AND SCOTCH REVIEWERS.

STILL must I hear ?—shall hoarse Fitzgerald bawl
His creaking couplets in a tavern hall,
And I not sing, lest, haply, Scotch reviews
Should dub me scribbler, and denounce my muse ?
Prepare for rhyme—I'll publish, right or wrong :
Fools are my theme, let satire be my song.

Oh! nature's noblest gift—my grey goose-quill !
Slave of my thoughts, obedient to my will,
Torn from thy parent bird to form a pen,
That mighty instrument of little men !
The pen ! foredoom'd to aid the mental throes
Of brains that labour, big with verse or prose,
Though nymphs forsake, and critics may deride,
The lover's solace, and the author's pride.
What wits, what poets dost thou daily raise !
How frequent is thy use, how small thy praise !
Condemn'd at length to be forgotten quite,
With all the pages which 't was thine to write.
But thou, at least, mine own especial pen !
Once laid aside, but now assumed again,
Our task complete, like Hamet's shall be free ;
Though spurn'd by others, yet beloved by me :
Then let us soar to-day ; no common theme,
No eastern vision, no distemper'd dream
Inspires—our path, though full of thorns, is plain ;
Smooth be the verse, and easy be the strain.

When Vice triumphant holds her sov'reign sway,
Obey'd by all who nought beside obey ;
When Folly, frequent harbinger of crime,
Bedecks her cap with bells of every clime ;
When knaves and fools combined o'er all prevail,
And weigh their justice in a golden scale ;
E'en then the boldest start from public sneers,
Afraid of shame, unknown to other fears,
More darkly sin, by satire kept in awe,
And shrink from ridicule, though not from law.

Such is the force of wit ! but not belong
To me the arrows of satiric song ;
The royal vices of our age demand
A keener weapon, and a mightier hand.
Still there are follies, e'en for me to chase,
And yield at least amusement in the race :

Laugh when I laugh, I seek no other fame ;
The cry is up, and scribblers are my game.
Speed, Pegasus !—ye strains of great and small,
Ode, epic, elegy, have at you all !
I too can scrawl, and once upon a time
I pour'd along the town a flood of rhyme,
A schoolboy freak, unworthy praise or blame ;
I printed—older children do the same.
'T is pleasant, sure, to see one's name in print ;
A book's a book, although there's nothing in't.
Not that a title's sounding charm can save
Or scrawl or scribbler from an equal grave :
This Lambe must own, since his patrician name
Fail'd to preserve the spurious farce from shame.
No matter, George continues still to write,
Though now the name is veil'd from public sight.
Moved by the great example, I pursue
The self-same road, but make my own review :
Not seek great Jeffrey's, yet, like him, will be
Self-constituted judge of poesy.

A man must serve his time to every trade
Save censure—critics all are ready made.
Take hackney'd jokes from Miller, got by rote,
With just enough of learning to misquote ;
A mind well skill'd to find or forge a fault ;
A turn for punning, call it Attic salt ;
To Jeffrey go, be silent and discreet,
His pay is just ten sterling pounds per sheet :
Fear not to lie, 'twill seem a sharper hit ;
Shrink not from blasphemy, 'twill pass for wit ;
Care not for feeling—pass your proper jest,
And stand a critic, hated yet caress'd.

And shall we own such judgment ? no—as soon
Seek roses in December—ice in June ;
Hope constancy in wind, or corn in chaff ;
Believe a woman or an epitaph,
Or any other thing that's false, before
You trust in critics, who themselves are sore ;
Or yield one single thought to be misled
By Jeffrey's heart, or Lambe's Bœotian head.
To these young tyrants, by themselves misplaced,
Combined usurpers on the throne of taste ;
To these, when authors bend in humble awe,
And hail their voice as truth, their word as law—

While these are censors, 't would be sin to
 spare;
While such are critics, why should I forbear?
But yet, so near all modern worthies run,
'T is doubtful whom to seek, or whom to
 shun;
Nor know we when to spare, or where to
 strike,
Our bards and censors are so much alike.

Then should you ask me, why I venture o'er
The path which Pope and Gifford trod before;
If not yet sicken'd, you can still proceed:
Go on; my rhyme will tell you as you read.
"But hold!" exclaims a friend, "here's some
 neglect:
This—that—and t' other line seem incorrect."
What then? the self-same blunder Pope has
 got,
And careless Dryden—"Ay, but Pye has
 not:"—
Indeed!—'t is granted, faith!—but what care
 I?
Better to err with Pope, than shine with Pye.

Time was, ere yet in these degenerate days
Ignoble themes obtain'd mistaken praise,
When sense and wit with poesy allied,
No fabled graces, flourish'd side by side;
From the same fount their inspiration drew,
And, rear'd by taste, bloom'd fairer as they
 grew.
Then, in this happy isle, a Pope's pure strain
Sought the rapt soul to charm, nor sought in
 vain;
A polish'd nation's praise aspired to claim,
And raised the people's, as the poet's fame.
Like him great Dryden pour'd the tide of
 song,
In stream less smooth, indeed, yet doubly
 strong.
Then Congreve's scenes could cheer, or Ot-
 way's melt—
For nature then an English audience felt.
But why these names, or greater still, retrace,
When all to feebler bards resign their place?
Yet to such times our lingering looks are cast,
When taste and reason with those times are
 past.
Now look around, and turn each trifling page,
Survey the precious works that please the
 age;
This truth at least let satire's self allow,
No dearth of bards can be complain'd of now.
The loaded press beneath her labour groans,
And printers' devils shake their weary bones;
While Southey's epics cram the creaking
 shelves,
And Little's lyrics shine in hot-press'd
 twelves.

Thus saith the Preacher: "Nought beneath
 the sun
Is new;" yet still from change to change we
 run:
What varied wonders tempt us as they pass:
The cow-pox, tractors, galvanism, and gas,
In turns appear, to make the vulgar stare,
Till the swoln bubble bursts—and all is air!
Nor less new schools of Poetry arise,
Where dull pretenders grapple for the prize:
O'er taste awhile these pseudo-bards prevail;
Each country book-club bows the knee to
 Baal,
And, hurling lawful genius from the throne,
Erects a shrine and idol of its own;
Some leaden calf—but whom it matters not,
From soaring Southey down to grovelling
 Stott.

Behold! in various throngs the scribbling
 crew,
For notice eager, pass in long review:
Each spurs his jaded Pegasus apace,
And rhyme and blank maintain an equal
 race;
Sonnets on sonnets crowd, and ode on ode;
And tales of terror jostle on the road;
Immeasurable measures move along;
For simpering folly loves a varied song,
To strange mysterious dulness still the friend,
Admires the strain she cannot comprehend.
Thus Lays of Minstrels—may they be the
 last!—
On half-strung harps whine mournful to the
 blast.
While mountain spirits prate to river sprites,
That dames may listen to the sound at
 nights;
And goblin brats, of Gilpin Horner's brood,
Decoy young border-nobles through the wood,
And skip at every step, Lord knows how
 high,
And frighten foolish babes, the Lord knows
 why;
While high-born ladies in their magic cell,
Forbidding knights to read who cannot spell,
Despatch a courier to a wizard's grave,
And fight with honest men to shield a knave.

Next view in state, proud prancing on his
 roan,
The golden-crested haughty Marmion,
Now forging scrolls, now foremost in the
 fight,
Not quite a felon, yet but half a knight,
The gibbet or the field prepared to grace;
A mighty mixture of the great and base.
And think'st thou, Scott! by vain conceit
 perchance,
On public taste to foist thy stale romance,

Though Murray with his Miller may combine
To yield thy muse just half-a-crown per line?
No! when the sons of song descend to trade,
Their bays are sear, their former laurels
 fade.
Let such forego the poet's sacred name,
Who rack their brains for lucre, not for
 fame:
Still for stern Mammon may they toil in
 vain!
And sadly gaze on gold they cannot gain!
Such be their meed, such still the just
 reward
Of prostituted muse and hireling bard!
For this we spurn Apollo's venal son,
And bid a long "good night to Marmion."

These are the themes that claim our plau-
 dits now;
These are the bards to whom the muse must
 bow;
While Milton, Dryden, Pope, alike forgot,
Resign their hallow'd bays to Walter Scott.

The time has been, when yet the muse was
 young,
When Homer swept the lyre, and Maro sung,
An epic scarce ten centuries could claim,
While awe-struck nations hail'd the magic
 name:
The work of each immortal bard appears
The single wonder of a thousand years.
Empires have moulder'd from the face of
 earth,
Tongues have expired with those who gave
 them birth,
Without the glory such a strain can give,
As even in ruin bids the language live.
Not so with us, though minor bards, conten
On one great work a life of labour spent:
With eagle pinion soaring to the skies,
Behold the ballad-monger Southey rise!
To him let Camoëns, Milton, Tasso yield,
Whose annual strains, like armies, take the
 field.
First in the ranks see Joan of Arc advance,
The scourge of England and the boast of
 France!
Though burnt by wicked Bedford for a witch,
Behold her statue placed in glory's niche;
Her fetters burst, and just released from
 prison,
A virgin phœnix from her ashes risen.
Next see tremendous Thalaba come on,
Arabia's monstrous, wild, and wondrous son;
Domdaniel's dread destroyer, who o'erthrew
More mad magicians than the world e'er
 knew.
Immortal hero! all thy foes o'ercome,
For ever reign—the rival of Tom Thumb!

Since startled metre fled before thy face,
Well wert thou doom'd the last of all thy
 race!
Well might triumphant genii bear thee hence,
Illustrious conqueror of common sense!
Now, last and greatest, Madoc spreads his
 sails,
Cacique in Mexico, and prince in Wales;
Tells us strange tales, as other travellers do,
More old than Mandeville's, and not so true.
Oh! Southey! Southey! cease thy varied
 song! ·
A bard may chant too often and too long:
As thou art strong in verse, in mercy, spare!
A fourth, alas! were more than we could
 bear.
But if, in spite of all the world can say,
Thou still wilt verseward plod thy weary
 way;
If still in Berkley ballads most uncivil,
Thou wilt devote old women to the devil,
The babe unborn thy dread intent may rue:
"God help thee," Southey, and thy readers
 too.

Next comes the dull disciple of thy school,
That mild apostate from poetic rule,
The simple Wordsworth, framer of a lay
As soft as evening in his favourite May,
Who warns his friend "to shake off toil and
 trouble,
And quit his books, for fear of growing
 double;"
Who, both by precept and example, shows
That prose is verse, and verse is merely
 prose;
Convincing all, by demonstration plain,
Poetic souls delight in prose insane;
And Christmas stories tortured into rhyme
Contain the essence of the true sublime.
Thus, when he tells the tale of Betty Foy,
The idiot mother of "an idiot boy;"
A moon-struck, silly lad, who lost his way,
And, like his bard, confounded night with
 day;
So close on each pathetic part he dwells,
And each adventure so sublimely tells,
That all who view the "idiot in his glory"
Conceive the bard the hero of the story.

Shall gentle Coleridge pass unnoticed here,
To turgid ode and tumid stanza dear?
Though themes of innocence amuse him best,
Yet still obscurity's a welcome guest.
If Inspiration should her aid refuse
To him who takes a pixy for a muse,
Yet none in lofty numbers can surpass
The bard who soars to elegise an ass.
So well the subject suits his noble mind,
He brays the laureat of the long-ear'd kind.

Oh! wonder-working Lewis! monk, or
 bard,
Who fain wouldst make Parnassus a church-
 yard!
Lo! wreaths of yew, not laurel, bind thy
 brow,
Thy muse a sprite, Apollo's sexton thou!
Whether on ancient tombs thou tak'st thy
 stand,
By gibb'ring spectres hail'd, thy kindred
 band;
Or tracest chaste descriptions on thy page,
To please the females of our modest age;
All hail, M.P.! from whose infernal brain
Thin-sheeted phantoms glide, a grisly train;
At whose command "grim women" throng in
 crowds,
And kings of fire, of water, and of clouds,
With "small gray men," "wild yagers," and
 what not,
To crown with honour thee and Walter
 Scott;
Again all hail! if tales like thine may
 please,
St. Luke alone can vanquish the disease;
Even Satan's self with thee might dread to
 dwell,
And in thy skull discern a deeper hell.

Who in soft guise, surrounded by a choir
Of virgins melting, not to Vesta's fire,
With sparkling eyes, and cheek by passion
 flush'd,
Strikes his wild lyre, whilst listening dames
 are hush'd?
'Tis Little! young Catullus of his day,
As sweet, but as immoral, in his lay!
Grieved to condemn, the muse must still be
 just,
Nor spare melodious advocates of lust.
Pure is the flame which o'er her altar burns;
From grosser incense with disgust she turns:
Yet kind to youth, this expiation o'er,
She bids thee "mend thy line and sin no
 more."

For thee, translator of the tinsel song,
To whom such glittering ornaments belong,
Hibernian Strangford! with thine eyes of
 blue,
And boasted locks of red or auburn hue,
Whose plaintive strain each love-sick miss
 admires,
And o'er harmonious fustian half expires,
Learn, if thou canst, to yield thine author's
 sense,
Nor vend thy sonnets on a false pretence.
Think'st thou to gain thy verse a higher
 place,
By dressing Camoëns in a suit of lace?

Mend, Strangford! mend thy morals and thy
 taste;
Be warm, but pure; be amorous, but be
 chaste;
Cease to deceive; thy pilfer'd harp restore,
Nor teach the Lusian bard to copy Moore.

Behold!—ye tarts!—one moment spare the
 text—
Hayley's last work, and worst—until his
 next;
Whether he spin poor couplets into plays,
Or damn the dead with purgatorial praise,
His style in youth or age is still the same,
For ever feeble and for ever tame.
Triumphant first see "Temper's Triumphs"
 shine!
At least I'm sure they triumph'd over mine.
Of "Music's Triumphs," all who read may
 swear
That luckless music never triumph'd there.

Moravians, rise! bestow some meet re-
 ward
On dull devotion—Lo! the Sabbath bard,
Sepulchral Grahame, pours his notes sub-
 lime
In mangled prose, nor e'en aspires to rhyme;
Breaks into blank the Gospel of St. Luke,
And boldly pilfers from the Pentateuch;
And, undisturb'd by conscientious qualms,
Perverts the Prophets, and purloins the
 Psalms.

Hail, Sympathy! thy soft idea brings
A thousand visions of a thousand things,
And shows, still whimpering through three-
 score of years,
The maudlin prince of mournful sonneteers.
And art thou not their prince, harmonious
 Bowles!
Thou first, great oracle of tender souls?
Whether thou sing'st with equal ease, and
 grief,
The fall of empires, or a yellow leaf;
Whether thy muse most lamentably tells
What merry sounds proceed from Oxford
 bells,
Or, still in bells delighting, finds a friend
In every chime that jingled from Ostend;
Ah! how much juster were thy muse's hap,
If to thy bells thou wouldst but add a cap!
Delightful Bowles! still blessing and still
 blest,
All love thy strain, but children like it best.
'Tis thine, with gentle Little's moral song,
To soothe the mania of the amorous throng!
With thee our nursery damsels shed their
 tears,
Ere miss as yet completes her infant years:

But in her teens thy whining powers are
　　vain;
She quits poor Bowles for Little's purer
　　strain.
Now to soft themes thou scornest to confine
The lofty numbers of a harp like thine;
"Awake a louder and a loftier strain,"
Such as none heard before, or will again!
Where all Discoveries jumbled from the
　　flood,
Since first the leaky ark reposed in mud,
By more or less, are sung in every book,
From Captain Noah down to Captain Cook.
Nor this alone; but, pausing on the road,
The bard sighs forth a gentle episode;
And gravely tells—attend, each beauteous
　　miss!—
When first Madeira trembled to a kiss.

Bowles! in thy memory let this precept
　　dwell,
Stick to thy sonnets, man!—at least they sell.
But if some new-born whim, or larger bribe,
Prompt thy crude brain, and claim thee for
　　a scribe;
If chance some bard, though once by dunces
　　fear'd,
Now, prone in dust, can only be revered;
If Pope, whose fame and genius, from the
　　first,
Have foil'd the best of critics, needs the
　　worst,
Do thou essay: each fault, each failing scan;
The first of poets was, alas! but man.
Rake from each ancient dunghill every pearl,
Consult Lord Fanny, and confide in Curll;
Let all the scandals of a former age
Perch on thy pen, and flutter o'er thy page;
Affect a candour which thou canst not feel,
Clothe envy in the garb of honest zeal;
Write, as if St. John's soul could still inspire,
And do from hate what Mallet did for hire.
Oh! hadst thou lived in that congenial time,
To rave with Dennis, and with Ralph to
　　rhyme;
Throng'd with the rest around his living
　　head,
Not raised thy hoof against the lion dead;
A meet reward had crown'd thy glorious
　　gains,
And link'd thee to the Dunciad for thy pains.

Another epic! Who inflicts again
More books of blank upon the sons of men?
Bœotian Cottle, rich Bristowa's boast,
Imports old stories from the Cambrian coast,
And sends his goods to market—all alive!
Lines forty thousand, cantos twenty-five?
Fresh fish from Helicon! who'll buy, who'll
　　buy?
The precious bargain's cheap—in faith, not I.

Your turtle-feeder's verse must needs be flat,
Though Bristol bloat him with the verdant
　　fat;
If Commerce fills the purse, she clogs the
　　brain,
And Amos Cottle strikes the lyre in vain.
In him an author's luckless lot behold,
Condemn'd to make the books which once
　　he sold.
Oh, Amos Cottle!—Phœbus! what a name
To fill the speaking trump of future fame!—
Oh, Amos Cottle! for a moment think
What meagre profits spring from pen and ink!
When thus devoted to poetic dreams,
Who will peruse thy prostituted reams?
Oh! pen perverted! paper misapplied!
Had Cottle still adorn'd the counter's side,
Bent o'er the desk, or, born to useful toils,
Been taught to make the paper which he
　　soils,
Plough'd, delved, or plied the oar with lusty
　　limb,
He had not sung of Wales, nor I of him.

As Sisyphus against the infernal steep
Rolls the huge rock whose motions ne'er
　　may sleep,
So up thy hill, ambrosial Richmond, heaves
Dull Maurice all his granite weight of leaves:
Smooth, solid monuments of mental pain!
The petrifactions of a plodding brain,
That, ere they reach the top, fall lumbering
　　back again.

With broken lyre, and cheek serenely pale,
Lo! sad Alcæus wanders down the vale;
Though fair they rose, and might have
　　bloom'd at last,
His hopes have perish'd by the northern
　　blast:
Nipp'd in the bud by Caledonian gales,
His blossoms wither as the blast prevails!
O'er his lost works let *classic* Sheffield weep;
May no rude hand disturb their early sleep!

Yet say! why should the bard at once
　　resign
His claim to favour from the sacred nine?
For ever startled by the mingled howl
Of northern wolves, that still in darkness
　　prowl;
A coward brood, which mangle as they prey,
By hellish instinct, all that cross their way;
Aged or young, the living or the dead,
No mercy find—these harpies must be fed.
Why do the injured unresisting yield
The calm possession of their native field?
Why tamely thus before their fangs retreat,
Nor hunt the blood-hounds back to Arthur's
　　Seat?

Health to immortal Jeffrey! once, in name,
England could boast a judge almost the same;
In soul so like, so merciful, yet just,
Some think that Satan has resign'd his trust,
And given the spirit to the world again,
To sentence letters, as he sentenced men.
With hand less mighty, but with heart as
 black,
With voice as willing to decree the rack;
Bred in the courts betimes, though all that
 law
As yet hath taught him is to find a flaw;
Since well instructed in the patriot school
To rail at party, though a party tool,
Who knows, if chance his patrons should
 restore
Back to the sway they forfeited before,
His scribbling toils some recompense may
 meet,
And raise this Daniel to the judgment-seat?
Let Jeffreys' shade indulge the pious hope,
And greeting thus, present him with a rope:
"Heir to my virtues! man of equal mind!
Skill'd to condemn as to traduce mankind,
This cord receive, for thee reserved with
 care,
To wield in judgment, and at length to wear."

Health to great Jeffrey! Heaven preserve
 his life,
To flourish on the fertile shores of Fife,
And guard it sacred in its future wars,
Since authors sometimes seek the field of
 Mars!
Can none remember that eventful day,
That ever-glorious, almost fatal fray,
When Little's leadless pistol met his eye,
And Bow-street myrmidons stood laughing
 by?
Oh, day disastrous! on her firm-set rock,
Dunedin's castle felt a secret shock;
Dark roll'd the sympathetic waves of Forth,
Low groan'd the startled whirlwinds of the
 north;
Tweed ruffled half his waves to form a tear,
The other half pursued its calm career;
Arthur's steep summit nodded to its base,
The surly Tolbooth scarcely kept her place.
The Tolbooth felt—for marble sometimes can,
On such occasions, feel as much as man—
The Tolbooth felt defrauded of his charms,
If Jeffrey died, except within her arms:
Nay last, not least, on that portentous morn,
The sixteenth story, where himself was
 born,
His patrimonial garret, fell to ground,
And pale Edina shudder'd at the sound:
Strew'd were the streets around with milk-
 white reams,
Flow'd all the Canongate with inky streams;

This of his candour seem'd the sable dew,
That of his valour show'd the bloodless hue;
And all with justice deem'd the two com-
 bined
The mingled emblems of his mighty mind.
But Caledonia's goddess hover'd o'er
The field, and saved him from the wrath of
 Moore;
From either pistol snatch'd the vengeful lead,
And straight restored it to her favourite's
 head;
That head, with greater than magnetic power,
Caught it, as Danaë caught the golden shower,
And, though the thickening dross will scarce
 refine,
Augments its ore, and is itself a mine.
"My son," she cried, "ne'er thirst for gore
 again,
Resign the pistol and resume the pen;
O'er politics and poesy preside,
Boast of thy country, and Britannia's guide!
For long as Albion's heedless sons submit,
Or Scottish taste decides on English wit,
So long shall last thine unmolested reign,
Nor any dare to take thy name in vain.
Behold, a chosen band shall aid thy plan,
And own thee chieftain of the critic clan.
First in the oat-fed phalanx shall be seen
The travell'd thane, Athenian Aberdeen.
Herbert shall wield Thor's hammer, and
 sometimes,
In gratitude, thou'lt praise his rugged rhymes.
Smug Sidney too thy bitter page shall seek,
And classic Hallam, much renown'd for Greek;
Scott may perchance his name and influence
 lend,
And paltry Pillans shall traduce his friend;
While gay Thalia's luckless votary, Lambe,
Damn'd like the devil, devil-like will damn.
Known be thy name, unbounded be thy sway!
Thy Holland's banquets shall each toil repay;
While grateful Britain yields the praise she
 owes
To Holland's hirelings and to learning's
 foes.
Yet mark one caution ere thy next Review
Spread its light wings of saffron and of blue,
Beware lest blundering Brougham destroy
 the sale,
Turn beef to bannocks, cauliflowers to kail."
Thus having said, the kilted goddess kiss'd
Her son, and vanish'd in a Scottish mist.

Then prosper, Jeffrey! pertest of the train
Whom Scotland pampers with her fiery grain!
Whatever blessing wait a genuine Scot,
In double portion swells thy glorious lot;
For thee Edina culls her evening sweets,
And showers their odours on thy candid
 sheets,

Whose hue and fragrance to thy work
 adhere—
This scents its pages, and that gilds its rear.
Lo! blushing Itch, coy nymph, enamour'd
 grown,
Forsakes the rest, and cleaves to thee alone;
And, too unjust to other Pictish men,
Enjoys thy person, and inspires thy pen!

Illustrious Holland! hard would be his lot,
His hirelings mention'd, and himself forgot!
Holland, with Henry Petty at his back,
The whipper-in and huntsman of the pack,
Blest be the banquets spread at Holland
 House,
Where Scotchmen feed, and critics may
 carouse!
Long, long beneath that hospitable roof
Shall Grub-street dine, while duns are kept
 aloof.
See honest Hallam lay aside his fork,
Resume his pen, review his Lordship's work,
And, grateful for the dainties on his plate,
Declare his landlord can at least translate!
Dunedin! view thy children with delight,
They write for food—and feed because they
 write:
And lest, when heated with the unusual
 grape,
Some glowing thoughts should to the press
 escape,
And tinge with red the female reader's cheek,
My lady skims the cream of each critique;
Breathes o'er the page her purity of soul,
Reforms each error, and refines the whole.

Now to the Drama turn—Oh! motley
 sight!
What precious scenes the wondering eyes
 invite!
Puns, and a prince within a barrel pent,
And Dibdin's nonsense yield complete con-
 tent.
Though now, thank Heaven! the Roscio-
 mania's o'er,
And full-grown actors are endured once more;
Yet what avail their vain attempts to please,
While British critics suffer scenes like these;
While Reynolds vents his "dammes!"
 "poohs!" and "zounds!"
And common-place and common sense con-
 founds?
While Kenney's "World"—ah! where is
 Kenney's wit?—
Tires the sad gallery, lulls the listless pit;
And Beaumont's pilfer'd Caratach affords
A tragedy complete in all but words?
Who but must mourn, while these are all the
 rage,
The degradation of our vaunted stage!

Heavens! is all sense of shame and talent
 gone?
Have we no living bard of merit?—none!
Awake, George Colman! Cumberland, awake!
Ring the alarum bell! let folly quake!
Oh, Sheridan! if aught can move thy pen,
Let Comedy assume her throne again;
Abjure the mummery of the German schools;
Leave new Pizarros to translating fools;
Give, as thy last memorial to the age,
One classic drama, and reform the stage.
Gods! o'er those boards shall Folly rear her
 head,
Where Garrick trod, and Siddons lives to
 tread?
On those shall Farce display Buffoon'ry's
 mask,
And Hook conceal his heroes in a cask?
Shall sapient managers new scenes produce
From Cherry, Skeffington, and Mother Goose?
While Shakspeare, Otway, Massinger, forgot,
On stalls must moulder, or in closets rot?
Lo! with what pomp the daily prints pro-
 claim
The rival candidates for Attic fame!
In grim array though Lewis' spectres rise,
Still Skeffington and Goose divide the prize.
And sure *great* Skeffington must claim our
 praise,
For skirtless coats and skeletons of plays
Renown'd alike; whose genius ne'er confines
Her flight to garnish Greenwood's gay de-
 signs;
Nor sleeps with "Sleeping Beauties," but
 anon
In five facetious acts comes thundering on,
While poor John Bull, bewilder'd with the
 scene
Stares, wondering what the devil it can
 mean;
But as some hands applaud, a venal few!
Rather than sleep, why John applauds it
 too.

Such are we now. Ah! wherefore should
 we turn
To what our fathers were, unless to mourn?
Degenerate Britons! are ye dead to shame,
Or, kind to dulness, do you fear to blame?
Well may the nobles of our present race
Watch each distortion of a Naldi's face;
Well may they smile on Italy's buffoons,
And worship Catalani's pantaloons,
Since their own drama yields no fairer trace
Of wit than puns, of humour than grimace.

Then let Ausonia, skill'd in every art
To soften manners, but corrupt the heart,
Pour her exotic follies o'er the town,
To sanction Vice, and hunt Decorum down:

Let wedded strumpets languish o'er Des-
hayes,
And bless the promise which his form dis-
plays;
While Gayton bounds before th' enraptured
looks
Of hoary marquises and stripling dukes:
Let high-born lechers eye the lively Présle
Twirl her light limbs, that spurn the needless
veil;
Let Angiolini bare her breast of snow,
Wave the white arm, and point the pliant
toe;
Collini trill her love-inspiring song,
Strain her fair neck, and charm the listen-
ing throng!
Whet not your scythe, suppressors of our
vice!
Reforming saints! too delicately nice!
By whose decrees, our sinful souls to save,
No Sunday tankards foam, no barbers shave;
And beer undrawn, and beards unmown,
display
Your holy reverence for the Sabbath-day.

Or hail at once the patron and the pile
Of vice and folly, Greville and Argyle!
Where yon proud palace, Fashion's hallow'd
fane,
Spreads wide her portals for the motley
train,
Behold the new Petronius of the day,
Our arbiter of pleasure and of play!
There the hired eunuch, the Hesperian choir,
The melting lute, the soft lascivious lyre,
The song from Italy, the step from France,
The midnight orgy, and the mazy dance,
The smile of beauty, and the flush of wine,
For fops, fools, gamesters, knaves, and lords
combine:
Each to his humour—Comus all allows;
Champaign, dice, music, or your neighbour's
spouse.
Talk not to us, ye starving sons of trade!
Of piteous ruin, which ourselves have made;
In plenty's sunshine Fortune's minions bask,
Nor think of poverty, except "en masque,"
When for the night some lately titled ass
Appears the beggar which his grandsire was.
The curtain dropp'd, the gay burletta o'er,
The audience take their turn upon the floor:
Now round the room the circling dow'gers
sweep,
Now in loose waltz the thin-clad daughters
leap;
The first in lengthen'd line majestic swim,
The last display the free unfetter'd limb!
Those for Hibernia's lusty sons repair
With art the charms which nature could not
spare;

These after husbands wing their eager flight,
Nor leave much mystery for the nuptial
night.

Oh! blest retreats of infamy and ease,
Where, all forgotten but the power to please,
Each maid may give a loose to genial
thought,
Each swain may teach new systems, or be
taught:
There the blithe youngster, just return'd
from Spain,
Cuts the light pack, or calls the rattling
main;
The jovial caster's set, and seven's the nick,
Or—done!—a thousand on the coming trick!
If, mad with loss, existence 'gins to tire,
And all your hope or wish is to expire,
Here's Powell's pistol ready for your life,
And, kinder still, two Pagets for your wife;
Fit consummation of an earthly race
Begun in folly, ended in disgrace;
While none but menials o'er the bed of
death,
Wash thy red wounds, or watch thy waver-
ing breath,
Traduced by liars, and forgot by all,
The mangled victim of a drunken brawl,
To live like Clodius, and like Falkland fall.

Truth! rouse some genuine bard, and guide
his hand
To drive this pestilence from out the land.
E'en I—least thinking of a thoughtless
throng,
Just skill'd to know the right and choose the
wrong,
Freed at that age when reason's shield is
lost,
To fight my course through passion's count-
less host,
Whom every path of pleasure's flowery way
Has lured in turn, and all have led astray—
E'en I must raise my voice, e'en I must
feel
Such scenes, such men, destroy the public
weal:
Although some kind, censorious friend will
say,
"What art thou better, meddling fool, than
they?"
And every brother rake will smile to see
That miracle, a moralist in me.
No matter—when some bard in virtue strong,
Gifford perchance, shall raise the chastening
song,
Then sleep my pen for ever! and my voice
Be only heard to hail him, and rejoice;
Rejoice, and yield my feeble praise, though I
May feel the lash that Virtue must apply.

As for the smaller fry, who swarm in
 shoals,
From silly Hafiz up to simple Bowles,
Why should we call them from their dark
 abode,
In broad St. Giles's or in Tottenham-road?
Or (since some men of fashion nobly dare
To scrawl in verse) from Bond-street or the
 Square?
If things of ton their harmless lays indite,
Most wisely doom'd to shun the public sight,
What harm? in spite of every critic elf,
Sir T. may read his stanzas to himself;
Miles Andrews still his strength in couplets
 try,
And live in prologues, though his dramas
 die:
Lords too are bards, such things at times
 befall,
And 'tis some praise in peers to write at all.
Yet, did or taste or reason sway the times,
Ah! who would take their titles with their
 rhymes?
Roscommon! Sheffield! with your spirits
 fled,
No future laurels deck a noble head;
No muse will cheer, with renovating smile,
The paralytic puling of Carlisle.
The puny schoolboy and his early lay
Men pardon, if his follies pass away;
But who forgives the senior's ceaseless verse,
Whose hairs grow hoary as his rhymes grow
 worse?
What heterogeneous honours deck the peer!
Lord, rhymester, petit-maitre, and pamphlet-
 eer!
So dull in youth, so drivelling in his age,
His scenes alone had damn'd our sinking
 stage;
But managers for once cried, "Hold, enough!"
Nor drugg'd their audience with the tragic
 stuff.
Yet at their judgment let his lordship laugh,
And case his volumes in congenial calf;
Yes! doff that covering, where morocco
 shines,
And hang a calf-skin on those recreant lines.

With you, ye Druids! rich in native lead,
Who daily scribble for your daily bread;
With you I war not: Gifford's heavy hand
Has crush'd, without remorse, your numerous
 band.
On "all the talents" vent your venal spleen;
Want is your plea, let pity be your screen.
Let monodies on Fox regale your crew,
And Melville's Mantle prove a blanket too!
One common Lethe waits each hapless bard,
And, peace be with you! 'tis your best
 reward.

Such damning fame as Dunciads only give
Could bid your lines beyond a morning live;
But now at once your fleeting labours close,
With names of greater note in blest repose.
Far be't from me unkindly to upbraid
The lovely Rosa's prose in masquerade,
Whose strains, the faithful echoes of her
 mind,
Leave wondering comprehension far behind.
Though Crusca's bards no more our journals
 fill,
Some stragglers skirmish round the columns
 still;
Last of the howling host which once was
 Bell's,
Matilda snivels yet, and Hafiz yells;
And Merry's metaphors appear anew,
Chain'd to the signature of O. P. Q.

When some brisk youth, the tenant of a
 stall,
Employs a pen less pointed than his awl,
Leaves his snug shop, forsakes his store of
 shoes,
St. Crispin quits, and cobbles for the muse,
Heavens! how the vulgar stare! how crowds
 applaud!
How ladies read, and literati laud!
If chance some wicked wag should pass his
 jest,
'Tis sheer ill-nature—don't the world know
 best?
Genius must guide when wits admire the
 rhyme,
And Capel Lofft declares 'tis quite sublime.
Hear, then, ye happy sons of needless trade!
Swains! quit the plough, resign the useless
 spade!
Lo! Burns and Bloomfield, nay, a greater
 far,
Gifford was born beneath an adverse star,
Forsook the labours of a servile state,
Stemm'd the rude storm, and triumph'd over
 fate:
Then why no more? if Phœbus smiled on
 you,
Bloomfield! why not on brother Nathan
 too?
Him too the mania, not the muse, has seized;
Not inspiration, but a mind diseased:
And now no boor can seek his last abode,
No common be enclosed without an ode.
Oh! since increased refinement deigns to
 smile
On Britain's sons, and bless our genial isle,
Let poesy go forth, pervade the whole,
Alike the rustic, and mechanic soul!
Ye tuneful cobblers! still your notes pro-
 long,
Compose at once a slipper and a song;

So shall the fair your handywork peruse,
Your sonnets sure shall please—perhaps your
shoes.
May Moorland weavers boast Pindaric skill,
And tailors' lays be longer than their bill!
While punctual beaux reward the grateful
notes,
And pay for poems—when they pay for
coats.

To the famed throng now paid the tribute
due,
Neglected genius! let me turn to you.
Come forth, oh Campbell! give thy talents
scope;
Who dares aspire if thou must cease to hope?
And thou, melodious Rogers! rise at last,
Recall the pleasing memory of the past;
Arise! let blest remembrance still inspire,
And strike to wonted tones thy hallow'd
lyre;
Restore Apollo to his vacant throne,
Assert thy country's honour and thine own.
What! must deserted Poesy still weep
Where her last hopes with pious Cowper
sleep?
Unless, perchance, from his cold bier she
turns,
To deck the turf that wraps her minstrel,
Burns!
No! though contempt hath mark'd the
spurious brood,
The race who rhyme from folly, or for food,
Yet still some genuine sons 't is hers to
boast,
Who, least affecting, still affect the most:
Feel as they write, and write but as they
feel—
Bear witness Gifford, Sotheby, Macneil.

"Why slumbers Gifford?" once was ask'd
in vain;
Why slumbers Gifford? let us ask again.
Are there no follies for his pen to purge?
Are there no fools whose backs demand the
scourge?
Are there no sins for satire's bard to greet?
Stalks not gigantic Vice in every street?
Shall peers or princes tread pollution's path,
And 'scape alike the law's and muse's wrath?
Nor blaze with guilty glare through future
time,
Eternal beacons of consummate crime?
Arouse thee, Gifford! be thy promise claim'd,
Make bad men better, or at least ashamed.

Unhappy White! while life was in its
spring,
And thy young muse just waved her joyous
wing,

The spoiler swept that soaring lyre away,
Which else had sounded an immortal lay.
Oh! what a noble heart was here undone,
When Science' self destroy'd her favourite
son!
Yes, she too much indulged thy fond pursuit,
She sow'd the seeds, but death has reap'd the
fruit.
'Twas thine own genius gave the final blow,
And help'd to plant the wound that laid thee
low:
So the struck eagle, stretch'd upon the plain,
No more through rolling clouds to soar again,
View'd his own feather on the fatal dart,
And wing'd the shaft that quiver'd in his
heart;
Keen were his pangs, but keener far to feel
He nursed the pinion which impell'd the
steel;
While the same plumage that had warm'd his
nest
Drank the last life-drop of his bleeding
breast.

There be who say, in these enlighten'd
days,
That splendid lies are all the poet's praise;
That strain'd invention, ever on the wing,
Alone impels the modern bard to sing:
'Tis true, that all who rhyme—nay, all who
write,
Shrink from that fatal word to genius—trite;
Yet Truth sometimes will lend her noblest
fires,
And decorate the verse herself inspires:
This fact in Virtue's name let Crabbe attest;
Though nature's sternest painter, yet the
best.

And here let Shee and Genius find a place,
Whose pen and pencil yield an equal grace;
To guide whose hand the sister arts combine,
And trace the poet's or the painter's line;
Whose magic touch can bid the canvas
glow,
Or pour the easy rhyme's harmonious flow;
While honours, doubly merited, attend
The poet's rival, but the painter's friend.

Blest is the man who dares approach the
bower
Where dwelt the muses at their natal hour;
Whose steps have press'd, whose eye has
mark'd afar,
The clime that nursed the sons of song and
war,
The scenes which glory still must hover o'er,
Her place of birth, her own Achaian shore.
But doubly blest is he whose heart expands
With hallow'd feelings for those classic lands;

Who rends the veil of ages long gone by,
And views their remnants with a poet's eye!
Wright! 'twas thy happy lot at once to view
Those shores of glory, and to sing them too;
And sure no common muse inspired thy pen
To hail the land of gods and godlike men.

And you, associate bards! who snatch'd to light
Those gems too long withheld from modern sight;
Whose mingling taste combined to cull the wreath
Where Attic flowers Aonion odours breathe,
And all their renovated fragrance flung
To grace the beauties of your native tongue;
Now let those minds, that nobly could transfuse
The glorious spirit of the Grecian muse,
Though soft the echo, scorn a borrow'd tone:
Resign Achaia's lyre, and strike your own.

Let these, or such as these, with just applause,
Restore the muse's violated laws;
But not in flimsy Darwin's pompous chime,
That mighty master of unmeaning rhyme,
Whose gilded cymbals, more adorn'd than clear,
The eye delighted, but fatigued the ear;
In show the simple lyre could once surpass,
But now, worn down, appear in native brass;
While all his train of hovering sylphs around
Evaporate in similes and sound:
Him let them shun, with him let tinsel die:
False glare attracts, but more offends the eye.

Yet let them not to vulgar Wordsworth stoop,
The meanest object of the lowly group,
Whose verse, of all but childish prattle void,
Seems blessed harmony to Lamb and Lloyd:
Let them—but hold, my muse, nor dare to teach
A strain far, far beyond thy humble reach:
The native genius with their being given
Will point the path, and peal their notes to heaven.

And thou, too, Scott! resign to minstrels rude
The wilder slogan of a border feud:
Let others spin their meagre lines for hire;
Enough for genius, if itself inspire!
Let Southey sing, although his teeming muse,
Prolific every spring, be too profuse;
Let simple Wordsworth chime his childish verse,
And brother Coleridge lull the babe at nurse;

Let spectre-mongering Lewis aim, at most,
To rouse the galleries, or to raise a ghost;
Let Moore still sigh; let Strangford steal from Moore,
And swear that Camoëns sang such notes of yore;
Let Hayley hobble on, Montgomery rave,
And godly Grahame chant a stupid stave:
Let sonneteering Bowles his strains refine,
And whine and whimper to the fourteenth line;
Let Stott, Carlisle, Matilda, and the rest
Of Grub Street, and of Grosvenor Place the best,
Scrawl on, till death release us from the strain,
Or Common Sense assert her rights again.
But thou, with powers that mock the aid of praise,
Shouldst leave to humbler bards ignoble lays:
Thy country's voice, the voice of all the nine,
Demand a hallow'd harp—that harp is thine.
Say! will not Caledonia's annals yield
The glorious record of some nobler field,
Than the wild foray of a plundering clan,
Whose proudest deeds disgrace the name of man?
Or Marmion's acts of darkness, fitter food
For Sherwood's outlaw tales of Robin Hood?
Scotland! still proudly claim thy native bard,
And be thy praise his first, his best reward!
Yet not with thee alone his name should live,
But own the vast renown a world can give:
Be known, perchance, when Albion is no more,
And tell the tale of what she was before;
To future times her faded fame recall,
And save her glory, though his country fall.

Yet what avails the sanguine poet's hope,
To conquer ages, and with time to cope?
New eras spread their wings, new nations rise,
And other victors fill the applauding skies;
A few brief generations fleet along,
Whose sons forget the poet and his song:
E'en now, what once-loved minstrels scarce may claim
The transient mention of a dubious name!
When fame's loud trump hath blown its noblest blast,
Though long the sound, the echo sleeps at last;
And glory, like the phœnix midst her fires,
Exhales her odours, blazes, and expires.

Shall hoary Granta call her sable sons,
Expert in science, more expert at puns?
Shall these approach the muse? ah, no! she flies,
Even from the tempting ore of Seaton's prize;

Though printers condescend the press to soil
With rhyme by Hoare, and epic blank by
 Hoyle :
Not him whose page, if still upheld by whist,
Requires no sacred theme to bid us list.
Ye ! who in Granta's honours would surpass,
Must mount her Pegasus, a full-grown ass ;
A foal well worthy of her ancient dam,
Whose Helicon is duller than her Cam.

There Clarke, still striving piteously " to
 please,"
Forgetting doggrel leads not to degrees,
A would-be satirist, a hired buffoon,
A monthly scribbler of some low lampoon,
Condemn'd to drudge, the meanest of the
 mean,
And furbish falsehoods for a magazine,
Devotes to scandal his congenial mind ;
Himself a living libel on mankind.

Oh ! dark asylum of a Vandal race !
At once the boast of learning, and disgrace !
So lost to Phœbus, that nor Hodgson's verse
Can make thee better, nor poor Hewson's
 worse.
But where fair Isis rolls her purer wave,
The partial muse delighted loves to lave ;
On her green banks a greener wreath she
 wove,
To crown the bards that haunt her classic
 grove :
Where Richards wakes a genuine poet's fires,
And modern Britons glory in their sires.

For me, who, thus unask'd, have dared to
 tell
My country what her sons should know too
 well,
Zeal for her honour bade me here engage
The host of idiots that infest her age ;
No just applause her honour'd name shall
 lose,
As first in freedom, dearest to the muse.
Oh ! would thy bards but emulate thy fame,
And rise more worthy, Albion, of thy name !
What Athens was in science, Rome in power,
What Tyre appear'd in her meridian hour,
'Tis thine at once, fair Albion ! to have been—
Earth's chief dictatress, ocean's lovely queen :
But Rome decay'd, and Athens strew'd the
 plain,
And Tyre's proud piers lie shatter'd in the
 main ;
Like these, thy strength may sink, in ruin
 hurl'd,
And Britain fall, the bulwark of the world.
But let me cease, and dread Cassandra's
 fate,
With warning ever scoff'd at, till too late ;

To themes less lofty still my lay confine,
And urge thy bards to gain a name like thine.

Then, hapless Britain ! be thy rulers blest,
The senate's oracles, the people's jest !
Still hear thy motley orators dispense
The flowers of rhetoric, though not of sense,
While Canning's colleagues hate him for his
 wit,
And old dame Portland fills the place of Pitt.

Yet once again, adieu ! ere this the sail
That wafts me hence is shivering in the gale ;
And Afric's coast and Calpe's adverse height,
And Stamboul's minarets must greet my
 sight :
Thence shall I stray through beauty's native
 clime,
Where Kaff is clad in rocks, and crown'd
 with snows sublime.
But should I back return, no tempting press
Shall drag my journal from the desk's recess ;
Let coxcombs, printing as they come from
 far,
Snatch his own wreath of ridicule from Carr ;
Let Aberdeen and Elgin still pursue
The shade of fame through regions of virtù ;
Waste useless thousands on their Phidian
 freaks,
Misshapen monuments and maim'd antiques ;
And make their grand saloons a general
 mart
For all the mutilated blocks of art :
Of Dardan tours let dilettanti tell,
I leave topography to rapid Gell ;
And, quite content, no more shall interpose
To stun the public ear—at least with prose.

Thus far I 've held my undisturb'd career,
Prepared for rancour, steel'd 'gainst selfish
 fear :
This thing of rhyme I ne'er disdain'd to own—
Though not obtrusive, yet not quite unknown :
My voice was heard again, though not so loud,
My page, though nameless, never disavow'd ;
And now at once I tear the veil away :—
Cheer on the pack ! the quarry stands at bay,
Unscared by all the din of Melbourne House,
By Lambe's resentment, or by Holland's
 spouse,
By Jeffrey's harmless pistol, Hallam's rage,
Edina's brawny sons and brimstone page.
Our men in buckram shall have blows enough,
And feel they too are " penetrable stuff : "
And though I hope not hence unscathed to go,
Who conquers me shall find a stubborn foe.
The time hath been, when no harsh sound
 would fall
From lips that now may seem imbued with
 gall ;

Nor fools nor follies tempt me to despise
The meanest thing that crawl'd beneath my
 eyes:
But now, so callous grown, so changed since
 youth,
I've learn'd to think, and sternly speak the
 truth;
Learn'd to deride the critic's starch decree,
And break him on the wheel he meant for
 me;
To spurn the rod a scribbler bids me kiss,
Nor care if courts and crowds applaud or
 hiss:
Nay more, though all my rival rhymesters
 frown,
I too can hunt a poetaster down;
And, arm'd in proof, the gauntlet cast at
 once
To Scotch marauder, and to southern dunce.
Thus much I've dared; if my incondite lay
Hath wrong'd these righteous times, let
 others say;
This, let the world, which knows not how to
 spare,
Yet rarely blames unjustly, now declare.

---••---

POSTSCRIPT TO THE SECOND EDITION.

I HAVE been informed, since the present edition
went to the press, that my trusty and well-beloved
cousins, the Edinburgh Reviewers, are preparing
a most vehement critique on my poor, gentle, *unre-
sisting* Muse, whom they have already so be-devilled
with their ungodly ribaldry:

 "Tantæne animis cœlestibus iræ!"

I suppose I must say of Jeffrey as Sir Andrew
Aguecheek saith, "An I had known he was so cun-
ning of fence, I had seen him damned ere I had
fought him." What a pity it is that I shall be
beyond the Bosphorus before the next number has
passed the Tweed! But I yet hope to light my pipe
with it in Persia.

My northern friends have accused me, with jus-
tice, of personality towards their great literary
anthropophagus, Jeffrey; but what else was to be
done with him and his dirty pack, who feed by
"lying and slandering," and slake their thirst by
"evil speaking"? I have adduced facts already
well known, and of Jeffrey's mind I have stated

my free opinion, nor has he thence sustained any
injury;—what scavenger was ever soiled by being
pelted with mud? It may be said that I quit Eng-
land because I have censured there "persons of
honour and wit about town;" but I am coming
back again, and their vengeance will keep hot till
my return. Those who know me can testify that
my motives for leaving England are very different
from fears, literary or personal: those who do not,
may one day be convinced. Since the publication
of this thing, my name has not been concealed; I
have been mostly in London, ready to answer for
my transgressions, and in daily expectation of
sundry cartels; but, alas! "the age of chivalry is
over," or, in the vulgar tongue, there is no spirit
now-a-days.

There is a youth ycleped Hewson Clarke (subaudi
esquire), a sizer of Emanuel College, and, I believe,
a denizen of Berwick-upon-Tweed, whom I have
introduced in these pages to much better company
than he has been accustomed to meet; he is,
notwithstanding, a very sad dog, and for no reason
that I can discover, except a personal quarrel
with a bear, kept by me at Cambridge to sit for
a fellowship, and whom the jealousy of his Trinity
contemporaries prevented from success, has been
abusing me, and, what is worse, the defenceless
innocent above mentioned, in "The Satirist," for
one year and some months. I am utterly uncon-
scious of having given him any provocation; indeed,
I am guiltless of having heard his name, till coupled
with "The Satirist." He has therefore no reason
to complain, and I dare say that, like Sir Fretful
Plagiary, he is rather *pleased* than otherwise.
I have now mentioned all who have done me the
honour to notice me and mine, that is, my bear
and my book, except the editor of "The Satirist,"
who, it seems, is a gentleman—God wot! I wish
he could impart a little of his gentility to his
subordinate scribblers. I hear that Mr. Jerning-
ham is about to take up the cudgels for his Mæcenas,
Lord Carlisle. I hope not: he was one of the few,
who, in the very short intercourse I had with him,
treated me with kindness when a boy; and what-
ever he may say or do, "pour on, I will endure."
I have nothing further to add, save a general note
of—thanksgiving to readers, purchasers, and pub-
lishers, and, in the words of Scott, I wish

 "To all and each a fair good night,
 And rosy dreams and slumbers light."

𝕳𝖎𝖓𝖙𝖘 𝖋𝖗𝖔𝖒 𝕳𝖔𝖗𝖆𝖈𝖊:

BEING AN ALLUSION IN ENGLISH VERSE TO THE EPISTLE "AD PISONES, DE ARTE POETICA," AND INTENDED AS A SEQUEL TO "ENGLISH BARDS AND SCOTCH REVIEWERS."

——•◆•——

——" Ergo fungar vice cotis, acutum
Reddere quae ferrum valet, exsors ipsa secandi"
HOR. *De Arte Poet.*
"Rhymes are difficult things—they are stubborn things, sir."
FIELDING'S *Amelia.*

——•◆•——

ATHENS: CAPUCHIN CONVENT,
March 12, 1811.

WHO would not laugh, if Lawrence, hired to grace
His costly canvas with each flatter'd face,
Abused his art, till Nature, with a blush,
Saw cits grow centaurs underneath his brush?
Or, should some limner join, for show or sale,
A maid of honour to a mermaid's tail?
Or low Dubost—as once the world has seen—
Degrade God's creatures in his graphic spleen?
Not all that forced politeness, which defends
Fools in their faults, could gag his grinning friends.
Believe me, Moschus, like that picture seems
The book which, sillier than a sick man's dreams,
Displays a crowd of figures incomplete,
Poetic nightmares, without head or feet.

Poets and painters, as all artists know,
May shoot a little with a lengthen'd bow;
We claim this mutual mercy for our task,
And grant in turn the pardon which we ask;
But make not monsters spring from gentle dams—
Birds breed not vipers, tigers nurse not lambs.

A labour'd, long exordium, sometimes tends
(Like patriot speeches) but to paltry ends;
And nonsense in a lofty note goes down,
As pertness passes with a legal gown:
Thus many a bard describes in pompous strain
The clear brook babbling through the goodly plain:
The groves of Granta, and her Gothic halls,
King's Coll., Cam's stream, stain'd windows, and old walls:
Or, in advent'rous numbers, neatly aims
To paint a rainbow, or—the river Thames.

You sketch a tree, and so perhaps may shine—
But daub a shipwreck like an alehouse sign;
You plan a *vase*—it dwindles to a *pot;*
Then glide down Grub-street—fasting and forgot;
Laugh'd into Lethe by some quaint Review,
Whose wit is never troublesome till—true.

In fine, to whatsoever you aspire,
Let it at least be simple and entire.

The greater portion of the rhyming tribe
(Give ear, my friend, for thou hast been a scribe)
Are led astray by some peculiar lure.
I labour to be brief—become obscure;

Humano capiti cervicem pictor equinam
Iungere si velit, et varias inducere plumas,
Undique collatis membris, ut turpiter atrum
Desinat in piscem mulier formosa superne:
Spectatum admissi risum teneatis, amici?
Credite, Pisones, isti tabulae fore librum
Persimilem, cuius, velut aegri somnia, vanae
Fingentur species; ut nec pes nec caput uni
Reddatur formae. Pictoribus atque poëtis
Quidlibet audendi semper fuit aequa potestas.
Scimus, et hanc veniam petimusque damusque vicissim;
Sed non ut placidis coëant immitia; non ut

Serpentes avibus geminentur, tigribus agni.
Incoeptis gravibus plerumque et magna professis,
Purpureus, late qui splendeat, unus et alter
Assuitur pannus; cum lucus et ara Dianae,
Et properantis aquae per amoenos ambitus agros,
Aut flumen Rhenum, aut pluvius describitur arcus.
Sed nunc non erat his locus: et fortasse cupressum
Scis simulare: quid hoc, si fractis enatat exspes
Navibus, aere dato qui pingitur? amphora coepit
Institui; currente rota cur urceus exit?
Denique sit quod vis, simplex duntaxat et unum.
Maxima pars vatum, pater et iuvenes patre digni,
Decipimur specie recti. Brevis esse laboro,

One falls while following elegance too fast;
Another soars, inflated with bombast;
Too low a third crawls on, afraid to fly,
He spins his subject to satiety;
Absurdly varying, he at last engraves
Fish in the woods, and boars beneath the
 waves!

Unless your care's exact, your judgment
 nice,
The flight from folly leads but into vice;
None are complete, all wanting in some part,
Like certain tailors, limited in art.
For galligaskins Slowshears is your man;
But coats must claim another artisan.
Now this to me, I own, seems much the same
As Vulcan's feet to bear Apollo's frame;
Or, with a fair complexion, to expose
Black eyes, black ringlets, but—a bottle nose!

Dear authors! suit your topics to your
 strength,
And ponder well your subject and its length;
Nor lift your load before you're quite aware
What weight your shoulders will, or will not,
 bear.
But lucid Order, and Wit's siren voice,
Await the poet, skilful in his choice;
With native eloquence he soars along,
Grace in his thoughts, and music in his song.

Let judgment teach them wisely to combine
With future parts the now omitted line:
This shall the author choose, or that reject,
Precise in style, and cautious to select;
Nor slight applause will candid pens afford
To him who furnishes a wanting word.
Then fear not, if 'tis needful, to produce
Some term unknown, or obsolete in use,
(As Pitt has furnish'd us a word or two,
Which lexicographers declined to do;)

So you indeed, with care,—(but be content
To take this license rarely)—may invent.
New words find credit in these latter days,
If neatly grafted on a Gallic phrase.
What Chaucer, Spenser did, we scarce refuse
To Dryden's or to Pope's maturer muse.
If you can add a little, say why not,
As well as William Pitt, and Walter Scott?
Since they, by force of rhyme and force of
 lungs,
Enrich'd our island's ill-united tongues;
'Tis then—and shall be—lawful to present
Reform in writing, as in parliament.

As forests shed their foliage by degrees,
So fade expressions which in season please;
And we and ours, alas! are due to fate,
And works and words but dwindle to a date.
Though as a monarch nods, and commerce calls,
Impetuous rivers stagnate in canals;
Though swamps subdued, and marshes
 drain'd, sustain
The heavy ploughshare and the yellow grain,
And rising ports along the busy shore
Protect the vessel from old Ocean's roar,
All, all, must perish; but, surviving last,
The love of letters half preserves the past.
True, some decay, yet not a few revive;
Though those shall sink, which now appear
 to thrive,
As custom arbitrates, whose shifting sway
Our life and language must alike obey.

The immortal wars which gods and angels
 wage,
Are they not shown in Milton's sacred page?
His strain will teach what numbers best belong
To themes celestial told in epic song.

The slow, sad stanza will correctly paint
The lover's anguish, or the friend's complaint.

Obscurus fio: sectantem levia, nervi
Deficiunt animique: professus grandia, turget:
Serpit humi, tutus nimium, timidusque procellae:
Qui variare cupit rem prodigialiter unam,
Delphinum sylvis appingit, fluctibus aprum.
In vitium ducit culpae fuga, si caret arte.
Aemilium circa ludum faber unus et ungues
Exprimet, et molles imitabitur aere capillos;
Infelix operis summa, quia ponere totum
Nesciet. Hunc ego me, si quid componere curem,
Non magis esse vellim, quam pravo vivere naso,
Spectandum nigris oculis nigroque capillo.
 Sumite materiam vestris, qui scribitis, aequam
Viribus; et versate diu quid ferre recusent
Quid valeant humeri. Cui lecta potenter erit res,
Nec facundia deseret hunc nec lucidus ordo.
 Ordinis haec virtus erit et venus, aut ego fallor,
Ut iam nunc dicat, iam nunc debentia dici
Pleraque differat, et praesens in tempus omittat;
 In verbis etiam tenuis cautusque serendis:
Hoc amet, hoc spernat promissi carminis auctor.
Dixeris egregio, notum si callida verbum
Reddiderit iunctura novum. Si forte necesse est
Indiciis monstrare recentibus abdita rerum,
Fingere cinctutis non exaudita Cethegis

Continget; dabiturque licentia sumpta pudenter;
Et nova fictaque nuper habebunt verba fidem, si
Graeco fonte cadant, parce detorta. Quid autem
Caecilio Plautoque dabit Romanus, ademptum
Virgilio Varioque? ego cur, acquirere pauca
Si possum, invideor; cum lingua Catonis et Enni
Sermonem patrium ditaverit, et nova rerum
Nomina protulerit? Licuit, semperque licebit,
Signatum praesente nota producere nomen.
 Ut silvae foliis pronos mutantur in annos:
Prima cadunt: ita verborum vetus interit aetas,
Et iuvenum ritu florent modo nata, vigentque.
Debemur morti nos, nostraque: sive receptus
Terra Neptunus classes Aquilonibus arcet,
Regis opus; sterilisque diu palus, aptaque remis
Vicinas urbes alit, et grave sentit aratrum:
Seu cursum mutavit iniquum frugibus amnis,
Doctus iter melius; mortalia facta peribunt:
Nedum sermonum stet honos, et gratia vivax.
Multa renascentur, quae iam cecidere; cadentque,
Quae nunc sunt in honore vocabula, si volet usus,
Quem penes arbitrium est, et ius, et norma loquendi.
 Res gestae regumque ducumque et tristia bella,
Quo scribi possent numero, monstravit Homerus.
Versibus impariter iunctis querimonia primum;

But which deserves the laurel—rhyme or
 blank?
Which holds on Helicon the higher rank?
Let squabbling critics by themselves dispute
This point, as puzzling as a Chancery suit.

Satiric rhyme first sprang from selfish
 spleen.
You doubt—see Dryden, Pope, St. Patrick's
 dean.

Blank verse is now, with one consent, allied
To Tragedy, and rarely quits her side.
Though mad Almanzor rhymed in Dryden's
 days,
No sing-song hero rants in modern plays;
While modest Comedy her verse foregoes
For jest and *pun* in very middling prose.
Not that our Bens or Beaumonts show the
 worse,
Or lose one point, because they wrote in
 verse.
But so Thalia pleases to appear,
Poor virgin! damn'd some twenty times
 a year!

Whate'er the scene, let this advice have
 weight:—
Adapt your language to your hero's state.
At times Melpomene forgets to groan,
And brisk Thalia takes a serious tone;
Nor unregarded will the act pass by
Where angry Townly lifts his voice on high.
Again our Shakspeare limits verse to kings,
When common prose will serve for common
 things;
And lively Hal resigns heroic ire,
To "hollowing Hotspur" and the sceptred
 sire.

'Tis not enough, ye bards, with all your art,
To polish poems; they must touch the heart:

Where'er the scene be laid, whate'er the
 song,
Still let it bear the hearer's soul along;
Command your audience or to smile or weep,
Whiche'er may please you—anything but
 sleep.
The poet claims our tears; but, by his leave,
Before I shed them, let me see him grieve.

If banish'd Romeo feign'd nor sigh nor
 tear,
Lull'd by his languor, I should sleep or sneer.
Sad words, no doubt, become a serious face,
And men look angry in the proper place.
At double meanings folks seem wondrous sly,
And sentiment prescribes a pensive eye;
For nature form'd at first the inward man,
And actors copy nature—when they can.
She bids the beating heart with rapture
 bound,
Raised to the stars, or levell'd with the
 ground;
And for expression's aid, 'tis said, or sung,
She gave our mind's interpreter—the tongue,
Who, worn with use, of late would fain
 dispense
(At least in theatres) with common sense;
O'erwhelm with sound the boxes, gallery, pit,
And raise a laugh with anything—but wit.

To skilful writers it will much import,
Whence spring their scenes, from common
 life or court;
Whether they seek applause by smile or tear,
To draw a "Lying Valet," or a "Lear,"
A sage, or rakish youngster wild from school,
A wandering "Peregrine," or plain "John
 Bull;"
All persons please when nature's voice
 prevails,
Scottish or Irish, born in Wilts or Wales.

Post etiam inclusa est voti sententia compos.
Quis tamen exiguos elegos emiserit auctor,
Grammatici certant, et adhuc sub iudice lis est.
 Archilochum proprio rabies armavit iambo;
Hunc socci cepere pedem grandesque cothurni,
Alternis aptum sermonibus, et populares
Vincentem strepitus, et natum rebus agendis.
 Musa dedit fidibus divos, puerosque deorum,
Et pugilem victorem, et equum certamine primum,
Et iuvenum curas, et libera vina referre.
 Descriptas servare vices, operumque colores,
Cur ego, si nequeo ignoroque, poeta salutor?
Cur nescire, pudens prave, quam discere malo?
 Versibus exponi tragicis res comica non vult;
Indignatur item privatis, ac prope socco
Dignis carminibus narrari coena Thyestae.
Singula quaeque locum teneant sortita decenter
Interdum tamen et vocem comoedia tollit,
Iratusque Chremes tumido delitigat ore;
Et tragicus plerumque dolet sermone pedestri.
Telephus et Peleus, cum pauper et exul, uterque
Proicit ampullas, et sesquipedalia verba,
Si curat cor spectantis tetigisse querela.
 Non satis est pulchra esse poemata; dulcia sunto,

Et quocunque volent, animum auditoris agunto.
Ut ridentibus arrident, ita flentibus adsunt
Humani vultus; si vis me flere dolendum est
Primum ipsi tibi; tunc tua me infortunia laedent
Telephe, vel Peleu, male si mandata loqueris
Aut dormitabo, aut ridebo: tristia moestum
Vultum verba decent; iratum, plena minarum;
Ludentem, lasciva; severum, seria dicta.
Format enim natura prius nos intus ad omnem
Fortunarum habitum; iuvat, aut impellit ad iram;
Aut ad humum moerore gravi deducit, et angit;
Post effert animi motus interprete lingua.
Si dicentis erunt fortunis absona dicta,
Romani tollent equites, peditesque cachinnum.
 Intererit multum, Davusne loquatur an heros;
Maturusne senex, an adhuc florente iuventa
Fervidus; an matrona potens, an sedula nutrix;
Mercatorne vagus, cultorne virentis agelli;
Colchus an Assyrius; Thebis nutritus, an Argis.
 Aut famam sequere, aut sibi convenientia finge,
Scriptor. Honoratum si forte reponis Achillem;
Impiger, iracundus, inexorabilis acer,
Iura neget sibi nata, nihil non arroget armis.
Sit Medea ferox invictaque; flebilis Ino;

Or follow common fame, or forge a plot;
Who cares if mimic heroes lived or not?
One precept serves to regulate the scene:—
Make it appear as if it *might* have *been*.

If some Drawcansir you aspire to draw,
Present him raving, and above all law:
If female furies in your scheme are plann'd,
Macbeth's fierce dame is ready to your hand;
For tears and treachery, for good and evil,
Constance, King Richard, Hamlet, and the
 Devil!
But if a new design you dare essay,
And freely wander from the beaten way,
True to your characters, till all be past,
Preserve consistency from first to last.

'Tis hard to venture where our betters fail,
Or lend fresh interest to a twice-told tale;
And yet, perchance, 'tis wiser to prefer
A hackney'd plot, than choose a new, and err;
Yet copy not too closely, but record,
More justly, thought for thought than word
 for word;
Nor trace your prototype through narrow ways,
But only follow where he merits praise.

For you, young bard! whom luckless fate
 may lead
To tremble on the nod of all who read,
Ere your first score of cantos time unrolls,
Beware—for God's sake, don't begin like
 Bowles!
" Awake a louder and a loftier strain,"—
And pray, what follows from his boiling
 brain?—
He sinks to Southey's level in a trice,
Whose epic mountains never fail in mice!
Not so of yore awoke your mighty sire
The temper'd warblings of his master-lyre;
Soft as the gentler breathing of the lute,
" Of man's first disobedience and the fruit "
He speaks, but, as his subject swells along,
Earth, Heaven, and Hades echo with the song.

Still to the midst of things he hastens on,
As if we witness'd all already done;
Leaves on his path whatever seems too mean
To raise the subject, or adorn the scene;
Gives, as each page improves upon the
 sight,
Not smoke from brightness, but from dark-
 ness—light;
And truth and fiction with such art com-
 pounds,
We know not where to fix their several
 bounds.
If you would please the public, deign to hear
What soothes the many-headed monster's ear:
If your heart triumph when the hands of all
Applaud in thunder at the curtain's fall,
Deserve those plaudits—study nature's page,
And sketch the striking traits of every age;
While varying man and varying years unfold
Life's little tale, so oft, so vainly told;
Observe his simple childhood's dawning days,
His pranks, his prate, his playmates, and his
 plays;
Till time at length the mannish tyro weans,
And prurient vice outstrips his tardy teens!

Behold him Freshman! forced no more to
 groan
O'er Virgil's devilish verses and his own;
Prayers are too tedious, lectures too abstruse,
He flies from Tavell's frown to "Fordham's
 Mews;"
(Unlucky Tavell! doom'd to daily cares
By pugilistic pupils, and by bears,)
Fines, tutors, tasks, conventions threat in vain,
Before hounds, hunters, and Newmarket
 plain.
Rough with his elders, with his equals rash,
Civil to sharpers, prodigal of cash;
Constant to nought—save hazard and a
 whore,
Yet cursing both—for both have made him
 sore;

Perfidus Ixion; Io vaga; tristis Orestes;
Si quid inexpertum scenae committis, et audes
Personam formare novam: servetur ad imum
Qualis ab incepto processerit, et sibi constet.
Difficile est proprie communia dicere: tuque
Rectius Iliacum carmen deducis in actus,
Quam si proferres ignota indictaque primus.
Publica materies privati iuris erit, si
Nec circa vilem patulumque moraberis orbem;
Nec verbum verbo curabis reddere fidus
Interpres, nec desilies imitator in arctum
Unde pedem proferre pudor vetet, aut operis lex.
Nec sic incipies, ut scriptor Cyclicus olim:
" Fortunam Priami cantabo, et nobile bellum."
Quid dignum tanto feret hic promissor hiatu?
Parturiunt montes: nascetur ridiculus mus.
Quanto rectius hic, qui nil molitur inepte!
" Dic mihi, Musa, virum, captae post tempora Troiae,
Qui mores hominum multorum vidit, et urbes."
Non fumum ex fulgore, sed ex fumo dare lucem
Cogitat, ut speciosa dehinc miracula promat,

Antiphaten, Scyllamque, et cum Cyclope Charybdin.
Nec reditum Diomedis ab interitu Meleagri,
Nec gemino bellum Troianum orditur ab ovo.
Semper ad eventum festinat; et in medias res
Non secus ac notas, auditorem rapit, et quae
Desperat tractata nitescere posse, relinquit:
Atque ita mentitur, sic veris falsa remiscet,
Primo ne medium, medio ne discrepet imum.
Tu, quid ego et populus mecum desideret, audi.
Si plausoris eges aulaea manentis, et usque
Sessuri, donec cantor, Vos plaudite, dicat;
Aetatis cuiusque notandi sunt tibi mores,
Mobilibusque decor naturis dandus et annis.
Reddere qui voces iam scit puer, et pede certo
Signat humum: gestit paribus colludere, et iram
Colligit ac ponit temere, et mutatur in horas.
Imberbus iuvenis, tandem custode remoto,
Gaudet equis canibusque, et aprici gramine campi;
Cereus in vitium flecti, monitoribus asper,
Utilium tardus provisor, prodigus aeris,
Sublimis, cupidusque, et amata relinquere pernix.

Unread (unless, since books beguile disease,
The p—x becomes his passage to degrees) ;
Fool'd, pillaged, dunn'd, he wastes his term
away,
And unexpell'd, perhaps, retires M.A. ;
Master of arts ! as *hells* and *clubs* proclaim,
Where scarce a blackleg bears a brighter
name !

Launch'd into life, extinct his early fire,
He apes the selfish prudence of his sire ;
Marries for money, chooses friends for rank,
Buys land, and shrewdly trusts not to the
Bank ;
Sits in the Senate ; gets a son and heir ;
Sends him to Harrow, for himself was there.
Mute, though he votes, unless when call'd to
cheer,
His son's so sharp—he'll see the dog a peer !

Manhood declines—age palsies every limb ;
He quits the scene—or else the scene quits
him ;
Scrapes wealth, o'er each departing penny
grieves,
And avarice seizes all ambition leaves ;
Counts cent. per cent., and smiles, or vainly
frets,
O'er hoards diminish'd by young Hopeful's
debts ;
Weighs well and wisely what to sell or buy,
Complete in all life's lessons—but to die ;
Peevish and spiteful, doting, hard to please,
Commending every time, save times like
these ;
Crazed, querulous, forsaken, half forgot,
Expires unwept—is buried—let him rot !

But from the Drama let me not digress,
Nor spare my precepts, though they please
you less.
Though woman weep, and hardest hearts are
stirr'd,
When what is done is rather seen than
heard,
Yet many deeds preserved in history's page
Are better told than acted on the stage ;
The ear sustains what shocks the timid eye,
And horror thus subsides to sympathy.
True Briton all beside, I here am French—
Bloodshed 'tis surely better to retrench ;

The gladiatorial gore we teach to flow
In tragic scene disgusts, though but in show ;
We hate the carnage while we see the trick,
And find small sympathy in being sick.
Not on the stage the regicide Macbeth
Appals an audience with a monarch's death ;
To gaze when sable Hubert threats to sear
Young Arthur's eyes, can *ours* or *nature* bear ?
A halter'd heroine Johnson sought to slay—
We saved Irene, but half damn'd the play,
And (Heaven be praised !) our tolerating
times
Stint metamorphoses to pantomimes ;
And Lewis' self, with all his sprites, would
quake
To change Earl Osmond's negro to a snake !
Because, in scenes exciting joy or grief,
We loathe the action which exceeds belief :
And yet, God knows ! what may not authors
do,
Whose postscripts prate of dyeing "heroines
blue ?"

Above all things, *Dan* Poet, if you can,
Eke out your acts, I pray, with mortal
man,
Nor call a ghost, unless some cursed scrape
Must open ten trap-doors for your escape.
Of all the monstrous things I'd fain forbid,
I loathe an opera worse than Dennis did ;
Where good and evil persons, right or wrong,
Rage, love, and aught but moralise, in song.
Hail, last memorial of our foreign friends,
Which Gaul allows, and still Hesperia lends !
Napoleon's edicts no embargo lay
On whores, spies, singers, wisely shipp'd
away.
Our giant capital, whose squares are spread
Where rustics earn'd, and now may beg, their
bread,
In all iniquity is grown so nice,
It scorns amusements which are not of price.
Hence the pert shopkeeper, whose throbbing
ear
Aches with orchestras which he pays to hear,
Whom shame, not sympathy, forbids to snore,
His anguish doubling by his own "encore ;"
Squeezed in "Fop's Alley," jostled by the
beaux,
Teased with his hat, and trembling for his
toes ;

Conversis studiis, aetas animusque virilis
Quaerit opes et amicitias, inservit honori ;
Commisisse cavet quod mox mutare laboret.
 Multa senem circumveniunt incommoda ; vel quod
Quaerit, et inventis miser abstinet, ac timet uti ;
Vel quod res omnes timide gelideque ministrat,
Dilator, spe longus, iners, avidusque futuri ;
Difficilis, querulus, laudator temporis acti
Se puero, castigator censorque minorum.
Multa ferunt anni venientes commoda secum,
Multa recedentes adimunt. Ne forte seniles

Mandentur iuveni partes, pueroque viriles,
Semper in adiunctis, aevoque morabimur aptis.
 Aut agitur res in scenis, aut acta refertur.
Segnius irritant animos demissa per aurem
Quam quae sunt oculis subiecta fidelibus, et quae
Ipse sibi tradit spectator. Non tamen intus
Digna geri, promes in scenam ; multaque tolles
Ex oculis, quae mox narret facundia praesens.
Ne pueros coram populo Medea trucidet ;
Aut humana palam coquat exta nefarius Atreus ;
Aut in avem Progne vertatur, Cadmus in anguem.

Scarce wrestles through the night, nor tastes
of ease,
Till the dropp'd curtain gives a glad release:
Why this, and more, he suffers — can ye
guess ?—
Because it costs him dear, and makes him
dress!

So prosper eunuchs from Etruscan schools;
Give us but fiddlers, and they're sure of
fools!
Ere scenes were play'd by many a reverend
clerk,
(What harm, if David danced before the
ark?)
In Christmas revels, simple country folks
Were pleased with morrice-mumm'ry and
coarse jokes.
Improving years, with things no longer
known,
Produced blithe Punch and merry Madame
Joan,
Who still frisk on with feats so lewdly low,
'T is strange Benvolio suffers such a show;
Suppressing peer! to whom each vice gives
place,
Oaths, boxing, begging,—all, save rout and
race.

Farce follow'd Comedy, and reach'd her
prime,
In ever-laughing Foote's fantastic time:
Mad wag! who pardon'd none, nor spared
the best,
And turn'd some very serious things to jest.
Nor church nor state escaped his public
sneers,
Arms nor the gown, priests, lawyers, volun-
teers:
"Alas, poor Yorick!" now for ever mute!
Whoever loves a laugh must sigh for Foote.

We smile, perforce, when histrionic scenes
Ape the swoln dialogue of kings and queens,
When "Chrononhotonthologos must die,"
And Arthur struts in mimic majesty.

Moschus! with whom once more I hope to
sit,
And smile at folly, if we can't at wit;
Yes, friend! for thee I 'll quit my cynic cell,
And bear Swift's motto, " Vive la bagatelle!"

Which charm'd our days in each Aegean
clime,
As oft at home, with revelry and rhyme.
Then may Euphrosyne, who sped the past,
Soothe thy life's scenes, nor leave thee in the
last;
But find in thine, like pagan Plato's bed,
Some merry manuscript of mimes, when
dead.

Now to the Drama let us bend our eyes,
Where fetter'd by whig Walpole low she
lies;
Corruption foil'd her, for she fear'd her
glance;
Decorum left her for an opera dance!
Yet Chesterfield, whose polish'd pen inveighs
'Gainst laughter, fought for freedom to our
plays;
Uncheck'd by megrims of patrician brains,
And damning dulness of lord chamberlains.
Repeal that act! again let Humour roam
Wild o'er the stage—we've time for tears at
home.
Let " Archer" plant the horns on " Sullen's"
brows,
And " Estifania" gull her " Copper" spouse;
The moral 's scant—but that may be excused,
Men go not to be lectured, but amused.
He whom our plays dispose to good or ill
Must wear a head in want of Willis' skill;
Ay, but Macheath's example — psha! — no
more!
It form'd no thieves—the thief was form'd
before;
And, spite of puritans and Collier's curse,
Plays make mankind no better, and no worse.
Then spare our stage, ye methodistic men!
Nor burn damn'd Drury if it rise again.
But why to brain-scorch'd bigots thus
appeal?
Can heavenly mercy dwell with earthly zeal?
For times of fire and faggot let them hope!
Times dear alike to puritan or pope.
As pious Calvin saw Servetus blaze,
So would new sects on newer victims gaze.
E'en now the songs of Solyma begin;
Faith cants, perplex'd apologist of sin!
While the Lord's servant chastens whom he
loves,
And Simeon kicks, where Baxter only
" shoves."

Quodcunque ostendis mihi sic, incredulus odi.
 Neve minor, neu sit quinto productior actu
Fabula, quae posci vult, et spectata reponi.
Nec deus intersit, nisi dignus vindice nodus
Inciderit,
 Ex noto fictum carmen sequar, ut sibi quivis
Speret idem: sudet multum frustraque laboret
Ausus idem: tantum series iuncturaque pollet;
Tantum de medio sumtis accedit honoris.
 Silvis deducti caveant, me iudice, Fauni,

Ne, velut innati triviis, ac pene forenses,
Aut nimium teneris iuventur versibus unquam,
Aut immunda crepent, ignominiosaque dicta.
Offenduntur enim, quibus est equus, et pater, et res:
Nec, si quid fricti ciceris probat et nucis emtor,
Aequis accipiunt animis, donantve corona.
 Syllaba longa brevi subiecta vocatur iambus,
Pes citus: unde etiam trimetris accrescere iussit
Nomen iambeis, cum senos redderet ictus,
Primus ad extremum similis sibi: non ita pridem,

Whom nature guides, so writes, that every
dunce,
Enraptured, thinks to do the same at once ;
But after inky thumbs and bitten nails,
And twenty scatter'd quires, the coxcomb
fails.

Let Pastoral be dumb ; for who can hope
To match the youthful eclogues of our
Pope?
Yet his and Phillips' faults, of different
kind,
For art too rude, for nature too refined,
Instruct how hard the medium 't is to hit
'Twixt too much polish and too coarse a wit.

A vulgar scribbler, certes, stands disgraced
In this nice age, when all aspire to taste ;
The dirty language, and the noisome jest,
Which pleased in Swift of yore, we now
detest ;
Proscribed not only in the world polite,
But even too nasty for a city knight !

Peace to Swift's faults ! his wit hath made
them pass,
Unmatch'd by all, save matchless Hudibras !
Whose author is perhaps the first we meet,
Who from our couplet lopp'd two final feet ;
Nor less in merit than the longer line,
This measure moves a favourite of the Nine.
Though at first view eight feet may seem in
vain
Form'd, save in ode, to bear a serious strain,
Yet Scott has shown our wondering isle of
late
This measure shrinks not from a theme of
weight,
And, varied skilfully, surpasses far
Heroic rhyme, but most in love and war,
Whose fluctuations, tender or sublime,
Are curb'd too much by long-recurring
rhyme.

But many a skilful judge abhors to see,
What few admire—irregularity.
This some vouchsafe to pardon ; but 't is
hard
When such a word contents a British bard.

And must the bard his glowing thoughts
confine,
Lest censure hover o'er some faulty line ?
Remove whate'er a critic may suspect,
To gain the paltry suffrage of *"correct"*?
Or prune the spirit of each daring phrase,
To fly from error, not to merit praise ?

Ye, who seek finish'd models, never cease,
By day and night, to read the works of
Greece.
But our good fathers never bent their brains
To heathen Greek, content with native
strains.
The few who read a page, or used a pen,
Were satisfied with Chaucer and old Ben ;
The jokes and numbers suited to their
taste
Were quaint and careless, anything but
chaste ;
Yet whether right or wrong the ancient rules,
It will not do to call our fathers fools !
Though you and I, who eruditely know
To separate the elegant and low,
Can also, when a hobbling line appears,
Detect with fingers, in default of ears.

In sooth I do not know, or greatly care
To learn, who our first English strollers
were ;
Or if, till roofs received the vagrant art,
Our Muse, like that of Thespis, kept a
cart ;
But this is certain, since our Shakspeare's
days,
There 's pomp enough, if little else, in plays ;
Nor will Melpomene ascend her throne
Without high heels, white plume, and Bristol
stone.

Old comedies still meet with much
applause,
Though too licentious for dramatic laws ;
At least, we moderns, wisely, 'tis confest,
Curtail, or silence, the lascivious jest.

Whate'er their follies, and their faults
beside,
Our enterprising bards pass nought untried ;

Tardior ut paulo graviorque veniret ad aures,
Spondeos stabiles in iura paterna recepit
Commodus et patiens ; non ut de sede secunda
Cederet aut quarta socialiter. Hic et in Acci
Nobilibus trimetris apparet rarus, et Enni.
In scenam missos magno cum pondere versus,
Aut operae celeris nimium, curaque carentis,
Aut ignoratae premit artis crimine turpi.
 Non quivis videt immodulata poemata iudex ;
Et data Romanis venia est indigna poetis.
Idcircone vager, scribamque licenter ? an omnes
Visuros peccata putem mea ; tutus, et intra
Spem veniae cautus ? vitavi denique culpam,
Non laudem merui. Vos exemplaria Graeca
Nocturna versate manu, versate diurna.

At vestri proavi Plautinos et numeros et
Laudavere sales ; nimium patienter utrumque,
Ne dicam stulte, mirati ; si modo ego et vos
Scimus inurbanum lepido seponere dicto,
Legitimumque sonum digitis callemus et aure.
 Ignotum tragicae genus invenisse Camoenae
Dicitur, et plaustris vexisse poemata Thespis,
Quae canerent agerentque peruncti faecibus ora.
Post hunc personae pallaeque repertor honestae
Aeschylus, et modicis instravit pulpita tignis,
Et docuit magnumque loqui, nitique cothurno.
 Successit vetus his comoedia, non sine multa
Laude ; sed in vitium libertas excidit, et vim
Dignam lege regi ; lex est accepta ; chorusque
Turpiter obticuit, sublato iure nocendi.

Nor do they merit slight applause who choose
An English subject for an English muse,
And leave to minds which never dare invent
French flippancy and German sentiment.
Where is that living language which could
 claim
Poetic more, as philosophic, fame,
If all our bards, more patient of delay,
Would stop, like Pope, to polish by the way?

Lords of the quill, whose critical assaults
O'erthrow whole quartos with their quires of
 faults,
Who soon detect, and mark where'er we fail,
And prove our marble with too nice a nail!
Democritus himself was not so bad;
He only _thought_, but _you_ would make, us mad!

But truth to say, most rhymers rarely guard
Against that ridicule they deem so hard;
In person negligent, they wear, from sloth,
Beards of a week, and nails of annual
 growth;
Reside in garrets, fly from those they meet,
And walk in alleys, rather than the street.

With little rhyme, less reason, if you please,
The name of poet may be got with ease,
So that not tuns of helleboric juice
Shall ever turn your head to any use;
Write but like Wordsworth, live beside a
 Lake,
And keep your bushy locks a year from
 Blake;
Then print your book, once more return to
 town,
And boys shall hunt your bardship up and
 down.

Am I not wise, if such some poets' plight,
To purge in spring—like Bayes—before I
 write?
If this precaution soften'd not my bile,
I know no scribbler with a madder style;

But since (perhaps my feelings are too nice)
I cannot purchase fame at such a price,
I'll labour gratis as a grinder's wheel,
And, blunt myself, give edge to others' steel,
Nor write at all, unless to teach the art
To those rehearsing for the poet's part;
From Horace show the pleasing paths of
 song,
And from my own example—what is wrong.

Though modern practice sometimes differs
 quite,
'T is just as well to think before you write;
Let every book that suits your theme be read,
So shall you trace it to the fountain-head.

He who has learn'd the duty which he owes
To friends and country, and to pardon foes;
Who models his deportment as may best
Accord with brother, sire, or stranger guest;
Who takes our laws and worship as they are,
Nor roars reform for senate, church, and bar;
In practice, rather than loud precept, wise,
Bids not his tongue, but heart, philosophise:
Such is the man the poet should rehearse,
As joint exemplar of his life and verse.

Sometimes a sprightly wit, and tale well
 told,
Without much grace, or weight, or art, will
 hold
A longer empire o'er the public mind
Than sounding trifles, empty, though refined.

Unhappy Greece! thy sons of ancient days
The muse may celebrate with perfect praise,
Whose generous children narrow'd not their
 hearts
With commerce, given alone to arms and arts.
Our boys (save those whom public schools
 compel
To "long and short" before they're taught
 to spell)
From frugal fathers soon imbibe by rote,
"A penny saved, my lad, 's a penny got."

Nil intentatum nostri liquere poetae;
Nec minimum meruere decus, vestigia Graeca
Ausi deserere, et celebrare domestica facta;
Vel qui praetextas, vel qui docuere togatas.
Nec virtute foret clarisve potentius armis,
Quam lingua, Latium, si non offenderet unum-
 quemque poetarum limae labor, et mora. Vos, o
Pompilius sanguis, carmen reprehendite, quod non
Multa dies et multa litura coercuit, atque
Praesectum decies non castigavit ad unguem.
 Ingenium misera quia fortunatius arte
Credit, et excludit sanos Helicone poetas
Democritus; bona pars non ungues ponere curat,
Non barbam; secreta petit loca, balnea vitat.
Nanciscetur enim pretium nomenque poetae,
Si tribus Anticyris caput insanabile nunquam
Tonsori Licino commiserit. O ego laevus,
Qui purgor bilem sub verni temporis horam!
Non alius faceret meliora poemata: verum
Nil tanti est: ergo fungar vice cotis, acutum
Reddere quae ferrum valet, exsors ipsa secandi:

Munus et officium, nil scribens ipse, docebo;
Unde parentur opes; quid alat formetque poetam;
Quid deceat, quid non; quo virtus, quo ferat error.
 Scribendi recte sapere est et principium et fons.
Rem tibi Socraticae poterunt ostendere chartae;
Verbaque provisam rem non invita sequentur:
Qui didicit patriae quid debeat, et quid amicis;
Quo sic amore parens, quo frater amandus, et
 hospes;
Quod sit conscripti, quod iudicis officium; quae
Partes in bellum missi ducis; ille profecto
Reddere personae scit convenientia cuique.
Respicere exemplar vitae morumque iubebo
Doctum imitatorem, et vivas hinc ducere voces.
 Interdum speciosa locis morataque recte
Fabula, nullius veneris, sine pondere et arte,
Valdius oblectat populum, meliusque moratur,
Quam, versus inopes rerum, nugaeque canorae.
 Graiis ingenium, Graiis dedit ore rotundo
Musa loqui, praeter laudem nullius avaris.
Romani pueri longis rationibus assem

Babe of a city birth! from sixpence take
The third, how much will the remainder
 make?—
"A groat."—"Ah, bravo! Dick hath done
 the sum!
He'll swell my fifty thousand to a plum."

They whose young souls receive this rust
 betimes,
'T is clear, are fit for anything but rhymes;
And Locke will tell you, that the father's right
Who hides all verses from his children's sight;
For poets (says this sage, and many more,)
Make sad mechanics with their lyric lore;
And Delphi now, however rich of old,
Discovers little silver, and less gold,
Because Parnassus, though a mount divine,
Is poor as Irus, or an Irish mine.

Two objects always should the poet move,
Or one or both,—to please or to improve.
Whate'er you teach, be brief, if you design
For our remembrance your didactic line;
Redundance places memory on the rack,
For brains may be o'erloaded, like the back.

Fiction does best when taught to look like
 truth,
And fairy fables bubble none but youth:
Expect no credit for too wondrous tales,
Since Jonas only springs alive from whales!

Young men with aught but elegance dispense;
Maturer years require a little sense.
To end at once:—that bard for all is fit
Who mingles well instruction with his wit;
For him reviews shall smile, for him o'erflow
The patronage of Paternoster-row;
His book, with Longman's liberal aid, shall pass
(Who ne'er despises books that bring him
 brass);
Through three long weeks the taste of London
 lead,
And cross St. George's Channel and the Tweed.

But everything has faults, nor is 't un-
 known
That harps and fiddles often lose their tone,
And wayward voices, at their owner's call,
With all his best endeavours, only squall;
Dogs blink their covey, flints withhold the
 spark,
And double-barrels (damn them!) miss their
 mark.

Where frequent beauties strike the reader's
 view,
We must not quarrel for a blot or two;
But pardon equally to books or men,
The slips of human nature, and the pen.

Yet if an author, spite of foe or friend,
Despises all advice too much to mend,
But ever twangs the same discordant string,
Give him no quarter, howsoe'er he sing.
Let Havard's fate o'ertake him, who, for
 once,
Produced a play too dashing for a dunce:
At first none deem'd it his; but when his
 name
Announced the fact—what then?—it lost its
 fame.
Though all deplore when Milton deigns to
 doze,
In a long work 't is fair to steal repose.

As pictures, so shall poems be; some stand
The critic eye, and please when near at
 hand;
But others at a distance strike the sight;
This seeks the shade, but that demands the
 light,
Nor dreads the connoisseur's fastidious view,
But, ten times scrutinised, is ten times new.

Parnassian pilgrims! ye whom chance or
 choice
Hath led to listen to the Muse's voice,

Discunt in partes centum diducere: dicat
Filius Albini, Si de quincunce remota est
Uncia, quid superat? poteras dixisse—Triens. Eu!
Rem poteris servare tuam. Redit uncia: quid
 fit?
Semis. An haec animos aerugo et cura peculi
Cum semel imbuerit, speramus carmina fingi
Posse linenda cedro, et levi servanda cupresso?
 Aut prodesse volunt, aut delectare poetae;
Aut simul et iucunda et idonea dicere vitae,
Quidquid praecipies, esto brevis: ut cito dicta
Percipiant animi dociles, teneantque fideles.
Omne supervacuum pleno de pectore manat.
 Ficta voluptatis causa sint proxima veris:
Nec, quodcunque volet, poscat sibi fabula credi:
Neu pransae Lamiae vivum puerum extrahat alvo.
 Centuriae seniorum agitant expertia frugis:
Celsi praetereunt austera poemata Rhamnes.
Omne tulit punctum, qui miscuit utile dulci:
Lectorem delectando pariterque monendo.
Hic meret aera liber Sosiis; hic et mare transit,
Et longum noto scriptori prorogat aevum.
 Sunt delicta tamen, quibus ignovisse velimus:

Nam neque chorda sonum reddit quem vult manus
 et mens,
Poscentique gravem persaepe remittit acutum;
Nec semper feriet quodcunque minabitur arcus.
Verum ubi plura nitent in carmine, non ego paucis
Offendar maculis, quas aut incuria fudit,
Aut humana parum cavit natura. Quid ergo est?
Ut scriptor si peccat idem librarius usque,
Quamvis est monitus, venia caret; ut citharoedus
Ridetur, chorda qui semper oberrat eadem:
Sic mihi, qui multum cessat, fit Choerilus ille,
Quem bis terve bonum cum risu miror; et idem
Indignor, quandoque bonus dormitat Homerus.
Verum operi longo fas est obrepere somnum.
 Ut pictura, poesis: erit quae, si propius stes,
Te capiat magis; et quaedam, si longius abstes:
Haec amat obscurum; volet haec sub luce videri,
Iudicis argutum quae non formidat acumen:
Haec placuit semel; haec decies repetita placebit.
 O maior iuvenum, quamvis et voce paterna
Fingeris ad rectum, et per te sapis, hoc tibi dictum
Tolle memor: certis medium et tolerabile rebus
Recte concedi: consultus iuris, et actor

Receive this counsel, and be timely wise;
Few reach the summit which before you
 lies.
Our church and state, our courts and camps,
 concede
Reward to very moderate heads indeed!
In these plain common sense will travel far;
All are not Erskines who mislead the bar:
But poesy between the best and worst
No medium knows; you must be last or
 first;
For middling poets' miserable volumes
Are damn'd alike by gods, and men, and
 columns.

Again, my Jeffrey!—as that sound in-
 spires,
How wakes my bosom to its wonted fires!
Fires, such as gentle Caledonians feel
When Southrons writhe upon their critic
 wheel,
Or mild Eclectics, when some, worse than
 Turks,
Would rob poor Faith to decorate "good
 works."
Such are the genial feelings thou canst
 claim—
My falcon flies not at ignoble game.
Mightiest of all Dunedin's beasts of chase!
For thee my Pegasus would mend his pace.
Arise, my Jeffrey! or my inkless pen
Shall never blunt its edge on meaner men;
Till thee or thine mine evil eye discerns,
Alas! "I cannot strike at wretched kernes."
Inhuman Saxon! wilt thou then resign
A muse and heart by choice so wholly thine?
Dear d——d contemner of my schoolboy
 songs,
Hast thou no vengeance for my manhood's
 wrongs?
If unprovoked thou once could bid me bleed,
Hast thou no weapon for my daring deed?
What! not a word!—and am I then so low?
Wilt thou forbear, who never spared a foe?
Hast thou no wrath, or wish to give it vent?
No wit for nobles, dunces by descent?
No jest on "minors," quibbles on a name,
Nor one facetious paragraph of blame?

Is it for this on Ilion I have stood,
And thought of Homer less than Holyrood!
On shore of Euxine or Aegean sea,
My hate, untravell'd, fondly turn'd to thee.
Ah! let me cease: in vain my bosom burns,
From Corydon unkind Alexis turns:
Thy rhymes are vain; thy Jeffrey then
 forego,
Nor woo that anger which he will not show.
What then?—Edina starves some lanker son,
To write an article thou canst not shun;
Some less fastidious Scotchman shall be
 found,
As bold in Billingsgate, though less renown'd.

As if at table some discordant dish
Should shock our optics, such as frogs for
 fish;
As oil in lieu of butter men decry,
And poppies please not in a modern pie;
If all such mixtures then be half a crime,
We must have excellence to relish rhyme.
Mere roast and boil'd no epicure invites;
Thus poetry disgusts, or else delights.

Who shoot not flying rarely touch a gun:
Will he who swims not to the river run?
And men unpractised in exchanging knocks
Must go to Jackson ere they dare to box.
Whate'er the weapon, cudgel, fist, or foil,
None reach expertness without years of toil;
But fifty dunces can, with perfect ease,
Tag twenty thousand couplets, when they
 please.
Why not?—shall I, thus qualified to sit
For rotten boroughs, never show my wit?
Shall I, whose fathers with the quorum sate,
And lived in freedom on a fair estate;
Who left me heir, with stables, kennels, packs,
To *all* their income, and to—*twice* its tax;
Whose form and pedigree have scarce a fault,
Shall I, I say, suppress my attic salt?

Thus think "the mob of gentlemen;" but
 you,
Besides all this, must have some genius too.
Be this your sober judgment, and a rule,
And print not piping hot from Southey's
 school,

Causarum mediocris abest virtute diserti
Messalae, nec scit quantum Cascellius Aulus:
Sed tamen in pretio est: mediocribus esse poetis
Non homines, non di, non concessere columnae.
Ut gratas inter mensas symphonia discors,
Et crassum unguentum, et Sardo cum melle papaver
Offendunt, poterat duci quia coena sine istis;
Sic animis natum inventumque poema iuvandis,
Si paulum a summo decessit, vergit ad imum.
 Ludere qui nescit, campestribus abstinet armis,
Indoctusque pilae, discive, trochive, quiescit,
Ne spissae risum tollant impune coronae:
Qui nescit, versus tamen audet fingere!—Quidni?
Liber et ingenuus praesertim census equestrem
Summam nummorum, vitioque remotus ab omni.

Tu nihil invita dices faciesve Minerva:
Id tibi iudicium est, ea mens: si quid tamen olim
Scripseris, in Metii descendat iudicis aures,
Et patris, et nostras, nonumque prematur in annum,
Membranis intus positis: delere licebit
Quod non edideris; nescit vox missa reverti.
 Sylvestres homines sacer interpresque deorum
Caedibus et victu foedo deterruit Orpheus:
Dictus ob hoc lenire tigres, rabidosque leones:
Dictus et Amphion, Thebanae conditor arcis,
Saxa movere sono testudinis, et prece blanda
Ducere quo vellet: fuit haec sapientia quondam,
Publica privatis secernere, sacra profanis;
Concubitu prohibere vago; dare iura maritis;
Oppida moliri; leges incidere ligno.

Who (ere another Thalaba appears)
I trust will spare us for at least nine years.
And hark 'ye, Southey! pray—but don't be
 vex'd—
Burn all your last three works—and half the
 next.
But why this vain advice? once published,
 books
Can never be recall'd—from pastry-cooks!
Though "Madoc," with "Pucelle," instead of
 punk,
May travel back to Quito—on a trunk!

Orpheus, we learn from Ovid and Lem-
 priere,
Led all wild beasts but women by the ear;
And had he fiddled at the present hour,
We'd seen the lions waltzing in the Tower;
And old Amphion, such were minstrels then,
Had built St. Paul's without the aid of Wren.
Verse too was justice, and the bards of
 Greece
Did more than constables to keep the peace;
Abolish'd cuckoldom with much applause,
Call'd county meetings, and enforced the
 laws,
Cut down crown influence with reforming
 scythes,
And served the church—without demanding
 tithes;
And hence, throughout all Hellas and the
 East,
Each poet was a prophet and a priest,
Whose old-establish'd board of joint controls
Included kingdoms in the cure of souls.

Next rose the martial Homer, Epic's
 prince,
And fighting's been in fashion ever since;
And old Tyrtæus, when the Spartans warr'd,
(A limping leader, but a lofty bard,)
Though wall'd Ithome had resisted long,
Reduced the fortress by the force of song.

When oracles prevail'd, in times of old,
In song alone Apollo's will was told.
Then if your verse is what all verse should be,
And gods were not ashamed on 't, why
 should we?

The Muse, like mortal females, may be
 woo'd;
In turns she 'll seem a Paphian, or a prude;

Fierce as a bride when first she feels affright,
Mild as the same upon the second night;
Wild as the wife of alderman or peer,
Now for his grace, and now a grenadier!
Her eyes beseem, her heart belies, her zone,
Ice in a crowd, and lava when alone.

If verse be studied with some show of art,
Kind Nature always will perform her part;
Though without genius, and a native vein
Of wit, we loathe an artificial strain,
Yet art and nature join'd will win the prize,
Unless they act like us and our allies.

The youth who trains to ride, or run a race,
Must bear privations with unruffled face,
Be call'd to labour when he thinks to dine,
And, harder still, leave wenching and his
 wine.
Ladies who sing, at least who sing at sight,
Have follow'd music through her farthest
 flight;
But rhymers tell you neither more nor less,
"I've got a pretty poem for the press;"
And that's enough; then write and print so
 fast;—
If Satan take the hindmost, who'd be last?
They storm the types, they publish, one
 and all,
They leap the counter, and they leave the
 stall.
Provincial maidens, men of high command,
Yea, baronets have ink'd the bloody hand!
Cash cannot quell them; Pollio play'd this
 prank,
(Then Phœbus first found credit in a bank!)
Not all the living only, but the dead,
Fool on, as fluent as an Orpheus' head;
Damn'd all their days, they posthumously
 thrive,
Dug up from dust, though buried when alive!
Reviews record this epidemic crime,
Those Books of Martyrs to the rage for
 rhyme,
Alas! woe worth the scribbler! often seen
In Morning Post or Monthly Magazine.
There lurk his earlier lays; but soon, hot
 press'd,
Behold a quarto!—Tarts must tell the rest.
Then leave, ye wise, the lyre's precarious
 chords
To muse-mad baronets, or madder lords,

Sic honor et nomen divinis vatibus atque
Carminibus venit. Post hos insignis Homerus
Tyrtaeusque mares animos in Martia bella
Versibus exacuit; dictae per carmina sortes:
Et vitae monstrata via est: et gratia regum
Pieriis tentata modis: ludusque repertus,
Et longorum operum finis: ne forte pudori
Sit tibi Musa lyrae solers, et cantor Apollo.
 Natura fieret laudabile carmen, an arte,
Quaesitum est: ego nec studium sine divite vena,

Nec rude quid possit video ingenium: alterius sic
Altera poscit opem res, et coniurat amice.
Qui studet optatam cursu contingere metam,
Multa tulit fecitque puer; sudavit et alsit;
Abstinuit Venere et vino; qui Pythia cantat
Tibicen, didicit prius, extimuitque magistrum.
Nunc satis est dixisse: ego mira poemata pango:
Occupet extremum scabies; mihi turpe relinqui est,
Et, quod non didici, sane nescire fateri.

Or country Crispins, now grown somewhat stale,
Twin Doric minstrels, drunk with Doric ale!
Hark to those notes, narcotically soft!
The cobbler-laureats sing to Capel Lofft!
Till, lo! that modern Midas, as he hears,
Adds an ell growth to his egregious ears!

There lives one druid, who prepares in time
'Gainst future feuds his poor revenge of rhyme;
Racks his dull memory, and his duller muse,
To publish faults which friendship should excuse.
If friendship's nothing, self-regard might teach
More polish'd usage of his parts of speech.
But what is shame, or what is aught to him?
He vents his spleen, or gratifies his whim.
Some fancied slight has roused his lurking hate,
Some folly cross'd, some jest, or some debate;
Up to his den Sir Scribbler hies, and soon
The gather'd gall is voided in lampoon.
Perhaps at some pert speech you've dared to frown,
Perhaps your poem may have pleased the town:
If so, alas! 'tis nature in the man—
May Heaven forgive you, for he never can!
Then be it so; and may his withering bays
Bloom fresh in satire, though they fade in praise!
While his lost songs no more shall steep and stink,
The dullest, fattest weeds on Lethe's brink,
But springing upwards from the sluggish mould,
Be (what they never were before) be—sold!
Should some rich bard (but such a monster now,
In modern physics, we can scarce allow),
Should some pretending scribbler of the court,
Some rhyming peer—there's plenty of the sort—
All but one poor dependent priest withdrawn,

(Ah! too regardless of his chaplain's yawn!)
Condemn the unlucky curate to recite
Their last dramatic work by candle-light,
How would the preacher turn each rueful leaf,
Dull as his sermons, but not half so brief!
Yet, since 't is promised at the rector's death,
He'll risk no living for a little breath.
Then spouts and foams, and cries at every line,
(The Lord forgive him!) "Bravo! grand! divine!"
Hoarse with those praises (which, by flatt'ry fed,
Dependence barters for her bitter bread),
He strides and stamps along with creaking boot;
Till the floor echoes his emphatic foot,
Then sits again, then rolls his pious eye,
As when the dying vicar will not die!
Nor feels, forsooth, emotion at his heart;—
But all dissemblers overact their part.

Ye, who aspire to "build the lofty rhyme,"
Believe not all who laud your false "sublime;"
But if some friend shall hear your work, and say,
"Expunge that stanza, lop that line away,"
And, after fruitless efforts, you return
Without amendment, and he answers, "Burn!"
That instant throw your paper in the fire,
Ask not his thoughts, or follow his desire;
But if (true bard!) you scorn to condescend,
And will not alter what you can't defend,
If you will breed this bastard of your brains,
We'll have no words—I've only lost my pains.

Yet, if you only prize your favourite thought,
As critics kindly do, and authors ought;
If your cool friend annoy you now and then,
And cross whole pages with his plaguy pen;
No matter, throw your ornaments aside,—
Better let him than all the world deride.
Give light to passages too much in shade,
Nor let a doubt obscure one verse you've made;

—— Si carmina condes,
Nunquam te fallant animi sub vulpe latentes.
Quintilio si quid recitares, Corrige, sodes,
Hoc (aiebat) et hoc: melius te posse negares,
Bis terque expertúm frustra, delere iubebat,
Et male tornatos incudi reddere versus.
Si defendere delictum quam vertere malles,

Nullum ultra verbum, aut operam insumebat inanem,
Quin sine rivali teque et tua solus amares.
Vir bonus et prudens versus reprehendet inertes;
Culpabit duros; incomptis allinet atrum
Transverso calamo signum; ambitiosa recidet
Ornamenta; parum claris lucem dare coget;
Arguet ambigue dictum; mutanda notabit;

Your friend's a "Johnson," not to leave one
 word,
However trifling, which may seem absurd;
Such erring trifles lead to serious ills,
And furnish food for critics, or their quills.

 As the Scotch fiddle, with its touching
 tune,
Or the sad influence of the angry moon,
All men avoid bad writers' ready tongues,
As yawning waiters fly Fitzscribble's lungs;
Yet on he mouths—ten minutes—tedious each
As prelate's homily, or placeman's speech;
Long as the last years of a lingering lease,
When riot pauses until rents increase.
While such a minstrel, muttering fustian,
 strays
O'er hedge and ditch, through unfrequented
 ways,
If by some chance he walks into a well,
And shouts for succour with stentorian yell,
"A rope! help, Christians, as ye hope for
 grace!"
Nor woman, man, nor child will stir a pace;
For there his carcass he might freely fling,
From frenzy, or the humour of the thing.
Though this has happen'd to more bards
 than one;
I'll tell you Budgell's story,—and have done.

Budgell, a rogue and rhymester, for no
 good,
(Unless his case be much misunderstood,)
When teased with creditors' continual claims,
"To die like Cato," leapt into the Thames!
And therefore be it lawful through the town
For any bard to poison, hang, or drown.
Who saves the intended suicide receives
Small thanks from him who loathes the life
 he leaves;
And, sooth to say, mad poets must not
 lose
The glory of that death they freely choose.

 Nor is it certain that some sorts of verse
Prick not the poet's conscience as a curse;
Dosed with vile drams on Sunday he was
 found,
Or got a child on consecrated ground!
And hence is haunted with a rhyming rage—
Fear'd like a bear just bursting from his
 cage.
If free, all fly his versifying fit,
Fatal at once to simpleton or wit:
But *him*, unhappy! whom he seizes,—*him*
He flays with recitation limb by limb;
Probes to the quick where'er he makes his
 breach,
And gorges like a lawyer—or a leech.

Fiet Aristarchus: nec dicet, Cur ego amicum
Offendam in nugis? hae nugae seria ducent
In mala derisum semel exceptumque sinistre.
 Ut mala quem scabies aut morbus regius urget,
Aut fanaticus error et iracunda Diana,
Vesanum tetigisse timent fugiuntque poetam,
Qui sapiunt; agitant pueri, incautique sequuntur.
Hic, dum sublimis versus ructatur, et errat,
Si veluti merulis intentus decidit auceps
In puteum, foveamve; licet, Succurrite, longum
Clamet, Io cives! non sit qui tollere curet.
Si quis curet opem ferre, et demittere funem,
Qui scis an prudens huc se deiecerit, atque
Servari nolit? dicam: Siculique poetae

Narrabo interitum. Deus immortalis haberi
Dum cupit Empedocles, ardentem frigidus Aet-
 nam
Insiluit. Sit ius liceatque perire poetis:
Invitum qui servat, idem facit occidenti.
Nec semel hoc fecit; nec, si retractus erit, iam
Fiet homo, et ponet famosae mortis amorem.
Nec satis apparet cur versus factitet; utrum
Minxerit in patrios cineres, an triste bidental
Moverit incestus: certe furit, ac velut ursus,
Obiectos caveae valuit si frangere clathros,
Indoctum doctumque fugat recitator acerbus.
Quem vero arripuit, tenet, occiditque legendo,
Non missura cutem, nisi plena cruoris, hirudo.

The Curse of Minerva.

——"Pallas te hoc vulnere, Pallas
Immolat, et poenam scelerato ex sanguine sumit."
Aeneid, lib. xii.

ATHENS: CAPUCHIN CONVENT,
March 17, 1811.

Slow sinks, more lovely ere his race be run,
Along Morea's hills the setting sun;
Not, as in northern climes, obscurely bright,
But one unclouded blaze of living light;
O'er the hush'd deep the yellow beam he throws,
Gilds the green wave that trembles as it glows;
On old Aegina's rock and Hydra's isle
The god of gladness sheds his parting smile;
O'er his own regions lingering loves to shine,
Though there his altars are no more divine.
Descending fast, the mountain-shadows kiss
Thy glorious gulf, unconquer'd Salamis!
Their azure arches through the long expanse,
More deeply purpled, meet his mellowing glance,
And tenderest tints, along their summits driven,
Mark his gay course, and own the hues of heaven;
Till, darkly shaded from the land and deep,
Behind his Delphian rock he sinks to sleep.

On such an eve his palest beam he cast
When, Athens! here thy wisest look'd his last,
How watch'd thy better sons his farewell ray,
That closed their murder'd sage's latest day!
Not yet—not yet—Sol pauses on the hill,
The precious hour of parting lingers still;
But sad his light to agonising eyes,
And dark the mountain's once delightful dyes;
Gloom o'er the lovely land he seem'd to pour,
The land where Phoebus never frown'd before;
But ere he sunk below Citheron's head,
The cup of woe was quaff'd—the spirit fled;
The soul of him that scorn'd to fear or fly,
Who lived and died as none can live or die.

But, lo! from high Hymettus to the plain
The queen of night asserts her silent reign;
No murky vapour, herald of the storm,
Hides her fair face, or girds her glowing form,
With cornice glimmering as the moonbeams play,
There the white column greets her grateful ray,
And bright around, with quivering beams beset,
Her emblem sparkles o'er the minaret:
The groves of olive scatter'd dark and wide,
Where meek Cephisus sheds his scanty tide,
The cypress saddening by the sacred mosque,
The gleaming turret of the gay kiosk,
And sad and sombre 'mid the holy calm,
Near Theseus' fane, yon solitary palm;
All, tinged with varied hues, arrest the eye;
And dull were his that pass'd them heedless by.

Again the Aegean, heard no more afar,
Lulls his chafed breast from elemental war:
Again his waves in milder tints unfold
Their long expanse of sapphire and of gold,
Mix'd with the shades of many a distant isle
That frown, where gentler ocean deigns to smile.

As thus, within the walls of Pallas' fane,
I mark'd the beauties of the land and main,
Alone, and friendless, on the magic shore,
Whose arts and arms but live in poets' lore;
Oft as the matchless dome I turn'd to scan,
Sacred to gods, but not secure from man,
The past return'd, the present seem'd to cease,
And Glory knew no clime beyond her Greece!

Hours roll'd along, and Dian's orb on high
Had gain'd the centre of her softest sky;
And yet unwearied still my footsteps trod
O'er the vain shrine of many a vanish'd god:

But chiefly, Pallas! thine, when Hecate's
glare,
Check'd by thy columns, fell more sadly fair
O'er the chill marble, where the startling
tread
Thrills the lone heart like echoes from the
dead.
Long had I mused, and treasured every
trace
The wreck of Greece recorded of her race,
When, lo! a giant form before me strode,
And Pallas hail'd me in her own abode!

Yes, 'twas Minerva's self; but, ah! how
changed,
Since o'er the Dardan field in arms she
ranged!
Not such as erst, by her divine command,
Her form appear'd from Phidias' plastic
hand:
Gone were the terrors of her awful brow,
Her idle aegis bore no Gorgon now;
Her helm was dinted, and the broken lance
Seem'd weak and shaftless e'en to mortal
glance;
The olive branch, which still she deign'd to
clasp,
Shrunk from her touch, and wither'd in her
grasp;
And, ah! though still the brightest of the
sky,
Celestial tears bedimm'd her large blue eye:
Round the rent casque her owlet circled
slow,
And mourn'd his mistress with a shriek of
woe!

"Mortal!"—'twas thus she spake—"that
blush of shame
Proclaims thee Briton, once a noble name;
First of the mighty, foremost of the free,
Now honour'd _less_ by all, and _least_ by me:
Chief of thy foes shall Pallas still be found.
Seek'st thou the cause of loathing?—look
around.
Lo! here, despite of war and wasting fire,
I saw successive tyrannies expire.
'Scaped from the ravage of the Turk and
Goth,
Thy country sends a spoiler worse than both.
Survey this vacant, violated fane;
Recount the relics torn that yet remain:
These Cecrops placed, _this_ Pericles adorn'd,
That Adrian rear'd when drooping Science
mourn'd.
What more I owe let gratitude attest—
Know, Alaric and Elgin did the rest.
That all may learn from whence the plunderer
came,
The insulted wall sustains his hated name:

For Elgin's fame thus grateful Pallas pleads,
Below, his name—above, behold his deeds!
Be ever hail'd with equal honour here
The Gothic monarch and the Pictish peer:
Arms gave the first his right, the last had
none,
But basely stole what less barbarians won.
So when the lion quits his fell repast,
Next prowls the wolf, the filthy jackal last:
Flesh, limbs, and blood the former make
their own,
The last poor brute securely gnaws the bone.
Yet still the gods are just, and crimes are
cross'd:
See here what Elgin won, and what he lost!
Another name with _his_ pollutes my shrine:
Behold where Dian's beams disdain to shine!
Some retribution still might Pallas claim,
When Venus half avenged Minerva's shame."

She ceased awhile, and thus I dared reply,
To soothe the vengeance kindling in her
eye:
"Daughter of Jove! in Britain's injured
name,
A true-born Briton may the deed disclaim.
Frown not on England; England owns him
not:
Athena, no! thy plunderer was a Scot.
Ask'st thou the difference? From fair Phyles'
towers
Survey Bœotia;—Caledonia's ours.
And well I know within that bastard land
Hath Wisdom's goddess never held command;
A barren soil, where Nature's germs, confined
To stern sterility, can stint the mind;
Whose thistle well betrays the niggard earth,
Emblem of all to whom the land gives
birth;
Each genial influence nurtured to resist;
A land of meanness, sophistry, and mist.
Each breeze from foggy mount and marshy
plain
Dilutes with drivel every drizzly brain,
Till, burst at length, each wat'ry head o'er-
flows,
Foul as their soil, and frigid as their snows:
Then thousand schemes of petulance and
pride
Despatch her scheming children far and
wide:
Some east, some west, some everywhere but
north,
In quest of lawless gain, they issue forth.
And thus—accursed be the day and year!
She sent a Pict to play the felon here.
Yet Caledonia claims some native worth,
As dull Bœotia gave a Pindar birth;
So may her few, the letter'd and the brave,
Bound to no clime, and victors of the grave,

Shake off the sordid dust of such a land,
And shine like children of a happier strand;
As once, of yore, in some obnoxious place,
Ten names (if found) had saved a wretched
race."

"Mortal!" the blue-eyed maid resumed,
"once more
Bear back my mandate to thy native shore.
Though fallen, alas! this vengeance yet is
mine,
To turn my counsels far from lands like
thine.
Hear then in silence Pallas' stern behest;
Hear and believe, for time will tell the rest.

"First on the head of him who did this
deed
My curse shall light,—on him and all his
seed:
Without one spark of intellectual fire,
Be all the sons as senseless as the sire:
If one with wit the parent brood disgrace,
Believe him bastard of a brighter race:
Still with his hireling artists let him prate,
And Folly's praise repay for Wisdom's hate;
Long of their patron's gusto let them tell,
Whose noblest, *native* gusto is—to sell:
To sell, and make—may shame record the
day!—
The state receiver of his pilfer'd prey.
Meantime, the flattering, feeble dotard, West,
Europe's worst dauber, and poor Britain's
best,
With palsied hand shall turn each model o'er,
And own himself an infant of fourscore.
Be all the bruisers cull'd from all St. Giles',
That art and nature may compare their
styles;
While brawny brutes in stupid wonder stare,
And marvel at his lordship's 'stone shop'
there.
Round the throng'd gate shall sauntering
coxcombs creep,
To lounge and lucubrate, to prate and peep;
While many a languid maid, with longing
sigh,
On giant statues casts the curious eye;
The room with transient glance appears to
skim
Yet marks the mighty back and length of
limb;
Mourns o'er the difference of *now* and *then;*
Exclaims, 'These Greeks indeed were proper
men!'
Draws slight comparisons of *these* with *those*,
And envies Laïs all her Attic beaux.
When shall a modern maid have swains like
these!
Alas! Sir Harry is no Hercules!

And last of all, amidst the gaping crew,
Some calm spectator, as he takes his view,
In silent indignation mix'd with grief,
Admires the plunder, but abhors the thief.
Oh, loath'd in life, nor pardon'd in the dust,
May hate pursue his sacrilegious lust!
Link'd with the fool that fired the Ephesian
dome,
Shall vengeance follow far beyond the tomb,
And Eratostratus and Elgin shine
In many a branding page and burning line;
Alike reserved for aye to stand accursed,
Perchance the second blacker than the first.

"So let him stand, through ages yet un-
born,
Fix'd statue on the pedestal of Scorn;
Though not for him alone revenge shall wait,
But fits thy country for her coming fate:
Hers were the deeds that taught her lawless
son
To do what oft Britannia's self had done.
Look to the Baltic—blazing from afar,
Your old ally yet mourns perfidious war.
Not to such deeds did Pallas lend her aid,
Or break the compact which herself had
made;
Far from such councils, from the faithless
field
She fled—but left behind her Gorgon shield;
A fatal gift that turn'd your friends to stone,
And left lost Albion hated and alone.

"Look to the East, where Ganges' swarthy
race
Shall shake your tyrant empire to its base;
Lo! there Rebellion rears her ghastly head,
And glares the Nemesis of native dead;
Till Indus rolls a deep purpureal flood
And claims his long arrear of northern blood.
So may ye perish! Pallas, when she gave
Your free-born rights, forbade ye to enslave.

"Look on your Spain!—she clasps the
hand she hates,
But boldly clasps, and thrusts you from her
gates.
Bear witness, bright Barossa! thou canst tell
Whose were the sons that bravely fought and
fell.
But Lusitania, kind and dear ally,
Can spare a few to fight, and sometimes fly.
Oh glorious field! by Famine fiercely won,
The Gaul retires for once, and all is done!
But when did Pallas teach, that one retreat
Retrieved three long olympiads of defeat?

"Look last at home—ye love not to look
there;
On the grim smile of comfortless despair:

Your city saddens: loud though Revel howls,
Here Famine faints, and yonder Rapine
 prowls.
See all alike of more or less bereft;
No misers tremble when there's nothing left.
'Blest paper credit;' who shall dare to sing?
It clogs like lead Corruption's weary wing.
Yet Pallas pluck'd each premier by the ear,
Who gods and men alike disdain'd to hear;
But one, repentant o'er a bankrupt state,
On Pallas calls,—but calls, alas! too late:
Then raves for . . . ; to that Mentor bends,
Though he and Pallas never yet were friends.
Him senates hear, whom never yet they
 heard,
Contemptuous once, and now no less absurd.
So, once of yore, each reasonable frog
Swore faith and fealty to his sovereign 'log.'
Thus hail'd your rulers their patrician clod,
As Egypt chose an onion for a god.

 "Now fare ye well! enjoy your little hour;
Go, grasp the shadow of your vanish'd power;
Gloss o'er the failure of each fondest scheme;
Your strength a name, your bloated wealth
 a dream.
Gone is that gold, the marvel of mankind,
And pirates barter all that's left behind.
No more the hirelings, purchased near and far,
Crowd to the ranks of mercenary war.
The idle merchant on the useless quay
Droops o'er the bales no bark may bear
 away;
Or, back returning, sees rejected stores
Rot piecemeal on his own encumber'd shores:
The starved mechanic breaks his rusting
 loom,
And desperate mans him 'gainst the coming
 doom.
Then in the senate of your sinking state
Show me the man whose counsels may have
 weight.
Vain is each voice where tones could once
 command;
E'en factions cease to charm a factious land:
Yet jarring sects convulse a sister isle,
And light with maddening hands the mutual
 pile.

 "'Tis done, 'tis past, since Pallas warns
 in vain;
The Furies seize her abdicated reign:
Wide o'er the realm they wave their kindling
 brands,
And wring her vitals with their fiery hands.
But one convulsive struggle still remains,
And Gaul shall weep ere Albion wear her
 chains.
The banner'd pomp of war, the glittering
 files,
O'er whose gay trappings stern Bellona
 smiles;
The brazen trump, the spirit-stirring drum,
That bid the foe defiance ere they come;
The hero bounding at his country's call,
The glorious death that consecrates his fall,
Swell the young heart with visionary charms,
And bid it antedate the joys of arms.
But know, a lesson you may yet be taught,
With death alone are laurels cheaply bought:
Not in the conflict Havoc seeks delight,
His day of mercy is the day of fight.
But when the field is fought, the battle
 won,
Though drench'd with gore, his woes are but
 begun:
His deeper deeds as yet ye know by name;
The slaughter'd peasant and the ravish'd
 dame,
The rifled mansion and the foe-reap'd field,
Ill suit with souls at home, untaught to yield.
Say with what eye along the distant down
Would flying burghers mark the blazing
 town?
How view the column of ascending flames
Shake his red shadow o'er the startled
 Thames?
Nay, frown not, Albion! for the torch was
 thine
That lit such pyres from Tagus to the
 Rhine:
Now should they burst on thy devoted coast,
Go, ask thy bosom who deserves them
 most.
The law of heaven and earth is life for life,
And she who raised, in vain regrets, the
 strife."

The Waltz:

AN APOSTROPHIC HYMN.

———◆◆———

"Qualis in Eurotae ripis, aut per iuga Cynthi,
Exercet Diana choros."—VIRGIL.

"Such on Eurota's banks, or Cynthia's height,
Diana seems: and so she charms the sight,
When in the dance the graceful goddess leads
The quire of nymphs, and overtops their heads."
DRYDEN'S VIRGIL.

———◆◆———

TO THE PUBLISHER.

SIR,

I AM a country gentleman of a midland county. I might have been a parliament man for a certain borough; having had the offer of as many votes as General T. at the general election in 1812*. But I was all for domestic happiness; as, fifteen years ago, on a visit to London, I married a middle-aged maid of honour. We lived happily at Hornem Hall till last season, when my wife and I were invited by the Countess of Waltzaway (a distant relation of my spouse) to pass the winter in town. Thinking no harm, and our girls being come to a marriageable (or, as they call it, *marketable*) age, and having besides a Chancery suit inveterately entailed upon the family estate, we came up in our old chariot,—of which, by the by, my wife grew so much ashamed in less than a week, that I was obliged to buy a second-hand barouche, of which I might mount the box, Mrs. H. says, if I could drive, but never see the inside—that place being reserved for the Honourable Augustus Tiptoe, her partner-general and opera-knight. Hearing great praises of Mrs. H.'s dancing (she was famous for birthnight minuets in the latter end of the last century), I unbooted, and went to a ball at the Countess's, expecting to see a country dance, or at most, cotillons, reels, and all the old paces to the newest tunes. But, judge of my surprise, on arriving, to see poor dear Mrs. Hornem with her arms half round the loins of a huge hussar-looking gentleman I never set eyes on before; and his, to say truth, rather more than half round her waist, turning round and round to a d——d see-saw up-and-down sort of tune, that reminded me of the "Black Joke," only more "*affettuoso*," till it made me quite giddy with wondering they were not so. By-and-by they stopped a bit, and I thought they

would sit or fall down:—but no; with Mrs. H.'s hand on his shoulder, "*quam familiariter**," (as Terence said, when I was at school,) they walked about a minute, and then at it again, like two cock-chafers spitted on the same bodkin. I asked what all this meant, when, with a loud laugh, a child no older than our Wilhelmina (a name I never heard but in the Vicar of Wakefield, though her mother would call her after the Princess of Swappenbach,) said, "Lord! Mr. Hornem, can't you see they're valtzing?" or waltzing (I forget which); and then up she got, and her mother and sister, and away they went, and round-abouted it till supper-time. Now, that I know what it is, I like it of all things, and so does Mrs. H. (though I have broken my shins, and four times overturned Mrs. Hornem's maid, in practising the preliminary steps in a morning). Indeed, so much do I like it, that having a turn for rhyme, tastily displayed in some election ballads, and songs in honour of all the victories (but till lately I have had little practice in that way), I sat down, and with the aid of William Fitzgerald, Esq., and a few hints from Dr. Busby, (whose recitations I attend, and am monstrous fond of Master Busby's manner of delivering his father's late successful "Drury Lane Address,") I composed the following hymn, wherewithal to make my sentiments known to the public; whom, nevertheless, I heartily despise, as well as the critics.

I am, Sir, yours, &c. &c.,

HORACE HORNEM.

———

* My Latin is all forgotten, if a man can be said to have forgotten what he never remembered; but I bought my title-page motto of a Catholic priest for a three-shilling bank token, after much haggling for the even sixpence. I grudged the money to a Papist, being all for the memory of Perceval and "No Popery," and quite regretting the downfall of the pope, because we can't burn him any more.

———

* State of the poll (last day) 5.

THE WALTZ.

MUSE of the many-twinkling feet! whose
 charms
Are now extended up from legs to arms;
Terpsichore!—too long misdeem'd a maid—
Reproachful term—bestow'd but to upbraid—
Henceforth in all the bronze of brightness
 shine,
The least a vestal of the virgin Nine.
Far be from thee and thine the name of prude:
Mock'd, yet triumphant; sneer'd at, un-
 subdued;
Thy legs must move to conquer as they fly,
If but thy coats are reasonably high;
Thy breast—if bare enough—requires no
 shield;
Dance forth—*sans armour* thou shalt take
 the field,
And own—impregnable to *most* assaults,
Thy not too lawfully begotten "Waltz."

Hail, nimble nymph! to whom the young
 hussar,
The whisker'd votary of waltz and war,
His night devotes, despite of spur and boots;
A sight unmatch'd since Orpheus and his
 brutes:
Hail, spirit-stirring Waltz!—beneath whose
 banners
A modern hero fought for modish manners;
On Hounslow's heath to rival Wellesley's fame,
Cock'd, fired, and miss'd his man—but gain'd
 his aim;
Hail, moving muse! to whom the fair one's
 breast
Gives all it can, and bids us take the rest.
Oh! for the flow of Busby, or of Fitz,
The latter's loyalty, the former's wits,
To "energise the object I pursue,"
And give both Belial and his dance their due!

Imperial Waltz! imported from the Rhine
(Famed for the growth of pedigrees and wine),
Long be thine import from all duty free,
And hock itself be less esteem'd than thee;
In some few qualities alike—for hock
Improves our cellar—*thou* our living stock.
The head to hock belongs—thy subtler art
Intoxicates alone the heedless heart:
Through the full veins thy gentler poison
 swims,
And wakes to wantonness the willing limbs.

Oh, Germany! how much to thee we owe,
As heaven-born Pitt can testify below,
Ere cursed confederation made thee France's,
And only left us thy d——d debts and dances!

Of subsidies and Hanover bereft,
We bless thee still—for George the Third is
 left!
Of kings the best—and last, not least in worth,
For graciously begetting George the Fourth.
To Germany, and highnesses serene,
Who owe us millions—don't we owe the
 queen?
To Germany, what owe we not besides?
So oft bestowing Brunswickers and brides;
Who paid for vulgar, with her royal blood,
Drawn from the stem of each Teutonic stud:
Who sent us—so be pardon'd all her faults—
A dozen dukes, some kings, a queen—and
 Waltz.

But peace to her—her emperor and diet,
Though now transferr'd to Buonaparte's
 "fiat!"
Back to my theme—O Muse of motion! say,
How first to Albion found thy Waltz her
 way!

Borne on the breath of hyperborean gales,
From Hamburg's port (while Hamburg yet
 had *mails*),
Ere yet unlucky Fame—compell'd to creep
To snowy Gottenburg—was chill'd to sleep;
Or, starting from her slumbers, deign'd arise,
Heligoland! to stock thy mart with lies;
While unburnt Moscow yet had news to send,
Nor owed her fiery exit to a friend,
She came—Waltz came—and with her certain
 sets
Of true despatches, and as true gazettes:
Then flamed of Austerlitz the blest despatch,
Which "Moniteur" nor "Morning Post" can
 match;
And—almost crush'd beneath the glorious
 news—
Ten plays, and forty tales of Kotzebue's;
One envoy's letters, six composers' airs,
And loads from Frankfort and from Leipsic
 fairs;
Meiner's four volumes upon womankind,
Like Lapland witches to insure a wind;
Brunck's heaviest tome for ballast, and, to
 back it,
Of Heyné, such as should not sink the packet.

Fraught with this cargo—and her fairest
 freight,
Delightful Waltz, on tiptoe for a mate,
The welcome vessel reach'd the genial strand,
And round her flock'd the daughters of the land:

Not decent David, when, before the ark,
His grand pas-seul excited some remark;
Not love-lorn Quixote, when his Sancho
 thought
The knight's fandango friskier than it ought;
Not soft Herodias, when, with winning tread,
Her nimble feet danced off another's head;
Not Cleopatra on her galley's deck,
Display'd so much of *leg*, or more of *neck*,
Than thou, ambrosial Waltz, when first the
 moon
Beheld thee twirling to a Saxon tune!

 To you, ye husbands of ten years! whose
 brows
Ache with the annual tributes of a spouse;
To you of nine years less, who only bear
The budding sprouts of those that you *shall*
 wear,
With added ornaments around them roll'd
Of native brass, or law-awarded gold;
To you, ye matrons, ever on the watch
To mar a son's, or make a daughter's match;
To you, ye children of—whom chance ac-
 cords—
Always the ladies, and *sometimes* their lords;
To you, ye single gentlemen, who seek
Torments for life, or pleasures for a week;
As Love or Hymen your endeavours guide,
To gain your own, or snatch another's
 bride;—
To one and all the lovely stranger came,
And every ball-room echoes with her name.

 Endearing Waltz!—to thy more melting
 tune
Bow Irish jig and ancient rigadoon.
Scotch reels, avaunt! and country-dance,
 forego
Your future claims to each fantastic toe!
Waltz—Waltz alone—both legs and arms
 demands,
Liberal of feet, and lavish of her hands;
Hands which may freely range in public
 sight
Where ne'er before—but—pray "put out the
 light."
Methinks the glare of yonder chandelier
Shines much too far—or I am much too
 near;
And true, though strange—Waltz whispers
 this remark,
"My slippery steps are safest in the dark!"
But here the Muse with due decorum halts,
And lends her longest petticoat to Waltz.

 Observant travellers of every time!
Ye quartos publish'd upon every clime!
O say, shall dull Romaika's heavy round,
Fandango's wriggles, or Bolero's bound;

Can Egypt's Almas—tantalising group—
Columbia's caperers to the warlike whoop—
Can aught from cold Kamschatka to Cape
 Horn
With Waltz compare, or after Waltz be
 borne?
Ah, no! from Morier's pages down to Galt's,
Each tourist pens a paragraph for "Waltz."

 Shades of those belles whose reign began
 of yore,
With George the Third's—and ended long
 before!—
Though in your daughters' daughters yet you
 thrive,
Burst from your lead, and be yourselves
 alive!
Back to the ball-room speed your spectred
 host,
Fool's Paradise is dull to that you lost.
No treacherous powder bids conjecture
 quake;
No stiff-starched stays make meddling-fingers
 ache;
(Transferr'd to those ambiguous things that
 ape
Goats in their visage, women in their shape;)
No damsel faints when rather closely press'd,
But more caressing seems when most ca-
 ress'd;
Superfluous hartshorn, and reviving salts,
Both banish'd by the sovereign cordial
 "Waltz."

 Seductive Waltz!—though on thy native
 shore
Even Werter's self proclaim'd thee half a
 whore;
Werter—to decent vice though much in-
 clined,
Yet warm, not wanton; dazzled, but not
 blind—
Though gentle Genlis, in her strife with
 Stael,
Would even proscribe thee from a Paris ball;
The fashion hails—from countesses to queens,
And maids and valets waltz behind the
 scenes;
Wide and more wide thy witching circle
 spreads,
And turns—if nothing else—at least our
 heads;
With thee even clumsy cits attempt to
 bounce,
And cockneys practise what they can't
 pronounce.
Gods! how the glorious theme my strain
 exalts,
And rhyme finds partner rhyme in praise of
 "Waltz!"

Blest was the time Waltz chose for her
　début;
The court, the Regent, like herself were
　new;
New face for friends, for foes some new
　rewards;
New ornaments for black and royal guards;
New laws to hang the rogues that roar'd for
　bread;
New coins (most new) to follow those that
　fled;
New victories—nor can we prize them less,
Though Jenky wonders at his own success;
New wars, because the old succeed so well,
That most survivors envy those who fell;
New mistresses—no, old—and yet 'tis true,
Though they be *old*, the *thing* is something
　new;
Each new, quite new—(except some ancient
　tricks),
New white-sticks, gold-sticks, broom-sticks,
　all new sticks!
With vests or ribands—deck'd alike in hue,
New troopers strut, new turncoats blush in
　blue:
So saith the muse: my ——, what say
　you?
Such was the time when Waltz might best
　maintain
Her new preferments in this novel reign;
Such was the time, nor ever yet was such;
Hoops are *no more*, and petticoats *not much;*
Morals and minuets, virtue and her stays,
And tell-tale powder—all have had their
　days.
The ball begins—the honours of the house
First duly done by daughter or by spouse,
Some potentate—or royal or serene—
With Kent's gay grace, or sapient Gloster's
　mien,
Leads forth the ready dame, whose rising
　flush
Might once have been mistaken for a blush.
From where the garb just leaves the bosom
　free,
That spot where hearts were once supposed
　to be;
Round all the confines of the yielded waist,
The strangest hand may wander undisplaced;
The lady's in return may grasp as much
As princely paunches offer to her touch.
Pleased round the chalky floor how well they
　trip,
One hand reposing on the royal hip;
The other to the shoulder no less royal
Ascending with affection truly loyal!
Thus front to front the partners move or
　stand,
The foot may rest, but none withdraw the
　hand;

And all in turn may follow in their rank,
The Earl of—Asterisk—and Lady—Blank;
Sir—Such-a-one—with those of fashion's
　host,
For whose blest surnames—vide "Morning
　Post."
(Or if for that impartial print too late,
Search Doctors' Commons six months from
　my date)—
Thus all and each, in movement swift or
　slow,
The genial contact gently undergo;
Till some might marvel, with the modest
　Turk,
If "nothing follows all this palming work?"
True, honest Mirza!—you may trust my
　rhyme—
Something does follow at a fitter time;
The breast thus publicly resign'd to man,
In private may resist him——if it can.

O ye who loved our grandmothers of yore,
Fitzpatrick, Sheridan, and many more!
And thou, my prince! whose sovereign taste
　and will
It is to love the lovely beldames still!
Thou ghost of Queensberry! whose judging
　sprite
Satan may spare to peep a single night,
Pronounce—if ever in your days of bliss
Asmodeus struck so bright a stroke as this;
To teach the young ideas how to rise,
Flush in the cheek, and languish in the eyes:
Rush to the heart, and lighten through the
　frame,
With half-told wish, and ill-dissembled flame,
For prurient nature still will storm the
　breast—
Who, tempted thus, can answer for the rest?

But ye—who never felt a single thought
For what our morals are to be, or ought;
Who wisely wish the charms you view to
　reap,
Say—would you make those beauties quite
　so cheap?
Hot from the hands promiscuously applied,
Round the slight waist, or down the glowing
　side,
Where were the rapture then to clasp the
　form
From this lewd grasp and lawless contact
　warm
At once love's most endearing thought resign,
To press the hand so press'd by none but
　thine;
To gaze upon that eye which never met
Another's ardent look without regret;
Approach the lip which all, without restraint,
Come near enough—if not to touch—to taint;

If such thou lovest—love her then no
more,
Or give—like her—caresses to a score;
Her mind with these is gone, and with it
go
The little left behind it to bestow.

 Voluptuous Waltz! and dare I thus
 blaspheme?
Thy bard forgot thy praises were his theme.

Terpsichore, forgive!—at every ball
My wife *now* waltzes—and my daughters
 shall;
My son—(or stop—'tis needless to inquire—
These little accidents should ne'er transpire;
Some ages hence our genealogic tree
Will wear as green a bough for him as me)—
Waltzing shall rear, to make our name
 amends,
Grandsons for me—in heirs to all his friends.

The Blues:

A LITERARY ECLOGUE.

"Nimium ne crede colori."—VIRGIL.

O trust not, ye beautiful creatures, to hue,
Though your *hair* were as *red* as your *stockings* are *blue*.

ECLOGUE THE FIRST.

London.—Before the Door of a Lecture Room.

 Enter TRACY, *meeting* INKEL.

Ink. You're too late.
Tra. Is it over?
Ink. Nor will be this hour.
But the benches are cramm'd like a garden
 in flower,
With the pride of our belles, who have made
 it the fashion;
So, instead of "beaux arts," we may say "la
 belle passion"
For learning, which lately has taken the
 lead in
The world, and set all the fine gentlemen
 reading.
 Tra. I know it too well, and have worn out
 my patience
With studying to study your new publications.
There's Vamp, Scamp, and Mouthy, and
 Wordswords and Co.
With their damnable——
 Ink. Hold, my good friend, do you know
 Whom you speak to?
 Tra. Right well, boy, and so does "the
 Row:"
You're an author—a poet—
 Ink. And think you that I
Can stand tamely in silence, to hear you
 decry
The Muses?

 Tra. Excuse me: I meant no offence
To the Nine; though the number who make
 some pretence
To their favours is such——but the subject
 to drop,
I am just piping hot from a publisher's shop,
(Next door to the pastry-cook's; so that
 when I
Cannot find the new volume I wanted to buy
On the bibliopole's shelves, it is only two paces,
As one finds every author in one of those places:)
Where I just had been skimming a charming
 critique,
So studded with wit, and so sprinkled with
 Greek!
Where your friend—you know who—has just
 got such a thrashing,
That it is, as the phrase goes, extremely
 "*refreshing*."
What a beautiful word!
 Ink. Very true; 'tis so soft
And so cooling—they use it a little too oft;
And the papers have got it at last—but no
 matter.
So they've cut up our friend then?
 Tra. Not left him a tatter—
Not a rag of his present or past reputation,
Which they call a disgrace to the age and
 the nation.
 Ink. I'm sorry to hear this! for friendship,
 you know——
Our poor friend!—but I thought it would
 terminate so.

Our friendship is such, I'll read nothing to
 shock it.
You don't happen to have the Review in
 your pocket?
 Tra. No; I left a round dozen of authors
 and others
(Very sorry, no doubt, since the cause is
 a brother's)
All scrambling and jostling, like so many
 imps,
And on fire with impatience to get the next
 glimpse.
 Ink. Let us join them.
 Tra. What, won't you return
 to the lecture?
 Ink. Why the place is so cramm'd, there's
 not room for a spectre.
Besides, our friend Scamp is to-day so
 absurd—
 Tra. How can you know that till you hear
 him?
 Ink. I heard
Quite enough; and, to tell you the truth, my
 retreat
Was from his vile nonsense, no less than the
 heat.
 Tra. I have had no great loss then?
 Ink. Loss!—such a palaver!
I'd inoculate sooner my wife with the slaver
Of a dog when gone rabid, than listen two hours
To the torrent of trash which around him he
 pours,
Pump'd up with such effort, disgorged with
 such labour,
That——come—do not make me speak ill of
 one's neighbour.
 Tra. *I* make you!
 Ink. Yes, you! I said nothing until
You compell'd me, by speaking the truth——
 Tra. *To speak ill!*
Is that your deduction?
 Ink. When speaking of Scamp ill,
I certainly *follow, not set* an example.
The fellow's a fool, an impostor, a zany.
 Tra. And the crowd of to-day shows that
 one fool makes many.
But we two will be wise.
 Ink. Pray, then, let us retire.
 Tra. I would, but——
 Ink. There must be attraction much
 higher
Than Scamp, or the Jew's harp he nicknames
 his lyre,
To call *you* to this hotbed.
 Tra. I own it—'tis true—
A fair lady——
 Ink. A spinster?
 Tra. Miss Lilac.
 Ink. The Blue!
The heiress!

 Tra. The angel!
 Ink. The devil! why, man,
Pray get out of this hobble as fast as you can.
You wed with Miss Lilac! 'twould be your
 perdition:
She's a poet, a chymist, a mathematician.
 Tra. I say she's an angel.
 Ink. Say rather an *angle*.
If you and she marry, you'll certainly
 wrangle.
I say she's a Blue, man, as blue as the ether.
 Tra. And is that any cause for not coming
 together?
 Ink. Humph! I can't say I know any
 happy alliance
Which has lately sprung up from a wedlock
 with science.
She's so learned in all things, and fond of
 concerning
Herself in all matters connected with learning,
 That——
 Tra. What?
 Ink. I perhaps may as well hold my
 tongue;
But there's five hundred people can tell you
 you're wrong.
 Tra. You forget Lady Lilac's as rich as
 a Jew.
 Ink. Is it miss or the cash of mamma you
 pursue?
 Tra. Why, Jack, I'll be frank with you—
 something of both.
The girl's a fine girl.
 Ink. And you feel nothing loth
To her good lady-mother's reversion; and yet
Her life is as good as your own, I will bet.
 Tra. Let her live, and as long as she
 likes; I demand
Nothing more than the heart of her daughter
 and hand.
 Ink. Why that heart's in the inkstand—
 that hand on the pen.
 Tra. A propos—Will you write me a song
 now and then?
 Ink. To what purpose?
 Tra. You know, my dear friend,
 that in prose
My talent is decent, as far as it goes;
But in rhyme——
 Ink. You're a terrible stick, to be sure.
 Tra. I own it: and yet, in these times,
 there's no lure
For the heart of the fair like a stanza or two;
And so, as I can't, will you furnish a few?
 Ink. In your name?
 Tra. In my name. I will copy
 them out,
To slip into her hand at the very next rout.
 Ink. Are you so far advanced as to hazard
 this?

Tra. Why,
Do you think me subdued by a Blue-stock-
ing's eye,
So far as to tremble to tell her in rhyme
What I've told her in prose, at the least, as
sublime?
Ink. *As sublime!* If it be so, no need of
my Muse.
Tra. But consider, dear Inkel, she's one
of the "Blues."
Ink. As sublime!—Mr. Tracy—I've no-
thing to say.
Stick to prose—As sublime!!—but I wish
you good day.
Tra. Nay, stay, my dear fellow—consider
—I'm wrong;
I own it; but, prithee, compose me the song.
Ink. *As* sublime!!
Tra. I but used the expression in haste.
Ink. That may be, Mr. Tracy, but shows
damn'd bad taste.
Tra. I own it—I know it—acknowledge
it—what
Can I say to you more?
Ink. I see what you'd be at:
You disparage my parts with insidious abuse,
Till you think you can turn them best to
your own use.
Tra. And is that not a sign I respect
them?
Ink. Why that
To be sure makes a difference.
Tra. I know what is what:
And you, who're a man of the gay world
no less
Than a poet of t'other, may easily guess
That I never could mean, by a word, to
offend
A genius like you, and moreover, my friend.
Ink. No doubt; you by this time should
know what is due
To a man of——but come—let us shake hands.
Tra. You knew,
And you *know*, my dear fellow, how heartily I
Whatever you publish, am ready to buy.
Ink. That's my bookseller's business; I
care not for sale;
Indeed the best poems at first rather fail.
There were Renegade's epics, and Botherby's
plays,
And my own grand romance——
Tra. Had its full share of praise.
I myself saw it puff'd in the "Old Girl's
Review."
Ink. What Review?
Tra. 'Tis the English "Journal de
Trevoux;"
A clerical work of our Jesuits at home.
Have you never yet seen it?
Ink. That pleasure's to come.

Tra. Make haste then.
Ink. Why so?
Tra. I have heard people say
That it threaten'd to give up the *ghost* t'other
day.
Ink. Well, that is a sign of some *spirit*.
Tra. No doubt.
Shall you be at the Countess of Fiddlecome's
rout?
Ink. I've a card, and shall go: but at
present, as soon
As friend Scamp shall be pleased to step
down from the moon
(Where he seems to be soaring in search of
his wits),
And an interval grants from his lecturing
fits,
I'm engaged to the Lady Bluebottle's
collation,
To partake of a luncheon and learn'd con-
versation:
'Tis a sort of reunion for Scamp, on the
days
Of his lecture, to treat him with cold tongue
and praise.
And I own, for my own part, that 'tis not
unpleasant.
Will you go? There's Miss Lilac will also
be present.
Tra. That "metal's attractive."
Ink. No doubt—to the pocket.
Tra. You should rather encourage my
passion than shock it.
But let us proceed; for I think by the
hum——
Ink. Very true; let us go, then, before
they can come,
Or else we'll be kept here an hour at their
levee,
On the rack of cross questions, by all the
blue bevy.
Hark! Zounds, they'll be on us; I know by
the drone
Of old Botherby's spouting ex-cathedrâ tone.
Ay! there he is at it. Poor Scamp! better
join
Your friends, or he'll pay you back in your
own coin.
Tra. All fair; 'tis but lecture for lecture.
Ink. That's clear.
But for God's sake let's go, or the Bore will
be here.
Come, come: nay, I'm off. [*Exit* INKEL.
Tra. You are right, and I'll follow;
'Tis high time for a "*Sic me servavit
Apollo.*"
And yet we shall have the whole crew on our
kibes,
Blues, dandies, and dowagers, and second-
hand scribes,

All flocking to moisten their exquisite throttles
With a glass of Madeira at Lady Blue-
bottle's. [Exit TRACY.

—◆◆—

ECLOGUE THE SECOND.

An Apartment in the House of LADY
BLUEBOTTLE.—*A Table prepared.*

SIR RICHARD BLUEBOTTLE *solus.*

WAS there ever a man who was married so
sorry?
Like a fool, I must needs do the thing in
a hurry.
My life is reversed, and my quiet destroy'd;
My days, which once pass'd in so gentle a
void,
Must now, every hour of the twelve, be
employ'd;
The twelve, do I say?—of the whole twenty-
four,
Is there one which I dare call my own any
more?
What with driving and visiting, dancing and
dining,
What with learning, and teaching, and scrib-
bling, and shining
In science and art, I'll be cursed if I know
Myself from my wife; for although we are
two,
Yet she somehow contrives that all things
shall be done
In a style which proclaims us eternally one.
But the thing of all things which distresses
me more
Than the bills of the week (though they
trouble me sore)
Is the numerous, humorous, backbiting crew
Of scribblers, wits, lecturers, white, black,
and blue,
Who are brought to my house as an inn, to
my cost—
For the bill here, it seems, is defray'd by the
host—
No pleasure! no leisure! no thought for my
pains,
But to hear a vile jargon which addles my
brains;
A smatter and chatter, glean'd out of reviews,
By the rag, tag, and bobtail, of those they
call "BLUES;"
A rabble who know not—But soft, here they
come!
Would to God I were deaf! as I'm not, I'll
be dumb.

Enter LADY BLUEBOTTLE, MISS LILAC, LADY
BLUEMOUNT, MR. BOTHERBY, INKEL, TRACY,
Miss MAZARINE, *and others, with* SCAMP *the
Lecturer, &c. &c.*

Lady Blueb. Ah! Sir Richard, good morn-
ing: I've brought you some friends.
Sir Rich. (*bows, and afterwards aside*). If
friends, they're the first.
Lady Blueb. But the luncheon attends.
I pray ye be seated, "*sans cérémonie.*"
Mr. Scamp, you're fatigued; take your chair
there next me. [*They all sit.*
Sir Rich. (*aside*). If he does, his fatigue
is to come.
Lady Blueb. Mr. Tracy—
Lady Bluemount—Miss Lilac—be pleased,
pray, to place ye;
And you, Mr. Botherby—
Both. Oh, my dear Lady,
I obey.
Lady Blueb. Mr. Inkel, I ought to up-
braid ye:
You were not at the lecture.
Ink. Excuse me, I was;
But the heat forced me out in the best
part—alas!
And when——
Lady Blueb. To be sure it was broiling;
but then
You have lost such a lecture!
Both. The best of the ten.
Tra. How can you know that? there are
two more.
Both. Because
I defy him to beat this day's wondrous
applause.
The very walls shook.
Ink. Oh, if that be the test,
I allow our friend Scamp has this day done
his best.
Miss Lilac, permit me to help you;—a wing?
Miss Lil. No more, sir, I thank you. Who
lectures next spring?
Both. Dick Dunder.
Ink. That is, if he lives.
Miss Lil. And why not?
Ink. No reason whatever, save that he's
a sot.
Lady Bluemount! a glass of Madeira?
Lady Bluem. With pleasure.
Ink. How does your friend Wordswords,
that Windermere treasure?
Does he stick to his lakes, like the leeches
he sings,
And their gatherers, as Homer sung warriors
and kings?
Lady Bluem. He has just got a place.
Ink. As a footman?

Lady Bluem. For shame!
Nor profane with your sneers so poetic a
 name.
Ink. Nay, I meant him no evil, but pitied
 his master;
For the poet of pedlars 't were, sure, no
 disaster
To wear a new livery; the more, as 't is not
The first time he has turn'd both his creed
 and his coat.
Lady Bluem. For shame! I repeat. If
 Sir George could but hear——
Lady Blueb. Never mind our friend Inkel;
 we all know, my dear,
'T is his way.
Sir Rich. But this place——
Ink. Is perhaps like friend Scamp's,
A lecturer's.
Lady Bluem. Excuse me—'t is one in the
 " Stamps:"
He is made a collector.
Tra. Collector!
Sir Rich. How?
Miss Lil. What?
Ink. I shall think of him oft when I buy
 a new hat:
There his works will appear——
Lady Bluem. Sir, they reach to the Ganges.
Ink. I shan't go so far—I can have them
 at Grange's.
Lady Bluem. Oh fie!
Miss Lil. And for shame!
Lady Bluem. You're too bad.
Both. Very good!
Lady Bluem. How good?
Lady Blueb. He means nought—'t is his
 phrase.
Lady Bluem. He grows rude.
Lady Blueb. He means nothing; nay, ask
 him.
Lady Bluem. Pray, Sir! did you mean
What you say?
Ink. Never mind if he did; 't will be seen
That whatever he means won't alloy what
 he says.
Both. Sir?
Ink. Pray be content with your por-
 tion of praise;
'T was in your defence.
Both. If you please, with submission,
I can make out my own.
Ink. It would be your perdition.
While you live, my dear Botherby, never
 defend
Yourself or your works; but leave both to
 a friend.
Apropos—Is your play then accepted at last?
Both. At last?
Ink. Why I thought—that's to say—
 there had pass'd

A few green-room whispers, which hinted,—
 you know
That the taste of the actors at best is so so.
Both. Sir, the green-room's in rapture,
 and so's the Committee.
Ink. Ay—yours are the plays for exciting
 our " pity
And fear," as the Greek says: for " purging
 the mind,"
I doubt if you'll leave us an equal behind.
Both. I have written the prologue, and
 meant to have pray'd
For a spice of your wit in an epilogue's aid.
Ink. Well, time enough yet, when the
 play's to be play'd.
Is it cast yet?
Both. The actors are fighting for parts,
As is usual in that most litigious of arts.
Lady Blueb. We'll all make a party, and
 go the *first* night.
Tra. And you promised the epilogue,
 Inkel.
Ink. Not quite.
However, to save my friend Botherby trouble,
I'll do what I can, though my pains must be
 double.
Tra. Why so?
Ink. To do justice to what goes before.
Both. Sir, I'm happy to say, I've no fears
 on that score.
Your parts, Mr. Inkel, are——
Ink. Never mind *mine;*
Stick to those of your play, which is quite
 your own line.
Lady Bluem. You're a fugitive writer, I
 think, sir, of rhymes?
Ink. Yes, ma'am; and a fugitive reader
 sometimes.
On Wordswords, for instance, I seldom alight,
Or on Mouthey, his friend, without taking to
 flight.
Lady Bluem. Sir, your taste is too com-
 mon; but time and posterity
Will right these great men, and this age's
 severity
Become its reproach.
Ink. I've no sort of objection,
So I'm not of the party to take the infection.
Lady Blueb. Perhaps you have doubts
 that they ever will *take?*
Ink. Not at all; on the contrary, those
 of the lake
Have taken already, and still will continue
To take—what they can, from a groat to a
 guinea,
Of pension or place;—but the subject's a
 bore.
Lady Bluem. Well, sir, the time's coming.
Ink. Scamp! don't you feel sore?
What say you to this?

Scamp. They have merit, I own;
Though their system's absurdity keeps it
 unknown.
Ink. Then why not unearth it in one of
 your lectures?
Scamp. It is only time past which comes
 under my strictures.
Lady Blueb. Come, a truce with all tart-
 ness;—the joy of my heart
Is to see Nature's triumph o'er all that is art.
Wild Nature!—Grand Shakspeare!
Both. And down Aristotle!
Lady Bluem. Sir George thinks exactly
 with Lady Bluebottle:
And my Lord Seventy-four, who protects our
 dear Bard,
And who gave him his place, has the greatest
 regard
For the poet, who, singing of pedlars and
 asses,
Has found out the way to dispense with
 Parnassus.
Tra. And you, Scamp!—
Scamp. I needs must confess I'm
 embarrass'd.
Ink. Don't call upon Scamp, who's already
 so harass'd
With old *schools*, and new *schools*, and no
 schools, and all *schools*.
Tra. Well, one thing is certain, that *some*
 must be fools.
I should like to know who.
Ink. And I should not be sorry
To know who are *not:*—it would save us
 some worry.
Lady Blueb. A truce with remark, and let
 nothing control
This "feast of our reason, and flow of the
 soul."
Oh! my dear Mr. Botherby! sympathise!—I
Now feel such a rapture, I'm ready to fly,
I feel so elastic—"*so buoyant—so buoyant!*"
Ink. Tracy! open the window.
Tra. I wish her much joy on 't.
Both. For God's sake, my Lady Blue-
 bottle, check not
This gentle emotion, so seldom our lot
Upon earth. Give it way: 't is an impulse
 which lifts
Our spirits from earth; the sublimest of gifts;
For which poor Prometheus was chain'd to
 his mountain:
'T is the source of all sentiment—feeling's
 true fountain;

'T is the Vision of Heaven upon Earth: 't is
 the gas
Of the soul: 'tis the seizing of shades as
 they pass,
And making them substance: 'tis something
 divine:—
Ink. Shall I help you, my friend, to a
 little more wine?
Both. I thank you; not any more, sir, till
 I dine.
Ink. Apropos—Do you dine with Sir Hum-
 phry to-day?
Tra. I should think with *Duke* Humphry
 was more in your way.
Ink. It might be of yore; but we authors
 now look
To the Knight, as a landlord, much more
 than the Duke.
The truth is, each writer now quite at his
 ease is,
And (except with his publisher) dines where
 he pleases.
But 'tis now nearly five, and I must to the
 Park.
Tra. And I'll take a turn with you there
 till 't is dark.
And you, Scamp—
Scamp. Excuse me! I must to my notes,
For my lecture next week.
Ink. He must mind whom he quotes
Out of "Elegant Extracts."
Lady Blueb. Well, now we break up;
But remember Miss Diddle invites us to sup.
Ink. Then at two hours past midnight we
 all meet again,
For the sciences, sandwiches, hock, and
 champagne!
Tra. And the sweet lobster salad!
Both. I honour that meal;
For 'tis then that our feelings most genuinely
 —feel.
Ink. True; feeling is truest *then*, far be-
 yond question:
I wish to the gods 't was the same with
 digestion!
Lady Blueb. Pshaw!—never mind that;
 for one moment of feeling
Is worth—God knows what.
Ink. 'T is at least worth concealing
For itself, or what follows——But here comes
 your carriage.
Sir Rich. (aside). I wish all these people
 were d——d with *my* marriage!
 [*Exeunt.*

The Vision of Judgment,

BY

QUEVEDO REDIVIVUS.

SUGGESTED BY THE COMPOSITION SO ENTITLED BY THE AUTHOR OF "WAT TYLER."

———◆◆———

"A Daniel come to judgment! yea, a Daniel!
I thank thee, Jew, for teaching me that word."

———◆◆———

PREFACE.

It hath been wisely said, that "One fool makes many;" and it hath been poetically observed—

"That fools rush in where angels fear to tread."—Pope.

If Mr. Southey had not rushed in where he had no business, and where he never was before, and never will be again, the following poem would not have been written. It is not impossible that it may be as good as his own, seeing that it cannot, by any species of stupidity, natural or acquired, be worse. The gross flattery, the dull impudence, the renegado intolerance, and impious cant, of the poem by the author of "Wat Tyler," are something so stupendous as to form the sublime of himself—containing the quintessence of his own attributes.

So much for his poem—a word on his preface. In this preface it has pleased the magnanimous Laureate to draw the picture of a supposed "Satanic School," the which he doth recommend to the notice of the legislature; thereby adding to his other laurels the ambition of those of an informer. If there exists anywhere, except in his imagination, such a School, is he not sufficiently armed against it by his own intense vanity? The truth is, that there are certain writers whom Mr. S. imagines, like Scrub, to have "talked of him; for they laughed consumedly."

I think I know enough of most of the writers to whom he is supposed to allude, to assert, that they, in their individual capacities, have done more good, in the charities of life, to their fellow-creatures, in any one year, than Mr. Southey has done harm to himself by his absurdities in his whole life; and this is saying a great deal. But I have a few questions to ask.

1stly, Is Mr. Southey the author of "Wat Tyler"?

2ndly, Was he not refused a remedy at law by the highest judge of his beloved England, because it was a blasphemous and seditious publication?

3rdly, Was he not entitled by William Smith, in full parliament, "a rancorous renegado?"

4thly, Is he not poet laureate, with his own lines on Martin the regicide staring him in the face?

And, 5thly, Putting the four preceding items together, with what conscience dare he call the attention of the laws to the publications of others, be they what they may?

I say nothing of the cowardice of such a proceeding, its meanness speaks for itself; but I wish to touch upon the motive, which is neither more nor less than that Mr. S. has been laughed at a little in some recent publications, as he was of yore in the "Anti-jacobin," by his present patrons. Hence all this "skimble-scamble stuff" about "Satanic," and so forth. However, it is worthy of him—"qualis ab incepto."

If there is anything obnoxious to the political opinions of a portion of the public in the following poem, they may thank Mr. Southey. He might have written hexameters, as he has written everything else, for aught that the writer cared—had they been upon another subject. But to attempt to canonise a monarch, who, whatever were his household virtues, was neither a successful nor a patriot king,—inasmuch as several years of his reign passed in war with America and Ireland, to say nothing of the aggression upon France,—like all other exaggeration, necessarily begets opposition. In whatever manner he may be spoken of in this new "Vision," his public career will not be more favourably transmitted by history. Of his private virtues (although a little expensive to the nation) there can be no doubt.

With regard to the supernatural personages treated of, I can only say that I know as much about them, and (as an honest man) have a better right to talk of them than Robert Southey. I have also treated them more tolerantly. The way in which that poor insane creature, the Laureate, deals about his judgments in the next world, is like his own judgment in this. If it was not completely ludicrous, it would be something worse. I don't think that there is much more to say at present.

QUEVEDO REDIVIVUS.

P.S.—It is possible that some readers may object, in these objectionable times, to the freedom with which saints, angels, and spiritual persons discourse in this "Vision." But, for precedents upon such points, I must refer him to Fielding's "Journey from this World to the next," and to the Visions of myself, the said Quevedo, in Spanish or translated. The reader is also requested to observe, that no doctrinal tenets are insisted upon or discussed; that the person of the Deity is carefully withheld from sight, which is more than can be said for the Laureate, who hath thought proper to make him talk, not "like a school-divine," but like the unscholarlike Mr. Southey. The whole action passes on the outside of heaven; and Chaucer's "Wife of Bath," Pulci's "Morgante Maggiore," Swift's "Tale of a Tub," and the other works above referred to, are cases in point of the freedom with which saints, &c. may be permitted to converse in works not intended to be serious.

Q. R.

₊ Mr. Southey being, as he says, a good Christian and vindictive, threatens, I understand, a reply to this our answer. It is to be hoped that his visionary faculties will in the mean time have acquired a little more judgment, properly so called: otherwise he will get himself into new dilemmas. These apostate Jacobins furnish rich rejoinders. Let him take a specimen. Mr. Southey laudeth grievously " one Mr. Landor," who cultivates much private renown in the shape of Latin verses; and not long ago, the poet laureate dedicated to him, it appeareth, one of his fugitive lyrics, upon the strength of a poem called "Gebir." Who could

suppose, that in this same Gebir the aforesaid Savage Landor (for such is his grim cognomen) putteth into the infernal regions no less a person than the hero of his friend Mr. Southey's heaven,—yea, even George the Third! See also how personal Savage becometh, when he hath a mind. The following is his portrait of our late gracious sovereign:

(Prince Gebir having descended into the infernal regions, the shades of his royal ancestors are, at his request, called up to his view; and he exclaims to his ghostly guide)—

" Aroar, what wretch that nearest us? what wretch
Is that with eyebrows white and slanting brow?
Listen! him yonder who, bound down supine,
Shrinks yelling from that sword there, engine-hung.
He too amongst my ancestors! I hate
The despot, but the dastard I despise.
Was he our countryman?"
 "Alas, O king!
Iberia bore him, but the breed accurst
Inclement winds blew blighting from north-east."
"He was a warrior then, nor fear'd the gods?"
" Gebir, he fear'd the demons, not the gods,
Though them indeed his daily face adored;
And was no warrior, yet the thousand lives
Squander'd, as stones to exercise a sling,
And the tame cruelty and cold caprice—
Oh madness of mankind! address'd, adored!"
 Gebir, p. 28.

I omit noticing some edifying Ithyphallics of Savagius, wishing to keep the proper veil over them, if his grave but somewhat indiscreet worshipper will suffer it; but certainly these teachers of "great moral lessons" are apt to be found in strange company.

THE VISION OF JUDGMENT.

I.

SAINT PETER sat by the celestial gate:
 His keys were rusty, and the lock was dull,
So little trouble had been given of late;
 Not that the place by any means was full,
But since the Gallic era "eighty-eight"
 The devils had ta'en a longer, stronger pull,
And "a pull altogether," as they say
At sea—which drew most souls another way.

II.

The angels all were singing out of tune,
 And hoarse with having little else to do,
Excepting to wind up the sun and moon,
 Or curb a runaway young star or two,
Or wild colt of a comet, which too soon
 Broke out of bounds o'er th' ethereal blue,
Splitting some planet with its playful tail,
As boats are sometimes by a wanton whale.

III.

The guardian seraphs had retired on high,
 Finding their charges past all care below;
Terrestrial business fill'd nought in the sky
 Save the recording angel's black bureau;
Who found, indeed, the facts to multiply
 With such rapidity of vice and woe,
That he had stripp'd off both his wings in quills,
And yet was in arrear of human ills.

IV.

His business so augmented of late years,
 That he was forced, against his will no doubt,
(Just like those cherubs, earthly ministers,)
 For some resource to turn himself about,

And claim the help of his celestial peers,
 To aid him ere he should be quite worn
 out
By the increased demand for his remarks:
Six angels and twelve saints were named his
 clerks.

V.

This was a handsome board—at least for
 heaven;
 And yet they had even then enough to do,
So many conquerors' cars were daily driven,
 So many kingdoms fitted up anew;
Each day too slew its thousands six or
 seven,
 Till at the crowning carnage, Waterloo,
They threw their pens down in divine
 disgust—
The page was so besmear'd with blood and
 dust.

VI.

This by the way; 'tis not mine to record
 What angels shrink from: even the very
 devil
On this occasion his own work abhorr'd,
 So surfeited with the infernal revel:
Though he himself had sharpen'd every
 sword,
 It almost quench'd his innate thirst of
 evil.
(Here Satan's sole good work deserves in-
 sertion—
'Tis, that he has both generals in reversion.)

VII.

Let's skip a few short years of hollow peace,
 Which peopled earth no better, hell as
 wont,
And heaven none—they form the tyrant's
 lease,
 With nothing but new names subscribed
 upon't;
'T will one day finish: meantime they in-
 crease,
 "With seven heads and ten horns," and
 all in front,
Like Saint John's foretold beast; but ours
 are born
Less formidable in the head than horn.

VIII.

In the first year of freedom's second dawn
 Died George the Third; although no
 tyrant, one
Who shielded tyrants, till each sense with-
 drawn
 Left him nor mental nor external sun:

A better farmer ne'er brush'd dew from
 lawn,
 A worse king never left a realm undone!
He died—but left his subjects still behind,
 One half as mad—and t'other no less blind.

IX.

He died! his death made no great stir on
 earth:
 His burial made some pomp; there was
 profusion
Of velvet, gilding, brass, and no great dearth
 Of aught but tears—save those shed by
 collusion.
For these things may be bought at their true
 worth;
 Of elegy there was the due infusion—
Bought also; and the torches, cloaks, and
 banners,
Heralds, and relics of old Gothic manners,

X.

Form'd a sepulchral melodrame. Of all
 The fools who flock'd to swell or see the
 show,
Who cared about the corpse? The funeral
 Made the attraction, and the black the woe.
There throbb'd not there a thought which
 pierced the pall;
 And when the gorgeous coffin was laid low,
It seem'd the mockery of hell to fold
The rottenness of eighty years in gold.

XI.

So mix his body with the dust! It might
 Return to what it *must* far sooner, were
The natural compound left alone to fight
 Its way back into earth, and fire, and air;
But the unnatural balsams merely blight
 What nature made him at his birth, as
 bare
As the mere million's base unmummied
 clay—
Yet all his spices but prolong decay.

XII.

He's dead—and upper earth with him has
 done;
 He's buried; save the undertaker's bill,
Or lapidary scrawl, the world is gone
 For him, unless he left a German will:
But where's the proctor who will ask his
 son?
 In whom his qualities are reigning still,
Except that household virtue, most un-
 common,
Of constancy to a bad, ugly woman.

XIII.

" God save the king!" It is a large economy
 In God to save the like; but if he will
Be saving, all the better; for not one am I
 Of those who think damnation better still:
I hardly know too if not quite alone am I
 In this small hope of bettering future ill
By circumscribing, with some slight restric-
 tion,
The eternity of hell's hot jurisdiction.

XIV.

I know this is unpopular; I know
 'Tis blasphemous; I know one may be
 damn'd
For hoping no one else may e'er be so;
 I know my catechism; I know we 're
 cramm'd
With the best doctrines till we quite o'erflow;
 I know that all save England's church
 have shamm'd,
And that the other twice two hundred
 churches
And synagogues have made a *damn'd* bad
 purchase.

XV.

God help us all! God help me too! I am,
 God knows, as helpless as the devil can
 wish,
And not a whit more difficult to damn,
 Than is to bring to land a late-hook'd fish,
Or to the butcher to purvey the lamb;
 Not that I'm fit for such a noble dish,
As one day will be that immortal fry
Of almost everybody born to die.

XVI.

Saint Peter sat by the celestial gate,
 And nodded o'er his keys; when, lo! there
 came
A wondrous noise he had not heard of late—
 A rushing sound of wind, and stream, and
 flame;
In short, a roar of things extremely great,
 Which would have made aught save a saint
 exclaim;
But he, with first a start and then a wink,
Said, "There's another star gone out, I
 think!"

XVII.

But ere he could return to his repose,
 A cherub flapp'd his right wing o'er his
 eyes—
At which St. Peter yawn'd, and rubb'd his
 nose:
 " Saint porter," said the angel, "prithee
 rise!"

Waving a goodly wing, which glow'd, as
 glows
 An earthly peacock's tail, with heavenly
 dyes:
To which the saint replied, "Well, what's
 the matter?
 " Is Lucifer come back with all this
 clatter?"

XVIII.

" No," quoth the cherub; " George the Third
 is dead."
 " And who *is* George the Third?" replied
 the apostle:
" *What George? what Third?*" "The king
 of England," said
The angel. "Well! he won't find kings
 to jostle
Him on his way; but does he wear his head?
 Because the last we saw here had a tustle,
And ne'er would have got into heaven's good
 graces,
Had he not flung his head in all our faces.

XIX.

" He was, if I remember, king of France;
 That head of his, which could not keep a
 crown
On earth, yet ventured in my face to advance
 A claim to those of martyrs—like my own:
If I had had my sword, as I had once
 When I cut ears off, I had cut him down;
But having but my *keys*, and not my brand,
I only knock'd his head from out his hand.

XX.

" And then he set up such a headless howl,
 That all the saints came out and took him
 in;
And there he sits by St. Paul, cheek by jowl;
 That fellow Paul—the parvenù! The skin
Of St. Bartholomew, which makes his cowl
 In heaven, and upon earth redeem'd his
 sin,
So as to make a martyr, never sped
Better than did this weak and wooden head.

XXI.

" But had it come up here upon its shoulders,
 There would have been a different tale to
 tell:
The fellow-feeling in the saint's beholders
 Seems to have acted on them like a spell,
And so this very foolish head heaven solders
 Back on its trunk: it may be very well,
And seems the custom here to overthrow
Whatever has been wisely done below."

XXII.

The angel answer'd, "Peter! do not pout:
 The king who comes has head and all
 entire,
And never knew much what it was about—
He did as doth the puppet—by its wire,
And will be judged like all the rest, no doubt:
 My business and your own is not to inquire
Into such matters, but to mind our cue—
Which is to act as we are bid to do."

XXIII.

While thus they spake, the angelic caravan,
 Arriving like a rush of mighty wind,
Cleaving the fields of space, as doth the swan
 Some silver stream (say Ganges, Nile, or
 Inde,
Or Thames, or Tweed), and 'midst them an
 old man
With an old soul, and both extremely blind,
Halted before the gate, and in his shroud
Seated their fellow traveller on a cloud.

XXIV.

But bringing up the rear of this bright host
 A Spirit of a different aspect waved
His wings, like thunder-clouds above some
 coast
 Whose barren beach with frequent wrecks
 is paved;
His brow was like the deep when tempest-
 toss'd;
 Fierce and unfathomable thoughts engraved
Eternal wrath on his immortal face,
And *where* he gazed a gloom pervaded space.

XXV.

As he drew near, he gazed upon the gate
 Ne'er to be enter'd more by him or Sin,
With such a glance of supernatural hate,
 As made Saint Peter wish himself within;
He patter'd with his keys at a great rate,
 And sweated through his apostolic skin:
Of course his perspiration was but ichor,
Or some such other spiritual liquor.

XXVI.

The very cherubs huddled all together,
 Like birds when soars the falcon; and
 they felt
A tingling to the tip of every feather,
 And form'd a circle like Orion's belt
Around their poor old charge; who scarce
 knew whither
 His guards had led him, though they gently
 dealt
With royal manes (for by many stories,
And true, we learn the angels all are Tories).

XXVII.

As things were in this posture, the gate flew
 Asunder, and the flashing of its hinges
Flung over space an universal hue
 Of many-colour'd flame, until its tinges
Reach'd even our speck of earth, and made a
 new
 Aurora borealis spread its fringes
O'er the North Pole; the same seen, when
 ice-bound,
By Captain Parry's crew, in "Melville's
 Sound."

XXVIII.

And from the gate thrown open issued
 beaming
 A beautiful and mighty Thing of Light,
Radiant with glory, like a banner streaming
 Victorious from some world-o'erthrowing
 fight:
My poor comparisons must needs be teeming
 With earthly likenesses, for here the night
Of clay obscures our best conceptions, saving
Johanna Southcote, or Bob Southey raving.

XXIX.

'Twas the archangel Michael; all men know
 The make of angels and archangels, since
There's scarce a scribbler has not one to show,
 From the fiends' leader to the angels'
 prince;
There also are some altar-pieces, though
 I really can't say that they much evince
One's inner notions of immortal spirits;
But let the connoisseurs explain *their* merits.

XXX.

Michael flew forth in glory and in good;
 A goodly work of him from whom all glory
And good arise; the portal past—he stood;
 Before him the young cherubs and saints
 hoary—
(I say *young*, begging to be understood
 By looks, not years; and should be very
 sorry
To state, they were not older than St. Peter,
But merely that they seem'd a little sweeter).

XXXI.

The cherubs and the saints bow'd down before
 That arch-angelic hierarch, the first
Of essences angelical, who wore
 The aspect of a god; but this ne'er nursed
Pride in his heavenly bosom, in whose core
 No thought, save for his Master's service,
 durst
Intrude, however glorified and high;
He knew him but the viceroy of the sky.

XXXII.

He and the sombre, silent Spirit met—
　They knew each other both for good
　　and ill;
Such was their power, that neither could
　　forget
　His former friend and future foe; but still
There was a high, immortal, proud regret
　In either's eye, as if 'twere less their will
Than destiny to make the eternal years
Their date of war, and their "champ clos"
　　the spheres.

XXXIII.

But here they were in neutral space: we
　　know
　From Job, that Satan hath the power to
　　pay
A heavenly visit thrice a year or so;
　And that the "sons of God," like those of
　　clay,
Must keep him company; and we might
　　show
　From the same book, in how polite a way
The dialogue is held between the Powers
Of Good and Evil—but 'twould take up
　　hours.

XXXIV.

And this is not a theologic tract,
　To prove with Hebrew and with Arabic,
If Job be allegory or a fact,
　But a true narrative; and thus I pick
From out the whole but such and such
　　an act
　As sets aside the slightest thought of trick.
'T is every tittle true, beyond suspicion,
And accurate as any other vision.

XXXV.

The spirits were in neutral space, before
　The gate of heaven; like eastern thres-
　　holds is
The place where Death's grand cause is
　　argued o'er,
　And souls despatch'd to that world or to
　　this;
And therefore Michael and the other wore
　A civil aspect: though they did not kiss,
Yet still between his Darkness and his
　　Brightness
There pass'd a mutual glance of great polite-
　　ness.

XXXVI.

The Archangel bow'd, not like a modern
　　beau,
　But with a graceful Oriental bend,
Pressing one radiant arm just where below
　The heart in good men is supposed to tend;

He turn'd as to an equal, not too low,
　But kindly; Satan met his ancient friend
With more hauteur, as might an old Castilian
Poor noble meet a mushroom rich civilian.

XXXVII.

He merely bent his diabolic brow
　An instant; and then raising it, he stood
In act to assert his right or wrong, and show
　Cause why King George by no means could
　　or should
Make out a case to be exempt from woe
　Eternal, more than other kings, endued
With better sense and hearts, whom history
　　mentions,
Who long have "paved hell with their good
　　intentions."

XXXVIII.

Michael began: "What wouldst thou with
　　this man,
　Now dead, and brought before the Lord?
　　What ill
Hath he wrought since his mortal race began,
　That thou canst claim him? Speak! and
　　do thy will,
If it be just: if in this earthly span
　He hath been greatly failing to fulfil
His duties as a king and mortal, say,
And he is thine; if not, let him have way."

XXXIX.

"Michael!" replied the Prince of Air, "even
　　here,
　Before the Gate of him thou servest, must
I claim my subject: and will make appear
　That as he was my worshipper in dust,
So shall he be in spirit, although dear
　To thee and thine, because nor wine nor lust
Were of his weaknesses; yet on the throne
He reign'd o'er millions to serve me alone.

XL.

"Look to *our* earth, or rather *mine;* it was,
　Once, more thy master's: but I triumph not
In this poor planet's conquest; nor, alas!
　Need he thou servest envy me my lot:
With all the myriads of bright worlds which
　　pass
　In worship round him, he may have forgot
Yon weak creation of such paltry things:
I think few worth damnation save their
　　kings,—

XLI.

"And these but as a kind of quit-rent, to
　Assert my right as lord: and even had
I such an inclination, 'twere (as you
　Well know) superfluous; they are grown
　　so bad,

That hell has nothing better left to do
 Than leave them to themselves: so much
 more mad
And evil by their own internal curse,
Heaven cannot make them better, nor I
 worse.

XLII.

"Look to the earth, I said, and say again:
 When this old, blind, mad, helpless, weak,
 poor worm
Began in youth's first bloom and flush to
 reign,
 The world and he both wore a different
 form,
And much of earth and all the watery plain
 Of ocean call'd him king: through many a
 storm
His isles had floated on the abyss of time;
For the rough virtues chose them for their
 clime.

XLIII.

"He came to his sceptre young; he leaves it
 old:
 Look to the state in which he found his
 realm,
And left it; and his annals too behold,
 How to a minion first he gave the helm;
How grew upon his heart a thirst for gold,
 The beggar's vice, which can but over-
 whelm
The meanest hearts; and for the rest, but
 glance
Thine eye along America and France.

XLIV.

" 'T is true, he was a tool from first to last
 (I have the workmen safe); but as a tool
So let him be consumed. From out the past
 Of ages, since mankind have known the
 rule
Of monarchs—from the bloody rolls amass'd
 Of sin and slaughter—from the Cæsar's
 school,
Take the worst pupil; and produce a reign
More drench'd with gore, more cumber'd
 with the slain.

XLV.

"He ever warr'd with freedom and the free:
 Nations as men, home subjects, foreign foes,
So that they utter'd the word 'Liberty!'
 Found George the Third their first op-
 ponent. Whose
History was ever stain'd as his will be
 With national and individual woes?
I grant his household abstinence; I grant
His neutral virtues, which most monarchs
 want;

XLVI.

"I know he was a constant consort; own
 He was a decent sire, and middling lord.
All this is much, and most upon a throne;
 As temperance, if at Apicius' board,
Is more than at an anchorite's supper shown.
 I grant him all the kindest can accord;
And this was well for him, but not for those
Millions who found him what oppression
 chose.

XLVII.

"The New World shook him off; the Old
 yet groans
 Beneath what he and his prepared, if not
Completed: he leaves heirs on many thrones
 To all his vices, without what begot
Compassion for him—his tame virtues;
 drones
 Who sleep, or despots who have now forgot
A lesson which shall be re-taught them,
 wake
Upon the thrones of earth; but let them
 quake!

XLVIII.

"Five millions of the primitive, who hold
 The faith which makes ye great on earth,
 implored
A *part* of that vast *all* they held of old,—
 Freedom to worship—not alone your Lord,
Michael, but you, and you, Saint Peter! Cold
 Must be your souls, if you have not
 abhorr'd
The foe to Catholic participation
In all the license of a Christian nation.

XLIX.

"True! he allow'd them to pray God; but as
 A consequence of prayer, refused the law
Which would have placed them upon the
 same base
 With those who did not hold the saints in
 awe."
But here Saint Peter started from his place,
 And cried, "You may the prisoner with-
 draw:
Ere heaven shall ope her portals to this
 Guelph,
While I am guard, may I be damn'd myself!

L.

"Sooner will I with Cerberus exchange
 My office (and *his* is no sinecure)
Than see this royal Bedlam bigot range
 The azure fields of heaven, of that be
 sure!"

" Saint!" replied Satan, "you do well to
avenge
 The wrongs he made your satellites en-
 dure;
And if to this exchange you should be given,
I'll try to coax *our* Cerberus up to heaven!"

LI.

Here Michael interposed: "Good saint! and
devil!
 Pray, not so fast; you both outrun dis-
 cretion.
Saint Peter! you were wont to be more civil!
Satan! excuse this warmth of his ex-
 pression,
And condescension to the vulgar's level:
 Even saints sometimes forget themselves
 in session.
Have you got more to say?"—"No."—"If
you please,
I'll trouble you to call your witnesses."

LII.

Then Satan turn'd and waved his swarthy
hand,
 Which stirr'd with its electric qualities
Clouds farther off than we can understand,
 Although we find him sometimes in our
 skies;
Infernal thunder shook both sea and land
 In all the planets, and hell's batteries
Let off the artillery, which Milton mentions
As one of Satan's most sublime inventions.

LIII.

This was a signal unto such damn'd souls
 As have the privilege of their damnation
Extended far beyond the mere controls
 Of worlds past, present, or to come; no
 station
Is theirs particularly in the rolls
 Of hell assign'd; but where their inclina-
 tion
Or business carries them in search of game,
They may range freely—being damn'd the
 same.

LIV.

They're proud of this—as very well they
may,
 It being a sort of knighthood, or gilt key
Stuck in their loins; or like to an "entré"
Up the back stairs, or such free-masonry.
I borrow my comparisons from clay,
 Being clay myself. Let not those spirits be
Offended with such base low likenesses;
We know their posts are nobler far than
 these.

LV.

When the great signal ran from heaven to
hell—
 About ten million times the distance reck-
 on'd
From our sun to its earth, as we can tell
 How much time it takes up, even to a
 second,
For every ray that travels to dispel
 The fogs of London, through which, dimly
 beacon'd,
The weathercocks are gilt some thrice a year,
If that the *summer* is not too severe:

LVI.

I say that I can tell—'twas half a minute;
 I know the solar beams take up more time
Ere, pack'd up for their journey, they begin it;
 But then their telegraph is less sublime,
And if they ran a race, they would not win it
 'Gainst Satan's couriers bound for their
 own clime.
The sun takes up some years for every ray
To reach its goal—the devil not half a day.

LVII.

Upon the verge of space, about the size
 Of half-a-crown, a little speck appear'd
(I've seen a something like it in the skies
 In the Ægean, ere a squall); it near'd,
And, growing bigger, took another guise;
 Like an aërial ship it tack'd, and steer'd,
Or *was* steer'd (I am doubtful of the grammar
 Of the last phrase, which makes the stanza
 stammer;—

LVIII.

But take your choice): and then it grew a
cloud;
 And so it was—a cloud of witnesses.
But such a cloud! No land e'er saw a crowd
 Of locusts numerous as the heavens saw
 these;
They shadow'd with their myriads space;
 their loud
 And varied cries were like those of wild
 geese
(If nations may be liken'd to a goose),
And realised the phrase of "hell broke loose."

LIX.

Here crash'd a sturdy oath of stout John Bull,
 Who damn'd away his eyes as heretofore:
There Paddy brogued "By Jasus!"—"What's
 your wull?"
 The temperate Scot exclaim'd: the French
 ghost swore

In certain terms I shan't translate in full,
 As the first coachman will; and 'midst the
 war,
The voice of Jonathan was heard to express,
" *Our* president is going to war, I guess."

LX.

Besides there were the Spaniard, Dutch, and
 Dane;
 In short, an universal shoal of shades,
From Otaheite's isle to Salisbury Plain,
 Of all climes and professions, years and
 trades,
Ready to swear against the good king's reign,
 Bitter as clubs in cards are against spades:
All summon'd by this grand " subpœna," to
Try if kings mayn't be damn'd like me or you.

LXI.

When Michael saw this host, he first grew
 pale,
 As angels can; next, like Italian twilight,
He turn'd all colours—as a peacock's tail,
 Or sunset streaming through a Gothic
 skylight
In some old abbey, or a trout not stale,
 Or distant lightning on the horizon *by* night,
Or a fresh rainbow, or a grand review
Of thirty regiments in red, green, and blue.

LXII.

Then he address'd himself to Satan : " Why—
 My good old friend, for such I deem you,
 though
Our different parties make us fight so shy,
 I ne'er mistake you for a *personal* foe ;
Our difference is *political*, and I
 Trust that, whatever may occur below,
You know my great respect for you: and this
Makes me regret whate'er you do amiss—

LXIII.

" Why, my dear Lucifer, would you abuse
 My call for witnesses? I did not mean
That you should half of earth and hell pro-
 duce ;
 'T is even superfluous, since two honest,
 clean,
True testimonies are enough: we lose
 Our time, nay, our eternity, between
The accusation and defence: if we
Hear both, 't will stretch our immortality."

LXIV.

Satan replied, " To me the matter is
 Indifferent, in a personal point of view :
I can have fifty better souls than this
 With far less trouble than we have gone
 through

Already ; and I merely argued his
 Late majesty of Britain's case with you
Upon a point of form: you may dispose
 Of him; I've kings enough below, God
 knows!"

LXV.

Thus spoke the Demon (late call'd "multi-
 faced"
 By multo-scribbling Southey). " Then we'll
 call
One or two persons of the myriads placed
 Around our congress, and dispense with all
The rest," quoth Michael: "Who may be so
 graced
 As to speak first? there's choice enough—
 who shall
It be?" Then Satan answer'd, "There are
 many;
But you may choose Jack Wilkes as well as
 any."

LXVI.

A merry, cock-eyed, curious-looking sprite
 Upon the instant started from the throng,
Dress'd in a fashion now forgotten quite;
 For all the fashions of the flesh stick long
By people in the next world; where unite
 All the costumes since Adam's, right or
 wrong,
From Eve's fig-leaf down to the petticoat,
Almost as scanty, of days less remote.

LXVII.

The spirit look'd around upon the crowds
 Assembled, and exclaim'd, " My friends
 of all
The spheres, we shall catch cold amongst
 these clouds;
 So let's to business: why this general call?
If those are freeholders I see in shrouds,
 And 'tis for an election that they bawl,
Behold a candidate with unturn'd coat !
Saint Peter, may I count upon your vote?"

LXVIII.

" Sir," replied Michael, "you mistake; these
 things
 Are of a former life, and what we do
Above is more august; to judge of kings
 Is the tribunal met: so now you know."
" Then I presume those gentlemen with
 wings,"
 Said Wilkes, "are cherubs; and that soul
 below
Looks much like George the Third, but to my
 mind
A good deal older—Bless me! is he blind?"

LXIX.

"He is what you behold him, and his doom
 Depends upon his deeds," the Angel said;
"If you have aught to arraign in him, the
 tomb
 Gives license to the humblest beggar's head
To lift itself against the loftiest."—" Some,"
 Said Wilkes, " don't wait to see them laid
 in lead,
For such a liberty—and I, for one,
Have told them what I thought beneath the
 sun."

LXX.

" *Above* the sun repeat, then, what thou hast
 To urge against him," said the Archangel.
 "Why,"
Replied the spirit, "since old scores are past,
 Must I turn evidence? In faith, not I.
Besides, I beat him hollow at the last,
 With all his Lords and Commons: in the
 sky
I don't like ripping up old stories, since
His conduct was but natural in a prince.

LXXI.

"Foolish, no doubt, and wicked, to oppress
 A poor unlucky devil without a shilling;
But then I blame the man himself much less
 Than Bute and Grafton, and shall be un-
 willing
To see him punish'd here for their excess,
 Since they were both damn'd long ago, and
 still in
Their place below: for me, I have forgiven,
And vote his ' habeas corpus ' into heaven."

LXXII.

" Wilkes," said the Devil, " I understand all
 this;
 You turn'd to half a courtier ere you died,
And seem to think it would not be amiss
 To grow a whole one on the other side
Of Charon's ferry; you forget that *his*
 Reign is concluded; whatsoe'er betide,
He won't be sovereign more: you've lost
 your labour,
For at the best he will but be your neighbour.

LXXIII.

"However, I knew what to think of it,
 When I beheld you in your jesting way,
Flitting and whispering round about the
 spit
 Where Belial, upon duty for the day,
With Fox's lard was basting William Pitt,
 His pupil; I knew what to think, I say:
That fellow even in hell breeds farther ills;
I'll have him *gagg'd*—'twas one of his own
 bills.

LXXIV.

"Call Junius!" From the crowd a shadow
 stalk'd,
 And at the name there was a general
 squeeze,
So that the very ghosts no longer walk'd
 In comfort, at their own aërial ease,
But were all ramm'd, and jamm'd (but to be
 balk'd,
 As we shall see), and jostled hands and
 knees,
Like wind compress'd and pent within a
 bladder,
Or like a human colic, which is sadder.

LXXV.

The shadow came—a tall, thin, grey-hair'd
 figure,
 That look'd as it had been a shade on earth;
Quick in its motions, with an air of vigour,
 But nought to mark its breeding or its
 birth;
Now it wax'd little, then again grew bigger,
 With now an air of gloom, or savage mirth;
But as you gazed upon its features, they
Changed every instant—to *what*, none could
 say.

LXXVI.

The more intently the ghosts gazed, the less
 Could they distinguish whose the features
 were;
The Devil himself seem'd puzzled even to
 guess;
 They varied like a dream—now here, now
 there;
And several people swore from out the press,
 They knew him perfectly; and one could
 swear
He was his father: upon which another
Was sure he was his mother's cousin's
 brother:

LXXVII.

Another, that he was a duke, or knight,
 An orator, a lawyer, or a priest,
A nabob, a man-midwife; but the wight
 Mysterious changed his countenance at
 least
As oft as they their minds; though in full sight
 He stood, the puzzle only was increased;
The man was a phantasmagoria in
Himself—he was so volatile and thin.

LXXVIII.

The moment that you had pronounced him *one*,
 Presto! his face changed, and he was
 another;
And when that change was hardly well put on,
 It varied, till I don't think his own mother

(If that he had a mother) would her son
 Have known, he shifted so from one to
 t' other;
Till guessing from a pleasure grew a task,
At this epistolary "Iron Mask."

LXXIX.

For sometimes he like Cerberus would seem—
 "Three gentlemen at once" (as sagely says
Good Mrs. Malaprop); then you might deem
 That he was not even *one ;* now many rays
Were flashing round him; and now a thick
 steam
 Hid him from sight—like fogs on London
 days :
Now Burke, now Tooke, he grew to people's
 fancies,
And certes often like Sir Philip Francis.

LXXX.

I've an hypothesis—'tis quite my own ;
 I never let it out till now, for fear
Of doing people harm about the throne,
 And injuring some minister or peer,
On whom the stigma might perhaps be blown;
 It is—my gentle public, lend thine ear !
'Tis, that what Junius we are wont to call
Was *really, truly,* nobody at all.

LXXXI.

I don't see wherefore letters should not be
 Written without hands, since we daily view
Them written without heads ; and books, we
 see,
 Are fill'd as well without the latter too :
And really till we fix on somebody
 For certain sure to claim them as his due,
Their author, like the Niger's mouth, will
 bother
The world to say if *there* be mouth or author.

LXXXII.

"And who and what art thou?" the Arch-
 angel said.
 "For *that* you may consult my title-page,"
Replied this mighty shadow of a shade :
 "If I have kept my secret half an age,
I scarce shall tell it now."—"Canst thou
 upbraid,"
 Continued Michael, "George Rex, or allege
Aught further?" Junius answer'd, "You
 had better
First ask him for *his* answer to my letter :

LXXXIII.

"My charges upon record will outlast
 The brass of both his epitaph and tomb."
"Repent'st thou not," said Michael, "of some
 past
 Exaggeration? something which may doom

Thyself if false, as him if true? Thou wast
 Too bitter—is it not so?—in thy gloom
Of passion?"—"Passion !" cried the phan-
 tom dim,
"I loved my country, and I hated him.

LXXXIV.

"What I have written, I have written : let
 The rest be on his head or mine !" So
 spoke
Old "Nominis Umbra ;" and while speaking
 yet,
 Away he melted in celestial smoke.
Then Satan said to Michael, "Don't forget
 To call George Washington, and John
 Horne Tooke,
And Franklin ;"—but at this time there was
 heard
A cry for room, though not a phantom stirr'd.

LXXXV.

At length with jostling, elbowing, and the
 aid
 Of cherubim appointed to that post,
The devil Asmodeus to the circle made
 His way, and look'd as if his journey cost
Some trouble. When his burden down he
 laid,
 "What's this ?" cried Michael ; "why,
 'tis not a ghost ?"
"I know it," quoth the incubus ; "but he
Shall be one, if you leave the affair to me.

LXXXVI.

"Confound the renegado ! I have sprain'd
 My left wing, he's so heavy; one would
 think
Some of his works about his neck were
 chain'd.
 But to the point ; while hovering o'er the
 brink
Of Skiddaw (where as usual it still rain'd),
 I saw a taper, far below me, wink,
And stooping, caught this fellow at a libel—
No less on history than the Holy Bible.

LXXXVII.

"The former is the devil's scripture, and
 The latter yours, good Michael: so the
 affair
Belongs to all of us, you understand.
 I snatch'd him up just as you see him
 there,
And brought him off for sentence out of
 hand :
I've scarcely been ten minutes in the air—
At least a quarter it can hardly be :
I dare say that his wife is still at tea."

LXXXVIII.

Here Satan said, "I know this man of old,
 And have expected him for some time here;
A sillier fellow you will scarce behold,
 Or more conceited in his petty sphere:
But surely it was not worth while to fold
 Such trash below your wing, Asmodeus
 dear:
We had the poor wretch safe (without being
 bored
With carriage) coming of his own accord.

LXXXIX.

"But since he's here, let's see what he has
 done."
 "Done!" cried Asmodeus, "he anticipates
The very business you are now upon,
 And scribbles as if head clerk to the Fates.
Who knows to what his ribaldry may run,
 When such an ass as this, like Balaam's,
 prates?"
"Let's hear," quoth Michael, "what he has
 to say:
You know we're bound to that in every way."

XC.

Now the bard, glad to get an audience, which
 By no means often was his case below,
Began to cough, and hawk, and hem, and pitch
 His voice into that awful note of woe
To all unhappy hearers within reach
 Of poets when the tide of rhyme's in flow;
But stuck fast with his first hexameter,
Not one of all whose gouty feet would stir.

XCI.

But ere the spavin'd dactyls could be spurr'd
 Into recitative, in great dismay
Both cherubim and seraphim were heard
 To murmur loudly through their long
 array;
And Michael rose ere he could get a word
 Of all his founder'd verses under way,
And cried, "For God's sake stop, my friend!
 'twere best—
Non Di, non homines—you know the rest."

XCII.

A general bustle spread throughout the
 throng,
 Which seem'd to hold all verse in detes-
 tation;
The angels had of course enough of song
 When upon service; and the generation
Of ghosts had heard too much in life, not long
 Before, to profit by a new occasion:
The monarch, mute till then, exclaim'd,
 "What! what!
Pye come again? No more—no more of that!"

XCIII.

The tumult grew; an universal cough
 Convulsed the skies, as during a debate,
When Castlereagh has been up long enough
 (Before he was first minister of state,
I mean—the *slaves hear now*); some cried
 "Off, off!"
As at a farce; till, grown quite desperate,
The bard Saint Peter pray'd to interpose
(Himself an author) only for his prose.

XCIV.

The varlet was not an ill-favour'd knave;
 A good deal like a vulture in the face,
With a hook nose and a hawk's eye, which
 gave
A smart and sharper-looking sort of grace
 To his whole aspect, which, though rather
 grave,
Was by no means so ugly as his case;
But that, indeed, was hopeless as can be,
Quite a poetic felony "*de se*."

XCV.

Then Michael blew his trump, and still'd the
 noise
 With one still greater, as is yet the mode
On earth besides; except some grumbling
 voice,
 Which now and then will make a slight
 inroad
Upon decorous silence, few will twice
 Lift up their lungs when fairly overcrow'd;
And now the bard could plead his own bad
 cause,
With all the attitudes of self-applause.

XCVI.

He said—(I only give the heads)—he said,
 He meant no harm in scribbling; 'twas
 his way
Upon all topics; 'twas, besides, his bread,
 Of which he butter'd both sides; 'twould
 delay
Too long the assembly (he was pleased to
 dread),
 And take up rather more time than a day,
To name his works—he would but cite a
 few—
"Wat Tyler"—"Rhymes on Blenheim"—
 "Waterloo."

XCVII.

He had written praises of a regicide;
 He had written praises of all kings what
 ever;
He had written for republics far and wide,
 And then against them bitterer than ever

For pantisocracy he once had cried
 Aloud, a scheme less moral than 't was
 clever;
Then grew a hearty anti-jacobin—
Had turn'd his coat—and would have turn'd
 his skin.

XCVIII.

He had sung against all battles, and again
 In their high praise and glory; he had
 call'd
Reviewing "the ungentle craft," and then
 Become as base a critic as e'er crawl'd—
Fed, paid, and pamper'd by the very men
 By whom his muse and morals had been
 maul'd:
He had written much blank verse, and blanker
 prose,
And more of both than anybody knows.

XCIX.

He had written Wesley's life:—here turning
 round
 To Satan, "Sir, I'm ready to write yours,
In two octavo volumes, nicely bound,
 With notes and preface, all that most al-
 lures
The pious purchaser; and there's no ground
 For fear, for I can choose my own re-
 viewers:
So let me have the proper documents,
That I may add you to my other saints."

C.

Satan bow'd, and was silent. "Well, if you,
 With amiable modesty, decline
My offer, what says Michael? There are few
 Whose memoirs could be render'd more
 divine.
Mine is a pen of all work; not so new
 As it was once, but I would make you
 shine
Like your own trumpet. By the way, my own
Has more of brass in it, and is as well blown.

CI.

"But talking about trumpets, here's my
 Vision!
 Now you shall judge, all people; yes, you
 shall
Judge with my judgment, and by my decision
 Be guided who shall enter heaven or fall.
I settle all these things by intuition,
 Times present, past, to come, heaven, hell,
 and all,
Like King Alfonso. When I thus see double,
I save the Deity some worlds of trouble."

CII.

He ceased, and drew forth an MS.; and no
 Persuasion on the part of devils, saints,
Or angels, now could stop the torrent; so
 He read the first three lines of the con-
 tents;
But at the fourth, the whole spiritual show
 Had vanish'd, with variety of scents,
Ambrosial and sulphureous, as they sprang,
Like lightning, off from his "melodious
 twang."

CIII.

Those grand heroics acted as a spell:
 The angels stopp'd their ears and plied
 their pinions;
The devils ran howling, deafen'd, down to hell;
 The ghosts fled, gibbering, for their own
 dominions—
(For 'tis not yet decided where they dwell,
 And I leave every man to his opinions);
Michael took refuge in his trump—but, lo!
His teeth were set on edge, he could not
 blow!

CIV.

Saint Peter, who has hitherto been known
 For an impetuous saint, upraised his keys,
And at the fifth line knock'd the poet down;
 Who fell like Phæton, but more at ease,
Into his lake, for there he did not drown;
 A different web being by the Destinies
Woven for the Laureate's final wreath, when-
 e'er
Reform shall happen either here or there.

CV.

He first sank to the bottom—like his works,
 But soon rose to the surface—like himself;
For all corrupted things are buoy'd like corks,
 By their own rottenness, light as an elf,
Or wisp that flits o'er a morass: he lurks,
 It may be, still, like dull books on a shelf,
In his own den, to scrawl some "Life" or
 "Vision,"
As Welborn says—"the devil turn'd pre-
 cisian."

CVI.

As for the rest, to come to the conclusion
 Of this true dream, the telescope is gone
Which kept my optics free from all delusion,
 And show'd me what I in my turn have
 shown;
All I saw farther, in the last confusion,
 Was, that King George slipp'd into heaven
 for one;
And when the tumult dwindled to a calm,
I left him practising the hundredth psalm.

The Age of Bronze;

OR,

CARMEN SECULARE ET ANNUS HAUD MIRABILIS.

———◆◆———

"Impar *Congressus* Achilli."

———◆◆———

I.

The "good old times"—all times when old
 are good—
Are gone; the present might be if they
 would;
Great things have been, and are, and greater
 still
Want little of mere mortals but their will:
A wider space, a greener field, is given
To those who play their "tricks before high
 heaven."
I know not if the angels weep, but men
Have wept enough—for what?—to weep
 again!

II.

All is exploded—be it good or bad.
Reader! remember when thou wert a lad,
Then Pitt was all; or, if not all, so much,
His very rival almost deem'd him such.
We, we have seen the intellectual race
Of giants stand, like Titans, face to face—
Athos and Ida, with a dashing sea
Of eloquence between, which flow'd all free,
As the deep billows of the Ægean roar
Betwixt the Hellenic and the Phrygian
 shore.
But where are they—the rivals! a few feet
Of sullen earth divide each winding sheet.
How peaceful and how powerful is the grave,
Which hushes all! a calm, unstormy wave,
Which oversweeps the world. The theme
 is old
Of "dust to dust;" but half its tale untold:
Time tempers not its terrors—still the worm
Winds its cold folds, the tomb preserves its
 form,
Varied above, but still alike below;
The urn may shine, the ashes will not glow,
Though Cleopatra's mummy cross the sea
O'er which from empire she lured Anthony;

Though Alexander's urn a show be grown
On shores he wept to conquer, though un-
 known—
How vain, how worse than vain, at length
 appear
The madman's wish, the Macedonian's tear!
He wept for worlds to conquer—half the
 earth
Knows not his name, or but his death, and
 birth,
And desolation; while his native Greece
Hath all of desolation, save its peace.
He "wept for worlds to conquer!" he who
 ne'er
Conceived the globe, he panted not to spare!
With even the busy Northern Isle unknown,
Which holds his urn, and never knew his
 throne.

III.

But where is he, the modern, mightier far,
Who, born no king, made monarchs draw
 his car;
The new Sesostris, whose unharness'd kings,
Freed from the bit, believe themselves with
 wings,
And spurn the dust o'er which they crawl'd
 of late,
Chain'd to the chariot of the chieftain's
 state?
Yes! where is he, the champion and the
 child
Of all that's great or little, wise or wild;
Whose game was empires, and whose stakes
 were thrones;
Whose table earth—whose dice were human
 bones?
Behold the grand result in yon lone isle,
And, as thy nature urges, weep or smile.
Sigh to behold the eagle's lofty rage
Reduced to nibble at his narrow cage;

Smile to survey the queller of the nations
Now daily squabbling o'er disputed rations;
Weep to perceive him mourning, as he dines,
O'er curtail'd dishes and o'er stinted wines;
O'er petty quarrels upon petty things.
Is this the man who scourged or feasted
　kings?
Behold the scales in which his fortune
　hangs,
A surgeon's statement, and an earl's ha-
　rangues!
A bust delayed, a book refused, can shake
The sleep of him who kept the world awake.
Is this indeed the tamer of the great,
Now slave of all could tease or irritate—
The paltry gaoler and the prying spy,
The staring stranger with his note-book
　nigh?
Plunged in a dungeon he had still been
　great;
How low, how little was this middle state,
Between a prison and a palace, where
How few could feel for what he had to bear!
Vain his complaint,—my lord presents his
　bill,
His food and wine were doled out duly still;
Vain was his sickness, never was a clime
So free from homicide—to doubt's a crime;
And the stiff surgeon, who maintain'd his
　cause,
Hath lost his place, and gain'd the world's
　applause.
But smile—though all the pangs of brain
　and heart
Disdain, defy, the tardy aid of art;
Though, save the few fond friends and
　imaged face
Of that fair boy his sire shall ne'er embrace,
None stand by his low bed—though even the
　mind
Be wavering, which long awed and awes
　mankind:
Smile—for the fetter'd eagle breaks his
　chain,
And higher worlds than this are his again.

IV.

How, if that soaring spirit still retain
A conscious twilight of his blazing reign,
How must he smile, on looking down, to see
The little that he was and sought to be!
What though his name a wider empire found
Than his ambition, though with scarce a
　bound;
Though first in glory, deepest in reverse,
He tasted empire's blessings and its curse;
Though kings, rejoicing in their late escape
From chains, would gladly be *their* tyrant's
　ape;

How must he smile, and turn to yon lone
　grave,
The proudest sea-mark that o'ertops the
　wave!
What though his gaoler, duteous to the last,
Scarce deem'd the coffin's lead could keep
　him fast,
Refusing one poor line along the lid,
To date the birth and death of all it hid;
That name shall hallow the ignoble shore,
A talisman to all save him who bore:
The fleets that sweep before the eastern
　blast
Shall hear their sea-boys hail it from the
　mast;
When Victory's Gallic column shall but rise,
Like Pompey's pillar, in a desert's skies,
The rocky isle that holds or held his dust,
Shall crown the Atlantic like the hero's bust,
And mighty nature o'er his obsequies
Do more than niggard envy still denies.
But what are these to him? Can glory's lust
Touch the freed spirit or the fetter'd dust?
Small care hath he of what his tomb con-
　sists;
Nought if he sleeps—nor more if he exists:
Alike the better-seeing shade will smile
On the rude cavern of the rocky isle,
As if his ashes found their latest home
In Rome's Pantheon or Gaul's mimic dome.
He wants not this; but France shall feel the
　want
Of this last consolation, though so scant:
Her honour, fame, and faith demand his
　bones,
To rear above a pyramid of thrones;
Or carried onward in the battle's van,
To form, like Guesclin's dust, her talisman.
But be it as it is—the time may come
His name shall beat the alarm, like Ziska's
　drum.

V.

Oh heaven! of which he was in power a
　feature;
Oh earth! of which he was a noble creature;
Thou isle! to be remember'd long and well,
That saw'st the unfledged eaglet chip his
　shell!
Ye Alps, which view'd him in his dawning
　flights
Hover, the victor of a hundred fights!
Thou Rome, who saw'st thy Cæsar's deeds
　outdone!
Alas! why pass'd he too the Rubicon—
The Rubicon of man's awaken'd rights,
To herd with vulgar kings and parasites?
Egypt! from whose all dateless tombs arose
Forgotten Pharaohs from their long repose,

And shook within their pyramids to hear
A new Cambyses thundering in their ear;
While the dark shades of forty ages stood
Like startled giants by Nile's famous flood;
Or from the pyramid's tall pinnacle
Beheld the desert peopled, as from hell,
With clashing hosts, who strew'd the barren
 sand,
To re-manure the uncultivated land!
Spain! which, a moment mindless of the
 Cid,
Beheld his banner flouting thy Madrid!
Austria! which saw thy twice-ta'en capital
Twice spared to be the traitress of his fall!
Ye race of Frederic!—Frederics but in name
And falsehood—heirs to all except his fame:
Who, crush'd at Jena, crouch'd at Berlin,
 fell
First, and but rose to follow! Ye who dwell
Where Kosciusko dwelt, remembering yet
The unpaid amount of Catherine's bloody
 debt!
Poland! o'er which the avenging angel
 pass'd,
But left thee as he found thee, still a waste,
Forgetting all thy still enduring claim,
Thy lotted people and extinguish'd name,
Thy sigh for freedom, thy long-flowing tear,
That sound that crashes in the tyrant's
 ear—
Kosciusko! On—on—on—the thirst of war
Gasps for the gore of serfs and of their czar.
The half barbaric Moscow's minarets
Gleam in the sun, but 'tis a sun that sets!
Moscow! thou limit of his long career,
For which rude Charles had wept his frozen
 tear
To see in vain—*he* saw thee—how? with
 spire
And palace fuel to one common fire.
To this the soldier lent his kindling match,
To this the peasant gave his cottage thatch,
To this the merchant flung his hoarded
 store,
The prince his hall—and Moscow was no
 more!
Sublimest of volcanos! Etna's flame
Pales before thine, and quenchless Hecla's
 tame;
Vesuvius shows his blaze, an usual sight
For gaping tourists, from his hackney'd
 height:
Thou stand'st alone unrivall'd, till the fire
To come, in which all empires shall expire!

Thou other element! as strong and stern,
To teach a lesson conquerors will not
 learn!—
Whose icy wing flapp'd o'er the faltering foe,
Till fell a hero with each flake of snow:

How did thy numbing beak and silent fang
Pierce, till hosts perish'd with a single pang!
In vain shall Seine look up along his banks
For the gay thousands of his dashing ranks!
In vain shall France recall beneath her vines
Her youth—their blood flows faster than her
 wines;
Or stagnant in their human ice remains
In frozen mummies on the Polar plains.
In vain will Italy's broad sun awaken
Her offspring chill'd; its beams are now
 forsaken.
Of all the trophies gather'd from the war,
What shall return? the conqueror's broken
 car!
The conqueror's yet unbroken heart! Again
The horn of Roland sounds, and not in vain.
Lutzen, where fell the Swede of victory,
Beholds him conquer, but, alas! not die:
Dresden surveys three despots fly once more
Before their sovereign,—sovereign as before;
But there exhausted Fortune quits the field,
And Leipsic's treason bids the unvanquish'd
 yield;
The Saxon jackal leaves the lion's side
To turn the bear's, and wolf's, and fox's guide;
And backward to the den of his despair
The forest monarch shrinks, but finds no lair!

 Oh ye! and each, and all! Oh France!
 who found
Thy long fair fields plough'd up as hostile
 ground,
Disputed foot by foot, till treason, still
His only victor, from Montmartre's hill
Look'd down o'er trampled Paris! and thou
 Isle,
Which seest Etruria from thy ramparts smile,
Thou momentary shelter of his pride,
Till woo'd by danger, his yet weeping bride!
Oh, France! retaken by a single march,
Whose path was through one long triumphal
 arch!
Oh, bloody and most bootless Waterloo!
Which proves how fools may have their
 fortune too,
Won half by blunder, half by treachery:
Oh, dull Saint Helen! with thy gaoler nigh—
Hear! hear Prometheus from his rock appeal
To earth, air, ocean, all that felt or feel
His power and glory, all who yet shall hear
A name eternal as the rolling year;
He teaches them the lesson taught so long,
So oft, so vainly—learn to do no wrong!
A single step into the right had made
This man the Washington of worlds betray'd:
A single step into the wrong has given
His name a doubt to all the winds of heaven;
The reed of Fortune, and of thrones the rod,
Of Fame the Moloch or the demigod;

His country's Cæsar, Europe's Hannibal,
Without their decent dignity of fall.
Yet Vanity herself had better taught
A surer path even to the fame he sought,
By pointing out on history's fruitless page
Ten thousand conquerors for a single sage.
While Franklin's quiet memory climbs to
 heaven,
Calming the lightning which he thence hath
 riven,
Or drawing from the no less kindled earth
Freedom and peace to that which boasts his
 birth;
While Washington's a watchword, such as
 ne'er
Shall sink while there's an echo left to air:
While even the Spaniard's thirst of gold and
 war
Forgets Pizarro to shout Bolivar!
Alas! why must the same Atlantic wave
Which wafted freedom gird a tyrant's grave—
The king of kings, and yet of slaves the
 slave,
Who burst the chains of millions to renew
The very fetters which his arm broke through,
And crush'd the rights of Europe and his own,
To flit between a dungeon and a throne?

VI.

But 't will not be—the spark's awaken'd—lo!
The swarthy Spaniard feels his former glow;
The same high spirit which beat back the
 Moor
Through eight long ages of alternate gore
Revives—and where? in that avenging clime
Where Spain was once synonymous with
 crime,
Where Cortes and Pizarro's banner flew,
The infant world redeems her name of "*New*."
'Tis the *old* aspiration breathed afresh,
To kindle souls within degraded flesh,
Such as repulsed the Persian from the shore
Where Greece *was*—No! she still is Greece
 once more.
One common cause makes myriads of one
 breast,
Slaves of the East, or helots of the West:
On Andes' and on Athos' peaks unfurl'd,
The self-same standard streams o'er either
 world:
The Athenian wears again Harmodius' sword;
The Chili chief abjures his foreign lord;
The Spartan knows himself once more a
 Greek,
Young Freedom plumes the crest of each
 cacique;
Debating despots, hemm'd on either shore,
Shrink vainly from the roused Atlantic's
 roar;

Through Calpe's strait the rolling tides ad-
 vance,
Sweep slightly by the half-tamed land of
 France,
Dash o'er the old Spaniard's cradle, and would
 fain
Unite Ausonia to the mighty main:
But driven from thence awhile, yet not for
 aye,
Break o'er th' Ægean, mindful of the day
Of Salamis!—there, there the waves arise,
Not to be lull'd by tyrant victories.
Lone, lost, abandon'd in their utmost need
By Christians, unto whom they gave their
 creed,
The desolated lands, the ravaged isle,
The foster'd feud encouraged to beguile,
The aid evaded, and the cold delay,
Prolong'd but in the hope to make a prey;—
These, these shall tell the tale, and Greece
 can show
The false friend worse than the infuriate foe.
But this is well: Greeks only should free
 Greece,
Not the barbarian, with his mask of peace.
How should the autocrat of bondage be
The king of serfs, and set the nations free?
Better still serve the haughty Mussulman,
Than swell the Cossaque's prowling caravan;
Better still toil for masters, than await,
The slave of slaves, before a Russian gate,—
Number'd by hordes, a human capital,
A live estate, existing but for thrall,
Lotted by thousands, as a meet reward
For the first courtier in the Czar's regard;
While their immediate owner never tastes
His sleep, *sans* dreaming of Siberia's wastes:
Better succumb even to their own despair,
And drive the camel than purvey the bear.

VII.

But not alone within the hoariest clime
Where Freedom dates her birth with that of
 Time,
And not alone where, plunged in night, a
 crowd
Of Incas darken to a dubious cloud,
The dawn revives: renown'd, romantic Spain
Holds back the invader from her soil again.
Not now the Roman tribe nor Punic horde
Demand her fields as lists to prove the sword;
Not now the Vandal or the Visigoth
Pollute the plains, alike abhorring both;
Nor old Pelayo on his mountain rears
The warlike fathers of a thousand years.
That seed is sown and reap'd, as oft the Moor
Sighs to remember on his dusky shore.
Long in the peasant's song or poet's page
Has dwelt the memory of Abencerrage;

The Zegri, and the captive victors, flung
Back to the barbarous realm from whence
 they sprung.
But these are gone—their faith, their swords,
 their sway,
Yet left more anti-christian foes than they;
The bigot monarch, and the butcher priest,
The Inquisition, with her burning feast,
The faith's red "auto," fed with human fuel,
While sate the catholic Moloch, calmly cruel,
Enjoying, with inexorable eye,
That fiery festival of agony!
The stern or feeble sovereign, one or both
By turns; the haughtiness whose pride was
 sloth;
The long degenerate noble; the debased
Hidalgo, and the peasant less disgraced,
But more degraded; the unpeopled realm;
The once proud navy which forgot the helm;
The once impervious phalanx disarray'd;
The idle forge that form'd Toledo's blade;
The foreign wealth that flow'd on ev'ry
 shore,
Save hers who earn'd it with the natives'
 gore;
The very language which might vie with
 Rome's,
And once was known to nations like their
 homes,
Neglected or forgotten :—such was Spain;
But such she is not, nor shall be again.
These worst, these *home* invaders, felt and
 feel
The new Numantine soul of old Castile.
Up! up again! undaunted Tauridor!
The bull of Phalaris renews his roar;
Mount, chivalrous Hidalgo! not in vain
Revive the cry!—"Iago! and close Spain!"
Yes, close her with your armed bosoms
 round,
And form the barrier which Napoleon found,—
The exterminating war, the desert plain,
The streets without a tenant, save the slain;
The wild sierra, with its wilder troop
Of vulture-plumed guerrillas, on the stoop
For their incessant prey; the desperate
 wall
Of Saragossa, mightiest in her fall;
The man nerved to a spirit, and the maid
Waving her more than Amazonian blade;
The knife of Arragon, Toledo's steel;
The famous lance of chivalrous Castile:
The unerring rifle of the Catalan;
The Andalusian courser in the van;
The torch to make a Moscow of Madrid;
And in each heart the spirit of the Cid:—
Such have been, such shall be, such are.
 Advance,
And win—not Spain! but thine own freedom,
 France!

VIII.

But lo! a Congress! What! that hallow'd
 name
Which freed the Atlantic! May we hope the
 same
For outworn Europe? With the sound arise,
Like Samuel's shade to Saul's monarchic
 eyes,
The prophets of young Freedom, summon'd
 far
From climes of Washington and Bolivar;
Henry, the forest-born Demosthenes,
Whose thunder shook the Philip of the seas;
And stoic Franklin's energetic shade,
Robed in the lightnings which his hand
 allay'd;
And Washington, the tyrant-tamer, wake,
To bid us blush for these old chains, or break.
But *who* compose this senate of the few
That should redeem the many? *Who* renew
This consecrated name, till now assign'd
To councils held to benefit mankind?
Who now assemble at the holy call?
The blest Alliance, which says three are all!
An earthly trinity! which wears the shape
Of heaven's, as man is mimick'd by the ape.
A pious unity! in purpose one—
To melt three fools to a Napoleon.
Why, Egypt's gods were rational to these;
Their dogs and oxen knew their own degrees,
And, quiet in their kennel or their shed,
Cared little, so that they were duly fed;
But these, more hungry, must have something
 more—
The power to bark and bite, to toss and gore.
Ah, how much happier were good Æsop's
 frogs
Than we! for ours are animated logs,
With ponderous malice swaying to and fro,
And crushing nations with a stupid blow;
All duly anxious to leave little work
Unto the revolutionary stork.

IX.

Thrice blest Verona! since the holy three
With their imperial presence shine on thee!
Honour'd by them, thy treacherous site forgets
The vaunted tomb of "all the Capulets;"
Thy Scaligers—for what was "Dog the
 Great,"
"Can Grande," (which I venture to translate,)
To these sublimer pugs? Thy poet too,
Catullus, whose old laurels yield to new;
Thine amphitheatre, where Romans sate;
And Dante's exile shelter'd by thy gate;
Thy good old man, whose world was all within
Thy wall, nor knew the country held him in;
Would that the royal guests it girds about
Were so far like, as never to get out!

Ay, shout! inscribe! rear monuments of
 shame,
To tell Oppression that the world is tame!
Crowd to the theatre with loyal rage,
The comedy is not upon the stage;
The show is rich in ribandry and stars,
Then gaze upon it through thy dungeon bars;
Clap thy permitted palms, kind Italy,
For thus much still thy fetter'd hands are
 free!

X.

Resplendent sight! Behold the coxcomb Czar,
The autocrat of waltzes and of war!
As eager for a plaudit as a realm,
And just as fit for flirting as the helm;
A Calmuck beauty with a Cossack wit,
And generous spirit, when 'tis not frost-bit;
Now half dissolving to a liberal thaw,
But harden'd back whene'er the morning's
 raw;
With no objection to true liberty,
Except that it would make the nations free.
How well the imperial dandy prates of peace!
How fain, if Greeks would be his slaves, free
 Greece!
How nobly gave he back the Poles their Diet,
Then told pugnacious Poland to be quiet!
How kindly would he send the mild Ukraine,
With all her pleasant pulks, to lecture Spain!
How royally show off in proud Madrid
His goodly person, from the South long hid!
A blessing cheaply purchased, the world
 knows,
By having Muscovites for friends or foes.
Proceed, thou namesake of great Philip's son!
La Harpe, thine Aristotle, beckons on;
And that which Scythia was to him of yore
Find with thy Scythians on Iberia's shore.
Yet think upon, thou somewhat aged youth,
Thy predecessor on the banks of Pruth;
Thou hast to aid thee, should his lot be
 thine,
Many an old woman, but no Catherine.
Spain, too, hath rocks, and rivers, and de-
 files—
The bear may rush into the lion's toils.
Fatal to Goths are Xeres' sunny fields;
Think'st thou to thee Napoleon's victor
 yields?
Better reclaim thy deserts, turn thy swords
To ploughshares, shave and wash thy Bash-
 kir hordes,
Redeem thy realms from slavery and the
 knout,
Than follow headlong in the fatal route,
To infest the clime whose skies and laws are
 pure
With thy foul legions. Spain wants no
 manure:

Her soil is fertile, but she feeds no foe:
Her vultures, too, were gorged not long ago;
And wouldst thou furnish them with fresher
 prey?
Alas! thou wilt not conquer, but purvey.
I am Diogenes, though Russ and Hun
Stand between mine and many a myriad's sun;
But were I not Diogenes, I'd wander
Rather a worm than *such* an Alexander!
Be slaves who will, the cynic shall be free;
His tub hath tougher walls than Sinopè:
Still will he hold his lantern up to scan
The face of monarchs for an "honest man."

XI.

And what doth Gaul, the all-prolific land
Of *ne plus ultra* ultras and their band
Of mercenaries? and her noisy chambers
And tribune, which each orator first clambers
Before he finds a voice, and when 'tis found,
Hears "the lie" echo for his answer round?
Our British Commons sometimes deign to
 "hear!"
A Gallic senate hath more tongue than ear;
Even Constant, their sole master of debate,
Must fight next day his speech to vindicate.
But this costs little to true Franks, who'd
 rather
Combat than listen, were it to their father.
What is the simple standing of a shot,
To listening long, and interrupting not?
Though this was not the method of old Rome,
When Tully fulmined o'er each vocal dome,
Demosthenes has sanction'd the transaction,
In saying eloquence meant "Action, action!"

XII.

But where's the monarch? hath he dined? or
 yet
Groans beneath indigestion's heavy debt?
Have revolutionary patés risen,
And turn'd the royal entrails to a prison?
Have discontented movements stirr'd the
 troops?
Or have *no* movements follow'd traitorous
 soups?
Have Carbonaro cooks not carbonadoed
Each course enough! or doctors dire dis-
 suaded
Repletion? Ah! in thy dejected looks
I read all France's treason in her cooks!
Good classic Louis! is it, canst thou say,
Desirable to be the "Desiré"?
Why wouldst thou leave calm Hartwell's
 green abode,
Apician table, and Horatian ode,
To rule a people who will not be ruled,
And love much rather to be scourged than
 school'd?

Ah! thine was not the temper or the taste
For thrones; the table sees thee better placed:
A mild Epicurean, form'd, at best,
To be a kind host and as good a guest,
To talk of letters, and to know by heart
One *half* the poet's, *all* the gourmand's art:
A scholar always, now and then a wit,
And gentle when digestion may permit;—
But not to govern lands enslaved or free;
The gout was martyrdom enough for thee.

XIII.

Shall noble Albion pass without a phrase
From a bold Briton in her wonted praise?
" Arts, arms, and George, and glory, and the
 isles,
And happy Britain, wealth, and Freedom's
 smiles,
White cliffs, that held invasion far aloof,
Contented subjects, all alike tax-proof,
Proud Wellington, with eagle beak so curl'd,
That nose, the hook where he suspends the
 world!
And Waterloo, and trade, and——(hush! not
 yet
A syllable of imposts or of debt)——
And ne'er (enough) lamented Castlereagh,
Whose penknife slit a goose-quill t'other
 day—
And 'pilots who have weather'd every
 storm'—
(But, no, not even for rhyme's sake, name
 Reform)."
These are the themes thus sung so oft before,
Methinks we need not sing them any more;
Found in so many volumes far and near,
There's no occasion you should find them
 here.
Yet something may remain perchance to
 chime
With reason, and what's stranger still, with
 rhyme.
Even this thy genius, Canning! may permit,
Who, bred a statesman, still wast born a wit,
And never, even in that dull House, couldst
 tame
To unleaven'd prose thine own poetic flame;
Our last, our best, our only orator,
Even I can praise thee—Tories do no more:
Nay, not so much;—they hate thee, man, be-
 cause
Thy spirit less upholds them than it awes.
The hounds will gather to their huntsman's
 hollo,
And where he leads the duteous pack will
 follow;
But not for love mistake their yelling cry;
Their yelp for game is not an eulogy;
Less faithful far than the four-footed pack,
A dubious scent would lure the bipeds back,

Thy saddle-girths are not yet quite secure,
Nor royal stallion's feet extremely sure;
The unwieldy old white horse is apt at last
To stumble, kick, and now and then stick
 fast
With his great self and rider in the mud;
But what of that? the animal shows blood.

XIV.

Alas, the country! how shall tongue or pen
Bewail her now *uncountry* gentlemen?
The last to bid the cry of warfare cease,
The first to make a malady of peace.
For what were all these country patriots
 born?
To hunt, and vote, and raise the price of
 corn?
But corn, like every mortal thing, must fall,
Kings, conquerors, and markets most of all.
And must ye fall with every ear of grain?
Why would you trouble Buonaparté's reign?
He was your great Triptolemus; his vices
Destroy'd but realms, and still maintain'd
 your prices;
He amplified to every lord's content
The grand agrarian alchymy, high *rent*.
Why did the tyrant stumble on the Tartars,
And lower wheat to such desponding quarters?
Why did you chain him on yon isle so lone?
The man was worth much more upon his
 throne.
True, blood and treasure boundlessly were
 spilt,
But what of that? the Gaul may bear the
 guilt;
But bread was high, the farmer paid his way,
And acres told upon the appointed day.
But where is now the goodly audit ale?
The purse-proud tenant, never known to fail?
The farm which never yet was left on hand?
The marsh reclaim'd to most improving land?
The impatient hope of the expiring lease?
The doubling rental? What an evil's peace!
In vain the prize excites the ploughman's
 skill,
In vain the Commons pass their patriot bill;
The *landed interest*—(you may understand
The phrase much better leaving out the
 land)—
The land self-interest groans from shore to
 shore,
For fear that plenty should attain the poor.
Up, up again, ye rents! exalt your notes,
Or else the ministry will lose their votes,
And patriotism, so delicately nice,
Her loaves will lower to the market price;
For ah! "the loaves and fishes," once so
 high,
Are gone—their oven closed, their ocean dry,

And nought remains of all the millions spent,
Excepting to grow moderate and content.
They who are not so, *had* their turn—and
 turn
About still flows from Fortune's equal urn;
Now let their virtue be its own reward,
And share the blessings which themselves
 prepared.
See these inglorious Cincinnati swarm,
Farmers of war, dictators of the farm;
Their ploughshare was the sword in hireling
 hands,
Their fields manured by gore of other lands;
Safe in their barns, these Sabine tillers sent
Their brethren out to battle—why? for
 rent!
Year after year they voted cent. per cent.,
Blood, sweat, and tear-wrung millions—why?
 for rent!
They roar'd, they dined, they drank, they
 swore they meant
To die for England—why then live?—for
 rent!
The peace has made one general malcontent
Of these high-market patriots; war was rent!
Their love of country, millions all misspent,
How reconcile? by reconciling rent!
And will they not repay the treasures lent?
No: down with everything, and up with rent!
Their good, ill, health, wealth, joy, or dis-
 content,
Being, end, aim, religion—rent, rent, rent!
Thou sold'st thy birthright, Esau! for a mess;
Thou shouldst have gotten more, or eaten
 less;
Now thou hast swill'd thy pottage, thy de-
 mands
Are idle; Israel says the bargain stands.
Such, landlords! was your appetite for war,
And gorged with blood, you grumble at a scar!
What! would they spread their earthquake
 even o'er cash?
And when land crumbles, bid firm paper
 crash?
So rent may rise, bid bank and nation fall,
And found on 'Change a *Fundling* Hospital?
Lo, Mother Church, while all religion writhes,
Like Niobe, weeps o'er her offspring, Tithes;
The prelates go to—where the saints have
 gone,
And proud pluralities subside to one;
Church, state, and faction wrestle in the dark,
Toss'd by the deluge in their common ark.
Shorn of her bishops, banks, and dividends,
Another Babel soars—but Britain ends.
And why? to pamper the self-seeking wants,
And prop the hill of these agrarian ants.
"Go to these ants, thou sluggard, and be
 wise;"
Admire their patience through each sacrifice,

Till taught to feel the lesson of their pride,
The price of taxes and of homicide;
Admire their justice, which would fain deny
The debt of nations:—pray, *who made it high?*

XV.

Or turn to sail between those shifting rocks,
The new Symplegades—the crushing Stocks,
Where Midas might again his wish behold
In real paper or imagined gold.
That magic palace of Alcina shows
More wealth than Britain ever had to lose,
Were all her atoms of unleaven'd ore,
And all her pebbles from Pactolus' shore.
There Fortune plays, while Rumour holds the
 stake,
And the world trembles to bid brokers break.
How rich is Britain! not indeed in mines,
Or peace or plenty, corn or oil, or wines;
No land of Canaan, full of milk and honey,
Nor (save in paper shekels) ready money:
But let us not to own the truth refuse,
Was ever Christian land so rich in Jews?
Those parted with their teeth to good King
 John,
And now, ye kings! they kindly draw your
 own;
All states, all things, all sovereigns they
 control,
And waft a loan "from Indus to the pole."
The banker, broker, baron, brethren, speed
To aid these bankrupt tyrants in their need.
Nor these alone; Columbia feels no less
Fresh speculations follow each success;
And philanthropic Israel deigns to drain
Her mild per-centage from exhausted Spain.
Not without Abraham's seed can Russia
 march;
'Tis gold, not steel, that rears the conqueror's
 arch.
Two Jews, a chosen people, can command
In every realm their scripture-promised
 land:—
Two Jews keep down the Romans, and up-
 hold
The accursed Hun, more brutal than of old:
Two Jews—but not Samaritans—direct
The world, with all the spirit of their sect.
What is the happiness of earth to them?
A congress forms their " New Jerusalem,"
Where baronies and orders both invite—
Oh, holy Abraham! dost thou see the sight?
Thy followers mingling with these royal
 swine,
Who spit not "on their Jewish gaberdine,"
But honour them as portion of the show—
(Where now, oh Pope! is thy forsaken toe?
Could it not favour Judah with some kicks?
Or has it ceased to "kick against the pricks?")

On Shylock's shore behold them stand afresh,
To cut from nations' hearts their "pound of flesh."

XVI.

Strange sight this Congress! destined to unite
All that's incongruous, all that's opposite.
I speak not of the sovereigns—they're alike,
A common coin as ever mint could strike;
But those who sway the puppets, pull the strings,
Have more of motley than their heavy kings.
Jews, authors, generals, charlatans, combine,
While Europe wonders at the vast design:
There Metternich, power's foremost parasite,
Cajoles; there Wellington forgets to fight;
There Chateaubriand forms new books of martyrs;
And subtle Greeks intrigue for stupid Tartars;
There Montmorenci, the sworn foe to charters,
Turns a diplomatist of great éclat,
To furnish articles for the "Débats;"
Of war so certain—yet not quite so sure
As his dismissal in the "Moniteur."
Alas! how could his cabinet thus err!
Can peace be worth an ultra-minister?
He falls indeed, perhaps to rise again,
"Almost as quickly as he conquer'd Spain."

XVII.

Enough of this—a sight more mournful woos
The averted eye of the reluctant muse.
The imperial daughter, the imperial bride,
The imperial victim—sacrifice to pride;
The mother of the hero's hope, the boy,
The young Astyanax of modern Troy;
The still pale shadow of the loftiest queen
That earth has yet to see, or e'er hath seen;
She flits amidst the phantoms of the hour,
The theme of pity, and the wreck of power.
Oh, cruel mockery! Could not Austria spare
A daughter? What did France's widow there?
Her fitter place was by St. Helen's wave,
Her only throne is in Napoleon's grave.
But, no—she still must hold a petty reign,
Flank'd by her formidable chamberlain;
The martial Argus, whose not hundred eyes
Must watch her through these paltry pageantries.
What though she share no more, and shared in vain,
A sway surpassing that of Charlemagne,

Which swept from Moscow to the southern seas!
Yet still she rules the pastoral realm of cheese,
Where Parma views the traveller resort,
To note the trappings of her mimic court.
But she appears! Verona sees her shorn
Of all her beams—while nations gaze and mourn—
Ere yet her husband's ashes have had time
To chill in their inhospitable clime;
(If e'er those awful ashes can grow cold;—
But no,—their embers soon will burst the mould;)
She comes!—the Andromache (but not Racine's,
Nor Homer's,)—Lo! on Pyrrhus' arm she leans!
Yes! the right arm, yet red from Waterloo,
Which cut her lord's half-shatter'd sceptre through,
Is offer'd and accepted? Could a slave
Do more? or less?—and *he* in his new grave!
Her eye, her cheek, betray no inward strife,
And the *ex*-empress grows as *ex* a wife!
So much for human ties in royal breasts!
Why spare men's feelings, when their own are jests?

XVIII.

But, tired of foreign follies, I turn home,
And sketch the group—the picture's yet to come.
My muse 'gan weep, but, ere a tear was spilt,
She caught Sir William Curtis in a kilt!
While throng'd the chiefs of every Highland clan
To hail their brother, Vich Ian Alderman!
Guildhall grows Gael, and echoes with Erse roar,
While all the Common Council cry "Claymore!"
To see proud Albyn's tartans as a belt
Gird the gross surloin of a city Celt,
She burst into a laughter so extreme,
That I awoke—and lo! it was *no* dream!

Here, reader, will we pause:—if there's no harm in
This first—you'll have, perhaps, a second "Carmen."

Childe Harold's Pilgrimage.

A ROMAUNT.

L'UNIVERS est une espèce de livre, dont on n'a lu que la première page quand on n'a vu que son pays. J'en ai feuilleté un assez grand nombre, que j'ai trouvé également mauvaises. Cet examen ne m'a point été infructueux. Je haïssais ma patrie. Toutes les impertinences des peuples divers, parmi lesquels j'ai vécu, m'ont réconcilié avec elle. Quand je n'aurais tiré d'autre bénéfice de mes voyages que celui-là, je n'en regretterais ni les frais ni les fatigues.—LE COSMOPOLITE.

PREFACE TO THE FIRST AND SECOND CANTOS.

THE following poem was written, for the most part, amidst the scenes which it attempts to describe. It was begun in Albania; and the parts relative to Spain and Portugal were composed from the author's observations in those countries. Thus much it may be necessary to state for the correctness of the descriptions. The scenes attempted to be sketched are in Spain, Portugal, Epirus, Acarnania, and Greece. There, for the present, the poem stops; its reception will determine whether the author may venture to conduct his readers to the capital of the East, through Ionia and Phrygia: these two cantos are merely experimental.

A fictitious character is introduced for the sake of giving some connexion to the piece; which, however, makes no pretension to regularity. It has been suggested to me by friends, on whose opinions I set a high value, that in this fictitious character, "Childe Harold," I may incur the suspicion of having intended some real personage: this I beg leave, once for all, to disclaim—Harold is the child of imagination, for the purpose I have stated. In some very trivial particulars, and those merely local, there might be grounds for such a notion; but in the main points, I should hope, none whatever.

It is almost superfluous to mention that the appellation "Childe," as "Childe Waters," "Childe Childers," &c., is used as more consonant with the old structure of versification which I have adopted. The "Good Night," in the beginning of the first canto, was suggested by "Lord Maxwell's Good Night," in the Border Minstrelsy, edited by Mr. Scott.

With the different poems which have been published on Spanish subjects, there may be found some slight coincidence in the first part, which treats of the Peninsula, but it can only be casual; as, with the exception of a few concluding stanzas, the whole of this poem was written in the Levant.

The stanza of Spenser, according to one of our most successful poets, admits of every variety. Dr.

Beattie makes the following observation:—"Not long ago, I began a poem in the style and stanza of Spenser, in which I propose to give full scope to my inclination, and be either droll or pathetic, descriptive or sentimental, tender or satirical, as the humour strikes me; for, if I mistake not, the measure which I have adopted admits equally of all these kinds of composition*."—Strengthened in my opinion by such authority, and by the example of some in the highest order of Italian poets, I shall make no apology for attempts at similar variations in the following composition; satisfied that if they are unsuccessful, their failure must be in the execution, rather than in the design, sanctioned by the practice of Ariosto, Thomson, and Beattie.

LONDON, *February*, 1812.

ADDITION TO THE PREFACE.

I HAVE now waited till almost all our periodical journals have distributed their usual portion of criticism. To the justice of the generality of their criticisms I have nothing to object: it would ill become me to quarrel with their very slight degree of censure, when, perhaps, if they had been less kind they had been more candid. Returning, therefore, to all and each my best thanks for their liberality, on one point alone shall I venture an observation. Amongst the many objections justly urged to the very indifferent character of the "vagrant Childe," (whom, notwithstanding many hints to the contrary, I still maintain to be a fictitious personage,) it has been stated, that, besides the anachronism, he is very *unknightly*, as the times of the Knights were times of Love, Honour, and so forth. Now, it so happens that the good old times, when "l'amour du bon vieux tems, l'amour antique," flourished, were the most profligate of all possible

* Beattie's Letters.

centuries. Those who have any doubts on this subject may consult Sainte-Palaye, *passim*, and more particularly vol. ii. p. 69. The vows of chivalry were no better kept than any other vows whatsoever; and the songs of the Troubadours were not more decent, and certainly were much less refined, than those of Ovid. The "Cours d'amour, parlemens d'amour, ou de courtesie et de gentilesse" had much more of love than of courtesy or gentleness. See Roland on the same subject with Sainte-Palaye. Whatever other objection may be urged to that most unamiable personage Childe Harold, he was so far perfectly knightly in his attributes—"No waiter, but a knight templar*." By the by, I fear that Sir Tristrem and Sir Lancelot were no better than they should be, although very poetical personages and true knights "sans peur," though not "sans réproche." If the story of the institution of the "Garter" be not a fable, the knights of that order have for several centuries borne the badge of a Countess of Salisbury, of indifferent memory. So much for chivalry. Burke need not have regretted that its days are over, though Marie-Antoinette was quite as chaste as most of those in whose honour lances were shivered, and knights unhorsed.

Before the days of Bayard, and down to those of Sir Joseph Banks (the most chaste and celebrated of ancient and modern times), few exceptions will be found to this statement; and I fear a little investigation will teach us not to regret these monstrous mummeries of the middle ages.

I now leave "Childe Harold" to live his day, such as he is; it had been more agreeable, and certainly more easy, to have drawn an amiable character. It had been easy to varnish over his faults, to make him do more and express less, but he never was intended as an example, further than to show, that early perversion of mind and morals leads to satiety of past pleasures and disappointment in new ones, and that even the beauties of nature and the stimulus of travel (except ambition, the most powerful of all excitements) are lost on a soul so constituted, or rather misdirected. Had I proceeded with the poem, this character would have deepened as he drew to the close; for the outline which I once meant to fill up for him was, with some exceptions, the sketch of a modern Timon, perhaps a poetical Zeluco.

LONDON, 1813.

* The Rovers, or the Double Arrangement.

TO IANTHE.

NoT in those climes where I have late been straying,
Though Beauty long hath there been matchless deem'd;
Not in those visions to the heart displaying
Forms which it sighs but to have only dream'd,
Hath aught like thee in truth or fancy seem'd:
Nor, having seen thee, shall I vainly seek
To paint those charms which varied as they beam'd—
To such as see thee not my words were weak;
To those who gaze on thee what language could they speak?

Ah! may'st thou ever be what now thou art,
Nor unbeseem the promise of thy spring,
As fair in form, as warm yet pure in heart,
Love's image upon earth without his wing,
And guileless beyond Hope's imagining!
And surely she who now so fondly rears
Thy youth, in thee, thus hourly brightening,
Beholds the rainbow of her future years,
Before whose heavenly hues all sorrow disappears.

Young Peri of the West!—'t is well for me
My years already doubly number thine;
My loveless eye unmoved may gaze on thee,
And safely view thy ripening beauties shine;
Happy, I ne'er shall see them in decline;
Happier, that while all younger hearts shall bleed,
Mine shall escape the doom thine eyes assign
To those whose admiration shall succeed,
But mix'd with pangs to Love's even loveliest hours decreed.

Oh! let that eye, which, wild as the Gazelle's,
Now brightly bold or beautifully shy,
Wins as it wanders, dazzles where it dwells,
Glance o'er this page, nor to my verse deny
That smile for which my breast might vainly sigh
Could I to thee be ever more than friend:
This much, dear maid, accord; nor question why
To one so young my strain I would commend,
But bid me with my wreath one matchless lily blend.

Such is thy name with this my verse
 entwined;
And long as kinder eyes a look shall cast
On Harold's page, Ianthe's here enshrined
Shall thus be first beheld, forgotten last:
My days once number'd, should this homage
 past

Attract thy fairy fingers near the lyre
Of him who hail'd thee, loveliest as thou
 wast,
Such is the most my memory may de-
 sire;
Though more than Hope can claim, could
 Friendship less require?

CHILDE HAROLD'S PILGRIMAGE.

Canto the First.

I.

OH, thou! in Hellas deem'd of heavenly
 birth,
Muse! form'd or fabled at the minstrel's
 will!
Since shamed full oft by later lyres on
 earth,
Mine dares not call thee from thy sacred
 hill:
Yet there I've wander'd by thy vaunted
 rill;
Yes! sigh'd o'er Delphi's long deserted
 shrine,
Where, save that feeble fountain, all is
 still;
Nor mote my shell awake the weary
 Nine
To grace so plain a tale—this lowly lay of
 mine.

II.

Whilome in Albion's isle there dwelt a
 youth,
Who ne in virtue's ways did take de-
 light;
But spent his days in riot most uncouth,
And vex'd with mirth the drowsy ear of
 Night.
Ah me! in sooth he was a shameless
 wight,
Sore given to revel and ungodly glee;
Few earthly things found favour in his
 sight
Save concubines and carnal companie,
And flaunting wassailers of high and low
 degree.

III.

Childe Harold was he hight:—but whence
 his name
And lineage long, it suits me not to say;
Suffice it, that perchance they were of
 fame,
And had been glorious in another day:
But one sad losel soils a name for aye,
However mighty in the olden time;
Nor all that heralds rake from coffin'd
 clay,
Nor florid prose, nor honeyed lies of
 rhyme,
Can blazon evil deeds, or consecrate a crime.

IV.

Childe Harold bask'd him in the noontide
 sun,
Disporting there like any other fly;
Nor deem'd before his little day was
 done
One blast might chill him into misery.
But long ere scarce a third of his pass'd
 by,
Worse than adversity the Childe befell;
He felt the fulness of satiety:
Then loathed he in his native land to
 dwell,
Which seem'd to him more lone than Erem-
 ite's sad cell.

V.

For he through Sin's long labyrinth had
 run,
Nor made atonement when he did amiss,
Had sigh'd to many though he loved but
 one,
And that loved one, alas! could ne'er
 be his.

Ah, happy she! to 'scape from him whose
kiss
Had been pollution unto aught so chaste;
Who soon had left her charms for vulgar
bliss,
And spoil'd her goodly lands to gild his
waste,
Nor calm domestic peace had ever deign'd to
taste.

VI.

And now Childe Harold was sore sick at
heart,
And from his fellow bacchanals would flee;
'T is said, at times the sullen tear would
start,
But Pride congeal'd the drop within his ee:
Apart he stalk'd in joyless reverie,
And from his native land resolved to go,
And visit scorching climes beyond the sea;
With pleasure drugg'd, he almost long'd
for woe,
And e'en for change of scene would seek the
shades below.

VII.

The Childe departed from his father's hall:
It was a vast and venerable pile;
So old, it seemed only not to fall,
Yet strength was pillar'd in each massy
aisle.
Monastic dome! condemn'd to uses vile!
Where Superstition once had made her den
Now Paphian girls were known to sing and
smile;
And monks might deem their time was
come agen,
If ancient tales say true, nor wrong these
holy men.

VIII.

Yet oft-times in his maddest mirthful
mood
Strange pangs would flash along Childe
Harold's brow,
As if the memory of some deadly feud
Or disappointed passion lurk'd below:
But this none knew, nor haply cared to
know;
For his was not that open, artless soul
That feels relief by bidding sorrow flow,
Nor sought he friend to counsel or condole,
Whate'er this grief mote be, which he could
not control.

IX.

And none did love him: though to hall and
bower
He gather'd revellers from far and near,
He knew them flatt'rers of the festal hour;
The heartless parasites of present cheer.

Yea! none did love him—not his lemans
dear—
But pomp and power alone are woman's
care,
And where these are light Eros finds a
feere;
Maidens, like moths, are ever caught by
glare,
And Mammon wins his way where Seraphs
might despair.

X.

Childe Harold had a mother—not forgot,
Though parting from that mother he did
shun;
A sister whom he loved, but saw her not
Before his weary pilgrimage begun:
If friends he had, he bade adieu to none.
Yet deem not thence his breast a breast of
steel:
Ye, who have known what 't is to dote
upon
A few dear objects, will in sadness feel
Such partings break the heart they fondly
hope to heal.

XI.

His house, his home, his heritage, his
lands,
The laughing dames in whom he did
delight,
Whose large blue eyes, fair locks, and
snowy hands,
Might shake the saintship of an anchorite,
And long had fed his youthful appetite;
His goblets brimm'd with every costly
wine,
And all that mote to luxury invite,
Without a sigh he left, to cross the brine,
And traverse Paynim shores, and pass Earth's
central line.

XII.

The sails were fill'd, and fair the light
winds blew,
As glad to waft him from his native home;
And fast the white rocks faded from his
view,
And soon were lost in circumambient foam:
And then, it may be, of his wish to roam
Repented he, but in his bosom slept
The silent thought, nor from his lips did
come
One word of wail, whilst others sate and
wept,
And to the reckless gales unmanly moaning
kept.

XIII.

But when the sun was sinking in the sea
He seized his harp, which he at times
 could string,
And strike, albeit with untaught melody,
When deem'd he no strange ear was
 listening:
And now his fingers o'er it he did fling,
And tuned his farewell in the dim twilight.
While flew the vessel on her snowy wing,
And fleeting shores receded from his sight,
Thus to the elements he pour'd his last
 "Good Night."

1.

ADIEU, adieu! my native shore
 Fades o'er the waters blue;
The night-winds sigh, the breakers roar,
 And shrieks the wild sea-mew.
Yon sun that sets upon the sea
 We follow in his flight;
Farewell awhile to him and thee,
 My native Land—Good Night!

2.

A few short hours and he will rise
 To give the morrow birth;
And I shall hail the main and skies,
 But not my mother earth.
Deserted is my own good hall,
 Its hearth is desolate;
Wild weeds are gathering on the wall;
 My dog howls at the gate.

3.

" Come hither, hither, my little page!
 Why dost thou weep and wail?
Or dost thou dread the billows' rage,
 Or tremble at the gale?
But dash the tear-drop from thine eye;
 Our ship is swift and strong:
Our fleetest falcon scarce can fly
 More merrily along."

4.

" Let winds be shrill, let waves roll high,
 I fear not wave nor wind:
Yet marvel not, Sir Childe, that I
 Am sorrowful in mind;
For I have from my father gone,
 A mother whom I love,
And have no friend, save these alone,
 But thee—and one above.

5.

" My father bless'd me fervently,
 Yet did not much complain;
But sorely will my mother sigh
 Till I come back again."—

 " Enough, enough, my little lad!
 Such tears become thine eye;
If I thy guileless bosom had,
 Mine own would not be dry.

6.

" Come hither, hither, my staunch yeoman,
 Why dost thou look so pale?
Or dost thou dread a French foeman?
 Or shiver at the gale?"—
" Deem'st thou I tremble for my life?
 Sir Childe, I'm not so weak;
But thinking on an absent wife
 Will blanch a faithful cheek.

7.

" My spouse and boys dwell near thy hall,
 Along the bordering lake,
And when they on their father call,
 What answer shall she make?"—
" Enough, enough, my yeoman good,
 Thy grief let none gainsay;
But I, who am of lighter mood,
 Will laugh to flee away."

8.

For who would trust the seeming sighs
 Of wife or paramour?
Fresh feeres will dry the bright blue eyes
 We late saw streaming o'er.
For pleasures past I do not grieve,
 Nor perils gathering near;
My greatest grief is that I leave
 No thing that claims a tear.

9.

And now I'm in the world alone,
 Upon the wide, wide sea:
But why should I for others groan,
 When none will sigh for me?
Perchance my dog will whine in vain,
 Till fed by stranger hands;
But long ere I come back again
 He'd tear me where he stands.

10.

With thee, my bark, I'll swiftly go
 Athwart the foaming brine;
Nor care what land thou bear'st me to,
 So not again to mine.
Welcome, welcome, ye dark-blue waves!
 And when you fail my sight,
Welcome, ye deserts and ye caves!
 My native Land—Good Night!

XIV.

On, on the vessel flies, the land is gone,
And winds are rude in Biscay's sleepless
 bay.
Four days are sped, but with the fifth,
 anon,
New shores descried make every bosom
 gay;
And Cintra's mountain greets them on
 their way,
And Tagus dashing onward to the deep,
His fabled golden tribute bent to pay;
And soon on board the Lusian pilots leap,
And steer 'twixt fertile shores where yet few
 rustics reap.

XV.

Oh, Christ! it is a goodly sight to see
What Heaven hath done for this delicious
 land:
What fruits of fragrance blush on every
 tree!
What goodly prospects o'er the hills
 expand!
But man would mar them with an impious
 hand:
And when the Almighty lifts his fiercest
 scourge
'Gainst those who most transgress his high
 command,
With treble vengeance will his hot shafts
 urge
Gaul's locust host, and earth from fellest
 foemen purge.

XVI.

What beauties doth Lisboa first unfold!
Her image floating on that noble tide,
Which poets vainly pave with sands of
 gold,
But now whereon a thousand keels did
 ride
Of mighty strength, since Albion was
 allied,
And to the Lusians did her aid afford:
A nation swoln with ignorance and pride,
Who lick yet loathe the hand that waves
 the sword
To save them from the wrath of Gaul's un-
 sparing lord.

XVII.

But whoso entereth within this town,
That, sheening far, celestial seems to be,
Disconsolate will wander up and down,
'Mid many things unsightly to strange ee;

For hut and palace show like filthily:
The dingy denizens are rear'd in dirt;
Ne personage of high or mean degree
Doth care for cleanness of surtout or shirt;
Though shent with Egypt's plague, unkempt,
 unwash'd, unhurt.

XVIII.

Poor, paltry slaves! yet born 'midst
 noblest scenes—
Why, Nature, waste thy wonders on such
 men?
Lo! Cintra's glorious Eden intervenes
In variegated maze of mount and glen.
Ah me! what hand can pencil guide, or pen,
To follow half on which the eye dilates
Through views more dazzling unto mortal
 ken
Than those whereof such things the bard
 relates,
Who to the awe-struck world unlock'd
 Elysium's gates?

XIX.

The horrid crags, by toppling convent
 crown'd,
The cork-trees hoar that clothe the shaggy
 steep,
The mountain-moss by scorching skies
 imbrown'd,
The sunken glen, whose sunless shrubs
 must weep,
The tender azure of the unruffled deep,
The orange tints that gild the greenest bough,
The torrents that from cliff to valley leap,
The vine on high, the willow branch below,
Mix'd in one mighty scene, with varied beauty
 glow.

XX.

Then slowly climb the many-winding way,
And frequent turn to linger as you go,
From loftier rocks new loveliness survey,
And rest ye at "Our Lady's house of woe;"
Where frugal monks their little relics show,
And sundry legends to the stranger tell:
Here impious men have punish'd been,
 and lo!
Deep in yon cave Honorius long did dwell,
In hope to merit Heaven by making earth
 a Hell.

XXI.

And here and there, as up the crags you
 spring,
Mark many rude-carved crosses near the
 path:
Yet deem not these devotion's offering—
These are memorials frail of murderous
 wrath:

For wheresoe'er the shrieking victim hath
 Pour'd forth his blood beneath the assas-
 sin's knife,
Some hand erects a cross of mouldering lath;
And grove and glen with thousand such
 are rife
Throughout this purple land, where law se-
 cures not life.

XXII.

On sloping mounds, or in the vale beneath,
Are domes where whilome kings did make
 repair;
But now the wild flowers round them only
 breathe;
Yet ruin'd splendour still is lingering there.
And yonder towers the Prince's palace fair:
There thou too, Vathek! England's wealthi-
 est son,
Once form'd thy Paradise, as not aware
When wanton Wealth her mightiest deeds
 hath done,
Meek Peace voluptuous lures was ever wont
 to shun.

XXIII.

Here didst thou dwell, here schemes of
 pleasure plan,
Beneath yon mountain's ever beauteous
 brow:
But now, as if a thing unblest by Man,
Thy fairy dwelling is as lone as thou!
Here giant weeds a passage scarce allow
To halls deserted, portals gaping wide:
Fresh lessons to the thinking bosom, how
Vain are the pleasaunces on earth supplied;
Swept into wrecks anon by Time's ungentle
 tide!

XXIV.

Behold the hall where chiefs were late
 convened!
Oh! dome displeasing unto British eye!
With diadem hight foolscap, lo! a fiend,
A little fiend that scoffs incessantly,
There sits in parchment robe array'd,
 and by
His side is hung a seal and sable scroll,
Where blazon'd glare names known to
 chivalry,
And sundry signatures adorn the roll,
Whereat the Urchin points and laughs with
 all his soul.

XXV.

Convention is the dwarfish demon styled
That foil'd the knights in Marialva's dome:
Of brains (if brains they had) he them
 beguiled,
And turn'd a nation's shallow joy to gloom.

Here Folly dash'd to earth the victor's
 plume,
And Policy regain'd what arms had lost:
For chiefs like ours in vain may laurels
 bloom!
Woe to the conqu'ring, not the conquer'd
 host,
Since baffled Triumph droops on Lusitania's
 coast!

XXVI.

And ever since that martial synod met,
Britannia sickens, Cintra! at thy name;
And folks in office at the mention fret,
And fain would blush, if blush they could,
 for shame.
How will posterity the deed proclaim!
Will not our own and fellow nations sneer,
To view these champions cheated of their
 fame,
By foes in fight o'erthrown, yet victors
 here,
Where Scorn her finger points through many
 a coming year?

XXVII.

So deem'd the Childe, as o'er the moun-
 tains he
Did take his way in solitary guise:
Sweet was the scene, yet soon he thought
 to flee,
More restless than the swallow in the skies:
Though here awhile he learn'd to moralize,
For Meditation fix'd at times on him;
And conscious Reason whisper'd to despise
His early youth, misspent in maddest
 whim;
But as he gazed on truth his aching eyes
 grew dim.

XXVIII.

To horse! to horse! he quits, for ever quits
A scene of peace, though soothing to his
 soul:
Again he rouses from his moping fits,
But seeks not now the harlot and the bowl.
Onward he flies, nor fix'd as yet the goal
Where he shall rest him on his pilgrimage;
And o'er him many changing scenes must
 roll
Ere toil his thirst for travel can assuage,
Or he shall calm his breast, or learn expe-
 rience sage.

XXIX.

Yet Mafra shall one moment claim delay,
Where dwelt of yore the Lusians' luckless
 queen;
And church and court did mingle their
 array,
And mass and revel were alternate seen;

Lordlings and freres—ill-sorted fry I ween!
But here the Babylonian whore hath built
A dome, where flaunts she in such glorious
 sheen,
That men forget the blood which she hath
 spilt,
And bow the knee to Pomp that loves to
 varnish guilt.

XXX.

O'er vales that teem with fruits, romantic
 hills,
(Oh, that such hills upheld a free-born
 race!)
Whereon to gaze the eye with joyaunce
 fills,
Childe Harold, wends through many a
 pleasant place.
Though sluggards deem it but a foolish
 chase,
And marvel men should quit their easy
 chair,
The toilsome way, and long, long league
 to trace,
Oh! there is sweetness in the mountain air,
And life, that bloated Ease can never hope
 to share.

XXXI.

More bleak to view the hills at length
 recede,
And, less luxuriant, smoother vales extend;
Immense horizon-bounded plains succeed!
Far as the eye discerns, withouten end,
Spain's realms appear whereon her shep-
 herds tend
Flocks, whose rich fleece right well the
 trader knows—
Now must the pastor's arm his lambs
 defend:
For Spain is compass'd by unyielding foes,
And all must shield their all, or share Sub-
 jection's woes.

XXXII.

Where Lusitania and her Sister meet,
Deem ye what bounds the rival realms
 divide?
Or ere the jealous queens of nations greet,
Doth Tayo interpose his mighty tide?
Or dark Sierras rise in craggy pride?
Or fence of art, like China's vasty wall?—
Ne barrier wall, ne river deep and wide,
Ne horrid crags, nor mountains dark and
 tall,
Rise like the rocks that part Hispania's land
 from Gaul:

XXXIII.

But these between a silver streamlet glides,
And scarce a name distinguisheth the
 brook,
Though rival kingdoms press its verdant
 sides.
Here leans the idle shepherd on his crook,
And vacant on the rippling waves doth
 look,
That peaceful still 'twixt bitterest foemen
 flow;
For proud each peasant as the noblest
 duke:
Well doth the Spanish hind the difference
 know
'Twixt him and Lusian slave, the lowest of
 the low.

XXXIV.

But ere the mingling bounds have far been
 pass'd,
Dark Guadiana rolls his power along
In sullen billows, murmuring and vast,
So noted ancient roundelays among.
Whilome upon his banks did legions
 throng
Of Moor and Knight, in mailed splendour
 drest:
Here ceased the swift their race, here sunk
 the strong;
The Paynim turban and the Christian crest
Mix'd on the bleeding stream, by floating
 hosts oppress'd.

XXXV.

Oh, lovely Spain! renown'd, romantic land!
Where is that standard which Pelagio
 bore,
When Cava's traitor-sire first call'd the
 band
That dyed thy mountain streams with
 Gothic gore?
Where are those bloody banners which
 of yore
Waved o'er thy sons, victorious to the gale,
And drove at last the spoilers to their
 shore?
Red gleam'd the cross, and waned the
 crescent pale,
While Afric's echoes thrill'd with Moorish
 matrons' wail.

XXXVI.

Teems not each ditty with the glorious
 tale?
Ah! such, alas! the hero's amplest fate!
When granite moulders and when records
 fail,
A peasant's plaint prolongs his dubious date.

Pride! bend thine eye from heaven to
thine estate,
See how the Mighty shrink into a song!
Can Volume, Pillar, Pile preserve thee
great?
Or must thou trust tradition's simple
tongue,
When Flattery sleeps with thee, and History
does thee wrong?

XXXVII.

Awake, ye sons of Spain! awake! advance!
Lo! Chivalry, your ancient goddess, cries,
But wields not, as of old, her thirsty lance,
Nor shakes her crimson plumage in the
skies:
Now on the smoke of blazing bolts she
flies,
And speaks in thunder through yon engine's roar:
In every peal she calls—"Awake! arise!"
Say, is her voice more feeble than of yore,
When her war-song was heard on Andalusia's
shore?

XXXVIII.

Hark! heard you not those hoofs of dreadful note?
Sounds not the clang of conflict on the
heath?
Saw ye not whom the reeking sabre smote,
Nor saved your brethren ere they sank
beneath
Tyrants and tyrants' slaves? the fires of
death,
The bale-fires flash on high:—from rock to
rock
Each volley tells that thousands cease to
breathe;
Death rides upon the sulphury Siroc,
Red Battle stamps his foot, and nations feel
the shock.

XXXIX.

Lo! where the Giant on the mountain
stands,
His blood-red tresses deep'ning in the sun,
With death-shot glowing in his fiery hands,
And eye that scorcheth all it glares upon;
Restless it rolls, now fix'd, and now anon
Flashing afar,—and at his iron feet
Destruction cowers, to mark what deeds
are done;
For on this morn three potent nations
meet,
To shed before his shrine the blood he deems
most sweet.

XL.

By Heaven! it is a splendid sight to see
(For one who hath no friend, no brother
there)
Their rival scarfs of mix'd embroidery,
Their various arms that glitter in the air!
What gallant war-hounds rouse them from
their lair,
And gnash their fangs, loud yelling for the
prey!
All join the chase, but few the triumph
share;
The Grave shall bear the chiefest prize
away,
And Havoc scarce for joy can number their
array.

XLI.

Three hosts combine to offer sacrifice;
Three tongues prefer strange orisons on
high;
Three gaudy standards flout the pale blue
skies;
The shouts are France, Spain, Albion,
Victory!
The foe, the victim, and the fond ally
That fights for all, but ever fights in vain,
Are met—as if at home they could not die—
To feed the crow on Talavera's plain,
And fertilize the field that each pretends
to gain.

XLII.

There shall they rot—Ambition's honour'd
fools!
Yes, Honour decks the turf that wraps
their clay!
Vain Sophistry! in these behold the tools,
The broken tools, that tyrants cast away
By myriads, when they dare to pave their
way
With human hearts—to what?—a dream
alone.
Can despots compass aught that hails their
sway?
Or call with truth one span of earth their
own,
Save that wherein at last they crumble bone
by bone?

XLIII.

Oh, Albuera! glorious field of grief!
As o'er thy plain the Pilgrim prick'd his
steed,
Who could foresee thee, in a space so
brief,
A scene where mingling foes should boast
and bleed!

Peace to the perish'd! may the warrior's
 meed
And tears of triumph their reward prolong!
Till others fall where other chieftains lead
Thy name shall circle round the gaping
 throng,
And shine in worthless lays the theme of
 transient song.

XLIV.

Enough of battle's minions! let them play
Their game of lives, and barter breath for
 fame:
Fame that will scarce reanimate their clay,
Though thousands fall to deck some single
 name.
In sooth 'twere sad to thwart their noble
 aim
Who strike, blest hirelings! for their
 country's good,
And die, that living might have proved her
 shame;
Perish'd, perchance, in some domestic
 feud,
Or in a narrower sphere wild Rapine's path
 pursued.

XLV.

Full swiftly Harold wends his lonely way
Where proud Sevilla triumphs unsubdued:
Yet is she free—the spoiler's wish'd-for
 prey!
Soon, soon shall Conquest's fiery foot
 intrude,
Blackening her lovely domes with traces
 rude.
Inevitable hour! 'Gainst fate to strive
Where Desolation plants her famish'd
 brood
Is vain, or Ilion, Tyre, might yet survive,
And Virtue vanquish all, and murder cease
 to thrive.

XLVI.

But all unconscious of the coming doom,
The feast, the song, the revel here
 abounds;
Strange modes of merriment the hours
 consume,
Nor bleed these patriots with their coun-
 try's wounds;
Nor here War's clarion, but Love's rebeck
 sounds;
Here Folly still his votaries inthrals;
And young-eyed Lewdness walks her mid-
 night rounds;
Girt with the silent crimes of Capitals,
Still to the last kind Vice clings to the
 tott'ring walls.

XLVII.

Not so the rustic—with his trembling mate
He lurks, nor casts his heavy eye afar,
Lest he should view his vineyard desolate,
Blasted below the dun hot breath of war.
No more beneath soft Eve's consenting star
Fandango twirls his jocund castanet:
Ah, monarchs! could ye taste the mirth ye
 mar,
Not in the toils of Glory would ye fret;
The hoarse dull drum would sleep, and Man
 be happy yet!

XLVIII.

How carols now the lusty muleteer?
Of love, romance, devotion is his lay,
As whilome he was wont the leagues to
 cheer,
His quick bells wildly jingling on the way?
No! as he speeds, he chants "Vivâ el
 Rey!"
And checks his song to execrate Godoy,
The royal wittol Charles, and curse the day
When first Spain's queen beheld the black-
 eyed boy,
And gore-faced Treason sprung from her
 adulterate joy.

XLIX.

On yon long, level plain, at distance
 crown'd
With crags, whereon those Moorish turrets
 rest,
Wide scatter'd hoof-marks dint the wound-
 ed ground;
And, scathed by fire, the greensward's
 darken'd vest
Tells that the foe was Andalusia's guest:
Here was the camp, the watch-flame, and
 the host,
Here the bold peasant storm'd the dragon's
 nest;
Still does he mark it with triumphant
 boast;
And points to yonder cliffs, which oft were
 won and lost.

L.

And whomsoe'er along the path you meet
Bears in his cap the badge of crimson hue,
Which tells you whom to shun and whom
 to greet.
Woe to the man that walks in public view
Without of loyalty this token true:
Sharp is the knife, and sudden is the stroke;
And sorely would the Gallic foeman rue,
If subtle poniards, wrapt beneath the cloke,
Could blunt the sabre's edge, or clear the
 cannon's smoke.

LI.

At every turn Morena's dusky height
Sustains aloft the battery's iron load;
And, far as mortal eye can compass sight,
The mountain-howitzer, the broken road,
The bristling palisade, the fosse o'erflow'd,
The station'd bands, the never-vacant watch,
The magazine in rocky durance stow'd,
The holster'd steed beneath the shed of
 thatch,
The ball-piled pyramid, the ever-blazing
 match,

LII.

Portend the deeds to come:—but he whose
 nod
Has tumbled feebler despots from their
 sway,
A moment pauseth ere he lifts the rod;
A little moment deigneth to delay:
Soon will his legions sweep through these
 their way;
The West must own the Scourger of the
 world.
Ah! Spain! how sad will be thy reckon-
 ing day,
When soars Gaul's Vulture, with his wings
 unfurl'd,
And thou shalt view thy sons in crowds to
 Hades hurl'd.

LIII.

And must they fall? the young, the proud,
 the brave,
To swell one bloated Chief's unwholesome
 reign?
No step between submission and a grave?
The rise of rapine and the fall of Spain?
And doth the Power that man adores ordain
Their doom, nor heed the suppliant's ap-
 peal?
Is all that desperate Valour acts in vain?
And Counsel sage, and patriotic Zeal,
The Veteran's skill, Youth's fire, and Man-
 hood's heart of steel?

LIV.

Is it for this the Spanish maid, aroused,
Hangs on the willow her unstrung guitar,
And, all unsex'd, the anlace hath espoused,
Sung the loud song, and dared the deed of
 war?
And she, whom once the semblance of a scar
Appall'd, an owlet's larum chill'd with
 dread,
Now views the column-scattering bay'net jar,
The falchion flash, and o'er the yet warm
 dead
Stalks with Minerva's step where Mars might
 quake to tread.

LV.

Ye who shall marvel when you hear her tale,
Oh! had you known her in her softer hour,
Mark'd her black eye that mocks her coal-
 black veil,
Heard her light, lively tones in Lady's
 bower,
Seen her long locks that foil the painter's
 power,
Her fairy form, with more than female grace,
Scarce would you deem that Saragoza's
 tower
Beheld her smile in Danger's Gorgon face,
Thin the closed ranks, and lead in Glory's
 fearful chase.

LVI.

Her lover sinks—she sheds no ill-timed
 tear;
Her chief is slain—she fills his fatal post;
Her fellows flee—she checks their base
 career;
The foe retires—she heads the sallying host:
Who can appease like her a lover's ghost?
Who can avenge so well a leader's fall?
What maid retrieve when man's flush'd
 hope is lost?
Who hang so fiercely on the flying Gaul,
Foil'd by a woman's hand, before a batter'd
 wall?

LVII.

Yet are Spain's maids no race of Amazons,
But form'd for all the witching arts of love:
Though thus in arms they emulate her sons,
And in the horrid phalanx dare to move,
'T is but the tender fierceness of the dove,
Pecking the hand that hovers o'er her mate:
In softness as in firmness far above
Remoter females, famed for sickening prate;
Her mind is nobler sure, her charms per-
 chance as great.

LVIII.

The seal Love's dimpling finger hath im-
 press'd
Denotes how soft that chin which bears his
 touch:
Her lips, whose kisses pout to leave their
 nest,
Bid man be valiant ere he merit such:
Her glance how wildly beautiful! how much
Hath Phœbus woo'd in vain to spoil her
 cheek,
Which glows yet smoother from his amorous
 clutch!
Who round the North for paler dames
 would seek?
How poor their forms appear! how languid,
 wan, and weak!

LIX.

Match me, ye climes! which poets love to
 laud;
Match me, ye harems of the land! where
 now
I strike my strain, far distant, to applaud
Beauties that ev'n a cynic must avow;
Match me those Houries, whom ye scarce
 allow
To taste the gale lest Love should ride the
 wind,
With Spain's dark-glancing daughters—
 deign to know,
There your wise Prophet's paradise we find,
His black-eyed maids of Heaven, angelic-
 ally kind.

LX.

Oh, thou Parnassus! whom I now survey,
Not in the phrensy of a dreamer's eye,
Not in the fabled landscape of a lay,
But soaring snow-clad through thy native
 sky,
In the wild pomp of mountain majesty!
What marvel if I thus essay to sing?
The humblest of thy pilgrims passing by
Would gladly woo thine Echoes with his
 string,
Though from thy heights no more one Muse
 will wave her wing.

LXI.

Oft have I dream'd of Thee! whose glorious
 name
Who knows not, knows not man's divinest
 lore:
And now I view thee, 't is, alas! with shame
That I in feeblest accents must adore.
When I recount thy worshippers of yore
I tremble, and can only bend the knee;
Nor raise my voice, nor vainly dare to soar,
But gaze beneath thy cloudy canopy
In silent joy to think at last I look on Thee!

LXII.

Happier in this than mightiest bards have
 been,
Whose fate to distant homes confined their
 lot,
Shall I unmoved behold the hallow'd scene,
Which others rave of, though they know it
 not?
Though here no more Apollo haunts his
 grot,
And thou, the Muses' seat, art now their
 grave,
Some gentle spirit still pervades the spot,
Sighs in the gale, keeps silence in the cave,
And glides with glassy foot o'er yon melodious
 wave.

LXIII.

Of thee hereafter.—Ev'n amidst my strain
I turn'd aside to pay my homage here;
Forgot the land, the sons, the maids of
 Spain;
Her fate, to every freeborn bosom dear;
And hail'd thee, not perchance without a
 tear.
Now to my theme—but from thy holy haunt
Let me some remnant, some memorial bear;
Yield me one leaf of Daphne's deathless
 plant,
Nor let thy votary's hope be deem'd an idle
 vaunt.

LXIV.

But ne'er didst thou, fair Mount, when
 Greece was young,
See round thy giant base a brighter choir,
Nor e'er did Delphi, when her priestess
 sung
The Pythian hymn with more than mortal
 fire,
Behold a train more fitting to inspire
The song of love, than Andalusia's maids,
Nurst in the glowing lap of soft desire:
Ah! that to these were given such peaceful
 shades
As Greece can still bestow, though Glory fly
 her glades.

LXV.

Fair is proud Seville; let her country boast
Her strength, her wealth, her site of ancient
 days;
But Cadiz, rising on the distant coast,
Calls forth a sweeter, though ignoble praise.
Ah, Vice! how soft are thy voluptuous
 ways!
While boyish blood is mantling, who can
 'scape
The fascination of thy magic gaze?
A Cherub-hydra round us dost thou gape,
And mould to every taste thy dear delusive
 shape.

LXVI.

When Paphos fell by Time—accursed Time!
The Queen who conquers all must yield to
 thee—
The Pleasures fled, but sought as warm a
 clime;
And Venus, constant to her native sea,
To nought else constant, hither deign'd to
 flee,
And fix'd her shrine within these walls of
 white;
Though not to one dome circumscribeth she
Her worship, but, devoted to her rite,
A thousand altars rise, for ever blazing bright.

LXVII.

From morn till night, from night till startled
 Morn
Peeps blushing on the revel's laughing
 crew,
The song is heard, the rosy garland worn ;
Devices quaint, and frolics ever new,
Tread on each other's kibes. A long adieu
He bids to sober joy that here sojourns :
Nought interrupts the riot, though in lieu
Of true devotion monkish incense burns,
And love and prayer unite, or rule the hour
 by turns.

LXVIII.

The Sabbath comes, a day of blessed rest :
What hallows it upon this Christian shore ?
Lo ! it is sacred to a solemn feast :
Hark ! heard you not the forest-monarch's
 roar ?
Crashing the lance, he snuffs the spouting
 gore
Of man and steed, o'erthrown beneath his
 horn ;
The throng'd arena shakes with shouts for
 more ;
Yells the mad crowd o'er entrails freshly
 torn,
Nor shrinks the female eye, nor ev'n affects
 to mourn.

LXIX.

The seventh day this ; the jubilee of man.
London ! right well thou know'st the day
 of prayer :
Then thy spruce citizen, wash'd artisan,
And smug apprentice gulp their weekly air :
Thy coach of hackney, whiskey, one-horse
 chair,
And humblest gig through sundry suburbs
 whirl ;
To Hampstead, Brentford, Harrow make
 repair ;
Till the tired jade the wheel forgets to hurl,
Provoking envious gibe from each pedestrian
 churl.

LXX.

Some o'er thy Thamis row the ribbon'd fair,
Others along the safer turnpike fly ;
Some Richmond-hill ascend, some scud to
 Ware,
And many to the steep of Highgate hie.
Ask ye, Bœotian shades ! the reason why ?
'T is to the worship of the solemn Horn,
Grasp'd in the holy hand of Mystery,
In whose dread name both men and maids
 are sworn,
And consecrate the oath with draught, and
 dance till morn.

LXXI.

All have their fooleries—not alike are thine,
Fair Cadiz, rising o'er the dark blue sea !
Soon as the matin bell proclaimeth nine,
Thy saint adorers count the rosary :
Much is the VIRGIN teased to shrive them
 free
(Well do I ween the only virgin there)
From crimes as numerous as her beads-
 men be ;
Then to the crowded circus forth they fare :
Young, old, high, low, at once the same diver-
 sion share.

LXXII.

The lists are oped, the spacious area clear'd,
Thousands on thousands piled are seated
 round ;
Long ere the first loud trumpet's note is
 heard,
Ne vacant space for lated wight is found :
Here dons, grandees, but chiefly dames
 abound,
Skill'd in the ogle of a roguish eye,
Yet ever well inclined to heal the wound ;
None through their cold disdain are doom'd
 to die,
As moon-struck bards complain, by Love's
 sad archery.

LXXIII.

Hush'd is the din of tongues—on gallant
 steeds,
With milk-white crest, gold spur, and light-
 poised lance,
Four cavaliers prepare for venturous deeds,
And lowly bending to the lists advance ;
Rich are their scarfs, their chargers featly
 prance :
If in the dangerous game they shine to-day,
The crowd's loud shout and ladies' lovely
 glance,
Best prize of better acts, they bear away,
And all that kings or chiefs e'er gain their
 toils repay.

LXXIV.

In costly sheen and gaudy cloak array'd,
But all afoot, the light-limb'd Matadore
Stands in the centre, eager to invade
The lord of lowing herds ; but not before
The ground, with cautious tread, is tra-
 versed o'er,
Lest aught unseen should lurk to thwart
 his speed :
His arms a dart, he fights aloof, nor more
Can man achieve without the friendly
 steed—
Alas ! too oft condemn'd for him to bear and
 bleed.

LXXV.

Thrice sounds the clarion; lo! the signal falls,
The den expands, and Expectation mute
Gapes round the silent circle's peopled walls.
Bounds with one lashing spring the mighty brute,
And, wildly staring, spurns, with sounding foot,
The sand, nor blindly rushes on his foe:
Here, there, he points his threatening front, to suit
His first attack, wide waving to and fro
His angry tail; red rolls his eye's dilated glow

LXXVI.

Sudden he stops; his eye is fix'd: away,
Away, thou heedless boy! prepare the spear:
Now is thy time to perish, or display
The skill that yet may check his mad career.
With well-timed croupe the nimble coursers veer;
On foams the bull, but not unscathed he goes;
Streams from his flank the crimson torrent clear:
He flies, he wheels, distracted with his throes;
Dart follows dart; lance, lance; loud bellowings speak his woes.

LXXVII.

Again he comes; nor dart nor lance avail,
Nor the wild plunging of the tortured horse;
Though man and man's avenging arms assail,
Vain are his weapons, vainer is his force.
One gallant steed is stretch'd a mangled corse;
Another, hideous sight! unseam'd appears,
His gory chest unveils life's panting source;
Though death-struck, still his feeble frame he rears;
Staggering, but stemming all, his lord unharm'd he bears.

LXXVIII.

Foil'd, bleeding, breathless, furious to the last,
Full in the centre stands the bull at bay,
Mid wounds, and clinging darts, and lances brast,
And foes disabled in the brutal fray;
And now the Matadores around him play,
Shake the red cloak and poise the ready brand:
Once more through all he bursts his thundering way—
Vain rage! the mantle quits the conynge hand,
Wraps his fierce eye—'t is past—he sinks upon the sand!

LXXIX.

Where his vast neck just mingles with the spine,
Sheathed in his form the deadly weapon lies.
He stops—he starts—disdaining to decline:
Slowly he falls, amidst triumphant cries,
Without a groan, without a struggle dies.
The decorated car appears—on high
The corse is piled—sweet sight for vulgar eyes—
Four steeds that spurn the rein, as swift as shy,
Hurl the dark bulk along, scarce seen in dashing by.

LXXX.

Such the ungentle sport that oft invites
The Spanish maid, and cheers the Spanish swain.
Nurtured in blood betimes, his heart delights
In vengeance, gloating on another's pain.
What private feuds the troubled village stain!
Though now one phalanx'd host should meet the foe,
Enough, alas! in humble homes remain,
To meditate 'gainst friends the secret blow,
For some slight cause of wrath whence life's warm stream must flow.

LXXXI.

But Jealousy has fled: his bars, his bolts,
His wither'd centinel, Duenna sage!
And all whereat the generous soul revolts,
Which the stern dotard deem'd he could encage,
Have pass'd to darkness with the vanish'd age.
Who late so free as Spanish girls were seen
(Ere War uprose in his volcanic rage),
With braided tresses bounding o'er the green,
While on the gay dance shone Night's lover-loving Queen?

LXXXII.

Oh! many a time and oft, had Harold
 loved,
Or dream'd he loved, since rapture is a
 dream;
But now his wayward bosom was unmoved,
For not yet had he drunk of Lethe's stream;
And lately had he learn'd with truth to
 deem
Love has no gift so grateful as his wings:
How fair, how young, how soft soe'er he
 seem,
Full from the fount of Joy's delicious
 springs
Some bitter o'er the flowers its bubbling
 venom flings.

LXXXIII.

Yet to the beauteous form he was not blind,
Though now it moved him as it moves the
 wise:
Not that Philosophy on such a mind
E'er deign'd to bend her chastely-awful
 eyes:
But Passion raves itself to rest, or flies;
And Vice, that digs her own voluptuous
 tomb,
Had buried long his hopes, no more to rise:
Pleasure's pall'd victim! life-abhorring
 gloom
Wrote on his faded brow curst Cain's un-
 resting doom.

LXXXIV.

Still he beheld, nor mingled with the
 throng;
But view'd them not with misanthropic
 hate:
Fain would he now have join'd the dance,
 the song;
But who may smile that sinks beneath his
 fate?
Nought that he saw his sadness could
 abate:
Yet once he struggled 'gainst the demon's
 sway,
And as in Beauty's bower he pensive sate,
Pour'd forth this unpremeditated lay,
To charms as fair as those that soothed his
 happier day.

TO INEZ.

1.

Nay, smile not at my sullen brow;
 Alas! I cannot smile again:
Yet Heaven avert that ever thou
 Shouldst weep, and haply weep in vain.

2.

And dost thou ask what secret woe
 I bear, corroding joy and youth?
And wilt thou vainly seek to know
 A pang, ev'n thou must fail to soothe?

3.

It is not love, it is not hate,
 Nor low Ambition's honours lost,
That bids me loathe my present state,
 And fly from all I prized the most:

4.

It is that weariness which springs
 From all I meet, or hear, or see:
To me no pleasure Beauty brings;
 Thine eyes have scarce a charm for me.

5.

It is that settled, ceaseless gloom
 The fabled Hebrew wanderer bore;
That will not look beyond the tomb,
 But cannot hope for rest before.

6.

What Exile from himself can flee?
 To zones though more and more remote,
Still, still pursues, where'er I be,
 The blight of life—the demon Thought.

7.

Yet others rapt in pleasure seem,
 And taste of all that I forsake;
Oh! may they still of transport dream,
 And ne'er, at least like me, awake!

8.

Through many a clime 'tis mine to go,
 With many a retrospection curst;
And all my solace is to know,
 Whate'er betides, I've known the worst.

9.

What is that worst? Nay, do not ask—
 In pity from the search forbear:
Smile on—nor venture to unmask
 Man's heart, and view the Hell that's there.

LXXXV.

Adieu, fair Cadiz! yea, a long adieu!
Who may forget how well thy walls have
 stood?
When all were changing, thou alone wert
 true,
First to be free, and last to be subdued:
And if amidst a scene, a shock so rude,
Some native blood was seen thy streets to dye
A traitor only fell beneath the feud:
Here all were noble, save Nobility!
None hugg'd a conqueror's chain, save fallen
 Chivalry!

LXXXVI.

Such be the sons of Spain, and strange her
 fate !
They fight for freedom who were never free,
A Kingless people for a nerveless state ;
Her vassals combat when their chieftains
 flee,
True to the veriest slaves of Treachery :
Fond of a land which gave them nought
 but life,
Pride points the path that leads to Liberty ;
Back to the struggle, baffled in the strife,
War, war is still the cry, "War even to the
 knife !"

LXXXVII.

Ye, who would more of Spain and Spaniards
 know,
Go, read whate'er is writ of bloodiest strife :
Whate'er keen Vengeance urged on foreign
 foe
Can act, is acting there against man's life :
From flashing scimitar to secret knife,
War mouldeth there each weapon to his
 need—
So may he guard the sister and the wife,
So may he make each curst oppressor
 bleed—
So may such foes deserve the most remorse-
 less deed !

LXXXVIII.

Flows there a tear of pity for the dead ?
Look o'er the ravage of the reeking plain ;
Look on the hands with female slaughter
 red ;
Then to the dogs resign the unburied slain,
Then to the vulture let each corse remain,
Albeit unworthy of the prey-bird's maw ;
Let their bleach'd bones, and blood's un-
 bleaching stain,
Long mark the battle-field with hideous
 awe :
Thus only may our sons conceive the scenes
 we saw !

LXXXIX.

Nor yet, alas ! the dreadful work is done ;
Fresh legions pour adown the Pyrenees :
It deepens still, the work is scarce begun,
Nor mortal eye the distant end foresees.
Fall'n nations gaze on Spain ; if freed, she
 frees
More than her fell Pizarros once enchain'd :
Strange retribution ! now Columbia's ease
Repairs the wrongs that Quito's sons sus-
 tain'd,
While o'er the parent clime prowls Murder
 unrestrain'd.

XC.

Not all the blood at Talavera shed,
Not all the marvels of Barossa's fight,
Not Albuera lavish of the dead,
Have won for Spain her well-asserted right.
When shall her Olive-Branch be free from
 blight ?
When shall she breathe her from the blush-
 ing toil ?
How many a doubtful day shall sink in
 night,
Ere the Frank robber turn him from his
 spoil,
And Freedom's stranger-tree grow native of
 the soil !

XCI.

And thou, my friend !—since unavailing
 woe
Bursts from my heart, and mingles with
 the strain—
Had the sword laid thee with the mighty
 low,
Pride might forbid e'en Friendship to
 complain :
But thus unlarrel'd to descend in vain,
By all forgotten, save the lonely breast,
And mix unbleeding with the boasted slain,
While Glory crowns so many a meaner
 crest !
What hadst thou done to sink so peacefully
 to rest ?

XCII.

Oh, known the earliest, and esteem'd the
 most !
Dear to a heart where nought was left so
 dear !
Though to my hopeless days for ever lost,
In dreams deny me not to see thee here !
And Morn in secret shall renew the tear
Of Consciousness awaking to her woes,
And Fancy hover o'er thy bloodless bier,
Till my frail frame return to whence it
 rose,
And mourn'd and mourner lie united in
 repose.

XCIII.

Here is one fytte of Harold's pilgrimage :
Ye who of him may further seek to know,
Shall find some tidings in a future page,
If he that rhymeth now may scribble moe.
Is this too much ? stern Critic ! say not so :
Patience ! and ye shall hear what he beheld
In other lands, where he was doom'd to go :
Lands that contain the monuments of Eld,
Ere Greece and Grecian arts by barbarous
 hands were quell'd.

Canto the Second.

I.

COME, blue-eyed maid of heaven!—but
 thou, alas!
Didst never yet one mortal song inspire—
Goddess of Wisdom! here thy temple was,
And is, despite of war and wasting fire,
And years, that bade thy worship to ex-
 pire:
But worse than steel, and flame, and ages
 slow,
Is the dread sceptre and dominion dire
Of men who never felt the sacred glow
That thoughts of thee and thine on polish'd
 breasts bestow.

II.

Ancient of days! august Athena! where,
Where are thy men of might? thy grand
 in soul?
Gone—glimmering through the dream of
 things that were:
First in the race that led to Glory's goal,
They won, and pass'd away—is this the
 whole?
A schoolboy's tale, the wonder of an hour!
The warrior's weapon and the sophist's
 stole
Are sought in vain, and o'er each moulder-
 ing tower,
Dim with the mist of years, gray flits the
 shade of power.

III.

Son of the morning, rise! approach you
 here!
Come—but molest not yon defenceless urn:
Look on this spot—a nation's sepulchre!
Abode of gods, whose shrines no longer
 burn.
Even gods must yield—religions take their
 turn:
'T was Jove's—'t is Mahomet's—and other
 creeds
Will rise with other years, till man shall
 learn
Vainly his incense soars, his victim bleeds
Poor child of Doubt and Death, whose hope
 is built on reeds.

IV.

Bound to the earth, he lifts his eye to
 heaven—
Is 't not enough, unhappy thing! to know
Thou art? Is this a boon so kindly given,
That being, thou wouldst be again, and go,

Thou know'st not, reck'st not, to what
 region, so
On earth no more, but mingled with the
 skies?
Still wilt thou dream on future joy and
 woe?
Regard and weigh yon dust before it flies:
That little urn saith more than thousand
 homilies.

V.

Or burst the vanish'd Hero's lofty mound;
Far on the solitary shore he sleeps:
He fell, and falling nations mourn'd
 around;
But now not one of saddening thousands
 weeps,
Nor warlike worshipper his vigil keeps
Where demi-gods appear'd, as records tell.
Remove yon skull from out the scatter'd
 heaps:
Is that a temple where a God may dwell?
Why ev'n the worm at last disdains her
 shatter'd cell!

VI.

Look on its broken arch, its ruin'd wall,
Its chambers desolate, and portals foul:
Yes, this was once Ambition's airy hall,
The dome of Thought, the palace of the
 Soul:
Behold through each lack-lustre, eyeless
 hole,
The gay recess of Wisdom and of Wit,
And Passion's host, that never brook'd
 control:
Can all saint, sage, or sophist ever writ,
People this lonely tower, this tenement refit?

VII.

Well didst thou speak, Athena's wisest
 son!
"All that we know is, nothing can be
 known."
Why should we shrink from what we can-
 not shun?
Each hath his pang, but feeble sufferers
 groan
With brain-born dreams of evil all their
 own.
Pursue what Chance or Fate proclaimeth
 best;
Peace waits us on the shores of Acheron:
There no forced banquet claims the sated
 guest,
But Silence spreads the couch of ever wel-
 come rest.

VIII.

Yet if, as holiest men have deem'd, there
 be
A land of souls beyond that sable shore,
To shame the doctrine of the Sadducee
And sophists, madly vain of dubious lore;
How sweet it were in concert to adore
With those who made our mortal labours
 light!
To hear each voice we fear'd to hear no
 more!
Behold each mighty shade reveal'd to
 sight,
The Bactrian, Samian sage, and all who
 taught the right!

IX.

There, thou!—whose love and life together
 fled,
Have left me here to love and live in vain—
Twined with my heart, and can I deem
 thee dead
When busy Memory flashes on my brain?
Well—I will dream that we may meet
 again,
And woo the vision to my vacant breast:
If aught of young Remembrance then re-
 main,
Be as it may Futurity's behest,
For me 't were bliss enough to know thy
 spirit blest!

X.

Here let me sit upon this massy stone,
The marble column's yet unshaken base;
Here, son of Saturn! was thy fav'rite
 throne:
Mightiest of many such! Hence let me trace
The latent grandeur of thy dwelling-place.
It may not be: nor ev'n can Fancy's eye
Restore what Time hath labour'd to de-
 face.
Yet these proud pillars claim no passing sigh;
Unmoved the Moslem sits, the light Greek
 carols by.

XI.

But who, of all the plunderers of yon fane
On high, where Pallas linger'd, loth to flee
The latest relic of her ancient reign;
The last, the worst, dull spoiler, who was
 he?
Blush, Caledonia! such thy son could be!
England! I joy no child he was of thine:
Thy free-born men should spare what once
 was free;
Yet they could violate each saddening
 shrine,
And bear these altars o'er the long-reluctant
 brine.

XII.

But most the modern Pict's ignoble boast,
To rive what Goth, and Turk, and Time
 hath spared:
Cold as the crags upon his native coast,
His mind as barren and his heart as hard,
Is he whose head conceived, whose hand
 prepared,
Aught to displace Athena's poor remains:
Her sons, too weak the sacred shrine to
 guard,
Yet felt some portion of their mother's
 pains,
And never knew, till then, the weight of
 Despot's chains.

XIII.

What! shall it e'er be said by British
 tongue,
Albion was happy in Athena's tears?
Though in thy name the slaves her bosom
 wrung,
Tell not the deed to blushing Europe's
 ears;
The ocean queen, the free Britannia, bears
The last poor plunder from a bleeding
 land:
Yes, she, whose gen'rous aid her name
 endears,
Tore down those remnants with a harpy's
 hand,
Which envious Eld forbore, and tyrants left
 to stand.

XIV.

Where was thine Ægis, Pallas! that ap-
 pall'd
Stern Alaric and Havoc on their way?
Where Peleus' son? whom Hell in vain
 inthrall'd,
His shade from Hades upon that dread
 day
Bursting to light in terrible array!
What! could not Pluto spare the chief
 once more,
To scare a second robber from his prey?
Idly he wander'd on the Stygian shore,
Nor now preserved the walls he loved to
 shield before.

XV.

Cold is the heart, fair Greece! that looks
 on thee,
Nor feels as lovers o'er the dust they
 loved;
Dull is the eye that will not weep to see
Thy walls defaced, thy mouldering shrines
 removed

By British hands, which it had best be-
hoved
To guard those relics ne'er to be restored.
Curst be the hour when from their isle
 they roved,
And once again thy hapless bosom gored,
And snatch'd thy shrinking Gods to northern
 climes abhorr'd!

XVI.

But where is Harold? shall I then forget
To urge the gloomy wanderer o'er the
 wave?
Little reck'd he of all that men regret;
No loved-one now in feign'd lament could
 rave;
No friend the parting hand extended gave,
Ere the cold stranger pass'd to other
 climes:
Hard is his heart whom charms may not
 enslave;
But Harold felt not as in other times,
And left without a sigh the land of war and
 crimes.

XVII.

He that has sail'd upon the dark blue sea
Has view'd at times, I ween, a full fair
 sight;
When the fresh breeze is fair as breeze
 may be,
The white sail set, the gallant frigate
 tight;
Masts, spires, and strand retiring to the
 right,
The glorious main expanding o'er the bow,
The convoy spread like wild swans in their
 flight,
The dullest sailer wearing bravely now,
So gaily curl the waves before each dashing
 prow.

XVIII.

And oh, the little warlike world within!
The well-reeved guns, the netted canopy,
The hoarse command, the busy humming
 din,
When, at a word, the tops are mann'd on
 high:
Hark, to the Boatswain's call, the cheering
 cry!
While through the seaman's hand the
 tackle glides;
Or schoolboy Midshipman that, standing
 by,
Strains his shrill pipe as good or ill betides,
And well the docile crew that skilful urchin
 guides.

XIX.

White is the glassy deck, without a stain,
Where on the watch the staid Lieutenant
 walks:
Look on that part which sacred doth re-
main
For the lone chieftain, who majestic stalks,
Silent and fear'd by all—not oft he talks
With aught beneath him, if he would pre-
 serve
That strict restraint, which broken, ever
 balks
Conquest and fame: but Britons rarely
 swerve
From law, however stern, which tends their
 strength to nerve.

XX.

Blow! swiftly blow, thou keel-compelling
 gale!
Till the broad sun withdraws his lessening
 ray;
Then must the pennant-bearer slacken
 sail,
That lagging barks may make their lazy
 way.
Ah! grievance sore, and listless dull delay,
To waste on sluggish hulks the sweetest
 breeze!
What leagues are lost, before the dawn of
 day,
Thus loitering pensive on the willing seas,
The flapping sail haul'd down to halt for logs
 like these!

XXI.

The moon is up; by Heaven, a lovely eve!
Long streams of light o'er dancing waves
 expand;
Now lads on shore may sigh, and maids
 believe:
Such be our fate when we return to land!
Meantime some rude Arion's restless hand
Wakes the brisk harmony that sailors love;
A circle there of merry listeners stand,
Or to some well-known measure featly
 move,
Thoughtless, as if on shore they still were
 free to rove.

XXII.

Through Calpe's straits survey the steepy
 shore;
Europe and Afric on each other gaze!
Lands of the dark-eyed Maid and dusky
 Moor
Alike beheld beneath pale Hecate's blaze:

How softly on the Spanish shore she plays,
Disclosing rock, and slope, and forest
 brown,
Distinct, though darkening with her waning
 phase;
But Mauritania's giant shadows frown,
From mountain-cliff to coast descending
 sombre down.

XXIII.

'T is night, when Meditation bids us feel
We once have loved, though love is at an
 end:
The heart, lone mourner of its baffled zeal,
Though friendless now, will dream it had
 a friend.
Who with the weight of years would wish
 to bend,
When Youth itself survives young Love
 and Joy?
Alas! when mingling souls forget to blend,
Death hath but little left him to destroy!
Ah! happy years! once more who would not
 be a boy?

XXIV.

Thus bending o'er the vessel's laving side,
To gaze on Dian's wave-reflected sphere,
The soul forgets her schemes of hope and
 pride,
And flies unconscious o'er each backward
 year.
None are so desolate but something dear,
Dearer than self, possesses or possess'd
A thought, and claims the homage of a
 tear;
A flashing pang! of which the weary breast
Would still, albeit in vain, the heavy heart
 divest.

XXV.

To sit on rocks, to muse o'er flood and fell,
To slowly trace the forest's shady scene,
Where things that own not man's dominion
 dwell,
And mortal foot hath ne'er or rarely been;
To climb the trackless mountain all unseen,
With the wild flock that never needs a fold;
Alone o'er steeps and foaming falls to lean;
This is not solitude; 't is but to hold
Converse with Nature's charms, and view her
 stores unroll'd.

XXVI.

But midst the crowd, the hum, the shock
 of men,
To hear, to see, to feel, and to possess,
And roam along, the world's tired denizen,
With none who bless us, none whom we
 can bless;

Minions of splendour shrinking from dis-
 tress!
None that, with kindred consciousness en-
 dued,
If we were not, would seem to smile the
 less,
Of all that flatter'd, follow'd, sought, and
 sued;
This is to be alone; this, this is solitude!

XXVII.

More blest the life of godly eremite,
Such as on lonely Athos may be seen,
Watching at eve upon the giant height,
Which looks o'er waves so blue, skies so
 serene,
That he who there at such an hour hath
 been
Will wistful linger on that hallow'd spot;
Then slowly tear him from the 'witching
 scene,
Sigh forth one wish that such had been his
 lot,
Then turn to hate a world he had almost
 forgot.

XXVIII.

Pass we the long, unvarying course, the
 track
Oft trod, that never leaves a trace behind;
Pass we the calm, the gale, the change, the
 tack,
And each well-known caprice of wave and
 wind;
Pass we the joys and sorrows sailors find,
Coop'd in their winged sea-girt citadel;
The foul, the fair, the contrary, the kind,
As breezes rise and fall and billows swell,
Till on some jocund morn—lo, land! and
 all is well.

XXIX.

But not in silence pass Calypso's isles,
The sister tenants of the middle deep;
There for the weary still a haven smiles,
Though the fair goddess long hath ceased
 to weep,
And o'er her cliffs a fruitless watch to keep
For him who dared prefer a mortal bride:
Here, too, his boy essay'd the dreadful leap
Stern Mentor urged from high to yonder
 tide;
While thus of both bereft, the nymph-queen
 doubly sigh'd.

XXX.

Her reign is past, her gentle glories gone:
But trust not this: too easy youth, beware!
A mortal sovereign holds her dangerous
 throne,
And thou mayst find a new Calypso there.

Sweet Florence! could another ever share
This wayward, loveless heart, it would be
 thine:
But check'd by every tie, I may not dare
To cast a worthless offering at thy shrine,
Nor ask so dear a breast to feel one pang for
 mine.

XXXI.

Thus Harold deem'd, as on that lady's eye
He look'd, and met its beam without a
 thought
Save admiration glancing harmless by:
Love kept aloof, albeit not far remote,
Who knew his votary often lost and caught,
But knew him as his worshipper no more,
And ne'er again the boy his bosom sought:
Since now he vainly urged him to adore,
Well deem'd the little God his ancient sway
 was o'er.

XXXII.

Fair Florence found, in sooth with some
 amaze,
One who, 'twas said, still sigh'd to all he
 saw,
Withstand, unmoved, the lustre of her gaze,
Which others hail'd with real or mimic awe,
Their hope, their doom, their punishment,
 their law;
All that gay Beauty from her bondsmen
 claims:
And much she marvell'd that a youth so
 raw
Nor felt, nor feign'd at least, the oft-told
 flames,
Which, though sometimes they frown, yet
 rarely anger dames.

XXXIII.

Little knew she that seeming marble heart,
Now mask'd in silence or withheld by pride,
Was not unskilful in the spoiler's art,
And spread its snares licentious far and
 wide;
Nor from the base pursuit had turn'd aside,
As long as aught was worthy to pursue:
But Harold on such arts no more relied;
And had he doted on those eyes so blue,
Yet never would he join the lover's whining
 crew.

XXXIV.

Not much he kens, I ween, of woman's
 breast,
Who thinks that wanton thing is won by
 sighs;
What careth she for hearts when once
 possess'd?
Do proper homage to thine idol's eyes;

But not too humbly, or she will despise
Thee and thy suit, though told in moving
 tropes:
Disguise ev'n tenderness, if thou art wise;
Brisk Confidence still best with woman
 copes:
Pique her and soothe in turn, soon Passion
 crowns thy hopes.

XXXV.

'Tis an old lesson; Time approves it true,
And those who know it best deplore it most;
When all is won that all desire to woo,
The paltry prize is hardly worth the cost:
Youth wasted, minds degraded, honour
 lost,
These are thy fruits, successful Passion!
 these!
If, kindly cruel, early hope is crost,
Still to the last it rankles, a disease,
Not to be cured when love itself forgets to
 please.

XXXVI.

Away! nor let me loiter in my song,
For we have many a mountain-path to tread,
And many a varied shore to sail along,
By pensive Sadness, not by Fiction, led—
Climes, fair withal as ever mortal head
Imagined in its little schemes of thought;
Or e'er in new Utopias were ared,
To teach man what he might be, or he
 ought;
If that corrupted thing could ever such be
 taught.

XXXVII.

Dear Nature is the kindest mother still,
Though always changing in her aspect mild;
From her bare bosom let me take my fill,
Her never-wean'd, though not her favour'd
 child.
Oh! she is fairest in her features wild,
Where nothing polish'd dares pollute her
 path:
To me by day or night she ever smiled,
Though I have mark'd her when none other
 hath,
And sought her more and more, and loved
 her best in wrath.

XXXVIII.

Land of Albania! where Iskander rose,
Theme of the young, and beacon of the wise,
And he his namesake, whose oft-baffled foes
Shrunk from his deeds of chivalrous em-
 prize:

Land of Albania! let me bend mine eyes
On thee, thou rugged nurse of savage men!
The cross descends, thy minarets arise,
And the pale crescent sparkles in the glen,
Through many a cypress grove within each
　city's ken.

XXXIX.

Childe Harold sail'd, and pass'd the barren
　spot,
Where sad Penelope o'erlook'd the wave;
And onward view'd the mount, not yet
　forgot,
The lover's refuge, and the Lesbian's grave.
Dark Sappho! could not verse immortal save
That breast imbued with such immortal fire?
Could she not live who life eternal gave?
If life eternal may await the lyre,
That only Heaven to which Earth's children
　may aspire.

XL.

'Twas on a Grecian autumn's gentle eve
Childe Harold hail'd Leucadia's cape afar;
A spot he longed to see, nor cared to leave:
Oft did he mark the scenes of vanish'd war,
Actium, Lepanto, fatal Trafalgar;
Mark them unmoved, for he would not
　delight
(Born beneath some remote inglorious star)
In themes of bloody fray, or gallant fight,
But loathed the bravo's trade, and laughed
　at martial wight.

XLI.

But when he saw the evening star above
Leucadia's far-projecting rock of woe,
And hail'd the last resort of fruitless love,
He felt, or deem'd he felt, no common glow:
And as the stately vessel glided slow
Beneath the shadow of that ancient mount,
He watch'd the billows' melancholy flow,
And, sunk albeit in thought as he was wont,
More placid seem'd his eye, and smooth his
　pallid front.

XLII.

Morn dawns: and with it stern Albania's
　hills,
Dark Suli's rocks, and Pindus' inland peak,
Robed half in mist, bedew'd with snowy rills,
Array'd in many a dun and purple streak,
Arise; and, as the clouds along them break,
Disclose the dwelling of the mountaineer;
Here roams the wolf, the eagle whets his
　beak,
Birds, beasts of prey, and wilder men
　appear,
And gathering storms around convulse the
　closing year.

XLIII.

Now Harold found himself at length alone,
And bade to Christian tongues a long adieu;
Now he adventured on a shore unknown,
Which all admire, but many dread to view:
His breast was arm'd 'gainst fate, his wants
　were few;
Peril he sought not, but ne'er shrank to
　meet:
The scene was savage, but the scene was
　new;
This made the ceaseless toil of travel sweet,
Beat back keen winter's blast, and welcomed
　summer's heat.

XLIV.

Here the red cross, for still the cross is here,
Though sadly scoff'd at by the circumcised,
Forgets that pride to pamper'd priesthood
　dear;
Churchman and votary alike despised.
Foul Superstition! howsoe'er disguised,
Idol, saint, virgin, prophet, crescent, cross,
For whatsoever symbol thou art prized,
Thou sacerdotal gain, but general loss!
Who from true worship's gold can separate
　thy dross?

XLV.

Ambracia's gulf behold, where once was
　lost
A world for woman, lovely, harmless thing!
In yonder rippling bay, their naval host
Did many a Roman chief and Asian king
To doubtful conflict, certain slaughter
　bring:
Look where the second Cæsar's trophies
　rose:
Now, like the hands that rear'd them,
　withering:
Imperial anarchs, doubling human woes!
God! was thy globe ordain'd for such to win
　and lose?

XLVI.

From the dark barriers of that rugged
　clime,
Ev'n to the centre of Illyria's vales,
Childe Harold pass'd o'er many a mount
　sublime,
Through lands scarce noticed in historic
　tales;
Yet in famed Attica such lovely dales
Are rarely seen; nor can fair Tempe boast
A charm they know not; loved Parnassus
　fails,
Though classic ground and consecrated
　most,
To match some spots that lurk within this
　lowering coast.

XLVII.

He pass'd bleak Pindus, Acherusia's lake,
And left the primal city of the land,
And onwards did his further journey take
To greet Albania's chief, whose dread command
Is lawless law; for with a bloody hand
He sways a nation, turbulent and bold;
Yet here and there some daring mountain-band
Disdain his power, and from their rocky hold
Hurl their defiance far, nor yield, unless to gold.

XLVIII.

Monastic Zitza! from thy shady brow,
Thou small but favour'd spot of holy ground!
Where'er we gaze, around, above, below,
What rainbow tints, what magic charms are found!
Rock, river, forest, mountain, all abound,
And bluest skies that harmonise the whole:
Beneath, the distant torrent's rushing sound
Tells where the volumed cataract doth roll
Between those hanging rocks, that shock yet please the soul.

XLIX.

Amidst the grove that crowns yon tufted hill,
Which, were it not for many a mountain nigh
Rising in lofty ranks, and loftier still,
Might well itself be deem'd of dignity,
The convent's white walls glisten fair on high:
Here dwells the caloyer, nor rude is he,
Nor niggard of his cheer; the passer by
Is welcome still; nor heedless will he flee
From hence, if he delight kind Nature's sheen to see.

L.

Here in the sultriest season let him rest,
Fresh is the green beneath those aged trees;
Here winds of gentlest wing will fan his breast,
From heaven itself he may inhale the breeze:
The plain is far beneath—oh! let him seize
Pure pleasure while he can; the scorching ray
Here pierceth not, impregnate with disease:
Then let his length the loitering pilgrim lay,
And gaze, untired, the morn, the noon, the eve away.

LI.

Dusky and huge, enlarging on the sight,
Nature's volcanic amphitheatre,
Chimæra's alps extend from left to right:
Beneath, a living valley seems to stir;
Flocks play, trees wave, streams flow, the mountain-fir
Nodding above; behold black Acheron!
Once consecrated to the sepulchre.
Pluto! if this be hell I look upon,
Close shamed Elysium's gates, my shade shall seek for none.

LII.

Ne city's towers pollute the lovely view;
Unseen is Yanina, though not remote,
Veil'd by the screen of hills: here men are few,
Scanty the hamlet, rare the lonely cot:
But, peering down each precipice, the goat
Browseth; and, pensive o'er his scatter'd flock,
The little shepherd in his white capote
Doth lean his boyish form along the rock,
Or in his cave awaits the tempest's short-lived shock.

LIII.

Oh! where, Dodona! is thine aged grove,
Prophetic fount, and oracle divine?
What valley echoed the response of Jove?
What trace remaineth of the Thunderer's shrine?
All, all forgotten—and shall man repine
That his frail bonds to fleeting life are broke?
Cease, fool! the fate of gods may well be thine:
Wouldst thou survive the marble or the oak?
When nations, tongues, and worlds must sink beneath the stroke!

LIV.

Epirus' bounds recede, and mountains fail;
Tired of up-gazing still, the wearied eye
Reposes gladly on as smooth a vale
As ever Spring yclad in grassy dye:
Ev'n on a plain no humble beauties lie,
Where some bold river breaks the long expanse,
And woods along the banks are waving high,
Whose shadows in the glassy waters dance,
Or with the moonbeam sleep in midnight's solemn trance.

LV.

The sun had sunk behind vast Tomerit,
And Laos wide and fierce came roaring by;
The shades of wonted night were gathering yet,
When, down the steep banks winding warily,

Childe Harold saw, like meteors in the sky,
The glittering minarets of Tepalen,
Whose walls o'erlook the stream; and
 drawing nigh,
He heard the busy hum of warrior-men
Swelling the breeze that sigh'd along the
 lengthening glen.

LVI.

He pass'd the sacred Haram's silent tower,
And underneath the wide o'erarching gate
Survey'd the dwelling of this chief of power,
Where all around proclaim'd his high estate.
Amidst no common pomp the despot sate,
While busy preparation shook the court,
Slaves, eunuchs, soldiers, guests, and san-
 tons wait;
Within, a palace, and, without, a fort:
Here men of every clime appear to make re-
 sort.

LVII.

Richly caparison'd, a ready row
Of armed horse, and many a warlike store,
Circled the wide-extending court below;
Above, strange groups adorn'd the corridore;
And oft-times through the area's echoing
 door,
Some high-capp'd Tartar spurr'd his steed
 away:
The Turk, the Greek, the Albanian, and the
 Moor,
Here mingled in their many-hued array,
While the deep war-drum's sound announced
 the close of day.

LVIII.

The wild Albanian kirtled to his knee,
With shawl-girt head and ornamented gun,
And gold-embroider'd garments, fair to see;
The crimson-scarfed men of Macedon;
The Delhi with his cap of terror on,
And crooked glaive; the lively, supple
 Greek;
And swarthy Nubia's mutilated son;
The bearded Turk, that rarely deigns to
 speak,
Master of all around, too potent to be meek,

LIX.

Are mix'd conspicuous: some recline in
 groups,
Scanning the motley scene that varies
 round;
There some grave Moslem to devotion
 stoops,
And some that smoke, and some that play,
 are found;

Here the Albanian proudly treads the
 ground;
Half whispering there the Greek is heard to
 prate;
Hark! from the mosque the nightly solemn
 sound,
The Muezzin's call doth shake the minaret,
" There is no god but God!—to prayer—lo!
 God is great!"

LX.

Just at this season Ramazani's fast
Through the long day its penance did main-
 tain:
But when the lingering twilight hour was
 past,
Revel and feast assumed the rule again:
Now all was bustle, and the menial train
Prepared and spread the plenteous board
 within;
The vacant gallery now seem'd made in
 vain,
But from the chambers came the mingling
 din,
As page and slave anon were passing out and
 in.

LXI.

Here woman's voice is never heard: apart,
And scarce permitted, guarded, veil'd, to
 move,
She yields to one her person and her heart,
Tamed to her cage, nor feels a wish to rove:
For, not unhappy in her master's love,
And joyful in a mother's gentlest cares,
Blest cares! all other feelings far above!
Herself more sweetly rears the babe she
 bears,
Who never quits the breast, no meaner passion
 shares.

LXII.

In marble-paved pavilion, where a spring
Of living water from the centre rose,
Whose bubbling did a genial freshness fling,
And soft voluptuous couches breathed re-
 pose,
ALI reclined, a man of war and woes:
Yet in his lineaments ye cannot trace,
While Gentleness her milder radiance
 throws
Along that aged venerable face,
The deeds that lurk beneath, and stain him
 with disgrace.

LXIII.

It is not that yon hoary lengthening beard
Ill suits the passions which belong to youth;
Love conquers age—so Hafiz hath averr'd,
So sings the Teian, and he sings in sooth—

But crimes that scorn the tender voice of
 ruth,
Beseeming all men ill, but most the man
In years, have mark'd him with a tiger's
 tooth;
Blood follows blood, and, through their
 mortal span,
In bloodier acts conclude those who with
 blood began.

LXIV.

'Mid many things most new to ear and eye
The pilgrim rested here his weary feet,
And gazed around on Moslem luxury,
Till quickly wearied with that spacious seat
Of Wealth and Wantonness, the choice
 retreat
Of sated Grandeur from the city's noise:
And were it humbler, it in sooth were sweet;
But Peace abhorreth artificial joys,
And Pleasure, leagued with Pomp, the zest of
 both destroys.

LXV.

Fierce are Albania's children, yet they lack
Not virtues, were those virtues more ma-
 ture.
Where is the foe that ever saw their back?
Who can so well the toil of war endure?
Their native fastnesses not more secure
Than they in doubtful time of troublous
 need:
Their wrath how deadly! but their friend-
 ship sure,
When Gratitude or Valour bids them bleed,
Unshaken rushing on where'er their chief may
 lead.

LXVI.

Childe Harold saw them in their chieftain's
 tower
Thronging to war in splendour and success;
And after view'd them, when, within their
 power,
Himself awhile the victim of distress;
That saddening hour when bad men hotlier
 press:
But these did shelter him beneath their roof,
When less barbarians would have cheer'd
 him less,
And fellow-countrymen have stood aloof—
In aught that tries the heart how few with-
 stand the proof!

LXVII.

It chanced that adverse winds once drove
 his bark
Full on the coast of Suli's shaggy shore,
When all around was desolate and dark;
To land was perilous, to sojourn more;

Yet for a while the mariners forbore,
Dubious to trust where treachery might
 lurk:
At length they ventured forth, though
 doubting sore
That those who loathe alike the Frank and
 Turk
Might once again renew their ancient butcher-
 work.

LXVIII.

Vain fear! the Suliotes stretch'd the wel-
 come hand,
Led them o'er rocks and past the dangerous
 swamp,
Kinder than polish'd slaves, though not so
 bland,
And piled the hearth, and wrung their
 garments damp,
And fill'd the bowl, and trimm'd the cheer-
 ful lamp,
And spread their fare; though homely, all
 they had:
Such conduct bears Philanthropy's rare
 stamp:
To rest the weary and to soothe the sad,
Doth lesson happier men, and shames at least
 the bad.

LXIX.

It came to pass, that when he did address
Himself to quit at length this mountain-
 land,
Combined marauders half-way barr'd
 egress,
And wasted far and near with glaive and
 brand;
And therefore did he take a trusty band
To traverse Acarnania's forest wide,
In war well season'd, and with labours
 tann'd,
Till he did greet white Achelous' tide,
And from his further bank Ætolia's wolds
 espied.

LXX.

Where lone Utraikey forms its circling cove,
And weary waves retire to gleam at rest,
How brown the foliage of the green hill's
 grove,
Nodding at midnight o'er the calm bay's
 breast,
As winds come lightly whispering from the
 west,
Kissing, not ruffling, the blue deep's
 serene:—
Here Harold was received a welcome guest;
Nor did he pass unmoved the gentle scene,
For many a joy could he from Night's soft
 presence glean.

LXXI.

On the smooth shore the night-fires brightly
 blazed,
The feast was done, the red wine circling
 fast,
And he that unawares had there ygazed
With gaping wonderment had stared aghast;
For ere night's midmost, stillest hour was
 past,
The native revels of the troop began;
Each Palikar his sabre from him cast,
And bounding hand in hand, man link'd to
 man,
Yelling their uncouth dirge, long daunced the
 kirtled clan.

LXXII.

Childe Harold at a little distance stood
And view'd, but not displeased, the revelrie,
Nor hated harmless mirth, however rude:
In sooth, it was no vulgar sight to see
Their barbarous, yet their not indecent, glee;
And, as the flames along their faces gleam'd,
Their gestures nimble, dark eyes flashing
 free,
The long wild locks that to their girdles
 stream'd,
While thus in concert they this lay half sang,
 half scream'd :—

1.

TAMBOURGI! Tambourgi! thy 'larum afar
Gives hope to the valiant, and promise of war;
All the sons of the mountains arise at the
 note,
Chimariot, Illyrian, and dark Suliote!

2.

Oh! who is more brave than a dark Suliote,
In his snowy camese and his shaggy capote?
To the wolf and the vulture he leaves his
 wild flock,
And descends to the plain like the stream
 from the rock.

3.

Shall the sons of Chimari, who never forgive
The fault of a friend, bid an enemy live?
Let those guns so unerring such vengeance
 forego?
What mark is so fair as the breast of a foe?

4.

Macedonia sends forth her invincible race;
For a time they abandon the cave and the
 chase;
But those scarfs of blood-red shall be redder,
 before
The sabre is sheathed and the battle is o'er.

5.

Then the pirates of Parga that dwell by the
 waves,
And teach the pale Franks what it is to be
 slaves,
Shall leave on the beach the long galley and
 oar,
And track to his covert the captive on shore.

6.

I ask not the pleasures that riches supply,
My sabre shall win what the feeble must
 buy;
Shall win the young bride with her long
 flowing hair,
And many a maid from her mother shall tear.

7.

I love the fair face of the maid in her youth,
Her caresses shall lull me, her music shall
 soothe;
Let her bring from the chamber her many-
 toned lyre,
And sing us a song on the fall of her sire.

8.

Remember the moment when Previsa fell,
The shrieks of the conquer'd, the conqueror's
 yell;
The roofs that we fired, and the plunder we
 shared,
The wealthy we slaughter'd, the lovely we
 spared.

9.

I talk not of mercy, I talk not of fear;
He neither must know who would serve the
 Vizier:
Since the days of our prophet the Crescent
 ne'er saw
A chief ever glorious like Ali Pashaw.

10.

Dark Muchtar his son to the Danube is sped,
Let the yellow-hair'd Giaours view his horse-
 tail with dread;
When his Delhis come dashing in blood o'er
 the banks,
How few shall escape from the Muscovite
 ranks!

11.

Selictar! unsheathe then our chief's scimitar;
Tambourgi! thy 'larum gives promise of war.
Ye mountains, that see us descend to the
 shore,
Shall view us as victors, or view us no more!

LXXIII.

Fair Greece! sad relic of departed worth!
Immortal, though no more; though fallen,
 great!
Who now shall lead thy scatter'd children
 forth,
And long accustom'd bondage uncreate?
Not such thy sons who whilome did await,
The hopeless warriors of a willing doom,
In bleak Thermopylæ's sepulchral strait—
Oh! who that gallant spirit shall resume,
Leap from Eurota's banks, and call thee from
 the tomb?

LXXIV.

Spirit of freedom! when on Phyle's brow
Thou sat'st with Thrasybulus and his train,
Couldst thou forebode the dismal hour
 which now
Dims the green beauties of thine Attic
 plain?
Not thirty tyrants now enforce the chain,
But every carle can lord it o'er thy land;
Nor rise thy sons, but idly rail in vain,
Trembling beneath the scourge of Turkish
 hand; -
From birth till death enslaved; in word, in
 deed, unmann'd.

LXXV.

In all save form alone, how changed! and
 who
That marks the fire still sparkling in each
 eye,
Who would but deem their bosoms burn'd
 anew
With thy unquenched beam, lost Liberty!
And many dream withal the hour is nigh
That gives them back their fathers' heritage:
For foreign arms and aid they fondly sigh,
Nor solely dare encounter hostile rage,
Or tear their name defiled from Slavery's
 mournful page.

LXXVI.

Hereditary bondsmen! know ye not
Who would be free themselves must strike
 the blow?
By their right arms the conquest must be
 wrought?
Will Gaul or Muscovite redress ye? no!
True, they may lay your proud despoilers
 low,
But not for you will Freedom's altars flame.
Shades of the Helots! triumph o'er your foe!
Greece! change thy lords, thy state is still
 the same;
Thy glorious day is o'er, but not thy years of
 shame.

LXXVII.

The city won for Allah from the Giaour,
The Giaour from Othman's race again may
 wrest;
And the Serai's impenetrable tower
Receive the fiery Frank, her former guest;
Or Wahab's rebel brood, who dared divest
The prophet's tomb of all its pious spoil,
May wind their path of blood along the
 West;
But ne'er will freedom seek this fated
 soil,
But slave succeed to slave through years of
 endless toil.

LXXVIII.

Yet mark their mirth—ere lenten days
 begin,
That penance which their holy rites prepare
To shrive from man his weight of mortal
 sin,
By daily abstinence and nightly prayer:
But ere his sackcloth garb Repentance
 wear,
Some days of joyaunce are decreed to all,
To take of pleasaunce each his secret
 share,
In motley robe to dance at masking ball,
And join the mimic train of merry Carnival.

LXXIX.

And whose more rife with merriment than
 thine,
Oh Stamboul! once the empress of their
 reign?
Though turbans now pollute Sophia's
 shrine,
And Greece her very altars eyes in vain:
(Alas! her woes will still pervade my
 strain!)
Gay were her minstrels once, for free her
 throng,
All felt the common joy they now must
 feign,
Nor oft I've seen such sight, nor heard
 such song,
As woo'd the eye, and thrill'd the Bosphorus
 along.

LXXX.

Loud was the lightsome tumult on the
 shore,
Oft Music changed, but never ceased her
 tone,
And timely echo'd back the measured oar,
And rippling waters made a pleasant
 moan:

The Queen of tides on high consenting
 shone,
And when a transient breeze swept o'er the
 wave,
'Twas, as if darting from her heavenly
 throne,
A brighter glance her form reflected gave,
Till sparkling billows seem'd to light the
 banks they lave.

LXXXI.

Glanced many a light caique along the
 foam,
Danced on the shore the daughters of the
 land,
No thought had man or maid of rest or
 home,
While many a languid eye and thrilling
 hand
Exchanged the look few bosoms may with-
 stand,
Or gently prest, return'd the pressure still:
Oh Love! young Love! bound in thy rosy
 band,
Let sage or cynic prattle as he will,
These hours, and only these, redeem Life's
 years of ill!

LXXXII.

But, midst the throng in merry masquer-
 ade,
Lurk there no hearts that throb with secret
 pain,
Even through the closest searment half
 betray'd?
To such the gentle murmurs of the main
Seem to re-echo all they mourn in vain;
To such the gladness of the gamesome crowd
Is source of wayward thought and stern
 disdain:
How do they loathe the laughter idly loud,
And long to change the robe of revel for the
 shroud!

LXXXIII.

This must he feel, the true-born son of
 Greece,
If Greece one true-born patriot still can
 boast:
Not such as prate of war, but skulk in peace,
The bondsman's peace, who sighs for all
 he lost,
Yet with smooth smile his tyrant can accost,
And wield the slavish sickle, not the sword:
Ah! Greece! they love thee least who owe
 thee most—
Their birth, their blood, and that sublime
 record
Of hero sires, who shame thy now degenerate
 horde!

LXXXIV.

When riseth Lacedemon's hardihood,
When Thebes Epaminondas rears again,
When Athens' children are with hearts
 endued,
When Grecian mothers shall give birth to
 men,
Then may'st thou be restored; but not till
 then.
A thousand years scarce serve to form a
 state;
An hour may lay it in the dust: and when
Can man its shatter'd splendour renovate,
Recall its virtues back, and vanquish Time
 and Fate?

LXXXV.

And yet how lovely in thine age of woe,
Land of lost gods and godlike men, art
 thou!
Thy vales of evergreen, thy hills of snow,
Proclaim thee Nature's varied favourite
 now;
Thy fanes, thy temples to thy surface bow,
Commingling slowly with heroic earth,
Broke by the share of every rustic plough:
So perish monuments of mortal birth,
So perish all in turn, save well-recorded
 Worth;

LXXXVI.

Save where some solitary column mourns
Above its prostrate brethren of the cave;
Save where Tritonia's airy shrine adorns
Colonna's cliff, and gleams along the wave;
Save o'er some warrior's half-forgotten
 grave,
Where the gray stones and unmolested
 grass
Ages, but not oblivion, feebly brave;
While strangers only not regardless pass,
Lingering like me, perchance, to gaze, and
 sigh "Alas!"

LXXXVII.

Yet are thy skies as blue, thy crags as wild;
Sweet are thy groves, and verdant are thy
 fields,
Thine olive ripe as when Minerva smiled,
And still his honey'd wealth Hymettus
 yields;
There the blithe bee his fragrant fortress
 builds,
The freeborn wanderer of thy mountain-
 air;
Apollo still thy long, long summer gilds,
Still in his beam Mendeli's marbles glare;
Art, Glory, Freedom fail, but Nature still is
 fair.

LXXXVIII.

Where'er we tread 't is haunted, holy
 ground;
No earth of thine is lost in vulgar mould,
But one vast realm of wonder spreads
 around,
And all the Muse's tales seem truly told,
Till the sense aches with gazing to behold
The scenes our earliest dreams have dwelt
 upon;
Each hill and dale, each deepening glen
 and wold
Defies the power which crush'd thy temples
 gone:
Age shakes Athena's tower, but spares gray
 Marathon.

LXXXIX.

The sun, the soil, but not the slave, the
 same;
Unchanged in all except its foreign lord;
Preserves alike its bounds and boundless
 fame
The Battle-field, where Persia's victim
 horde
First bow'd beneath the brunt of Hellas'
 sword,
As on the morn to distant Glory dear,
When Marathon became a magic word;
Which utter'd, to the hearer's eye appear
The camp, the host, the fight, the conqueror's
 career,

XC.

The flying Mede, his shaftless broken bow;
The fiery Greek, his red pursuing spear;
Mountains above, Earth's, Ocean's plain
 below;
Death in the front, Destruction in the
 rear!
Such was the scene—what now remaineth
 here?
What sacred trophy marks the hallow'd
 ground,
Recording Freedom's smile and Asia's
 tear?
The rifled urn, the violated mound,
The dust thy courser's hoof, rude stranger!
 spurns around.

XCI.

Yet to the remnants of thy splendour past
Shall pilgrims, pensive, but unwearied,
 throng;
Long shall the voyager, with th' Ionian
 blast,
Hail the bright clime of battle and of song;

Long shall thine annals and immortal
 tongue
Fill with thy fame the youth of many a
 shore;
Boast of the aged! lesson of the young!
Which sages venerate and bards adore,
As Pallas and the Muse unveil their awful lore.

XCII.

The parted bosom clings to wonted home,
If aught that's kindred cheer the welcome
 hearth;
He that is lonely, hither let him roam,
And gaze complacent on congenial earth.
Greece is no lightsome land of social
 mirth:
But he whom Sadness sootheth may abide,
And scarce regret the region of his birth,
When wandering slow by Delphi's sacred
 side,
Or gazing o'er the plains where Greek and
 Persian died.

XCIII.

Let such approach this consecrated land,
And pass in peace along the magic waste;
But spare its relics—let no busy hand
Deface the scenes, already how defaced!
Not for such purpose were these altars
 placed:
Revere the remnants nations once revered:
So may our country's name be undisgraced,
So may'st thou prosper where thy youth
 was rear'd,
By every honest joy of love and life endear'd!

XCIV.

For thee, who thus in too protracted song
Hast soothed thine idlesse with inglorious
 lays,
Soon shall thy voice be lost amid the
 throng
Of louder minstrels in these later days:
To such resign the strife for fading bays—
Ill may such contest now the spirit move
Which heeds nor keen reproach nor partial
 praise,
Since cold each kinder heart that might
 approve,
And none are left to please when none are
 left to love.

XCV.

Thou too art gone, thou loved and lovely
 one!
Whom youth and youth's affections bound
 to me;
Who did for me what none beside have
 done,
Nor shrank from one albeit unworthy thee.

What is my being? thou hast ceased to be!
Nor staid to welcome here thy wanderer
 home,
Who mourns o'er hours which we no more
 shall see—
Would they had never been, or were to
 come!
Would he had ne'er return'd to find fresh
 cause to roam!

XCVI.

Oh! ever loving, lovely, and beloved!
How selfish Sorrow ponders on the past,
And clings to thoughts now better far
 removed!
But Time shall tear thy shadow from me
 last.
All thou couldst have of mine, stern Death!
 thou hast;
The parent, friend, and now the more than
 friend;
Ne'er yet for one thine arrows flew so
 fast,
And grief with grief continuing still to
 blend,
Hath snatch'd the little joy that life had yet
 to lend.

XCVII.

Then must I plunge again into the crowd,
And follow all that Peace disdains to seek?
Where Revel calls, and Laughter, vainly
 loud,
False to the heart, distorts the hollow
 cheek,
To leave the flagging spirit doubly weak;
Still o'er the features, which perforce they
 cheer,
To feign the pleasure or conceal the pique?
Smiles form the channel of a future tear,
Or raise the writhing lip with ill-dissembled
 sneer.

XCVIII.

What is the worst of woes that wait on
 age?
What stamps the wrinkle deeper on the
 brow?
To view each loved one blotted from life's
 page,
And be alone on earth, as I am now.
Before the Chastener humbly let me bow,
O'er hearts divided and o'er hopes de-
 stroy'd:
Roll on, vain days! full reckless may ye
 flow,
Since Time hath reft whate'er my soul
 enjoy'd,
And with the ills of Eld mine earlier years
 alloy'd.

Canto the Third.

"Afin que cette application vous forçât de penser
à autre chose; il n'y a en vérité de remède que
celui-là et le temps."
Lettre du Roi de Prusse à D'Alembert, Sept. 7, 1776.

I.

Is thy face like thy mother's, my fair
 child!
ADA! sole daughter of my house and heart?
When last I saw thy young blue eyes they
 smiled,
And then we parted,—not as now we part,
But with a hope.—
 Awaking with a start,
The waters heave around me; and on
 high
The winds lift up their voices: I depart,
Whither I know not; but the hour's
 gone by,
When Albion's lessening shores could grieve
 or glad mine eye.

II.

Once more upon the waters! yet once
 more!
And the waves bound beneath me as a
 steed
That knows his rider. Welcome to their
 roar!
Swift be their guidance, wheresoe'er it
 lead!
Though the strain'd mast should quiver
 as a reed,
And the rent canvas fluttering strew the
 gale,
Still must I on; for I am as a weed,
Flung from the rock, on Ocean's foam
 to sail
Where'er the surge may sweep, the tempest's
 breath prevail.

III.

In my youth's summer I did sing of One,
The wandering outlaw of his own dark
 mind;
Again I seize the theme, then but begun,
And bear it with me, as the rushing wind
Bears the cloud onwards: in that Tale
 I find
The furrows of long thought, and dried-up
 tears,
Which, ebbing, leave a sterile track behind,
O'er which all heavily the journeying years
Plod the last sands of life,—where not a
 flower appears.

IV.

Since my young days of passion—joy, or
 pain,
Perchance my heart and harp have lost
 a string,
And both may jar: it may be, that in vain
I would essay as I have sung to sing.
Yet, though a dreary strain, to this I cling;
So that it wean me from the weary dream
Of selfish grief or gladness—so it fling
Forgetfulness around me—it shall seem
To me, though to none else, a not ungrateful
 theme.

V.

He, who grown aged in this world of woe,
In deeds, not years, piercing the depths
 of life,
So that no wonder waits him; nor below
Can love or sorrow, fame, ambition, strife,
Cut to his heart again with the keen knife
Of silent, sharp endurance: he can tell
Why thought seeks refuge in lone caves,
 yet rife
With airy images, and shapes which dwell
Still unimpair'd, though old, in the soul's
 haunted cell.

VI.

'T is to create, and in creating live
A being more intense that we endow
With form our fancy, gaining as we give
The life we image, even as I do now.
What am I? Nothing: but not so art thou,
Soul of my thought! with whom I traverse
 earth,
Invisible but gazing, as I glow
Mix'd with thy spirit, blended with thy
 birth,
And feeling still with thee in my crush'd
 feelings' dearth.

VII.

Yet must I think less wildly:—I *have*
 thought
Too long and darkly, till my brain became,
In its own eddy boiling and o'erwrought,
A whirling gulf of phantasy and flame:
And thus, untaught in youth my heart
 to tame,
My springs of life were poison'd. 'T is
 too late!
Yet am I changed; though still enough
 the same
In strength to bear what time cannot
 abate,
And feed on bitter fruits without accusing
 Fate.

VIII.

Something too much of this:—but now
 't is past,
And the spell closes with its silent seal.
Long absent HAROLD re-appears at last;
He of the breast which fain no more would
 feel,
Wrung with the wounds which kill not,
 but ne'er heal;
Yet Time, who changes all, had alter'd
 him
In soul and aspect as in age: years steal
Fire from the mind as vigour from the
 limb;
And life's enchanted cup but sparkles near
 the brim.

IX.

His had been quaff'd too quickly, and he
 found
The dregs were wormwood; but he fill'd
 again,
And from a purer fount, on holier ground,
And deem'd its spring perpetual; but in
 vain!
Still round him clung invisibly a chain
Which gall'd for ever, fettering though
 unseen,
And heavy though it clank'd not; worn
 with pain,
Which pined although it spoke not, and
 grew keen,
Entering with every step he took through
 many a scene.

X.

Secure in guarded coldness, he had mix'd
Again in fancied safety with his kind,
And deem'd his spirit now so firmly fix'd
And sheath'd with an invulnerable mind,
That, if no joy, no sorrow lurk'd behind;
And he, as one, might 'midst the many
 stand
Unheeded, searching through the crowd to
 find
Fit speculation; such as in strange land
He found in wonder-works of God and
 Nature's hand.

XI.

But who can view the ripen'd rose, nor
 seek
To wear it? who can curiously behold
The smoothness and the sheen of beauty's
 cheek,
Nor feel the heart can never all grow
 old?

Who can contemplate Fame through clouds
 unfold
The star which rises o'er her steep, nor
 climb?
Harold, once more within the vortex, roll'd
On with the giddy circle, chasing Time,
Yet with a nobler aim than in his youth's
 fond prime.

XII.

But soon he knew himself the most unfit
Of men to herd with Man; with whom he
 held
Little in common; untaught to submit
His thoughts to others, though his soul
 was quell'd
In youth by his own thoughts; still un-
 compell'd,
He would not yield dominion of his mind
To spirits against whom his own rebell'd;
Proud though in desolation; which could
 find
A life within itself, to breathe without man-
 kind.

XIII.

Where rose the mountains, there to him
 were friends;
Where roll'd the ocean, thereon was his
 home;
Where a blue sky, and glowing clime,
 extends,
He had the passion and the power to
 roam;
The desert, forest, cavern, breaker's foam,
Were unto him companionship; they spake
A mutual language, clearer than the tome
Of his land's tongue, which he would oft
 forsake
For Nature's pages glass'd by sunbeams on
 the lake.

XIV.

Like the Chaldean, he could watch the
 stars,
Till he had peopled them with beings
 bright
As their own beams; and earth, and earth-
 born jars,
And human frailties, were forgotten quite:
Could he have kept his spirit to that flight
He had been happy; but this clay will
 sink
Its spark immortal, envying it the light
To which it mounts, as if to break the
 link
That keeps us from yon heaven which woos
 us to its brink.

XV.

But in Man's dwellings he became a thing
Restless and worn, and stern and weari-
 some,
Droop'd as a wild-born falcon with clipt
 wing,
To whom the boundless air alone were
 home:
Then came his fit again, which to o'er-
 come,
As eagerly the barr'd-up bird will beat
His breast and beak against his wiry dome
Till the blood tinge his plumage, so the
 heat
Of his impeded soul would through his bosom
 eat.

XVI.

Self-exiled Harold wanders forth again,
With nought of hope left, but with less
 of gloom;
The very knowledge that he lived in vain,
That all was over on this side the tomb,
Had made Despair a smilingness assume,
Which, though 'twere wild,—as on the
 plunder'd wreck
When mariners would madly meet their
 doom
With draughts intemperate on the sinking
 deck,—
Did yet inspire a cheer, which he forbore to
 check.

XVII.

Stop!—for thy tread is on an Empire's
 dust!
An Earthquake's spoil is sepulchred below!
Is the spot mark'd with no colossal bust?
Nor column trophied for triumphal show?
None; but the moral's truth tells simpler so,
As the ground was before, thus let it be;—
How that red rain hath made the harvest
 grow!
And is this all the world has gain'd by thee,
Thou first and last of fields! king-making
 Victory?

XVIII.

And Harold stands upon this place of skulls,
The grave of France, the deadly Waterloo!
How in an hour the power which gave
 annuls
Its gifts, transferring fame as fleeting too!
In "pride of place" here last the eagle flew,
Then tore with bloody talon the rent plain,
Pierced by the shaft of banded nations
 through;
Ambition's life and labours all were vain;
He wears the shatter'd links of the world's
 broken chain.

XIX.

Fit retribution! Gaul may champ the bit
And foam in fetters;—but is Earth more
 free?
Did nations combat to make *One* submit;
Or league to teach all kings true sove-
 reignty?
What! shall reviving Thraldom again be
The patch'd-up idol of enlighten'd days?
Shall we, who struck the Lion down, shall we
Pay the Wolf homage? proffering lowly gaze
And servile knees to thrones? No; *prove*
 before ye praise!

XX.

If not, o'er one fallen despot boast no
 more!
In vain fair cheeks were furrow'd with hot
 tears
For Europe's flowers long rooted up before
The trampler of her vineyards; in vain
 years
Of death, depopulation, bondage, fears,
Have all been borne, and broken by the
 accord
Of roused-up millions; all that most endears
Glory, is when the myrtle wreathes a
 sword
Such as Harmodius drew on Athens' tyrant
 lord.

XXI.

There was a sound of revelry by night,
And Belgium's capital had gather'd then
Her Beauty and her Chivalry, and bright
The lamps shone o'er fair women and
 brave men;
A thousand hearts beat happily; and when
Music arose with its voluptuous swell,
Soft eyes look'd love to eyes which spake
 again,
And all went merry as a marriage bell;
But hush! hark! a deep sound strikes like
 a rising knell!

XXII.

Did ye not hear it?—No; 't was but the
 wind,
Or the car rattling o'er the stony street;
On with the dance! let joy be unconfined;
No sleep till morn, when Youth and Plea-
 sure meet
To chase the glowing Hours with flying
 feet—
But hark!—that heavy sound breaks in
 once more,
As if the clouds its echo would repeat;
And nearer, clearer, deadlier than before!
Arm! Arm! it is—it is—the cannon's opening
 roar!

XXIII.

Within a window'd niche of that high hall
Sate Brunswick's fated chieftain; he did
 hear
That sound the first amidst the festival,
And caught its tone with Death's prophetic
 ear;
And when they smiled because he deem'd
 it near,
His heart more truly knew that peal too
 well
Which stretch'd his father on a bloody
 bier,
And roused the vengeance blood alone could
 quell;
He rush'd into the field, and, foremost fight-
 ing, fell.

XXIV.

Ah! then and there was hurrying to and
 fro,
And gathering tears, and tremblings of
 distress,
And cheeks all pale, which but an hour ago
Blush'd at the praise of their own loveli-
 ness;
And there were sudden partings, such as
 press
The life from out young hearts, and choking
 sighs
Which ne'er might be repeated; who could
 guess
If ever more should meet those mutual eyes,
Since upon night so sweet such awful morn
 could rise!

XXV.

And there was mounting in hot haste: the
 steed,
The mustering squadron, and the clattering
 car,
Went pouring forward with impetuous
 speed,
And swiftly forming in the ranks of war;
And the deep thunder peal on peal afar;
And near, the beat of the alarming drum
Roused up the soldier ere the morning star;
While throng'd the citizens with terror
 dumb,
Or whispering, with white lips—"The foe!
 they come! they come!"

XXVI.

And wild and high the "Cameron's gather-
 ing" rose!
The war-note of Lochiel, which Albyn's hills
Have heard, and heard, too, have her Saxon
 foes:—
How in the noon of night that pibroch
 thrills,

Savage and shrill! But with the breath
 which fills
Their mountain-pipe, so fill the moun-
 taineers
With the fierce native daring which instils
The stirring memory of a thousand years,
And Evan's, Donald's fame rings in each
 clansman's ears!

XXVII.

And Ardennes waves above them her green
 leaves,
Dewy with nature's tear-drops as they
 pass,
Grieving, if aught inanimate e'er grieves,
Over the unreturning brave,—alas!
Ere evening to be trodden like the grass
Which now beneath them, but above shall
 grow
In its next verdure, when this fiery mass
Of living valour, rolling on the foe
And burning with high hope shall moulder
 cold and low.

XXVIII.

Last noon beheld them full of lusty life,
Last eve in Beauty's circle proudly gay,
The midnight brought the signal-sound of
 strife,
The morn the marshalling in arms,—the
 day
Battle's magnificently stern array!
The thunder-clouds close o'er it, which
 when rent
The earth is cover'd thick with other clay,
Which her own clay shall cover, heap'd
 and pent,
Rider and horse,—friend, foe,—in one red
 burial blent!

XXIX.

Their praise is hymn'd by loftier harps
 than mine:
Yet one I would select from that proud
 throng,
Partly because they blend me with his
 line,
And partly that I did his sire some wrong,
And partly that bright names will hallow
 song;
And his was of the bravest, and when
 shower'd
The death-bolts deadliest the thinn'd files
 along,
Even where the thickest of war's tempest
 lower'd,
They reach'd no nobler breast than thine,
 young gallant Howard!

XXX.

There have been tears and breaking hearts
 for thee,
And mine were nothing had I such to give;
But when I stood beneath the fresh green
 tree,
Which living waves where thou didst cease
 to live,
And saw around me the wide field revive
With fruits and fertile promise, and the
 Spring
Came forth her work of gladness to contrive,
With all her reckless birds upon the wing,
I turn'd from all she brought to those she
 could not bring.

XXXI.

I turn'd to thee, to thousands, of whom each
And one as all a ghastly gap did make
In his own kind and kindred, whom to teach
Forgetfulness were mercy for their sake;
The Archangel's trump, not Glory's, must
 awake
Those whom they thirst for; though the
 sound of Fame
May for a moment soothe, it cannot slake
The fever of vain longing, and the name
So honour'd but assumes a stronger, bitterer
 claim.

XXXII.

They mourn, but smile at length; and,
 smiling,
The tree will wither long before it fall;
The hull drives on, though mast and sail
 be torn;
The roof-tree sinks, but moulders on the
 hall
In massy hoariness; the ruin'd wall
Stands when its wind-worn battlements are
 gone;
The bars survive the captive they enthral;
The day drags through, though storms
 keep out the sun;
And thus the heart will break, yet brokenly
 live on:

XXXIII.

Even as a broken mirror, which the glass
In every fragment multiplies; and makes
A thousand images of one that was,
The same, and still the more, the more it
 breaks;
And thus the heart will do which not
 forsakes,
Living in shatter'd guise; and still, and cold,
And bloodless, with its sleepless sorrow
 aches,
Yet withers on till all without is old,
Showing no visible sign, for such things
 are untold.

XXXIV.

There is a very life in our despair,
Vitality of poison,—a quick root
Which feeds these deadly branches; for it
 were
As nothing did we die; but Life will suit
Itself to Sorrow's most detested fruit,
Like to the apples on the Dead Sea's shore,
All ashes to the taste: Did man compute
Existence by enjoyment, and count o'er
Such hours 'gainst years of life,—say, would
 he name threescore?

XXXV.

The Psalmist number'd out the years of man:
They are enough; and if thy tale be *true*,
Thou, who didst grudge him even that
 fleeting span,
More than enough, thou fatal Waterloo!
Millions of tongues record thee, and anew
Their children's lips shall echo them, and
 say—
"Here, where the sword united nations
 drew,
Our countrymen were warring on that day!"
And this is much, and all which will not
 pass away.

XXXVI.

There sunk the greatest, nor the worst of men,
Whose spirit, antithetically mixt,
One moment of the mightiest, and again
On little objects with like firmness fixt;
Extreme in all things! hadst thou been
 betwixt,
Thy throne had still been thine, or never
 been;
For daring made thy rise as fall: thou
 seek'st
Even now to re-assume the imperial mien,
And shake again the world, the Thunderer
 of the scene!

XXXVII.

Conqueror and captive of the earth art thou!
She trembles at thee still, and thy wild
 name
Was ne'er more bruited in men's minds
 than now
That thou art nothing, save the jest of
 Fame,
Who woo'd thee once, thy vassal, and
 became
The flatterer of thy fierceness, till thou wert
A god unto thyself; nor less the same
To the astounded kingdoms all inert,
Who deem'd thee for a time whate'er thou
 didst assert.

XXXVIII.

Oh, more or less than man—in high or
 low,
Battling with nations, flying from the field;
Now making monarchs' necks thy footstool,
 now
More than thy meanest soldier taught to
 yield;
An empire thou couldst crush, command,
 rebuild,
But govern not thy pettiest passion, nor,
However deeply in men's spirits skill'd,
Look through thine own, nor curb the lust
 of war,
Nor learn that tempted Fate will leave the
 loftiest star.

XXXIX.

Yet well thy soul hath brook'd the turning
 tide
With that untaught innate philosophy,
Which, be it wisdom, coldness, or deep
 pride,
Is gall and wormwood to an enemy,
When the whole host of hatred stood
 hard by,
To watch and mock thee shrinking, thou
 hast smiled
With a sedate and all-enduring eye;—
When Fortune fled her spoil'd and favourite
 child,
He stood unbow'd beneath the ills upon him
 piled.

XL.

Sager than in thy fortunes; for in them
Ambition steel'd thee on too far to show
That just habitual scorn, which could
 contemn
Men and their thoughts; 't was wise to feel,
 not so
To wear it ever on thy lip and brow,
And spurn the instruments thou wert to
 use
Till they were turn'd unto thine overthrow:
'Tis but a worthless world to win or lose;
So hath it proved to thee, and all such lot
 who choose.

XLI.

If, like a tower upon a headland rock,
Thou hadst been made to stand or fall
 alone,
Such scorn of man had help'd to brave the
 shock;
But men's thoughts were the steps which
 paved thy throne,

Their admiration thy best weapon shone;
The part of Philip's son was thine, not then
(Unless aside thy purple had been thrown)
Like stern Diogenes to mock at men;
For sceptred cynics earth were far too wide
　　a den.

XLII.

But quiet to quick bosoms is a hell,
　　And *there* hath been thy bane; there is a
　　　　fire
And motion of the soul which will not
　　dwell
In its own narrow being, but aspire
Beyond the fitting medium of desire;
And, but once kindled, quenchless ever-
　　more,
Preys upon high adventure, nor can tire
Of aught but rest; a fever at the core,
Fatal to him who bears, to all who ever bore.

XLIII.

This makes the madmen who have made
　　men mad
By their contagion; Conquerors and Kings,
Founders of sects and systems, to whom
　　add
Sophists, Bards, Statesmen, all unquiet
　　things
Which stir too strongly the soul's secret
　　springs,
And are themselves the fools to those they
　　fool;
Envied, yet how unenviable! what stings
Are theirs! One breast laid open were a
　　school
Which would unteach mankind the lust to
　　shine or rule:

XLIV.

Their breath is agitation, and their life
A storm whereon they ride, to sink at last,
And yet so nursed and bigoted to strife,
That should their days, surviving perils
　　past,
Melt to calm twilight, they feel overcast
With sorrow and supineness, and so die;
Even as a flame unfed, which runs to waste
With its own flickering, or a sword laid by,
Which eats into itself, and rusts ingloriously.

XLV.

He who ascends to mountain-tops, shall
　　find
The loftiest peaks most wrapt in clouds
　　and snow;
He who surpasses or subdues mankind,
Must look down on the hate of those below.

Though high *above* the sun of glory glow,
And far *beneath* the earth and ocean spread,
Round him are icy rocks, and loudly blow
Contending tempests on his naked head,
And thus reward the toils which to those
　　summits led.

XLVI.

Away with these! true Wisdom's world
　　will be
Within its own creation, or in thine,
Maternal Nature! for who teems like thee,
Thus on the banks of thy majestic Rhine?
There Harold gazes on a work divine,
A blending of all beauties; streams and dells,
Fruit, foliage, crag, wood, cornfield, moun-
　　tain, vine,
And chiefless castles breathing stern fare-
　　wells
From gray but leafy walls, where Ruin
　　greenly dwells.

XLVII.

And there they stand, as stands a lofty
　　mind,
Worn, but unstooping to the baser crowd,
All tentantless, save to the crannying wind,
Or holding dark communion with the crowd.
There was a day when they were young
　　and proud;
Banners on high, and battles pass'd below;
But they who fought are in a bloody shroud,
And those which waved are shredless dust
　　ere now,
And the bleak battlements shall bear no
　　future blow.

XLVIII.

Beneath those battlements, within those
　　walls,
Power dwelt amidst her passions; in proud
　　state
Each robber chief upheld his armed halls,
Doing his evil will, nor less elate
Than mightier heroes of a longer date.
What want these outlaws conquerors should
　　have
But history's purchased page to call them
　　great?
A wider space, an ornamented grave?
Their hopes were not less warm, their souls
　　were full as brave.

XLIX.

In their baronial feuds and single fields,
What deeds of prowess unrecorded died!
And Love, which lent a blazon to their
　　shields,
With emblems well devised by amorous
　　pride,

Through all the mail of iron hearts would
 glide;
But still their flame was fierceness, and
 drew on
Keen contest and destruction near allied,
And many a tower for some fair mischief
 won,
Saw the discolour'd Rhine beneath its ruin
 run.

L.

But Thou, exulting and abounding river!
Making thy waves a blessing as they flow
Through banks whose beauty would endure
 for ever
Could man but leave thy bright creation so,
Nor its fair promise from the surface mow
With the sharp scythe of conflict,—then
 to see
Thy valley of sweet waters, were to know
Earth paved like Heaven; and to seem
 such to me,
Even now what wants thy stream?—that it
 should Lethe be.

LI.

A thousand battles have assail'd thy banks,
But these and half their fame have pass'd
 away,
And Slaughter heap'd on high his welter-
 ing ranks;
Their very graves are gone, and what are
 they?
Thy tide wash'd down the blood of yester-
 day,
And all was stainless, and on thy clear
 stream
Glass'd, with its dancing light, the sunny
 ray;
But o'er the blacken'd memory's blighting
 dream
Thy waves would vainly roll, all sweeping
 as they seem.

LII.

Thus Harold inly said, and pass'd along,
Yet not insensible to all which here
Awoke the jocund birds to early song
In glens which might have made even
 exile dear:
Though on his brow were graven lines
 austere,
And tranquil sternness, which had ta'en
 the place
Of feelings fierier far but less severe,
Joy was not always absent from his face,
But o'er it in such scenes would steal with
 transient trace.

LIII.

Nor was all love shut from him, though
 his days
Of passion had consumed themselves to
 dust.
It is in vain that we would coldly gaze
On such as smile upon us; the heart must
Leap kindly back to kindness, though dis-
 gust
Hath wean'd it from all worldlings: thus
 he felt,
For there was soft remembrance, and sweet
 trust
In one fond breast, to which his own would
 melt,
And in its tenderer hour on that his bosom
 dwelt.

LIV.

And he had learn'd to love,—I know not
 why,
For this in such as him seems strange of
 mood,—
The helpless looks of blooming infancy,
Even in its earliest nurture; what subdued,
To change like this, a mind so far imbued
With scorn of man, it little boots to know;
But thus it was; and though in solitude
Small power the nipp'd affections have to
 grow,
In him this glow'd when all beside had ceased
 to glow.

LV.

And there was one soft breast, as hath
 been said,
Which unto his was bound by stronger ties
Than the church links withal; and, though
 unwed,
That love was pure, and, far above disguise,
Had stood the test of mortal enmities
Still undivided, and cemented more
By peril, dreaded most in female eyes;
But this was firm, and from a foreign shore
Well to that heart might his these absent
 greetings pour!

1.

The castled crag of Drachenfels
Frowns o'er the wide and winding Rhine,
Whose breast of waters broadly swells
Between the banks which bear the vine,
And hills all rich with blossom'd trees,
And fields which promise corn and wine,
And scatter'd cities crowning these,
Whose far white walls along them shine,
Have strew'd a scene, which I should see
With double joy wert *thou* with me.

2.

And peasant girls, with deep blue eyes,
And hands which offer early flowers,
Walk smiling o'er this paradise;
Above, the frequent feudal towers
Through green leaves lift their walls of
gray;
And many a rock which steeply lowers,
And noble arch in proud decay,
Look o'er this vale of vintage-bowers;
But one thing want these banks of
Rhine,—
Thy gentle hand to clasp in mine!

3.

I send the lilies given to me;
Though long before thy hand they touch,
I know that they must wither'd be,
But yet reject them not as such;
For I have cherish'd them as dear,
Because they yet may meet thine eye,
And guide thy soul to mine even here,
When thou behold'st them drooping nigh,
And know'st them gather'd by the Rhine,
And offer'd from my heart to thine!

4.

The river nobly foams and flows,
The charm of this enchanted ground,
And all its thousand turns disclose
Some fresher beauty varying round:
The haughtiest breast its wish might
bound
Through life to dwell delighted here;
Nor could on earth a spot be found
To nature and to me so dear,
Could thy dear eyes in following mine
Still sweeten more these banks of Rhine!

LVI.

By Coblentz, on a rise of gentle ground,
There is a small and simple pyramid,
Crowning the summit of the verdant
mound;
Beneath its base are heroes' ashes hid,
Our enemy's—but let not that forbid
Honour to Marceau! o'er whose early tomb
Tears, big tears, gush'd from the rough
soldier's lid,
Lamenting and yet envying such a doom,
Falling for France, whose rights he battled
to resume.

LVII.

Brief, brave, and glorious was his young
career,—
His mourners were two hosts, his friends
and foes;
And fitly may the stranger lingering here
Pray for his gallant spirit's bright repose;

For he was Freedom's champion, one of
those,
The few in number, who had not o'erstept
The charter to chastise which she bestows
On such as wield her weapons; he had
kept
The whiteness of his soul, and thus men o'er
him wept.

LVIII.

Here Ehrenbreitstein, with her shatter'd
wall
Black with the miner's blast, upon her
height
Yet shows of what she was, when shell
and ball
Rebounding idly on her strength did light:
A tower of victory! from whence the flight
Of baffled foes was watch'd along the plain:
But Peace destroy'd what War could never
blight,
And laid those proud roofs bare to Sum-
mer's rain—
On which the iron shower for years had
pour'd in vain.

LIX.

Adieu to thee, fair Rhine! How long de-
lighted
The stranger fain would linger on his way!
Thine is a scene alike where souls united
Or lonely Contemplation thus might stray;
And could the ceaseless vultures cease to
prey
On self-condemning bosoms, it were here,
Where Nature, nor too sombre nor too gay,
Wild but not rude, awful yet not austere,
Is to the mellow Earth as Autumn to the year.

LX.

Adieu to thee again! a vain adieu!
There can be no farewell to scene like
thine;
The mind is colour'd by thy every hue;
And if reluctantly the eyes resign
Their cherish'd gaze upon thee, lovely
Rhine!
'Tis with the thankful heart of parting
praise;
More mighty spots may rise, more glaring
shine,
But none unite in one attaching maze
The brilliant, fair, and soft,—the glories of
old days.

LXI.

The negligently grand, the fruitful bloom
Of coming ripeness, the white city's sheen,
The rolling stream, the precipice's gloom,
The forest's growth, and Gothic walls
between,

The wild rocks shaped as they had turrets
 been,
In mockery of man's art; and these withal
A race of faces happy as the scene,
Whose fertile bounties here extend to all,
Still springing o'er thy banks, though Em-
 pires near them fall.

LXII.

But these recede. Above me are the Alps,
 The palaces of Nature, whose vast walls
Have pinnacled in clouds their snowy
 scalps,
And throned Eternity in icy halls
Of cold sublimity, where forms and falls
The avalanche—the thunderbolt of snow!
All that expands the spirit, yet appals,
Gather around these summits, as to show
How Earth may pierce to Heaven, yet leave
 vain man below.

LXIII.

But ere these matchless heights I dare to
 scan,
There is a spot should not be pass'd in
 vain,—
Morat! the proud, the patriot field! where
 man
May gaze on ghastly trophies of the slain,
Nor blush for those who conquer'd on that
 plain;
Here Burgundy bequeath'd his tombless
 host,
A bony heap, through ages to remain,
 Themselves their monument;—the Stygian
 coast
Unsepulchred they roam'd, and shriek'd
 each wandering ghost.

LXIV.

While Waterloo with Cannæ's carnage
 vies,
Morat and Marathon twin names shall
 stand;
They were true Glory's stainless victories,
Won by the unambitious heart and hand
Of a proud, brotherly, and civic band,
All unbought champions in no princely
 cause
Of vice-entail'd Corruption; they no land
Doom'd to bewail the blasphemy of laws
Making kings' rights divine, by some Draconic
 clause.

LXV.

By a lone wall a lonelier column rears
A gray and grief-worn aspect of old days;
'Tis the last remnant of the wreck of years,
And looks as with the wild-bewilder'd
 gaze

Of one to stone converted by amaze,
Yet still with consciousness; and there it
 stands
Making a marvel that it not decays,
When the coeval pride of human hands,
Levell'd Adventicum, hath strew'd her sub-
 ject lands.

LXVI.

And there—oh! sweet and sacred be the
 name!—
Julia—the daughter, the devoted—gave
Her youth to Heaven; her heart, beneath
 a claim
Nearest to Heaven's, broke o'er a father's
 grave.
Justice is sworn 'gainst tears, and hers
 would crave
The life she lived in; but the judge was
 just,
And then she died on him she could not save.
Their tomb was simple, and without a bust,
And held within their urn one mind, one
 heart, one dust.

LXVII.

But these are deeds which should not pass
 away,
And names that must not wither, though
 the earth
Forgets her empires with a just decay,
The enslavers and the enslaved, their
 death and birth;
The high, the mountain-majesty of worth
Should be, and shall, survivor of its woe,
And from its immortality look forth
In the sun's face, like yonder Alpine snow,
Imperishably pure beyond all things below.

LXVIII.

Lake Leman woos me with its crystal face,
The mirror where the stars and mountains
 view
The stillness of their aspect in each trace
Its clear depth yields of their far height
 and hue:
There is too much of man here, to look
 through
With a fit mind the might which I behold;
But soon in me shall Loneliness renew
Thoughts hid, but not less cherish'd than
 of old,
Ere mingling with the herd had penn'd me in
 their fold.

LXIX.

To fly from, need not be to hate, mankind:
All are not fit with them to stir and toil,
Nor is it discontent to keep the mind
Deep in its fountain, lest it overboil

In the hot throng, where we become the
 spoil
Of our infection, till too late and long
We may deplore and struggle with the coil,
In wretched interchange of wrong for
 wrong
Midst a contentious world, striving where
 none are strong.

LXX.

There, in a moment we may plunge our
 years
In fatal penitence, and in the blight
Of our own soul turn all our blood to tears,
And colour things to come with hues of
 Night;
The race of life becomes a hopeless flight
To those that walk in darkness: on the
 sea
The boldest steer but where their ports
 invite;
But there are wanderers o'er Eternity
Whose bark drives on and on, and anchor'd
 ne'er shall be.

LXXI.

Is it not better, then, to be alone,
And love Earth only for its earthly sake?
By the blue rushing of the arrowy Rhone,
Or the pure bosom of its nursing lake,
Which feeds it as a mother who doth make
A fair but froward infant her own care,
Kissing its cries away as these awake;—
Is it not better thus our lives to wear,
Than join the crushing crowd, doom'd to
 inflict or bear?

LXXII.

I live not in myself, but I become
Portion of that around me; and to me
High mountains are a feeling, but the hum
Of human cities torture: I can see
Nothing to loathe in nature, save to be
A link reluctant in a fleshly chain,
Class'd among creatures, when the soul
 can flee,
And with the sky, the peak, the heaving
 plain
Of ocean, or the stars, mingle, and not in
 vain.

LXXIII.

And thus I am absorb'd, and this is life:
I look upon the peopled desert past,
As on a place of agony and strife,
Where, for some sin, to sorrow I was
 cast,

To act and suffer, but remount at last
With a fresh pinion; which I feel to
 spring,
Though young, yet waxing vigorous as the
 blast
Which it would cope with, on delighted
 wing,
Spurning the clay-cold bonds which round
 our being cling.

LXXIV.

And when, at length, the mind shall be all
 free
From what it hates in this degraded form,
Reft of its carnal life, save what shall be
Existent happier in the fly and worm,—
When elements to elements conform,
And dust is as it should be, shall I not
Feel all I see, less dazzling, but more
 warm?
The bodiless thought? the Spirit of each
 spot?
Of which, even now, I share at times the
 immortal lot?

LXXV.

Are not the mountains, waves, and skies,
 a part
Of me and of my soul, as I of them?
Is not the love of these deep in my heart
With a pure passion? should I not con-
 temn
All objects, if compared with these? and
 stem
A tide of suffering, rather than forego
Such feelings for the hard and worldly
 phlegm
Of those whose eyes are only turn'd below,
Gazing upon the ground, with thoughts which
 dare not glow?

LXXVI.

But this is not my theme; and I return
To that which is immediate, and require
Those who find contemplation in the urn,
To look on One, whose dust was once all
 fire,
A native of the land where I respire
The clear air for a while—a passing guest,
Where he became a being,—whose desire
Was to be glorious; 'twas a foolish quest,
The which to gain and keep, he sacrificed all
 rest.

LXXVII.

Here the self-torturing sophist, wild Rous-
 seau,
The apostle of affliction, he who threw
Enchantment over passion, and from woe
Wrung overwhelming eloquence, first drew

The breath which made him wretched; yet
 he knew
How to make madness beautiful, and cast
O'er erring deeds and thoughts a heavenly
 hue
Of words, like sunbeams, dazzling as they
 past
The eyes, which o'er them shed tears feel-
 ingly and fast.

LXXVIII.

His love was passion's essence:—as a tree
On fire by lightning, with ethereal flame
Kindled he was, and blasted; for to be
Thus, and enamour'd, were in him the
 same.
But his was not the love of living dame,
Nor of the dead who rise upon our dreams,
But of ideal beauty, which became
In him existence, and o'erflowing teems
Along his burning page, distemper'd though
 it seems.

LXXIX.

This breathed itself to life in Julie, *this*
Invested her with all that's wild and
 sweet;
This hallow'd, too, the memorable kiss
Which every morn his fever'd lip would
 greet,
From hers, who but with friendship his
 would meet;
But to that gentle touch through brain and
 breast
Flash'd the thrill'd spirit's love-devouring
 heat;
In that absorbing sigh perchance more
 blest
Than vulgar minds may be with all they
 seek possest.

LXXX.

His life was one long war with self-sought
 foes,
Or friends by him self-banish'd; for his
 mind
Had grown Suspicion's sanctuary, and
 chose,
For its own cruel sacrifice, the kind,
'Gainst whom he raged with fury strange
 and blind.
But he was phrensied,—wherefore, who
 may know?
Since cause might be which skill could
 never find;
But he was phrensied by disease or woe,
To that worst pitch of all, which wears a
 reasoning show.

LXXXI.

For then he was inspired, and from him
 came,
As from the Pythian's mystic cave of yore,
Those oracles which set the world in flame,
Nor ceased to burn till kingdoms were no
 more:
Did he not this for France? which lay
 before
Bow'd to the inborn tyranny of years?
Broken and trembling to the yoke she
 bore,
Till by the voice of him and his compeers
Roused up to too much wrath, which follows
 o'ergrown fears?

LXXXII.

They made themselves a fearful monu-
 ment!
The wreck of old opinions—things which
 grew,
Breathed from the birth of time: the veil
 they rent,
And what behind it lay, all earth shall
 view.
But good with ill they also overthrew,
Leaving but ruins, wherewith to rebuild
Upon the same foundation, and renew
Dungeons and thrones, which the same
 hour refill'd,
As heretofore, because ambition was self-
 will'd.

LXXXIII.

But this will not endure, nor be endured!
Mankind have felt their strength, and made
 it felt.
They might have used it better, but, allured
By their new vigour, sternly have they
 dealt
On one another; pity ceased to melt
With her once natural charities. But they,
Who in oppression's darkness caved had
 dwelt,
They were not eagles, nourish'd with the
 day;
What marvel then, at times, if they mistook
 their prey?

LXXXIV.

What deep wounds ever closed without a
 scar?
The heart's bleed longest, and but heal to
 wear
That which disfigures it; and they who
 war
With their own hopes, and have been van-
 quish'd, bear

Silence, but not submission: in his lair
Fix'd Passion holds his breath, until the
　　hour
Which shall atone for years; none need
　　despair:
It came, it cometh, and will come,—the
　　power
To punish or forgive—in *one* we shall be
　　slower.

LXXXV.

Clear, placid Leman! thy contrasted lake,
With the wild world I dwelt in, is a thing
Which warns me, with its stillness, to
　　forsake
Earth's troubled waters for a purer spring.
This quiet sail is as a noiseless wing
To waft me from distraction; once I loved
Torn ocean's roar, but thy soft murmuring
Sounds sweet as if a Sister's voice reproved,
That I with stern delights should e'er have
　　been so moved.

LXXXVI.

It is the hush of night, and all between
Thy margin and the mountains, dusk, yet
　　clear,
Mellow'd and mingling, yet distinctly seen,
Save darken'd Jura, whose capt heights
　　appear
Precipitously steep; and drawing near,
There breathes a living fragrance from the
　　shore,
Of flowers yet fresh with childhood; on
　　the ear
Drops the light drip of the suspended oar,
Or chirps the grasshopper one good-night
　　carol more;

LXXXVII.

He is an evening reveller, who makes
His life an infancy, and sings his fill;
At intervals, some bird from out the brakes
Starts into voice a moment, then is still.
There seems a floating whisper on the hill,
But that is fancy, for the starlight dews
All silently their tears of love instil,
Weeping themselves away, till they infuse
Deep into nature's breast the spirit of her
　　hues.

LXXXVIII.

Ye stars! which are the poetry of heaven!
If in your bright leaves we would read the
　　fate
Of men and empires,—'tis to be forgiven,
That in our aspirations to be great,

Our destinies o'erleap their mortal state,
And claim a kindred with you; for ye are
A beauty and a mystery, and create
In us such love and reverence from afar,
That fortune, fame, power, life, have named
　　themselves a star.

LXXXIX.

All heaven and earth are still—though not
　　in sleep,
But breathless, as we grow when feeling
　　most;
And silent, as we stand in thoughts too
　　deep:—
All heaven and earth are still: From the
　　high host
Of stars, to the lull'd lake and mountain-
　　coast,
All is concenter'd in a life intense,
Where not a beam, nor air, nor leaf is lost,
But hath a part of being, and a sense
Of that which is of all Creator and defence.

XC.

Then stirs the feeling infinite, so felt
In solitude, where we are *least* alone;
A truth, which through our being then doth
　　melt,
And purifies from self: it is a tone,
The soul and source of music, which makes
　　known
Eternal harmony, and sheds a charm
Like to the fabled Cytherea's zone,
Binding all things with beauty;—'t would
　　disarm
The spectre Death, had he substantial power
　　to harm.

XCI.

Not vainly did the early Persian make
His altar the high places, and the peak
Of earth-o'ergazing mountains, and thus
　　take
A fit and unwall'd temple, there to seek
The Spirit, in whose honour shrines are
　　weak,
Uprear'd of human hands. Come, and
　　compare
Columns and idol-dwellings, Goth or Greek,
With Nature's realms of worship, earth
　　and air,
Nor fix on fond abodes to circumscribe thy
　　pray'r!

XCII.

The sky is changed!—and such a change!
　　Oh night,
And storm, and darkness, ye are wondrous
　　strong,
Yet lovely in your strength, as is the light
Of a dark eye in woman! Far along,

From peak to peak, the rattling crags
 among
Leaps the live thunder! Not from one lone
 cloud,
But every mountain now hath found a
 tongue,
And Jura answers, through her misty
 shroud,
Back to the joyous Alps, who call to her
 aloud!

XCIII.

And this is in the night:—Most glorious
 night!
Thou wert not sent for slumber! let me be
A sharer in thy fierce and far delight,—
A portion of the tempest and of thee!
How the lit lake shines, a phosphoric sea,
And the big rain comes dancing to the
 earth!
And now again 't is black,—and now, the
 glee
Of the loud hills shakes with its mountain-
 mirth,
As if they did rejoice o'er a young earth-
 quake's birth.

XCIV.

Now, where the swift Rhone cleaves his
 way between
Heights which appear as lovers who have
 parted
In hate, whose mining depths so intervene,
That they can meet no more, though
 broken-hearted;
Though in their souls, which thus each
 other thwarted,
Love was the very root of the fond rage
Which blighted their life's bloom, and then
 departed:
Itself expired, but leaving them an age
Of years all winters,—war within themselves
 to wage.

XCV.

Now, where the quick Rhone thus hath
 cleft his way,
The mightiest of the storms hath ta'en his
 stand:
For here, not one, but many, make their
 play,
And fling their thunder-bolts from hand to
 hand,
Flashing and cast around; of all the band,
The brightest through these parted hills
 hath fork'd
His lightnings,—as if he did understand,
That in such gaps as desolation work'd,
There the hot shaft should blast whatever
 therein lurk'd.

XCVI.

Sky, mountains, river, winds, lake, light-
 nings! ye!
With night, and clouds, and thunder, and
 a soul
To make these felt and feeling, well may be
Things that have made me watchful; the
 far roll
Of your departing voices, is the knoll
Of what in me is sleepless,—if I rest.
But where of ye, O tempests! is the
 goal?
Are ye like those within the human breast?
Or do ye find, at length, like eagles, some
 high nest?

XCVII.

Could I embody and unbosom now
That which is most within me,—could
 I wreak
My thoughts upon expression, and thus
 throw
Soul, heart, mind, passions, feelings, strong
 or weak,
All that I would have sought, and all I
 seek,
Bear, know, feel, and yet breathe—into *one*
 word,
And that one word were Lightning, I would
 speak;
But as it is, I live and die unheard,
With a most voiceless thought, sheathing it
 as a sword.

XCVIII.

The morn is up again, the dewy morn,
With breath all incense, and with cheek all
 bloom,
Laughing the clouds away with playful
 scorn,
And living as if earth contain'd no tomb,—
And glowing into day: we may resume
The march of our existence: and thus I,
Still on thy shores, fair Leman! may find
 room
And food for meditation, nor pass by
Much, that may give us pause, if ponder'd
 fittingly.

XCIX.

Clarens! sweet Clarens, birthplace of deep
 Love!
Thine air is the young breath of passionate
 thought;
Thy trees take root in Love; the snows
 above
The very Glaciers have his colours caught,

And sun-set into rose-hues sees them
 wrought
By rays which sleep there lovingly: the
 rocks,
The permanent crags, tell here of Love,
 who sought
In them a refuge from the worldly shocks,
Which stir and sting the soul with hope that
 woos, then mocks.

C.

Clarens! by heavenly feet thy paths are
 trod,—
Undying Love's, who here ascends a throne
To which the steps are mountains; where
 the god
Is a pervading life and light,—so shown
Not on those summits solely, nor alone
In the still cave and forest; o'er the flower
His eye is sparkling, and his breath hath
 blown,
His soft and summer breath, whose tender
 power
Passes the strength of storms in their most
 desolate hour.

CI.

All things are here of *him;* from the black
 pines,
Which are his shade on high, and the loud
 roar
Of torrents, where he listeneth, to the
 vines
Which slope his green path downward to
 the shore,
Where the bow'd waters meet him, and
 adore,
Kissing his feet with murmurs; and the
 wood,
The covert of old trees, with trunks all
 hoar,
But light leaves, young as joy, stands
 where it stood,
Offering to him, and his, a populous solitude.

CII.

A populous solitude of bees and birds,
And fairy-form'd and many-colour'd things,
Who worship him with notes more sweet
 than words,
And innocently open their glad wings,
Fearless and full of life: the gush of springs,
And fall of lofty fountains, and the bend
Of stirring branches, and the bud which
 brings
The swiftest thought of beauty, here extend,
Mingling, and made by Love, unto one mighty
 end.

CIII.

He who hath loved not, here would learn
 that lore,
And make his heart a spirit; he who knows
That tender mystery, will love the more;
For this is Love's recess, where vain men's
 woes,
And the world's waste, have driven him far
 from those,
For 'tis his nature to advance or die;
He stands not still, but or decays, or grows
Into a boundless blessing, which may vie
With the immortal lights, in its eternity!

CIV.

'Twas not for fiction chose Rousseau this
 spot,
Peopling it with affections; but he found
It was the scene which Passion must allot
To the mind's purified beings; 'twas the
 ground
Where early Love his Psyche's zone un-
 bound,
And hallow'd it with loveliness: 'tis lone,
And wonderful, and deep, and hath a sound,
And sense, and sight of sweetness; here
 the Rhone
Hath spread himself a couch, the Alps have
 rear'd a throne.

CV.

Lausanne! and Ferney! ye have been the
 abodes
Of names which unto you bequeath'd a name;
Mortals, who sought and found, by danger-
 ous roads,
A path to perpetuity of fame:
They were gigantic minds, and their steep
 aim
Was, Titan-like, on daring doubts to pile
Thoughts which should call down thunder,
 and the flame
Of Heaven again assail'd, if Heaven the while
On man and man's research could deign do
 more than smile.

CVI.

The one was fire and fickleness, a child
Most mutable in wishes, but in mind
A wit as various,—gay, grave, sage, or
 wild,—
Historian, bard, philosopher, combined;
He multiplied himself among mankind,
The Proteus of their talents: But his own
Breathed most in ridicule,—which, as the
 wind,
Blew where it listed, laying all things
 prone,—
Now to o'erthrow a fool, and now to shake
 a throne.

CVII.

The other, deep and slow, exhausting
 thought,
And hiving wisdom with each studious year,
In meditation dwelt, with learning wrought,
And shaped his weapon with an edge severe,
Sapping a solemn creed with solemn sneer;
The lord of irony,—that master-spell,
Which stung his foes to wrath, which grew
 from fear,
And doom'd him to the zealot's ready Hell,
Which answers to all doubts so eloquently
 well.

CVIII.

Yet, peace be with their ashes,—for by
 them,
If merited, the penalty is paid;
It is not ours to judge,—far less condemn;
The hour must come when such things
 shall be made
Known unto all, or hope and dread allay'd
By slumber, on one pillow, in the dust,
Which, thus much we are sure, must lie
 decay'd;
And when it shall revive, as is our trust,
'Twill be to be forgiven, or suffer what is
 just.

CIX.

But let me quit man's works, again to read
His Maker's, spread around me, and suspend
This page, which from my reveries I feed,
Until it seems prolonging without end.
The clouds above me to the white Alps tend,
And I must pierce them, and survey what-
 e'er
May be permitted, as my steps I bend
To their most great and growing region,
 where
The earth to her embrace compels the powers
 of air.

CX.

Italia! too, Italia! looking on thee,
Full flashes on the soul the light of ages,
Since the fierce Carthaginian almost won
 thee,
To the last halo of the chiefs and sages
Who glorify thy consecrated pages;
Thou wert the throne and grave of empires;
 still,
The fount at which the panting mind as-
 suages
Her thirst of knowledge, quaffing there her
 fill,
Flows from the eternal source of Rome's im-
 perial hill.

CXI.

Thus far have I proceeded in a theme
Renew'd with no kind auspices:—to feel
We are not what we have been, and to
 deem
We are not what we should be, and to steel
The heart against itself; and to conceal,
With a proud caution, love, or hate, or
 aught,—
Passion or feeling, purpose, grief or zeal,—
Which is the tyrant spirit of our thought,
Is a stern task of soul:—No matter,—it is
 taught.

CXII.

And for these words, thus woven into song,
It may be that they are a harmless wile,—
The colouring of the scenes which fleet
 along,
Which I would seize, in passing, to beguile
My breast, or that of others, for a while.
Fame is the thirst of youth, but I am not
So young as to regard men's frown or smile,
As loss or guerdon of a glorious lot;
I stood and stand alone,—remember'd or
 forgot.

CXIII.

I have not loved the world, nor the world
 me;
I have not flatter'd its rank breath, nor
 bow'd
To its idolatries a patient knee,
Nor coin'd my cheek to smiles, nor cried
 aloud
In worship of an echo; in the crowd
They could not deem me one of such; I
 stood
Among them, but not of them; in a shroud
Of thoughts which were not their thoughts,
 and still could,
Had I not filed my mind, which thus itself
 subdued.

CXIV.

I have not loved the world, nor the world
 me,—
But let us part fair foes; I do believe,
Though I have found them not, that there
 may be
Words which are things, hopes which will
 not deceive,
And virtues which are merciful, nor weave
Snares for the failing; I would also deem
O'er others' griefs that some sincerely
 grieve;
That two, or one, are almost what they seem,
That goodness is no name, and happiness no
 dream.

CXV.

My daughter! with thy name this song
 begun;
My daughter! with thy name thus much
 shall end;
I see thee not, I hear thee not, but none
Can be so wrapt in thee; thou art the
 friend
To whom the shadows of far years extend:
Albeit my brow thou never shouldst behold,
My voice shall with thy future visions blend,
And reach into thy heart, when mine is cold,
A token and a tone, even from thy father's
 mould.

CXVI.

To aid thy mind's development, to watch
Thy dawn of little joys, to sit and see
Almost thy very growth, to view thee catch
Knowledge of objects,—wonders yet to thee!
To hold thee lightly on a gentle knee,
And print on thy soft cheek a parent's
 kiss,—
This, it should seem, was not reserved for
 me;
Yet this was in my nature: as it is,
I know not what is there, yet something like
 to this.

CXVII.

Yet, though dull Hate as duty should be
 taught,
I know that thou wilt love me; though my
 name
Should be shut from thee, as a spell still
 fraught
With desolation, and a broken claim:
Though the grave closed between us,—
 'twere the same,
I know that thou wilt love me; though to
 drain
My blood from out thy being were an aim,
And an attainment,—all would be in vain,—
Still thou wouldst love me, still that more
 than life retain.

CXVIII.

The child of love, though born in bitterness,
And nurtured in convulsion. Of thy sire
These were the elements, and thine no less.
As yet such are around thee, but thy fire
Shall be more temper'd, and thy hope far
 higher.
Sweet be thy cradled slumbers! O'er the
 sea
And from the mountains where I now
 respire,
Fain would I waft such blessing upon thee,
As, with a sigh, I deem thou might'st have
 been to me.

Canto the Fourth.

———

"Visto ho Toscana, Lombardia, Romagna,
 Quel Monte che divide, e quel che serra
Italia, e un mare e l' altro, che la bagna."
 Ariosto, Satira iii.

———

TO

JOHN HOBHOUSE, ESQ., A.M., F.R.S.,

&c. &c. &c.

VENICE, *January* 2, 1818.

MY DEAR HOBHOUSE,

AFTER an interval of eight years between the composition of the first and last cantos of Childe Harold, the conclusion of the poem is about to be submitted to the public. In parting with so old a friend, it is not extraordinary that I should recur to one still older and better,—to one who has beheld the birth and death of the other, and to whom I am far more indebted for the social advantages of an enlightened friendship, than—though not ungrateful—I can, or could be, to Childe Harold, for any public favour reflected through the poem on the poet,—to one, whom I have known long and accompanied far, whom I have found wakeful over my sickness and kind in my sorrow, glad in my prosperity and firm in my adversity, true in counsel and trusty in peril,—to a friend often tried and never found wanting;—to yourself.

In so doing, I recur from fiction to truth; and in dedicating to you in its complete, or at least concluded state, a poetical work which is the longest, the most thoughtful and comprehensive of my compositions, I wish to do honour to myself by the record of many years' intimacy with a man of learning, of talent, of steadiness, and of honour. It is not for minds like ours to give or to receive flattery; yet the praises of sincerity have ever been permitted to the voice of friendship; and it is not for you, nor even for others, but to relieve a heart which has not elsewhere, or lately, been so much accustomed to the encounter of good-will as to withstand the shock firmly, that I thus attempt to commemorate your good qualities, or rather the advantages which I have derived from their exertion. Even the recurrence of the date of this letter, the anniversary of the most unfortunate day of my past existence*, but which cannot poison my future while I retain the resource of your friendship, and of my own faculties, will henceforth have a more agreeable recollection for both, inasmuch as it will remind us of this my attempt to thank you for an indefatigable regard, such as few men have experienced, and no one could experience without thinking better of his species and of himself.

———

* His marriage.

It has been our fortune to traverse together, at various periods, the countries of chivalry, history, and fable—Spain, Greece, Asia Minor, and Italy; and what Athens and Constantinople were to us a few years ago, Venice and Rome have been more recently. The poem also, or the pilgrim, or both, have accompanied me from first to last; and perhaps it may be a pardonable vanity which induces me to reflect with complacency on a composition which in some degree connects me with the spot where it was produced, and the objects it would fain describe; and however unworthy it may be deemed of those magical and memorable abodes, however short it may fall of our distant conceptions and immediate impressions, yet as a mark of respect for what is venerable, and of feeling for what is glorious, it has been to me a source of pleasure in the production, and I part with it with a kind of regret, which I hardly suspected that events could have left me for imaginary objects.

With regard to the conduct of the last canto, there will be found less of the pilgrim than in any of the preceding, and that little slightly, if at all, separated from the author speaking in his own person. The fact is, that I had become weary of drawing a line which every one seemed determined not to perceive: like the Chinese in Goldsmith's "Citizen of the World," whom nobody would believe to be a Chinese, it was in vain that I asserted, and imagined that I had drawn, a distinction between the author and the pilgrim; and the very anxiety to preserve this difference, and disappointment at finding it unavailing, so far crushed my efforts in the composition, that I determined to abandon it altogether—and have done so. The opinions which have been, or may be, formed on that subject are *now* a matter of indifference; the work is to depend on itself, and not on the writer; and the author, who has no resources in his own mind beyond the reputation, transient or permanent, which is to arise from his literary efforts, deserves the fate of authors.

In the course of the following canto it was my intention, either in the text or in the notes, to have touched upon the present state of Italian literature, and perhaps of manners. But the text, within the limits I proposed, I soon found hardly sufficient for the labyrinth of external objects, and the consequent reflections; and for the whole of the notes, excepting a few of the shortest, I am indebted to yourself, and these were necessarily limited to the elucidation of the text.

It is also a delicate, and no very grateful task, to dissert upon the literature and manners of a nation so dissimilar; and requires an attention and impartiality which would induce us—though perhaps no inattentive observers, nor ignorant of the language or customs of the people amongst whom we have recently abode—to distrust, or at least defer our judgment, and more narrowly examine our information. The state of literary, as well as political party, appears to run, or to *have* run, so high, that for a stranger to steer impartially between them is next to impossible. It may be enough, then, at least for my purpose, to quote from their own beautiful language—"Mi pare che in un paese tutto poetico, che vanta la lingua la più nobile ed insieme la più dolce, tutte tutte le vie diverse si possono tentare, e che sinche la patria di Alfieri e di Monti non ha perduto l' antico valore, in tutte essa dovrebbe essere la prima." Italy has great names still—Canova, Monti, Ugo Foscolo, Pindemonte, Visconti, Morelli, Cicognara, Albrizzi, Mezzophanti, Mai, Mustoxidi, Aglietti, and Vacca, will secure to the present generation an honourable place in most of the departments of Art, Science, and Belles Lettres; and in some the very highest—Europe—the World—has but one Canova.

It has been somewhere said by Alfieri, that "La pianta uomo nasce più robusta in Italia che in qualunque altra terra—e che gli stessi atroci delitti che vi si commettono ne sono una prova." Without subscribing to the latter part of his proposition, a dangerous doctrine, the truth of which may be disputed on better grounds, namely, that the Italians are in no respect more ferocious than their neighbours, that man must be wilfully blind, or ignorantly heedless, who is not struck with the extraordinary capácity of this people, or, if such a word be admissible, their *capabilities*, the facility of their acquisitions, the rapidity of their conceptions, the fire of their genius, their sense of beauty, and, amidst all the disadvantages of repeated revolutions, the desolation of battles, and the despair of ages, their still unquenched "longing after immortality,"—the immortality of independence. And when we ourselves, in riding round the walls of Rome, heard the simple lament of the labourers' chorus, "Roma! Roma! Roma! Roma non è più come era prima," it was difficult not to contrast this melancholy dirge with the bacchanal roar of the songs of exultation still yelled from the London taverns, over the carnage of Mont St. Jean, and the betrayal of Genoa, of Italy, of France, and of the world, by men whose conduct you yourself have exposed in a work worthy of the better days of our history. For me,—

> "Non movero mai corda
> Ove la turba di sue ciance assorda."

What Italy has gained by the late transfer of nations, it were useless for Englishmen to inquire, till it becomes ascertained that England has acquired something more than a permanent army and a suspended Habeas Corpus; it is enough for them to look at home. For what they have done abroad, and especially in the South, "Verily they *will have* their reward," and at no very distant period.

Wishing you, my dear Hobhouse, a safe and agreeable return to that country whose real welfare can be dearer to none than to yourself, I dedicate to you this poem in its completed state; and repeat once more how truly I am ever

Your obliged and affectionate friend,

BYRON.

I.

I STOOD in Venice, on the Bridge of Sighs;
A palace and a prison on each hand:
I saw from out the wave her structures rise
As from the stroke of the enchanter's wand:
A thousand years their cloudy wings expand
Around me, and a dying Glory smiles
O'er the far times, when many a subject land
Look'd to the winged Lion's marble piles,
Where Venice sate in state, throned on her hundred isles!

II.

She looks a sea Cybele, fresh from ocean,
Rising with her tiara of proud towers
At airy distance, with majestic motion,
A ruler of the waters and their powers:
And such she was;—her daughters had their dowers
From spoils of nations, and the exhaustless East
Pour'd in her lap all gems in sparkling showers.
In purple was she robed, and of her feast
Monarchs partook, and deem'd their dignity increased.

III.

In Venice Tasso's echoes are no more,
And silent rows the songless gondolier;
Her palaces are crumbling to the shore,
And music meets not always now the ear:
Those days are gone—but Beauty still is here.
States fall, arts fade—but Nature doth not die,
Nor yet forget how Venice once was dear,
The pleasant place of all festivity,
The revel of the earth, the masque of Italy!

IV.

But unto us she hath a spell beyond
Her name in story, and her long array
Of mighty shadows, whose dim forms despond
Above the dogeless city's vanish'd sway;
Ours is a trophy which will not decay
With the Rialto; Shylock and the Moor,
And Pierre, cannot be swept or worn away—
The keystones of the arch! though all were o'er,
For us repeopled were the solitary shore.

V.

The beings of the mind are not of clay;
Essentially immortal, they create
And multiply in us a brighter ray
And more beloved existence: that which Fate
Prohibits to dull life, in this our state
Of mortal bondage, by these spirits supplied,
First exiles, then replaces what we hate;
Watering the heart whose early flowers have died,
And with a fresher growth replenishing the void.

VI.

Such is the refuge of our youth and age,
The first from Hope, the last from Vacancy;
And this worn feeling peoples many a page,
And, may be, that which grows beneath mine eye:
Yet there are things whose strong reality
Outshines our fairy-land; in shape and hues
More beautiful than our fantastic sky,
And the strange constellations which the Muse
O'er her wild universe is skilful to diffuse:

VII.

I saw or dream'd of such,—but let them go,—
They came like truth, and disappear'd like dreams;
And whatsoe'er they were—are now but so:
I could replace them if I would; still teems
My mind with many a form which aptly seems
Such as I sought for, and at moments found;
Let these too go—for waking Reason deems
Such overweening phantasies unsound,
And other voices speak, and other sights surround.

VIII.

I've taught me other tongues, and in strange eyes
Have made me not a stranger; to the mind
Which is itself, no changes bring surprise;
Nor is it harsh to make, nor hard to find
A country with—ay, or without mankind;
Yet was I born where men are proud to be,—
Not without cause; and should I leave behind
The inviolate island of the sage and free,
And seek me out a home by a remoter sea,

IX.

Perhaps I loved it well: and should I lay
My ashes in a soil which is not mine,
My spirit shall resume it—if we may
Unbodied choose a sanctuary. I twine
My hopes of being remember'd in my line
With my land's language: if too fond and
 far
These aspirations in their scope incline,—
If my fame should be, as my fortunes are,
Of hasty growth and blight, and dull Oblivion
 bar

X.

My name from out the temple where the
 dead
Are honour'd by the nations—let it be—
And light the laurels on a loftier head!
And be the Spartan's epitaph on me—
" Sparta hath many a worthier son than
 he."
Meantime I seek no sympathies, nor need;
The thorns which I have reap'd are of the
 tree
I planted: they have torn me, and I bleed:
I should have known what fruit would spring
 from such a seed.

XI.

The spouseless Adriatic mourns her lord;
And, annual marriage now no more re-
 new'd,
The Bucentaur lies rotting unrestored,
Neglected garment of her widowhood!
St. Mark yet sees his lion where he stood
Stand, but in mockery of his wither'd
 power,
Over the proud Place where an Emperor
 sued,
And monarchs gazed and envied in the
 hour
When Venice was a queen with an unequall'd
 dower.

XII.

The Suabian sued, and now the Austrian
 reigns—
An Emperor tramples where an Emperor
 knelt;
Kingdoms are shrunk to provinces, and
 chains
Clank over sceptred cities; nations melt
From power's high pinnacle, when they
 have felt
The sunshine for a while, and downward go
Like lauwine loosen'd from the mountain's
 belt;
Oh for one hour of blind old Dandolo!
Th' octogenarian chief, Byzantium's conquer-
 ing foe.

XIII.

Before St. Mark still glow his steeds of
 brass,
Their gilded collars glittering in the sun;
But is not Doria's menace come to pass?
Are they not *bridled?*—Venice, lost and
 won,
Her thirteen hundred years of freedom
 done,
Sinks, like a seaweed, into whence she rose!
Better be whelm'd beneath the waves, and
 shun,
Even in destruction's depth, her foreign
 foes,
From whom submission wrings an infamous
 repose.

XIV.

In youth she was all glory,—a new Tyre;
Her very by-word sprung from victory,
The " Planter of the Lion," which through
 fire
And blood she bore o'er subject earth and
 sea;
Though making many slaves, herself still
 free,
And Europe's bulwark 'gainst the Ottomite;
Witness Troy's rival, Candia! Vouch it, ye
Immortal waves that saw Lepanto's fight!
For ye are names no time nor tyranny can
 blight.

XV.

Statues of glass—all shiver'd—the long file
Of her dead Doges are declined to dust;
But where they dwelt, the vast and sump-
 tuous pile
Bespeaks the pageant of their splendid
 trust;
Their sceptre broken, and their sword in
 rust,
Have yielded to the stranger: empty halls,
Thin streets, and foreign aspects, such as
 must
Too oft remind her who and what inthrals,
Have flung a desolate cloud o'er Venice'
 lovely walls.

XVI.

When Athens' armies fell at Syracuse,
And fetter'd thousands bore the yoke of war,
Redemption rose up in the Attic Muse,
Her voice their only ransom from afar:
See! as they chant the tragic hymn, the car
Of the o'ermaster'd victor stops, the reins
Fall from his hands, his idle scimitar
Starts from its belt—he rends his captive's
 chains,
And bids him thank the bard for freedom and
 his strains.

XVII.

Thus, Venice, if no stronger claim were thine,
Were all thy proud historic deeds forgot,
Thy choral memory of the Bard divine,
Thy love of Tasso, should have cut the knot
Which ties thee to thy tyrants; and thy lot
Is shameful to the nations,—most of all,
Albion! to thee: the Ocean queen should not
Abandon Ocean's children; in the fall
Of Venice think of thine, despite thy watery wall.

XVIII.

I loved her from my boyhood; she to me
Was as a fairy city of the heart,
Rising like water-columns from the sea,
Of joy the sojourn, and of wealth the mart;
And Otway, Radcliffe, Schiller, Shakspeare's art,
Had stamp'd her image in me, and even so,
Although I found her thus, we did not part;
Perchance even dearer in her day of woe,
Than when she was a boast, a marvel, and a show.

XIX.

I can repeople with the past—and of
The present there is still for eye and thought,
And meditation chasten'd down, enough;
And more, it may be, than I hoped or sought;
And of the happiest moments which were wrought
Within the web of my existence, some
From thee, fair Venice! have their colours caught:
There are some feelings Time cannot benumb,
Nor Torture shake, or mine would now be cold and dumb.

XX.

But from their nature will the tannen grow
Loftiest on loftiest and least shelter'd rocks,
Rooted in barrenness, where nought below
Of soil supports them 'gainst the Alpine shocks
Of eddying storms; yet springs the trunk, and mocks
The howling tempest, till its height and frame
Are worthy of the mountains from whose blocks
Of bleak, gray granite into life it came,
And grew a giant tree;—the mind may grow the same.

XXI.

Existence may be borne, and the deep root
Of life and sufferance make its firm abode
The bare and desolated bosoms: mute
The camel labours with the heaviest load,
And the wolf dies in silence,—not bestow'd
In vain should such example be; if they,
Things of ignoble or of savage mood,
Endure and shrink not, we of nobler clay
May temper it to bear,—it is but for a day.

XXII.

All suffering doth destroy, or is destroy'd,
Even by the sufferer; and, in each event,
Ends: Some, with hope replenish'd and rebuoy'd,
Return to whence they came—with like intent,
And weave their web again; some, bow'd and bent,
Wax gray and ghastly, withering ere their time,
And perish with the reed on which they leant;
Some seek devotion, toil, war, good or crime,
According as their souls were form'd to sink or climb.

XXIII.

But ever and anon of griefs subdued
There comes a token like a scorpion's sting,
Scarce seen, but with fresh bitterness imbued;
And slight withal may be the things which bring
Back on the heart the weight which it would fling
Aside for ever: it may be a sound—
A tone of music—summer's eve—or spring—
A flower—the wind—the ocean—which shall wound,
Striking the electric chain wherewith we are darkly bound;

XXIV.

And how and why we know not, nor can trace
Home to its cloud this lightning of the mind,
But feel the shock renew'd, nor can efface
The blight and blackening which it leaves behind,
Which out of things familiar, undesign'd,
When least we deem of such, calls up to view
The spectres whom no exorcism can bind,—
The cold, the changed, perchance the dead—anew,
The mourn'd, the loved, the lost—too many! yet how few!

XXV.

But my soul wanders; I demand it back
To meditate amongst decay, and stand
A ruin amidst ruins; there to track
Fall'n states and buried greatness, o'er a
 land
Which *was* the mightiest in its old com-
 mand,
And *is* the loveliest, and must ever be
The master-mould of Nature's heavenly
 hand;
Wherein were cast the heroic and the free,
The beautiful, the brave, the lords of earth
 and sea,

XXVI.

The commonwealth of kings, the men of
 Rome!
And even since, and now, fair Italy!
Thou art the garden of the world, the home
Of all Art yields, and Nature can decree;
Even in thy desert, what is like to thee?
Thy very weeds are beautiful, thy waste
More rich than other climes' fertility;
Thy wreck a glory, and thy ruin graced
With an immaculate charm which cannot be
 defaced.

XXVII.

The moon is up, and yet it is not night;
Sunset divides the sky with her; a sea
Of glory streams along the Alpine height
Of blue Friuli's mountains; Heaven is free
From clouds, but of all colours seems to
 be,—
Melted to one vast Iris of the West,—
Where the Day joins the past Eternity,
While, on the other hand, meek Dian's crest
Floats through the azure air—an island of the
 blest!

XXVIII.

A single star is at her side, and reigns
With her o'er half the lovely heaven; but still
Yon sunny sea heaves brightly, and remains
Roll'd o'er the peak of the far Rhætian hill,
As Day and Night contending were, until
Nature reclaim'd her order:—gently flows
The deep-dyed Brenta, where their hues
 instil
The odorous purple of a new-born rose,
Which streams upon her stream, and glass'd
 within it glows,

XXIX.

Fill'd with the face of heaven, which, from
 afar,
Comes down upon the waters; all its hues,
From the rich sunset to the rising star,
Their magical variety diffuse:

And now they change; a paler shadow
 strews
Its mantle o'er the mountains; parting day
Dies like the dolphin, whom each pang im-
 bues
With a new colour as it gasps away,
The last still loveliest,—till—'t is gone—and
 all is gray.

XXX.

There is a tomb in Arqua;—rear'd in air,
Pillar'd in their sarcophagus, repose
The bones of Laura's lover: here repair
Many familiar with his well-sung woes,
The pilgrims of his genius. He arose
To raise a language, and his land reclaim
From the dull yoke of her barbaric foes:
Watering the tree which bears his lady's
 name
With his melodious tears, he gave himself to
 fame.

XXXI.

They keep his dust in Arqua, where he died;
The mountain-village where his latter days
Went down the vale of years; and 't is their
 pride—
An honest pride—and let it be their praise,
To offer to the passing stranger's gaze
His mansion and his sepulchre; both plain
And venerably simple, such as raise
A feeling more accordant with his strain
Than if a pyramid form'd his monumental
 fane.

XXXII.

And the soft quiet hamlet where he dwelt
Is one of that complexion which seems
 made
For those who their mortality have felt,
And sought a refuge from their hopes de-
 cay'd
In the deep umbrage of a green hill's shade,
Which shows a distant prospect far away
Of busy cities, now in vain display'd,
For they can lure no further; and the ray
Of a bright sun can make sufficient holiday,

XXXIII.

Developing the mountains, leaves, and
 flowers,
And shining in the brawling brook, where-
 by,
Clear as its current, glide the sauntering
 hours
With a calm languor, which, though to the
 eye

Idlesse it seem, hath its morality.
If from society we learn to live,
'T is solitude should teach us how to die ;
It hath no flatterers ; vanity can give
No hollow aid ; alone—man with his God must
 strive :

XXXIV.

Or, it may be, with demons, who impair
The strength of better thoughts, and seek
 their prey
In melancholy bosoms, such as were
Of moody texture from their earliest day,
And loved to dwell in darkness and dismay,
Deeming themselves predestined to a doom
Which is not of the pangs that pass away ;
Making the sun like blood, the earth a tomb,
The tomb a hell, and hell itself a murkier
 gloom.

XXXV.

Ferrara ! in thy wide and grass-grown
 streets,
Whose symmetry was not for solitude,
There seems as 't were a curse upon the
 seats
Of former sovereigns, and the antique brood
Of Este, which for many an age made good
Its strength within thy walls, and was of
 yore
Patron or tyrant, as the changing mood
Of petty power impell'd, of those who wore
The wreath which Dante's brow alone had
 worn before.

XXXVI.

And Tasso is their glory and their shame.
Hark to his strain ! and then survey his cell !
And see how dearly earn'd Torquato's fame,
And where Alfonso bade his poet dwell :
The miserable despot could not quell
The insulted mind he sought to quench, and
 blend
With the surrounding maniacs, in the hell
Where he had plunged it. Glory without end
Scatter'd the clouds away ; and on that name
 attend

XXXVII.

The tears and praises of all time ; while
 thine
Would rot in its oblivion—in the sink
Of worthless dust, which from thy boasted
 line
Is shaken into nothing—but the link
Thou formest in his fortunes bids us think
Of thy poor malice, naming thee with scorn :
Alfonso ! how thy ducal pageants shrink
From thee ! if in another station born,
Scarce fit to be the slave of him thou madest
 to mourn :

XXXVIII.

Thou ! form'd to eat, and be despised, and
 die,
Even as the beasts that perish, save that
 thou
Hadst a more splendid trough and wider sty :
He ! with a glory round his furrow'd brow,
Which emanated then, and dazzles now,
In face of all his foes, the Cruscan quire,
And Boileau, whose rash envy could allow
No strain which shamed his country's
 creaking lyre,
That whetstone of the teeth—monotony in
 wire !

XXXIX.

Peace to Torquato's injured shade ! 't was his
In life and death to be the mark where
 Wrong
Aim'd with her poison'd arrows,—but to
 miss.
Oh, victor unsurpass'd in modern song !
Each year brings forth its millions ; but
 how long
The tide of generations shall roll on,
And not the whole combined and countless
 throng
Compose a mind like thine ? though all in one
Condensed their scatter'd rays, they would
 not form a sun.

XL.

Great as thou art, yet parallel'd by those,
Thy countrymen, before thee born to shine,
The Bards of Hell and Chivalry : first
 rose
The Tuscan father's comedy divine ;
Then, not unequal to the Florentine,
The southern Scott, the minstrel who call'd
 forth
A new creation with his magic line,
And, like the Ariosto of the North,
Sang ladye-love and war, romance and knightly
 worth.

XLI.

The lightning rent from Ariosto's bust
The iron crown of laurel's mimick'd leaves ;
Nor was the ominous element unjust,
For the true laurel-wreath which Glory
 weaves
Is of the tree no bolt of thunder cleaves,
And the false semblance but disgraced his
 brow ;
Yet still, if fondly Superstition grieves,
Know, that the lightning sanctifies below
Whate'er it strikes ;—yon head is doubly
 sacred now.

XLII.

Italia! oh Italia! thou who hast
The fatal gift of beauty, which became
A funeral dower of present woes and past,
On thy sweet brow is sorrow plough'd by
 shame,
And annals graved in characters of flame.
Oh, God! that thou wert in thy nakedness
Less lovely or more powerful, and couldst
 claim
Thy right, and awe the robbers back, who
 press
To shed thy blood, and drink the tears of thy
 distress;

XLIII.

Then might'st thou more appal; or, less
 desired,
Be homely and be peaceful, undeplored
For thy destructive charms; then, still un-
 tired,
Would not be seen the armed torrents pour'd
Down the deep Alps; nor would the hostile
 horde
Of many-nation'd spoilers from the Po
Quaff blood and water; nor the stranger's
 sword
Be thy sad weapon of defence, and so,
Victor or vanquish'd, thou the slave of friend
 or foe.

XLIV.

Wandering in youth, I traced the path of him,
The Roman friend of Rome's least-mortal
 mind,
The friend of Tully: as my bark did skim
The bright blue waters with a fanning wind,
Came Megara before me, and behind
Ægina lay, Piræus on the right,
And Corinth on the left; I lay reclined
Along the prow, and saw all these unite
In ruin, even as he had seen the desolate sight;

XLV.

For Time hath not rebuilt them, but up-
 rear'd
Barbaric dwellings on their shatter'd site,
Which only make more mourn'd and more
 endear'd
The few last rays of their far-scatter'd light,
And the crush'd relics of their vanish'd
 might.
The Roman saw these tombs in his own age,
These sepulchres of cities, which excite
Sad wonder, and his yet surviving page
The moral lesson bears, drawn from such
 pilgrimage.

XLVI.

That page is now before me, and on mine
His country's ruin added to the mass
Of perish'd states he mourn'd in their
 decline,
And I in desolation: all that *was*
Of them destruction *is;* and now, alas!
Rome—Rome imperial, bows her to the
 storm,
In the same dust and blackness, and we
 pass
The skeleton of her Titanic form,
Wrecks of another world, whose ashes still
 are warm.

XLVII.

Yet, Italy! through every other land
Thy wrongs should ring, and shall, from
 side to side;
Mother of Arts! as once of arms; thy hand
Was then our guardian, and is still our
 guide;
Parent of our religion! whom the wide
Nations have knelt to for the keys of
 heaven!
Europe, repentant of her parricide,
Shall yet redeem thee, and, all backward
 driven,
Roll the barbarian tide, and sue to be for-
 given.

XLVIII.

But Arno wins us to the fair white walls,
Where the Etrurian Athens claims and
 keeps
A softer feeling for her fairy halls.
Girt by her theatre of hills, she reaps
Her corn, and wine, and oil, and Plenty
 leaps
To laughing life, with her redundant horn.
Along the banks where smiling Arno sweeps
Was modern Luxury of Commerce born,
And buried Learning rose, redeem'd to a new
 morn.

XLIX.

There, too, the Goddess loves in stone, and
 fills
The air around with beauty; we inhale
The ambrosial aspect, which, beheld, instils
Part of its immortality; the veil
Of heaven is half undrawn; within the pale
We stand, and in that form and face behold
What Mind can make, when Nature's self
 would fail;
And to the fond idolaters of old
Envy the innate flash which such a soul could
 mould:

L.

We gaze and turn away, and know not
 where,
Dazzled and drunk with beauty, till the
 heart
Reels with its fulness; there—for ever
 there—
Chain'd to the chariot of triumphal Art,
We stand as captives, and would not depart.
Away!—there need no words nor terms
 precise,
The paltry jargon of the marble mart,
Where Pedantry gulls Folly—we have eyes:
Blood, pulse, and breast confirm the Dardan
 Shepherd's prize.

LI.

Appear'dst thou not to Paris in this guise?
Or to more deeply blest Anchises? or,
In all thy perfect goddess-ship, when lies
Before thee thy own vanquish'd Lord of
 War?
And gazing in thy face as toward a star,
Laid on thy lap, his eyes to thee upturn,
Feeding on thy sweet cheek! while thy
 lips are
With lava kisses melting while they burn,
Shower'd on his eyelids, brow, and mouth, as
 from an urn?

LII.

Glowing, and circumfused in speechless love
Their full divinity inadequate
That feeling to express, or to improve,
The gods become as mortals, and man's fate
Has moments like their brightest; but the
 weight
Of earth recoils upon us;—let it go!
We can recall such visions, and create,
From what has been, or might be, things
 which grow
Into thy statue's form, and look like gods
 below.

LIII.

I leave to learned fingers and wise hands,
The artist and his ape, to teach and tell
How well his connoisseurship understands
The graceful bend, and the voluptuous
 swell:
Let these describe the undescribable:
I would not their vile breath should crisp
 the stream
Wherein that image shall for ever dwell;
The unruffled mirror of the loveliest dream
That ever left the sky on the deep soul to
 beam.

LIV.

In Santa Croce's holy precincts lie
Ashes which make it holier, dust which is
Even in itself an immortality,
Though there were nothing save the past,
 and this,
The particle of those sublimities
Which have relapsed to chaos: here repose
Angelo's, Alfieri's bones, and his,
The starry Galileo, with his woes;
Here Machiavelli's earth return'd to whence
 it rose.

LV.

These are four minds, which, like the
 elements,
Might furnish forth creation:—Italy!
Time, which hath wrong'd thee with ten
 thousand rents
Of thine imperial garment, shall deny,
And hath denied, to every other sky,
Spirits which soar from ruin: thy decay
Is still impregnate with divinity,
Which gilds it with revivifying ray;
Such as the great of yore, Canova is to-day.

LVI.

But where repose the all Etruscan three—
Dante, and Petrarch, and, scarce less than
 they,
The Bard of Prose, creative spirit! he
Of the Hundred Tales of love—where did
 they lay
Their bones, distinguish'd from our common
 clay
In death as life? Are they resolved to dust,
And have their country's marbles nought
 to say?
Could not her quarries furnish forth one
 bust?
Did they not to her breast their filial earth
 intrust?

LVII.

Ungrateful Florence! Dante sleeps afar,
Like Scipio, buried by the upbraiding shore:
Thy factions, in their worse than civil war,
Proscribed the bard whose name for ever-
 more
Their children's children would in vain
 adore
With the remorse of ages; and the crown
Which Petrarch's laureate brow supremely
 wore,
Upon a far and foreign soil had grown,
His life, his fame, his grave, though rifled—
 not thine own.

LVIII.

Boccaccio to his parent earth bequeath'd
His dust,—and lies it not her great among,
With many a sweet and solemn requiem
 breathed
O'er him who form'd the Tuscan's siren
 tongue?
That music in itself, whose sounds are song,
The poetry of speech? No;—even his tomb
Uptorn, must bear the hyæna bigot's wrong,
No more amidst the meaner dead find room,
Nor claim a passing sigh, because it told for
 whom!

LIX.

And Santa Croce wants their mighty dust;
Yet for this want more noted, as of yore
The Cæsar's pageant, shorn of Brutus'
 bust,
Did but of Rome's best Son remind her
 more:
Happier Ravenna! on thy hoary shore,
Fortress of falling empire! honour'd sleeps
The immortal exile;—Arqua, too, her store
Of tuneful relics proudly claims and keeps,
While Florence vainly begs her banish'd dead
 and weeps.

LX.

What is her pyramid of precious stones?
Of porphyry, jasper, agate, and all hues
Of gem and marble, to incrust the bones
Of merchant-dukes? the momentary dews
Which, sparkling to the twilight stars,
 infuse
Freshness in the green turf that wraps the
 dead,
Whose names are mausoleums of the Muse,
Are gently prest with far more reverent
 tread
Than ever paced the slab which paves the
 princely head.

LXI.

There be more things to greet the heart
 and eyes
In Arno's dome of Art's most princely
 shrine,
Where Sculpture with her rainbow sister
 vies;
There be more marvels yet—but not for
 mine;
For I have been accustom'd to entwine
My thoughts with Nature rather in the
 fields,
Than Art in galleries; though a work divine
Calls for my spirit's homage, yet it yields
Less than it feels, because the weapon which
 it wields

LXII.

Is of another temper, and I roam
By Thrasimene's lake, in the defiles
Fatal to Roman rashness, more at home;
For there the Carthaginian's warlike wiles
Come back before me, as his skill beguiles
The host between the mountains and the
 shore,
Where Courage falls in her despairing files,
And torrents, swoll'n to rivers with their
 gore,
Reek through the sultry plain, with legions
 scatter'd o'er,

LXIII.

Like to a forest fell'd by mountain winds;
And such the storm of battle on this day,
And such the frenzy, whose convulsion
 blinds
To all save carnage, that, beneath the fray,
An earthquake reel'd unheededly away!
None felt stern Nature rocking at his feet,
And yawning forth a grave for those who
 lay
Upon their bucklers for a winding-sheet;
Such is the absorbing hate when warring
 nations meet!

LXIV.

The Earth to them was as a rolling bark
Which bore them to Eternity; they saw
The Ocean round, but had no time to mark
The motions of their vessel; Nature's law,
In them suspended, reck'd not of the awe
Which reigns when mountains tremble,
 and the birds
Plunge in the clouds for refuge, and with-
 draw
From their down-toppling nests; and bel-
 lowing herds
Stumble o'er heaving plains, and man's dread
 hath no words.

LXV.

Far other scene is Thrasimene now;
Her lake a sheet of silver, and her plain
Rent by no ravage save the gentle plough;
Her aged trees rise thick as once the slain
Lay where their roots are; but a brook
 hath ta'en—
A little rill of scanty stream and bed—
A name of blood from that day's sanguine
 rain;
And Sanguinetto tells ye where the dead
Made the earth wet, and turn'd the unwilling
 waters red.

LXVI.

But thou, Clitumnus! in thy sweetest wave
Of the most living crystal that was e'er
The haunt of river nymph, to gaze and lave
Her limbs where nothing hid them, thou
dost rear
Thy grassy banks whereon the milk-white
steer
Grazes; the purest god of gentle waters!
And most serene of aspect, and most clear;
Surely that stream was unprofaned by
slaughters,
A mirror and a bath for Beauty's youngest
daughters!

LXVII.

And on thy happy shore a Temple still,
Of small and delicate proportion, keeps,
Upon a mild declivity of hill,
Its memory of thee; beneath it sweeps
Thy current's calmness; oft from out it
leaps
The finny darter with the glittering scales,
Who dwells and revels in thy glassy deeps;
While, chance, some scatter'd water-lily
sails
Down where the shallower wave still tells its
bubbling tales.

LXVIII.

Pass not unblest the Genius of the place!
If through the air a zephyr more serene
Win to the brow, 't is his; and if ye trace
Along his margin a more eloquent green,
If on the heart the freshness of the scene
Sprinkle its coolness, and from the dry
dust
Of weary life a moment lave it clean
With Nature's baptism,—'t is to him ye
must
Pay orisons for this suspension of disgust.

LXIX.

The roar of waters!—from the headlong
height
Velino cleaves the wave-worn precipice;
The fall of waters! rapid as the light
The flashing mass foams shaking the abyss;
The hell of waters! where they howl and
hiss,
And boil in endless torture; while the sweat
Of their great agony, wrung out from this
Their Phlegethon, curls round the rocks of
jet
That guard the gulf around, in pitiless horror
set,

LXX.

And mounts in spray the skies, and thence
again
Returns in an unceasing shower, which
round,
With its unemptied cloud of gentle rain,
Is an eternal April to the ground,
Making it all one emerald:—how profound
The gulf! and how the giant element
From rock to rock leaps with delirious bound,
Crushing the cliffs, which, downward worn
and rent
With his fierce footsteps, yield in chasms a
fearful vent!

LXXI.

To the broad column which rolls on, and
shows
More like the fountain of an infant sea
Torn from the womb of mountains by the
throes
Of a new world, than only thus to be
Parent of rivers, which flow gushingly,
With many windings, through the vale:—
Look back!
Lo! where it comes like an eternity,
As if to sweep down all things in its track,
Charming the eye with dread,—a matchless
cataract,

LXXII.

Horribly beautiful! but on the verge,
From side to side, beneath the glittering
morn,
An Iris sits, amidst the infernal surge,
Like Hope upon a death-bed, and, unworn
Its steady dyes, while all around is torn
By the distracted waters, bears serene
Its brilliant hues with all their beams un-
shorn:
Resembling, 'mid the torture of the scene,
Love watching Madness with unalterable
mien.

LXXIII.

Once more upon the woody Apennine,
The infant Alps, which—had I not before
Gazed on their mightier parents, where the
pine
Sits on more shaggy summits, and where
roar
The thundering lauwine—might be wor-
shipp'd more;
But I have seen the soaring Jungfrau rear
Her never-trodden snow, and seen the hoar
Glaciers of bleak Mont Blanc both far and
near,
And in Chimari heard the thunder-hills of fear,

LXXIV.

Th' Acroceraunian mountains of old name;
And on Parnassus seen the eagles fly
Like spirits of the spot, as 'twere for fame,
For still they soared unutterably high:
I've look'd on Ida with a Trojan's eye;
Athos, Olympus, Ætna, Atlas, made
These hills seem things of lesser dignity,
All, save the lone Soracte's height, display'd
Not *now* in snow, which asks the lyric
 Roman's aid

LXXV.

For our remembrance, and from out the
 plain
Heaves like a long-swept wave about to
 break,
And on the curl hangs pausing: not in vain
May he, who will, his recollections rake,
And quote in classic raptures, and awake
The hills with Latian echoes; I abhorr'd
Too much, to conquer for the poet's sake,
The drill'd dull lesson, forced down word
 by word
In my repugnant youth, with pleasure to
 record

LXXVI.

Aught that recalls the daily drug which
 turn'd
My sickening memory; and, though Time
 hath taught
My mind to meditate what then it learn'd,
Yet such the fix'd inveteracy wrought
By the impatience of my early thought,
That, with the freshness wearing out before
My mind could relish what it might have
 sought,
If free to choose, I cannot now restore
Its health; but what it then detested, still
 abhor.

LXXVII.

Then farewell, Horace; whom I hated so,
Not for thy faults, but mine; it is a curse
To understand, not feel thy lyric flow,
To comprehend, but never love thy verse:
Although no deeper Moralist rehearse
Our little life, nor Bard prescribe his art,
Nor livelier Satirist the conscience pierce,
Awakening without wounding the touch'd
 heart,
Yet fare thee well—upon Soracte's ridge we
 part.

LXXVIII.

Oh Rome! my country! city of the soul!
The orphans of the heart must turn to thee,
Lone mother of dead empires! and control
In their shut breasts their petty misery.

What are our woes and sufferance? Come
 and see
The cypress, hear the owl, and plod your
 way
O'er steps of broken thrones and temples,
 Ye!
Whose agonies are evils of a day—
A world is at our feet as fragile as our clay.

LXXIX.

The Niobe of nations! there she stands,
Childless and crownless, in her voiceless
 woe;
An empty urn within her wither'd hands,
Whose holy dust was scatter'd long ago;
The Scipios' tomb contains no ashes now;
The very sepulchres lie tenantless
Of their heroic dwellers: dost thou flow,
Old Tiber! through a marble wilderness?
Rise, with thy yellow waves, and mantle her
 distress.

LXXX.

The Goth, the Christian, Time, War, Flood,
 and Fire,
Have dealt upon the seven-hill'd city's
 pride;
She saw her glories star by star expire,
And up the steep barbarian monarchs ride,
Where the car climb'd the Capitol; far and
 wide
Temple and tower went down, nor left a
 site:
Chaos of ruins! who shall trace the void,
O'er the dim fragments cast a lunar light,
And say, "here was, or is," where all is
 doubly night?

LXXXI.

The double night of ages, and of her,
Night's daughter, Ignorance, hath wrapt
 and wrap
All round us: we but feel our way to err:
The ocean hath its chart, the stars their
 map,
And Knowledge spreads them on her ample
 lap;
But Rome is as the desert, where we steer
Stumbling o'er recollections; now we clap
Our hands, and cry "Eureka!" it is clear—
When but some false mirage of ruin rises near.

LXXXII.

Alas! the lofty city! and alas!
The trebly hundred triumphs! and the day
When Brutus made the dagger's edge sur-
 pass
The conqueror's sword in bearing fame
 away!

Alas, for Tully's voice, and Virgil's lay,
And Livy's pictured page!—but these shall
 be
Her resurrection; all beside—decay.
Alas, for Earth, for never shall we see
That brightness in her eye she bore when
 Rome was free!

LXXXIII.

Oh thou, whose chariot roll'd on Fortune's
 wheel,
Triumphant Sylla! Thou, who didst subdue
Thy country's foes ere thou wouldst pause
 to feel
The wrath of thy own wrongs, or reap the
 due
Of hoarded vengeance till thine eagles flew
O'er prostrate Asia;—thou, who with thy
 frown
Annihilated senates—Roman, too,
With all thy vices, for thou didst lay down
With an atoning smile a more than earthly
 crown—

LXXXIV.

The dictatorial wreath—couldst thou divine
To what would one day dwindle that which
 made
Thee more than mortal? and that so supine
By aught than Romans Rome should thus
 be laid?
She who was named Eternal, and array'd
Her warriors but to conquer—she who veil'd
Earth with her haughty shadow, and dis-
 play'd,
Until the o'er-canopied horizon fail'd,
Her rushing wings—Oh! she who was Al-
 mighty hail'd!

LXXXV.

Sylla was first of victors; but our own,
The sagest of usurpers, Cromwell!—he
Too swept off senates while he hew'd the
 throne
Down to a block—immortal rebel! See
What crimes it costs to be a moment free,
And famous through all ages! but beneath
His fate the moral lurks of destiny;
His day of double victory and death
Beheld him win two realms, and, happier,
 yield his breath.

LXXXVI.

The third of the same moon whose former
 course
Had all but crown'd him, on the self-same
 day
Deposed him gently from his throne of force,
And laid him with the earth's preceding
 clay.

And show'd not Fortune thus how fame and
 sway,
And all we deem delightful, and consume
Our souls to compass through each arduous
 way,
Are in her eyes less happy than the tomb?
Were they but so in man's, how different were
 his doom!

LXXXVII.

And thou, dread statue! yet existent in
The austerest form of naked majesty,
Thou who beheldest, 'mid the assassins' din,
At thy bathed base the bloody Cæsar lie,
Folding his robe in dying dignity,
An offering to thine altar from the queen
Of gods and men, great Nemesis! did he
 die,
And thou, too, perish, Pompey? have ye
 been
Victors of countless kings, or puppets of
 a scene?

LXXXVIII.

And thou, the thunder-stricken nurse of
 Rome!
She-wolf! whose brazen-imaged dugs im-
 part
The milk of conquest yet within the dome
Where, as a monument of antique art,
Thou standest:—Mother of the mighty
 heart,
Which the great founder suck'd from thy
 wild teat,
Scorch'd by the Roman Jove's ethereal dart,
And thy limbs black with lightning—dost
 thou yet
Guard thine immortal cubs, nor thy fond
 charge forget?

LXXXIX.

Thou dost; but all thy foster-babes are
 dead—
The men of iron: and the world hath
 rear'd
Cities from out their sepulchres: men bled
In imitation of the things they fear'd,
And fought and conquer'd, and the same
 course steer'd,
At apish distance; but as yet none have,
Nor could, the same supremacy have near'd,
Save one vain man, who is not in the grave,
But, vanquish'd by himself, to his own slaves
 a slave—

XC.

The fool of false dominion—and a kind
Of bastard Cæsar, following him of old
With steps unequal; for the Roman's mind
Was modell'd in a less terrestrial mould,

With passions fiercer, yet a judgment cold,
And an immortal instinct which redeem'd
The frailties of a heart so soft, yet bold,
Alcides with the distaff now he seem'd
At Cleopatra's feet,—and now himself he
 beam'd,

XCI.

And came—and saw—and conquer'd! But
 the man
Who would have tamed his eagles down to
 flee,
Like a train'd falcon, in the Gallic van,
Which he, in sooth, long led to victory,
With a deaf heart which never seem'd to be
A listener to itself, was strangely framed ;
With but one weakest weakness—vanity,
Coquettish in ambition, still he aim'd—
At what ? can he avouch, or answer what he
 claim'd ?

XCII.

And would be all or nothing—nor could wait
For the sure grave to level him ; few years
Had fix'd him with the Cæsars in his fate,
On whom we tread : For *this* the conqueror
 rears
The arch of triumph ! and for this the tears
And blood of earth flow on as they have
 flow'd,
An universal deluge, which appears
Without an ark for wretched man's abode,
And ebbs but to reflow! Renew thy rainbow,
 God !

XCIII.

What from this barren being do we reap ?
Our senses narrow, and our reason frail,
Life short, and truth a gem which loves the
 deep,
And all things weigh'd in custom's falsest
 scale ;
Opinion an omnipotence,—whose veil
Mantles the earth with darkness, until right
And wrong are accidents, and men grow
 pale
Lest their own judgments should become
 too bright,
And their free thoughts be crimes, and earth
 have too much light.

XCIV.

And thus they plod in sluggish misery,
Rotting from sire to son, and age to age,
Proud of their trampled nature, and so
 die,
Bequeathing their hereditary rage

To the new race of inborn slaves, who
 wage
War for their chains, and rather than be
 free,
Bleed gladiator-like, and still engage
Within the same arena where they see
Their fellows fall before, like leaves of the
 same tree.

XCV.

I speak not of men's creeds—they rest
 between
Man and his Maker—but of things allow'd,
Averr'd, and known, and daily, hourly
 seen—
The yoke that is upon us doubly bow'd,
And the intent of tyranny avow'd,
The edict of Earth's rulers, who are grown
The apes of him who humbled once the
 proud,
And shook them from their slumbers on
 the throne :
Too glorious, were this all his mighty arm
 had done.

XCVI.

Can tyrants but by tyrants conquer'd be,
And Freedom find no champion and no
 child
Such as Columbia saw arise when she
Sprung forth a Pallas, arm'd and un-
 defiled ?
Or must such minds be nourish'd in the
 wild,
Deep in the unpruned forest, 'midst the
 roar
Of cataracts, where nursing Nature smiled
On infant Washington ? Has Earth no
 more
Such seeds within her breast, or Europe no
 such shore ?

XCVII.

But France got drunk with blood to vomit
 crime,
And fatal have her Saturnalia been
To Freedom's cause, in every age and
 clime ;
Because the deadly days which we have
 seen,
And vile Ambition, that built up between
Man and his hopes an adamantine wall,
And the base pageant last upon the scene,
Are grown the pretext for the eternal
 thrall
Which nips life's tree, and dooms man's
 worst—his second fall.

XCVIII.

Yet, Freedom! yet thy banner, torn, but
 flying,
Streams like the thunder-storm *against*
 the wind;
Thy trumpet voice, though broken now
 and dying,
The loudest still the tempest leaves behind;
Thy tree hath lost its blossoms, and the
 rind,
Chopp'd by the axe, looks rough and little
 worth,
But the sap lasts,—and still the seed
 we find
Sown deep, even in the bosom of the
 North;
So shall a better spring less bitter fruit bring
 forth.

XCIX.

There is a stern round tower of other days,
Firm as a fortress, with its fence of stone,
Such as an army's baffled strength delays,
Standing with half its battlements alone,
And with two thousand years of ivy grown,
The garland of eternity, where wave
The green leaves over all by time o'er-
 thrown;—
What was this tower of strength? within
 its cave
What treasure lay so lock'd. so hid?—A
 woman's grave.

C

But who was she, the lady of the dead.
Tomb'd in a palace? Was she chaste and
 fair?
Worthy a king's, or more—a Roman's bed?
What race of chiefs and heroes did she bear?
What daughter of her beauties was the heir?
How lived, how loved, how died she? Was
 she not
So honoured—and conspicuously there,
Where meaner relics must not dare to rot,
Placed to commemorate a more than mortal
 lot?

CI.

Was she as those who love their lords, or
 they
Who love the lords of others? such have
 been
Even in the olden time, Rome's annals say.
Was she a matron of Cornelia's mien,
Or the light air of Egypt's graceful queen,
Profuse of joy—or 'gainst it did she war
Inveterate in virtue? Did she lean
To the soft side of the heart, or wisely bar
Love from amongst her griefs?—for such
 the affections are.

CII.

Perchance she died in youth: it may be,
 bow'd
With woes far heavier than the ponderous
 tomb
That weigh'd upon her gentle dust, a cloud
Might gather o'er her beauty, and a gloom
In her dark eye, prophetic of the doom
Heaven gives its favourites—early death;
 yet shed
A sunset charm around her, and illume
With hectic light, the Hesperus of the dead,
Of her consuming cheek the autumnal leaf-
 like red.

CIII.

Perchance she died in age—surviving all,
Charms, kindred, children—with the silver
 gray
On her long tresses, which might yet recall,
It may be, still a something of the day
When they were braided, and her proud
 array
And lovely form were envied, praised, and
 eyed
By Rome—But whither would Conjecture
 stray?
Thus much alone we know—Metella died,
The wealthiest Roman's wife: Behold his
 love or pride!

CIV.

I know not why—but standing thus by
 thee
It seems as if I had thine inmate known,
Thou Tomb! and other days come back
 on me
With recollected music, though the tone
Is changed and solemn, like the cloudy
 groan
Of dying thunder on the distant wind;
Yet could I seat me by this ivied stone
Till I had bodied forth the heated mind
Forms from the floating wreck which Ruin
 leaves behind;

CV.

And from the planks, far shatter'd o'er
 the rocks,
Built me a little bark of hope, once more
To battle with the ocean and the shocks
Of the loud breakers, and the ceaseless roar
Which rushes on the solitary shore
Where all lies founder'd that was ever dear:
But could I gather from the wave-worn
 store
Enough for my rude boat, where should
 I steer?
There woos no home, nor hope, nor life, save
 what is here.

CVI.

Then let the winds howl on! their
 harmony
Shall henceforth be my music, and the
 night
The sound shall temper with the owlets'
 cry,
As I now hear them, in the fading light
Dim o'er the bird of darkness' native site,
Answering each other on the Palatine,
With their large eyes, all glistening gray
 and bright,
And sailing pinions.—Upon such a shrine
What are our petty griefs?—let me not
 number mine.

CVII.

Cypress and ivy, weed and wallflower
 grown
Matted and mass'd together, hillocks heap'd
On what were chambers, arch crush'd,
 column strown
In fragments, choked up vaults, and frescos
 steep'd
In subterranean damps, where the owl
 peep'd,
Deeming it midnight:—Temples, baths,
 or halls?
Pronounce who can; for all that Learning
 reap'd
From her research hath been, that these
 are walls—
Behold the Imperial Mount! 't is thus the
 mighty falls.

CVIII.

There is the moral of all human tales;
'Tis but the same rehearsal of the past,
First Freedom, and then Glory—when
 that fails,
Wealth, vice, corruption,—barbarism at
 last.
And History, with all her volumes vast,
Hath but *one* page,—'t is better written
 here
Where gorgeous Tyranny hath thus a-
 mass'd
All treasures, all delights, that eye or ear,
Heart, soul could seek, tongue ask—Away
 with words! draw near,

CIX.

Admire, exult, despise, laugh, weep,—for
 here
There is such matter for all feeling:—
 Man!
Thou pendulum betwixt a smile and tear,
Ages and realms are crowded in this span,

This mountain, whose obliterated plan
The pyramid of empires pinnacled,
Of Glory's gewgaws shining in the van
Till the sun's rays with added flame were
 fill'd!
Where are its golden roofs? where those
 who dared to build?

CX.

Tully was not so eloquent as thou,
Thou nameless column with the buried
 base!
What are the laurels of the Cæsar's brow?
Crown me with ivy from his dwelling-
 place.
Whose arch or pillar meets me in the
 face,
Titus or Trajan's? No—'t is that of Time:
Triumph, arch, pillar, all he doth dis-
 place
Scoffing; and apostolic statues climb
To crush the imperial urn, whose ashes slept
 sublime,

CXI.

Buried in air, the deep blue sky of Rome,
And looking to the stars: they had con-
 tain'd
A spirit which with these would find a
 home,
The last of those who o'er the whole earth
 reign'd,
The Roman globe, for after none sustain'd,
But yielded back his conquests:—he was
 more
Than a mere Alexander, and, unstain'd
With household blood and wine, serenely
 wore
His sovereign virtues—still we Trajan's name
 adore.

CXII.

Where is the rock of Triumph, the high
 place
Where Rome embraced her heroes? where
 the steep
Tarpeian? fittest goal of Treason's race,
The promontory whence the Traitor's Leap
Cured all ambition. Did the conquerors
 heap
Their spoils here? Yes; and in yon field
 below,
A thousand years of silenced factions
 sleep—
The Forum, where the immortal accents
 glow,
And still the eloquent air breathes—burns
 with Cicero!

CXIII.

The field of freedom, faction, fame, and blood:
Here a proud people's passions were exhaled,
From the first hour of empire in the bud
To that when further worlds to conquer fail'd;
But long before had Freedom's face been veil'd,
And Anarchy assumed her attributes;
Till every lawless soldier who assail'd
Trod on the trembling senate's slavish mutes,
Or raised the venal voice of baser prostitutes.

CXIV.

Then turn we to her latest tribune's name,
From her ten thousand tyrants turn to thee,
Redeemer of dark centuries of shame—
The friend of Petrarch—hope of Italy—
Rienzi! last of Romans! While the tree
Of freedom's wither'd trunk puts forth a leaf
Even for thy tomb a garland let it be—
The forum's champion, and the people's chief—
Her new-born Numa thou—with reign, alas! too brief.

CXV.

Egeria! sweet creation of some heart
Which found no mortal resting-place so fair
As thine ideal breast; whate'er thou art
Or wert,—a young Aurora of the air,
The nympholepsy of some fond despair;
Or, it might be, a beauty of the earth,
Who found a more than common votary there
Too much adoring; whatsoe'er thy birth,
Thou wert a beautiful thought, and softly bodied forth.

CXVI.

The mosses of thy fountain still are sprinkled
With thine Elysian water-drops; the face
Of thy cave-guarded spring with years unwrinkled,
Reflects the meek-eyed genius of the place,
Whose green, wild margin now no more erase
Art's works; nor must the delicate waters sleep,
Prison'd in marble, bubbling from the base
Of the cleft statue, with a gentle leap
The rill runs o'er, and round fern, flowers, and ivy creep,

CXVII.

Fantastically tangled: the green hills
Are clothed with early blossoms, through the grass
The quick-eyed lizard rustles, and the bills
Of summer-birds sing welcome as ye pass;
Flowers fresh in hue, and many in their class,
Implore the pausing step, and with their dyes,
Dance in the soft breeze in a fairy mass;
The sweetness of the violet's deep blue eyes,
Kiss'd by the breath of heaven seems colour'd by its skies.

CXVIII.

Here didst thou dwell, in this enchanted cover,
Egeria! thy all heavenly bosom beating
For the far footsteps of thy mortal lover;
The purple Midnight veil'd that mystic meeting
With her most starry canopy, and seating
Thyself by thine adorer, what befell?
This cave was surely shaped out for the greeting
Of an enamour'd Goddess, and the cell
Haunted by holy Love—the earliest oracle!

CXIX.

And didst thou not, thy breast to his replying,
Blend a celestial with a human heart;
And Love, which dies as it was born, in sighing,
Share with immortal transports? could thine art
Make them indeed immortal, and impart
The purity of heaven to earthly joys,
Expel the venom and not blunt the dart—
The dull satiety which all destroys—
And root from out the soul the deadly weed which cloys?

CXX.

Alas! our young affections run to waste,
Or water but the desert; whence arise
But weeds of dark luxuriance, tares of haste,
Rank at the core, though tempting to the eyes,
Flowers whose wild odours breathe but agonies,
And trees whose gums are poisons; such the plants
Which spring beneath her steps as Passion flies
O'er the world's wilderness, and vainly pants
For some celestial fruit forbidden to our wants.

CXXI.

Oh Love! no habitant of earth thou art—
An unseen seraph, we believe in thee,—
A faith whose martyrs are the broken
 heart,—
But never yet hath seen, nor e'er shall see
The naked eye, thy form, as it should be;
The mind hath made thee, as it peopled
 heaven,
Even with its own desiring phantasy,
And to a thought such shape and image
 given,
As haunts the unquench'd soul—parch'd,
 wearied, wrung, and riven.

CXXII.

Of its own beauty is the mind diseased,
And fevers into false creation:—where,
Where are the forms the sculptor's soul
 hath seiz'd?
In him alone. Can Nature show so fair?
Where are the charms and virtues which
 we dare
Conceive in boyhood and pursue as men,
The unreach'd Paradise of our despair,
Which o'er-informs the pencil and the pen,
And overpowers the page where it would
 bloom again?

CXXIII.

Who loves, raves—'t is youth's frenzy—but
 the cure
Is bitterer still, as charm by charm un-
 winds
Which robed our idols, and we see too sure
Nor worth nor beauty dwells from out the
 mind's
Ideal shape of such; yet still it binds
The fatal spell, and still it draws us on,
Reaping the whirlwind from the oft-sown
 winds;
The stubborn heart, its alchemy begun,
Seems ever near the prize—wealthiest when
 most undone.

CXXIV.

We wither from our youth, we gasp away—
Sick—sick; unfound the boon, unslaked
 the thirst,
Though to the last, in verge of our decay,
Some phantom lures, such as we sought at
 first—
But all too late,—so are we doubly curst.
Love, fame, ambition, avarice—'t is the
 same,
Each idle, and all ill, and none the worst—
For all are meteors with a different name,
And Death the sable smoke where vanishes
 the flame.

CXXV.

Few—none—find what they love or could
 have loved,
Though accident, blind contact, and the
 strong
Necessity of loving, have removed
Antipathies—but to recur, ere long,
Envenom'd with irrevocable wrong;
And Circumstance, that unspiritual god
And miscreator, makes and helps along
Our coming evils with a crutch-like rod,
Whose touch turns Hope to dust,—the dust
 we all have trod.

CXXVI.

Our life is a false nature: 'tis not in
The harmony of things,—this hard decree,
This uneradicable taint of sin,
This boundless upas, this all-blasting tree,
Whose root is earth, whose leaves and
 branches be
The skies which rain their plagues on men
 like dew—
Disease, death, bondage—all the woes we
 see,
And worse, the woes we see not—which
 throb through
The immedicable soul, with heart-aches ever
 new.

CXXVII.

Yet let us ponder boldly—'t is a base
Abandonment of reason to resign
Our right of thought—our last and only place
Of refuge; this, at least, shall still be
 mine:
Though from our birth the faculty divine
Is chain'd and tortured—cabin'd, cribb'd,
 confined,
And bred in darkness, lest the truth should
 shine
Too brightly on the unprepared mind,
The beam pours in, for time and skill will
 couch the blind.

CXXVIII.

Arches on arches! as it were that Rome,
Collecting the chief trophies of her line,
Would build up all her triumphs in one
 dome,
Her Coliseum stands; the moonbeams
 shine
As 'twere its natural torches, for divine
Should be the light which streams here to
 illume
This long-explored but still exhaustless
 mine
Of contemplation; and the azure gloom
Of an Italian night, where the deep skies
 assume

CXXIX.

Hues which have words, and speak to ye
 of heaven,
Floats o'er this vast and wondrous monu-
 ment,
And shadows forth its glory. There is given
Unto the things of earth, which Time hath
 bent,
A spirit's feeling, and where he hath leant
His hand, but broke his scythe, there is a
 power
And magic in the ruin'd battlement,
For which the palace of the present hour
Must yield its pomp, and wait till ages are its
 dower.

CXXX.

Oh Time! the beautifier of the dead,
Adorner of the ruin, comforter
And only healer when the heart hath bled;
Time! the corrector where our judgments
 err,
The test of truth, love—sole philosopher,
For all beside are sophists—from thy thrift,
Which never loses though it doth defer—
Time, the avenger! unto thee I lift
My hands, and eyes, and heart, and crave of
 thee a gift:

CXXXI.

Amidst this wreck, where thou hast made a
 shrine
And temple more divinely desolate,
Among thy mightier offerings here are mine,
Ruins of years, though few, yet full of fate:
If thou hast ever seen me too elate,
Hear me not; but if calmly I have borne
Good, and reserved my pride against the
 hate
Which shall not whelm me, let me not
 have worn
This iron in my soul in vain—shall *they* not
 mourn?

CXXXII.

And thou, who never yet of human wrong
Left the unbalanced scale, great Nemesis!
Here, where the ancient paid thee homage
 long—
Thou who didst call the Furies from the
 abyss,
And round Orestes bade them howl and
 hiss
For that unnatural retribution—just,
Had it but been from hands less near—in
 this
Thy former realm, I call thee from the
 dust!
Dost thou not hear my heart?—Awake!
 thou shalt, and must.

CXXXIII.

It is not that I may not have incurr'd
For my ancestral faults or mine the wound
I bleed withal, and, had it been conferr'd
With a just weapon, it had flow'd unbound;
But now my blood shall not sink in the
 ground;
To thee I do devote it—*thou* shalt take
The vengeance, which shall yet be sought
 and found,
Which if *I* have not taken for the sake——
But let that pass—I sleep, but thou shalt yet
 awake.

CXXXIV.

And if my voice break forth, 't is not that
 now
I shrink from what is suffer'd: let him
 speak
Who hath beheld decline upon my brow,
Or seen my mind's convulsion leave it
 weak;
But in this page a record will I seek.
Not in the air shall these my words dis-
 perse,
Though I be ashes; a far hour shall wreak
The deep prophetic fulness of this verse,
And pile on human heads the mountain of
 my curse!

CXXXV.

That curse shall be Forgiveness.—Have
 I not—
Hear me, my mother Earth! behold it,
 Heaven!
Have I not had to wrestle with my lot?
Have I not suffer'd things to be forgiven?
Have I not had my brain sear'd, my heart
 riven,
Hopes sapp'd, name blighted, Life's life
 lied away?
And only not to desperation driven,
Because not altogether of such clay
As rots into the souls of those whom I
 survey.

CXXXVI.

From mighty wrongs to petty perfidy
Have I not seen what human things could
 do?
From the loud roar of foaming calumny
To the small whisper of the as paltry few,
And subtler venom of the reptile crew,
The Janus glance of whose significant eye,
Learning to lie with silence, would *seem*
 true,
And without utterance, save the shrug or
 sigh,
Deal round to happy fools its speechless
 obloquy.

CXXXVII.

But I have lived, and have not lived in
　　vain:
My mind may lose its force, my blood its
　　fire,
And my frame perish even in conquering
　　pain;
But there is that within me which shall
　　tire
Torture and Time, and breathe when I
　　expire;
Something unearthly, which they deem
　　not of,
Like the remember'd tone of a mute lyre,
Shall on their soften'd spirits sink, and
　　move
In hearts all rocky now the late remorse of
　　love.

CXXXVIII.

The seal is set.—Now welcome, thou dread
　　power!
Nameless, yet thus omnipotent, which here
Walk'st in the shadow of the midnight
　　hour
With a deep awe, yet all distinct from fear;
Thy haunts are ever where the dead walls
　　rear
Their ivy mantles, and the solemn scene
Derives from thee a sense so deep and
　　clear
That we become a part of what has been,
And grow unto the spot, all-seeing but
　　unseen.

CXXXIX.

And here the buzz of eager nations ran,
In murmur'd pity, or loud-roar'd applause,
As man was slaughter'd by his fellow-
　　man.
And wherefore slaughter'd? wherefore, but
　　because
Such were the bloody Circus' genial laws,
And the imperial pleasure.—Wherefore
　　not?
What matters where we fall to fill the
　　maws
Of worms—on battle-plains or listed spot?
Both are but theatres where the chief actors
　　rot.

CXL.

I see before me the Gladiator lie:
He leans upon his hand—his manly brow
Consents to death, but conquers agony,
And his droop'd head sinks gradually
　　low—

And through his side the last drops, ebbing
　　slow
From the red gash, fall heavy, one by one,
Like the first of a thunder-shower; and
　　now
The arena swims around him—he is gone,
Ere ceased the inhuman shout which hail'd
　　the wretch who won.

CXLI.

He heard it, but he heeded not—his eyes
Were with his heart, and that was far
　　away;
He reck'd not of the life he lost nor prize,
But where his rude hut by the Danube lay,
There were his young barbarians all at
　　play,
There was their Dacian mother—he, their
　　sire,
Butcher'd to make a Roman holiday—
All this rush'd with his blood—Shall he
　　expire
And unavenged? Arise! ye Goths, and glut
　　your ire!

CXLII.

But here, where Murder breathed her
　　bloody steam;
And here, where buzzing nations choked
　　the ways,
And roar'd or murmur'd like a mountain
　　stream
Dashing or winding as its torrent strays;
Here, where the Roman million's blame or
　　praise
Was death or life, the playthings of a
　　crowd,
My voice sounds much—and fall the stars'
　　faint rays
On the arena void—seats crush'd—walls
　　bow'd—
And galleries, where my steps seem echoes
　　strangely loud.

CXLIII.

A ruin—yet what ruin! from its mass
Walls, palaces, half-cities, have been rear'd;
Yet oft the enormous skeleton ye pass,
And marvel where the spoil could have
　　appear'd.
Hath it indeed been plunder'd, or but
　　clear'd?
Alas! developed, opens the decay,
When the colossal fabric's form is near'd:
It will not bear the brightness of the day,
Which streams too much on all years, man,
　　have reft away.

CXLIV.

But when the rising moon begins to climb
Its topmost arch, and gently pauses there;
When the stars twinkle through the loops
of time,
And the low night-breeze waves along the air
The garland-forest, which the gray walls
wear,
Like laurels on the bald first Cæsar's head;
When the light shines serene but doth not
glare,
Then in this magic circle raise the dead:
Heroes have trod this spot—'t is on their
dust ye tread.

CXLV.

"While stands the Coliseum, Rome shall
stand;
"When falls the Coliseum, Rome shall fall;
"And when Rome falls—the World."
From our own land
Thus spake the pilgrims o'er this mighty wall
In Saxon times, which we are wont to call
Ancient; and these three mortal things
are still
On their foundations, and unalter'd all;
Rome and her Ruin past Redemption's skill,
The World, the same wide den—of thieves,
or what ye will.

CXLVI.

Simple, erect, severe, austere, sublime—
Shrine of all saints and temple of all gods,
From Jove to Jesus—spared and blest by
time;
Looking tranquillity, while falls or nods
Arch, empire, each thing round thee, and
man plods
His way through thorns to ashes—glorious
dome!
Shalt thou not last? Time's scythe and
tyrants' rods
Shiver upon thee—sanctuary and home
Of art and piety—Pantheon!—pride of Rome!

CXLVII.

Relic of nobler days, and noblest arts!
Despoil'd yet perfect, with thy circle
spreads
A holiness appealing to all hearts—
To art a model; and to him who treads
Rome for the sake of ages, Glory sheds
Her light through thy sole aperture; to
those
Who worship, here are altars for their
beads;
And they who feel for genius may repose
Their eyes on honour'd forms, whose busts
around them close.

CXLVIII.

There is a dungeon, in whose dim drear
light
What do I gaze on? Nothing: Look again!
Two forms are slowly shadow'd on my
sight—
Two insulated phantoms of the brain:
It is not so; I see them full and plain—
An old man, and a female young and fair,
Fresh as a nursing mother, in whose vein
The blood is nectar:—but what doth she
there,
With her unmantled neck, and bosom white
and bare?

CXLIX.

Full swells the deep pure fountain of young
life,
Where *on* the heart and *from* the heart we
took
Our first and sweetest nurture, when the
wife,
Blest into mother, in the innocent look,
Or even the piping cry of lips that brook
No pain and small suspense, a joy perceives
Man knows not, when from out its cradled
nook
She sees her little bud put forth its leaves—
What may the fruit be yet? I know not—
Cain was Eve's.

CL.

But here youth offers to old age the food,
The milk of his own gift: it is her sire
To whom she renders back the debt of blood
Born with her birth. No; he shall not
expire
While in those warm and lovely veins the
fire
Of health and holy feeling can provide
Great Nature's Nile, whose deep stream
rises higher
Than Egypt's river: from that gentle side
Drink, drink and live, old man! Heaven's
realm holds no such tide.

CLI.

The starry fable of the milky way
Has not thy story's purity; it is
A constellation of a sweeter ray,
And sacred Nature triumphs more in this
Reverse of her decree, than in the abyss
Where sparkle distant worlds:—Oh, holiest
nurse!
No drop of that clear stream its way shall
miss
To thy sire's heart, replenishing its source
With life, as our freed souls rejoin the uni-
verse.

CLII.

Turn to the mole which Hadrian rear'd on
 high,
Imperial mimic of old Egypt's piles,
Colossal copyist of deformity
Whose travell'd phantasy from the far Nile's
Enormous model, doom'd the artist's toils
To build for giants, and for his vain earth,
His shrunken ashes, raise this dome: How
 smiles
The gazer's eye with philosophic mirth,
To view the huge design which sprung from
 such a birth!

CLIII.

But lo! the dome—the vast and wondrous
 dome,
To which Diana's marvel was a cell—
Christ's mighty shrine above his martyr's
 tomb!
I have beheld the Ephesian's miracle;—
Its columns strew the wilderness, and dwell
The hyæna and the jackal in their shade;
I have beheld Sophia's bright roofs swell
Their glittering mass i' the sun, and have
 survey'd
Its sanctuary the while the usurping Moslem
 pray'd;

CLIV.

But thou, of temples old, or altars new,
Standest alone, with nothing like to thee—
Worthiest of God, the holy and the true.
Since Zion's desolation, when that He
Forsook his former city, what could be,
Of earthly structures, in his honour piled,
Of a sublimer aspect? Majesty,
Power, Glory, Strength, and Beauty all
 are aisled
In this eternal ark of worship undefiled.

CLV.

Enter: its grandeur overwhelms thee not;
And why? It is not lessen'd; but thy mind,
Expanded by the genius of the spot,
Has grown colossal, and can only find
A fit abode wherein appear enshrined
Thy hopes of immortality; and thou
Shalt one day, if found worthy, so defined,
See thy God face to face, as thou dost now
His Holy of Holies, nor be blasted by his brow.

CLVI.

Thou movest, but increasing with the ad-
 vance,
Like climbing some great Alp, which still
 doth rise,
Deceived by its gigantic elegance;
Vastness which grows, but grows to har-
 monise—

All musical in its immensities;
Rich marbles, richer painting—shrines
 where flame
The lamps of gold—and haughty dome
 which vies
In air with Earth's chief structures, though
 their frame
Sits on the firm-set ground, and this the
 clouds must claim.

CLVII.

Thou seest not all; but piecemeal thou
 must break,
To separate contemplation, the great whole;
And as the ocean many bays will make
That ask the eye—so here condense thy
 soul
To more immediate objects, and control
Thy thoughts until thy mind hath got by
 heart
Its eloquent proportions, and unroll
In mighty graduations, part by part,
The glory which at once upon thee did not
 dart,

CLVIII.

Not by its fault—but thine: Our outward
 sense
Is but of gradual grasp—and as it is
That what we have of feeling most in-
 tense
Outstrips our faint expression; even so
 this
Outshining and o'erwhelming edifice
Fools our fond gaze, and greatest of the
 great
Defies at first our Nature's littleness,
Till, growing with its growth, we thus
 dilate
Our spirits to the size of that they contem-
 plate.

CLIX.

Then pause, and be enlighten'd; there is
 more
In such a survey than the sating gaze
Of wonder pleased, or awe which would
 adore
The worship of the place, or the mere
 praise
Of art and its great masters, who could
 raise
What former time, nor skill, nor thought
 could plan;
The fountain of sublimity displays
Its depth, and thence may draw the mind
 of man
Its golden sands, and learn what great con-
 ceptions can.

CLX.

Or, turning to the Vatican, go see
Laocoön's torture dignifying pain—
A father's love and mortal's agony
With an immortal's patience blending:
 Vain
The struggle; vain, against the coiling
 strain
And gripe, and deepening of the dragon's
 grasp,
The old man's clench; the long envenom'd
 chain
Rivets the living links,—the enormous asp
Enforces pang on pang, and stifles gasp on
 gasp.

CLXI.

Or view the Lord of the unerring bow,
The God of life, and poesy, and light—
The Sun in human limbs array'd, and brow
All radiant from his triumph in the fight;
The shaft hath just been shot—the arrow
 bright
With an immortal's vengeance; in his eye
And nostril beautiful disdain, and might
And majesty, flash their full lightnings by,
Developing in that one glance the Deity.

CLXII.

But in his delicate form—a dream of Love,
Shaped by some solitary nymph, whose
 breast
Long'd for a deathless lover from above,
And madden'd in that vision—are exprest
All that ideal beauty ever bless'd
The mind with in its most unearthly mood,
When each conception was a heavenly
 guest—
A ray of immortality—and stood
Starlike, around, until they gather'd to a
 god!

CLXIII.

And if it be Prometheus stole from Heaven
The fire which we endure, it was repaid
By him to whom the energy was given
Which this poetic marble hath array'd
With an eternal glory—which, if made
By human hands, is not of human thought;
And Time himself hath hallow'd it, nor laid
One ringlet in the dust—nor hath it caught
A tinge of years, but breathes the flame with
 which 't was wrought.

CLXIV.

But where is he, the Pilgrim of my song,
The being who upheld it through the past?
Methinks he cometh late and tarries long.
He is no more—these breathings are his
 last;

His wanderings done, his visions ebbing
 fast,
And he himself as nothing :—if he was
Aught but a phantasy, and could be class'd
With forms which live and suffer—let that
 pass—
His shadow fades away into Destruction's
 mass.

CLXV.

Which gathers shadow, substance, life, and
 all
That we inherit in its mortal shroud,
And spreads the dim and universal pall
Through which all things grow phantoms;
 and the cloud
Between us sinks and all which ever glow'd,
Till Glory's self is twilight, and displays
A melancholy halo scarce allow'd
To hover on the verge of darkness; rays
Sadder than saddest night, for they distract
 the gaze,

CLXVI.

And send us prying into the abyss,
To gather what we shall be when the frame
Shall be resolved to something less than
 this
Its wretched essence; and to dream of
 fame,
And wipe the dust from off the idle name
We never more shall hear,—but never more,
Oh, happier thought! can we be made the
 same:
It is enough in sooth that *once* we bore
These fardels of the heart—the heart whose
 sweat was gore.

CLXVII.

Hark! forth from the abyss a voice proceeds,
A long low distant murmur of dread sound,
Such as arises when a nation bleeds
With some deep and immedicable wound;
Through storm and darkness yawns the
 rending ground,
The gulf is thick with phantoms, but the
 chief
Seems royal still, though with her head
 discrown'd,
And pale, but lovely, with maternal grief
She clasps a babe, to whom her breast yields
 no relief.

CLXVIII.

Scion of chiefs and monarchs, where art
 thou?
Fond hope of many nations, art thou dead?
Could not the grave forget thee, and lay
 low
Some less majestic, less beloved head?

In the sad midnight, while thy heart still
 bled,
The mother of a moment, o'er thy boy,
Death hush'd that pang for ever: with thee
 fled
The present happiness and promised joy
Which fill'd the imperial isles so full it
 seem'd to cloy.

CLXIX.

Peasants bring forth in safety.—Can it
 be,
Oh thou that wert so happy, so adored!
Those who weep not for kings shall weep
 for thee,
And Freedom's heart, grown heavy, cease
 to hoard
Her many griefs for ONE; for she had
 pour'd
Her orisons for thee, and o'er thy head
Beheld her Iris.—Thou, too, lonely lord,
And desolate consort—vainly wert thou
 wed!
The husband of a year! the father of the
 dead!

CLXX.

Of sackcloth was thy wedding garment
 made;
Thy bridal's fruit is ashes: in the dust
The fair-hair'd Daughter of the Isles is
 laid,
The love of millions! How we did intrust
Futurity to her! and, though it must
Darken above our bones, yet fondly deem'd
Our children should obey her child, and
 bless'd
Her and her hoped-for seed, whose promise
 seem'd
Like stars to shepherd's eyes:—'twas but a
 meteor beam'd.

CLXXI.

Woe unto us, not her; for she sleeps well:
The fickle reek of popular breath, the
 tongue
Of hollow counsel, the false oracle,
Which from the birth of monarchy hath
 rung
Its knell in princely ears, till the o'erstung
Nations have arm'd in madness, the strange
 fate
Which tumbles mightiest sovereigns, and
 hath flung
Against their blind omnipotence a weight
Within the opposing scale, which crushes
 soon or late,—

CLXXII.

These might have been her destiny; but
 no,
Our hearts deny it: and so young, so fair,
Good without effort, great without a foe;
But now a bride and mother—and now
 there!
How many ties did that stern moment
 tear!
From thy Sire's to his humblest subject's
 breast
Is link'd the electric chain of that despair,
Whose shock was as an earthquake's, and
 opprest
The land which loved thee so that none
 could love thee best.

CLXXIII.

Lo, Nemi! navell'd in the woody hills
So far, that the uprooting wind which tears
The oak from his foundation, and which
 spills
The ocean o'er its boundary, and bears
Its form against the skies, reluctant spares
The oval mirror of thy glassy lake;
And calm as cherish'd hate, its surface
 wears
A deep cold settled aspect nought can
 shake,
All coil'd into itself and round, as sleeps the
 snake.

CLXXIV.

And near, Albano's scarce divided waves
Shine from a sister valley;—and afar
The Tiber winds, and the broad ocean laves
The Latian coast where sprung the Epic
 war,
"Arms and the man," whose re-ascending
 star
Rose o'er an empire:—but beneath thy
 right
Tully reposed from Rome;—and where
 yon bar
Of girdling mountains intercepts the sight
The Sabine farm was till'd, the weary bard's
 delight.

CLXXV.

But I forget.—My Pilgrim's shrine is won,
And he and I must part,—so let it be,—
His task and mine alike are nearly done;
Yet once more let us look upon the sea;
The midland ocean breaks on him and me,
And from the Alban Mount we now behold
Our friend of youth, that Ocean, which
 when we
Beheld it last by Calpe's rock unfold
Those waves, we follow'd on till the dark
 Euxine roll'd

CLXXVI.

Upon the blue Symplegades: long years—
Long, though not very many—since have
 done
Their work on both; some suffering and
 some tears
Have left us nearly where we had begun:
Yet not in vain our mortal race hath run;
We have had our reward, and it is here,—
That we can yet feel gladden'd by the sun,
And reap from earth, sea, joy almost as
 dear
As if there were no man to trouble what is
 clear.

CLXXVII.

Oh! that the Desert were my dwelling-
 place,
With one fair Spirit for my minister,
That I might all forget the human race,
And, hating no one, love but only her!
Ye elements!—in whose ennobling stir
I feel myself exalted—Can ye not
Accord me such a being? Do I err
In deeming such inhabit many a spot?
Though with them to converse can rarely be
 our lot.

CLXXVIII.

There is a pleasure in the pathless woods,
There is a rapture on the lonely shore,
There is society, where none intrudes,
By the deep Sea, and music in its roar:
I love not Man the less, but Nature more,
From these our interviews, in which I steal
From all I may be, or have been before,
To mingle with the Universe, and feel
What I can ne'er express, yet cannot all con-
 ceal.

CLXXIX.

Roll on, thou deep and dark blue Ocean—
 roll!
Ten thousand fleets sweep over thee in
 vain;
Man marks the earth with ruin—his con-
 trol
Stops with the shore; upon the watery
 plain
The wrecks are all thy deed, nor doth re-
 main
A shadow of man's ravage, save his own,
When, for a moment, like a drop of rain,
He sinks into thy depths with bubbling
 groan,
Without a grave, unknell'd, uncoffin'd, and
 unknown.

CLXXX.

His steps are not upon thy paths,—thy
 fields
Are not a spoil for him,—thou dost arise
And shake him from thee; the vile strength
 he wields
For earth's destruction thou dost all de-
 spise,
Spurning him from thy bosom to the skies,
And send'st him, shivering in thy playful
 spray
And howling, to his Gods, where haply lies
His petty hope in some near port or bay,
And dashest him again to earth:—there let
 him lay.

CLXXXI.

The armaments which thunderstrike the
 walls
Of rock-built cities, bidding nations quake,
And monarchs tremble in their capitals,
The oak leviathans, whose huge ribs make
Their clay creator the vain title take
Of lord of thee, and arbiter of war—
These are thy toys, and, as the snowy
 flake,
They melt into thy yeast of waves, which
 mar
Alike the Armada's pride or spoils of Tra-
 falgar.

CLXXXII.

Thy shores are empires, changed in all
 save thee—
Assyria, Greece, Rome, Carthage, what are
 they?
Thy waters wash'd them power while they
 were free,
And many a tyrant since; their shores
 obey
The stranger, slave, or savage; their decay
Has dried up realms to deserts:—not so
 thou;—
Unchangeable, save to thy wild waves' play,
Time writes no wrinkle on thine azure
 brow:
Such as creation's dawn beheld, thou rollest
 now.

CLXXXIII.

Thou glorious mirror, where the Almighty's
 form
Glasses itself in tempests; in all time,—
Calm or convulsed, in breeze, or gale, or
 storm,
Icing the pole, or in the torrid clime

Dark-heaving—boundless, endless, and
 sublime,
The image of eternity, the throne
Of the Invisible; even from out thy slime
The monsters of the deep are made; each
 zone
Obeys thee; thou goest forth, dread, fathom-
 less, alone.

CLXXXIV.

And I have loved thee, Ocean! and my joy
Of youthful sports was on thy breast to be
Borne, like thy bubbles, onward: from a boy
I wanton'd with thy breakers—they to me
Were a delight; and if the freshening sea
Made them a terror—'t was a pleasing fear,
For I was as it were a child of thee,
And trusted to thy billows far and near,
And laid my hand upon thy mane—as I do
 here.

CLXXXV.

My task is done, my song hath ceased, my
 theme
Has died into an echo; it is fit
The spell should break of this protracted
 dream.
The torch shall be extinguish'd which hath
 lit
My midnight lamp—and what is writ, is
 writ;
Would it were worthier! but I am not
 now
That which I have been—and my visions
 flit
Less palpably before me—and the glow
Which in my spirit dwelt is fluttering, faint,
 and low.

CLXXXVI.

Farewell! a word that must be, and hath
 been—
A sound which makes us linger;—yet—
 farewell!
Ye! who have traced the Pilgrim to the
 scene
Which is his last, if in your memories
 dwell
A thought which once was his, if on ye
 swell
A single recollection, not in vain
He wore his sandal-shoon and scallop-
 shell;
Farewell! with *him* alone may rest the
 pain,
If such there were—with *you*, the moral of
 his strain.

TALES.

𝕿𝖍𝖊 𝕲𝖎𝖆𝖔𝖚𝖗:

A FRAGMENT OF A TURKISH TALE.

<div align="center">

"One fatal remembrance—one sorrow that throws
Its bleak shade alike o'er our joys and our woes—
To which Life nothing darker nor brighter can bring,
For which joy hath no balm—and affliction no sting."—MOORE.

</div>

<div align="center">

TO

SAMUEL ROGERS, ESQ.

AS A SLIGHT BUT MOST SINCERE TOKEN OF ADMIRATION FOR HIS GENIUS, RESPECT FOR
HIS CHARACTER, AND GRATITUDE FOR HIS FRIENDSHIP,

THIS PRODUCTION IS INSCRIBED,

BY HIS OBLIGED AND AFFECTIONATE SERVANT,

BYRON.

</div>

LONDON, *May*, 1813.

ADVERTISEMENT.

THE tale which these disjointed fragments present is founded upon circumstances now less common in the East than formerly; either because the ladies are more circumspect than in the "olden time," or because the Christians have better fortune, or less enterprise.

The story, when entire, contained the adventures of a female slave, who was thrown, in the Mussulman manner, into the sea for infidelity, and avenged by a young Venetian, her lover, at the time the Seven Islands were possessed by the Republic of Venice, and soon after the Arnauts were beaten back from the Morea, which they had ravaged for some time subsequent to the Russian invasion. The desertion of the Mainotes, on being refused the plunder of Misitra, led to the abandonment of that enterprise, and to the desolation of the Morea; during which the cruelty exercised on all sides was unparalleled even in the annals of the faithful.

THE GIAOUR.

No breath of air to break the wave
That rolls below the Athenian's grave,
That tomb which, gleaming o'er the cliff,
First greets the homeward-veering skiff,
High o'er the land he saved in vain;
When shall such hero live again?

.

Fair clime! where every season smiles
Benignant o'er those blessed isles,
Which, seen from far Colonna's height,
Make glad the heart that hails the sight,
And lend to loneliness delight.

There mildly dimpling, Ocean's cheek
Reflects the tints of many a peak
Caught by the laughing tides that lave
These Edens of the eastern wave:
And if at times a transient breeze
Break the blue crystal of the seas,
Or sweep one blossom from the trees,
How welcome is each gentle air
That wakes and wafts the odours there!
For there the Rose, o'er crag or vale,
Sultana of the Nightingale,
　The maid for whom his melody,
　His thousand songs are heard on high,

Blooms blushing to her lover's tale:
His queen, the garden queen, his Rose,
Unbent by winds, unchill'd by snows,
Far from the winters of the west,
By every breeze and season blest,
Returns the sweets by nature given
In softest incense back to heaven;
And grateful yields that smiling sky
Her fairest hue and fragrant sigh.
And many a summer flower is there,
And many a shade that love might share,
And many a grotto, meant for rest,
That holds the pirate for a guest;
Whose bark in sheltering cove below
Lurks for the passing peaceful prow,
Till the gay mariner's guitar
Is heard, and seen the evening star;
Then stealing with the muffled oar,
Far shaded by the rocky shore,
Rush the night-prowlers on the prey,
And turn to groans his roundelay.
Strange—that where Nature loved to trace,
As if for gods, a dwelling-place,
And every charm and grace hath mix'd
Within the paradise she fix'd,
There man, enamour'd of distress,
Should mar it into wilderness,
And trample, brute-like, o'er each flower
That tasks not one laborious hour;
Nor claims the culture of his hand
To bloom along the fairy land,
But springs as to preclude his care,
And sweetly woos him—but to spare!
Strange—that where all is peace beside,
There passion riots in her pride,
And lust and rapine wildly reign
To darken o'er the fair domain.
It is as though the fiends prevail'd
Against the seraphs they assail'd,
And, fix'd on heavenly thrones, should dwell
The freed inheritors of hell;
So soft the scene, so form'd for joy,
So curst the tyrants that destroy!

He who hath bent him o'er the dead
Ere the first day of death is fled,
The first dark day of nothingness,
The last of danger and distress,
(Before Decay's effacing fingers
Have swept the lines where beauty lingers,)
And mark'd the mild angelic air,
The rapture of repose that's there,
The fix'd yet tender traits that streak
The languor of the placid cheek,
And—but for that sad shrouded eye,
That fires not, wins not, weeps not, now,
And but for that chill, changeless brow,
Where cold Obstruction's apathy
Appals the gazing mourner's heart,
As if to him it could impart

The doom he dreads, yet dwells upon;
Yes, but for these and these alone,
Some moments, ay, one treacherous hour,
He still might doubt the tyrant's power;
So fair, so calm, so softly seal'd,
The first, last look by death reveal'd!
Such is the aspect of this shore;
'T is Greece, but living Greece no more!
So coldly sweet, so deadly fair,
We start, for soul is wanting there.
Hers is the loveliness in death,
That parts not quite with parting breath;
But beauty with that fearful bloom,
That hue which haunts it to the tomb,
Expression's last receding ray,
A gilded halo hovering round decay,
The farewell beam of Feeling pass'd away!
Spark of that flame, perchance of heavenly birth,
Which gleams, but warms no more its cher-
 ish'd earth!

Clime of the unforgotten brave!
Whose land from plain to mountain-cave
Was Freedom's home or Glory's grave!
Shrine of the mighty! can it be,
That this is all remains of thee?
Approach, thou craven crouching slave:
 Say, is not this Thermopylæ?
These waters blue that round you lave,—
 Oh servile offspring of the free,
Pronounce what sea, what shore is this?
The gulf, the rock of Salamis!
These scenes, their story not unknown,
Arise, and make again your own;
Snatch from the ashes of your sires
The embers of their former fires;
And he who in the strife expires
Will add to theirs a name of fear
That Tyranny shall quake to hear,
And leave his sons a hope, a fame,
They too will rather die than shame:
For Freedom's battle once begun,
Bequeath'd by bleeding Sire to Son,
Though baffled oft is ever won.
Bear witness, Greece, thy living page!
Attest it many a deathless age!
While kings, in dusty darkness hid,
Have left a nameless pyramid,
Thy heroes, though the general doom
Hath swept the column from their tomb,
A mightier monument command,
The mountains of their native land!
There points thy Muse to stranger's eye
The graves of those that cannot die!
'T were long to tell, and sad to trace,
Each step from splendour to disgrace;
Enough—no foreign foe could quell
Thy soul, till from itself it fell;
Yes! Self-abasement paved the way
To villain-bonds and despot sway.

What can he tell who treads thy shore?
 No legend of thine olden time,
No theme on which the Muse might soar
High as thine own in days of yore,
 When man was worthy of thy clime.
The hearts within thy valleys bred,
The fiery souls that might have led
 Thy sons to deeds sublime,
Now crawl from cradle to the grave,
Slaves—nay, the bondsmen of a slave,
 And callous, save to crime;
Stain'd with each evil that pollutes
Mankind, where least above the brutes;
Without even savage virtue blest,
Without one free or valiant breast,
Still to the neighbouring ports they waft
Proverbial wiles and ancient craft;
In this the subtle Greek is found,
For this, and this alone, renown'd.
In vain might Liberty invoke
The spirit to its bondage broke,
Or raise the neck that courts the yoke:
No more her sorrows I bewail,
Yet this will be a mournful tale,
And they who listen may believe,
Who heard it first had cause to grieve.

· · · · · ·

Far, dark, along the blue sea glancing,
The shadows of the rocks advancing
Start on the fisher's eye like boat
Of island-pirate or Mainote;
And fearful for his light caïque,
He shuns the near but doubtful creek:
Though worn and weary with his toil,
And cumber'd with his scaly spoil,
Slowly, yet strongly, plies the oar,
Till Port Leone's safer shore
Receives him by the lovely light
That best becomes an Eastern night.

· · · · · ·

Who thundering comes on blackest steed,
With slacken'd bit and hoof of speed?
Beneath the clattering iron's sound
The cavern'd echoes wake around
In lash for lash, and bound for bound;
The foam that streaks the courser's side
Seems gather'd from the ocean-tide:
Though weary waves are sunk to rest,
There's none within his rider's breast;
And though to-morrow's tempest lower,
'Tis calmer than thy heart, young Giaour!
I know thee not, I loathe thy race,
But in thy lineaments I trace
What time shall strengthen, not efface:
Though young and pale, that sallow front
Is scathed by fiery passion's brunt;
Though bent on earth thine evil eye,
As meteor-like thou glidest by,

Right well I view and deem thee one
Whom Othman's sons should slay or shun.

On—on he hasten'd, and he drew
My gaze of wonder as he flew:
Though like a demon of the night
He pass'd, and vanish'd from my sight,
His aspect and his air impress'd
A troubled memory on my breast,
And long upon my startled ear
Rung his dark courser's hoofs of fear.
He spurs his steed; he nears the steep,
That, jutting, shadows o'er the deep;
He winds around; he hurries by;
The rock relieves him from mine eye;
For well I ween unwelcome he
Whose glance is fix'd on those that flee;
And not a star but shines too bright
On him who takes such timeless flight.
He wound along; but ere he pass'd,
One glance he snatch'd, as if his last,
A moment check'd his wheeling steed,
A moment breathed him from his speed,
A moment on his stirrup stood—
Why looks he o'er the olive wood?
The crescent glimmers on the hill,
The Mosque's high lamps are quivering still:
Though too remote for sound to wake
In echoes of the far tophaike,
The flashes of each joyous peal
Are seen to prove the Moslem's zeal.
To-night, set Rhamazani's sun;
To-night, the Bairam feast's begun;
To-night—but who and what art thou
Of foreign garb and fearful brow?
And what are these to thine or thee,
That thou shouldst either pause or flee?

He stood—some dread was on his face,
Soon Hatred settled in its place:
It rose not with the reddening flush
Of transient Anger's hasty blush,
But pale as marble o'er the tomb,
Whose ghastly whiteness aids its gloom.
His brow was bent, his eye was glazed;
He raised his arm, and fiercely raised,
And sternly shook his hand on high,
As doubting to return or fly;
Impatient of his flight delay'd,
Here loud his raven charger neigh'd—
Down glanced that hand, and grasp'd his
 blade;
That sound had burst his waking dream,
As Slumber starts at owlet's scream,
The spur hath lanced his courser's sides;
Away, away, for life he rides:
Swift as the hurl'd on high jerreed
Springs to the touch his startled steed:
The rock is doubled, and the shore
Shakes with the clattering tramp no more;

The crag is won, no more is seen
His Christian crest and haughty mien.
'Twas but an instant he restrain'd
That fiery barb so sternly rein'd;
'Twas but a moment that he stood,
Then sped as if by death pursued;
But in that instant o'er his soul
Winters of Memory seem'd to roll,
And gather in that drop of time
A life of pain, an age of crime.
O'er him who loves, or hates, or fears,
Such moment pours the grief of years:
What felt *he* then, at once opprest
By all that most distracts the breast?
That pause, which ponder'd o'er his fate,
Oh, who its dreary length shall date!
Though in Time's record nearly nought,
It was Eternity to Thought!
For infinite as boundless space
The thought that Conscience must embrace,
Which in itself can comprehend
Woe without name, or hope, or end.

The hour is past, the Giaour is gone;
And did he fly or fall alone?
Woe to that hour he came or went!
The curse for Hassan's sin was sent
To turn a palace to a tomb;
He came, he went, like the simoom,
That harbinger of fate and gloom,
Beneath whose widely-wasting breath
The very cypress droops to death—
Dark tree, still sad when others' grief is fled,
The only constant mourner o'er the dead!

The steed is vanish'd from the stall;
No serf is seen in Hassan's hall;
The lonely spider's thin gray pall
Waves slowly widening o'er the wall;
The bat builds in his haram bower,
And in the fortress of his power
The owl usurps the beacon-tower;
The wild-dog howls o'er the fountain's brim,
With baffled thirst, and famine, grim;
For the stream has shrunk from its marble bed,
Where the weeds and the desolate dust are spread.
'Twas sweet of yore to see it play
And chase the sultriness of day,
As springing high the silver dew
In whirls fantastically flew,
And flung luxurious coolness round
The air, and verdure o'er the ground.
'Twas sweet, when cloudless stars were bright,
To view the wave of watery light,
And hear its melody by night.
And oft had Hassan's Childhood play'd
Around the verge of that cascade;

And oft upon his mother's breast
That sound had harmonized his rest;
And oft had Hassan's Youth along
Its bank been soothed by Beauty's song;
And softer seem'd each melting tone
Of Music mingled with its own.
But ne'er shall Hassan's Age repose
Along the brink at twilight's close:
The stream that fill'd that font is fled—
The blood that warm'd his heart is shed!
And here no more shall human voice
Be heard to rage, regret, rejoice.
The last sad note that swell'd the gale
Was woman's wildest funeral wail:
That quench'd in silence, all is still,
But the lattice that flaps when the wind is shrill:
Though raves the gust, and floods the rain,
No hand shall close its clasp again.
On desert sands 'twere joy to scan
The rudest steps of fellow man,
So here the very voice of Grief
Might wake an Echo like relief—
At least 'twould say, "All are not gone;
There lingers Life, though but in one"—
For many a gilded chamber's there,
Which Solitude might well forbear;
Within that dome as yet Decay
Hath slowly work'd her cankering way—
But gloom is gather'd o'er the gate,
Nor there the Fakir's self will wait;
Nor there will wandering Dervise stay,
For bounty cheers not his delay;
Nor there will weary stranger halt
To bless the sacred "bread and salt."
Alike must Wealth and Poverty
Pass heedless and unheeded by,
For Courtesy and Pity died
With Hassan on the mountain side.
His roof, that refuge unto men,
Is Desolation's hungry den.
The guest flies the hall, and the vassal from labour,
Since his turban was cleft by the infidel's sabre!

· · · · · · ·

I hear the sound of coming feet,
But not a voice mine ear to greet;
More near—each turban I can scan,
And silver-sheathed ataghan;
The foremost of the band is seen
An Emir by his garb of green:
"Ho! who art thou?"—"This low salam
Replies of Moslem faith I am."
"The burthen ye so gently bear
Seems one that claims your utmost care,
And, doubtless, holds some precious freight,
My humble bark would gladly wait."

"Thou speakest sooth: thy skiff unmoor,
And waft us from the silent shore;
Nay, leave the sail still furl'd, and ply
The nearest oar that's scatter'd by,
And midway to those rocks where sleep
The channell'd waters dark and deep.
Rest from your task—so—bravely done,
Our course has been right swiftly run;
Yet 'tis the longest voyage, I trow,
That one of— "

Sullen it plunged, and slowly sank,
The calm wave rippled to the bank;
I watch'd it as it sank, methought
Some motion from the current caught
Bestirr'd it more,—'twas but the beam
That checker'd o'er the living stream:
I gazed, till vanishing from view,
Like lessening pebble it withdrew;
Still less and less, a speck of white
That gemm'd the tide, then mock'd the sight;
And all its hidden secrets sleep,
Known but to Genii of the deep,
Which, trembling in their coral caves,
They dare not whisper to the waves.

As rising on its purple wing
The insect queen of eastern spring,
O'er emerald meadows of Kashmeer
Invites the young pursuer near,
And leads him on from flower to flower
A weary chase and wasted hour,
Then leaves him as it soars on high,
With panting heart and tearful eye:
So Beauty lures the full-grown child,
With hue as bright, and wing as wild;
A chase of idle hopes and fears,
Begun in folly, closed in tears.
If won, to equal ills betray'd,
Woe waits the insect and the maid;
A life of pain, the loss of peace,
From infant's play, and man's caprice:
The lovely toy so fiercely sought
Hath lost its charm by being caught,
For every touch that woo'd its stay
Hath brush'd its brightest hues away,
Till charm, and hue, and beauty gone,
'Tis left to fly or fall alone.
With wounded wing, or bleeding breast,
Ah! where shall either victim rest?
Can this with faded pinion soar
From rose to tulip as before?
Or Beauty, blighted in an hour,
Find joy within her broken bower?
No: gayer insects fluttering by
Ne'er droop the wing o'er those that die,
And lovelier things have mercy shown
To every failing but their own,
And every woe a tear can claim
Except an erring sister's shame.

The Mind, that broods o'er guilty woes,
Is like the Scorpion girt by fire;
In circle narrowing as it glows,
The flames around their captive close,
Till inly search'd by thousand throes,
 And maddening in her ire,
One sad and sole relief she knows,
The sting she nourish'd for her foes,
Whose venom never yet was vain,
Gives but one pang and cures all pain,
And darts into her desperate brain:
So do the dark in soul expire,
Or live like Scorpion girt by fire;
So writhes the mind Remorse hath riven,
Unfit for earth, undoom'd for heaven,
Darkness above, despair beneath,
Around it flame, within it death!

Black Hassan from the Haram flies,
Nor bends on woman's form his eyes;
The unwonted chase each hour employs,
Yet shares he not the hunter's joys.
Not thus was Hassan wont to fly
When Leila dwelt in his Serai.
Doth Leila there no longer dwell?
That tale can only Hassan tell:
Strange rumours in our city say
Upon that eve she fled away
When Rhamazan's last sun was set,
And flashing from each minaret
Millions of lamps proclaim'd the feast
Of Bairam through the boundless East.
'Twas then she went as to the bath,
Which Hassan vainly search'd in wrath;
For she was flown her master's rage
In likeness of a Georgian page,
And far beyond the Moslem's power
Had wrong'd him with the faithless Giaour.
Somewhat of this had Hassan deem'd;
But still so fond, so fair she seem'd,
Too well he trusted to the slave
Whose treachery deserved a grave:
And on that eve had gone to mosque,
And thence to feast in his kiosk.
Such is the tale his Nubians tell,
Who did not watch their charge too well,
But others say, that on that night,
By pale Phingari's trembling light,
The Giaour upon his jet-black steed
Was seen, but seen alone to speed
With bloody spur along the shore,
Nor maid nor page behind him bore.

Her eye's dark charm 't were vain to tell,
But gaze on that of the Gazelle,
It will assist thy fancy well;
As large, as languishingly dark,
But Soul beam'd forth in every spark
That darted from beneath the lid,
Bright as the jewel of Giamschid.
Yea, *Soul*, and should our prophet say
That form was nought but breathing clay,
By Alla! I would answer nay;
Though on Al-Sirat's arch I stood,
Which totters o'er the fiery flood,
With Paradise within my view,
And all his Houris beckoning through.
Oh! who young Leila's glance could read
And keep that portion of his creed
Which saith that woman is but dust,
A soulless toy for tyrant's lust?
On her might Muftis gaze, and own
That through her eye the Immortal shone;
On her fair cheek's unfading hue
The young pomegranate's blossoms strew
Their bloom in blushes ever new;
Her hair in hyacinthine flow,
When left to roll its folds below,
As midst her handmaids in the hall
She stood superior to them all,
Hath swept the marble where her feet
Gleam'd whiter than the mountain sleet
Ere from the cloud that gave it birth
It fell, and caught one stain of earth.
The cygnet nobly walks the water;
So moved on earth Circassia's daughter,
The loveliest bird of Franguestan!
As rears her crest the ruffled Swan,
 And spurns the waves with wings of pride,
When pass the steps of stranger man
 Along the banks that bound her tide;
Thus rose fair Leila's whiter neck:—
Thus arm'd with beauty would she check
Intrusion's glance, till Folly's gaze
Shrunk from the charms it meant to praise.
Thus high and graceful was her gait;
Her heart as tender to her mate;
Her mate—stern Hassan, who was he?
Alas! that name was not for thee!

.

Stern Hassan hath a journey ta'en
With twenty vassals in his train,
Each arm'd, as best becomes a man,
With arquebuss and ataghan;
The chief before, as deck'd for war,
Bears in his belt the scimitar
Stain'd with the best of Arnaut blood,
When in the pass the rebels stood,
And few return'd to tell the tale
Of what befell in Parne's vale.
The pistols which his girdle bore
Were those that once a pasha wore,

Which still, though gemm'd and boss'd with
 gold,
Even robbers tremble to behold.
'T is said he goes to woo a bride
More true than her who left his side;
The faithless slave that broke her bower,
And, worse than faithless, for a Giaour!

.

The sun's last rays are on the hill,
And sparkle in the fountain rill,
Whose welcome waters, cool and clear,
Draw blessings from the mountaineer:
Here may the loitering merchant Greek
Find that repose 'twere vain to seek
In cities lodged too near his lord,
And trembling for his secret hoard—
Here may he rest where none can see,
In crowds a slave, in deserts free;
And with forbidden wine may stain
The bowl a Moslem must not drain.

.

The foremost Tartar's in the gap
Conspicuous by his yellow cap;
The rest in lengthening line the while
Wind slowly through the long defile:
Above, the mountain rears a peak,
Where vultures whet the thirsty beak,
And theirs may be a feast to-night,
Shall tempt them down ere morrow's light;
Beneath, a river's wintry stream
Has shrunk before the summer beam,
And left a channel bleak and bare,
Save shrubs that spring to perish there;
Each side the midway path there lay
Small broken crags of granite gray,
By time, or mountain lightning, riven
From summits clad in mists of heaven;
For where is he that hath beheld
The peak of Liakura unveil'd?

.

They reach the grove of pine at last;
"Bismillah! now the peril's past;
For yonder view the opening plain,
And there we'll prick our steeds amain:"
The Chiaus spake, and as he said,
A bullet whistles o'er his head;
The foremost Tartar bites the ground!
 Scarce had they time to check the rein,
Swift from their steeds the riders bound;
 But three shall never mount again:
Unseen the foes that gave the wound,
 The dying ask revenge in vain.
With steel unsheath'd, and carbine bent,
Some o'er their courser's harness leant,
 Half shelter'd by the steed;
Some fly behind the nearest rock,
And there await the coming shock,

Nor tamely stand to bleed
Beneath the shaft of foes unseen,
Who dare not quit their craggy screen.
Stern Hassan only from his horse
Disdains to light, and keeps his course,
Till fiery flashes in the van
Proclaim too sure the robber-clan
Have well secured the only way
Could now avail the promised prey;
Then curl'd his very beard with ire,
And glared his eye with fiercer fire;
"Though far and near the bullets hiss,
I've scaped a bloodier hour than this."
And now the foe their covert quit,
And call his vassals to submit;
But Hassan's frown and furious word
Are dreaded more than hostile sword,
Nor of his little band a man
Resign'd carbine or ataghan,
Nor raised the craven cry, Amaun!
In fuller sight, more near and near,
The lately ambush'd foes appear,
And issuing from the grove, advance
Some who on battle-charger prance.
Who leads them on with foreign brand
Far flashing in his red right hand?
"'Tis he! 'tis he! I know him now;
I know him by his pallid brow;
I know him by the evil eye
That aids his envious treachery;
I know him by his jet-black barb;
Though now array'd in Arnaut garb,
Apostate from his own vile faith,
It shall not save him from the death:
'Tis he! well met in any hour,
Lost Leila's love, accursed Giaour!"

As rolls the river into ocean,
In sable torrent wildly streaming;
As the sea-tide's opposing motion,
In azure column proudly gleaming,
Beats back the current many a rood,
In curling foam and mingling flood,
While eddying whirl, and breaking wave,
Roused by the blast of winter, rave;
Through sparkling spray, in thundering clash,
The lightnings of the waters flash
In awful whiteness o'er the shore,
That shines and shakes beneath the roar;
Thus—as the stream and ocean greet,
With waves that madden as they meet—
Thus join the bands, whom mutual wrong,
And fate, and fury, drive along.
The bickering sabres' shivering jar;
And pealing wide or ringing near
Its echoes on the throbbing ear,
The deathshot hissing from afar;
The shock, the shout, the groan of war,
Reverberate along that vale,
More suited to the shepherd's tale:

Though few the numbers—theirs the strife,
That neither spares nor speaks for life!
Ah! fondly youthful hearts can press,
To seize and share the dear caress;
But Love itself could never pant
For all that Beauty sighs to grant
With half the fervour Hate bestows
Upon the last embrace of foes,
When grappling in the fight they fold
Those arms that ne'er shall lose their
 hold:
Friends meet to part; Love laughs at faith;
True foes, once met, are join'd till death!

.

With sabre shiver'd to the hilt,
Yet dripping with the blood he spilt;
Yet strain'd within the sever'd hand
Which quivers round that faithless brand;
His turban far behind him roll'd,
And cleft in twain its firmest fold;
His flowing robe by falchion torn,
And crimson as those clouds of morn
That, streak'd with dusky red, portend
The day shall have a stormy end;
A stain on every bush that bore
A fragment of his palampore;
His breast with wounds unnumber'd riven,
His back to earth, his face to heaven,
Fall'n Hassan lies—his unclosed eye
Yet lowering on his enemy,
As if the hour that seal'd his fate
Surviving left his quenchless hate;
And o'er him bends that foe with brow
As dark as his that bled below.—

"Yes, Leila sleeps beneath the wave,
But his shall be a redder grave;
Her spirit pointed well the steel
Which taught that felon heart to feel.
He call'd the Prophet, but his power
Was vain against the vengeful Giaour:
He call'd on Alla, but the word
Arose unheeded or unheard.
Thou Paynim fool! could Leila's prayer
Be pass'd, and thine accorded there?
I watch'd my time, I leagued with these,
The traitor in his turn to seize;
My wrath is wreak'd, the deed is done,
And now I go—but go alone."

.

The browsing camels' bells are tinkling:
His mother look'd from her lattice high—
 She saw the dews of eve besprinkling
The pasture green beneath her eye,
 She saw the planets faintly twinkling:
"'T is twilight—sure his train is nigh."

She could not rest in the garden-bower,
But gazed through the grate of his steepest
 tower:
"Why comes he not? his steeds are fleet,
Nor shrink they from the summer heat;
Why sends not the Bridegroom his promised
 gift?
Is his heart more cold, or his barb less
 swift?
Oh, false reproach! yon Tartar now
Has gain'd our nearest mountain's brow,
And warily the steep descends,
And now within the valley bends;
And he bears the gift at his saddle-bow—
How could I deem his courser slow?
Right well my largess shall repay
His welcome speed and weary way."

The Tartar lighted at the gate,
But scarce upheld his fainting weight:
His swarthy visage spake distress,
But this might be from weariness;
His garb with sanguine spots was dyed,
But these might be from his courser's side;
He drew the token from his vest—
Angel of Death! 'tis Hassan's cloven crest!
His calpac rent—his caftan red—
"Lady, a fearful bride thy son hath wed:
Me, not from mercy, did they spare,
But this empurpled pledge to bear.
Peace to the brave! whose blood is spilt:
Woe to the Giaour! for his the guilt."

A turban carved in coarsest stone,
A pillar with rank weeds o'ergrown,
Whereon can now be scarcely read
The Koran verse that mourns the dead,
Point out the spot where Hassan fell
A victim in that lonely dell.
There sleeps as true an Osmanlie
As e'er at Mecca bent the knee;
As ever scorn'd forbidden wine,
Or pray'd with face towards the shrine,
In orisons resumed anew
At solemn sound of "Alla Hu!"
Yet died he by a stranger's hand,
And stranger in his native land;
Yet died he as in arms he stood,
And unavenged, at least in blood.
But him the maids of Paradise
 Impatient to their halls invite,
And the dark heaven of Houris' eyes
 On him shall glance for ever bright;
They come—their kerchiefs green they
 wave,
And welcome with a kiss the brave!
Who falls in battle 'gainst a Giaour
Is worthiest an immortal bower.

But thou, false Infidel! shalt writhe
Beneath avenging Monkir's scythe;
And from its torment 'scape alone
To wander round lost Eblis' throne;
And fire unquench'd, unquenchable,
Around, within, thy heart shall dwell;
Nor ear can hear nor tongue can tell
The tortures of that inward hell!
But first, on earth as Vampire sent,
Thy corse shall from its tomb be rent:
Then ghastly haunt thy native place,
And suck the blood of all thy race;
There from thy daughter, sister, wife,
At midnight drain the stream of life;
Yet loathe the banquet which perforce
Must feed thy livid living corse:
Thy victims ere they yet expire
Shall know the demon for their sire,
As cursing thee, thou cursing them,
Thy flowers are wither'd on the stem.
But one that for thy crime must fall,
The youngest, most beloved of all,
Shall bless thee with a *father's* name—
That word shall wrap thy heart in flame!
Yet must thou end thy task, and mark
Her cheek's last tinge, her eye's last spark,
And the last glassy glance must view
Which freezes o'er its lifeless blue;
Then with unhallow'd hand shalt tear
The tresses of her yellow hair,
Of which in life a lock when shorn,
Affection's fondest pledge was worn,
But now is borne away by thee,
Memorial of thine agony!
Wet with thine own best blood shall drip
Thy gnashing tooth and haggard lip;
Then stalking to thy sullen grave,
Go—and with Gouls and Afrits rave;
Till these in horror shrink away
From spectre more accursed than they!

"How name ye yon lone Caloyer?
 His features I have scann'd before
In mine own land: 'tis many a year,
 Since, dashing by the lonely shore,
I saw him urge as fleet a steed
As ever served a horseman's need.
But once I saw that face, yet then
It was so mark'd with inward pain,
I could not pass it by again;
It breathes the same dark spirit now,
As death were stamp'd upon his brow.

"'Tis twice three years at summer tide
 Since first among our freres he came;
And here it soothes him to abide
 For some dark deed he will not name.
But never at our vesper prayer,
Nor e'er before confession chair

Kneels he, nor recks he when arise
Incense or anthem to the skies,
But broods within his cell alone,
His faith and race alike unknown.
The sea from Paynim land he crost,
And here ascended from the coast;
Yet seems he not of Othman race,
But only Christian in his face:
I'd judge him some stray renegade,
Repentant of the change he made,
Save that he shuns our holy shrine,
Nor tastes the sacred bread and wine.
Great largess to these walls he brought,
And thus our abbot's favour bought;
But were I prior, not a day
Should brook such stranger's further stay,
Or pent within our penance cell
Should doom him there for aye to dwell.
Much in his visions mutters he
Of maiden whelm'd beneath the sea;
Of sabres clashing, foemen flying,
Wrongs avenged, and Moslem dying.
On cliff he hath been known to stand,
And rave as to some bloody hand
Fresh sever'd from its parent limb,
Invisible to all but him,
Which beckons onward to his grave,
And lures to leap into the wave."

.
. . . .

Dark and unearthly is the scowl
That glares beneath his dusky cowl.
The flash of that dilating eye
Reveals too much of times gone by;
Though varying, indistinct its hue,
Oft will his glance the gazer rue,
For in it lurks that nameless spell,
Which speaks, itself unspeakable,
A spirit yet unquell'd and high,
That claims and keeps ascendency;
And like the bird whose pinions quake,
But cannot fly the gazing snake,
Will others quail beneath his look,
Nor 'scape the glance they scarce can brook.
From him the half-affrighted Friar
When met alone would fain retire,
As if that eye and bitter smile
Transferr'd to others fear and guile:
Not oft to smile descendeth he,
And when he doth 'tis sad to see
That he but mocks at Misery.
How that pale lip will curl and quiver!
Then fix once more as if for ever;
As if his sorrow or disdain
Forbade him e'er to smile again.
Well were it so—such ghastly mirth
From joyaunce ne'er derived its birth.
But sadder still it were to trace
What once were feelings in that face:

Time hath not yet the features fix'd,
But brighter traits with evil mix'd;
And there are hues not always faded,
Which speak a mind not all degraded
Even by the crimes through which it waded:
The common crowd but see the gloom
Of wayward deeds, and fitting doom;
The close observer can espy
A noble soul, and lineage high:
Alas! though both bestow'd in vain,
Which Grief could change, and Guilt could
	stain,
It was no vulgar tenement
To which such lofty gifts were lent,
And still with little less than dread
On such the sight is riveted.
The roofless cot, decay'd and rent,
	Will scarce delay the passer by;
The tower by war or tempest bent,
While yet may frown one battlement,
	Demands and daunts the stranger's eye;
Each ivied arch, and pillar lone,
Pleads haughtily for glories gone!

His floating robe around him folding,
	Slow sweeps he through the column'd aisle;
With dread beheld, with gloom beholding
	The rites that sanctify the pile.
But when the anthem shakes the choir,
And kneel the monks, his steps retire;
By yonder lone and wavering torch
His aspect glares within the porch;
There will he pause till all is done—
And hear the prayer, but utter none.
See—by the half-illumined wall
His hood fly back, his dark hair fall,
That pale brow wildly wreathing round,
As if the Gorgon there had bound
The sablest of the serpent-braid
That o'er her fearful forehead stray'd:
For he declines the convent oath,
And leaves those locks unhallow'd growth,
But wears our garb in all beside;
And, not from piety but pride,
Gives wealth to walls that never heard
Of his one holy vow nor word.
Lo!—mark ye, as the harmony
Peals louder praises to the sky,
That livid cheek, that stony air
Of mix'd defiance and despair!
Saint Francis, keep him from the shrine!
Else may we dread the wrath divine
Made manifest by awful sign.
If ever evil angel bore
The form of mortal, such he wore;
By all my hope of sins forgiven,
Such looks are not of earth nor heaven!"

To love the softest hearts are prone,
But such can ne'er be all his own;

Too timid in his woes to share,
Too meek to meet, or brave despair;
And sterner hearts alone may feel
The wound that time can never heal.
The rugged metal of the mine
Must burn before its surface shine,
But plunged within the furnace-flame,
It bends and melts—though still the same;
Then temper'd to thy want, or will,
'T will serve thee to defend or kill;
A breastplate for thine hour of need,
Or blade to bid thy foeman bleed;
But if a dagger's form it bear,
Let those who shape its edge beware!
Thus passion's fire, and woman's art,
Can turn and tame the sterner heart;
From these its form and tone are ta'en,
And what they metal make it, must remain,
But break—before it bend again.

If solitude succeed to grief,
Release from pain is slight relief;
The vacant bosom's wilderness
Might thank the pang that made it less.
We loathe what none are left to share:
Even bliss—'twere woe alone to bear;
The heart once thus left desolate
Must fly at last for ease—to hate.
It is as if the dead could feel
The icy worm around them steal,
And shudder, as the reptiles creep
To revel o'er their rotting sleep,
Without the power to scare away
The cold consumers of their clay!
It is as if the desert bird,
 Whose beak unlocks her bosom's stream
To still her famish'd nestlings' scream,
Nor mourns a life to them transferr'd,
Should rend her rash devoted breast,
And find them flown her empty nest.
The keenest pangs the wretched find
 Are rapture to the dreary void,
The leafless desert of the mind,
 The waste of feelings unemploy'd.
Who would be doom'd to gaze upon
A sky without a cloud or sun?
Less hideous far the tempest's roar
Than ne'er to brave the billows more—
Thrown, when the war of winds is o'er,
A lonely wreck on fortune's shore,
'Mid sullen calm, and silent bay,
Unseen to drop by dull decay;—
Better to sink beneath the shock
Than moulder piecemeal on the rock!

"Father! thy days have pass'd in peace,
 'Mid counted beads, and countless prayer;
To bid the sins of others cease,

Thyself without a crime or care,
Save transient ills that all must bear,
Has been thy lot from youth to age;
And thou wilt bless thee from the rage
Of passions fierce and uncontroll'd,
Such as thy penitents unfold,
Whose secret sins and sorrows rest
Within thy pure and pitying breast.
My days, though few, have pass'd below
In much of joy, but more of woe;
Yet still in hours of love or strife,
I've 'scaped the weariness of life:
Now leagued with friends, now girt by foes,
I loathed the languor of repose.
Now nothing left to love or hate,
No more with hope or pride elate,
I'd rather be the thing that crawls
Most noxious o'er a dungeon's walls,
Than pass my dull, unvarying days,
Condemn'd to meditate and gaze.
Yet, lurks a wish within my breast
For rest—but not to feel 'tis rest.
Soon shall my fate that wish fulfil;
 And I shall sleep without the dream
Of what I was, and would be still,
 Dark as to thee my deeds may seem:
My memory now is but the tomb
Of joys long dead; my hope, their doom:
Though better to have died with those
Than bear a life of lingering woes.
My spirit shrunk not to sustain
The searching throes of ceaseless pain;
Nor sought the self-accorded grave
Of ancient fool and modern knave:
Yet death I have not fear'd to meet;
And in the field it had been sweet,
Had danger woo'd me on to move
The slave of glory, not of love.
I've braved it—not for honour's boast;
I smile at laurels won or lost;
To such let others carve their way,
For high renown, or hireling pay:
But place again before my eyes
Aught that I deem a worthy prize—
The maid I love, the man I hate—
And I will hunt the steps of fate,
To save or slay, as these require,
Through rending steel and rolling fire:
Nor need'st thou doubt this speech from one
Who would but do—what he *hath* done.
Death is but what the haughty brave,
The weak must bear, the wretch must crave;
Then let life go to Him who gave:
I have not quail'd to danger's brow
When high and happy—need I *now?*

"I loved her, Friar! nay, adored—
But these are words that all can use—
I proved it more in deed than word;
There's blood upon that dinted sword,
A stain its steel can never lose:
'Twas shed for her, who died for me,
It warm'd the heart of one abhorr'd:
Nay, start not—no—nor bend thy knee,
Nor midst my sins such act record;
Thou wilt absolve me from the deed,
For he was hostile to thy creed!
The very name of Nazarene
Was wormwood to his Paynim spleen.
Ungrateful fool! since but for brands
Well wielded in some hardy hands,
And wounds by Galileans given,
The surest pass to Turkish heaven,
For him his Houris still might wait
Impatient at the Prophet's gate.
I loved her—love will find its way
Through paths where wolves would fear to prey;
And if it dares enough, 'twere hard
If passion met not some reward—
No matter how, or where, or why,
I did not vainly seek, nor sigh:
Yet sometimes, with remorse, in vain
I wish she had not loved again.
She died—I dare not tell thee how;
But look—'tis written on my brow!
There read of Cain the curse and crime,
In characters unworn by time:
Still, ere thou dost condemn me, pause;
Not mine the act, though I the cause.
Yet did he but what I had done
Had she been false to more than one.
Faithless to him, he gave the blow;
But true to me, I laid him low:
Howe'er deserved her doom might be,
Her treachery was truth to me;
To me she gave her heart, that all
Which tyranny can ne'er enthral:
And I, alas! too late to save!
Yet all I then could give, I gave,
'Twas some relief, our foe a grave.
His death sits lightly; but her fate
Has made me—what thou well may'st hate.
His doom was seal'd—he knew it well,
Warn'd by the voice of stern Taheer,
Deep in whose darkly boding ear
The deathshot peal'd of murder near
As filed the troop to where they fell!
He died too in the battle broil,
A time that heeds nor pain nor toil;
One cry to Mahomet for aid,
One prayer to Alla all he made:
He knew and cross'd me in the fray—
I gazed upon him where he lay,
And watch'd his spirit ebb away;
Though pierced like pard by hunter s steel,
He felt not half that now I feel.

I search'd, but vainly search'd, to find
The workings of a wounded mind;
Each feature of that sullen corse
Betray'd his rage, but no remorse.
Oh, what had Vengeance given to trace
Despair upon his dying face!
The late repentance of that hour,
When Penitence hath lost her power
To tear one terror from the grave,
And will not soothe, and cannot save.

. . . .

"The cold in clime are cold in blood,
Their love can scarce deserve the name;
But mine was like the lava flood
That boils in Ætna's breast of flame.
I cannot prate in puling strain
Of ladye-love and beauty's chain:
If changing cheek, and scorching vein,
Lips taught to writhe, but not complain,
If bursting heart, and madd'ning brain,
And daring deed, and vengeful steel,
And all that I have felt, and feel,
Betoken love—that love was mine,
And shown by many a bitter sign.
'Tis true, I could not whine nor sigh,
I knew but to obtain or die.
I die—but first I have possess'd,
And come what may, I *have been* bless'd.
Shall I the doom I sought upbraid?
No—reft of all, yet undismay'd
But for the thought of Leila slain,
Give me the pleasure with the pain,
So would I live and love again.
I grieve, but not, my holy guide!
For him who dies, but her who died:
She sleeps beneath the wandering wave—
Ah! had she but an earthly grave,
This breaking heart and throbbing head
Should seek and share her narrow bed.
She was a form of life and light,
That, seen, became a part of sight;
And rose, where'er I turn'd mine eye,
The Morning-star of Memory!

"Yes, Love indeed is light from hea-
 ven;
 A spark of that immortal fire
With angels shared, by Alla given,
 To lift from earth our low desire.
Devotion wafts the mind above,
But Heaven itself descends in love;
A feeling from the Godhead caught,
To wean from self each sordid thought;
A Ray of him who form'd the whole;
A Glory circling round the soul!
I grant *my* love imperfect, all
That mortals by the name miscall;
Then deem it evil, what thou wilt;
But say, oh say, *hers* was not guilt!

She was my life's unerring light:
That quench'd, what beam shall break my
 night?
Oh! would it shone to lead me still,
Although to death or deadliest ill!
Why marvel ye, if they who lose
 This present joy, this future hope,
 No more with sorrow meekly cope;
In phrensy then their fate accuse;
In madness do those fearful deeds
 That seem to add but guilt to woe?
Alas! the breast that inly bleeds
 Hath nought to dread from outward
 blow:
Who falls from all he knows of bliss,
Cares little into what abyss.
Fierce as the gloomy vulture's now
 To thee, old man, my deeds appear:
I read abhorrence on thy brow,
 And this too was I born to bear!
'Tis true, that, like that bird of prey,
With havoc have I mark'd my way:
But this was taught me by the dove,
To die—and know no second love.
This lesson yet hath man to learn,
Taught by the thing he dares to spurn:
The bird that sings within the brake,
The swan that swims upon the lake,
One mate, and one alone, will take.
And let the fool still prone to range,
And sneer on all who cannot change,
Partake his jest with boasting boys;
I envy not his varied joys,
But deem such feeble, heartless man
Less than yon solitary swan;
Far, far beneath the shallow maid
He left believing and betray'd.
Such shame at least was never mine—
Leila! each thought was only thine!
My good, my guilt, my weal, my woe,
My hope on high—my all below.
Earth holds no other like to thee,
Or, if it doth, in vain for me:
For worlds I dare not view the dame
Resembling thee, yet not the same.
The very crimes that mar my youth,
This bed of death—attest my truth!
'Tis all too late—thou wert, thou art
The cherish'd madness of my heart!

"And she was lost—and yet I breathed,
 But not the breath of human life:
A serpent round my heart was wreathed,
 And stung my every thought to strife.
Alike all time, abhorr'd all place,
Shuddering I shrunk from Nature's face,
Where every hue that charm'd before
The blackness of my bosom wore.
The rest thou dost already know,
And all my sins, and half my woe.

But talk no more of penitence;
Thou seest I soon shall part from hence:
And if thy holy tale were true,
The deed that's done canst *thou* undo?
Think me not thankless—but this grief
Looks not to priesthood for relief.
My soul's estate in secret guess:
But wouldst thou pity more, say less.
When thou canst bid my Leila live,
Then will I sue thee to forgive;
Then plead my cause in that high place
Where purchased masses proffer grace.
Go, when the hunter's hand hath wrung
From forest-cave her shrieking young,
And calm the lonely lioness:
But soothe not—mock not *my* distress!

"In earlier days, and calmer hours,
 When heart with heart delights to blend,
Where bloom my native valley's bowers,
 I had—Ah! have I now?—a friend!
To him this pledge I charge thee send,
 Memorial of a youthful vow;
I would remind him of my end:
 Though souls absorb'd like mine allow
Brief thought to distant friendship's claim,
Yet dear to him my blighted name.
'Tis strange—he prophesied my doom,
 And I have smiled—I then could smile—
When Prudence would his voice assume,
 And warn—I reck'd not what—the while:
But now remembrance whispers o'er
Those accents scarcely mark'd before.
Say—that his bodings came to pass,
And he will start to hear their truth,
And wish his words had not been sooth:
Tell him, unheeding as I was,
 Through many a busy bitter scene
 Of all our golden youth had been,
In pain, my faltering tongue had tried
To bless his memory ere I died;
But Heaven in wrath would turn away
If Guilt should for the guiltless pray.
I do not ask him not to blame,
Too gentle he to wound my name;
And what have I to do with fame?
I do not ask him not to mourn,
Such cold request might sound like scorn;
And what than friendship's manly tear
May better grace a brother's bier?
But bear this ring, his own of old,
And tell him—what thou dost behold!
The wither'd frame, the ruin'd mind,
The wrack by passion left behind,
A shrivell'd scroll, a scatter'd leaf,
Sear'd by the autumn blast of grief!

"Tell me no more of fancy's gleam,
No, father, no, 'twas not a dream;

Alas! the dreamer first must sleep,
I only watch'd, and wish'd to weep,
But could not, for my burning brow
Throbb'd to the very brain as now:
I wish'd but for a single tear,
As something welcome, new, and dear:
I wish'd it then, I wish it still;
Despair is stronger than my will.
Waste not thine orison, despair
Is mightier than thy pious prayer:
I would not, if I might, be blest;
I want no paradise, but rest.
'T was then, I tell thee, father! then
I saw her; yes, she lived again;
And shining in her white symar,
As through yon pale gray cloud the star
Which now I gaze on, as on her,
Who look'd and looks far lovelier;
Dimly I view its trembling spark;
To-morrow's night shall be more dark;
And I, before its rays appear,
That lifeless thing the living fear.
I wander, father! for my soul
Is fleeting towards the final goal.
I saw her, friar! and I rose
Forgetful of our former woes;
And rushing from my couch, I dart,
And clasp her to my desperate heart;
I clasp—what is it that I clasp?
No breathing form within my grasp,
No heart that beats reply to mine—
Yet, Leila! yet the form is thine!
And art thou, dearest, changed so much
As meet my eye, yet mock my touch?
Ah! were thy beauties e'er so cold,
I care not so my arms enfold
The all they ever wish'd to hold.
Alas! around a shadow prest
They shrink upon my lonely breast;
Yet still 't is there! In silence stands,

And beckons with beseeching hands!
With braided hair, and bright-black eye-
I knew 't was false—she could not die!
But he is dead! within the dell
I saw him buried where he fell;
He comes not, for he cannot break
From earth; why then art thou awake?
They told me wild waves roll'd above
The face I view, the form I love;
They told me—'t was a hideous tale!—
I'd tell it, but my tongue would fail:
If true, and from thine ocean-cave
Thou com'st to claim a calmer grave,
Oh! pass thy dewy fingers o'er
This brow that then will burn no more;
Or place them on my hopeless heart:
But, shape or shade! whate'er thou art,
In mercy ne'er again depart!
Or farther with thee bear my soul
Than winds can waft or waters roll!

.

" Such is my name, and such my tale.
 Confessor! to thy secret ear
I breathe the sorrows I bewail,
 And thank thee for the generous tear
This glazing eye could never shed.
Then lay me with the humblest dead,
And, save the cross above my head,
Be neither name nor emblem spread,
By prying stranger to be read,
Or stay the passing pilgrim's tread."

 He pass'd—nor of his name and race
Hath left a token or a trace,
Save what the father must not say
Who shrived him on his dying day:
This broken tale was all we knew
Of her he loved, or him he slew.

The Bride of Abydos:

A TURKISH TALE.

"Had we never loved so kindly,
Had we never loved so blindly,
Never met or never parted,
We had ne'er been broken-hearted."—BURNS.

TO

THE RIGHT HON. LORD HOLLAND,

THIS TALE IS INSCRIBED,

WITH EVERY SENTIMENT OF REGARD AND RESPECT,
BY HIS GRATEFULLY OBLIGED AND SINCERE FRIEND,

BYRON.

Canto the First.

I.

KNOW ye the land where the cypress and
 myrtle
 Are emblems of deeds that are done in their
 clime?
Where the rage of the vulture, the love of the
 turtle,
 Now melt into sorrow, now madden to
 crime!
Know ye the land of the cedar and vine,
Where the flowers ever blossom, the beams
 ever shine;
Where the light wings of Zephyr, oppress'd
 with perfume,
Wax faint o'er the gardens of Gúl in her
 bloom;
Where the citron and olive are fairest of
 fruit,
And the voice of the nightingale never is
 mute;
Where the tints of the earth, and the hues of
 the sky,
In colour though varied, in beauty may
 vie,
And the purple of ocean is deepest in dye;
Where the virgins are soft as the roses they
 twine,
And all, save the spirit of man, is divine?
'T is the clime of the East; 't is the land of
 the Sun—
Can he smile on such deeds as his children
 have done?

Oh! wild as the accents of lovers' farewell
Are the hearts which they bear, and the tales
 which they tell.

II.

Begirt with many a gallant slave,
Apparell'd as becomes the brave,
Awaiting each his lord's behest
To guide his steps, or guard his rest,
Old Giaffir sate in his Divan:
 Deep thought was in his aged eye;
And though the face of Mussulman
 Not oft betrays to standers by
The mind within, well skill'd to hide
All but unconquerable pride,
His pensive cheek and pondering brow
Did more than he was wont avow.

III.

"Let the chamber be clear'd."—The train
 disappear'd.—
"Now call me the chief of the Haram guard."
With Giaffir is none but his only son,
And the Nubian awaiting the sire's award.
 "Haroun—when all the crowd that wait
 Are pass'd beyond the outer gate,
 (Woe to the head whose eye beheld
 My child Zuleika's face unveil'd!)
Hence, lead my daughter from her tower;
Her fate is fix'd this very hour:
Yet not to her repeat my thought;
By me alone be duty taught!"

"Pacha! to hear is to obey."
No more must slave to despot say—
Then to the tower had ta'en his way,

But here young Selim silence brake,
 First lowly rendering reverence meet;
And downcast look'd, and gently spake,
 Still standing at the Pacha's feet:
For son of Moslem must expire,
Ere dare to sit before his sire!

"Father! for fear that thou shouldst chide
My sister, or her sable guide,
Know—for the fault, if fault there be,
Was mine, then fall thy frowns on me—
So lovelily the morning shone,
 That—let the old and weary sleep—
I could not; and to view alone
 The fairest scenes of land and deep,
With none to listen and reply
To thoughts with which my heart beat high
Were irksome—for whate'er my mood,
In sooth I love not solitude;
I on Zuleika's slumber broke,
 And, as thou knowest that for me
 Soon turns the Haram's grating key,
Before the guardian slaves awoke
We to the cypress groves had flown,
And made earth, main, and heaven our
 own!
There linger'd we, beguiled too long
With Mejnoun's tale, or Sadi's song;
Till I, who heard the deep tambour
Beat thy Divan's approaching hour,
To thee, and to my duty true,
Warn'd by the sound, to greet thee flew:
But there Zuleika wanders yet—
Nay, Father, rage not—nor forget
That none can pierce that secret bower
But those who watch the women's tower."

IV.

"Son of a slave"—the Pacha said—
"From unbelieving mother bred,
Vain were a father's hope to see
Aught that beseems a man in thee.
Thou, when thine arm should bend the
 bow,
 And hurl the dart, and curb the steed,
 Thou, Greek in soul if not in creed,
Must pore where babbling waters flow,
And watch unfolding roses blow.
Would that yon orb, whose matin glow
Thy listless eyes so much admire,
Would lend thee something of his fire!
Thou, who wouldst see this battlement
By Christian cannon piecemeal rent;
Nay, tamely view old Stambol's wall
Before the dogs of Moscow fall,
Nor strike one stroke for life and death
Against the curse of Nazareth!
Go—let thy less than woman's hand
Assume the distaff—not the brand.

But, Haroun!—to my daughter speed;
And hark—of thine own head take heed—
If thus Zuleika oft takes wing—
Thou see'st yon bow—it hath a string!"

V.

No sound from Selim's lip was heard,
 At least that met old Giaffir's ear,
But every frown and every word
Pierced keener than a Christian's sword.
 "Son of a slave!—reproach'd with fear!
 Those gibes had cost another dear.
Son of a slave!—and *who* my sire?"
Thus held his thoughts their dark career;
And glances ev'n of more than ire
Flash forth, then faintly disappear.
Old Giaffir gazed upon his son
 And started; for within his eye
He read how much his wrath had done;
 He saw rebellion there begun:
 "Come hither, boy—what, no reply?
I mark thee—and I know thee too;
But there be deeds thou dar'st not do:
But if thy beard had manlier length,
And if thy hand had skill and strength,
I'd joy to see thee break a lance,
Albeit against my own perchance."

As sneeringly these accents fell,
On Selim's eye he fiercely gazed:
 That eye return'd him glance for glance,
And proudly to his sire's was raised,
 Till Giaffir's quail'd and shrunk askance—
And why—he felt, but durst not tell.
"Much I misdoubt this wayward boy
Will one day work me more annoy:
I never loved him from his birth,
And—but his arm is little worth,
And scarcely in the chase could cope
With timid fawn or antelope,
Far less would venture into strife
Where man contends for fame and life—
I would not trust that look or tone:
No—nor the blood so near my own.
That blood—he hath not heard—no more—
I'll watch him closer than before.
He is an Arab to my sight,
Or Christian crouching in the fight—
But hark!—I hear Zuleika's voice;
 Like Houris' hymn it meets mine ear:
She is the offspring of my choice;
 Oh! more than ev'n her mother dear,
With all to hope, and nought to fear—
My Peri! ever welcome here!
Sweet, as the desert fountain's wave
To lips just cool'd in time to save—
 Such to my longing sight art thou;
Nor can they waft to Mecca's shrine
More thanks for life, than I for thine,
 Who blest thy birth and bless thee now."

VI.

Fair, as the first that fell of womankind,
 When on that dread yet lovely serpent
 smiling,
Whose image then was stamp'd upon her
 mind—
 But once beguil'd—and ever more be-
 guiling;
Dazzling, as that, oh! too transcendent vision
 To Sorrow's phantom-peopled slumber
 given,
When heart meets heart again in dreams
 Elysian,
 And paints the lost on Earth revived in
 Heaven;
Soft, as the memory of buried love;
Pure, as the prayer which Childhood wafts
 above,
Was she—the daughter of that rude old Chief,
Who met the maid with tears—but not of
 grief.

Who hath not proved how feebly words essay
To fix one spark of Beauty's heavenly ray?
Who doth not feel, until his failing sight
Faints into dimness with its own delight,
His changing cheek, his sinking heart confess
The might, the majesty of Loveliness?
Such was Zuleika, such around her shone
The nameless charms unmark'd by her
 alone—
The light of love, the purity of grace,
The mind, the Music breathing from her face,
The heart whose softness harmonized the
 whole,
And oh! that eye was in itself a Soul!

 Her graceful arms in meekness bending
 Across her gently-budding breast;
 At one kind word those arms extending
 To clasp the neck of him who blest
 His child caressing and carest,
Zuleika came—and Giaffir felt
His purpose half within him melt:
Not that against her fancied weal
His heart though stern could ever feel;
Affection chain'd her to that heart;
Ambition tore the links apart.

VII.

"Zuleika! child of gentleness!
 How dear this very day must tell,
When I forget my own distress,
 In losing what I love so well,
 To bid thee with another dwell:
Another! and a braver man
Was never seen in battle's van.
We Moslem reck not much of blood;
 But yet the line of Carasman
Unchanged, unchangeable hath stood

First of the bold Timariot bands
That won and well can keep their lands.
Enough that he who comes to woo
Is kinsman of the Bey Oglou:
His years need scarce a thought employ;
I would not have thee wed a boy.
And thou shalt have a noble dower:
And his and my united power
Will laugh to scorn the death-firman,
Which others tremble but to scan,
And teach the messenger what fate
The bearer of such boon may wait.
And now thou know'st thy father's will:
All that thy sex hath need to know:
'Twas mine to teach obedience still—
The way to love, thy lord may show."

VIII.

In silence bow'd the virgin's head;
 And if her eye was fill'd with tears
That stifled feeling dare not shed,
 And changed her cheek from pale to red,
 And red to pale, as through her ears
Those winged words like arrows sped,
 What could such be but maiden fears?
So bright the tear in Beauty's eye,
Love half regrets to kiss it dry;
So sweet the blush of Bashfulness,
Even Pity scarce can wish it less!

Whate'er it was the sire forgot;
Or if remember'd, mark'd it not;
Thrice clapp'd his hands, and call'd his
 steed,
 Resign'd his gem-adorn'd chibouque,
And mounting featly for the mead,
 With Maugrabee and Mamaluke,
 His way amid his Delis took,
To witness many an active deed
With sabre keen, or blunt jerreed.
The Kislar only and his Moors
Watch well the Haram's massy doors.

IX.

His head was leant upon his hand,
 His eye look'd o'er the dark blue water
That swiftly glides and gently swells
Between the winding Dardanelles;
But yet he saw nor sea nor strand,
Nor even his Pacha's turban'd band
 Mix in the game of mimic slaughter,
Careering cleave the folded felt,
With sabre stroke right sharply dealt;
Nor mark'd the javelin-darting crowd
Nor heard their Ollahs wild and loud—
 He thought but of old Giaffir's daughter!

X.

No word from Selim's bosom broke;
One sigh Zuleika's thought bespoke:

Still gazed he through the lattice grate,
Pale, mute, and mournfully sedate.
To him Zuleika's eye was turn'd,
But little from his aspect learn'd:
Equal her grief, yet not the same;
Her heart confess'd a gentler flame:
But yet that heart, alarm'd or weak,
She knew not why, forbade to speak.
Yet speak she must—but when essay?
"How strange he thus should turn away!
Not thus we e'er before have met;
Nor thus shall be our parting yet."
Thrice paced she slowly through the room,
 And watch'd his eye—it still was fix'd:
She snatch'd the urn wherein was mix'd
The Persian Atar-gul's perfume,
And sprinkled all its odours o'er
The pictured roof and marble floor:
The drops, that through his glittering vest
The playful girl's appeal address'd,
Unheeded o'er his bosom flew,
As if that breast were marble too.
"What, sullen yet? it must not be—
Oh! gentle Selim, this from thee!"
She saw in curious order set
 The fairest flowers of eastern land—
"He loved them once; may touch them yet,
 If offer'd by Zuleika's hand."
The childish thought was hardly breathed
Before the rose was pluck'd and wreathed;
The next fond moment saw her seat
Her fairy form at Selim's feet:
"This rose to calm my brother's cares
A message from the Bulbul bears;
It says to-night he will prolong
For Selim's ear his sweetest song;
And though his note is somewhat sad,
He'll try for once a strain more glad,
With some faint hope his alter'd lay
May sing these gloomy thoughts away.

XI.

"What! not receive my foolish flower?
 Nay then I am indeed unblest:
On me can thus thy forehead lower?
 And know'st thou not who loves thee best?
Oh, Selim dear! oh, more than dearest!
Say, is it me thou hat'st or fearest?
Come, lay thy head upon my breast,
And I will kiss thee into rest,
Since words of mine, and songs must fail,
Ev'n from my fabled nightingale.
I knew our sire at times was stern,
But this from thee had yet to learn:
Too well I know he loves thee not;
But is Zuleika's love forgot?
Ah! deem I right? the Pacha's plan—
This kinsman Bey of Carasman
Perhaps may prove some foe of thine.
If so, I swear by Mecca's shrine,—

If shrines that ne'er approach allow
To woman's step admit her vow,—
Without thy free consent, command,
The Sultan should not have my hand!
Think'st thou that I could bear to part
With thee, and learn to halve my heart?
Ah! were I sever'd from thy side,
Where were thy friend—and who my guide?
Years have not seen, Time shall not see,
The hour that tears my soul from thee:
Ev'n Azrael, from his deadly quiver
 When flies that shaft, and fly it must,
That parts all else, shall doom for ever
 Our hearts to undivided dust!"

XII.

He lived, he breathed, he moved, he felt;
He raised the maid from where she knelt;
His trance was gone, his keen eye shone
With thoughts that long in darkness dwelt;
With thoughts that burn—in rays that melt.
As the stream late conceal'd
 By the fringe of its willows,
When it rushes reveal'd
 In the light of its billows;
As the bolt bursts on high
 From the black cloud that bound it,
Flash'd the soul of that eye
 Through the long lashes round it.
A war-horse at the trumpet's sound,
A lion roused by heedless hound,
A tyrant waked to sudden strife
By graze of ill-directed knife,
Starts not to more convulsive life
Than he, who heard that vow, display'd,
And all, before repress'd, betray'd:
"Now thou art mine, for ever mine,
With life to keep, and scarce with life resign;
Now thou art mine, that sacred oath,
Though sworn by one, hath bound us both.
Yes, fondly, wisely hast thou done;
That vow hath saved more heads than one:
But blench not thou—thy simplest tress
Claims more from me than tenderness;
I would not wrong the slenderest hair
That clusters round thy forehead fair,
For all the treasures buried far
Within the caves of Istakar.
This morning clouds upon me lower'd,
Reproaches on my head were shower'd,
And Giaffir almost call'd me coward!
Now I have motive to be brave;
The son of his neglected slave,
Nay, start not, 'twas the term he gave,
May show, though little apt to vaunt,
A heart his words nor deeds can daunt.
His son, indeed!—yet, thanks to thee,
Perchance I am, at least shall be;
But let our plighted secret vow
Be only known to us as now.

I know the wretch who dares demand.
From Giaffir thy reluctant hand;
More ill-got wealth, a meaner soul
Holds not a Musselim's control:
Was he not bred in Egripo?
A viler race let Israel show!
But let that pass—to none be told
Our oath; the rest shall time unfold.
To me and mine leave Osman Bey;
I've partisans for peril's day:
Think not I am what I appear;
I've arms, and friends, and vengeance
　　near."

XIII.

"Think not thou art what thou appearest!
　My Selim, thou art sadly changed:
This morn I saw thee gentlest, dearest;
　But now thou'rt from thyself estranged.
My love thou surely knew'st before,
It ne'er was less, nor can be more.
To see thee, hear thee, near thee stay,
　And hate the night I know not why,
Save that we meet not but by day;
　With thee to live, with thee to die,
I dare not to my hope deny:
Thy cheek, thine eyes, thy lips to kiss,
Like this—and this—no more than this;
For, Allah! sure thy lips are flame:
　What fever in thy veins is flushing?
My own have nearly caught the same,
　At least I feel my cheek, too, blushing.
To soothe thy sickness, watch thy health,
Partake, but never waste thy wealth,
Or stand with smiles unmurmuring by,
And lighten half thy poverty;
Do all but close thy dying eye,
For that I could not live to try;
To these alone my thoughts aspire:
More can I do? or thou require?
But, Selim, thou must answer why
We need so much of mystery?
The cause I cannot dream nor tell,
But be it, since thou say'st 'tis well;
Yet what thou mean'st by 'arms' and
　'friends,'
Beyond my weaker sense extends.
I meant that Giaffir should have heard
　The very vow I plighted thee;
His wrath would not revoke my word:
　But surely he would leave me free.
　Can this fond wish seem strange in me,
To be what I have ever been?
What other hath Zuleika seen
From simple childhood's earliest hour?
　What other can she seek to see
Than thee, companion of her bower,
　The partner of her infancy?
These cherish'd thoughts with life begun,
　Say, why must I no more avow?

What change is wrought to make me shun
　The truth; my pride, and thine till now?
To meet the gaze of stranger's eyes
Our law, our creed, our God denies;
Nor shall one wandering thought of mine
At such, our Prophet's will, repine:
No! happier made by that decree,
He left me all in leaving thee.
Deep were my anguish, thus compell'd
To wed with one I ne'er beheld:
This wherefore should I not reveal?
Why wilt thou urge me to conceal?
I know the Pacha's haughty mood
To thee hath never boded good;
And he so often storms at nought,
Allah! forbid that e'er he ought!
And why I know not, but within
My heart concealment weighs like sin.
If then such secrecy be crime,
　And such it feels while lurking here;
Oh, Selim! tell me yet in time,
　Nor leave me thus to thoughts of fear.
Ah! yonder see the Tchocadar,
My father leaves the mimic war;
I tremble now to meet his eye—
Say, Selim, canst thou tell me why?"

XIV.

"Zuleika—to thy tower's retreat
Betake thee—Giaffir I can greet:
And now with him I fain must prate
Of firmans, imposts, levies, state.
There's fearful news from Danube's banks,
Our Vizier nobly thins his ranks,
For which the Giaour may give him thanks!
Our Sultan hath a shorter way
Such costly triumph to repay.
But, mark me, when the twilight drum
　Hath warn'd the troops to food and sleep.
Unto thy cell with Selim come:
　Then softly from the Haram creep
　Where we may wander by the deep:
　Our garden battlements are steep;
Nor these will rash intruder climb
To list our words, or stint our time;
And if he doth, I want not steel
Which some have felt, and more may feel.
Then shalt thou learn of Selim more
Than thou hast heard or thought before:
Trust me, Zuleika—fear not me!
Thou know'st I hold a Haram key."
"Fear thee, my Selim! ne'er till now
Did word like this——"
　　　　　　　　　"Delay not thou;
I keep the key—and Haroun's guard
Have some, and hope of more reward.
To-night, Zuleika, thou shalt hear
My tale, my purpose, and my fear:
I am not, love! what I appear."

Canto the Second.

I.

The winds are high on Helle's wave,
 As on that night of stormy water
When Love, who sent, forgot to save
The young, the beautiful, the brave,
 The lonely hope of Sestos' daughter.
Oh! when alone along the sky
Her turret-torch was blazing high,
Though rising gale, and breaking foam,
And shrieking sea-birds warn'd him home;
And clouds aloft and tides below,
With signs and sounds, forbade to go,
He could not see, he would not hear,
Or sound or sign foreboding fear;
His eye but saw that light of love,
The only star it hail'd above;
His ear but rang with Hero's song,
"Ye waves, divide not lovers long!"—
That tale is old, but love anew
May nerve young hearts to prove as true.

II.

The winds are high, and Helle's tide
 Rolls darkly heaving to the main;
And Night's descending shadows hide
 That field with blood bedew'd in vain,
The desert of old Priam's pride;
 The tombs, sole relics of his reign,
All—save immortal dreams that could beguile
The blind old man of Scio's rocky isle!

III.

Oh! yet—for there my steps have been;
 These feet have press'd the sacred shore,
These limbs that buoyant wave hath borne—
Minstrel! with thee to muse, to mourn,
 To trace again those fields of yore,
Believing every hillock green
 Contains no fabled hero's ashes,
And that around the undoubted scene
 Thine own "broad Hellespont" still
 dashes,
Be long my lot! and cold were he
Who there could gaze denying thee!

IV.

The night hath closed on Helle's stream,
 Nor yet hath risen on Ida's hill.
That moon, which shone on his high theme:
No warrior chides her peaceful beam,
 But conscious shepherds bless it still.
Their flocks are grazing on the mound
 Of him who felt the Dardan's arrow:
That mighty heap of gather'd ground
Which Ammon's son ran proudly round,
By nations raised, by monarchs crown'd,
 Is now a lone and nameless barrow!
Within—thy dwelling-place how narrow!

Without—can only strangers breathe
The name of him that *was* beneath:
Dust long outlasts the storied stone;
But Thou—thy very dust is gone!

V.

Late, late to-night will Dian cheer
The swain, and chase the boatman's fear;
Till then—no beacon on the cliff
May shape the course of struggling skiff;
The scatter'd lights that skirt the bay,
All, one by one, have died away;
The only lamp of this lone hour
Is glimmering in Zuleika's tower.
Yes! there is light in that lone chamber,
 And o'er her silken ottoman
Are thrown the fragrant beads of amber,
 O'er which her fairy fingers ran;
Near these, with emerald rays beset,
(How could she thus that gem forget?)
Her mother's sainted amulet,
Whereon engraved the Koorsee text,
Could smooth this life, and win the next;
And by her comboloio lies
A Koran of illumined dyes;
And many a bright emblazon'd rhyme
By Persian scribes redeem'd from time;
And o'er those scrolls, not oft so mute,
Reclines her now neglected lute;
And round her lamp of fretted gold
Bloom flowers in urns of China's mould;
The richest work of Iran's loom,
And Sheeraz' tribute of perfume;
All that can eye or sense delight
 Are gather'd in that gorgeous room:
But yet it hath an air of gloom.
She, of this Peri cell the sprite,
What doth she hence, and on so rude
 a night?

VI.

Wrapt in the darkest sable vest,
 Which none save noblest Moslem wear,
To guard from winds of heaven the breast
 As heaven itself to Selim dear,
With cautious steps the thicket threading,
 And starting oft, as through the glade
The gust its hollow moanings made,
Till on the smoother pathway treading,
More free her timid bosom beat,
 The maid pursued her silent guide;
And though her terror urged retreat,
How could she quit her Selim's side?
How teach her tender lips to chide?

VII.

They reach'd at length a grotto, hewn
 By nature, but enlarged by art,
Where oft her lute she wont to tune,
 And oft her Koran conn'd apart;

And oft in youthful reverie
She dream'd what Paradise might be :
Where woman's parted soul shall go
Her Prophet had disdain'd to show ;
But Selim's mansion was secure,
Nor deem'd she, could he long endure
His bower in other worlds of bliss
Without *her*, most beloved in this !
Oh ! who so dear with him could dwell ?
What Houri soothe him half so well ?

VIII.

Since last she visited the spot
Some change seem'd wrought within the grot:
It might be only that the night
Disguised things seen by better light :
That brazen lamp but dimly threw
A ray of no celestial hue ;
But in a nook within the cell
Her eye on stranger objects fell.
There arms were piled, not such as wield
The turban'd Delis in the field ;
But brands of foreign blade and hilt,
And one was red—perchance with guilt !
Ah ! how without can blood be spilt ?
A cup too on the board was set
That did not seem to hold sherbet.
What may this mean ? she turn'd to see
Her Selim—" Oh ! can this be he ? "

IX.

His robe of pride was thrown aside,
 His brow no high-crown'd turban bore,
But in its stead a shawl of red,
 Wreathed lightly round, his temples
 wore :
That dagger, on whose hilt the gem
Were worthy of a diadem,
No longer glitter'd at his waist,
Where pistols unadorn'd were braced ;
And from his belt a sabre swung,
And from his shoulder loosely hung
The cloak of white, the thin capote
That decks the wandering Candiote ;
Beneath—his golden plated vest
Clung like a cuirass to his breast ;
The greaves below his knee that wound
With silvery scales were sheathed and
 bound.
But were it not that high command
Spake in his eye, and tone, and hand,
All that a careless eye could see
In him was some young Galiongée.

X.

" I said I was not what I seem'd ;
 And now thou see'st my words were
 true :
I have a tale thou hast not dream'd,
 If sooth—its truth must others rue.

My story now 't were vain to hide,
I must not see thee Osman's bride :
But had not thine own lips declared
How much of that young heart I shared,
I could not, must not, yet have shown
The darker secret of my own.
In this I speak not now of love ;
That, let time, truth, and peril prove :
But first—Oh ! never wed another—
Zuleika ! I am not thy brother ! "

XI.

" Oh ! not my brother !—yet unsay—
 God ! am I left alone on earth
To mourn—I dare not curse—the day
 That saw my solitary birth ?
Oh ! thou wilt love me now no more !
 My sinking heart foreboded ill ;
But know *me* all I was before,
 Thy sister—friend—Zuleika still.
Thou led'st me here perchance to kill ;
 If thou hast cause for vengeance, see !
My breast is offer'd—take thy fill !
 Far better with the dead to be
Than live thus nothing now to thee !
Perhaps far worse, for now I know
Why Giaffir always seem'd thy foe ;
And I, alas ! am Giaffir's child,
For whom thou wert contemn'd, reviled.
If not thy sister—wouldst thou save
My life, oh ! bid me be thy slave ! "

XII.

" My slave, Zuleika !—nay, I 'm thine :
 But, gentle love, this transport calm,
Thy lot shall yet be link'd with mine ;
I swear it by our Prophet's shrine,
 And be that thought thy sorrow's balm.
So may the Koran verse display'd
Upon its steel direct my blade,
In danger's hour to guard us both,
As I preserve that awful oath !
The name in which thy heart hath prided
 Must change ; but, my Zuleika, know,
That tie is widen'd, not divided,
 Although thy Sire 's my deadliest foe.
My father was to Giaffir all
That Selim late was deem'd to thee :
That brother wrought a brother's fall,
 But spared, at least, my infancy ;
And lull'd me with a vain deceit
That yet a like return may meet.
He rear'd me, not with tender help,
 But like the nephew of a Cain ;
He watch'd me like a lion's whelp,
 That gnaws and yet may break his chain.
My father's blood in every vein
Is boiling ; but, for thy dear sake
No present vengeance will I take ;
 Though here I must no more remain.

But first, beloved Zuleika! hear
How Giaffir wrought this deed of fear.

XIII.

"How first their strife to rancour grew,
 If love or envy made them foes,
It matters little if I knew;
 In fiery spirits, slights, though few
 And thoughtless, will disturb repose.
In war Abdallah's arm was strong,
Remember'd yet in Bosniac song,
And Paswan's rebel hordes attest
How little love they bore such guest:
His death is all I need relate,
The stern effect of Giaffir's hate;
And how my birth disclosed to me,
Whate'er beside it makes, hath made me free.

XIV.

" When Paswan, after years of strife,
At last for power, but first for life,
In Widdin's walls too proudly sate,
Our Pachas rallied round the state;
Nor last nor least in high command,
Each brother led a separate band;
They gave their horse-tails to the wind,
 And mustering in Sophia's plain
Their tents were pitch'd, their post assign'd;
 To one, alas! assign'd in vain!
What need of words! the deadly bowl,
 By Giaffir's order drugged and given,
With venom subtle as his soul,
 Dismiss'd Abdallah's hence to heaven.
Reclined and feverish in the bath,
 He, when the hunter's sport was up,
But little deem'd a brother's wrath
 To quench his thirst had such a cup:
The bowl a bribed attendant bore;
He drank one draught, nor needed more!
If thou my tale, Zuleika, doubt,
Call Haroun—he can tell it out.

XV.

"The deed once done, and Paswan's feud
In part suppress'd, though ne'er subdued,
 Abdallah's Pachalick was gain'd :—
Thou know'st not what in our Divan
Can wealth procure for worse than man—
 Abdallah's honours were obtain'd
By him a brother's murder stain'd;
'T is true, the purchase nearly drain'd
His ill got treasure, soon replaced.
Wouldst question whence? Survey the
 waste,
And ask the squalid peasant how
His gains repay his broiling brow!—
Why me the stern usurper spared,
Why thus with me his palace shared,
I know not. Shame, regret, remorse,
And little fear from infant's force;

Besides, adoption as a son
By him whom Heaven accorded none,
Or some unknown cabal, caprice,
Preserved me thus ;—but not in peace :
He cannot curb his haughty mood,
Nor I forgive a father's blood.

XVI.

"Within thy father's house are foes ;
 Not all who break his bread are true :
To these should I my birth disclose,
 His days, his very hours were few :
They only want a heart to lead,
A hand to point them to the deed.
But Haroun only knows, or knew,
 This tale, whose close is almost nigh :
He in Abdallah's palace grew,
 And held that post in his Serai
 Which holds he here—he saw him die :
But what could single slavery do?
Avenge his lord ? alas! too late;
Or save his son from such a fate?
He chose the last, and when elate
 With foes subdued, or friends betray'd,
Proud Giaffir in high triumph sate,
He led me helpless to his gate,
 And not in vain it seems essay'd
 To save the life for which he pray'd.
The knowledge of my birth secured
 From all and each, but most from me ;
Thus Giaffir's safety was insured.
 Removed he too from Roumelie
To this our Asiatic side,
Far from our seats by Danube's tide,
 With none but Haroun, who retains
Such knowledge—and that Nubian feels
 A tyrant's secrets are but chains,
From which the captive gladly steals,
And this and more to me reveals:
Such still to guilt just Alla sends—
Slaves, tools, accomplices—no friends !

XVII.

" All this, Zuleika, harshly sounds ;
 But harsher still my tale must be :
Howe'er my tongue thy softness wounds,
 Yet I must prove all truth to thee.
I saw thee start this garb to see,
Yet is it one I oft have worn,
 And long must wear : this Galiongée,
To whom thy plighted vow is sworn,
 Is leader of those pirate hordes,
 Whose laws and lives are on their swords;
To hear whose desolating tale
Would make thy waning cheek more pale :
Those arms thou see'st my band have
 brought,
The hands that wield are not remote;

This cup too for the rugged knaves
Is fill'd—once quaff'd, they ne'er repine:
Our Prophet might forgive the slaves;
They're only infidels in wine.

XVIII.

"What could I be? Proscribed at home,
And taunted to a wish to roam;
And listless left—for Giaffir's fear
Denied the courser and the spear—
Though oft—Oh, Mahomet! how oft!—
In full Divan the despot scoff'd,
As if *my* weak unwilling hand
Refused the bridle or the brand:
He ever went to war alone,
And pent me here untried—unknown;
To Haroun's care with women left,
By hope unblest, of fame bereft,
While thou—whose softness long endear'd,
Though it unmann'd me, still had cheer'd—
To Brusa's walls for safety sent,
Awaited'st there the field's event.
Haroun, who saw my spirit pining
 Beneath inaction's sluggish yoke,
His captive, though with dread resigning,
 My thraldom for a season broke,
On promise to return before
The day when Giaffir's charge was o'er.
'T is vain—my tongue cannot impart
My almost drunkenness of heart,
When first this liberated eye
Survey'd Earth, Ocean, Sun, and Sky,
As if my spirit pierced them through,
And all their inmost wonders knew!
One word alone can paint to thee
That more than feeling—I was Free!
E'en for thy presence ceased to pine;
The World—nay, Heaven itself was mine!

XIX.

"The shallop of a trusty Moor
Convey'd me from this idle shore;
I long'd to see the isles that gem
Old Ocean's purple diadem:
I sought by turns, and saw them all;
 But when and where I join'd the crew,
With whom I'm pledged to rise or fall,
 When all that we design to do
Is done, 'twill then be time more meet
To tell thee, when the tale's complete.

XX.

"'T is true, they are a lawless brood,
But rough in form, nor mild in mood;
And every creed, and every race,
With them hath found—may find a place;
But open speech, and ready hand,
Obedience to their chief's command;
A soul for every enterprise,
That never sees with terror's eyes;

Friendship for each, and faith to all,
And vengeance vow'd for those who fall,
Have made them fitting instruments
For more than ev'n my own intents.
And some—and I have studied all
 Distinguish'd from the vulgar rank,
But chiefly to my council call
 The wisdom of the cautious Frank—
And some to higher thoughts aspire,
 The last of Lambro's patriots there
Anticipated freedom share;
And oft around the cavern fire
On visionary schemes debate,
To snatch the Rayahs from their fate.
So let them ease their hearts with prate
Of equal rights, which man ne'er knew;
I have a love for freedom too.
Ay! let me like the ocean-Patriarch roam,
Or only know on land the Tartar's home!
My tent on shore, my galley on the sea,
Are more than cities and Serais to me:
Borne by my steed, or wafted by my sail,
Across the desert, or before the gale,
Bound where thou wilt, my barb! or glide,
 my prow!
But be the star that guides the wanderer,
 Thou!
Thou, my Zuleika, share and bless my bark;
The Dove of peace and promise to mine ark!
Or, since that hope denied in worlds of strife,
Be thou the rainbow to the storms of life!
The evening beam that smiles the clouds away,
And tints to-morrow with prophetic ray!
Blest—as the Muezzin's strain from Mecca's
 wall
To pilgrims pure and prostrate at his call;
Soft—as the melody of youthful days,
That steals the trembling tear of speechless
 praise;
Dear—as his native song to Exile's ears,
Shall sound each tone thy long-loved voice
 endears.
For thee in those bright isles is built a bower
Blooming as Aden in its earliest hour.
A thousand swords, with Selim's heart and
 hand,
Wait—wave—defend—destroy—at thy com-
 mand!
Girt by my band, Zuleika at my side,
The spoil of nations shall bedeck my bride.
The Haram's languid years of listless ease
Are well resign'd for cares—for joys like these:
Not blind to fate, I see, where'er I rove,
Unnumber'd perils—but one only love!
Yet well my toils shall that fond breast repay,
Though fortune frown, or falser friends be-
 tray.
How dear the dream in darkest hours of ill,
Should all be changed, to find thee faithful
 still!

Be but thy soul, like Selim's, firmly shown;
To thee be Selim's tender as thine own;
To soothe each sorrow, share in each delight,
Blend every thought, do all—but disunite!
Once free, 'tis mine our horde again to
 guide;
Friends to each other, foes to aught beside:
Yet there we follow but the bent assign'd
By fatal Nature to man's warring kind:
Mark! where his carnage and his conquests
 cease!
He makes a solitude, and calls it—peace!
I, like the rest, must use my skill or strength,
But ask no land beyond my sabre's length:
Power sways but by division—her resource
The blest alternative of fraud or force!
Ours be the last; in time deceit may come
When cities cage us in a social home:
There ev'n thy soul might err—how oft the
 heart
Corruption shakes which peril could not part!
And woman, more than man, when death or
 woe,
Or even Disgrace, would lay her lover low,
Sunk in the lap of Luxury will shame—
Away suspicion!—*not* Zuleika's name!
But life is hazard at the best; and here
No more remains to win, and much to fear:
Yes, fear! the doubt, the dread of losing
 thee,
By Osman's power, and Giaffir's stern decree.
That dread shall vanish with the favouring
 gale,
Which Love to-night hath promised to my
 sail:
No danger daunts the pair his smile hath
 blest,
Their steps still roving, but their hearts at
 rest.
With thee all toils are sweet, each clime hath
 charms;
Earth—sea alike—our world within our arms!
Ay—let the loud winds whistle o'er the deck,
So that those arms cling closer round my
 neck:
The deepest murmur of this lip shall be,
No sigh for safety, but a prayer for thee!
The war of elements no fears impart
To Love, whose deadliest bane is human Art:
There lie the only rocks our course can
 check;
Here moments menace—*there* are years of
 wreck!
But hence ye thoughts that rise in Horror's
 shape!
This hour bestows, or ever bars escape.
Few words remain of mine my tale to close;
Of thine but *one* to waft us from our foes;
Yea—foes—to me will Giaffir's hate decline?
And is not Osman, who would part us, thine?

XXI.

"His head and faith from doubt and death
Return'd in time my guard to save;
Few heard, none told, that o'er the wave
From isle to isle I roved the while;
And since, though parted from my band
Too seldom now I leave the land,
No deed they've done, nor deed shall do,
Ere I have heard and doom'd it too:
I form the plan, decree the spoil,
'Tis fit I oftener share the toil.
But now too long I've held thine ear;
Time presses, floats my bark, and here
We leave behind but hate and fear.
To-morrow Osman with his train
Arrives—to-night must break thy chain:
And wouldst thou save that haughty Bey,—
 Perchance *his* life who gave thee thine,—
With me this hour away—away!
But yet, though thou art plighted mine,
Wouldst thou recall thy willing vow,
Appall'd by truths imparted now,
Here rest I—not to see thee wed:
But be that peril on *my* head!"

XXII.

Zuleika, mute and motionless,
Stood like that statue of distress,
When, her last hope for ever gone,
The mother harden'd into stone:
All in the maid that eye could see
Was but a younger Niobé.
But ere her lip, or even her eye,
Essay'd to speak, or look reply,
Beneath the garden's wicket porch
Far flash'd on high a blazing torch!
Another—and another—and another—
"Oh! fly—no more—yet now my more
 than brother!"
Far, wide, through every thicket spread
The fearful lights are gleaming red;
Nor these alone—for each right hand
Is ready with a sheathless brand.
They part, pursue, return, and wheel
With searching flambeau, shining steel;
And last of all, his sabre waving,
Stern Giaffir in his fury raving:
And now almost they touch the cave—
Oh! must that grot be Selim's grave?

XXIII.

Dauntless he stood—"'Tis come—soon
 past—
One kiss, Zuleika—'tis my last:
But yet my band not far from shore
May hear this signal, see the flash;
Yet now too few—the attempt were rash:
No matter—yet one effort more."

Forth to the cavern mouth he stept;
　His pistol's echo rang on high,
Zuleika started not, nor wept,
　Despair benumb'd her breast and eye!—
" They hear me not, or if they ply
Their oars, 'tis but to see me die ;
That sound hath drawn my foes more nigh.
Then forth my father's scimitar,
Thou ne'er hast seen less equal war !
Farewell, Zuleika !—sweet ! retire :
　Yet stay within—here linger safe,
　At thee his rage will only chafe.
Stir not—lest even to thee perchance
Some erring blade or ball should glance.
Fear'st thou for him ?—may I expire
If in this strife I seek thy sire !
No—though by him that poison pour'd ;
No—though again he call me coward !
But tamely shall I meet their steel ?
No—as each crest save *his* may feel !"

XXIV.

One bound he made, and gain'd the sand :
　Already at his feet hath sunk
The foremost of the prying band,
　A gasping head, a quivering trunk :
Another falls—but round him close
A swarming circle of his foes ;
From right to left his path he cleft,
　And almost met the meeting wave :
His boat appears—not five oars' length—
His comrades strain with desperate
　　　strength—
　Oh ! are they yet in time to save ?
His feet the foremost breakers lave ;
His band are plunging in the bay,
Their sabres glitter through the spray ;
Wet—wild—unwearied to the strand
They struggle—now they touch the land !
They come—'tis but to add to slaughter—
His heart's best blood is on the water.

XXV.

Escaped from shot, unharm'd by steel,
Or scarcely grazed its force to feel,
Had Selim won, betray'd, beset,
To where the strand and billows met ;
There as his last step left the land—
And the last death-blow dealt his hand—
Ah ! wherefore did he turn to look
　For her his eye but sought in vain ?
That pause, that fatal gaze he took,
　Hath doom'd his death, or fix'd his chain.
Sad proof, in peril and in pain,
How late will Lover's hope remain !
His back was to the dashing spray ;
Behind, but close, his comrades lay,
When, at the instant, hiss'd the ball—
" So may the foes of Giaffir fall !"
Whose voice is heard ? whose carbine rang ?
Whose bullet through the night-air sang,

Too nearly, deadly aim'd to err ?
'T is thine—Abdallah's Murderer !
The father slowly rued thy hate,
The son hath found a quicker fate :
Fast from his breast the blood is bubbling,
The whiteness of the sea-foam troubling—
If aught his lips essay'd to groan,
The rushing billows choked the tone !

XXVI.

Morn slowly rolls the clouds away ;
　Few trophies of the fight are there :
The shouts that shook the midnight-bay
Are silent ; but some signs of fray
　That strand of strife may bear,
And fragments of each shiver'd brand ;
Steps stamp'd ; and dash'd into the sand
The print of many a struggling hand
　May there be mark'd ; nor far remote
　A broken torch, an oarless boat ;
And tangled on the weeds that heap
The beach where shelving to the deep
　There lies a white capote !
'T is rent in twain—one dark-red stain
The wave yet ripples o'er in vain ;
　　But where is he who wore ?
Ye ! who would o'er his relics weep,
Go, seek them where the surges sweep
Their burthen round Sigæum's steep
　　And cast on Lemnos' shore :
The sea-birds shriek above the prey,
O'er which their hungry beaks delay,
As shaken on his restless pillow,
His head heaves with the heaving billow ;
That hand, whose motion is not life,
Yet feebly seems to menace strife,
Flung by the tossing tide on high,
　Then levell'd with the wave—
What recks it, though that corse shall lie
　Within a living grave ?
The bird that tears that prostrate form
Hath only robb'd the meaner worm ;
The only heart, the only eye
Had bled or wept to see him die,
Had seen those scatter'd limbs composed,
　And mourn'd above his turban-stone,
That heart hath burst—that eye was closed—
　Yea—closed before his own !

XXVII.

By Helle's stream there is a voice of wail !
And woman's eye is wet—man's cheek is pale :
Zuleika ! last of Giaffir's race,
　Thy destined lord is come too late :
He sees not—ne'er shall see thy face !
　　Can he not hear
The loud Wul-wulleh warn his distant ear ?
　Thy handmaids weeping at the gate,
　The Koran-chanters of the hymn of fate,
　The silent slaves with folded arms that wait,

Sighs in the hall, and shrieks upon the gale,
 Tell him thy tale!
Thou didst not view thy Selim fall!
 That fearful moment when he left the cave
 Thy heart grew chill:
He was thy hope—thy joy—thy love—thine all,
And that last thought on him thou couldst
 not save
 Sufficed to kill;
Burst forth in one wild cry—and all was still.
 Peace to thy broken heart, and virgin
 grave!
Ah! happy! but of life to lose the worst!
That grief—though deep—though fatal—was
 thy first!
Thrice happy ne'er to feel nor fear the force
Of absence, shame, pride, hate, revenge,
 remorse!
And, oh! that pang where more than mad-
 ness lies!
The worm that will not sleep—and never dies;
Thought of the gloomy day and ghastly
 night,
That dreads the darkness, and yet loathes
 the light,
That winds around, and tears the quivering
 heart!
Ah! wherefore not consume it—and depart!
Woe to thee, rash and unrelenting chief!
 Vainly thou heap'st the dust upon thy head,
 Vainly the sackcloth o'er thy limbs dost
 spread:
By that same hand Abdallah—Selim bled.
Now let it tear thy beard in idle grief:
Thy pride of heart, thy bride for Osman's bed,
She, whom thy sultan had but seen to wed,
 Thy Daughter's dead!
 Hope of thine age, thy twilight's lonely
 beam,
 The Star hath set that shone on Helle's
 stream.
What quench'd its ray?—the blood that thou
 hast shed!
Hark! to the hurried question of Despair:
"Where is my child?"—an Echo answers—
 "Where?"

XXVIII.

Within the place of thousand tombs
 That shine beneath, while dark above
The sad but living cypress glooms
 And withers not, though branch and leaf
Are stamp'd with an eternal grief,
 Like early unrequited Love,
One spot exists, which ever blooms,
 Ev'n in that deadly grove—
A single rose is shedding there
 Its lonely lustre, meek and pale:
It looks as planted by Despair—
 So white—so faint—the slightest gale

Might whirl the leaves on high;
 And yet, though storms and blight assail,
And hands more rude than wintry sky
 May wring it from the stem—in vain—
 To-morrow sees it bloom again:
The stalk some spirit gently rears,
And waters with celestial tears;
 For well may maids of Helle deem
That this can be no earthly flower,
Which mocks the tempest's withering hour,
And buds unshelter'd by a bower;
Nor droops though Spring refuse her
 shower,
 Nor woos the summer beam:
To it the livelong night there sings
 A bird unseen—but not remote:
Invisible his airy wings,
But soft as harp that Houri strings
 His long entrancing note!
It were the Bulbul; but his throat,
 Though mournful, pours not such a
 strain:
For they who listen cannot leave
 The spot, but linger there and grieve,
 As if they loved in vain!
And yet so sweet the tears they shed,
'Tis sorrow so unmix'd with dread,
They scarce can bear the morn to break
 That melancholy spell,
And longer yet would weep and wake,
 He sings so wild and well!
But when the day-blush bursts from high
 Expires that magic melody.
And some have been who could believe,
(So fondly youthful dreams deceive,
 Yet harsh be they that blame,)
That note so piercing and profound
Will shape and syllable its sound
 Into Zuleika's name.
'Tis from her cypress summit heard,
That melts in air the liquid word:
'Tis from her lowly virgin earth
That white rose takes its tender birth.
There late was laid a marble stone;
Eve saw it placed—the Morrow gone!
It was no mortal arm that bore
That deep-fix'd pillar to the shore;
For there, as Helle's legends tell,
Next morn 'twas found where Selim fell;
Lash'd by the tumbling tide, whose wave
Denied his bones a holier grave:
And there by night, reclined, 'tis said,
Is seen a ghastly turban'd head:
 And hence extended by the billow,
 'Tis named the "Pirate-phantom's pil-
 low!"
 Where first it lay that mourning flower
 Hath flourish'd; flourisheth this hour,
Alone and dewy, coldly pure and pale;
As weeping Beauty's cheek at Sorrow's tale!

The Corsair:

A TALE.

————"I suoi pensieri in lui dormir non ponno."
TASSO, *Gerusalemme Liberata*, canto x.

TO

THOMAS MOORE, ESQ.

MY DEAR MOORE,

I DEDICATE to you the last production with which I shall trespass on public patience, and your indulgence, for some years; and I own that I feel anxious to avail myself of this latest and only opportunity of adorning my pages with a name, consecrated by unshaken public principle, and the most undoubted and various talents. While Ireland ranks you among the firmest of her patriots; while you stand alone the first of her bards in her estimation, and Britain repeats and ratifies the decree, permit one, whose only regret, since our first acquaintance, has been the years he had lost before it commenced, to add the humble but sincere suffrage of friendship to the voice of more than one nation. It will at least prove to you, that I have neither forgotten the gratification derived from your society, nor abandoned the prospect of its renewal, whenever your leisure or inclination allows you to atone to your friends for too long an absence. It is said among those friends, I trust truly, that you are engaged in the composition of a poem whose scene will be laid in the East; none can do those scenes so much justice. The wrongs of your own country, the magnificent and fiery spirit of her sons, the beauty and feeling of her daughters, may there be found; and Collins, when he denominated his Oriental his Irish Eclogues, was not aware how true, at least, was a part of his parallel. Your imagination will create a warmer sun, and less clouded sky; but wildness, tenderness, and originality, are part of your national claim of oriental descent, to which you have already thus far proved your title more clearly than the most zealous of your country's antiquarians.

May I add a few words on a subject on which all men are supposed to be fluent, and none agreeable? —Self. I have written much, and published more than enough to demand a longer silence than I now meditate; but, for some years to come, it is my intention to tempt no further the award of "Gods, men, nor columns." In the present composition I have attempted not the most difficult, but, perhaps, the best adapted measure to our language, the good old and now neglected heroic couplet. The stanza of Spenser is perhaps too slow and dignified for narrative; though, I confess, it is the measure most after my own heart: Scott alone, of the present generation, has hitherto completely triumphed over the fatal facility of the octo-syllabic verse; and this is not the least victory of his fertile and mighty genius: in blank verse, Milton, Thomson, and our dramatists, are the beacons that shine along the deep, but warn us from the rough and barren rock on which they are kindled. The heroic couplet is not the most popular measure certainly; but as I did not deviate into the other from a wish to flatter what is called public opinion, I shall quit it without further apology, and take my chance once more with that versification, in which I have hitherto published nothing but compositions whose former circulation is part of my present, and will be of my future regret.

With regard to my story, and stories in general, I should have been glad to have rendered my personages more perfect and amiable, if possible, inasmuch as I have been sometimes criticised, and considered no less responsible for their deeds and qualities than if all had been personal. Be it so—if I have deviated into the gloomy vanity of "drawing from self," the pictures are probably like, since they are unfavourable; and if not, those who know me are undeceived, and those who do not, I have little interest in undeceiving. I have no particular desire that any but my acquaintance should think the author better than the beings of his imagining; but I cannot help a little surprise, and perhaps amusement, at some odd critical exceptions in the present instance, when I see several bards (far more deserving, I allow) in very reputable plight, and quite exempted from all participation in the faults of those heroes, who, nevertheless, might be found with little more morality than "The Giaour," and perhaps—but no— I must admit Childe Harold to be a very repulsive personage; and as to his identity, those who like it must give him whatever "alias" they please.

If, however, it were worth while to remove the impression, it might be of some service to me, that the man who is alike the delight of his readers and his friends, the poet of all circles, and the idol of his own, permits me here and elsewhere to subscribe myself,

Most truly,
And affectionately,
His obedient servant,
BYRON.

January 2, 1814.

THE CORSAIR.

Canto the First.

"————nessun maggior dolore,
Che ricordarsi del tempo felice
*Nella miseria,————"—*DANTE.

I.

"O'ER the glad waters of the dark blue sea,
Our thoughts as boundless, and our souls as
 free,
Far as the breeze can bear, the billows foam,
Survey our empire, and behold our home!
These are our realms, no limits to their
 sway—
Our flag the sceptre all who meet obey.
Ours the wild life in tumult still to range
From toil to rest, and joy in every change.
Oh, who can tell? not thou, luxurious slave!
Whose soul would sicken o'er the heaving
 wave;
Not thou, vain lord of wantonness and ease!
Whom slumber soothes not—pleasure cannot
 please—
Oh, who can tell, save he whose heart hath
 tried,
And danced in triumph o'er the waters wide,
The exulting sense—the pulse's maddening
 play,
That thrills the wanderer of that trackless
 way?
That for itself can woo the approaching fight,
And turn what some deem danger to delight;
That seeks what cravens shun with more
 than zeal,
And where the feebler faint can only feel—
Feel—to the rising bosom's inmost core,
Its hope awaken and its spirit soar?
No dread of death if with us die our foes—
Save that it seems even duller than repose:
Come when it will—we snatch the life of life—
When lost—what recks it but disease or
 strife?
Let him who crawls enamour'd of decay,
Cling to his couch, and sicken years away:
Heave his thick breath, and shake his
 palsied head;
Ours—the fresh turf, and not the feverish bed.
While gasp by gasp he falters forth his soul,
Ours with one pang—one bound—escapes
 control.
His corse may boast its urn and narrow cave,
And they who loath'd his life may gild his
 grave:

Ours are the tears, though few, sincerely shed,
When Ocean shrouds and sepulchres our dead.
For us, even banquets fond regret supply
In the red cup that crowns our memory;
And the brief epitaph in danger's day,
When those who win at length divide the
 prey,
And cry, Remembrance saddening o'er each
 brow,
How had the brave who fell exulted *now!*"

II.

Such were the notes that from the Pirate's isle
Around the kindling watch-fire rang the
 while:
Such were the sounds that thrill'd the rocks
 along,
And unto ears as rugged seem'd a song!
In scatter'd groups upon the golden sand,
They game—carouse—converse—or whet the
 brand:
Select the arms—to each his blade assign,
And careless eye the blood that dims its
 shine;
Repair the boat, replace the helm or oar,
While others straggling muse along the
 shore;
For the wild bird the busy springes set,
Or spread beneath the sun the dripping net;
Gaze where some distant sail a speck supplies,
With all the thirsting eye of Enterprise;
Tell o'er the tales of many a night of toil,
And marvel where they next shall seize a
 spoil:
No matter where—their chief's allotment
 this;
Theirs, to believe no prey nor plan amiss.
But who that CHIEF? his name on every
 shore
Is famed and fear'd—they ask and know no
 more.
With these he mingles not but to command;
Few are his words, but keen his eye and
 hand.
Ne'er seasons he with mirth their jovial mess,
But they forgive his silence for success.
Ne'er for his lip the purpling cup they fill,
That goblet passes him untasted still—
And for his fare—the rudest of his crew
Would that, in turn, have pass'd untasted
 too;
Earth's coarsest bread, the garden's home-
 liest roots,
And scarce the summer luxury of fruits,

His short repast in humbleness supply
With all a hermit's board would scarce deny.
But while he shuns the grosser joys of sense,
His mind seems nourish'd by that abstinence.
"Steer to that shore!"—they sail. "Do
 this!"—'t is done:
"Now form and follow me!"—the spoil is
 won.
Thus prompt his accents and his actions still,
And all obey and few inquire his will;
To such, brief answer and contemptuous eye
Convey reproof, nor further deign reply.

III.

"A sail!—a sail!"—a promised prize to
 Hope!
Her nation—flag—how speaks the telescope?
No prize, alas! but yet a welcome sail:
The blood-red signal glitters in the gale.
Yes—she is ours—a home-returning bark—
Blow fair, thou breeze!—she anchors ere the
 dark.
Already doubled is the cape—our bay
Receives that prow which proudly spurns the
 spray.
How gloriously her gallant course she goes!
Her white wings flying—never from her
 foes—
She walks the waters like a thing of life,
And seems to dare the elements to strife.
Who would not brave the battle-fire, the
 wreck,
To move the monarch of her peopled deck?

IV.

Hoarse o'er her side the rustling cable rings;
The sails are furl'd; and anchoring round
 she swings;
And gathering loiterers on the land discern
Her boat descending from the latticed stern.
'T is mann'd—the oars keep concert to the
 strand,
Till grates her keel upon the shallow sand.
Hail to the welcome shout!—the friendly
 speech!
When hand grasps hand uniting on the
 beach;
The smile, the question, and the quick reply,
And the heart's promise of festivity!

V.

The tidings spread, and gathering grows the
 crowd;
The hum of voices, and the laughter loud,
And woman's gentler anxious tone is heard—
Friends', husbands', lovers' names in each
 dear word:
"Oh! are they safe? we ask not of success—
But shall we see them? will their accents
 bless?

From where the battle roars, the billows
 chafe,
They doubtless boldly did—but who are safe?
Here let them haste to gladden and surprise,
And kiss the doubt from these delighted
 eyes!"

VI.

"Where is our chief? for him we bear re-
 port—
And doubt that joy—which hails our coming—
 short;
Yet thus sincere, 't is cheering, though so
 brief:
But, Juan! instant guide us to our chief:
Our greeting paid, we'll feast on our return,
And all shall hear what each may wish to
 learn."
Ascending slowly by the rock-hewn way,
To where his watch-tower beetles o'er the
 bay,
By bushy brake, and wild flowers blossoming,
And freshness breathing from each silver
 spring,
Whose scatter'd streams from granite basins
 burst,
Leap into life, and sparkling woo your thirst;
From crag to cliff they mount—Near yonder
 cave,
What lonely straggler looks along the wave?
In pensive posture leaning on the brand,
Not oft a resting-staff to that red hand?
"'T is he—'t is Conrad—here, as wont, alone;
On—Juan!—on—and make our purpose
 known.
The bark he views—and tell him we would
 greet
His ear with tidings he must quickly meet:
We dare not yet approach—thou know'st his
 mood
When strange or uninvited steps intrude."

VII.

Him Juan sought, and told of their intent;—
He spake not, but a sign exprest assent.
These Juan calls—they come—to their salute
He bends him slightly, but his lips are
 mute.
"These letters, Chief, are from the Greek—
 the spy,
Who still proclaims our spoil or peril nigh:
Whate'er his tidings, we can well report,
Much that"—"Peace, peace!"—he cuts their
 prating short.
Wondering they turn, abash'd, while each to
 each
Conjecture whispers in his muttering speech:
They watch his glance with many a stealing
 look,
To gather how that eye the tidings took;

But, this as if he guess'd, with head aside,
Perchance from some emotion, doubt, or
 pride,
He read the scroll—"My tablets, Juan, hark—
Where is Gonsalvo?"
 "In the anchor'd bark."
"There let him stay—to him this order bear—
Back to your duty—for my course prepare:
Myself this enterprise to-night will share."

"To-night, Lord Conrad!"
 "Ay! at set of sun:
The breeze will freshen when the day is done.
My corslet, cloak—one hour and we are gone.
Sling on thy bugle—see that free from rust
My carbine-lock springs worthy of my trust;
Be the edge sharpen'd of my boarding-brand,
And give its guard more room to fit my hand.
This let the armourer with speed dispose;
Last time, it more fatigued my arm than foes:
Mark that the signal-gun be duly fired,
To tell us when the hour of stay's expired."

VIII.

They make obeisance, and retire in haste,
Too soon to seek again the watery waste:
Yet they repine not—so that Conrad guides;
And who dare question aught that he decides?
That man of loneliness and mystery,
Scarce seen to smile, and seldom heard to
 sigh;
Whose name appals the fiercest of his crew,
And tints each swarthy cheek with sallower
 hue;
Still sways their souls with that commanding
 art
That dazzles, leads, yet chills the vulgar
 heart.
What is that spell, that thus his lawless
 train
Confess and envy, yet oppose in vain?
What should it be, that thus their faith can
 bind?
The power of Thought—the magic of the
 Mind!
Link'd with success, assumed and kept with
 skill,
That moulds another's weakness to its will;
Wields with their hands, but, still to these
 unknown,
Makes even their mightiest deeds appear his
 own.
Such hath it been—shall be—beneath the sun
The many still must labour for the one!
'Tis Nature's doom—but let the wretch who
 toils
Accuse not, hate not *him* who wears the
 spoils.
Oh! if he knew the weight of splendid chains,
How light the balance of his humbler pains!

IX.

Unlike the heroes of each ancient race,
Demons in act, but Gods at least in face,
In Conrad's form seems little to admire,
Though his dark eyebrow shades a glance of
 fire:
Robust but not Herculean—to the sight
No giant frame sets forth his common
 height;
Yet, in the whole, who paused to look again,
Saw more than marks the crowd of vulgar
 men;
They gaze and marvel how—and still con-
 fess
That thus it is, but why they cannot guess.
Sun-burnt his cheek, his forehead high and
 pale
The sable curls in wild profusion veil;
And oft perforce his rising lip reveals
The haughtier thought it curbs, but scarce
 conceals.
Though smooth his voice, and calm his
 general mien,
Still seems there something he would not
 have seen:
His features' deepening lines and varying
 hue
At times attracted, yet perplex'd the view,
As if within that murkiness of mind
Work'd feelings fearful, and yet undefined;
Such might it be—that none could truly
 tell—
Too close inquiry his stern glance would
 quell.
There breathe but few whose aspect might
 defy
The full encounter of his searching eye;
He had the skill, when Cunning's gaze would
 seek
To probe his heart and watch his changing
 cheek,
At once the observer's purpose to espy,
And on himself roll back his scrutiny,
Lest he to Conrad rather should betray
Some secret thought, than drag that chief's
 to day.
There was a laughing Devil in his sneer,
That raised emotions both of rage and fear;
And where his frown of hatred darkly fell,
Hope withering fled, and Mercy sigh'd fare-
 well!

X.

Slight are the outward signs of evil thought,
Within—within—'twas there the spirit
 wrought!
Love shows all changes—Hate, Ambition,
 Guile,
Betray no further than the bitter smile;

The lip's least curl, the lightest paleness
thrown
Along the govern'd aspect, speak alone
Of deeper passions; and to judge their mien,
He, who would see, must be himself unseen.
Then—with the hurried tread, the upward
eye,
The clenched hand, the pause of agony,
That listens, starting, lest the step too near
Approach intrusive on that mood of fear;
Then—with each feature working from the
heart,
With feelings, loosed to strengthen—not
depart,
That rise, convulse, contend—that freeze, or
glow,
Flush in the cheek, or damp upon the brow;
Then, Stranger! if thou canst, and tremblest
not,
Behold his soul—the rest that soothes his
lot!
Mark how that lone and blighted bosom
sears
The scathing thought of execrated years!
Behold—but who hath seen, or e'er shall see,
Man as himself—the secret spirit free?

XI.

Yet was not Conrad thus by Nature sent
To lead the guilty—guilt's worse instru-
ment—
His soul was changed, before his deeds had
driven
Him forth to war with man and forfeit
heaven.
Warp'd by the world in Disappointment's
school,
In words too wise, in conduct *there* a fool;
Too firm to yield, and far too proud to stoop,
Doom'd by his very virtues for a dupe,
He cursed those virtues as the cause of ill,
And not the traitors who betray'd him still;
Nor deem'd that gifts bestow'd on better men
Had left him joy, and means to give again.
Fear'd, shunn'd, belied, ere youth had lost
her force,
He hated man too much to feel remorse,
And thought the voice of wrath a sacred call,
To pay the injuries of some on all.
He knew himself a villain—but he deem'd
The rest no better than the thing he seem'd;
And scorn'd the best as hypocrites who hid
Those deeds the bolder spirit plainly did.
He knew himself detested, but he knew
The hearts that loath'd him, crouch'd and
dreaded too.
Lone, wild, and strange, he stood alike
exempt
From all affection and from all contempt:

His name could sadden, and his acts surprise;
But they that fear'd him dared not to despise:
Man spurns the worm, but pauses ere he
wake
The slumbering venom of the folded snake:
The first may turn, but not avenge the blow;
The last expires, but leaves no living foe;
Fast to the doom'd offender's form it clings,
And he may crush—not conquer—still it
stings!

XII.

None are all evil—quickening round his heart
One softer feeling would not yet depart;
Oft could he sneer at others as beguiled
By passions worthy of a fool or child;
Yet 'gainst that passion vainly still he strove,
And even in him it asks the name of Love!
Yes, it was love—unchangeable—unchanged,
Felt but for one from whom he never ranged;
Though fairest captives daily met his eye,
He shunn'd, nor sought, but coldly pass'd
them by;
Though many a beauty droop'd in prison'd
bower,
None ever sooth'd his most unguarded hour.
Yes—it was Love—if thoughts of tenderness
Tried in temptation, strengthen'd by distress,
Unmoved by absence, firm in every clime,
And yet—oh more than all! untired by time;
Which nor defeated hope, nor baffled wile,
Could render sullen were she near to smile,
Nor rage could fire, nor sickness fret to vent
On her one murmur of his discontent;
Which still would meet with joy, with calm-
ness part,
Lest that his look of grief should reach her
heart;
Which nought removed, nor menaced to re-
move—
If there be love in mortals—this was love!
He was a villain—ay, reproaches shower
On him—but not the passion, nor its power,
Which only proved, all other virtues gone,
Not guilt itself could quench this loveliest
one!

XIII.

He paused a moment—till his hastening men
Pass'd the first winding downward to the
glen.
"Strange tidings!—many a peril have I
pass'd,
Nor know I why this next appears the last!
Yet so my heart forebodes, but must not fear,
Nor shall my followers find me falter here.
'T is rash to meet, but surer death to wait
Till here they hunt us to undoubted fate;
And, if my plan but hold, and Fortune smile,
We'll furnish mourners for our funeral pile.

Ay, let them slumber—peaceful be their
 dreams!
Morn ne'er awoke them with such brilliant
 beams
As kindle high to-night (but blow, thou
 breeze!)
To warm these slow avengers of the seas.
Now to Medora—Oh! my sinking heart,
Long may her own be lighter than thou art!
Yet was I brave—mean boast where all are
 brave!
Ev'n insects sting for aught they seek to save.
This common courage which with brutes we
 share,
That owes its deadliest efforts to despair,
Small merit claims—but 't was my nobler
 hope
To teach my few with numbers still to cope;
Long have I led them—not to vainly bleed:
No medium now—we perish or succeed;
So let it be—it irks not me to die;
But thus to urge them whence they cannot
 fly.
My lot hath long had little of my care,
But chafes my pride thus baffled in the
 snare:
Is this my skill? my craft? to set at last
Hope, power, and life upon a single cast?
Oh, Fate!—accuse thy folly, not thy fate!
She may redeem thee still, nor yet too late."

XIV.

Thus with himself communion held he, till
He reach'd the summit of his tower-crown'd
 hill:
There at the portal paused—for wild and soft
He heard those accents never heard too oft;
Through the high lattice far yet sweet they
 rung,
And these the notes his bird of beauty sung:

1.

"Deep in my soul that tender secret dwells,
 Lonely and lost to light for evermore,
Save when to thine my heart responsive
 swells,
 Then trembles into silence as before.

2.

"There, in its centre, a sepulchral lamp
 Burns the slow flame, eternal, but unseen;
Which not the darkness of despair can damp,
 Though vain its ray as it had never been.

3.

"Remember me—Oh! pass not thou my grave
 Without one thought whose relics there
 recline:
The only pang my bosom dare not brave
 Must be to find forgetfulness in thine.

4.

"My fondest, faintest, latest accents hear—
 Grief for the dead not virtue can reprove;
Then give me all I ever ask'd—a tear,
 The first—last—sole reward of so much
 love!"

He pass'd the portal, cross'd the corridor,
And reach'd the chamber as the strain gave
 o'er:
"My own Medora! sure thy song is sad—"

"In Conrad's absence wouldst thou have it
 glad?
Without thine ear to listen to my lay,
Still must my song my thoughts, my soul
 betray:
Still must each action to my bosom suit,
My heart unhush'd, although my lips were
 mute!
Oh! many a night on this lone couch reclined,
My dreaming fear with storms hath wing'd
 the wind,
And deem'd the breath that faintly fann'd
 thy sail
The murmuring prelude of the ruder gale;
Though soft, it seem'd the low prophetic dirge,
That mourn'd thee floating on the savage
 surge;
Still would I rise to rouse the beacon fire,
Lest spies less true should let the blaze
 expire;
And many a restless hour outwatch'd each
 star,
And morning came—and still thou wert afar.
Oh! how the chill blast on my bosom blew,
And day broke dreary on my troubled view,
And still I gazed and gazed—and not a prow
Was granted to my tears, my truth, my vow!
At length 't was noon—I hail'd and blest the
 mast
That met my sight—it near'd—Alas! it pass'd!
Another came—Oh God! 't was thine at last!
Would that those days were over! wilt thou
 ne'er,
My Conrad! learn the joys of peace to share?
Sure thou hast more than wealth, and many
 a home
As bright as this invites us not to roam:
Thou know'st it is not peril that I fear,
I only tremble when thou art not here;
Then not for mine, but that far dearer life,
Which flies from love and languishes for
 strife—
How strange that heart, to me so tender still,
Should war with nature and its better will!"

"Yea, strange indeed—that heart hath long
 been changed;
Worm-like 't was trampled, adder-like avenged,

Without one hope on earth beyond thy love,
And scarce a glimpse of mercy from above.
Yet the same feeling which thou dost con-
 demn,
My very love to thee is hate to them,
So closely mingling here, that disentwined,
I cease to love thee when I love mankind:
Yet dread not this—the proof of all the past
Assures the future that my love will last;
But—oh, Medora! nerve thy gentler heart:
This hour again—but not for long—we part."
" This hour we part—my heart foreboded this:
Thus ever fade my fairy dreams of bliss.
This hour—it cannot be—this hour away!
Yon bark hath hardly anchor'd in the bay:
Her consort still is absent, and her crew
Have need of rest before they toil anew:
My love! thou mock'st my weakness; and
 wouldst steel
My breast before the time when it must feel;
But trifle now no more with my distress,
Such mirth hath less of play than bitterness.
Be silent, Conrad!—dearest! come and share
The feast these hands delighted to prepare;
Light toil! to cull and dress thy frugal fare!
See, I have pluck'd the fruit that promised
 best,
And where not sure, perplex'd, but pleased,
 I guess'd
At such as seem'd the fairest; thrice the hill
My steps have wound to try the coolest rill;
Yes! thy sherbet to-night will sweetly flow,
See how it sparkles in its vase of snow!
The grapes' gay juice thy bosom never cheers;
Thou more than Moslem when the cup ap-
 pears:
Think not I mean to chide—for I rejoice
What others deem a penance is thy choice.
But come, the board is spread; our silver
 lamp
Is trimm'd, and heeds not the sirocco's damp:
Then shall my handmaids while the time
 along,
And join with me the dance, or wake the
 song;
Or my guitar, which still thou lov'st to
 hear,
Shall soothe or lull—or, should it vex thine
 ear,
We 'll turn the tale, by Ariosto told,
Of fair Olympia loved and left of old.
Why, thou wert worse than he who broke
 his vow
To that lost damsel, shouldst thou leave me
 now;
Or even that traitor chief—I've seen thee
 smile,
When the clear sky show'd Ariadne's Isle,
Which I have pointed from these cliffs the
 while:

And thus half sportive, half in fear, I said,
Lest time should raise that doubt to more
 than dread,
Thus Conrad, too, will quit me for the main;
And he deceived me—for he came again!"

" Again, again—and oft again—my love!
If there be life below, and hope above,
He will return—but now, the moments bring
The time of parting with redoubled wing:
The why, the where—what boots it now to
 tell?
Since all must end in that wild word—fare-
 well!
Yet would I fain—did time allow—disclose—
Fear not—these are no formidable foes;
And here shall watch a more than wonted
 guard,
For sudden siege and long defence prepared:
Nor be thou lonely, though thy lord's away,
Our matrons and thy handmaids with thee
 stay;
And this thy comfort—that, when next we
 meet,
Security shall make repose more sweet.
List!—'t is the bugle!"—Juan shrilly blew—
" One kiss—one more—another—Oh! Adieu!"

She rose—she sprung—she clung to his em-
 brace,
Till his heart heaved beneath her hidden face:
He dared not raise to his that deep-blue eye,
Which downcast droop'd in tearless agony.
Her long fair hair lay floating o'er his arms,
In all the wildness of dishevell'd charms;
Scarce beat that bosom where his image dwelt
So full—*that* feeling seem'd almost unfelt!
Hark—peals the thunder of the signal-gun!
It told 'twas sunset, and he cursed that sun.
Again—again—that form he madly press'd,
Which mutely clasp'd imploringly caress'd!
And tottering to the couch his bride he bore,
One moment gazed, as if to gaze no more;
Felt that for him earth held but her alone,
Kiss'd her cold forehead—turn'd—is Conrad
 gone?

XV.

" And is he gone?" on sudden solitude
How oft that fearful question will intrude!
" 'T was but an instant past—and here he
 stood!
And now"—without the portal's porch she
 rush'd,
And then at length her tears in freedom
 gush'd;
Big, bright, and fast, unknown to her they
 fell;
But still her lips refused to send—" Fare-
 well!"

For in that word—that fatal word—howe'er
We promise, hope, believe, there breathes
despair.
O'er every feature of that still, pale face,
Had sorrow fix'd what time can ne'er erase:
The tender blue of that large loving eye
Grew frozen with its gaze on vacancy,
Till—Oh, how far!—it caught a glimpse of
him,
And then it flow'd, and phrensied seem'd to
swim,
Through those long, dark, and glistening
lashes dew'd
With drops of sadness oft to be renew'd.
"He's gone!"—against her heart that hand
is driven,
Convulsed and quick—then gently raised to
heaven:
She look'd and saw the heaving of the main;
The white sail set—she dared not look again;
But turn'd with sickening soul within the
gate—
"It is no dream—and I am desolate!"

XVI.

From crag to crag descending, swiftly sped
Stern Conrad down, nor once he turn'd his
head;
But shrunk whene'er the windings of his way
Forced on his eye what he would not survey,
His lone but lovely dwelling on the steep,
That hail'd him first when homeward from
the deep:
And she—the dim and melancholy star,
Whose ray of beauty reach'd him from afar,
On her he must not gaze, he must not think,
There he might rest—but on Destruction's
brink:
Yet once almost he stopp'd, and nearly gave
His fate to chance, his projects to the wave:
But no—it must not be—a worthy chief
May melt, but not betray to woman's grief.
He sees his bark, he notes how fair the wind,
And sternly gathers all his might of mind:
Again he hurries on—and as he hears
The clang of tumult vibrate on his ears,
The busy sounds, the bustle of the shore,
The shout, the signal, and the dashing oar;
As marks his eye the seaboy on the mast,
The anchors rise, the sails unfurling fast,
The waving kerchiefs of the crowd that urge
That mute adieu to those who stem the surge;
And more than all, his blood-red flag aloft,
He marvell'd how his heart could seem so
soft.
Fire in his glance, and wildness in his breast,
He feels of all his former self possest;
He bounds—he flies—until his footsteps reach
The verge where ends the cliff, begins the
beach,

There checks his speed; but pauses less to
breathe
The breezy freshness of the deep beneath,
Than there his wonted statelier step renew;
Nor rush, disturb'd by haste, to vulgar view:
For well had Conrad learn'd to curb the
crowd,
By arts that veil, and oft preserve the proud;
His was the lofty port, the distant mien,
That seems to shun the sight—and awes if
seen:
The solemn aspect, and the high-born eye,
That checks low mirth, but lacks not courtesy;
All these he wielded to command assent:
But where he wish'd to win, so well unbent,
That kindness cancell'd fear in those who
heard,
And others' gifts show'd mean beside his
word,
When echo'd to the heart as from his own
His deep yet tender melody of tone:
But such was foreign to his wonted mood,
He cared not what he soften'd, but subdued:
The evil passions of his youth had made
Him value less who loved—than what obey'd.

XVII.

Around him mustering ranged his ready guard,
Before him Juan stands—"Are all prepared?"

"They are—nay more—embark'd: the latest
boat
Waits but my chief——"
 "My sword, and my capote."
Soon firmly girded on, and lightly slung,
His belt and cloak were o'er his shoulders
flung:
"Call Pedro here!" He comes—and Conrad
bends,
With all the courtesy he deign'd his friends;
"Receive these tablets, and peruse with care,
Words of high trust and truth are graven
there;
Double the guard, and when Anselmo's bark
Arrives, let him alike these orders mark:
In three days (serve the breeze) the sun shall
shine
On our return—till then all peace be thine!"
This said, his brother Pirate's hand he wrung,
Then to his boat with haughty gesture sprung.
Flash'd the dipt oars, and sparkling with the
stroke,
Around the waves' phosphoric brightness
broke;
They gain the vessel—on the deck he stands,—
Shrieks the shrill whistle, ply the busy
hands—
He marks how well the ship her helm obeys,
How gallant all her crew, and deigns to
praise.

His eyes of pride to young Gonsalvo turn—
Why doth he start, and inly seem to mourn?
Alas! those eyes beheld his rocky tower,
And live a moment o'er the parting hour;
She—his Medora—did she mark the prow?
Ah! never loved he half so much as now!
But much must yet be done ere dawn of day—
Again he mans himself and turns away;
Down to the cabin with Gonsalvo bends,
And there unfolds his plan, his means, and
　　ends;
Before them burns the lamp, and spreads the
　　chart,
And all that speaks and aids the naval art;
They to the midnight watch protract debate;
To anxious eyes what hour is ever late?
Meantime, the steady breeze serenely blew,
And fast and falcon-like the vessel flew;
Pass'd the high headlands of each clustering
　　isle,
To gain their port—long—long ere morning
　　smile:
And soon the night-glass through the narrow
　　bay
Discovers where the Pacha's galleys lay.
Count they each sail, and mark how there
　　supine
The lights in vain o'er heedless Moslem shine.
Secure, unnoted, Conrad's prow pass'd by,
And anchor'd where his ambush meant to lie;
Screen'd from espial by the jutting cape,
That rears on high its rude fantastic shape.
Then rose his band to duty—not from sleep—
Equipp'd for deeds alike on land or deep;
While lean'd their leader o'er the fretting
　　flood,
And calmly talk'd—and yet he talk'd of
　　blood!

———◆◆———

Canto the Second.

"Conosceste i dubiosi desiri?"—DANTE.

I.

IN Coron's bay floats many a galley light,
Through Coron's lattices the lamps are
　　bright,
For Seyd, the Pacha, makes a feast to-night:
A feast for promised triumph yet to come,
When he shall drag the fetter'd Rovers home;
This hath he sworn by Alla and his sword,
And faithful to his firman and his word,
His summon'd prows collect along the coast,
And great the gathering crews, and loud the
　　boast;
Already shared the captives and the prize,
Though far the distant foe they thus despise;
'Tis but to sail—no doubt to-morrow's Sun
Will see the Pirates bound, their haven won!

Meantime the watch may slumber, if they will,
Nor only wake to war, but dreaming kill.
Though all, who can, disperse on shore and
　　seek
To flesh their glowing valour on the Greek;
How well such deed becomes the turban'd
　　brave—
To bare the sabre's edge before a slave!
Infest his dwelling—but forbear to slay,
Their arms are strong, yet merciful to-day,
And do not deign to smite because they may!
Unless some gay caprice suggests the blow,
To keep in practice for the coming foe.
Revel and rout the evening hours beguile,
And they who wish to wear a head must
　　smile;
For Moslem mouths produce their choicest
　　cheer,
And hoard their curses, till the coast is clear.

II.

High in his hall reclines the turban'd Seyd;
Around—the bearded chiefs he came to lead.
Removed the banquet, and the last pilaff—
Forbidden draughts, 'tis said, he dared to
　　quaff,
Though to the rest the sober berry's juice
The slaves bear round for rigid Moslems' use;
The long chibouque's dissolving cloud supply,
While dance the Almas to wild minstrelsy.
The rising morn will view the chiefs embark;
But waves are somewhat treacherous in the
　　dark:
And revellers may more securely sleep
On silken couch than o'er the rugged deep:
Feast there who can—nor combat till they
　　must,
And less to conquest than to Korans trust:
And yet the numbers crowded in his host
Might warrant more than even the Pacha's
　　boast.

III.

With cautious reverence from the outer gate
Slow stalks the slave, whose office there to
　　wait,
Bows his bent head, his hand salutes the
　　floor,
Ere yet his tongue the trusted tidings bore:
"A captive Dervise, from the pirate's nest
Escaped, is here—himself would tell the
　　rest."
He took the sign from Seyd's assenting eye,
And led the holy man in silence nigh.
His arms were folded on his dark-green vest,
His step was feeble, and his look deprest;
Yet worn he seem'd of hardship more than
　　years,
And pale his cheek with penance, not from
　　fears.

Vow'd to his God—his sable locks he wore,
And these his lofty cap rose proudly o'er :
Around his form his loose long robe was
 thrown,
And wrapt a breast bestow'd on heaven alone ;
Submissive, yet with self-possession mann'd,
He calmly met the curious eyes that scann'd ;
And question of his coming fain would seek,
Before the Pacha's will allow'd to speak.

IV.

"Whence com'st thou, Dervise ? "
 "From the outlaw's den,
A fugitive—"
 "Thy capture where and when ?"
"From Scalanovo's port to Scio's isle,
The Saick was bound ; but Allah did not smile
Upon our course—the Moslem merchant's
 gains
The Rovers won ; our limbs have worn their
 chains.
I had no death to fear, nor wealth to boast,
Beyond the wandering freedom which I lost ;
At length a fisher's humble boat by night
Afforded hope, and offer'd chance of flight ;
I seized the hour, and find my safety here—
With thee—most mighty Pacha ! who can
 fear ?"

"How speed the outlaws ? stand they well
 prepared,
Their plunder'd wealth, and robber's rock, to
 guard ?
Dream they of this our preparation, doom'd
To view with fire their scorpion nest con-
 sumed ?"

"Pacha ! the fetter'd captive's mourning eye,
That weeps for flight, but ill can play the spy ;
I only heard the reckless waters roar,
Those waves that would not bear me from
 the shore ;
I only mark'd the glorious sun and sky,
Too bright, too blue, for my captivity ;
And felt that all which Freedom's bosom
 cheers,
Must break my chain before it dried my tears.
This may'st thou judge, at least, from my
 escape,
They little deem of aught in peril's shape ;
Else vainly had I pray'd or sought the chance
That leads me here—if eyed with vigilance :
The careless guard that did not see me fly
May watch as idly when thy power is nigh.
Pacha ! my limbs are faint—and nature
 craves
Food for my hunger, rest from tossing waves :
Permit my absence—peace be with thee !
 Peace
With all around !—now grant repose—re-
 lease."

"Stay, Dervise ! I have more to question—
 stay,
I do command thee—sit—dost hear ?—obey !
More I must ask, and food the slaves shall
 bring ;
Thou shalt not pine where all are banqueting :
The supper done—prepare thee to reply,
Clearly and full—I love not mystery."
'T were vain to guess what shook the pious
 man,
Who look'd not lovingly on that Divan ;
Nor show'd high relish for the banquet prest,
And less respect for every fellow guest.
'T was but a moment's peevish hectic pass'd
Along his cheek, and tranquillised as fast :
He sate him down in silence, and his look
Resumed the calmness which before forsook :
The feast was usher'd in, but sumptuous fare
He shunn'd as if some poison mingled there.
For one so long condemn'd to toil and fast,
Methinks he strangely spares the rich repast.

"What ails thee, Dervise ? eat—dost thou
 suppose
This feast a Christian's ? or my friends thy
 foes ?
Why dost thou shun the salt ? that sacred
 pledge,
Which, once partaken, blunts the sabre's edge,
Makes ev'n in contending tribes in peace unite,
And hated hosts seem brethren to the sight !"

"Salt seasons dainties—and my food is still
The humblest root, my drink the simplest rill ;
And my stern vow and order's laws oppose
To break or mingle bread with friends or foes ;
It may seem strange—if there be aught to
 dread,
That peril rests upon my single head ;
But for thy sway—nay more—thy Sultan's
 throne,
I taste nor bread nor banquet—save alone ;
Infringed our order's rule, the Prophet's rage
To Mecca's dome might bar my pilgrimage."

"Well—as thou wilt—ascetic as thou art—
One question answer ; then in peace depart.
How many ?—Ha ! it cannot sure be day ?
What star—what sun is bursting on the bay ?
It shines a lake of fire !—away—away !
Ho ! treachery ! my guards ! my scimitar !
The galleys feed the flames—and I afar !
Accursed Dervise !—these thy tidings—thou
Some villain spy—seize—cleave him—slay
 him now !"

Up rose the Dervise with that burst of light,
Nor less his change of form appall'd the sight :
Up rose that Dervise—not in saintly garb,
But like a warrior bounding on his barb,

Dash'd his high cap, and tore his robe away—
Shone his mail'd breast, and flash'd his
 sabre's ray!
His close but glittering casque, and sable
 plume,
More glittering eye, and black brow's sabler
 gloom,
Glared on the Moslems' eyes some Afrit
 sprite,
Whose demon death-blow left no hope for
 fight.
The wild confusion, and the swarthy glow
Of flames on high, and torches from below;
The shriek of terror, and the mingling yell—
For swords began to clash, and shouts to
 swell—
Flung o'er that spot of earth the air of hell!
Distracted, to and fro, the flying slaves
Behold but bloody shore and fiery waves;
Nought heeded they the Pacha's angry cry,
They seize that Dervise!—seize on Zatanai!
He saw their terror—check'd the first despair
That urged him but to stand and perish there,
Since far too early and too well obey'd,
The flame was kindled ere the signal made;
He saw their terror—from his baldric drew
His bugle—brief the blast—but shrilly blew;
'T is answered—" Well ye speed, my gallant
 crew!
Why did I doubt their quickness of career?
And deem design had left me single here?"
Sweeps his long arm—that sabre's whirling
 sway
Sheds fast atonement for its first delay;
Completes his fury what their fear begun,
And makes the many basely quail to one.
The cloven turbans o'er the chamber spread,
And scarce an arm dare rise to guard its
 head:
Even Seyd, convulsed, o'erwhelm'd, with
 rage, surprise,
Retreats before him, though he still defies.
No craven he—and yet he dreads the blow,
So much Confusion magnifies his foe!
His blazing galleys still distract his sight,
He tore his beard, and foaming fled the
 fight;
For now the pirates pass'd the Haram gate,
And burst within—and it were death to
 wait;
Where wild Amazement shrieking—kneeling
 throws
The sword aside—in vain—the blood o'er-
 flows!
The Corsairs pouring, haste to where within
Invited Conrad's bugle, and the din
Of groaning victims, and wild cries for life,
Proclaim'd how well he did the work of strife,
They shout to find him grim and lonely there,
A glutted tiger mangling in his lair!

But short their greeting, shorter his reply—
" 'T is well—but Seyd escapes, and he must
 die—
Much hath been done, but more remains to
 do—
Their galleys blaze—why not their city too?"

V.

Quick at the word they seized him each a
 torch,
And fire the dome from minaret to porch.
A stern delight was fix'd in Conrad's eye,
But sudden sunk—for on his ear the cry
Of women struck, and like a deadly knell
Knock'd at that heart unmoved by battle's
 yell.
" Oh! burst the Haram—wrong not on your
 lives
One female form—remember—*we* have wives.
On them such outrage Vengeance will repay;
Man is our foe, and such 'tis ours to slay:
But still we spared—must spare the weaker
 prey.
Oh! I forgot—but Heaven will not forgive
If at my word the helpless cease to live;
Follow who will—I go—we yet have time
Our souls to lighten of at least a crime."
He climbs the crackling stair, he bursts the
 door,
Nor feels his feet glow scorching with the
 floor;
His breath choked gasping with the volumed
 smoke,
But still from room to room his way he
 broke.
They search—they find—they save: with
 lusty arms
Each bears a prize of unregarded charms;
Calm their loud fears; sustain their sinking
 frames
With all the care defenceless beauty claims:
So well could Conrad tame their fiercest
 mood,
And check the very hands with gore imbrued.
But who is she? whom Conrad's arms convey
From reeking pile and combat's wreck away—
Who but the love of him he dooms to bleed?
The Haram queen—but still the slave of
 Seyd!

VI.

Brief time had Conrad now to greet Gulnare,
Few words to re-assure the trembling fair;
For in that pause compassion snatch'd from
 war,
The foe before retiring, fast and far,
With wonder saw their footsteps unpursued,
First slowlier fled—then rallied—then with-
 stood.

This Seyd perceives, then first perceives how
few,
Compared with his, the Corsair's roving
crew,
And blushes o'er his error, as he eyes
The ruin wrought by panic and surprise.
Alla il Alla! Vengeance swells the cry—
Shame mounts to rage that must atone or
die!
And flame for flame and blood for blood must
tell,
The tide of triumph ebbs that flow'd too
well—
When wrath returns to renovated strife,
And those who fought for conquest strike for
life.
Conrad beheld the danger—he beheld
His followers faint by freshening foes re-
pell'd:
"One effort—one—to break the circling
host!"
They form—unite—charge—waver—all is
lost!
Within a narrower ring compress'd, beset,
Hopeless, not heartless, strive and struggle
yet—
Ah! now they fight in firmest file no more,
Hemm'd in, cut off, cleft down, and trampled
o'er,
But each strikes singly, silently, and home,
And sinks outwearied rather than o'ercome,
His last faint quittance rendering with his
breath,
Till the blade glimmers in the grasp of death!

VII.

But first, ere came the rallying host to blows,
And rank to rank, and hand to hand oppose,
Gulnare and all her Haram handmaids freed,
Safe in the dome of one who held their creed,
By Conrad's mandate safely were bestow'd,
And dried those tears for life and fame that
flow'd:
And when that dark-eyed lady, young
Gulnare,
Recall'd those thoughts late wandering in
despair,
Much did she marvel o'er the courtesy
That smooth'd his accents; soften'd in his
eye:
'Twas strange—*that* robber thus with gore
bedew'd
Seem'd gentler then than Seyd in fondest
mood.
The Pacha woo'd as if he deem'd the slave
Must seem delighted with the heart he gave;
The Corsair vow'd protection, soothed af-
fright,
As if his homage were a woman's right.

"The wish is wrong—nay, worse for female—
vain:
Yet much I long to view that chief again;
If but to thank for, what my fear forgot,
The life my loving lord remember'd not!"

VIII.

And him she saw, where thickest carnage
spread,
But gather'd breathing from the happier
dead;
Far from his band, and battling with a host
That deem right dearly won the field he lost,
Fell'd—bleeding—baffled of the death he
sought,
And snatch'd to expiate all the ills he
wrought;
Preserved to linger and to live in vain,
While Vengeance ponder'd o'er new plans of
pain,
And stanch'd the blood she saves to shed
again—
But drop for drop, for Seyd's unglutted eye
Would doom him ever dying—ne'er to die!
Can this be he? triumphant late she saw,
When his red hand's wild gesture waved,
a law!
'Tis he indeed—disarm'd but undeprest,
His sole regret the life he still possest;
His wounds too slight, though taken with
that will,
Which would have kiss'd the hand that then
could kill.
Oh were there none, of all the many given,
To send his soul—he scarcely ask'd to
heaven?
Must he alone of all retain his breath,
Who more than all had striven and struck
for death?
He deeply felt—what mortal hearts must
feel,
When thus reversed on faithless fortune's
wheel,
For crimes committed, and the victor's threat
Of lingering tortures to repay the debt—
He deeply, darkly felt; but evil pride
That led to perpetrate, now serves to hide.
Still in his stern and self-collected mien
A conqueror's more than captive's air is
seen,
Though faint with wasting toil and stiffening
wound,
But few that saw—so calmly gazed around:
Though the far shouting of the distant
crowd,
Their tremors o'er, rose insolently loud,
The better warriors who beheld him near,
Insulted not the foe who taught them fear;
And the grim guards that to his durance led,
In silence eyed him with a secret dread.

IX.

The Leech was sent—but not in mercy—
 there,
To note how much the life yet left could
 bear;
He found enough to load with heaviest chain,
And promise feeling for the wrench of pain;
To-morrow—yea—to-morrow's evening sun
Will sinking see impalement's pangs begun,
And rising with the wonted blush of morn
Behold how well or ill those pangs are borne.
Of torments this the longest and the worst,
Which adds all other agony to thirst,
That day by day death still forbears to slake,
While famish'd vultures flit around the stake.
"Oh! water—water!"—smiling Hate denies
The victim's prayer, for if he drinks he dies.
This was his doom;—the Leech, the guard
 were gone,
And left proud Conrad fetter'd and alone.

X.

'T were vain to paint to what his feelings
 grew—
It even were doubtful if their victim knew.
There is a war, a chaos of the mind,
When all its elements convulsed, combined,
Lie dark and jarring with perturbed force,
And gnashing with impenitent Remorse—
That juggling fiend, who never spake before,
But cries "I warn'd thee!" when the deed
 is o'er.
Vain voice! the spirit burning but unbent,
May writhe, rebel—the weak alone repent!
Even in that lonely hour when most it feels,
And, to itself, all, all that self reveals,—
No single passion, and no ruling thought
That leaves the rest, as once, unseen, un-
 sought,
But the wild prospect when the soul reviews,
All rushing through their thousand avenues.
Ambition's dreams expiring, love's regret,
Endanger'd glory, life itself beset;
The joy untasted, the contempt or hate
'Gainst those who fain would triumph in our
 fate;
The hopeless past, the hasting future driven
Too quickly on to guess of hell or heaven;
Deeds, thoughts, and words, perhaps remem-
 ber'd not
So keenly till that hour, but ne'er forgot;
Things light or lovely in their acted time,
But now to stern reflection each a crime;
The withering sense of evil unreveal'd,
Not cankering less because the more con-
 ceal'd—
All, in a word, from which all eyes must
 start,
That opening sepulchre—the naked heart

Bares with its buried woes, till Pride awake,
To snatch the mirror from the soul—and
 break.
Ay, Pride can veil, and Courage brave it
 all—
All—all—before—beyond—the deadliest fall.
Each hath some fear, and he who least
 betrays,
The only hypocrite deserving praise:
Not the loud recreant wretch who boasts and
 flies;
But he who looks on death—and silent dies.
So steel'd by pondering o'er his far career,
He half-way meets him should he menace
 near!

XI.

In the high chamber of his highest tower
Sate Conrad, fetter'd in the Pacha's power.
His palace perish'd in the flame—this fort
Contain'd at once his captive and his court.
Not much could Conrad of his sentence
 blame,
His foe, if vanquish'd, had but shared the
 same:—
Alone he sate—in solitude had scann'd
His guilty bosom, but that breast he mann'd:
One thought alone he could not—dared not
 meet—
"Oh, how these tidings will Medora greet?"
Then—only then—his clanking hands he
 raised,
And strain'd with rage the chain on which he
 gazed;
But soon he found, or feign'd, or dream'd
 relief,
And smiled in self-derision of his grief,
"And now come torture when it will—or
 may,
More need of rest to nerve me for the day!"
This said, with languor to his mat he crept,
And, whatsoe'er his visions, quickly slept.
'T was hardly midnight when that fray
 begun,
For Conrad's plans matured, at once were
 done:
And Havoc loathes so much the waste of time,
She scarce had left an uncommitted crime.
One hour beheld him since the tide he
 stemm'd—
Disguised, discover'd, conquering, ta'en, con-
 demn'd—
A chief on land, an outlaw on the deep—
Destroying, saving, prison'd, and asleep!

XII.

He slept in calmest seeming, for his breath
Was hush'd so deep—Ah! happy if in death!
He slept—Who o'er his placid slumber bends?
His foes are gone, and here he hath no friends;

Is it some seraph sent to grant him grace?
No, 'tis an earthly form with heavenly face!
Its white arm raised a lamp—yet gently hid,
Lest the ray flash abruptly on the lid
Of that closed eye, which opens but to pain,
And once unclosed—but once may close again.
That form, with eye so dark, and cheek so fair,
And auburn waves of gemm'd and braided
　　hair;
With shape of fairy lightness—naked foot,
That shines like snow, and falls on earth as
　　mute—
Through guards and dunnest night how came
　　it there?
Ah! rather ask what will not woman dare?
Whom youth and pity lead like thee, Gulnare!
She could not sleep—and while the Pacha's
　　rest
In muttering dreams yet saw his pirate-guest,
She left his side—his signet-ring she bore,
Which oft in sport adorn'd her hand before—
And with it, scarcely question'd, won her way
Through drowsy guards that must that sign
　　obey.
Worn out with toil, and tired with changing
　　blows,
Their eyes had envied Conrad his repose;
And chill and nodding at the turret door,
They stretch their listless limbs, and watch
　　no more;
Just raised their heads to hail the signet-ring,
Nor ask or what or who the sign may bring.

XIII.

She gazed in wonder, "Can he calmly sleep,
While other eyes his fall or ravage weep?
And mine in restlessness are wandering here—
What sudden spell hath made this man so
　　dear?
True—'tis to him my life, and more, I owe,
And me and mine he spared from worse than
　　woe:
'Tis late to think—but soft, his slumber
　　breaks—
How heavily he sighs!—he starts—awakes!"

He raised his head, and dazzled with the
　　light,
His eye seem'd dubious if it saw aright:
He moved his hand—the grating of his chain
Too harshly told him that he lived again.
"What is that form? if not a shape of air,
Methinks, my jailor's face shows wondrous
　　fair!"

"Pirate! thou know'st me not—but I am one,
Grateful for deeds thou hast too rarely done;
Look on me—and remember her, thy hand
Snatch'd from the flames, and thy more fear-
　　ful band.

I come through darkness—and I scarce know
　　why—
Yet not to hurt—I would not see thee die."
"If so, kind lady! thine the only eye
That would not here in that gay hope delight:
Theirs is the chance—and let them use their
　　right.
But still I thank their courtesy or thine,
That would confess me at so fair a shrine!"
Strange though it seem—yet with extremest
　　grief
Is link'd a mirth—it doth not bring relief—
That playfulness of Sorrow ne'er beguiles,
And smiles in bitterness—but still it smiles;
And sometimes with the wisest and the best,
Till even the scaffold echoes with their jest!
Yet not the joy to which it seems akin—
It may deceive all hearts, save that within.
Whate'er it was that flash'd on Conrad, now
A laughing wildness half unbent his brow:
And these his accents had a sound of mirth,
As if the last he could enjoy on earth;
Yet 'gainst his nature—for through that short
　　life,
Few thoughts had he to spare from gloom and
　　strife.

XIV.

"Corsair! thy doom is named—but I have
　　power
To soothe the Pacha in his weaker hour.
Thee would I spare—nay more—would save
　　thee now,
But this—time—hope—nor even thy strength
　　allow;
But all I can, I will: at least, delay
The sentence that remits thee scarce a day.
More now were ruin—even thyself were loth
The vain attempt should bring but doom to
　　both."

"Yes! loth indeed:—my soul is nerved to all,
Or fall'n too low to fear a further fall:
Tempt not thyself with peril—me with hope
Of flight from foes with whom I could not
　　cope:
Unfit to vanquish, shall I meanly fly,
The one of all my band that would not die?
Yet there is one to whom my memory clings,
Till to these eyes her own wild softness
　　springs.
My sole resources in the path I trod
Were these—my bark, my sword, my love, my
　　God!
The last I left in youth!—he leaves me now—
And Man but works his will to lay me low.
I have no thought to mock his throne with
　　prayer
Wrung from the coward crouching of despair;
It is enough—I breathe, and I can bear.

My sword is shaken from the worthless hand
That might have better kept so true a brand;
My bark is sunk or captive—but my love—
For her in sooth my voice would mount above:
Oh! she is all that still to earth can bind—
And this will break a heart so more than
 kind,
And blight a form—till thine appear'd,
 Gulnare!
Mine eye ne'er ask'd if others were as fair."

"Thou lov'st another then?—but what to me
Is this—'t is nothing—nothing e'er can be:
But yet—thou lov'st—and—Oh! I envy those
Whose hearts on hearts as faithful can repose,
Who never feel the void—the wandering
 thought
That sighs o'er visions—such as mine hath
 wrought."

"Lady, methought thy love was his, for whom
This arm redeem'd thee from a fiery tomb."

"My love stern Seyd's! Oh—No—No—not
 my love—
Yet much this heart, that strives no more, once
 strove
To meet his passion—but it would not be.
I felt—I feel—love dwells with—with the free.
I am a slave, a favour'd slave at best,
To share his splendour, and seem very blest!
Oft must my soul the question undergo,
Of—'Dost thou love?' and burn to answer,
 'No!'
Oh! hard it is that fondness to sustain,
And struggle not to feel averse in vain;
But harder still the heart's recoil to bear,
And hide from one—perhaps another there.
He takes the hand I give not, nor withhold—
Its pulse nor check'd, nor quicken'd—calmly
 cold:
And when resign'd, it drops a lifeless weight
From one I never loved enough to hate.
No warmth these lips return by his imprest,
And chill'd remembrance shudders o'er the
 rest.
Yes—had I ever proved that passion's zeal,
The change to hatred were at least to feel:
But still he goes unmourn'd, returns unsought,
And oft when present—absent from my
 thought.
Or when reflection comes—and come it must—
I fear that henceforth 't will but bring disgust;
I am his slave—but, in despite of pride,
'T were worse than bondage to become his
 bride.
Oh! that this dotage of his breast would
 cease:
Or seek another and give mine release,
But yesterday—I could have said, to peace!

Yes, if unwonted fondness now I feign,
Remember, captive! 't is to break thy chain;
Repay the life that to thy hand I owe;
To give thee back to all endear'd below,
Who share such love as I can never know.
Farewell, morn breaks, and I must now away:
'T will cost me dear—but dread no death
 to-day!"

XV.

She press'd his fetter'd fingers to her heart,
And bow'd her head, and turn'd her to de-
 part,
And noiseless as a lovely dream is gone.
And was she here? and is he now alone?
What gem hath dropp'd and sparkles o'er his
 chain?
The tear most sacred, shed for others' pain,
That starts at once—bright—pure—from
 Pity's mine,
Already polish'd by the hand divine!

Oh! too convincing—dangerously dear—
In woman's eye the unanswerable tear!
That weapon of her weakness she can wield,
To save, subdue—at once her spear and
 shield:
Avoid it—Virtue ebbs and Wisdom errs,
Too fondly gazing on that grief of hers!
What lost a world, and bade a hero fly?
The timid tear in Cleopatra's eye.
Yet be the soft triumvir's fault forgiven;
By this—how many lose not earth—but
 heaven!
Consign their souls to man's eternal foe,
And seal their own to spare some wanton's
 woe!

XVI.

'T is morn, and o'er his alter'd features play
The beams—without the hope of yesterday.
What shall he be ere night? perchance a
 thing
O'er which the raven flaps her funeral wing,
By his closed eye unheeded and unfelt;
While sets that sun, and dews of evening
 melt,
Chill, wet, and misty round each stiffen'd
 limb,
Refreshing earth—reviving all but him!

———•———

Canto the Third.

"Come vedi—ancor non m'abbandona."—DANTE.

I.

SLOW sinks, more lovely ere his race be run,
Along Morea's hills the setting sun;
Not, as in Northern climes, obscurely bright,
But one unclouded blaze of living light!

O'er the hush'd deep the yellow beam he
 throws,
Gilds the green wave, that trembles as it
 glows.
On old Ægina's rock and Idra's isle,
The god of gladness sheds his parting smile;
O'er his own regions lingering, loves to
 shine,
Though there his altars are no more divine.
Descending fast the mountain shadows kiss
Thy glorious gulf, unconquer'd Salamis!
Their azure arches through the long expanse
More deeply purpled meet his mellowing
 glance,
And tenderest tints, along their summits
 driven,
Mark his gay course, and own the hues of
 heaven;
Till, darkly shaded from the land and deep,
Behind his Delphian cliff he sinks to sleep.

On such an eve, his palest beam he cast,
When—Athens! here thy Wisest look'd his
 last.
How watch'd thy better sons his farewell ray,
That closed their murder'd sage's latest day!
Not yet—not yet—Sol pauses on the hill—
The precious hour of parting lingers still;
But sad his light to agonising eyes,
And dark the mountain's once delightful
 dyes:
Gloom o'er the lovely land he seem'd to pour,
The land, where Phœbus never frown'd be-
 fore;
But ere he sank below Cithæron's head,
The cup of woe was quaff'd—the spirit fled;
The soul of him who scorn'd to fear or fly—
Who lived and died, as none can live or die!

But lo! from high Hymettus to the plain,
The queen of night asserts her silent reign.
No murky vapour, herald of the storm,
Hides her fair face, nor girds her glowing
 form;
With cornice glimmering as the moonbeams
 play,
There the white column greets her grateful
 ray,
And, bright around with quivering beams
 beset,
Her emblem sparkles o'er the minaret:
The groves of olive scatter'd dark and wide
Where meek Cephisus pours his scanty tide,
The cypress saddening by the sacred mosque,
The gleaming turret of the gay kiosk,
And, dun and sombre 'mid the holy calm,
Near Theseus' fane yon solitary palm,
All tinged with varied hues arrest the eye—
And dull were his that pass'd them heed-
 less by.

Again the Ægean, heard no more afar,
Lulls his chafed breast from elemental war;
Again his waves in milder tints unfold
Their long array of sapphire and of gold,
Mix'd with the shades of many a distant isle,
That frown—where gentler ocean seems to
 smile.

II.

Not now my theme—why turn my thoughts
 to thee?
Oh! who can look along thy native sea,
Nor dwell upon thy name, whate'er the tale,
So much its magic must o'er all prevail?
Who that beheld that Sun upon thee set,
Fair Athens! could thine evening face forget?
Not he—whose heart nor time nor distance
 frees,
Spell-bound within the clustering Cyclades!
Nor seems this homage foreign to its strain,
His Corsair's isle was once thine own do-
 main—
Would that with freedom it were thine again!

III.

The Sun hath sunk—and, darker than the night,
Sinks with its beam upon the beacon height
Medora's heart—the third day 's come and
 gone—
With it he comes not—sends not—faithless
 one!
The wind was fair though light; and storms
 were none.
Last eve Anselmo's bark return'd, and yet
His only tidings that they had not met!
Though wild, as now, far different were the
 tale
Had Conrad waited for that single sail.

The night-breeze freshens—she that day had
 pass'd
In watching all that Hope proclaim'd a mast;
Sadly she sate on high—Impatience bore
At last her footsteps to the midnight shore,
And there she wander'd, heedless of the spray
That dash'd her garments oft, and warn'd
 away:
She saw not, felt not this—nor dared depart,
Nor deem'd it cold—her chill was at her
 heart;
Till grew such certainty from that suspense—
His very sight had shock'd from life or sense!

It came at last—a sad and shatter'd boat,
Whose inmates first beheld whom first they
 sought;
Some bleeding—all most wretched—these
 the few—
Scarce knew they how escaped—*this* all they
 knew.

In silence, darkling, each appear'd to wait
His fellow's mournful guess at Conrad's fate:
Something they would have said; but seem'd
 to fear
To trust their accents to Medora's ear.
She saw at once, yet sunk not—trembled not—
Beneath that grief, that loneliness of lot,
Within that meek fair form, were feelings
 high,
That deem'd not till they found their energy.
While yet it was Hope they soften'd, flutter'd,
 wept—
All lost—that softness died not—but it slept;
And o'er its slumber rose that Strength
 which said,
"With nothing left to love, there's nought to
 dread."
'Tis more than nature's; like the burning
 might
Delirium gathers from the fever's height.

"Silent you stand—nor would I hear you tell
What—speak not—breathe not—for I know
 it well—
Yet would I ask—almost my lip denies
The—quick your answer—tell me where he
 lies."

"Lady! we know not—scarce with life we fled;
But here is one denies that he is dead:
He saw him bound; and bleeding—but alive."

She heard no further—'t was in vain to
 strive—
So throbb'd each vein—each thought—till
 then withstood;
Her own dark soul—these words at once
 subdued:
She totters—falls—and senseless had the
 wave
Perchance but snatched her from another
 grave,
But that with hands though rude, yet weep-
 ing eyes,
They yield such aid as Pity's haste supplies;
Dash o'er her deathlike cheek the ocean
 dew,
Raise, fan, sustain—till life returns anew;
Awake her handmaids, with the matrons leave
That fainting form o'er which they gaze and
 grieve;
Then seek Anselmo's cavern, to report
The tale too tedious—when the triumph
 short.

IV.

In that wild council words wax'd warm and
 strange
With thoughts of ransom, rescue, and re-
 venge;

All, save repose or flight: still lingering there
Breathed Conrad's spirit, and forbade despair;
Whate'er his fate—the breasts he form'd and
 led
Will save him living, or appease him dead.
Woe to his foes! there yet survive a few,
Whose deeds are daring, as their hearts are
 true.

V.

Within the Haram's secret chamber sate
Stern Seyd, still pondering o'er his Captive's
 fate;
His thoughts on love and hate alternate
 dwell,
Now with Gulnare, and now in Conrad's
 cell;
Here at his feet the lovely slave reclined
Surveys his brow—would soothe his gloom
 of mind;
While many an anxious glance her large
 dark eye
Sends in its idle search for sympathy,
His only bends in seeming o'er his beads,
But inly views his victim as he bleeds.
"Pacha! the day is thine; and on thy crest
Sits Triumph—Conrad taken—fall'n the rest!
His doom is fix'd—he dies: and well his fate
Was earn'd—yet much too worthless for thy
 hate:
Methinks, a short release, for ransom told
With all his treasure, not unwisely sold;
Report speaks largely of his pirate-hoard—
Would that of this my Pacha were the lord!
While baffled, weaken'd by this fatal fray—
Watch'd—follow'd—he were then an easier
 prey;
But once cut off—the remnant of his band
Embark their wealth, and seek a safer
 strand."

"Gulnare!—if for each drop of blood a gem
Were offer'd rich as Stamboul's diadem;
If for each hair of his a massy mine
Of virgin ore should supplicating shine;
If all our Arab tales divulge or dream
Of wealth were here—that gold should not
 redeem!
It had not now redeem'd a single hour,
But that I know him fetter'd, in my power;
And, thirsting for revenge, I ponder still
On pangs that longest rack, and latest kill."

"Nay, Seyd! I seek not to restrain thy rage,
Too justly moved for mercy to assuage;
My thoughts were only to secure for thee
His riches—thus released, he were not free:
Disabled, shorn of half his might and band,
His capture could but wait thy first com-
 mand."

"His capture *could!*—and shall I then resign
One day to him—the wretch already mine?
Release my foe!—at whose remonstrance?—
thine!
Fair suitor!—to thy virtuous gratitude,
That thus repays this Giaour's relenting
mood,
Which thee and thine alone of all could
spare,
No doubt—regardless if the prize were fair,
My thanks and praise alike are due—now
hear!
I have a counsel for thy gentler ear:
I do mistrust thee, woman! and each word
Of thine stamps truth on all Suspicion heard.
Borne in his arms through fire from yon
Serai—
Say, wert thou lingering there with him
to fly?
Thou need'st not answer—thy confession
speaks,
Already reddening on thy guilty cheeks;
Then, lovely dame, bethink thee! and be-
ware:
'Tis not *his* life alone may claim such care!
Another word and—nay—I need no more.
Accursed was the moment when he bore
Thee from the flames, which better far—
but no—
I then had mourn'd thee with a lover's woe—
Now 'tis thy lord that warns—deceitful
thing!
Know'st thou that I can clip thy wanton
wing?
In words alone I am not wont to chafe:
Look to thyself, nor deem thy falsehood
safe!"

He rose—and slowly, sternly thence with-
drew,
Rage in his eye and threats in his adieu:
Ah! little reck'd that chief of womanhood—
Which frowns ne'er quell'd, nor menaces
subdued;
And little deem'd he what thy heart, Gul-
nare!
When soft could feel, and when incensed
could dare.
His doubts appear'd to wrong—nor yet she
knew
How deep the root from whence compassion
grew—
She was a slave—from such may captives
claim
A fellow-feeling, differing but in name;
Still half unconscious—heedless of his wrath,
Again she ventured on the dangerous path,
Again his rage repell'd—until arose
That strife of thought, the source of woman's
woes!

VI.

Meanwhile long, anxious, weary, still the
same
Roll'd day and night: his soul could terror
tame—
This fearful interval of doubt and dread,
When every hour might doom him worse
than dead,
When every step that echo'd by the gate,
Might entering lead where axe and stake
await;
When every voice that grated on his ear
Might be the last that he could ever hear;
Could terror tame—that spirit stern and high
Had proved unwilling as unfit to die;
'Twas worn—perhaps decay'd—yet silent
bore
That conflict, deadlier far than all before:
The heat of fight, the hurry of the gale,
Leave scarce one thought inert enough to
quail;
But bound and fix'd in fetter'd solitude,
To pine, the prey of every changing mood;
To gaze on thine own heart; and meditate
Irrevocable faults, and coming fate—
Too late the last to shun—the first to mend—
To count the hours that struggle to thine end,
With not a friend to animate, and tell
To other ears that death became thee well;
Around thee foes to forge the ready lie,
And blot life's latest scene with calumny;
Before thee tortures, which the soul can dare,
Yet doubts how well the shrinking flesh may
bear;
But deeply feels a single cry would shame,
To valour's praise thy last and dearest claim;
The life thou leav'st below, denied above
By kind monopolists of heavenly love;
And more than doubtful paradise—thy heaven
Of earthly hope—thy loved one from thee
riven.
Such were the thoughts that outlaw must
sustain,
And govern pangs surpassing mortal pain:
And those sustain'd he—boots it well or ill?
Since not to sink beneath, is something still!

VII.

The first day pass'd—he saw not her—
Gulnare—
The second, third—and still she came not
there;
But what her words avouch'd, her charms
had done,
Or else he had not seen another sun.
The fourth day roll'd along, and with the
night
Came storm and darkness in their mingling
might.

Oh! how he listen'd to the rushing deep,
That ne'er till now so broke upon his sleep;
And his wild spirit wilder wishes sent,
Roused by the roar of his own element!
Oft had he ridden on that winged wave,
And loved its roughness for the speed it gave;
And now its dashing echo'd on his ear,
A long known voice—alas! too vainly near!
Loud sung the wind above; and, doubly loud,
Shook o'er his turret cell the thunder-cloud;
And flash'd the lightning by the latticed bar,
To him more genial than the midnight star:
Close to the glimmering grate he dragg'd his chain;
And hoped *that* peril might not prove in vain.
He raised his iron hand to Heaven, and pray'd
One pitying flash to mar the form it made:
His steel and impious prayer attract alike—
The storm roll'd onward, and disdain'd to strike;
Its peal wax'd fainter—ceased—he felt alone,
As if some faithless friend had spurn'd his groan?

VIII.

The midnight pass'd, and to the massy door
A light step came—it paused—it moved once more;
Slow turns the grating bolt and sullen key:
'Tis as his heart foreboded—that fair she!
Whate'er her sins, to him a guardian saint,
And beauteous still as hermit's hope can paint;
Yet changed since last within that cell she came,
More pale her cheek, more tremulous her frame:
On him she cast her dark and hurried eye,
Which spoke before her accents—"Thou must die!
Yes, thou must die—there is but one resource,
The last—the worst—if torture were not worse."

"Lady! I look to none; my lips proclaim
What last proclaim'd they—Conrad still the same:
Why shouldst thou seek an outlaw's life to spare,
And change the sentence I deserve to bear?
Well have I earn'd—nor here alone—the meed
Of Seyd's revenge, by many a lawless deed."

"Why should I seek? because—Oh! didst thou not
Redeem my life from worse than slavery's lot?

Why should I seek?—hath misery made thee blind
To the fond workings of a woman's mind?
And must I say?—albeit my heart rebel
With all that woman feels, but should not tell—
Because, despite thy crimes, that heart is moved:
It fear'd thee, thank'd thee, pitied, madden'd, loved.
Reply not, tell not now thy tale again,
Thou lov'st another, and I love in vain:
Though fond as mine her bosom, form more fair,
I rush through peril which she would not dare.
If that thy heart to hers were truly dear,
Were I thine own thou wert not lonely here:
An outlaw's spouse and leave her lord to roam!
What hath such gentle dame to do with home?
But speak not now—o'er thine and o'er my head
Hangs the keen sabre by a single thread;
If thou hast courage still, and wouldst be free,
Receive this poniard—rise and follow me!"

"Ay in my chains! my steps will gently tread,
With these adornments, o'er each slumbering head!
Thou hast forgot—is this a garb for flight?
Or is that instrument more fit for fight?"

"Misdoubting Corsair! I have gain'd the guard,
Ripe for revolt, and greedy for reward.
A single word of mine removes that chain:
Without some aid how here could I remain?
Well, since we met, hath sped my busy time,
If in aught evil, for thy sake the crime:
The crime—'tis none to punish those of Seyd.
That hated tyrant, Conrad—he must bleed!
I see thee shudder, but my soul is changed—
Wrong'd, spurn'd, reviled, and it shall be avenged—
Accused of what till now my heart disdain'd—
Too faithful, though to bitter bondage chain'd.
Yes, smile!—but he had little cause to sneer,
I was not treacherous then, nor thou too dear:
But he has said it—and the jealous well—
Those tyrants, teasing, tempting to rebel—
Deserve the fate their fretting lips foretell.
I never loved—he bought me—somewhat high—
Since with me came a heart he could not buy.
I was a slave unmurmuring; he hath said,
But for his rescue I with thee had fled.

'Twas false thou know'st—but let such
 augurs rue,
Their words are omens insult renders true.
Nor was thy respite granted to my prayer;
This fleeting grace was only to prepare
New torments for thy life, and my despair.
Mine too he threatens; but his dotage still
Would fain reserve me for his lordly will:
When wearier of these fleeting charms and
 me,
There yawns the sack, and yonder rolls the
 sea!
What, am I then a toy for dotard's play,
To wear but till the gilding frets away?
I saw thee—loved thee—owe thee all—would
 save,
If but to show how grateful is a slave.
But had he not thus menaced fame and life—
(And well he keeps his oaths pronounced in
 strife)—
I still had saved thee, but the Pacha spared.
Now I am all thine own, for all prepared:
Thou lov'st me not, nor know'st—or but the
 worst.
Alas! *this* love—*that* hatred—are the first—
Oh! couldst thou prove my truth, thou
 wouldst not start,
Nor fear the fire that lights an Eastern heart;
'Tis now the beacon of thy safety—now
It points within the port a Mainote prow:
But in one chamber, where our path must
 lead,
There sleeps—he must not wake—the op-
 pressor Seyd!"

" Gulnare—Gulnare—I never felt till now
My abject fortune, wither'd fame so low:
Seyd is mine enemy; had swept my band
From earth with ruthless but with open
 hand,
And therefore came I, in my bark of war,
To smite the smiter with the scimitar;
Such is my weapon—not the secret knife;
Who spares a woman's seeks not slumber's
 life.
Thine saved I gladly, Lady—not for this;
Let me not deem that mercy shown amiss.
Now fare thee well—more peace be with thy
 breast!
Night wears apace, my last of earthly rest!"

"Rest! rest! by sunrise must thy sinews
 shake,
And thy limbs writhe around the ready stake.
I heard the order—saw—I will not see—
If thou wilt perish, I will fall with thee.
My life, my love, my hatred—all below
Are on this cast—Corsair! 'tis but a blow!
Without it flight were idle—how evade
His sure pursuit?—my wrongs too unrepaid,

My youth disgraced, the long, long wasted
 years,
One blow shall cancel with our future fears;
But since the dagger suits thee less than
 brand,
I'll try the firmness of a female hand.
The guards are gain'd—one moment all were
 o'er—
Corsair! we meet in safety or no more;
If errs my feeble hand, the morning cloud
Will hover o'er thy scaffold, and my shroud."

IX.

She turn'd, and vanish'd ere he could reply,
But his glance follow'd far with eager eye;
And gathering, as he could, the links that
 bound
His form, to curl their length, and curb their
 sound,
Since bar and bolt no more his steps pre-
 clude,
He, fast as fetter'd limbs allow, pursued.
'Twas dark and winding, and he knew not
 where
That passage led; nor lamp nor guard was
 there:
He sees a dusky glimmering—shall he seek
Or shun that ray so indistinct and weak?
Chance guides his steps—a freshness seems
 to bear
Full on his brow, as if from morning air;
He reach'd an open gallery—on his eye
Gleam'd the last star of night, the clearing
 sky:
Yet scarcely heeded these—another light
From a lone chamber struck upon his sight.
Towards it he moved; a scarcely closing
 door
Reveal'd the ray within, but nothing more.
With hasty step a figure outward pass'd,
Then paused, and turn'd—and paused—'tis
 she at last!
No poniard in that hand, nor sign of ill—
" Thanks to that softening heart—she could
 not kill!"
Again he look'd, the wildness of her eye
Starts from the day abrupt and fearfully.
She stopp'd—threw back her dark far-float-
 ing hair,
That nearly veil'd her face and bosom fair,
As if she late had bent her leaning head
Above some object of her doubt or dread.
They meet—upon her brow—unknown, for-
 got—
Her hurrying hand had left—'t was but a
 spot—
Its hue was all he saw, and scarce with-
 stood—
Oh! slight but certain pledge of crime—'tis
 blood!

X.

He had seen battle—he had brooded lone
O'er promised pangs to sentenced guilt fore-
 shown;
He had been tempted, chasten'd, and the chain
Yet on his arms might ever there remain:
But ne'er from strife, captivity, remorse—
From all his feelings in their inmost force—
So thrill'd, so shudder'd every creeping vein,
As now they froze before that purple stain.
That spot of blood, that light but guilty
 streak,
Had banish'd all the beauty from her cheek!
Blood he had view'd, could view unmoved—
 but then
It flow'd in combat, or was shed by men!

XI.

" 'Tis done—he nearly waked—but it is done.
Corsair! he perish'd—thou art dearly won.
All words would now be vain—away—away!
Our bark is tossing—'tis already day.
The few gain'd over, now are wholly mine,
And these thy yet surviving band shall join:
Anon my voice shall vindicate my hand,
When once our sail forsakes this hated
 strand."

XII.

She clapp'd her hands, and through the gallery
 pour,
Equipp'd for flight, her vassals—Greek and
 Moor;
Silent but quick they stoop, his chains un-
 bind;
Once more his limbs are free as mountain
 wind!
But on his heavy heart such sadness sate,
As if they there transferr'd that iron weight.
No words are utter'd—at her sign, a door
Reveals the secret passage to the shore:
The city lies behind—they speed, they reach
The glad waves dancing on the yellow beach;
And Conrad following, at her beck, obey'd,
Nor cared he now if rescued or betray'd;
Resistance were as useless as if Seyd
Yet lived to view the doom his ire decreed.

XIII.

Embark'd, the sail unfurl'd, the light breeze
 blew—
How much had Conrad's memory to review!
Sunk he in contemplation, till the cape
Where last he anchor'd rear'd its giant shape.
Ah! since that fatal night, though brief the
 time,
Had swept an age of terror, grief, and crime.
As its far shadow frown'd above the mast,
He veil'd his face, and sorrow'd as he pass'd;

He thought of all—Gonsalvo and his band,
His fleeting triumph and his failing hand;
He thought on her afar, his lonely bride:
He turn'd and saw—Gulnare, the homicide!

XIV.

She watch'd his features till she could not
 bear
Their freezing aspect and averted air;
And that strange fierceness, foreign to her
 eye,
Fell quench'd in tears, too late to shed or
 dry.
She knelt beside him and his hand she
 press'd,
"Thou may'st forgive, though Allah's self
 detest;
But for that deed of darkness what wert
 thou?
Reproach me—but not yet—Oh! spare me
 now!
I am not what I seem—this fearful night
My brain bewilder'd—do not madden quite!
If I had never loved, though less my guilt,
Thou hadst not lived to—hate me—if thou
 wilt."

XV.

She wrongs his thoughts, they more himself
 upbraid
Than her, though undesign'd, the wretch he
 made;
But speechless all, deep, dark, and unexprest,
They bleed within that silent cell—his breast.
Still onward, fair the breeze, nor rough the
 surge,
The blue waves sport around the stern they
 urge;
Far on the horizon's verge appears a speck,
A spot—a mast—a sail—an armed deck!
Their little bark her men of watch descry,
And ampler canvas woos the wind from high;
She bears her down majestically near,
Speed on her prow, and terror in her tier;
A flash is seen—the ball beyond their bow
Booms harmless, hissing to the deep below.
Uprose keen Conrad from his silent trance,
A long, long absent gladness in his glance;
" 'Tis mine—my blood-red flag! again—
 again—
I am not all deserted on the main!"
They own the signal, answer to the hail,
Hoist out the boat at once, and slacken sail.
" 'Tis Conrad! Conrad!" shouting from the
 deck,
Command nor duty could their transport
 check!
With light alacrity and gaze of pride,
They view him mount once more his vessel's
 side;

A smile relaxing in each rugged face,
Their arms can scarce forbear a rough embrace.
He, half forgetting danger and defeat,
Returns their greeting as a chief may greet,
Wrings with a cordial grasp Anselmo's hand,
And feels he yet can conquer and command!

XVI.

These greetings o'er, the feelings that o'erflow,
Yet grieve to win him back without a blow;
They sail'd prepared for vengeance—had they known
A woman's hand secured that deed her own,
She were their queen—less scrupulous are they
Than haughty Conrad how they win their way.
With many an asking smile, and wondering stare,
They whisper round, and gaze upon Gulnare;
And her—at once above—beneath her sex,
Whom blood appall'd not, their regards perplex.
To Conrad turns her faint imploring eye,
She drops her veil, and stands in silence by;
Her arms are meekly folded on that breast,
Which—Conrad safe—to fate resign'd the rest.
Though worse than frenzy could that bosom fill,
Extreme in love or hate, in good or ill,
The worst of crimes had left her woman still!

XVII.

This Conrad mark'd, and felt—ah! could he less?—
Hate of that deed, but grief for her distress;
What she has done no tears can wash away,
And Heaven must punish on its angry day:
But—it was done: he knew, whate'er her guilt,
For him that poniard smote, that blood was spilt;
And he was free! and she for him had given
Her all on earth, and more than all in heaven!
And now he turn'd him to that dark-eyed slave
Whose brow was bow'd beneath the glance he gave,
Who now seem'd changed and humbled, faint and meek,
But varying oft the colour of her cheek
To deeper shades of paleness—all its red
That fearful spot which stain'd it from the dead!

He took that hand—it trembled—now too late—
So soft in love, so wildly nerved in hate;
He clasp'd that hand—it trembled—and his own
Had lost its firmness, and his voice its tone.
"Gulnare!"—but she replied not—"dear Gulnare!"
She raised her eye—her only answer there—
At once she sought and sunk in his embrace:
If he had driven her from that resting-place,
His had been more or less than mortal heart,
But—good or ill—it bade her not depart.
Perchance, but for the bodings of his breast,
His latest virtue then had join'd the rest.
Yet even Medora might forgive the kiss
That ask'd from form so fair no more than this,
The first, the last that Frailty stole from Faith—
To lips where Love had lavish'd all his breath,
To lips—whose broken sighs such fragrance fling,
As he had fann'd them freshly with his wing!

XVIII.

They gain by twilight's hour their lonely isle.
To them the very rocks appear to smile;
The haven hums with many a cheering sound,
The beacons blaze their wonted stations round,
The boats are darting o'er the curly bay,
And sportive dolphins bend them through the spray;
Even the hoarse sea-bird's shrill, discordant shriek
Greets like the welcome of his tuneless beak!
Beneath each lamp that through its lattice gleams,
Their fancy paints the friends that trim the beams.
Oh! what can sanctify the joys of home,
Like Hope's gay glance from Ocean's troubled foam?

XIX.

The lights are high on beacon and from bower,
And 'midst them Conrad seeks Medora's tower:
He looks in vain—'t is strange—and all remark,
Amid so many, hers alone is dark.
'T is strange—of yore its welcome never fail'd,
Nor now, perchance, extinguish'd, only veil'd.
With the first boat descends he for the shore,
And looks impatient on the lingering oar.

Oh! for a wing beyond the falcon's flight,
To bear him like an arrow to that height!
With the first pause the resting rowers gave,
He waits not, looks not—leaps into the wave,
Strives through the surge, bestrides the
 beach, and high
Ascends the path familiar to his eye.
He reach'd his turret door—he paused—no
 sound
Broke from within; and all was night
 around.
He knock'd, and loudly—footstep nor reply
Announced that any heard or deem'd him
 nigh;
He knock'd, but faintly—for his trembling
 hand
Refused to aid his heavy heart's demand.
The portal opens—'t is a well-known face,
But not the form he panted to embrace.
Its lips are silent—twice his own essay'd,
And fail'd to frame the question they delay'd;
He snatch'd the lamp—its light will answer
 all—
It quits his grasp, expiring in the fall.
He would not wait for that reviving ray—
As soon could he have linger'd there for day;
But, glimmering through the dusky corridor,
Another chequers o'er the shadow'd floor;
His steps the chamber gain—his eyes behold
All that his heart believed not—yet foretold!

XX.

He turn'd not—spoke not—sunk not—fix'd
 his look,
And set the anxious frame that lately shook:
He gazed—how long we gaze despite of pain,
And know, but dare not own, we gaze in
 vain!
In life itself she was so still and fair,
That death with gentler aspect wither'd
 there;
And the cold flowers her colder hand con-
 tain'd,
In that last grasp as tenderly were strain'd
As if she scarcely felt, but feign'd a sleep,
And made it almost mockery yet to weep:
The long dark lashes fringed her lids of
 snow,
And veil'd—thought shrinks from all that
 lurk'd below—
Oh! o'er the eye Death most exerts his
 might,
And hurls the spirit from her throne of light;
Sinks those blue orbs in that long last
 eclipse,
But spares, as yet, the charm around her
 lips—
Yet, yet they seem as they forbore to smile,
And wish'd repose,—but only for a while;

But the white shroud, and each extended
 tress,
Long, fair—but spread in utter lifelessness,
Which, late the sport of every summer wind,
Escaped the baffled wreath that strove to
 bind;
These—and the pale pure cheek, became the
 bier—
But she is nothing—wherefore is he here?

XXI.

He ask'd no question—all were answer'd now
By the first glance on that still, marble brow.
It was enough—she died—what reck'd it how
The love of youth, the hope of better years,
The source of softest wishes, tenderest fears,
The only living thing he could not hate,
Was reft at once—and he deserved his fate,
But did not feel it less;—the good explore,
For peace, those realms where guilt can
 never soar:
The proud, the wayward—who have fix'd
 below
Their joy, and find this earth enough for woe,
Lose in that one their all—perchance a
 mite—
But who in patience parts with all delight?
Full many a stoic eye and aspect stern
Mask hearts where grief hath little left to
 learn;
And many a withering thought lies hid, not
 lost,
In smiles that least befit who wear them
 most.

XXII.

By those, that deepest feel, is ill exprest
The indistinctness of the suffering breast;
Where thousand thoughts begin to end in
 one,
Which seeks from all the refuge found in
 none;
No words suffice the secret soul to show,
For Truth denies all eloquence to Woe.
On Conrad's stricken soul exhaustion prest,
And stupor almost lull'd it into rest;
So feeble now—his mother's softness crept
To those wild eyes, which like an infant's
 wept:
It was the very weakness of his brain,
Which thus confess'd without relieving pain.
None saw his trickling tears—perchance, if
 seen,
That useless flood of grief had never been:
Nor long they flow'd—he dried them to
 depart,
In helpless—hopeless—brokenness of heart:
The sun goes forth, but Conrad's day is dim;
And the night cometh—ne'er to pass from
 him.

There is no darkness like the cloud of mind,
On Grief's vain eye—the blindest of the
 blind!
Which may not—dare not see—but turns
 aside
To blackest shade—nor will endure a guide!

XXIII.

His heart was form'd for softness—warp'd to
 wrong;
Betray'd too early, and beguiled too long;
Each feeling pure—as falls the dropping dew
Within the grot—like that had harden'd too;
Less clear, perchance, its earthly trials
 pass'd,
But sunk, and chill'd, and petrified at last.
Yet tempests wear, and lightning cleaves the
 rock;
If such his heart, so shatter'd it the shock.
There grew one flower beneath its rugged
 brow,
Though dark the shade—it shelter'd—saved
 till now.
The thunder came—that bolt hath blasted
 both,
The Granite's firmness, and the Lily's
 growth:
The gentle plant hath left no leaf to tell
Its tale, but shrunk and wither'd where it
 fell;

And of its cold protector, blacken round
But shiver'd fragments on the barren ground!

XXIV.

'Tis morn—to venture on his lonely hour
Few dare; though now Anselmo sought his
 tower.
He was not there, nor seen along the shore;
Ere night, alarm'd, their isle is traversed
 o'er:
Another morn—another bids them seek,
And shout his name till echo waxeth weak;
Mount, grotto, cavern, valley search'd in vain,
They find on shore a sea-boat's broken chain:
Their hope revives—they follow o'er the
 main.
'Tis idle all—moons roll on moons away,
And Conrad comes not, came not since that
 day:
Nor trace, nor tidings of his doom declare
Where lives his grief, or perish'd his despair!
Long mourn'd his band whom none could
 mourn beside;
And fair the monument they gave his bride:
For him they raise not the recording stone—
His death yet dubious, deeds too widely
 known;
He left a Corsair's name to other times,
Link'd with one virtue, and a thousand
 crimes.

Lara.

Canto the First.

I.

THE Serfs are glad through Lara's wide
 domain,
And Slavery half forgets her feudal chain;
He, their unhoped, but unforgotten lord,
The long self-exiled chieftain, is restored,
There be bright faces in the busy hall,
Bowls on the board, and banners on the
 wall;
Far checkering o'er the pictured window,
 plays
The unwonted faggot's hospitable blaze;
And gay retainers gather round the hearth,
With tongues all loudness, and with eyes all
 mirth.

II.

The chief of Lara is return'd again:
And why had Lara cross'd the bounding
 main?
Left by his sire, too young such loss to know,
Lord of himself,—that heritage of woe,
That fearful empire which the human breast
But holds to rob the heart within of rest!—
With none to check, and few to point in time
The thousand paths that slope the way to
 crime;
Then, when he most required commandment,
 then
Had Lara's daring boyhood govern'd men.
It skills not, boots not step by step to trace
His youth through all the mazes of its
 race;

Short was the course his restlessness had
 run,
But long enough to leave him half undone.

III.

And Lara left in youth his father-land;
But from the hour he waved his parting
 hand
Each trace wax'd fainter of his course, till all
Had nearly ceased his memory to recall.
His sire was dust, his vassals could declare,
'Twas all they knew, that Lara was not
 there;
Nor sent, nor came he, till conjecture grew
Cold in the many, anxious in the few.
His hall scarce echoes with his wonted name,
His portrait darkens in its fading frame,
Another chief consoled his destined bride,
The young forgot him, and the old had died;
"Yet doth he live!" exclaims the impatient
 heir,
And sighs for sables which he must not
 wear.
A hundred scutcheons deck with gloomy
 grace
The Laras' last and longest dwelling-place;
But one is absent from the mouldering file,
That now were welcome in that Gothic pile.

IV.

He comes at last in sudden loneliness,
And whence they know not, why they need
 not guess;
They more might marvel, when the greeting's
 o'er,
Not that he came, but came not long before:
No train is his beyond a single page,
Of foreign aspect, and of tender age.
Years had roll'd on, and fast they speed
 away
To those that wander as to those that stay;
But lack of tidings from another clime
Had lent a flagging wing to weary Time.
They see, they recognise, yet almost deem
The present dubious, or the past a dream.

He lives, nor yet is past his manhood's prime,
Though sear'd by toil, and something touch'd
 by time;
His faults, whate'er they were, if scarce for-
 got,
Might be untaught him by his varied lot;
Nor good nor ill of late were known, his name
Might yet uphold his patrimonial fame:
His soul in youth was haughty, but his sins
No more than pleasure from the stripling
 wins;
And such, if not yet harden'd in their course,
Might be redeem'd, nor ask a long remorse.

V.

And they indeed were changed—'t is quickly
 seen,
Whate'er he be, 't was not what he had been:
That brow in furrow'd lines had fix'd at last,
And spake of passions, but of passion past:
The pride, but not the fire, of early days,
Coldness of mien, and carelessness of praise;
A high demeanour, and a glance that took
Their thoughts from others by a single look;
And that sarcastic levity of tongue,
The stinging of a heart the world hath stung,
That darts in seeming playfulness around,
And makes those feel that will not own the
 wound;
All these seem'd his, and something more
 beneath
Than glance could well reveal, or accent breathe
Ambition, glory, love, the common aim,
That some can conquer, and that all would
 claim,
Within his breast appear'd no more to strive,
Yet seem'd as lately they had been alive;
And some deep feeling it were vain to trace
At moments lighten'd o'er his livid face.

VI.

Not much he loved long question of the past,
Nor told of wondrous wilds, and deserts vast,
In those far lands where he had wander'd lone,
And—as himself would have it seem—un-
 known;
Yet these in vain his eye could scarcely scan,
Nor glean experience from his fellow man;
But what he had beheld he shunn'd to show,
As hardly worth a stranger's care to know;
If still more prying such inquiry grew,
His brow fell darker, and his words more few.

VII.

Not unrejoiced to see him once again,
Warm was his welcome to the haunts of men;
Born of high lineage, link'd in high command,
He mingled with the magnates of his land;
Join'd the carousals of the great and gay,
And saw them smile or sigh their hours away;
But still he only saw, and did not share,
The common pleasure or the general care;
He did not follow what they all pursued
With hope still baffled, still to be renew'd;
Nor shadowy honour, nor substantial gain,
Nor beauty's preference, and the rival's pain:
Around him some mysterious circle thrown
Repell'd approach, and show'd him still alone;
Upon his eye sat something of reproof,
That kept at least frivolity aloof;
And things more timid that beheld him near
In silence gazed, or whisper'd mutual fear;
And they the wiser, friendlier few confess'd
They deem'd him better than his air express'd.

VIII.

'Twas strange—in youth all action and all life,
Burning for pleasure, not averse from strife;
Woman, the field, the ocean, all that gave
Promise of gladness, peril of a grave,
In turn he tried—he ransack'd all below,
And found his recompense in joy or woe,
No tame, trite medium; for his feelings sought
In that intenseness an escape from thought:
The tempest of his heart in scorn had gazed
On that the feebler elements had raised;
The rapture of his heart had look'd on high,
And ask'd if greater dwelt beyond the sky:
Chain'd to excess, the slave of each extreme,
How woke he from the wildness of that dream?
Alas! he told not—but he did awake
To curse the wither'd heart that would not
 break.

IX.

Books, for his volume heretofore was Man,
With eye more curious he appear'd to scan,
And oft, in sudden mood, for many a day,
From all communion he would start away:
And then, his rarely call'd attendants said,
Through night's long hours would sound his
 hurried tread
O'er the dark gallery, where his fathers
 frown'd
In rude but antique portraiture around:
They heard, but whisper'd—"*that* must not
 be known—
The sound of words less earthly than his own.
Yes, they who chose might smile, but some
 had seen
They scarce knew what, but more than
 should have been.
Why gazed he so upon the ghastly head
Which hands profane had gather'd from the
 dead,
That still beside his open'd volume lay,
As if to startle all save him away?
Why slept he not when others were at rest?
Why heard no music, and received no guest?
All was not well, they deem'd—but where
 the wrong?
Some knew perchance—but 'twere a tale too
 long;
And such besides were too discreetly wise,
To more than hint their knowledge in sur-
 mise;
But if they would—they could "—around the
 board
Thus Lara's vassals prattled of their lord.

X.

It was the night—and Lara's glassy stream
The stars are studding, each with imaged
 beam;

So calm, the waters scarcely seem to stray,
And yet they glide like happiness away;
Reflecting far and fairy-like from high
The immortal lights that live along the sky:
Its banks are fringed with many a goodly tree,
And flowers the fairest that may feast the bee;
Such in her chaplet infant Dian wove,
And Innocence would offer to her love.
These deck the shore; the waves their chan-
 nel make
In windings bright and mazy like the snake.
All was so still, so soft in earth and air,
You scarce would start to meet a spirit there;
Secure that nought of evil could delight
To walk in such a scene, on such a night!
It was a moment only for the good:
So Lara deem'd, nor longer there he stood,
But turn'd in silence to his castle-gate;
Such scene his soul no more could con-
 template:
Such scene reminded him of other days,
Of skies more cloudless, moons of purer
 blaze,
Of nights more soft and frequent, hearts that
 now—
No—no—the storm may beat upon his brow,
Unfelt, unsparing—but a night like this,
A night of beauty, mock'd such breast as his.

XI.

He turn'd within his solitary hall,
And his high shadow shot along the wall:
There were the painted forms of other times,
'Twas all they left of virtues or of crimes,
Save vague tradition; and the gloomy vaults
That hid their dust, their foibles, and their
 faults;
And half a column of the pompous page,
That speeds the specious tale from age to age;
Where history's pen its praise or blame
 supplies,
And lies like truth, and still most truly lies.
He wandering mused, and as the moonbeam
 shone
Through the dim lattice or the floor of stone,
And the high fretted roof, and saints, that
 there
O'er Gothic windows knelt in pictured prayer,
Reflected in fantastic figures grew,
Like life, but not like mortal life to view:
His bristling locks of sable, brow of gloom,
And the wide waving of his shaken plume,
Glanced like a spectre's attributes, and gave
His aspect all that terror gives the grave.

XII.

'Twas midnight—all was slumber; the lone
 light
Dimm'd in the lamp, as loth to break the
 night.

Hark! there be murmurs heard in Lara's
 hall—
A sound, a voice, a shriek, a fearful call!
A long, loud shriek—and silence—did they
 hear
That frantic echo burst the sleeping ear?
They heard and rose, and, tremulously brave,
Rush where the sound invoked their aid to
 save;
They come with half-lit tapers in their hands,
And snatch'd in startled haste unbelted
 brands.

XIII.

Cold as the marble where his length was laid,
Pale as the beam that o'er his features play'd,
Was Lara stretch'd; his half-drawn sabre
 near,
Dropp'd it should seem in more than nature's
 fear;
Yet he was firm, or had been firm till now,
And still defiance knit his gather'd brow;
Though mix'd with terror, senseless as he lay,
There lived upon his lip the wish to slay;
Some half-form'd threat in utterance there
 had died,
Some imprecation of despairing pride;
His eye was almost seal'd, but not forsook,
Even in its trance, the gladiator's look,
That oft awake his aspect could disclose,
And now was fix'd in horrible repose.
They raise him—bear him:—hush! he
 breathes, he speaks,
The swarthy blush recolours in his cheeks,
His lip resumes its red, his eye, though dim,
Rolls wide and wild, each slowly quivering
 limb
Recalls its function, but his words are strung
In terms that seem not of his native tongue;
Distinct but strange, enough they understand
To deem them accents of another land;
And such they were, and meant to meet an
 ear
That hears him not—alas! that cannot hear!

XIV.

His page approach'd, and he alone appear'd
To know the import of the words they heard;
And, by the changes of his cheek and brow,
They were not such as Lara should avow,
Nor he interpret,—yet with less surprise
Than those around their chieftain's state he
 eyes,
But Lara's prostrate form he bent beside,
And in that tongue which seem'd his own
 replied,
And Lara heeds those tones that gently seem
To soothe away the horrors of his dream—
If dream it were that thus could overthrow
A breast that needed not ideal woe.

XV.

Whate'er his frenzy dream'd or eye beheld,—
If yet remember'd ne'er to be reveal'd,—
Rests at his heart: the custom'd morning
 came,
And breathed new vigour in his shaken frame;
And solace sought he none from priest nor
 leech,
And soon the same in movement and in speech,
As heretofore he fill'd the passing hours,
Nor less he smiles, nor more his forehead
 lowers,
Than these were wont; and if the coming
 night
Appear'd less welcome now to Lara's sight,
He to his marvelling vassals show'd it not,
Whose shuddering proved *their* fear was less
 forgot.
In trembling pairs (alone they dared not)
 crawl
The astonish'd slaves, and shun the fated hall;
The waving banner, and the clapping door,
The rustling tapestry, and the echoing floor;
The long dim shadows of surrounding trees,
The flapping bat, the night song of the breeze;
Aught they behold or hear their thought
 appals,
As evening saddens o'er the dark grey walls.

XVI.

Vain thought! that hour of ne'er unravell'd
 gloom
Came not again, or Lara could assume
A seeming of forgetfulness, that made
His vassals more amazed nor less afraid.
Had memory vanish'd then with sense re-
 stored?
Since word, nor look, nor gesture of their lord
Betray'd a feeling that recall'd to these
That fever'd moment of his mind's disease.
Was it a dream? was his the voice that spoke
Those strange wild accents; his the cry that
 broke
Their slumber? his the oppress'd, o'erlabour'd
 heart
That ceased to beat, the look that made them
 start?
Could he who thus had suffer'd so forget,
When such as saw that suffering shudder yet?
Or did that silence prove his memory fix'd
Too deep for words, indelible, unmix'd
In that corroding secrecy which gnaws
The heart to show the effect, but not the
 cause?
Not so in him; his breast had buried both,
Nor common gazers could discern the growth
Of thoughts that mortal lips must leave half
 told;
They choke the feeble words that would
 unfold.

XVII.

In him inexplicably mix'd appear'd
Much to be loved and hated, sought and
 fear'd;
Opinion varying o'er his hidden lot,
In praise or railing ne'er his name forgot:
His silence form'd a theme for others' prate—
They guess'd, they gazed, they fain would
 know his fate.
What had he been? what was he, thus un-
 known,
Who walk'd their world, his lineage only
 known?
A hater of his kind? yet some would say,
With them he could seem gay amidst the gay;
But own'd that smile, if oft observed and
 near,
Waned in its mirth, and wither'd to a sneer;
That smile might reach his lip, but pass'd
 not by,
None e'er could trace its laughter to his eye:
Yet there was softness too in his regard,
At times, a heart as not by nature hard,
But once perceived, his spirit seem'd to chide
Such weakness, as unworthy of its pride,
And steel'd itself, as scorning to redeem
One doubt from others' half withheld esteem;
In self-inflicted penance of a breast
Which tenderness might once have wrung
 from rest;
In vigilance of grief that would compel
The soul to hate for having loved too well.

XVIII.

There was in him a vital scorn of all:
As if the worst had fall'n which could befall,
He stood a stranger in this breathing world,
An erring spirit from another hurl'd;
A thing of dark imaginings, that shaped
By choice the perils he by chance escaped;
But 'scaped in vain, for in their memory yet
His mind would half exult and half regret:
With more capacity for love than earth
Bestows on most of mortal mould and birth,
His early dreams of good outstripp'd the
 truth,
And troubled manhood follow'd baffled youth;
With thought of years in phantom chase mis-
 spent,
And wasted powers for better purpose lent;
And fiery passions that had pour'd their
 wrath
In hurried desolation o'er his path,
And left the better feelings all at strife
In wild reflection o'er his stormy life;
But haughty still, and loth himself to blame,
He call'd on Nature's self to share the shame,

And charged all faults upon the fleshly form
She gave to clog the soul, and feast the worm;
Till he at last confounded good and ill,
And half mistook for fate the acts of will:
Too high for common selfishness, he could
At times resign his own for others' good,
But not in pity, not because he ought,
But in some strange perversity of thought,
That sway'd him onward with a secret pride
To do what few or none would do beside;
And this same impulse would, in tempting
 time,
Mislead his spirit equally to crime;
So much he soar'd beyond, or sunk beneath,
The men with whom he felt condemn'd to
 breathe,
And long'd by good or ill to separate
Himself from all who shared his mortal state;
His mind abhorring this, had fix'd her throne
Far from the world, in regions of her own:
Thus coldly passing all that pass'd below,
His blood in temperate seeming now would
 flow:
Ah! happier if it ne'er with guilt had glow'd,
But ever in that icy smoothness flow'd!
'Tis true, with other men their path he walk'd,
And like the rest in seeming did and talk'd,
Nor outraged Reason's rules by flaw nor start,
His madness was not of the head, but heart;
And rarely wander'd in his speech, or drew
His thoughts so forth as to offend the view.

XIX.

With all that chilling mystery of mien,
And seeming gladness to remain unseen,
He had (if 'twere not nature's boon) an art
Of fixing memory on another's heart:
It was not love perchance, nor hate, nor aught
That words can image to express the thought;
But they who saw him did not see in vain,
And once beheld, would ask of him again:
And those to whom he spake remember'd
 well,
And on the words, however light, would
 dwell:
None knew nor how, nor why, but he en-
 twined
Himself perforce around the hearer's mind;
There he was stamp'd, in liking, or in hate,
If greeted once; however brief the date
That friendship, pity, or aversion knew,
Still there within the inmost thought he grew.
You could not penetrate his soul, but found,
Despite your wonder, to your own he wound;
His presence haunted still; and from the
 breast
He forced an all unwilling interest:
Vain was the struggle in that mental net,
His spirit seem'd to dare you to forget!

XX.

There is a festival, where knights and dames,
And aught that wealth or lofty lineage claims,
Appear—a high-born and a welcome guest
To Otho's hall came Lara with the rest.
The long carousal shakes the illumined hall,
Well speeds alike the banquet and the ball;
And the gay dance of bounding Beauty's train
Links grace and harmony in happiest chain:
Blest are the early hearts and gentle hands
That mingle there in well according bands;
It is a sight the careful brow might smooth,
And make Age smile, and dream itself to youth,
And Youth forget such hour was past on earth,
So springs the exulting bosom to that mirth!

XXI.

And Lara gazed on these, sedately glad,
His brow belied him if his soul was sad;
And his glance follow'd fast each fluttering fair,
Whose steps of lightness woke no echo there:
He lean'd against the lofty pillar nigh,
With folded arms and long attentive eye,
Nor mark'd a glance so sternly fix'd on his—
Ill brook'd high Lara scrutiny like this:
At length he caught it, 'tis a face unknown,
But seems as searching his, and his alone;
Prying and dark, a stranger's by his mien,
Who still till now had gazed on him unseen:
At length encountering meets the mutual gaze
Of keen inquiry, and of mute amaze;
On Lara's glance emotion gathering grew,
As if distrusting that the stranger threw;
Along the stranger's aspect, fix'd and stern,
Flash'd more than thence the vulgar eye could learn.

XXII.

"'Tis he!" the stranger cried, and those that heard
Re-echoed fast and far the whisper'd word.
"'Tis he!"—"'Tis who?" they question far and near,
Till louder accents rung on Lara's ear;
So widely spread, few bosoms well could brook
The general marvel, or that single look:
But Lara stirr'd not, changed not, the surprise
That sprung at first to his arrested eyes
Seem'd now subsided, neither sunk nor raised
Glanced his eye round, though still the stranger gazed;
And drawing nigh, exclaim'd, with haughty sneer,
"'Tis he! how came he thence?—what doth he here?"

XXIII.

It were too much for Lara to pass by
Such questions, so repeated fierce and high;
With look collected, but with accent cold,
More mildly firm than petulantly bold,
He turn'd, and met the inquisitorial tone—
"My name is Lara!—when thine own is known,
Doubt not my fitting answer to requite
The unlook'd for courtesy of such a knight.
'Tis Lara!—further wouldst thou mark or ask?
I shun no question, and I wear no mask."

"Thou shunn'st no question! Ponder—is there none
Thy heart must answer, though thine ear would shun?
And deem'st thou me unknown too? Gaze again!
At least thy memory was not given in vain.
Oh! never canst thou cancel half her debt,
Eternity forbids thee to forget."
With slow and searching glance upon his face
Grew Lara's eyes, but nothing there could trace
They knew, or chose to know—with dubious look
He deign'd no answer, but his head he shook,
And half contemptuous turn'd to pass away;
But the stern stranger motion'd him to stay.
"A word!—I charge thee stay, and answer here
To one, who, wert thou noble, were thy peer,
But as thou wast and art—nay, frown not, lord,
If false, 'tis easy to disprove the word—
But as thou wast and art, on thee looks down,
Distrusts thy smiles, but shakes not at thy frown.
Art thou not he? whose deeds——"
 "Whate'er I be,
Words wild as these, accusers like to thee,
I list no further; those with whom they weigh
May hear the rest, nor venture to gainsay
The wondrous tale no doubt thy tongue can tell,
Which thus begins so courteously and well.
Let Otho cherish here his polish'd guest,
To him my thanks and thoughts shall be express'd."
And here their wondering host hath interposed—
"Whate'er there be between you undisclosed,
This is no time nor fitting place to mar
The mirthful meeting with a wordy war.
If thou, Sir Ezzelin, hast aught to show
Which it befits Count Lara's ear to know,

To-morrow, here, or elsewhere, as may best
Beseem your mutual judgment, speak the rest;
I pledge myself for thee, as not unknown,
Though, like Count Lara, now return'd alone
From other lands, almost a stranger grown;
And if from Lara's blood and gentle birth
I augur right of courage and of worth,
He will not that untainted line belie,
Nor aught that knighthood may accord,
 deny."

" To-morrow be it," Ezzelin replied,
" And here our several worth and truth be
 tried;
I gage my life, my falchion to attest
My words, so may I mingle with the blest!"
What answers Lara? to its centre shrunk
His soul, in deep abstraction sudden sunk;
The words of many, and the eyes of all
That there were gather'd, seem'd on him to
 fall;
But his were silent, his appear'd to stray
In far forgetfulness away—away—
Alas! that heedlessness of all around
Bespoke remembrance only too profound.

XXIV.

" To-morrow!—ay, to-morrow!" further word
Than those repeated none from Lara heard:
Upon his brow no outward passion spoke;
From his large eye no flashing anger broke;
Yet there was something fix'd in that low
 tone,
Which show'd resolve, determined, though
 unknown.
He seized his cloak—his head he slightly
 bow'd,
And passing Ezzelin, he left the crowd;
And as he pass'd him, smiling met the frown
With which that chieftain's brow would bear
 him down:
It was nor smile of mirth. nor struggling
 pride
That curbs to scorn the wrath it cannot hide;
But that of one in his own heart secure
Of all that he would do, or could endure.
Could this mean peace? the calmness of the
 good?
Or guilt grown old in desperate hardihood?
Alas! too like in confidence are each,
For man to trust to mortal look or speech;
From deeds, and deeds alone, may he discern
Truths which it wrings the unpractised heart
 to learn.

XXV.

And Lara call'd his page, and went his way—
Well could that stripling word or sign obey:
His only follower from those climes afar,
Where the soul glows beneath a brighter star;

For Lara left the shore from whence he
 sprung,
In duty patient, and sedate though young;
Silent as him he served, his faith appears
Above his station, and beyond his years.
Though not unknown the tongue of Lara's.
 land,
In such from him he rarely heard command;
But fleet his step, and clear his tones would
 come,
When Lara's lip breathed forth the words
 of home:
Those accents, as his native mountains dear,
Awake their absent echoes in his ear,
Friends', kindred's, parents' wonted voice
 recall,
Now lost, abjured, for one—his friend, his
 all:
For him earth now disclosed no other guide;
What marvel then he rarely left his side?

XXVI.

Light was his form, and darkly delicate
That brow whereon his native sun had sate,
But had not marr'd, though in his beams he
 grew,
The cheek where oft the unbidden blush
 shone through;
Yet not such blush as mounts when health
 would show
All the heart's hue in that delighted glow;
But 'twas a hectic tint of secret care
That for a burning moment fever'd there;
And the wild sparkle of his eye seem'd
 caught
From high, and lighten'd with electric
 thought,
Though its black orb those long low lashes'
 fringe
Had temper'd with a melancholy tinge;
Yet less of sorrow than of pride was there,
Or, if 'twere grief, a grief that none should
 share:
And pleased not him the sports that please
 his age,
The tricks of youth, the frolics of the page;
For hours on Lara he would fix his glance,
As all-forgotten in that watchful trance;
And from his chief withdrawn, he wander'd
 lone,
Brief were his answers, and his questions
 none;
His walk the wood, his sport some foreign
 book;
His resting-place the bank that curbs the
 brook;
He seem'd, like him he served, to live apart
From all that lures the eye, and fills the
 heart;

To know no brotherhood, and take from
 earth
No gift beyond that bitter boon—our birth.

XXVII.

If aught he loved, 'twas Lara; but was
 shown
His faith in reverence and in deeds alone;
In mute attention; and his care, which
 guess'd
Each wish, fulfill'd it ere the tongue ex-
 press'd.
Still there was haughtiness in all he did,
A spirit deep that brook'd not to be chid;
His zeal, though more than that of servile
 hands,
In act alone obeys, his air commands;
As if 'twas Lara's less than *his* desire
That thus he served, but surely not for hire.
Slight were the tasks enjoin'd him by his
 lord,
To hold the stirrup, or to bear the sword;
To tune his lute, or, if he will'd it more,
On tomes of other times and tongues to pore;
But ne'er to mingle with the menial train,
To whom he show'd nor deference nor dis-
 dain,
But that well-worn reserve which proved he
 knew
No sympathy with that familiar crew:
His soul, whate'er his station or his stem,
Could bow to Lara, not descend to them.
Of higher birth he seem'd, and better days,
Nor mark of vulgar toil that hand betrays,
So femininely white it might bespeak
Another sex, when match'd with that smooth
 cheek,
But for his garb, and something in his gaze,
More wild and high than woman's eye be-
 trays;
A latent fierceness that far more became
His fiery climate than his tender frame:
True, in his words it broke not from his
 breast,
But from his aspect might be more than
 guess'd.
Kaled his name, though rumour said he bore
Another ere he left his mountain-shore;
For sometimes he would hear, however nigh,
That name repeated loud without reply,
As unfamiliar, or, if roused again,
Start to the sound, as but remember'd then;
Unless 'twas Lara's wonted voice that spake,
For then, ear, eyes, and heart would all
 awake.

XXVIII.

He had look'd down upon the festive hall,
And mark'd that sudden strife so mark'd of
 all:

And when the crowd around and near him
 told
Their wonder at the calmness of the bold,
Their marvel how the high-born Lara bore
Such insult from a stranger, doubly sore,
The colour of young Kaled went and came,
The lip of ashes, and the cheek of flame;
And o'er his brow the dampening heart-drops
 threw
The sickening iciness of that cold dew,
That rises as the busy bosom sinks
With heavy thoughts from which reflection
 shrinks.
Yes—there be things which we must dream
 and dare,
And execute ere thought be half aware:
Whate'er might Kaled's be, it was enow
To seal his lip, but agonise his brow.
He gazed on Ezzelin till Lara cast
That sidelong smile upon the knight he
 pass'd;
When Kaled saw that smile his visage fell,
As if on something recognised right well:
His memory read in such a meaning more
Than Lara's aspect unto others wore:
Forward he sprung—a moment, both were
 gone,
And all within that hall seem'd left alone;
Each had so fix'd his eye on Lara's mien,
All had so mix'd their feelings with that
 scene,
That when his long dark shadow through
 the porch
No more relieves the glare of yon high torch,
Each pulse beats quicker, and all bosoms
 seem
To bound as doubting from too black a
 dream,
Such as we know is false, yet dread in sooth,
Because the worst is ever nearest truth.
And they are gone—but Ezzelin is there,
With thoughtful visage and imperious air;
But long remain'd not; ere an hour expired
He waved his hand to Otho and retired.

XXIX.

The crowd are gone, the revellers at rest;
The courteous host, and all-approving guest,
Again to that accustom'd couch must creep
Where joy subsides, and sorrow sighs to
 sleep,
And man, o'erlabour'd with his being's strife,
Shrinks to that sweet forgetfulness of life:
There lie love's feverish hope, and cunning's
 guile,
Hate's working brain, and lull'd ambition's
 wile;
O'er each vain eye oblivion's pinions wave,
And quench'd existence crouches in a grave.

What better name may slumber's bed be-
come?
Night's sepulchre, the universal home,
Where weakness, strength, vice, virtue, sunk
supine,
Alike in naked helplessness recline;
Glad for a while to heave unconscious breath,
Yet wake to wrestle with the dread of death,
And shun, though day but dawn on ills in-
creased,
That sleep, the loveliest, since it dreams
the least.

——◆——

Canto the Second.

I.

NIGHT wanes—the vapours round the moun-
tains curl'd
Melt into morn, and Light awakes the world,
Man has another day to swell the past,
And lead him near to little, but his last:
But mighty Nature bounds as from her birth,
The sun is in the heavens, and life on earth;
Flowers in the valley, splendour in the beam,
Health on the gale, and freshness in the
stream.
Immortal man! behold her glories shine,
And cry, exulting inly, "They are thine!"
Gaze on, while yet thy gladden'd eye may
see:
A morrow comes when they are not for thee:
And grieve what may above thy senseless
bier,
Nor earth nor sky will yield a single tear;
Nor cloud shall gather more, nor leaf shall
fall,
Nor gale breathe forth one sigh for thee,
for all;
But creeping things shall revel in their spoil,
And fit thy clay to fertilise the soil.

II.

'Tis morn—'tis noon—assembled in the hall,
The gather'd chieftains come to Otho's call;
'Tis now the promised hour, that must pro-
claim
The life or death of Lara's future fame;
When Ezzelin his charge may here unfold,
And whatsoe'er the tale, it must be told.
His faith was pledged, and Lara's promise
given,
To meet it in the eye of man and heaven.
Why comes he not? Such truths to be di-
vulged,
Methinks the accuser's rest is long indulged.

III.

The hour is past, and Lara too is there,
With self-confiding, coldly patient air;

Why comes not Ezzelin? The hour is past,
And murmurs rise, and Otho's brow's o'er-
cast.
"I know my friend! his faith I cannot fear,
If yet he be on earth, expect him here;
The roof that held him in the valley stands
Between my own and noble Lara's lands;
My halls from such a guest had honour
gain'd,
Nor had Sir Ezzelin his host disdain'd,
But that some previous proof forbade his stay,
And urged him to prepare against to-day;
The word I pledged for his I pledge again,
Or will myself redeem his knighthood's
stain."

He ceased—and Lara answered, "I am here
To lend at thy demand a listening ear
To tales of evil from a stranger's tongue,
Whose words already might my heart have
wrung,
But that I deem'd him scarcely less than mad,
Or, at the worst, a foe ignobly bad.
I know him not—but me it seems he knew
In lands where—but I must not trifle too:
Produce this babbler—or redeem the pledge;
Here in thy hold, and with thy falchion's
edge."

Proud Otho on the instant, reddening, threw
His glove on earth, and forth his sabre flew.
"The last alternative befits me best,
And thus I answer for mine absent guest."
With cheek unchanging from its sallow
gloom,
However near his own or other's tomb;
With hand, whose almost careless coolness
spoke
Its grasp well used to deal the sabre-stroke;
With eye, though calm, determin'd not to
spare,
Did Lara too his willing weapon bare.
In vain the circling chieftains round them
closed,
For Otho's frenzy would not be opposed;
And from his lip those words of insult fell—
His sword is good who can maintain them
well.

IV.

Short was the conflict; furious, blindly rash,
Vain Otho gave his bosom to the gash:
He bled, and fell; but not with deadly wound,
Stretch'd by a dexterous sleight along the
ground.
"Demand thy life!" He answer'd not: and
then
From that red floor he ne'er had risen again,
For Lara's brow upon the moment grew
Almost to blackness in its demon hue;

And fiercer shook his angry falchion now
Than when his foe's was levell'd at his brow;
Then all was stern collectedness and art,
Now rose the unleaven'd hatred of his heart;
So little sparing to the foe he fell'd,
That when the approaching crowd his arm withheld,
He almost turn'd the thirsty point on those
Who thus for mercy dared to interpose;
But to a moment's thought that purpose bent;
Yet look'd he on him still with eye intent,
As if he loathed the ineffectual strife
That left a foe, howe'er o'ercome, with life;
As if to search how far the wound he gave
Had sent its victim onward to his grave.

V.

They raised the bleeding Otho, and the Leech
Forbade all present question, sign, and speech:
The others met within a neighbouring hall,
And he, incensed, and heedless of them all,
The cause and conqueror in this sudden fray,
In haughty silence slowly strode away;
He back'd his steed, his homeward path he took,
Nor cast on Otho's towers a single look.

VI.

But where was he? that meteor of a night,
Who menaced but to disappear with light.
Where was this Ezzelin? who came and went,
To leave no other trace of his intent.
He left the dome of Otho long ere morn,
In darkness, yet so well the path was worn
He could not miss it: near his dwelling lay;
But there he was not, and with coming day
Came fast inquiry, which unfolded nought,
Except the absence of the chief it sought.
A chamber tenantless, a steed at rest,
His host alarm'd, his murmuring squires distress'd:
Their search extends along, around the path,
In dread to meet the marks of prowlers' wrath:
But none are there, and not a brake hath borne
Nor gout of blood, nor shred of mantle torn;
Nor fall nor struggle hath defaced the grass,
Which still retains a mark where murder was;
Nor dabbling fingers left to tell the tale,
The bitter print of each convulsive nail,
When agonised hands that cease to guard,
Wound in that pang the smoothness of the sward.
Some such had been, if here a life was reft,
But these were not; and doubting hope is left;

And strange suspicion, whispering Lara's name,
Now daily mutters o'er his blacken'd fame;
Then sudden silent when his form appear'd,
Awaits the absence of the thing it fear'd
Again its wonted wondering to renew,
And dye conjecture with a darker hue.

VII.

Days roll along, and Otho's wounds are heal'd,
But not his pride; and hate no more conceal'd:
He was a man of power, and Lara's foe,
The friend of all who sought to work him woe,
And from his country's justice now demands
Account of Ezzelin at Lara's hands.
Who else than Lara could have cause to fear
His presence? who had made him disappear,
If not the man on whom his menaced charge
Had sate too deeply were he left at large?
The general rumour ignorantly loud,
The mystery dearest to the curious crowd;
The seeming friendlessness of him who strove
To win no confidence, and wake no love;
The sweeping fierceness which his soul betray'd,
The skill with which he wielded his keen blade;
Where had his arm unwarlike caught that art?
Where had that fierceness grown upon his heart?
For it was not the blind capricious rage
A word can kindle and a word assuage;
But the deep working of a soul unmix'd
With aught of pity where its wrath had fix'd;
Such as long power and overgorged success
Concentrates into all that's merciless:
These, link'd with that desire which ever sways
Mankind, the rather to condemn than praise,
'Gainst Lara gathering raised at length a storm,
Such as himself might fear, and foes would form,
And he must answer for the absent head
Of one that haunts him still, alive or dead.

VIII.

Within that land was many a malcontent,
Who cursed the tyranny to which he bent;
That soil full many a wringing despot saw
Who work'd his wantonness in form of law;
Long war without and frequent broil within
Had made a path for blood and giant sin,
That waited but a signal to begin

New havoc, such as civil discord blends,
Which knows no neuter, owns but foes or
　friends;
Fix'd in his feudal fortress each was lord,
In word and deed obey'd, in soul abhorr'd.
Thus Lara had inherited his lands,
And with them pining hearts and sluggish
　hands;
But that long absence from his native clime
Had left him stainless of oppression's crime,
And now, diverted by his milder sway,
All dread by slow degrees had worn away.
The menials felt their usual awe alone,
But more for him than them that fear was
　grown;
They deem'd him now unhappy, though at
　first
Their evil judgment augur'd of the worst,
And each long restless night, and silent
　mood,
Was traced to sickness, fed by solitude:
And though his lonely habits threw of late
Gloom o'er his chamber, cheerful was his
　gate;
For thence the wretched ne'er unsoothed
　withdrew,
For them, at least, his soul compassion knew.
Cold to the great, contemptuous to the high,
The humble pass'd not his unheeding eye;
Much he would speak not, but beneath his
　roof
They found asylum oft, and ne'er reproof.
And they who watch'd might mark that, day
　by day,
Some new retainers gather'd to his sway;
But most of late, since Ezzelin was lost,
He play'd the courteous lord and bounteous
　host:
Perchance his strife with Otho made him
　dread
Some snare prepared for his obnoxious head;
Whate'er his view, his favour more obtains
With these, the people, than his fellow
　thanes.
If this were policy, so far 't was sound,
The million judged but of him as they found;
From him by sterner chiefs to exile driven
They but required a shelter, and 't was
　given.
By him no peasant mourn'd his rifled cot,
And scarce the Serf could murmur o'er his
　lot;
With him old avarice found its hoard secure,
With him contempt forbore to mock the
　poor;
Youth present cheer and promised recom-
　pense
Detain'd, till all too late to part from thence:
To hate he offer'd, with the coming change,
The deep reversion of delay'd revenge;

To love, long baffled by the unequal match,
The well-won charms success was sure to
　snatch.
All now was ripe, he waits but to proclaim
That slavery nothing which was still a name.
The moment came, the hour when Otho
　thought
Secure at last the vengence which he
　sought:
His summons found the destined criminal
Begirt by thousands in his swarming hall,
Fresh from their feudal fetters newly riven,
Defying earth, and confident of heaven.
That morning he had freed the soil-bound
　slaves,
Who dig no land for tyrants but their graves!
Such is their cry—some watchword for the
　fight
Must vindicate the wrong, and warp the
　right;
Religion — freedom — vengeance — what you
　will,
A word's enough to raise mankind to kill;
Some factious phrase by cunning caught and
　spread,
That guilt may reign, and wolves and worms
　be fed!

IX.

Throughout that clime the feudal chiefs had
　gain'd
Such sway, their infant monarch hardly
　reign'd;
Now was the hour for faction's rebel growth,
The Serfs contemn'd the one, and hated
　both:
They waited but a leader, and they found
One to their cause inseparably bound;
By circumstance compell'd to plunge again,
In self-defence, amidst the strife of men.
Cut off by some mysterious fate from those
Whom birth and nature meant not for his
　foes,
Had Lara from that night, to him accurst,
Prepared to meet, but not alone, the worst:
Some reason urged, whate'er it was, to shun
Inquiry into deeds at distance done;
By mingling with his own the cause of all,
E'en if he fail'd, he still delay'd his fall.
The sullen calm that long his bosom kept,
The storm that once had spent itself and
　slept,
Roused by events that seem'd foredoom'd to
　urge
His gloomy fortunes to their utmost verge,
Burst forth, and made him all he once had
　been,
And is again; he only changed the scene.
Light care had he for life, and less for fame,
But not less fitted for the desperate game:

He deem'd himself mark'd out for others'
　　hate,
And mock'd at ruin so they shared his fate.
What cared he for the freedom of the crowd?
He raised the humble but to bend the proud.
He had hoped quiet in his sullen lair,
But man and destiny beset him there:
Inured to hunters, he was found at bay;
And they must kill, they cannot snare the
　　prey.
Stern, unambitious, silent, he had been
Henceforth a calm spectator of life's scene;
But dragg'd again upon the arena, stood
A leader not unequal to the feud;
In voice, mien, gesture, savage nature spoke,
And from his eye the gladiator broke.

X.

What boots the oft-repeated tale of strife,
The feast of vultures, and the waste of life?
The varying fortune of each separate field,
The fierce that vanquish, and the faint that
　　yield?
The smoking ruin, and the crumbled wall?
In this the struggle was the same with all;
Save that distemper'd passions lent their
　　force
In bitterness that banish'd all remorse.
None sued, for Mercy knew her cry was vain,
The captive died upon the battle-slain:
In either cause, one rage alone possess'd
The empire of the alternate victor's breast;
And they that smote for freedom or for sway,
Deem'd few were slain, while more remain'd
　　to slay.
It was too late to check the wasting brand,
And Desolation reap'd the famish'd land;
The torch was lighted, and the flame was
　　spread,
And Carnage smiled upon her daily dead.

XI.

Fresh with the nerve the new-born impulse
　　strung,
The first success to Lara's numbers clung:
But that vain victory hath ruin'd all;
They form no longer to their leader's call:
In blind confusion on the foe they press,
And think to snatch is to secure success.
The lust of booty, and the thirst of hate,
Lure on the broken brigands to their fate:
In vain he doth whate'er a chief may do,
To check the headlong fury of that crew;
In vain their stubborn ardour he would tame,
The hand that kindles cannot quench the
　　flame;
The wary foe alone hath turn'd their mood,
And shown their rashness to that erring
　　brood:

The feign'd retreat, the nightly ambuscade,
The daily harass, and the fight delay'd,
The long privation of the hoped supply,
The tentless rest beneath the humid sky,
The stubborn wall that mocks the leaguer's
　　art,
And palls the patience of his baffled heart,
Of these they had not deem'd: the battle-day
They could encounter as a veteran may;
But more preferr'd the fury of the strife,
And present death, to hourly suffering life:
And famine wrings, and fever sweeps away
His numbers melting fast from their array;
Intemperate triumph fades to discontent,
And Lara's soul alone seems still unbent:
But few remain to aid his voice and hand,
And thousands dwindled to a scanty band:
Desperate, though few, the last and best
　　remain'd
To mourn the discipline they late disdain'd.
One hope survives, the frontier is not far,
And thence they may escape from native
　　war;
And bear within them to the neighbouring
　　state
An exile's sorrows, or an outlaw's hate:
Hard is the task their father-land to quit,
But harder still to perish or submit.

XII.

It is resolved—they march—consenting Night
Guides with her star their dim and torchless
　　flight;
Already they perceive its tranquil beam
Sleep on the surface of the barrier stream;
Already they descry—Is yon the bank?
Away! 'tis lined with many a hostile rank.
Return or fly!—What glitters in the rear?
'Tis Otho's banner—the pursuer's spear!
Are those the shepherds' fires upon the
　　height?
Alas! they blaze too widely for the flight:
Cut off from hope, and compass'd in the toil,
Less blood perchance hath bought a richer
　　spoil!

XIII.

A moment's pause—'tis but to breathe their
　　band,
Or shall they onward press, or here with-
　　stand?
It matters little—if they charge the foes
Who by their border-stream their march
　　oppose,
Some few, perchance, may break and pass
　　the line,
However link'd to baffle such design.
"The charge be ours! to wait for their
　　assault
Were fate well worthy of a coward's halt."

Forth flies each sabre, rein'd is every steed,
And the next word shall scarce outstrip the
deed:
In the next tone of Lara's gathering breath
How many shall but hear the voice of death!

XIV.

His blade is bared,—in him there is an air
As deep, but far too tranquil for despair;
A something of indifference more than then
Becomes the bravest, if they feel for men.
He turn'd his eye on Kaled, ever near,
And still too faithful to betray one fear;
Perchance 'twas but the moon's dim twilight
threw
Along his aspect an unwonted hue
Of mournful paleness, whose deep tint ex-
press'd
The truth, and not the terror of his breast.
This Lara mark'd, and laid his hand on his:
It trembled not in such an hour as this;
His lip was silent, scarcely beat his heart,
His eye alone proclaim'd, "We will not part!
Thy band may perish, or thy friends may flee,
Farewell to life, but not adieu to thee!"

The word hath pass'd his lips, and onward
driven,
Pours the link'd band through ranks asunder
riven:
Well has each steed obey'd the armed heel,
And flash the scimitars, and rings the steel;
Outnumber'd, not outbraved, they still oppose
Despair to daring, and a front to foes;
And blood is mingled with the dashing stream,
Which runs all redly till the morning beam.

XV.

Commanding, aiding, animating all,
Where foe appear'd to press, or friend to fall,
Cheers Lara's voice, and waves or strikes his
steel,
Inspiring hope himself had ceased to feel.
None fled, for well they knew that flight were
vain;
But those that waver turn to smite again,
While yet they find the firmest of the foe
Recoil before their leader's look and blow:
Now girt with numbers, now almost alone,
He foils their ranks, or re-unites his own;
Himself he spared not—once they seem'd to
fly—
Now was the time, he waved his hand on
high,
And shook—Why sudden droops that plumed
crest?
The shaft is sped—the arrow's in his breast!
That fatal gesture left the unguarded side,
And Death has stricken down yon arm of
pride.

The word of triumph fainted from his tongue;
That hand, so raised, how droopingly it hung!
But yet the sword instinctively retains,
Though from its fellow shrink the falling
reins;
These Kaled snatches: dizzy with the blow,
And senseless bending o'er his saddle-bow,
Perceives not Lara that his anxious page
Beguiles his charger from the combat's rage:
Meantime his followers charge, and charge
again;
Too mix'd the slayers now to heed the slain!

XVI.

Day glimmers on the dying and the dead,
The cloven cuirass and the helmless head;
The war-horse masterless is on the earth,
And that last gasp hath burst his bloody
girth;
And near, yet quivering with what life re-
main'd,
The heel that urged him and the hand that
rein'd;
And some too near that rolling torrent lie,
Whose waters mock the lip of those that die;
That panting thirst which scorches in the
breath
Of those that die the soldier's fiery death,
In vain impels the burning mouth to crave
One drop—the last—to cool it for the grave;
With feeble and convulsive effort swept,
Their limbs along the crimson'd turf have
crept;
The faint remains of life such struggles waste,
But yet they reach the stream and bend to
taste:
They feel its freshness, and almost partake—
Why pause? No further thirst have they to
slake—
It is unquench'd, and yet they feel it not;
It was an agony—but now forgot!

XVII.

Beneath a lime, remoter from the scene,
Where but for him that strife had never been,
A breathing but devoted warrior lay:
'Twas Lara bleeding fast from life away.
His follower once, and now his only guide,
Kneels Kaled watchful o'er his welling side,
And with his scarf would stanch the tides
that rush,
With each convulsion, in a blacker gush;
And then, as his faint breathing waxes low,
In feebler, not less fatal tricklings flow:
He scarce can speak, but motions him 'tis
vain,
And merely adds another throb to pain.
He clasps the hand that pang which would
assuage,
And sadly smiles his thanks to that dark page,

Who nothing fears, nor feels, nor heeds, nor
 sees,
Save that damp brow which rests upon his
 knees;
Save that pale aspect, where the eye, though
 dim,
Held all the light that shone on earth for him.

XVIII.

The foe arrives, who long had search'd the
 field,
Their triumph nought till Lara too should
 yield:
They would remove him, but they see 't were
 vain,
And he regards them with a calm disdain,
That rose to reconcile him with his fate,
And that escape to death from living hate:
And Otho comes, and leaping from his steed,
Looks on the bleeding foe that made him
 bleed,
And questions of his state; he answers not,
Scarce glances on him as on one forgot,
And turns to Kaled:—each remaining word
They understood not, if distinctly heard;
His dying tones are in that other tongue,
To which some strange remembrance wildly
 clung.
They spake of other scenes, but what—is
 known
To Kaled, whom their meaning reach'd alone;
And he replied, though faintly, to their sound,
While gazed the rest in dumb amazement
 round:
They seem'd even then—that twain—unto
 the last
To half forget the present in the past;
To share between themselves some separate
 fate,
Whose darkness none beside should penetrate.

XIX.

Their words though faint were many—from
 the tone
Their import those who heard could judge
 alone;
From this, you might have deem'd young
 Kaled's death
More near than Lara's by his voice and
 breath,
So sad, so deep, and hesitating broke
The accents his scarce-moving pale lips
 spoke;
But Lara's voice, though low, at first was
 clear
And calm, till murmuring death gasp'd
 hoarsely near;
But from his visage little could we guess,
So unrepentant, dark, and passionless,

Save that when struggling nearer to his last,
Upon that page his eye was kindly cast;
And once, as Kaled's answering accents
 ceased,
Rose Lara's hand, and pointed to the East:
Whether (as then the breaking sun from high
Roll'd back the clouds) the morrow caught
 his eye,
Or that 't was chance, or some remember'd
 scene,
That raised his arm to point where such had
 been,
Scarce Kaled seem'd to know, but turn'd
 away,
As if his heart abhorr'd that coming day,
And shrunk his glance before that morning
 light,
To look on Lara's brow—where all grew
 night,
Yet sense seem'd left, though better were its
 loss;
For when one near display'd the absolving
 cross,
And proffer'd to his touch the holy bead,
Of which his parting soul might own the need,
He look'd upon it with an eye profane,
And smiled—Heaven pardon! if 't were with
 disdain:
And Kaled, though he spoke not, nor with-
 drew
From Lara's face his fix'd despairing view,
With brow repulsive, and with gesture swift,
Flung back the hand which held the sacred
 gift,
As if such but disturb'd the expiring man,
Nor seem'd to know his life but *then* began,
That life of Immortality, secure
To none, save them whose faith in Christ is
 sure.

XX.

But gasping heaved the breath that Lara
 drew,
And dull the film along his dim eye grew;
His limbs stretch'd fluttering, and his head
 droop'd o'er
The weak yet still untiring knee that bore;
He press'd the hand he held upon his heart—
It beats no more, but Kaled will not part
With the cold grasp, but feels, and feels in
 vain,
For that faint throb which answers not again.
"It beats!"—Away, thou dreamer! he is
 gone—
It once was Lara which thou look'st upon.

XXI.

He gazed, as if not yet had pass'd away
The haughty spirit of that humble clay;

And those around have roused him from his
 trance,
But cannot tear from thence his fixed glance;
And when, in raising him from where he bore
Within his arms the form that felt no more,
He saw the head his breast would still sustain,
Roll down like earth to earth upon the plain;
He did not dash himself thereby, nor tear
The glossy tendrils of his raven hair,
But strove to stand and gaze, but reel'd and
 fell,
Scarce breathing more than that he loved so
 well.
Than that *he* loved! Oh! never yet beneath
The breast of man such trusty love may
 breathe!
That trying moment hath at once reveal'd
The secret long and yet but half conceal'd;
In baring to revive that lifeless breast,
Its grief seem'd ended, but the sex confess'd;
And life return'd, and Kaled felt no shame—
What now to her was Womanhood or Fame?

XXII.

And Lara sleeps not where his fathers sleep,
But where he died his grave was dug as deep;
Nor is his mortal slumber less profound,
Though priest nor bless'd nor marble deck'd
 the mound,
And he was mourn'd by one whose quiet
 grief,
Less loud, outlasts a people's for their chief.
Vain was all question ask'd her of the past,
And vain e'en menace—silent to the last;
She told nor whence, nor why she left
 behind
Her all for one who seem'd but little kind.
Why did she love him? Curious fool!—be
 still—
Is human love the growth of human will?
To her he might be gentleness; the stern
Have deeper thoughts than your dull eyes
 discern,
And when they love, your smilers guess not
 how
Beats the strong heart, though less the lips
 avow.
They were not common links, that form'd the
 chain
That bound to Lara Kaled's heart and brain;
But that wild tale she brook'd not to unfold,
And seal'd is now each lip that could have
 told.

XXIII.

They laid him in the earth, and on his breast,
Besides the wound that sent his soul to rest,
They found the scatter'd dints of many a scar,
Which were not planted there in recent war;

Where'er had pass'd his summer years of life,
It seems they vanish'd in a land of strife;
But all unknown his glory or his guilt,
These only told that somewhere blood was
 spilt,
And Ezzelin, who might have spoke the past,
Return'd no more—that night appear'd his
 last.

XXIV.

Upon that night (a peasant's is the tale)
A Serf that cross'd the intervening vale,
When Cynthia's light almost gave way to
 morn,
And nearly veil'd in mist her waning horn;
A Serf, that rose betimes to thread the wood,
And hew the bough that brought his children's
 food,
Pass'd by the river that divides the plain
Of Otho's lands and Lara's broad domain:
He heard a tramp—a horse and horseman
 broke
From out the wood—before him was a cloak
Wrapt round some burthen at his saddle-bow,
Bent was his head, and hidden was his brow.
Roused by the sudden sight at such a time,
And some foreboding that it might be crime,
Himself unheeded watch'd the stranger's
 course,
Who reach'd the river, bounded from his
 horse,
And lifting thence the burthen which he
 bore,
Heaved up the bank, and dash'd it from the
 shore,
Then paused, and look'd, and turn'd, and
 seem'd to watch,
And still another hurried glance would snatch,
And follow with his step the stream that
 flow'd,
As if even yet too much its surface show'd;
At once he started, stoop'd, around him
 strown
The winter floods had scatter'd heaps of
 stone;
Of these the heaviest thence he gather'd
 there,
And slung them with a more than common
 care.
Meantime the Serf had crept to where unseen
Himself might safely mark what this might
 mean;
He caught a glimpse, as of a floating breast,
And something glitter'd starlike on the vest;
But ere he well could mark the buoyant
 trunk,
A massy fragment smote it, and it sunk:
It rose again, but indistinct to view,
And left the waters of a purple hue.

Then deeply disappear'd : the horseman gazed
Till ebb'd the latest eddy it had raised ;
Then turning, vaulted on his pawing steed,
And instant spurr'd him into panting speed.
His face was mask'd—the features of the dead,
If dead it were, escaped the observer's dread ;
But if in sooth a star its bosom bore,
Such is the badge that knighthood ever wore,
And such 'tis known Sir Ezzelin had worn
Upon the night that led to such a morn.
If thus he perish'd, Heaven receive his soul !
His undiscover'd limbs to ocean roll ;
And charity upon the hope would dwell
It was not Lara's hand by which he fell.

XXV.

And Kaled—Lara—Ezzelin, are gone,
Alike without their monumental stone !
The first, all efforts vainly strove to wean
From lingering where her chieftain's blood
 had been :
Grief had so tamed a spirit once too proud,
Her tears were few, her wailing never loud ;
But furious would you tear her from the spot
Where yet she scarce believed that he was not,

Her eye shot forth with all the living fire
That haunts the tigress in her whelpless ire ;
But left to waste her weary moments there,
She talk'd all idly unto shapes of air,
Such as the busy brain of Sorrow paints,
And woos to listen to her fond complaints:
And she would sit beneath the very tree
Where lay his drooping head upon her knee :
And in that posture where she saw him fall,
His words, his looks, his dying grasp recall ;
And she had shorn, but sayed her raven hair,
And oft would snatch it from her bosom
 there,
And fold, and press it gently to the ground,
As if she staunch'd anew some phantom's
 wound.
Herself would question, and for him reply ;
Then rising, start, and beckon him to fly
From some imagined spectre in pursuit ;
Then seat her down upon some linden's root,
And hide her visage with her meagre hand,
Or trace strange characters along the sand.
This could not last—she lies by him she
 loved ;
Her tale untold, her truth too dearly proved.

The Siege of Corinth.

TO

JOHN HOBHOUSE, ESQ.,

THIS POEM IS INSCRIBED BY HIS

January 22nd, 1816. FRIEND.

ADVERTISEMENT.

"The grand army of the Turks (in 1715), under the Prime Vizier, to open to themselves a way into the heart of the Morea, and to form the siege of Napoli di Romania, the most considerable place in all that country *, thought it best in the first place to attack Corinth, upon which they made several storms. The garrison being weakened, and the governor seeing it was impossible to hold out against so mighty a force, thought it fit to beat a parley : but while they were treating about the articles, one of the magazines in the Turkish camp, wherein they had six hundred barrels of powder, blew up by accident, whereby six or seven hundred men were killed ; which so enraged the infidels, that they would not grant any capitulation, but stormed the place with so much fury, that they took it, and put most of the garrison, with Signior Minotti, the governor, to the sword. The rest, with Antonio Bembo, proveditor extraordinary, were made prisoners of war." —*History of the Turks*, vol. iii. p. 151.

* Napoli di Romania is not now the most considerable place in the Morea, but Tripolitza, where the Pacha resides, and maintains his government. Napoli is near Argos. I visited all three in 1810-11 ; and, in the course of journeying through the country from my first arrival in 1809, I crossed the Isthmus eight times in my way from Attica to the Morea, over the mountains ; or in the other direction, when passing from the Gulf of Athens to that of Lepanto. Both the routes are picturesque and beautiful, though very different : that by sea has more sameness ; but the voyage being always within sight of land, and often very near it, presents many attractive views of the islands Salamis, Ægina, Poros, &c., and the coast of the Continent.

THE SIEGE OF CORINTH.

In the year since Jesus died for men,
Eighteen hundred years and ten,
We were a gallant company,
Riding o'er land, and sailing o'er sea.
Oh! but we went merrily!
We forded the river, and clomb the high
 hill,
Never our steeds for a day stood still;
Whether we lay in the cave or the shed,
Our sleep fell soft on the hardest bed:
Whether we couch'd in our rough capote,
On the rougher plank of our gliding boat,
Or stretch'd on the beach, or our saddles
 spread
As a pillow beneath the resting head,
Fresh we woke upon the morrow:
 All our thoughts and words had scope,
 We had health, and we had hope,
Toil and travel, but no sorrow.
We were of all tongues and creeds;—
Some were those who counted beads,
Some of mosque, and some of church,
 And some, or I mis-say, of neither;
Yet through the wide world might ye search,
 Nor find a motlier crew nor blither.
But some are dead, and some are gone,
And some are scatter'd and alone,
And some are rebels on the hills
 That look along Epirus' valleys,
 Where freedom still at moments rallies,
And pays in blood oppression's ills;
 And some are in a far countree,
And some all restlessly at home;
 But never more, oh! never, we
Shall meet to revel and to roam.

But those hardy days flew cheerily!
And when they now fall drearily,
My thoughts, like swallows, skim the main,
And bear my spirit back again
Over the earth, and through the air,
A wild bird and a wanderer.
'Tis this that ever wakes my strain,
And oft, too oft, implores again
The few who may endure my lay,
To follow me so far away.
Stranger—wilt thou follow now,
And sit with me on Acro-Corinth's brow?

I.

Many a vanish'd year and age,
And tempest's breath, and battle's rage,
Have swept o'er Corinth; yet she stands,
A fortress form'd to Freedom's hands.

The whirlwind's wrath, the earthquake's
 shock,
Have left untouch'd her hoary rock,
The keystone of a land, which still,
Though fall'n, looks proudly on that hill,
The landmark to the double tide
That purpling rolls on either side,
As if their waters chafed to meet,
Yet pause and crouch beneath her feet.
But could the blood before her shed
Since first Timoleon's brother bled,
Or baffled Persia's despot fled,
Arise from out the earth which drank
The stream of slaughter as it sank,
That sanguine ocean would o'erflow
Her isthmus idly spread below:
Or could the bones of all the slain,
Who perish'd there, be piled again,
That rival pyramid would rise
More mountain-like, through those clear skies,
Than yon tower-capp'd Acropolis,
Which seems the very clouds to kiss.

II.

On dun Cithæron's ridge appears
The gleam of twice ten thousand spears;
And downward to the Isthmian plain,
From shore to shore of either main,
The tent is pitch'd, the crescent shines
Along the Moslem's leaguering lines;
And the dusk Spahi's bands advance
Beneath each bearded pacha's glance;
And far and wide as eye can reach
The turban'd cohorts throng the beach;
And there the Arab's camel kneels,
And there his steed the Tartar wheels;
The Turcoman hath left his herd,
The sabre round his loins to gird;
And there the volleying thunders pour,
Till waves grow smoother to the roar.
The trench is dug, the cannon's breath
Wings the far hissing globe of death;
Fast whirl the fragments from the wall,
Which crumbles with the ponderous ball;
And from that wall the foe replies,
O'er dusty plain and smoky skies,
With fires that answer fast and well
The summons of the Infidel.

III.

But near and nearest to the wall
Of those who wish and work its fall,
With deeper skill in war's black art
Than Othman's sons, and high of heart

As any chief that ever stood
Triumphant in the fields of blood;
From post to post, and deed to deed,
Fast spurring on his reeking steed,
Where sallying ranks the trench assail,
And make the foremost Moslem quail;
Or where the battery, guarded well,
Remains as yet impregnable,
Alighting cheerly to inspire
The soldier slackening in his fire;
The first and freshest of the host
Which Stamboul's sultan there can boast,
To guide the follower o'er the field,
To point the tube, the lance to wield,
Or whirl around the bickering blade;—
Was Alp, the Adrian renegade!

IV.

From Venice—once a race of worth
His gentle sires—he drew his birth;
But late an exile from her shore,
Against his countrymen he bore
The arms they taught to bear; and now
The turban girt his shaven brow.
Through many a change had Corinth pass'd
With Greece to Venice' rule at last;
And here, before her walls, with those
To Greece and Venice equal foes,
He stood a foe, with all the zeal
Which young and fiery converts feel,
Within whose heated bosom throngs
The memory of a thousand wrongs.
To him had Venice ceased to be
Her ancient civic boast—" the Free;"
And in the palace of St. Mark
Unnamed accusers in the dark
Within the "Lion's mouth " had placed
A charge against him uneffaced:
He fled in time, and saved his life,
To waste his future years in strife,
That taught his land how great her loss
In him who triumph'd o'er the Cross,
'Gainst which he rear'd the Crescent high,
And battled to avenge or die.

V.

Coumourgi—he whose closing scene
Adorn'd the triumph of Eugene,
When on Carlowitz' bloody plain,
The last and mightiest of the slain,
He sank, regretting not to die,
But cursed the Christian's victory—
Coumourgi—can his glory cease,
That latest conqueror of Greece,
Till Christian hands to Greece restore
The freedom Venice gave of yore?
A hundred years have roll'd away
Since he refix'd the Moslem's sway;
And now he led the Mussulman,
And gave the guidance of the van

To Alp, who well repaid the trust
By cities levell'd with the dust;
And proved, by many a deed of death,
How firm his heart in novel faith.

VI.

The walls grew weak; and fast and hot
Against them pour'd the ceaseless shot,
With unabating fury sent
From battery to battlement;
And thunder-like the pealing din
Rose from each heated culverin;
And here and there some crackling dome
Was fired before the exploding bomb;
And as the fabric sank beneath
The shattering shell's volcanic breath,
In red and wreathing columns flash'd
The flame, as loud the ruin crash'd,
Or into countless meteors driven,
Its earth-stars melted into heaven;
Whose clouds that day grew doubly dun,
Impervious to the hidden sun,
With volumed smoke that slowly grew
To one wide sky of sulphurous hue.

VII.

But not for vengeance, long delay'd,
Alone, did Alp, the renegade,
The Moslem warriors sternly teach
His skill to pierce the promised breach:
Within these walls a maid was pent
His hope would win, without consent
Of that inexorable sire,
Whose heart refused him in its ire,
When Alp, beneath his Christian name,
Her virgin hand aspired to claim.
In happier mood, and earlier time,
While unimpeach'd for traitorous crime,
Gayest in gondola or hall,
He glitter'd through the Carnival;
And tuned the softest serenade
That e'er on Adria's waters play'd
At midnight to Italian maid.

VIII.

And many deem'd her heart was won!
For sought by numbers, given to none,
Had young Francesca's hand remain'd
Still by the church's bonds unchain'd:
And when the Adriatic bore
Lanciotto to the Paynim shore,
Her wonted smiles were seen to fail,
And pensive wax'd the maid and pale;
More constant at confessional,
More rare at masque and festival;
Or seen at such, with downcast eyes,
Which conquer'd hearts they ceased to prize:
With listless look she seems to gaze:
With humbler care her form arrays·

Her voice less lively in the song;
Her step, though light, less fleet among
The pairs, on whom the Morning's glance
Breaks, yet unsated with the dance.

IX.

Sent by the state to guard the land,
(Which, wrested from the Moslem's hand,
While Sobięski tamed his pride
By Buda's wall and Danube's side,
The chiefs of Venice wrung away
From Patra to Euboea's bay,)
Minotti held in Corinth's towers
The Doge's delegated powers,
While yet the pitying eye of Peace
Smiled o'er her long forgotten Greece:
And ere that faithless truce was broke
Which freed her from the unchristian yoke,
With him his gentle daughter came;
Nor there, since Menelaus' dame
Forsook her lord and land, to prove
What woes await on lawless love,
Had fairer form adorn'd the shore
Than she, the matchless stranger, bore.

X.

The wall is rent, the ruins yawn;
And with to-morrow's earliest dawn,
O'er the disjointed mass shall vault
The foremost of the fierce assault.
The bands are rank'd; the chosen van
Of Tartar and of Mussulman,
The full of hope, misnamed "forlorn,"
Who hold the thought of death in scorn,
And win their way with falchion's force,
Or pave the path with many a corse,
O'er which the following brave may rise,
Their stepping-stone—the last who dies !

XI.

'Tis midnight: on the mountains brown
The cold, round moon shines deeply down;
Blue roll the waters, blue the sky
Spreads like an ocean hung on high,
Bespangled with those isles of light,
So wildly, spiritually bright;
Who ever gazed upon them shining
And turn'd to earth without repining,
Nor wish'd for wings to flee away,
And mix with their eternal ray?
The waves on either shore lay there
Calm, clear, and azure as the air;
And scarce their foam the pebbles shook,
But murmur'd meekly as the brook.
The winds were pillow'd on the waves;
The banners droop'd along their staves,
And, as they fell around them furling,
Above them shone the crescent curling;
And that deep silence was unbroke,
Save where the watch his signal spoke,

Save where the steed neigh'd oft and shrill,
And echo answer'd from the hill,
And the wide hum of that wild host
Rustled like leaves from coast to coast,
As rose the Muezzin's voice in air
In midnight call to wonted prayer;
It rose, that chanted mournful strain,
Like some lone spirit's o'er the plain:
'Twas musical, but sadly sweet,
Such as when winds and harp-strings meet,
And take a long unmeasured tone,
To mortal minstrelsy unknown.
It seem'd to those within the wall
A cry prophetic of their fall:
It struck even the besieger's ear
With something ominous and drear,
An undefined and sudden thrill,
Which makes the heart a moment still,
Then beat with quicker pulse, ashamed
Of that strange sense its silence framed;
Such as a sudden passing-bell
Wakes, though but for a stranger's knell.

XII.

The tent of Alp was on the shore;
The sound was hush'd, the prayer was o'er,
The watch was set, the night-round made,
All mandates issued and obey'd:
'Tis but another anxious night,
His pains the morrow may requite
With all revenge and love can pay,
In guerdon for their long delay.
Few hours remain, and he hath need
Of rest, to nerve for many a deed
Of slaughter; but within his soul
The thoughts like troubled waters roll.
He stood alone among the host;
Not his the loud fanatic boast
To plant the crescent o'er the cross,
Or risk a life with little loss,
Secure in paradise to be
By Houris loved immortally:
Nor his, what burning patriots feel,
The stern exaltedness of zeal,
Profuse of blood, untired in toil,
When battling on the parent soil.
He stood alone—a renegade
Against the country he betray'd;
He stood alone amidst his band,
Without a trusted heart or hand:
They follow'd him, for he was brave,
And great the spoil he got and gave;
They crouch'd to him, for he had skill
To warp and wield the vulgar will:
But still his Christian origin
With them was little less than sin.
They envied even the faithless fame
He earn'd beneath a Moslem name;
Since he, their mightiest chief, had been
In youth a bitter Nazarene.

They did not know how pride can stoop,
When baffled feelings withering droop;
They did not know how hate can burn
In hearts once changed from soft to stern;
Nor all the false and fatal zeal
The convert of revenge can feel.
He ruled them—man may rule the worst,
By ever daring to be first:
So lions o'er the jackal sway;
The jackal points, he fells the prey,
Then on the vulgar yelling press,
To gorge the relics of success.

XIII.

His head grows fever'd, and his pulse
The quick successive throbs convulse:
In vain from side to side he throws
His form, in courtship of repose;
Or if he dozed, a sound, a start
Awoke him with a sunken heart.
The turban on his hot brow press'd,
The mail weigh'd lead-like on his breast,
Though oft and long beneath its weight
Upon his eyes had slumber sate,
Without or couch or canopy,
Except a rougher field and sky
Than now might yield a warrior's bed,
Than now along the heaven was spread.
He could not rest, he could not stay
Within his tent to wait for day,
But walk'd him forth along the sand,
Where thousand sleepers strew'd the strand.
What pillow'd them? and why should he
More wakeful than the humblest be,
Since more their peril, worse their toil?
And yet they fearless dream of spoil;
While he alone, where thousands pass'd
A night of sleep, perchance their last,
In sickly vigil wander'd on,
And envied all he gazed upon.

XIV.

He felt his soul become more light
Beneath the freshness of the night.
Cool was the silent sky, though calm,
And bathed his brow with airy balm:
Behind, the camp—before him lay,
In many a winding creek and bay,
Lepanto's gulf; and, on the brow
Of Delphi's hill, unshaken snow,
High and eternal, such as shone
Through thousand summers brightly gone,
Along the gulf, the mount, the clime;
It will not melt, like man, to time:
Tyrant and slave are swept away,
Less form'd to wear before the ray;
But that white veil, the lightest, frailest,
Which on the mighty mount thou hailest,
While tower and tree are torn and rent,
Shines o'er its craggy battlement;

In form a peak, in height a cloud,
In texture like a hovering shroud,
Thus high by parting Freedom spread,
As from her fond abode she fled,
And linger'd on the spot, where long
Her prophet spirit spake in song.
Oh! still her step at moments falters
O'er wither'd fields, and ruin'd altars,
And fain would wake, in souls too broken,
By pointing to each glorious token:
But vain her voice, till better days
Dawn in those yet remember'd rays,
Which shone upon the Persian flying,
And saw the Spartan smile in dying.

XV.

Not mindless of these mighty times
Was Alp, despite his flight and crimes;
And through this night, as on he wander'd,
And o'er the past and present ponder'd,
And thought upon the glorious dead
Who there in better cause had bled,
He felt how faint and feebly dim
The fame that could accrue to him,
Who cheer'd the band, and waved the sword,
A traitor in a turban'd horde;
And led them to the lawless siege,
Whose best success were sacrilege.
Not so had those his fancy number'd,
The chiefs whose dust around him slumber'd;
Their phalanx marshall'd on the plain,
Whose bulwarks were not then in vain.
They fell devoted, but undying;
The very gale their name seem'd sighing;
The waters murmur'd of their name;
The woods were peopled with their fame;
The silent pillar, lone and grey,
Claim'd kindred with their sacred clay;
Their spirits wrapp'd the dusky mountain,
Their memory sparkled o'er the fountain;
The meanest rill, the mightiest river
Roll'd mingling with their fame for ever.
Despite of every yoke she bears,
That land is glory's still and theirs!
'Tis still a watchword to the earth:
When man would do a deed of worth
He points to Greece, and turns to tread,
So sanction'd, on the tyrant's head:
He looks to her, and rushes on
Where life is lost, or freedom won.

XVI.

Still by the shore Alp mutely mused,
And woo'd the freshness Night diffused.
There shrinks no ebb in that tideless sea,
Which changeless rolls eternally;
So that wildest of waves, in their angriest
　　mood,
Scarce break on the bounds of the land for
　　a rood;

And the powerless moon beholds them flow,
Heedless if she come or go:
Calm or high, in main or bay,
On their course she hath no sway.
The rock unworn its base doth bare,
And looks o'er the surf, but it comes not
 there;
And the fringe of the foam may be seen below,
On the line that it left long ages ago:
A smooth short space of yellow sand
Between it and the greener land·

He wander'd on along the beach,
Till within the range of a carbine's reach
Of the leaguer'd wall; but they saw him not,
Or how could he 'scape from the hostile shot?
Did traitors lurk in the Christians' hold?
Were their hands grown stiff, or their hearts
 wax'd cold?
I know not, in sooth; but from yonder wall
There flash'd no fire, and there hiss'd no ball,
Though he stood beneath the bastion's frown,
That flank'd the sea-ward gate of the town;
Though he heard the sound, and could almost
 tell
The sullen words of the sentinel,
As his measured step on the stone below
Clank'd, as he paced it to and fro;
And he saw the lean dogs beneath the wall
Hold o'er the dead their carnival,
Gorging and growling o'er carcass and limb;
They were too busy to bark at him!
From a Tartar's skull they had stripp'd the
 flesh,
As ye peel the fig when its fruit is fresh;
And their white tusks crunch'd o'er the whiter
 skull,
As it slipp'd through their jaws, when their
 edge grew dull,
As they lazily mumbled the bones of the dead,
When they scarce could rise from the spot
 where they fed;
So well had they broken a lingering fast
With those who had fallen for that night's
 repast.
And Alp knew, by the turbans that roll'd on
 the sand,
The foremost of these were the best of his
 band:
Crimson and green were the shawls of their
 wear,
And each scalp had a single long tuft of hair,
All the rest was shaven and bare.
The scalps were in the wild dog's maw,
The hair was tangled round his jaw:
But close by the shore, on the edge of the
 gulf,
There sat a vulture flapping a wolf,
Who had stolen from the hills, but kept away,
Scared by the dogs, from the human prey;

But he seized on his share of a steed that lay,
Pick'd by the birds, on the sands of the bay.

XVII.

Alp turn'd him from the sickening sight:
Never had shaken his nerves in fight;
But he better could brook to behold the dying,
Deep in the tide of their warm blood lying,
Scorch'd with the death-thirst, and writhing
 in vain,
Than the perishing dead who are past all
 pain.
There is something of pride in the perilous
 hour,
Whate'er be the shape in which death may
 lower;
For Fame is there to say who bleeds,
And Honour's eye on daring deeds!
But when all is past, it is humbling to tread
O'er the weltering field of the tombless dead,
And see worms of the earth, and fowls of the
 air,
Beasts of the forest, all gathering there;
All regarding man as their prey,
All rejoicing in his decay.

XVIII.

There is a temple in ruin stands,
Fashion'd by long forgotten hands;
Two or three columns, and many a stone,
Marble and granite, with grass o'ergrown!
Out upon Time! it will leave no more
Of the things to come than the things before!
Out upon Time! who for ever will leave
But enough of the past for the future to grieve
O'er that which hath been, and o'er that
 which must be:
What we have seen, our sons shall see;
Remnants of things that have pass'd away,
Fragments of stone rear'd by creatures of
 clay!

XIX.

He sate him down at a pillar's base,
And pass'd his hand athwart his face;
Like one in dreary musing mood,
Declining was his attitude;
His head was drooping on his breast,
Fever'd, throbbing, and oppress'd;
And o'er his brow, so downward bent,
Oft his beating fingers went,
Hurriedly, as you may see
Your own run over the ivory key,
Ere the measured tone is taken
By the chords you would awaken.
There he sate all heavily,
As he heard the night-wind sigh.
Was it the wind through some hollow stone
Sent that soft and tender moan?

He lifted his head, and he look'd on the sea,
But it was unrippled as glass may be;
He look'd on the long grass—it waved not
 a blade;
How was that gentle sound convey'd?
He look'd to the banners—each flag lay still,
So did the leaves on Cithæron's hill,
And he felt not a breath come over his cheek;
What did that sudden sound bespeak?
He turn'd to the left—is he sure of sight?
There sate a lady, youthful and bright!

XX.

He started up with more of fear
Than if an armed foe were near.
"God of my fathers! what is here?
Who art thou? and wherefore sent
So near a hostile armament?"
His trembling hands refused to sign
The cross he deem'd no more divine:
He had resumed it in that hour,
But conscience wrung away the power.
He gazed, he saw: he knew the face
Of beauty, and the form of grace;
It was Francesca by his side,
The maid who might have been his bride!

The rose was yet upon her cheek,
But mellow'd with a tenderer streak:
Where was the play of her soft lips fled?
Gone was the smile that enliven'd their red.
The ocean's calm within their view,
Beside her eye had less of blue;
But like that cold wave it stood still,
And its glance, though clear, was chill.
Around her form a thin robe twining,
Nought conceal'd her bosom shining;
Through the parting of her hair,
Floating darkly downward there,
Her rounded arm show'd white and bare:
And ere yet she made reply,
Once she raised her hand on high;
It was so wan, and transparent of hue,
You might have seen the moon shine
 through.

XXI.

"I come from my rest to him I love best,
That I may be happy, and he may be bless'd.
I have pass'd the guards, the gate, the wall;
Sought thee in safety through foes and all.
'Tis said the lion will turn and flee
From a maid in the pride of her purity;
And the Power on high, that can shield the
 good
Thus from the tyrant of the wood,
Hath extended its mercy to guard me as well
From the hands of the leaguering infidel.
I come—and if I come in vain,
Never, oh never, we meet again!

Thou hast done a fearful deed
In falling away from thy fathers' creed:
But dash that turban to earth, and sign
The sign of the cross, and for ever be mine;
Wring the black drop from thy heart,
And to-morrow unites us no more to part."

"And where should our bridal couch be
 spread?
In the midst of the dying and the dead?
For to-morrow we give to the slaughter and
 flame
The sons and the shrines of the Christian
 name.
None, save thou and thine, I've sworn,
Shall be left upon the morn:
But thee will I bear to a lovely spot,
Where our hands shall be join'd, and our
 sorrow forgot.
There thou yet shalt be my bride,
When once again I've quell'd the pride
Of Venice; and her hated race
Have felt the arm they would debase
Scourge, with a whip of scorpions, those
Whom vice and envy made my foes."

Upon his hand she laid her own—
Light was the touch, but it thrill'd to the
 bone,
And shot a chillness to his heart,
Which fix'd him beyond the power to start.
Though slight was that grasp so mortal cold,
He could not loose him from its hold;
But never did clasp of one so dear
Strike on the pulse with such feeling of fear,
As those thin fingers, long and white,
Froze through his blood by their touch that
 night.
The feverish glow of his brow was gone,
And his heart sank so still that it felt like
 stone,
As he look'd on the face, and beheld its hue,
So deeply changed from what he knew:
Fair but faint—without the ray
Of mind, that made each feature play
Like sparkling waves on a sunny day;
And her motionless lips lay still as death,
And her words came forth without her breath,
And there rose not a heave o'er her bosom's
 swell,
And there seem'd not a pulse in her veins to
 dwell.
Though her eye shone out, yet the lids were
 fix'd,
And the glance that it gave was wild and
 unmix'd
With aught of change, as the eyes may seem
Of the restless who walk in a troubled dream;
Like the figures on arras, that gloomily glare,
Stirr'd by the breath of the wintry air,

So seen by the dying lamp's fitful light,
Lifeless, but life-like, and awful to sight;
As they seem, through the dimness, about to
 come down
From the shadowy wall where their images
 frown;
Fearfully flitting to and fro,
As the gusts on the tapestry come and go.

"If not for love of me be given
Thus much, then, for the love of heaven,—
Again I say—that turban tear
From off thy faithless brow, and swear
Thine injured country's sons to spare,
Or thou art lost; and never shalt see—
Not earth—that 's past—but heaven or me.
If this thou dost accord, albeit
A heavy doom 'tis thine to meet,
That doom shall half absolve thy sin,
And mercy's gate may receive thee within:
But pause one moment more, and take
The curse of Him thou didst forsake;
And look once more to heaven, and see
Its love for ever shut from thee.
There is a light cloud by the moon—
'Tis passing, and will pass full soon—
If, by the time its vapoury sail
Hath ceased her shaded orb to veil,
Thy heart within thee is not changed,
Then God and man are both avenged;
Dark will thy doom be, darker still
Thine immortality of ill."

Alp look'd to heaven, and saw on high
The sign she spake of in the sky;
But his heart was swollen, and turn'd
 aside,
By deep interminable pride.
This first false passion of his breast
Roll'd like a torrent o'er the rest.
He sue for mercy! *He* dismay'd
By wild words of a timid maid!
He, wrong'd by Venice, vow to save
Her sons, devoted to the grave!
No—though that cloud were thunder's
 worst,
And charged to crush him—let it burst!

He look'd upon it earnestly,
Without an accent of reply;
He watch'd it passing; it is flown:
Full on his eye the clear moon shone,
And thus he spake—"Whate'er my fate,
I am no changeling—'tis too late:
The reed in storms may bow and quiver,
Then rise again; the tree must shiver.
What Venice made me, I must be,
Her foe in all, save love to thee:
But thou art safe: oh, fly with me!"

He turn'd, but she is gone!
Nothing is there but the column stone.
Hath she sunk in the earth, or melted in air?
He saw not—he knew not—but nothing is
 there.

XXII.

The night is past, and shines the sun
As if that morn were a jocund one.
Lightly and brightly breaks away
The Morning from her mantle grey,
And the noon will look on a sultry day.
Hark to the trump, and the drum,
And the mournful sound of the barbarous
 horn,
And the flap of the banners, that flit as
 they're borne,
And the neigh of the steed, and the multi-
 tude's hum,
And the clash, and the shout, "They come!
 they come!"
The horsetails are pluck'd from the ground,
 and the sword
From its sheath; and they form, and but
 wait for the word.
Tartar, and Spahi, and Turcoman,
Strike your tents, and throng to the van;
Mount ye, spur ye, skirr the plain,
That the fugitive may flee in vain,
When he breaks from the town; and none
 escape,
Aged or young, in the Christian shape;
While your fellows on foot, in a fiery mass,
Bloodstain the breach through which they
 pass.
The steeds are all bridled, and snort to the
 rein;
Curved is each neck, and flowing each mane;
White is the foam of their champ on the bit;
The spears are uplifted; the matches are lit;
The cannon are pointed, and ready to roar,
And crush the wall they have crumbled
 before:
Forms in his phalanx each janizar;
Alp at their head; his right arm is bare,
So is the blade of his scimitar;
The khan and the pachas are all at their
 post;
The vizier himself at the head of the host.
When the culverin's signal is fired, then on;
Leave not in Corinth a living one—
A priest at her altars, a chief in her halls,
A hearth in her mansions, a stone on her
 walls.
God and the prophet—Alla Hu!
Up to the skies with that wild halloo!
"There the breach lies for passage, the
 ladder to scale;
And your hands on your sabres, and how
 should ye fail?

He who first downs with the red cross may
 crave
His heart's dearest wish; let him ask it, and
 have!"
Thus utter'd Coumourgi, the dauntless vizier;
The reply was the brandish of sabre and
 spear,
And the shout of fierce thousands in joyous
 ire:—
Silence—hark to the signal—fire!

XXIII.

As the wolves, that headlong go
On the stately buffalo,
Though with fiery eyes, and angry roar,
And hoofs that stamp, and horns that gore,
He tramples on earth, or tosses on high
The foremost, who rush on his strength
 but to die:
Thus against the wall they went,
Thus the first were backward bent;
Many a bosom, sheathed in brass,
Strew'd the earth like broken glass,
Shiver'd by the shot, that tore
The ground whereon they moved no more:
Even as they fell, in files they lay,
Like the mower's grass at the close of day,
When his work is done on the levell'd
 plain;
Such was the fall of the foremost slain.

XXIV.

As the spring-tides, with heavy plash,
From the cliffs invading dash
Huge fragments, sapp'd by the ceaseless
 flow,
Till white and thundering down they go,
Like the avalanche's snow
On the Alpine vales below;
Thus at length, outbreathed and worn,
Corinth's sons were downward borne
By the long and oft renew'd
Charge of the Moslem multitude.
In firmness they stood, and in masses they
 fell,
Heap'd by the host of the infidel,
Hand to hand, and foot to foot:
Nothing there, save death, was mute:
Stroke, and thrust, and flash, and cry
For quarter or for victory,
Mingle there with the volleying thunder,
Which makes the distant cities wonder
How the sounding battle goes,
If with them, or for their foes;
If they must mourn, or may rejoice
In that annihilating voice,
Which pierces the deep hills through and
 through
With an echo dread and new:

You might have heard it, on that day,
O'er Salamis and Megara;
(We have heard the hearers say,)
Even unto Piræus' bay.

XXV.

From the point of encountering blades to
 the hilt,
Sabres and swords with blood were gilt;
But the rampart is won, and the spoil
 begun,
And all but the after carnage done.
Shriller shrieks now mingling come
From within the plunder'd dome:
Hark to the haste of flying feet,
That splash in the blood of the slippery
 street;
But here and there, where 'vantage ground
Against the foe may still be found,
Desperate groups, of twelve or ten,
Make a pause, and turn again—
With banded backs against the wall,
Fiercely stand, or fighting fall.

There stood an old man—his hairs were
 white,
But his veteran arm was full of might:
So gallantly bore he the brunt of the fray,
The dead before him, on that day,
In a semicircle lay;
Still he combated unwounded,
Though retreating, unsurrounded.
Many a scar of former fight
Lurk'd beneath his corslet bright;
But of every wound his body bore,
Each and all had been ta'en before:
Though aged, he was so iron of limb,
Few of our youth could cope with him,
And the foes, whom he singly kept at bay,
Outnumber'd his thin hairs of silver grey.
From right to left his sabre swept;
Many an Othman mother wept
Sons that were unborn, when dipp'd
His weapon first in Moslem gore,
Ere his years could count a score.
Of all he might have been the sire
Who fell that day beneath his ire:
For, sonless left long years ago,
His wrath made many a childless foe;
And since the day, when in the strait
His only boy had met his fate,
His parent's iron hand did doom
More than a human hecatomb.
If shades by carnage be appeased,
Patroclus' spirit less was pleased
Than his, Minotti's son, who died
Where Asia's bounds and ours divide.
Buried he lay, where thousands before
For thousands of years were inhumed on
 the shore;

What of them is left, to tell
Where they lie, and how they fell?
Not a stone on their turf, nor a bone in their
 graves;
But they live in the verse that immortally
 saves.

XXVI.

Hark to the Allah shout! a band
Of the Mussulman bravest and best is at
 hand;
Their leader's nervous arm is bare,
Swifter to smite, and never to spare—
Unclothed to the shoulder it waves them
 on;
Thus in the fight is he ever known:
Others a gaudier garb may show,
To tempt the spoil of the greedy foe;
Many a hand's on a richer hilt,
But none on a steel more ruddily gilt;
Many a loftier turban may wear,—
Alp is but known by the white arm bare;
Look through the thick of the fight, 'tis
 there!
There is not a standard on that shore
So well advanced the ranks before;
There is not a banner in Moslem war
Will lure the Delhis half so far;
It glances like a falling star!
Where'er that mighty arm is seen,
The bravest be, or late have been;
There the craven cries for quarter
Vainly to the vengeful Tartar;
Or the hero, silent lying,
Scorns to yield a groan in dying;
Mustering his last feeble blow
'Gainst the nearest levell'd foe,
Though faint beneath the mutual wound,
Grappling on the gory ground.

XXVII.

Still the old man stood erect,
And Alp's career a moment check'd.
"Yield thee, Minotti; quarter take,
For thine own, thy daughter's sake."

"Never, renegado, never!
Though the life of thy gift would last for
 ever."

"Francesca!—Oh, my promised bride!
Must she too perish by thy pride?"

"She is safe."—"Where? where?"—"In
 heaven;
From whence thy traitor soul is driven—
Far from thee, and undefiled."
Grimly then Minotti smiled,
As he saw Alp staggering bow
Before his words, as with a blow.

"Oh God! when died she?"—"Yester-
 night—
Nor weep I for her spirit's flight:
None of my pure race shall be
Slaves to Mahomet and thee—
Come on!"—That challenge is in vain—
Alp's already with the slain!
While Minotti's words were wreaking
More revenge in bitter speaking
Than his falchion's point had found,
Had the time allow'd to wound,
From within the neighbouring porch
Of a long defended church,
Where the last and desperate few
Would the failing fight renew,
The sharp shot dash'd Alp to the ground;
Ere an eye could view the wound
That crash'd through the brain of the
 infidel,
Round he spun, and down he fell;
A flash like fire within his eyes
Blazed, as he bent no more to rise,
And then eternal darkness sunk
Through all the palpitating trunk;
Nought of life left, save a quivering
Where his limbs were slightly shivering:
They turn'd him on his back; his breast
And brow were stain'd with gore and dust,
And through his lips the life-blood oozed,
From its deep veins lately loosed:
But in his pulse there was no throb,
Nor on his lips one dying sob;
Sigh, nor word, nor struggling breath
Heralded his way to death;
Ere his very thought could pray,
Unanel'd he pass'd away,
Without a hope from mercy's aid,—
To the last a Renegade.

XXVIII.

Fearfully the yell arose
Of his followers, and his foes;
These in joy, in fury those:
Then again in conflict mixing,
Clashing swords, and spears transfixing,
Interchanged the blow and thrust,
Hurling warriors in the dust.
Street by street, and foot by foot,
Still Minotti dares dispute
The latest portion of the land
Left beneath his high command;
With him, aiding heart and hand,
The remnant of his gallant band.
Still the church is tenable,
 Whence issued late the fated ball
 That half avenged the city's fall,
When Alp, her fierce assailant, fell:
Thither bending sternly back,
They leave before a bloody track;

And, with their faces to the foe,
Dealing wounds with every blow,
The chief, and his retreating train,
Join to those within the fane;
There they yet may breathe awhile,
Shelter'd by the massy pile.

XXIX.

Brief breathing-time! the turban'd host,
With added ranks and raging boast,
Press onwards with such strength and heat,
Their numbers balk their own retreat;
For narrow the way that led to the spot
Where still the Christians yielded not;
And the foremost, if fearful, may vainly try
Through the massy column to turn and fly;
They perforce must do or die.
They die; but ere their eyes could close,
Avengers o'er their bodies rose;
Fresh and furious, fast they fill
The ranks unthinn'd, though slaughter'd
 still;
And faint the weary Christians wax
Before the still renew'd attacks;
And now the Othmans gain the gate;
Still resists its iron weight,
And still, all deadly aim'd and hot,
From every crevice comes the shot;
From every shatter'd window pour
The volleys of the sulphurous shower:
But the portal wavering grows and weak—
The iron yields, the hinges creak—
It bends—it falls—and all is o'er;
Lost Corinth may resist no more!

XXX.

Darkly, sternly, and all alone,
Minotti stood o'er the altar-stone:
Madonna's face upon him shone,
Painted in heavenly hues above,
With eyes of light and looks of love;
And placed upon that holy shrine
To fix our thoughts on things divine,
When pictured there, we kneeling see
Her, and the boy-God on her knee,
Smiling sweetly on each prayer
To heaven, as if to waft it there.
Still she smiled; even now she smiles,
Though slaughter streams along her aisles:
Minotti lifted his aged eye,
And made the sign of a cross with a sigh,
Then seized a torch which blazed thereby;
And still he stood, while with steel and flame
Inward and onward the Mussulman came.

XXXI.

The vaults beneath the mosaic stone
Contain'd the dead of ages gone;
Their names were on the graven floor,
But now illegible with gore;

The carved crests, and curious hues
The varied marble's vein diffuse,
Were smear'd, and slippery,—stain'd, and
 strown
With broken swords, and helms o'erthrown:
There were dead above, and the dead below
Lay cold in many a coffin'd row;
You might see them piled in sable state,
By a pale light through a gloomy grate;
But War had enter'd their dark caves,
And stored along the vaulted graves
Her sulphurous treasures, thickly spread
In masses by the fleshless dead:
 Here, throughout the siege, had been
 The Christians' chiefest magazine;
To these a late form'd train now led,
Minotti's last and stern resource
Against the foe's o'erwhelming force.

XXXII.

The foe came on, and few remain
To strive, and those must strive in vain:
For lack of further lives, to slake
The thirst of vengeance now awake,
With barbarous blows they gash the dead,
And lop the already lifeless head,
And fell the statues from their niche,
And spoil the shrines of offerings rich,
And from each other's rude hands wrest
The silver vessels saints had bless'd.
To the high altar on they go;
Oh, but it made a glorious show!
On its table still behold
The cup of consecrated gold;
Massy and deep, a glittering prize,
Brightly it sparkles to plunderers' eyes:
That morn it held the holy wine,
Converted by Christ to his blood so divine,
Which his worshippers drank at the break
 of day,
To shrive their souls ere they join'd in the
 fray.
Still a few drops within it lay:
And round the sacred table glow
Twelve lofty lamps, in splendid row,
From the purest metal cast;
A spoil—the richest, and the last.

XXXIII.

So near they came, the nearest stretch'd
To grasp the spoil he almost reach'd,
 When old Minotti's hand
Touch'd with the torch the train—
 'Tis fired!
Spire, vaults, the shrine, the spoil, the slain,
 The turban'd victors, the Christian band,
All that of living or dead remain,
Hurl'd on high with the shiver'd fane,
 In one wild roar expired!

The shatter'd town—the walls thrown
 down—
The waves a moment backward bent—
The hills that shake, although unrent,
 As if an earthquake pass'd—
The thousand shapeless things all driven
In cloud and flame athwart the heaven,
 By that tremendous blast—
Proclaim'd the desperate conflict o'er
On that too long afflicted shore:
Up to the sky like rockets go
All that mingled there below:
Many a tall and goodly man,
Scorch'd and shrivell'd to a span,
When he fell to earth again
Like a cinder strew'd the plain:
Down the ashes shower like rain;
Some fell in the gulf, which received the
 sprinkles
With a thousand circling wrinkles;
Some fell on the shore, but, far away,
Scatter'd o'er the isthmus lay;
Christian or Moslem, which be they?
Let their mothers see and say!
When in cradled rest they lay,
And each nursing mother smiled
On the sweet sleep of her child,
Little deem'd she such a day
Would rend those tender limbs away.
Not the matrons that them bore
Could discern their offspring more;

That one moment left no trace
More of human form or face
Save a scatter'd scalp or bone:
And down came blazing rafters, strown
Around, and many a falling stone,
 Deeply dinted in the clay,
All blacken'd there and reeking lay.
All the living things that heard
That deadly earth-shock disappear'd:
The wild birds flew; the wild dogs fled,
And howling left the unburied dead;
The camels from their keepers broke;
The distant steer forsook the yoke—
The nearer steed plunged o'er the plain,
And burst his girth, and tore his rein;
The bull-frog's note, from out the marsh,
Deep-mouth'd arose, and doubly harsh;
The wolves yell'd on the cavern'd hill
Where echo roll'd in thunder still;
The jackals' troop, in gather'd cry,
Bay'd from afar complainingly,
With a mix'd and mournful sound,
Like crying babe, and beaten hound:
With sudden wing, and ruffled breast,
The eagle left his rocky nest,
And mounted nearer to the sun,
The clouds beneath him seem'd so
 dun;
Their smoke assail'd his startled beak,
And made him higher soar and shriek—
 Thus was Corinth lost and won!

Parisina.

TO

SCROPE BERDMORE DAVIES, ESQ.

THE FOLLOWING POEM IS INSCRIBED,

BY ONE WHO HAS LONG ADMIRED HIS TALENTS, AND VALUED HIS FRIENDSHIP.

January 22, 1816.

ADVERTISEMENT.

THE following poem is grounded on a circumstance mentioned in Gibbon's "Antiquities of the House of Brunswick." I am aware, that in modern times the delicacy or fastidiousness of the reader may deem such subjects unfit for the purposes of poetry. The Greek dramatists, and some of the best of our old English writers, were of a different opinion: as Alfieri and Schiller have also been, more recently, upon the Continent. The following extract will explain the facts on which the story is founded. The name of *Azo* is substituted for Nicholas, as more metrical.

"Under the reign of Nicholas III. Ferrara was polluted with a domestic tragedy. By the testimony of an attendant, and his own observation, the Marquis of Este discovered the incestuous loves of his wife Parisina, and Hugo his bastard son, a beautiful and valiant youth. They were beheaded in the castle by the sentence of a father and husband, who published his shame, and survived their execution. He was unfortunate, if they were guilty: if they were innocent, he was still more unfortunate; nor is there any possible situation in which I can sincerely approve the last act of the justice of a parent."—GIBBON'S *Miscellaneous Works*, vol. iii. p. 470.

PARISINA.

I.

It is the hour when from the boughs
 The nightingale's high note is heard;
It is the hour when lovers' vows
 Seem sweet in every whisper'd word;
And gentle winds, and waters near,
Make music to the lonely ear.
Each flower the dews have lightly wet,
And in the sky the stars are met,
And on the wave is deeper blue,
And on the leaf a browner hue,
And in the heaven that clear obscure,
So softly dark, and darkly pure,
Which follows the decline of day,
As twilight melts beneath the moon away.

II.

But it is not to list to the waterfall
That Parisina leaves her hall,
And it is not to gaze on the heavenly light
That the lady walks in the shadow of night;
And if she sits in Este's bower,
'T is not for the sake of its full-blown flower;
She listens—but not for the nightingale—
Though her ear expects as soft a tale.
There glides a step through the foliage thick,
And her cheek grows pale, and her heart
 beats quick.
There whispers a voice through the rustling
 leaves,
And her blush returns, and her bosom heaves:
A moment more and they shall meet—
'T is past—her lover's at her feet.

III.

And what unto them is the world beside,
 With all its change of time and tide?
Its living things, its earth and sky,
Are nothing to their mind and eye.
And heedless as the dead are they
 Of aught around, above, beneath;
As if all else had pass'd away,
 They only for each other breathe;
Their very sighs are full of joy
 So deep, that did it not decay,
That happy madness would destroy
 The hearts which feel its fiery sway:
Of guilt, of peril, do they deem
In that tumultuous tender dream?
Who that have felt that passion's power,
Or paused, or fear'd in such an hour?
Or thought how brief such moments last?
But yet—they are already past!
Alas! we must awake before
We know such vision comes no more.

IV.

With many a lingering look they leave
 The spot of guilty gladness past:
And though they hope and vow, they grieve,
 As if that parting were the last.
The frequent sigh—the long embrace—
 The lip that there would cling for ever,
While gleams on Parisina's face
 The Heaven she fears will not forgive her,
As if each calmly conscious star
Beheld her frailty from afar—
The frequent sigh, the long embrace,
Yet binds them to their trysting place.
But it must come, and they must part
In fearful heaviness of heart,
With all the deep and shuddering chill
Which follows fast the deeds of ill.

V.

And Hugo is gone to his lonely bed,
 To covet there another's bride;
But she must lay her conscious head
 A husband's trusting heart beside.
But fever'd in her sleep she seems,
And red her cheek with troubled dreams,
 And mutters she in her unrest
A name she dare not breathe by day,
 And clasps her lord unto the breast
Which pants for one away:
And he to that embrace awakes,
And, happy in the thought, mistakes
The dreaming sigh, and warm caress,
For such as he was wont to bless;
And could in very fondness weep
O'er her who loves him even in sleep.

VI.

He clasp'd her sleeping to his heart,
 And listen'd to each broken word:
He hears—Why doth Prince Azo start,
 As if the Archangel's voice he heard?
And well he may—a deeper doom
Could scarcely thunder o'er his tomb,
When he shall wake to sleep no more,
And stand the eternal throne before.
And well he may—his earthly peace
Upon that sound is doom'd to cease.
That sleeping whisper of a name
Bespeaks her guilt and Azo's shame.
And whose that name? that o'er his pillow
Sounds fearful as the breaking billow,
Which rolls the plank upon the shore,
 And dashes on the pointed rock
The wretch who sinks to rise no more,—
 So came upon his soul the shock.

And whose that name? 't is Hugo's,—his—
In sooth he had not deem'd of this!—
'T is Hugo's,—he, the child of one
He loved—his own all-evil son—
The offspring of his wayward youth,
When he betray'd Bianca's truth,
The maid whose folly could confide
In him who made her not his bride.

VII.

He pluck'd his poniard in its sheath,
 But sheath'd it ere the point was bare—
Howe'er unworthy now to breathe,
 He could not slay a thing so fair—
 At least, not smiling—sleeping—there:
Nay more :—he did not wake her then,
 But gazed upon her with a glance
 Which, had she roused her from her
 trance,
Had frozen her sense to sleep again;
And o'er his brow the burning lamp
Gleam'd on the dew-drops big and damp.
She spake no more—but still she slum-
 ber'd—
While, in his thought, her days are num-
 ber'd.

VIII.

And with the morn he sought and found,
In many a tale from those around,
The proof of all he fear'd to know,
Their present guilt, his future woe;
The long-conniving damsels seek
 To save themselves, and would transfer
 The guilt—the shame—the doom—to her:
Concealment is no more—they speak
All circumstance which may compel
Full credence to the tale they tell:
And Azo's tortured heart and ear
Have nothing more to feel or hear.

IX.

He was not one who brook'd delay:
 Within the chamber of his state,
The chief of Este's ancient sway
 Upon his throne of judgment sate;
His nobles and his guards are there,—
Before him is the sinful pair;
Both young,—and *one* how passing fair!
With swordless belt, and fetter'd hand,
Oh, Christ! that thus a son should stand
 Before a father's face!
Yet thus must Hugo meet his sire,
And hear the sentence of his ire,
 The tale of his disgrace!
And yet he seems not overcome,
Although, as yet, his voice be dumb.

X.

And still, and pale, and silently
 Did Parisina wait her doom;
How changed since last her speaking
 eye
 Glanced gladness round the glittering
 room,
Where high-born men were proud to wait,
Where Beauty watch'd to imitate
 Her gentle voice, her lovely mien,
And gather from her air and gait
 The graces of its queen!
Then,—had her eye in sorrow wept,
A thousand warriors forth had leapt,
A thousand swords had sheathless shone,
And made her quarrel all their own.
Now,—what is she? and what are they?
Can she command, or these obey?
All silent and unheeding now,
With downcast eyes and knitting brow,
And folded arms, and freezing air,
And lips that scarce their scorn forbear,
Her knights and dames, her court—is
 there:
And he, the chosen one, whose lance
Had yet been couch'd before her glance,
Who—were his arm a moment free—
Had died or gain'd her liberty;
The minion of his father's bride,—
He, too, is fetter'd by her side;
Nor sees her swoln and full eye swim
Less for her own despair than him:
Those lids—o'er which the violet vein
Wandering, leaves a tender stain,
Shining through the smoothest white
That e'er did softest kiss invite—
Now seem'd with hot and livid glow
To press, not shade, the orbs below;
Which glance so heavily, and fill,
As tear on tear grows gathering still.

XI.

And he for her had also wept,
 But for the eyes that on him gazed:
His sorrow, if he felt it, slept;
 Stern and erect his brow was raised.
Whate'er the grief his soul avow'd,
He would not shrink before the crowd;
But yet he dared not look on her;
Remembrance of the hours that were—
His guilt, his love, his present state—
His father's wrath, all good men's hate—
His earthly, his eternal fate—
And hers,—oh, hers! he dared not throw
One look upon that death-like brow!
Else had his rising heart betray'd
Remorse for all the wreck it made.

XII.

And Azo spake:—" But yesterday
 I gloried in a wife and son ;
That dream this morning pass'd away ;
 Ere day declines, I shall have none.
My life must linger on alone ;
Well,—let that pass,—there breathes not one
Who would not do as I have done :
Those ties are broken—not by me ;
 Let that too pass ;—the doom's prepared !
Hugo, the priest awaits on thee,
 And then—thy crime's reward !
Away ! address thy prayers to Heaven,
 Before its evening stars are met—
Learn if thou there canst be forgiven ;
 Its mercy may absolve thee yet.
But here, upon the earth beneath,
 There is no spot where thou and I
Together for an hour could breathe :
 Farewell ! I will not see thee die—
But thou, frail thing ! shalt view his head—
 Away ! I cannot speak the rest :
Go ! woman of the wanton breast ;
Not I, but thou his blood dost shed :
Go ! if that sight thou canst outlive,
And joy thee in the life I give."

XIII.

And here stern Azo hid his face—
 For on his brow the swelling vein
Throbb'd as if back upon his brain
 The hot blood ebb'd and flow'd again ,
And therefore bow'd he for a space,
 And pass'd his shaking hand along
His eye, to veil it from the throng :
While Hugo raised his chained hands,
And for a brief delay demands
His father's ear : the silent sire
Forbids not what his words require.

 " It is not that I dread the death—
For thou hast seen me by thy side
All redly through the battle ride,
And that—not once a useless brand—
Thy slaves have wrested from my hand
Hath shed more blood in cause of thine,
Than e'er can stain the axe of mine :
 Thou gav'st, and may'st resume my breath,
A gift for which I thank thee not ;
Nor are my mother's wrongs forgot,
 Her slighted love and ruin'd name,
 Her offspring's heritage of shame ;
But she is in the grave, where he,
 Her son, thy rival, soon shall be.
Her broken heart—my sever'd head—
 Shall witness for thee from the dead
How trusty and how tender were
Thy youthful love—paternal care.

'Tis true that I have done thee wrong—
 But wrong for wrong :—this,—deem'd thy bride,
 The other victim of thy pride,—
Thou know'st for me was destined long ;
Thou saw'st, and coveted'st her charms ;
 And with thy very crime—my birth—
 Thou tauntedst me, as little worth ;
A match ignoble for her arms,
Because, forsooth, I could not claim
The lawful heirship of thy name,
Nor sit on Este's lineal throne ;
 Yet, were a few short summers mine,
 My name should more than Este's shine
With honours all my own.
I had a sword—and have a breast
That should have won as haught a crest
As ever waved along the line
Of all these sovereign sires of thine.
Not always knightly spurs are worn
The brightest by the better born ;
And mine have lanced my courser's flank
Before proud chiefs of princely rank,
When charging to the cheering cry
Of ' Este and of Victory ! '
I will not plead the cause of crime,
Nor sue thee to redeem from time
A few brief hours or days that must
At length roll o'er my reckless dust ;—
Such maddening moments as my past,
They could not, and they did not, last.
Albeit my birth and name be base,
And thy nobility of race
Disdain'd to deck a thing like me—
 Yet in my lineaments they trace
 Some features of my father's face,
And in my spirit—all of thee.
From thee this tamelessness of heart—
From thee,—nay, wherefore dost thou start?—
From thee in all their vigour came
My arm of strength, my soul of flame ;
Thou didst not give me life alone,
But all that made me more thine own.
See what thy guilty love hath done !
Repaid thee with too like a son !
I am no bastard in my soul,
For that, like thine, abhorr'd control ;
And for my breath, that hasty boon
Thou gav'st and wilt resume so soon,
I valued it no more than thou,
When rose thy casque above thy brow,
And we, all side by side, have striven,
And o'er the dead our coursers driven :
The past is nothing—and at last
The future can but be the past ;
Yet would I that I then had died :
 For though thou work'dst my mother's ill,
And made thy own my destined bride,
 I feel thou art my father still :

And harsh as sounds thy hard decree,
'T is not unjust, although from thee.
Begot in sin, to die in shame,
My life begun and ends the same:
As err'd the sire, so err'd the son,
And thou must punish both in one.
My crime seems worst to human view,
But God must judge between us too ! "

XIV.

He ceased—and stood with folded arms,
 On which the circling fetters sounded ;
 And not an ear but felt as wounded,
 Of all the chiefs that there were rank'd,
 When those dull chains in meeting
 clank'd :
Till Parisina's fatal charms
Again attracted every eye—
Would she thus hear him doom'd to die !
She stood, I said, all pale and still,
The living cause of Hugo's ill:
Her eyes unmoved, but full and wide,
Not once had turn'd to either side—
Nor once did those sweet eyelids close,
Or shade the glance o'er which they rose,
But round their orbs of deepest blue
The circling white dilated grew—
And there with glassy gaze she stood
As ice were in her curdled blood ;
But every now and then a tear
 So large and slowly gather'd slid
 From the long dark fringe of that fair lid,
It was a thing to see, not hear !
And those who saw, it did surprise,
Such drops could fall from human eyes.
To speak she thought—the imperfect note
Was choked within her swelling throat,
Yet seem'd in that low hollow groan
Her whole heart gushing in the tone.
It ceased—again she thought to speak,
Then burst her voice in one long shriek,
And to the earth she fell like stone
Or statue from its base o'erthrown,
More like a thing that ne'er had life,—
A monument of Azo's wife,—
Than her, that living guilty thing,
Whose every passion was a sting,
Which urged to guilt, but could not bear
That guilt's detection and despair.
But yet she lived—and all too soon
Recover'd from that death-like swoon—
But scarce to reason—every sense
Had been o'erstrung by pangs intense ;
And each frail fibre of her brain
(As bowstrings, when relax'd by rain,
The erring arrow launch aside)
Sent forth her thoughts all wild and wide—
The past a blank, the future black,
With glimpses of a dreary track,

Like lightning on the desert path,
When midnight storms are mustering
 wrath.
She fear'd—she felt that something ill
Lay on her soul, so deep and chill ;
That there was sin and shame she knew,
That some one was to die—but who ?
She had forgotten :—did she breathe ?
Could this be still the earth beneath,
The sky above, and men around ;
Or were they fiends who now so frown'd
On one, before whose eyes each eye
Till then had smiled in sympathy ?
All was confused and undefined
To her all-jarr'd and wandering mind ;
A chaos of wild hopes and fears :
And now in laughter, now in tears,
But madly still in each extreme,
She strove with that convulsive dream ;
For so it seem'd on her to break :
Oh ! vainly must she strive to wake !

XV.

The Convent bells are ringing,
 But mournfully and slow ;
In the grey square turret swinging,
 With a deep sound, to and fro.
Heavily to the heart they go !
Hark ! the hymn is singing—
 The song for the dead below,
Or the living who shortly shall be so !
For a departing being's soul
The death-hymn peals and the hollow bells
 knoll :
He is near his mortal goal ;
Kneeling at the Friar's knee,
Sad to hear, and piteous to see—
Kneeling on the bare cold ground,
With the block before and the guards
 around—
And the headsman with his bare arm
 ready,
That the blow may be both swift and
 steady,
Feels if the axe be sharp and true
Since he set its edge anew :
While the crowd in a speechless circle
 gather
To see the Son fall by the doom of the
 Father !

XVI.

It is a lovely hour as yet
Before the summer sun shall set,
Which rose upon that heavy day,
And mock'd it with his steadiest ray ;
And his evening beams are shed
Full on Hugo's fated head,
As his last confession pouring
To the monk, his doom deploring

In penitential holiness,
He bends to hear his accents bless
With absolution such as may
Wipe our mortal stains away.
That high sun on his head did glisten
As he there did bow and listen,
And the rings of chestnut hair
Curl'd half down his neck so bare;
But brighter still the beam was thrown
Upon the axe which near him shone
With a clear and ghastly glitter—
Oh! that parting hour was bitter!
Even the stern stood chill'd with awe:
Dark the crime, and just the law—
Yet they shudder'd as they saw.

XVII.

The parting prayers are said and over
Of that false son, and daring lover!
His beads and sins are all recounted,
His hours to their last minute mounted;
His mantling cloak before was stripp'd,
His bright brown locks must now be
 clipp'd;
'Tis done—all closely are they shorn;
The vest which till this moment worn—
The scarf which Parisina gave—
Must not adorn him to the grave.
Even that must now be thrown aside,
And o'er his eyes the kerchief tied;
But no—that last indignity
Shall ne'er approach his haughty eye.
All feelings seemingly subdued,
In deep disdain were half renew'd,
When headsman's hands prepared to bind
Those eyes which would not brook such
 blind,
As if they dared not look on death.
"No—yours my forfeit blood and breath;
These hands are chain'd, but let me die
At least with an unshackled eye—
Strike:"—and as the word he said,
Upon the block he bow'd his head;
These the last accents Hugo spoke:
"Strike"—and flashing fell the stroke—
Roll'd the head—and, gushing, sunk
Back the stain'd and heaving trunk,
In the dust, which each deep vein
Slaked with its ensanguined rain;
His eyes and lips a moment quiver,
Convulsed and quick—then fix for ever.

He died, as erring man should die,
 Without display, without parade;
 Meekly had he bow'd and pray'd,
 As not disdaining priestly aid,
Nor desperate of all hope on high.
And while before the Prior kneeling,
His heart was wean'd from earthly feeling;

His wrathful sire, his paramour—
What were they in such an hour?
No more reproach, no more despair,
No thought but heaven, no word but
 prayer—
Save the few which from him broke,
When, bared to meet the headsman's stroke,
He claim'd to die with eyes unbound,
His sole adieu to those around.

XVIII.

Still as the lips that closed in death,
Each gazer's bosom held his breath:
But yet, afar, from man to man,
A cold electric shiver ran,
As down the deadly blow descended
On him whose life and love thus ended;
And, with a hushing sound compress'd,
A sigh shrunk back on every breast;
But no more thrilling noise rose there,
 Beyond the blow that to the block
 Pierced through with forced and sullen
 shock,
Save one:—what cleaves the silent air
So madly shrill, so passing wild?
That, as a mother's o'er her child,
Done to death by sudden blow,
To the sky these accents go,
Like a soul's in endless woe.
Through Azo's palace-lattice driven,
That horrid voice ascends to heaven,
And every eye is turn'd thereon:
But sound and sight alike are gone!
It was a woman's shriek—and ne'er
In madlier accents rose despair;
And those who heard it, as it pass'd,
In mercy wish'd it were the last.

XIX.

Hugo is fallen; and, from that hour,
No more in palace, hall, or bower,
Was Parisina heard or seen:
Her name—as if she ne'er had been—
Was banish'd from each lip and ear,
Like words of wantonness or fear;
And from Prince Azo's voice, by none
Was mention heard of wife or son;
No tomb, no memory had they;
Theirs was unconsecrated clay—
At least the knight's who died that day.
But Parisina's fate lies hid
Like dust beneath the coffin lid:
Whether in convent she abode,
And won to heaven her dreary road
By blighted and remorseful years
Of scourge, and fast, and sleepless tears;
Or if she fell by bowl or steel,
For that dark love she dared to feel;
Or if, upon the moment smote,
She died by tortures less remote,

Like him she saw upon the block,
With heart that shared the headsman's
 shock,
In quicken'd brokenness that came,
In pity, o'er her shatter'd frame,
None knew—and none can ever know:
But whatsoe'er its end below,
Her life began and closed in woe!

XX.

And Azo found another bride,
And goodly sons grew by his side;
But none so lovely and so brave
As him who wither'd in the grave;
Or if they were—on his cold eye
Their growth but glanced unheeded by,
Or noticed with a smother'd sigh.
But never tear his cheek descended,
And never smile his brow unbended;
And o'er that fair broad brow were wrought
The intersected lines of thought;
Those furrows which the burning share
Of Sorrow ploughs untimely there;
Scars of the lacerating mind
Which the Soul's war doth leave behind,
He was past all mirth or woe:
Nothing more remain'd below
But sleepless nights and heavy days,
A mind all dead to scorn or praise,
A heart which shunn'd itself—and yet
That would not yield, nor could forget,
Which, when it least appear'd to melt,
Intently thought, intensely felt:

The deepest ice which ever froze
Can only o'er the surface close;
The living stream lies quick below,
And flows, and cannot cease to flow.
Still was his seal'd-up bosom haunted
By thoughts which Nature hath implanted;
Too deeply rooted thence to vanish,
Howe'er our stifled tears we banish;
When, struggling as they rise to start,
We check those waters of the heart,
They are not dried—those tears unshed
But flow back to the fountain head,
And resting in their spring more pure,
For ever in its depth endure,
Unseen, unwept, but uncongeal'd,
And cherish'd most where least reveal'd.
With inward starts of feeling left,
To throb o'er those of life bereft,
Without the power to fill again
The desert gap which made his pain;
Without the hope to meet them where
United souls shall gladness share;
With all the consciousness that he
Had only pass'd a just decree;
That they had wrought their doom of ill;
Yet Azo's age was wretched still.
The tainted branches of the tree,
 If lopp'd with care, a strength may give,
 By which the rest shall bloom and live
All greenly fresh and wildly free:
But if the lightning, in its wrath,
The waving boughs with fury scathe,
The massy trunk the ruin feels,
And never more a leaf reveals.

The Prisoner of Chillon.

SONNET ON CHILLON.

ETERNAL Spirit of the chainless Mind!
 Brightest in dungeons, Liberty! thou art,
 For there thy habitation is the heart—
The heart which love of thee alone can bind;
And when thy sons to fetters are consign'd—
 To fetters, and the damp vault's dayless gloom,
 Their country conquers with their martyrdom,
And Freedom's fame finds wings on every wind.
Chillon! thy prison is a holy place,
 And thy sad floor an altar—for 't was trod,
Until his very steps have left a trace
 Worn, as if thy cold pavement were a sod,
By Bonnivard! May none those marks efface!
 For they appeal from tyranny to God.

ADVERTISEMENT.

WHEN this poem was composed, I was not suffi-
ciently aware of the history of Bonnivard, or I
should have endeavoured to dignify the subject by
an attempt to celebrate his courage and his virtues.
With some account of his life I have been furnished,
by the kindness of a citizen of that republic, which
is still proud of the memory of a man worthy of the
best age of ancient freedom :—

"François de Bonnivard, fils de Louis de Bonni-
vard, originaire de Seyssel et Seigneur de Lunes,
naquit en 1496. Il fit ses études à Turin : en 1510
Jean Aimé de Bonnivard, son oncle, lui résigna le
Prieuré de St. Victor, qui aboutissait aux murs de
Genève, et qui formait un bénéfice considérable.

"Ce grand homme—(Bonnivard mérite ce titre
par la force de son âme, la droiture de son cœur, la
noblesse de ses intentions, la sagesse de ses con-
seils, le courage de ses démarches, l'étendue de ses
connaissances, et la vivacité de son esprit),—ce
grand homme, qui excitera l'admiration de tous
ceux qu'une vertu héroïque peut encore émouvoir,
inspirera encore la plus vive reconnaissance dans
les cœurs des Génévois qui aiment Genève. Bon-
nivard en fut toujours un des plus fermes appuis :
pour assurer la liberté de notre République, il ne
craignit pas de perdre souvent la sienne ; il oublia
son repos ; il méprisa ses richesses ; il ne négligea

rien pour affermir le bonheur d'une patrie qu'il
honora de son choix : dès ce moment il la chérit
comme le plus zélé de ses citoyens ; il la servit avec
l'intrépidité d'un héros, et il écrivit son Histoire
avec la naïveté d'un philosophe et la chaleur d'un
patriote.

"Il dit dans le commencement de son Histoire
de Genève, que, *dès qu'il eut commencé de lire
l'histoire des nations, il se sentit entraîné par son
goût pour les Républiques, dont il épousa toujours
les intérêts :* c'est ce goût pour la liberté qui lui fit
sans doute adopter Genève pour sa patrie.

"Bonnivard, encore jeune, s'annonça hautement
comme le défenseur de Genève contre le Duc de
Savoye et l'Evêque.

"En 1519, Bonnivard devient le martyr de sa
patrie. Le Duc de Savoye étant entré dans Genève
avec cinq cent hommes, Bonnivard craint le res-
sentiment du Duc ; il voulut se retirer à Fribourg
pour en éviter les suites ; mais il fut trahi par deux
hommes qui l'accompagnaient, et conduit par ordre
du Prince à Grolée, où il resta prisonnier pendant
deux ans. Bonnivard était malheureux dans ses
voyages : comme ses malheurs n'avaient point ra-
lenti son zèle pour Genève, il était toujours un
ennemi redoutable pour ceux qui la menaçaient,
et par conséquent il devait être exposé à leurs coups.
Il fut rencontré en 1530 sur le Jura par des voleurs,

qui le dépouillèrent et qui le mirent encore entre les mains du Duc de Savoye: ce Prince le fit enfermer dans le Château de Chillon, où il resta sans être interrogé jusques en 1536; il fut alors delivré par les Bernois, qui s'emparèrent du Pays de Vaud.

"Bonnivard, en sortant de sa captivité, eut le plaisir de trouver Genève libre et réformée: la République s'empressa de lui témoigner sa reconnaissance, et de le dédommager des maux qu'il avoit soufferts; elle le reçut Bourgeois de la ville au mois de Juin, 1536; elle lui donna la maison habitée autrefois par le Vicaire-Général, et elle lui assigna une pension de deux cent écus d'or tant qu'il séjournerait à Genève. Il fut admis dans le Conseil de Deux-Cent en 1537.

"Bonnivard n'a pas fini d'être utile: après avoir travaillé à rendre Genève libre, il réussit à la rendre tolérante. Bonnivard engagea le Conseil à accorder aux ecclésiastiques et aux paysans un tems suffisant pour examiner les propositions qu'on leur faisait; il réussit par sa douceur: on prêche toujours le Christianisme avec succès quand on le prêche avec charité.

"Bonnivard fut savant: ses manuscrits, qui sont dans la bibliothèque publique, prouvent qu'il avait bien lu les auteurs classiques Latins, et qu'il avait approfondi la théologie et l'histoire. Ce grand homme aimait les sciences, et il croyait qu'elles pouvaient faire la gloire de Genève; aussi il ne négligea rien pour les fixer dans cette ville naissante; en 1551 il donna sa bibliothèque au public; elle fut le commencement de notre bibliothèque publique; et ces livres sont en partie les rares et belles éditions du quinzième siècle qu'on voit dans notre collection. Enfin, pendant la même année, ce bon patriote institua la République son héritière, à condition qu'elle employerait ses biens à entretenir le collège dont on projettait la fondation.

"Il parait que Bonnivard mourut en 1570; mais on ne peut l'assurer, parcequ'il y a une lacune dans le Nécrologe depuis le mois de Juillet, 1570, jusques en 1571."

THE PRISONER OF CHILLON.

I.

My hair is grey, but not with years,
 Nor grew it white
 In a single night,
As men's have grown from sudden fears:
My limbs are bow'd, though not with toil,
 But rusted with a vile repose,
For they have been a dungeon's spoil,
 And mine has been the fate of those
To whom the goodly earth and air
Are bann'd, and barr'd—forbidden fare:
But this was for my father's faith
I suffer'd chains and courted death;
That father perish'd at the stake
For tenets he would not forsake;
And for the same his lineal race
In darkness found a dwelling-place;
We were seven—who now are one,
 Six in youth, and one in age,
Finish'd as they had begun,
 Proud of Persecution's rage;
One in fire, and two in field,
Their belief with blood have seal'd,
Dying as their father died,
For the God their foes denied;
Three were in a dungeon cast,
Of whom this wreck is left the last.

II.

There are seven pillars of Gothic mould,
In Chillon's dungeons deep and old,
There are seven columns, massy and grey,
Dim with a dull imprison'd ray,
A sunbeam which hath lost its way,
And through the crevice and the cleft
Of the thick wall is fallen and left;
Creeping o'er the floor so damp,
Like a marsh's meteor lamp:
And in each pillar there is a ring,
 And in each ring there is a chain;
That iron is a cankering thing,
 For in these limbs its teeth remain,
With marks that will not wear away,
Till I have done with this new day,
Which now is painful to these eyes,
Which have not seen the sun so rise
For years—I cannot count them o'er,
I lost their long and heavy score,
When my last brother droop'd and died,
And I lay living by his side.

III.

They chain'd us each to a column stone,
And we were three—yet, each alone;
We could not move a single pace,
We could not see each other's face,
But with that pale and livid light
That made us strangers in our sight:
And thus together—yet apart,
Fetter'd in hand, but join'd in heart,
'Twas still some solace, in the dearth
Of the pure elements of earth,
To hearken to each other's speech,
And each turn comforter to each
With some new hope, or legend old,
Or song heroically bold;
But even these at length grew cold.
Our voices took a dreary tone,
An echo of the dungeon stone,

A grating sound, not full and free,
As they of yore were wont to be:
It might be fancy, but to me
They never sounded like our own.

IV.

I was the eldest of the three,
And to uphold and cheer the rest
I ought to do—and did my best—
And each did well in his degree.
The youngest, whom my father loved,
Because our mother's brow was given
To him, with eyes as blue as heaven—
For him my soul was sorely moved;
And truly might it be distress'd
To see such bird in such a nest;
For he was beautiful as day—
(When day was beautiful to me
As to young eagles, being free)—
A polar day, which will not see
A sunset till its summer's gone,
Its sleepless summer of long light,
The snow-clad offspring of the sun:
And thus he was as pure and bright,
And in his natural spirit gay,
With tears for nought but others' ills,
And then they flow'd like mountain rills,
Unless he could assuage the woe
Which he abhorr'd to view below.

V.

The other was as pure of mind,
But form'd to combat with his kind;
Strong in his frame, and of a mood
Which 'gainst the world in war had stood,
And perish'd in the foremost rank
With joy:—but not in chains to pine:
His spirit wither'd with their clank,
I saw it silently decline—
And so perchance in sooth did mine:
But yet I forced it on to cheer
Those relics of a home so dear.
He was a hunter of the hills,
Had follow'd there the deer and wolf;
To him his dungeon was a gulf,
And fetter'd feet the worst of ills.

VI.

Lake Leman lies by Chillon's walls:
A thousand feet in depth below
Its massy waters meet and flow;
Thus much the fathom-line was sent
From Chillon's snow-white battlement,
Which round about the wave inthrals:
A double dungeon wall and wave
Have made—and like a living grave
Below the surface of the lake
The dark vault lies wherein we lay,
We heard it ripple night and day;
Sounding o'er our heads it knock'd;
And I have felt the winter's spray
Wash through the bars when winds were
high
And wanton in the happy sky;
And then the very rock hath rock'd,
And I have felt it shake, unshock'd,
Because I could have smiled to see
The death that would have set me free.

VII.

I said my nearer brother pined,
I said his mighty heart declined,
He loathed and put away his food;
It was not that 'twas coarse and rude,
For we were used to hunter's fare,
And for the like had little care:
The milk drawn from the mountain goat
Was changed for water from the moat,
Our bread was such as captives' tears
Have moisten'd many a thousand years,
Since man first pent his fellow men
Like brutes within an iron den;
But what were these to us or him?
These wasted not his heart or limb;
My brother's soul was of that mould
Which in a palace had grown cold,
Had his free breathing been denied
The range of the steep mountain's side;
But why delay the truth?—he died.
I saw, and could not hold his head,
Nor reach his dying hand—nor dead,—
Though hard I strove, but strove in vain,
To rend and gnash my bonds in twain.
He died, and they unlock'd his chain,
And scoop'd for him a shallow grave
Even from the cold earth of our cave,
I begg'd them as a boon to lay
His corse in dust whereon the day
Might shine—it was a foolish thought,
But then within my brain it wrought,
That even in death his freeborn breast
In such a dungeon could not rest.
I might have spared my idle prayer—
They coldly laugh'd, and laid him there:
The flat and turfless earth above
The being we so much did love;
His empty chain above it leant,
Such murder's fitting monument!

VIII.

But he, the favourite and the flower,
Most cherish'd since his natal hour,
His mother's image in fair face,
The infant love of all his race,
His martyr'd father's dearest thought,
My latest care, for whom I sought
To hoard my life, that his might be
Less wretched now, and one day free;

He, too, who yet had held untired
A spirit natural or inspired—
He, too, was struck, and day by day
Was wither'd on the stalk away.
Oh, God! it is a fearful thing
To see the human soul take wing
In any shape, in any mood:
I've seen it rushing forth in blood,
I've seen it on the breaking ocean
Strive with a swoln convulsive motion,
I've seen the sick and ghastly bed
Of Sin delirious with its dread;
But these were horrors—this was woe
Unmix'd with such—but sure and slow:
He faded, and so calm and meek,
So softly worn, so sweetly weak,
So tearless, yet so tender, kind,
And grieved for those he left behind;
With all the while a cheek whose bloom
Was as a mockery of the tomb,
Whose tints as gently sunk away
As a departing rainbow's ray;
An eye of most transparent light,
That almost made the dungeon bright,
And not a word of murmur, not
A groan o'er his untimely lot,—
A little talk of better days,
A little hope my own to raise,
For I was sunk in silence—lost
In this last loss, of all the most;
And then the sighs he would suppress
Of fainting nature's feebleness,
More slowly drawn, grew less and less:
I listen'd, but I could not hear;
I call'd, for I was wild with fear;
I knew 't was hopeless, but my dread
Would not be thus admonished;
I call'd, and thought I heard a sound—
I burst my chain with one strong bound,
And rush'd to him:—I found him not,
I only stirr'd in this black spot,
I only lived, *I* only drew
The accursed breath of dungeon-dew;
The last, the sole, the dearest link
Between me and the eternal brink,
Which bound me to my failing race,
Was broken in this fatal place.
One on the earth, and one beneath—
My brothers—both had ceased to breathe:
I took that hand which lay so still,
Alas! my own was full as chill;
I had not strength to stir, or strive,
But felt that I was still alive—
A frantic feeling, when we know
That what we love shall ne'er be so.
 I know not why
 I could not die,
I had no earthly hope but faith,
And that forbade a selfish death.

IX.

What next befell me then and there
 I know not well—I never knew—
First came the loss of light, and air,
 And then of darkness too:
I had no thought, no feeling—none—
Among the stones I stood a stone,
And was, scarce conscious what I wist,
As shrubless crags within the mist;
For all was blank, and bleak, and grey;
It was not night, it was not day;
It was not even the dungeon-light,
So hateful to my heavy sight,
But vacancy absorbing space,
And fixedness without a place;
There were no stars, no earth, no time,
No check, no change, no good, no crime,
But silence, and a stirless breath
Which neither was of life nor death;
A sea of stagnant idleness,
Blind, boundless, mute, and motionless!

X.

A light broke in upon my brain,—
 It was the carol of a bird;
It ceased, and then it came again,
 The sweetest song ear ever heard,
And mine was thankful till my eyes
Ran over with the glad surprise,
And they that moment could not see
I was the mate of misery;
But then by dull degrees came back
My senses to their wonted track;
I saw the dungeon walls and floor
Close slowly round me as before,
I saw the glimmer of the sun
Creeping as it before had done,
But through the crevice where it came
That bird was perch'd, as fond and tame,
 And tamer than upon the tree;
A lovely bird, with azure wings,
And song that said a thousand things,
 And seem'd to say them all for me!
I never saw its like before,
I ne'er shall see its likeness more:
It seem'd like me to want a mate,
But was not half so desolate,
And it was come to love me when
None lived to love me so again,
And cheering from my dungeon's brink,
Had brought me back to feel and think.
I know not if it late were free,
 Or broke its cage to perch on mine,
But knowing well captivity,
 Sweet bird! I could not wish for thine!
Or if it were, in winged guise,
A visitant from Paradise;
For—Heaven forgive that thought! the while
 Which made me both to weep and smile—

I sometimes deem'd that it might be
My brother's soul come down to me;
But then at last away it flew,
And then 'twas mortal well I knew,
For he would never thus have flown,
And left me twice so doubly lone,
Lone as the corse within its shroud,
Lone as a solitary cloud,—
 A single cloud on a sunny day,
While all the rest of heaven is clear,
A frown upon the atmosphere,
That hath no business to appear
 When skies are blue, and earth is gay.

XI.

A kind of change came in my fate,
My keepers grew compassionate;
I know not what had made them so,
They were inured to sights of woe,
But so it was:—my broken chain
With links unfasten'd did remain,
And it was liberty to stride
Along my cell from side to side,
And up and down, and then athwart,
And tread it over every part;
And round the pillars one by one,
Returning where my walk begun,
Avoiding only, as I trod,
My brothers' graves without a sod;
For if I thought with heedless tread
My step profaned their lowly bed,
My breath came gaspingly and thick,
And my crush'd heart fell blind and sick.

XII.

I made a footing in the wall,
 It was not therefrom to escape,
For I had buried one and all
 Who loved me in a human shape;
And the whole earth would henceforth be
A wider prison unto me:
No child, no sire, no kin had I,
No partner in my misery;
I thought of this, and I was glad,
For thought of them had made me mad;
But I was curious to ascend
To my barr'd windows, and to bend
Once more, upon the mountains high,
The quiet of a loving eye.

XIII.

I saw them, and they were the same,
They were not changed like me in frame;
I saw their thousand years of snow
On high—their wide long lake below,
And the blue Rhone in fullest flow;

I heard the torrents leap and gush
O'er channell'd rock and broken bush;
I saw the white-wall'd distant town,
And whiter sails go skimming down;
And then there was a little isle,
Which in my very face did smile,
 The only one in view;
A small green isle, it seem'd no more,
Scarce broader than my dungeon floor,
But in it there were three tall trees,
And o'er it blew the mountain breeze,
And by it there were waters flowing,
And on it there were young flowers growing,
 Of gentle breath and hue.
The fish swam by the castle wall,
And they seem'd joyous each and all;
The eagle rode the rising blast,
Methought he never flew so fast
As then to me he seem'd to fly;
And then new tears came in my eye,
And I felt troubled—and would fain
I had not left my recent chain;
And when I did descend again,
The darkness of my dim abode
Fell on me as a heavy load;
It was as is a new-dug grave,
Closing o'er one we sought to save,—
And yet my glance, too much opprest,
Had almost need of such a rest.

XIV.

It might be months, or years, or days,
 I kept no count, I took no note,
I had no hope my eyes to raise,
 And clear them of their dreary mote;
At last men came to set me free;
 I ask'd not why, and reck'd not where;
It was at length the same to me,
Fetter'd or fetterless to be,
 I learn'd to love despair.
And thus when they appear'd at last,
And all my bonds aside were cast,
These heavy walls to me had grown
A hermitage—and all my own!
And half I felt as they were come
To tear me from a second home:
With spiders I had friendship made,
And watch'd them in their sullen trade,
Had seen the mice by moonlight play,
And why should I feel less than they?
We were all inmates of one place,
And I, the monarch of each race,
Had power to kill—yet, strange to tell!
In quiet we had learn'd to dwell;
My very chains and I grew friends,
So much a long communion tends
To make us what we are:—even I
Regain'd my freedom with a sigh.

Mazeppa.

ADVERTISEMENT.

" CELUI qui remplissait alors cette place était un gentilhomme Polonais, nommé Mazeppa, né dans le palatinat de Podolie : il avait été élevé page de Jean Casimir, et avait pris à sa cour quelque teinture des belles-lettres. Une intrigue qu'il eut dans sa jeunesse avec la femme d'un gentilhomme Polonais ayant été découverte, le mari le fit lier tout nu sur un cheval farouche, et le laissa aller en cet état. Le cheval, qui était du pays de l'Ukraine, y retourna, et y porta Mazeppa, demi-mort de fatigue et de faim. Quelques paysans le secoururent : il resta longtems parmi eux, et se signala dans plusieurs courses contre les Tartares. La supériorité de ses lumières lui donna une grande considération parmi les Cosaques : sa réputation s'augmentant de jour en jour obligea le Czar à le faire Prince de l'Ukraine."—VOLTAIRE, *Hist. de Charles XII.* p. 196.

"Le roi fuyant, et poursuivi, eut son cheval tué sous lui ; le Colonel Gieta, blessé, et perdant tout son sang, lui donna le sien. Ainsi on remit deux fois à cheval, dans sa fuite, ce conquérant qui n'avait pu y monter pendant la bataille."—P. 216.

"Le roi alla par un autre chemin avec quelques cavaliers. Le carrosse, où il était, rompit dans la marche ; on le remit à cheval. Pour comble de disgrace, il s'égara pendant la nuit dans un bois ; là, son courage ne pouvant plus suppléer à ses forces épuisées, les douleurs de sa blessure devenues plus insupportables par la fatigue, son cheval étant tombé de lassitude, il se coucha quelques heures au pied d'un arbre, en danger d'être surpris à tout moment par les vainqueurs, qui le cherchaient de tous côtés."—P. 218.

I.

'TWAS after dread Pultowa's day,
 When fortune left the royal Swede,
Around a slaughter'd army lay,
 No more to combat and to bleed.
The power and glory of the war,
Faithless as their vain votaries, men,
Had pass'd to the triumphant Czar,
 And Moscow's walls were safe again,
Until a day more dark and drear,
And a more memorable year,
Should give to slaughter and to shame
A mightier host and haughtier name ;
A greater wreck, a deeper fall,
A shock to one—a thunderbolt to all.

II.

Such was the hazard of the die ;
The wounded Charles was taught to fly
By day and night through field and flood,
Stain'd with his own and subjects' blood ;
For thousands fell that flight to aid :
And not a voice was heard t'upbraid
Ambition in his humbled hour,
When truth had nought to dread from
 power.

His horse was slain, and Gieta gave
His own—and died the Russians' slave.
This too sinks after many a league
Of well sustain'd but vain fatigue ;
And in the depth of forests, darkling
The watch-fires in the distance sparkling—
 The beacons of surrounding foes—
A king must lay his limbs at length.
Are these the laurels and repose
For which the nations strain their strength ?
They laid him by a savage tree,
In outworn nature's agony ;
His wounds were stiff, his limbs were stark ;
The heavy hour was chill and dark ;
The fever in his blood forbade
A transient slumber's fitful aid :
And thus it was ; but yet through all,
Kinglike the monarch bore his fall,
And made, in this extreme of ill,
His pangs the vassals of his will :
All silent and subdued were they,
As once the nations round him lay.

III.

A band of chiefs !—alas ! how few,
 Since but the fleeting of a day
Had thinn'd it ; but this wreck was true
 And chivalrous : upon the clay

Each sate him down, all sad and mute,
　Beside his monarch and his steed;
For danger levels man and brute,
　And all are fellows in their need.
Among the rest, Mazeppa made
His pillow in an old oak's shade—
Himself as rough, and scarce less old,
The Ukraine's Hetman, calm and bold;
But first, outspent with this long course,
The Cossack prince rubb'd down his horse,
And made for him a leafy bed,
　And smooth'd his fetlocks and his mane,
　　And slack'd his girth, and stripp'd his
　　　rein,
And joy'd to see how well he fed;
For until now he had the dread
His wearied courser might refuse
To browse beneath the midnight dews:
But he was hardy as his lord,
And little cared for bed and board;
But spirited and docile too,
Whate'er was to be done, would do.
Shaggy and swift, and strong of limb,
All Tartar-like he carried him;
Obey'd his voice, and came to call,
And knew him in the midst of all:
Though　thousands　were　around,—and
　Night,
Without a star, pursued her flight,—
That steed from sunset until dawn
His chief would follow like a fawn.

IV.

This done, Mazeppa spread his cloak,
And laid his lance beneath his oak,
Felt if his arms in order good
The long day's march had well withstood—
If still the powder fill'd the pan,
　And flints unloosen'd kept their lock—
His sabre's hilt and scabbard felt,
And whether they had chafed his belt;
And next the venerable man,
From out his havresack and can,
　Prepared and spread his slender stock;
And to the monarch and his men
The whole or portion offer'd then
With far less of inquietude
Than courtiers at a banquet would.
And Charles of this his slender share
With smiles partook a moment there,
To force of cheer a greater show,
And seem above both wounds and woe;
And then he said—"Of all our band,
Though firm of heart and strong of hand,
In skirmish, march, or forage, none
Can less have said or more have done
Than thee, Mazeppa! on the earth
So fit a pair had never birth,
Since Alexander's days till now,
As thy Bucephalus and thou:

All Scythia's fame to thine should yield
For pricking on o'er flood and field."
Mazeppa answer'd—"Ill betide
The school wherein I learn'd to ride!"
Quoth Charles—"Old Hetman, wherefore so,
Since thou hast learn'd the art so well?"
Mazeppa said—"'Twere long to tell;
And we have many a league to go,
With every now and then a blow,
And ten to one at least the foe,
Before our steeds may graze at ease
Beyond the swift Borysthenes:
And, Sire, your limbs have need of rest,
　And I will be the sentinel
Of this your troop."—"But I request,"
　Said Sweden's monarch, "thou wilt tell
This tale of thine, and I may reap,
Perchance, from this the boon of sleep;
For at this moment from my eyes
The hope of present slumber flies."

"Well, Sire, with such a hope, I'll track
My seventy years of memory back:
I think 'twas in my twentieth spring,—
Ay, 'twas,—when Casimir was king—
John Casimir,—I was his page
Six summers, in my earlier age:
A learned monarch, faith! was he,
And most unlike your majesty;
He made no wars, and did not gain
New realms to lose them back again;
And (save debates in Warsaw's diet)
He reign'd in most unseemly quiet;
Not that he had no cares to vex;
He loved the muses and the sex;
And sometimes these so froward are,
They made him wish himself at war;
But soon his wrath being o'er, he took
Another mistress, or new book:
And then he gave prodigious fêtes—
All Warsaw gather'd round his gates
To gaze upon his splendid court,
And dames, and chiefs, of princely port:
He was the Polish Solomon,
So sung his poets, all but one,
Who, being unpension'd, made a satire,
And boasted that he could not flatter.
It was a court of jousts and mimes,
Where every courtier tried at rhymes;
Even I for once produced some verses,
And sign'd my odes 'Despairing Thyrsis.'
There was a certain Palatine,
　A count of far and high descent,
Rich as a salt or silver mine;
And he was proud, ye may divine,
　As if from heaven he had been sent:
He had such wealth in blood and ore
　As few could match beneath the throne;
And he would gaze upon his store,
And o'er his pedigree would pore,

Until by some confusion led,
Which almost look'd like want of head,
 He thought their merits were his own.
His wife was not of his opinion;
 His junior she by thirty years,
Grew daily tired of his dominion;
 And, after wishes, hopes, and fears,
 To virtue a few farewell tears,
A restless dream or two, some glances
At Warsaw's youth, some songs, and
 dances,
Awaited but the usual chances,
Those happy accidents which render
The coldest dames so very tender,
To deck her Count with titles given,
'Tis said, as passports into heaven;
But, strange to say, they rarely boast
Of these, who have deserved them most.

V.

"I was a goodly stripling then;
 At seventy years I so may say,
That there were few, or boys or men,
 Who, in my dawning time of day,
Of vassal or of knight's degree,
Could vie in vanities with me;
For I had strength, youth, gaiety,
A port, not like to this ye see,
But smooth, as all is rugged now;
 For time, and care, and war, have
 plough'd
My very soul from out my brow;
 And thus I should be disavow'd
By all my kind and kin, could they
Compare my day and yesterday;
This change was wrought, too, long ere
 age
Had ta'en my features for his page;
With years, ye know, have not declined
My strength, my courage, or my mind,
Or at this hour I should not be
Telling old tales beneath a tree,
With starless skies my canopy.
 But let me on: Theresa's form—
Methinks it glides before me now,
Between me and yon chestnut's bough,
 The memory is so quick and warm;
And yet I find no words to tell
The shape of her I loved so well:
She had the Asiatic eye,
 Such as our Turkish neighbourhood
 Hath mingled with our Polish blood,
Dark as above us is the sky;
But through it stole a tender light,
Like the first moonrise of midnight;
Large, dark, and swimming in the stream,
Which seem'd to melt to its own beam;
All love, half languor, and half fire,
Like saints that at the stake expire,

And lift their raptured looks on high,
As though it were a joy to die.
A brow like a midsummer lake,
 Transparent with the sun therein,
When waves no murmur dare to make,
 And heaven beholds her face within.
A cheek and lip—but why proceed?
 I loved her then, I love her still;
And such as I am, love indeed
 In fierce extremes—in good and ill.
But still we love even in our rage,
And haunted to our very age
With the vain shadow of the past,
As is Mazeppa to the last.

VI.

"We met—we gazed—I saw, and sigh'd,
She did not speak, and yet replied;
There are ten thousand tones and signs
We hear and see, but none defines—
Involuntary sparks of thought,
Which strike from out the heart o'er-
 wrought,
And form a strange intelligence,
Alike mysterious and intense,
Which link the burning chain that binds,
Without their will, young hearts and
 minds:
Conveying, as the electric wire,
We know not how, the absorbing fire.
I saw, and sigh'd—in silence wept,
And still reluctant distance kept,
Until I was made known to her,
And we might then and there confer
Without suspicion—then, even then,
 I long'd, and was resolved to speak;
But on my lips they died again,
 The accents tremulous and weak,
Until one hour.—There is a game,
 A frivolous and foolish play,
 Wherewith we while away the day;
It is—I have forgot the name—
And we to this, it seems, were set,
By some strange chance, which I forget:
I reck'd not if I won or lost,
 It was enough for me to be
 So near to hear, and oh! to see
The being whom I loved the most.
I watch'd her as a sentinel,
(May ours this dark night watch as well!)
 Until I saw, and thus it was,
That she was pensive, nor perceived
 Her occupation, nor was grieved
Nor glad to lose or gain; but still
Play'd on for hours, as if her will
Yet bound her to the place, though not
That hers might be the winning lot.
 Then through my brain the thought did
 pass

Even as a flash of lightning there,
Tnat there was something in her air
Which would not doom me to despair;
And on the thought my words broke forth,
 All incoherent as they were;
Their eloquence was little worth,
But yet she listen'd—'tis enough—
 Who listens once will listen twice;
 Her heart, be sure, is not of ice,
And one refusal no rebuff.

VII.

" I loved, and was beloved again—
 They tell me, Sire, you never knew
 Those gentle frailties ; if 'tis true,
I shorten all my joy or pain;
To you 'twould seem absurd as vain;
But all men are not born to reign,
Or o'er their passions, or as you
Thus o'er themselves and nations too.
I am—or rather was—a prince,
 A chief of thousands, and could lead
 Them on where each would foremost
 bleed ;
But could not o'er myself evince
The like control—But to resume:
 I loved, and was beloved again ;
In sooth, it is a happy doom,
 But yet where happiest ends in pain.
We met in secret, and the hour
Which led me to that lady's bower
Was fiery Expectation's dower.
My days and nights were nothing—all
Except that hour, which doth recall,
In the long lapse from youth to age,
 No other like itself: I'd give
 The Ukraine back again to live
It o'er once more, and be a page,
The happy page, who was the lord
Of one soft heart, and his own sword,
And had no other gem nor wealth
Save nature's gift of youth and health.
We met in secret—doubly sweet,
Some say, they find it so to meet;
I know not that—I would have given
My life but to have call'd her mine
In the full view of earth and heaven;
 For I did oft and long repine
That we could only meet by stealth.

VIII.

" For lovers there are many eyes,
 And such there were on us ; the devil
On such occasions should be civil—
The devil!—I'm loth to do him wrong,
 It might be some untoward saint,
Who would not be at rest too long,
 But to his pious bile gave vent—
But one fair night, some lurking spies

Surprised and seized us both.
The Count was something more than
 wroth—
I was unarm'd ; but if in steel,
All cap-à-pie from head to heel,
What 'gainst their numbers could I do ?
'Twas near his castle, far away
 From city or from succour near,
And almost on the break of day;
I did not think to see another,
 My moments seem'd reduced to few;
And with one prayer to Mary Mother,
 And, it may be, a saint or two,
As I resign'd me to my fate,
They led me to the castle gate:
 Theresa's doom I never knew,
Our lot was henceforth separate.
An angry man, ye may opine,
Was he, the proud Count Palatine;
And he had reason good to be,
 But he was most enraged lest such
 An accident should chance to touch
Upon his future pedigree ;
Nor less amazed, that such a blot
His noble 'scutcheon should have got,
While he was highest of his line;
 Because unto himself he seem'd
 The first of men, nor less he deem'd
In others' eyes, and most in mine.
'Sdeath! with a page—perchance a king
Had reconciled him to the thing;
But with a stripling of a page—
I felt, but cannot paint his rage.

IX.

" ' Bring forth the horse !'—the horse was
 brought ;
 In truth, he was a noble steed,
 A Tartar of the Ukraine breed,
Who look'd as though the speed of thought
Were in his limbs ; but he was wild,
 Wild as the wild deer, and untaught,
With spur and bridle undefiled—
 'Twas but a day he had been caught;
And snorting, with erected mane,
And struggling fiercely, but in vain,
In the full foam of wrath and dread
To me the desert-born was led :
They bound me on, that menial throng;
Upon his back with many a thong;
Then loosed him with a sudden lash—
Away !—away !— and on we dash !
Torrents less rapid and less rash.

X.

" Away !—away ! My breath was gone,
I saw not where he hurried on :
'Twas scarcely yet the break of day,
And on he foam'd—away !—away !

type="header_navigation">(Mazeppa. 335

The last of human sounds which rose,
As I was darted from my foes,
Was the wild shout of savage laughter,
Which on the wind came roaring after
A moment from that rabble rout :
With sudden wrath I wrench'd my head,
 And snapp'd the cord, which to the mane
 Had bound my neck in lieu of rein,
And, writhing half my form about,
Howl'd back my curse; but 'midst the tread,
The thunder of my courser's speed,
Perchance they did not hear nor heed :
It vexes me—for I would fain
Have paid their insult back again.
I paid it well in after days :
There is not of that castle gate,
Its drawbridge and portcullis' weight,
Stone, bar, moat, bridge, or barrier left ;
Nor of its fields a blade of grass,
 Save what grows on a ridge of wall,
 Where stood the hearth-stone of the hall;
And many a time ye there might pass,
Nor dream that e'er that fortress was.
I saw its turrets in a blaze,
Their crackling battlements all cleft,
 And the hot lead pour down like rain
From off the scorch'd and blackening roof,
Whose thickness was not vengeance-proof.
 They little thought that day of pain,
When launch'd, as on the lightning's flash,
They bade me to destruction dash,
 That one day I should come again,
With twice five thousand horse, to thank
 The Count for his uncourteous ride.
They play'd me then a bitter prank,
 When, with the wild horse for my guide,
They bound me to his foaming flank :
At length I play'd them one as frank
For time at last sets all things even—
 And if we do but watch the hour,
 There never yet was human power
Which could evade, if unforgiven,
The patient search and vigil long
Of him who treasures up a wrong.

XI.

"Away, away, my steed and I,
 Upon the pinions of the wind,
 All human dwellings left behind ;
We sped like meteors through the sky,
When with its crackling sound the night
Is chequer'd with the northern light :
Town—village—none were on our track,
 But a wild plain of far extent,
And bounded by a forest black ;
 And, save the scarce seen battlement
On distant heights of some strong hold,
Against the Tartars built of old,
No trace of man. The year before
A Turkish army had march'd o'er ;

And where the Spahi's hoof hath trod,
The verdure flies the bloody sod :
The sky was dull, and dim, and gray,
 And a low breeze crept moaning by—
 I could have answer'd with a sigh—
But fast we fled, away, away,
And I could neither sigh nor pray ;
And my cold sweat-drops fell like rain
Upon the courser's bristling mane ;
But, snorting still with rage and fear,
He flew upon his far career :
At times I almost thought, indeed,
He must have slacken'd in his speed ;
But no—my bound and slender frame
 Was nothing to his angry might,
And merely like a spur became :
Each motion which I made to free
My swoln limbs from their agony
 Increased his fury and affright :
I tried my voice,—'twas faint and low,
But yet he swerved as from a blow ;
And, starting to each accent, sprang
As from a sudden trumpet's clang :
Meantime my cords were wet with gore,
Which, oozing through my limbs, ran o'er ;
And in my tongue the thirst became
A something fierier far than flame.

XII.

"We near'd the wild wood—'twas so wide,
I saw no bounds on either side ;
'Twas studded with old sturdy trees,
That bent not to the roughest breeze
Which howls down from Siberia's waste,
And strips the forest in its haste,—
But these were few and far between,
Set thick with shrubs more young and
 green,
Luxuriant with their annual leaves,
Ere strown by those autumnal eves
That nip the forest's foliage dead,
Discolour'd with a lifeless red,
Which stands thereon like stiffen'd gore
Upon the slain when battle's o'er,
And some long winter's night hath shed
Its frost o'er every tombless head,
So cold and stark the raven's beak
May peck unpierced each frozen cheek :
'Twas a wild waste of underwood,
And here and there a chestnut stood,
The strong oak, and the hardy pine ;
 But far apart—and well it were,
Or else a different lot were mine—
 The boughs gave way, and did not tear
My limbs; and I found strength to bear
My wounds, already scarr'd with cold ;
My bonds forbade to loose my hold.
We rustled through the leaves like wind,
Left shrubs, and trees, and wolves behind ;

By night I heard them on the track,
Their troop came hard upon our back,
With their long gallop, which can tire
The hound's deep hate, and hunter's fire:
Where'er we flew they follow'd on,
Nor left us with the morning sun;
Behind I saw them, scarce a rood,
At day-break winding through the wood,
And through the night had heard their feet
Their stealing, rustling step repeat.
Oh! how I wish'd for spear or sword,
At least to die amidst the horde,
And perish—if it must be so—
At bay, destroying many a foe!
When first my courser's race begun,
I wish'd the goal already won;
But now I doubted strength and speed.
Vain doubt! his swift and savage breed
Had nerved him like the mountain-roe;
Nor faster falls the blinding snow
Which whelms the peasant near the door
Whose threshold he shall cross no more,
Bewilder'd with the dazzling blast,
Than through the forest-paths he pass'd—
Untired, untamed, and worse than wild;
All furious as a favour'd child
Balk'd of its wish; or fiercer still—
A woman piqued—who has her will.

XIII.

"The wood was past; 'twas more than
 noon,
But chill the air, although in June;
Or it might be my veins ran cold—
Prolong'd endurance tames the bold;
And I was then not what I seem,
But headlong as a wintry stream,
And wore my feelings out before
I well could count their causes o'er:
And what with fury, fear, and wrath,
The tortures which beset my path,
Cold, hunger, sorrow, shame, distress,
Thus bound in nature's nakedness;
Sprung from a race whose rising blood,
When stirr'd beyond its calmer mood,
And trodden hard upon, is like
The rattle-snake's, in act to strike,
What marvel if this worn-out trunk
Beneath its woes a moment sunk?
The earth gave way, the skies roll'd round,
I seem'd to sink upon the ground;
But err'd, for I was fastly bound.
My heart turn'd sick, my brain grew sore,
And throbb'd awhile, then beat no more:
The skies spun like a mighty wheel;
I saw the trees like drunkards reel,
And a slight flash sprang o'er my eyes,
Which saw no farther: he who dies
Can die no more than then I died.
O'ertortured by that ghastly ride,

I felt the blackness come and go,
 And strove to wake; but could not make
My senses climb up from below:
I felt as on a plank at sea,
When all the waves that dash o'er thee,
At the same time upheave and whelm,
And hurl thee towards a desert realm
My undulating life was as
The fancied lights that flitting pass
Our shut eyes in deep midnight, when
Fever begins upon the brain;
But soon it pass'd, with little pain,
 But a confusion worse than such:
I own that I should deem it much,
Dying, to feel the same again;
And yet I do suppose we must
Feel far more ere we turn to dust:
No matter; I have bared my brow
Full in Death's face—before—and now.

XIV.

"My thoughts came back; where was I? Cold,
 And numb, and giddy: pulse by pulse
Life reassumed its lingering hold,
And throb by throb,—till grown a pang
 Which for a moment would convulse,
My blood reflow'd, though thick and chill;
My ear with uncouth noises rang,
 My heart began once more to thrill;
My sight return'd, though dim; alas!
And thicken'd, as it were, with glass.
Methought the dash of waves was nigh;
There was a gleam too of the sky,
Studded with stars;—it is no dream;
The wild horse swims the wilder stream!
The bright broad river's gushing tide
Sweeps, winding onward, far and wide,
And we are half-way, struggling o'er
To yon unknown and silent shore.
The waters broke my hollow trance,
And with a temporary strength
 My stiffen'd limbs were rebaptized.
My courser's broad breast proudly braves,
And dashes off the ascending waves,
And onward we advance!
We reach the slippery shore at length,
 A haven I but little prized,
For all behind was dark and drear,
And all before was night and fear.
How many hours of night or day
In those suspended pangs I lay,
I could not tell; I scarcely knew
If this were human breath I drew.

XV.

"With glossy skin, and dripping mane,
 And reeling limbs, and reeking flank,
The wild steed's sinewy nerves still strain
 Up the repelling bank.
We gain the top: a boundless plain

Spreads through the shadow of the night;
 And onward, onward, onward, seems,
 Like precipices in our dreams,
To stretch beyond the sight;
And here and there a speck of white,
 Or scatter'd spot of dusky green,
In masses broke into the light,
 As rose the moon upon my right:
 But nought distinctly seen
In the dim waste would indicate
The omen of a cottage gate;
No twinkling taper from afar
Stood like a hospitable star;
Not even an ignis-fatuus rose
To make him merry with my woes:
 That very cheat had cheer'd me then!
Although detected, welcome still,
Reminding me, through every ill,
 Of the abodes of men.

XVI.

"Onward we went—but slack and slow;
 His savage force at length o'erspent,
The drooping courser, faint and low,
 All feebly foaming went.
A sickly infant had had power
To guide him forward in that hour:
 But useless all to me:
His new-born tameness nought avail'd—
My limbs were bound; my force had fail'd,
 Perchance, had they been free.
With feeble effort still I tried
To rend the bonds so starkly tied,
 But still it was in vain;
My limbs were only wrung the more,
And soon the idle strife gave o'er,
 Which but prolong'd their pain:
The dizzy race seem'd almost done,
Although no goal was nearly won:
 Some streaks announced the coming sun—
 How slow, alas! he came!
Methought that mist of dawning gray
Would never dapple into day;
How heavily it roll'd away—
 Before the eastern flame
Rose crimson, and deposed the stars,
And call'd the radiance from their cars,
And fill'd the earth, from his deep throne,
With lonely lustre, all his own.

XVII.

"Up rose the sun; the mists were curl'd
Back from the solitary world
Which lay around, behind, before.
What booted it to traverse o'er
Plain, forest, river? Man nor brute,
Nor dint of hoof, nor print of foot,
Lay in the wild luxuriant soil;
No sign of travel, none of toil;
The very air was mute;

And not an insect's shrill small horn,
Nor matin bird's new voice was borne
From herb nor thicket. Many a werst,
Panting as if his heart would burst,
The weary brute still stagger'd on;
And still we were—or seem'd—alone.
At length, while reeling on our way,
Methought I heard a courser neigh,
From out yon tuft of blackening firs.
Is it the wind those branches stirs?
No, no! from out the forest prance
 A trampling troop; I see them come!
In one vast squadron they advance!
I strove to cry—my lips were dumb.
The steeds rush on in plunging pride;
But where are they the reins to guide?
A thousand horse, and none to ride!
With flowing tail, and flying mane,
Wide nostrils never stretch'd by pain,
Mouths bloodless to the bit or rein,
And feet that iron never shod,
And flanks unscarr'd by spur or rod,
A thousand horse, the wild, the free,
Like waves that follow o'er the sea,
 Came thickly thundering on,
As if our faint approach to meet;
The sight re-nerved my courser's feet,
A moment staggering, feebly fleet,
A moment, with a faint low neigh,
 He answer'd, and then fell;
With gasps and glazing eyes he lay,
 And reeking limbs immoveable,
 His first and last career is done!
On came the troop—they saw him stoop,
 They saw me strangely bound along
 His back with many a bloody thong:
They stop, they start, they snuff the
 air,
Gallop a moment here and there,
Approach, retire, wheel round and round,
Then plunging back with sudden bound,
Headed by one black mighty steed,
Who seem'd the patriarch of his breed,
 Without a single speck or hair
Of white upon his shaggy hide;
They snort, they foam, neigh, swerve aside,
And backward to the forest fly,
By instinct, from a human eye.
 They left me there to my despair,
Link'd to the dead and stiffening wretch,
Whose lifeless limbs beneath me stretch,
Relieved from that unwonted weight,
From whence I could not extricate
Nor him nor me—and there we lay,
 The dying on the dead!
I little deem'd another day
 Would see my houseless, helpless head.

"And there from morn to twilight bound,
I felt the heavy hours toil round,

With just enough of life to see
My last of suns go down on me,
In hopeless certainty of mind,
That makes us feel at length resign'd
To that which our foreboding years
Present the worst and last of fears:
Inevitable—even a boon,
Nor more unkind for coming soon,
Yet shunn'd and dreaded with such care,
As if it only were a snare
 That prudence might escape:
At times both wish'd for and implored,
At times sought with self-pointed sword,
Yet still a dark and hideous close
To even intolerable woes,
 And welcome in no shape.
And, strange to say, the sons of pleasure,
They who have revell'd beyond measure
In beauty, wassail, wine, and treasure,
Die calm, or calmer, oft than he
Whose heritage was misery:
For he who hath in turn run through
All that was beautiful and new,
 Hath nought to hope, and nought to leave;
And, save the future, (which is view'd
Not quite as men are base or good,
But as their nerves may be endued,)
 With nought perhaps to grieve:
The wretch still hopes his woes must end,
And Death, whom he should deem his friend,
Appears, to his distemper'd eyes,
Arrived to rob him of his prize,
The tree of his new Paradise.
To-morrow would have given him all,
Repaid his pangs, repair'd his fall;
To-morrow would have been the first
Of days no more deplored or curst,
But bright, and long, and beckoning years,
Seen dazzling through the mist of tears,
Guerdon of many a painful hour;
To-morrow would have given him power
To rule, to shine, to smite, to save—
And must it dawn upon his grave?

XVIII.

"The sun was sinking—still I lay
 Chain'd to the chill and stiffening steed;
I thought to mingle there our clay,
 And my dim eyes of death had need;
 No hope arose of being freed:
I cast my last looks up the sky,
 And there between me and the sun
I saw the expecting raven fly,
Who scarce would wait till both should die,
 Ere his repast begun;
He flew, and perch'd, then flew once more,
And each time nearer than before;
I saw his wing through twilight flit,
And once so near me he alit

I could have smote, but lack'd the
 strength;
But the slight motion of my hand,
And feeble scratching of the sand,
The exerted throat's faint struggling noise,
Which scarcely could be called a voice,
 Together scared him off at length.
I know no more—my latest dream
 Is something of a lovely star
 Which fix'd my dull eyes from afar,
And went and came with wandering beam,
And of the cold, dull, swimming, dense
Sensation of recurring sense,
And then subsiding back to death,
And then again a little breath,
A little thrill, a short suspense,
An icy sickness curdling o'er
My heart, and sparks that cross'd my
 brain—
A gasp, a throb, a start of pain,
A sigh, and nothing more.

XIX.

"I woke—where was I?—Do I see
A human face look down on me?
And doth a roof above me close?
Do these limbs on a couch repose?
Is this a chamber where I lie?
And is it mortal yon bright eye,
That watches me with gentle glance?
 I closed my own again once more,
As doubtful that my former trance
 Could not as yet be o'er.
A slender girl, long-hair'd, and tall,
Sate watching by the cottage wall;
The sparkle of her eye I caught,
Even with my first return of thought;
For ever and anon she threw
 A prying, pitying glance on me
With her black eyes so wild and free:
I gazed, and gazed, until I knew
 No vision it could be,—
But that I lived, and was released
From adding to the vulture's feast:
And when the Cossack maid beheld
My heavy eyes at length unseal'd,
She smiled—and I essay'd to speak,
 But fail'd—and she approach'd, and made
With lip and finger signs that said,
I must not strive as yet to break
The silence, till my strength should be
Enough to leave my accents free;
And then her hand on mine she laid,
And smooth'd the pillow for my head,
And stole along on tiptoe tread,
 And gently oped the door, and spake
In whispers—ne'er was voice so sweet!
Even music follow'd her light feet:
 But those she call'd were not awake,

And she went forth; but, ere she pass'd,
Another look on me she cast,
 Another sign she made, to say,
That I had nought to fear, that all
Were near, at my command or call,
 And she would not delay
Her due return:—while she was gone,
Methought I felt too much alone.

XX.

"She came with mother and with sire—
What need of more?—I will not tire
With long recital of the rest,
Since I became the Cossack's guest.
They found me senseless on the plain,
 They bore me to the nearest hut,
They brought me into life again—
Me—one day o'er their realm to reign!
 Thus the vain fool who strove to glut
His rage, refining on my pain,

Sent me forth to the wilderness,
Bound, naked, bleeding, and alone,
To pass the desert to a throne,—
 What mortal his own doom may guess?
Let none despond, let none despair!
To-morrow the Borysthenes
May see our coursers graze at ease
Upon his Turkish bank, and never
Had I such welcome for a river
 As I shall yield when safely there.
Comrades, good night!"—The Hetman threw
 His length beneath the oak-tree shade,
 With leafy couch already made,
A bed nor comfortless nor new
To him, who took his rest whene'er
The hour arrived, no matter where:
 His eyes the hastening slumbers steep,
And if ye marvel Charles forgot
To thank his tale, *he* wonder'd not,—
 The king had been an hour asleep.

𝕿𝖍𝖊 𝕴𝖘𝖑𝖆𝖓𝖉;

OR,

CHRISTIAN AND HIS COMRADES.

ADVERTISEMENT.

THE foundation of the following story will be found partly in Lieutenant Bligh's "Narrative of the Mutiny and Seizure of the Bounty, in the South Seas, in 1789;" and partly in "Mariner's Account of the Tonga Islands."

Genoa, 1823.

Canto the First.

I.

THE morning watch was come; the vessel lay
Her course, and gently made her liquid way;
The cloven billow flash'd from off her prow
In furrows form'd by that majestic plough;
The waters with their world were all before;
Behind, the South Sea's many an islet shore.
The quiet night, now dappling, 'gan to wane,
Dividing darkness from the dawning main;
The dolphins, not unconscious of the day,
Swam high, as eager of the coming ray;
The stars from broader beams began to creep,
And lift their shining eyelids from the deep;
The sail resumed its lately shadow'd white,
And the wind flutter'd with a freshening flight:

The purpling ocean owns the coming sun,
But ere he break—a deed is to be done.

II.

The gallant chief within his cabin slept,
Secure in those by whom the watch was kept:
His dreams were of Old England's welcome shore,
Of toils rewarded, and of dangers o'er;
His name was added to the glorious roll
Of those who search the storm-surrounded Pole.
The worst was over, and the rest seem'd sure,
And why should not his slumber be secure?
Alas! his deck was trod by unwilling feet,
And wilder hands would hold the vessel's sheet;

Young hearts, which languish'd for some
 sunny isle,
Where summer years and summer women
 smile;
Men without country, who, too long estranged,
Had found no native home, or found it
 changed,
And, half uncivilised, preferr'd the cave
Of some soft savage to the uncertain wave—
The gushing fruits that nature gave untill'd;
The wood without a path but where they
 will'd;
The field o'er which promiscuous Plenty
 pour'd
Her horn; the equal land without a lord;
The wish—which ages have not yet sub-
 dued
In man—to have no master save his mood;
The earth, whose mine was on its face, un-
 sold,
The glowing sun and produce all its gold;
The freedom which can call each grot a
 home;
The general garden, where all steps may
 roam,
Where Nature owns a nation as her child,
Exulting in the enjoyment of the wild;
Their shells, their fruits, the only wealth
 they know,
Their unexploring navy, the canoe;
Their sport, the dashing breakers and the
 chase;
Their strangest sight, an European face:—
Such was the country which these strangers
 yearn'd
To see again; a sight they dearly earn'd.

III.

Awake, bold Bligh! the foe is at the gate!
Awake! awake!——Alas! it is too late!
Fiercely beside thy cot the mutineer
Stands, and proclaims the reign of rage and
 fear.
Thy limbs are bound, the bayonet at thy
 breast;
The hands, which trembled at thy voice,
 arrest;
Dragg'd o'er the deck, no more at thy com-
 mand
The obedient helm shall veer, the sail ex-
 pand;
That savage spirit, which would lull by
 wrath
Its desperate escape from duty's path,
Glares round thee, in the scarce believing
 eyes
Of those who fear the chief they sacrifice:
For ne'er can man his conscience all assuage,
Unless he drain the wine of passion—rage.

IV.

In vain, not silenced by the eye of death,
Thou call'st the loyal with thy menaced
 breath:—
They come not; they are few, and, overawed,
Must acquiesce, while sterner hearts applaud.
In vain thou dost demand the cause: a curse
Is all the answer, with the threat of worse.
Full in thine eyes is waved the glittering
 blade,
Close to thy throat the pointed bayonet laid.
The levell'd muskets circle round thy breast
In hands as steel'd to do the deadly rest.
Thou dar'st them to their worst, exclaiming—
 "Fire!"
But they who pitied not could yet admire;
Some lurking remnant of their former awe
Restrain'd them longer than their broken law;
They would not dip their souls at once in
 blood,
But left thee to the mercies of the flood.

V.

"Hoist out the boat!" was now the leader's
 cry;
And who dare answer "No!" to Mutiny,
In the first dawning of the drunken hour,
The Saturnalia of unhoped-for power?
The boat is lower'd with all the haste of hate,
With its slight plank between thee and thy
 fate;
Her only cargo such a scant supply
As promises the death their hands deny;
And just enough of water and of bread
To keep, some days, the dying from the dead:
Some cordage, canvas, sails, and lines, and
 twine,
But treasures all to hermits of the brine,
Were added after, to the earnest prayer
Of those who saw no hope, save sea and air;
And last, that trembling vassal of the Pole—
The feeling compass—Navigation's soul.

VI.

And now the self-elected chief finds time
To stun the first sensation of his crime,
And raise it in his followers—"Ho! the
 bowl!"
Lest passion should return to reason's shoal.
"Brandy for heroes!" Burke could once ex-
 claim—
No doubt a liquid path to epic fame;
And such the new-born heroes found it here,
And drain'd the draught with an applauding
 cheer.
"Huzza! for Otaheite!" was the cry.
How strange such shouts from sons of
 Mutiny!

The gentle island, and the genial soil,
The friendly hearts, the feasts without a toil,
The courteous manners but from nature caught,
The wealth unhoarded, and the love unbought;
Could these have charms for rudest sea-boys, driven
Before the mast by every wind of heaven?
And now, even now prepared with others' woes
To earn mild Virtue's vain desire, repose?
Alas! such is our nature! all but aim
At the same end by pathways not the same;
Our means, our birth, our nation, and our name,
Our fortune, temper, even our outward frame,
Are far more potent o'er our yielding clay
Than aught we know beyond our little day.
Yet still there whispers the small voice within,
Heard through Gain's silence, and o'er Glory's din:
Whatever creed be taught, or land be trod,
Man's conscience is the oracle of God.

VII.

The launch is crowded with the faithful few
Who wait their chief, a melancholy crew:
But some remain'd reluctant on the deck
Of that proud vessel—now a moral wreck—
And view'd their captain's fate with piteous eyes:
While others scoff'd his augur'd miseries,
Sneer'd at the prospect of his pigmy sail,
And the slight bark so laden and so frail.
The tender nautilus, who steers his prow,
The sea-born sailor of his shell canoe,
The ocean Mab, the fairy of the sea,
Seems far less fragile, and, alas! more free.
He, when the lightning-wing'd tornados sweep
The surge, is safe—his port is in the deep—
And triumphs o'er the armadas of mankind,
Which shake the world, yet crumble in the wind.

VIII.

When all was now prepared, the vessel clear
Which hail'd her master in the mutineer,
A seaman, less obdurate than his mates,
Show'd the vain pity which but irritates;
Watch'd his late chieftain with exploring eye,
And told, in signs, repentant sympathy;
Held the moist shaddock to his parched mouth,
Which felt exhaustion's deep and bitter drouth.
But soon observed, this guardian was withdrawn,
Nor further mercy clouds rebellion's dawn.

Then forward stepp'd the bold and froward boy
His chief had cherish'd only to destroy,
And, pointing to the helpless prow beneath,
Exclaim'd, "Depart at once! delay is death!"
Yet then, even then, his feelings ceased not all:
In that last moment could a word recall
Remorse for the black deed as yet half done,
And what he hid from many show'd to one:
When Bligh in stern reproach demanded where
Was now his grateful sense of former care?
Where all his hopes to see his name aspire,
And blazon Britain's thousand glories higher?
His feverish lips thus broke their gloomy spell,
"'Tis that! 'tis that! I am in hell! in hell!"
No more he said: but urging to the bark
His chief, commits him to his fragile ark;
These the sole accents from his tongue that fell,
But volumes lurk'd below his fierce farewell.

IX.

The arctic sun rose broad above the wave;
The breeze now sank, now whisper'd from his cave;
As on the Æolian harp, his fitful wings
Now swell'd, now flutter'd o'er his ocean strings.
With slow, despairing oar, the abandon'd skiff
Ploughs its drear progress to the scarce seen cliff,
Which lifts its peak a cloud above the main:
That boat and ship shall never meet again!

But 'tis not mine to tell their tale of grief,
Their constant peril, and their scant relief;
Their days of danger, and their nights of pain;
Their manly courage even when deem'd in vain;
The sapping famine, rendering scarce a son
Known to his mother in the skeleton;
The ills that lessen'd still their little store,
And starved even Hunger till he wrung no more;
The varying frowns and favours of the deep,
That now almost ingulfs, then leaves to creep
With crazy oar and shatter'd strength along
The tide that yields reluctant to the strong;
The incessant fever of that arid thirst
Which welcomes, as a well, the clouds that burst
Above their naked bones, and feels delight
In the cold drenching of the stormy night,

And from the outspread canvas gladly wrings
A drop to moisten life's all-gasping springs;
The savage foe escaped, to seek again
More hospitable shelter from the main;
The ghastly spectres which were doom'd at
last
To tell as true a tale of dangers past,
As ever the dark annals of the deep
Disclosed for man to dread or woman weep.

X.

We leave them to their fate, but not un-
known
Nor unredress'd. Revenge may have her
own:
Roused discipline aloud proclaims their
cause,
And injured navies urge their broken laws.
Pursue we on his track the mutineer,
Whom distant vengeance had not taught to
fear.
Wide o'er the wave—away! away! away!
Once more his eyes shall hail the welcome
bay;
Once more the happy shores without a law
Receive the outlaws whom they lately saw;
Nature, and Nature's goddess—woman—
woos
To lands where, save their conscience, none
accuse;
Where all partake the earth without dispute,
And bread itself is gather'd as a fruit;
Where none contest the fields, the woods,
the streams:—
The goldless age, where gold disturbs no
dreams,
Inhabits or inhabited the shore,
Till Europe taught them better than before:
Bestow'd her customs, and amended theirs,
But left her vices also to their heirs,
Away with this! behold them as they were,
Do good with Nature, or with Nature err,
"Huzza! for Otaheite!" was the cry,
As stately swept the gallant vessel by.
The breeze springs up; the lately flapping
sail
Extends its arch before the growing gale;
In swifter ripples stream aside the seas,
Which her bold bow flings off with dashing
ease.
Thus Argo plough'd the Euxine's virgin
foam,
But those she wafted still look'd back to
home:
These spurn their country with their rebel
bark,
And fly her as the raven fled the ark;
And yet they seek to nestle with the dove,
And tame their fiery spirits down to love.

Canto the Second.

I.

How pleasant were the songs of Toobonai,
When summer's sun went down the coral
bay!
Come, let us to the islet's softest shade,
And hear the warbling birds! the damsel
said:
The wood-dove from the forest-depth shall
coo,
Like voices of the gods from Bolotoo,
We'll cull the flowers that grow above the
dead,
For these most bloom where rests the war-
rior's head;
And we will sit in twilight's face, and see
The sweet moon glancing through the tooa
tree,
The lofty accents of whose sighing bough
Shall sadly please us as we lean below;
Or climb the steep, and view the surf in vain
Wrestle with rocky giants o'er the main,
Which spurn in columns back the baffled
spray.
How beautiful are these! how happy they,
Who, from the toil and tumult of their lives,
Steal to look down where nought but ocean
strives!
Even he too loves at times the blue lagoon,
And smooths his ruffled mane beneath the
moon.

II.

Yes—from the sepulchre we'll gather flowers,
Then feast like spirits in their promised
bowers,
Then plunge and revel in the rolling surf,
Then lay our limbs along the tender turf,
And, wet and shining from the sportive toil,
Anoint our bodies with the fragrant oil,
And plait our garlands gather'd from the
grave,
And wear the wreaths that sprung from out
the brave.
But lo! night comes, the Mooa woos us back,
The sound of mats are heard along our
track;
Anon the torchlight dance shall fling its
sheen
In flashing mazes o'er the Marly's green;
And we too will be there; we too recall
The memory bright with many a festival,
Ere Fiji blew the shell of war, when foes
For the first time were wafted in canoes.
Alas! for them the flower of mankind bleeds;
Alas! for them our fields are rank with
weeds:
Forgotten is the rapture, or unknown,
Of wandering with the moon and love alone.

But be it so:—*they* taught us how to wield
The club, and rain our arrows o'er the field:
Now let them reap the harvest of their art!
But feast to-night! to-morrow we depart.
Strike up the dance! the cava bowl fill high!
Drain every drop!—to-morrow we may die.
In summer garments be our limbs array'd;
Around our waists the tappa's white display'd;
Thick wreaths shall form our coronal, like
 spring's,
And round our necks shall glance the hooni
 strings;
So shall their brighter hues contrast the glow
Of the dusk bosoms that beat high below.

III.

But now the dance is o'er—yet stay awhile;
Ah, pause! nor yet put out the social smile.
To-morrow for the Mooa we depart,
But not to-night—to-night is for the heart.
Again bestow the wreaths we gently woo,
Ye young enchantresses of gay Licoo!
How lovely are your forms! how every sense
Bows to your beauties, soften'd, but intense,
Like to the flowers on Mataloco's steep,
Which fling their fragrance far athwart the
 deep!—
We too will see Licoo; but—oh! my heart!—
What do I say?—to-morrow we depart!

IV.

Thus rose a song—the harmony of times
Before the winds blew Europe o'er these
 climes.
True, they had vices—such are Nature's
 growth—
But only the barbarian's—we have both;
The sordor of civilisation, mix'd
With all the savage which man's fall hath
 fix'd.
Who hath not seen Dissimulation's reign,
The prayers of Abel link'd to deeds of Cain?
Who such would see may from his lattice view
The Old World more degraded than the
 New,—
Now *new* no more, save where Columbia
 rears
Twin giants, born by Freedom to her sphéres,
Where Chimborazo, over air, earth, wave,
Glares with his Titan eye, and sees no slave.

V.

Such was this ditty of Tradition's days,
Which to the dead a lingering fame conveys
In song, where fame as yet hath left no sign
Beyond the sound whose charm is half
 divine;
Which leaves no record to the sceptic eye,
But yields young history all to harmony;

A boy Achilles, with the centaur's lyre
In hand, to teach him to surpass his sire.
For one long-cherish'd ballad's simple stave,
Rung from the rock, or mingled with the
 wave,
Or from the bubbling streamlet's grassy side,
Or gathering mountain echoes as they glide,
Hath greater power o'er each true heart
 and ear,
Than all the columns Conquest's minions
 rear;
Invites, when hieroglyphics are a theme
For sages' labours, or the student's dream;
Attracts, when History's volumes are a toil,—
The first, the freshest bud of Feeling's soil.
Such was this rude rhyme—rhyme is of the
 rude—
But such inspired the Norseman's solitude,
Who came and conquer'd; such, wherever
 rise
Lands which no foe destroy or civilise,
Exist: and what can our accomplish'd art
Of verse do more than reach the awaken'd
 heart?

VI.

And sweetly now those untaught melodies
Broke the luxurious silence of the skies,
The sweet siesta of a summer day,
The tropic afternoon of Toobonai,
When every flower was bloom, and air was
 balm,
And the first breath began to stir the palm,
The first yet voiceless wind to urge the wave
All gently to refresh the thirsty cave,
Where sat the songstress with the stranger
 boy,
Who taught her passion's desolating joy,
Too powerful over every heart, but most
O'er those who know not how it may be lost;
O'er those who, burning in the new-born fire,
Like martyrs revel in their funeral pyre,
With such devotion to their ecstasy,
That life knows no such rapture as to die:
And die they do; for earthly life has nought
Match'd with that burst of nature, even in
 thought;
And all our dreams of better life above
But close in one eternal gush of love.

VII.

There sat the gentle savage of the wild,
In growth a woman, though in years a child,
As childhood dates within our colder clime,
Where nought is ripen'd rapidly save crime;
The infant of an infant world, as pure
From nature—lovely, warm, and premature;
Dusky like night, but night with all her
 stars,
Or cavern sparkling with its native spars;

With eyes that were a language and a spell,
A form like Aphrodite's in her shell,
With all her loves around her on the deep,
Voluptuous as the first approach of sleep;
Yet full of life—for through her tropic cheek
The blush would make its way, and all but
speak:
The sun-born blood suffused her neck, and
threw
O'er her clear nut-brown skin a lucid hue,
Like coral reddening through the darken'd
wave,
Which draws the diver to the crimson cave.
Such was this daughter of the southern seas,
Herself a billow in her energies,
To bear the bark of others' happiness,
Nor feel a sorrow till their joy grew less:
Her wild and warm yet faithful bosom knew
No joy like what it gave; her hopes ne'er drew
Aught from experience, that chill touchstone,
whose
Sad proof reduces all things from their hues:
She fear'd no ill, because she knew it not,
Or what she knew was soon—too soon—
forgot:
Her smiles and tears had pass'd, as light
winds pass
O'er lakes to ruffle, not destroy, their glass,
Whose depths unsearch'd, and fountains
from the hill,
Restore their surface, in itself so still,
Until the earthquake tear the naiad's cave,
Root up the spring, and trample on the
wave,
And crush the living waters to a mass,
The amphibious desert of the dank morass!
And must their fate be hers? The eternal
change
But grasps humanity with quicker range;
And they who fall but fall as worlds will fall,
To rise, if just, a spirit o'er them all.

VIII.

And who is he? the blue-eyed northern child
Of isles more known to man, but scarce less
wild;
The fair-hair'd offspring of the Hebrides,
Where roars the Pentland with its whirling
seas;
Rock'd in his cradle by the roaring wind,
The tempest-born in body and in mind,
His young eyes opening on the ocean-foam,
Had from that moment deem'd the deep his
home,
The giant comrade of his pensive moods,
The sharer of his craggy solitudes,
The only Mentor of his youth, where'er
His bark was borne; the sport of wave and
air;

A careless thing, who placed his choice in
chance,
Nursed by the legends of his land's romance;
Eager to hope, but not less firm to bear,
Acquainted with all feelings save despair.
Placed in the Arab's clime, he would have
been
As bold a rover as the sands have seen,
And braved their thirst with as enduring lip
As Ishmael, wafted on his desert-ship;
Fix'd upon Chili's shore, a proud cacique;
On Hellas' mountains, a rebellious Greek;
Born in a tent, perhaps a Tamerlane;
Bred to a throne, perhaps unfit to reign.
For the same soul that rends its path to
sway,
If rear'd to such, can find no further prey
Beyond itself, and must retrace its way,
Plunging for pleasure into pain: the same
Spirit which made a Nero, Rome's worst
shame,
A humbler state and discipline of heart,
Had form'd his glorious namesake's counter-
part;
But grant his vices, grant them all his own,
How small their theatre without a throne!

IX.

Thou smilest:—these comparisons seem high
To those who scan all things with dazzled
eye;
Link'd with the unknown name of one whose
doom
Has nought to do with glory or with Rome,
With Chili, Hellas, or with Araby;
Thou smilest?—Smile; 'tis better thus than
sigh;
Yet such he might have been; he was a man,
A soaring spirit, ever in the van,
A patriot hero or despotic chief,
To form a nation's glory or its grief,
Born under auspices which make us more
Or less than we delight to ponder o'er.
But these are visions; say, what was he
here?
A blooming boy, a truant mutineer.
The fair-hair'd Torquil, free as ocean's spray,
The husband of the bride of Toobonai.

X.

By Neuha's side he sate, and watch'd the
waters,—
Neuha, the sun-flower of the island daughters,
Highborn, (a birth at which the herald smiles,
Without a scutcheon for these secret isles,)
Of a long race, the valiant and the free,
The naked knights of savage chivalry,
Whose grassy cairns ascend along the shore;
And thine—I've seen—Achilles! do no more.

She, when the thunder-bearing strangers came,
In vast canoes, begirt with bolts of flame,
Topp'd with tall trees, which, loftier than the palm,
Seem'd rooted in the deep amidst its calm:
But when the winds awaken'd, shot forth wings
Broad as the cloud along the horizon flings,
And sway'd the waves like cities of the sea,
Making the very billows look less free;—
She, with her paddling oar and dancing prow,
Shot through the surf, like reindeer through the snow,
Swift-gliding o'er the breaker's whitening edge,
Light as a nereid in her ocean sledge,
And gazed and wonder'd at the giant hulk,
Which heaved from wave to wave its trampling bulk,
The anchor dropp'd; it lay along the deep,
Like a huge lion in the sun asleep,
While round it swarm'd the proas' flitting chain,
Like summer bees that hum around his mane.

XI.

The white man landed! need the rest be told?
The New World stretch'd its dusk hand to the Old;
Each was to each a marvel, and the tie
Of wonder warm'd to better sympathy.
Kind was the welcome of the sun-born sires,
And kinder still their daughters' gentler fires.
Their union grew: the children of the storm
Found beauty link'd with many a dusky form;
While these in turn admired the paler glow,
Which seem'd so white in climes that knew no snow.
The chase, the race, the liberty to roam,
The soil where every cottage show'd a home;
The sea-spread net, the lightly launch'd canoe,
Which stemm'd the studded archipelago,
O'er whose blue bosom rose the starry isles;
The healthy slumber, earn'd by sportive toils;
The palm, the loftiest dryad of the woods,
Within whose bosom infant Bacchus broods,
While eagles scarce build higher than the crest
Which shadows o'er the vineyard in her breast;
The cava feast, the yam, the cocoa's root,
Which bears at once the cup, and milk, and fruit;
The bread-tree, which, without the plough-share, yields
The unreap'd harvest of unfurrow'd fields,

And bakes its unadulterated loaves
Without a furnace in unpurchased groves,
And flings off famine from its fertile breast,
A priceless market for the gathering guest;—
These, with the luxuries of seas and woods,
The airy joys of social solitudes,
Tamed each rude wanderer to the sympathies
Of those who were more happy, if less wise,
Did more than Europe's discipline had done,
And civilised Civilisation's son!

XII.

Of these, and there was many a willing pair,
Neuha and Torquil were not the least fair:
Both children of the isles, though distant far;
Both born beneath a sea-presiding star;
Both nourish'd amidst nature's native scenes,
Loved to the last, whatever intervenes
Between us and our childhood's sympathy,
Which still reverts to what first caught the eye.
He who first met the Highlands' swelling blue
Will love each peak that shows a kindred hue,
Hail in each crag a friend's familiar face,
And clasp the mountain in his mind's embrace.
Long have I roamed through lands which are not mine,
Adored the Alp, and loved the Apennine,
Revered Parnassus, and beheld the steep
Jove's Ida and Olympus crown the deep:
But 't was not all long ages' lore, nor all
Their nature held me in their thrilling thrall;
The infant rapture still survived the boy,
And Loch-na-gar with Ida look'd o'er Troy,
Mix'd Celtic memories with the Phrygian mount,
And Highland linns with Castalie's clear fount.
Forgive me, Homer's universal shade!
Forgive me, Phœbus! that my fancy stray'd;
The north and nature taught me to adore
Your scenes sublime, from those beloved before.

XIII.

The love which maketh all things fond and fair,
The youth which makes one rainbow of the air,
The dangers past, that make even man enjoy
The pause in which he ceases to destroy,
The mutual beauty, which the sternest feel
Strike to their hearts like lightning to the steel,
United the half savage and the whole,
The maid and boy in one absorbing soul.
No more the thundering memory of the fight
Wrapp'd his wean'd bosom in its dark delight:

No more the irksome restlessness of rest
Disturb'd him like the eagle in her nest,
Whose whetted beak and far-pervading eye
Darts for a victim over all the sky:
His heart was tamed to that voluptuous state,
At once Elysian and effeminate,
Which leaves no laurels o'er the hero's urn;—
These wither when for aught save blood they
 burn;
Yet when their ashes in their nook are laid,
Doth not the myrtle leave as sweet a shade?
Had Cæsar known but Cleopatra's kiss,
Rome had been free, the world had not been
 his.
And what have Cæsar's deeds and Cæsar's
 fame
Done for the earth? We feel them in our
 shame:
The gory sanction of his glory stains
The rust which tyrants cherish on our chains.
Though Glory, Nature, Reason, Freedom, bid
Roused millions do what single Brutus did—
Sweep these mere mock-birds of the despot's
 song
From the tall bough where they have perch'd
 so long,—
Still are we hawk'd at by such mousing owls,
And take for falcons those ignoble fowls,
When but a word of freedom would dispel
These bugbears, as their terrors show too
 well.

XIV.

Rapt in the fond forgetfulness of life,
Neuha, the South Sea girl, was all a wife,
With no distracting world to call her off
From love; with no society to scoff
At the new transient flame; no babbling
 crowd
Of coxcombry in admiration loud,
Or with adulterous whisper to alloy
Her duty, and her glory, and her joy:
With faith and feelings naked as her form,
She stood as stands a rainbow in a storm,
Changing its hues with bright variety,
But still expanding lovelier o'er the sky,
Howe'er its arch may swell, its colours move,
The cloud-compelling harbinger of love.

XV.

Here, in this grotto of the wave-worn shore,
They pass'd the tropic's red meridian o'er;
Nor long the hours—they never paused o'er
 time,
Unbroken by the clock's funereal chime,
Which deals the daily pittance of our span,
And points and mocks with iron laugh at man.
What deem'd they of the future or the past?
The present, like a tyrant, held them fast:

Their hour-glass was the sea-sand, and the
 tide,
Like her smooth billow, saw their moments
 glide;
Their clock the sun, in his unbounded tow'r;
They reckon'd not, whose day was but an
 hour;
The nightingale, their only vesper-bell,
Sung sweetly to the rose the day's farewell;
The broad sun set, but not with lingering
 sweep,
As in the north he mellows o'er the deep;
But fiery, full, and fierce, as if he left
The world for ever, earth of light bereft,
Plunged with red forehead down along the
 wave,
As dives a hero headlong to his grave.
Then rose they, looking first along the skies,
And then for light into each other's eyes,
Wondering that summer show'd so brief a
 sun,
And asking if indeed the day were done.

XVI.

And let not this seem strange: the devotee
Lives not in earth, but in his ecstasy;
Around him days and worlds are heedless
 driven,
His soul is gone before his dust to heaven.
Is love less potent? No—his path is trod,
Alike uplifted gloriously to God;
Or link'd to all we know of heaven below,
The other better self, whose joy or woe
Is more than ours; the all-absorbing flame
Which, kindled by another, grows the same,
Wrapt in one blaze; the pure, yet funeral pile,
Where gentle hearts, like Bramins, sit and
 smile.
How often we forget all time, when lone,
Admiring Nature's universal throne,
Her woods, her wilds, her waters, the in-
 tense
Reply of *hers* to our intelligence!
Live not the stars and mountains? Are the
 waves
Without a spirit? Are the dropping caves
Without a feeling in their silent tears?
No, no;—they woo and clasp us to their
 spheres,
Dissolve this clog and clod of clay before
Its hour, and merge our soul in the great
 shore.
Strip off this fond and false identity!—
Who thinks of self when gazing on the sky?
And who, though gazing lower, ever thought,
In the young moments ere the heart is
 taught
Time's lesson, of man's baseness or his own?
All nature is his realm, and love his throne.

XVII.

Neuha arose, and Torquil: twilight's hour
Came sad and softly to their rocky bower,
Which, kindling by degrees its dewy spars,
Echoed their dim light to the mustering
 stars.
Slowly the pair, partaking nature's calm,
Sought out their cottage, built beneath the
 palm;
Now smiling and now silent, as the scene;
Lovely as Love—the spirit!—when serene.
The Ocean scarce spoke louder with his
 swell,
Than breathes his mimic murmurer in the
 shell,
As, far divided from his parent deep,
The sea-born infant cries, and will not sleep,
Raising his little plaint in vain, to rave
For the broad bosom of his nursing wave:
The woods droop'd darkly, as inclined to rest,
The tropic bird wheel'd rockward to his nest,
And the blue sky spread round them like a
 lake
Of peace, where Piety her thirst might slake.

XVIII.

But through the palm and plantain, hark, a
 voice!
Not such as would have been a lover's
 choice,
In such an hour, to break the air so still;
No dying night-breeze, harping o'er the hill,
Striking the strings of nature, rock and tree,
Those best and earliest lyres of harmony,
With Echo for their chorus; nor the alarm
Of the loud war-whoop to dispel the charm;
Nor the soliloquy of the hermit owl,
Exhaling all his solitary soul,
The dim though large-eyed winged anchorite,
Who peals his dreary pæan o'er the night;
But a loud, long, and naval whistle, shrill
As ever started through a sea-bird's bill;
And then a pause, and then a hoarse,
 "Hillo!
Torquil, my boy! what cheer? Ho! brother,
 ho!"
"Who hails?" cried Torquil, following with
 his eye
The sound. "Here's one," was all the brief
 reply.

XIX.

But here the herald of the self-same mouth
Came breathing o'er the aromatic south,
Not like a "bed of violets" on the gale,
But such as wafts its cloud o'er grog or ale,
Borne from a short frail pipe, which yet had
 blown
Its gentle odours over either zone,
And, puff'd where'er winds rise or waters roll,
Had wafted smoke from Portsmouth to the
 Pole,
Opposed its vapour as the lightning flash'd,
And reek'd, 'midst mountain-billows, un-
 abash'd,
To Æolus a constant sacrifice,
Through every change of all the varying
 skies.
And what was he who bore it?—I may err,
But deem him sailor or philosopher.
Sublime tobacco! which from east to west
Cheers the tar's labour or the Turkman's
 rest;
Which on the Moslem's ottoman divides
His hours, and rivals opium and his brides;
Magnificent in Stamboul, but less grand,
Though not less loved, in Wapping or the
 Strand;
Divine in hookas, glorious in a pipe,
When tipp'd with amber, mellow, rich, and
 ripe;
Like other charmers, wooing the caress,
More dazzlingly when daring in full dress;
Yet thy true lovers more admire by far
Thy naked beauties—Give me a cigar!

XX.

Through the approaching darkness of the
 wood
A human figure broke the solitude,
Fantastically, it may be, array'd,
A seaman in a savage masquerade;
Such as appears to rise out from the deep
When o'er the line the merry vessels sweep,
And the rough saturnalia of the tar
Flock o'er the deck, in Neptune's borrow'd
 car;
And, pleased, the god of ocean sees his name
Revive once more, though but in mimic
 game
Of his true sons, who riot in the breeze
Undreamt of in his native Cyclades.
Still the old god delights, from out the main,
To snatch some glimpses of his ancient reign.
Our sailor's jacket, though in ragged trim,
His constant pipe, which never yet burn'd
 dim,
His foremast air, and somewhat rolling gait,
Like his dear vessel, spoke his former state;
But then a sort of kerchief round his head,
Not over-tightly bound, nor nicely spread;
And, 'stead of trowsers (ah! too early torn!
For even the mildest woods will have their
 thorn),
A curious sort of somewhat scanty mat
Now served for inexpressibles and hat;
His naked feet and neck, and sunburnt face,
Perchance might suit alike with either race.

His arms were all his own, our Europe's growth,
Which two worlds bless for civilising both;
The musket swung behind his shoulders broad,
And somewhat stoop'd by his marine abode,
But brawny as the boar's; and hung beneath,
His cutlass droop'd, unconscious of a sheath,
Or lost or worn away; his pistols were
Link'd to his belt, a matrimonial pair—
(Let not this metaphor appear a scoff,
Though one miss'd fire, the other would go off);
These, with a bayonet, not so free from rust
As when the arm-chest held its brighter trust,
Completed his accoutrements, as Night
Survey'd him in his garb heteroclite.

XXI.

"What cheer, Ben Bunting?" cried (when in full view
Our new acquaintance) Torquil. "Aught of new?"
"Ey, ey!" quoth Ben, "not new, but news enow;
A strange sail in the offing."—"Sail! and how?
What! could you make her out? It cannot be;
I've seen no rag of canvas on the sea."
"Belike," said Ben, "you might not from the bay,
But from the bluff-head, where I watch'd to-day,
I saw her in the doldrums; for the wind
Was light and baffling."—"When the sun declined
Where lay she? had she anchor'd?"—"No, but still
She bore down on us, till the wind grew still."
"Her flag?"—"I had no glass: but fore and aft,
Egad! she seem'd a wicked-looking craft."
"Arm'd?"—"I expect so;—sent on the look-out:
'Tis time, belike, to put our helm about."
"About?—Whate'er may have us now in chase,
We'll make no running fight, for that were base;
We will die at our quarters, like true men."
"Ey, ey! for that 'tis all the same to Ben."
"Does Christian know this?"—"Ay; he has piped all hands
To quarters. They are furbishing the stands

Of arms; and we have got some guns to bear,
And scaled them. You are wanted."—"That's but fair;
And if it were not, mine is not the soul
To leave my comrades helpless on the shoal.
My Neuha! ah! and must my fate pursue
Not me alone, but one so sweet and true?
But whatsoe'er betide, ah, Neuha! now
Unman me not; the hour will not allow
A tear; I'm thine whatever intervenes!"
"Right," quoth Ben; "that will do for the marines."

Canto the Third.

I.

THE fight was o'er; the flashing through the gloom,
Which robes the cannon as he wings a tomb,
Had ceased; and sulphury vapours upward driven
Had left the earth, and but polluted heaven:
The rattling roar which rung in every volley
Had left the echoes to their melancholy;
No more they shriek'd their horror, boom for boom;
The strife was done, the vanquish'd had their doom;
The mutineers were crush'd, dispers'd, or ta'en,
Or lived to deem the happiest were the slain.
Few, few escaped, and these were hunted o'er
The isle they loved beyond their native shore.
No further home was theirs, it seem'd, on earth,
Once renegades to that which gave them birth;
Track'd like wild beasts, like them they sought the wild,
As to a mother's bosom flies the child;
But vainly wolves and lions seek their den,
And still more vainly men escape from men.

II.

Beneath a rock whose jutting base protrudes
Far over ocean in its fiercest moods,
When scaling his enormous crag the wave
Is hurl'd down headlong like the foremost brave,
And falls back on the foaming crowd behind,
Which fight beneath the banners of the wind,
But now at rest, a little remnant drew
Together, bleeding, thirsty, faint, and few;
But still their weapons in their hands, and still
With something of the pride of former will,

As men not all unused to meditate,
And strive much more than wonder at their
　fate.
Their present lot was what they had fore-
　seen,
And dared as what was likely to have been;
Yet still the lingering hope, which deem'd
　their lot
Not pardon'd, but unsought for or forgot,
Or trusted that, if sought, their distant caves
Might still be miss'd amidst the world of
　waves,
Had wean'd their thoughts in part from what
　they saw
And felt, the vengeance of their country's
　law.
Their sea-green isle, their guilt-won paradise,
No more could shield their virtue or their
　vice:
Their better feelings, if such were, were
　thrown
Back on themselves,—their sins remain'd
　alone.
Proscribed even in their second country, they
Were lost; in vain the world before them
　lay;
All outlets seem'd secured. Their new allies
Had fought and bled in mutual sacrifice;
But what avail'd the club and spear, and arm
Of Hercules, against the sulphury charm,
The magic of the thunder, which destroy'd
The warrior ere his strength could be em-
　ploy'd?
Dug, like a spreading pestilence, the grave
No less of human bravery than the brave!
Their own scant numbers acted all the few
Against the many oft will dare and do;
But though the choice seems native to die
　free,
Even Greece can boast but one Thermopylæ,
Till *now*, when she has forged her broken
　chain
Back to a sword, and dies and lives again!

III.

Beside the jutting rock the few appear'd,
Like the last remnant of the red-deer's herd;
Their eyes were feverish, and their aspect
　worn,
But still the hunter's blood was on their
　horn,
A little stream came tumbling from the
　height,
And straggling into ocean as it might,
Its bounding crystal frolick'd in the ray,
And gush'd from cliff to crag with saltless
　spray;
Close on the wild, wide ocean, yet as pure
And fresh as innocence, and more secure,

Its silver torrent glitter'd o'er the deep,
As the shy chamois' eye o'erlooks the steep,
While far below the vast and sullen swell
Of ocean's alpine azure rose and fell.
To this young spring they rush'd,—all feel-
　ings first
Absorb'd in passion's and in nature's thirst,—
Drank as they do who drink their last, and
　threw
Their arms aside to revel in its dew;
Cool'd their scorch'd throats, and wash'd the
　gory stains
From wounds whose only bandage might be
　chains;
Then, when their drought was quench'd,
　look'd sadly round,
As wondering how so many still were found
Alive and fetterless:—but silent all,
Each sought his fellow's eyes, as if to call
On him for language which his lips denied,
As though their voices with their cause had
　died.

IV.

Stern, and aloof a little from the rest,
Stood Christian, with his arms across his
　chest.
The ruddy, reckless, dauntless hue once
　spread
Along his cheek was livid now as lead;
His light-brown locks, so graceful in their
　flow,
Now rose like startled vipers o'er his brow.
Still as a statue, with his lips comprest
To stifle even the breath within his breast,
Fast by the rock, all menacing, but mute,
He stood; and, save a slight beat of his foot,
Which deepen'd now and then the sandy
　dint
Beneath his heel, his form seem'd turn'd to
　flint.
Some paces further Torquil lean'd his head
Against a bank, and spoke not, but he bled,—
Not mortally:—his worst wound was within;
His brow was pale, his blue eyes sunken in,
And blood-drops, sprinkled o'er his yellow
　hair,
Show'd that his faintness came not from
　despair,
But nature's ebb. Beside him was another,
Rough as a bear, but willing as a brother,—
Ben Bunting, who essay'd to wash, and wipe,
And bind his wound—then calmly lit his pipe,
A trophy which survived a hundred fights,
A beacon which had cheer'd ten thousand
　nights.
The fourth and last of this deserted group
Walk'd up and down—at times would stand,
　then stoop

To pick a pebble up—then let it drop—
Then hurry as in haste—then quickly stop—
Then cast his eyes on his companions—then
Half whistle half a tune, and pause again—
And then his former movements would re-
 double,
With something between carelessness and
 trouble.
This is a long description, but applies
To scarce five minutes pass'd before the eyes;
But yet *what* minutes! Moments like to these
Rend men's lives into immortalities.

V.

At length Jack Skyscrape, a mercurial man,
Who flutter'd over all things like a fan,
More brave than firm, and more disposed to
 dare
And die at once than wrestle with despair,
Exclaim'd, " G—d damn!"—those syllables
 intense,—
Nucleus of England's native eloquence,
As the Turk's "Allah!" or the Roman's
 more
Pagan "Proh Jupiter!" was wont of yore
To give their first impressions such a vent,
By way of echo to embarrassment.
Jack was embarrass'd,—never hero more,
And as he knew not what to say, he swore:
Nor swore in vain; the long congenial sound
Revived Ben Bunting from his pipe pro-
 found;
He drew it from his mouth, and look'd full
 wise,
But merely added to the oath his *eyes;*
Thus rendering the imperfect phrase com-
 plete,
A peroration I need not repeat.

VI.

But Christian, of a higher order, stood
Like an extinct volcano in his mood;
Silent, and sad, and savage,—with the trace
Of passion reeking from his clouded face;
Till lifting up again his sombre eye,
It glanced on Torquil, who lean'd faintly by.
"And is it thus?" he cried, "unhappy boy!
And thee, too, *thee*—my madness must de-
 stroy!"
He said, and strode to where young Torquil
 stood,
Yet dabbled with his lately flowing blood;
Seized his hand wistfully, but did not press,
And shrunk as fearful of his own caress;
Inquired into his state; and when he heard
The wound was slighter than he deem'd or
 fear'd,
A moment's brightness pass'd along his brow,
As much as such a moment would allow.

"Yes," he exclaim'd, "we're taken. in the
 toil,
But not a coward or a common spoil;
Dearly they've bought us—dearly still may
 buy,—
And I must fall; but have you strength to
 fly?
'T would be some comfort still, could you
 survive;
Our dwindled band is now too few to strive.
Oh! for a sole canoe! though but a shell,
To bear you hence to where a hope may
 dwell!
For me, my lot is what I sought; to be,
In life or death, the fearless and the free."

VII.

Even as he spoke, around the promontory,
Which nodded o'er the billows high and
 hoary,
A dark speck dotted ocean: on it flew
Like to the shadow of a roused sea-mew;
Onward it came—and, lo! a second follow'd—
Now seen—now hid—where ocean's vale was
 hollow'd;
And near, and nearer, till their dusky crew
Presented well-known aspects to the view,
Till on the surf their skimming paddles play,
Buoyant as wings, and flitting through the
 spray;—
Now perching on the wave's high curl, and
 now
Dash'd downward in the thundering foam
 below,
Which flings it broad and boiling sheet on
 sheet,
And slings its high flakes, shiver'd into sleet:
But floating still through surf and swell,
 drew nigh
The barks, like small birds through a lower-
 ing sky.
Their art seem'd nature—such the skill to
 sweep
The wave of these born playmates of the
 deep.

VIII.

And who the first that, springing on the
 strand,
Leap'd like a nereid from her shell to land,
With dark but brilliant skin, and dewy eye
Shining with love, and hope, and constancy?
Neuha—the fond, the faithful, the adored—
Her heart on Torquil's like a torrent pour'd;
And smiled, and wept, and near, and nearer
 clasp'd,
As if to be assured 't was *him* she grasp'd;
Shudder'd to see his yet warm wound, and
 then,
To find it trivial, smiled and wept again.

She was a warrior's daughter, and could bear
Such sights, and feel, and mourn, but not
 despair.
Her lover lived,—nor foes nor fears could
 blight
That full-blown moment in its all delight:
Joy trickled in her tears, joy fill'd the sob
That rock'd her heart till almost heard to
 throb;
And paradise was breathing in the sigh
Of nature's child in nature's ecstasy.

IX.

The sterner spirits who beheld that meeting
Were not unmoved; who are, when hearts
 are greeting?
Even Christian gazed upon the maid and boy
With tearless eye, but yet a gloomy joy
Mix'd with those bitter thoughts the soul
 arrays
In hopeless visions of our better days,
When all's gone—to the rainbow's latest ray.
"And but for me!" he said, and turn'd
 away;
Then gazed upon the pair, as in his den
A lion looks upon his cubs again;
And then relapsed into his sullen guise,
As headless of his further destinies.

X.

But brief their time for good or evil thought;
The billows round the promontory brought
The plash of hostile oars.—Alas! who made
That sound a dread? All around them seem'd
 array'd
Against them, save the bride of Toobonai:
She, as she caught the first glimpse o'er the
 bay
Of the arm'd boats, which hurried to complete
The remnant's ruin with their flying feet,
Beckon'd the natives round her to their
 prows,
Embark'd their guests and launch'd their
 light canoes,
In one placed Christian and his comrades
 twain;
But she and Torquil must not part again.
She fix'd him in her own.—Away! away!
They clear the breakers, dart along the bay,
And towards a group of islets, such as bear
The sea-bird's nest and seal's surf-hollow'd
 lair,
They skim the blue tops of the billows; fast
They flew, and fast their fierce pursuers
 chased.
They gain upon them—now they lose again,—
Again make way and menace o'er the main;
And now the two canoes in chase divide,
And follow different courses o'er the tide,

To baffle the pursuit.—Away! away!
As life is on each paddle's flight to-day,
And more than life or lives to Neuha: Love
Freights the frail bark and urges to the cove;
And now the refuge and the foe are nigh—
Yet, yet a moment: Fly, thou light ark, fly!

Canto the Fourth.

I.

White as a white sail on a dusky sea,
When half the horizon's clouded and half free,
Fluttering between the dun wave and the sky,
Is hope's last gleam in man's extremity.
Her anchor parts! but still her snowy sail
Attracts our eye amidst the rudest gale:
Though every wave she climbs divides us
 more,
The heart still follows from the loneliest
 shore.

II.

Not distant from the isle of Toobonai,
A black rock rears its bosom o'er the spray,
The haunt of birds, a desert to mankind,
Where the rough seal reposes from the wind,
And sleeps unwieldy in his cavern dun,
Or gambols with huge frolic in the sun:
There shrilly to the passing oar is heard
The startled echo of the ocean bird,
Who rears on its bare breast her callow
 brood,
The feather'd fishers of the solitude.
A narrow segment of the yellow sand
On one side forms the outline of a strand;
Here the young turtle, crawling from his
 shell,
Steals to the deep wherein his parents dwell;
Chipp'd by the beam, a nursling of the day,
But hatch'd for ocean by the fostering ray;
The rest was one bleak precipice, as e'er
Gave mariners a shelter and despair;
A spot to make the saved regret the deck
Which late went down, and envy the lost
 wreck.
Such was the stern asylum Neuha chose
To shield her lover from his following foes;
But all its secret was not told; she knew
In this a treasure hidden from the view.

III.

Ere the canoes divided, near the spot,
The men that mann'd what held her Torquil's
 lot,
By her command removed, to strengthen
 more
The skiff which wafted Christian from the
 shore.

This he would have opposed; but with a smile
She pointed calmly to the craggy isle,
And bade him "speed and prosper." *She* would take
The rest upon herself for Torquil's sake.
They parted with this added aid; afar
The proa darted like a shooting star,
And gain'd on the pursuers, who now steer'd
Right on the rock which she and Torquil near'd.
They pull'd; her arm, though delicate, was free
And firm as ever grappled with the sea,
And yielded scarce to Torquil's manlier strength.
The prow now almost lay within its length
Of the crag's steep, inexorable face,
With nought but soundless waters for its base;
Within a hundred boats' length was the foe,
And now what refuge but their frail canoe?
This Torquil ask'd with half upbraiding eye,
Which said—"Has Neuha brought me here to die?
Is this a place of safety, or a grave,
And yon huge rock the tombstone of the wave?"

IV.

They rested on their paddles, and uprose
Neuha, and pointing to the approaching foes,
Cried, "Torquil, follow me, and fearless follow!"
Then plunged at once into the ocean's hollow.
There was no time to pause—the foes were near—
Chains in his eye, and menace in his ear;
With vigour they pull'd on, and as they came,
Hail'd him to yield, and by his forfeit name.
Headlong he leapt—to him the swimmer's skill
Was native, and now all his hope from ill:
But how, or where? He dived, and rose no more;
The boat's crew look'd amazed o'er sea and shore.
There was no landing on that precipice,
Steep, harsh, and slippery as a berg of ice.
They watch'd awhile to see him float again,
But not a trace rebubbled from the main:
The wave roll'd on, no ripple on its face,
Since their first plunge recall'd a single trace;
The little whirl which eddied, and slight foam,
That whiten'd o'er what seem'd their latest home,
White as a sepulchre above the pair
Who left no marble (mournful as an heir)

The quiet proa wavering o'er the tide
Was all that told of Torquil and his bride;
And but for this alone the whole might seem
The vanish'd phantom of a seaman's dream.
They paused and search'd in vain, then pull'd away;
Every superstition now forbade their stay.
Some said he had not plunged into the wave,
But vanish'd like a corpse-light from a grave;
Others, that something supernatural
Glared in his figure, more than mortal tall;
While all agreed that in his cheek and eye
There was a dead hue of eternity.
Still as their oars receded from the crag,
Round every weed a moment would they lag,
Expectant of some token of their prey;
But no—he had melted from them like the spray.

V.

And where was he the pilgrim of the deep,
Following the nereid? Had they ceased to weep
For ever? or, received in coral caves,
Wrung life and pity from the softening waves?
Did they with ocean's hidden sovereigns dwell,
And sound with mermen the fantastic shell?
Did Neuha with the mermaids comb her hair
Flowing o'er ocean as it stream'd in air?
Or had they perish'd, and in silence slept
Beneath the gulf wherein they boldly leapt?

VI.

Young Neuha plunged into the deep, and he
Follow'd: her track beneath her native sea
Was as a native's of the element,
So smoothly, bravely, brilliantly she went,
Leaving a streak of light behind her heel,
Which struck and flash'd like an amphibious steel.
Closely, and scarcely less expert to trace
The depths where divers hold the pearl in chase,
Torquil, the nursling of the northern seas,
Pursued her liquid steps with heart and ease.
Deep—deeper for an instant Neuha led
The way—then upward soar'd—and as she spread
Her arms, and flung the foam from off her locks,
Laugh'd, and the sound was answer'd by the rocks.
They had gain'd a central realm of earth again,
But look'd for tree, and field, and sky, in vain.
Around she pointed to a spacious cave,
Whose only portal was the keyless wave,

(A hollow archway by the sun unseen,
Save through the billows' glassy veil of green,
In some transparent ocean holiday,
When all the finny people are at play,)
Wiped with her hair the brine from Torquil's
 eyes,
And clapp'd her hands with joy at his sur-
 prise;
Led him to where the rock appear'd to jut,
And form a something like a Triton's hut;
For all was darkness for a space, till day
Through clefts above let in a sober'd ray;
As in some old cathedral's glimmering aisle
The dusty monuments from light recoil,
Thus sadly in their refuge submarine
The vault drew half her shadow from the
 scene.

VII.

Forth from her bosom the young savage
 drew
A pine torch, strongly girded with gnatoo;
A plantain-leaf o'er all, the more to keep
Its latent sparkle from the sapping deep.
This mantle kept it dry; then from a nook
Of the same plantain-leaf a flint she took,
A few shrunk wither'd twigs, and from the
 blade
Of Torquil's knife struck fire, and thus
 array'd
The grot with torchlight. Wide it was and
 high,
And show'd a self-born Gothic canopy;
The arch uprear'd by nature's architect,
The architrave some earthquake might erect;
The buttress from some mountain's bosom
 hurl'd,
When the Poles crash'd, and water was the
 world;
Or harden'd from some earth-absorbing fire,
While yet the globe reek'd from its funeral
 pyre;
The fretted pinnacle, the aisle, the nave,
Were there, all scoop'd by Darkness from
 her cave.
There, with a little tinge of phantasy,
Fantastic faces mop'd and mow'd on high,
And then a mitre or a shrine would fix
The eye upon its seeming crucifix.
Thus Nature play'd with the stalactites,
And built herself a chapel of the seas.

VIII.

And Neuha took her Torquil by the hand,
And waved along the vault her kindled brand,
And led him into each recess, and show'd
The secret places of their new abode.
Nor these alone, for all had been prepared
Before, to soothe the lover's lot she shared:

The mat for rest; for dress the fresh gnatoo,
And sandal oil to fence against the dew;
For food the cocoa-nut, the yam, the bread
Born of the fruit; for board the plantain
 spread
With its broad leaf, or turtle-shell which bore
A banquet in the flesh it cover'd o'er;
The gourd with water recent from the rill,
The ripe banana from the mellow hill;
A pine-torch pile to keep undying light,
And she herself, as beautiful as night,
To fling her shadowy spirit o'er the scene,
And make their subterranean world serene.
She had foreseen, since first the stranger's
 sail
Drew to their isle, that force or flight might
 fail,
And form'd a refuge of the rocky den
For Torquil's safety from his countrymen.
Each dawn had wafted there her light canoe,
Laden with all the golden fruits that grew;
Each eve had seen her gliding through the
 hour
With all could cheer or deck their sparry
 bower;
And now she spread her little store with
 smiles,
The happiest daughter of the loving isles.

IX.

She, as he gazed with grateful wonder,
 press'd
Her shelter'd love to her impassion'd breast;
And suited to her soft caresses, told
An olden tale of love,—for love is old,
Old as eternity, but not outworn
With each new being born or to be born:
How a young chief, a thousand moons ago,
Diving for turtle in the depths below,
Had risen, in tracking fast his ocean prey,
Into the cave which round and o'er them lay;
How in some desperate feud of after-time
He shelter'd there a daughter of the clime,
A foe beloved, and offspring of a foe,
Saved by his tribe but for a captive's woe;
How, when the storm of war was still'd, he led
His island clan to where the waters spread
Their deep-green shadow o'er the rocky door,
Then dived—it seem'd as if to rise no more:
His wondering mates, amazed within their
 bark,
Or deem'd him mad, or prey to the blue
 shark;
Row'd round in sorrow the sea-girded rock,
Then paused upon their paddles from the
 shock;
When, fresh and springing from the deep,
 they saw
A goddess rise—so deem'd they in their awe;

And their companion, glorious by her side,
Proud and exulting in his mermaid bride:
And how, when undeceived, the pair they
 bore
With sounding conchs and joyous shouts to
 shore;
How they had gladly lived and calmly died,
And why not also Torquil and his bride?
Not mine to tell the rapturous caress
Which follow'd wildly in that wild recess
This tale; enough that all within that cave
Was love, though buried strong as in the grave
Where Abelard, through twenty years of
 death,
When Eloïsa's form was lower'd beneath
Their nuptial vault, his arms outstretch'd,
 and press'd
The kindling ashes to his kindled breast.
The waves without sang round their couch,
 their roar
As much unheeded as if life were o'er;
Within, their hearts made all their harmony,
Love's broken murmur and more broken sigh.

X.

And they, the cause and sharers of the shock
Which left them exiles of the hollow rock,
Where were they? O'er the sea for life they
 plied,
To seek from Heaven the shelter men denied.
Another course had been their choice—but
 where?
The wave which bore them still their foes
 would bear,
Who, disappointed of their former chase,
In search of Christian now renew'd their race.
Eager with anger, their strong arms made
 way,
Like vultures baffled of their previous prey.
They gain'd upon them, all whose safety lay
In some bleak crag or deeply-hidden bay:
No further chance or choice remain'd; and
 right
For the first further rock which met their sight
They steer'd, to take their latest view of land,
And yield as victims, or die sword in hand;
Dismiss'd the natives and their shallop, who
Would still have battled for that scanty crew;
But Christian bade them seek their shore
 again,
Nor add a sacrifice which were in vain;
For what were simple bow and savage spear
Against the arms which must be wielded
 here?

XI.

They landed on a wild but narrow scene,
Where few but Nature's footsteps yet had
 been;

Prepared their arms, and with that gloomy
 eye,
Stern and sustain'd, of man's extremity,
When hope is gone, nor glory's self remains
To cheer resistance against death or chains,—
They stood, the three, as the three hundred
 stood
Who dyed Thermopylæ with holy blood.
But, ah! how different! 'tis the *cause* makes
 all,
Degrades or hallows courage in its fall.
O'er them no fame, eternal and intense,
Blazed through the clouds of death and
 beckon'd hence;
No grateful country, smiling through her
 tears,
Begun the praises of a thousand years;
No nation's eyes would on their tomb be bent,
No heroes envy them their monument;
However boldly their warm blood was spilt,
Their life was shame, their epitaph was guilt.
And this they knew and felt, at least the one,
The leader of the band he had undone;
Who, born perchance for better things, had set
His life upon a cast which linger'd yet:
But now the die was to be thrown, and all
The chances were in favour of his fall:
And such a fall! But still he faced the shock,
Obdurate as a portion of the rock
Whereon he stood, and fix'd his levell'd gun,
Dark as a sullen cloud before the sun.

XII.

The boat drew nigh, well arm'd, and firm the
 crew
To act whatever duty bade them do;
Careless of danger, as the onward wind
Is of the leaves it strews, nor looks behind.
And yet perhaps they rather wish'd to go
Against a nation's than a native foe,
And felt that this poor victim of self-will,
Briton no more, had once been Britain's still.
They hail'd him to surrender—no reply;
Their arms were poised, and glitter'd in the
 sky.
They hail'd again—no answer; yet once more
They offer'd quarter louder than before.
The echoes only, from the rock's rebound,
Took their last farewell of the dying sound.
Then flash'd the flint, and blazed the volley-
 ing flame,
And the smoke rose between them and their
 aim,
While the rock rattled with the bullets' knell,
Which peal'd in vain, and flatten'd as they
 fell;
Then flew the only answer to be given
By those who had lost all hope in earth or
 heaven.

After the first fierce peal, as they pull'd
 nigher,
They heard the voice of Christian shout,
 " Now, fire ! "
And ere the word upon the echo died,
Two fell ; the rest assail'd the rock's rough side,
And, furious at the madness of their foes,
Disdain'd all further efforts, save to close.
But steep the crag, and all without a path,
Each step opposed a bastion to their wrath,
While, placed 'midst clefts the least acces-
 sible,
Which Christian's eye was train'd to mark
 full well,
The three maintain'd a strife which must not
 yield,
In spots where eagles might have chosen to
 build.
Their every shot told ; while the assailant
 fell,
Dash'd on the shingles like the limpet shell ;
But still enough survived, and mounted still,
Scattering their numbers here and there,
 until
Surrounded and commanded, though not nigh
Enough for seizure, near enough to die,
The desperate trio held aloof their fate
But by a thread, like sharks who've gorged
 the bait ;
Yet to the very last they battled well,
And not a groan inform'd their foes *who* fell.
Christian died last—twice wounded ; and
 once more
Mercy was offer'd when they saw his gore ;
Too late for life, but not too late to die,
With, though a hostile hand, to close his eye.
A limb was broken, and he droop'd along
The crag, as doth a falcon reft of young.
The sound revived him, or appear'd to wake
Some passion which a weakly gesture spake :
He beckon'd to the foremost, who drew nigh,
But, as they near'd, he rear'd his weapon
 high—
His last ball had been aim'd, but from his
 breast
He tore the topmost button from his vest,
Down the tube dash'd it, levell'd, fired, and
 smiled
As his foe fell ; then, like a serpent, coil'd
His wounded, weary form, to where the steep
Look'd desperate as himself along the deep ;
Cast one glance back, and clench'd his hand,
 and shook
His last rage 'gainst the earth which he for-
 sook ;
Then plunged : the rock below received like
 glass
His body crush'd into one gory mass,
With scarce a shred to tell of human form,
Or fragment for the sea-bird or the worm ;

A fair-hair'd scalp, besmear'd with blood and
 weeds,
Yet reek'd, the remnant of himself and deeds ;
Some splinters of his weapons (to the last,
As long as hand could hold, he held them
 fast)
Yet glitter'd, but at distance—hurl'd away
To rust beneath the dew and dashing spray.
The rest was nothing—save a life mis-spent,
And soul—but who shall answer where it
 went ?
'Tis ours to bear, not judge the dead ; and
 they
Who doom to hell, themselves are on the
 way,
Unless these bullies of eternal pains
Are pardon'd their bad hearts for their worse
 brains.

XIII.

The deed was over ! All were gone or ta'en,
The fugitive, the captive, or the slain.
Chain'd on the deck, where once, a gallant
 crew,
They stood with honour, were the wretched
 few
Survivors of the skirmish on the isle ;
But the last rock left no surviving spoil.
Cold lay they where they fell, and weltering,
While o'er them flapp'd the sea-birds' dewy
 wing,
Now wheeling nearer from the neighbouring
 surge,
And screaming high their harsh and hungry
 dirge :
But calm and careless heaved the wave below,
Eternal with unsympathetic flow ;
Far o'er its face the dolphins sported on,
And sprung the flying fish against the sun,
Till its dried wing relapsed from its brief
 height,
To gather moisture for another flight.

XIV.

'Twas morn ; and Neuha, who by dawn of
 day
Swam smoothly forth to catch the rising ray,
And watch if aught approach'd the amphi-
 bious lair
Where lay her lover, saw a sail in air :
It flapp'd, it fill'd, and to the growing gale
Bent its broad arch : her breath began to fail
With fluttering fear, her heart beat thick and
 high,
While yet a doubt sprung where its course
 might lie,
But no ! it came not ; fast and far away
The shadow lessen'd as it clear'd the bay.

She gazed. and flung the sea-foam from her
 eyes,
To watch as for a rainbow in the skies.
On the horizon verged the distant deck,
Diminish'd, dwindled to a very speck—
Then vanish'd. All was ocean, all was joy!
Down plunged she through the cave to rouse
 her boy;
Told all she had seen, and all she hoped, and
 all
That happy love could augur or recall;
Sprung forth again, with Torquil following
 free
His bounding nereid over the broad sea;
Swam round the rock, to where a shallow
 cleft
Hid the canoe that Neuha there had left
Drifting along the tide, without an oar,
That eve the strangers chased them from the
 shore;
But when these vanish'd, she pursued her
 prow,
Regain'd, and urged to where they found it
 now;
Nor ever did more love and joy embark,
Than now were wafted in that slender ark.

XV.

Again their own shore rises on the view,
No more polluted with a hostile hue;
No sullen ship lay bristling o'er the foam,
A floating dungeon:—all was hope and home!
A thousand proas darted o'er the bay,
With sounding shells, and heralded their
 way;
The chiefs came down, around the people
 pour'd,
And welcomed Torquil as a son restored;
The women throng'd, embracing and em-
 braced
By Neuha, asking where they had been
 chased,
And how escaped? The tale was told; and then
One acclamation rent the sky again;
And from that hour a new tradition gave
Their sanctuary the name of "Neuha's Cave."
A hundred fires, far flickering from the height,
Blazed o'er the general revel of the night,
The feast in honour of the guest, return'd
To peace and pleasure, perilously earn'd;
A night succeeded by such happy days
As only the yet infant world displays.

The Lament of Tasso.

ADVERTISEMENT.

At Ferrara, in the Library, are preserved the original MSS. of Tasso's Gierusalemme and of Guarini's Pastor Fido, with letters of Tasso, one from Titian to Ariosto, and the inkstand and chair, the tomb and the house, of the latter. But, as misfortune has a greater interest for posterity, and little or none for the cotemporary, the cell where Tasso was confined in the hospital of St. Anna attracts a more fixed attention than the residence or the monument of Ariosto—at least it had this effect on me. There are two inscriptions, one on the outer gate, the second over the cell itself, inviting, unnecessarily, the wonder and the indignation of the spectator. Ferrara is much decayed and depopulated: the castle still exists entire; and I saw the court where Parisina and Hugo were beheaded, according to the annal of Gibbon.

I.

Long years!—It tries the thrilling frame to
 bear
And eagle-spirit of a child of Song—
Long years of outrage, calumny, and wrong;
Imputed madness, prison'd solitude,
And the mind's canker in its savage mood,
When the impatient thirst of light and air
Parches the heart; and the abhorred grate,
Marring the sunbeams with its hideous shade,

Works through the throbbing eyeball to the
 brain,
With a hot sense of heaviness and pain;
And bare, at once, Captivity display'd
Stands scoffing through the never-open'd gate,
Which nothing through its bars admits, save
 day,
And tasteless food, which I have eat alone
Till its unsocial bitterness is gone;
And I can banquet like a beast of prey,
Sullen and lonely, couching in the cave
Which is my lair, and—it may be—my grave.

All this hath somewhat worn me, and may
 wear,
But must be borne. I stoop not to despair;
For I have battled with mine agony,
And made me wings wherewith to overfly
The narrow circus of my dungeon wall,
And freed the Holy Sepulchre from thrall;
And revell'd among men and things divine,
And pour'd my spirit over Palestine,
In honour of the sacred war for Him,
The God who was on earth and is in heaven,
For he has strengthen'd me in heart and limb.
That through this sufferance I might be for-
 given,
I have employ'd my penance to record
How Salem's shrine was won, and how adored.

II.

But this is o'er—my pleasant task is done :—
My long-sustaining friend of many years !
If I do blot thy final page with tears,
Know, that my sorrows have wrung from me
 none.
But thou, my young creation ! my soul's child !
Which ever playing round me came and
 smiled,
And woo'd me from myself with thy sweet
 sight,
Thou too art gone—and so is my delight :
And therefore do I weep and inly bleed
With this last bruise upon a broken reed.
Thou too art ended—what is left me now ?
For I have anguish yet to bear—and how ?
I know not that—but in the innate force
Of my own spirit shall be found resource.
I have not sunk, for I had no remorse,
Nor cause for such : they call'd me mad—and
 why ?
Oh Leonora ! wilt not *thou* reply ?
I was indeed delirious in my heart
To lift my love so lofty as thou art ;
But still my frenzy was not of the mind :
I knew my fault, and feel my punishment
Not less because I suffer it unbent.
That thou wert beautiful, and I not blind,
Hath been the sin which shuts me from
 mankind ;
But let them go, or torture as they will,
My heart can multiply thine image still ;
Successful love may sate itself away ;
The wretched are the faithful ; 'tis their fate
To have all feeling, save the one, decay,
And every passion into one dilate,
As rapid rivers into ocean pour ;
But ours is fathomless, and hath no shore.

III.

Above me, hark ! the long and maniac cry
Of minds and bodies in captivity.

And hark ! the lash and the increasing howl,
And the half-inarticulate blasphemy !
There be some here with worse than frenzy
 foul,
Some who do still goad on the o'er-labour'd
 mind,
And dim the little light that's left behind
With needless torture, as their tyrant will
Is wound up to the lust of doing ill :
With these and with their victims am I
 class'd,
'Mid sounds and sights like these long years
 have pass'd ;
'Mid sights and sounds like these my life may
 close :
So let it be—for then I shall repose.

IV.

I have been patient, let me be so yet ;
I had forgotten half I would forget,
But it revives—Oh ! would it were my lot
To be forgetful as I am forgot !
Feel I not wroth with those who bade me
 dwell
In this vast lazar-house of many woes ?
Where laughter is not mirth, nor thought the
 mind,
Nor words a language, nor ev'n men man-
 kind ;
Where cries reply to curses, shrieks to blows,
And each is tortured in his separate hell—
For we are crowded in our solitudes—
Many, but each divided by the wall,
Which echoes Madness in her babbling moods ;
While all can hear, none heed his neighbour's
 call—
None! save that One, the veriest wretch of
 all,
Who was not made to be the mate of these,
Nor bound between Distraction and Disease.
Feel I not wroth with those who placed me
 here ?
Who have debased me in the minds of men,
Debarring me the usage of my own,
Blighting my life in best of its career,
Branding my thoughts as things to shun and
 fear ?
Would I not pay them back these pangs again,
And teach them inward Sorrow's stifled groan?
The struggle to be calm, and cold distress,
Which undermines our Stoical success ?
No!—still too proud to be vindictive—I
Have pardon'd princes' insults, and would
 die.
Yes, Sister of my Sovereign ! for thy sake
I weed all bitterness from out my breast,
It hath no business where *thou* art a guest :
Thy brother hates—but I cannot detest ;
Thou pitiest not—but I cannot forsake.

V.

Look on a love which knows not to despair,
But all unquench'd is still my better part,
Dwelling deep in my shut and silent heart,
As dwells the gather'd lightning in its cloud,
Encompass'd with its dark and rolling shroud,
Till struck,—forth flies the all-ethereal dart!
And thus at the collision of thy name,
The vivid thought still flashes through my
 frame,
And for a moment all things as they were
Flit by me; they are gone—I am the same.
And yet my love without ambition grew;
I knew thy state, my station, and I knew
A Princess was no love-mate for a bard;
I told it not, I breathed it not, it was
Sufficient to itself, its own reward;
And if my eyes reveal'd it, they, alas!
Were punish'd by the silentness of thine,
And yet I did not venture to repine.
Thou wert to me a crystal-girded shrine,
Worshipp'd at holy distance, and around
Hallow'd and meekly kiss'd the saintly ground;
Not for thou wert a princess, but that Love
Had robed thee with a glory, and array'd
Thy lineaments in beauty that dismay'd—
Oh! not dismay'd—but awed, like One above!
And in that sweet severity there was
A something which all softness did surpass;
I know not how—thy genius master'd mine;
My star stood still before thee: if it were
Presumptuous thus to love without design,
That sad fatality hath cost me dear;
But thou art dearest still, and I should be
Fit for this cell, which wrongs me—but for
 thee.
The very love which lock'd me to my chain
Hath lighten'd half its weight; and for the
 rest,
Though heavy, lent me vigour to sustain,
And look to thee with undivided breast,
And foil the ingenuity of Pain.

VI.

It is no marvel—from my very birth
My soul was drunk with love, which did per-
 vade
And mingle with whate'er I saw on earth:
Of objects all inanimate I made
Idols, and out of wild and lonely flowers,
And rocks, whereby they grew, a paradise,
Where I did lay me down within the shade
Of waving trees, and dreamed uncounted
 hours,
Though I was chid for wandering; and the
 wise
Shook their white aged heads o'er me and
 said,
Of such materials wretched men were made,

And such a truant boy would end in woe,
And that the only lesson was a blow;
And then they smote me, and I did not weep,
But cursed them in my heart, and to my
 haunt
Return'd and wept alone, and dream'd again
The visions which arise without a sleep,
And with my years my soul began to pant
With feelings of strange tumult and soft pain;
And the whole heart exhaled into One Want,
But undefined and wandering, till the day
I found the thing I sought—and that was
 thee;
And then I lost my being, all to be
Absorb'd in thine; the world was past away;
Thou didst annihilate the earth to me!

VII.

I loved all Solitude, but little thought
To spend I know not what of life, remote
From all communion with existence, save
The maniac and his tyrant; had I been
Their fellow, many years ere this had seen
My mind like theirs corrupted to its grave.
But who hath seen me writhe, or heard me
 rave?
Perchance in such a cell we suffer more
Than the wreck'd sailor on his desert shore;
The world is all before him—*mine* is *here*,
Scarce twice the space they must accord my
 bier.
What though *he* perish, he may lift his eye.
And with a dying glance upbraid the sky;
I will not raise my own in such reproof,
Although 'tis clouded by my dungeon roof

VIII.

Yet do I feel at times my mind decline,
But with a sense of its decay: I see
Unwonted lights along my prison shine,
And a strange demon, who is vexing me
With pilfering pranks and petty pains, below
The feeling of the healthful and the free;
But much to One, who long hath suffer'd so,
Sickness of heart, and narrowness of place,
And all that may be borne, or can debase,
I thought mine enemies had been but Man,
But Spirits may be leagued with them; all
 Earth
Abandons, Heaven forgets me: in the dearth
Of such defence the Powers of Evil can,
It may be, tempt me further,—and prevail
Against the outworn creature they assail.
Why in this furnace is my spirit proved,
Like steel in tempering fire? because I
 loved?
Because I loved what not to love, and see,
Was more or less than mortal, and than me.

IX.

I once was quick in feeling—that is o'er ;
My scars are callous, or I should have dash'd
My brain against these bars, as the sun
 flash'd
In mockery through them : If I bear and
 bore
The much I have recounted, and the more
Which hath no words,—'t is that I would
 not die
And sanction with self-slaughter the dull lie
Which snared me here, and with the brand
 of shame
Stamp Madness deep into my memory,
And woo Compassion to a blighted name,
Sealing the sentence which my foes pro-
 claim.
No—it shall be immortal! and I make
A future temple of my present cell,
Which nations yet shall visit for my sake.
While thou, Ferrara! when no longer dwell
The ducal chiefs within thee, shalt fall down,
And crumbling piecemeal view thy hearthless
 halls,
A poet's wreath shall be thine only crown,—
A poet's dungeon thy most far renown,
While strangers wonder o'er thy unpeopled
 walls !

And thou, Leonora! thou—who wert
 ashamed
That such as I could love—who blush'd to
 hear
To less than monarchs that thou couldst be
 dear,
Go! tell thy brother, that my heart, untamed
By grief, years, weariness,—and it may be
A taint of that he would impute to me—
From long infection of a den like this,
Where the mind rots congenial with the
 abyss,—
Adores thee still; and add—that when the
 towers
And battlements which guard his joyous
 hours
Of banquet, dance, and revel, are forgot,
Or left untended in a dull repose,—
This, this, shall be a consecrated spot!
But *Thou*—when all that Birth and Beauty
 throws
Of magic round thee is extinct—shalt have
One half the laurel which o'ershades my
 grave.
No power in death can tear our names apart,
As none in life could rend thee from my
 heart.
Yes, Leonora! it shall be our fate
To be entwined for ever—but too late !

The Prophecy of Dante.

"'Tis the sunset of life gives me mystical lore,
And coming events cast their shadows before."
CAMPBELL.

DEDICATION.

LADY! if for the cold and cloudy clime,
　　Where I was born, but where I would not die,
　　Of the great Poet-Sire of Italy
I dare to build the imitative rhyme,
Harsh Runic copy of the South's sublime,
　　THOU art the cause; and howsoever I
　　Fall short of his immortal harmony,
Thy gentle heart will pardon me the crime.
Thou, in the pride of Beauty and of Youth,
　　Spakest; and for thee to speak and be obey'd
Are one; but only in the sunny South
　　Such sounds are uttered, and such charms display'd,
So sweet a language from so fair a mouth—
　　Ah! to what effort would it not persuade?

RAVENNA, *June* 21, 1819.

PREFACE.

IN the course of a visit to the city of Ravenna in the summer of 1819, it was suggested to the author that having composed something on the subject of Tasso's confinement, he should do the same on Dante's exile,—the tomb of the poet forming one of the principal objects of interest in that city, both to the native and to the stranger.

"On this hint I spake," and the result has been the following four cantos, in terza rima, now offered to the reader. If they are understood and approved, it is my purpose to continue the poem, in various other cantos, to its natural conclusion in the present age. The reader is requested to suppose that Dante addresses him in the interval between the conclusion of the Divina Commedia and his death, and shortly before the latter event, foretelling the fortunes of Italy in general in the ensuing centuries. In adopting this plan I have had in my mind the Cassandra of Lycophron, and the Prophecy of Nereus by Horace, as well as the Prophecies of Holy Writ. The measure adopted is the terza rima of Dante, which I am not aware to have seen hitherto tried in our language, except it may be by Mr. Hayley, of whose translation I never saw but one extract, quoted in the notes to Caliph Vathek; so that—if I do not err—this poem may be considered as a metrical experiment. The cantos are short, and about the same length of those of the poet, whose name I have borrowed, and most probably taken in vain.

Amongst the inconveniences of authors in the present day, it is difficult for any who have a name, good or bad, to escape translation. I have had the fortune to see the fourth canto of "Childe Harold" translated into Italian versi sciolti,—that is, a poem written in the *Spenserean stanza* into *blank verse*, without regard to the natural divisions of the stanza or of the sense. If the present poem, being on a national topic, should chance to undergo the same fate, I would request the Italian reader to remember that when I have failed in the imitation of his great "Padre Alighier," I have failed in imitating that which all study and few understand, since to this very day it is not yet settled what was the meaning of the allegory in the first canto of the Inferno, unless Count Marchetti's ingenious and probable conjecture may be considered as having decided the question.

He may also pardon my failure the more, as I am not quite sure that he would be pleased with my success, since the Italians, with a pardonable nationality, are particularly jealous of all that is left them as a nation,—their literature; and in the present bitterness of the classic and romantic war, are but ill disposed to permit a foreigner even to approve or imitate them, without finding some fault with his ultramontane presumption. I can easily enter into all this, knowing what would be thought in England of an Italian imitator of Milton, or if a translation of Monti, or Pindemonte, or Arici, should be held up to the rising generation as a model for their future poetical essays. But I perceive that I am deviating into an address to the Italian reader, when my business is with the English one; and be they few or many, I must take my leave of both.

THE PROPHECY OF DANTE.

Canto the First.

ONCE more in man's frail world! which I
 had left
So long that 'twas forgotten; and I feel
The weight of clay again,—too soon bereft
Of the immortal vision which could heal
 My earthly sorrows, and to God's own
 skies
 Lift me from that deep gulf without re-
 peal,
Where late my ears rung with the damned
 cries
 Of souls in hopeless bale; and from that
 place
Of lesser torment, whence men may arise
Pure from the fire to join the angelic race;
 Midst whom my own bright Beatrice
 bless'd
My spirit with her light; and to the base
Of the eternal Triad! first, last, best,
 Mysterious, three, sole, infinite, great God!
 Soul universal! led the mortal guest,
Unblasted by the glory, though he trod
 From star to star to reach the almighty
 throne.
Oh Beatrice! whose sweet limbs the sod
So long hath press'd, and the cold marble
 stone,
Thou sole pure seraph of my earliest love,
Love so ineffable, and so alone,
That nought on earth could more my bosom
 move,
 And meeting thee in heaven was but to
 meet
 That without which my soul, like the
 arkless dove,
Had wander'd still in search of, nor her
 feet
 Relieved her wing till found: without thy
 light
My paradise had still been incomplete.
Since my tenth sun gave summer to my
 sight
 Thou wert my life, the essence of my
 thought,
 Loved ere I knew the name of love, and
 bright
Still in these dim old eyes, now overwrought
 With the world's war, and years, and
 banishment,
 And tears for thee, by other woes un-
 taught;

For mine is not a nature to be bent
 By tyrannous faction, and the brawling
 crowd,
 And though the long, long conflict hath
 been spent
In vain,—and never more, save when the
 cloud
 Which overhangs the Apennine my mind's
 eye
Pierces to fancy Florence, once so proud
Of me, can I return, though but to die,
 Unto my native soil,—they have not yet
 Quench'd the old exile's spirit, stern and
 high.
But the sun, though not overcast, must set,
 And the night cometh; I am old in days,
 And deeds, and contemplation, and have
 met
Destruction face to face in all his ways.
 The world hath left me, what it found me,
 pure,
 And if I have not gather'd yet its praise,
I sought it not by any baser lure;
 Man wrongs, and Time avenges, and my
 name
May form a monument not all obscure,
Though such was not my ambition's end or
 aim,
 To add to the vain-glorious list of those
 Who dabble in the pettiness of fame,
And make men's fickle breath the wind that
 blows
 Their sail, and deem it glory to be class'd
 With conquerors, and virtue's other foes,
In bloody chronicles of ages past.
 I would have had my Florence great and
 free;
 Oh Florence! Florence! unto me thou
 wast
Like that Jerusalem which the Almighty He
 Wept over, "but thou wouldst not;" as
 the bird
 Gathers its young, I would have gather'd
 thee
Beneath a parent pinion, hadst thou heard
 My voice; but as the adder, deaf and
 fierce,
 Against the breast that cherish'd thee was
 stirr'd
Thy venom, and my state thou didst amerce,
 And doom this body forfeit to the fire.
 Alas! how bitter is his country's curse
To him who *for* that country would expire,
 But did not merit to expire *by* her,
 And loves her, loves her even in her ire!

The day may come when she will cease to err,
 The day may come she would be proud to have
The dust she dooms to scatter, and transfer
Of him, whom she denied a home, the grave.
 But this shall not be granted; let my dust
Lie where it falls; nor shall the soil which gave
Me breath, but in her sudden fury thrust
 Me forth to breathe elsewhere, so reassume
My indignant bones, because her angry gust
Forsooth is over, and repeal'd her doom;.
 No,—she denied me what was mine—my roof,
And shall not have what is not hers—my tomb.
Too long her armed wrath hath kept aloof
 The breast which would have bled for her, the heart
That beat, the mind that was temptation proof,
The man who fought, toil'd, travell'd, and each part
 Of a true citizen fulfill'd, and saw
For his reward the Guelf's ascendant art.
Pass his destruction even into a law.
 These things are not made for forgetfulness,
Florence shall be forgotten first; too raw
The wound, too deep the wrong, and the distress
 Of such endurance too prolong'd to make
My pardon greater, her injustice less,
Though late repented; yet—yet for her sake
 I feel some fonder yearnings, and for thine,
My own Beatrice, I would hardly take
Vengeance upon the land which once was mine,
 And still is hallow'd by thy dust's return,
Which would protect the murderess like a shrine,
And save ten thousand foes by thy sole urn.
 Though, like old Marius from Minturnæ's marsh
And Carthage ruins, my lone breast may burn
At times with evil feelings hot and harsh,
 And sometimes the last pangs of a vile foe
Writhe in a dream before me, and o'erarch
My brow with hopes of triumph,—let them go!
 Such are the last infirmities of those
Who long have suffer'd more than mortal woe,
And yet being mortal still have no repose.
 But on the pillow of Revenge—Revenge,
Who sleeps to dream of blood, and waking glows

With the oft-baffled slakeless thirst of change,
 When we shall mount again, and they that trod
Be trampled on, while Death and Até range
O'er humbled heads and sever'd necks—
 Great God!
Take these thoughts from me—to thy hands I yield
 My many wrongs, and thine almighty rod
Will fall on those who smote me,—be my shield!
 As thou hast been in peril, and in pain,
In turbulent cities, and the tented field—
In toil, and many troubles borne in vain
 For Florence,—I appeal from her to Thee!
Thee whom I late saw in thy loftiest reign,
Even in that glorious vision, which to see
 And live was never granted until now,
And yet thou hast permitted this to me.
Alas! with what a weight upon my brow
 The sense of earth and earthly things come back,
Corrosive passions, feelings dull and low,
The heart's quick throb upon the mental rack,
 Long day, and dreary night; the retrospect
Of half a century bloody and black,
And the frail few years I may yet expect
 Hoary and hopeless, but less hard to bear,
For I have been too long and deeply wreck'd
On the lone rock of desolate Despair,
 To lift my eyes more to the passing sail
Which shuns that reef so horrible and bare;
Nor raise my voice—for who would heed my wail?
 I am not of this people, nor this age,
And yet my harpings will unfold a tale
Which shall preserve these times when not a page
 Of their perturbed annals could attract
An eye to gaze upon their civil rage,
Did not my verse embalm full many an act
 Worthless as they who wrought it: 'tis the doom
Of spirits of my order to be rack'd
In life, to wear their hearts out, and consume
 Their days in endless strife, and die alone;
Then future thousands crowd around their tomb,
And pilgrims come from climes where they have known
 The name of him—who now is but a name,
And wasting homage o'er the sullen stone,
Spread his—by him unheard, unheeded, fame;
 And mine at least hath cost me dear: to die
Is nothing; but to wither thus—to tame

My mind down from its own infinity—
 To live in narrow ways with little men,
 A common sight to every common eye,
A wanderer, while even wolves can find a
 den,
 Ripp'd from all kindred, from all home, all
 things
 That make communion sweet, and soften
 pain—
To feel me in the solitude of kings
 Without the power that makes them bear
 a crown—
 To envy every dove his nest and wings
Which waft him where the Apennine looks
 down
 On Arno, till he perches, it may be,
 Within my all inexorable town,
Where yet my boys are, and that fatal she,
 Their mother, the cold partner who hath
 brought
 Destruction for a dowry—this to see
And feel, and know without repair, hath
 taught
 A bitter lesson; but it leaves me free:
 I have not vilely found, nor basely sought,
They made an Exile—not a slave of me.

—⊷—

Canto the Second.

THE Spirit of the fervent days of Old,
 When words were things that came to
 pass, and thought
 Flash'd o'er the future, bidding men be-
 hold
Their children's children's doom already
 brought
 Forth from the abyss of time which is to
 be,
 The chaos of events, where lie half-wrought
Shapes that must undergo mortality;
 What the great Seers of Israel wore within,
 That spirit was on them, and is on me,
And if, Cassandra-like, amidst the din
 Of conflict none will hear, or hearing heed
 This voice from out the Wilderness, the
 sin
Be theirs, and my own feelings be my meed,
 The only guerdon I have ever known.
 Hast thou not bled? and hast thou still to
 bleed,
Italia? Ah! to me such things, foreshown
 With dim sepulchral light, bid me forget
 In thine irreparable wrongs my own;
We can have but one country, and even yet
 Thou 'rt mine—my bones shall be within
 thy breast,
 My soul within thy language, which once
 set

With our old Roman sway in the wide
 West;
 But I will make another tongue arise
 As lofty and more sweet, in which ex-
 press'd
The hero's ardour, or the lover's sighs,
 Shall find alike such sounds for every
 theme
 That every word, as brilliant as thy skies,
Shall realise a poet's proudest dream,
 And make thee Europe's nightingale of
 song;
 So that all present speech to thine shall
 seem
The note of meaner birds, and every
 tongue
 Confess its barbarism when compared with
 thine.
 This shalt thou owe to him thou didst so
 wrong,
Thy Tuscan bard, the banish'd Ghibelline.
 Woe! woe! the veil of coming centuries
 Is rent,—a thousand years which yet su-
 pine
Lie like the ocean waves ere winds arise,
 Heaving in dark and sullen undulation,
 Float from eternity into these eyes;
The storms yet sleep, the clouds still keep
 their station,
 The unborn earthquake yet is in the
 womb,
 The bloody chaos yet expects creation,
But all things are disposing for thy doom;
 The elements await but for the word,
 "Let there be darkness!" and thou grow'st
 a tomb!
Yes! thou, so beautiful, shalt feel the
 sword,
 Thou, Italy! so fair that Paradise,
 Revived in thee, blooms forth to man
 restored:
Ah! must the sons of Adam lose it twice?
 Thou, Italy! whose ever golden fields,
 Plough'd by the sunbeams solely, would
 suffice
For the world's granary; thou, whose sky
 heaven gilds
 With brighter stars, and robes with deeper
 blue;
 Thou, in whose pleasant places Summer
 builds
Her palace, in whose cradle Empire grew,
 And form'd the Eternal City's ornaments
 From spoils of kings whom freemen over-
 threw;
Birthplace of heroes, sanctuary of saints,
 Where earthly first, then heavenly glory
 made
 Her home; thou, all which fondest fancy
 paints,

And finds her prior vision but portray'd
　In feeble colours, when the eye—from the
　　Alp
　Of horrid snow, and rock, and shaggy
　　shade
Of desert-loving pine, whose emerald scalp
　Nods to the storm—dilates and dotes o'er
　　thee,
　And wistfully implores, as 'twere for help
To see thy sunny fields, my Italy,
　Nearer and nearer yet, and dearer still
　The more approach'd, and dearest were
　　they free,
Thou—thou must wither to each tyrant's
　will:
　The Goth hath been,—the German, Frank,
　　and Hun
Are yet to come,—and on the imperial hill
Ruin, already proud of the deeds done
　By the old barbarians, there awaits the
　　new,
　Throned on the Palatine, while lost and won
Rome at her feet lies bleeding; and the hue
Of human sacrifice and Roman slaughter
Troubles the clotted air, of late so blue,
And deepens into red the saffron water
　Of Tiber, thick with dead; the helpless
　　priest,
　And still more helpless nor less holy
　　daughter,
Vow'd to their God, have shrieking fled, and
　ceased
　Their ministry: the nations take their prey,
　Iberian, Almain, Lombard, and the beast
And bird, wolf, vulture, more human than
　they
　Are; these but gorge the flesh and lap the
　　gore
　Of the departed, and then go their way;
But those, the human savages, explore
All paths of torture, and insatiate yet,
　With Ugolino hunger prowl for more.
Nine moons shall rise o'er scenes like this
　and set;
　The chiefless army of the dead, which late
Beneath the traitor Prince's banner met,
Hath left its leader's ashes at the gate;
　Had but the royal Rebel lived, perchance
　Thou hadst been spared, but his involved
　　thy fate.
Oh! Rome, the spoiler or the spoil of France,
　From Brennus to the Bourbon, never,
　　never
　Shall foreign standard to thy walls ad-
　　vance,
But Tiber shall become a mournful river.
　Oh! when the strangers pass the Alps
　　and Po,
　Crush them, ye rocks! floods whelm them,
　　and for ever!

Why sleep the idle avalanches so,
　To topple on the lonely pilgrim's head?
　Why doth Eridanus but overflow
The peasant's harvest from his turbid bed?
　Were not each barbarous horde a nobler
　　prey?
　Over Cambyses' host the desert spread
Her sandy ocean, and the sea-waves' sway
　Roll'd over Pharaoh and his thousands,—
　　why,
　Mountains and waters, do ye not as they?
And you, ye men! Romans who dare not
　die,
　Sons of the conquerors who overthrew
　Those who o'erthrew proud Xerxes, where
　　yet lie
The dead whose tomb Oblivion never knew,
　Are the Alps weaker than Thermopylæ?
　Their passes more alluring to the view
Of an invader? is it they, or ye,
　That to each host the mountain-gate unbar,
　And leave the march in peace, the passage
　　free?

Why, Nature's self detains the victor's car,
　And makes your land impregnable, if earth
　Could be so; but alone she will not war,
Yet aids the warrior worthy of his birth
　In a soil where the mothers bring forth
　　men:
　Not so with those whose souls are little
　　worth;
For them no fortress can avail,—the den
　Of the poor reptile which preserves its
　　sting
　Is more secure than walls of adamant,
　　when
The hearts of those within are quivering.
　Are ye not brave? Yes, yet the Ausonian
　　soil
　Hath hearts, and hands, and arms, and hosts
　　to bring
Against Oppression; but how vain the toil,
　While still Division sows the seeds of woe
　And weakness, till the stranger reaps the
　　spoil!
Oh! my own beauteous land! so long laid
　low,
　So long the grave of thy own children's
　　hopes,
　When there is but required a single blow
To break the chain, yet—yet the Avenger
　stops,
　And Doubt and Discord step 'twixt thine
　　and thee,
　And join their strength to that which with
　　thee copes;
What is there wanting then to set thee free,
　And show thy beauty in its fullest light?
　To make the Alps impassable; and we,
Her sons, may do this with *one* deed——Unite.

Canto the Third.

From out the mass of never-dying ill,
　　The Plague, the Prince, the Stranger, and
　　the Sword,
　　Vials of wrath but emptied to refill
And flow again, I cannot all record
　　That crowds on my prophetic eye : the
　　earth
　　And ocean written o'er would not afford
Space for the annal, yet it shall go forth;
　　Yes, all, though not by human pen, is
　　graven,
　　There where the farthest suns and stars
　　have birth,
Spread like a banner at the gate of heaven,
　　The bloody scroll of our millennial wrongs
　　Waves, and the echo of our groans is driven
Athwart the sound of archangelic songs,
　　And Italy, the martyr'd nation's gore,
　　Will not in vain arise to where belongs
Omnipotence and mercy evermore :
　　Like to a harp-string stricken by the wind,
　　The sound of her lament shall, rising o'er
The seraph voices, touch the Almighty Mind.
　　Meantime I, humblest of thy sons, and of
　　Earth's dust by immortality refined
To sense and suffering, though the vain may
　　scoff,
　　And tyrants threat, and meeker victims
　　bow
　　Before the storm because its breath is
　　rough,
To thee, my country ! whom before, as now,
　　I loved and love, devote the mournful lyre
　　And melancholy gift high powers allow
To read the future ; and if now my fire
　　Is not as once it shone o'er thee, forgive !
　　I but foretell thy fortunes—then expire ;
Think not that I would look on them and
　　live.
　　A spirit forces me to see and speak,
　　And for my guerdon grants *not* to survive :
My heart shall be pour'd over thee and break :
　　Yet for a moment, ere I must resume
　　Thy sable web of sorrow, let me take
Over the gleams that flash athwart thy gloom
　　A softer glimpse; some stars shine through
　　thy night,
　　And many meteors, and above thy tomb
Leans sculptured Beauty, which Death cannot
　　blight :
　　And from thine ashes boundless spirits rise
　　To give thee honour, and the earth delight ;
Thy soil shall still be pregnant with the wise,
　　The gay, the learn'd, the generous, and the
　　brave,
　　Native to thee as summer to thy skies,

Conquerors on foreign shores, and the far
　　wave,
　　Discoverers of new worlds, which take their
　　name ;
　　For *thee* alone they have no arm to save,
And all thy recompense is in their fame,
　　A noble one to them, but not to thee—
　　Shall they be glorious, and thou still the
　　same ?
Oh ! more than these illustrious far shall be
　　The being—and even yet he may be born—
　　The mortal saviour who shall set thee free,
And see thy diadem, so changed and worn
　　By fresh barbarians, on thy brow replaced ;
　　And the sweet sun replenishing thy morn,
Thy moral morn, too long with clouds de-
　　faced,
　　And noxious vapours from Avernus risen,
　　Such as all they must breathe who are de-
　　based
By servitude, and have the mind in prison.
　　Yet through this centuried eclipse of woe
　　Some voices shall be heard, and earth shall
　　listen :
Poets shall follow in the path I show,
　　And make it broader : the same brilliant sky
　　Which cheers the birds to song shall bid
　　them glow,
And raise their notes as natural and high ;
　　Tuneful shall be their numbers ; they shall
　　sing
　　Many of love, and some of liberty,
But few shall soar upon that eagle's wing,
　　And look in the sun's face with eagle's
　　gaze,
　　All free and fearless as the feather'd king,
But fly more near the earth ; how many
　　a phrase
　　Sublime shall lavish'd be on some small
　　prince
　　In all the prodigality of praise !
And language, eloquently false, evince
　　The harlotry of genius, which, like beauty,
　　Too oft forgets its own self-reverence,
And looks on prostitution as a duty.
　　He who once enters in a tyrant's hall
　　As guest is slave, his thoughts become
　　a booty,
And the first day which sees the chain en-
　　thral
　　A captive, sees his half of manhood gone—
　　The soul's emasculation saddens all
His spirit ; thus the Bard too near the throne
　　Quails from his inspiration, bound to
　　please,—
　　How servile is the task to please alone !
To smooth the verse to suit his sovereign's
　　ease
　　And royal leisure, nor too much prolong
　　Aught save his eulogy, and find, and seize,

Or force, or forge fit argument of song!
 Thus trammell'd, thus condemn'd to
 Flattery's trebles,
 He toils through all, still trembling to be
 wrong:
For fear some noble thoughts, like heavenly
 rebels,
 Should rise up in high treason to his brain,
 He sings, as the Athenian spoke, with
 pebbles
In's mouth, lest truth should stammer through
 his strain.

 But out of the long file of sonneteers
 There shall be some who will not sing in
 vain,
And he, their prince, shall rank among my
 peers,
 And love shall be his torment; but his grief
 Shall make an immortality of tears,
And Italy shall hail him as the Chief
 Of Poet-lovers, and his higher song
 Of Freedom wreathe him with as green
 a leaf.

But in a farther age shall rise along
 The banks of Po two greater still than he;
 The world which smiled on him shall do
 them wrong
Till they are ashes, and repose with me.
 The first will make an epoch with his lyre,
 And fill the earth with feats of chivalry:
His fancy like a rainbow, and his fire,
 Like that of Heaven, immortal, and his
 thought
Borne onward with a wing that cannot tire;
 Pleasure shall, like a butterfly new caught,
 Flutter her lovely pinions o'er his theme,
 And Art itself seem into Nature wrought
By the transparency of his bright dream.—
 The second, of a tenderer, sadder mood,
 Shall pour his soul out o'er Jerusalem;
He, too, shall sing of arms, and Christian
 blood
 Shed where Christ bled for man; and his
 high harp
 Shall, by the willow over Jordan's flood,
Revive a song of Sion, and the sharp
 Conflict, and final triumph of the brave
 And pious, and the strife of hell to warp
Their hearts from their great purpose, until
 wave
 The red-cross banners where the first red
 Cross
 Was crimson'd from his veins who died to
 save,
Shall be his sacred argument; the loss
 Of years, of favour, freedom, even of fame
 Contested for a time, while the smooth gloss
Of courts would slide o'er his forgotten name
 And call captivity a kindness, meant
 To shield him from insanity or shame,

Such shall be his meet guerdon! who was sent
 To be Christ's Laureate—they reward him
 well!
 Florence dooms me but death or banishment,
Ferrara him a pittance and a cell,
 Harder to bear and less deserved, for I
 Had stung the factions which I strove to
 quell;
But this meek man, who with a lover's eye
 Will look on earth and heaven, and who will
 deign
 To embalm with his celestial flattery,
As poor a thing as e'er was spawn'd to reign,
 What will *he* do to merit such a doom?
 Perhaps he'll *love*,—and is not love in vain
Torture enough without a living tomb?
 Yet it will be so—he and his compeer,
 The Bard of Chivalry, will both consume
In penury and pain too many a year,
 And, dying in despondency, bequeath
 To the kind world, which scarce will yield
 a tear,
A heritage enriching all who breathe
 With the wealth of a genuine poet's soul,
 And to their country a redoubled wreath,
Unmatch'd by time; not Hellas can unroll
 Through her olympiads two such names,
 though one
 Of hers be mighty;—and is this the whole
Of such men's destiny beneath the sun?
 Must all the finer thoughts, the thrilling
 sense,
 The electric blood with which their arteries
 run,
Their body's self turned soul with the intense
 Feeling of that which is, and fancy of
 That which should be, to such a recompense
Conduct? shall their bright plumage on the
 rough
 Storm be still scatter'd? Yes, and it must
 be;
 For, form'd of far too penetrable stuff,
These birds of Paradise but long to flee
 Back to their native mansion, soon they find
 Earth's mist with their pure pinions not
 agree,
And die or are degraded; for the mind
 Succumbs to long infection, and despair,
 And vulture passions flying close behind,
Await the moment to assail and tear;
 And when at length the winged wanderers
 stoop,
 Then is the prey-birds' triumph, then they
 share
The spoil, o'erpower'd at length by one fell
 swoop.
 Yet some have been untouch'd who learn'd
 to bear,
 Some whom no power could ever force to
 droop,

Who could resist themselves even, hardest
 care!
 And task most hopeless; but some such
 have been,
 And if my name amongst the number were,
That destiny austere, and yet serene,
 Were prouder than more dazzling fame un-
 bless'd;
 The Alp's snow summit nearer heaven is
 seen
Than the volcano's fierce eruptive crest,
 Whose splendour from the black abyss is
 flung,
 While the scorch'd mountain, from whose
 burning breast
A temporary torturing flame is wrung,
 Shines for a night of terror, then repels
 Its fire back to the hell from whence it
 sprung,
The hell which in its entrails ever dwells.

—————

Canto the Fourth.

MANY are poets who have never penn'd
 Their inspiration, and perchance the best:
 They felt, and loved, and died, but would
 not lend
Their thoughts to meaner beings; they com-
 press'd
 The god within them, and rejoin'd the stars
Unlaurell'd upon earth, but far more bless'd
Than those who are degraded by the jars
 Of passion, and their frailties link'd to fame,
 Conquerors of high renown, but full of
 scars.
Many are poets but without the name,
 For what is poesy but to create
 From overfeeling good or ill; and aim
At an external life beyond our fate,
 And be the new Prometheus of new men,
 Bestowing fire from heaven, and then, too
 late,
Finding the pleasure given repaid with pain,
 And vultures to the heart of the bestower,
 Who, having lavish'd his high gift in vain,
Lies chain'd to his lone rock by the sea-shore?
 So be it: we can bear.—But thus all they
 Whose intellect is an o'ermastering power
Which still recoils from its encumbering clay
 Or lightens it to spirit, whatsoe'er
 The form which their creations may essay,
Are bards; the kindled marble's bust may
 wear
More poesy upon its speaking brow
Than aught less than the Homeric page may
 bear;

One noble stroke with a whole life may
 glow,
 Or deify the canvas till it shine
 With beauty so surpassing all below,
That they who kneel to idols so divine
 Break no commandment, for high heaven
 is there
 Transfused, transfigurated: and the line
Of poesy, which peoples but the air
 With thought and beings of our thought
 reflected,
 Can do no more: then let the artist share
The palm, he shares the peril, and dejected
 Faints o'er the labour unapproved—Alas!
 Despair and Genius are too oft connected.
Within the ages which before me pass
 Art shall resume and equal even the sway
 Which with Apelles and old Phidias
She held in Hellas' unforgotten day.
 Ye shall be taught by Ruin to revive
 The Grecian forms at least from their
 decay,
And Roman souls at last again shall live
 In Roman works wrought by Italian hands,
 And temples, loftier than the old temples,
 give
New wonders to the world; and while still
 stands
 The austere Pantheon, into heaven shall
 soar
A dome, its image, while the base expands
 Into a fane surpassing all before,
 Such as all flesh shall flock to kneel in:
 ne'er
Such sight hath been unfolded by a door
 As this, to which all nations shall repair
 And lay their sins at this huge gate of
 heaven.
And the bold Architect unto whose care
 The daring charge to raise it shall be given,
 Whom all hearts shall acknowledge as
 their lord,
 Whether into the marble chaos driven
His chisel bid the Hebrew, at whose word
 Israel left Egypt, stop the waves in stone,
 Or hues of Hell be by his pencil pour'd
Over the damn'd before the Judgment-
 throne,
 Such as I saw them, such as all shall see,
 Or fanes be built of grandeur yet unknown,
The stream of his great thoughts shall spring
 from me,
 The Ghibelline, who traversed the three
 realms
 Which form the empire of eternity.
Amidst the clash of swords, and clang of
 helms,
 The age which I anticipate, no less
 Shall be the Age of Beauty, and while
 whelms,

Calamity the nations with distress,
　The genius of my country shall arise,
　A Cedar towering o'er the Wilderness,
Lovely in all its branches to all eyes,
　Fragrant as fair, and recognised afar,
　Wafting its native incense through the
　　skies.

Sovereigns shall pause amidst their sport of
　　war,
　Wean'd for an hour from blood, to turn
　　and gaze
　On canvas or on stone; and they who mar
All beauty upon earth, compell'd to praise,
　Shall feel the power of that which they
　　destroy;
　And Art's mistaken gratitude shall raise
To tyrants who but take her for a toy,
　Emblems and monuments, and prostitute
　Her charms to pontiffs proud, who but em-
　　ploy

The man of genius as the meanest brute
　To bear a burthen, and to serve a need,
　To sell his labours, and his soul to boot.
Who toils for nations may be poor indeed,
　But free; who sweats for monarchs is no
　　more
　Than the gilt chamberlain, who, clothed
　　and fee'd,
Stands sleek and slavish, bowing at his
　　door.

Oh, Power that rulest and inspirest! how
　Is it that they on earth, whose earthly
　　power
Is likest thine in heaven in outward show,
　Least like to thee in attributes divine,
　Tread on the universal necks that bow,
And then assure us that their rights are
　　thine?
　And how is it that they, the sons of fame,
　Whose inspiration seems to them to shine
From high, they whom the nations oftest
　　name,
　Must pass their days in penury or pain,
　Or step to grandeur through the paths of
　　shame,
And wear a deeper brand and gaudier chain?
　Or if their destiny be born aloof
　From lowliness, or tempted thence in vain,
In their own souls sustain a harder proof,
　The inner war of passions deep and fierce?
　Florence! when thy harsh sentence razed
　　my roof,
I loved thee; but the vengeance of my verse,
　The hate of injuries which every year
　Makes greater, and accumulates my curse,

Shall live, outliving all thou holdest dear,
　Thy pride, thy wealth, thy freedom, and
　　even *that*,
　The most infernal of all evils here,
The sway of petty tyrants in a state;
　For such sway is not limited to kings,
　And demagogues yield to them but in date,
As swept off sooner; in all deadly things,
　Which make men hate themselves, and one
　　another,
　In discord, cowardice, cruelty, all that
　　springs,
From Death the Sin-born's incest with his
　　mother,
　In rank oppression in its rudest shape,
　The faction Chief is but the Sultan's
　　brother,
And the worst despot's far less human ape:
　Florence! when this lone spirit, which so
　　long
　Yearn'd, as the captive toiling at escape,
To fly back to thee in despite of wrong,
　An exile, saddest of all prisoners,
　Who has the whole world for a dungeon
　　strong,
Seas, mountains, and the horizon's verge for
　　bars,
　Which shut him from the sole small spot
　　of earth,
　Where—whatsoe'er his fate—he still were
　　hers,
His country's, and might die where he had
　　birth—
　Florence! when this lone spirit shall re-
　　turn
　To kindred spirits, thou wilt feel my worth,
And seek to honour with an empty urn
　The ashes thou shalt ne'er obtain—Alas!
　"What have I done to thee, my people?"
　　Stern
Are all thy dealings, but in this they pass
　The limits of man's common malice, for
　All that a citizen could be I was;
Raised by thy will, all thine in peace or war,
　And for this thou hast warr'd with me—
　　'Tis done:
　I may not overleap the eternal bar
Built up between us, and will die alone,
　Beholding with the dark eye of a seer
　The evil days to gifted souls foreshown,
Foretelling them to those who will not hear.
　As in the old time, till the hour be come
　When Truth shall strike their eyes through
　　many a tear,
And make them own the Prophet in his tomb

The Morgante Maggiore

OF PULCI.

ADVERTISEMENT.

The Morgante Maggiore, of the first canto of which this translation is offered, divides with the Orlando Innamorato the honour of having formed and suggested the style and story of Ariosto. The great defects of Boiardo were his treating too seriously the narratives of chivalry, and his harsh style. Ariosto, in his continuation, by a judicious mixture of the gaiety of Pulci, has avoided the one; and Berni, in his reformation of Boiardo's poem, has corrected the other. Pulci may be considered as the precursor and model of Berni altogether, as he has partly been to Ariosto, however inferior to both his copyists. He is no less the founder of a new style of poetry very lately sprung up in England. I allude to that of the ingenious Whistlecraft. The serious poems on Roncesvalles in the same language, and more particularly the excellent one of Mr. Merivale, are to be traced to the same source. It has never yet been decided entirely whether Pulci's intention was or was not to deride the religion which is one of his favourite topics. It appears to me, that such an intention would have been no less hazardous to the poet than to the priest, particularly in that age and country; and the permission to publish the poem, and its reception among the classics of Italy, prove that it neither was nor is so interpreted. That he intended to ridicule the monastic life, and suffered his imagination to play with the simple dulness of his converted giant, seems evident enough; but surely it were as unjust to accuse him of irreligion on this account, as to denounce Fielding for his Parson Adams, Barnabas, Thwackum, Supple, and the Ordinary in Jonathan Wild,—or Scott, for the exquisite use of his Covenanters in the "Tales of my Landlord."

In the following translation I have used the liberty of the original with the proper names: as Pulci uses Gan, Ganellon, or Ganellone; Carlo, Carlomagno, or Carlomano; Rondel, or Rondello, &c., as it suits his convenience; so has the translator. In other respects the version is faithful to the best of the translator's ability in combining his interpretation of the one language with the not very easy task of reducing it to the same versification in the other. The reader, on comparing it with the original, is requested to remember that the antiquated language of Pulci, however pure, is not easy to the generality of Italians themselves, from its great mixture of Tuscan proverbs; and he may therefore be more indulgent to the present attempt. How far the translator has succeeded, and whether or no he shall continue the work, are questions which the public will decide. He was induced to make the experiment partly by his love for, and partial intercourse with, the Italian language, of which it is so easy to acquire a slight knowledge, and with which it is so nearly impossible for a foreigner to become accurately conversant. The Italian language is like a capricious beauty, who accords her smiles to all, her favours to few, and sometimes least to those who have courted her longest. The translator wished also to present in an English dress a part at least of a poem never yet rendered into a northern language; at the same time that it has been the original of some of the most celebrated productions on this side of the Alps, as well as of those recent experiments in poetry in England which have been already mentioned.

Canto the First.

I.

In the beginning was the Word next God;
　God was the Word, the Word no less was he:
This was in the beginning, to my mode
　Of thinking, and without him nought could
　be:
Therefore, just Lord! from out thy high abode,
　Benign and pious, bid an angel flee,
One only, to be my companion, who
　Shall help my famous, worthy, old song
　through.

II.

And thou, oh Virgin! daughter, mother, bride
　Of the same Lord, who gave to you each
　key
Of heaven, and hell, and everything beside,
　The day thy Gabriel said "All hail!" to
　thee,
Since to thy servants pity's ne'er denied,
　With flowing rhymes, a pleasant style and
　free,
Be to my verses then benignly kind,
And to the end illuminate my mind.

III.

'T was in the season when sad Philòmel
 Weeps with her sister, who remembers
 and
Deplores the ancient woes which both befell,
 And makes the nymphs enamour'd, to the
 hand
Of Phaëton by Phœbus loved so well
 His car (but temper'd by his sire's com-
 can do)
Was given, and on the horizon's verge just
 now
Appear'd, so that Tithonus scratch'd his
 brow:

IV.

When I prepared my bark first to obey,
 As it should still obey, the helm, my mind,
And carry prose or rhyme, and this my lay
 Of Charles the Emperor, whom you will find
By several pens already praised; but they
 Who to diffuse his glory were inclined,
For all that I can see in prose or verse,
Have understood Charles badly, and wrote
 worse.

V.

Leonardo Aretino said already,
 That if, like Pepin, Charles had had a
 writer
Of genius quick, and diligently steady,
 No hero would in history look brighter;
He in the cabinet being always ready,
 And in the field a most victorious fighter,
Who for the church and Christian faith had
 wrought,
Certes, far more than yet is said or thought.

VI.

You still may see at St. Liberatore,
 The abbey, no great way from Manopell,
Erected in the Abruzzi to his glory,
 Because of the great battle in which fell
A pagan king, according to the story,
 And felon people whom Charles sent to hell:
And there are bones so many, and so many,
Near them Giusaffa's would seem few, if any.

VII.

But the world, blind and ignorant, don't prize
 His virtues as I wish to see them: thou,
Florence, by his great bounty don't arise,
 And hast, and may have, if thou wilt allow,
All proper customs and true courtesies:
 Whate'er thou hast acquired from then till
 now,
With knightly courage, treasure, or the lance,
Is sprung from out the noble blood of France.

VIII.

Twelve paladins had Charles in court, of
 whom
 The wisest and most famous was Orlando;
Him traitor Gan conducted to the tomb
 In Roncesvalles, as the villain plann'd too,
While the horn rang so loud, and knell'd the
 doom
 Of their sad rout, though he did all knight
 can do;
And Dante in his comedy has given
To him a happy seat with Charles in heaven.

IX.

'T was Christmas-day; in Paris all his court
 Charles held; the chief, I say, Orlando was,
The Dane; Astolfo there too did resort,
 Also Ansuigi, the gay time to pass
In festival and in triumphal sport,
 The much renown'd St. Dennis being the
 cause;
Angiolin of Bayonne, and Oliver,
And gentle Belinghieri too came there:

X.

Avolio, and Arino, and Othone
 Of Normandy, and Richard Paladin,
Wise Hamo, and the ancient Salamone,
 Walter of Lion's Mount and Baldovin,
Who was the son of the sad Ganellone,
 Were there, exciting too much gladness in
The son of Pepin:—when his knights came
 hither,
He groan'd with joy to see them all together.

XI.

But watchful Fortune, lurking, takes good
 heed
 Ever some bar 'gainst our intents to bring,
While Charles reposed him thus, in word and
 deed,
 Orlando ruled court, Charles, and every-
 thing;
Curst Gan, with envy bursting, had such need
 To vent his spite, that thus with Charles the
 king
One day he openly began to say,
" Orlando must we always then obey?

XII.

" A thousand times I've been about to say,
 Orlando too presumptuously goes on;
Here are we, counts, kings, dukes, to own thy
 sway,
 Hamo, and Otho, Ogier, Solomon,
Each have to honour thee and to obey;
 But he has too much credit near the throne,
Which we won't suffer, but are quite decided
By such a boy to be no longer guided.

XIII.

" And even at Aspramont thou didst begin
 To let him know he was a gallant knight,
And by the fount did much the day to win ;
 But I know *who* that day had won the fight
If it had not for good Gherardo been;
 The victory was Almonte's else ; his sight
He kept upon the standard, and the laurels
In fact and fairness are his earning, Charles.

XIV.

" If thou rememberest being in Gascony,
 When there advanced the nations out of
 Spain,
The Christian cause had suffer'd shamefully,
 Had not his valour driven them back again.
Best speak the truth when there's a reason
 why :
Know then, oh Emperor! that all complain :
As for myself, I shall repass the mounts
O'er which I cross'd with two and sixty counts.

XV.

* 'T is fit thy grandeur should dispense relief,
 So that each here may have his proper part,
For the whole court is more or less in grief :
 Perhaps thou deem'st this lad a Mars in
 heart ? "
Orlando one day heard this speech in brief,
 As by himself it chanced he sate apart :
Displeased he was with Gan because he said it,
But much more still that Charles should give
 him credit.

XVI.

And with the sword he would have murder'd
 Gan,
 But Oliver thrust in between the pair,
And from his hand extracted Durlindan,
 And thus at length they separated were.
Orlando, angry too with Carloman,
 Wanted but little to have slain him there ;
Then forth alone from Paris went the chief,
And burst and madden'd with disdain and
 grief.

XVII.

From Ermellina, consort of the Dane,
 He took Cortana, and then took Rondell,
And on towards Brara prick'd him o'er the
 plain ;
 And when she saw him coming, Aldabelle
Stretch'd forth her arms to clasp her lord
 again :
Orlando, in whose brain all was not well,
As " Welcome, my Orlando, home," she said,
Raised up his sword to smite her on the head,

XVIII.

Like him a fury counsels ; his revenge
 On Gan in that rash act he seem'd to take,
Which Aldabella thought extremely strange ;
 But soon Orlando found himself awake ;
And his spouse took his bridle on this change,
 And he dismounted from his horse, and
 spake
Of everything which pass'd without demur,
And then reposed himself some days with her.

XIX.

Then full of wrath departed from the place,
 And far as pagan countries roam'd astray,
And while he rode, yet still at every pace
 The traitor Gan remember'd by the way ;
And wandering on in error a long space,
 An abbey which in a lone desert lay,
'Midst glens obscure, and distant lands, he
 found,
Which form'd the Christian's and the pagan's
 bound.

XX.

The abbot was call'd Clermont, and by blood
 Descended from Anglante : under cover
Of a great mountain's brow the abbey stood,
 But certain savage giants look'd him over ;
One Passamont was foremost of the brood,
 And Alabaster and Morgante hover
Second and third, with certain slings, and
 throw
In daily jeopardy the place below.

XXI.

The monks could pass the convent gate no
 more,
 Nor leave their cells for water or for wood;
Orlando knock'd, but none would ope, before
 Unto the prior it at length seem'd good ;
Enter'd, he said that he was taught to adore
 Him who was born of Mary's holiest blood,
And was baptized a Christian ; and then
 show'd
How to the abbey he had found his road.

XXII.

Said the abbot, "You are welcome ; what is
 mine
 We give you freely, since that you believe
With us in Mary Mother's Son divine ;
 And that you may not, cavalier, conceive
The cause of our delay to let you in
 To be rusticity, you shall receive
The reason why our gate was barr'd to you :
Thus those who in suspicion live must do.

XXIII.

" When hither to inhabit first we came
 These mountains, albeit that they are ob-
 scure,
As you perceive, yet without fear or blame
 They seem'd to promise an asylum sure :
From savage brutes alone, too fierce to tame,
 'T was fit our quiet dwelling to secure ;
But now, if here we 'd stay, we needs must
 guard
Against domestic beasts with watch and ward.

XXIV.

"These make us stand, in fact, upon the
 watch ;
 For late there have appear'd three giants
 rough ;
What nation or what kingdom bore the batch
 I know not, but they are all of savage stuff ;
When force and malice with some genius
 match,
 You know, they can do all—*we* are not
 enough :
And these so much our orisons derange,
I know not what to do, till matters change.

XXV.

" Our ancient fathers living the desert in,
 For just and holy works were duly fed ;
Think not they lived on locusts sole, 't is
 certain
 That manna was rain'd down from heaven
 instead ;
But here 't is fit we keep on the alert in
 Our bounds, or taste the stones shower'd
 down for bread,
From off yon mountain daily raining faster,
And flung by Passamont and Alabaster.

XXVI.

" The third, Morgante,'s savagest by far ; he
 Plucks up pines, beeches, poplar-trees, and
 oaks,
And flings them, our community to bury ;
 And all that I can do but more provokes."
While thus they parley in the cemetery,
 A stone from one of their gigantic strokes,
Which nearly crush'd Rondell, came tumbling
 over,
So that he took a long leap under cover.

XXVII.

" For God-sake, cavalier, come in with speed ;
 The manna 's falling now," the abbot cried.
" This fellow does not wish my horse should
 feed,
 Dear Abbot," Roland unto him replied.
" Of restiveness he 'd cure him had he need ;
 That stone seems with good will and aim
 applied."

The holy father said, " I don't deceive ;
They 'll one day fling the mountain, I believe."

XXVIII.

Orlando bade them take care of Rondello,
 And also made a breakfast of his own :
" Abbot," he said, "I want to find that fellow
 Who flung at my good horse yon corner-
 stone."
Said the abbot, "Let not my advice seem
 shallow ;
 As to a brother dear I speak alone ;
I would dissuade you, baron, from this strife,
As knowing sure that you will lose your life.

XXIX.

" That Passamont has in his hand three
 darts—
 Such slings, clubs, ballast-stones, that yield
 you must :
You know that giants have much stouter
 hearts
 Than us, with reason, in proportion just :
If go you will, guard well against their arts,
 For these are very barbarous and robust."
Orlando answer'd, " This I 'll see, be sure,
And walk the wild on foot to be secure."

XXX.

The abbot sign'd the great cross on his front,
 " Then go you with God's benison and
 mine :"
Orlando, after he had scaled the mount,
 As the abbot had directed, kept the line
Right to the usual haunt of Passamont ;
 Who, seeing him alone in this design,
Survey'd him fore and aft with eyes obser-
 vant,
Then ask'd him, "If he wish'd to stay as
 servant ?"

XXXI.

And promised him an office of great ease.
 But said Orlando, " Saracen insane !
I come to kill you, if it shall so please
God, not to serve as footboy in your train ;
You with his monks so oft have broke the
 peace—
Vile dog ! 'tis past his patience to sustain."
The giant ran to fetch his arms, quite furious,
When he received an answer so injurious.

XXXII.

And being return'd to where Orlando stood,
 Who had not moved him from the spot,
 and swinging
The cord, he hurl'd a stone with strength so
 rude,
 As show'd a sample of his skill in slinging ;

It roll'd on Count Orlando's helmet good
　　And head, and set both head and helmet
　　　　ringing,
So that he swoon'd with pain as if he died,
But more than dead, he seem'd so stupified.

XXXIII.

Then Passamont, who thought him slain out-
　　　right,
　　Said, "I will go, and while he lies along,
Disarm me: why such craven did I fight?"
　　But Christ his servants ne'er abandons
　　　long,
Especially Orlando, such a knight,
　　As to desert would almost be a wrong.
While the giant goes to put off his defences,
Orlando has recall'd his force and senses:

XXXIV.

And loud he shouted, "Giant, where dost
　　　go?"
　　Thou thought'st me doubtless for the bier
　　　outlaid;
To the right about—without wings thou'rt
　　　too slow
　　To fly my vengeance—currish renegade?
'Twas but by treachery thou laid'st me low."
　　The giant his astonishment betray'd,
And turn'd about, and stopp'd his journey on,
And then he stoop'd to pick up a great stone.

XXXV.

Orlando had Cortana bare in hand;
　　To split the head in twain was what he
　　　schemed:
Cortana clave the skull like a true brand,
　　And pagan Passamont died unredeem'd,
Yet harsh and haughty, as he lay he bann'd,
　　And most devoutly Macon still blasphemed;
But while his crude, rude blasphemies he
　　　heard,
Orlando thank'd the Father and the Word,—

XXXVI.

Saying, "What grace to me thou'st this day
　　　given!
　　And I to thee, O Lord! am ever bound.
I know my life was saved by thee from
　　　heaven,
　　Since by the giant I was fairly down'd.
All things by thee are measured just and
　　even;
　　Our power without thine aid would nought
　　　be found:
I pray thee take heed of me, till I can
At least return once more to Carloman."

XXXVII.

And having said thus much, he went his way;
　　And Alabaster he found out below,
Doing the very best that in him lay
　　To root from out a bank a rock or two.
Orlando, when he reach'd him, loud 'gan say,
　　"How think'st thou, glutton, such a stone
　　　to throw?"
When Alabaster heard his deep voice ring,
He suddenly betook him to his sling,

XXXVIII.

And hurl'd a fragment of a size so large,
　　That if it had in fact fulfill'd its mission,
And Roland not avail'd him of his targe,
　　There would have been no need of a
　　　physician.
Orlando set himself in turn to charge,
　　And in his bulky bosom made incision
With all his sword. The lout fell; but o'er-
　　　thrown, he
However by no means forgot Macone.

XXXIX.

Morgante had a palace in his mode,
　　Composed of branches, logs of wood, and
　　　earth,
And stretch'd himself at ease in this abode,
　　And shut himself at night within his berth.
Orlando knock'd, and knock'd again, to goad
　　The giant from his sleep; and he came forth,
The door to open, like a crazy thing,
　　For a rough dream had shook him slumber-
　　　ing.

XL.

He thought that a fierce serpent had attack'd
　　　him;
　　And Mahomet he call'd; but Mahomet
Is nothing worth, and not an instant back'd him;
　　But praying blessed Jesu, he was set
At liberty from all the fears which rack'd him;
　　And to the gate he came with great regret—
"Who knocks here?" grumbling all the while,
　　　said he.
"That," said Orlando, "you will quickly see:

XLI.

"I come to preach to you, as to your brothers,
　　Sent by the miserable monks—repentance;
For Providence divine, in you and others,
　　Condemns the evil done my new acquaint-
　　　ance.
'Tis writ on high—your wrong must pay
　　　another's:
　　From heaven itself is issued out this sen-
　　　tence.
Know then, that colder now than a pilaster
I left your Passamont and Alabaster."

XLII.

Morgante said, " Oh, gentle cavalier !
 Now by thy God say me no villany ;
The favour of your name I fain would hear,
 And if a Christian, speak for courtesy."
Replied Orlando, " So much to your ear
 I by my faith disclose contentedly ;
Christ I adore, who is the genuine Lord,
And, if you please, by you may be adored."

XLIII.

The Saracen rejoin'd in humble tone,
 " I have had an extraordinary vision ;
A savage serpent fell on me alone,
 And Macon would not pity my condition ;
Hence to thy God, who for ye did atone
 Upon the cross, preferr'd I my petition ;
His timely succour set me safe and free,
And I a Christian am disposed to be."

XLIV.

Orlando answer'd, " Baron just and pious,
 If this good wish your heart can really
 move
To the true God, you will not then deny us
 Eternal honour, you will go above,
And, if you please, as friends we will ally
 us,
 And I will love you with a perfect love.
Your idols are vain liars, full of fraud :
The only true God is the Christians' God.

XLV.

" The Lord descended to the virgin breast
 Of Mary Mother, sinless and divine ;
If you acknowledge the Redeemer blest,
 Without whom neither sun nor star can
 shine,
Abjure bad Macon's false and felon test,
 Your renegado god, and worship mine,
Baptize yourself with zeal, since you re-
 pent."
To which Morgante answer'd, " I 'm content."

XLVI.

And then Orlando to embrace him flew,
 And made much of his convert, as he
 cried,
" To the abbey I will gladly marshal you."
 To whom Morgante, " Let us go," replied ;
" I to the friars have for peace to sue."
 Which thing Orlando heard with inward
 pride,
Saying, " My brother, so devout and good,
Ask the abbot pardon, as I wish you would :

XLVII.

" Since God has granted your illumination,
 Accepting you in mercy for his own,
Humility should be your first oblation."
 Morgante said, " For goodness' sake, make
 known,—
Since that your God is to be mine—your
 station,
 And let your name in verity be shown ;
Then will I everything at your command do."
On which the other said, he was Orlando.

XLVIII.

"Then," quoth the giant, " blessed be Jesu
 A thousand times with gratitude and
 praise !
Oft, perfect baron ! have I heard of you
 Through all the different periods of my days :
And, as I said, to be your vassal too
 I wish, for your great gallantry always."
Thus reasoning, they continued much to say,
And onwards to the abbey went their way.

XLIX.

And by the way about the giants dead
 Orlando with Morgante reason'd : " Be,
For their decease, I pray you, comforted ;
 And, since it is God's pleasure, pardon me ;
A thousand wrongs unto the monks they bred,
 And our true Scripture soundeth openly,
Good is rewarded, and chastised the ill,
Which the Lord never faileth to fulfil :

L.

" Because his love of justice unto all
 Is such, he wills his judgment should de-
 vour
All who have sin, however great or small ;
 But good he well remembers to restore.
Nor without justice holy could we call
 Him, whom I now require you to adore.
All men must make his will their wishes
 sway,
And quickly and spontaneously obey.

LI.

" And here our doctors are of one accord,
 Coming on this point to the same con-
 clusion,
That in their thoughts who praise in heaven
 the Lord
If pity e'er was guilty of intrusion
For their unfortunate relations stored
 In hell below, and damn'd in great con-
 fusion,
Their happiness would be reduced to nought,
And thus unjust the Almighty's self be
 thought.

LII.

"But they in Christ have firmest hope, and all
 Which seems to him, to them too must
 appear
Well done; nor could it otherwise befall;
 He never can in any purpose err.
If sire or mother suffer endless thrall,
 They don't disturb themselves for him or
 her:
What pleases God to them must joy inspire;—
Such is the observance of the eternal choir."

LIII.

"A word unto the wise," Morgante said,
 "Is wont to be enough, and you shall see
How much I grieve about my brethren dead;
 And if the will of God seem good to me,
Just, as you tell me, 'tis in heaven obey'd—
 Ashes to ashes,—merry let us be!
I will cut off the hands from both their
 trunks,
And carry them unto the holy monks.

LIV.

"So that all persons may be sure and certain
 That they are dead, and have no further fear
To wander solitary this desert in,
 And that they may perceive my spirit clear
By the Lord's grace, who hath withdrawn
 the curtain
 Of darkness, making his bright realm
 appear."
He cut his brethren's hands off at these
 words,
And left them to the savage beasts and birds.

LV.

Then to the abbey they went on together,
 Where waited them the abbot in great
 doubt.
The monks, who knew not yet the fact, ran
 thither,
 To their superior, all in breathless rout,
Saying with tremor, "Please to tell us
 whether
 You wish to have this person in or out?"
The abbot, looking through upon the giant,
Too greatly fear'd, at first, to be compliant.

LVI.

Orlando, seeing him thus agitated,
 Said quickly, "Abbot, be thou of good cheer;
He Christ believes, as Christian must be
 rated,
 And hath renounced his Macon false;"
 which here
Morgante with the hands corroborated,
 A proof of both the giants' fate quite clear:

Thence, with due thanks, the abbot God
 adored,
Saying, "Thou hast contented me, oh Lord!"

LVII.

He gazed; Morgante's height he calculated,
 And more than once contemplated his size;
And then he said, "Oh giant celebrated!
 Know, that no more my wonder will arise,
How you could tear and fling the trees you
 late did,
 When I behold your form with my own
 eyes.
You now a true and perfect friend will show
Yourself to Christ, as once you were a foe.

LVIII.

"And one of our apostles, Saul once named,
 Long persecuted sore the faith of Christ,
Till, one day, by the Spirit being inflamed,
 'Why dost thou persecute me thus?' said
 Christ;
And then from his offence he was reclaim'd,
 And went for ever after preaching Christ,
And of the faith became a trump, whose
 sounding
O'er the whole earth is echoing and re-
 bounding.

LIX.

"So, my Morgante, you may do likewise:
 He who repents—thus writes the Evan-
 gelist—
Occasions more rejoicing in the skies
 Than ninety-nine of the celestial list.
You may be sure, should each desire arise
 With just zeal for the Lord, that you'll
 exist
Among the happy saints for evermore;
But you were lost and damn'd to hell before!"

LX.

And thus great honour to Morgante paid
 The abbot: many days they did repose.
One day, as with Orlando they both stray'd,
 And saunter'd here and there, where'er
 they chose,
The abbot show'd a chamber, where array'd
 Much armour was, and hung up certain
 bows;
And one of these Morgante for a whim
Girt on, though useless, he believed, to him.

LXI.

There being a want of water in the place,
 Orlando, like a worthy brother, said,
"Morgante, I could wish you in this case
 To go for water." "You shall be obey'd

In all commands," was the reply, " straight-
　　ways."
Upon his shoulder a great tub he laid,
And went out on his way unto a fountain,
Where he was wont to drink below the
　　mountain.

LXII.

Arrived there, a prodigious noise he hears,
　Which suddenly along the forest spread;
Whereat from out his quiver he prepares
　An arrow for his bow, and lifts his head;
And lo! a monstrous herd of swine appears,
　And onward rushes with tempestuous tread,
And to the fountain's brink precisely pours;
So that the giant's join'd by all the boars.

LXIII.

Morgante at a venture shot an arrow,
　Which pierced a pig precisely in the ear,
And pass'd unto the other side quite thorough;
　So that the boar, defunct, lay tripp'd up
　　near.
Another, to revenge his fellow farrow,
　Against the giant rush'd in fierce career,
And reach'd the passage with so swift a foot,
Morgante was not now in time to shoot.

LXIV.

Perceiving that the pig was on him close,
　He gave him such a punch upon the head,
As floor'd him so that he no more arose,
　Smashing the very bone; and he fell dead
Next to the other. Having seen such blows,
　The other pigs along the valley fled;
Morgante on his neck the bucket took,
Full from the spring, which neither swerved
　　nor shook.

LXV.

The tub was on one shoulder, and there were
　The hogs on t' other, and he brush'd apace
On to the abbey, though by no means near,
　Nor spilt one drop of water in his race.
Orlando, seeing him so soon appear
　With the dead boars, and with that brim-
　　ful vase,
Marvell'd to see his strength so very great;
So did the abbot, and set wide the gate.

LXVI.

The monks, who saw the water fresh and
　　good,
　Rejoiced, but much more to perceive the
　　pork;
All animals are glad at sight of food:
　They lay their breviaries to sleep, and
　　work

With greedy pleasure, and in such a mood,
　That the flesh needs no salt beneath their
　　fork.
Of rankness and of rot there is no fear,
For all the fasts are now left in arrear.

LXVII.

As though they wish'd to burst at once, they
　　ate;
　And gorged so that, as if the bones had been
In water, sorely grieved the dog and cat,
　Perceiving that they all were pick'd too
　　clean.
The abbot, who to all did honour great,
　A few days after this convivial scene,
Gave to Morgante a fine horse, well train'd,
Which he long time had for himself main-
　　tain'd.

LXVIII.

The horse Morgante to a meadow led,
　To gallop, and to put him to the proof,
Thinking that he a back of iron had,
　Or to skim eggs unbroke was light enough;
But the horse, sinking with the pain, fell dead,
　And burst, while cold on earth lay head
　　and hoof.
Morgante said, " Get up, thou sulky cur!"
And still continued pricking with the spur.

LXIX.

But finally he thought fit to dismount,
　And said, " I am as light as any feather,
And he has burst;—to this what say you,
　　count?"
　Orlando answer'd, "Like a ship's mast
　　rather
You seem to me, and with the truck for front:
　Let him go! Fortune wills that we together
Should march, but you on foot Morgante
　　still."
To which the giant answer'd, " So I will.

LXX.

" When there shall be occasion, you will see
　How I approve my courage in the fight."
Orlando said, " I really think you'll be,
　If it should prove God's will, a goodly
　　knight;
Nor will you napping there discover me.
　But never mind your horse, though out of
　　sight
'T were best to carry him into some wood,
If but the means or way I understood."

LXXI.

The giant said, " Then carry him I will,
　Since that to carry me he was so slack—
To render, as the gods do, good for ill;
　But lend a hand to place him on my back.'

Orlando answer'd, " If my counsel still
 May weigh, Morgante, do not undertake
To lift or carry this dead courser, who,
As you have done to him, will do to you.

LXXII.

" Take care he don't revenge himself, though
 dead,
 As Nessus did of old beyond all cure.
I don't know if the fact you've heard or
 read ;
 But he will make you burst, you may be
 sure."
" But help him on my back," Morgante said,
 " And you shall see what weight I can
 endure.
In place, my gentle Roland, of this palfrey,
With all the bells, I'd carry yonder belfry."

LXXIII.

The abbot said, " The steeple may do well,
 But, for the bells, you've broken them, I
 wot."
Morgante answer'd, " Let them pay in hell
 The penalty who lie dead in yon grot ;"
And hoisting up the horse from where he fell,
 He said, " Now look if I the gout have got,
Orlando, in the legs—or if I have force ;"—
And then he made two gambols with the
 horse

LXXIV.

Morgante was like any mountain framed ;
 So if he did this 't is no prodigy ;
But secretly himself Orlando blamed,
 Because he was one of his family ;
And fearing that he might be hurt or maim'd,
 Once more he bade him lay his burden by :
" Put down, nor bear him further the desert
 in."
Morgante said, " I'll carry him for certain."

LXXV.

He did ; and stow'd him in some nook away,
 And to the abbey then return'd with speed.
Orlando said, " Why longer do we stay ?
 Morgante, here is nought to do indeed."
The abbot by the hand he took one day,
 And said, with great respect, he had agreed
To leave his reverence ; but for this decision
He wish'd to have his pardon and permission.

LXXVI.

The honours they continued to receive
 Perhaps exceeded what his merits claim'd :
He said, " I mean, and quickly, to retrieve
 The lost days of time past, which may be
 blamed ;

Some days ago I should have ask'd your
 leave,
 Kind father, but I really was ashamed,
And know not how to show my sentiment,
So much I see you with our stay content.

LXXVII.

" But in my heart I bear through every clime
 The abbot, abbey, and this solitude—
So much I love you in so short a time ;
 For me, from heaven reward you with all
 good
The God so true, the eternal Lord sublime !
 Whose kingdom at the last hath open
 stood.
Meantime we stand expectant of your bless-
 ing,
And recommend us to your prayers with
 pressing."

LXXVIII.

Now when the abbot Count Orlando heard,
 His heart grew soft with inner tenderness,
Such fervour in his bosom bred each word ;
 And, "Cavalier," he said, "if I have less
Courteous and kind to your great worth
 appear'd,
 Than fits me for such gentle blood to ex-
 press,
I know I have done too little in this case ;
But blame our ignorance, and this poor place.

LXXIX.

" We can indeed but honour you with masses,
 And sermons, thanksgivings, and pater-
 nosters,
Hot suppers, dinners (fitting other places
 In verity much rather than the cloisters) ;
But such a love for you my heart embraces,
 For thousand virtues which your bosom
 fosters,
That wheresoe'er you go I too shall be,
And, on the other part, you rest with me.

LXXX.

" This may involve a seeming contradiction ;
 But you I know are sage, and feel, and
 taste,
And understand my speech, with full con-
 viction.
 For your just pious deeds may you be
 graced
With the Lord's great reward and benedic-
 tion,
 By whom you were directed to this waste :
To his high mercy is our freedom due,
For which we render thanks to him and
 you.

LXXXI.

"You saved at once our life and soul: such fear
 The giants caused us, that the way was lost
By which we could pursue a fit career
 In search of Jesus and the saintly host;
And your departure breeds such sorrow here,
 That comfortless we all are to our cost;
But months and years you would not stay in sloth,
Nor are you form'd to wear our sober cloth,

LXXXII.

"But to bear arms, and wield the lance; indeed,
 With these as much is done as with this cowl;
In proof of which the Scriptures you may read.
 This giant up to heaven may bear his soul
By your compassion: now in peace proceed.
 Your state and name I seek not to unroll;
But, if I'm ask'd, this answer shall be given,
That here an angel was sent down from heaven.

LXXXIII.

"If you want armour or aught else, go in,
 Look o'er the wardrobe, and take what you choose,
And cover with it o'er this giant's skin."
 Orlando answer'd, "If there should lie loose
Some armour, ere our journey we begin,
 Which might be turn'd to my companion's use,
The gift would be acceptable to me."
The abbot said to him, "Come in and see."

LXXXIV.

And in a certain closet, where the wall
 Was cover'd with old armour like a crust,
The abbot said to them, "I give you all."
 Morgante rummaged piecemeal from the dust
The whole, which, save one cuirass, was too small,
 And that too had the mail inlaid with rust.
They wonder'd how it fitted him exactly,
Which ne'er has suited others so compactly.

LXXXV.

'Twas an immeasurable giant's, who
 By the great Milo of Agrante fell
Before the abbey many years ago.
 The story on the wall was figured well;
In the last moment of the abbey's foe,
 Who long had waged a war implacable:
Precisely as the war occurr'd they drew him,
And there was Milo as he overthrew him.

LXXXVI.

Seeing this history, Count Orlando said
 In his heart, "Oh God, who in the sky
Know'st all things! how was Milo hither led?
 Who caused the giant in this place to die?"
And certain letters, weeping, then he read,
 So that he could not keep his visage dry,—
As I will tell in the ensuing story.
From evil keep you the high King of glory!

Francesca of Rimini.

FROM THE INFERNO OF DANTE.

CANTO THE FIFTH.

"THE land where I was born sits by the
 seas,
 Upon that shore to which the Po descends,
 With all his followers, in search of peace.
Love, which the gentle heart soon appre-
 hends,
 Seized him for the fair person which was
 ta'en
 From me, and me even yet the mode
 offends.
Love, who to none beloved to love again
 Remits, seized me with wish to please, so
 strong,
 That, as thou seest, yet, yet it doth remain.
Love to one death conducted us along,
 But Caina waits for him our life who
 ended:"
 These were the accents utter'd by her
 tongue.—
Since I first listen'd to these souls offended,
 I bow'd my visage, and so kept it till—
 "What think'st thou," said the bard; when
 I unbended,
And recommenced: "Alas! unto such ill
 How many sweet thoughts, what strong
 ecstasies,
 Led these their evil fortune to fulfil!"

And then I turn'd unto their side my eyes,
 And said, "Francesca, thy sad destinies
 Have made me sorrow till the tears arise.
But tell me, in the season of sweet sighs,
 By what and how thy love to passion rose,
 So as his dim desires to recognise?"
Then she to me: "The greatest of all woes
 Is to remind us of our happy days
 In misery, and that thy teacher knows.
But if to learn our passion's first root preys
 Upon thy spirit with such sympathy,
 I will do even as he who weeps and says.
We read one day for pastime, seated nigh,
 Of Lancilot, how love enchain'd him too.
 We were alone, quite unsuspiciously.
But oft our eyes met, and our cheeks in
 hue
 All o'er discolour'd by that reading were;
 But one point only wholly us o'erthrew;
When we read the long-sigh'd-for smile of
 her,
 To be thus kiss'd by such devoted lover,
 He who from me can be divided ne'er
Kiss'd my mouth, trembling in the act all
 over:
 Accursed was the book and he who wrote!
 That day no further leaf we did uncover."
While thus one spirit told us of their lot,
 The other wept, so that with pity's thralls
 I swoon'd, as if by death I had been smote,
And fell down even as a dead body falls.

DRAMAS.

Manfred:

A DRAMATIC POEM.

"There are more things in heaven and earth, Horatio,
Than are dreamt of in your philosophy."

Dramatis Personæ.

MANFRED.

CHAMOIS HUNTER.

ABBOT OF ST. MAURICE.

MANUEL.

HERMAN.

WITCH OF THE ALPS.

ARIMANES.

NEMESIS.

THE DESTINIES.

SPIRITS, &c.

The Scene of the Drama is amongst the Higher Alps—partly in the Castle of Manfred, and partly in the Mountains.

Act I.

Scene I.—MANFRED *alone.—Scene, a Gothic Gallery.—Time, Midnight.*

Man. The lamp must be replenish'd, but even then
It will not burn so long as I must watch:
My slumbers—if I slumber—are not sleep,
But a continuance of enduring thought,
Which then I can resist not: in my heart
There is a vigil, and these eyes but close
To look within; and yet I live, and bear
The aspect and the form of breathing men.
But grief should be the instructor of the wise;
Sorrow is knowledge: they who know the most
Must mourn the deepest o'er the fatal truth,
The Tree of Knowledge is not that of Life.
Philosophy and science, and the springs
Of wonder, and the wisdom of the world,
I have essay'd, and in my mind there is
A power to make these subject to itself—
But they avail not: I have done men good,
And I have met with good even among men—
But this avail'd not: I have had my foes,
And none have baffled, many fallen before me—

But this avail'd not:—Good, or evil, life,
Powers, passions, all I see in other beings,
Have been to me as rain unto the sands,
Since that all-nameless hour. I have no dread,
And feel the curse to have no natural fear,
Nor fluttering throb, that beats with hopes or wishes,
Or lurking love of something on the earth.
Now to my task.—
 Mysterious agency!
Ye spirits of the unbounded Universe!
Whom I have sought in darkness and in light—
Ye, who do compass earth about, and dwell
In subtler essence—ye, to whom the tops
Of mountains inaccessible are haunts,
And earth's and ocean's caves familiar things—
I call upon ye by the written charm
Which gives me power upon you—Rise! Appear!
 [*A pause.*
They come not yet.—Now by the voice of him
Who is the first among you—by this sign,
Which makes you tremble—by the claims of him
Who is undying,—Rise! Appear!——Appear!
 [*A pause.*

If it be so—Spirits of earth and air,
Ye shall not thus elude me : by a power,
Deeper than all yet urged, a tyrant-spell,
Which had its birthplace in a star con-
 demn'd,
The burning wreck of a demolish'd world,
A wandering hell in the eternal space ;
By the strong curse which is upon my
 soul,
The thought which is within me and around
 me,
I do compel ye to my will—Appear !

 [*A star is seen at the darker end of the
 gallery: it is stationary; and a voice
 is heard singing.*

FIRST SPIRIT.

Mortal ! to thy bidding bow'd,
From my mansion in the cloud,
Which the breath of twilight builds,
And the summer's sunset gilds
With the azure and vermilion,
Which is mix'd for my pavilion ;
Though thy quest may be forbidden,
On a star-beam I have ridden :
To thine adjuration bow'd,
Mortal—be thy wish avow'd !

Voice of the SECOND SPIRIT.

Mont Blanc is the monarch of mountains ;
 They crown'd him long ago
On a throne of rocks, in a robe of clouds,
 With a diadem of snow.
Around his waist are forests braced,
 The Avalanche in his hand ;
But ere it fall, that thundering ball
 Must pause for my command.
The Glacier's cold and restless mass
 Moves onward day by day ;
But I am he who bids it pass,
 Or with its ice delay.
I am the spirit of the place,
 Could make the mountain bow
And quiver to his cavern'd base—
 And what with me wouldst *Thou?*

Voice of the THIRD SPIRIT.

In the blue depth of the waters,
 Where the wave hath no strife,
Where the wind is a stranger,
 And the sea-snake hath life,
Where the Mermaid is decking
 Her green hair with shells,
Like the storm on the surface
 Came the sound of thy spells ;

O'er my calm Hall of Coral
 The deep echo roll'd—
To the Spirit of Ocean
 Thy wishes unfold!

FOURTH SPIRIT.

Where the slumbering earthquake
 Lies pillow'd on fire,
And the lakes of bitumen
 Rise boilingly higher ;
Where the roots of the Andes
 Strike deep in the earth,
As their summits to heaven
 Shoot soaringly forth ;
I have quitted my birthplace,
 Thy bidding to bide—
Thy spell hath subdued me,
 Thy will be my guide !

FIFTH SPIRIT.

I am the Rider of the wind,
 The Stirrer of the storm ;
The hurricane I left behind
 Is yet with lightning warm ;
To speed to thee, o'er shore and sea
 I swept upon the blast :
The fleet I met sail'd well, and yet
 'Twill sink ere night be past.

SIXTH SPIRIT.

My dwelling is the shadow of the night,
Why doth thy magic torture me with light ?

SEVENTH SPIRIT.

The star which rules thy destiny
Was ruled, ere earth began, by me :
It was a world as fresh and fair
As e'er revolved round sun in air ;
Its course was free and regular,
Space bosom'd not a lovelier star.
The hour arrived—and it became
A wandering mass of shapeless flame,
A pathless comet, and a curse,
The menace of the universe ;
Still rolling on with innate force,
Without a sphere, without a course,
A bright deformity on high,
The monster of the upper sky !
And thou ! beneath its influence born—
Thou worm ! whom I obey and scorn—
Forced by a power (which is not thine,
And lent thee but to make thee mine)
For this brief moment to descend,
Where these weak spirits round thee bend
And parley with a thing like thee—
What wouldst thou, Child of Clay ! with
 me ?

The SEVEN SPIRITS.

Earth, ocean, air, night, mountains, winds,
　　thy star,
Are at thy beck and bidding, Child of Clay!
Before thee at thy quest their spirits are—
　　What wouldst thou with us, son of mor-
　　tals—say?

Man. Forgetfulness——
First Spirit. Of what—of whom—and why?
Man. Of that which is within me; read it
　　there—
Ye know it, and I cannot utter it.
Spirit. We can but give thee that which
　　we possess:
Ask of us subjects, sovereignty, the power
O'er earth—the whole, or portion—or a sign
Which shall control the elements, whereof
We are the dominators,—each and all,
These shall be thine.
Man. 　　　　　　Oblivion, self-oblivion!
Can ye not wring from out the hidden realms
Ye offer so profusely what I ask?
Spirit. It is not in our essence, in our
　　skill;
But—thou may'st die.
Man. 　　　　Will death bestow it on me?
Spirit. We are immortal, and do not for-
　　get;
We are eternal; and to us the past
Is, as the future, present. Art thou an-
　　swer'd?
Man. Ye mock me—but the power which
　　brought ye here
Hath made you mine. Slaves, scoff not at
　　my will!
The mind, the spirit, the Promethean spark,
The lightning of my being, is as bright,
Pervading, and far darting as your own,
And shall not yield to yours, though coop'd
　　in clay!
Answer, or I will teach you what I am.
Spirit. We answer as we answer'd; our
　　reply
Is even in thine own words.
Man. 　　　　　　　Why say ye so?
Spirit. If, as thou say'st, thine essence be
　　as ours,
We have replied in telling thee, the thing
Mortals call death hath nought to do with us.
Man. I then have call'd ye from your
　　realms in vain;
Ye cannot, or ye will not, aid me.
Spirit. 　　　　　　　　　　Say,
What we possess we offer; it is thine:
Bethink ere thou dismiss us; ask again;
Kingdom, and sway, and strength, and length
　　of days——

Man. Accursed! what have I to do with
　　days?
They are too long already.—Hence—begone!
Spirit. Yet pause: being here, our will
　　would do thee service;
Bethink thee, is there then no other gift
Which we can make not worthless in thine
　　eyes?
Man. No, none: yet stay—one moment,
　　ere we part,
I would behold ye face to face. I hear
Your voices, sweet and melancholy sounds,
As music on the waters; and I see
The steady aspect of a clear large star;
But nothing more. Approach me as ye are,
Or one, or all, in your accustom'd forms.
Spirit. We have no forms, beyond the
　　elements
Of which we are the mind and principle:
But choose a form—in that we will appear.
Man. I have no choice; there is no form
　　on earth
Hideous or beautiful to me. Let him,
Who is most powerful of ye, take such aspect
As unto him may seem most fitting—Come!
Seventh Spirit (*appearing in the shape of
　　a beautiful female figure*). Behold!
Man. Oh God! if it be thus, and *thou*
Art not a madness and a mockery,
I yet might be most happy, I will clasp
　　thee,
And we again will be——
　　　　　　　　　　[*The figure vanishes.*
　　　　　　　　　My heart is crush'd!
　　　　　　　　　[MANFRED *falls senseless.*

(*A voice is heard in the Incantation which
　　follows.*)

When the moon is on the wave,
　　And the glow-worm in the grass,
And the meteor on the grave,
　　And the wisp on the morass;
When the falling stars are shooting,
And the answer'd owls are hooting,
And the silent leaves are still
In the shadow of the hill,
Shall my soul be upon thine,
With a power and with a sign.

Though thy slumber may be deep,
Yet thy spirit shall not sleep;
There are shades which will not vanish,
There are thoughts thou canst not banish;
By a power to thee unknown,
Thou canst never be alone;
Thou art wrapt as with a shroud,
Thou art gather'd in a cloud;
And for ever shalt thou dwell
In the spirit of this spell.

Though thou seest me not pass by,
Thou shalt feel me with thine eye
As a thing that, though unseen,
Must be near thee, and hath been;
And when in that secret dread
Thou hast turn'd around thy head,
Thou shalt marvel I am not
As thy shadow on the spot,
And the power which thou dost feel
Shall be what thou must conceal.

And a magic voice and verse
Hath baptized thee with a curse;
And a spirit of the air
Hath begirt thee with a snare;
In the wind there is a voice
Shall forbid thee to rejoice;
And to thee shall night deny
All the quiet of her sky;
And the day shall have a sun,
Which shall make thee wish it done.

From thy false tears I did distil
An essence which hath strength to kill;
From thy own heart I then did wring
The black blood in its blackest spring;
From thy own smile I snatch'd the snake,
For there it coil'd as in a brake;
From thy own lip I drew the charm
Which gave all these their chiefest harm;
In proving every poison known,
I found the strongest was thine own.

By thy cold breast and serpent smile,
By thy unfathom'd gulfs of guile,
By that most seeming virtuous eye,
By thy shut soul's hypocrisy;
By the perfection of thine art
Which pass'd for human thine own heart;
By thy delight in others' pain,
And by thy brotherhood of Cain,
I call upon thee! and compel
Thyself to be thy proper Hell!

And on thy head I pour the vial
Which doth devote thee to this trial;
Nor to slumber, nor to die,
Shall be in thy destiny;
Though thy death shall still seem near
To thy wish, but as a fear;
Lo! the spell now works around thee,
And the clankless chain hath bound thee;
O'er thy heart and brain together
Hath the word been pass'd—now wither!

Scene II.

*The Mountain of the Jungfrau.—Time, Morn-
ing.—*MANFRED *alone upon the Cliffs.*

Man. The spirits I have raised abandon
 me,
The spells which I have studied baffle me,
The remedy I reck'd of tortured me;
I lean no more on superhuman aid;
It hath no power upon the past, and for
The future, till the past be gulf'd in darkness,
It is not of my search.—My mother Earth!
And thou fresh breaking Day, and you, ye
 Mountains,
Why are ye beautiful? I cannot love ye.
And thou, the bright eye of the universe,
That openest over all, and unto all
Art a delight—thou shin'st not on my heart.
And you, ye crags, upon whose extreme edge
I stand, and on the torrent's brink beneath
Behold the tall pines dwindled as to shrubs
In dizziness of distance; when a leap,
A stir, a motion, even a breath, would bring
My breast upon its rocky bosom's bed
To rest for ever—wherefore do I pause?
I feel the impulse—yet I do not plunge;
I see the peril—yet do not recede;
And my brain reels—and yet my foot is firm:
There is a power upon me which withholds,
And makes it my fatality to live,—
If it be life to wear within myself
This barrenness of spirit, and to be
My own soul's sepulchre, for I have ceased
To justify my deeds unto myself—
The last infirmity of evil. Ay,
Thou winged and cloud-cleaving minister,
 [*An eagle passes.*
Whose happy flight is highest into heaven,
Well may'st thou swoop so near me—I
 should be
Thy prey, and gorge thine eaglets; thou art
 gone
Where the eye cannot follow thee; but thine
Yet pierces downward, onward, or above,
With a pervading vision.—Beautiful!
How beautiful is all this visible world!
How glorious in its action and itself!
But we, who name ourselves its sovereigns,
 we,
Half dust, half deity, alike unfit
To sink or soar, with our mix'd essence make
A conflict of its elements, and breathe
The breath of degradation and of pride,
Contending with low wants and lofty will,
Till our mortality predominates,
And men are—what they name not to them-
 selves,
And trust not to each other. Hark! the
 note, [*The Shepherd's pipe in the
 distance is heard.*
The natural music of the mountain reed—
For here the patriarchal days are not
A pastoral fable—pipes in the liberal air,
Mix'd with the sweet bells of the sauntering
 herd;
My soul would drink those echoes. Oh, that
 I were

The viewless spirit of a lovely sound,
A living voice, a breathing harmony,
A bodiless enjoyment—born and dying
With the blest tone which made me !

Enter from below a CHAMOIS HUNTER.

Chamois Hunter. Even so
This way the chamois leapt: her nimble
 feet
Have baffled me ; my gains to-day will scarce
Repay my break-neck travail.—What is here ?
Who seems not of my trade, and yet hath
 reach'd
A height which none even of our moun-
 taineers,
Save our best hunters, may attain : his garb
Is goodly, his mien manly, and his air
Proud as a free-born peasant's, at this dis-
 tance :
I will approach him nearer.
 Man. (*not perceiving the other*). To be
 thus—
Grey-hair'd with anguish, like these blasted
 pines,
Wrecks of a single winter, barkless, branch-
 less,
A blighted trunk upon a cursed root,
Which but supplies a feeling to decay—
And to be thus, eternally but thus,
Having been otherwise ! Now furrow'd o'er
With wrinkles, plough'd by moments,—not
 by years,—
And hours, all tortured into ages—hours
Which I outlive !—Ye toppling crags of ice !
Ye avalanches, whom a breath draws down
In mountainous o'erwhelming, come and
 crush me !
I hear ye momently above, beneath,
Crash with a frequent conflict; but ye pass,
And only fall on things that still would live ;
On the young flourishing forest, or the hut
And hamlet of the harmless villager.
 C. Hun. The mists begin to rise from up
 the valley;
I 'll warn him to descend, or he may chance
To lose at once his way and life together.
 Man. The mists boil up around the
 glaciers ; clouds
Rise curling fast beneath me, white and
 sulphury,
Like foam from the roused ocean of deep
 Hell,
Whose every wave breaks on a living shore,
Heap'd with the damn'd like pebbles.—I am
 giddy.
 C. Hun. I must approach him cautiously;
 if near,
A sudden step will startle him, and he
Seems tottering already.

 Man. Mountains have fallen,
Leaving a gap in the clouds, and with the
 shock
Rocking their Alpine brethren ; filling up
The ripe green valleys with destruction's
 splinters ;
Damming the rivers with a sudden dash,
Which crush'd the waters into mist and
 made
Their fountains find another channel—thus,
Thus, in its old age, did Mount Rosenberg—
Why stood I not beneath it ?
 C. Hun. Friend ! have a care,
Your next step may be fatal !—for the love
Of him who made you, stand not on that
 brink !
 Man. (*not hearing him*). Such would have
 been for me a fitting tomb;
My bones had then been quiet in their depth;
They had not then been strewn upon the
 rocks
For the wind's pastime—as thus—thus they
 shall be—
In this one plunge.—Farewell, ye opening
 heavens !
Look not upon me thus reproachfully—
You were not meant for me—Earth ! take
 these atoms !
 [*As* MANFRED *is in act to spring from the
 cliff, the* CHAMOIS HUNTER *seizes and
 retains him with a sudden grasp.*
 C. Hun. Hold, madman !—though aweary
 of thy life,
Stain not our pure vales with thy guilty
 blood :
Away with me ——— I will not quit my hold.
 Man. I am most sick at heart—nay, grasp
 me not—
I am all feebleness—the mountains whirl
Spinning around me —— I grow blind ——
 What art thou ?
 C. Hun. I 'll answer that anon. Away
 with me—
The clouds grow thicker —— there—now lean
 on me—
Place your foot here—here, take this staff,
 and cling
A moment to that shrub—now give me your
 hand,
And hold fast by my girdle—softly—well—
The Chalet will be gain'd within an hour :
Come on, we 'll quickly find a surer footing,
And something like a pathway, which the
 torrent
Hath wash'd since winter.—Come, 't is bravely
 done—
You should have been a hunter.—Follow
 me.
 [*As they descend the rocks with
 difficulty, the scene closes.*

Act II.

Scene I.—*A Cottage amongst the Bernese
Alps.*

MANFRED *and the* CHAMOIS HUNTER.

C. Hun. No, no—yet pause—thou must
not yet go forth:
Thy mind and body are alike unfit
To trust each other, for some hours, at least;
When thou art better, I will be thy guide—
But whither?
Man.　　It imports not: I do know
My route full well, and need no further
guidance.
C. Hun. Thy garb and gait bespeak thee
of high lineage—
One of the many chiefs, whose castled crags
Look o'er the lower valleys—which of these
May call thee lord? I only know their
portals;
My way of life leads me but rarely down
To bask by the huge hearths of those old
halls,
Carousing with the vassals; but the paths,
Which step from out our mountains to their
doors,
I know from childhood—which of these is
thine?
Man. No matter.
C. Hun.　　Well, sir, pardon me the
question,
And be of better cheer. Come, taste my
wine;
'Tis of an ancient vintage; many a day
'Thas thaw'd my veins among our glaciers,
now
Let it do thus for thine—Come, pledge me
fairly.
Man. Away, away! there's blood upon the
brim!
Will it then never—never sink in the earth?
C. Hun. What dost thou mean? thy senses
wander from thee.
Man. I say 'tis blood—my blood! the pure
warm stream
Which ran in the veins of my fathers, and in
ours
When we were in our youth, and had one
heart,
And loved each other as we should not love,
And this was shed: but still it rises up,
Colouring the clouds, that shut me out from
heaven,
Where thou art not—and I shall never be.
C. Hun. Man of strange words, and some
half-maddening sin,
Which makes thee people vacancy, whate'er

Thy dread and sufferance be, there's comfort
yet—
The aid of holy men, and heavenly pa-
tience—
Man. Patience and patience! Hence—that
word was made
For brutes of burthen, not for birds of prey;
Preach it to mortals of a dust like thine,—
I am not of thine order.
C. Hun.　　　　Thanks to heaven!
I would not be of thine for the free fame
Of William Tell; but whatsoe'er thine ill,
It must be borne, and these wild starts are
useless.
Man. Do I not bear it?—Look on me—I
live.
C. Hun. This is convulsion, and no health-
ful life.
Man. I tell thee, man! I have lived many
years,
Many long years, but they are nothing now
To those which I must number: ages—ages—
Space and eternity—and consciousness,
With the fierce thirst of death—and still
unslaked!
C. Hun. Why, on thy brow the seal of
middle age
Hath scarce been set; I am thine elder far.
Man. Think'st thou existence doth depend
on time?
It doth; but actions are our epochs: mine
Have made my days and nights imperishable,
Endless, and all alike, as sands on the shore,
Innumerable atoms; and one desert,
Barren and cold, on which the wild waves
break,
But nothing rests, save carcasses and wrecks,
Rocks, and the salt-surf weeds of bitterness.
C. Hun. Alas! he's mad—but yet I must
not leave him.
Man. I would I were—for then the things
I see
Would be but a distemper'd dream.
C. Hun.　　　　　What is it
That thou dost see, or think thou look'st
upon?
Man. Myself, and thee—a peasant of the
Alps—
Thy humble virtues, hospitable home,
And spirit patient, pious, proud, and free;
Thy self-respect, grafted on innocent thoughts;
Thy days of health, and nights of sleep; thy
toils,
By danger dignified, yet guiltless; hopes
Of cheerful old age and a quiet grave,
With cross and garland over its green turf,
And thy grandchildren's love for epitaph;
This do I see—and then I look within—
It matters not—my soul was scorch'd al-
ready!

C. Hun. And wouldst thou then exchange
 thy lot for mine?
 Man. No, friend! I would not wrong thee,
 nor exchange
My lot with living being: I can bear—
However wretchedly, 'tis still to bear—
In life what others could not brook to dream,
But perish in their slumber.
 C. Hun. And with this—
This cautious feeling for another's pain,
Canst thou be black with evil?—say not so.
Can one of gentle thoughts have wreak'd
 revenge
Upon his enemies?
 Man. Oh! no, no, no!
My injuries came down on those who loved
 me—
On those whom I best loved: I never quell'd
An enemy, save in my just defence—
But my embrace was fatal.
 C. Hun. Heaven give thee rest!
And penitence restore thee to thyself;
My prayers shall be for thee.
 Man. I need them not—
But can endure thy pity. I depart—
'Tis time—farewell!—Here's gold, and thanks
 for thee—
No words—it is thy due.—Follow me not—
I know my path—the mountain peril's past:
And once again I charge thee, follow not!
 [*Exit* MANFRED.

Scene II.

A lower Valley in the Alps.—A Cataract.

Enter MANFRED.

It is not noon—the sunbow's rays still arch
The torrent with the many hues of heaven,
And roll the sheeted silver's waving column
O'er the crag's headlong perpendicular,
And fling its lines of foaming light along,
And to and fro, like the pale courser's tail,
The Giant steed, to be bestrode by Death,
As told in the Apocalypse. No eyes
But mine now drink this sight of loveliness;
I should be sole in this sweet solitude,
And with the Spirit of the place divide
The homage of these waters.—I will call her.
 [MANFRED *takes some of the water into*
 the palm of his hand, and flings it
 into the air, muttering the adjuration.
 After a pause, the WITCH OF THE
 ALPS *rises beneath the arch of the*
 sunbow of the torrent.
Beautiful Spirit! with thy hair of light,
And dazzling eyes of glory, in whose form
The charms of earth's least mortal daughters
 grow
To an unearthly stature, in an essence

Of purer elements; while the hues of youth,—
Carnation'd like a sleeping infant's cheek,
Rock'd by the beating of her mother's heart,
Or the rose tints, which summer's twilight
 leaves
Upon the lofty glacier's virgin snow,
The blush of earth embracing with her hea-
 ven,—
Tinge thy celestial aspect, and make tame
The beauties of the sunbow which bends o'er
 thee.
Beautiful Spirit! in thy calm clear brow,
Wherein is glass'd serenity of soul,
Which of itself shows immortality,
I read that thou wilt pardon to a Son
Of Earth, whom the abstruser powers permit
At times to commune with them—if that he
Avail him of his spells—to call thee thus,
And gaze on thee a moment.
 Witch. Son of Earth!
I know thee, and the powers which give thee
 power;
I know thee for a man of many thoughts,
And deeds of good and ill, extreme in both,
Fatal and fated in thy sufferings.
I have expected this—what wouldst thou
 with me?
 Man. To look upon thy beauty—nothing
 further.
The face of the earth hath madden'd me,
 and I
Take refuge in her mysteries, and pierce
To the abodes of those who govern her—
But they can nothing aid me. I have sought
From them what they could not bestow, and
 now
I search no further.
 Witch. What could be the quest
Which is not in the power of the most power-
 ful,
The rulers of the invisible?
 Man. A boon;
But why should I repeat it? 't were in vain.
 Witch. I know not that; let thy lips utter
 it.
 Man. Well, though it torture me, 'tis but
 the same;
My pang shall find a voice. From my youth
 upwards
My spirit walk'd not with the souls of men,
Nor look'd upon the earth with human eyes;
The thirst of their ambition was not mine,
The aim of their existence was not mine;
My joys, my griefs, my passions, and my
 powers,
Made me a stranger; though I wore the
 form,
I had no sympathy with breathing flesh,
Nor midst the creatures of clay that girded
 me

Was there but one who—but of her anon.
I said with men, and with the thoughts of
 men,
I held but slight communion ; but instead,
My joy was in the wilderness,—to breathe
The difficult air of the iced mountain's top,
Where the birds dare not build, nor insect's
 wing
Flit o'er the herbless granite ; or to plunge
Into the torrent, and to roll along
On the swift whirl of the new breaking wave
Of river-stream, or ocean, in their flow.
In these my early strength exulted ; or
To follow through the night the moving
 moon,
The stars and their development ; or catch
The dazzling lightnings till my eyes grew
 dim ;
Or to look, list'ning, on the scatter'd leaves,
While Autumn winds were at their evening
 song.
These were my pastimes, and to be alone ;
For if the beings, of whom I was one,—
Hating to be so,—cross'd me in my path,
I felt myself degraded back to them,
And was all clay again. And then I dived,
In my lone wanderings, to the caves of death,
Searching its cause in its effect ; and drew
From wither'd bones, and skulls, and heap'd
 up dust,
Conclusions most forbidden. Then I pass'd
The nights of years in sciences untaught,
Save in the old time ; and with time and toil,
And terrible ordeal, and such penance
As in itself hath power upon the air,
And spirits that do compass air and earth,
Space, and the peopled infinite, I made
Mine eyes familiar with Eternity,
Such as, before me, did the Magi, and
He who from out their fountain dwellings
 raised
Eros and Anteros, at Gadara,
As I do thee ;—and with my knowledge grew
The thirst of knowledge, and the power and
 joy
Of this most bright intelligence, until—
 Witch. Proceed.
 Man. Oh ! I but thus prolong'd my words,
Boasting these idle attributes, because
As I approach the core of my heart's grief—
But to my task. I have not named to thee
Father or mother, mistress, friend, or being,
With whom I wore the chain of human
 ties ;
If I had such, they seem'd not such to me ;
Yet there was one—
 Witch. Spare not thyself—proceed.
 Man. She was like me in lineaments ; her
 eyes,
Her hair, her features, all, to the very tone

Even of her voice, they said were like to
 mine ;
But soften'd all, and temper'd into beauty :
She had the same lone thoughts and wander-
 ings,
The quest of hidden knowledge, and a mind
To comprehend the universe : nor these
Alone, but with them gentler powers than
 mine,
Pity, and smiles, and tears—which I had not ;
And tenderness—but that I had for her ;
Humility—and that I never had.
Her faults were mine—her virtues were her
 own—
I loved her, and destroy'd her !
 Witch. With thy hand ?
 Man. Not with my hand, but heart, which
 broke her heart ;
It gazed on mine, and wither'd. I have shed
Blood, but not hers—and yet her blood was
 shed ;
I saw—and could not stanch it.
 Witch. And for this—
A being of the race thou dost despise,
The order, which thine own would rise
 above,
Mingling with us and ours,—thou dost forego
The gifts of our great knowledge, and shrink'st
 back
To recreant mortality——Away !
 Man. Daughter of Air ! I tell thee, since
 that hour—
But words are breath—look on me in my
 sleep,
Or watch my watchings—Come and sit by
 me !
My solitude is solitude no more,
But peopled with the Furies ;—I have gnash'd
My teeth in darkness till returning morn,
Then cursed myself till sunset ;—I have
 pray'd
For madness as a blessing—'t is denied me.
I have affronted death—but in the war
Of elements the waters shrunk from me,
And fatal things pass'd harmless ; the cold
 hand
Of an all-pitiless demon held me back,
Back by a single hair, which would not break,
In fantasy, imagination, all
The affluence of my soul—which one day
 was
A Crœsus in creation—I plunged deep,
But, like an ebbing wave, it dash'd me back
Into the gulf of my unfathom'd thought.
I plunged amidst mankind—Forgetfulness
I sought in all, save where 'tis to be found,
And that I have to learn ; my sciences,
My long-pursued and superhuman art,
Is mortal here : I dwell in my despair—
And live—and live for ever.

Witch. It may be
That I can aid thee.

Man. To do this thy power
Must wake the dead, or lay me low with
them.
Do so—in any shape—in any hour—
With any torture—so it be the last.

Witch. That is not in my province; but if
thou
Wilt swear obedience to my will, and do
My bidding, it may help thee to thy wishes.

Man. I will not swear—Obey! and whom?
the spirits
Whose presence I command, and be the slave
Of those who served me—Never!

Witch. Is this all?
Hast thou no gentler answer?—Yet bethink
thee,
And pause ere thou rejectest.

Man. I have said it.

Witch. Enough! I may retire then—say!

Man. Retire!
 [*The* WITCH *disappears.*

Man. (*alone*). We are the fools of time and
terror: Days
Steal on us, and steal from us; yet we live,
Loathing our life, and dreading still to die.
In all the days of this detested yoke—
This vital weight upon the struggling heart,
Which sinks with sorrow, or beats quick with
pain,
Or joy that ends in agony or faintness—
In all the days of past and future, for
In life there is no present, we can number
How few—how less than few—wherein the
soul
Forbears to pant for death, and yet draws
back
As from a stream in winter, though the chill
Be but a moment's. I have one resource
Still in my science—I can call the dead,
And ask them what it is we dread to be:
The sternest answer can but be the Grave,
And that is nothing. If they answer not——
The buried Prophet answered to the Hag
Of Endor; and the Spartan Monarch drew
From the Byzantine maid's unsleeping spirit
An answer and his destiny—he slew
That which he loved, unknowing what he slew,
And died unpardon'd—though he call'd in aid
The Phyxian Jove, and in Phigalia roused
The Arcadian Evocators to compel
The indignant shadow to depose her wrath,
Or fix her term of vengeance—she replied
In words of dubious import, but fulfill'd.
If I had never lived, that which I love
Had still been living; had I never loved,
That which I love would still be beautiful,
Happy and giving happiness. What is she?
What is she now?—a sufferer for my sins—

A thing I dare not think upon—or nothing.
Within few hours I shall not call in vain—
Yet in this hour I dread the thing I dare:
Until this hour I never shrunk to gaze
On spirit, good or evil—now I tremble,
And feel a strange cold thaw upon my heart.
But I can act even what I most abhor,
And champion human fears.—The night ap-
proaches. [*Exit.*

Scene III.

The Summit of the Jungfrau Mountain.

Enter FIRST DESTINY.

The moon is rising broad, and round, and
bright;
And here on snows, where never human foot
Of common mortal trod, we nightly tread,
And leave no traces: o'er the savage sea,
The glassy ocean of the mountain ice,
We skim its rugged breakers, which put on
The aspect of a tumbling tempest's foam,
Frozen in a moment—a dead whirlpool's
image:
And this most steep fantastic pinnacle,
The fretwork of some earthquake—where the
clouds
Pause to repose themselves in passing by—
Is sacred to our revels, or our vigils;
Here do I wait my sisters, on our way
To the Hall of Arimanes, for to-night
Is our great festival—'tis strange they come
not.

A Voice without, singing.

The Captive Usurper,
Hurl'd down from the throne,
Lay buried in torpor,
Forgotten and lone;
I broke through his slumbers,
I shiver'd his chain,
I leagued him with numbers—
He's Tyrant again!
With the blood of a million he'll answer my
care,
With a nation's destruction—his flight and
despair.

Second Voice, without.

The ship sail'd on, the ship sail'd fast,
But I left not a sail, and I left not a mast;
There is not a plank of the hull or the deck,
And there is not a wretch to lament o'er his
wreck;
Save one, whom I held, as he swam, by the
hair,
And he was a subject well worthy my care;
A traitor on land, and a pirate at sea—
But I saved him to wreak further havoc for
me!

FIRST DESTINY, *answering.*

The city lies sleeping;
 The morn, to deplore it,
May dawn on it weeping:
 Sullenly, slowly,
The black plague flew o'er it—
 Thousands lie lowly;
Tens of thousands shall perish;
 The living shall fly from
The sick they should cherish;
 But nothing can vanquish
The touch that they die from.
 Sorrow and anguish,
And evil and dread,
 Envelope a nation;
The blest are the dead,
 Who see not the sight
Of their own desolation;
 This work of a night—
This wreck of a realm—this deed of my
 doing—
For ages I've done, and shall still be re-
 newing!

Enter the SECOND *and* THIRD DESTINIES.

The Three.

Our hands contain the hearts of men,
 Our footsteps are their graves;
We only give to take again
 The spirits of our slaves!

First Des. Welcome!—Where's Nemesis?
Second Des. At some great work;
But what I know not, for my hands were
 full.
Third Des. Behold she cometh.

Enter NEMESIS.

First Des. Say, where hast thou been?
My sisters and thyself are slow to-night.
 Nem. I was detain'd repairing shatter'd
 thrones,
Marrying fools, restoring dynasties,
Avenging men upon their enemies,
And making them repent their own revenge;
Goading the wise to madness; from the
 dull
Shaping out oracles to rule the world
Afresh, for they were waxing out of date,
And mortals dared to ponder for them-
 selves,
To weigh kings in the balance, and to speak
Of freedom, the forbidden fruit.—Away!
We have outstay'd the hour—mount we our
 clouds! [*Exeunt.*

Scene IV.

*The Hall of Arimanes—Arimanes on his
Throne, a Globe of Fire, surrounded by
the Spirits.*

Hymn of the SPIRITS.

Hail to our Master!—Prince of Earth and
 Air!
 Who walks the clouds and waters—in his
 hand
The sceptre of the elements, which tear
 Themselves to chaos at his high command!
He breatheth—and a tempest shakes the sea;
 He speaketh—and the clouds reply in
 thunder;
He gazeth—from his glance the sunbeams
 flee;
 He moveth—earthquakes rend the world
 asunder.
Beneath his footsteps the volcanoes rise;
 His shadow is the Pestilence; his path
The comets herald through the crackling
 skies;
 And planets turn to ashes at his wrath.
To him War offers daily sacrifice;
 To him Death pays his tribute; Life is
 his,
With all its infinite of agonies—
 And his the spirit of whatever is!

Enter the DESTINIES *and* NEMESIS.

First Des. Glory to Arimanes! on the
 earth
His power increaseth—both my sisters did
His bidding, nor did I neglect my duty!
 Second Des. Glory to Arimanes! we who
 bow
The necks of men, bow down before his
 throne!
Third Des. Glory to Arimanes! we await
His nod!
 Nem. Sovereign of Sovereigns! we are
 thine,
And all that liveth, more or less, is ours,
And most things wholly so; still to increase
Our power, increasing thine, demands our
 care,
And we are vigilant. Thy late commands
Have been fulfill'd to the utmost.

Enter MANFRED.

A Spirit. What is here?
A mortal!—Thou most rash and fatal wretch,
Bow down and worship!
 Second Spirit. I do know the man—
A Magian of great power, and fearful skill!
 Third Spirit. Bow down and worship,
 slave!—
 What, know'st thou not

Thine and our Sovereign?—Tremble, and
 obey!
 All the Spirits. Prostrate thyself, and thy
 condemned clay,
Child of the Earth! or dread the worst.
 Man. I know it;
And yet ye see I kneel not.
 Fourth Spirit. 'T will be taught thee.
 Man. 'T is taught already;—many a night
 on the earth,
On the bare ground, have I bow'd down my
 face,
And strew'd my head with ashes; I have
 known
The fulness of humiliation, for
I sunk before my vain despair, and knelt
To my own desolation.
 Fifth Spirit. Dost thou dare
Refuse to Arimanes on his throne
What the whole earth accords, beholding not
The terror of his glory?—Crouch, I say.
 Man. Bid *him* bow down to that which is
 above him,
The overruling Infinite—the Maker
Who made him not for worship—let him
 kneel,
And we will kneel together.
 The Spirits. Crush the worm!
Tear him in pieces!—
 First Des. Hence! avaunt!—he's mine.
Prince of the Powers invisible! This man
Is of no common order, as his port
And presence here denote; his sufferings
Have been of an immortal nature, like
Our own; his knowledge, and his powers
 and will,
As far as is compatible with clay,
Which clogs the ethereal essence, have been
 such
As clay hath seldom borne; his aspirations
Have been beyond the dwellers of the earth,
And they have only taught him what we
 know—
That knowledge is not happiness, and science
But an exchange of ignorance for that
Which is another kind of ignorance.
This is not all—the passions, attributes
Of earth and heaven, from which no power,
 nor being,
Nor breath from the worm upwards is
 exempt,
Have pierced his heart, and in their conse-
 quence
Made him a thing which I, who pity not,
Yet pardon those who pity. He is mine,
And thine, it may be; be it so, or not,
No other Spirit in this region hath
A soul like his—or power upon his soul.
 Nem. What doth he here then?
 First Des. Let him answer that.

 Man. Ye know what I have known; and
 without power
I could not be amongst ye: but there are
Powers deeper still beyond—I come in quest
Of such, to answer unto what I seek.
 Nem. What wouldst thou?
 Man. Thou canst not reply to me.
Call up the dead—my question is for them.
 Nem. Great Arimanes, doth thy will a-
 vouch
The wishes of this mortal?
 Ari. Yea.
 Nem. Whom wouldst thou
Uncharnel?
 Man. One without a tomb—call up
Astarte.

NEMESIS.

Shadow! or Spirit!
 Whatever thou art,
Which still doth inherit
 The whole or a part
Of the form of thy birth,
 Of the mould of thy clay,
Which return'd to the earth,
 Re-appear to the day!
Bear what thou borest,
 The heart and the form,
And the aspect thou worest
 Redeem from the worm.
Appear!—Appear!—Appear!
Who sent thee there requires thee here!

 [*The Phantom of* ASTARTE *rises
 and stands in the midst.*

 Man. Can this be death? there's bloom
 upon her cheek;
But now I see it is no living hue,
But a strange hectic—like the unnatural red
Which Autumn plants upon the perish'd leaf.
It is the same! Oh, God! that I should
 dread
To look upon the same—Astarte!—No,
I cannot speak to her—but bid her speak—
Forgive me or condemn me.

NEMESIS.

By the power which hath broken
 The grave which enthrall'd thee,
Speak to him who hath spoken,
 Or those who have call'd thee!

 Man. She is silent,
And in that silence I am more than answer'd.
 Nem. My power extends no further. Prince
 of Air!
It rests with thee alone—command her voice.
 Ari. Spirit—obey this sceptre!
 Nem. Silent still!
She is not of our order, but belongs
To the other powers. Mortal! thy quest is vain,
And we are baffled also.

Man. Hear me, hear me—
Astarte! my beloved! speak to me:
I have so much endured—so much endure—
Look on me! the grave hath not changed
 thee more
Than I am changed for thee. Thou lovedst
 me
Too much, as I loved thee: we were not
 made
To torture thus each other, though it were
The deadliest sin to love as we have loved.
Say that thou loath'st me not—that I do
 bear
This punishment for both—that thou wilt be
One of the blessed—and that I shall die;
For hitherto all hateful things conspire
To bind me in existence—in a life
Which makes me shrink from immortality—
A future like the past. I cannot rest.
I know not what I ask, nor what I seek:
I feel but what thou art, and what I am;
And I would hear yet once before I perish
The voice which was my music—Speak to
 me!
For I have call'd on thee in the still night,
Startled the slumbering birds from the hush'd
 boughs,
And woke the mountain wolves, and made
 the caves
Acquainted with thy vainly echoed name,
Which answer'd me—many things answer'd
 me—
Spirits and men—but thou wert silent all.
Yet speak to me! I have outwatch'd the
 stars,
And gazed o'er heaven in vain in search of
 thee.
Speak to me! I have wander'd o'er the earth,
And never found thy likeness—Speak to me!
Look on the fiends around—they feel for
 me:
I fear them not, and feel for thee alone—
Speak to me! though it be in wrath;—but
 say—
I reck not what—but let me hear thee once—
This once—once more!
Phantom of Astarte. Manfred!
Man. Say on, say on—
I live but in the sound—it is thy voice!
 Phan. Manfred! To-morrow ends thine
 earthly ills.
Farewell!
 Man. Yet one word more—am I forgiven?
 Phan. Farewell!
 Man. Say, shall we meet again?
 Phan. Farewell!
 Man. One word for mercy! Say, thou
 lovest me.
 Phan. Manfred!
 [*The Spirit of* ASTARTE *disappears.*

Nem. She's gone, and will not be recall'd;
Her words will be fulfill'd. Return to the
 earth.
 A Spirit. He is convulsed.—This is to be
 a mortal
And seek the things beyond mortality.
 Another Spirit. Yet, see, he mastereth
 himself, and makes
His torture tributary to his will.
Had he been one of us, he would have made
An awful spirit.
 Nem. Hast thou further question
Of our great sovereign, or his worshippers?
 Man. None.
 Nem. Then for a time farewell.
 Man. We meet then! Where? On the
 earth?—
Even as thou wilt: and for the grace ac-
 corded
I now depart a debtor. Fare ye well!
 [*Exit* MANFRED.
 (*Scene closes.*)

Act III.

Scene I.—*A Hall in the Castle of Manfred.*

MANFRED *and* HERMAN.

Man. What is the hour?
 Her. It wants but one till sunset,
And promises a lovely twilight.
 Man. Say,
Are all things so disposed of in the tower
As I directed?
 Her. All, my lord, are ready:
Here is the key and casket.
 Man. It is well:
Thou may'st retire. [*Exit* HERMAN.
 Man. (*alone*). There is a calm upon me—
Inexplicable stillness! which till now
Did not belong to what I knew of life.
If that I did not know philosophy
To be of all our vanities the motliest,
The merest worthat ever fool'd the ear
From out the schoolman's jargon, I should
 deem
The golden secret, the sought "Kalon," found,
And seated in my soul. It will not last,
But it is well to have known it, though but
 once:
It hath enlarged my thoughts with a new
 sense,
And I within my tablets would note down
That there is such a feeling. Who is there?

Re-enter HERMAN.

Her. My lord, the abbot of St. Maurice
 craves
To greet your presence.

Enter the ABBOT OF ST. MAURICE.

Abbot. Peace be with Count Manfred !
Man. Thanks, holy father ! welcome to
 these walls ;
Thy presence honours them, and blesseth
 those
Who dwell within them.
Abbot. Would it were so, Count !—
But I would fain confer with thee alone.
Man. Herman, retire.—What would my
 reverend guest ?
Abbot. Thus, without prelude :—Age and
 zeal, my office,
And good intent, must plead my privilege ;
Our near, though not acquainted neighbour-
 hood,
May also be my herald. Rumours strange,
And of unholy nature, are abroad,
And busy with thy name ; a noble name
For centuries : may he who bears it now
Transmit it unimpair'd !
Man. Proceed,—I listen.
Abbot. 'Tis said thou holdest converse with
 the things
Which are forbidden to the search of man ;
That with the dwellers of the dark abodes,
The many evil and unheavenly spirits
Which walk the valley of the shade of death,
Thou communest. I know that with mankind,
Thy fellows in creation, thou dost rarely
Exchange thy thoughts, and that thy solitude
Is as an anchorite's, were it but holy.
Man. And what are they who do avouch
 these things ?
Abbot. My pious brethren—the scared
 peasantry—
Even thy own vassals—who do look on thee
With most unquiet eyes. Thy life's in peril.
Man. Take it.
Abbot. I come to save, and not destroy :
I would not pry into thy secret soul ;
But if these things be sooth, there still is time
For penitence and pity : reconcile thee
With the true church, and through the church
 to heaven.
Man. I hear thee. This is my reply : what-
 e'er
I may have been, or am, doth rest between
Heaven and myself. I shall not choose a
 mortal
To be my mediator. Have I sinn'd
Against your ordinances ? prove and punish !
Abbot. My son ! I did not speak of punish-
 ment,
But penitence and pardon ;—with thyself
The choice of such remains—and for the last,
Our institutions and our strong belief
Have given me power to smooth the path from
 sin

To higher hope and better thoughts ; the first
I leave to heaven,—"Vengeance is mine
 alone ! "
So saith the Lord, and with all humbleness
His servant echoes back the awful word.
Man. Old man ! there is no power in holy
 men,
Nor charm in prayer, nor purifying form
Of penitence, nor outward look, nor fast,
Nor agony—nor, greater than all these,
The innate tortures of that deep despair,
Which is remorse without the fear of hell,
But all in all sufficient to itself
Would make a hell of heaven—can exorcise
From out the unbounded spirit the quick
 sense
Of its own sins, wrongs, sufferance, and re-
 venge
Upon itself ; there is no future pang
Can deal that justice on the self-condemn'd
He deals on his own soul.
Abbot. All this is well ;
For this will pass away, and be succeeded
By an auspicious hope, which shall look up
With calm assurance to that blessed place,
Which all who seek may win, whatever be
Their earthly errors, so they be atoned :
And the commencement of atonement is
The sense of its necessity. Say on—
And all our church can teach thee shall be
 taught ;
And all we can absolve thee shall be pardon'd.
Man. When Rome's sixth emperor was
 near his last,
The victim of a self-inflicted wound,
To shun the torments of a public death
From senates once his slaves, a certain soldier,
With show of loyal pity, would have stanch'd
The gushing throat with his officious robe ;
The dying Roman thrust him back, and said—
Some empire still in his expiring glance—
"It is too late—is this fidelity ? "
Abbot. And what of this ?
Man. I answer with the Roman—
"It is too late ! "
Abbot. It never can be so,
To reconcile thyself with thy own soul,
And thy own soul with heaven. Hast thou
 no hope ?
'Tis strange—even those who do despair above,
Yet shape themselves some fantasy on earth,
To which frail twig they cling, like drowning
 men.
Man. Ay—father ! I have had those earthly
 visions,
And noble aspirations in my youth,
To make my own the mind of other men,
The enlightener of nations ; and to rise
I knew not whither—it might be to fall ;
But fall, even as the mountain-cataract,

Which having leapt from its more dazzling
 height,
Even in the foaming strength of its abyss,
(Which casts up misty columns that become
Clouds raining from the re-ascended skies,)
Lies low but mighty still.—But this is past,
My thoughts mistook themselves.

 Abbot. And wherefore so ?
 Man. I could not tame my nature down;
 for he
Must serve who fain would sway ; and soothe,
 and sue,
And watch all time, and pry into all place,
And be a living lie, who would become
A mighty thing amongst the mean, and such
The mass are ; I disdain'd to mingle with
A herd, though to be leader—and of wolves.
The lion is alone, and so am I.

 Abbot. And why not live and act with other
 men ?
 Man. Because my nature was averse from
 life ;
And yet not cruel ; for I would not make,
But find a desolation. Like the wind,
The red-hot breath of the most lone simoom,
Which dwells but in the desert, and sweeps
 o'er
The barren sands which bear no shrubs to
 blast,
And revels o'er their wild and arid waves,
And seeketh not, so that it is not sought,
But being met is deadly,—such hath been
The course of my existence ; but there came
Things in my path which are no more.

 Abbot. Alas !
I 'gin to fear that thou art past all aid
From me and from my calling ; yet so young,
I still would—

 Man. Look on me ! there is an order
Of mortals on the earth, who do become
Old in their youth, and die ere middle age,
Without the violence of warlike death ;
Some perishing of pleasure, some of study,
Some worn with toil, some of mere weariness,
Some of disease, and some insanity,
And some of wither'd or of broken hearts ;
For this last is a malady which slays
More than are number'd in the lists of Fate,
Taking all shapes, and bearing many names.
Look upon me ! for even of all these things
Have I partaken ; and of all these things,
One were enough ; then wonder not that I
Am what I am, but that I ever was,
Or having been, that I am still on earth.

 Abbot. Yet, hear me still——
 Man. Old man ! I do respect
Thine order, and revere thine years ; I deem
Thy purpose pious, but it is in vain :
Think me not churlish ; I would spare thy-
 self,

Far more than me, in shunning at this time
All further colloquy—and so—farewell.
 [*Exit* Manfred.
 Abbot. This should have been a noble
 creature : he
Hath all the energy which would have made
A goodly frame of glorious elements,
Had they been wisely mingled ; as it is,
It is an awful chaos—light and darkness,
And mind and dust, and passions and pure
 thoughts
Mix'd, and contending without end or order,—
All dormant or destructive : he will perish,
And yet he must not ; I will try once more.
For such are worth redemption ; and my duty
Is to dare all things for a righteous end.
I 'll follow him—but cautiously, though surely.
 [*Exit* Abbot.

Scene II.

Another Chamber.

Manfred *and* Herman.

 Her. My lord, you bade me wait on you at
 sunset :
He sinks behind the mountain.

 Man. Doth he so ?
I will look on him. [Manfred *advances to the*
 Window of the Hall.
 Glorious Orb ! the idol
Of early nature, and the vigorous race
Of undiseased mankind, the giant sons
Of the embrace of angels, with a sex
More beautiful than they, which did draw down
The erring spirits who can ne'er return.—
Most glorious orb ! that wert a worship, ere
The mystery of thy making was reveal'd !
Thou earliest minister of the Almighty,
Which gladden'd, on their mountain tops, the
 hearts
Of the Chaldean shepherds, till they pour'd
Themselves in orisons ! Thou material God !
And representative of the Unknown—
Who chose thee for his shadow ! Thou chief
 star !
Centre of many stars ! which mak'st our
 earth
Endurable, and temperest the hues
And hearts of all who walk within thy rays !
Sire of the seasons ! Monarch of the climes,
And those who dwell in them ! for near or
 far,
Our inborn spirits have a tint of thee
Even as our outward aspects ;—thou dost
 rise,
And shine, and set in glory. Fare thee well !
I ne'er shall see thee more. As my first
 glance
Of love and wonder was for thee, then take
My latest look ; thou wilt not beam on one

To whom the gifts of life and warmth have
been
Of a more fatal nature. He is gone:
I follow. [*Exit* MANFRED.

Scene III.

*The Mountains—The Castle of Manfred at
some distance—A Terrace before a Tower—
Time, Twilight.*

HERMAN, MANUEL, *and other Dependants of*
MANFRED.

Her. 'Tis strange enough; night after
night, for years,
He hath pursued long vigils in this tower,
Without a witness. I have been within it,—
So have we all been oft-times; but from it,
Or its contents, it were impossible
To draw conclusions absolute, of aught
His studies tend to. To be sure, there is
One chamber where none enter: I would give
The fee of what I have to come these three
 years,
To pore upon its mysteries.
Manuel. 'T were dangerous;
Content thyself with what thou know'st
already.
Her. Ah! Manuel! thou art elderly and
wise,
And couldst say much; thou hast dwelt
within the castle—
How many years is 't?
Manuel. Ere Count Manfred's birth,
I served his father, whom he nought re-
sembles.
Her. There be more sons in like pre-
dicament.
But wherein do they differ?
Manuel. I speak not
Of features or of form, but mind and habits;
Count Sigismund was proud, but gay and
free,—
A warrior and a reveller; he dwelt not
With books and solitude, nor made the night
A gloomy vigil, but a festal time,
Merrier than day; he did not walk the rocks
And forests like a wolf, nor turn aside
From men and their delights.
Her. Beshrew the hour,
But those were jocund times! I would that
such
Would visit the old walls again; they look
As if they had forgotten them.
Manuel. These walls
Must change their chieftain first. Oh! I
have seen
Some strange things in them, Herman.
Her. Come, be friendly;
Relate me some to while away our watch:

I've heard thee darkly speak of an event
Which happen'd hereabouts, by this same
tower.
Manuel. That was a night indeed! I do
remember
'T was twilight, as it may be now, and such
Another evening;—yon red cloud, which
rests
On Eigher's pinnacle, so rested then,—
So like that it might be the same; the wind
Was faint and gusty, and the mountain
snows
Began to glitter with the climbing moon;
Count Manfred was, as now, within his
tower,—
How occupied, we knew not, but with him
The sole companion of his wanderings
And watchings—her, whom of all earthly
things
That lived, the only thing he seem'd to
love,—
As he, indeed, by blood was bound to do,
The lady Astarte, his—
Hush! who comes here?

Enter the ABBOT.

Abbot. Where is your master?
Her. Yonder in the tower.
Abbot. I must speak with him.
Manuel. 'Tis impossible;
He is most private, and must not be thus
Intruded on.
Abbot. Upon myself I take
The forfeit of my fault, if fault there be—
But I must see him.
Her. Thou hast seen him once
This eve already.
Abbot. Herman! I command thee,
Knock, and apprize the Count of my approach.
Her. We dare not.
Abbot. Then it seems I must be herald
Of my own purpose.
Manuel. Reverend father, stop—
I pray you pause.
Abbot. Why so?
Manuel. But step this way,
And I will tell you further. [*Exeunt.*

Scene IV.

Interior of the Tower.

MANFRED *alone.*

The stars are forth, the moon above the tops
Of the snow-shining mountains.—Beautiful!
I linger yet with Nature, for the Night
Hath been to me a more familiar face
Than that of man; and in her starry shade
Of dim and solitary loveliness,
I learn'd the language of another world.

I do remember me, that in my youth,
When I was wandering,—upon such a night
I stood within the Coliseum's wall,
'Midst the chief relics of almighty Rome;
The trees which grew along the broken
 arches
Waved dark in the blue midnight, and the
 stars
Shone through the rents of ruin; from afar
The watch-dog bay'd beyond the Tiber; and
More near from out the Cæsars' palace came
The owl's long cry, and, interruptedly,
Of distant sentinels the fitful song
Begun and died upon the gentle wind.
Some cypresses beyond the time-worn breach
Appear'd to skirt the horizon, yet they stood
Within a bowshot. Where the Cæsars dwelt,
And dwell the tuneless birds of night, amidst
A grove which springs through levell'd
 battlements,
And twines its roots with the imperial
 hearths,
Ivy usurps the laurel's place of growth;
But the gladiators' bloody Circus stands,
A noble wreck in ruinous perfection,
While Cæsar's chambers, and the Augustan
 halls,
Grovel on earth in indistinct decay.
And thou didst shine, thou rolling moon,
 upon
All this, and cast a wide and tender light,
Which soften'd down the hoar austerity
Of rugged desolation, and fill'd up,
As 't were anew, the gaps of centuries;
Leaving that beautiful which still was so,
And making that which was not, till the place
Became religion, and the heart ran o'er
With silent worship of the great of old,—
The dead but sceptred sovereigns, who still
 rule
Our spirits from their urns.
 'T was such a night!
'T is strange that I recall it at this time;
But I have found our thoughts take wildest
 flight
Even at the moment when they should array
Themselves in pensive order.

Enter the ABBOT.

Abbot. My good lord!
I crave a second grace for this approach;
But yet let not my humble zeal offend
By its abruptness—all it hath of ill
Recoils on me; its good in the effect
May light upon your head—could I say
 heart—
Could I touch *that*, with words or prayers,
 I should
Recall a noble spirit which hath wander'd;
But is not yet all lost.

Man. Thou know'st me not;
My days are number'd, and my deeds re-
 corded:
Retire, or 't will be dangerous—Away!
 Abbot. Thou dost not mean to menace me?
 Man. Not I;
I simply tell thee peril is at hand,
And would preserve thee.
 Abbot. What dost thou mean?
 Man. Look there!
What dost thou see?
 Abbot. Nothing.
 Man. Look there I say,
And stedfastly;—now tell me what thou
 seest?
 Abbot. That which should shake me, but
 I fear it not:
I see a dusk and awful figure rise,
Like an infernal god, from out the earth;
His face wrapt in a mantle, and his form
Robed as with angry clouds: he stands be-
 tween
Thyself and me—but I do fear him not.
 Man. Thou hast no cause—he shall not
 harm thee—but'
His sight may shock thine old limbs into
 palsy.
I say to thee—Retire!
 Abbot. And I reply—
Never—till I have battled with this fiend:—
What doth he here?
 Man. Why—ay—what doth he here?
I did not send for him,—he is unbidden.
 Abbot. Alas! lost mortal! what with guests
 like these
Hast thou to do? I tremble for thy sake:
Why doth he gaze on thee, and thou on him?
Ah! he unveils his aspect: on his brow
The thunder-scars are graven: from his eye
Glares forth the immortality of hell—
Avaunt!—
 Man. Pronounce—what is thy mission?
 Spirit. Come!
 Abbot. What art thou, unknown being?
 answer!—speak!
 Spirit. The genius of this mortal.—Come!
 'tis time.
 Man. I am prepared for all things, but
 deny
The power which summons me. Who sent
 thee here?
 Spirit. Thou 'lt know anon—Come! come!
 Man. I have commanded
Things of an essence greater far than thine,
And striven with thy masters. Get thee
 hence!
 Spirit. Mortal! thine hour is come—Away!
 I say.
 Man. I knew, and know my hour is come,
 but not

To render up my soul to such as thee:
Away! I'll die as I have lived—alone.
　　Spirit. Then I must summon up my bre-
　　　　thren.—Rise!
　　　　　　　　[*Other Spirits rise up.*
　　Abbot. Avaunt! ye evil ones!—Avaunt!
　　　　I say!
Ye have no power where piety hath power,
And I do charge ye in the name——
　　Spirit. 　　　　　　　　Old man!
We know ourselves, our mission, and thine
　　　　order;
Waste not thy holy words on idle uses,
It were in vain: this man is forfeited.
Once more I summon him—Away! Away!
　　Man. I do defy ye,—though I feel my soul
Is ebbing from me, yet I do defy ye;
Nor will I hence, while I have earthly breath
To breathe my scorn upon ye—earthly
　　　　strength
To wrestle, though with spirits; what ye take
Shall be ta'en limb by limb.
　　Spirit. 　　　　　Reluctant mortal!
Is this the Magian who would so pervade
The world invisible, and make himself
Almost our equal? Can it be that thou
Art thus in love with life? the very life
Which made thee wretched!
　　Man. 　　　　Thou false fiend, thou liest!
My life is in its last hour,—*that* I know,
Nor would redeem a moment of that hour;
I do not combat against death, but thee
And thy surrounding angels; my past power,
Was purchased by no compact with thy
　　　　crew,
But by superior science—penance, daring,
And length of watching, strength of mind,
　　　　and skill
In knowledge of our fathers—when the earth
Saw men and spirits walking side by side,
And gave ye no supremacy: I stand
Upon my strength—I do defy—deny—
Spurn back, and scorn ye!—
　　Spirit. 　　　　But thy many crimes
Have made thee——

　　Man. 　　　What are they to such as thee?
Must crimes be punish'd but by other crimes,
And greater criminals?—Back to thy hell!
Thou hast no power upon me, *that* I feel;
Thou never shalt possess me, *that* I know:
What I have done is done; I bear within
A torture which could nothing gain from
　　　　thine:
The mind which is immortal makes itself
Requital for its good or evil thoughts,—
Is its own origin of ill and end
And its own place and time: its innate sense,
When stripp'd of this mortality, derives
No colour from the fleeting things without,
But is absorb'd in sufferance or in joy,
Born from the knowledge of its own desert.
Thou didst not tempt me, and thou couldst
　　　　not tempt me;
I have not been thy dupe, nor am thy prey—
But was my own destroyer, and will be
My own hereafter.—Back, ye baffled fiends!—
The hand of death is on me—but not yours!
　　　　　　　　[*The Demons disappear.*
　　Abbot. Alas! how pale thou art—thy lips
　　　　are white—
And thy breast heaves—and in thy gasping
　　　　throat
The accents rattle: Give thy prayers to hea-
　　　　ven—
Pray—albeit but in thought,—but die not
　　　　thus.
　　Man. 'Tis over—my dull eyes can fix thee
　　　　not;
But all things swim around me, and the earth
Heaves as it were beneath me. Fare thee
　　　　well!
Give me thy hand.
　　Abbot. 　　Cold—cold—even to the heart—
But yet one prayer—Alas! how fares it with
　　　　thee?
　　Man. Old man! 'tis not so difficult to die.
　　　　　　　　　　　　[Manfred *expires.*
　　Abbot. He's gone—his soul hath ta'en its
　　　　earthless flight;
Whither? I dread to think—but he is gone.

Marino Faliero, Doge of Venice:

AN HISTORICAL TRAGEDY,

IN FIVE ACTS.

"Dux inquieti turbidus Adriæ."—HORACE.

PREFACE.

THE conspiracy of the Doge Marino Faliero is one of the most remarkable events in the annals of the most singular government, city, and people of modern history. It occurred in the year 1355. Everything about Venice is, or was, extraordinary—her aspect is like a dream, and her history is like a romance. The story of this Doge is to be found in all her Chronicles, and particularly detailed in the "Lives of the Doges," by Marin Sanuto, which is given in the Appendix. It is simply and clearly related, and is perhaps more dramatic in itself than any scenes which can be founded upon the subject.

Marino Faliero appears to have been a man of talents and of courage. I find him commander-in-chief of the land forces at the siege of Zara, where he beat the King of Hungary and his army of eighty thousand men, killing eight thousand men, and keeping the besieged at the same time in check; an exploit to which I know none similar in history, except that of Cæsar at Alesia, and of Prince Eugene at Belgrade. He was afterwards commander of the fleet in the same war. He took Capo d'Istria. He was ambassador at Genoa and Rome,—at which last he received the news of his election to the dukedom; his absence being a proof that he sought it by no intrigue, since he was apprised of his predecessor's death and his own succession at the same moment. But he appears to have been of an ungovernable temper. A story is told by Sanuto, of his having, many years before, when podesta and captain at Treviso, boxed the ears of the bishop, who was somewhat tardy in bringing the Host. For this, honest Sanuto "saddles him with a judgment," as Thwackum did Square; but he does not tell us whether he was punished or rebuked by the Senate for this outrage at the time of its commission. He seems, indeed, to have been afterwards at peace with the church, for we find him ambassador at Rome, and invested with the fief of Val di Marino, in the march of Treviso, and with the title of count, by Lorenzo Count-bishop of Ceneda. For these facts my authorities are Sanuto, Vettor Sandi, Andrea Navagero, and the account of the siege of Zara, first published by the indefatigable

Abate Morelli, in his "Monumenti Veneziani di varia Letteratura," printed in 1796, all of which I have looked over in the original language. The moderns, Darù, Sismondi, and Laugier, nearly agree with the ancient chroniclers. Sismondi attributes the conspiracy to his *jealousy*; but I find this nowhere asserted by the national historians. Vettor Sandi, indeed, says, that "Altri scrissero che dalla gelosa suspizion di esso Doge siasi fatto (Michel Steno) staccar con violenza," &c. &c.; but this appears to have been by no means the general opinion, nor is it alluded to by Sanuto, or by Navagero: and Sandi himself adds, a moment after, that "per altre Veneziane memorie traspiri, che non il *solo* desiderio di vendetta lo dispose alla congiura ma anche la innata abituale ambizion sua, per cui anelava a farsi principe independente." The first motive appears to have been excited by the gross affront of the words written by Michel Steno on the ducal chair, and by the light and inadequate sentence of the Forty on the offender, who was one of their "tre Capi." The attentions of Steno himself appear to have been directed towards one of her damsels, and not to the "Dogaressa" herself, against whose fame not the slightest insinuation appears, while she is praised for her beauty, and remarked for her youth. Neither do I find it asserted (unless the hint of Sandi be an assertion), that the Doge was actuated by jealousy of his wife; but rather by respect for her, and for his own honour, warranted by his past services and present dignity.

I know not that the historical facts are alluded to in English, unless by Dr. Moore in his View of Italy. His account is false and flippant, full of stale jests about old men and young wives, and wondering at so great an effect from so slight a cause. How so acute and severe an observer of mankind as the author of Zeluco could wonder at this is inconceivable. He knew that a basin of water spilt on Mrs. Masham's gown deprived the Duke of Marlborough of his command, and led to the inglorious peace of Utrecht—that Louis XIV. was plunged into the most desolating wars, because his minister was nettled at his

finding fault with a window, and wished to give him another occupation—that Helen lost Troy—that Lucretia expelled the Tarquins from Rome—and that Cava brought the Moors to Spain—that an insulted husband led the Gauls to Clusium, and thence to Rome—that a single verse of Frederick II. of Prussia on the Abbé de Bernis, and a jest on Madame de Pompadour, led to the battle of Rosbach—that the elopement of Dearbhorgil with Mac Murchad conducted the English to the slavery of Ireland—that a personal pique between Maria Antoinette and the Duke of Orleans precipitated the first expulsion of the Bourbons—and, not to multiply instances, that Commodus, Domitian, and Caligula fell victims not to their public tyranny, but to private vengeance—and that an order to make Cromwell disembark from the ship in which he would have sailed to America destroyed both King and Commonwealth. After these instances, on the least reflection, it is indeed extraordinary in Dr. Moore to seem surprised that a man used to command, who had served and swayed in the most important offices, should fiercely resent, in a fierce age, an unpunished affront, the grossest that can be offered to a man, be he prince or peasant. The age of Faliero is little to the purpose, unless to favour it—

 "The young man's wrath is like straw on fire,
 But like red-hot steel is the old man's ire."

 "Young men soon give and soon forget affronts,
 Old age is slow at both."

Laugier's reflections are more philosophical:— "Tale fù il fine ignominioso di un' uomo, che la sua nascità, la sua età, il suo carattere dovevano tener lontano dalle passioni produttrici di grandi delitti. I suoi *talenti* per lungo tempo esercitati ne' maggiori impieghi, la sua capacità sperimentata ne' governi e nelle ambasciate, gli avevano acquistato la stima e la fiducia de' cittadini, ed avevano uniti i suffragj per collocarlo alla testa della republica, Innalzato ad un grado che terminava gloriosamente la sua vita, il risentimento di un' ingiuria leggiera insinuò nel suo cuore tal veleno che bastò a corrompere le antiche sue qualità, e a condurlo al termine dei scellerati ; serio esempio, che prova *non esservi età, in cui la prudenza umana sia sicura, e che nell' uomo restano sempre passioni capaci a disonorarlo, quando non invigili sopra se stesso ×*".

Where did Dr. Moore find that Marino Faliero begged his life ? I have searched the chroniclers, and find nothing of the kind : it is true that he avowed all. He was conducted to the place of torture, but there is no mention made of any application for mercy on his part ; and the very circumstance of their having taken him to the rack seems to argue anything but his having shown a want of firmness, which would doubtless have been also mentioned by those minute historians, who by no means favour him: such, indeed, would be contrary to his character as a soldier, to the age in which he lived, and

* Laugier, Hist. de la Répub. de Venise.

at which he died, as it is to the truth of history. I know no justification, at any distance of time, for calumniating an historical character : surely truth belongs to the dead, and to the unfortunate : and they who have died upon a scaffold have generally had faults enough of their own, without attributing to them that which the very incurring of the perils which conducted them to their violent death renders, of all others, the most improbable. The black veil which is painted over the place of Marino Faliero amongst the Doges, and the Giants' Staircase where he was crowned, and discrowned, and decapitated, struck forcibly upon my imagination ; as did his fiery character and strange story. I went, in 1819, in search of his tomb more than once to the church San Giovanni e San Paolo ; and, as I was standing before the monument of another family, a priest came up to me and said, " I can show you finer monuments than that." I told him that I was in search of that of the Faliero family, and particularly of the Doge Marino's. "Oh," said he, "I will show it you ;" and conducting me to the outside, pointed out a sarcophagus in the wall with an illegible inscription. He said that it had been in a convent adjoining, but was removed after the French came, and placed in its present situation ; that he had seen the tomb opened at its removal ; there were still some bones remaining, but no positive vestige of the decapitation. The equestrian statue of which I have made mention in the third act as before that church is not, however, of a Faliero, but of some other now obsolete warrior, although of a later date. There were two other Doges of this family prior to Marino ; Ordelafo, who fell in battle at Zara, in 1117 (where his descendant afterwards conquered the Huns), and Vital Faliero, who reigned in 1082. The family, originally from Fano, was of the most illustrious in blood and wealth in the city of once the most wealthy and still the most ancient families in Europe. The length I have gone into on this subject will show the interest I have taken in it. Whether I have succeeded or not in the tragedy, I have at least transferred into our language an historical fact worthy of commemoration.

It is now four years that I have meditated this work ; and before I had sufficiently examined the records, I was rather disposed to have made it turn on a jealousy in Faliero. But, perceiving no foundation for this in historical truth, and aware that jealousy is an exhausted passion in the drama, I have given it a more historical form. I was, besides, well advised by the late Matthew Lewis on that point, in talking with him of my intention at Venice in 1817. " If you make him jealous," said he, "recollect that you have to contend with established writers, to say nothing of Shakspeare, and an exhausted subject :—stick to the old fiery Doge's natural character, which will bear you out, if properly drawn : and make your plot as regular as you can." Sir William Drummond gave me nearly the same counsel. How far I have followed these instructions, or whether they have availed me, is not for me to decide. I have had no view to the stage ;

in its present state it is, perhaps, not a very exalted object of ambition; besides, I have been too much behind the scenes to have thought it so at any time. And I cannot conceive any man of irritable feeling putting himself at the mercies of an audience. The sneering reader, and the loud critic, and the tart review, are scattered and distant calamities; but the trampling of an intelligent or of an ignorant audience on a production which, be it good or bad, has been a mental labour to the writer, is a palpable and immediate grievance, heightened by a man's doubt of their competency to judge, and his certainty of his own imprudence in electing them his judges. Were I capable of writing a play which could be deemed stage-worthy, success would give me no pleasure, and failure great pain. It is for this reason that, even during the time of being one of the committee of one of the theatres, I never made the attempt, and never will. But surely there is dramatic power somewhere, where Joanna Baillie, and Milman, and John Wilson exist. The "City of the Plague" and the "Fall of Jerusalem" are full of the best *materiel* for tragedy that has been seen since Horace Walpole, except passages of Ethwald and De Montfort. It is the fashion to underrate Horace Walpole; firstly, because he was a nobleman, and secondly, because he was a gentleman; but, to say

nothing of the composition of his incomparable letters, and of the "Castle of Otranto," he is the "Ultimus Romanorum," the author of the "Mysterious Mother," a tragedy of the highest order, and not a puling love-play. He is the father of the first romance and of the last tragedy in our language, and surely worthy of a higher place than any living writer, be he who he may.

In speaking of the drama of "Marino Faliero," I forgot to mention, that the desire of preserving, though still too remote, a nearer approach to unity than the irregularity, which is the reproach of the English theatrical compositions, permits, has induced me to represent the conspiracy as already formed, and the Doge acceding to it; whereas, in fact, it was of his own preparation, and that of Israel Bertuccio. The other characters (except that of the Duchess), incidents, and almost the time, which was wonderfully short for such a design in real life, are strictly historical, except that all the consultations took place in the palace. Had I followed this, the unity would have been better preserved; but I wished to produce the Doge in the full assembly of the conspirators, instead of monotonously placing him always in dialogue with the same individuals. For the real facts, I refer to the Appendix.

MARINO FALIERO, DOGE OF VENICE.

Dramatis Personæ.

MEN.

MARINO FALIERO, *Doge of Venice.*
BERTUCCIO FALIERO, *Nephew of the Doge.*
LIONI, *a Patrician and Senator.*
BENINTENDE, *Chief of the Council of Ten.*
MICHEL STENO, *One of the three Capi of the Forty.*
ISRAEL BERTUCCIO, *Chief of the Arsenal.*
PHILIP CALENDARO, ⎫
DAGOLINO, ⎬ *Conspirators.*
BERTRAM, ⎭

Signor of the Night, ⎫ *"Signore di Notte," one of the Officers belonging to the Republic.*

First Citizen.
Second Citizen.
Third Citizen.
VINCENZO, ⎫
PIETRO, ⎬ *Officers belonging to the Ducal Palace.*
BATTISTA, ⎭
Secretary of the Council of Ten.
Guards, Conspirators, Citizens, The Council of Ten, The Giunta, &c., &c.

WOMEN.

ANGIOLINA, *Wife to the Doge.*
MARIANNA, *her Friend.*

Female Attendants, &c.

Scene.—VENICE *in the year* 1355.

Act I.

Scene I.—*An Antechamber in the Ducal Palace.*

PIETRO *speaks, in entering, to* BATTISTA.

Pie. Is not the messenger return'd?
Bat. Not yet;
I have sent frequently, as you commanded,
But still the Signory is deep in council,
And long debate on Steno's accusation.
Pie. Too long—at least so thinks the Doge.
Bat. How bears he
These moments of suspense?
Pie. With struggling patience.
Placed at the ducal table, cover'd o'er
With all the apparel of the state; petitions,
Despatches, judgments, acts, reprieves, reports,
He sits as rapt in duty; but whene'er
He hears the jarring of a distant door,
Or aught that intimates a coming step,
Or murmur of a voice, his quick eye wanders,
And he will start up from his chair, then pause,
And seat himself again, and fix his gaze
Upon some edict; but I have observed
For the last hour he has not turned a leaf.

Bat. 'Tis said he is much moved,—and doubtless 'twas
Foul scorn in Steno to offend so grossly.
Pie. Ay, if a poor man: Steno's a patrician,
Young, galliard, gay, and haughty.
Bat. Then you think
He will not be judged hardly?
Pie. 'Twere enough
He be judged justly, but 'tis not for us
To anticipate the sentence of the Forty.
Bat. And here it comes.—What news, Vincenzo?

Enter VINCENZO.

Vin. 'Tis
Decided; but as yet his doom's unknown:
I saw the president in act to seal
The parchment which will bear the Forty's judgment
Unto the Doge, and hasten to inform him.
[*Exeunt.*

Scene II.

The Ducal Chamber.

MARINO FALIERO, *Doge; and his Nephew,* BERTUCCIO FALIERO.

Ber. F. It cannot be but they will do you justice.

Doge. Ay, such as the Avogadori did,
Who sent up my appeal unto the Forty
To try him by his peers, his own tribunal.

Ber. F. His peers will scarce protect him;
 such an act
Would bring contempt on all authority.

Doge. Know you not Venice? Know you
 not the Forty?
But we shall see anon.

Ber. F. (*addressing* VINCENZO, *then enter-
 ing*). How now—what tidings?

Vin. I am charged to tell his highness that
 the court
Has pass'd its resolution, and that, soon
As the due forms of judgment are gone
 through,
The sentence will be sent up to the Doge;
In the mean time the Forty doth salute
The Prince of the Republic, and entreat
His acceptation of their duty.

Doge. Yes—
They are wondrous dutiful, and ever humble.
Sentence is pass'd, you say?

Vin. It is, your highness:
The president was sealing it, when I
Was call'd in, that no moment might be
 lost
In forwarding the intimation due
Not only to the Chief of the Republic,
But the complainant, both in one united.

Ber. F. Are you aware, from aught you
 have perceived,
Of their decision?

Vin. No, my lord; you know
The secret custom of the courts in Venice.

Ber. F. True; but there still is something
 given to guess,
Which a shrewd gleaner and quick eye would
 catch at;
A whisper, or a murmur, or an air
More or less solemn spread o'er the tribu-
 nal.
The Forty are but men—most worthy men,
And wise, and just, and cautious—this I
 grant—
And secret as the grave to which they doom
The guilty: but with all this, in their as-
 pects—
At least in some, the juniors of the number—
A searching eye, an eye like yours, Vincenzo,
Would read the sentence ere it was pro-
 nounced.

Vin. My lord, I came away upon the mo-
 ment,
And had no leisure to take note of that
Which pass'd among the judges, even in
 seeming;
My station near the accused too, Michel
 Steno,
Made me—

Doge (*abruptly*). And how look'd he? de-
 liver that.

Vin. Calm, but not overcast, he stood re-
 sign'd
To the decree, whate'er it were;—but lo!
It comes, for the perusal of his highness.

Enter the SECRETARY *of the Forty.*

Sec. The high tribunal of the Forty sends
Health and respect to the Doge Faliero,
Chief magistrate of Venice, and requests
His highness to peruse and to approve
The sentence pass'd on Michel Steno, born
Patrician, and arraign'd upon the charge
Contain'd, together with its penalty,
Within the rescript which I now present.

Doge. Retire, and wait without.
 [*Exeunt* SECRETARY *and* VINCENZO.
 Take thou this paper:
The misty letters vanish from my eyes;
I cannot fix them.

Ber. F. Patience, my dear uncle:
Why do you tremble thus?—nay, doubt not,
 all
Will be as could be wish'd.

Doge. Say on.

Ber. F. (*reading*). "Decreed
In council, without one dissenting voice,
That Michel Steno, by his own confession,
Guilty on the last night of Carnival
Of having graven on the ducal throne
The following words——"

Doge. Wouldst thou repeat them?
Wouldst *thou* repeat them—*thou*, a Faliero,
Harp on the deep dishonour of our house,
Dishonour'd in its chief—that chief the
 prince
Of Venice, first of cities?—To the sentence.

Ber. F. Forgive me, my good lord; I will
 obey—
(*Reads*). "That Michel Steno be detain'd a
 month
In close arrest."

Doge. Proceed.

Ber. F. My Lord, 'tis finish'd.

Doge. How say you?—finish'd! Do I
 dream?—'tis false—
Give me the paper—(*Snatches the paper and
 reads*)—"'Tis decreed in council
That Michael Steno"——Nephew, thine arm!

Ber. F. Nay,
Cheer up, be calm; this transport is uncall'd
 for—
Let me seek some assistance.

Doge. Stop, sir—Stir not—
'Tis past.

Ber. F. I cannot but agree with you
The sentence is too slight for the offence;
It is not honourable in the Forty
To affix so slight a penalty to that

Which was a foul affront to you, and even
To them, as being your subjects; but 'tis not
Yet without remedy: you can appeal
To them once more, or to the Avogadori,
Who, seeing that true justice is withheld,
Will now take up the cause they once de-
　clined,
And do you right upon the bold delinquent.
Think you not thus, good uncle? why do you
　stand
So fix'd? You heed me not:—I pray you,
　hear me!

　*Doge (dashing down the ducal bonnet, and
　　offering to trample upon it, exclaims, as
　　he is withheld by his nephew).*
Oh! that the Saracen were in St. Mark's!
Thus would I do him homage.
　Ber. F.　　　　　　　For the sake
Of Heaven and all its saints, my lord ——
　Doge.　　　　　　　　Away!
Oh, that the Genoese were in the port!
Oh, that the Huns whom I o'erthrew at Zara
Were ranged around the palace!
　Ber. F.　　　　　　'T is not well
In Venice' Duke to say so.
　Doge.　　　　　　Venice' Duke!
Who now is Duke in Venice? let me see him,
That he may do me right.
　Ber. F.　　　　　If you forget
Your office, and its dignity and duty,
Remember that of man, and curb this passion.
The Duke of Venice ——
　Doge (interrupting him).　There is no such
　　thing—
It is a word—nay, worse—a worthless by-
　word:
The most despised, wrong'd, outraged, help-
　less wretch,
Who begs his bread, if 'tis refused by one,
May win it from another kinder heart!
But he, who is denied his right by those
Whose place it is to do no wrong, is poorer
Than the rejected beggar—he's a slave—
And that am I, and thou, and all our house,
Even from this hour; the meanest artisan
Will point the finger, and the haughty noble
May spit upon us:—where is our redress?
　Ber. F. The law, my prince ——
　Doge (interrupting him).　You see what it
　　has done;
I ask'd no remedy but from the law,
I sought no vengeance but redress by law,
I call'd no judges but those named by law;
As sovereign, I appeal'd unto my subjects,
The very subjects who had made me sovereign,
And gave me thus a double right to be so.
The rights of place and choice, of birth and
　service,
Honours and years, these scars, these hoary
　hairs,

The travel, toil, the perils, the fatigues,
The blood and sweat of almost eighty years,
Were weigh'd i' the balance, 'gainst the foulest
　stain,
The grossest insult, most contemptuous crime
Of a rank, rash patrician—and found wanting!
And this is to be borne!
　Ber. F.　　　　I say not that:—
In case your fresh appeal should be rejected,
We will find other means to make all even.
　Doge. Appeal again! art thou my brother's
　　son?
A scion of the house of Faliero?
The nephew of a Doge? and of that blood
Which hath already given three dukes to
　Venice?
But thou say'st well—we must be humble now.
　Ber. F. My princely uncle! you are too
　　much moved;—
I grant it was a gross offence, and grossly
Left without fitting punishment: but still
This fury doth exceed the provocation,
Or any provocation: if we are wrong'd,
We will ask justice; if it be denied,
We'll take it; but may do all this in calm-
　ness—
Deep Vengeance is the daughter of deep
　Silence.
I have yet scarce a third part of your years,
I love our house, I honour you, its chief,
The guardian of my youth, and its instructor—
But though I understand your grief, and enter
In part of your disdain, it doth appal me
To see your anger, like our Adrian waves,
O'ersweep all bounds, and foam itself to air.
　Doge. I tell thee—*must* I tell thee—what
　　thy father
Would have required no words to compre-
　hend?
Hast thou no feeling save the external sense
Of torture from the touch? hast thou no
　soul—
No pride—no passion—no deep sense of
　honour?
　Ber. F. 'T is the first time that honour has
　　been doubted,
And were the last, from any other sceptic.
　Doge. You know the full offence of this born
　　villain,
This creeping, coward, rank, acquitted felon,
Who threw his sting into a poisonous libel,
And on the honour of—Oh God! my wife,
The nearest, dearest part of all men's honour,
Left a base slur to pass from mouth to mouth
Of loose mechanics, with all coarse foul com-
　ments,
And villainous jests, and blasphemies obscene;
While sneering nobles, in more polish'd
　guise,
Whisper'd the tale, and smiled upon the lie

Which made me look like them—a courteous
 wittol,
Patient—ay, proud, it may be, of dishonour.
 Ber. F. But still it was a lie—you knew it
 false,
And so did all men.
 Doge. Nephew, the high Roman
Said, " Cæsar's wife must not even be sus-
 pected,"
And put her from him.
 Ber. F. True—but in those days——
 Doge. What is it that a Roman would not
 suffer,
That a Venetian prince must bear ? old Dan-
 dolo
Refused the diadem of all the Cæsars,
And wore the ducal cap I trample on,
Because 'tis now degraded.
 Ber. F. 'Tis even so.
 Doge. It is—it is ;—I did not visit on
The innocent creature thus most vilely slan-
 der'd
Because she took an old man for her lord,
For that he had been long her father's friend
And patron of her house, as if there were
No love in woman's heart but lust of youth
And beardless faces ;—I did not for this
Visit the villain's infamy on her,
But craved my country's justice on his head,
The justice due unto the humblest being
Who hath a wife whose faith is sweet to him,
Who hath a home whose hearth is dear to him,
Who hath a name whose honour's all to him,
When these are tainted by the accursing breath
Of calumny and scorn.
 Ber. F. And what redress
Did you expect as his fit punishment ?
 Doge. Death ! Was I not the sovereign of
 the state—
Insulted on his very throne, and made
A mockery to the men who should obey me ?
Was I not injured as a husband ? scorn'd
As man ? reviled, degraded, as a prince ?
Was not offence like his a complication
Of insult and of treason ?—and he lives !
Had he instead of on the Doge's throne
Stamp'd the same brand upon a peasant's
 stool,
His blood had gilt the threshold ; for the
 carle
Had stabb'd him on the instant.
 Ber. F. Do not doubt it,
He shall not live till sunset—leave to me
The means, and calm yourself.
 Doge. Hold, nephew : this
Would have sufficed but yesterday ; at present
I have no further wrath against this man.
 Ber. F. What mean you ? is not the offence
 redoubled
By this most rank—I will not say—acquittal ;

For it is worse, being full acknowledgment
Of the offence, and leaving it unpunish'd ?
 Doge. It is *redoubled*, but not now by him :
The Forty hath decreed a month's arrest—
We must obey the Forty.
 Ber. F. Obey *them !*
Who have forgot their duty to the sovereign ?
 Doge. Why yes ;—boy, you perceive it then
 at last :
Whether as fellow citizen who sues
For justice, or as sovereign who commands it,
They have defrauded me of both my rights
(For here the sovereign is a citizen) ;
But, notwithstanding, harm not thou a hair
Of Steno's head—he shall not wear it long.
 Ber. F. Not twelve hours longer, had you
 left to me
The mode and means : if you had calmly
 heard me,
I never meant this miscreant should escape,
But wish'd you to repress such gusts of
 passion,
That we more surely might devise together
His taking off.
 Doge. No, nephew, he must live ;
At least, just now—a life so vile as his
Were nothing at this hour ; in th' olden time
Some sacrifices ask'd a single victim,
Great expiations had a hecatomb.
 Ber. F. Your wishes are my law : and yet
 I fain
Would prove to you how near unto my heart
The honour of our house must ever be.
 Doge. Fear not ; you shall have time and
 place of proof :
But be not thou too rash, as I have been.
I am ashamed of my own anger now ;
I pray you, pardon me.
 Ber. F. Why, that's my uncle !
The leader, and the statesman, and the chief
Of commonwealths, and sovereign of himself !
I wonder'd to perceive you so forget
All prudence in your fury at these years,
Although the cause——
 Doge. Ay, think upon the cause—
Forget it not :—When you lie down to rest,
Let it be black among your dreams ; and
 when
The morn returns, so let it stand between
The sun and you, as an ill-omen'd cloud
Upon a summer day of festival :
So will it stand to me ;—but speak not, stir
 not,—
Leave all to me ; we shall have much to do,
And you shall have a part.—But now retire,
'Tis fit I were alone.
 *Ber. F. (taking up and placing the ducal
 bonnet on the table).* Ere I depart,
I pray you to resume what you have spurn'd,
Till you can change it haply for a crown.

And now I take my leave, imploring you
In all things to rely upon my duty
As doth become your near and faithful kins-
man,
And not less loyal citizen and subject.
 [*Exit* Bertuccio Faliero.
Doge (*solus*). Adieu, my worthy nephew.—
 Hollow bauble?
 [*Taking up the ducal cap.*
Beset with all the thorns that line a crown,
Without investing the insulted brow
With the all-swaying majesty of kings;
Thou idle, gilded, and degraded toy,
Let me resume thee as I would a vizor.
 [*Puts it on.*
How my brain aches beneath thee! and my
 temples
Throb feverish under thy dishonest weight.
Could I not turn thee to a diadem?
Could I not shatter the Briarean sceptre
Which in this hundred-handed senate rules,
Making the people nothing, and the prince
A pageant? In my life I have achieved
Tasks not less difficult—achieved for them,
Who thus repay me! Can I not requite them?
Oh for one year! Oh! but for even a day
Of my full youth, while yet my body served
My soul as serves the generous steed his lord,
I would have dash'd amongst them, asking
 few
In aid to overthrow these swoln patricians;
But now I must look round for other hands
To serve this hoary head;—but it shall plan
In such a sort as will not leave the task
Herculean, though as yet 't is but a chaos
Of darkly brooding thoughts: my fancy is
In her first work, more nearly to the light
Holding the sleeping images of things
For the selection of the pausing judgment.—
The troops are few in——

Enter Vincenzo.

Vin. There is one without
Craves audience of your highness.
Doge. I'm unwell—
I can see no one, not even a patrician—
Let him refer his business to the council.
Vin. My lord, I will deliver your reply;
It cannot much import—he's a plebeian,
The master of a galley, I believe.
 Doge. How! did you say the patron of a
 galley?
That is—I mean—a servant of the state:
Admit him, he may be on public service.
 [*Exit* Vincenzo.
Doge (*solus*). This patron may be sounded;
 I will try him.
I know the people to be discontented:
They have cause, since Sapienza's adverse
 day,

When Genoa conquer'd: they have further
 cause,
Since they are nothing in the state, and in
The city worse than nothing—mere machines,
To serve the nobles' most patrician pleasure.
The troops have long arrears of pay, oft
 promised,
And murmur deeply—any hope of change
Will draw them forward: they shall pay
 themselves
With plunder:—but the priests—I doubt the
 priesthood
Will not be with us; they have hated me
Since that rash hour, when, madden'd with
 the drone,
I smote the tardy bishop at Treviso,
Quickening his holy march; yet ne'ertheless,
They may be won, at least their chief at Rome,
By some well-timed concessions; but, above
All things, I must be speedy: at my hour
Of twilight little light of life remains.
Could I free Venice, and avenge my wrongs,
I had lived too long, and willingly would
 sleep
Next moment with my sires; and, wanting
 this,
Better that sixty of my fourscore years
Had been already where—how soon, I care
 not—
The whole must be extinguish'd; better that
They ne'er had been, than drag me on to be
The thing these arch-oppressors fain would
 make me.
Let me consider—of efficient troops
There are three thousand posted at——

Enter Vincenzo *and* Israel Bertuccio.

Vin. May it please
Your highness, the same patron whom I
 spake of
Is here to crave your patience.
 Doge. Leave the chamber,
Vincenzo.— [*Exit* Vincenzo.
 Sir, you may advance—what
 would you?
I. Ber. Redress.
Doge. Of whom?
I. Ber. Of God and of the Doge.
Doge. Alas! my friend, you seek it of the
 twain
Of least respect and interest in Venice.
You must address the council.
I. Ber. 'T were in vain;
For he who injured me is one of them.
 Doge. There's blood upon thy face—how
 came it there?
I. Ber. 'T is mine, and not the first I've
 shed for Venice,
But the first shed by a Venetian hand:
A noble smote me.

Doge. Doth he live?

I. Ber. Not long—
But for the hope I had and have, that you,
My prince, yourself a soldier, will redress
Him, whom the laws of discipline and Venice
Permit not to protect himself :—if not—
I say no more.

Doge. But something you would do—
Is it not so?

I. Ber. I am a man, my lord.

Doge. Why so is he who smote you.

I. Ber. He is call'd so;
Nay, more, a noble one—at least, in Venice:
But since he hath forgotten that I am
one,
And treats me like a brute, the brute may
turn—
'T is said the worm will.

Doge. Say—his name and lineage?

I. Ber. Barbaro.

Doge. What was the cause? or
the pretext?

I. Ber. I am the chief of the arsenal, em-
ploy'd
At present in repairing certain galleys
But roughly used by the Genoese last year.
This morning comes the noble Barbaro
Full of reproof, because our artisans
Had left some frivolous order of his house,
To execute the state's decree: I dared
To justify the men—he raised his hand;—
Behold my blood! the first time it e'er flow'd
Dishonourably.

Doge. Have you long time served?

I. Ber. So long as to remember Zara's
siege,
And fight beneath the chief who beat the
Huns there,
Sometime my general, now the Doge Fa-
liero.—

Doge. How! are we comrades?—the state's
ducal robes
Sit newly on me, and you were appointed
Chief of the arsenal ere I came from Rome;
So that I recognised you not. Who placed
you?

I. Ber. The late Doge; keeping still my
old command
As patron of a galley: my new office
Was given as the reward of certain scars
(So was your predecessor pleased to say):
I little thought his bounty would conduct me
To his successor as a helpless plaintiff;
At least, in such a cause.

Doge. Are you much hurt?

I. Ber. Irreparably in my self-esteem.

Doge. Speak out; fear nothing: being
stung at heart,
What would you do to be revenged on this
man?

I. Ber. That which I dare not name, and
yet will do.

Doge. Then wherefore came you here?

I. Ber. I come for justice,
Because my general is Doge, and will not
See his old soldier trampled on. Had any,
Save Faliero, fill'd the ducal throne,
This blood had been wash'd out in other
blood.

Doge. You come to me for justice—unto
me!
The Doge of Venice, and I cannot give it;
I cannot even obtain it—'t was denied
To me most solemnly an hour ago!

I. Ber. How says your highness?

Doge. Steno is condemn'd
To a month's confinement.

I. Ber. What! the same who dared
To stain the ducal throne with those foul
words,
That have cried shame to every ear in
Venice?

Doge. Ay, doubtless they have echo'd o'er
the arsenal,
Keeping due time with every hammer's clink
As a good jest to jolly artisans;
Or making chorus to the creaking oar,
In the vile tune of every galley-slave,
Who, as he sung the merry stave, exulted
He was not a shamed dotard like the Doge.

I. Ber. Is 't possible? a month's imprison-
ment!
No more for Steno?

Doge. You have heard the offence,
And now you know his punishment; and
then
You ask redress of *me!* Go to the Forty,
Who pass'd the sentence upon Michel Steno;
They 'll do as much by Barbaro, no doubt.

I. Ber. Ah! dared I speak my feelings!

Doge. Give them breath.
Mine have no further outrage to endure.

I. Ber. Then in a word, it rests but on your
word
To punish and avenge—I will not say
My petty wrong, for what is a mere blow,
However vile, to such a thing as I am?—
But the base insult done your state and
person.

Doge. You overrate my power, which is a
pageant.
This cap is not the monarch's crown; these
robes
Might move compassion, like a beggar's rags;
Nay, more, a beggar's are his own, and
these
But lent to the poor puppet, who must play
Its part with all its empire in this ermine.

I. Ber. Wouldst thou be king?

Doge. Yes—of a happy people.

I. Ber. Wouldst thou be sovereign lord of
 Venice?
Doge. Ay,
If that the people shared that sovereignty,
So that nor they nor I were further slaves
To this o'ergrown aristocratic Hydra,
The poisonous heads of whose envenom'd
 body
Have breathed a pestilence upon us all.
I. Ber. Yet, thou wast born, and still hast
 lived, patrician.
Doge. In evil hour was I so born; my birth
Hath made me Doge to be insulted: but
I lived and toil'd a soldier and a servant
Of Venice and her people, not the senate;
Their good and my own honour were my
 guerdon.
I have fought and bled; commanded, ay,
 and conquer'd;
Have made and marr'd peace oft in em-
 bassies,
As it might chance to be our country's
 'vantage;
Have traversed land and sea in constant
 duty,
Through almost sixty years, and still for
 Venice,
My fathers' and my birthplace, whose dear
 spires,
Rising at distance o'er the blue Lagoon,
It was reward enough for me to view
Once more; but not for any knot of men,
Nor sect, nor faction, did I bleed or sweat!
But would you know why I have done all
 this?
Ask of the bleeding pelican why she
Hath ripp'd her bosom? Had the bird a
 voice,
She'd tell thee 'twas for *all* her little ones.
I. Ber. And yet they made thee duke.
Doge. *They made* me so;
I sought it not, the flattering fetters met me
Returning from my Roman embassy,
And never having hitherto refused
Toil, charge, or duty for the state, I did not,
At these late years, decline what was the
 highest
Of all in seeming, but of all most base
In what we have to do and to endure:
Bear witness for me thou, my injured sub-
 ject,
When I can neither right myself nor thee.
I. Ber. You shall do both, if you possess
 the will;
And many thousands more not less oppress'd,
Who wait but for a signal—will you give it?
Doge. You speak in riddles.
I. Ber. Which shall soon be read
At peril of my life, if you disdain not
To lend a patient ear.

Doge. Say on.
I. Ber. Not thou,
Nor I alone, are injured and abused,
Contemn'd and trampled on; but the whole
 people
Groan with the strong conception of their
 wrongs;
The foreign soldiers in the senate's pay
Are discontented for their long arrears;
The native mariners, and civic troops,
Feel with their friends; for who is he
 amongst them
Whose brethren, parents, children, wives,
 or sisters,
Have not partook oppression, or pollution,
From the patricians? And the hopeless war
Against the Genoese, which is still main-
 tain'd
With the plebeian blood, and treasure wrung
From their hard earnings, has inflamed them
 further:
Even now—but, I forget that speaking thus,
Perhaps I pass the sentence of my death!
Doge. And suffering what thou hast done—
 fear'st thou death?
Be silent then, and live on, to be beaten
By those for whom thou hast bled.
I. Ber. No, I will speak
At every hazard; and if Venice' Doge
Should turn delator, be the shame on him,
And sorrow too; for he will lose far more
Than I.
Doge. From me fear nothing; out with it!
I. Ber. Know then, that there are met and
 sworn in secret
A band of brethren, valiant hearts and true;
Men who have proved all fortunes, and have
 long
Grieved over that of Venice, and have right
To do so; having served her in all climes,
And having rescued her from foreign foes,
Would do the same from those within her
 walls.
They are not numerous, nor yet too few
For their great purpose; they have arms,
 and means,
And hearts, and hopes, and faith, and patient
 courage.
Doge. For what then do they pause?
I. Ber. An hour to strike.
Doge (*aside*). Saint Mark's shall strike
 that hour!
I. Ber. I now have placed
My life, my honour, all my earthly hopes
Within thy power, but in the firm belief
That injuries like ours, sprung from one
 cause,
Will generate one vengeance: should it
 be so,
Be our chief now—our sovereign hereafter.

Doge. How many are ye?
I. Ber. I'll not answer that
Till I am answer'd.
Doge. How, sir! do you menace?
I. Ber. No; I affirm. I have betray'd
 myself;
But there's no torture in the mystic wells
Which undermine your palace, nor in those
Not less appalling cells, the "leaden roofs,"
To force a single name from me of others.
The Pozzi and the Piombi were in vain;
They might wring blood from me, but
 treachery never.
And I would pass the fearful "Bridge of
 Sighs,"
Joyous that mine must be the last that e'er
Would echo o'er the Stygian wave which
 flows
Between the murderers and the murder'd,
 washing
The prison and the palace walls: there are
Those who would live to think on't, and
 avenge me.
Doge. If such your power and purpose,
 why come here
To sue for justice, being in the course
To do yourself due right?
I. Ber. Because the man,
Who claims protection from authority,
Showing his confidence and his submission
To that authority, can hardly be
Suspected of combining to destroy it.
Had I sate down too humbly with this blow,
A moody brow and mutter'd threats had
 made me
A mark'd man to the Forty's inquisition;
But loud complaint, however angrily
It shapes its phrase, is little to be fear'd,
And less distrusted. But, besides all this,
I had another reason.
Doge. What was that?
I. Ber. Some rumours that the Doge was
 greatly moved
By the reference of the Avogadori
Of Michel Steno's sentence to the Forty
Had reach'd me. I had served you, honour'd
 you,
And felt that you were dangerously insulted,
Being of an order of such spirits, as
Requite tenfold both good and evil: 'twas
My wish to prove and urge you to redress.
Now you know all; and that I speak the
 truth,
My peril be the proof.
Doge. You have deeply ventured;
But all must do so who would greatly win:
Thus far I'll answer you—your secret's safe.
I. Ber. And is this all?
Doge. Unless with all intrusted,
What would you have me answer?

I. Ber. I would have you
Trust him who leaves his life in trust with
 you.
Doge. But I must know your plan, your
 names, and numbers;
The last may then be doubled, and the
 former
Matured and strengthen'd.
I. Ber. We're enough already;
You are the sole ally we covet now.
Doge. But bring me to the knowledge of
 your chiefs.
I. Ber. That shall be done upon your
 formal pledge
To keep the faith that we will pledge to you.
Doge. When? where?
I. Ber. This night I'll bring to your
 apartment
Two of the principals: a greater number
Were hazardous.
Doge. Stay, I must think of this.—
What if I were to trust myself amongst you,
And leave the palace?
I. Ber. You must come alone.
Doge. With but my nephew.
I. Ber. Not were he your son.
Doge. Wretch! darest thou name my son?
 He died in arms
At Sapienza for this faithless state.
Oh! that he were alive, and I in ashes!
Or that he were alive ere I be ashes!
I should not need the dubious aid of
 strangers.
I. Ber. Not one of all those strangers
 whom thou doubtest,
But will regard thee with a filial feeling,
So that thou keep'st a father's faith with
 them.
Doge. The die is cast. Where is the place
 of meeting?
I. Ber. At midnight I will be alone and
 mask'd
Where'er your highness pleases to direct me,
To wait your coming, and conduct you where
You shall receive our homage, and pronounce
Upon our project.
Doge. At what hour arises
The moon?
I. Ber. Late, but the atmosphere is thick
 and dusky,
'T is a sirocco.
Doge. At the midnight hour, then,
Near to the church where sleep my sires;
 the same,
Twin-named from the apostles John and
 Paul;
A gondola, with one oar only, will
Lurk in the narrow channel which glides by.
Be there.
I. Ber. I will not fail.

Doge. And now retire——
I. Ber. In the full hope your highness
 will not falter
In your great purpose. Prince, I take my
 leave. [*Exit* ISRAEL BERTUCCIO.
Doge (*solus*). At midnight, by the church
 Saints John and Paul,
Where sleep my noble fathers, I repair—
To what? to hold a council in the dark
With common ruffians leagued to ruin states!
And will not my great sires leap from the
 vault,
Where lie two doges who preceded me,
And pluck me down amongst them? Would
 they could!
For I should rest in honour with the honour'd.
Alas! I must not think of them, but those
Who have made me thus unworthy of
 a name
Noble and brave as aught of consular
On Roman marbles; but I will redeem it
Back to its antique lustre in our annals,
By sweet revenge on all that's base in
 Venice,
And freedom to the rest, or leave it black
To all the growing calumnies of time,
Which never spare the fame of him who
 fails,
But try the Cæsar, or the Catiline,
By the true touchstone of desert—success.

————◆————

Act II.

Scene I.—*An Apartment in the Ducal Palace.*

ANGIOLINA (*wife of the* DOGE) *and* MARIANNA.

Ang. What was the Doge's answer?
Mar. That he was
That moment summon'd to a conference.
But 'tis by this time ended. I perceived
Not long ago the senators embarking;
And the last gondola may now be seen
Gliding into the throng of barks which stud
The glittering waters.
Ang. Would he were return'd!
He has been much disquieted of late;
And Time, which has not tamed his fiery
 spirit,
Nor yet enfeebled even his mortal frame,
Which seems to me more nourish'd by a soul
So quick and restless that it would consume
Less hardy clay—Time has but little power
On his resentments or his griefs. Unlike
To other spirits of his order, who,
In the first burst of passion, pour away
Their wrath or sorrow, all things wear in
 him

An aspect of eternity: his thoughts,
His feelings, passions, good or evil, all
Have nothing of old age; and his bold brow
Bears but the scars of mind, the thoughts of
 years,
Not their decrepitude: and he of late
Has been more agitated than his wont.
Would he were come! for I alone have
 power
Upon his troubled spirit.
Mar. It is true,
His highness has of late been greatly moved
By the affront of Steno, and with cause:
But the offender doubtless even now
Is doom'd to expiate his rash insult with
Such chastisement as will enforce respect
To female virtue, and to noble blood.
Ang. 'Twas a gross insult; but I heed it
 not
For the rash scorner's falsehood in itself,
But for the effect, the deadly deep impression
Which it has made upon Faliero's soul,
The proud, the fiery, the austere—austere
To all save me: I tremble when I think
To what it may conduct.
Mar. Assuredly
The Doge cannot suspect you?
Ang. Suspect *me*!
Why Steno dared not: when he scrawl'd his
 lie,
Grovelling by stealth in the moon's glimmer-
 ing light,
His own still conscience smote him for the
 act,
And every shadow on the walls frown'd
 shame
Upon his coward calumny.
Mar. 'T were fit
He should be punish'd grievously.
Ang. He is so.
Mar. What! is the sentence pass'd? is he
 condemn'd?
Ang. I know not that, but he has been
 detected.
Mar. And deem you this enough for such
 foul scorn?
Ang. I would not be a judge in my own
 cause,
Nor do I know what sense of punishment
May reach the soul of ribalds such as Steno;
But if his insults sink no deeper in
The minds of the inquisitors than they
Have ruffled mine, he will, for all acquittance,
Be left to his own shamelessness or shame.
Mar. Some sacrifice is due to slander'd
 virtue.
Ang. Why, what is virtue if it needs a
 victim?
Or if it must depend upon men's words?
The dying Roman said, "'t was but a name:"

It were indeed no more, if human breath
Could make or mar it.
 Mar. Yet full many a dame,
Stainless and faithful, would feel all the
 wrong
Of such a slander; and less rigid ladies,
Such as abound in Venice, would be loud
And all-inexorable in their cry
For justice.
 Ang. This but proves it is the name
And not the quality they prize: the first
Have found it a hard task to hold their
 honour,
If they require it to be blazon'd forth;
And those who have not kept it, seek its
 seeming
As they would look out for an ornament
Of which they feel the want, but not because
They think it so; they live in others' thoughts,
And would seem honest as they must seem
 fair.
 Mar. You have strange thoughts for a
 patrician dame.
 Ang. And yet they were my father's; with
 his name,
The sole inheritance he left.
 Mar. You want none;
Wife to a prince, the chief of the Republic.
 Ang. I should have sought none though
 a peasant's bride,
But feel not less the love and gratitude
Due to my father, who bestow'd my hand
Upon his early, tried, and trusted friend,
The Count Val di Marino, now our Doge.
 Mar. And with that hand did he bestow
 your heart?
 Ang. He did so, or it had not been
 bestow'd.
 Mar. Yet this strange disproportion in
 your years,
And, let me add, disparity of tempers,
Might make the world doubt whether such
 an union
Could make you wisely, permanently happy.
 Ang. The world will think with world-
 lings; but my heart
Has still been in my duties, which are many,
But never difficult.
 Mar. And do you love him?
 Ang. I love all noble qualities which merit
Love, and I loved my father, who first
 taught me
To single out what we should love in others,
And to subdue all tendency to lend
The best and purest feelings of our nature
To baser passions. He bestow'd my hand
Upon Faliero: he had known him noble,
Brave, generous; rich in all the qualities
Of soldier, citizen, and friend; in all
Such have I found him as my father said.

His faults are those that dwell in the high
 bosoms
Of men who have commanded; too much
 pride,
And the deep passions fiercely foster'd by
The uses of patricians, and a life
Spent in the storms of state and war; and
 also
From the quick sense of honour, which
 becomes
A duty to a certain sign, a vice
When overstrain'd, and this I fear in him.
And then he has been rash from his youth
 upwards,
Yet temper'd by redeeming nobleness
In such sort, that the wariest of republics
Has lavish'd all its chief employs upon him,
From his first fight to his last embassy,
From which on his return the dukedom met
 him.
 Mar. But previous to this marriage, had
 your heart
Ne'er beat for any of the noble youth,
Such as in years had been more meet to
 match
Beauty like yours? or since have you ne'er
 seen
One, who, if your fair hand were still to
 give,
Might now pretend to Loredano's daughter?
 Ang. I answer'd your first question when
 I said
I married.
 Mar. And the second?
 Ang. Needs no answer.
 Mar. I pray you pardon, if I have offended.
 Ang. I feel no wrath, but some surprise:
 I knew not
That wedded bosoms could permit themselves
To ponder upon what they *now* might choose,
Or aught save their past choice.
 Mar. 'Tis their past choice
That far too often makes them deem they
 would
Now choose more wisely, could they cancel it.
 Ang. It may be so. I knew not of such
 thoughts.
 Mar. Here comes the Doge—shall I
 retire?
 Ang. It may
Be better you should quit me; he seems
 wrapt
In thought—How pensively he takes his way!
 [*Exit* MARIANNA.

 Enter the DOGE *and* PIETRO.

 Doge (*musing*). There is a certain Philip
 Calendaro
Now in the Arsenal, who holds command
Of eighty men, and has great influence

Besides on all the spirits of his comrades:
This man, I hear, is bold and popular,
Sudden and daring, and yet secret; 't would
Be well that he were won: I needs must
 hope
That Israel Bertuccio has secured him,
But fain would be——
 Pie. My lord, pray pardon me
For breaking in upon your meditation;
The Senator Bertuccio, your kinsman,
Charged me to follow and inquire your plea-
 sure
To fix an hour when he may speak with you.
 Doge. At sunset.—Stay a moment—let me
 see—
Say in the second hour of night. [*Exit* PIETRO.
 Ang. My lord!
 Doge. My dearest child, forgive me—why
 delay
So long approaching me?—I saw you not.
 Ang. You were absorb'd in thought, and
 he who now
Has parted from you might have words of
 weight
To bear you from the senate.
 Doge. From the senate?
 Ang. I would not interrupt him in his duty
And theirs.
 Doge. The senate's duty! you mistake;
'T is we who owe all service to the senate.
 Ang. I thought the Duke had held com-
 mand in Venice.
 Doge. He shall.—But let that pass.—We
 will be jocund.
How fares it with you? have you been
 abroad?
The day is overcast, but the calm wave
Favours the gondolier's light skimming oar;
Or have you held a levee of your friends?
Or has your music made you solitary?
Say—is there aught that you would will
 within
The little sway now left the Duke? or aught
Of fitting splendour, or of honest pleasure,
Social or lonely, that would glad your heart,
To compensate for many a dull hour, wasted
On an old man oft moved with many cares?
Speak, and 't is done.
 Ang. You're ever kind to me.
I have nothing to desire, or to request,
Except to see you oftener and calmer.
 Doge. Calmer?
 Ang. Ay, calmer, my good lord.—Ah, why
Do you still keep apart, and walk alone,
And let such strong emotions stamp your
 brow,
As not betraying their full import, yet
Disclose too much?
 Doge. Disclose too much!—of what?
What is there to disclose?

 Ang. A heart so ill
At ease.
 Doge. 'Tis nothing, child.—But in the state
You know what daily cares oppress all those
Who govern this precarious commonwealth;
Now suffering from the Genoese without,
And malcontents within—'t is this which
 makes me
More pensive and less tranquil than my wont.
 Ang. Yet this existed long before, and
 never
Till in these late days did I see you thus.
Forgive me; there is something at your heart
More than the mere discharge of public duties,
Which long use and a talent like to yours
Have render'd light, nay, a necessity,
To keep your mind from stagnating. 'T is not
In hostile states, nor perils, thus to shake
 you,—
You, who have stood all storms and never
 sunk,
And climb'd up to the pinnacle of power
And never fainted by the way, and stand
Upon it, and can look down steadily
Along the depth beneath, and ne'er feel dizzy.
Were Genoa's galleys riding in the port,
Were civil fury raging in Saint Mark's,
You are not to be wrought on, but would
 fall,
As you have risen, with an unalter'd brow:
Your feelings now are of a different kind;
Something has stung your pride, not patriot-
 ism.
 Doge. Pride! Angiolina? Alas! none is
 left me.
 Ang. Yes—the same sin that overthrew
 the angels,
And of all sins most easily besets
Mortals the nearest to the angelic nature:
The vile are only vain; the great are proud.
 Doge. I *had* the pride of honour, of *your*
 honour,
Deep at my heart—But let us change the
 theme.
 Ang. Ah no!—As I have ever shared your
 kindness
In all things else, let me not be shut out
From your distress: were it of public import,
You know I never sought, would never seek
To win a word from you; but feeling now
Your grief is private, it belongs to me
To lighten or divide it. Since the day
When foolish Steno's ribaldry detected
Unfix'd your quiet, you are greatly changed,
And I would soothe you back to what you were.
 Doge. To what I was!—have you heard
 Steno's sentence?
 Ang. No.
 Doge. A month's arrest.
 Ang. Is it not enough?

Doge. Enough!—yes, for a drunken galley slave,
Who, stung by stripes, may murmur at his master;
But not for a deliberate, false, cool villain,
Who stains a lady's and a prince's honour
Even on the throne of his authority.

Ang. There seems to me enough in the conviction
Of a patrician guilty of a falsehood:
All other punishment were light unto
His loss of honour.

Doge. Such men have no honour;
They have but their vile lives—and these are spared.

Ang. You would not have him die for this offence?

Doge. Not *now :*—being still alive, I'd have him live
Long as *he* can; he has ceased to merit death;
The guilty saved hath damn'd his hundred judges,
And he is pure, for now his crime is theirs.

Ang. Oh! had this false and flippant libeller
Shed his young blood for his absurd lampoon,
Ne'er from that moment could this breast have known
A joyous hour, or dreamless slumber more.

Doge. Does not the law of Heaven say blood for blood?
And he who *taints* kills more than he who sheds it.
Is it the *pain* of blows, or *shame* of blows,
That makes such deadly to the sense of man?
Do not the laws of man say blood for honour,—
And, less than honour, for a little gold?
Say not the laws of nations blood for treason?
Is't nothing to have fill'd these veins with poison
For their once healthful current? is it nothing
To have stain'd your name and mine—the noblest names?
Is't nothing to have brought into contempt
A prince before his people? to have fail'd
In the respect accorded by mankind
To youth in woman, and old age in man?
To virtue in your sex, and dignity
In ours?—But let them look to it who have saved him.

Ang. Heaven bids us to forgive our enemies.

Doge. Doth Heaven forgive her own? Is Satan saved
From wrath eternal?

Ang. Do not speak thus wildly—
Heaven will alike forgive you and your foes.

Doge. Amen! May Heaven forgive them!

Ang. And will you?

Doge. Yes, when they are in heaven!

Ang. And not till then?

Doge. What matters my forgiveness? an old man's,
Worn out, scorn'd, spurn'd, abused; what matters then
My pardon more than my resentment, both
Being weak and worthless? I have lived too long;
But let us change the argument.—My child!
My injured wife, the child of Loredano,
The brave, the chivalrous, how little deem'd
Thy father, wedding thee unto his friend,
That he was linking thee to shame!—Alas!
Shame without sin, for thou art faultless. Hadst thou
But had a different husband, *any* husband
In Venice save the Doge, this blight, this brand,
This blasphemy had never fallen upon thee.
So young, so beautiful, so good, so pure,
To suffer this, and yet be unavenged!

Ang. I am too well avenged, for you still love me,
And trust, and honour me; and all men know
That you are just, and I am true: what more
Could I require, or you command?

Doge. 'Tis well,
And may be better; but whate'er betide,
Be thou at least kind to my memory.

Ang. Why speak you thus?

Doge. It is no matter why;
But I would still, whatever others think,
Have your respect both now and in my grave.

Ang. Why should you doubt it? has it ever fail'd?

Doge. Come hither, child; I would a word with you.
Your father was my friend; unequal fortune
Made him my debtor for some courtesies
Which bind the good more firmly: when, oppress'd
With his last malady, he will'd our union,
It was not to repay me, long repaid
Before by his great loyalty in friendship;
His object was to place your orphan beauty
In honourable safety from the perils
Which, in this scorpion nest of vice, assail
A lonely and undower'd maid. I did not
Think with him, but would not oppose the thought
Which soothed his death-bed.

Ang. I have not forgotten
The nobleness with which you bade me speak
If my young heart held any preference
Which would have made me happier; nor your offer
To make my dowry equal to the rank
Of aught in Venice, and forego all claim

My father's last injunction gave you.

Doge. Thus,
'Twas not a foolish dotard's vile caprice,
Nor the false edge of aged appetite,
Which made me covetous of girlish beauty,
And a young bride: for in my fieriest youth
I sway'd such passions; nor was this my age
Infected with that leprosy of lust
Which taints the hoariest years of vicious
 men,
Making them ransack to the very last
The dregs of pleasure for their vanish'd joys;
Or buy in selfish marriage some young victim,
Too helpless to refuse a state that's honest,
Too feeling not to know herself a wretch.
Our wedlock was not of this sort; you had
Freedom from me to choose, and urged in
 answer
Your father's choice.

Ang. I did so; I would do so
In face of earth and heaven; for I have never
Repented for my sake; sometimes for yours,
In pondering o'er your late disquietudes.

Doge. I knew my heart would never treat
 you harshly;
I knew my days could not disturb you
 long;
And then the daughter of my earliest friend,
His worthy daughter, free to choose again,
Wealthier and wiser, in the ripest bloom
Of womanhood, more skilful to select
By passing these probationary years
Inheriting a prince's name and riches,
Secured, by the short penance of enduring
An old man for some summers, against all
That law's chicane or envious kinsmen might
Have urged against her right; my best
 friend's child
Would choose more fitly in respect of years,
And not less truly in a faithful heart.

Ang. My lord, I look'd but to my father's
 wishes,
Hallow'd by his last words, and to my heart
For doing all its duties, and replying
With faith to him with whom I was affianced.
Ambitious hopes ne'er cross'd my dreams;
 and should
The hour you speak of come, it will be seen
 so.

Doge. I do believe you; and I know you
 true:
For love, romantic love, which in my youth
I knew to be illusion, and ne'er saw
Lasting, but often fatal, it had been
No lure for me, in my most passionate days,
And could not be so now, did such exist.
But such respect, and mildly paid regard
As a true feeling for your welfare, and
A free compliance with all honest wishes,—
A kindness to your virtues, watchfulness

Not shown, but shadowing o'er such little
 failings
As youth is apt in, so as not to check
Rashly, but win you from them ere you knew
You had been won, but thought the change
 your choice;
A pride not in your beauty, but your conduct;
A trust in you; a patriarchal love,
And not a doting homage · friendship, faith,—
Such estimation in your eyes as these
Might claim, I hoped for.

Ang. And have ever had.

Doge. I think so. For the difference in
 our years
You knew it, choosing me, and chose: I
 trusted
Not to my qualities, nor would have faith
In such, nor outward ornaments of nature,
Were I still in my five and twentieth spring;
I trusted to the blood of Loredano
Pure in your veins; I trusted to the soul
God gave you—to the truths your father
 taught you—
To your belief in Heaven—to your mild vir-
 tues—
To your own faith and honour, for my own.

Ang. You have done well.—I thank you
 for that trust,
Which I have never for one moment ceased
To honour you the more for.

Doge. Where is honour,
Innate and precept-strengthen'd, 'tis the rock
Of faith connubial: where it is not—where
Light thoughts are lurking, or the vanities
Of worldly pleasure rankle in the heart,
Or sensual throbs convulse it, well I know
'T were hopeless for humanity to dream
Of honesty in such infected blood,
Although 't were wed to him it covets most:
An incarnation of the poet's god
In all his marble-chisell'd beauty, or
The demi-deity, Alcides, in
His majesty of superhuman manhood,
Would not suffice to bind where virtue is not;
It is consistency which forms and proves it:
Vice cannot fix, and virtue cannot change.
The once fall'n woman must for ever fall;
For vice must have variety, while virtue
Stands like the sun, and all which rolls
 around
Drinks life, and light, and glory from her
 aspect.

Ang. And seeing, feeling thus this truth
 in others,
(I pray you pardon me;) but wherefore yield
 you
To the most fierce of fatal passions, and
Disquiet your great thoughts with restless
 hate
Of such a thing as Steno?

Doge. You mistake me.
It is not Steno who could move me thus;
Had it been so, he should——but let that
 pass.
Ang. What is 't you feel so deeply, then,
 even now?
Doge. The violated majesty of Venice,
At once insulted in her lord and laws.
Ang. Alas! why will you thus consider it?
Doge. I have thought on 't till——but let
 me lead you back
To what I urged; all these things being
 noted,
I wedded you; the world then did me justice
Upon the motive, and my conduct proved
They did me right, while yours was all to
 praise:
You had all freedom, all respect, all trust
From me and mine; and, born of those who
 made
Princes at home, and swept kings from their
 thrones
On foreign shores, in all things you appear'd
Worthy to be our first of native dames.
Ang. To what does this conduct?
Doge. To thus much—that
A miscreant's angry breath may blast it all—
A villain, whom for his unbridled bearing,
Even in the midst of our great festival,
I caused to be conducted forth, and taught
How to demean himself in ducal chambers;
A wretch like this may leave upon the
 wall
The blighting venom of his sweltering heart,
And this shall spread itself in general poison;
And woman's innocence, man's honour, pass
Into a by-word; and the doubly felon
(Who first insulted your virgin modesty
By a gross affront to your attendant damsels
Amidst the noblest of our dames in public)
Requite himself for his most just expulsion
By blackening publicly his sovereign's con-
 sort,
And be absolved by his upright compeers.
Ang. But he has been condemn'd into
 captivity.
Doge. For such as him a dungeon were
 acquittal;
And his brief term of mock-arrest will pass
Within a palace. But I 've done with him;
The rest must be with you.
Ang. With me, my lord?
Doge. Yes, Angiolina. Do not marvel; I
Have let this prey upon me till I feel
My life cannot be long; and fain would have
 you
Regard the injunctions you will find within
This scroll (*Giving her a paper*)——Fear not;
 they are for your advantage:
Read them hereafter at the fitting hour.

Ang. My lord, in life, and after life, you
 shall
Be honour'd still by me: but may your days
Be many yet—and happier than the present!
This passion will give way, and you will be
Serene, and what you should be—what you
 were.
Doge. I will be what I should be, or be
 nothing;
But never more—oh! never, never more,
O'er the few days or hours which yet await
The blighted old age of Faliero, shall
Sweet quiet shed her sunset! Never more
Those summer shadows rising from the past
Of a not ill-spent nor inglorious life,
Mellowing the last hours as the night
 approaches,
Shall soothe me to my moment of long rest.
I had but little more to ask, or hope,
Save the regards due to the blood and sweat,
And the soul's labour through which I had
 toil'd
To make my country honour'd. As her ser-
 vant—
Her servant, though her chief—I would have
 gone
Down to my fathers with a name serene
And pure as theirs; but this has been denied
 me.—
Would I had died at Zara!
Ang. There you saved
The state; then live to save her still. A day,
Another day like that would be the best
Reproof to them, and sole revenge for you.
Doge. But one such day occurs within an
 age;
My life is little less than one, and 't is
Enough for Fortune to have granted *once*,
That which scarce one more favour'd citizen
May win in many states and years. But why
Thus speak I? Venice has forgot that day—
Then why should I remember it?—Farewell,
Sweet Angiolina! I must to my cabinet;
There's much for me to do—and the hour
 hastens.
Ang. Remember what you were.
Doge. It were in vain!
Joy's recollection is no longer joy,
While sorrow's memory is a sorrow still.
Ang. At least, whate'er may urge, let me
 implore
That you will take some little pause of rest:
Your sleep for many nights has been so
 turbid,
That it had been relief to have awaked you,
Had I not hoped that Nature would o'erpower
At length the thoughts which shock your
 slumbers thus.
An hour of rest will give you to your toils
With fitter thoughts and freshen'd strength.

Doge.　　　　　　　　　　　I cannot—
I must not, if I could; for never was
Such reason to be watchful: yet a few—
Yet a few days and dream-perturbed nights,
And I shall slumber well—but where?—no
　　　matter.
Adieu, my Angiolina.
　　Ang.　　　　　　　　Let me be
An instant—yet an instant your companion!
I cannot bear to leave you thus.
　　Doge.　　　　　　　　Come then,
My gentle child—forgive me; thou wert made
For better fortunes than to share in mine,
Now darkling in their close toward the deep
　　　vale
Where Death sits robed in his all-sweeping
　　　shadow.
When I am gone—it may be sooner than
Even these years warrant, for there is that
　　　stirring
Within, above, around, that in this city
Will make the cemeteries populous
As e'er they were by pestilence or war,—
When I *am* nothing, let that which I *was*
Be still sometimes a name on thy sweet lips,
A shadow in thy fancy, of a thing
Which would not have thee mourn it, but
　　　remember.
Let us begone, my child—the time is pressing.
　　　　　　　　　　　　　　　[*Exeunt.*

Scene II.

A retired spot near the Arsenal.

ISRAEL BERTUCCIO *and* PHILIP CALENDARO.

　Cal. How sped you, Israel, in your late
　　　complaint?
　I. Ber. Why, well.
　Cal. Is't possible! will he be punish'd?
　I. Ber.　　　　　　　　　　　Yes.
　Cal. With what? a mulct or an arrest?
　I. Ber.　　　　　　　　　With death!
　Cal. Now you rave, or must intend re-
　　　venge,
Such as I counsell'd you, with your own
　　　hand.
　I. Ber. Yes; and for one sole draught of
　　　hate, forego
The great redress we meditate for Venice,
And change a life of hope for one of exile;
Leaving one scorpion crush'd, and thousands
　　　stinging
My friends, my family, my countrymen!
No, Calendaro; these same drops of blood,
Shed shamefully, shall have the whole of his
For their requital——but not only his;
We will not strike for private wrongs alone:
Such are for selfish passions and rash men,
But are unworthy a tyrannicide.

　Cal. You have more patience than I care
　　　to boast.
Had I been present when you bore this in-
　　　sult,
I must have slain him, or expired myself
In the vain effort to repress my wrath.
　I. Ber. Thank Heaven you were not—all
　　　had else been marr'd:
As 't is, our cause looks prosperous still.
　Cal.　　　　　　　　　　　You saw
The Doge—what answer gave he?
　I. Ber.　　　　　　　　That there was
No punishment for such as Barbaro.
　Cal. I told you so before, and that 't was
　　　idle
To think of justice from such hands.
　I. Ber.　　　　　　　　　At least,
It lull'd suspicion, showing confidence.
Had I been silent, not a sbirro but
Had kept me in his eye, as meditating
A silent, solitary, deep revenge.
　Cal. But wherefore not address you to
　　　the Council?
The Doge is a mere puppet, who can scarce
Obtain right for himself. Why speak to him?
　I. Ber. You shall know that hereafter.
　Cal.　　　　　　　　　Why not now?
　I. Ber. Be patient but till midnight. Get
　　　your musters,
And bid our friends prepare their companies:
Set all in readiness to strike the blow,
Perhaps in a few hours; we have long waited
For a fit time—that hour is on the dial,
It may be, of to-morrow's sun: delay
Beyond may breed us double danger. See
That all be punctual at our place of meeting,
And arm'd, excepting those of the Sixteen,
Who will remain among the troops to wait
The signal.
　Cal.　　　These brave words have breathed
　　　new life
Into my veins; I'm sick of these protracted
And hesitating councils: day on day
Crawl'd on, and added but another link
To our long fetters, and some fresher wrong
Inflicted on our brethren or ourselves,
Helping to swell our tyrants' bloated strength.
Let us but deal upon them, and I care not
For the result, which must be death or free
　　　dom!
I'm weary to the heart of finding neither.
　I. Ber. We will be free in life or death!
　　　the grave
Is chainless. Have you all the musters ready?
And are the sixteen companies completed
To sixty?
　Cal. All save two, in which there are
Twenty-five wanting to make up the number.
　I. Ber. No matter; we can do without.
　　　Whose are they?

Cal. Bertram's and old Soranzo's, both of whom
Appear less forward in the cause than we are.

I. Ber. Your fiery nature makes you deem all those
Who are not restless cold : but there exists
Oft in concentred spirits not less daring
Than in more loud avengers. Do not doubt them.

Cal. I do not doubt the elder; but in Bertram
There is a hesitating softness, fatal
To enterprise like ours : I've seen that man
Weep like an infant o'er the misery
Of others, heedless of his own, though greater;
And in a recent quarrel I beheld him
Turn sick at sight of blood, although a villain's.

I. Ber. The truly brave are soft of heart and eyes,
And feel for what their duty bids them do.
I have known Bertram long; there doth not breathe
A soul more full of honour.

Cal. It may be so :
I apprehend less treachery than weakness;
Yet as he has no mistress, and no wife
To work upon his milkiness of spirit,
He may go through the ordeal; it is well
He is an orphan, friendless save in us :
A woman or a child had made him less
Than either in resolve.

I. Ber. Such ties are not
For those who are call'd to the high destinies
Which purify corrupted commonwealths;
We must forget all feelings save the *one*,
We must resign all passions save our purpose,
We must behold no object save our country,
And only look on death as beautiful,
So that the sacrifice ascend to heaven,
And draw down freedom on her evermore.

Cal. But if we fail——

I. Ber. They never fail who die
In a great cause : the block may soak their gore;
Their heads may sodden in the sun; their limbs
Be strung to city gates and castle walls—
But still their spirit walks abroad. Though years
Elapse, and others share as dark a doom,
They but augment the deep and sweeping thoughts
Which overpower all others, and conduct
The world at last to freedom. What were we,
If Brutus had not lived? He died in giving
Rome liberty, but left a deathless lesson—
A name which is a virtue, and a soul
Which multiplies itself throughout all time,
When wicked men wax mighty, and a state
Turns servile. He and his high friend were styled
"The last of Romans !" Let us be the first
Of true Venetians, sprung from Roman sires.

Cal. Our fathers did not fly from Attila
Into these isles, where palaces have sprung
On banks redeem'd from the rude ocean's ooze,
To own a thousand despots in his place.
Better bow down before the Hun, and call
A Tartar lord, than these swoln silkworms masters !
The first at least was man, and used his sword
As sceptre : these unmanly creeping things
Command our swords, and rule us with a word
As with a spell.

I. Ber. It shall be broken soon.
You say that all things are in readiness;
To-day I have not been the usual round,
And why thou knowest; but thy vigilance
Will better have supplied my care : these orders
In recent council to redouble now
Our efforts to repair the galleys, have
Lent a fair colour to the introduction
Of many of our cause into the arsenal,
As new artificers for their equipment,
Or fresh recruits obtained in haste to man
The hoped-for fleet.—Are all supplied with arms?

Cal. All who were deem'd trustworthy : there are some
Whom it were well to keep in ignorance
Till it be time to strike, and then supply them;
When in the heat and hurry of the hour
They have no opportunity to pause,
But needs must on with those who will surround them.

I. Ber. You have said well. Have you remark'd all such ?

Cal. I've noted most; and caused the other chiefs
To use like caution in their companies.
As far as I have seen, we are enough
To make the enterprise secure, if 'tis
Commenced to-morrow; but, till 'tis begun,
Each hour is pregnant with a thousand perils.

I. Ber. Let the Sixteen meet at the wonted hour,
Except Soranzo, Nicoletto Blondo,
And Marco Giuda, who will keep their watch
Within the arsenal, and hold all ready,
Expectant of the signal we will fix on.

Cal. We will not fail.
I. Ber. Let all the rest be there;
I have a stranger to present to them.
 Cal. A stranger! doth he know the secret?
 I. Ber. Yes.
 Cal. And have you dared to peril your
 friends' lives
On a rash confidence in one we know not?
 I. Ber. I have risk'd no man's life except
 my own—
Of that be certain: he is one who may
Make our assurance doubly sure, according
His aid; and if reluctant, he no less
Is in our power: he comes alone with me,
And cannot 'scape us; but he will not swerve.
 Cal. I cannot judge of this until I know
 him:
Is he one of our order?
 I. Ber. Ay, in spirit,
Although a child of greatness; he is one—
Who would become a throne, or overthrow
 one—
One who has done great deeds, and seen
 great changes;
No tyrant, though bred up to tyranny;
Valiant in war, and sage in council: noble
In nature, although haughty; quick, yet
 wary:
Yet for all this, so full of certain passions,
That if once stirr'd and baffled, as he has
 been
Upon the tenderest points, there is no Fury
In Grecian story like to that which wrings
His vitals with her burning hands, till he
Grows capable of all things for revenge;
And add too, that his mind is liberal,
He sees and feels the people are oppress'd,
And shares their sufferings. Take him all in
 all,
We have need of such, and such have need of
 us.
 Cal. And what part would you have him
 take with us?
 I. Ber. It may be, that of chief.
 Cal. What! and resign
Your own command as leader?
 I. Ber. Even so.
My object is to make your cause end well,
And not to push myself to power. Ex-
 perience,
Some skill, and your own choice, had mark'd
 me out
To act in trust as your commander, till
Some worthier should appear: if I have
 found such
As you yourselves shall own more worthy,
 think you
That I would hesitate from selfishness,
And, covetous of brief authority,
Stake our deep interest on my single thoughts,

Rather than yield to one above me in
All leading qualities? No, Calendaro,
Know your friend better; but you all shall
 judge.
Away! and let us meet at the fix'd hour.
Be vigilant, and all will yet go well.
 Cal. Worthy Bertuccio, I have known
 you ever
Trusty and brave, with head and heart to
 plan
What I have still been prompt to execute.
For my own part, I seek no other chief;
What the rest will decide I know not, but
I am with you, as I have ever been,
In all our undertakings. Now farewell,
Until the hour of midnight sees us meet.
 [*Exeunt.*

Act III.

Scene I.—*Scene, the Space between the Canal
and the Church of San Giovanni e San
Paolo. An equestrian Statue before it.—
A Gondola lies in the Canal at some dis-
tance.*

Enter the Doge *alone, disguised.*

Doge (*solus*). I am before the hour, the
 hour whose voice,
Pealing into the arch of night, might strike
These palaces with ominous tottering,
And rock their marbles to the corner-stone,
Waking the sleepers from some hideous
 dream
Of indistinct but awful augury
Of that which will befall them. Yes, proud
 city!
Thou must be cleansed of the black blood
 which makes thee
A lazar-house of tyranny: the task
Is forced upon me, I have sought it not;
And therefore was I punish'd, seeing this
Patrician pestilence spread on and on,
Until at length it smote me in my slumbers,
And I am tainted, and must wash away
The plague spots in the healing wave. Tall
 fane!
Where sleep my fathers, whose dim statues
 shadow
The floor which doth divide us from the dead,
Where all the pregnant hearts of our bold
 blood,
Moulder'd into a mite of ashes, hold
In one shrunk heap what once made many
 heroes,
When what is now a handful shook the
 earth—
Fane of the tutelar saints who guard our
 house!

Vault where two Doges rest—my sires! who
 died
The one of toil, the other in the field,
With a long race of other lineal chiefs
And sages, whose great labours, wounds, and
 state
I have inherited,—let the graves gape,
Till all thine aisles be peopled with the dead,
And pour them from thy portals to gaze
 on me!
I call them up, and them and thee to witness
What it hath been which put me to this
 task—
Their pure high blood, their blazon-roll of
 glories,
Their mighty name dishonour'd all *in* me,
Not *by* me, but by the ungrateful nobles
We fought to make our equals, not our
 lords:
And chiefly thou, Ordelafo the brave,
Who perish'd in the field, where I since
 conquer'd,
Battling at Zara, did the hecatombs
Of thine and Venice' foes, there offer'd up
By thy descendant, merit such acquittance?
Spirits! smile down upon me; for my cause
Is yours, in all life now can be of yours,—
Your fame, your name, all mingled up in
 mine,
And in the future fortunes of our race!
Let me but prosper, and I make this city
Free and immortal, and our house's name
Worthier of what you were, now and here-
 after.

 Enter ISRAEL BERTUCCIO

I. Ber. Who goes there?
Doge. A friend to Venice.
I. Ber. 'Tis he.
Welcome, my lord,—you are before the time.
Doge. I am ready to proceed to your
 assembly.
I. Ber. Have with you.—I am proud and
 pleased to see
Such confident alacrity. Your doubts
Since our last meeting, then, are all dispell'd?
Doge. Not so—but I have set my little
 left
Of life upon this cast: the die was thrown
When I first listen'd to your treason.—Start
 not!
That is the word; I cannot shape my tongue
To syllable black deeds into smooth names,
Though I be wrought on to commit them.
 When
I heard you tempt your sovereign, and
 forbore
To have you dragg'd to prison, I became
Your guiltiest accomplice: now you may,
If it so please you, do as much by me.

I. Ber. Strange words, my lord, and most
 unmerited;
I am no spy, and neither are we traitors.
Doge. We—*We!*—no matter—you have
 earn'd the right
To talk of *us.*—But to the point.—If this
Attempt succeeds, and Venice, render'd free
And flourishing, when we are in our graves,
Conducts her generations to our tombs,
And makes her children with their little
 hands
Strew flowers o'er her deliverers' ashes, then
The consequence will sanctify the deed,
And we shall be like the two Bruti in
The annals of hereafter; but if not,
If we should fail, employing bloody means
And secret plot, although to a good end,
Still we are traitors, honest Israel;—thou
No less than he who was thy sovereign
Six hours ago, and now thy brother rebel.
I. Ber. 'Tis not the moment to consider
 thus,
Else I could answer.—Let us to the meeting,
Or we may be observed in lingering here.
Doge. We *are* observed, and have been.
I. Ber. We observed!
Let me discover—and this steel——
Doge. Put up;
Here are no human witnesses: look there—
What see you?
I. Ber. Only a tall warrior's statue
Bestriding a proud steed, in the dim light
Of the dull moon.
Doge. That warrior was the sire
Of my sire's fathers, and that statue was
Decreed to him by the twice rescued city:—
Think you that he looks down on us or no?
I. Ber. My lord, these are mere fantasies;
 there are
No eyes in marble.
Doge. But there are in Death.
I tell thee, man, there is a spirit in
Such things that acts and sees, unseen,
 though felt;
And, if there be a spell to stir the dead,
'Tis in such deeds as we are now upon.
Deem'st thou the souls of such a race as
 mine
Can rest, when he, their last descendant
 chief,
Stands plotting on the brink of their pure
 graves
With stung plebeians?
I. Ber. It had been as well
To have pondered this before,—ere you em-
 bark'd
In our great enterprise.—Do you repent?
Doge. No—but I *feel*, and shall do to the
 last.
I cannot quench a glorious life at once

Nor dwindle to the thing I now must be,
And take men's lives by stealth, without
 some pause:
Yet doubt me not; it is this very feeling,
And knowing *what* has wrung me to be thus,
Which is your best security. There's not
A roused mechanic in your busy plot
So wrong'd as I, so fall'n, so loudly call'd
To his redress: the very means I am forced
By these fell tyrants to adopt is such,
That I abhor them doubly for the deeds
Which I must do to pay them back for theirs.

I. Ber. Let us away—hark—the hour
 strikes.

Doge. On—on—
It is our knell, or that of Venice—On.

I. Ber. Say rather, 'tis her freedom's
 rising peal
Of triumph.—This way—we are near the
 place. [*Exeunt.*

Scene II.

The House where the Conspirators meet.

DAGOLINO, DORO, BERTRAM, FEDELE TREVI-
SANO, CALENDARO, ANTONIO DELLE BENDE,
&c. &c.

Cal. (*entering*). Are all here?

Dag. All with you; except the three
On duty, and our leader Israel,
Who is expected momently.

Cal. Where's Bertram?

Ber. Here!

Cal. Have you not been able to
 complete
The number wanting in your company?

Ber. I had mark'd out some: but I have
 not dared
To trust them with the secret, till assured
That they were worthy faith.

Cal. There is no need
Of trusting to their faith; *who*, save ourselves
And our more chosen comrades, is aware
Fully of our intent? they think themselves
Engaged in secret to the Signory,
To punish some more dissolute young nobles
Who have defied the law in their excesses;
But once drawn up, and their new swords
 well flesh'd
In the rank hearts of the more odious
 senators,
They will not hesitate to follow up
Their blow upon the others, when they see
The example of their chiefs, and I for one
Will set them such, that they for very shame
And safety will not pause till all have perish'd.

Ber. How say you? *all!*

Cal. Whom wouldst thou spare?

Ber. *I spare?*
I have no power to spare. I only question'd,

Thinking that even amongst these wicked
 men
There might be some, whose age and qualities
Might mark them out for pity.

Cal. Yes, such pity
As when the viper hath been cut to pieces,
The separate fragments quivering in the sun.
In the last energy of venomous life,
Deserve and have. Why, I should think as
 soon
Of pitying some particular fang which made
One in the jaw of the swoln serpent, as
Of saving one of these: they form but links
Of one long chain; one mass, one breath,
 one body; .
They eat, and drink, and live, and breed
 together,
Revel, and lie, oppress, and kill in concert,—
So let them die as *one!*

Dag. Should *one* survive,
He would be dangerous as the whole; it is
 not
Their number, be it tens or thousands, but
The spirit of this aristocracy
Which must be rooted out; and if there were
A single shoot of the old tree in life,
'Twould fasten in the soil, and spring again
To gloomy verdure and to bitter fruit.
Bertram, we must be firm!

Cal. Look to it well,
Bertram; I have an eye upon thee.

Ber. Who
Distrusts me?

Cal. Not I; for if I did so,
Thou wouldst not now be there to talk of
 trust:
It is thy softness, not thy want of faith,
Which makes thee to be doubted.

Ber. You should know
Who hear me, who and what I am; a man
Roused like yourselves to overthrow oppres-
 sion;
A kind man, I am apt to think, as some
Of you have found me; and if brave or no,
You, Calendaro, can pronounce, who have
 seen me
Put to the proof; or, if you should have
 doubts,
I'll clear them on your person!

Cal. You are welcome,
When once our enterprise is o'er, which
 must not
Be interrupted by a private brawl.

Ber. I am no brawler; but can bear my-
 self
As far among the foe as any he
Who hears me; else why have I been selected
To be of your chief comrades? but no less
I own my natural weakness; I have not
Yet learn'd to think of indiscriminate murder

Without some sense of shuddering; and the
 sight
Of blood which spouts through hoary scalps
 is not
To me a thing of triumph, nor the death
Of men surprised a glory. Well—too well
I know that we must do such things on those
Whose acts have raised up such avengers;
 but
If there were some of these who could be
 saved
From out this sweeping fate, for our own
 sakes
And for our honour, to take off some stain
Of massacre, which else pollutes it wholly,
I had been glad; and see no cause in this
For sneer, nor for suspicion!
 Dag. Calm thee, Bertram,
For we suspect thee not, and take good heart.
It is the cause, and not our will, which asks
Such actions from our hands: we'll wash
 away
All stains in Freedom's fountain!

Enter Israel Bertuccio, *and the* Doge,
 disguised.

 Dag. Welcome, Israel.
 Consp. Most welcome.—Brave Bertuccio,
 thou art late—
Who is this stranger?
 Cal. It is time to name him.
Our comrades are even now prepared to
 greet him
In brotherhood, as I have made it known
That thou wouldst add a brother to our
 cause,
Approved by thee, and thus approved by all,
Such is our trust in all thine actions. Now
Let him unfold himself.
 I. Ber. Stranger, step forth!
 [*The Doge discovers himself.*
 Consp. To arms!—we are betray'd—it is
 the Doge!
Down with them both! our traitorous cap-
 tain, and
The tyrant he hath sold us to.
 Cal. (*drawing his sword*). Hold! hold!
Who moves a step against them dies. Hold!
 hear
Bertuccio—What! are you appall'd to see
A lone, unguarded, weaponless old man
Amongst you?—Israel, speak; what means
 this mystery?
 I. Ber. Let them advance and strike at
 their own bosoms,
Ungrateful suicides! for on our lives
Depend their own, their fortunes, and their
 hopes.
 Doge. Strike!—If I dreaded death, a death
 more fearful

Than any your rash weapons can inflict,
I should not now be here: Oh, noble Courage!
The eldest born of Fear, which makes you
 brave
Against this solitary hoary head!
See the bold chiefs, who would reform a state
And shake down senates, mad with wrath
 and dread
At sight of one patrician! Butcher me!
You can, I care not.—Israel, are these men
The mighty hearts you spoke of? look upon
 them!
 Cal. Faith! he hath shamed us, and
 deservedly.
Was this your trust in your true chief
 Bertuccio,
To turn your swords against him and his
 guest?
Sheathe them, and hear him.
 I. Ber. I disdain to speak.
They might and must have known a heart
 like mine
Incapable of treachery; and the power
They gave me to adopt all fitting means
To further their design was ne'er abused.
They might be certain that whoe'er was
 brought
By me into this council had been led
To take his choice—as brother, or as victim.
 Doge. And which am I to be? your actions
 leave
Some cause to doubt the freedom of the
 choice.
 I. Ber. My lord, we would have perish'd
 here together,
Had these rash men proceeded; but, behold,
They are ashamed of that mad moment's
 impulse,
And droop their heads; believe me, they
 are such
As I described them.—Speak to them.
 Cal. Ay, speak;
We are all listening in wonder.
 I. Ber. (*addressing the conspirators*). You
 are safe,
Nay, more, almost triumphant—listen then,
And know my words for truth.
 Doge. You see me here,
As one of you hath said, an old, unarm'd,
Defenceless man; and yesterday you saw me
Presiding in the hall of ducal state,
Apparent sovereign of our hundred isles,
Robed in official purple, dealing out
The edicts of a power which is not mine,
Nor yours, but of our masters—the patri-
 cians.
Why I was there you know, or think you
 know;
Why I am *here*, he who hath been most
 wrong'd,

He who among you hath been most insulted,
Outraged, and trodden on, until he doubt
If he be worm or no, may answer for me,
Asking of his own heart what brought him
 here ?
You know my recent story, all men know it,
And judge of it far differently from those
Who sate in judgment to heap scorn on
 scorn.
But spare me the recital—it is here,
Here at my heart the outrage—but my words,
Already spent in unavailing plaints,
Would only show my feebleness the more,
And I come here to strengthen even the
 strong,
And urge them on to deeds, and not to war
With woman's weapons ; but I need not
 urge you.
Our private wrongs have sprung from public
 vices,
In this—I cannot call it commonwealth,
Nor kingdom, which hath neither prince nor
 people,
But all the sins of the old Spartan state
Without its virtues—temperance and valour.
The Lords of Lacedæmon were true soldiers,
But ours are Sybarites, while we are Helots,
Of whom I am the lowest, most enslaved ;
Although dress'd out to head a pageant, as
The Greeks of yore made drunk their slaves
 to form
A pastime for their children. You are met
To overthrow this monster of a state,
This mockery of a government, this spectre,
Which must be exorcised with blood,—and
 then
We will renew the times of truth and justice,
Condensing in a fair free commonwealth
Not rash equality but equal rights,
Proportion'd like the columns to the temple,
Giving and taking strength reciprocal,
And making firm the whole with grace and
 beauty,
So that no part could be removed without
Infringement of the general symmetry.
In operating this great change, I claim
To be one of you—if you trust in me ;
If not, strike home,—my life is compromised,
And I would rather fall by freemen's hands
Than live another day to act the tyrant
As delegate of tyrants : such I am not,
And never have been—read it in our annals ;
I can appeal to my past government
In many lands and cities ; they can tell you
If I were an oppressor, or a man
Feeling and thinking for my fellow men.
Haply had I been what the senate sought,
A thing of robes and trinkets, dizen'd out
To sit in state as for a sovereign's picture ;
A popular scourge, a ready sentence-signer,

A stickler for the Senate and "the Forty,"
A sceptic of all measures which had not
The sanction of "the Ten," a council-fawner,
A tool, a fool, a puppet,—they had ne'er
Foster'd the wretch who stung me. What I
 suffer
Has reach'd me through my pity for the
 people ;
That many know, and they who know not
 yet
Will one day learn : meantime I do devote,
Whate'er the issue, my last days of life—
My present power such as it is, not that
Of Doge, but of a man who has been great
Before he was degraded to a Doge,
And still has individual means and mind ;
I stake my fame (and I had fame)—my
 breath—
(The least of all, for its last hours are nigh)
My heart, my hope, my soul, upon this cast !
Such as I am, I offer me to you
And to your chiefs ; accept me or reject me,—
A Prince who fain would be a citizen
Or nothing, and who has left his throne to
 be so.
 Cal. Long live Faliero !—Venice shall be
 free !
 Consp. Long live Faliero !
 I. Ber. Comrades ! did I well ?
Is not this man a host in such a cause ?
 Doge. This is no time for eulogies, nor
 place
For exultation. Am I one of you ?
 Cal. Ay, and the first among us, as thou
 hast been
Of Venice—be our general and chief.
 Doge. Chief !—general !—I was general at
 Zara,
And chief in Rhodes and Cyprus, prince in
 Venice :
I cannot stoop——that is, I am not fit
To lead a band of——patriots : when I lay
Aside the dignities which I have borne,
'Tis not to put on others, but to be
Mate to my fellows—but now to the point ;
Israel has stated to me your whole plan—
'Tis bold, but feasible if I assist it,
And must be set in motion instantly.
 Cal. E'en when thou wilt. Is it not so, my
 friends ?
I have disposed all for a sudden blow ;
When shall it be then ?
 Doge. At sunrise.
 Ber. So soon ?
 Doge. So soon ?—so late—each hour ac-
 cumulates
Peril on peril, and the more so now
Since I have mingled with you ;—know you not
The Council, and "the Ten ?" the spies, the
 eyes

Of the patricians dubious of their slaves,
And now more dubious of the prince they have
 made one?
I tell you, you must strike, and suddenly,
Full to the Hydra's heart—its heads will
 follow.
 Cal. With all my soul and sword, I yield
 assent;
Our companies are ready, sixty each,
And all now under arms by Israel's order;
Each at their different place of rendezvous,
And vigilant, expectant of some blow;
Let each repair for action to his post!
And now, my lord, the signal?
 Doge. When you hear
The great bell of St. Mark's, which may not be
Struck without special order of the Doge
(The last poor privilege they leave their
 prince),
March on Saint Mark's!
 I. Ber. And there?—
 Doge. By different routes
Let your march be directed, every sixty
Entering a separate avenue, and still
Upon the way let your cry be of war
And of the Genoese fleet, by the first dawn
Discern'd before the port; form round the
 palace,
Within whose court will be drawn out in arms
My nephew and the clients of our house,
Many and martial; while the bell tolls on,
Shout ye, " Saint Mark!—the foe is on our
 waters!"
 Cal. I see it now—but on, my noble lord.
 Doge. All the patricians flocking to the
 Council,
(Which they dare not refuse, at the dread
 signal
Pealing from out their patron saint's proud
 tower),
Will then be gather'd in unto the harvest,
And we will reap them with the sword for
 sickle.
If some few should be tardy or absent them.
'Twill be but to be taken faint and single,
When the majority are put to rest.
 Cal. Would that the hour were come! we
 will not scotch,
But kill.
 Ber. Once more, sir, with your pardon, I
Would now repeat the question which I ask'd
Before Bertuccio added to our cause
This great ally who renders it more sure,
And therefore safer, and as such admits
Some dawn of mercy to a portion of
Our victims—must all perish in this slaugh-
 ter?
 Cal. All who encounter me and mine, be
 sure,
The mercy they have shown, I show.

 Consp. All! all!
Is this a time to talk of pity? when
Have they e'er shown, or felt, or feign'd it?
 I. Ber. Bertram,
This false compassion is a folly, and
Injustice to thy comrades and thy cause!
Dost thou not see, that if we single out
Some for escape, they live but to avenge
The fallen? and how distinguish now the
 innocent
From out the guilty? all their acts are *one*—
A single emanation from one body,
Together knit for our oppression! 'Tis
Much that we let their children live; I doubt
If all of these even should be set apart:
The hunter may reserve some single cub
From out the tiger's litter, but who e'er
Would seek to save the spotted sire or dam,
Unless to perish by their fangs? however,
I will abide by Doge Faliero's counsel:
Let him decide if any should be saved.
 Doge. Ask me not—tempt me not with
 such a question—
Decide yourselves.
 I. Ber. You know their private virtues
Far better than we can, to whom alone
Their public vices, and most foul oppression,
Have made them deadly; if there be amongst
 them
One who deserves to be repeal'd, pronounce.
 Doge. Dolfino's father was my friend, and
 Lando
Fought by my side, and Marc Cornaro shared
My Genoese embassy: I saved the life
Of Veniero—shall I save it twice?
Would that I could save them and Venice
 also!
All these men, or their fathers, were my
 friends
Till they became my subjects; then fell
 from me
As faithless leaves drop from the o'erblown
 flower,
All left me a lone blighted thorny stalk,
Which, in its solitude, can shelter nothing;
So, as they let me wither, let them perish.
 Cal. They cannot co-exist with Venice'
 freedom!
 Doge. Ye, though you know and feel our
 mutual mass
Of many wrongs, even ye are ignorant
What fatal poison to the springs of life,
To human ties, and all that's good and dear,
Lurks in the present institutes of Venice:
All these men were my friends: I loved them,
 they
Requited honourably my regards;
We served and fought; we smiled and wept
 in concert;
We revell'd or we sorrow'd side by side;

We made alliances of blood and marriage;
We grew in years and honours fairly,—till
Their own desire, not my ambition, made
Them choose me for their prince, and then
 farewell!
Farewell all social memory! all thoughts
In common! and sweet bonds which link old
 friendships,
When the survivors of long years and actions,
Which now belong to history, soothe the
 days
Which yet remain by treasuring each other,
And never meet, but each beholds the mirror
Of half a century on his brother's brow,
And sees a hundred beings, now in earth,
Flit round them whispering of the days gone
 by,
And seeming not all dead, as long as two
Of the brave, joyous, reckless, glorious band,
Which once were one and many, still retain
A breath to sigh for them, a tongue to speak
Of deeds that else were silent, save on
 marble——
Oime! Oime!—and must I do this deed?
 I. Ber. My lord, you are much moved: it
 is not now
That such things must be dwelt upon.
 Doge. Your patience
A moment—I recede not: mark with me
The gloomy vices of this government.
From the hour they made me Doge, the *Doge*
 THEY *made* me—
Farewell the past! I died to all that had been,
Or rather they to me: no friends, no kindness,
No privacy of life—all were cut off:
They came not near me, such approach gave
 umbrage;
They could not love me, such was not the
 law;
They thwarted me, 'twas the state's policy;
They baffled me, 'twas a patrician's duty;
They wrong'd me, for such was to right the
 state;
They could not right me, that would give
 suspicion;
So that I was a slave to my own subjects;
So that I was a foe to my own friends;
Begirt with spies for guards, with robes for
 power,
With pomp for freedom, gaolers for a council,
Inquisitors for friends, and hell for life!
I had one only fount of quiet left,
And *that* they poison'd! My pure household
 gods
Were shiver'd on my hearth, and o'er their
 shrine
Sate grinning Ribaldry and sneering Scorn.
 I. Ber. You have been deeply wrong'd,
 and now shall be
Nobly avenged before another night

 Doge. I had borne all—it hurt me, but I
 bore it—
Till this last running over of the cup
Of bitterness—until this last loud insult,
Not only unredress'd, but sanction'd; then,
And thus, I cast all further feelings from me—
The feelings which they crush'd for me, long,
 long
Before, even in their oath of false allegiance!
Even in that very hour and vow, they ab-
 jured
Their friend and made a sovereign, as boys
 make
Playthings, to do their pleasure—and be
 broken!
I from that hour have seen but senators
In dark suspicious conflict with the Doge,
Brooding with him in mutual hate and fear;
They dreading he should snatch the tyranny
From out their grasp, and he abhorring ty-
 rants.
To me, then, these men have no *private* life,
Nor claim to ties they have cut off from others;
As senators for arbitrary acts
Amenable, I look on them—as such
Let them be dealt upon.
 Cal. And now to action!
Hence, brethren, to our posts, and may this be
The last night of mere words: I'd fain be
 doing!
Saint Mark's great bell at dawn shall find me
 wakeful!
 I. Ber. Disperse then to your posts: be
 firm and vigilant;
Think on the wrongs we bear, the rights we
 claim.
This day and night shall be the last of peril!
Watch for the signal, and then march. I go
To join my band; let each be prompt to
 marshal
His separate charge: the Doge will now
 return
To the palace to prepare all for the blow.
We part to meet in freedom and in glory!
 Cal. Doge, when I greet you next, my
 homage to you
Shall be the head of Steno on this sword!
 Doge. No; let him be reserved unto the
 last,
Nor turn aside to strike at such a prey,
Till nobler game is quarried: his offence
Was a mere ebullition of the vice,
The general corruption generated
By the foul aristocracy: he could not—
He dared not in more honourable days
Have risk'd it. I have merged all private
 wrath
Against him in the thought of our great pur-
 pose.
A slave insults me—I require his punishment

From his proud master's hands; if he refuse it,
The offence grows his, and let him answer it.
 Cal. Yet, as the immediate cause of the
 alliance
Which consecrates our undertaking more,
I owe him such deep gratitude, that fain
I would repay him as he merits; may I?
 Doge. You would but lop the hand, and I
 the head;
You would but smite the scholar, I the master;
You would but punish Steno, I the senate.
I cannot pause on individual hate,
In the absorbing, sweeping, whole revenge,
Which, like the sheeted fire from heaven, must
 blast
Without distinction, as it fell of yore,
Where the Dead Sea hath quench'd two cities'
 ashes.
 I. Ber. Away, then, to your posts! I but
 remain
A moment to accompany the Doge
To our late place of tryst, to see no spies
Have been upon the scout, and thence I hasten
To where my allotted band is under arms.
 Cal. Farewell, then,—until dawn!
 I. Ber. Success go with you!
 Consp. We will not fail—Away! My lord,
 farewell!
 [*The Conspirators salute the* Doge *and* Is-
 rael Bertuccio, *and retire, headed by*
 Philip Calendaro. *The* Doge *and* Is-
 rael Bertuccio *remain.*
 I. Ber. We have them in the toil—it can-
 not fail!
Now thou 'rt indeed a sovereign, and wilt make
A name immortal greater than the greatest:
Free citizens have struck at kings ere now;
Cæsars have fallen, and even patrician hands
Have crush'd dictators, as the popular steel
Has reach'd patricians: but, until this hour,
What prince has plotted for his people's
 freedom?
Or risk'd a life to liberate his subjects?
For ever, and for ever, they conspire
Against the people, to abuse their hands
To chains, but laid aside to carry weapons
Against the fellow nations, so that yoke
On yoke, and slavery and death may whet,
Not glut, the never-gorged Leviathan!
Now, my lord, to our enterprise;—'t is
 great,
And greater the reward; why stand you rapt?
A moment back, and you were all im-
 patience!
 Doge. And is it then decided! must they
 die?
 I. Ber. Who?
 Doge. My own friends by blood and
 courtesy,
And many deeds and days—the senators?

 I. Ber. You pass'd their sentence, and it
 is a just one.
 Doge. Ay, so it seems, and so it is to
 you;
You are a patriot, plebeian Gracchus—
The rebels' oracle, the people's tribune—
I blame you not—you act in your vocation;
They smote you, and oppress'd you, and
 despised you;
So they have *me*: but *you* ne'er spake with
 them;
You never broke their bread, nor shared their
 salt;
You never had their wine-cup at your lips;
You grew not up with them, nor laugh'd,
 nor wept,
Nor held a revel in their company;
Ne'er smiled to see them smile, nor claim'd
 their smile
In social interchange for yours, nor trusted
Nor wore them in your heart of hearts, as
 I have:
These hairs of mine are grey, and so are
 theirs,
The elders of the Council: I remember
When all our locks were like the raven's
 wing,
As we went forth to take our prey around
The isles wrung from the false Mahometan;
And can I see them dabbled o'er with blood?
Each stab to them will seem my suicide.
 I. Ber. Doge! Doge! this vacillation is
 unworthy
A child; if you are not in second childhood,
Call back your nerves to your own purpose,
 nor
Thus shame yourself and me. By heavens!
 I 'd rather
Forego even now, or fail in our intent,
Than see the man I venerate subside
From high resolves into such shallow weak-
 ness!
You have seen blood in battle, shed it, both
Your own and that of others; can you shrink
 then
From a few drops from veins of hoary
 vampires,
Who but give back what they have drain'd
 from millions?
 Doge. Bear with me! Step by step, and
 blow on blow,
I will divide with you; think not I waver:
Ah! no; it is the *certainty* of all
Which I must do doth make me tremble
 thus.
But let these last and lingering thoughts
 have way,
To which you only and the night are con-
 scious,
And both regardless: when the hour arrives,

'T is mine to sound the knell, and strike
 the blow,
Which shall unpeople many palaces,
And hew the highest genealogic trees
Down to the earth, strew'd with their bleed-
 ing fruit,
And crush their blossoms into barrenness:
This will I—must I—have I sworn to do,
Nor aught can turn me from my destiny;
But still I quiver to behold what I
Must be, and think what I have been! Bear
 with me.
 I. Ber. Re-man your breast; I feel no such
 remorse,
I understand it not: why should you change?
You acted, and you act, on your free will.
 Doge. Ay, there it is—*you* feel not, nor
 do I,
Else I should stab thee on the spot, to save
A thousand lives, and killing, do no murder;
You *feel* not—*you* go to this butcher-work
As if these high-born men were steers for
 shambles:
When all is over, you'll be free and merry,
And calmly wash those hands incarnadine;
But I, outgoing thee and all thy fellows
In this surpassing massacre, shall be,
Shall see and feel—oh God! oh God! 't is
 true,
And thou dost well to answer that it was
"My own free will and act," and yet you err,
For I *will* do this! Doubt not—fear not; I
Will be your most unmerciful accomplice!
And yet I act no more on my free will,
Nor my own feelings—both compel me back;
But there is *hell* within me and around,
And like the demon who believes and
 trembles
Must I abhor and do. Away! away!
Get thee unto thy fellows, I will hie me
To gather the retainers of our house.
Doubt not, St. Mark's great bell shall wake
 all Venice,
Except her slaughtered senate: ere the sun
Be broad upon the Adriatic there
Shall be a voice of weeping, which shall
 drown
The roar of waters in the cry of blood!
I am resolved—come on.
 I. Ber. With all my soul!
Keep a firm rein upon these bursts of
 passion;
Remember what these men have dealt to
 thee,
And that this sacrifice will be succeeded
By ages of prosperity and freedom
To this unshackled city: a true tyrant
Would have depopulated empires, nor
Have felt the strange compunction which
 hath wrung you

To punish a few traitors to the people.
Trust me, such were a pity more misplaced
Than the late mercy of the state to Steno.
 Doge. Man, thou hast struck upon the
 chord which jars
All nature from my heart. Hence to our
 task! [*Exeunt.*

———•·•———

Act IV.

Scene I.—*Palazzo of the Patrician* LIONI.
LIONI *laying aside the mask and cloak
which the Venetian Nobles wore in public,
attended by a Domestic.*

 Lioni. I will to rest, right weary of this
 revel,
The gayest we have held for many moons,
And yet, I know not why, it cheer'd me not;
There came a heaviness across my heart,
Which, in the lightest movement of the
 dance,
Though eye to eye, and hand in hand united
Even with the lady of my love, oppress'd me,
And through my spirit chill'd my blood, until
A damp like death rose o'er my brow; I
 strove
To laugh the thought away, but 't would
 not be;
Through all the music ringing in my ears
A knell was sounding as distinct and clear,
Though low and far, as e'er the Adrian wave
Rose o'er the city's murmur in the night,
Dashing against the outward Lido's bul-
 wark:
So that I left the festival before
It reach'd its zenith, and will woo my pillow
For thoughts more tranquil, or forgetfulness.
Antonio, take my mask and cloak, and light
The lamp within my chamber.
 Ant. Yes, my lord:
Command you no refreshment?
 Lioni. Nought, save sleep,
Which will not be commanded. Let me
 hope it, [*Exit* ANTONIO.
Though my breast feels too anxious; I will
 try
Whether the air will calm my spirits: 't is
A goodly night; the cloudy wind which blew
From the Levant hath crept into its cave,
And the broad moon has brighten'd. What
 a stillness! [*Goes to an open lattice.*
And what a contrast with the scene I left,
Where the tall torches' glare, and silver
 lamps'
More pallid gleam along the tapestried walls,
Spread over the reluctant gloom which
 haunts

Those vast and dimly-latticed galleries
A dazzling mass of artificial light,
Which show'd all things, but nothing as they
 were.
There Age essaying to recall the past,
After long striving for the hues of youth
At the sad labour of the toilet, and
Full many a glance at the too faithful
 mirror,
Prank'd forth in all the pride of ornament,
Forgot itself, and trusting to the falsehood
Of the indulgent beams, which show, yet
 hide,
Believed itself forgotten, and was fool'd.
There Youth, which needed not, nor thought
 of such
Vain adjuncts, lavish'd its true bloom, and
 health,
And bridal beauty, in the unwholesome press
Of flush'd and crowded wassailers, and
 wasted
Its hours of rest in dreaming this was
 pleasure,
And so shall waste them till the sunrise
 streams
On sallow cheeks and sunken eyes, which
 should not
Have worn this aspect yet for many a year.
The music, and the banquet, and the wine,
The garlands, the rose odours, and the
 flowers,
The sparkling eyes, and flashing ornaments,
The white arms and the raven hair, the braids
And bracelets; swanlike bosoms, and the
 necklace,
An India in itself, yet dazzling not
The eye like what it circled; the thin robes,
Floating like light clouds 'twixt our gaze
 and heaven;
The many-twinkling feet so small and sylph-
 like,
Suggesting the more secret symmetry
Of the fair forms which terminate so well—
All the delusion of the dizzy scene,
Its false and true enchantments—art and
 nature,
Which swam before my giddy eyes, that
 drank
The sight of beauty as the parch'd pilgrim's
On Arab sands the false mirage, which offers
A lucid lake to his eluded thirst,
Are gone. Around me are the stars and
 waters—
Worlds mirror'd in the ocean, goodlier sight
Than torches glared back by a gaudy glass;
And the great element, which is to space
What ocean is to earth, spreads its blue
 depths,
Soften'd with the first breathings of the
 spring;

The high moon sails upon her beauteous way,
Serenely smoothing o'er the lofty walls
Of those tall piles and sea-girt palaces,
Whose porphyry pillars, and whose costly
 fronts,
Fraught with the orient spoil of many
 marbles,
Like altars ranged along the broad canal,
Seem each a trophy of some mighty deed
Rear'd up from out the waters, scarce less
 strangely
Than those more massy and mysterious
 giants
Of architecture, those Titanian fabrics,
Which point in Egypt's plains to times that
 have
No other record. All is gentle : nought
Stirs rudely; but, congenial with the night,
Whatever walks is gliding like a spirit.
The tinklings of some vigilant guitars
Of sleepless lovers to a wakeful mistress,
And cautious opening of the casement, show-
 ing
That he is not unheard; while her young
 hand,
Fair as the moonlight of which it seems part,
So delicately white, it trembles in
The act of opening the forbidden lattice,
To let in love through music, makes his heart
Thrill like his lyre-strings at the sight; the
 dash
Phosphoric of the oar, or rapid twinkle
Of the far lights of skimming gondolas,
And the responsive voices of the choir
Of boatmen answering back with verse for
 verse;
Some dusky shadow checkering the Rialto;
Some glimmering palace roof, or tapering
 spire,
Are all the sights and sounds which here
 pervade
The ocean-born and earth-commanding city—
How sweet and soothing is this hour of
 calm !
I thank thee, Night! for thou hast chased
 away
Those horrid bodements which, amidst the
 throng,
I could not dissipate : and with the blessing
Of thy benign and quiet influence,
Now will I to my couch, although to rest
Is almost wronging such a night as this.——
 [*A knocking is heard from without.*
Hark ! what is that? or who at such a
 moment ?

Enter ANTONIO.

Ant. My lord, a man without, on urgent
 business,
Implores to be admitted.

Lioni.　　　　　　　　Is he a stranger?
Ant. His face is muffled in his cloak, but
　　both
His voice and gestures seem familiar to me;
I craved his name, but this he seem'd
　　reluctant
To trust, save to yourself; most earnestly
He sues to be permitted to approach you.
Lioni. 'Tis a strange hour, and a suspi-
　　cious bearing!
And yet there is slight peril: 't is not in
Their houses noble men are struck at; still,
Although I know not that I have a foe
In Venice, 't will be wise to use some
　　caution.
Admit him, and retire; but call up quickly
Some of thy fellows, who may wait with-
　　out.—
Who can this man be?
　　　　　[*Exit* ANTONIO, *and returns with*
　　　　　　　　　BERTRAM *muffled.*
Ber.　　　　　　My good lord Lioni,
I have no time to lose, nor thou,—dismiss
This menial hence; I would be private with
　　you.
Lioni. It seems the voice of Bertram—
　　Go, Antonio.　　　[*Exit* ANTONIO.
Now, stranger, what would you at such an
　　hour?
Ber. (*discovering himself*). A boon, my
　　noble patron; you have granted
Many to your poor client, Bertram; add
This one, and make him happy.
Lioni.　　　　　Thou hast known me
From boyhood, ever ready to assist thee
In all fair objects of advancement, which
Beseem one of thy station; I would promise
Ere thy request was heard, but that the hour,
Thy bearing, and this strange and hurried
　　mode
Of suing, gives me to suspect this visit
Hath some mysterious import—but say on—
What has occurred, some rash and sudden
　　broil?—
A cup too much, a scuffle, and a stab?—
Mere things of every day; so that thou hast
　　not
Spilt noble blood, I guarantee thy safety;
But then thou must withdraw, for angry
　　friends
And relatives, in the first burst of vengeance,
Are things in Venice deadlier than the laws.
Ber. My lord, I thank you; but——
Lioni.　　　　　But what? You have not
Raised a rash hand against one of our
　　order?
If so, withdraw and fly, and own it not;
I would not slay—but then I must not save
　　thee!
He who has shed patrician blood——

Ber.　　　　　　　　　I come
To save patrician blood, and not to shed it!
And thereunto I must be speedy, for
Each minute lost may lose a life; since Time
Has changed his slow scythe for the two-
　　edged sword,
And is about to take, instead of sand,
The dust from sepulchres to fill his hour-
　　glass!—
Go not *thou* forth to-morrow!
Lioni.　　　　　　　Wherefore not?
What means this menace?
Ber.　　　　　Do not seek its meaning,
But do as I implore thee;—stir not forth,
Whate'er be stirring; though the roar of
　　crowds—
The cry of women, and the shrieks of babes—
The groans of men—the clash of arms—the
　　sound
Of rolling drum, shrill trump, and hollow bell,
Peal in one wide alarum!—Go not forth,
Until the tocsin's silent, nor even then
Till I return!
Lioni. Again, what does this mean?
Ber. Again, I tell thee, ask not; but by all
Thou holdest dear on earth or heaven—by all
The souls of thy great fathers, and thy hope
To emulate them, and to leave behind
Descendants worthy both of them and thee—
By all thou hast of bless'd in hope or me-
　　mory—
By all thou hast to fear here or hereafter—
By all the good deeds thou hast done to me,
Good I would now repay with greater good,
Remain within—trust to thy household gods,
And to my word for safety, if thou dost
As I now counsel—but if not, thou art lost!
Lioni. I am indeed already lost in wonder;
Surely thou ravest! what have *I* to dread?
Who are my foes? or if there be such, *why*
Art *thou* leagued with them? *thou!* or if so
　　leagued,
Why comest thou to tell me at this hour,
And not before?
Ber.　　　　I cannot answer this.
Wilt thou go forth despite of this true warn-
　　ing?
Lioni. I was not born to shrink from idle
　　threats,
The cause of which I know not: at the hour
Of council, be it soon or late, I shall not
Be found among the absent.
Ber.　　　　　　Say not so!
Once more, art thou determined to go forth?
Lioni. I am. Nor is there aught which
　　shall impede me!
Ber. Then, Heaven have mercy on thy
　　soul!—Farewell!　　　　[*Going.*
Lioni. Stay—there is more in this than
　　my own safety

Which makes me call thee back; we must
 not part thus:
Bertram, I have known thee long.
 Ber. From childhood, signor,
You have been my protector: in the days
Of reckless infancy, when rank forgets,
Or, rather, is not yet taught to remember,
Its cold prerogative, we play'd together;
Our sports, our smiles, our tears, were min-
 gled oft;
My father was your father's client, I
His son's scarce less than foster-brother;
 years
Saw us together—happy, heart-full hours!
Oh God! the difference 'twixt those hours
 and this!
 Lioni. Bertram, 'tis thou who hast for-
 gotten them.
 Ber. Nor now, nor ever; whatsoe'er betide,
I would have saved you: when to manhood's
 growth
We sprung, and you, devoted to the state,
As suits your station, the more humble Ber-
 tram
Was left unto the labours of the humble,
Still you forsook me not; and if my fortunes
Have not been towering, 'twas no fault of
 him
Who ofttimes rescued and supported me,
When struggling with the tides of circum-
 stance,
Which bear away the weaker: noble blood
Ne'er mantled in a nobler heart than thine
Has proved to me, the poor plebeian Bertram.
Would that thy fellow senators were like
 thee!
 Lioni. Why, what hast thou to say against
 the senate?
 Ber. Nothing.
 Lioni. I know that there are angry spirits
And turbulent mutterers of stifled treason,
Who lurk in narrow places, and walk out
Muffled to whisper curses to the night;
Disbanded soldiers, discontented ruffians,
And desperate libertines who brawl in ta-
 verns;
Thou herdest not with such: 'tis true, of late
I have lost sight of thee, but thou wert wont
To lead a temperate life, and break thy bread
With honest mates, and bear a cheerful
 aspect.
What hath come to thee? in thy hollow eye
And hueless cheek, and thine unquiet motions,
Sorrow and shame and conscience seem at
 war
To waste thee.
 Ber. Rather shame and sorrow light
On the accursed tyranny which rides
The very air in Venice, and makes men
Madden as in the last hours of the plague

Which sweeps the soul deliriously from life!
 Lioni. Some villains have been tampering
 with thee, Bertram;
This is not thy old language, nor own
 thoughts;
Some wretch has made thee drunk with dis-
 affection:
But thou must not be lost so; thou *wert* good
And kind, and art not fit for such base acts
As vice and villainy would put thee to:
Confess—confide in me—thou know'st my
 nature.
What is it thou and thine are bound to do,
Which should prevent thy friend, the only son
Of him who was a friend unto thy father,
So that our good-will is a heritage
We should bequeath to our posterity
Such as ourselves received it, or augmented;
I say, what is it thou must do, that I
Should deem thee dangerous, and keep the
 house
Like a sick girl?
 Ber. Nay, question me no further:
I must be gone.——
 Lioni. And I be murder'd!—say,
Was it not thus thou said'st, my gentle Ber-
 tram?
 Ber. Who talks of murder? what said I
 of murder?
'Tis false! I did not utter such a word.
 Lioni. Thou didst not; but from out thy
 wolfish eye,
So changed from what I knew it, there glares
 forth
The gladiator. If *my* life's thine object,
Take it—I am unarm'd,—and then away!
I would not hold my breath on such a tenure
As the capricious mercy of such things
As thou and those who have set thee to thy
 taskwork.
 Ber. Sooner than spill thy blood, I peril
 mine;
Sooner than harm a hair of thine, I place
In jeopardy a thousand heads, and some
As noble, nay, even nobler than thine own.
 Lioni. Ay, is it even so? Excuse me,
 Bertram;
I am not worthy to be singled out
From such exalted hecatombs—who are they
That *are* in danger, and that *make* the danger?
 Ber. Venice, and all that she inherits, are
Divided like a house against itself,
And so will perish ere to-morrow's twilight!
 Lioni. More mysteries, and awful ones!
 But now,
Or thou, or I, or both, it may be, are
Upon the verge of ruin; speak once out,
And thou art safe and glorious; for 'tis more
Glorious to save than slay, and slay i' the
 dark too—

Fie, Bertram! that was not a craft for thee!
How would it look to see upon a spear
The head of him whose heart was open to
thee,
Borne by thy hand before the shuddering
people?
And such may be my doom; for here I swear,
Whate'er the peril or the penalty
Of thy denunciation, I go forth,
Unless thou dost detail the cause, and show
The consequence of all which led thee here!

 Ber. Is there no way to save thee? mi-
nutes fly,
And thou art lost!—*thou!* my sole benefactor,
The only being who was constant to me
Through every change. Yet, make me not a
traitor!
Let me save thee—but spare my honour!

 Lioni. Where
Can lie the honour in a league of murder?
And who are traitors save unto the state?

 Ber. A league is still a compact, and more
binding
In honest hearts when words must stand for
law;
And in my mind, there is no traitor like
He whose domestic treason plants the poniard
Within the breast which trusted to his
truth.

 Lioni. And *who* will strike the steel to
mine?

 Ber. Not I;
I could have wound my soul up to all things
Save this. *Thou* must not die! and think
how dear
Thy life is, when I risk so many lives,
Nay, more, the life of lives, the liberty
Of future generations, *not* to be
The assassin thou miscall'st me:—once, once
more
I do adjure thee, pass not o'er thy threshold!

 Lioni. It is in vain—this moment I go
forth.

 Ber. Then perish Venice rather than my
friend!
I will disclose—ensnare—betray—destroy—
Oh, what a villain I become for thee!

 Lioni. Say, rather, thy friend's saviour
and the state's!—
Speak—pause not—all rewards, all pledges
for
Thy safety and thy welfare; wealth such as
The state accords her worthiest servants;
nay,
Nobility itself I guarantee thee,
So that thou art sincere and penitent.

 Ber. I have thought again: it must not
be—I love thee—
Thou know'st it—that I stand here is the
proof,

Not least though last; but having done my
duty
By thee, I now must do it by my country!
Farewell—we meet no more in life!—farewell!

 Lioni. What, ho!—Antonio—Pedro—to
the door!
See that none pass—arrest this man!—

Enter ANTONIO *and other armed Domestics,*
who seize BERTRAM.

 Lioni (*continues*). Take care
He hath no harm; bring me my sword and
cloak,
And man the gondola with four oars—quick—
 [*Exit* ANTONIO.
We will unto Giovanni Gradenigo's,
And send for Marc Cornaro:—fear not, Ber-
tram;
This needful violence is for thy safety,
No less than for the general weal.

 Ber. Where wouldst thou
Bear me a prisoner?

 Lioni. Firstly to "the Ten;"
Next to the Doge.

 Ber. To the Doge?

 Lioni. Assuredly:
Is he not chief of the state?

 Ber. Perhaps at sunrise—

 Lioni. What mean you?—but we'll know
anon.

 Ber. Art sure?

 Lioni. Sure as all gentle means can
make; and if
They fail, you know "the Ten" and their
tribunal,
And that St. Mark's has dungeons, and the
dungeons
A rack.

 Ber. Apply it then before the dawn
Now hastening into heaven.—One more such
word,
And you shall perish piecemeal, by the death
You think to doom to me.

Re-enter ANTONIO.

 Ant. The bark is ready,
My lord, and all prepared.

 Lioni. Look to the prisoner.
Bertram, I'll reason with thee as we go
To the Magnifico's, sage Gradenigo.
 [*Exeunt.*

Scene II.

The Ducal Palace.—The Doge's Apartment.

The DOGE *and his Nephew* BERTUCCIO
FALIERO.

 Doge. Are all the people of our house in
muster?

Ber. F. They are array'd, and eager for
the signal,
Within our palace precincts at San Polo.
I come for your last orders.
Doge. It had been
As well had there been time to have got
together,
From my own fief, Val di Marino, more
Of our retainers—but it is too late.
Ber. F. Methinks, my lord, 'tis better as
it is:
A sudden swelling of our retinue
Had waked suspicion; and, though fierce
and trusty,
The vassals of that district are too rude
And quick in quarrel to have long maintain'd
The secret discipline we need for such
A service, till our foes are dealt upon.
Doge. True; but when once the signal
has been given,
These are the men for such an enterprise;
These city slaves have all their private bias
Their prejudice *against* or *for* this noble,
Which may induce them to o'erdo or spare
Where mercy may be madness; the fierce
peasants,
Serfs of my county of Val di Marino,
Would do the bidding of their lord without
Distinguishing for love or hate his foes;
Alike to them Marcello or Cornaro,
A Gradenigo or a Foscari;
They are not used to start at those vain
names,
Nor bow the knee before a civic senate;
A chief in armour is their Suzerain,
And not a thing in robes.
Ber. F. We are enough;
And for the dispositions of our clients
Against the senate I will answer.
Doge. Well,
The die is thrown; but for a warlike service,
Done in the field, commend me to my pea-
sants:
They made the sun shine through the host
of Huns
When sallow burghers slunk back to their
tents,
And cower'd to hear their own victorious
trumpet.
If there be small resistance you will find
These citizens all lions, like their standard;
But if there's much to do, you'll wish, with
me,
A band of iron rustics at our backs.
Ber. F. Thus thinking, I must marvel
you resolve
To strike the blow so suddenly.
Doge. Such blows
Must be struck suddenly or never. When
I had o'ermaster'd the weak false remorse

Which yearn'd about my heart, too fondly
yielding
A moment to the feelings of old days,
I was most fain to strike; and, firstly, that
I might not yield again to such emotions;
And, secondly, because of all these men,
Save Israel and Philip Calendaro,
I know not well the courage or the faith:
To-day might find 'mongst them a traitor
to us,
As yesterday a thousand to the senate;
But once in, with their hilts hot in their
hands,
They must *on* for their own sakes: one
stroke struck,
And the mere instinct of the first-born Cain,
Which ever lurks somewhere in human
hearts,
Though circumstance may keep it in abey-
ance,
Will urge the rest on like to wolves; the
sight
Of blood to crowds begets the thirst of more,
As the first wine-cup leads to the long revel;
And you will find a harder task to quell
Than urge them when they *have* commenced,
but *till*
That moment, a mere voice, a straw, a
shadow,
Are capable of turning them aside.—
How goes the night?
 Ber. F. Almost upon the dawn.
 Doge. Then it is time to strike upon the
bell.
Are the men posted?
 Ber. F. By this time they are;
But they have orders not to strike, until
They have command from you through me
in person.
 Doge. 'Tis well.—Will the morn never
put to rest
These stars which twinkle yet o'er all the
heavens?
I am settled and bound up, and being so,
The very effort which it cost me to
Resolve to cleanse this commonwealth with
fire,
Now leaves my mind more steady. I have
wept
And trembled at the thought of this dread
duty;
But now I have put down all idle passion,
And look the growing tempest in the face,
As doth the pilot of an admiral galley:
Yet (wouldst thou think it, kinsman?) it hath
been
A greater struggle to me, than when nations
Beheld their fate merged in the approaching
fight,
Where I was leader of a phalanx, where

Thousands were sure to perish—Yes, to spill
The rank polluted current from the veins
Of a few bloated despots needed more
To steel me to a purpose such as made
Timoleon immortal, than to face
The toils and dangers of a life of war.
 Ber. F. It gladdens me to see your former
 wisdom
Subdue the furies which so wrung you ere
You were decided.
 Doge. It was ever thus
With me; the hour of agitation came
In the first glimmerings of a purpose, when
Passion had too much room to sway; but in
The hour of action I have stood as calm
As were the dead who lay around me: this
They knew who made me what I am, and
 trusted
To the subduing power which I preserved
Over my mood, when its first burst was spent.
But they were not aware that there are
 things
Which make revenge a virtue by reflection,
And not an impulse of mere anger; though
The laws sleep, justice wakes, and injured
 souls
Oft do a public right with private wrong,
And justify their deeds unto themselves.—
Methinks the day breaks—is it not so? look,
Thine eyes are clear with youth;—the air
 puts on
A morning freshness, and, at least to me,
The sea looks greyer through the lattice.
 Ber. F. True,
The morn is dappling in the sky.
 Doge. Away then!
See that they strike without delay, and with
The first toll from St. Mark's, march on the
 palace
With all our house's strength; here I will
 meet you;
The Sixteen and their companies will move
In separate columns at the self-same mo-
 ment:
Be sure you post yourself at the great gate:
I would not trust "the Ten" except to us—
The rest, the rabble of patricians, may
Glut the more careless swords of those
 leagued with us.
Remember that the cry is still "Saint Mark!
The Genoese are come—ho! to the rescue!
Saint Mark and Liberty!"—Now—now to
 action!
 Ber. F. Farewell then, noble uncle! we
 will meet
In freedom and true sovereignty, or never!
 Doge. Come hither, my Bertuccio—one
 embrace;
Speed, for the day grows broader; send me
 soon

A messenger to tell me how all goes
When you rejoin our troops, and then sound—
 sound
The storm-bell from St. Mark's!
 [*Exit* BERTUCCIO FALIERO.
 Doge (solus). He is gone,
And on each footstep moves a life. 'Tis done.
Now the destroying angel hovers o'er
Venice, and pauses ere he pours the vial,
Even as the eagle overlooks his prey,
And for a moment, poised in middle air,
Suspends the motion of his mighty wings,
Then swoops with his unerring beak. Thou
 day!
That slowly walk'st the waters! march—
 march on—
I would not smite i' the dark, but rather see
That no stroke errs. And you, ye blue sea
 waves!
I have seen you dyed ere now, and deeply too,
With Genoese, Saracen, and Hunnish gore,
While that of Venice flow'd too, but vic-
 torious,
Now thou must wear an unmix'd crimson; no
Barbaric blood can reconcile us now
Unto that horrible incarnadine,
But friend or foe will roll in civic slaughter.
And have I lived to fourscore years for this?
I, who was named Preserver of the City?
I, at whose name the million's caps were
 flung
Into the air, and cries from tens of thousands
Rose up, imploring Heaven to send me
 blessings,
And fame, and length of days—to see this
 day?
But this day, black within the calendar,
Shall be succeeded by a bright millennium.
Doge Dandolo survived to ninety summers
To vanquish empires, and refuse their crown;
I will resign a crown, and make the state
Renew its freedom—but oh! by what means?
The noble end must justify them. What
Are a few drops of human blood? 'tis false,
The blood of tyrants is not human; they,
Like to incarnate Molochs, feed on ours,
Until 'tis time to give them to the tombs
Which they have made so populous.—Oh
 world!
Oh men! what are ye, and our best designs,
That we must work by crime to punish
 crime?
And slay as if Death had but this one gate,
When a few years would make the sword
 superfluous?
And I, upon the verge of th' unknown realm,
Yet send so many heralds on before me?—
I must not ponder this. [*A pause.*
 Hark! was there not
A murmur as of distant voices, and

The tramp of feet in martial unison?
What phantoms even of sound our wishes
 raise!
It cannot be—the signal hath not rung—
Why pauses it? My nephew's messenger
Should be upon his way to me, and he
Himself perhaps even now draws grating
 back
Upon its ponderous hinge the steep tower
 portal,
Where swings the sullen huge oracular bell,
Which never knells but for a princely death,
Or for a state in peril, pealing forth
Tremendous bodements; let it do its office,
And be this peal its awfullest and last
Sound till the strong tower rock!—What!
 silent still?
I would go forth, but that my post is here,
To be the centre of re-union to
The oft discordant elements which form
Leagues of this nature, and to keep compact
The wavering of the weak, in case of conflict;
For if they should do battle, 'twill be here,
Within the palace, that the strife will thicken:
Then here must be my station, as becomes
The master-mover.——Hark! he comes—he
 comes,
My nephew, brave Bertuccio's messenger.—
What tidings? Is he marching? hath he
 sped?
They here!—all's lost—yet will I make an
 effort.

Enter a SIGNOR OF THE NIGHT, *with*
Guards, &c. &c.

Sig. Doge, I arrest thee of high treason!
Doge. Me!
Thy prince, of treason?—Who are they that
 dare
Cloak their own treason under such an order?
Sig. (*showing his order*). Behold my order
 from the assembled Ten.
Doge. And *where* are they, and *why* as-
 sembled? no
Such council can be lawful, till the prince
Preside there, and that duty's mine: on
 thine
I charge thee, give me way, or marshal me
To the council chamber.
Sig. Duke! it may not be:
Nor are they in the wonted Hall of Council,
But sitting in the convent of Saint Saviour's.
Doge. You dare to disobey me, then?
Sig. I serve
The state, and needs must serve it faithfully;
My warrant is the will of those who rule it.
Doge. And till that warrant has my sig-
 nature
It is illegal, and, as *now* applied,

Rebellious. Hast thou weigh'd well thy life's
 worth,
That thus you dare assume a lawless func-
 tion?
Sig. 'Tis not my office to reply, but act—
I am placed here as guard upon thy person,
And not as judge to hear or to decide.
Doge (*aside*). I must gain time. So that
 the storm-bell sound,
All may be well yet.—Kinsman, speed—
 speed—speed!—
Our fate is trembling in the balance, and
Woe to the vanquish'd! be they prince and
 people,
Or slaves and senate—
 [*The great bell of St. Mark's tolls.*
 Lo! it sounds—it tolls!
(*Aloud*). Hark, Signor of the Night! and
 you, ye hirelings,
Who wield your mercenary staves in fear,
It is your knell—Swell on, thou lusty peal!
Now, knaves, what ransom for your lives?
Sig. Confusion!
Stand to your arms, and guard the door—
 all's lost
Unless that fearful bell be silenced soon.
The officer hath miss'd his path or purpose,
Or met some unforeseen and hideous obstacle.
Anselmo, with thy company proceed
Straight to the tower; the rest remain with
 me. [*Exit part of the Guard.*
Doge. Wretch! if thou wouldst have thy
 vile life, implore it;
It is not now a lease of sixty seconds.
Ay, send thy miserable ruffians forth;
They never shall return.
Sig. So let it be!
They die then in their duty, as will I.
Doge. Fool! the high eagle flies at nobler
 game
Than thou and thy base myrmidons,—live on,
So thou provok'st not peril by resistance,
And learn (if souls so much obscured can
 bear
To gaze upon the sunbeams) to be free.
Sig. And learn thou to be captive. It
 hath ceased, [*The bell ceases to toll.*
The traitorous signal, which was to have
 set
The bloodhound mob on their patrician
 prey—
The knell hath rung, but it is not the senate's!
Doge (*after a pause*). All's silent, and all's
 lost!
Sig. Now, Doge, denounce me
As rebel slave of a revolted council!
Have I not done my duty?
Doge. Peace, thou thing!
Thou hast done a worthy deed, and earn'd
 the price

Of blood, and they who use thee will reward
 thee.
But thou wert sent to watch, and not to
 prate,
As thou said'st even now—then do thine
 office,
But let it be in silence, as behoves thee,
Since, though thy prisoner, I am thy prince.
 Sig. I did not mean to fail in the respect
Due to your rank: in this I shall obey you.
 Doge (aside). There now is nothing left
 me save to die;
And yet how near success! I would have
 fallen,
And proudly, in the hour of triumph, but
To miss it thus!——

Enter other SIGNORS OF THE NIGHT, *with*
 BERTUCCIO FALIERO *prisoner.*

 2nd Sig. We took him in the act
Of issuing from the tower, where, at his
 order,
As delegated from the Doge, the signal
Had thus begun to sound.
 1st Sig. Are all the passes
Which lead up to the palace well secured?
 2nd Sig. They are — besides, it matters
 not; the chiefs
Are all in chains, and some even now on
 trial—
Their followers are dispersed, and many
 taken.
 Ber. F. Uncle!
 Doge. It is in vain to war with Fortune;
The glory hath departed from our house.
 Ber. F. Who would have deem'd it?—
 Ah! one moment sooner!
 Doge. That moment would have changed
 the face of ages;
This gives us to eternity—We'll meet it
As men whose triumph is not in success,
But who can make their own minds all in all,
Equal to every fortune. Droop not, 'tis
But a brief passage—I would go alone,
Yet if they send us, as 'tis like, together,
Let us go worthy of our sires and selves.
 Ber. F. I shall not shame you, uncle.
 1st Sig. Lords, our orders
Are to keep guard on both in separate
 chambers,
Until the council call ye to your trial.
 Doge. Our trial! will they keep their
 mockery up
Even to the last? but let them deal upon us,
As we had dealt on them, but with less pomp.
'Tis but a game of mutual homicides,
Who have cast lots for the first death, and
 they
Have won with false dice.—Who hath been
 our Judas?

 1st Sig. I am not warranted to answer
 that.
 Ber. F. I'll answer for thee—'tis a cer-
 tain Bertram,
Even now deposing to the secret giunta.
 Doge. Bertram, the Bergamask! With
 what vile tools
We operate to slay or save! This creature,
Black with a double treason, now will earn
Rewards and honours, and be stamp'd in
 story
With the geese in the Capitol, which gabbled
Till Rome awoke, and had an annual triumph,
While Manlius, who hurl'd down the Gauls,
 was cast
From the Tarpeian.
 1st Sig. He aspired to treason,
And sought to rule the state.
 Doge. He saved the state,
And sought but to reform what he revived—
But this is idle——Come, sirs, do your work.
 1st Sig. Noble Bertuccio, we must now
 remove you
Into an inner chamber.
 Ber. F. Farewell, uncle!
If we shall meet again in life I know not,
But they perhaps will let our ashes mingle.
 Doge. Yes, and our spirits, which shall
 yet go forth,
And do what our frail clay, thus clogg'd, hath
 fail'd in!
They cannot quench the memory of those
Who would have hurl'd them from their
 guilty thrones,
And such examples will find heirs, though
 distant.

——◆——

Act V.

Scene I.—*The Hall of the Council of Ten,
assembled with the additional Senators,
who, on the Trials of the Conspirators for
the Treason of* MARINO FALIERO, *composed
what was called the Giunta.*—*Guards,
Officers, &c. &c.*—ISRAEL BERTUCCIO *and*
PHILIP CALENDARO *as Prisoners.*—BER-
TRAM, LIONI, *and Witnesses, &c.*

 The Chief of the Ten, BENINTENDE.

 Ben. There now rests, after such con-
 viction of
Their manifold and manifest offences,
But to pronounce on these obdurate men
The sentence of the law:—a grievous task
To those who hear, and those who speak.
 Alas!
That it should fall to me! and that my days

Of office should be stigmatised through all
The years of coming time, as bearing record
To this most foul and complicated treason
Against a just and free state, known to all
The earth as being the Christian bulwark
 'gainst
The Saracen and the schismatic Greek,
The savage Hun, and not less barbarous
 Frank;
A city which has open'd India's wealth
To Europe; the last Roman refuge from
O'erwhelming Attila; the ocean's queen;
Proud Genoa's prouder rival! 'Tis to sap
The throne of such a city, these lost men
Have risk'd and forfeited their worthless
 lives—
So let them die the death.
 I. Ber. We are prepared;
Your racks have done that for us. Let us
 die.
 Ben. If ye have that to say which would
 obtain
Abatement of your punishment, the Giunta
Will hear you; if you have aught to confess,
Now is your time, perhaps it may avail ye.
 I. Ber. We stand to hear, and not to
 speak.
 Ben. Your crimes
Are fully proved by your accomplices,
And all which circumstance can add to aid
 them;
Yet we would hear from your own lips com-
 plete
Avowal of your treason: on the verge
Of that dread gulf which none repass, the
 truth
Alone can profit you on earth or heaven—
Say, then, what was your motive?
 I. Ber. Justice!
 Ben. What
Your object?
 I. Ber. Freedom!
 Ben. You are brief, sir.
 I. Ber. So my life grows: I
Was bred a soldier, not a senator.
 Ben. Perhaps you think by this blunt
 brevity
To brave your judges to postpone the sen-
 tence?
 I. Ber. Do you be brief as I am, and be-
 lieve me,
I shall prefer that mercy to your pardon.
 Ben. Is this your sole reply to the tribunal?
 I. Ber. Go, ask your racks what they have
 wrung from us,
Or place us there again; we have still some
 blood left,
And some slight sense of pain in these
 wrench'd limbs:
But this ye dare not do; for if we die there—

And you have left us little life to spend
Upon your engines, gorged with pangs al-
 ready—
Ye lose the public spectacle, with which
You would appal your slaves to further
 slavery!
Groans are not words, nor agony assent,
Nor affirmation truth, if nature's sense
Should overcome the soul into a lie,
For a short respite—must we bear or die?
 Ben. Say, who were your accomplices?
 I. Ber. The Senate.
 Ben. What do you mean?
 I. Ber. Ask of the suffering people,
Whom your patrician crimes have driven
 to crime.
 Ben. You know the Doge?
 I. Ber. I served with him at Zara
In the field, when *you* were pleading here
 your way
To present office; we exposed our lives,
While you but hazarded the lives of others,
Alike by accusation or defence;
And for the rest, all Venice knows her Doge,
Through his great actions, and the Senate's
 insults.
 Ben. You have held conference with him?
 I. Ber. I am weary—
Even wearier of your questions than your
 tortures:
I pray you pass to judgment.
 Ben. It is coming.
And you, too, Philip Calendaro, what
Have you to say why you should not be
 doomed?
 Cal. I never was a man of many words,
And now have few left worth the utterance.
 Ben. A further application of yon engine
May change your tone.
 Cal. Most true, it *will* do so;
A former application did so; but
It will not change my words, or, if it did—
 Ben. What then?
 Cal. Will my avowal on yon rack
Stand good in law?
 Ben. Assuredly.
 Cal. Whoe'er
The culprit be whom I accuse of treason?
 Ben. Without doubt, he will be brought
 up to trial.
 Cal. And on this testimony would he
 perish?
 Ben. So your confession be detail'd and full,
He will stand here in peril of his life.
 Cal. Then look well to thy proud self,
 President!
For by the eternity which yawns before me,
I swear that *thou*, and only thou, shalt be
The traitor I denounce upon that rack,
If I be stretch'd there for the second time.

One of the Giunta. Lord President,'twere
　　best proceed to judgment;
There is no more to be drawn from these
　　men.
　Ben. Unhappy men! prepare for instant
　　death.
The nature of your crime, our law, and peril
The state now stands in, leave not an hour's
　　respite.
Guards! lead them forth, and upon the
　　balcony
Of the red columns, where, on festal Thurs-
　　day,
The Doge stands to behold the chase of bulls,
Let them be justified: and leave exposed
Their wavering relics, in the place of judg-
　　ment,
To the full view of the assembled people!
And Heaven have mercy on their souls!
　The Giunta.　　　　　　　　Amen!
　I. Ber. Signors, farewell! we shall not
　　all again
Meet in one place.
　Ben.　　　　And lest they should essay
To stir up the distracted multitude—
Guards! let their mouths be gagg'd even in
　　the act
Of execution. Lead them hence!
　Cal.　　　　　　　What! must we
Not even say farewell to some fond friend,
Nor leave a last word with our confessor?
　Ben. A priest is waiting in the ante-
　　chamber;
But, for your friends, such interviews would
　　be
Painful to them, and useless all to you.
　Cal. I knew that we were gagg'd in life;
　　at least
All those who had not heart to risk their
　　lives
Upon their open thoughts; but still I deem'd
That in the last few moments, the same
　　idle
Freedom of speech accorded to the dying,
Would not now be denied to us; but since——
　I. Ber. Even let them have their way,
　　brave Calendaro!
What matter a few syllables? let's die
Without the slightest show of favour from
　　them;
So shall our blood more readily arise
To Heaven against them, and more testify
To their atrocities, than could a volume
Spoken or written of our dying words!
They tremble at our voices—nay, they dread
Our very silence—let them live in fear!
Leave them unto their thoughts, and let us
　　now
Address our own above!—Lead on; we are
　　ready.

　Cal. Israel, hadst thou but hearken'd
　　unto me
It had not now been thus; and yon pale
　　villain,
The coward Bertram, would—
　I. Ber.　　　　　　Peace, Calendaro!
What brooks it now to ponder upon this?
　Bert. Alas! I fain you died in peace
　　with me:
I did not seek this task; 'twas forced upon
　　me:
Say, you forgive me, though I never can
Retrieve my own forgiveness—frown not
　　thus!
　I. Ber. I die and pardon thee!
　Cal. (*spitting at him*).　　　I die and
　　scorn thee!
　　　　[*Exeunt* ISRAEL BERTUCCIO *and* PHILIP
　　　　　　　　　　CALENDARO, *Guards, &c.*
　Ben. Now that these criminals have been
　　disposed of,
'Tis time that we proceed to pass our sen-
　　tence
Upon the greatest traitor upon record
In any annals, the Doge Faliero!
The proofs and process are complete; the
　　time
And crime require a quick procedure: shall
He now be call'd in to receive the award?
　The Giunta. Ay, ay.
　Ben.　　　Avogadori, order that the Doge
Be brought before the council.
　One of the Giunta.　　　And the rest,
When shall they be brought up?
　Ben.　　　　When all the chiefs
Have been disposed of. Some have fled to
　　Chiozza;
But there are thousands in pursuit of them,
And such precaution ta'en on terra firma,
As well as in the islands, that we hope
None will escape to utter in strange lands
His libellous tale of treasons 'gainst the
　　senate.

　　　　Enter the DOGE *as Prisoner, with*
　　　　　　　Guards, &c. &c.

　Ben. Doge—for such still you are, and by
　　the law
Must be consider'd, till the hour shall come
When you must doff the ducal bonnet from
That head, which could not wear a crown
　　more noble
Than empires can confer, in quiet honour,
But it must plot to overthrow your peers,
Who made you what you are, and quench in
　　blood
A city's glory—we have laid already
Before you in your chamber at full length,
By the Avogadori, all the proofs

Which have appear'd against you; and more
 ample
Ne'er rear'd their sanguinary shadows to
Confront a traitor. What have you to say
In your defence?
 Doge. What shall I say to ye,
Since my defence must be your condemna-
 tion?
You are at once offenders and accusers,
Judges and executioners!—Proceed
Upon your power.
 Ben. Your chief accomplices
Having confess'd, there is no hope for you.
 Doge. And who be they?
 Ben. In number many; but
The first now stands before you and the court,
Bertram, of Bergamo,—would you question
 him?
 Doge (looking at him contemptuously). No.
 Ben. And two others, Israel Bertuccio
And Philip Calendaro, have admitted
Their fellowship in treason with the Doge!
 Doge. And where are they?
 Ben. Gone to their place, and now
Answering to Heaven for what they did on
 earth.
 Doge. Ah! the plebeian Brutus, is he
 gone?
And the quick Cassius of the arsenal?—
How did they meet their doom?
 Ben. Think of your own:
It is approaching. You decline to plead,
 then?
 Doge. I cannot plead to my inferiors, nor
Can recognise your legal power to try me.
Show me the law!
 Ben. On great emergencies
The law must be remodell'd or amended:
Our fathers had not fix'd the punishment
Of such a crime, as on the old Roman tables
The sentence against parricide was left
In pure forgetfulness; they could not render
That penal, which had neither name nor
 thought
In their great bosoms; who would have
 foreseen
That nature could be filed to such a crime
As sons 'gainst sires, and princes 'gainst
 their realms?
Your sin hath made us make a law which will
Become a precedent 'gainst such haught
 traitors,
As would with treason mount to tyranny;
Not even contented with a sceptre, till
They can convert it to a two-edged sword!
Was not the place of Doge sufficient for ye?
What's nobler than the signory of Venice?
 Doge. The signory of Venice! You be-
 tray'd me—
You—you, who sit there, traitors as ye are!

From my equality with you in birth,
And my superiority in action,
You drew me from my honourable toils
In distant lands—on flood, in field, in cities—
You singled me out like a victim to
Stand crown'd, but bound and helpless, at
 the altar
Where you alone could minister. I knew not,
I sought not, wish'd not, dream'd not the
 election,
Which reach'd me first at Rome, and I
 obey'd;
But found on my arrival, that, besides
The jealous vigilance which always led you
To mock and mar your sovereign's best in-
 tents,
You had, even in the interregnum of
My journey to the capital, curtail'd
And mutilated the few privileges
Yet left the duke: all this I bore, and would
Have borne, until my very hearth was stain'd
By the pollution of your ribaldry,
And he, the ribald, whom I see amongst you—
Fit judge in such a tribunal!——
 Ben. (interrupting him). Michel Steno
Is here in virtue of his office, as
One of the Forty; "the Ten" having craved
A Giunta of patricians from the senate
To aid our judgment in a trial arduous
And novel as the present: he was set
Free from the penalty pronounced upon him,
Because the Doge, who should protect the law,
Seeking to abrogate all law, can claim
No punishment of others by the statutes
Which he himself denies and violates!
 Doge. *His* punishment! I rather see him
 there,
Where he now sits, to glut him with my
 death,
Than in the mockery of castigation,
Which your foul, outward, juggling show of
 justice
Decreed as sentence! Base as was his crime,
'Twas purity compared with your protection.
 Ben. And can it be, that the great Doge
 of Venice,
With three parts of a century of years
And honours on his head, could thus allow
His fury, like an angry boy's, to master
All feeling, wisdom, faith, and fear, on such
A provocation as a young man's petulance?
 Doge. A spark creates the flame—'tis the
 last drop
Which makes the cup run o'er, and mine
 was full
Already: you oppress'd the prince and people;
I would have freed both, and have fail'd in
 both:
The price of such success would have been
 glory,

Vengeance, and victory, and such a name
As would have made Venetian history
Rival to that of Greece and Syracuse
When they were freed, and flourish'd ages
 after,
And mine to Gelon and to Thrasybulus:—
Failing, I know the penalty of failure
Is present infamy and death—the future
Will judge, when Venice is no more, or free;
Till then, the truth is in abeyance. Pause
 not;
I would have shown no mercy, and I seek
 none;
My life was staked upon a mighty hazard,
And being lost, take what I would have
 taken!
I would have stood alone amidst your tombs:
Now you may flock round mine, and trample
 on it,
As you have done upon my heart while living.
 Ben. You do confess then, and admit the
 justice
Of our tribunal?
 Doge. I confess to have fail'd;
Fortune is female: from my youth her favours
Were not withheld, the fault was mine to
 hope
Her former smiles again at this late hour.
 Ben. You do not then in aught arraign
 our equity?
 Doge. Noble Venetians! stir me not with
 questions.
I am resign'd to the worst; but in me still
Have something of the blood of brighter days,
And am not over-patient. Pray you, spare
 me
Further interrogation, which boots nothing,
Except to turn a trial to debate.
I shall but answer that which will offend
 you,
And please your enemies—a host already;
'Tis true, these sullen walls should yield no
 echo:
But walls have ears—nay, more, they have
 tongues; and if
There were no other way for truth to o'er-
 leap them,
You who condemn me, you who fear and
 slay me,
Yet could not bear in silence to your graves
What you would hear from me of good or
 evil;
The secret were too mighty for your souls:
Then let it sleep in mine, unless you court
A danger which would double that you escape.
Such my defence would be, had I full scope
To make it famous; for true *words* are *things*,
And dying men's are things which long out-
 live,
And oftentimes avenge them; bury mine,

If ye would fain survive me: take this
 counsel,
And though too oft ye made me live in wrath,
Let me die calmly; you may grant me this;
I deny nothing, defend nothing, nothing
I ask of you, but silence for myself,
And sentence from the court!
 Ben. This full admission
Spares us the harsh necessity of ordering
The torture to elicit the whole truth.
 Doge. The torture! you have put me
 there already,
Daily since I was Doge; but if you will
Add the corporeal rack, you may: these limbs
Will yield with age to crushing iron; but
There's that within my heart shall strain
 your engines.

Enter an OFFICER.

 Officer. Noble Venetians! Duchess Faliero
Requests admission to the Giunta's presence.
 Ben. Say, conscript fathers, shall she be
 admitted?
 One of the Giunta. She may have revela-
 tions of importance
Unto the state, to justify compliance
With her request.
 Ben. Is this the general will?
 All. It is.
 Doge. Oh, admirable laws of Venice!
Which would admit the wife, in the full hope
That she might testify against the husband.
What glory to the chaste Venetian dames!
But such blasphemers 'gainst all honour, as
Sit here, do well to act in their vocation.
Now, villain Steno! if this woman fail,
I'll pardon thee thy lie, and thy escape,
And my own violent death, and thy vile life.

The DUCHESS enters.

 Ben. Lady! this just tribunal has resolved,
Though the request be strange, to grant it,
 and
Whatever be its purport, to accord
A patient hearing with the due respect
Which fits your ancestry, your rank, and
 virtues:
But you turn pale—ho! there, look to the
 lady!
Place a chair instantly.
 Ang. A moment's faintness—
'Tis past; I pray you pardon me,—I sit not
In presence of my prince and of my husband,
While he is on his feet.
 Ben. Your pleasure, lady?
 Ang. Strange rumours, but most true, if
 all I hear
And see be sooth, have reach'd me, and I
 come

To know the worst, even at the worst; for-
 give
The abruptness of my entrance and my
 bearing.
Is it ——I cannot speak—I cannot shape
The question—but you answer it ere spoken,
With eyes averted, and with gloomy brows—
Oh God! this is the silence of the grave!
 Ben. (after a pause). Spare us, and spare
 thyself the repetition
Of our most awful, but inexorable
Duty to Heaven and man!
 Ang. Yet speak; I cannot—
I cannot—no—even now believe these things.
Is *he* condemned?
 Ben. Alas!
 Ang. And was he guilty?
 Ben. Lady! the natural distraction of
Thy thoughts at such a moment makes the
 question
Merit forgiveness; else a doubt like this
Against a just and paramount tribunal
Were deep offence. But question even the
 Doge,
And if he can deny the proofs, believe him
Guiltless as thy own bosom.
 Ang. Is it so?
My lord, my sovereign, my poor father's
 friend,
The mighty in the field, the sage in council,
Unsay the words of this man!—Thou art
 silent!
 Ben. He hath already own'd to his own
 guilt,
Nor, as thou see'st, doth he deny it now.
 Ang. Ay, but he must not die! Spare his
 few years,
Which grief and shame will soon cut down to
 days!
One day of baffled crime must not efface
Near sixteen lustres crowded with brave acts.
 Ben. His doom must be fulfill'd without
 remission
Of time or penalty—'t is a decree.
 Ang. He hath been guilty, but there may
 be mercy.
 Ben. Not in this case with justice.
 Ang. Alas! signor,
He who is only just is cruel; who
Upon the earth would live were all judged
 justly?
 Ben. His punishment is safety to the state.
 Ang. He was a subject, and hath served
 the state;
He was your general, and hath saved the
 state;
He is your sovereign, and hath ruled the
 state.
 One of the Council. He is a traitor, and
 betray'd the state.

 Ang. And, but for him, there now had
 been no state
To save or to destroy; and you, who sit
There to pronounce the death of your de-
 liverer,
Had now been groaning at a Moslem oar,
Or digging in the Hunnish mines in fetters!
 One of the Council. No, lady, there are
 others who would die
Rather than breathe in slavery!
 Ang. If there are so
Within *these* walls, *thou* art not of the
 number:
The truly brave are generous to the fallen!—
Is there no hope?
 Ben. Lady, it cannot be.
 Ang. (turning to the Doge). Then die,
 Faliero! since it must be so;
But with the spirit of my father's friend.
Thou hast been guilty of a great offence,
Half cancell'd by the harshness of these men.
I would have sued to them, have pray'd to
 them,
Have begg'd as famish'd mendicants for
 bread,
Have wept as they will cry unto their God
For mercy, and be answer'd as they answer,—
Had it been fitting for thy name or mine,
And if the cruelty in their cold eyes
Had not announced the heartless wrath
 within.
Then, as a prince, address thee to thy doom!
 Doge. I have lived too long not to know
 how to die!
Thy suing to these men were but the bleating
Of the lamb to the butcher, or the cry
Of seamen to the surge: I would not take
A life eternal, granted at the hands
Of wretches, from whose monstrous villainies
I sought to free the groaning nations!
 Michel Steno. Doge,
A word with thee, and with this noble lady,
Whom I have grievously offended. Would
Sorrow, or shame, or penance on my part,
Could cancel the inexorable past!
But since that cannot be, as Christians let us
Say farewell, and in peace: with full con-
 trition
I crave, not pardon, but compassion from
 you,
And give, however weak, my prayers for
 both.
 Ang. Sage Benintende, now chief judge
 of Venice,
I speak to thee in answer to yon signor.
Inform the ribald Steno, that his words
Ne'er weigh'd in mind with Loredano's
 daughter,
Further than to create a moment's pity
For such as he is: would that others had

Despis'd him as I pity! I prefer
My honour to a thousand lives, could such
Be multiplied in mine, but would not have
A single life of others lost for that
Which nothing human can impugn—the
 sense
Of virtue, looking not to what is call'd
A good name for reward, but to itself.
To me the scorner's words were as the wind
Unto the rock: but as there are—alas!
Spirits more sensitive, on which such things
Light as the whirlwind on the waters; souls
To whom dishonour's shadow is a substance
More terrible than death, here and hereafter;
Men whose vice is to start at vice's scoffing,
And who, though proof against all blandish-
 ments
Of pleasure, and all pangs of pain, are feeble
When the proud name on which they pin-
 nacled
Their hopes is breathed on, jealous as the
 eagle
Of her high aiery; let what we now
Behold, and feel, and suffer, be a lesson
To wretches how they tamper in their spleen
With beings of a higher order. Insects
Have made the lion mad ere now; a shaft
I' the heel o'erthrew the bravest of the brave;
A wife's dishonour was the bane of Troy;
A wife's dishonour unking'd Rome for ever;
An injured husband brought the Gauls to
 Clusium,
And thence to Rome, which perish'd for a
 time;
An obscene gesture cost Caligula
His life, while Earth yet bore his cruelties;
A virgin's wrong made Spain a Moorish pro-
 vince;
And Steno's lie, couch'd in two worthless
 lines,
Hath decimated Venice, put in peril
A senate which hath stood eight hundred
 years,
Discrown'd a prince, cut off his crownless
 head,
And forged new fetters for a groaning people!
Let the poor wretch, like to the courtesan
Who fired Persepolis, be proud of this,
If it so please him—'t were a pride fit for him!
But let him not insult the last hours of
Him, who, whate'er he now is, *was* a hero,
By the intrusion of his very prayers;
Nothing of good can come from such a source,
Nor would we aught with him, nor now, nor
 ever:
We leave him to himself, that lowest depth
Of human baseness. Pardon is for men,
And not for reptiles—we have none for Steno,
And no resentment: things like him must
 sting,

And higher beings suffer; 'tis the charter
Of life. The man who dies by the adder's
 fang
May have the crawler crush'd, but feels no
 anger:
'T was the worm's nature; and some men
 are worms
In soul more than the living things of tombs.
 Doge (to Ben.). Signor! complete that
 which you deem your duty.
 Ben. Before we can proceed upon that
 duty, ,
We would request the princess to withdraw;
'T will move her too much to be witness to it.
 Ang. I know it will, and yet I must en-
 dure it,
For 'tis a part of mine—I will not quit,
Except by force, my husband's side.—Pro-
 ceed!
Nay, fear not either shriek, or sigh, or tear;
Though my heart burst it shall be silent.—
 Speak!
I have that within which shall o'ermaster all.
 Ben. Marino Faliero, Doge of Venice,
Count of Val di Marino, Senator,
And some time General of the Fleet and
 Army,
Noble Venetian, many times and oft
Intrusted by the state with high employ-
 ments,
Even to the highest, listen to the sentence.
Convict by many witnesses and proofs,
And by thine own confession, of the guilt
Of treachery and treason, yet unheard of
Until this trial—the decree is death.
Thy goods are confiscate unto the state,
Thy name is razed from out her records, save
Upon a public day of thanksgiving
For this our most miraculous deliverance,
When thou art noted in our calendars
With earthquakes, pestilence, and foreign
 foes,
And the great enemy of man, as subject
Of grateful masses for Heaven's grace in
 snatching
Our lives and country from thy wickedness.
The place wherein as Doge thou shouldst be
 painted,
With thine illustrious predecessors, is
To be left vacant, with a death-black veil
Flung over these dim words engraved be-
 neath,—
" This place is of Marino Faliero,
Decapitated for his crimes."
 Doge. " His crimes!"
But let it be so;—it will be in vain.
The veil which blackens o'er this blighted
 name,
And hides, or seems to hide, these linea-
 ments,

Shall draw more gazers than the thousand
 portraits
Which glitter round it in their pictured
 trappings—
Your delegated slaves—the people's tyrants!
"Decapitated for his crimes!"—*What* crimes?
Were it not better to record the facts,
So that the contemplator might approve,
Or at the least learn *whence* the crimes arose?
When the beholder knows a Doge conspired,
Let him be told the cause—it is your history.
 Ben. Time must reply to that; our sons
 will judge
Their fathers' judgment, which I now pro-
 nounce.
As Doge, clad in the ducal robes and cap,
Thou shalt be led hence to the Giant's Stair-
 case,
Where thou and all our princes are invested;
And there, the ducal crown being first re-
 sumed
Upon the spot where it was first assumed,
Thy head shall be struck off; and Heaven
 have mercy
Upon thy soul!
 Doge. Is this the Giunta's sentence?
 Ben. It is.
 Doge. I can endure it.—And the time?
 Ben. Must be immediate.—Make thy peace
 with God:
Within an hour thou must be in His pre-
 sence.
 Doge. I am already; and my blood will
 rise
To Heaven before the souls of those who
 shed it.
Are all my lands confiscated?
 Ben. They are;
And goods, and jewels, and all kind of trea-
 sure,
Except two thousand ducats—these dispose of.
 Doge. That's harsh.—I would have fain
 reserved the lands
Near to Treviso, which I hold by investment
From Laurence the Count-bishop of Ceneda,
In fief perpetual to myself and heirs,
To portion them (leaving my city spoil,
My palace and my treasures, to your forfeit)
Between my consort and my kinsmen.
 Ben. These
Lie under the state's ban; their chief, thy
 nephew,
In peril of his own life; but the council
Postpones his trial for the present. If
Thou will'st a state unto thy widow'd prin-
 cess,
Fear not, for we will do her justice.
 Ang. Signors,
I share not in your spoil! From henceforth,
 know

I am devoted unto God alone,
And take my refuge in the cloister.
 Doge. Come!
The hour may be a hard one, but 'twill end.
Have I aught else to undergo save death?
 Ben. You have nought to do, except con-
 fess and die.
The priest is robed, the scimitar is bare,
And both await without. But, above all,
Think not to speak unto the people; they
Are now by thousands swarming at the gates,
But these are closed: the Ten, the Avogadori,
The Giunta, and the chief men of the Forty,
Alone will be beholders of thy doom,
And they are ready to attend the Doge.
 Doge. The Doge!
 Ben. Yes, Doge, thou hast lived
 and thou shalt die
A sovereign; till the moment which precedes
The separation of that head and trunk,
That ducal crown and head shall be united.
Thou hast forgot thy dignity in deigning
To plot with petty traitors; not so we,
Who in the very punishment acknowledge
The prince. Thy vile accomplices have died
The dog's death, and the wolf's; but thou
 shalt fall
As falls the lion by the hunters, girt
By those who feel a proud compassion for
 thee,
And mourn even the inevitable death
Provoked by thy wild wrath and regal fierce-
 ness.
Now we remit thee to thy preparation:
Let it be brief, and we ourselves will be
Thy guides unto the place where first we
 were
United to thee as thy subjects, and
Thy senate; and must now be parted from
 thee
As such for ever, on the self-same spot.
Guards! form the Doge's escort to his
 chamber. [*Exeunt.*

Scene II.

The Doge's Apartment.

The Doge *as Prisoner, and the* Duchess
 attending him.

 Doge. Now, that the priest is gone, 't were
 useless all
To linger out the miserable minutes;
But one pang more, the pang of parting from
 thee,
And I will leave the few last grains of sand
Which yet remain of the accorded hour,
Still falling—I have done with Time.

Ang. Alas!
And I have been the cause, the unconscious
 cause;
And for this funeral marriage, this black
 union,
Which thou, compliant with my father's
 wish,
Didst promise at *his* death, thou hast seal'd
 thine own.
 Doge. Not so; there was that in my spirit
 ever
Which shaped out for itself some great
 reverse;
The marvel is, it came not until now—
And yet it was foretold me.
 Ang. How foretold you?
 Doge. Long years ago—so long, they are
 a doubt
In memory, and yet they live in annals:
When I was in my youth, and served the
 senate
And signory as podesta and captain
Of the town of Treviso, on a day
Of festival, the sluggish bishop who
Convey'd the Host aroused my rash young
 anger
By strange delay, and arrogant reply
To my reproof: I raised my hand and smote
 him,
Until he reel'd beneath his holy burthen;
And as he rose from earth again, he raised
His tremulous hands in pious wrath towards
 Heaven.
Thence pointing to' the Host, which had
 fallen from him,
He turn'd to me, and said, " The hour will
 come
When he thou hast o'erthrown shall over-
 throw thee:
The glory shall depart from out thy house,
The wisdom shall be shaken from thy soul,
And in thy best maturity of mind
A madness of the heart shall seize upon
 thee;
Passion shall tear thee when all passions
 cease
In other men, or mellow into virtues;
And majesty, which decks all other heads,
Shall crown to leave thee headless; honours
 shall
But prove to thee the heralds of destruction,
And hoary hairs of shame, and both of death,
But not such death as fits an aged man."
Thus saying, he pass'd on.—That hour is
 come.
 Ang. And with this warning couldst thou
 not have striven
To avert the fatal moment, and atone,
By penitence, for that which thou hadst
 done?

 Doge. I own the words went to my heart,
 so much
That I remember'd them amid the maze
Of life, as if they form'd a spectral voice,
Which shook me in a supernatural dream;
And I repented; but 'twas not for me
To pull in resolution: what must be
I could not change, and would not fear.—
 Nay more,
Thou canst not have forgot, what all re-
 member,
That on my day of landing here as Doge,
On my return from Rome, a mist of such
Unwonted density went on before
The Bucentaur, like the columnar cloud
Which usher'd Israel out of Egypt, till
The pilot was misled, and disembark'd us
Between the pillars of Saint Mark's, where
 'tis
The custom of the state to put to death
Its criminals, instead of touching at
The Riva della Paglia, as the wont is,—
So that all Venice shudder'd at the omen.
 Ang. Ah! little boots it now to recollect
Such things.
 Doge. And yet I find a comfort in
The thought, that these things are the work
 of Fate;
For I would rather yield to gods than men,
Or cling to any creed of destiny,
Rather than deem these mortals, most of
 whom
I know to be as worthless as the dust,
And weak as worthless, more than instru-
 ments
Of an o'erruling power; they in themselves
Were all incapable—they could not be
Victors of him who oft had conquer'd for
 them.
 Ang. Employ the minutes left in aspira-
 tions
Of a more healing nature, and in peace
Even with these wretches take thy flight to
 heaven.
 Doge. I *am* at peace: the peace of cer-
 tainty
That a sure hour will come, when their
 sons' sons,
And this proud city, and these azure waters,
And all which makes them eminent and
 bright,
Shall be a desolation and a curse,
A hissing and a scoff unto the nations,
A Carthage, and a Tyre, an Ocean Babel.
 Ang. Speak not thus now: the surge of
 passion still
Sweeps o'er thee to the last; thou dost
 deceive
Thyself, and canst not injure them—be
 calmer.

Doge. I stand within eternity, and see
Into eternity, and I behold—
Ay, palpable as I see thy sweet face
For the last time—the days which I de-
　　nounce
Unto all time against these wave-girt walls,
And they who are indwellers.
　　Guard (coming forward). Doge of Venice,
The Ten are in attendance on your highness.
　　Doge. Then farewell, Angiolina!—one
　　embrace—
Forgive the old man who hath been to thee
A fond but fatal husband—love my memory—
I would not ask so much for me still living,
But thou canst judge of me more kindly now,
Seeing my evil feelings are at rest.
Besides, of all the fruit of these long years,
Glory, and wealth, and power, and fame,
　　and name,
Which generally leave some flowers to bloom
Even o'er the grave, I have nothing left,
　　not even
A little love, or friendship, or esteem,
No, not enough to extract an epitaph
From ostentatious kinsmen; in one hour
I have uprooted all my former life,
And outlived everything, except thy heart,
The pure, the good, the gentle, which will oft
With unimpair'd but not a clamorous grief
Still keep—Thou turn'st so pale!—Alas! she
　　faints,
She has no breath, no pulse!—Guards! lend
　　your aid—
I cannot leave her thus, and yet 't is better,
Since every lifeless moment spares a pang.
When she shakes off this temporary death,
I shall be with the Eternal.—Call her
　　women—
One look!—how cold her hand!—as cold as
　　mine
Shall be ere she recovers.—Gently tend her,
And take my last thanks——I am ready now.
　　[*The Attendants of* Angiolina *enter, and
　　surround their Mistress, who has fainted.
　　—Exeunt the* Doge, *Guards, &c. &c.*

Scene III.

*The Court of the Ducal Palace; the outer
gates are shut against the people.—The
Doge enters in his ducal robes, in pro-
cession with the Council of Ten and other
Patricians, attended by the Guards, till
they arrive at the top of the "Giants' Stair-
case" (where the Doges took the oaths); the
Executioner is stationed there with his
sword.—On arriving, a Chief of the Ten
takes off the ducal cap from the Doge's
head.*

　　Doge. So now the Doge is nothing, and at
　　last

I am again Marino Faliero:
'T is well to be so, though but for a moment.
Here was I crown'd, and here, bear witness,
　　Heaven!
With how much more contentment I resign
That shining mockery, the ducal bauble,
Than I received the fatal ornament.
　　One of the Ten. Thou tremblest, Faliero!
　　Doge. 'T is with age, then.
　　Ben. Faliero! hast thou aught further to
　　commend,
Compatible with justice, to the senate?
　　Doge. I would commend my nephew to
　　their mercy,
My consort to their justice; for methinks
My death, and such a death, might settle all
Between the state and me.
　　Ben. They shall be cared for;
Even notwithstanding thine unheard-of
　　crime.
　　Doge. Unheard of! ay, there's not a
　　history
But shows a thousand crown'd conspirators
Against the people; but to set them free,
One sovereign only died, and one is dying.
　　Ben. And who were they who fell in such
　　a cause?
　　Doge. The King of Sparta and the Doge
　　of Venice—
Agis and Faliero!
　　Ben. Hast thou more
To utter or to do?
　　Doge. May I speak?
　　Ben. Thou may'st;
But recollect the people are without,
Beyond the compass of the human voice.
　　Doge. I speak to Time and to Eternity,
Of which I grow a portion, not to man.
Ye elements! in which to be resolved
I hasten, let my voice be as a spirit
Upon you! Ye blue waves! which bore my
　　banner,
Ye winds! which flutter'd o'er as if you
　　loved it,
And fill'd my swelling sails as they were
　　wafted
To many a triumph! Thou, my native earth,
Which I have bled for! and thou, foreign
　　earth,
Which drank this willing blood from many
　　a wound!
Ye stones, in which my gore will not sink,
　　but
Reek up to heaven! Ye skies, which will
　　receive it!
Thou sun! which shinest on these things,
　　and Thou!
Who kindlest and who quenchest suns!—
　　Attest!
I am not innocent—but are these guiltless?

I perish, but not unavenged : far ages
Float up from the abyss of time to be,
And show these eyes, before they close, the
 doom
Of this proud city, and I leave my curse
On her and hers for ever !——Yes, the hours
Are silently engendering of the day,
When she, who built 'gainst Attila a bul-
 wark,
Shall yield, and bloodlessly and basely yield,
Unto a bastard Attila, without
Shedding so much blood in her last defence,
As these old veins, oft drain'd in shielding
 her,
Shall pour in sacrifice.—She shall be bought
And sold, and be an appanage to those
Who shall despise her !—She shall stoop
 to be
A province for an empire, petty town
In lieu of capital, with slaves for senates,
Beggars for nobles, panders for a people !
Then when the Hebrew's in thy palaces,
The Hun in thy high places, and the Greek
Walks o'er thy mart, and smiles on it for
 his :
When thy patricians beg their bitter bread
In narrow streets, and in their shameful
 need
Make their nobility a plea for pity ;
Then, when the few who still retain a wreck
Of their great fathers' heritage shall fawn
Round a barbarian Vice of Kings' Vice-
 gerent,
Even in the palace where they sway'd as
 sovereigns,
Even in the palace where they slew their
 sovereign,
Proud of some name they have disgraced, or
 sprung
From an adulteress boastful of her guilt
With some large gondolier or foreign soldier,
Shall bear about their bastardy in triumph
To the third spurious generation ;—when
Thy sons are in the lowest scale of being,
Slaves turn'd o'er to the vanquish'd by the
 victors,
Despised by cowards for greater cowardice,
And scorn'd even by the vicious for such
 vices
As in the monstrous grasp of their con-
 ception
Defy all codes to image or to name them ;
Then, when of Cyprus, now thy subject
 kingdom,
All thine inheritance shall be her shame
Entail'd on thy less virtuous daughters,
 grown
A wider proverb for worse prostitution ;—
When all the ills of conquer'd states shall
 cling thee,

Vice without splendour, sin without relief
Even from the gloss of love to smooth it o'er,
But in its stead, coarse lusts of habitude,
Prurient yet passionless, cold studied lewd-
 ness,
Depraving nature's frailty to an art ;—
When these and more are heavy on thee,
 when
Smiles without mirth, and pastimes without
 pleasure,
Youth without honour, age without respect,
Meanness and weakness, and a sense of woe
'Gainst which thou wilt not strive, and dar'st
 not murmur,
Have made thee last and worst of peopled
 deserts,
Then, in the last gasp of thine agony,
Amidst thy many murders, think of *mine !*
Thou den of drunkards with the blood of
 princes !
Gehenna of the waters ! thou sea Sodom !
Thus I devote thee to the infernal gods !
Thee and thy serpent seed !
 [*Here the* Doge *turns and addresses
 the Executioner.*
 Slave, do thine office !
Strike as I struck the foe ! Strike as I would
Have struck those tyrants ! Strike deep as my
 curse !
Strike—and but once !
 [*The* Doge *throws himself upon his
 knees, and as the Executioner raises
 his sword the scene closes.*

Scene IV.

*The Piazza and Piazzetta of St Mark's.—The
 people in crowds gathered round the grated
 gates of the Ducal Palace, which are shut.*

 First Citizen. I have gain'd the gate, and
 can discern the Ten,
Robed in their gowns of state, ranged round
 the Doge.
 Second Cit. I cannot reach thee with mine
 utmost effort.
How is it ? let us hear at least, since sight
Is thus prohibited unto the people,
Except the occupiers of those bars.
 First Cit. One has approach'd the Doge,
 and now they strip
The ducal bonnet from his head—and now
He raises his keen eyes to heaven ; I see
Them glitter, and his lips move—Hush ! hush !
 —no,
'Twas but a murmur—Curse upon the dis-
 tance !
His words are inarticulate, but the voice
Swells up like mutter'd thunder ; would we
 could
But gather a sole sentence !

Second Cit. Hush! we perhaps may catch
　　the sound.
First Cit. 　　'Tis vain,
I cannot hear him.—How his hoary hair
Streams on the wind like foam upon the
　　wave!
Now—now—he kneels—and now they form a
　　circle
Round him, and all is hidden—but I see
The lifted sword in air——Ah! hark! it falls!
　　　　　　　　　[*The people murmur.*
Third Cit. Then they have murder'd him
　　who would have freed us.
Fourth Cit. He was a kind man to the
　　commons ever.
Fifth Cit. Wisely they did to keep their
　　portals barr'd.
Would we had known the work they were
　　preparing

Ere we were summon'd here—we would have
　　brought
Weapons, and forced them!
Sixth Cit. 　　　Are you sure he's dead?
First Cit. I saw the sword fall—Lo! what
　　have we here?

*Enter on the Balcony of the Palace which fronts
St. Mark's Place a* CHIEF OF THE TEN, *with
a bloody sword. He waves it thrice before
the People, and exclaims,*

"Justice hath dealt upon the mighty Traitor!"

　　[*The gates are opened; the populace rush in
　　towards the "Giants' Staircase," where
　　the execution has taken place. The fore-
　　most of them exclaims to those behind,*

"The gory head rolls down the Giants'
　　Steps!" 　　　[*The curtain falls.*

Sardanapalus:

A TRAGEDY.

TO

THE ILLUSTRIOUS GOETHE

A STRANGER PRESUMES TO OFFER THE HOMAGE OF A
LITERARY VASSAL TO HIS LIEGE LORD, THE FIRST OF EXISTING WRITERS,
WHO HAS CREATED THE LITERATURE OF HIS OWN COUNTRY,
AND ILLUSTRATED THAT OF EUROPE.

THE UNWORTHY PRODUCTION
WHICH THE AUTHOR VENTURES TO INSCRIBE TO HIM IS ENTITLED,

SARDANAPALUS.

PREFACE.

IN publishing the following Tragedies * I have only to repeat, that they were not composed with the most remote view to the stage. On the attempt made by the managers in a former instance, the public opinion has been already expressed. With regard to my own private feelings, as it seems that they are to stand for nothing, I shall say nothing.

For the historical foundation of the following compositions the reader is referred to the Notes.

The Author has in one instance attempted to preserve, and in the other to approach, the "unities;" conceiving that with any very distant departure from them, there may be poetry, but can be no

drama. He is aware of the unpopularity of this notion in present English literature; but it is not a system of his own, being merely an opinion, which, not very long ago, was the law of literature throughout the world, and is still so in the more civilized parts of it. But "nous avons changé tout cela," and are reaping the advantages of the change. The writer is far from conceiving that anything he can adduce by personal precept or example can at all approach his regular, or even irregular, predecessors: he is merely giving a reason why he preferred the more regular formation of a structure, however feeble, to an entire abandonment of all rules whatsoever. Where he has failed, the failure is in the architect,—and not in the art.

* "Sardanapalus" and "The Two Foscari."

SARDANAPALUS.

Dramatis Personæ.

<table>
<tr><td align="center">MEN.</td><td align="center">WOMEN.</td></tr>
<tr><td>SARDANAPALUS, King of Nineveh and Assyria, &c.</td><td>ZARINA, the Queen.</td></tr>
<tr><td>ARBACES, the Mede who aspired to the Throne.</td><td></td></tr>
<tr><td>BELESES, a Chaldean and Soothsayer.</td><td>MYRRHA, an Ionian female Slave, and the Favourite of SARDANAPALUS.</td></tr>
<tr><td>SALEMENES, the King's Brother-in-Law.</td><td></td></tr>
<tr><td>ALTADA, an Assyrian Officer of the Palace.</td><td></td></tr>
<tr><td>PANIA.</td><td></td></tr>
<tr><td>ZAMES.</td><td>Women composing the Harem of SARDA-</td></tr>
<tr><td>SFERO.</td><td>NAPALUS, Guards, Attendants, Chal-</td></tr>
<tr><td>BALEA.</td><td>dean Priests, Medes, &c. &c.</td></tr>
</table>

Scene.—*A Hall in the Royal Palace of Nineveh.*

In this tragedy it has been my intention to follow the account of Diodorus Siculus; reducing it, however, to such dramatic regularity as I best could, and trying to approach the unities. I therefore suppose the rebellion to explode and succeed in one day by a sudden conspiracy, instead of the long war of the history.

Act I.

Scene I.—*A Hall in the Palace.*

Salemenes (solus). He hath wrong'd his
 queen, but still he is her lord ;
He hath wrong'd my sister, still he is my
 brother ;
He hath wrong'd his people, still he is their
 sovereign,
And I must be his friend as well as subject·
He must not perish thus. I will not see
The blood of Nimrod and Semiramis
Sink in the earth, and thirteen hundred years
Of empire ending like a shepherd's tale ;
He must be roused. In his effeminate heart
There is a careless courage which corruption
Has not all quench'd, and latent energies,
Repress'd by circumstance, but not de-
 stroy'd—
Steep'd, but not drown'd, in deep voluptuous-
 ness.
If born a peasant, he had been a man
To have reach'd an empire : to an empire born,
He will bequeath none ; nothing but a name,
Which his sons will not prize in heritage :
Yet, not all lost, even yet he may redeem
His sloth and shame, by only being that

Which he should be, as easily as the thing
He should not be and is. Were it less toil
To sway his nations than consume his life ?
To head an army than to rule a harem ?
He sweats in palling pleasures, dulls his soul,
And saps his goodly strength, in toils which
 yield not
Health like the chase, nor glory like the
 war—
He must be roused. Alas ! there is no sound
 [*Sound of soft music heard from within.*
To rouse him short of thunder. Hark ! the
 lute,
The lyre, the timbrel ; the lascivious tinklings
Of lulling instruments, the softening voices
Of women, and of beings less than women,
Must chime in to the echo of his revel,
While the great king of all we know of earth
Lolls crown'd with roses, and his diadem
Lies negligently by to be caught up
By the first manly hand which dares to snatch
 it.
Lo, where they come ! already I perceive
The reeking odours of the perfumed trains,
And see the bright gems of the glittering girls,
At once his chorus and his council, flash
Along the gallery, and amidst the damsels,
As femininely garb'd, and scarce less female,
The grandson of Semiramis, the man-queen.—

He comes! Shall I await him? yes, and front
 him,
And tell him what all good men tell each other,
Speaking of him and his. They come, the
 slaves
Led by the monarch subject to his slaves.

Scene II.

Enter SARDANAPALUS *effeminately dressed, his
Head crowned with Flowers, and his Robe
negligently flowing, attended by a Train of
Women and young Slaves.*

 Sar. (*speaking to some of his attendants*). Let
 the pavilion over the Euphrates
Be garlanded, and lit, and furnish'd forth
For an especial banquet; at the hour
Of midnight we will sup there: see nought
 wanting,
And bid the galley be prepared. There is
A cooling breeze which crisps the broad clear
 river:
We will embark anon. Fair nymphs, who
 deign
To share the soft hours of Sardanapalus,
We'll meet again in that the sweetest hour,
When we shall gather like the stars above us,
And you will form a heaven as bright as theirs;
Till then, let each be mistress of her time,
And thou, my own Ionian Myrrha, choose
Wilt thou along with them or me?
 Myr. My lord——
 Sar. My lord, my life! why answerest
 thou so coldly?
It is the curse of kings to be so answer'd.
Rule thy own hours, thou rulest mine—say,
 wouldst thou
Accompany our guests, or charm away
The moments from me?
 Myr. The king's choice is mine.
 Sar. I pray thee say not so: my chiefest
 joy
Is to contribute to thine every wish.
I do not dare to breathe my own desire,
Lest it should clash with thine; for thou art
 still
Too prompt to sacrifice thy thoughts for
 others.
 Myr. I would remain: I have no happiness
Save in beholding thine; yet——
 Sar. Yet! what YET?
Thy own sweet will shall be the only barrier
Which ever rises betwixt thee and me.
 Myr. I think the present is the wonted
 hour
Of council; it were better I retire.
 Sal. (*comes forward and says*). The Ionian
 slave says well: let her retire.
 Sar. Who answers? How now, brother?

 Sal. The *queen's* brother,
And your most faithful vassal, royal lord.
 Sar. (*addressing his train*). As I have
 said, let all dispose their hours
Till midnight, when again we pray your
 presence. [*The court retiring.*
(*To* MYRRHA, *who is going*). Myrrha! I
 thought *thou* wouldst remain.
 Myr. Great king,
Thou didst not say so.
 Sar. But *thou* lookedst it:
I know each glance of those Ionic eyes,
Which said thou wouldst not leave me.
 Myr. Sire! your brother——
 Sal. His *consort's* brother, minion of Ionia!
How darest *thou* name *me* and not blush?
 Sar. Not blush!
Thou hast no more eyes than heart to make
 her crimson
Like to the dying day on Caucasus,
Where sunset tints the snow with rosy
 shadows,
And then reproach her with thine own cold
 blindness,
Which will not see it. What! in tears, my
 Myrrha?
 Sal. Let them flow on; she weeps for
 more than one,
And is herself the cause of bitterer tears.
 Sar. Cursed be he who caused those tears
 to flow!
 Sal. Curse not thyself—millions do that
 already.
 Sar. Thou dost forget thee: make me not
 remember
I am a monarch.
 Sal. Would thou couldst!
 Myr. My sovereign,
I pray, and thou, too, prince, permit my
 absence.
 Sar. Since it must be so, and this churl
 has check'd
Thy gentle spirit, go; but recollect
That we must forthwith meet: I had rather
 lose
An empire than thy presence.
 [*Exit* MYRRHA.
 Sal. It may be
Thou wilt lose both, and both for ever!
 Sar. Brother!
I can at least command myself, who listen
To language such as this: yet urge me not
Beyond my easy nature.
 Sal. 'T is beyond
That easy, far too easy, idle nature,
Which I would urge thee. O that I could
 rouse thee!
Though 't were against myself.
 Sar. By the god Baal!
The man would make me tyrant.

Sal. So thou art.
Think'st thou there is no tyranny but that
Of blood and chains? The despotism of vice,
The weakness and the wickedness of luxury,
The negligence, the apathy, the evils
Of sensual sloth—produce ten thousand
 tyrants,
Whose delegated cruelty surpasses
The worst acts of one energetic master,
However harsh and hard in his own bearing.
The false and fond examples of thy lusts
Corrupt no less than they oppress, and sap
In the same moment all thy pageant power
And those who should sustain it; so that
 whether
A foreign foe invade, or civil broil
Distract within, both will alike prove fatal:
The first thy subjects have no heart to
 conquer;
The last they rather would assist than
 vanquish.
 Sar. Why, what makes thee the mouth-
 piece of the people?
 Sal. Forgiveness of the queen's, my
 sister's wrongs;
A natural love unto my infant nephews;
Faith to the king, a faith he may need
 shortly,
In more than words; respect for Nimrod's
 line;
Also, another thing thou knowest not.
 Sar. What's that?
 Sal. To thee an unknown word.
 Sar. Yet speak it;
I love to learn.
 Sal. Virtue.
 Sar. Not know the word!
Never was word yet rung so in my ears—
Worse than the rabble's shout, or splitting
 trumpet:
I've heard thy sister talk of nothing else.
 Sal. To change the irksome theme, then
 hear of vice.
 Sar. From whom?
 Sal. Even from the winds, if thou
 couldst listen
Unto the echoes of the nation's voice.
 Sar. Come, I'm indulgent, as thou know-
 est, patient,
As thou hast often proved—speak out, what
 moves thee?
 Sal. Thy peril.
 Sar. Say on.
 Sal. Thus, then: all the nations,
For they are many, whom thy father left
In heritage, are loud in wrath against thee.
 Sar. 'Gainst *me!* What would the slaves?
 Sal. A king.
 Sar. And what
Am I then?

 Sal. In their eyes a nothing; but
In mine a man who might be something still.
 Sar. The railing drunkards! why, what
 would they have?
Have they not peace and plenty?
 Sal. Of the first
More than is glorious; of the last, far less
Than the king recks of.
 Sar. Whose then is the crime,
But the false satraps, who provide no better?
 Sal. And somewhat in the monarch who
 ne'er looks
Beyond his palace walls, or if he stirs
Beyond them, 'tis but to some mountain
 palace,
Till summer heats wear down. O glorious
 Baal!
Who built up this vast empire, and wert
 made
A god, or at the least shinest like a god
Through the long centuries of thy renown,
This, thy presumed descendant, ne'er beheld
As king the kingdoms thou didst leave as
 hero,
Won with thy blood, and toil, and time, and
 peril!
For what? to furnish imposts for a revel,
Or multiplied extortions for a minion.
 Sar. I understand thee—thou wouldst
 have me go
Forth as a conqueror. By all the stars
Which the Chaldeans read—the restless
 slaves
Deserve that I should curse them with their
 wishes,
And lead them forth to glory.
 Sal. Wherefore not?
Semiramis—a woman only—led
These our Assyrians to the solar shores
Of Ganges.
 Sar. 'Tis most true. And *how* re-
 turn'd?
 Sal. Why, like a *man*—a hero; baffled, but
Not vanquish'd. With but twenty guards,
 she made
Good her retreat to Bactria.
 Sar. And how many
Left she behind in India to the vultures?
 Sal. Our annals say not.
 Sar. Then I will say for them—
That she had better woven within her palace
Some twenty garments, than with twenty
 guards
Have fled to Bactria, leaving to the ravens,
And wolves, and men—the fiercer of the
 three,
Her myriads of fond subjects. Is *this* glory?
Then let me live in ignominy ever.
 Sal. All warlike spirits have not the same
 fate.

Semiramis, the glorious parent of
A hundred kings, although she fail'd in
 India,
Brought Persia, Media, Bactria, to the realm
Which she once sway'd—and thou *might'st*
 sway.
 Sar. I *sway* them—
She but subdued them.
 Sal. It may be ere long
That they will need her sword more than
 your sceptre.
 Sar. There was a certain Bacchus, was
 there not?
I've heard my Greek girls speak of such—
 they say
He was a god, that is, a Grecian god,
An idol foreign to Assyria's worship,
Who conquer'd this same golden realm of Ind
Thou prat'st of, where Semiramis was
 vanquish'd.
 Sal. I have heard of such a man; and
 thou perceiv'st
That he is deem'd a god for what he did.
 Sar. And in his godship I will honour
 him—
Not much as man. What, ho! my cupbearer?
 Sal. What means the king?
 Sar. To worship your new god
And ancient conqueror. Some wine, I say.

 Enter Cupbearer.

 Sar. (*addressing the Cupbearer*). Bring
 me the golden goblet, thick with gems,
Which bears the name of Nimrod's chalice.
 Hence,
Fill full, and bear it quickly.
 [*Exit Cupbearer.*
 Sal. Is this moment
A fitting one for the resumption of
Thy yet unslept-off revels?

 Re-enter Cupbearer, with wine.

 Sar. (*taking the cup from him*). Noble
 kinsman,
If these barbarian Greeks of the far shores
And skirts of these our realms lie not, this
 Bacchus
Conquer'd the whole of India, did he not?
 Sal. He did, and thence was deem'd a
 deity.
 Sar. Not so:—of all his conquests a few
 columns
Which may be his, and might be mine, if I
Thought them worth purchase and convey-
 ance, are
The landmarks of the seas of gore he shed,
The realms he wasted, and the hearts he
 broke.
But here, here in this goblet is his title

To immortality—the immortal grape
From which he first express'd the soul, and
 gave
To gladden that of man, as some atonement
For the victorious mischiefs he had done.
Had it not been for this, he would have
 been
A mortal still in name as in his grave;
And, like my ancestor Semiramis,
A sort of semi-glorious human monster.
Here's that which deified him—let it now
Humanise thee; my surly, chiding brother
Pledge me to the Greek god!
 Sal. For all thy realms
I would not so blaspheme our country's
 creed.
 Sar. That is to say, thou thinkest him
 a hero,
That he shed blood by oceans; and no god,
Because he turn'd a fruit to an enchantment,
Which cheers the sad, revives the old,
 inspires
The young, makes weariness forget his toil,
And fear her danger; opens a new world
When this, the present, palls. Well, then
 I pledge thee
And *him* as a true man, who did his utmost
In good or evil to surprise mankind. [*Drinks.*
 Sal. Wilt thou resume a revel at this
 hour?
 Sar. And if I did, 't were better than a
 trophy,
Being bought without a tear. But that is
 not
My present purpose: since thou wilt not
 pledge me,
Continue what thou pleasest.
 (*To the Cupbearer.*) Boy, retire.
 [*Exit Cupbearer.*
 Sal. I would but have recall'd thee from
 thy dream;
Better by me awaken'd than rebellion.
 Sar. Who should rebel? or why? what
 cause? pretext?
I am the lawful king, descended from
A race of kings who knew no predecessors.
What have I done to thee, or to the people,
That thou shouldst rail, or they rise up
 against me?
 Sal. Of what thou hast done to me, I
 speak not.
 Sar. But
Thou think'st that I have wrong'd the queen:
 is't not so?
 Sal. *Think!* Thou hast wrong'd her!
 Sar. Patience, prince, and hear me.
She has all power and splendour of her
 station,
Respect, the tutelage of Assyria's heirs,
The homage and the appanage of sovereignty.

I married her as monarchs wed—for state,
And loved her as most husbands love their
wives.
If she or thou supposedst I could link me
Like a Chaldean peasant to his mate,
Ye knew nor me, nor monarchs, nor man-
kind.
 Sal. I pray thee, change the theme: my
 blood disdains
Complaint, and Salemenes' sister seeks not
Reluctant love even from Assyria's lord!
Nor would she deign to accept divided pas-
sion
With foreign strumpets and Ionian slaves.
The queen is silent.
 Sar. And why not her brother?
 Sal. I only echo thee the voice of empires,
Which he who long neglects not long will
 govern.
 Sar. The ungrateful and ungracious
 slaves! they murmur
Because I have not shed their blood, nor led
 them
To dry into the desert's dust by myriads,
Or whiten with their bones the banks of
 Ganges;
Nor decimated them with savage laws,
Nor sweated them to build up pyramids,
Or Babylonian walls.
 Sal. Yet these are trophies
More worthy of a people and their prince
Than songs, and lutes, and feasts, and con-
cubines,
And lavish'd treasures, and contemned vir-
tues.
 Sar. Or for my trophies I have founded
 cities:
There's Tarsus and Anchialus, both built
In one day—what could that blood-loving
 beldame,
My martial grandam, chaste Semiramis,
Do more, except destroy them?
 Sal. 'Tis most true;
I own thy merit in those founded cities,
Built for a whim, recorded with a verse,
Which shames both them and thee to coming
 ages.
 Sar. Shame me! By Baal, the cities,
 though well built,
Are not more goodly than the verse! Say
 what
Thou wilt 'gainst me, my mode of life or rule,
But nothing 'gainst the truth of that brief
 record.
Why, those few lines contain the history
Of all things human: hear—" Sardanapalus,
The king, and son of Anacyndaraxes,
In one day built Anchialus and Tarsus.
Eat, drink, and love; the rest's not worth a
 fillip."

 Sal. A worthy moral, and a wise inscrip-
 tion,
For a king to put up before his subjects!
 Sar. Oh, thou wouldst have me doubtless
 set up edicts—
" Obey the king—contribute to his treasure—
Recruit his phalanx—spill your blood at bid-
ding—
Fall down and worship, or get up and toil."
Or thus—" Sardanapalus on this spot
Slew fifty thousand of his enemies.
These are their sepulchres, and this his
 trophy."
I leave such things to conquerors; enough
For me, if I can make my subjects feel
The weight of human misery less, and glide
Ungroaning to the tomb: I take no licence
Which I deny to them. We all are men.
 Sal. Thy sires have been revered as
 gods—
 Sar. In dust
And death, where they are neither gods nor
 men.
Talk not of such to me! the worms are gods;
At least they banqueted upon your gods,
And died for lack of further nutriment.
Those gods were merely men; look to their
 issue—
I feel a thousand mortal things about me,
But nothing godlike,—unless it may be
The thing which you condemn, a disposition
To love and to be merciful, to pardon
The follies of my species, and (that's human)
To be indulgent to my own.
 Sal. Alas!
The doom of Nineveh is seal'd.—Woe—woe
To the unrivall'd city!
 Sar. What dost dread?
 Sal. Thou art guarded by thy foes: in a
 few hours
The tempest may break out which over-
 whelms thee,
And thine and mine; and in another day
What *is* shall be the past of Belus' race.
 Sar. What must we dread?
 Sal. Ambitious treachery,
Which has environ'd thee with snares; but yet
There is resource: empower me with thy
 signet
To quell the machinations, and I lay
The heads of thy chief foes before thy feet.
 Sar. The heads—how many?
 Sal. Must I stay to number
When even thine own's in peril? Let me go;
Give me thy signet—trust me with the rest.
 Sar. I will trust no man with unlimited
 lives.
When we take those from others, we nor
 know
What we have taken, nor the thing we give.

Sal. Wouldst thou not take their lives
 who seek for thine?
Sar. That's a hard question—But I an-
 swer, Yes.
Cannot the thing be done without? Who are
 they
Whom thou suspectest?—Let them be ar-
 rested.
Sal. I would thou wouldst not ask me;
 the next moment
Will send my answer through thy babbling
 troop
Of paramours, and thence fly o'er the palace,
Even to the city, and so baffle all.—
Trust me.
Sar. Thou knowest I have done so ever;
Take thou the signet. [*Gives the signet.*
Sal. I have one more request.
Sar. Name it.
Sal. That thou this night forbear the
 banquet
In the pavilion over the Euphrates.
Sar. Forbear the banquet! Not for all
 the plotters
That ever shook a kingdom! Let them come,
And do their worst: I shall not blench for
 them;
Nor rise the sooner; nor forbear the goblet;
Nor crown me with a single rose the less;
Nor lose one joyous hour.—I fear them not.
Sal. But thou wouldst arm thee, wouldst
 thou not, if needful?
Sar. Perhaps. I have the goodliest ar-
 mour, and
A sword of such a temper; and a bow
And javelin, which might furnish Nimrod
 forth:
A little heavy, but yet not unwieldy.
And now I think on't, 'tis long since I've
 used them,
Even in the chase. Hast ever seen them,
 brother?
Sal. Is this a time for such fantastic tri-
 fling?—
If need be, wilt thou wear them?
Sar. Will I not?
Oh! if it must be so, and these rash slaves
Will not be ruled with less, I'll use the sword
Till they shall wish it turn'd into a distaff.
Sal. They say thy sceptre's turn'd to that
 already.
Sar. That's false! but let them say so:
 the old Greeks, .
Of whom our captives often sing, related
The same of their chief hero, Hercules,
Because he loved a Lydian queen: thou
 seest
The populace of all the nations seize
Each calumny they can to sink their sove-
 reigns.

Sal. They did not speak thus of thy
 fathers.
Sar. No;
They dared not. They were kept to toil and
 combat;
And never changed their chains but for their
 armour:
Now they have peace and pastime, and the
 licence
To revel and to rail; it irks me not.
I would not give the smile of one fair girl
For all the popular breath that e'er divided
A name from nothing. What are the rank
 tongues
Of this vile herd, grown insolent with feeding,
That I should prize their noisy praise, or
 dread
Their noisome clamour?
Sal. You have said they are men;
As such their hearts are something.
Sar. So my dogs' are;
And better, as more faithful:—but, proceed;
Thou hast my signet:—since they are tumul-
 tuous,
Let them be temper'd, yet not roughly, till
Necessity enforce it. I hate all pain,
Given or received; we have enough within
 us,
The meanest vassal as the loftiest monarch,
Not to add to each other's natural burthen
Of mortal misery, but rather lessen,
By mild reciprocal alleviation,
The fatal penalties imposed on life:
But this they know not, or they will not know.
I have, by Baal! done all I could to soothe
 them:
I made no wars, I added no new imposts,
I interfered not with their civic lives,
I let them pass their days as best might suit
 them:
Passing my own as suited me.
Sal. Thou stopp'st
Short of the duties of a king; and therefore
They say thou art unfit to be a monarch.
Sar. They lie.—Unhappily, I am unfit
To be aught save a monarch; else for me
The meanest Mede might be the king instead.
Sal. There is one Mede, at least, who seeks
 to be so.
Sar. What mean'st thou?—'t is thy secret;
 thou desirest
Few questions, and I'm not of curious nature.
Take the fit steps; and, since necessity
Requires, I sanction and support thee. Ne'er
Was man who more desired to rule in peace
The peaceful only: if they rouse me, better
They had conjured up stern Nimrod from his
 ashes,
"The mighty hunter." I will turn these
 realms

To one wide desert chase of brutes, who *were*,
But *would* no more, by their own choice, be
 human.
What they have found me, they belie; *that
 which*
They yet may find me—shall defy their wish
To speak it worse; and let them thank them-
 selves.
 Sal. Then thou at last canst feel?
 Sar. Feel! who feels not
Ingratitude?
 Sal. I will not pause to answer
With words, but deeds. Keep thou awake
 that energy
Which sleeps at times, but is not dead within
 thee,
And thou may'st yet be glorious in thy reign,
As powerful in thy realm. Farewell!
 [*Exit* SALEMENES.
 Sar. (*solus*). Farewell!
He's gone; and on his finger bears my signet,
Which is to him a sceptre. He is stern
As I am heedless; and the slaves deserve
To feel a master. What may be the danger,
I know not: he hath found it, let him quell
 it.
Must I consume my life—this little life—
In guarding against all may make it less?
It is not worth so much! It were to die
Before my hour, to live in dread of death,
Tracing revolt; suspecting all about me,
Because they are near; and all who are
 remote,
Because they are far. But if it should be
 so—
If they should sweep me off from earth and
 empire,
Why, what is earth or empire of the earth?
I have loved, and lived, and multiplied my
 image;
To die is no less natural than those
Acts of this clay! 'Tis true I have not shed
Blood as I might have done, in oceans, till
My name became the synonyme of death—
A terror and a trophy. But for this
I feel no penitence; my life is love:
If I must shed blood, it shall be by force.
Till now, no drop from an Assyrian vein
Hath flow'd for me, nor hath the smallest
 coin
Of Nineveh's vast treasures e'er been lavish'd
On objects which could cost her sons a tear:
If then they hate me, 'tis because I hate not:
If they rebel, 'tis because I oppress not.
Oh, men! ye must be ruled with scythes, not
 sceptres,
And mow'd down like the grass, else all we
 reap
Is rank abundance, and a rotten harvest
Of discontents infecting the fair soil,

Making a desert of fertility.—
I'll think no more.——Within there, ho!

 Enter an ATTENDANT.

 Sar. Slave, tell
The Ionian Myrrha we could crave her pre-
 sence.
 Attend. King, she is here.

 MYRRHA *enters.*

 Sar. (*apart to Attendant*). Away!
(*Addressing* MYRRHA). Beautiful being!
Thou dost almost anticipate my heart;
It throbb'd for thee, and here thou comest:
 let me
Deem that some unknown influence, some
 sweet oracle,
Communicates between us, though unseen,
In absence, and attracts us to each other.
 Myr. There doth.
 Sar. I know there doth, but not its
 name:
What is it?
 Myr. In my native land a God,
And in my heart a feeling like a God's,
Exalted; yet I own 'tis only mortal;
For what I feel is humble, and yet happy—
That is, it would be happy; but——
 [MYRRHA *pauses.*
 Sar. There comes
For ever something between us and what
We deem our happiness: let me remove
The barrier which that hesitating accent
Proclaims to thine, and mine is seal'd.
 Myr. My lord!
 Sar. My lord—my king—sire—sovereign;
 thus it is—
For ever thus, address'd with awe. I ne'er
Can see a smile, unless in some broad
 banquet's
Intoxicating glare, when the buffoons
Have gorged themselves up to equality,
Or I have quaff'd me down to their abase-
 ment.
Myrrha, I can hear all these things, these
 names,
Lord—king—sire—monarch—nay, time was
 I prized them;
That is, I suffer'd them—from slaves and
 nobles;
But when they falter from the lips I love,
The lips which have been press'd to mine,
 a chill
Comes o'er my heart, a cold sense of the
 falsehood
Of this my station, which represses feeling
In those for whom I have felt most, and
 makes me
Wish that I could lay down the dull tiara,
And share a cottage on the Caucasus

With thee, and wear no crowns but those
of flowers.
Myr. Would that we could!
Sar. And dost *thou* feel this?—Why?
Myr. Then thou wouldst know what thou
canst never know.
Sar. And that is——
Myr. The true value of a heart;
At least, a woman's.
Sar. I have proved a thousand—
A thousand, and a thousand.
Myr. Hearts?
Sar. I think so.
Myr. Not one! the time may come thou
may'st.
Sar. It will.
Hear, Myrrha; Salemenes has declared—
Or why or how he hath divined it, Belus,
Who founded our great realm, knows more
than I—
But Salemenes hath declared my throne
In peril.
Myr. He did well.
Sar. And say'st *thou* so?
Thou whom he spurn'd so harshly, and now
dared
Drive from our presence with his savage jeers,
And made thee weep and blush?
Myr. I should do both
More frequently, and he did well to call me
Back to my duty. But thou spak'st of
peril—
Peril to thee——
Sar. Ay, from dark plots and snares
From Medes—and discontented troops and
nations,
I know not what—a labyrinth of things—
A maze of mutter'd threats and mysteries:
Thou know'st the man—it is his usual
custom.
But he is honest. Come, we'll think no
more on't—
But of the midnight festival.
Myr. 'Tis time
To think of aught save festivals. Thou hast
not
Spurn'd his sage cautions?
Sar. What?—and dost thou fear?
Myr. Fear!—I'm a Greek, and how should
I fear death?
A slave, and wherefore should I dread my
freedom?
Sar. Then wherefore dost thou turn so
pale?
Myr. I love.
Sar. And do not I? I love thee far—far
more
Than either the brief life or the wide realm,
Which, it may be, are menaced;—yet I
blench not.

Myr. That means thou lovest nor thyself
nor me;
For he who loves another loves himself,
Even for that other's sake. This is too rash:
Kingdoms and lives are not to be so lost.
Sar. Lost!—why, who is the aspiring
chief who dared
Assume to win them?
Myr. Who is he should dread
To try so much? When he who is their ruler
Forgets himself, will they remember him?
Sar. Myrrha!
Myr. Frown not upon me; you have
smiled
Too often on me not to make those frowns
Bitterer to bear than any punishment
Which they may augur.—King, I am your
subject!
Master, I am your slave! Man, I have loved
you!—
Loved you, I know not by what fatal weak-
ness,
Although a Greek, and born a foe to
monarchs—
A slave, and hating fetters—an Ionian,
And, therefore, when I love a stranger, more
Degraded by that passion than by chains!
Still I have loved you. If that love were
strong
Enough to overcome all former nature,
Shall it not claim the privilege to save
you?
Sar. Save me, my beauty! Thou art very
fair,
And what I seek of thee is love—not safety.
Myr. And without love where dwells
security?
Sar. I speak of woman's love.
Myr. The very first
Of human life must spring from woman's
breast,
Your first small words are taught you from
her lips,
Your first tears quench'd by her, and your
last sighs
Too often breathed out in a woman's hearing,
When men have shrunk from the ignoble
care
Of watching the last hour of him who led
them.
Sar. My eloquent Ionian! thou speak'st
music;
The very chorus of the tragic song
I have heard thee talk of as the favourite
pastime
Of thy far father-land. Nay, weep not—calm
thee.
Myr. I weep not.—But I pray thee, do not
speak
About my fathers or their land.

Sar.　　　　　Yet oft
Thou speakest of them.

Myr.　　　True—true : constant thought
Will overflow in words unconsciously ;
But when another speaks of Greece, it wounds
　me.

Sar. Well, then, how wouldst thou *save*
　me, as thou saidst ?

Myr. By teaching thee to save thyself,
　and not
Thyself alone, but these vast realms, from
　all
The rage of the worst war—the war of
　brethren.

Sar. Why, child, I loathe all war and
　warriors ;
I live in peace and pleasure : what can man
Do more ?

Myr. Alas ! my lord, with common men
There needs too oft the show of war to keep
The substance of sweet peace ; and, for a king,
'T is sometimes better to be fear'd than loved.

Sar. And I have never sought but for the
　last.

Myr. And now art neither.

Sar.　　　　Dost *thou* say so, Myrrha ?

Myr. I speak of civic popular-love, *self-*
　love,
Which means that men are kept in awe and
　law,
Yet not oppress'd—at least they must not
　think so,
Or if they think so, deem it necessary,
To ward off worse oppression, their own
　passions.
A king of feasts, and flowers, and wine, and
　revel,
And love, and mirth, was never king of glory.

Sar. Glory ! what 's that ?

Myr. Ask of the gods thy fathers.

Sar. They cannot answer ;. when the
　priests speak for them,
'T is for some small addition to the temple.

Myr. Look to the annals of thine empire's
　founders.

Sar. They are so blotted o'er with blood,
　I cannot.
But what wouldst have ? the empire *has been*
　founded.
I cannot go on multiplying empires.

Myr. Preserve thine own.

Sar.　　　　At least, I will enjoy it.
Come, Myrrha, let us go on to the Euphrates :
The hour invites, the galley is prepared,
And the pavilion, deck'd for our return,
In fit adornment for the evening banquet,
Shall blaze with beauty and with light, until
It seems unto the stars which are above us
Itself an opposite star ; and we will sit
Crown'd with fresh flowers like—

Myr.　　Victims.

Sar.　　　　　No, like sovereigns,
The shepherd kings of patriarchal times,
Who knew no brighter gems than summer
　wreaths,
And none but tearless triumphs.　Let us on.

Enter PANIA.

Pan. May the king live for ever !

Sar.　　　　　Not an hour
Longer than he can live.　How my soul hates
This language, which makes life itself a lie,
Flattering dust with eternity !　Well, Pania !
Be brief.

Pan. I am charged by Salemenes to
Reiterate his prayer unto the king,
That for this day, at least, he will not quit
The palace : when the general returns,
He will adduce such reasons as will warrant
His daring, and perhaps obtain the pardon
Of his presumption.

Sar.　　　　What ! am I then coop'd ?
Already captive ? can I not even breathe
The breath of heaven ? Tell prince Salemenes,
Were all Assyria raging round the walls
In mutinous myriads, I would still go forth.

Pan. I must obey you, and yet——

Myr.　　　　Oh, monarch, listen.—
How many a day and moon thou hast reclined
Within these palace walls in silken dalliance,
And never shown thee to thy people's longing ;
Leaving thy subjects' eyes ungratified,
The satraps uncontroll'd, the gods unwor-
　shipp'd,
And all things in the anarchy of sloth,
Till all, save evil, slumber'd through the
　realm !
And wilt thou not now tarry for a day,—
A day which may redeem thee ? Wilt thou
　not
Yield to the few still faithful a few hours,
For them, for thee, for thy past fathers' race,
And for thy sons' inheritance ?

Pan.　　　　　'T is true !
From the deep urgency with which the prince
Despatch'd me to your sacred presence, I
Must dare to add my feeble voice to that
Which now has spoken.

Sar.　　　　No, it must not be.

Myr. For the sake of thy realm !

Sar.　　　　Away !

Pan.　　　　For that
Of all thy faithful subjects, who will rally
Round thee and thine.

Sar.　　　　These are mere fantasies :
There is no peril :—'t is a sullen scheme
Of Salemenes, to approve his zeal,
And show himself more necessary to us.

Myr. By all that 's good and glorious take
　this counsel.

Sar. Business to-morrow.

Myr. Ay, or death to-night.

Sar. Why let it come then unexpectedly,
'Midst joy and gentleness, and mirth and
love;
So let me fall like the pluck'd rose!—far
better
Thus than be wither'd.

Myr. Then thou wilt not yield,
Even for the sake of all that ever stirr'd
A monarch into action, to forego
A trifling revel.

Sar. No.

Myr. Then yield for *mine*;
For my sake!

Sar. Thine, my Myrrha!

Myr. 'T is the first
Boon which I ever ask'd Assyria's king.

Sar. That's true, and were't my kingdom,
must be granted.
Well, for thy sake, I yield me. Pania, hence!
Thou hear'st me.

Pan. And obey. [*Exit* PANIA.

Sar. I marvel at thee.
What is thy motive, Myrrha, thus to urge me?

Myr. Thy safety; and the certainty that
nought
Could urge the prince thy kinsman to require
Thus much from thee, but some impending
danger.

Sar. And if I do not dread it, why shouldst
thou?

Myr. Because *thou* dost not fear, I fear
for *thee*.

Sar. To-morrow thou wilt smile at these
vain fancies.

Myr. If the worst come, I shall be where
none weep,
And that is better than the power to smile.
And thou?

Sar. I shall be king, as heretofore.

Myr. Where?

Sar. With Baal, Nimrod, and Semiramis,
Sole in Assyria, or with them elsewhere.
Fate made me what I am—may make me
nothing—
But either that or nothing must I be:
I will not live degraded.

Myr. Hadst thou felt
Thus always, none would ever dare degrade
thee.

Sar. And who will do so now?

Myr. Dost thou suspect none?

Sar. Suspect!—that's a spy's office. Oh!
we lose
Ten thousand precious moments in vain
words,
And vainer fears. Within there!—ye slaves,
deck
The hall of Nimrod for the evening revel:

If I must make a prison of our palace,
At least we'll wear our fetters jocundly;
If the Euphrates be forbid us, and
The summer dwelling on its beauteous bor-
der,
Here we are still unmenaced. Ho! within
there! [*Exit* SARDANAPALUS.

Myr. (*sola.*) Why do I love this man? My
country's daughters
Love none but heroes. But I have no
country!
The slave hath lost all save her bonds. I
love him;
And that's the heaviest link of the long
chain—
To love whom we esteem not. Be it so:
The hour is coming when he'll need all
love,
And find none. To fall from him now were
baser
Than to have stabb'd him on his throne when
highest
Would have been noble in my. country's
creed:
I was not made for either. Could I save him,
I should not love *him* better, but myself;
And I have need of the last, for I have fallen
In my own thoughts, by loving this soft
stranger:
And yet methinks I love him more, perceiv-
ing
That he is hated of his own barbarians,
The natural foes of all the blood of Greece.
Could I but wake a single thought like those
Which even the Phrygians felt when battling
long
'Twixt Ilion and the sea, within his heart,
He would tread down the barbarous crowds,
and triumph.
He loves me, and I love him; the slave loves
Her master, and would free him from his
vices.
If not, I have a means of freedom still,
And if I cannot teach him how to reign,
May show him how alone a king can leave
His throne. I must not lose him from my
sight. [*Exit.*

———◆◆———

Act II.

Scene I.—*The Portal of the same Hall
of the Palace.*

Beleses (*solus*). The sun goes down: me-
thinks he sets more slowly,
Taking his last look of Assyria's empire.
How red he glares amongst those deepening
clouds,
Like the blood he predicts! If not in vain,

Thou sun that sinkest, and ye stars which
 rise,
I have outwatch'd ye, reading ray by ray
The edicts of your orbs, which make Time
 tremble
For what he brings the nations, 'tis the
 furthest
Hour of Assyria's years. And yet how calm!
An earthquake should announce so great a
 fall—
A summer's sun discloses it. Yon disk,
To the star-read Chaldean, bears upon
Its everlasting page the end of what
Seem'd everlasting; but oh! thou true sun!
The burning oracle of all that live,
As fountain of all life, and symbol of
Him who bestows it, wherefore dost thou limit
Thy lore unto calamity? Why not
Unfold the rise of days more worthy thine
All-glorious burst from ocean? why not dart
A beam of hope athwart the future years,
As of wrath to its days? Hear me! oh, hear
 me!
I am thy worshipper, thy priest, thy servant—
I have gazed on thee at thy rise and fall,
And bow'd my head beneath thy mid-day
 beams,
When my eye dared not meet thee. I have
 watch'd
For thee, and after thee, and pray'd to thee,
And sacrificed to thee, and read, and fear'd
 thee,
And ask'd of thee, and thou hast answer'd—
 but
Only to thus much: while I speak, he sinks—
Is gone—and leaves his beauty, not his know-
 ledge,
To the delighted west, which revels in
Its hues of dying glory. Yet what is
Death, so it be but glorious? 'Tis a sunset;
And mortals may be happy to resemble
The gods but in decay.

Enter ARBACES *by an inner door.*

Arb. Beleses, why
So rapt in thy devotions? Dost thou stand
Gazing to trace thy disappearing god
Into some realm of undiscover'd day?
Our business is with night—'tis come.
 Bel. But not
Gone.
 Arb. Let it roll on—we are ready.
 Bel. Yes.
Would it were over!
 Arb. Does the prophet doubt,
To whom the very stars shine victory?
 Bel. I do not doubt of victory—but the
 victor.
 Arb. Well, let thy science settle that.
 Meantime

I have prepared as many glittering spears
As will out-sparkle our allies—your planets.
There is no more to thwart us. The she-
 king,
That less than woman, is even now upon
The waters with his female mates. The
 order
Is issued for the feast in the pavilion.
The first cup which he drains will be the last
Quaff'd by the line of Nimrod.
 Bel. 'Twas a brave one.
 Arb. And is a weak one—'tis worn out—
 we'll mend it.
 Bel. Art sure of that?
 Arb. Its founder was a hunter—
I am a soldier—what is there to fear?
 Bel. The soldier.
 Arb. And the priest, it may be: but
If you thought thus, or think, why not retain
Your king of concubines? why stir me up?
Why spur me to this enterprise? your own
No less than mine?
 Bel. Look to the sky!
 Arb. I look.
 Bel. What seest thou?
 Arb. A fair summer's twilight, and
The gathering of the stars.
 Bel. And midst them, mark
Yon earliest, and the brightest, which so
 quivers,
As it would quit its place in the blue ether.
 Arb. Well!
 Bel. 'Tis thy natal ruler—thy birth planet.
 Arb. (*touching his scabbard*). My star is in
 this scabbard: when it shines,
It shall out-dazzle comets. Let us think
Of what is to be done to justify
Thy planets and their portents. When we
 conquer,
They shall have temples—ay, and priests—
 and thou
Shalt be the pontiff of—what gods thou wilt;
For I observe that they are ever just,
And own the bravest for the most devout.
 Bel. Ay, and the most devout for brave—
 thou hast not
Seen me turn back from battle.
 Arb. No; I own thee
As firm in fight as Babylonia's captain,
As skilful in Chaldea's worship: now,
Will it but please thee to forget the priest,
And be the warrior?
 Bel. Why not both?
 Arb. The better;
And yet it almost shames me, we shall
 have
So little to effect. This woman's warfare
Degrades the very conqueror. To have
 pluck'd
A bold and bloody despot from his throne,

And grappled with him, clashing steel with
 steel,
That were heroic or to win or fall;
But to upraise my sword against this silk-
 worm,
And hear him whine, it may be——
 Bel. Do not deem it:
He has that in him which may make you
 strife yet;
And were he all you think, his guards are
 hardy,
And headed by the cool, stern Salemenes.
 Arb. They'll not resist.
 Bel. Why not? they are soldiers.
 Arb. True,
And therefore need a soldier to command
 them.
 Bel. That Salemenes is.
 Arb. But not their king.
Besides, he hates the effeminate thing that
 governs,
For the queen's sake, his sister. Mark you
 not
He keeps aloof from all the revels?
 Bel. But
Not from the council—there he is ever con-
 stant.
 Arb. And ever thwarted: what would you
 have more
To make a rebel out of? A fool reigning,
His blood dishonour'd, and himself disdain'd:
Why, it is *his* revenge we work for.
 Bel. Could
He but be brought to think so: this I doubt
 of.
 Arb. What, if we sound him?
 Bel. Yes—if the time served.

Enter BALEA.

 Bal. Satraps! The king commands your
 presence at
The feast to-night.
 Bel. To hear is to obey.
In the pavilion?
 Bal. No; here in the palace.
 Arb. How! in the palace? it was not thus
 order'd.
 Bal. It is so order'd now.
 Arb. And why?
 Bal. I know not.
May I retire?
 Arb. Stay.
 Bel. (*to Arb. aside*). Hush! let him go his
 way.
(*Alternately to Bal*). Yes, Balea, thank the
 monarch, kiss the hem
Of his imperial robe, and say, his slaves
Will take the crumbs he deigns to scatter
 from
His royal table at the hour—was't midnight?

 Bal. It was: the place, the hall of Nimrod.
 Lords,
I humble me before you, and depart.
 [*Exit* BALEA.
 Arb. I like not this same sudden change
 of place;
There is some mystery: wherefore should he
 change it?
 Bel. Doth he not change a thousand times
 a day?
Sloth is of all things the most fanciful—
And moves more parasangs in its intents
Than generals in their marches, when they
 seek
To leave their foe at fault.—Why dost thou
 muse?
 Arb. He loved that gay pavilion,—it was
 ever
His summer dotage.
 Bel. And he loved his queen—
And thrice a thousand harlotry besides—
And he has loved all things by turns, except
Wisdom and glory.
 Arb. Still—I like it not.
If he has changed—why, so must we: the
 attack
Were easy in the isolated bower,
Beset with drowsy guards and drunken
 courtiers;
But in the hall of Nimrod——
 Bel. Is it so?
Methought the haughty soldier fear'd to
 mount
A throne too easily—does it disappoint thee
To find there is a slipperier step or two
Than what was counted on?
 Arb. When the hour comes,
Thou shalt perceive how far I fear or no.
Thou hast seen my life at stake—and gaily
 play'd for:
But here is more upon the die—a kingdom.
 Bel. I have foretold already—thou wilt
 win it:
Then on, and prosper.
 Arb. Now were I a soothsayer,
I would have boded so much to myself.
But be the stars obey'd—I cannot quarrel
With them, nor their interpreter. Who's
 here?

Enter SALEMENES.

 Sal. Satraps!
 Bel. My prince!
 Sal. Well met—I sought ye both,
But elsewhere than the palace.
 Arb. Wherefore so?
 Sal. 'Tis not the hour.
 Arb. The hour!—what hour?
 Sal. Of midnight.
 Bel. Midnight, my lord!

Sal. What, are you not invited?

Bel. Oh! yes—we had forgotten.

Sal. Is it usual
Thus to forget a sovereign's invitation?

Arb. Why—we but now received it.

Sal. Then why here?

Arb. On duty.

Sal. On what duty?

Bel. On the state's.
We have the privilege to approach the
 presence;
But found the monarch absent.

Sal. And I too
Am upon duty.

Arb. May we crave its purport?

Sal. To arrest two traitors. Guards!
Within there!

Enter Guards.

Sal. (*continuing*). Satraps,
Your swords.

Bel. (*delivering his*). My lord, behold
my scimitar.

Arb. (*drawing his sword*). Take mine.

Sal. (*advancing*). I will.

Arb. But in your heart the blade—
The hilt quits not this hand.

Sal. (*drawing*). How! dost thou brave
me?
'T is well—this saves a trial, and false mercy.
Soldiers, hew down the rebel!

Arb. Soldiers! Ay—
Alone you dare not.

Sal. Alone! foolish slave—
What is there in thee that a prince should
 shrink from
Of open force? We dread thy treason, not
Thy strength: thy tooth is nought without
 its venom—
The serpent's, not the lion's. Cut him down.

Bel. (*interposing*). Arbaces! are you mad?
Have I not render'd
My sword? Then trust like me our sove-
reign's justice.

Arb. No—I will sooner trust the stars
thou prat'st of,
And this slight arm, and die a king at least
Of my own breath and body—so far that
None else shall chain them.

Sal. (*to the Guards*). You hear *him* and
me.
Take him not,—kill.
 [*The Guards attack* ARBACES, *who de-
 fends himself valiantly and dex-
 terously till they waver.*

Sal. Is it even so; and must
I do the hangman's office? Recreants! see
How you should fell a traitor.
 [SALEMENES *attacks* ARBACES.

Enter SARDANAPALUS *and Train.*

Sar. Hold your hands—
Upon your lives, I say. What, deaf or
 drunken?
My sword! O fool, I wear no sword: here,
 fellow,
Give me thy weapon. [*To a Guard.*
 [SARDANAPALUS *snatches a sword from
 one of the soldiers, and rushes between
 the combatants—they separate.*

Sar. In my very palace!
What hinders me from cleaving you in twain,
Audacious brawlers?

Bel. Sire, your justice.

Sal. Or—
Your weakness.

Sar. (*raising the sword*). How?

Sal. Strike! so the blow's repeated
Upon yon traitor—whom you spare a mo-
 ment,
I trust, for torture—I'm content.

Sar. What—him!
Who dares assail Arbaces?

Sal. I!

Sar. Indeed!
Prince, you forget yourself. Upon what war-
 rant?

Sal. (*showing the signet*). Thine.

Arb. (*confused*). The king's!

Sal. Yes! and let the king confirm it.

Sar. I parted not from this for such a
 purpose.

Sal. You parted with it for your safety—I
Employ'd it for the best. Pronounce in
 person.
Here I am but your slave—a moment past
I was your representative.

Sar. Then sheathe
Your swords.
 [ARBACES *and* SALEMENES *return their
 swords to the scabbards.*

Sal. Mine's sheathed: I pray you sheathe
 not yours:
'Tis the sole sceptre left you now with
 safety.

Sar. A heavy one; the hilt, too, hurts my
 hand.
(*To a Guard*). Here, fellow, take thy weapon
 back. Well, sirs,
What doth this mean?

Bel. The prince must answer that.

Sal. Truth upon my part, treason upon
 theirs.

Sar. Treason—Arbaces! treachery and
 Beleses!
That were an union I will not believe.

Bel. Where is the proof?

Sal. I'll answer that, if once
The king demands your fellow-traitor's sword.

Arb. (to Sal.). A sword which hath been
 drawn as oft as thine
Against his foes.
 Sal. And now against his brother,
And in an hour or so against himself.
 Sar. That is not possible: he dared not;
 no—
No—I'll not hear of such things.—These
 vain bickerings
Are spawn'd in courts by base intrigues, and
 baser
Hirelings, who live by lies on good men's
 lives.
You must have been deceived, my brother.
 Sal. First
Let him deliver up his weapon, and
Proclaim himself your subject by that duty,
And I will answer all.
 Sar. Why, if I thought so—
But no, it cannot be: the Mede Arbaces—
The trusty, rough, true soldier—the best cap-
 tain
Of all who discipline our nations——No,
I'll not insult him thus, to bid him render
The scimitar to me he never yielded
Unto our enemies. Chief, keep your weapon.
 Sal. (delivering back the signet). Monarch,
 take back your signet.
 Sar. No, retain it;
But use it with more moderation.
 Sal. Sire,
I used it for your honour, and restore it
Because I cannot keep it with my own.
Bestow it on Arbaces.
 Sar. So I should
He never ask'd it.
 Sal. Doubt not, he will have it,
Without that hollow semblance of respect.
 Bel. I know not what hath prejudiced the
 prince
So strongly 'gainst two subjects, than whom
 none
Have been more zealous for Assyria's weal.
 Sal. Peace, factious priest, and faithless
 soldier! thou
Unitest in thy own person the worst vices
Of the most dangerous orders of mankind.
Keep thy smooth words and juggling homilies
For those who know thee not. Thy fellow's
 sin
Is, at the least, a bold one, and not temper'd
By the tricks taught thee in Chaldea.
 Bel. Hear him,
My liege—the son of Belus! he blasphemes
The worship of the land, which bows the knee
Before your fathers.
 Sar. Oh! for that I pray you
Let him have absolution. I dispense with
The worship of dead men; feeling that I
Am mortal, and believing that the race

From whence I sprung are—what I see them
 —ashes.
 Bel. King! do not deem so: they are with
 the stars,
And——
 Sar. You shall join them ere they will
 rise,
If you preach further.—Why, *this* is rank
 treason.
 Sal. My lord!
 Sar. To school me in the worship of
Assyria's idols! Let him be released—
Give him his sword.
 Sal. My lord, and king, and brother,
I pray ye pause.
 Sar. Yes, and be sermonised,
And dinn'd, and deafen'd with dead men and
 Baal,
And all Chaldea's starry mysteries.
 Bel. Monarch! respect them.
 Sar. Oh! for that—I love them;
I love to watch them in the deep blue vault,
And to compare them with my Myrrha's eyes;
I love to see their rays redoubled in
The tremulous silver of Euphrates' wave,
As the light breeze of midnight crisps the broad
And rolling water, sighing through the sedges
Which fringe his banks: but whether they
 may be
Gods, as some say, or the abodes of gods,
As others hold, or simply lamps of night,
Worlds, or the lights of worlds, I know nor
 care not.
There's something sweet in my uncertainty
I would not change for your Chaldean lore;
Besides, I know of these all clay can know
Of aught above it, or below it—nothing.
I see their brilliancy and feel their beauty—
When they shine on my grave I shall know
 neither.
 Bel. For *neither*, sire, say *better*.
 Sar. I will wait,
If it so please you, pontiff, for that knowledge.
In the mean time receive your sword, and
 know
That I prefer your service militant
Unto your ministry—not loving either.
 Sal. (aside). His lusts have made him
 mad. Then must I save him,
Spite of himself.
 Sar. Please you to hear me, Satraps!
And chiefly thou, my priest, because I doubt
 thee
More than the soldier; and would doubt thee
 all
Wert thou not half a warrior: let us part
In peace—I'll not say pardon—which must be
Earn'd by the guilty; this I'll not pronounce
 ye,
Although upon this breath of mine depends

Your own; and, deadlier for ye, on my fears.
But fear not—for that I am soft, not fearful—
And so live on. Were I the thing some think
　me,
Your heads would now be dripping the last
　drops
Of their attainted gore from the high gates
Of this our palace, into the dry dust,
Their only portion of the coveted kingdom
They would be crown'd to reign o'er—let that
　pass.
As I have said, I will not *deem* ye guilty,
Nor *doom* ye guiltless. Albeit better men
Than ye or I stand ready to arraign you;
And should I leave your fate to sterner judges,
And proofs of all kinds, I might sacrifice
Two men, who, whatsoe'er they now are, were
Once honest. Ye are free, sirs.

　　Arb.　　　　　Sire, this clemency—
　　Bel. (*interrupting him*). Is worthy of your-
　　　self; and, although innocent,
We thank——
　　Sar. Priest! keep your thanksgivings for
　　　Belus;
His offspring needs none.
　　Bel.　　　　　But being innocent——
　　Sar. Be silent.—Guilt is loud. If ye are
　　　loyal,
Ye are injured men, and should be sad, not
　grateful.
　　Bel. So we should be, were justice always
　　　done
By earthly power omnipotent; but innocence
Must oft receive her right as a mere favour.
　　Sar. That's a good sentence for a homily,
Though not for this occasion. Prithee keep it
To plead thy sovereign's cause before his
　people.
　　Bel. I trust there is no cause.
　　Sar.　　　　　No *cause*, perhaps;
But many causers:—if ye meet with such
In the exercise of your inquisitive function
On earth, or should you read of it in heaven
In some mysterious twinkle of the stars,
Which are your chronicles, I pray you note,
That there are worse things betwixt earth
　and heaven
Than him who ruleth many and slays none;
And, hating not himself, yet loves his fellows
Enough to spare even those who would not
　spare him
Were they once masters—but that's doubtful.
　Satraps!
Your swords and persons are at liberty
To use them as ye will—but from this hour
I have no call for either. Salemenes!
Follow me.
　　[*Exeunt* SARDANAPALUS, SALEMENES,
　　　and the Train, &c., leaving ARBACES
　　　and BELESES.

　　Arb.　　　Beleses!
　　Bel.　　　　　Now, what think you?
　　Arb. That we are lost.
　　Bel.　　　That we have won the kingdom.
　　Arb. What? thus suspected—with the
　　　sword slung o'er us
But by a single hair, and that still wavering,
To be blown down by his imperious breath
Which spared us—why, I know not.
　　Bel.　　　　　Seek not why;
But let us profit by the interval.
The hour is still our own—our power the
　same—
The night the same we destined. He hath
　changed
Nothing except our ignorance of all
Suspicion into such a certainty
As must make madness of delay.
　　Arb.　　　　　And yet——
　　Bel. What, doubting still?
　　Arb.　　　He spared our lives, nay, more,
Saved them from Salemenes.
　　Bel.　　　　　And how long
Will he so spare? till the first drunken
　minute.
　　Arb. Or sober, rather. Yet he did it
　　　nobly;
Gave royally what we had forfeited
Basely——
　　Bel.　　　Say bravely.
　　Arb.　　　Somewhat of both, perhaps,
But it has touch'd me, and, whate'er betide,
I will no further on.
　　Bel.　　　　　And lose the world!
　　Arb. Lose anything except my own esteem.
　　Bel. I blush that we should owe our lives
　　　to such
A king of distaffs!
　　Arb.　　　But no less we owe them;
And I should blush far more to take the
　grantor's!
　　Bel. Thou may'st endure whate'er thou
　　　wilt—the stars
Have written otherwise.
　　Arb.　　　Though they came down,
And marshall'd me the way in all their
　brightness,
I would not follow.
　　Bel.　　　This is weakness—worse
Than a scared beldam's dreaming of the
　dead,
And waking in the dark.—Go to—go to.
　　Arb. Methought he look'd like Nimrod as
　　　he spoke,
Even as the proud imperial statue stands
Looking the monarch of the kings around it,
And sways, while they but ornament, the
　temple.
　　Bel. I told you that you had too much
　　　despised him.

And that there was some royalty within
 him—
What then? he is the nobler foe.
 Arb. But we
The meaner.—Would he had not spared us!
 Bel. So—
Wouldst thou be sacrificed thus readily?
 Arb. No—but it had been better to have
 died
Than live ungrateful.
 Bel. Oh, the souls of some men!
Thou wouldst digest what some call treason,
 and
Fools treachery—and, behold, upon the sud-
 den,
Because for something or for nothing, this
Rash reveller steps, ostentatiously,
'Twixt thee and Salemenes, thou art turn'd
Into—what shall I say?—Sardanapalus!
I know no name more ignominious.
 Arb. But
An hour ago, who dared to term me such
Had held his life but lightly—as it is,
I must forgive you, even as he forgave us—
Semiramis herself would not have done it.
 Bel. No—the queen liked no sharers of
 the kingdom,
Not even a husband.
 Arb. I must serve him truly——
 Bel. And humbly?
 Arb. No, sir, proudly—being honest.
I shall be nearer thrones than you to heaven;
And if not quite so haughty, yet more lofty.
You may do your own deeming—you have
 codes,
And mysteries, and corollaries of
Right and wrong, which I lack for my direc-
 tion,
And must pursue but what a plain heart
 teaches.
And now you know me.
 Bel. Have you finish'd?
 Arb. Yes—
With you.
 Bel. And would, perhaps, betray as well
As quit me?
 Arb. That's a sacerdotal thought
And not a soldier's.
 Bel. Be it what you will—
Truce with these wranglings, and but hear me.
 Arb. No—
There is more peril in your subtle spirit
Than in a phalanx.
 Bel. If it must be so—
I'll on alone.
 Arb. Alone!
 Bel. Thrones hold but one.
 Arb. But this is fill'd.
 Bel. With worse than vacancy—
A despised monarch. Look to it, Arbaces:

I have still aided, cherish'd, loved, and urged
 you;
Was willing even to serve you, in the hope
To serve and save Assyria. Heaven itself
Seem'd to consent, and all events were
 friendly
Even to the last, till that your spirit shrunk
Into a shallow softness; but now, rather
Than see my country languish, I will be
Her saviour or the victim of her tyrant,
Or one or both, for sometimes both are one;
And if I win, Arbaces is my servant.
 Arb. Your servant!
 Bel. Why not? better than be slave,
The *pardon'd* slave of *she* Sardanapalus!

Enter PANIA.

 Pan. My lords, I bear an order from the
 king.
 Arb. It is obey'd ere spoken.
 Bel. Notwithstanding,
Let's hear it.
 Pan. Forthwith, on this very night,
Repair to your respective satrapies
Of Babylon and Media.
 Bel. With our troops?
 Pan. My order is unto the satraps and
Their household train.
 Arb. But——
 Bel. It must be obey'd:
Say, we depart.
 Pan. My order is to see you
Depart, and not to bear your answer.
 Bel. (aside). Ay!
Well, sir, we will accompany you hence.
 Pan. I will retire to marshal forth the
 guard
Of honour which befits your rank, and wait
Your leisure, so that it the hour exceeds not.
 [*Exit* PANIA.
 Bel. Now then obey!
 Arb. Doubtless.
 Bel. Yes, to the gates
That grate the palace, which is now our
 prison—
No further.
 Arb. Thou hast harp'd the truth indeed!
The realm itself, in all its wide extension,
Yawns dungeons at each step for thee and me.
 Bel. Graves!
 Arb. If I thought so, this good sword
 should dig
One more than mine.
 Bel. It shall have work enough.
Let me hope better than thou augurest;
At present, let us hence as best we may.
Thou dost agree with me in understanding
This order as a sentence?
 Arb. Why, what other
Interpretation should it bear? it is

The very policy of orient monarchs—
Pardon and poison—favours and a sword—
A distant voyage, and an eternal sleep.
How many satraps in his father's time—
For he I own is, or at least *was*, bloodless—
 Bel. But *will* not, *can* not be so now.
 Arb. I doubt it.
How many satraps have I seen set out
In his sire's day for mighty vice-royalties,
Whose tombs are on their path! I know not
 how,
But they all sicken'd by the way, it was
So long and heavy.
 Bel. Let us but regain
The free air of the city, and we'll shorten
The journey.
 Arb. 'Twill be shorten'd at the gates,
It may be.
 Bel. No; they hardly will risk that.
They mean us to die privately, but not
Within the palace or the city walls,
Where we are known, and may have partisans:
If they had meant to slay us here, we were
No longer with the living. Let us hence.
 Arb. If I but thought he did not mean
 my life——
 Bel. Fool! hence—what else should des-
potism alarm'd
Mean? Let us but rejoin our troops, and
 march.
 Arb. Towards our provinces?
 Bel. No; towards your kingdom.
There's time, there's heart, and hope, and
 power, and means,
Which their half measures leave us in full
 scope.—
Away!
 Arb. And I even yet repenting must
Relapse to guilt!
 Bel. Self-defence is a virtue,
Sole bulwark of all right. Away, I say!
Let's leave this place, the air grows thick
 and choking,
And the walls have a scent of night-shade—
 hence!
Let us not leave them time for further council.
Our quick departure proves our civic zeal;
Our quick departure hinders our good escort,
The worthy Pania, from anticipating
The orders of some parasangs from hence:
Nay, there's no other choice, but——hence,
 I say. [*Exit with* ARBACES, *who*
 follows reluctantly.

Enter SARDANAPALUS *and* SALEMENES.

 Sar. Well, all is remedied, and without
 bloodshed,
That worst of mockeries of a remedy;
We are now secure by these men's exile.

 Sal. Yes,
As he who treads on flowers is from the
 adder
Twined round their roots.
 Sar. Why, what wouldst have me do?
 Sal. Undo what you have done.
 Sar. Revoke my pardon?
 Sal. Replace the crown now tottering on
 your temples.
 Sar. That were tyrannical.
 Sal. But sure.
 Sar. We are so.
What danger can they work upon the fron-
 tier?
 Sal. They are not there yet—never should
 they be so,
Were I well listen'd to.
 Sar. Nay, I *have* listen'd
Impartially to thee—why not to them?
 Sal. You may know that hereafter; as
 it is,
I take my leave to order forth the guard.
 Sar. And you will join us at the banquet?
 Sal. Sire,
Dispense with me—I am no wassailer:
Command me in all service save the Bac-
 chant's.
 Sar. Nay, but 'tis fit to revel now and
 then.
 Sal. And fit that some should watch for
 those who revel
Too oft. Am I permitted to depart?
 Sar. Yes——Stay a moment, my good
 Salemenes,
My brother, my best subject, better prince
Than I am king. You should have been the
 monarch,
And I—I know not what, and care not; but
Think not I am insensible to all
Thine honest wisdom, and thy rough yet
 kind,
Though oft reproving, sufferance of my follies.
If I have spared these men against thy
 counsel,
That is, their lives—it is not that I doubt
The advice was sound; but, let them live:
 we will not
Cavil about their lives—so let them mend
 them.
Their banishment will leave me still sound
 sleep,
Which their death had not left me.
 Sal. Thus you run
The risk to sleep for ever, to save traitors—
A moment's pang now changed for years of
 crime.
Still let them be made quiet.
 Sar. Tempt me not;
My word is past.
 Sal. But it may be recall'd.

Sar. 'Tis royal.
Sal. And should therefore be decisive.
This half indulgence of an exile serves
But to provoke—a pardon should be full,
Or it is none.
Sar. And who persuaded me
After I had repeal'd them, or at least
Only dismiss'd them from our presence, who
Urged me to send them to their satrapies?
Sal. True; that I had forgotten; that is,
 sire,
If they e'er reach'd their satrapies—why,
 then,
Reprove me more for my advice.
Sar. And if
They do not reach them—look to it!—in
 safety,
In safety, mark me—and security—
Look to thine own.
Sal. Permit me to depart;
Their *safety* shall be cared for.
Sar. Get thee hence, then;
And, prithee, think more gently of thy bro-
 ther.
Sal. Sire, I shall ever duly serve my
 sovereign. [*Exit* SALEMENES.
Sar. (*solus*). That man is of a temper too
 severe;
Hard but as lofty as the rock, and free
From all the taints of common earth—while I
Am softer clay, impregnated with flowers :
But as our mould is, must the produce be.
If I have err'd this time, 't is on the side
Where error sits most lightly on that sense,
I know not what to call it; but it reckons
With me ofttimes for pain, and sometimes
 pleasure;
A spirit which seems placed about my heart
To count its throbs, not quicken them, and
 ask
Questions which mortal never dared to ask
 me,
Nor Baal, though an oracular deity—
Albeit his marble face majestical
Frowns as the shadows of the evening dim
His brows to changed expression, till at times
I think the statue looks in act to speak.
Away with these vain thoughts, I will be
 joyous—
And here comes Joy's true herald.

Enter MYRRHA.

Myr. King! the sky
Is overcast, and musters muttering thunder,
In clouds that seem approaching fast, and
 show
In forked flashes a commanding tempest.
Will you then quit the palace?
Sar. Tempest, say'st thou?
Myr. Ay, my good lord.

Sar. For my own part, I should be
Not ill content to vary the smooth scene,
And watch the warring elements; but this
Would little suit the silken garments and
Smooth faces of our festive friends. Say,
 Myrrha,
Art thou of those who dread the roar of
 clouds?
Myr. In my own country we respect their
 voices
As auguries of Jove.
Sar. Jove!—ay, your Baal—
Ours also has a property in thunder,
And ever and anon some falling bolt
Proves his divinity,—and yet sometimes
Strikes his own altars.
Myr. That were a dread omen.
Sar. Yes—for the priests. Well, we will
 not go forth
Beyond the palace walls to-night, but make
Our feast within.
Myr. Now, Jove be praised! that he
Hath heard the prayer thou wouldst not hear.
 The gods
Are kinder to thee than thou to thyself,
And flash this storm between thee and thy
 foes,
To shield thee from them.
Sar. Child, if there be peril,
Methinks it is the same within these walls
As on the river's brink.
Myr. Not so; these walls
Are high and strong, and guarded. Treason
 has
To penetrate through many a winding way,
And massy portal; but in the pavilion
There is no bulwark.
Sar. No, nor in the palace,
Nor in the fortress, nor upon the top
Of cloud-fenced Caucasus, where the eagle
 sits
Nested in pathless clefts, if treachery be:
Even as the arrow finds the airy king,
The steel will reach the earthly. But be
 calm;
The men, or innocent or guilty, are
Banish'd, and far upon their way.
Myr. They live, then?
Sar. So sanguinary? *Thou!*
Myr. I would not shrink
From just infliction of due punishment
On those who seek your life: were't other-
 wise,
I should not merit mine. Besides, you heard
The princely Salemenes.
Sar. This is strange;
The gentle and the austere are both against
 me,
And urge me to revenge.
Myr. 'T is a Greek virtue.

Sar. But not a kingly one—I'll none on't;
 or
If ever I indulge in't, it shall be
With kings—my equals.
 Myr. These men sought to be so.
 Sar. Myrrha, this is too feminine, and
 springs
From fear——
 Myr. For you.
 Sar. No matter, still 'tis fear.
I have observed your sex, once roused to
 wrath,
Are timidly vindictive to a pitch
Of perseverance, which I would not copy.
I thought you were exempt from this, as from
The childish helplessness of Asian women.
 Myr. My lord, I am no boaster of my love,
Nor of my attributes; I have shared your
 splendour,
And will partake your fortunes. You may
 live
To find one slave more true than subject
 myriads:
But this the gods avert! I am content
To be beloved on trust for what I feel,
Rather than prove it to you in your griefs,
Which might not yield to any cares of mine.
 Sar. Grief cannot come where perfect love
 exists,
Except to heighten it, and vanish from
That which it could not scare away. Let's
 in—
The hour approaches, and we must prepare
To meet the invited guests who grace our
 feast. [*Exeunt.*

—————

Act III.

Scene I.—*The Hall of the Palace illuminated*
—Sardanapalus *and his Guests at Table.*—
*A storm without, and Thunder occasionally
heard during the Banquet.*

 Sar. Fill full! why this is as it should be:
 here
Is my true realm, amidst bright eyes and
 faces
Happy as fair! Here sorrow cannot reach.
 Zam. Nor elsewhere—where the king is,
 pleasure sparkles.
 Sar. Is not this better now than Nimrod's
 huntings,
Or my wild grandam's 'chase in search of
 kingdoms
She could not keep when conquer'd?
 Alt. Mighty though
They were, as all thy royal line have been,
Yet none of these who went before have
 reach'd
The acmé of Sardanapalus, who

Has placed his joy in peace—the sole true
 glory.
 Sar. And pleasure, good Altada, to which
 glory
Is but the path. What is it that we seek?
Enjoyment! We have cut the way short to it,
And not gone tracking it through human ashes,
Making a grave with every footstep.
 Zam. No;
All hearts are happy, and all voices bless
The king of peace, who holds a world in
 jubilee.
 Sar. Art sure of that? I have heard other-
 wise;
Some say that there be traitors.
 Zam. Traitors they
Who dare to say so!—'T is impossible.
What cause?
 Sar. What cause? true,—fill the goblet up;
We will not think of them: there are none such,
Or if there be, they are gone.
 Alt. Guests, to my pledge!
Down on your knees, and drink a measure to
The safety of the king—the monarch, say I?
The god Sardanapalus!
 [Zames *and the Guests kneel, and ex-
 claim—*
 Mightier than
His father Baal, the god Sardanapalus!
 [*It thunders as they kneel; some start
 up in confusion.*
 Zam. Why do you rise, my friends? in that
 strong peal
His father gods consented.
 Myr. Menaced, rather.
King, wilt thou bear this mad impiety?
 Sar. Impiety!—nay, if the sires who
 reign'd
Before me can be gods, I'll not disgrace
Their lineage. But arise, my pious friends;
Hoard your devotion for the thunderer there:
I seek but to be loved, not worshipp'd.
 Alt. Both—
Both you must ever be by all true subjects.
 Sar. Methinks the thunders still increase:
 it is
An awful night.
 Myr. Oh yes, for those who have
No palace to protect their worshippers.
 Sar. That's true, my Myrrha; and could
 I convert
My realm to one wide shelter for the wretched,
I'd do it.
 Myr. Thou'rt no god then, not to be
Able to work a will so good and general,
As thy wish would imply.
 Sar. And your gods, then,
Who can, and do not?
 Myr. Do not speak of that,
Lest we provoke them.

Sar. True, they love not censure
Better than mortals. Friends, a thought has
 struck me:
Were there no temples, would there, think
 ye, be
Air worshippers? that is, when it is angry,
And pelting as even now.
Myr. The Persian prays
Upon his mountain.
Sar. Yes, when the sun shines.
Myr. And I would ask if this your palace
 were
Unroof'd and desolate, how many flatterers
Would lick the dust in which the king lay
 low?
Alt. The fair Ionian is too sarcastic
Upon a nation whom she knows not well;
The Assyrians know no pleasure but their
 king's,
And homage is their pride.
Sar. Nay, pardon, guests,
The fair Greek's readiness of speech.
Alt. Pardon! sire:
We honour her of all things next to thee.
Hark! what was that?
Zam. That! nothing but the jar
Of distant portals shaken by the wind.
Alt. It sounded like the clash of—hark
 again!
Zam. The big rain pattering on the roof.
Sar. No more.
Myrrha, my love, hast thou thy shell in order?
Sing me a song of Sappho, her, thou know'st,
Who in thy country threw——

Enter Pania, *with his sword and garments
bloody, and disordered. The guests rise in
confusion.*

Pan.(to the Guards). Look to the portals;
And with your best speed to the walls with-
 out.
Your arms! To arms! The king's in danger.
 Monarch,
Excuse this haste,—'t is faith.
Sar. Speak on.
Pan. It is
As Salemenes fear'd; the faithless satraps——
Sar. You are wounded—give some wine.
 Take breath, good Pania.
Pan. 'T is nothing—a mere flesh wound.
 I am worn
More with my speed to warn my sovereign,
Than hurt in his defence.
Myr. Well, sir, the rebels?
Pan. Soon as Arbaces and Beleses reach'd
Their stations in the city, they refused
To march; and on my attempt to use the
 power
Which I was delegated with, they call'd
Upon their troops, who rose in fierce defiance.

Myr. All?
Pan. Too many.
Sar. Spare not of thy free speech,
To spare mine ears the truth.
Pan. My own slight guard
Were faithful, and what 's left of it is still so.
Myr. And are these all the force still faith-
 ful?
Pan. No—
The Bactrians, now led on by Salemenes,
Who even then was on his way, still urged
By strong suspicion of the Median chiefs,
Are numerous, and make strong head against
The rebels, fighting inch by inch, and forming
An orb around the palace, where they mean
To centre all their force, and save the king.
(He hesitates) I am charged to——
Myr. 'T is no time for hesitation.
Pan. Prince Salemenes doth implore the
 king
To arm himself, although but for a moment,
And show himself unto the soldiers: his
Sole presence in this instance might do more
Than hosts can do in his behalf.
Sar. What, ho!
My armour there.
Myr. And wilt thou?
Sar. Will I not?
Ho, there!—but seek not for the buckler:
 't is
Too heavy:—a light cuirass and my sword.
Where are the rebels?
Pan. Scarce a furlong's length
From the outward wall the fiercest conflict
 rages.
Sar. Then I may charge on horseback.
 Sfero, ho!
Order my horse out.—There is space enough
Even in our courts, and by the outer gate,
To marshal half the horsemen of Arabia.
 [*Exit* Sfero *for the armour.*
Myr. How I do love thee!
Sar. I ne'er doubted it.
Myr. But now I know thee.
Sar. (to his Attendant). Bring down my
 spear too.—
Where 's Salemenes?
Pan. Where a soldier should be,
In the thick of the fight.
Sar. Then hasten to him——Is
The path still open, and communication
Left 'twixt the palace and the phalanx?
Pan. 'T was
When I late left him, and I have no fear:
Our troops were steady, and the phalanx
 form'd.
Sar. Tell him to spare his person for the
 present,
And that I will not spare my own—and say,
I come.

Pan. There's victory in the very word.
[*Exit* PANIA.

Sar. Altada—Zames—forth, and arm ye!
There
Is all in readiness in the armoury.
See that the women are bestow'd in safety
In the remote apartments: let a guard
Be set before them, with strict charge to quit
The post but with their lives—command it,
Zames.
Altada, arm yourself, and return here;
Your post is near our person.
[*Exeunt* ZAMES, ALTADA, *and all save*
MYRRHA.

Enter SFERO *and others with the King's
Arms, &c.*

Sfe. King! your armour.
Sar. (*arming himself*). Give me the cuirass
—so: my baldric; now
My sword: I had forgot the helm—where
is it?
That's well—no, 'tis too heavy: you mis-
take, too—
It was not this I meant, but that which bears
A diadem around it.
Sfe. Sire, I deem'd
That too conspicuous from the precious stones
To risk your sacred brow beneath—and trust
me,
This is of better metal, though less rich.
Sar. You deem'd! Are you too turn'd a
rebel? Fellow!
Your part is to obey: return, and—no—
It is too late—I will go forth without it.
Sfe. At least, wear this.
Sar. Wear Caucasus! why, 'tis
A mountain on my temples.
Sfe. Sire, the meanest
Soldier goes not forth thus exposed to battle.
All men will recognise you—for the storm
Has ceased, and the moon breaks forth in
her brightness.
Sar. I go forth to be recognised, and thus
Shall be so sooner. Now—my spear! I'm
arm'd.
[*In going stops short, and turns to* SFERO.
Sfero—I had forgotten—bring the mirror.
Sfe. The mirror, sire?
Sar. Yes, sir, of polish'd brass,
Brought from the spoils of India—but be
speedy. [*Exit* SFERO.
Sar. Myrrha, retire unto a place of safety.
Why went you not forth with the other
damsels?
Myr. Because my place is here.
Sar. And when I am gone——
Myr. I follow.
Sar. You! to battle?

Myr. If it were so,
'Twere not the first Greek girl had trod the
path.
I will await here your *return.*
Sar. The place
Is spacious, and the first to be sought out,
If they prevail; and, if it be so,
And I return not——
Myr. Still we meet again.
Sar. How?
Myr. In the spot where all must meet at
last—
In Hades! if there be, as I believe,
A shore beyond the Styx; and if there be
not,
In ashes.
Sar. Darest thou so much?
Myr. I dare all things
Except survive what I have loved, to be
A rebel's booty: forth, and do your bravest.

Re-enter SFERO *with the mirror.*

Sar. (*looking at himself*). This cuirass fits
me well, the baldric better,
And the helm not at all. Methinks I seem
[*Flings away the helmet after trying
it again.*
Passing well in these toys; and now to
prove them.
Altada! Where's Altada?
Sfe. Waiting, sire,
Without: he has your shield in readiness.
Sar. True; I forgot he is my shield-bearer
By right of blood, derived from age to age.
Myrrha, embrace me; yet once more—once
more—
Love me, whate'er betide. My chiefest glory
Shall be to make me worthier of your love.
Myr. Go forth, and conquer!
[*Exeunt* SARDANAPALUS *and* SFERO.
Now, I am alone,
All are gone forth, and of that all how few
Perhaps return! Let him but vanquish, and
Me perish! If he vanquish not, I perish;
For I will not outlive him. He has wound
About my heart, I know not how nor why.
Not for that he is king; for now his kingdom
Rocks underneath his throne, and the earth
yawns
To yield him no more of it than a grave;
And yet I love him more. Oh, mighty Jove!
Forgive this monstrous love for a barbarian,
Who knows not of Olympus! yes, I love him
Now, now, far more than——Hark—to the
war shout!
Methinks it nears me. If it should be so,
[*She draws forth a small vial.*
This cunning Colchian poison, which my
father

Learn'd to compound on Euxine shores, and
 taught me
How to preserve, shall free me! It had
 freed me
Long ere this hour, but that I loved, until
I half forgot I was a slave:—where all
Are slaves save one, and proud of servitude,
So they are served in turn by something
 lower
In the degree of bondage, we forget
That shackles worn like ornaments no less
Are chains. Again that shout! and now the
 clash
Of arms—and now—and now—

Enter ALTADA.

Alt. Ho, Sfero, ho!
Myr. He is not here; what wouldst thou
 with him? How
Goes on the conflict?
 Alt. Dubiously and fiercely.
Myr. And the king?
Alt. Like a king. I must find Sfero,
And bring him a new spear and his own
 helmet.
He fights till now bare-headed, and by far
Too much exposed. The soldiers knew his
 face,
And the foe too; and in the moon's broad
 light,
His silk tiara and his flowing hair
Make him a mark too royal. Every arrow
Is pointed at the fair hair and fair features,
And the broad fillet which crowns both.
 Myr. Ye gods,
Who fulminate o'er my father's land, protect
 him!
Were you sent by the king?
Alt. By Salemenes,
Who sent me privily upon this charge,
Without the knowledge of the careless
 sovereign.
The king! the king fights as he revels! ho!
What, Sfero! I will seek the armoury—
He must be there. [*Exit* ALTADA.
 Myr. 'Tis no dishonour—no—
'Tis no dishonour to have loved this man.
I almost wish now, what I never wish'd
Before, that he were Grecian. If Alcides
Were shamed in wearing Lydian Omphale's
She-garb, and wielding her vile distaff; surely
He, who springs up a Hercules at once,
Nursed in effeminate arts from youth to
 manhood,
And rushes from the banquet to the battle,
As though it were a bed of love, deserves
That a Greek girl should be his paramour,
And a Greek bard his minstrel, a Greek tomb
His monument. How goes the strife, sir?

Enter an Officer.

Officer. Lost,
Lost almost past recovery. Zames! Where
Is Zames?
 Myr. Posted with the guard appointed
To watch before the apartment of the women.
 [*Exit Officer.*
 Myr. (*sola*). He's gone; and told no more
 than that all's lost!
What need have I to know more? In those
 words,
Those little words, a kingdom and a king,
A line of thirteen ages, and the lives
Of thousands, and the fortune of all left
With life, are merged; and I, too, with the
 great,
Like a small bubble breaking with the wave
Which bore it, shall be nothing. At the
 least,
My fate is in my keeping: no proud victor
Shall count me with his spoils.

Enter PANIA.

Pan. Away with me,
Myrrha, without delay; we must not lose
A moment—all that's left us now.
 Myr. The king?
 Pan. Sent me here to conduct you hence,
 beyond
The river, by a secret passage.
 Myr. Then
He lives—
 Pan. And charged me to secure your life,
And beg you to live on for his sake, till
He can rejoin you.
 Myr. Will he then give way?
 Pan. Not till the last. Still, still he does
 whate'er
Despair can do; and step by step disputes
The very palace.
 Myr. They are here, then:—ay,
Their shouts come ringing through the an-
 cient halls,
Never profaned by rebel echoes till
This fatal night. Farewell, Assyria's line!
Farewell to all of Nimrod! Even the name
Is now no more.
 Pan. Away with me—away!
 Myr. No: I'll die here!—Away, and tell
 your king
I loved him to the last.

Enter SARDANAPALUS *and* SALEMENES *with
 Soldiers.* PANIA *quits* MYRRHA, *and ranges
 himself with them.*

Sar. Since it is thus,
We'll die where we were born—in our own
 halls.

Serry your ranks—stand firm. I have de-
 spatch'd
A trusty satrap for the guard of Zames,
All fresh and faithful; they'll be here anon.
All is not over.—Pania, look to Myrrha.
 [Pania *returns towards* Myrrha.
 Sal. We have breathing time; yet once
 more charge, my friends—
One for Assyria!
 Sar. Rather say for Bactria!
My faithful Bactrians, I will henceforth be
King of your nation, and we'll hold together
This realm as province.
 Sal. Hark! they come—they come.

Enter Beleses *and* Arbaces *with the Rebels.*

 Arb. Set on, we have them in the toil.
 Charge! charge!
 Bel. On! on!—Heaven fights for us, and
 with us—On!
 [*They charge the King and* Salemenes
 *with their troops, who defend themselves
 till the arrival of* Zames *with the Guard
 before mentioned. The Rebels are then
 driven off, and pursued by* Salemenes,
 *&c. As the King is going to join the
 pursuit,* Beleses *crosses him.*
 Bel. Ho! tyrant—*I* will end this war.
 Sar. Even so,
My warlike priest, and precious prophet, and
Grateful and trusty subject: yield, I pray
 thee.
I would reserve thee for a fitter doom,
Rather than dip my hands in holy blood.
 Bel. Thine hour is come.
 Sar. No, thine.—I've lately read,
Though but a young astrologer, the stars;
And ranging round the zodiac, found thy fate
In the sign of the Scorpion, which proclaims
That thou wilt now be crush'd.
 Bel. But not by thee.
 [*They fight;* Beleses *is wounded and
 disarmed.*
 Sar. (*raising his sword to despatch him,
 exclaims*)—
Now call upon thy planets, will they shoot
From the sky to preserve their seer and
 credit?
 [*A party of Rebels enter and rescue* Be-
 leses. *They assail the King, who, in
 turn, is rescued by a Party of his
 Soldiers, who drive the Rebels off.*
The villain was a prophet after all.
Upon them—ho! there—victory is ours.
 [*Exit in pursuit.*
 Myr. (*to Pan.*) Pursue! Why stand'st thou
 here, and leav'st the ranks
Of fellow-soldiers conquering without thee?
 Pan. The king's command was not to
 quit thee.

 Myr. Me!
Think not of me—a single soldier's arm
Must not be wanting now. I ask no guard,
I need no guard: what, with a world at
 stake,
Keep watch upon a woman? Hence, I say,
Or thou art shamed! Nay, then, *I* will go
 forth,
A feeble female, 'midst their desperate strife,
And bid thee guard me *there*—where thou
 shouldst shield
Thy sovereign. [*Exit* Myrrha.
 Pan. Yet stay, damsel!—She is gone.
If aught of ill betide her, better I
Had lost my life. Sardanapalus holds her
Far dearer than his kingdom, yet he fights
For that too; and can I do less than he,
Who never flash'd a scimitar till now?
Myrrha, return, and I obey you, though
In disobedience to the monarch. [*Exit* Pania.

Enter Altada *and* Sfero *by an opposite door.*

 Alt. Myrrha!
What, gone? yet she was here when the fight
 raged,
And Pania also. Can aught have befallen
 them?
 Sfe. I saw both safe, when late the rebels
 fled;
They probably are but retired to make
Their way back to the harem.
 Alt. If the king
Prove victor, as it seems even now he must,
And miss his own Ionian, we are doom'd
To worse than captive rebels.
 Sfe. Let us trace them;
She cannot be fled far; and, found, she makes
A richer prize to our soft sovereign
Than his recover'd kingdom.
 Alt. Baal himself
Ne'er fought more fiercely to win empire,
 than
His silken son to save it: he defies
All augury of foes or friends; and like
The close and sultry summer's day, which
 bodes
A twilight tempest, bursts forth in such
 thunder
As sweeps the air and deluges the earth.
The man's inscrutable.
 Sfe. Not more than others.
All are the sons of circumstance: away—
Let's seek the slave out, or prepare to be
Tortured for his infatuation, and
Condemn'd without a crime. [*Exeunt.*

Enter Salemenes *and Soldiers, &c.*

 Sal. The triumph is
Flattering: they are beaten backward from
 the palace,

And we have open'd regular access
To the troops station'd on the other side
Euphrates, who may still be true; nay, must
 be,
When they hear of our victory.—But where
Is the chief victor? where's the king?

Enter SARDANAPALUS, *cum suis, &c. and*
 MYRRHA.

Sar. Here, brother.
Sal. Unhurt, I hope.
Sar. Not quite; but let it pass.
We've clear'd the palace——
Sal. And I trust the city.
Our numbers gather; and I've order'd on-
 ward
A cloud of Parthians, hitherto reserved,
All fresh and fiery, to be pour'd upon them
In their retreat, which soon will be a flight.
Sar. It is already, or at least they march'd
Faster than I could follow with my Bactrians,
Who spared no speed. I am spent: give me
 a seat.
Sal. There stands the throne, sire.
Sar. 'Tis no place to rest on,
For mind nor body: let me have a couch,
 [*They place a seat.*
A peasant's stool, I care not what: so—now
I breathe more freely.
Sal. This great hour has proved
The brightest and most glorious of your life.
Sar. And the most tiresome. Where's my
 cupbearer?
Bring me some water.
Sal. (smiling). 'Tis the first time he
Ever had such an order: even I,
Your most austere of counsellors, would now
Suggest a purpler beverage.
Sar. Blood—doubtless.
But there's enough of that shed; as for wine,
I have learn'd to-night the price of the pure
 element:
Thrice have I drank of it, and thrice renew'd,
With greater strength than the grape ever
 gave me,
My charge upon the rebels. Where's the
 soldier
Who gave me water in his helmet?
One of the Guards. Slain, sire!
An arrow pierced his brain, while, scattering
The last drops from his helm, he stood in act
To place it on his brows.
Sar. Slain! unrewarded!
And slain to serve my thirst: that's hard,
 poor slave!
Had he but lived, I would have gorged him
 with
Gold: all the gold of earth could ne'er repay
The pleasure of that draught; for I was
 parch'd

As I am now. [*They bring water—he drinks.*
 I live again—from henceforth
The goblet I reserve for hours of love,
But war on water.
Sal. And that bandage, sire,
Which girds your arm?
Sar. A scratch from brave Beleses.
Myr. Oh! he is wounded!
Sar. · Not too much of that;
And yet it feels a little stiff and painful,
Now I am cooler.
Myr. You have bound it with—
Sar. The fillet of my diadem: the first
 time
That ornament was ever aught to me
Save an encumbrance.
Myr. (to the Attendants). Summon speedily
A leech of the most skilful: pray, retire:
I will unbind your wound and tend it.
Sar. Do so,
For now it throbs sufficiently: but what
Know'st thou of wounds? yet wherefore do
 I ask?
Know'st thou, my brother, where I lighted
 on
This minion?
Sal. Herding with the other females,
Like frighten'd antelopes.
Sar. No: like the dam
Of the young lion, femininely raging
(And femininely meaneth furiously,
Because all passions in excess are female)
Against the hunter flying with her cub,
She urged on with her voice and gesture, and
Her floating hair and flashing eyes, the
 . soldiers,
In the pursuit.
Sal. Indeed!
Sar. You see, this night
Made warriors of more than me. I paused
To look upon her, and her kindled cheek;
Her large black eyes, that flash'd through
 her long hair
As it stream'd o'er her; her blue veins that
 rose
Along her most transparent brow; her nos-
 tril
Dilated from its symmetry; her lips
Apart; her voice that clove through all the
 din,
As a lute pierceth through the cymbals'
 clash,
Jarr'd but not drown'd by the loud brattling;
 her
Waved arms, more dazzling with their own
 born whiteness
Than the steel her hand held, which she
 caught up
From a dead soldier's grasp;—all these things
 made

Her seem unto the troops a prophetess
Of victory, or Victory herself,
Come down to hail us hers.
　　Sal. (aside.)　　　　　　This is too much.
Again the love-fit's on him, and all's lost,
Unless we turn his thoughts.
　　　　　(Aloud.) But pray thee, sire,
Think of your wound—you said even now
　　't was painful.
　　Sar. That's true, too; but I must not
　　　　think of it.
　　Sal. I have look'd to all things needful,
　　　　and will now
Receive reports of progress made in such
Orders as I had given, and then return
To hear your further pleasure.
　　Sar.　　　　　　　　Be it so.
　　Sal. (in retiring). Myrrha!
　　Myr.　　　　　　　　Prince!
　　Sal.　　　　You have shown a soul to-night,
Which, were he not my sister's lord——But
　　now
I have no time: thou lovest the king?
　　Myr.　　　　　　　　　　I love
Sardanapalus.
　　Sal.　　But wouldst have him king still?
　　Myr. I would not have him less than
　　　　what he should be.
　　Sal. Well then, to have him king, and
　　　　yours, and all
He should, or should not be; to have him
　　live,
Let him not sink back into luxury.
You have more power upon his spirit than
Wisdom within these walls, or fierce re-
　　bellion
Raging without: look well that he relapse
　　not.
　　Myr. There needed not the voice of Sa-
　　　　lemenes
To urge me on to this: I will not fail.
All that a woman's weakness can——
　　Sal.　　　　　　　　　　Is power
Omnipotent o'er such a heart as his:
Exert it wisely.　　　　*[Exit* SALEMENES.
　　Sar.　　　　Myrrha! what, at whispers
With my stern brother? I shall soon be
　　jealous.
　　Myr. (smiling). You have cause, sire; for
　　　　on the earth there breathes not
A man more worthy of a woman's love,
A soldier's trust, a subject's reverence,
A king's esteem—the whole world's admira-
　　tion!
　　Sar. Praise him, but not so warmly. I
　　　　must not
Hear those sweet lips grow eloquent in
　　aught
That throws me into shade; yet you speak
　　truth.

　　Myr. And now retire, to have your wound
　　　　look'd to.
Pray lean on me.
　　Sar.　　　Yes, love! but not from pain.
　　　　　　　　　　　　　　[Exeunt omnes.

* * *

Act IV.

SCENE I.—SARDANAPALUS *discovered sleeping
upon a Couch, and occasionally disturbed in
his slumbers, with* MYRRHA *watching.*

　　Myr. (sola, gazing). I have stolen upon
　　　　his rest, if rest it be,
Which thus convulses slumber: shall I wake
　　him?
No, he seems calmer. Oh, thou God of Quiet!
Whose reign is o'er seal'd eyelids and soft
　　dreams,
Or deep, deep sleep, so as to be unfathom'd,
Look like thy brother, Death,—so still, so
　　stirless—
For then we are happiest, as it may be, we
Are happiest of all within the realm
Of thy stern, silent, and unwakening twin.
Again he moves—again the play of pain
Shoots o'er his features, as the sudden gust
Crisps the reluctant lake that lay so calm
Beneath the mountain shadow; or the blast
Ruffles the autumn leaves, that drooping
　　cling
Faintly and motionless to their loved boughs.
I must awake him—yet not yet; who knows
From what I rouse him? It seems pain;
　　but if
I quicken him to heavier pain? The fever
Of this tumultuous night, the grief too of
His wound, though slight, may cause all this,
　　and shake
Me more to see than him to suffer. No:
Let Nature use her own maternal means,
And I await to second, not disturb her.
　　Sar. (awakening). Not so—although ye
　　　　multiplied the stars,
And gave them to me as a realm to share
From you and with you! I would not so
　　purchase
The empire of eternity. Hence—hence—
Old hunter of the earliest brutes! and ye,
Who hunted fellow-creatures as if brutes!
Once bloody mortals—and now bloodier idols,
If your priests lie not! And thou, ghastly
　　beldame!
Dripping with dusky gore, and trampling on
The carcasses of Inde—away! away!
Where am I? Where the spectres? Where——
　　No—that
Is no false phantom: I should know it 'midst

All that the dead dare gloomily raise up
From their black gulf to daunt the living.
 Myrrha!
 Myr. Alas! thou art pale, and on thy
 brow the drops
Gather like night dew. My beloved, hush—
Calm thee. Thy speech seems of another
 world,
And thou art lord of this. Be of good cheer;
All will go well.
 Sar. Thy *hand*—so—'t is thy hand;
'Tis flesh; grasp—clasp—yet closer, till I feel
Myself that which I was.
 Myr. At least know me
For what I am, and ever must be—thine.
 Sar. I know it now. I know this life
 again.
Ah, Myrrha! I have been where we shall be.
 Myr. My lord!
 Sar. I've been i' the grave—where worms
 are lords,
And kings are——But I did not deem it so;
I thought 't was nothing.
 Myr. So it is; except
Unto the timid, who anticipate
That which may never be.
 Sar. Oh, Myrrha! if
Sleep shows such things, what may not death
 disclose?
 Myr. I know no evil death can show,
 which life
Has not already shown to those who live
Embodied longest. If there be indeed
A shore where mind survives, 't will be as mind,
All unincorporate: or if there flits
A shadow of this cumbrous clog of clay,
Which stalks, methinks, between our souls
 and heaven,
And fetters us to earth—at least the phantom,
Whate'er it have to fear, will not fear death.
 Sar. I fear it not; but I have felt—have
 seen—
A legion of the dead.
 Myr. And so have I.
The dust we tread upon was once alive,
And wretched. But proceed: what hast thou
 seen?
Speak it, 't will lighten thy dimm'd mind.
 Sar. Methought——
 Myr. Yet pause, thou art tired—in pain—
 exhausted; all
Which can impair both strength and spirit:
 seek
Rather to sleep again.
 Sar. Not now—I would not
Dream; though I know it now to be a dream
What I have dreamt:—and canst thou bear
 to hear it?
 Myr. I can bear all things, dreams of life
 or death,

Which I participate with you in semblance
Or full reality.
 Sar. And this look'd real,
I tell you: after that these eyes were open,
I saw them in their flight—for then they fled.
 Myr. Say on.
 Sar. I saw, that is, I dream'd myself
Here—here—even where we are, guests as
 we were,
Myself a host that deem'd himself but guest,
Willing to equal all in social freedom;
But, on my right hand and my left, instead
Of thee and Zames, and our custom'd meeting,
Was ranged on my left hand a haughty, dark,
And deadly face; I could not recognise it,
Yet I had seen it, though I knew not where:
The features were a giant's, and the eye
Was still, yet lighted; his long locks curl'd
 down
On his vast bust, whence a huge quiver rose
With shaft-heads feather'd from the eagle's
 wing,
That peep'd up bristling through his serpent
 hair.
I invited him to fill the cup which stood
Between us, but he answer'd not; I fill'd it;
He took it not, but stared upon me, till
I trembled at the fix'd glare of his eye:
I frown'd upon him as a king should frown;
He frown'd not in his turn, but look'd upon
 me
With the same aspect, which appall'd me
 more,
Because it changed not; and I turn'd for
 refuge
To milder guests, and sought them on the
 right,
Where thou wert wont to be. But——
 [*He pauses.*
 Myr. What instead?
 Sar. In thy own chair—thy own place in
 the banquet—
I sought thy sweet face in the circle—but
Instead—a grey-hair'd, wither'd, bloody-eyed,
And bloody-handed, ghastly, ghostly thing,
Female in garb, and crown'd upon the brow,
Furrow'd with years, yet sneering with the
 passion
Of vengeance, leering too with that of lust,
Sate:—my veins curdled.
 Myr. Is this all?
 Sar. Upon
Her right hand—her lank, bird-like right
 hand—stood
A goblet, bubbling o'er with blood; and on
Her left, another, fill'd with—what I saw not,
But turn'd from it and her. But all along
The table sate a range of crowned wretches,
Of various aspects, but of one expression.
 Myr. And felt you not this a mere vision?

Sar. No:
It was so palpable, I could have touch'd them.
I turn'd from one face to another, in
The hope to find at last one which I knew
Ere I saw theirs: but no—all turn'd upon me,
And stared, but neither ate nor drank, but
 stared,
Till I grew stone, as they seem'd half to be,
Yet breathing stone, for I felt life in them,
And life in me: there was a horrid kind
Of sympathy between us, as if they
Had lost a part of death to come to me,
And I the half of life to sit by them.
We were in an existence all apart
From heaven or earth——And rather let me
 see
Death all than such a being!
 Myr. And the end?
 Sar. At last I sate, marble, as they, when
 rose
The hunter and the crone; and smiling on
 me—
Yes, the enlarged but noble aspect of
The hunter smiled upon me—I should say,
His lips, for his eyes moved not—and the
 woman's
Thin lips relax'd to something like a smile.
Both rose, and the crown'd figures on each
 hand
Rose also, as if aping their chief shades—
Mere mimics even in death—but I sate still:
A desperate courage crept through every
 limb,
And at the last I fear'd them not, but laugh'd
Full in their phantom faces. But then—then
The hunter laid his hand on mine: I took it,
And grasp'd it—but it melted from my own;
While he too vanish'd, and left nothing but
The memory of a hero, for he look'd so.
 Myr. And was: the ancestor of heroes, too,
And thine no less.
 Sar. Ay, Myrrha, but the woman,
The female who remain'd, she flew upon me,
And burnt my lips up with her noisome
 kisses;
And, flinging down the goblets on each hand,
Methought their poisons flow'd around us,
 till
Each form'd a hideous river. Still she clung;
The other phantoms, like a row of statues,
Stood dull as in our temples, but she still
Embraced me, while I shrunk from her, as if,
In lieu of her remote descendant, I
Had been the son who slew her for her incest.
Then—then—a chaos of all loathsome things
Throng'd thick and shapeless: I was dead,
 yet feeling—
Buried, and raised again—consumed by
 worms,
Purged by the flames, and wither'd in the air!

I can fix nothing further of my thoughts,
Save that I long'd for thee, and sought for
 thee,
In all these agonies,—and woke and found
 thee.
 Myr. So shalt thou find me ever at thy
 side,
Here and hereafter, if the last may be.
But think not of these things—the mere
 creations
Of late events, acting upon a frame
Unused to toil, yet over-wrought by toil
Such as might try the sternest.
 Sar. I am better.
Now that I see thee once more, what was seen
Seems nothing.

 Enter SALEMENES.

 Sal. Is the king so soon awake?
 Sar. Yes, brother, and I would I had not
 slept;
For all the predecessors of our line
Rose up, methought, to drag me down to
 them.
My father was amongst them, too; but he,
I know not why, kept from me, leaving me
Between the hunter-founder of our race,
And her, the homicide and husband-killer,
Whom you call glorious.
 Sal. So I term you also,
Now you have shown a spirit like to hers.
By day-break I propose that we set forth,
And charge once more the rebel crew, who still
Keep gathering head, repulsed, but not quite
 quell'd.
 Sar. How wears the night?
 Sal. There yet remain some hours
Of darkness: use them for your further rest.
 Sar. No, not to-night, if 'tis not gone:
 methought
I pass'd hours in that vision.
 Myr. Scarcely one;
I watch'd by you: it was a heavy hour,
But an hour only.
 Sar. Let us then hold council;
To-morrow we set forth.
 Sal. But ere that time,
I had a grace to seek.
 Sar. 'T is granted.
 Sal. Hear it
Ere you reply too readily; and 't is
For *your* ear only.
 Myr. Prince, I take my leave.
 [*Exit* MYRRHA.
 Sal. That slave deserves her freedom.
 Sar. Freedom only!
That slave deserves to share a throne.
 Sal. Your patience—
'T is not yet vacant, and 't is of its partner
I come to speak with you.

Sar.　　　　　How! of the queen?

Sal. Even so. I judged it fitting for their safety

That, ere the dawn, she sets forth with her children

For Paphlagonia, where our kinsman Cotta

Governs; and there at all events secure

My nephews and your sons their lives, and with them

Their just pretensions to the crown in case——

Sar. I perish — as is probable: well thought—

Let them set forth with a sure escort.

Sal.　　　　　　　　　That

Is all provided, and the galley ready

To drop down the Euphrates: but ere they

Depart, will you not see——

Sar.　　　　　　My sons? It may

Unman my heart, and the poor boys will weep;

And what can I reply to comfort them,

Save with some hollow hopes and ill-worn smiles?

You know I cannot feign.

Sal.　　　　　　But you can feel!

At least, I trust so; in a word, the queen

Requests to see you ere you part—for ever.

Sar. Unto what end? what purpose? I will grant

Aught—all that she can ask—but such a meeting.

Sal. You know, or ought to know, enough of women,

Since you have studied them so steadily,

That what they ask in aught that touches on

The heart, is dearer to their feelings or

Their fancy than the whole external world.

I think as you do of my sister's wish;

But 't was her wish—she is my sister—you

Her husband—will you grant it?

Sar.　　　　　　　'T will be useless:

But let her come.

Sal. I go.　　　[*Exit* SALEMENES.

Sar.　　　　We have lived asunder

Too long to meet again—and *now* to meet!

Have I not cares enow, and pangs enow,

To bear alone, that we must mingle sorrows,

Who have ceased to mingle love?

Re-enter SALEMENES *and* ZARINA.

Sal.　　　　　My sister! Courage:

Shame not our blood with trembling, but remember

From whence we sprung. The queen is present, sire.

Zar. I pray thee, brother, leave me.

Sal.　　　　　Since you ask it.

　　　　　　　　　　　[*Exit* SALEMENES.

Zar. Alone with him! How many a year has pass'd,

Though we are still so young, since we have met,

Which I have worn in widowhood of heart!

He loved me not: yet he seems little changed—

Changed to me only—would the change were mutual!

He speaks not—scarce regards me—not a word,

Nor look—yet he *was* soft of voice and aspect,

Indifferent, not austere. My lord!

Sar.　　　　　　　　Zarina!

Zar. No, *not* Zarina—do not say Zarina.

That tone—that word—annihilate long years,

And things which make them longer.

Sar.　　　　　　　'T is too late

To think of these past dreams. Let 's not reproach—

That is, reproach me not—for the *last* time——

Zar. And *first*. I ne'er reproach'd you.

Sar.　　　　　　　'T is most true;

And that reproof comes heavier on my heart

Than—— But our hearts are not in our own power.

Zar. Nor hands; but I gave both.

Sar.　　　　　　Your brother said

It was your will to see me ere you went

From Nineveh with —— (*He hesitates*).

Zar.　　　　　Our children: it is true.

I wish'd to thank you that you have not divided

My heart from all that's left it now to love—

Those who are yours and mine, who look like you,

And look upon me as you look'd upon me

Once —— But they have not changed.

Sar.　　　　　　Nor ever will.

I fain would have them dutiful.

Zar.　　　　　　I cherish

Those infants, not alone from the blind love

Of a fond mother, but as a fond woman.

They are now the only tie between us.

Sar.　　　　　　Deem not

I have not done you justice: rather make them

Resemble your own line than their own sire.

I trust them with you—to you: fit them for

A throne, or, if that be denied — You have heard

Of this night's tumults?

Zar.　　　　I had half forgotten,

And could have welcomed any grief save yours,

Which gave me to behold your face again.

Sar. The throne—I say it not in fear— but 't is

In peril: they perhaps may never mount it;

But let them not for this lose sight of it.
I will dare all things to bequeath it them;
But if I fail, then they must win it back
Bravely—and, won, wear it wisely, not as I
Have wasted down my royalty.
Zar. They ne'er
Shall know from me of aught but what may
 honour
Their father's memory.
Sar. Rather let them hear
The truth from you than from a trampling
 world.
If they be in adversity, they'll learn
Too soon the scorn of crowds for crownless
 princes,
And find that all their father's sins are theirs.
My boys!—I could have borne it were I
 childless.
Zar. Oh! do not say so—do not poison
 all
My peace left, by unwishing that thou wert
A father. If thou conquerest, they shall
 reign,
And honour him who saved the realm for
 them,
So little cared for as his own; and if——
Sar. 'Tis lost, all earth will cry out,
 thank your father!
And they will swell the echo with a curse.
Zar. That they shall never do; but rather
 honour
The name of him, who, dying like a king,
In his last hours did more for his own
 memory
Than many monarchs in a length of days,
Which date the flight of time, but make no
 annals.
Sar. Our annals draw perchance unto
 their close;
But at the least, whate'er the past, their end
Shall be like their beginning—memorable.
Zar. Yet be not rash—be careful of your
 life,
Live but for those who love.
Sar. And who are they?
A slave, who loves from passion—I'll not say
Ambition—she has seen thrones shake, and
 loves;
A few friends who have revell'd till we are
As one, for they are nothing if I fall;
A brother I have injured—children whom
I have neglected, and a spouse ——
Zar. Who loves.
Sar. And pardons?
Zar. I have never thought of this,
And cannot pardon till I have condemn'd.
Sar. My wife!
Zar. Now blessings on thee for
 that word!
I never thought to hear it more—from thee.

Sar. Oh! thou wilt hear it from my
 subjects. Yes—
These slaves whom I have nurtured, pam-
 per'd, fed,
And swoln with peace, and gorged with
 plenty, till
They reign themselves—all monarchs in
 their mansions—
Now swarm forth in rebellion, and demand
His death, who made their lives a jubilee;
While the few upon whom I have no claim
Are faithful! This is true, yet monstrous.
Zar. 'Tis
Perhaps too natural; for benefits
Turn poison in bad minds.
Sar. And good ones make
Good out of evil. Happier than the bee,
Which hives not but from wholesome flowers.
Zar. Then reap
The honey, nor inquire whence 't is derived.
Be satisfied—you are not all abandon'd.
Sar. My life insures me that. How long,
 bethink you,
Were not I yet a king, should I be mortal;
That is, where mortals are, not where they
 must be?
Zar. I know not. But yet live for my—
 that is,
Your children's sake!
Sar. My gentle, wrong'd Zarina!
I am the very slave of circumstance
And impulse—borne away with every breath!
Misplaced upon the throne—misplaced in
 life.
I know not what I could have been, but feel
I am not what I should be—let it end.
But take this with thee: if I was not form'd
To prize a love like thine, a mind like thine,
Nor dote even on thy beauty—as I've doted
On lesser charms, for no cause save that
 such
Devotion was a duty, and I hated
All that look'd like a chain for me or others
(This even rebellion must avouch); yet hear
These words, perhaps among my last—that
 none
E'er valued more thy virtues, though he
 knew not
To profit by them—as the miner lights
Upon a vein of virgin ore, discovering
That which avails him nothing: he hath
 found it,
But 'tis not his—but some superior's, who
Placed him to dig, but not divide the wealth
Which sparkles at his feet; nor dare he lift
Nor poise it, but must grovel on, upturning
The sullen earth.
Zar. Oh! if thou hast at length
Discover'd that my love is worth esteem,
I ask no more—but let us hence together,

And *I*—let me say *we*—shall yet be happy.
Assyria is not all the earth—we'll find
A world out of our own—and be more bless'd
Than I have ever been, or thou, with all
An empire to indulge thee.

Enter SALEMENES.

Sal. I must part ye—
The moments, which must not be lost, are
 passing.
Zar. Inhuman brother! wilt thou thus
 weigh out
Instants so high and blest?
Sal. Blest!
Zar. He hath been
So gentle with me, that I cannot think
Of quitting.
Sal. So—this feminine farewell
Ends as such partings end, in *no* departure.
I thought as much, and yielded against all
My better bodings. But it must not be.
Zar. Not be?
Sal. Remain, and perish——
Zar. With my husband——
Sal. And children.
Zar. Alas!
Sal. Hear me, sister, like
My sister:—all's prepared to make your
 safety
Certain, and of the boys too, our last hopes;
'T is not a single question of mere feeling,
Though that were much—but 't is a point of
 state:
The rebels would do more to seize upon
The offspring of their sovereign, and so
 crush——
Zar. Ah! do not name it.
Sal. Well, then, mark me: when
They are safe beyond the Median's grasp, the
 rebels
Have miss'd their chief aim—the extinction of
The line of Nimrod. Though the present
 king
Fall, his sons live for victory and vengeance.
Zar. But could not I remain, alone?
Sal. What! leave
Your children, with two parents and yet
 orphans—
In a strange land—so young, so distant?
Zar. No—
My heart will break.
Sal. Now you know all—decide.
Sar. Zarina, he hath spoken well, and we
Must yield awhile to this necessity.
Remaining here, you may lose all; departing,
You save the better part of what is left,
To both of us, and to such loyal hearts
As yet beat in these kingdoms.
Sal. The time presses.

Sar. Go, then. If e'er we meet again,
 perhaps
I may be worthier of you—and, if not,
Remember that my faults, though not atoned
 for,
Are *ended.* Yet, I dread thy nature will
Grieve more about the blighted name and
 ashes
Which once were mightiest in Assyria—
 than—
But I grow womanish again, and must not;
I must learn sternness now. My sins have
 all
Been of the softer order——*hide* thy tears—
I do not bid thee *not* to shed them—'t were
Easier to stop Euphrates at its source
Than one tear of a true and tender heart—
But let me not behold them; they unman
 me
Here when I had remann'd myself. My
 brother,
Lead her away.
Zar. Oh, God! I never shall
Behold him more!
Sal. (*striving to conduct her*). Nay, sister,
 I *must* be obey'd.
Zar. I must remain—away! you shall
 not hold me.
What, shall he die alone?—*I* live alone?
Sal. He shall *not die alone;* but lonely
 you
Have lived for years.
Zar. That's false! I knew *he* lived,
And lived upon his image—let me go!
Sal. (*conducting her off the stage*). Nay,
 then, I must use some fraternal force,
Which you will pardon.
Zar. Never. Help me! Oh!
Sardanapalus, wilt thou thus behold me
Torn from thee?
Sal. Nay—then all is lost again,
If that this moment is not gain'd.
Zar. My brain turns—
My eyes fail—where is he? [*She faints.*
Sar. (*advancing*). No—set her down;
She's dead—and you have slain her.
Sal. 'Tis the mere
Faintness of o'erwrought passion: in the air
She will recover. Pray, keep back.—
 [*Aside*] I must
Avail myself of this sole moment to
Bear her to where her children are embark'd,
I' the royal galley on the river.
 [SALEMENES *bears her off.*
Sar. (*solus*). This, too—
And this too must I suffer—I, who never
Inflicted purposely on human hearts
A voluntary pang! But that is false—
She loved me, and I loved her.—Fatal
 passion!

Why dost thou not expire *at once* in hearts
Which thou hast lighted up at once? Zarina!
I must pay dearly for the desolation
Now brought upon thee. Had I never loved
But thee, I should have been an unopposed
Monarch of honouring nations. To what
 gulfs
A single deviation from the track
Of human duties leads even those who claim
The homage of mankind as their born due,
And find it, till they forfeit it themselves!

Enter MYRRHA.

Sar. You here! Who call'd you?
Myr. No one—but I heard
Far off a voice of wail and lamentation,
And thought——
Sar. It forms no portion of your duties
To enter here till sought for.
Myr. Though I might,
Perhaps, recall some softer words of yours
(Although they *too were chiding*), which
 reproved
Because I ever dreaded to intrude;
Resisting my own wish and your injunction
To heed no time nor presence, but approach
 you
Uncall'd for:—I retire.
Sar. Yet stay—being here.
I pray you pardon me: events have sour'd
 me
Till I wax peevish—heed it not: I shall
Soon be myself again.
Myr. I wait with patience.
What I shall see with pleasure.
Sar. Scarce a moment
Before your entrance in this hall, Zarina,
Queen of Assyria, departed hence.
Myr. Ah!
Sar. Wherefore do you start?
Myr. Did I do so?
Sar. 'Twas well you enter'd by another
 portal,
Else you had met. That pang at least is
 spared her!
Myr. I know to feel for her.
Sar. That is too much,
And beyond nature—'tis nor mutual
Nor possible. You cannot pity her,
Nor she aught but——
Myr. Despise the favourite slave?
Not more than I have ever scorn'd myself.
Sar. Scorn'd! what, to be the envy of
 your sex,
And lord it o'er the heart of the world's
 lord?
Myr. Were you the lord of twice ten thou-
 sand worlds—
As you are like to lose the one you sway'd—
I did abase myself as much in being

Your paramour, as though you were a
 peasant—
Nay, more, if that the peasant were a Greek.
Sar. You talk it well——
Myr. And truly.
Sar. In the hour
Of man's adversity all things grow daring
Against the falling; but as I am not
Quite fall'n, nor now disposed to bear
 reproaches,
Perhaps because I merit them too often,
Let us then part while peace is still between
 us.
Myr. Part!
Sar. Have not all past human be-
 ings parted,
And must not all the present one day part?
Myr. Why?
Sar. For your safety, which I will have
 look'd to,
With a strong escort to your native land;
And such gifts, as, if you had not been all
A queen, shall make your dowry worth a
 kingdom.
Myr. I pray you talk not thus.
Sar. The queen is gone:
You need not shame to follow. I would fall
Alone—I seek no partners but in pleasure.
Myr. And I no pleasure but in parting
 not.
You shall not force me from you.
Sar. Think well of it—
It soon may be too late.
Myr. So let it be;
For then you cannot separate me from you.
Sar. And will not; but I thought you
 wish'd it.
Myr. I!
Sar. You spoke of your abasement.
Myr. And I feel it
Deeply—more deeply than all things but
 love.
Sar. Then fly from it.
Myr. 'Twill not recall the past—
'Twill not restore my honour, nor my heart.
No—here I stand or fall. If that you
 conquer,
I live to joy in your great triumph: should
Your lot be different, I'll not weep, but
 share it.
You did not doubt me a few hours ago.
Sar. Your courage never—nor your love
 till now;
And none could make me doubt it save
 yourself.
Those words——
Myr. Were words. I pray you, let the
 proofs
Be in the past acts you were pleased to
 praise

This very night, and in my further bearing,
Beside, wherever you are borne by fate.

　Sar.　I am content: and, trusting in my
　　　cause,
Think we may yet be victors and return
To peace—the only victory I covet.
To me war is no glory—conquest no
Renown. To be forced thus to uphold my
　　　right
Sits heavier on my heart than all the wrongs
These men would bow me down with. Never,
　　　never
Can I forget this night, even should I live
To add it to the memory of others.
I thought to have made mine inoffensive
　　　rule
An era of sweet peace 'midst bloody annals,
A green spot amidst desert centuries,
On which the future would turn back and
　　　smile,
And cultivate, or sigh when it could not
Recall Sardanapalus' golden reign.
I thought to have made my realm a paradise,
And every moon an epoch of new pleasures.
I took the rabble's shouts for love—the
　　　breath
Of friends for truth—the lips of woman for
My only guerdon—so they are, my Myrrha:
　　　　　　　　　　　　[*He kisses her.*
Kiss me. Now let them take my realm and
　　　life!
They shall have both, but never thee!

　Myr.　　　　　　　　No, never!
Man may despoil his brother man of all
That's great or glittering—kingdoms fall,
　　　hosts yield,
Friends fail, slaves fly, and all betray—and,
　　　more
Than all, the most indebted—but a heart
That loves without self-love! 'Tis here—now
　　　prove it.

　　　　　　　Enter SALEMENES.

　Sal.　I sought you—How! *she* here again?
　Sar.　　　　　　　　　　　Return not
Now to reproof: methinks your aspect speaks
Of higher matter than a woman's presence.
　Sal.　The only woman whom it much
　　　imports me
At such a moment now is safe in absence—
The queen's embark'd.
　Sar.　　　　　　And well? say that much.
　Sal.　　　　　　　　　　　　Yes.
Her transient weakness has pass'd o'er; at
　　　least,
It settled into tearless silence: her
Pale face and glittering eye, after a glance
Upon her sleeping children, were still fix'd
Upon the palace towers as the swift galley

Stole down the hurrying stream beneath the
　　　starlight;
But she said nothing.
　Sar.　　　　　　Would I felt no more
Than she has said!
　Sal.　　　　　　'Tis now too late to feel.
Your feelings cannot cancel a sole pang:
To change them, my advices bring sure
　　　tidings
That the rebellious Medes and Chaldees,
　　　marshall'd
By their two leaders, are already up
In arms again; and, serrying their ranks,
Prepare to attack: they have apparently
Been join'd by other satraps.
　Sar.　　　　　　What! more rebels?
Let us be first, then.
　Sal.　　　　　　That were hardly prudent
Now, though it was our first intention. If
By noon to-morrow we are join'd by those
I've sent for by sure messengers, we shall be
In strength enough to venture an attack,
Ay, and pursuit too; but, till then, my voice
Is to await the onset.
　Sar.　　　　　　I detest
That waiting; though it seems so safe to
　　　fight
Behind high walls, and hurl down foes into
Deep fosses, or behold them sprawl on spikes
Strew'd to receive them, still I like it not—
My soul seems lukewarm; but when I set on
　　　them,
Though they were piled on mountains, I
　　　would have
A pluck at them, or perish in hot blood!—
Let me then charge.
　Sal.　　　　　You talk like a young soldier.
　Sar.　I am no soldier, but a man: speak not
Of soldiership, I loathe the word, and those
Who pride themselves upon it; but direct me
Where I may pour upon them.
　Sal.　　　　　　　You must spare
To expose your life too hastily: 'tis not
Like mine or any other subject's breath;
The whole war turns upon it—with it; this
Alone creates it, kindles, and may quench it—
Prolong it—end it.
　Sar.　　　　　Then let us end both!
'Twere better thus, perhaps, than prolong
　　　either;
I'm sick of one, perchance of both.
　　　　　　　　[*A trumpet sounds without.*
　Sal.　　　　　　　　　　Hark!
　Sar.　　　　　　　　　　Let us
Reply, not listen.
　Sal.　　　　　And your wound!
　Sar.　　　　　　　　　'Tis bound—
'Tis heal'd—I had forgotten it. Away!
A leech's lancet would have scratch'd me
　　　deeper;

The slave that gave it might be well ashamed
To have struck so weakly.

Sal. Now, may none this hour
Strike with a better aim!

Sar. Ay, if we conquer;
But if not, they will only leave to me
A task they might have spared their king.
Upon them! [*Trumpet sounds again.*

Sal. I am with you.

Sar. Ho, my arms! again, my arms!
[*Exeunt.*

—◆—

Act V.

Scene I.—*The same Hall in the Palace.*

MYRRHA *and* BALEA.

Myr. (*at a window*). The day at last has
broken. What a night
Hath usher'd it! how beautiful in heaven!
Though varied with a transitory storm,
More beautiful in that variety!
How hideous upon earth! where peace and
hope,
And love and revel, in an hour were trampled
By human passions to a human chaos,
Not yet resolved to separate elements—
'Tis warring still! And can the sun so rise,
So bright, so rolling back the clouds into
Vapours more lovely than the unclouded sky,
With golden pinnacles, and snowy moun-
tains,
And billows purpler than the ocean's, making
In heaven a glorious mockery of the earth,
So like we almost deem it permanent;
So fleeting, we can scarcely call it aught
Beyond a vision, 't is so transiently
Scatter'd along the eternal vault: and yet
It dwells upon the soul, and soothes the soul,
And blends itself into the soul, until
Sunrise and sunset form the haunted epoch
Of sorrow and of love; which they who mark
not,
Know not the realms where those twin genii
(Who chasten and who purify our hearts,
So that we would not change their sweet
rebukes,
For all the boisterous joys that ever shook
The air with clamour) build the palaces
Where their fond votaries repose and breathe
Briefly;—but in that brief cool calm inhale
Enough of heaven to enable them to bear
The rest of common, heavy, human hours,
And dream them through in placid sufferance,
Though seemingly employ'd like all the rest
Of toiling breathers in allotted tasks
Of pain or pleasure, *two* names for *one*
feeling,

Which our internal, restless agony
Would vary in the sound, although the sense
Escapes our highest efforts to be happy.

Bal. You muse right calmly: and can you
so watch
The sunrise which may be our last?

Myr. It is
Therefore that I so watch it, and reproach
Those eyes, which never may behold it more,
For having look'd upon it oft, too oft,
Without the reverence and the rapture due
To that which keeps all earth from being as
fragile
As I am in this form. Come, look upon it,
The Chaldee's god, which when I gaze upon
I grow almost a convert to your Baal.

Bal. As now he reigns in heaven, so once
on earth
He sway'd.

Myr. He sways it now far more, then;
never
Had earthly monarch half the power and
glory
Which centres in a single ray of his.

Bal. Surely he is a god!

Myr. So we Greeks deem too;
And yet I sometimes think that gorgeous orb
Must rather be the abode of gods than one
Of the immortal sovereigns. Now he breaks
Through all the clouds, and fills my eyes
with light
That shuts the world out. I can look no
more.

Bal. Hark! heard you not a sound?

Myr. No, 't was mere fancy;
They battle it beyond the wall, and not
As in late midnight conflict in the very
Chambers: the palace has become a fortress
Since that insidious hour; and here, within
The very centre, girded by vast courts
And regal halls of pyramid proportions,
Which must be carried one by one before
They penetrate to where they then arrived,
We are as much shut in even from the sound
Of peril as from glory.

Bal. But they reach'd
Thus far before.

Myr. Yes, by surprise, and were
Beat back by valour: now at once we have
Courage and vigilance to guard us.

Bal. May they
Prosper!

Myr. That is the prayer of many, and
The dread of more: it is an anxious hour;
I strive to keep it from my thoughts. Alas!
How vainly!

Bal. It is said the king's demeanour
In the late action scarcely more appall'd
The rebels than astonish'd his true subjects.

Myr. 'Tis easy to astonish or appal

The vulgar mass which moulds a horde of
 slaves;
But he did bravely.
 Bal. Slew he not Beleses?
I heard the soldiers say he struck him down.
 Myr. The wretch was overthrown, but
 rescued to
Triumph, perhaps, o'er one who vanquish'd
 him
In fight, as he had spared him in his peril;
And by that heedless pity risk'd a crown.
 Bal. Hark!
 Myr. You are right; some steps approach,
 but slowly.

Enter Soldiers, bearing in SALEMENES *wound-
 ed, with a broken javelin in his side:
 they seat him upon one of the couches
 which furnish the Apartment.*

 Myr. Oh, Jove!
 Bal. Then all is over.
 Sal. That is false.
Hew down the slave who says so, if a soldier.
 Myr. Spare him—he's none: a mere court
 butterfly,
That flutters in the pageant of a monarch.
 Sal. Let him live on, then.
 Myr. So wilt thou, I trust.
 Sal. I fain would live this hour out, and
 the event,
But doubt it. Wherefore did ye bear me here?
 Sol. By the king's order. When the jave-
 lin struck you,
You fell and fainted: 'twas his strict command
To bear you to this hall.
 Sal. 'Twas not ill done:
For seeming slain in that cold dizzy trance,
The sight might shake our soldiers—but—
 'tis vain,
I feel it ebbing!
 Myr. Let me see the wound;
I am not quite skilless: in my native land
'Tis part of our instruction. War being
 constant,
We are nerved to look on such things.
 Sol. Best extract
The javelin.
 Myr. Hold! no, no, it cannot be.
 Sal. I am sped, then!
 Myr. With the blood that fast must follow
The extracted weapon, I do fear thy life.
 Sal. And I *not* death. Where was the
 king when you
Convey'd me from the spot where I was
 stricken?
 Sol. Upon the same ground, and en-
 couraging
With voice and gesture the dispirited troops
Who had seen you fall, and falter'd back.
 Sal. Whom heard ye

Named next to the command?
 Sol. I did not hear.
 Sal. Fly then, and tell him, 'twas my last
 request
That Zames take my post until the junction,
So hoped for, yet delay'd, of Ofratanes,
Satrap of Susa. Leave me here: our troops
Are not so numerous as to spare your absence.
 Sol. But, prince——
 Sal. Hence, I say! Here's a courtier and
A woman, the best chamber company.
As you would not permit me to expire
Upon the field, I'll have no idle soldiers
About my sick couch. Hence! and do my
 bidding! [*Exeunt the Soldiers.*
 Myr. Gallant and glorious spirit! must
 the earth
So soon resign thee?
 Sal. Gentle Myrrha, 'tis
The end I would have chosen, had I saved
The monarch or the monarchy by this;
As 'tis, I have not outlived them.
 Myr. You wax paler.
 Sal. Your hand; this broken weapon but
 prolongs
My pangs, without sustaining life enough
To make me useful: I would draw it forth
And my life with it, could I but hear how
The fight goes.

Enter SARDANAPALUS *and Soldiers.*

 Sar. My best brother!
 Sal. And the battle
Is lost?
 Sar. (*despondingly*). You see *me* here.
 Sal. I'd rather see you *thus!*
 [*He draws out the weapon from the
 wound, and dies.*
 Sar. And *thus* I will be seen; unless the
 succour,
The last frail reed of our beleaguer'd hopes,
Arrive with Ofratanes.
 Myr. Did you not
Receive a token from your dying brother,
Appointing Zames chief?
 Sar. I did.
 Myr. Where's Zames?
 Sar. Dead.
 Myr. And Altada?
 Sar. Dying.
 Myr. Pania? Sfero?
 Sar. Pania yet lives: but Sfero's fled or
 captive.
I am alone.
 Myr. And is all lost?
 Sar. Our walls,
Though thinly mann'd, may still hold out
 against
Their present force, or aught save treachery:
But i' the field——

Myr. I thought 't was the intent
Of Salemenes not to risk a sally
Till ye were strengthen'd by the expected
 succours.
Sar. *I* overruled him.
Myr. Well, the fault's a brave one.
 Sar. But fatal. Oh, my brother! I would
 give
These realms, of which thou wert the orna-
 ment,
The sword and shield, the sole-redeeming
 honour,
To call back——But I will not weep for thee;
Thou shalt be mourn'd for as thou wouldst
 be mourn'd.
It grieves me most that thou couldst quit
 this life
Believing that I could survive what thou
Hast died for—our long royalty of race.
If I redeem it, I will give thee blood
Of thousands, tears of millions, for atone-
 ment
(The tears of all the good are thine already).
If not, we meet again soon,—if the spirit
Within us lives beyond ;—thou readest mine,
And dost me justice now. Let me once clasp
That yet warm hand, and fold that throbless
 heart [*Embraces the body.*
To this which beats so bitterly. Now, bear
The body hence.
 Soldier. Where?
 Sar. To my proper chamber.
Place it beneath my canopy, as though
The king lay there: when this is done, we
 will
Speak further of the rites due to such ashes.
 [*Exeunt Soldiers with the body of* SA-
 LEMENES.

Enter PANIA.

 Sar. Well, Pania! have you placed the
 guards, and issued
The orders fix'd on?
 Pan. Sire, I have obey'd.
 Sar. And do the soldiers keep their hearts
 up?
 Pan. Sire?
 Sar. I'm answer'd! When a king asks
 twice, and has
A question as an answer to *his* question,
It is a portent. What! they are dishearten'd?
 Pan. The death of Salemenes, and the
 shouts
Of the exulting rebels on his fall,
Have made them——
 Sar. Rage—not droop—it should have
 been.
We 'll find the means to rouse them.
 Pan. Such a loss
Might sadden even a victory.

 Sar. Alas!
Who can so feel it as I feel? but yet,
Though coop'd within these walls, they are
 strong, and we
Have those without will break their way
 through hosts,
To make their sovereign's dwelling what it
 was—
A palace; not a prison, nor a fortress.

Enter an Officer, hastily.

 Sar. Thy face seems ominous. Speak!
 Offi. I dare not.
 Sar. Dare not?
While millions dare revolt with sword in
 hand!
That's strange. I pray thee break that loyal
 silence
Which loathes to shock its sovereign; we
 can hear
Worse than thou hast to tell.
 Pan. Proceed, thou hearest.
 Offi. The wall which skirted near the
 river's brink
Is thrown down by the sudden inundation
Of the Euphrates, which now rolling, swoln
From the enormous mountains where it rises,
By the late rains of that tempestuous region,
O'erfloods its banks, and hath destroy'd the
 bulwark.
 Pan. That's a black augury! it has been
 said
For ages, "That the city ne'er should yield
To man, until the river grew its foe."
 Sar. I can forgive the omen, not the
 ravage.
How much is swept down of the wall?
 Offi. About
Some twenty stadia.
 Sar. And all this is left
Pervious to the assailants?
 Offi. For the present
The river's fury must impede the assault;
But when he shrinks into his wonted channel,
And may be cross'd by the accustom'd barks,
The palace is their own.
 Sar. That shall be never.
Though men, and gods, and elements, and
 omens,
Have risen up 'gainst one who ne'er pro-
 voked them,
My fathers' house shall never be a cave
For wolves to horde and howl in.
 Pan. With your sanction,
I will proceed to the spot, and take such
 measures
For the assurance of the vacant space
As time and means permit.
 Sar. About it straight,
And bring me back, as speedily as full.

And fair investigation may permit,
Report of the true state of this irruption
Of waters. [*Exeunt* PANIA *and the Officer.*
 Myr. Thus the very waves rise up
Against you.
 Sar. They are not my subjects, girl,
And may be pardon'd, since they can't be
 punish'd.
 Myr. I joy to see this portent shakes you
 not.
 Sar. I am past the fear of portents: they
 can tell me
Nothing I have not told myself since mid-
 night:
Despair anticipates such things.
 Myr. Despair!
 Sar. No; not despair precisely. When we
 know
All that can come, and how to meet it, our
Resolves, if firm, may merit a more noble
Word than this is to give it utterance.
But what are words to us? we have well
 nigh done
With them and all things.
 Myr. Save *one deed*—the last
And greatest to all mortals; crowning act
Of all that was, or is, or is to be—
The only thing common to all mankind,
So different in their births, tongues, sexes,
 natures,
Hues, features, climes, times, feelings, in-
 tellects,
Without one point of union save in this,
To which we tend, for which we're born, and
 thread
The labyrinth of mystery, call'd life.
 Sar. Our clew being well nigh wound out,
 let's be cheerful.
They who have nothing more to fear may
 well
Indulge a smile at that which once appall'd;
As children at discover'd bugbears.

<center>*Re-enter* PANIA.</center>

 Pan. 'T is
As was reported: I have order'd there
A double guard, withdrawing from the wall
Where it was strongest the required addition
To watch the breach occasion'd by the waters.
 Sar. You have done your duty faithfully,
 and as
My worthy Pania! further ties between us
Draw near a close—I pray you take this key:
 [*Gives a key.*
It opens to a secret chamber, placed
Behind the couch in my own chamber. (Now
Press'd by a nobler weight than e'er it bore—
Though a long line of sovereigns have lain
 down
Along its golden frame—as bearing for

A time what late was Salemenes). Search
The secret covert to which this will lead you;
'T is full of treasure; take it for yourself
And your companions: there's enough to
 load ye,
Though ye be many. Let the slaves be freed,
 too;
And all the inmates of the palace, of
Whatever sex, now quit it in an hour.
Thence launch the regal barks, once form'd
 for pleasure,
And now to serve for safety, and embark.
The river's broad and swoln, and uncom-
 manded
(More potent than a king) by these besiegers.
Fly! and be happy!
 Pan. Under your protection!
So you accompany your faithful guard.
 Sar. No, Pania! that must not be; get
 thee hence,
And leave me to my fate.
 Pan. 'T is the first time
I ever disobey'd: but now——
 Sar. So all men
Dare beard me now, and Insolence within
Apes Treason from without. Question no
 further;
'T is my command, my last command. Wilt
 thou
Oppose it? *thou!*
 Pan. But yet—not yet.
 Sar. Well, then,
Swear that you will obey when I shall give
The signal.
 Pan. With a heavy but true heart,
I promise.
 Sar. 'T is enough. Now order here
Faggots, pine-nuts, and wither'd leaves, and
 such
Things as catch fire and blaze with one sole
 spark;
Bring cedar, too, and precious drugs, and
 spices,
And mighty planks, to nourish a tall pile;
Bring frankincense and myrrh, too, for it is
For a great sacrifice I build the pyre!
And heap them round yon throne.
 Pan. My lord!
 Sar. I have said it,
And *you* have *sworn.*
 Pan. And could keep my faith
Without a vow. [*Exit* PANIA.
 Myr. What mean you?
 Sar. You shall know
Anon—what the whole earth shall ne'er for-
 get.

<center>PANIA, *returning with a Herald.*</center>

 Pan. My king, in going forth upon my
 duty,

This herald has been brought before me,
craving
An audience.
Sar. Let him speak.
Her. The *King* Arbaces——
Sar. What, crown'd already?—But, pro-
ceed.
Her. Beleses,
The anointed high-priest——
Sar. Of what god or demon?
With new kings rise new altars. But, proceed;
You are sent to prate your master's will, and
not
Reply to mine.
Her. And Satrap Ofratanes——
Sar. Why, *he* is ours.
Her. (*showing a ring*). Be sure that he is
now
In the camp of the conquerors; behold
His signet ring.
Sar. 'T is his. A worthy triad!
Poor Salemenes! thou hast died in time
To see one treachery the less: this man
Was thy true friend and my most trusted
subject.
Proceed.
Her. They offer thee thy life, and freedom
Of choice to single out a residence
In any of the further provinces,
Guarded and watch'd, but not confined in
person,
Where thou shalt pass thy days in peace;
but on
Condition that the three young princes are
Given up as hostages.
Sar. (*ironically*). The generous victors!
Her. I wait the answer.
Sar. Answer, slave! How long
Have slaves decided on the doom of kings?
Her. Since they were free.
Sar. Mouthpiece of mutiny!
Thou at the least shalt learn the penalty
Of treason, though its proxy only. Pania!
Let his head be thrown from our walls within
The rebels' lines, his carcass down the river.
Away with him!
[PANIA *and the Guards seizing him.*
Pan. I never yet obey'd
Your orders with more pleasure than the
present.
Hence with him, soldiers! do not soil this
hall
Of royalty with treasonable gore;
Put him to rest without.
Her. A single word:
My office, king, is sacred.
Sar. And what's *mine*?
That thou shouldst come and dare to ask of
me
To lay it down?

Her. I but obey'd my orders,
At the same peril if refused, as now
Incurr'd by my obedience.
Sar. So there are
New monarchs of an hour's growth as despotic
As sovereigns swathed in purple, and en-
throned
From birth to manhood!
Her. My life waits your breath.
Yours (I speak humbly)—but it may be—
yours
May also be in danger scarce less imminent:
Would it then suit the last hours of a line
Such as is that of Nimrod, to destroy
A peaceful herald, unarm'd, in his office;
And violate not only all that man
Holds sacred between man and man—but that
More holy tie which links us with the gods?
Sar. He's right.—Let him go free.—My
life's last act
Shall not be one of wrath. Here, fellow, take
[*Gives him a golden cup from a table near.*
This golden goblet, let it hold your wine,
And think of *me;* or melt it into ingots,
And think of nothing but their weight and
value.
Her. I thank you doubly for my life, and
this
Most gorgeous gift, which renders it more
precious.
But must I bear no answer?
Sar. Yes,—I ask
An hour's truce to consider.
Her. But an hour's?
Sar. An hour's: if at the expiration of
That time your masters hear no further
from me,
They are to deem that I reject their terms,
And act befittingly.
Her. I shall not fail
To be a faithful legate of your pleasure.
Sar. And hark! a word more.
Her. I shall not forget it,
Whate'er it be.
Sar. Commend me to Beleses;
And tell him, ere a year expire, I summon
Him hence to meet me.
Her. Where?
Sar. At Babylon.
At least from thence he will depart to meet me.
Her. I shall obey you to the letter.
[*Exit Herald.*
Sar. Pania!—
Now, my good Pania!—quick—with what I
order'd.
Pan. My lord,—the soldiers are already
charged.
And see! they enter.
[*Soldiers enter, and form a Pile about
the Throne, &c.*

Sar. Higher, my good soldiers,
And thicker yet; and see that the foundation
Be such as will not speedily exhaust
Its own too subtle flame; nor yet be quench'd
With aught officious aid would bring to
 quell it.
Let the throne form the *core* of it; I would not
Leave that, save fraught with fire unquench-
 able,
To the new comers. Frame the whole as if
'T were to enkindle the strong tower of our
Inveterate enemies. Now it bears an aspect!
How say you, Pania, will this pile suffice
For a king's obsequies?
Pan. Ay, for a kingdom's.
I understand you, now.
Sar. And blame me?
Pan. No—
Let me but fire the pile, and share it with you.
Myr. That duty's mine.
Pan. A woman's!
Myr. 'T is the soldier's
Part to die *for* his sovereign, and why not
The woman's with her lover?
Pan. 'T is most strange!
Myr. But not so rare, my Pania, as thou
 think'st it.
In the mean time, live thou.—Farewell! the
 pile
Is ready.
Pan. I should shame to leave my sovereign
With but a single female to partake
His death.
Sar. Too many far have heralded
Me to the dust already. Get thee hence:
Enrich thee.
Pan. And live wretched!
Sar. Think upon
Thy vow:—'tis sacred and irrevocable.
Pan. Since it is so, farewell.
Sar. Search well my chamber,
Feel no remorse at bearing off the gold;
Remember, what you leave you leave the
 slaves
Who slew me: and when you have borne
 away
All safe off to your boats, blow one long
 blast
Upon the trumpet as you quit the palace.
The river's brink is too remote, its stream
Too loud at present to permit the echo
To reach distinctly from its banks. Then
 fly,—
And as you sail, turn back; but still keep on
Your way along the Euphrates: if you reach
The land of Paphlagonia, where the queen
Is safe with my three sons in Cotta's court,
Say, what you *saw* at parting, and request
That she remember what I *said* at one
Parting more mournful still.

Pan. That royal hand!
Let me then once more press it to my lips;
And these poor soldiers who throng round
 you, and
Would fain die with you!
 [*The Soldiers and* PANIA *throng round
 him, kissing his hand and the hem of
 his robe.*
Sar. My best! my last friends!
Let 's not unman each other: part at once:
All farewells should be sudden, when for ever,
Else they make an eternity of moments,
And clog the last sad sands of life with tears.
Hence, and be happy: trust me, I am not
Now to be pitied; or far more for what
Is past than present; for the future, 'tis
In the hands of the deities, if such
There be: I shall know soon Farewell—
 Farewell.
 [*Exeunt* PANIA *and Soldiers.*
Myr. These men were honest: it is com-
 fort still
That our last looks should be on loving faces.
Sar. And *lovely* ones, my beautiful! but
 hear me!
If at this moment—for we now are on
The brink—thou feel'st an inward shrinking
 from
This leap through flame into the future,
 say it:
I shall not love thee less; nay, perhaps more,
For yielding to thy nature; and there's time
Yet for thee to escape hence.
Myr. Shall I light
One of the torches which lie heap'd beneath
The ever-burning lamp that burns without,
Before Baal's shrine, in the adjoining hall?
Sar. Do so. Is that thy answer?
Myr. Thou shalt see.
 [*Exit* MYRRHA.
Sar. (*solus*). She's firm. My fathers!
 whom I will rejoin,
It may be, purified by death from some
Of the gross stains of too material being,
I would not leave your ancient first abode
To the defilement of usurping bondmen;
If I have not kept your inheritance
As ye bequeath'd it, this bright part of it, ·
Your treasure, your abode, your sacred relics
Of arms and records, monuments, and spoils,
In which *they* would have revell'd, I bear
 with me
To you in that absorbing element,
Which most personifies the soul as leaving
The least of matter unconsumed before
Its fiery workings:—and the light of this
Most royal of funereal pyres shall be
Not a mere pillar form'd of cloud and flame,
A beacon in the horizon for a day,
And then a mount of ashes, but a light

To lesson ages, rebel nations, and
Voluptuous princes. Time shall quench full
 many
A people's records, and a hero's acts;
Sweep empire after empire, like this first
Of empires, into nothing; but even then
Shall spare this deed of mine, and hold it up
A problem few dare imitate, and none
Despise—but, it may be, avoid the life
Which led to such a consummation.

MYRRHA *returns with a lighted Torch in one
 Hand, and a Cup in the other.*

Myr. Lo!
I've lit the lamp which lights us to the stars.
 Sar. And the cup?
 Myr. 'Tis my country's custom to
Make a libation to the gods.
 Sar. And mine
To make libations amongst men. I've not
Forgot the custom; and although alone,
Will drain one draught in memory of many
A joyous banquet past.
 [SARDANAPALUS *takes the cup, and after
 drinking and tinkling the reversed cup,
 as a drop falls, exclaims—*
 And this libation
Is for the excellent Beleses.
 Myr. Why
Dwells thy mind rather upon that man's
 name
Than on his mate's in villainy?
 Sar. The one
Is a mere soldier, a mere tool, a kind
Of human sword in a friend's hand; the
 other
Is master-mover of his warlike puppet;
But I dismiss them from my mind.—Yet
 pause,
My Myrrha! dost thou truly follow me,
Freely and fearlessly?
 Myr. And dost thou think
A Greek girl dare not do for love, that which
An Indian widow braves for custom?
 Sar. Then
We but await the signal.
 Myr. It is long
In sounding.
 Sar. Now, farewell; one last embrace.
 Myr. Embrace, but *not* the last; there is
 one more.

 Sar. True, the commingling fire will mix
 our ashes.
 Myr. And pure as is my love to thee, shall
 they,
Purged from the dross of earth, and earthly
 passion,
Mix pale with thine. A single thought yet
 irks me.
 Sar. Say it.
 Myr. It is that no kind hand will
 gather
The dust of both into one urn.
 Sar. The better:
Rather let them be borne abroad upon
The winds of heaven, and scatter'd into air,
Than be polluted more by human hands
Of slaves and traitors. In this blazing palace,
And its enormous walls of reeking ruin,
We leave a nobler monument than Egypt
Hath piled in her brick mountains, o'er dead
 kings,
Or *kine*, for none know whether those proud
 piles
Be for their monarch or their ox-god Apis:
So much for monuments that have forgotten
Their very record!
 Myr. Then farewell, thou earth!
And loveliest spot of earth! farewell, Ionia!
Be thou still free and beautiful, and far
Aloof from desolation! My last prayer
Was for thee, my last thoughts, save *one*, were
 of thee!
 Sar. And that?
 Myr. Is yours.
 [*The trumpet of* PANIA *sounds without.*
 Sar. Hark!
 Myr. Now!
 Sar. Adieu, Assyria!
I loved thee well, my own, my fathers' land,
And better as my country than my kingdom.
I sated thee with peace and joys; and this
Is my reward! and now I owe thee nothing,
Not even a grave. [*He mounts the pile.*
 Now, Myrrha!
 Myr. Art thou ready?
 Sar. As the torch in thy grasp.
 [MYRRHA *fires the pile.*
 Myr. 'Tis fired! I come.
 [*As* MYRRHA *springs forward to throw
 herself into the flames, the Curtain
 falls.*

The Two Foscari.

AN HISTORICAL TRAGEDY.

—◆◆—

"The *father* softens, but the *governor*'s resolved."—CRITIC.

—◆◆—

Dramatis Personæ.

MEN.

FRANCIS FOSCARI, *Doge of Venice.*
JACOPO FOSCARI, *Son of the Doge.*
JAMES LOREDANO, *a Patrician.*
MARCO MEMMO, *a Chief of the Forty.*
BARBARIGO, *a Senator.*
Other Senators, The Council of Ten, Guards, Attendants, &c. &c.

WOMAN.

MARINA, *Wife of young* FOSCARI.

Scene.—*The Ducal Palace, Venice.*

———

Act I.

Scene I.—*A Hall in the Ducal Palace.*

Enter LOREDANO *and* BARBARIGO, *meeting.*

Lor. Where is the prisoner?
Bar. Reposing from
The Question.
Lor. The hour's past—fix'd yesterday
For the resumption of his trial.—Let us
Rejoin our colleagues in the council, and
Urge his recall.
Bar. Nay, let him profit by
A few brief minutes for his tortured limbs;
He was o'erwrought by the Question yester-
 day,
And may die under it if now repeated.
Lor. Well?
Bar. I yield not to you in love of justice,
Or hate of the ambitious Foscari,
Father and son, and all their noxious race;
But the poor wretch has suffer'd beyond
 nature's
Most stoical endurance.
Lor. Without owning
His crime?
Bar. Perhaps without committing any.
But he avow'd the letter to the Duke

Of Milan, and his sufferings half atone for
Such weakness.
Lor. We shall see.
Bar. You, Loredano,
Pursue hereditary hate too far.
Lor. How far?
Bar. To extermination.
Lor. When they are
Extinct, you may say this.—Let's in to coun-
 cil.
Bar. Yet pause—the number of our col-
 leagues is not
Complete yet; two are wanting ere we can
Proceed.
Lor. And the chief judge, the Doge?
Bar. No—he,
With more than Roman fortitude, is ever
First at the board in this unhappy process
Against his last and only son.
Lor. True—true—
His *last.*
Bar. Will nothing move you?
Lor. Feels he, think you?
Bar. He shows it not.
Lor. I have mark'd *that*—the wretch!
Bar. But yesterday, I hear, on his return
To the ducal chambers, as he pass'd the
 threshold
The old man fainted.
Lor. It begins to work, then.

Bar. The work is half your own.
Lor. And should be *all* mine—
My father and my uncle are no more.
Bar. I have read their epitaph, which
 says they died
By poison.
Lor. When the Doge declared that he
Should never deem himself a sovereign till
The death of Peter Loredano, both
The brothers sicken'd shortly:—he *is* sove-
 reign.
Bar. A wretched one.
Lor. What should they be who make
Orphans?
Bar. But *did* the Doge make you so?
Lor. Yes.
Bar. What solid proofs?
Lor. When princes set themselves
To work in secret, proofs and process are
Alike made difficult; but I have such
Of the first, as shall make the second need-
 less.
Bar. But you will move by law?
Lor. By all the laws
Which he would leave us.
Bar. They are such in this
Our state as render retribution easier
Than 'mongst remoter nations. Is it true
That you have written in your books of com-
 ·merce
(The wealthy practice of our highest nobles),
"Doge Foscari, my debtor for the deaths
Of Marco and Pietro Loredano,
My sire and uncle?"
Lor. It is written thus.
Bar. And will you leave it unerased?
Lor. Till balanced.
Bar. And how?
 [*Two Senators pass over the stage, as
 in their way to "the Hall of the
 Council of Ten."*
Lor. You see the number is complete.
Follow me. [*Exit* LOREDANO.
Bar. (*solus*). Follow *thee!* I have follow'd
 long
Thy path of desolation, as the wave
Sweeps after that before it, alike whelming
The wreck that creaks to the wild winds, and
 wretch
Who shrieks within its riven ribs, as gush
The waters through them; but this son and
 sire
Might move the elements to pause, and yet
Must I on hardily like them—Oh! would
I could as blindly and remorselessly!—
Lo, where he comes!—Be still, my heart!
 they are
Thy foes, must be thy victims: wilt thou
 beat
For those who almost broke thee?

Enter Guards, with young FOSCARI *as
 prisoner, &c.*

Guard. Let him rest.
Signor, take time.
Jac. Fos. I thank thee, friend, I'm feeble;
But thou may'st stand reproved.
Guard. I'll stand the hazard.
Jac. Fos. That's kind:—I meet some pity,
 but no mercy;
This is the first.
Guard. And might be the last, did they
Who rule behold us.
Bar. (*advancing to the Guard*). There is
 one who does:
Yet fear not; I will neither be thy judge
Nor thy accuser; though the hour is past,
Wait their last summons—I am of "the Ten,"
And waiting for that summons, sanction you
Even by my presence: when the last call
 sounds,
We'll in together.—Look well to the prisoner!
Jac. Fos. What voice is that?—'T is Bar-
 barigo's! Ah!
Our house's foe, and one of my few judges.
Bar. To balance such a foe, if such there
 be,
Thy father sits amongst thy judges.
Jac. Fos. True,
He judges.
Bar. Then deem not the laws too harsh
Which yield so much indulgence to a sire,
As to allow his voice in such high matter
As the state's safety——
Jac. Fos. And his son's. I'm faint;
Let me approach, I pray you, for a breath
Of air, yon window which o'erlooks the waters.

Enter an Officer, who whispers BARBARIGO.

Bar. (*to the Guard*). Let him approach.
 I must not speak with him
Further than thus: I have transgress'd my
 duty
In this brief parley, and must now redeem it
Within the Council Chamber.
 [*Exit* BARBARIGO.
 [*Guard conducting* JACOPO FOSCARI *to
 the window.*
Guard. There, sir, 't is
Open.—How feel you?
Jac. Fos. Like a boy—Oh Venice!
Guard. And your limbs?
Jac. Fos. Limbs! how often have they
 borne me
Bounding o'er yon blue tide, as I have
 skimm'd
The gondola along in childish race,
And, masqued as a young gondolier, amidst
My gay competitors, noble as I,

Raced for our pleasure, in the pride of
　　strength;
While the fair populace of crowding beauties,
Plebeian as patrician, cheer'd us on
With dazzling smiles, and wishes audible,
And waving kerchiefs, and applauding hands,
Even to the goal!—How many a time have I
Cloven with arm still lustier, breast more
　　daring,
The wave all roughen'd; with a swimmer's
　　stroke
Flinging the billows back from my drench'd
　　hair,
And laughing from my lip the audacious
　　brine,
Which kiss'd it like a wine-cup, rising o'er
The waves as they arose, and prouder still
The loftier they uplifted me; and oft,
In wantonness of spirit, plunging down
Into their green and glassy gulfs, and making
My way to shells and sea-weed, all unseen
By those above, till they wax'd fearful; then
Returning with my grasp full of such tokens
As show'd that I had search'd the deep:
　　exulting,
With a far-dashing stroke, and drawing deep
The long-suspended breath, again I spurn'd
The foam which broke around me, and pur-
　　sued
My track like a sea-bird.—I was a boy then.
　　Guard. Be a man now: there never was
　　more need
Of manhood's strength.
　　Jac. Fos. (*looking from the lattice*). My
　　beautiful, my own,
My only Venice—*this is breath!* Thy breeze,
Thine Adrian sea-breeze, how it fans my face!
Thy very winds feel native to my veins,
And cool them into calmness! How unlike
The hot gales of the horrid Cyclades,
Which howled about my Candiote dungeon,
　　and
Made my heart sick!
　　Guard.　　　　I see the colour comes
Back to your cheek: Heaven send you
　　strength to bear
What more may be imposed!—I dread to
　　think on 't.
　　Jac. Fos. They will not banish me again?—
　　No—no,
Let them wring on; I am strong yet.
　　Guard.　　　　　　Confess.
And the rack will be spared you.
　　Jac. Fos.　　　　　I confess'd
Once—twice before: both times they exiled me.
　　Guard. And the third time will slay you.
　　Jac. Fos.　　　　Let them do so,
So I be buried in my birth-place: better
Be ashes here than aught that lives else-
　　where.

　　Guard. And can you so much love the
　　soil which hates you?
　　Jac. Fos. The soil!—Oh no, it is the seed
　　of the soil
Which persecutes me; but my native earth
Will take me as a mother to her arms.
I ask no more than a Venetian grave,
A dungeon, what they will, so it be here.

　　　　　　Enter an Officer.

　　Offi. Bring in the prisoner!
　　Guard.　　Signor, you hear the order.
　　Jac. Fos. Ay, I am used to such a sum-
　　mons: 't is
The third time they have tortured me:—then
　　lend me
Thine arm.　　　　　　[*To the Guard.*
　　Offi.　　Take mine, sir; 't is my duty to
Be nearest to your person.
　　Jac. Fos.　　　　You!—you are he
Who yesterday presided o'er my pangs—
Away!—I'll walk alone.
　　Offi.　　　　As you please, signor;
The sentence was not of my signing, but
I dared not disobey the Council when
They——
　　Jac. Fos. Bade thee stretch me on their
　　horrid engine.
I pray thee touch me not—that is, just now;
The time will come they will renew that
　　order,
But keep off from me till 't is issued. As
I look upon thy hands my curdling limbs
Quiver with the anticipated wrenching,
And the cold drops strain through my brow,
　　as if——
But onward—I have borne it—I can bear it.—
How looks my father?
　　Offi.　　　　With his wonted aspect.
　　Jac. Fos. So does the earth, and sky, the
　　blue of ocean,
The brightness of our city, and her domes,
The mirth of her Piazza, even now
Its merry hum of nations pierces here,
Even here, into these chambers of the un-
　　known
Who govern, and the unknown and the
　　unnumber'd
Judged and destroy'd in silence,—all things
　　wear
The self-same aspect, to my very sire!
Nothing can sympathise with Foscari,
Not even a Foscari.—Sir, I attend you.
　　　　[*Exeunt* JACOPO FOSCARI, *Officer, &c.*

　　　Enter MEMMO *and another Senator.*

　　Mem. He's gone—we are too late:—think
　　you "the Ten"
Will sit for any length of time to-day?

Sen. They say the prisoner is most ob-
 durate,
Persisting in his first avowal; but
More I know not.
 Mem. And that is much; the secrets
Of yon terrific chamber are as hidden
From us, the premier nobles of the state,
As from the people.
 Sen. Save the wonted rumours,
Which—like the tales of spectres,that are rife
Near ruin'd buildings—never have been
 proved,
Nor wholly disbelieved: men know as little
Of the state's real acts as of the grave's
Unfathom'd mysteries.
 Mem. But with length of time
We gain a step in knowledge, and I look
Forward to be one day of the decemvirs.
 Sen. Or Doge?
 Mem. Why, no; not if I can avoid it.
 Sen. 'T is the first station of the state, and
 may
Be lawfully desired, and lawfully
Attain'd by noble aspirants.
 Mem. To such
I leave it; though born noble, my ambition
Is limited: I'd rather be an unit
Of an united and imperial "Ten,"
Than shine a lonely though a gilded cipher.—
Whom have we here? the wife of Foscari?

Enter MARINA, *with a female Attendant.*

 Mar. What, no one?—I am wrong, there
 still are two;
But they are senators.
 Mem. Most noble lady,
Command us.
 Mar. *I command!*—Alas! my life
Has been one long entreaty, and a vain one.
 Mem. I understand thee, but I must not
answer.
 Mar. (*fiercely*). True—none dare answer
 here save on the rack,
Or question save those——
 Mem. (*interrupting her*). High-born dame!
 bethink thee
Where thou now art.
 Mar. Where I now am!—It was
My husband's father's palace.
 Mem. The Duke's palace.
 Mar. And his son's prison!—True, I have
 not forgot it;
And if there were no other nearer, bitterer
Remembrances, would thank the illustrious
 Memmo
For pointing out the pleasures of the place.
 Mem. Be calm!
 Mar. (*looking up towards heaven*). I am;
 but oh, thou eternal God!

Canst *thou* continue so, with such a world?
 Mem. Thy husband yet may be absolved.
 Mar. He is,
In heaven. I pray you, signor senator,
Speak not of that; you are a man of office,
So is the Doge; he has a son at stake
Now, at this moment, and I have a husband,
Or had; they are there within, or were at least
An hour since, face to face, as judge and
 culprit:
Will *he* condemn *him?*
 Mem. I trust not.
 Mar. But if
He does not, there are those will sentence
 both.
 Mem. They can.
 Mar. And with them power and will
 are one
In wickedness:—my husband's lost!
 Mem. Not so;
Justice is judge in Venice.
 Mar. If it were so,
There now would be no Venice. But let it
Live on, so the good die not, till the hour
Of nature's summons; but "the Ten's" is
 quicker,
And we must wait on't. Ah! a voice of wail!
 [*A faint cry within.*
 Sen. Hark!
 Mem. 'T was a cry of—
 Mar. No, no; not my husband's—
Not Foscari's.
 Mem. The voice was—
 Mar. Not his: no.
He shriek! No; that should be his father's
 part,
Not his—not his—he'll die in silence.
 [*A faint groan again within.*
 Mem. What!
Again?
 Mar. *His* voice! it seem'd so: I will not
Believe it. Should he shrink, I cannot cease
To love; but—no—no—no—it must have been
A fearful pang, which wrung a groan from
 him.
 Sen. And, feeling for thy husband's
 wrongs, wouldst thou
Have him bear more than mortal pain in
 silence?
 Mar. We all must bear our tortures. I
 have not
Left barren the great house of Foscari,
Though they sweep both the Doge and son
 from life;
I have endured as much in giving life
To those who will succeed them, as they can
In leaving it: but mine were joyful pangs:
And yet they wrung me till I *could* have
 shriek'd,
But did not; for my hope was to bring forth

Heroes, and would not welcome them with tears.

Mem. All's silent now.

Mar. Perhaps all's over; but
I will not deem it: he hath nerved himself,
And now defies them.

Enter an Officer hastily.

Mem. How now, friend, what seek you?

Off. A leech. The prisoner has fainted.
 [*Exit Officer.*

Mem. Lady,
'T were better to retire.

Sen. (*offering to assist her*). I pray thee
 do so.

Mar. Off! *I* will tend him.

Mem. You! Remember, lady!
Ingress is given to none within those
 chambers,
Except "the Ten," and their familiars.

Mar. Well,
I know that none who enter there return
As they have enter'd—many never; but
They shall not balk my entrance.

Mem. ` Alas! this
Is but to expose yourself to harsh repulse,
And worse suspense.

Mar. Who shall oppose me?

Mem. They
Whose duty 't is to do so.

Mar. 'T is *their* duty
To trample on all human feelings, all
Ties which bind man to man, to emulate
The fiends who will one day requite them in
Variety of torturing! Yet I'll pass.

Mem. It is impossible.

Mar. That shall be tried.
Despair defies even despotism: there is
That in my heart would make its way through
 hosts
With levell'd spears; and think you a few
 jailors
Shall put me from my path? Give me, then,
 way;
This is the Doge's palace; I am wife
Of the Duke's son, the *innocent* Duke's son,
And they shall hear this!

Mem. ` It will only serve
More to exasperate his judges.

Mar. What
Are *judges* who give way to anger? they
Who do so are assassins. Give me way.
 [*Exit* MARINA.

Sen. Poor lady!

Mem. 'T is mere desperation: she
Will not be admitted o'er the threshold.

Sen. And
Even if she be so, cannot save her husband.
But see, the officer returns.
 [*The Officer passes over the stage with
 another person.*

Mem. I hardly
Thought that "the Ten" had even this touch
 of pity,
Or would permit assistance to this sufferer.

Sen. Pity! Is't pity to recall to feeling
The wretch too happy to escape to death
By the compassionate trance, poor nature's
 last
Resource against the tyranny of pain?

Mem. I marvel they condemn him not at
 once.

· *Sen.* That's not their policy: they'd have
 him live,
Because he fears not death; and banish him,
Because all earth, except his native land,
To him is one wide prison, and each breath
Of foreign air he draws seems a slow poison,
Consuming but not killing.

Mem. Circumstance
Confirms his crimes, but he avows them not.

Sen. None, save the Letter, which he says
 was written,
Address'd to Milan's duke, in the full know-
 ledge
That it would fall into the senate's hands,
And thus he should be re-conveyed to Venice.

Mem. But as a culprit.

Sen. Yes, but to his country;
And that was all he sought,—so he avouches.

Mem. The accusation of the bribes was
 proved.

Sen. Not clearly, and the charge of homi-
 cide
Has been annull'd by the death-bed con-
 fession
Of Nicolas Erizzo, who slew the late
Chief of "the Ten."

Mem. Then why not clear him?

Sen. That
They ought to answer; for it is well known
That Almoro Donato, as I said,
Was slain by Erizzo for private vengeance.

Mem. There must be more in this strange
 process than
The apparent crimes of the accused disclose—
But here come two of "the Ten;" let us
 retire. [*Exeunt* MEMMO *and Senator.*

Enter LOREDANO *and* BARBARIGO.

Bar. (*addressing* LOR.). That were too
 much: believe me, 'twas not meet `
The trial should go further at this moment.

Lor. And so the Council must break up,
 and Justice
Pause in her full career, because a woman
Breaks in on our deliberations?

Bar. No,
That's not the cause; you saw the prisoner's
 state.

Lor. And had he not recover'd?

Bar. To relapse
Upon the least renewal.
 Lor. 'T was not tried.
 Bar. 'T is vain to murmur; the majority
In council were against you.
 Lor. Thanks to you, sir,
And the old ducal dotard, who combined
The worthy voices which o'er-ruled my own.
 Bar. I am a judge; but must confess that
 part
Of our stern duty, which prescribes the
 Question,
And bids us sit and see its sharp infliction,
Makes me wish——
 Lor. What?
 Bar. That *you* would *sometimes* feel,
As I do always.
 Lor. Go to, you 're a child,
Infirm of feeling as of purpose, blown
About by every breath, shook by a sigh,
And melted by a tear—a precious judge
For Venice! and a worthy statesman to
Be partner in my policy.
 Bar. He shed
No tears.
 Lor. He cried out twice.
 Bar. A saint had done so,
Even with the crown of glory in his eye,
At such inhuman artifice of pain
As was forced on him; but he did not cry
For pity; not a word nor groan escaped him,
And those two shrieks were not in suppli-
 cation,
But wrung from pangs, and follow'd by no
 prayers.
 Lor. He mutter'd many times between
 his teeth,
But inarticulately.
 Bar. That I heard not;
You stood more near him.
 Lor. I did so.
 Bar. Methought,
To my surprise too, you were touch'd with
 mercy,
And were the first to call out for assistance
When he was failing.
 Lor. I believed that swoon
His last.
 Bar. And have I not oft heard thee name
His and his father's death your nearest wish?
 Lor. If he dies innocent, that is to say,
With his guilt unavow'd, he 'll be lamented.
 Bar. What, wouldst thou slay his memory?
 Lor. Wouldst thou have
His state descend to his children, as it
 must,
If he die unattainted?
 Bar. War with *them* too?
 Lor. With all their house, till theirs or
 mine are nothing.

 Bar. And the deep agony of his pale wife,
And the repress'd convulsion of the high
And princely brow of his old father, which
Broke forth in a slight shuddering, though
 rarely,
Or in some clammy drops, soon wiped away
In stern serenity; these moved you not?
 [*Exit* LOREDANO.
He 's silent in his hate, as Foscari
Was in his suffering; and the poor wretch
 moved me
More by his silence than a thousand outcries
Could have effected. 'T was a dreadful sight
When his distracted wife broke through into
The hall of our tribunal, and beheld
What we could scarcely look upon, long used
To such sights. I must think no more of
 this,
Lest I forget in this compassion for
Our foes, their former injuries, and lose
The hold of vengeance Loredano plans
For him and me; but mine would be content
With lesser retribution than he thirsts for,
And I would mitigate his deeper hatred
To milder thoughts; but for the present,
 Foscari
Has a short hourly respite, granted at
The instance of the elders of the Council,
Moved doubtless by his wife's appearance in
The hall, and his own sufferings.—Lo! they
 come:
How feeble and forlorn! I cannot bear
To look on them again in this extremity:
I 'll hence, and try to soften Loredano.
 [*Exit* BARBARIGO.

Act II.

Scene I.—*A Hall in the* DOGE's *palace.*

The DOGE *and a* SENATOR.

 Sen. Is it your pleasure to sign the report
Now, or postpone it till to-morrow?
 Doge. Now;
I overlook'd it yesterday: it wants
Merely the signature. Give me the pen—
 [*The* DOGE *sits down and signs the paper.*
There, signor.
 Sen. (*looking at the paper*). You have for-
 got; it is not signed.
 Doge. Not sign'd? Ah, I perceive my
 eyes begin
To wax more weak with age. I did not see
That I had dipp'd the pen without effect.
 Sen. (*dipping the pen into the ink, and
 placing the paper before the* DOGE).
 Your hand, too, shakes, my lord: allow
 me, thus—

Doge. 'Tis done, I thank you.
Sen.　　　　　Thus the act confirm'd
By you and by "the Ten" gives peace to
　　Venice.
Doge. 'Tis long since she enjoyed it: may
　　it be
As long ere she resume her arms!
Sen.　　　　　　　　'Tis almost
Thirty-four years of nearly ceaseless warfare
With the Turk, or the powers of Italy;
The state had need of some repose.
Doge.　　　　　　No doubt:
I found her Queen of Ocean, and I leave her
Lady of Lombardy; it is a comfort
That I have added to her diadem
The gems of Brescia and Ravenna; Crema
And Bergamo no less are hers; her realm
By land has grown by thus much in my
　　reign,
While her sea-sway has not shrunk.
Sen.　　　　　　'Tis most true,
And merits all our country's gratitude.
Doge. Perhaps so.
Sen.　　Which should be made manifest.
Doge. I have not complain'd, sir.
Sen.　　　　My good lord, forgive me.
Doge. For what?
Sen.　　　My heart bleeds for you.
Doge.　　　　　For me, signor?
Sen. And for your——
Doge.　　　　Stop!
Sen.　　　It must have way, my lord:
I have too many duties towards you
And all your house, for past and present
　　kindness,
Not to feel deeply for your son.
Doge.　　　　　Was this
In your commission?
Sen.　　　What, my lord?
Doge.　　　　　This prattle
Of things you know not: but the treaty's
　　sign'd;
Return with it to them who sent you.
Sen.　　　　　　　　　I
Obey. I had in charge, too, from the Council
That you would fix an hour for their reunion.
Doge. Say, when they will—now, even at
　　this moment,
If it so please them: I am the state's ser-
　　vant.
Sen. They would accord some time for
　　your repose.
Doge. I have no repose, that is, none which
　　shall cause
The loss of an hour's time unto the state.
Let them meet when they will, I shall be
　　found
Where I should be, and *what* I have been
　　ever. 　[*Exit* SENATOR. *The* DOGE
　　　　　　　remains in silence.

Enter an Attendant.

Att. Prince!
Doge. Say on.
Att.　　　　The illustrious lady Foscari
Requests an audience.
Doge.　　　　Bid her enter. Poor
Marina! 　[*Exit Attendant. The* DOGE
　　　　　remains in silence as before.

Enter MARINA.

Mar. I have ventured, father, on
Your privacy.
Doge.　　I have none from you, my child.
Command my time, when not commanded by
The state.
Mar. I wish'd to speak to you of *him.*
Doge. Your husband?
Mar.　　　　And your son.
Doge.　　　　　Proceed, my daughter!
Mar. I had obtain'd permission from "the
　　Ten"
To attend my husband for a limited number
Of hours.
Doge. You had so.
Mar.　　　　'Tis revoked.
Doge.　　　　　By whom?
Mar. "The Ten."—When we had reach'd
　　"the Bridge of Sighs,"
Which I prepared to pass with Foscari,
The gloomy guardian of that passage first
Demurr'd: a messenger was sent back to
"The Ten;"—but as the court no longer sate,
And no permission had been given in writing,
I was thrust back, with the assurance that
Until that high tribunal re-assembled
The dungeon walls must still divide us.
Doge.　　　　　True,
The form has been omitted in the haste
With which the court adjourn'd; and till it
　　meets,
'Tis dubious.
Mar.　　Till it meets! and when it meets,
They'll torture him again; and he and I
Must purchase by renewal of the rack
The interview of husband and of wife,
The holiest tie beneath the heavens!—Oh
　　God!
Dost thou see this?
Doge.　　Child—child——
Mar. (*abruptly*). 　Call *me* not "child!"
You soon will have no children—you deserve
　　none—
You, who can talk thus calmly of a son
In circumstances which would call forth tears
Of blood from Spartans! Though these did
　　not weep
Their boys who died in battle, is it written
That they beheld them perish piecemeal, nor
Stretch'd forth a hand to save them?

Doge. You behold me:
I cannot weep—I would I could; but if
Each white hair on this head were a young
　　life,
This ducal cap the diadem of earth,
This ducal ring with which I wed the waves
A talisman to still them—I'd give all
For him.
　　Mar. With less he surely might be saved.
　　Doge. That answer only shows you know
　　　not Venice.
Alas! how should you? she knows not herself,
In all her mystery. Hear me—they who aim
At Foscari, no less at his father;
The sire's destruction would not save the son;
They work by different means to the same
　　end,
And that is——but they have not conquer'd
　　yet.
　　Mar. But they have crush'd.
　　Doge. Nor crush'd as yet—I live.
　　Mar. And your son,—how long will he
　　　live?
　　Doge. I trust,
For all that yet is past, as many years
And happier than his father. The rash boy,
With womanish impatience to.return,
Hath ruin'd all by that detected letter:
A high crime, which I neither can deny
Nor palliate, as parent or as Duke:
Had he but borne a little, little longer
His Candiote exile, I had hopes——he has
　　quench'd them—
He must return.
　　Mar. To exile?
　　Doge. I have said it.
　　Mar. And can I not go with him?
　　Doge. You well know
This prayer of yours was twice denied before
By the assembled "Ten," and hardly now
Will be accorded to a third request,
Since aggravated errors on the part
Of your lord renders them still more austere.
　　Mar. Austere? Atrocious! The old human
　　　fiends,
With one foot in the grave, with dim eyes,
　　strange
To tears save drops of dotage, with long white
And scanty hairs, and shaking hands, and
　　heads
As palsied as their hearts are hard, they
　　counsel,
Cabal, and put men's lives out, as if life
Were no more than the feelings long extin-
　　guish'd
In their accursed bosoms.
　　Doge. You know not—
　　Mar. I do—I do—and so should you, me-
　　　thinks—
That these are demons: could it be else that

Men, who have been of women born and
　　suckled—
Who have loved, or talk'd at least of love—
　　have given
Their hands in sacred vows—have danced
　　their babes
Upon their knees, perhaps have mourn'd
　　above them—
In pain, in peril, or in death—who are,
Or were at least in seeming, human, could
Do as they have done by yours, and you
　　yourself—
You, who abet them?
　　Doge. I forgive this, for
You know not what you say.
　　Mar. *You* know it well,
And feel it nothing.
　　Doge. I have borne so much,
That words have ceased to shake me.
　　Mar. Oh, no doubt!
You have seen your son's blood flow, and
　　your flesh shook not;
And after that, what are a woman's words?
No more than woman's tears, that they should
　　shake you.
　　Doge. Woman, this clamorous grief of
　　　thine, I tell thee,
Is no more in the balance weigh'd with that
Which——but I pity thee, my poor Marina!
　　Mar. Pity my husband, or I cast it from me;
Pity thy son! *Thou* pity!—'t is a word
Strange to thy heart—how came it on thy lips?
　　Doge. I must bear these reproaches, though
　　　they wrong me.
Couldst thou but read——
　　Mar. 'T is not upon thy brow,
Nor in thine eyes,nor in thine acts,—where then
Should I behold this sympathy? or shall?
　　Doge. (*pointing downwards*). There.
　　Mar. In the earth?
　　Doge. To which I am tending: when
It lies upon this heart, far lightlier, though
Loaded with marble, than the thoughts which
　　press it
Now, you will know me better.
　　Mar. Are you, then,
Indeed, thus to be pitied?
　　Doge. Pitied! None
Shall ever use that base word, with which men
Cloak their soul's hoarded triumph, as a fit one
To mingle with my name; that name shall be,
As far as *I* have borne it, what it was
When I received it.
　　Mar. But for the poor children
Of him thou canst not, or thou wilt not save
You were the last to bear it.
　　Doge. Would it were so!
Better for him he never had been born;
Better for me.—I have seen our house dis-
　　honour'd.

Mar. That's false! A truer, nobler,
　　trustier heart,
More loving, or more loyal, never beat
Within a human breast. I would not change
My exiled, persecuted, mangled husband,
Oppress'd but not disgraced, crush'd, over-
　　whelm'd,
Alive, or dead, for prince or paladin
In story or in fable, with a world
To back his suit. Dishonour'd!—*he* dis-
　　honour'd!
I tell thee, Doge, 'tis Venice is dishonour'd!
His name shall be her foulest, worst reproach,
For what he suffers, not for what he did.
'Tis ye who are all traitors, tyrant!—ye!
Did you but love your country like this victim
Who totters back in chains to tortures, and
Submits to all things rather than to exile,
You'd fling yourselves before him, and implore
His grace for your enormous guilt.

Doge. 　　　　　　　He was
Indeed all you have said. I better bore
The deaths of the two sons Heaven took
　　from me,
Than Jacopo's disgrace.

Mar. 　　　　　That word again?

Doge. Has he not been condemn'd?

Mar. 　　　　　Is none but guilt so?

Doge. Time may restore his memory—I
　　would hope so.
He was my pride, my——but 't is useless
　　now—
I am not given to tears, but wept for joy
When he was born: those drops were ominous.

Mar. I say he's innocent! And were he
　　not so,
Is our own blood and kin to shrink from us
In fatal moments?

Doge. 　　　　I shrank not from him:
But I have other duties than a father's;
The state would not dispense me from those
　　duties;
Twice I demanded it, but was refused':
They must then be fulfill'd.

Enter an Attendant.

Att. 　　　　A message from
" The Ten."

Doge. Who bears it?

Att. 　　　　Noble Loredano.

Doge. He!—but admit him.

　　　　　　　[*Exit Attendant.*

Mar. 　　　　Must I then retire?

Doge. Perhaps it is not requisite, if this
Concerns your husband, and if not——Well,
　　signor,
Your pleasure?　　[*To* LOREDANO *entering.*

Lor. I bear that of " the Ten."

Doge. 　　　　　　　　They
Have chosen well their envoy.

Lor. 　　　　　　'Tis *their* choice
Which leads me here.

Doge. 　　　It does their wisdom honour,
And no less to their courtesy.—Proceed.

Lor. We have decided.

Doge. 　　　　　　We?

Lor. 　　　　" The Ten " in council.

Doge. What! have they met again, and
　　met without
Apprising me?

Lor. They wish'd to spare your feelings,
No less than age.

Doge. That's new—when spared they
　　either?
I thank them, notwithstanding.

Lor. 　　　　　You know well
That they have power to act at their discretion,
With or without the presence of the Doge.

Doge. 'T is some years since I learn'd this.
　　long before
I became Doge, or dream'd of such advance-
　　ment.
You need not school me, signor; I sate in
That council when you were a young patrician.

Lor. True, in my father's time; I have
　　heard him and
The admiral, his brother, say as much.
Your highness may remember them; they both
Died suddenly.

Doge. 　　And if they did so, better
So die than live on lingeringly in pain.

Lor. No doubt: yet most men like to live
　　their days out.

Doge. And did not they?

Lor. 　　The grave knows best: they died,
As I said, suddenly.

Doge. 　　　Is that so strange,
That you repeat the word emphatically?

Lor. So far from strange, that never was
　　there death
In my mind half so natural as theirs.
Think *you* not so?

Doge. 　　What should I think of mortals?

Lor. That they have mortal foes.

Doge. 　　　I understand you;
Your sires were mine, and you are heir in all
　　things.

Lor. You best know if I should be so.

Doge. 　　　　　　　　I do.
Your fathers were my foes, and I have heard
Foul rumours were abroad; I have also read
Their epitaph, attributing their deaths
To poison. 'Tis perhaps as true as most
Inscriptions upon tombs, and yet no less
A fable.

Lor. Who dares say so?

Doge. 　　　　I!—'Tis true
Your fathers were mine enemies, as bitter
As their son e'er can be, and I no less
Was theirs; but I was *openly* their foe:

I never work'd by plot in council, nor
Cabal in commonwealth, nor secret means
Of practice against life by steel or drug.
The proof is, your existence.

 Lor. I fear not.

 Doge. You have no cause, being what
 I am ; but were I
That you would have me thought, you long
 ere now
Were past the sense of fear. Hate on ; I care
 not.

 Lor. I never yet knew that a noble's life
In Venice had to dread a Doge's frown,
That is, by open means.

 Doge. But I, good signor,
Am, or at least *was*, more than a mere duke,
In blood, in mind, in means ; and that they
 know
Who dreaded to elect me, and have since
Striven all they dare to weigh me down : be
 sure,
Before or since that period, had I held you
At so much price as to require your absence,
A word of mine had set such spirits to work
As would have made you nothing. But in all
 things
I have observed the strictest reverence ;
Not for the laws alone, for those *you* have
 strain'd
(I do not speak of *you* but as a single
Voice of the many) somewhat beyond what
I could enforce for my authority,
Were I disposed to brawl ; but, as I said,
I have observed with veneration, like
A priest's for the high altar, even unto
The sacrifice of my own blood and quiet,
Safety, and all save honour, the decrees,
The health, the pride, and welfare of the state.
And now, sir, to your business.

 Lor. 'T is decreed,
That, without further repetition of
The Question, or continuance of the trial,
Which only tends to show how stubborn
 guilt is
("The Ten," dispensing with the stricter law
Which still prescribes the Question till a full
Confession, and the prisoner partly having
Avow'd his crime in not denying that
The letter to the Duke of Milan's his),
James Foscari return to banishment,
And sail in the same galley which convey'd
 him.

 Mar. Thank God ! At least they will not
 drag him more
Before that horrible tribunal. Would he
But think so, to my mind the happiest doom,
Not he alone, but all who dwell here, could
Desire, were to escape from such a land.

 Doge. That is not a Venetian thought, my
 daughter.

 Mar. No, 't was too human. May I share
 his exile ?

 Lor. Of this "the Ten" said nothing.

 Mar. So I thought !
That were too human, also. But it was not
Inhibited ?

 Lor. It was not named.

 Mar. (*to the Doge*). Then, father,
Surely you can obtain or grant me thus much :
 [*To* LOREDANO.
And you, sir, not oppose my prayer to be
Permitted to accompany my husband.

 Doge. I will endeavour.

 Mar. And you, signor ?

 Lor. Lady !
'T is not for me to anticipate the pleasure
Of the tribunal.

 Mar. Pleasure ! what a word
To use for the decrees of ——

 Doge. Daughter, know you
In what a presence you pronounce these
 things ?

 Mar. A prince's and his subject's.

 Lor. Subject !

 Mar. Oh !
It galls you :—well, you are his equal, as
You think ; but that you are not, nor would
 be,
Were he a peasant :—well, then, you 're a
 prince,
A princely noble ; and what then am I ?

 Lor. The offspring of a noble house.

 Mar. And wedded
To one as noble. What, or whose, then, is
The presence that should silence my free
 thoughts ?

 Lor. The presence of your husband's
 judges.

 Doge. And
The deference due even to the lightest word
That falls from those who rule in Venice.

 Mar. Keep
Those maxims for your mass of scared me-
 chanics,
Your merchants, your Dalmatian and Greek
 slaves,
Your tributaries, your dumb citizens,
And mask'd nobility, your sbirri, and
Your spies, your galley and your other slaves,
To whom your midnight carryings off and
 drownings,
Your dungeons next the palace roofs, or
 under
The water's level ; your mysterious meetings,
And unknown dooms, and sudden executions,
Your "Bridge of Sighs," your strangling
 chamber, and
Your torturing instruments, have made ye
 seem
The beings of another and worse world !

Keep such for them: I fear ye not. I know
 ye;
Have known and proved your worst, in the
 infernal
Process of my poor husband! Treat me as
Ye treated him:—you did so, in so dealing
With him. Then what have I to fear *from*
 you,
Even if I were of fearful nature, which
I trust I am not?
 Doge. You hear, she speaks wildly.
 Mar. Not wisely, yet not wildly.
 Lor. Lady! words
Utter'd within these walls I bear no further
Than to the threshold, saving such as pass
Between the Duke and me on the state's
 service.
Doge! have you aught in answer?
 Doge. Something from
The Doge; it may be also from a parent.
 Lor. My mission *here* is to the *Doge.*
 Doge. Then say
The Doge will choose his own ambassador,
Or state in person what is meet; and for
The father——
 Lor. I remember *mine.*—Farewell!
I kiss the hands of the illustrious lady,
And bow me to the Duke. [*Exit* LOREDANO.
 Mar. Are you content?
 Doge. I am what you behold.
 Mar. And that's a mystery.
 Doge. All things are so to mortals; who
 can read them
Save he who made? or, if they can, the few
And gifted spirits, who have studied long
That loathsome volume—man, and pored
 upon
Those black and bloody leaves, his heart and
 brain,
But learn a magic which recoils upon
The adept who pursues it: all the sins
We find in others, nature made our own;
All our advantages are those of fortune;
Birth, wealth, health, beauty, are her acci-
 dents,
And when we cry out against Fate, 't were
 well
We should remember Fortune can take
 nought
Save what she *gave*—the rest was nakedness,
And lusts, and appetites, and vanities,
The universal heritage, to battle
With as we may, and least in humblest
 stations,
Where hunger swallows all in one low want,
And the original ordinance, that man
Must sweat for his poor pittance, keeps all
 passions
Aloof, save fear of famine! All is low,
And false, and hollow—clay from first to last,

The prince's urn no less than potter's vessel.
Our fame is in men's breath, our lives upon
Less than their breath; our durance upon
 days,
Our days on seasons; our whole being on
Something which is not *us!*—So, we are
 slaves,
The greatest as the meanest—nothing rests
Upon our will; the will itself no less
Depends upon a straw than on a storm;
And when we think we lead, we are most led,
And still towards death, a thing which comes
 as much
Without our act or choice as birth, so that
Methinks we must have sinn'd in some old
 world,
And *this* is hell: the best is, that it is not
 Eternal.
 Mar. These are things we cannot judge
On earth.
 Doge. And how then shall we judge each
 other,
Who are all earth, and I, who am call'd upon
To judge my son? I have administer'd
My country faithfully—victoriously—
I dare them to the proof, the *chart* of what
She was and is: my reign has doubled realms;
And, in reward, the gratitude of Venice
Has left, or is about to leave, *me* single.
 Mar. And Foscari? I do not think of such
 things,
So I be left with him.
 Doge. You shall be so;
Thus much they cannot well deny.
 Mar. And if
They should, I will fly with him.
 Doge. That can ne'er be.
And whither would you fly?
 Mar. I know not, reck not—
To Syria, Egypt, to the Ottoman—
Anywhere, where we might respire unfetter'd,
And live nor girt by spies, nor liable
To edicts of inquisitors of state.
 Doge. What, wouldst thou have a rene-
 gade for husband,
And turn him into traitor?
 Mar. He is none!
The country is the traitress, which thrusts
 forth
Her best and bravest from her. Tyranny
Is far the worst of treasons. Dost thou deem
None rebels except subjects? The prince who
Neglects or violates his trust is more
A brigand than the robber-chief.
 Doge. I cannot
Charge me with such a breach of faith.
 Mar. No; thou
Observ'st, obey'st such laws as make old
 Draco's
A code of mercy by comparison.

Doge. I found the law; I did not make it.
　　　Were I
A subject, still I might find parts and portions
Fit for amendment; but as prince, I never
Would change, for the sake of my house, the
　　　charter
Left by our fathers.
　Mar.　　　　　Did they make it for
The ruin of their children?
　Doge.　　　　Under such laws, Venice
Has risen to what she is—a state to rival
In deeds, and days, and sway, and, let me
　　　add,
In glory (for we have had Roman spirits
Amongst us), all that history has bequeath'd
Of Rome and Carthage in their best times,
　　　when
The people sway'd by senates.
　Mar.　　　　　Rather say,
Groan'd under the stern oligarchs.
　Doge.　　　　　Perhaps so;
But yet subdued the world: in such a state
An individual, be he richest of
Such rank as is permitted, or the meanest,
Without a name, is alike nothing, when
The policy, irrevocably tending
To one great end, must be maintain'd in
　　　vigour.
　Mar. This means that you are more a
　　　Doge than father.
　Doge. It means, I am more citizen than
　　　either.
If we had not for many centuries
Had thousands of such citizens, and shall,
I trust, have still such, Venice were no city.
　Mar. Accursed be the city where the laws
Would stifle nature's!
　Doge.　　　　Had I as many sons
As I have years, I would have given them
　　　all,
Not without feeling, but I would have given
　　　them
To the state's service, to fulfil her wishes
On the flood, in the field, or, if it must be,
As it, alas! has been, to ostracism,
Exile, or chains, or whatsoever worse
She might decree.
　Mar.　　　　And this is patriotism?
To me it seems the worst barbarity.
Let me seek out my husband: the sage "Ten,"
With all its jealousy, will hardly war
So far with a weak woman as deny me
A moment's access to his dungeon.
　Doge.　　　　　I'll
So far take on myself, as order that
You may be admitted.
　Mar.　　　And what shall I say
To Foscari from his father?
　Doge.　　　　　That he obey
The laws.

Mar.　　　And nothing more? Will you
　　　not see him
Ere he depart? It may be the last time.
　Doge. The last!—my boy!—the last time
　　　I shall see
My last of children! Tell him I will come.
　　　　　　　　　　　　　[*Exeunt.*

Act III.

Scene I.—*The Prison of* JACOPO FOSCARI.

　Jac. Fos. (*solus*). No light, save yon faint
　　　gleam which shows me walls
Which never echo'd but to sorrow's sounds,
The sigh of long imprisonment, the step
Of feet on which the iron clank'd, the groan
Of death, the imprecation of despair!
And yet for this I have return'd to Venice,
With some faint hope, 't is true, that time,
　　　which wears
The marble down, had worn away the hate
Of men's hearts; but I knew them not, and
　　　here
Must I consume my own, which never beat
For Venice but with such a yearning as
The dove has for her distant nest, when
　　　wheeling
High in the air on her return to greet
Her callow brood. What letters are these
　　　which　　　[*Approaching the wall.*
Are scrawl'd along the inexorable wall?
Will the gleam let me trace them? Ah! the
　　　names
Of my sad predecessors in this place,
The dates of their despair, the brief words of
A grief too great for many. This stone page
Holds like an epitaph their history;
And the poor captive's tale is graven on
His dungeon barrier, like the lover's record
Upon the bark of some tall tree, which bears
His own and his beloved's name. Alas!
I recognise some names familiar to me,
And blighted like to mine, which I will add,
Fittest for such a chronicle as this,
Which only can be read, as writ, by wretches.
　　　　　　　　　　[*He engraves his name.*

Enter a Familiar of "*the Ten.*"

　Fam. I bring you food.
　Jac. Fos.　　　　I pray you set it down;
I am past hunger: but my lips are parch'd—
The water!　　　　　　　　　　　＼
　Fam.　　　There.
　Jac. Fos. (*after drinking*). I thank you: I
　　　am better.
　Fam. I am commanded to inform you that
Your further trial is postponed.
　Jac. Fos.　　　　　　Till when?

Fam. I know not.—It is also in my orders
That your illustrious lady be admitted.
 Jac. Fos. Ah! they relent, then—I had
 ceased to hope it:
'T was time.

 Enter MARINA.

 Mar. My best beloved!
 Jac. Fos. (*embracing her*). My true wife,
And only friend! What happiness!
 Mar. We'll part
No more.
 Jac. Fos. How! wouldst thou share a
 dungeon?
 Mar. Ay,
The rack, the grave, all—anything with thee,
But the tomb last of all, for there we shall
Be ignorant of each other, yet I will
Share that—all things except new separation;
It is too much to have survived the first.
How dost thou? How are those worn limbs?
 Alas!
Why do I ask? Thy paleness——
 Jac. Fos. 'T is the joy
Of seeing thee again so soon, and so
Without expectancy, has sent the blood
Back to my heart, and left my cheeks like thine,
For thou art pale too, my Marina!
 Mar. 'T is
The gloom of this eternal cell, which never
Knew sunbeam, and the sallow sullen glare
Of the familiar's torch, which seems akin
To darkness more than light, by lending to
The dungeon vapours its bituminous smoke,
Which cloud whate'er we gaze on, even thine
 eyes—
No, not thine eyes—they sparkle—how they
 sparkle!
 Jac. Fos. And thine!—but I am blinded
 by the torch.
 Mar. As I had been without it. Couldst
 thou see here?
 Jac. Fos. Nothing at first; but use and
 time had taught me
Familiarity with what was darkness;
And the grey twilight of such glimmerings as
Glide through the crevices made by the winds
Was kinder to mine eyes than the full sun,
When gorgeously o'ergilding any towers
Save those of Venice: but a moment ere
Thou camest hither I was busy writing.
 Mar. What?
 Jac. Fos. My name: look, 'tis there—
 recorded next
The name of him who here preceded me,
If dungeon dates say true.
 Mar. And what of him?
 Jac. Fos. These walls are silent of men's
 ends; they only

Seem to hint shrewdly of them. Such stern
 walls
Were never piled on high save o'er the dead,
Or those who soon must be so.—*What of*
 him?
Thou askest.—What of me? may soon be
 ask'd,
With the like answer—doubt and dreadful
 surmise—
Unless thou tell'st my tale.
 Mar. *I speak* of thee!
 Jac. Fos. And wherefore not? All then
 shall speak of me:
The tyranny of silence is not lasting,
And, though events be hidden, just men's
 groans
Will burst all cerement, even a living grave's!
I do not *doubt* my memory, but my life;
And neither do I fear.
 Mar. Thy life is safe.
 Jac. Fos. And liberty?
 Mar. The mind should make its own.
 Jac. Fos. That has a noble sound; but 'tis
 a sound,
A music most impressive, but too transient:
The mind is much, but is not all. The mind
Hath nerved me to endure the risk of death,
And torture positive, far worse than death
(If death be a deep sleep), without a groan,
Or with a cry which rather shamed my judges
Than me; but 'tis not all, for there are things
More woful—such as this small dungeon,
 where
I may breathe many years.
 Mar. Alas! and this
Small dungeon is all that belongs to thee
Of this wide realm, of which thy sire is
 prince.
 Jac. Fos. That thought would scarcely aid
 me to endure it.
My doom is common; many are in dungeons,
But none like mine, so near their father's
 palace;
But then my heart is sometimes high, and
 hope
Will stream along those moted rays of light
Peopled with dusty atoms, which afford
Our only day: for, save the gaoler's torch,
And a strange firefly, which was quickly caught
Last night in yon enormous spider's net,
I ne'er saw aught here like a ray. Alas!
I know if mind may bear us up, or no,
For I have such, and shown it before men;
It sinks in solitude: my soul is social.
 Mar. I will be with thee.
 Jac. Fos. Ah! if it were so!
But *that* they never granted—nor will grant,
And I shall be alone: no men; no books—
Those lying likenesses of lying men.
I ask'd for even those outlines of their kind,

Which they term annals, history, what you
 will,
Which men bequeath as portraits, and they
 were
Refused me,—so these walls have been my
 study,
More faithful pictures of Venetian story,
With all their blank, or dismal stains, than is
The Hall not far from hence, which bears on
 high
Hundreds of doges, and their deeds and dates.
 Mar. I come to tell thee the result of their
Last council on thy doom.
 Jac. Fos. I know it—look!
 [*He points to his limbs, as referring to the*
 Question which he had undergone.
 Mar. No—no—no more of that : even they
 relent
From that atrocity.
 Jac. Fos. What then ?
 Mar. That you
Return to Candia.
 Jac. Fos. Then my last hope's gone.
I could endure my dungeon, for 't was Venice;
I could support the torture, there was some-
 thing
In my native air that buoy'd my spirits up
Like a ship on the ocean toss'd by storms,
But proudly still bestriding the high waves,
And holding on its course ; but *there*, afar,
In that accursed isle of slaves and captives,
And unbelievers, like a stranded wreck,
My very soul seem'd mouldering in my bosom,
And piecemeal I shall perish, if remanded.
 Mar. And *here* ?
 Jac. Fos. At once—by better means, as
 briefer.
What! would they even deny me my sire's
 sepulchre,
As well as home and heritage ?
 Mar. My husband!
I have sued to accompany thee hence,
And not so hopelessly. This love of thine
For an ungrateful and tyrannic soil
Is passion, and not patriotism ; for me,
So I could see thee with a quiet aspect,
And the sweet freedom of the earth and air,
I would not cavil about climes or regions.
This crowd of palaces and prisons is not
A paradise ; its first inhabitants
Were wretched exiles.
 Jac. Fos. Well I know *how* wretched !
 Mar. And yet you see how, from their
 banishment
Before the Tartar into these salt isles,
Their antique energy of mind, all that
Remain'd of Rome for their inheritance,
Created by degrees an ocean Rome ;
And shall an evil, which so often leads
To good, depress thee thus ?

 Jac. Fos. Had I gone forth
From my own land, like the old patriarchs,
 seeking
Another region, with their flocks and herds ;
Had I been cast out like the Jews from Zion,
Or like our fathers, driven by Attila
From fertile Italy, to barren islets,
I would have given some tears to my late
 country,
And many thoughts ; but afterwards address'd
Myself, with those about me, to create
A new home and fresh state : perhaps I could
Have borne this—though I know not.
 Mar. Wherefore not ?
It was the lot of millions, and must be
The fate of myriads more.
 Jac. Fos. Ay—we but hear
Of the survivors' toil in their new lands,
Their numbers and success ; but who can
 number
The hearts which broke in silence at that
 parting,
Or after their departure ; of that malady
Which calls up green and native fields to view
From the rough deep, with such identity
To the poor exile's fever'd eye, that he
Can scarcely be restrained from treading them?
That melody, which out of tones and tunes
Collects such pasture for the longing sorrow
Of the sad mountaineer, when far away
From his snow canopy of cliffs and clouds,
That he feeds on the sweet, but poisonous
 thought,
And dies. You call this *weakness !* It is
 strength,
I say,—the parent of all honest, feeling.
He who loves not his country, can love nothing.
 Mar. Obey her, then : 't is she that puts
 thee forth.
 Jac. Fos. Ay, there it is ; 't is like a
 mother's curse
Upon my soul—the mark is set upon me.
The exiles you speak of went forth by
 nations,
Their hands upheld each other by the way,
Their tents were pitch'd together—I'm alone.
 Mar. You shall be so no more—I will go
 with thee.
 Jac. Fos. My best Marina !—and our
 children ?
 Mar. They,
I fear, by the prevention of the state's
Abhorrent policy (which holds all ties
As threads, which may be broken at her
 pleasure),
Will not be suffer'd to proceed with us.
 Jac. Fos. And canst thou leave them ?
 Mar. Yes. With many a pang.
But—I *can* leave them, children as they are,
To teach you to be less a child. From this

Learn you to sway your feelings, when
　　exacted
By duties paramount; and 'tis our first
On earth to bear.
　　Jac. Fos.　　　Have I not borne?
　　Mar.　　　　　　　Too much
From tyrannous injustice, and enough
To teach you not to shrink now from a lot,
Which, as compared with what you have
　　undergone
Of late, is mercy.
　　Jac. Fos.　　　Ah! you never yet
Were far away from Venice, never saw
Her beautiful towers in the receding distance,
While every furrow of the vessel's track
Seem'd ploughing deep into your heart; you
　　never
Saw day go down upon your native spires
So calmly with its gold and crimson glory,
And after dreaming a disturbed vision
Of them and theirs, awoke and found them
　　not.
　　Mar. I will divide this with you. Let us
　　think
Of our departure from this much-loved city
(Since you must *love* it, as it seems), and this
Chamber of state, her gratitude allots you.
Our children will be cared for by the Doge,
And by my uncles: we must sail ere night.
　　Jac. Fos. That's sudden. Shall I not
　　behold my father?
　　Mar. You will.
　　Jac. Fos.　　　Where?
　　Mar.　　　Here, or in the ducal chamber—
He said not which. I would that you could
　　bear
Your exile as he bears it.
　　Jac. Fos.　　　Blame him not.
I sometimes murmur for a moment; but
He could not now act otherwise. A show
Of feeling or compassion on his part
Would have but drawn upon his aged head
Suspicion from "the Ten," and upon mine
Accumulated ills.
　　Mar.　　　Accumulated!
What pangs are those they have spared you?
　　Jac. Fos.　　　That of leaving
Venice without beholding him or you,
Which might have been forbidden now, as
　　't was
Upon my former exile.
　　Mar.　　　That is true,
And thus far I am also the state's debtor,
And shall be more so when I see us both
Floating on the free waves—away—away—
Be it to the earth's end, from this abhorr'd,
Unjust, and——
　　Jac. Fos. Curse it not. If I am silent,
Who dares accuse my country?
　　Mar.　　　Men and angels!

The blood of myriads reeking up to heaven,
The groans of slaves in chains, and men in
　　dungeons,
Mothers, and wives, and sons, and sires, and
　　subjects,
Held in the bondage of ten bald-heads; and
Though last, not least, *thy silence! Couldst
　　thou* say
Aught in its favour, who would praise like
　　thee?
　　Jac. Fos. Let us address us then, since so
　　it must be,
To our departure. Who comes here?

Enter LOREDANO, *attended by Familiars.*

　　Lor. (*to the Familiars*).　　　Retire,
But leave the torch.
　　　　　　　[*Exeunt the two Familiars.*
　　Jac. Fos. Most welcome, noble signor.
I did not deem this poor place could have
　　drawn
Such presence hither.
　　Lor.　　　'Tis not the first time
I have visited these places.
　　Mar.　　　Nor would be
The last, were all men's merits well re-
　　warded.
Came you here to insult us, or remain
As spy upon us, or as hostage for us?
　　Lor. Neither are of my office, noble lady!
I am sent hither to your husband, to
Announce "the Ten's" decree.
　　Mar.　　　That tenderness
Has been anticipated: it is known.
　　Lor. As how?
　　Mar. I have inform'd him, not so gently,
Doubtless, as your nice feelings would pre-
　　scribe,
The indulgence of your colleagues; but he
　　knew it.
If you come for our thanks, take them, and
　　hence!
The dungeon gloom is deep enough without
　　you,
And full of reptiles, not less loathsome,
　　though
Their sting is honester.
　　Jac. Fos.　　　I pray you, calm you:
What can avail such words?
　　Mar.　　　To let him know
That he is known.
　　Lor.　　　Let the fair dame preserve
Her sex's privilege.
　　Mar.　　　I have some sons, sir,
Will one day thank you better.
　　Lor.　　　You do well
To nurse them wisely. Foscari—you know
Your sentence, then?
　　Jac. Fos.　　　Return to Candia?

Lor. True—
For life.

Jac. Fos. Not long.

Lor. I said—for *life*.

Jac. Fos. And I
Repeat—not long.

Lor. A year's imprisonment
In Canea—afterwards the freedom of
The whole isle.

Jac. Fos. Both the same to me: the after
Freedom as is the first imprisonment.
Is't true my wife accompanies me?

Lor. Yes,
If she so wills it.

Mar. Who obtain'd that justice?

Lor. One who wars not with women.

Mar. But oppresses
Men: howsoever let him have *my* thanks
For the only boon I would have ask'd or
 taken
From him or such as he is.

Lor. He receives them
As they are offer'd.

Mar. May they thrive with him
So much!—no more.

Jac. Fos. Is this, sir, your whole mission?
Because we have brief time for preparation,
And you perceive your presence doth disquiet
This lady, of a house noble as yours.

Mar. Nobler!

Lor. How nobler?

Mar. As more generous!
We say the "generous steed" to express the
 purity
Of his high blood. Thus much I've learnt,
 although
Venetian (who see few steeds save of bronze),
From those Venetians who have skimm'd the
 coasts
Of Egypt and her neighbour Araby:
And why not say as soon the "*generous
 man?*"
If race be aught, it is in qualities
More than in years; and mine, which is as
 old
As yours, is better in its product, nay—
Look not so stern—but get you back, and
 pore
Upon your genealogic tree's most green
Of leaves and most mature of fruits, and
 there
Blush to find ancestors, who would have
 blush'd
For such a son—thou cold inveterate hater!

Jac. Fos. Again, Marina!

Mar. Again! *still*, Marina.
See you not, he comes here to glut his hate
With a last look upon our misery?
Let him partake it!

Jac. Fos. That were difficult.

Mar. Nothing more easy. He partakes it
 now—
Ay, he may veil beneath a marble brow
And sneering lip the pang, but he partakes it.
A few brief words of truth shame the devil's
 servants
No less than master; I have probed his soul
A moment, as the eternal fire, ere long,
Will reach it always. See how he shrinks
 from me!
With death, and chains, and exile in his
 hand,
To scatter o'er his kind as he thinks fit;
They are his weapons, not his armour, for
I have pierced him to the core of his cold
 heart.
I care not for his frowns! We can but die,
And he but live, for him the very worst
Of destinies: each day secures him more
His tempter's.

Jac. Fos. This is mere insanity.

Mar. It may be so; and *who* hath made
 us *mad?*

Lor. Let her go on; it irks not me.

Mar. That's false!
You came here to enjoy a heartless triumph
Of cold looks upon manifold griefs! You
 came
To be sued to in vain—to mark our tears,
And hoard our groans—to gaze upon the
 wreck
Which you have made a prince's son—my
 husband;
In short, to trample on the fallen—an office
The hangman shrinks from, as all men from
 him!
How have you sped? We are wretched,
 signor, as
Your plots could make, and vengeance could
 desire us,
And how *feel you?*

Lor. As rocks.

Mar. By thunder blasted:
They feel not, but no less are shiver'd.
 Come,
Foscari; now let us go, and leave this felon,
The sole fit habitant of such a cell,
Which he has peopled often, but ne'er fitly
Till he himself shall brood in it alone.

Enter the DOGE.

Jac. Fos. My father!

Doge (*embracing him*). Jacopo! my son—
 my son!

Jac. Fos. My father still! How long it is
 since I
Have heard thee name my name—*our* name!

Doge. My boy!
Couldst thou but know——

Jac. Fos. I rarely, sir, have murmur'd.

Doge. I feel too much thou hast not.
Mar. Doge, look there!
 [*She points to* LOREDANO.
Doge. I see the man—what mean'st thou?
Mar. Caution!
Lor. Being
The virtue which this noble lady most
May practise, she doth well to recommend it.
Mar. Wretch! 'tis no virtue, but the
 policy
Of those who fain must deal perforce with
 vice:
As such I recommend it, as I would
To one whose foot was on an adder's path.
Doge. Daughter, it is superfluous; I have
 long
Known Loredano.
Lor. You may know him better.
Mar. Yes: *worse* he could not.
Jac. Fos. Father, let not these
Our parting hours be lost in listening to
Reproaches, which boot nothing. Is it—is it,
Indeed, our last of meetings?
Doge. You behold
These white hairs!
Jac. Fos. And I feel, besides, that mine
Will never be so white. Embrace me, father!
I loved you ever—never more than now.
Look to my children—to your last child's
 children:
Let them be all to you which he was once,
And never be to you what I am now.
May I not see *them* also?
Mar. No—not *here.*
Jac. Fos. They might behold their parent
 anywhere.
Mar. I would that they beheld their
 father in
A place which would not mingle fear with
 love,
To freeze their young blood in its natural
 current.
They have fed well, slept soft, and knew not
 that
Their sire was a mere hunted outlaw. Well,
I know his fate may one day be their
 heritage;
But let it only be their *heritage,*
And not their present fee. Their senses,
 though
Alive to love, are yet awake to terror;
And these vile damps, too, and yon *thick
green* wave
Which floats above the place where we now
 stand—
A cell so far below the water's level,
Sending its pestilence through every crevice,
Might strike them: *this is not their* atmo-
 sphere,
However you—and you—and most of all,

As worthiest—*you*, sir, noble Loredano!
May breathe it without prejudice.
Jac. Fos. I have not
Reflected upon this, but acquiesce.
I shall depart, then, without meeting them?
Doge. Not so: they shall await you in my
 chamber.
Jac. Fos. And must I leave them—*all?*
Lor. You must.
Jac. Fos. Not one?
Lor. They are the state's.
Mar. I thought they had been mine.
Lor. They are, in all maternal things.
Mar. That is
In all things painful. If they 're sick, they
 will
Be left to me to tend them; should they die,
To me to bury and to mourn; but if
They live, they 'll make you soldiers, senators,
Slaves, exiles—what *you* will; or if they are
Females with portions, brides and *bribes* for
 nobles!
Behold the state's care for its sons and
 mothers!
Lor. The hour approaches, and the wind
 is fair.
Jac. Fos. How know you that here, where
 the genial wind
Ne'er blows in all its blustering freedom?
Lor. 'Twas so
When I came here. The galley floats within
A bow-shot of the "Riva di Schiavoni."
Jac. Fos. Father! I pray you to precede
 me, and
Prepare my children to behold their father.
Doge. Be firm, my son!
Jac. Fos. I will do my endeavour.
Mar. Farewell! at least to this detested
 dungeon,
And him to whose good offices you owe
In part your past imprisonment.
Lor. And present
Liberation.
Doge. He speaks truth.
Jac. Fos. No doubt! but 'tis
Exchange of chains for heavier chains I owe
 him.
He knows this, or he had not sought to change
 them.
But I reproach not.
Lor. The time narrows, signor.
Jac. Fos. Alas! I little thought so linger-
 ingly
To leave abodes like this: but when I feel
That every step I take, even from this cell,
Is one away from Venice, I look back
Even on these dull damp walls, and——
Doge. Boy! no tears.
Mar. Let them flow on: he wept not on
 the rack

To shame him, and they cannot shame him
　　now.
They will relieve his heart—that too kind
　　heart—
And I will find an hour to wipe away
Those tears, or add my own. I could weep
　　now,
But would not gratify yon wretch so far.
Let us proceed. Doge, lead the way.
　　Lor. (*to the Familiar*).　The torch, there !
　　Mar.　Yes, light us on, as to a funeral pyre,
With Loredano mourning like an heir.
　　Doge.　My son, you are feeble; take this
　　hand.
　　Jac. Fos.　Alas !
Must youth support itself on age, and I
Who ought to be the prop of yours ?
　　Lor.　　　　　　　　　Take mine.
　　Mar.　Touch it not, Foscari; 't will sting
　　you. Signor,
Stand off ! be sure, that if a grasp of yours
Would raise us from the gulf wherein we are
　　plunged,
No hand of ours would stretch itself to meet it.
Come, Foscari, take the hand the altar gave
　　you,
It could not save, but will support you ever.
　　　　　　　　　　　　　　　　[*Exeunt.*

————◆————

Act IV.

Scene I,—*A Hall in the Ducal Palace.*

Enter LOREDANO *and* BARBARIGO.

　　Bar.　And have you confidence in such a
　　project ?
　　Lor.　I have.
　　Bar.　　　　'T is hard upon his years.
　　Lor.　　　　　　　　Say rather
Kind to relieve him from the cares of state.
　　Bar.　'T will break his heart.
　　Lor.　　　　　Age has no heart to break.
He has seen his son's half broken, and, except
A start of feeling in his dungeon, never
Swerved.
　　Bar.　In his countenance, I grant you, never;
But I have seen him sometimes in a calm
So desolate, that the most clamorous grief
Had nought to envy him within. Where is
　　he ?
　　Lor.　In his own portion of the palace,
　　with
His son, and the whole race of Foscaris.
　　Bar.　Bidding farewell.
　　Lor.　　　　　A last. As soon he shall
Bid to his dukedom.
　　Bar.　　　　When embarks the son ?

　　Lor.　Forthwith—when this long leave is
　　taken. 'T is
Time to admonish them again.
　　Bar.　　　　　　　　Forbear;
Retrench not from their moments.
　　Lor.　　　　　　　　Not I, now
We have higher business for our own. This
　　day
Shall be the last of the old Doge's reign,
As the first of his son's last banishment,
And that is vengeance.
　　Bar.　　　　In my mind, too deep.
　　Lor.　'T is moderate—not even life for life,
　　the rule
Denounced of retribution from all time;
They owe me still my father's and my uncle's.
　　Bar.　Did not the Doge deny this strongly ?
　　Lor.　　　　　　　　　Doubtless.
　　Bar.　And did not this shake your suspicion?
　　Lor.　　　　　　　　　　　No.
　　Bar.　But if this deposition should take place
By our united influence in the Council,
It must be done with all the deference
Due to his years, his station, and his deeds.
　　Lor.　As much of ceremony as you will,
So that the thing be done. You may, for aught
I care, depute the Council on their knees
(Like Barbarossa to the Pope), to beg him
To have the courtesy to abdicate.
　　Bar.　What if he will not ?
　　Lor.　　　　　We'll elect another,
And make him null.
　　Bar.　　　But will the laws uphold us ?
　　Lor.　What laws ?—"The Ten" are laws ;
　　and if they were not,
I will be legislator in this business.
　　Bar.　At your own peril ?
　　Lor.　　　　There is none, I tell you,
Our powers are such.
　　Bar.　　　　But he has twice already
Solicited permission to retire,
And twice it was refused.
　　Lor.　　　　　The better reason
To grant it the third time.
　　Bar.　　　　　Unask'd ?
　　Lor.　　　　　　　It shows
The impression of his former instances :
If they were from his heart, he may be thank-
　　ful :
If not, 't will punish his hypocrisy.
Come, they are met by this time ; let us join
　　them,
And be *thou* fix'd in purpose for this once.
I have prepared such arguments as will not
Fail to move them, and to remove him : since
Their thoughts, their objects, have been
　　sounded, do not
You, with your wonted scruples, teach us
　　pause,
And all will prosper.

Bar. Could I but be certain
This is no prelude to such persecution
Of the sire as has fallen upon the son,
I would support you.
 Lor. He is safe, I tell you;
His fourscore years and five may linger on
As long as he can drag them : 'tis his throne
Alone is aim'd at.
 Bar. But discarded princes
Are seldom long of life.
 Lor. And men of eighty
More seldom still.
 Bar.. And why not wait these few years?
 Lor. Because we have waited long enough,
 and he
Lived longer than enough. Hence! in to
council !
 [*Exeunt* LOREDANO *and* BARBARIGO.

 Enter MEMMO *and a Senator.*

 Sen. A summons to "the Ten !" why so?
 Mem. "The Ten"
Alone can answer; they are rarely wont
To let their thoughts anticipate their purpose
By previous proclamation. We are sum-
 mon'd—
That is enough.
 Sen. For them, but not for us;
I would know why.
 Mem. You will know why anon,
If you obey: and, if not, you no less
Will know why you should have obey'd.
 Sen. I mean not
To oppose them, *but*——
 Mem. In Venice "*but*"'s a traitor.
But me no "*buts*," unless you would pass o'er
The Bridge which few repass.
 Sen. I am silent.
 Mem. Why
Thus hesitate? "The Ten" have call'd in aid
Of their deliberation five and twenty
Patricians of the senate—you are one,
And I another; and it seems to me
Both honour'd by the choice or chance which
 leads us
To mingle with a body so august.
 Sen. Most true. I say no more.
 Mem. As we hope, signor,
And all may honestly, (that is, all those
Of noble blood may,) one day hope to be
Decemvir, it is surely for the senate's
Chosen delegates a school of wisdom, to
Be thus admitted, though as novices,
To view the mysteries.
 Sen. Let us view them : they,
No doubt, are worth it.
 Mem. Being worth our lives
If we divulge them, doubtless they are worth
Something, at least to you or me.

 Sen. I sought not
A place within the sanctuary; but being
Chosen, however reluctantly so chosen,
I shall fulfil my office.
 Mem. Let us not
Be latest in obeying " the Ten's " summons.
 Sen. All are not met, but I am of your
 thought
So far—let's in.
 Mem. The earliest are most welcome
In earnest councils—we will not be least so.
 [*Exeunt.*

Enter the DOGE, JACOPO FOSCARI, *and* MARINA.

 Jac. Fos. Ah, father! though I must and
 will depart,
Yet—yet—I pray you to obtain for me
That I once more return unto my home,
Howe'er remote the period. Let there be
A point of time, as beacon to my heart,
With any penalty annex'd they please,
But let me still return.
 Doge. Son Jacopo,
Go and obey our country's will : 'tis not
For us to look beyond.
 Jac. Fos. But still I must
Look back. I pray you think of me.
 Doge. Alas!
You ever were my dearest offspring, when
They were more numerous, nor can be less
 so
Now you are last; but did the state demand
The exile of the disinterred ashes
Of your three goodly brothers, now in earth,
And their desponding shades came flitting
 round
To impede the act, I must no less obey
A duty, paramount to every duty.
 Mar. My husband! let us on: this but
 prolongs
Our sorrow.
 Jac. Fos. But we are not summon'd yet;
The galley's sails are not unfurl'd :—who
 knows?
The wind may change.
 Mar. And if it do, it will not
Change *their* hearts, or your lot: the galley's
 oars
Will quickly clear the harbour.
 Jac. Fos. O ye elements !
Where are your storms?
 Mar. In human breasts. Alas!
Will nothing calm you?
 Jac. Fos. Never yet did mariner
Put up to patron saint such prayers for
 prosperous
And pleasant breezes, as I call upon you,
Ye tutelar saints of my own city! which
Ye love not with more holy love than I,

To lash up from the deep the Adrian waves,
And waken Auster, sovereign of the tempest!
Till the sea dash me back on my own shore
A broken corse upon the barren Lido,
Where I may mingle with the sands which
 skirt
The land I love, and never shall see more!
 Mar. And wish you this with *me* beside
 you?
 Jac. Fos. No—
No—not for thee, too good, too kind! May'st
 thou
Live long to be a mother to those children
Thy fond fidelity for a time deprives
Of such support! But for myself alone,
May all the winds of heaven howl down the
 Gulf,
And tear the vessel, till the mariners,
Appall'd, turn their despairing eyes on me,
As the Phenicians did on Jonah, then
Cast me out from amongst them, as an
 offering
To appease the waves. The billow which
 destroys me
Will be more merciful than man, and bear me
Dead, but *still bear* me to a native grave,
From fishers' hands, upon the desolate
 strand,
Which, of its thousand wrecks, hath ne'er
 received
One lacerated like the heart which then
Will be.—But wherefore breaks it not? why
 live I?
 Mar. To man thyself, I trust, with time,
 to master
Such useless passion. Until now thou wert
A sufferer, but not a loud one: why
What is this to the things thou hast borne in
 silence—
Imprisonment and actual torture?
 Jac. Fos. Double,
Triple, and tenfold torture! But you are
 right,
It must be borne. Father, your blessing.
 Doge. Would
It could avail thee! but no less thou hast it.
 Jac. Fos. Forgive ——
 Doge. What?
 Jac. Fos. My poor mother, for my birth,
And me for having lived, and you yourself
(As I forgive you), for the gift of life,
Which you bestow'd upon me as my sire.
 Mar. What hast thou done?
 Jac Fos. Nothing. I cannot charge
My memory with much save sorrow: but
I have been so beyond the common lot
Chasten'd and visited, I needs must think
That I was wicked. If it be so, may
What I have undergone here keep me from
A like hereafter!

 Mar. Fear not: *that*'s reserved
For your oppressors.
 Jac. Fos. Let me hope not.
 Mar. Hope not?
 Jac. Fos. I cannot wish them *all* they have
 inflicted.
 Mar. All! the consummate fiends! A
 thousand-fold
May the worm which ne'er dieth feed upon
 them!
 Jac. Fos. They may repent.
 Mar. And if they do, Heaven will not
Accept the tardy penitence of demons.

Enter an Officer and Guards.

 Offi. Signor! the boat is at the shore—the
 wind
Is rising—we are ready to attend you.
 Jac. Fos. And I to be attended. Once
 more, father,
Your hand!
 Doge. Take it. Alas! how thine own
 trembles!
 Jac. Fos. No—you mistake; 't is yours
 that shakes, my father.
Farewell!
 Doge. Farewell! Is there aught else?
 Jac. Fos. No—nothing.
 [To the Officer.
Lend me your arm, good signor.
 Offi. You turn pale—
Let me support you—paler—ho! some aid
 there!
Some water!
 Mar. Ah, he is dying!
 Jac. Fos. Now, I'm ready—
My eyes swim strangely—where's the door?
 Mar. Away!
Let me support him—my best love! Oh,
 God!
How faintly beats this heart—this pulse!
 Jac. Fos. The light!
Is it the light?—I am faint.
 [Officer presents him with water.
 Offi. He will be better,
Perhaps, in the air.
 Jac. Fos. I doubt not. Father—wife—
Your hands!
 Mar. There's death in that damp, clammy
 grasp.
Oh, God!—My Foscari, how fare you?
 Jac. Fos. Well! *[He dies.*
 Offi. He's gone!
 Doge. He's free.
 Mar. No—no, he is not dead;
There must be life yet in that heart—he
 could not
Thus leave me.
 Doge. Daughter!

Mar. Hold thy peace, old man!
I am no daughter now—thou hast no son.
Oh, Foscari!
Offi. We must remove the body.
Mar. Touch it not, dungeon miscreants!
 your base office
Ends with his life, and goes not beyond
 murder,
Even by your murderous laws. Leave his
 remains
To those who know to honour them.
Offi. I must
Inform the signory, and learn their pleasure.
Doge. Inform the signory from *me*, the
 Doge,
They have no further power upon those
 ashes:
While he lived, he was theirs, as fits a
 subject—
Now he is *mine*—my broken-hearted boy!
 [*Exit Officer.*
Mar. And I must live!
Doge. Your children live, Marina.
Mar. My children! true—they live, and I
 must live
To bring them up to serve the state, and die
As died their father. Oh! what best of
 blessings
Were barrenness in Venice! Would my
 mother
Had been so!
Doge. My unhappy children!
Mar. What!
You feel it then at last—*you!*—Where is now
The stoic of the state?
Doge (*throwing himself down by the body*).
 Here!
Mar. Ay, weep on!
I thought you had no tears—you hoarded
 them
Until they are useless; but weep on! he
 never
Shall weep more—never, never more.

Enter LOREDANO *and* BARBARIGO.

Lor. What's here?
Mar. Ah! the devil come to insult the
 dead! Avaunt!
Incarnate Lucifer! 'tis holy ground.
A martyr's ashes now lie there, which make
 it
A shrine. Get thee back to thy place of
 torment!
Bar. Lady, we knew not of this sad
 event,
But pass'd here merely on our path from
 council.
Mar. Pass on.
Lor. We sought the Doge.

Mar. (*pointing to the Doge, who is still on
 the ground by his son's body*).
 He's busy, look,
About the business *you* provided for him.
Are ye content?
Bar. We will not interrupt
A parent's sorrows.
Mar. No, ye only make them,
Then leave them.
Doge. (*rising*). Sirs, I am ready.
Bar. No—not now.
Lor. Yet 'twas important.
Doge. If 't was so, I can
Only repeat—I am ready.
Bar. It shall not be
Just now, though Venice totter'd o'er the deep
Like a frail vessel. I respect your griefs.
Doge. I thank you. If the tidings which
 you bring
Are evil, you may say them; nothing further
Can touch me more than him thou look'st on
 there;
If they be good, say on; you need not *fear*
That they can *comfort* me.
Bar. I would they could!
Doge. I spoke not to *you*, but to Loredano.
He understands me.
Mar. Ah! I thought it would be so.
Doge. What mean you?
Mar. Lo! there is the blood beginning
To flow through the dead lips of Foscari—
The body bleeds in presence of the assassin.
 [*To* LOREDANO.
Thou cowardly murderer by law, behold
How death itself bears witness to thy deeds!
Doge. My child! this is a phantasy of
 grief.
Bear hence the body. [*To his attendants.*]
 Signors, if it please you,
Within an hour I'll hear you.
 [*Exeunt* DOGE, MARINA, *and attendants
 with the body. Manent* LOREDANO
 and BARBARIGO.
Bar. He must not
Be troubled now.
Lor. He said himself that nought
Could give him trouble further.
Bar. These are words;
But grief is lonely, and the breaking in
Upon it barbarous.
Lor. Sorrow preys upon
Its solitude, and nothing more diverts it
From its sad visions of the other world,
Than calling it at moments back to this.
The busy have no time for tears.
Bar. And therefore
You would deprive this old man of all
 business?
Lor. The thing's decreed. The Giunta
 and "the Ten"

Have made it law—who shall oppose that
　law?

Bar. Humanity!

Lor.　　　　　Because his son is dead?

Bar. And yet unburied.

Lor.　　　　Had we known this when
The act was passing, it might have suspended
Its passage, but impedes it not—once past.

Bar. I'll not consent.

Lor.　　　　　You have consented to
All that's essential—leave the rest to me.

Bar. Why press his abdication now?

Lor.　　　　　The feelings
Of private passion may not interrupt
The public benefit; and what the state
Decides to-day must not give way before
To-morrow for a natural accident.

Bar. You have a son.

Lor.　　　　I *have*—and *had* a father.

Bar. Still so inexorable?

Lor.　　　　　Still.

Bar.　　　　　But let him
Inter his son before we press upon him
This edict.

Lor.　　Let him call up into life
My sire and uncle—I consent. Men may,
Even aged men, be, or appear to be,
Sires of a hundred sons, but cannot kindle
An atom of their ancestors from earth.
The victims are not equal; he has seen
His sons expire by natural deaths, and I
My sires by violent and mysterious maladies.
I used no poison, bribed no subtle master
Of the destructive art of healing, to
Shorten the path to the eternal cure.
His sons—and he had four—are dead, without
My dabbling in vile drugs.

Bar.　　　　　And art thou sure
He dealt in such?

Lor.　　Most sure.

Bar.　　　　And yet he seems
All openness.

Lor.　　And so he seem'd not long
Ago to Carmagnuola.

Bar.　　　　The attainted
And foreign traitor?

Lor.　　　Even so: when *he*,
After the very night in which "the Ten"
(Join'd with the Doge) decided his destruc-
　tion,
Met the great Duke at daybreak with a jest,
Demanding whether he should augur him
"The good day or good night?" his Doge-
　ship answer'd,
"That he in truth had pass'd a night of vigil,
In which (he added with a gracious smile),
There often has been question about you."
'Twas true; the question was the death
　resolved
Of Carmagnuola, eight months ere he died;

And the old Doge, who knew him doom'd,
　smiled on him
With deadly cozenage, eight long months
　beforehand—
Eight months of such hypocrisy as is
Learnt but in eighty years. Brave Car-
　magnuola
Is dead; so is young Foscari and his brethren—
I never *smiled* on *them*.

Bar.　　　　　Was Carmagnuola
Your friend?

Lor.　　He was the safeguard of the city.
In early life its foe, but, in his manhood,
Its saviour first, then victim.

Bar.　　　　　Ah! that seems
The penalty of saving cities. He
Whom we now act against not only saved
Our own, but added others to our sway.

Lor. The Romans (and we ape them) gave
　a crown
To him who took a city; and they gave
A crown to him who saved a citizen
In battle: the rewards are equal. Now,
If we should measure forth the cities taken
By the Doge Foscari, with citizens
Destroy'd by him, or *through* him, the account
Were fearfully against him, although narrow'd
To private havoc, such as between him
And my dead father.

Bar.　　　　Are you then thus fix'd?

Lor. Why, what should change me?

Bar.　　　　That which changes me:
But you, I know, are marble to retain
A feud. But when all is accomplish'd, when
The old man is deposed, his name degraded,
His sons all dead, his family depress'd,
And you and yours triumphant, shall you
　sleep?

Lor. More soundly.

Bar. That's an error, and you'll find it
Ere you sleep with your fathers.

Lor.　　　　　They sleep not
In their accelerated graves, nor will
Till Foscari fills his. Each night I see them
Stalk frowning round my couch, and, pointing
　towards
The ducal palace, marshal me to vengeance.

Bar. Fancy's distemperature! There is
　no passion
More spectral or fantastical than Hate;
Not even its opposite, Love, so peoples air
With phantoms, as this madness of the heart.

Enter an Officer.

Lor. Where go you, sirrah?

Offi.　　　　　By the ducal order
To forward the preparatory rites
For the late Foscari's interment.

Bar.　　　　　Their
Vault has been often open'd of late years.

Lor. 'T will be full soon, and may be closed
 for ever.
Offi. May I pass on?
Lor. You may.
Bar. How bears the Doge
This last calamity?
Offi. With desperate firmness.
In presence of another he says little,
But I perceive his lips move now and then;
And once or twice I heard him, from the
 adjoining
Apartment, mutter forth the words—"My
 son!"
Scarce audibly. I must proceed.
 [Exit Officer.
Bar. This stroke
Will move all Venice in his favour.
Lor. Right!
We must be speedy: let us call together
The delegates appointed to convey
The Council's resolution.
Bar. I protest
Against it at this moment.
Lor. As you please—
I'll take their voices on it ne'ertheless,
And see whose most may sway them, yours
 or mine.
 [Exeunt BARBARIGO *and* LOREDANO.

———•———

Act V.

Scene I.—*The* DOGE'S *Apartment.*

The DOGE *and Attendants.*

Att. My lord, the deputation is in waiting;
But add, that if another hour would better
Accord with your will, they will make it theirs.
Doge. To me all hours are like. Let them
 approach. *[Exit Attendant.*
An Officer. Prince! I have done your
 bidding.
Doge. What command?
Offi. A melancholy one—to call the atten-
 dance
Of——
Doge. True—true—true; I crave your
 pardon. I
Begin to fail in apprehension, and
Wax very old—old almost as my years.
Till now I fought them off, but they begin
To overtake me.

*Enter the Deputation, consisting of six of the
Signory and the Chief of the Ten.*

 Noble men, your pleasure!
Chief of the Ten. In the first place, the
 Council doth condole
With the Doge on his late and private grief.

Doge. No more—no more of that.
Chief of the Ten. Will not the Duke
Accept the homage of respect?
Doge. I do
Accept it as 'tis given—proceed.
Chief of the Ten. 'The Ten,'
With a selected Giunta from the senate
Of twenty-five of the best born patricians,
Having deliberated on the state
Of the republic, and the o'erwhelming cares
Which, at this moment, doubly must oppress
Your years, so long devoted to your country,
Have judged it fitting, with all reverence,
Now to solicit from your wisdom (which
Upon reflection must accord in this),
The resignation of the ducal ring,
Which you have worn so long and venerably:
And to prove that they are not ungrateful, nor
Cold to your years and services, they add
An appanage of twenty hundred golden
Ducats, to make retirement not less splendid
Than should become a sovereign's retreat.
Doge. Did I hear rightly?
Chief of the Ten. Need I say again?
Doge. No—Have you done?
Chief of the Ten. I have spoken. Twenty-
 four
Hours are accorded you to give an answer.
Doge. I shall not need so many seconds.
Chief of the Ten. We
Will now retire.
Doge. Stay! four and twenty hours
Will alter nothing which I have to say.
Chief of the Ten. Speak!
Doge. When I twice before reiterated
My wish to abdicate, it was refused me:
And not alone refused, but ye exacted
An oath from me that I would never more
Renew this instance. I have sworn to die
In full exertion of the functions which
My country call'd me here to exercise,
According to my honour and my conscience—
I cannot break *my* oath.
Chief of the Ten. Reduce us not
To the alternative of a decree,
Instead of your compliance.
Doge. Providence
Prolongs my days to prove and chasten me;
But ye have no right to reproach my length
Of days, since every hour has been the
 country's.
I am ready to lay down my life for her,
As I have laid down dearer things than life:
But for my dignity—I hold it of
The *whole* republic: when the *general* will
Is manifest, then you shall all be answer'd.
Chief of the Ten. We grieve for such an
 answer; but it cannot
Avail you aught.
Doge. I can submit to all things,

But nothing will advance; no, not a moment.
What you decree—decree.

Chief of the Ten. With this, then, must we
Return to those who sent us?

Doge. You have heard me.

Chief of the Ten. With all due reverence
we retire.

[*Exeunt the Deputation, &c.*

Enter an Attendant.

Att. My lord,
The noble dame Marina craves an audience.

Doge. My time is hers.

Enter MARINA.

Mar. My lord, if I intrude—
Perhaps you fain would be alone?

Doge. Alone!
Alone, come all the world around me, I
Am now and evermore. But we will bear it.

Mar. We will, and for the sake of those
who are,
Endeavour——Oh, my husband!

Doge. Give it way:
I cannot comfort thee.

Mar. He might have lived,
So form'd for gentle privacy of life,
So loving, so beloved; the native of
Another land, and who so blest and blessing
As my poor Foscari? Nothing was wanting
Unto his happiness and mine save not
To be Venetian.

Doge. Or a prince's son.

Mar. Yes; all things which conduce to
other men's
Imperfect happiness or high ambition,
By some strange destiny, to him proved deadly.
The country and the people whom he loved,
The prince of whom he was the elder born,
And ——

Doge. Soon may be a prince no longer.

Mar. How?

Doge. They have taken my son from me,
and now aim
At my too long worn diadem and ring.
Let them resume the gewgaws!

Mar. Oh, the tyrants!
In such an hour too!

Doge. 'Tis the fittest time;
An hour ago I should have felt it.

Mar. And
Will you not now resent it?—Oh, for venge-
ance!
But he, who, had he been enough protected,
Might have repaid protection in this moment,
Cannot assist his father.

Doge. Nor should do so
Against his country, had he a thousand lives
Instead of that——

Mar. They tortured from him. This

May be pure patriotism. I am a woman:
To me my husband and my children were
Country and home. I loved *him*—how I loved
him!
I have seen him pass through such an ordeal as
The old martyrs would have shrunk from: he
is gone,
And I, who would have given my blood for him,
Have nought to give but tears! But could I
compass
The retribution of his wrongs!—Well, well!
I have sons, who shall be men.

Doge. Your grief distracts you.

Mar. I thought I could have borne it, when
I saw him
Bow'd down by such oppression; yes, I
thought
That I would rather look upon his corse
Than his prolong'd captivity:—I am punish'd
For that thought now. Would I were in his
grave!

Doge. I must look on him once more.

Mar. Come with me!

Doge. Is he——

Mar. Our bridal bed is now his bier.

Doge. And he is in his shroud!

Mar. Come, come, old man!

[*Exeunt the* DOGE *and* MARINA.

Enter BARBARIGO *and* LOREDANO.

Mar. (to an Attendant). Where is the Doge?

Att. This instant retired hence,
With the illustrious lady his son's widow.

Lor. Where?

Att. To the chamber where the body lies.

Bar. Let us return, then.

Lor. You forget, you cannot.
We have the implicit order of the Giunta
To await their coming here, and join them in
Their office: they'll be here soon after us.

Bar. And will they press their answer on
the Doge?

Lor. 'Twas his own wish that all should
be done promptly.
He answer'd quickly, and must so be
answer'd;
His dignity is look'd to, his estate
Cared for—what would he more?

Bar. Die in his robes:
He could not have lived long; but I have
done
My best to save his honours, and opposed
This proposition to the last, though vainly.
Why would the general vote compel me
hither?

Lor. 'Twas fit that some one of such
different thoughts
From ours should be a witness, lest false
tongues

Should whisper that a harsh majority
Dreaded to have its acts beheld by others.

 Bar. And not less, I must needs think,
 for the sake
Of humbling me for my vain opposition.
You are ingenious, Loredano, in
Your modes of vengeance, nay, poetical,
A very Ovid in the art of *hating ;*
'T is thus (although a secondary object,
Yet hate his microscopic eyes), to you
I owe by way of foil to the more zealous,
This undesired association in
Your Giunta's duties.

 Lor. How !—*my* Giunta !
 Bar. *Yours !*
They speak your language, watch your nod,
 approve
Your plans, and do your work. Are they not
 yours ?

 Lor. You talk unwarily. 'T were best
 they hear not
This from you.

 Bar. Oh ! they 'll hear as much one day
From louder tongues than mine ; they have
 gone beyond
Even their exorbitance of power : and when
This happens in the most contemn'd and
 abject
States, stung humanity will rise to check it.

 Lor. You talk but idly.
 Bar. That remains for proof.
Here come our colleagues.

 Enter the Deputation as before.

 Chief of the Ten. Is the Duke aware
We seek his presence ?

 Att. He shall be inform'd.
 [*Exit Attendant.*

 Bar. The Duke is with his son.
 Chief of the Ten. If it be so,
We will remit him till the rites are over.
Let us return. 'T is time enough to-morrow.

 Lor. (aside to Bar.) Now the rich man's
 hell-fire upon your tongue,
Unquench'd, unquenchable ! I'll have it torn
From its vile babbling roots, till you shall
 utter
Nothing but sobs through blood, for this !
 Sage signors,
I pray ye be not hasty. [*Aloud to the others.*
 Bar. But be human !
 Lor. See, the Duke comes !

 Enter the DOGE.

 Doge. I have obey'd your summons.
 Chief of the Ten. We come once more to
 urge our past request.
 Doge. And I to answer.
 Chief of the Ten. What ?
 Doge. My only answer.

You have heard it.

 Chief of the Ten. Hear *you* then the last
 decree,
Definitive and absolute !

 Doge. To the point—
To the point ! I know of old the forms of
 office,
And gentle preludes to strong acts.—Go on !

 Chief of the Ten. You are no longer Doge ;
 you are released
From your imperial oath as sovereign ;
Your ducal robes must be put off ; but for
Your services, the state allots the appanage
Already mention'd in our former congress.
Three days are left you to remove from hence,
Under the penalty to see confiscated
All your own private fortune.

 Doge. That last clause,
I am proud to say, would not enrich the
 treasury.

 Chief of the Ten. Your answer, Duke !
 Lor. Your answer, Francis Foscari !
 Doge. If I could have foreseen that my
 old age
Was prejudicial to the state, the chief
Of the republic never would have shown
Himself so far ungrateful, as to place
His own high dignity before his country ;
But this *life* having been so many years
Not useless to that country, I would fain
Have consecrated my last moments to her.
But the decree being render'd, I obey.

 Chief of the Ten. If you would have the
 three days named extended,
We willingly will lengthen them to eight,
As sign of our esteem.

 Doge. Not eight hours, signor,
Nor even eight minutes—there 's the ducal
 ring, [*Taking off his ring and cap.*
And there the ducal diadem. And so
The Adriatic 's free to wed another.

 Chief of the Ten. Yet go not forth so
 quickly.

 Doge. I am old, sir,
And even to move but slowly must begin
To move betimes. Methinks I see amongst
 you
A face I know not.—Senator ! your name,
You, by your garb, Chief of the Forty !

 Mem. Signor,
I am the son of Marco Memmo.

 Doge. Ah !
Your father was my friend.—But *sons* and
 fathers !—
What, ho ! my servants there !

 Atten. My prince !
 Doge. No prince—
There are the princes of the prince ! [*Pointing
 to the Ten's Deputation.*]—Prepare
To part from hence upon the instant.

Chief of the Ten. Why
So rashly? 'twill give scandal.
Doge. Answer that;
 [*To the Ten.*
It is your province.—Sirs, bestir yourselves:
 [*To the Servants.*
There is one burthen which I beg you bear
With care, although 'tis past all further
 harm—
But I will look to that myself.
Bar. He means
The body of his son.
Doge. And call Marina,
My daughter!

 Enter MARINA.

Doge. Get thee ready, we must mourn
Elsewhere.
Mar. And everywhere.
Doge. True; but in freedom,
Without these jealous spies upon the great.
Signors, you may depart: what would you
 more?
We are going: do you fear that we shall bear
The palace with us? Its *old* walls, ten times
As *old* as I am, and I'm very old,
Have served you, so have I, and I and they
Could tell a tale; but I invoke them not
To fall upon you! else they would, as erst
The pillars of stone Dagon's temple on
The Israelite and his Philistine foes.
Such power I do believe there might exist
In such a curse as mine, provoked by such
As you; but I curse not. Adieu, good
 signors!
May the next duke be better than the
 present!
Lor. The *present* duke is Paschal Malipiero.
Doge. Not till I pass the threshold of
 these doors.
Lor. St. Mark's great bell is soon about
 to toll
For his inauguration.
Doge. Earth and heaven!
Ye will reverberate this peal; and I
Live to hear this!—the first Doge who e'er
 heard
Such sound for his successor: happier he,
My attainted predecessor, stern Faliero—
This insult at the least was spared him
Lor. What!
Do you regret a traitor?
Doge. No—I merely
Envy the dead.
 Chief of the Ten. My lord, if you indeed
Are bent upon this rash abandonment
Of the state's palace, at the least retire
By the private staircase, which conducts you
 towards
The landing-place of the canal.

Doge. No. I
Will now descend the stairs by which I
 mounted
To sovereignty—the Giants' Stairs, on whose
Broad eminence I was invested duke.
My services have called me up those steps,
The malice of my foes will drive me down
 them.
There five and thirty years ago was I
Install'd, and traversed these same halls,
 from which
I never thought to be divorced except
A corse—a corse, it might be, fighting for
 them—
But not push'd hence by fellow-citizens.
But come; my son and I will go together—
He to his grave, and I to pray for mine.
 Chief of the Ten. What! thus in public?
Doge. I was publicly
Elected, and so will I be deposed.
Marina! art thou willing?
 Mar. Here's my arm!
 Doge. And here my *staff:* thus propp'd
 will I go forth.
 Chief of the Ten. It must not be—the
 people will perceive it.
 Doge. The people!—There's no people,
 you well know it,
Else you dare not deal thus by them or me.
There is a *populace,* perhaps, whose looks
May shame you; but they dare not groan nor
 curse you,
Save with their hearts and eyes.
 Chief of the Ten. You speak in passion,
Else——
 Doge. You have reason. I have spoken
 much
More than my wont: it is a foible which
Was not of mine, but more excuses you,
Inasmuch as it shows that I approach
A dotage which may justify this deed
Of yours, although the law does not, nor
 will.
Farewell, sirs!
 Bar. You shall not depart without
An escort fitting past and present rank.
We will accompany, with due respect,
The Doge unto his private palace. Say!
My brethren, will we not?
 Different voices. Ay!—Ay!
 Doge. You shall not
Stir—in my train, at least. I enter'd here
As sovereign—I go out as citizen
By the same portals, but as citizen.
All these vain ceremonies are base insults,
Which only ulcerate the heart the more,
Applying poisons there as antidotes.
Pomp is for princes—I am *none!*—That's
 false,
I *am,* but only to these gates.—Ah!

Lor.　　　　　　　　　　　Hark!

[*The great bell of St. Mark's tolls.*

Bar. The bell!

Chief of the Ten.　St. Mark's, which tolls
for the election

Of Malipiero.

Doge.　　Well I recognise

The sound! I heard it once, but once before,

And that is five and thirty years ago;

Even *then* I *was not young.*

Bar.　　　　　Sit down, my lord!

You tremble.

Doge.　　'T is the knell of my poor boy!

My heart aches bitterly.

Bar.　　　　I pray you sit.

Doge.　No; my seat here has been a throne
till now.

Marina! let us go.

Mar.　　　Most readily.

Doge (walks a few steps, then stops).　I feel
athirst—will no one bring me here

A cup of water?

Bar.　　I——

Mar.　　　And I——

Lor.　　　　　And I——

[*The Doge takes a goblet from the hand
of* LOREDANO.

Doge.　I take *yours*, Loredano, from the
hand

Most fit for such an hour as this.

Lor.　　　　　Why so?

Doge.　'T is said that our Venetian crystal
has

Such pure antipathy to poisons as

To burst, if aught of venom touches it.

You bore this goblet, and it is not broken.

Lor.　Well, sir!

Doge.　　Then it is false, or you are true.

For my own part, I credit neither; 't is

An idle legend.

Mar.　　　You talk wildly, and

Had better now be seated, nor as yet

Depart. Ah! now you look as look'd my
husband!

Bar.　He sinks!—support him!—quick—a
chair—support him!

Doge.　The bell tolls on!—let's hence—my
brain's on fire!

Bar.　I do beseech you, lean upon us!

Doge.　　　　　　　　　　No!

A sovereign should die standing. My poor
boy!—

Off with your arms!—*That bell!*

[*The* DOGE *drops down and dies.*

Mar.　　　My God! My God!

Bar. (to Lor.).　Behold! your work's com-
pleted!

Chief of the Ten.　Is there then

No aid? Call in assistance!

Att.　　　　　'T is all over.

Chief of the Ten.　If it be so, at least his
obsequies

Shall be such as befits his name and nation,

His rank and his devotion to the duties

Of the realm, while his age permitted him

To do himself and them full justice. Breth-
ren,

Say, shall it not be so?

Bar.　　　　He has not had

The misery to die a subject where

He reign'd: then let his funeral rites be
princely.

Chief of the Ten.　We are agreed, then?

All, except Lor., answer,　　　　Yes.

Chief of the Ten.　Heaven's peace be with
him!

Mar.　Signors, your pardon: this is mock-
ery.

Juggle no more with that poor remnant,
which,

A moment since, while yet it had a soul,

(A soul by whom you have increased your
empire,

And made your power as proud as was his
glory,)

You banish'd from his palace, and tore down

From his high place, with such relentless
coldness;

And now, when he can neither know these
honours,

Nor would accept them if he could, you,
signors,

Purpose, with idle and superfluous pomp,

To make a pageant over what you trampled.

A princely funeral will be your reproach,

And not his honour.

Chief of the Ten.　Lady, we revoke not

Our purposes so readily.

Mar.　　　　I know it,

As far as touches torturing the living.

I thought the dead had been beyond even
you,

Though (some, no doubt) consign'd to powers
which may

Resemble that you exercise on earth.

Leave him to me; you would have done so for

His dregs of life, which you have kindly
snorten'd:

It is my last of duties, and may prove

A dreary comfort in my desolation.

Grief is fantastical, and loves the dead,

And the apparel of the grave.

Chief of the Ten.　　　　Do you

Pretend still to this office?

Mar.　　　　I do, signor.

Though his possessions have been all con-
sumed

In the state's service, I have still my dowry,

Which shall be consecrated to his rites,

And those of——　[*She stops with agitation.*

Chief of the Ten. Best retain it for your children.

Mar. Ay, they are fatherless, I thank you.

Chief of the Ten. We
Cannot comply with your request. His relics
Shall be exposed with wonted pomp, and follow'd
Unto their home by the new Doge, not clad
As *Doge*, but simply as a senator.

Mar. I have heard of murderers, who have interr'd
Their victims; but ne'er heard, until this hour,
Of so much splendour in hypocrisy
O'er those they slew. I've heard of widows' tears—
Alas! I have shed some—always thanks to you!
I've heard of *heirs* in sables—you have left none
To the deceased, so you would act the part
Of such. Well, sirs, your will be done! as one day,
I trust, Heaven's will be done too!

Chief of the Ten. Know you, lady,
To whom ye speak, and perils of such speech?

Mar. I know the former better than yourselves;
The latter—like yourselves; and can face both.
Wish you more funerals?

Bar. Heed not her rash words;
Her circumstances must excuse her bearing.

Chief of the Ten. We will not note them down.

Bar. (*turning to Lor., who is writing upon his tablets*). What art thou writing,
With such an earnest brow, upon thy tablets?

Lor. (*pointing to the Doge's body.*) That *he* has paid me!

Chief of the Ten. What debt did he owe you?

Lor. A long and just one; Nature's debt and *mine.*

 [*Curtain falls.*

Cain:

A MYSTERY.

<hr>

Now the Serpent was more subtil than any beast of the field which the LORD God had made.—*Gen.* iii. 1.

<hr>

TO

SIR WALTER SCOTT, BART.,

THIS MYSTERY OF CAIN IS INSCRIBED,

BY HIS OBLIGED FRIEND AND FAITHFUL SERVANT,

THE AUTHOR.

<hr>

PREFACE.

THE following scenes are entitled "A Mystery," in conformity with the ancient title annexed to dramas upon similar subjects, which were styled "Mysteries, or Moralities." The author has by no means taken the same liberties with his subject which were common formerly, as may be seen by any reader curious enough to refer to those very profane productions, whether in English, French, Italian, or Spanish. The author has endeavoured to preserve the language adapted to his characters; and where it is (and this is but rarely) taken from actual *Scripture*, he has made as little alteration, even of words, as the rhythm would permit. The reader will recollect that the book of Genesis does not state that Eve was tempted by a demon, but by "the Serpent;" and that only because he was "the most subtil of all the beasts of the field." Whatever interpretation the Rabbins and the Fathers may have put upon this, I take the words as I find them, and reply, with Bishop Watson upon similar occasions, when the Fathers were quoted to him, as Moderator in the schools of Cambridge, "Behold the Book!"—holding up the Scripture. It is to be recollected, that my present subject has nothing to do with the *New Testament*, to which no reference can be here made without anachronism. With the poems upon similar topics I have not been recently familiar. Since I was twenty I have never read Milton; but I had read him so frequently before, that this may make little difference. Gesner's "Death of Abel" I have never read since I was eight years of age, at Aberdeen. The general impression of my recollection is delight; but of the contents I remember only that Cain's wife was called Mahala, and Abel's Thirza; in the following pages I have called them "Adah" and "Zillah," the earliest female names which occur in Genesis; they were those of Lamech's wives: those of Cain and Abel are not called by their names. Whether, then, a coincidence of subject may have caused the same in expression, I know nothing, and care as little.

The reader will please to bear in mind (what few choose to recollect), that there is no allusion to a future state in any of the books of Moses, nor indeed in the Old Testament. For a reason for this extraordinary omission he may consult Warburton's "Divine Legation;" whether satisfactory or not, no better has yet been assigned. I have therefore supposed it new to Cain, without, I hope, any perversion of Holy Writ.

With regard to the language of Lucifer, it was difficult for me to make him talk like a clergyman upon the same subjects; but I have done what I could to restrain him within the bounds of spiritual politeness. If he disclaims having tempted Eve in the shape of the Serpent, it is only because the book of Genesis has not the most distant allusion to anything of the kind, but merely to the Serpent in his serpentine capacity.

Note.—The reader will perceive that the author has partly adopted in this poem the notion of Cuvier, that the world had been destroyed several times before the creation of man. This speculation, derived from the different strata and the bones of enormous and unknown animals found in them, is not contrary to the Mosaic account, but rather confirms it; as no human bones have yet been discovered in those strata, although those of many known animals are found near the remains of the unknown. The assertion of Lucifer, that the pre-Adamite world was also peopled by rational beings much more intelligent than man, and proportionably powerful to the mammoth, &c., &c., is, of course, a poetical fiction to help him to make out his case.

I ought to add, that there is a "tramelogedia' of Alfieri, called "Abele." I have never read that, nor any other of the posthumous works of the writer, except his Life.

RAVENNA, *Sept.* 20, 1821.

CAIN: A MYSTERY.

Dramatis Personæ.

MEN.	WOMEN.
ADAM.	EVE.
CAIN.	ADAH.
ABEL.	ZILLAH.

SPIRITS.

ANGEL OF THE LORD.

LUCIFER.

Act I.

Scene I.—*The Land without Paradise.—
 Time, Sunrise.*

ADAM, EVE, CAIN, ABEL, ADAH, ZILLAH,
 offering a Sacrifice.

Adam. God, the Eternal! Infinite! All-
 wise!—
Who out of darkness on the deep didst make
Light on the waters with a word—all hail!
Jehovah, with returning light, all hail!
 Eve. God! who didst name the day, and
 separate
Morning from night, till then divided never—
Who didst divide the wave from wave, and
 call
Part of thy work the firmament—all hail!
 Abel. God! who didst call the elements
 into
Earth, ocean, air, and fire, and with the day
And night, and worlds which these illuminate,
Or shadow, madest beings to enjoy them,
And love both them and thee—all hail! all
 hail!
 Adah. God, the Eternal! Parent of all
 things!
Who didst create these best and beauteous
 beings,
To be beloved, more than all, save thee—
Let me love thee and them:—All hail! all
 hail!
 Zillah. Oh, God! who loving, making,
 blessing all,
Yet didst permit the serpent to creep in,
And drive my father forth from Paradise,
Keep us from further evil:—Hail! all hail!
 Adam. Son Cain, my first-born, where-
 fore art thou silent?
 Cain. Why should I speak?

Adam. To pray.
Cain. Have ye not pray'd?
Adam. We have, most fervently.
Cain. And loudly: I
Have heard you.
 Adam. So will God, I trust.
 Abel. Amen!
 Adam. But thou, my eldest born, art
 silent still.
 Cain. 'Tis better I should be so.
 Adam. Wherefore so?
 Cain. I have nought to ask.
 Adam. Nor aught to thank for!
 Cain. No.
 Adam. Dost thou not live?
 Cain. Must I not die?
 Eve. Alas!
The fruit of our forbidden tree begins
To fall.
 Adam. And we must gather it again.
Oh, God! why didst thou plant the tree of
 knowledge?
 Cain. And wherefore pluck'd ye not the
 tree of life?
Ye might have then defied him.
 Adam. Oh! my son,
Blaspheme not: these are serpent's words.
 Cain. Why not?
The snake spoke *truth;* it *was* the tree of
 knowledge;
It *was* the tree of life: knowledge is good,
And life is good; and how can both be evil?
 Eve. My boy! thou speakest as I spoke,
 in sin,
Before thy birth: let me not see renew'd
My misery in thine. I have repented.
Let me not see my offspring fall into
The snares beyond the walls of Paradise,
Which e'en in Paradise destroy'd his parents.
Content thee with what *is*. Had we been so,
Thou now hadst been contented.—Oh, my
 son!

Adam. Our orisons completed, let us hence,
Each to his task of toil—not heavy, though
Needful: the earth is young, and yields us kindly
Her fruits with little labour.
Eve. Cain, my son,
Behold thy father cheerful and resign'd,
And do as he doth. [*Exeunt* ADAM *and* EVE.
Zillah. Wilt thou not, my brother?
Abel. Why wilt thou wear this gloom
upon thy brow,
Which can avail thee nothing, save to rouse
The Eternal anger?
Adah. My beloved Cain,
Wilt thou frown even on me?
Cain. No, Adah! no;
I fain would be alone a little while.
Abel, I'm sick at heart; but it will pass;
Precede me, brother—I will follow shortly.
And you, too, sisters, tarry not behind:
Your gentleness must not be harshly met;
I'll follow you anon.
Adah. If not, I will
Return to seek you here.
Abel. The peace of God
Be on your spirit, brother!
 [*Exeunt* ABEL, ZILLAH, *and* ADAH.
Cain (solus). And this is
Life!—Toil! and wherefore should I toil?—
because
My father could not keep his place in Eden.
What had *I* done in this?—I was unborn:
I sought not to be born; nor love the state
To which that birth has brought me. Why
did he
Yield to the serpent and the woman? or,
Yielding, why suffer? What was there in
this?
The tree was planted, and why not for him?
If not, why place him near it, where it grew,
The fairest in the centre? They have but
One answer to all questions, "'Twas *his*
will,
And *he* is good." How know I that? Be-
cause
He is all-powerful, must all-good, too, follow?
I judge but by the fruits—and they are
bitter—
Which I must feed on for a fault not mine.
Whom have we here?—A shape like to the
angels,
Yet of a sterner and a sadder aspect
Of spiritual essence: why do I quake?
Why should I fear him more than other
spirits,
Whom I see daily wave their fiery swords
Before the gates round which I linger oft,
In twilight's hour, to catch a glimpse of those
Gardens which are my just inheritance,

Ere the night closes o'er the inhibited walls
And the immortal trees which overtop
The cherubim-defended battlements?
If I shrink not from these, the fire-arm'd
angels,
Why should I quail from him who now
approaches?
Yet he seems mightier far than them, nor
less
Beauteous, and yet not all as beautiful
As he hath been, and might be: sorrow seems
Half of his immortality. And is it
So? and can aught grieve save humanity?
He cometh.

 Enter LUCIFER.

Lucifer. Mortal!
Cain. Spirit, who art thou?
Lucifer. Master of Spirits.
Cain. And being so, canst thou
Leave them, and walk with dust?
Lucifer. I know the thoughts
Of dust, and feel for it, and with you.
Cain. How!
You know my thoughts?
Lucifer. They are the thoughts of all
Worthy of thought;—'tis your immortal part
Which speaks within you.
Cain. What immortal part?
This has not been reveal'd: the tree of life
Was withheld from us by my father's folly,
While that of knowledge, by my mother's
haste,
Was pluck'd too soon; and all the fruit is
death!
Lucifer. They have deceived thee; thou
shalt live.
Cain. I live,
But live to die; and, living, see no thing
To make death hateful, save an innate cling-
ing,
A loathsome, and yet all invincible
Instinct of life, which I abhor, as I
Despise myself, yet cannot overcome—
And so I live. Would I had never lived!
Lucifer. Thou livest, and must live for
ever: think not
The earth, which is thine outward cov'ring, is
Existence—it will cease, and thou wilt be
No less than thou art now.
Cain. No *less!* and why
No more?
Lucifer. It may be thou shalt be as we.
Cain. And ye?
Lucifer. Are everlasting.
Cain. Are ye happy?
Lucifer. We are mighty.
Cain. Are ye happy?
Lucifer. No: art thou?
Cain. How should I be so? Look on me!

Lucifer. Poor clay!
And thou pretendest to be wretched! Thou!
 Cain. I am:—and thou, with all thy
 might, what art thou?
 Lucifer. One who aspired to be what
 made thee, and
Would not have made thee what thou art.
 Cain. Ah!
Thou look'st almost a god; and——
 Lucifer. I am none:
And having fail'd to be one, would be nought
Save what I am. He conquer'd; let him
 reign!
 Cain. Who?
 Lucifer. Thy sire's Maker, and the earth's.
 Cain. And heaven's,
And all that in them is. So I have heard
His seraphs sing; and so my father saith.
 Lucifer. They say—what they must sing
 and say, on pain
Of being that which I am—and thou art—
Of spirits and of men.
 Cain. And what is that?
 Lucifer. Souls who dare use their im-
 mortality—
Souls who dare look the Omnipotent tyrant
 in
His everlasting face, and tell him that
His evil is not good! If he has made,
As he saith—which I know not, nor believe—
But, if he made us—he cannot unmake:
We are immortal! nay, he'd *have* us so,
That he may torture:—let him! He is great—
But, in his greatness, is no happier than
We in our conflict: Goodness would not
 make
Evil; and what else hath he made? But let
 him
Sit on his vast and solitary throne,
Creating worlds, to make eternity
Less burthensome to his immense existence
And unparticipated solitude;
Let him crowd orb on orb: he is alone
Indefinite, indissoluble tyrant;
Could he but crush himself, 'twere the best
 boon
He ever granted: but let him reign on,
And multiply himself in misery!
Spirits and Men, at least we sympathise—
And, suffering in concert, make our pangs
Innumerable more endurable,
By the unbounded sympathy of all
With all! But *He!* so wretched in his
 height,
So restless in his wretchedness, must still
Create, and re-create——
 Cain. Thou speak'st to me of things
 which long have swum
In visions through my thought: I never
 could

Reconcile what I saw with what I heard.
My father and my mother talk to me
Of serpents, and of fruits and trees: I see
The gates of what they call their Paradise
Guarded by fiery-sworded cherubim,
Which shut them out and me: I feel the
 weight
Of daily toil, and constant thought: I look
Around a world where I seem nothing, with
Thoughts which arise within me, as if they
Could master all things—but I thought alone
This misery was *mine.* My father is
Tamed down; my mother has forgot the
 mind
Which made her thirst for knowledge at the
 risk,
Of an eternal curse; my brother is
A watching shepherd boy, who offers up
The firstlings of the flock to him who bids
The earth yield nothing to us without sweat;
My sister Zillah sings an earlier hymn
Than the birds' matins; and my Adah, my
Own and beloved, she, too, understands not
The mind which overwhelms me: never till
Now met I aught to sympathise with me.
'Tis well—I rather would consort with
 spirits.
 Lucifer. And hadst thou not been fit by
 thine own soul
For such companionship, I would not now
Have stood before thee as I am: a serpent
Had been enough to charm ye, as before.
 Cain. Ah! didst *thou* tempt my mother?
 Lucifer. I tempt none,
Save with the truth: was not the tree the
 tree
Of knowledge? and was not the tree of life
Still fruitful? Did *I* bid her pluck them not?
Did *I* plant things prohibited within
The reach of beings innocent, and curious
By their own innocence? I would have made
 ye
Gods; and even He who thrust ye forth, so
 thrust ye
Because "ye should not eat the fruits of
 life,
And become gods as we." Were those his
 words?
 Cain. They were, as I have heard from
 those who heard them,
In thunder.
 Lucifer. Then who was the demon? He
Who would not let ye live, or he who would
Have made ye live for ever in the joy
And power of knowledge?
 Cain. Would they had snatch'd both
The fruits, or neither!
 Lucifer. One is yours already,
The other may be still.
 Cain. How so?

Lucifer. By being
Yourselves, in your resistance. Nothing can
Quench the mind, if the mind will be itself
And centre of surrounding things—'t is made
To sway.
 Cain. But didst thou tempt my parents?
 Lucifer. I?
Poor clay! what should I tempt them for, or
 how?
 Cain. They say the serpent was a spirit.
 Lucifer. Who
Saith that? It is not written so on high:
The proud One will not so far falsify,
Though man's vast fears and little vanity
Would make him cast upon the spiritual
 nature
His own low failing. The snake *was* the
 snake—
No more; and yet not less than those he
 tempted,
In nature being earth also—*more* in *wisdom*,
Since he could overcome them, and fore-
 knew
The knowledge fatal to their narrow joys.
Think'st thou I'd take the shape of things
 that die?
 Cain. But the thing had a demon?
 Lucifer. He but woke one
In those he spake to with his forky tongue.
I tell thee that the serpent was no more
Than a mere serpent : ask the cherubim
Who guard the tempting tree. When thou-
 sand ages
Have roll'd o'er your dead ashes, and your
 seed's,
The seed of the then world may thus array
Their earliest fault in fable, and attribute
To me a shape I scorn, as I scorn all
That bows to him, who made things but to
 bend
Before his sullen, sole eternity;
But we, who see the truth, must speak it. Thy
Fond parents listen'd to a creeping thing,
And fell. For what should spirits tempt
 them? What
Was there to envy in the narrow bounds
Of Paradise, that spirits who pervade
Space——but I speak to thee of what thou
 know'st not,
With all thy tree of knowledge.
 Cain. But thou canst not
Speak aught of knowledge which I would not
 know,
And do not thirst to know, and bear a mind
To know.
 Lucifer. And heart to look on?
 Cain. Be it proved.
 Lucifer. Darest thou look on Death?
 Cain. He has not yet
Been seen.

 Lucifer. But must be undergone.
 Cain. My father
Says he is something dreadful, and my
 mother
Weeps when he 's named; and Abel lifts his
 eyes
To heaven, and Zillah casts hers to the earth,
And sighs a prayer; and Adah looks on me,
And speaks not.
 Lucifer. And thou?
 Cain. Thoughts unspeakable
Crowd in my breast to burning, when I hear
Of this almighty Death, who is, it seems,
Inevitable. Could I wrestle with him?
I wrestled with the lion, when a boy,
In play, till he ran roaring from my gripe.
 Lucifer. It has no shape; but will absorb
 all things
That bear the form of earth-born being.
 Cain. Ah!
I thought it was a being: who could do
Such evil things to beings save a being?
 Lucifer. Ask the Destroyer.
 Cain. Who?
 Lucifer. The Maker—call him
Which name thou wilt: he makes but to
 destroy.
 Cain. I knew not that, yet thought it, since
 I heard
Of death: although I know not what it is,
Yet it seems horrible. I have look'd out
In the vast desolate night in search of him;
And when I saw gigantic shadows in
The umbrage of the walls of Eden, chequer'd
By the far-flashing of the cherubs' swords,
I watch'd for what I thought his coming: for
With fear rose longing in my heart to know
What 't was which shook us all—but nothing
 came.
And then I turn'd my weary eyes from off
Our native and forbidden Paradise,
Up to the lights above us, in the azure,
Which are so beautiful · shall they, too, die?
 Lucifer. Perhaps—but long outlive both
 thine and thee.
 Cain. I'm glad of that: I would not have
 them die—
They are so lovely. What is death? I fear,
I feel, it is a dreadful thing; but what,
I cannot compass: 't is denounced against us,
Both them who sinn'd and sinn'd not, as an
 ill—
What ill?
 Lucifer. To be resolved into the earth.
 Cain. But shall I know it?
 Lucifer. As I know not death,
I cannot answer.
 Cain. Were I quiet earth,
That were no evil: would I ne'er had been
Aught else but dust!

Lucifer.　　　　That is a grovelling wish,
Less than thy father's, for he wish'd to know.
　Cain. But not to live, or wherefore
　　pluck'd he not
The life-tree?
　Lucifer. He was hinder'd.
　Cain.　　　　　　　　Deadly error!
Not to snatch first that fruit:—but ere he
　　pluck'd
The knowledge, he was ignorant of death.
Alas! I scarcely now know what it is,
And yet I fear it—fear I know not what!
　Lucifer. And I, who know all things, fear
　　nothing; see
What is true knowledge.
　Cain.　　　　Wilt thou teach me all?
　Lucifer. Ay, upon one condition.
　Cain.　　　　　　　　Name it.
　Lucifer.　　　　　　　　That
Thou dost fall down and worship me—thy
　　Lord.
　Cain. Thou art not the Lord my father
　　worships.
　Lucifer. No.
　Cain. His equal?
　Lucifer. No;—I have nought in common
　　with him!
Nor would: I would be aught above—be-
　　neath—
Aught save a sharer or a servant of
His power. I dwell apart; but I am great:—
Many there are who worship me, and more
Who shall—be thou amongst the first.
　Cain.　　　　　　　　I never
As yet have bow'd unto my father's God,
Although my brother Abel oft implores
That I would join with him in sacrifice:—
Why should I bow to thee?
　Lucifer.　　　Hast thou ne'er bow'd
To him?
　Cain. Have I not said it?—need I say it?
Could not thy mighty knowledge teach thee
　　that?
　Lucifer. He who bows not to him has
　　bow'd to me.
　Cain. But I will bend to neither.
　Lucifer.　　　　　　Ne'er the less,
Thou art my worshipper; not worshipping
Him makes thee mine the same.
　Cain.　　　　　And what is that?
　Lucifer. Thou 'lt know here—and here-
　　after.
　Cain.　　　　　　　Let me but
Be taught the mystery of my being.
　Lucifer.　　　　　　Follow
Where I will lead thee.
　Cain.　　　　But I must retire
To till the earth—for I had promised—
　Lucifer.　　　　　　　What?
　Cain. To cull some first-fruits.

　Lucifer.　　　　　　Why?
　Cain.　　　　　　To offer up
With Abel on an altar.
　Lucifer.　　　　Said'st thou not
Thou ne'er hadst bent to him who made
　　thee?
　Cain.　　Yes—
But Abel's earnest prayer has wrought upon
　　me.
The offering is more his than mine—and
　　Adah——
　Lucifer. Why dost thou hesitate?
　Cain.　　　　She is my sister,
Born on the same day, of the same womb;
　　and
She wrung from me, with tears, this promise;
　　and
Rather than see her weep, I would, methinks,
Bear all—and worship aught.
　Lucifer.　　　　　Then follow me!
　Cain. I will.

Enter ADAH.

　Adah. My brother, I have come for thee;
It is our hour of rest and joy—and we
Have less without thee. Thou hast labour'd
　　not
This morn; but I have done thy task: the
　　fruits
Are ripe, and glowing as the light which
　　ripens:
Come away.
　Cain. Seest thou not?
　Adah.　　　　　I see an angel;
We have seen many: will he share our hour
Of rest?—he is welcome.
　Cain.　　　　But he is not like
The angels we have seen.
　Adah.　　　　Are there, then, others?
But he is welcome, as they were: they
　　deign'd
To be our guests—will he?
　Cain (to Lucifer).　　　Wilt thou?
　Lucifer.　　　　　　I ask
Thee to be mine.
　Cain.　　　I must away with him.
　Adah. And leave us?
　Cain.　　　　Ay.
　Adah.　　　　　　And *me?*
　Cain.　　　　　Beloved Adah!
　Adah. Let me go with thee.
　Lucifer.　　　No, she must not.
　Adah.　　　　　　Who
Art thou that steppest between heart and
　　heart?
　Cain. He is a god.
　Adah.　　　How know'st thou?
　Cain.　　　　　He speaks like
A god.
　Adah. So did the serpent, and it lied.

Lucifer. Thou errest, Adah!—was not the tree that
Of knowledge?
Adah. Ay—to our eternal sorrow.
Lucifer. And yet that grief is know-
 ledge—so he lied not:
And if he did betray you, 't was with truth;
And truth in its own essence cannot be
But good.
Adah. But all we know of it has gather'd
Evil on ill; expulsion from our home,
And dread, and toil, and sweat, and heavi-
 ness;
Remorse of that which was—and hope of that
Which cometh not. Cain! walk not with
 this spirit.
Bear with what we have borne, and love
 me—I
Love thee.
Lucifer. More than thy mother, and thy
 sire?
Adah. I do. Is that a sin, too?
Lucifer. No, not yet;
It one day will be in your children.
Adah. What!
Must not my daughter love her brother
 Enoch?
Lucifer. Not as thou lovest Cain.
Adah. Oh, my God!
Shall they not love and bring forth things
 that love
Out of their love? have they not drawn their
 milk
Out of this bosom? was not he, their father,
Born of the same sole womb, in the same
 hour
With me? did we not love each other? and
In multiplying our being multiply
Things which will love each other as we love
Them?—And as I love thee, my Cain! go not
Forth with this spirit; he is not of ours.
Lucifer. The sin I speak of is not of my
 making,
And cannot be a sin in you—whate'er
It seem in those who will replace ye in
Mortality.
Adah. What is the sin which is not
Sin in itself? Can circumstance make sin
Or virtue?—if it doth, we are the slaves
Of——
Lucifer. Higher things than ye are slaves:
 and higher
Than them or ye would be so, did they not
Prefer an independency of torture
To the smooth agonies of adulation,
In hymns and harpings, and self-seeking
 prayers,
To that which is omnipotent, because
It is omnipotent, and not from love,
But terror and self-hope.

Adah. Omnipotence
Must be all goodness.
Lucifer. Was it so in Eden?
Adah. Fiend! tempt me not with beauty;
 thou art fairer
Than was the serpent, and as false.
Lucifer. As true.
Ask Eve, your mother: bears she not the
 knowledge
Of good and evil?
Adah. Oh, my mother! thou
Hast pluck'd a fruit more fatal to thine off-
 spring
Than to thyself; thou at the least hast
 pass'd
Thy youth in Paradise, in innocent
And happy intercourse with happy spirits:
But we, thy children, ignorant of Eden,
Are girt about by demons, who assume
The words of God, and tempt us with our
 own
Dissatisfied and curious thoughts—as thou
Wert work'd on by the snake, in thy most
 flush'd
And heedless, harmless wantonness of bliss.
I cannot answer this immortal thing
Which stands before me; I cannot abhor
 him;
I look upon him with a pleasing fear,
And yet I fly not from him: in his eye
There is a fastening attraction which
Fixes my fluttering eyes on his; my heart
Beats quick; he awes me, and yet draws me
 near,
Nearer and nearer:—Cain—Cain—save me
 from him!
Cain. What dreads my Adah? This is no
 ill spirit.
Adah. He is not God—nor God's: I have
 beheld
The cherubs and the seraphs; he looks not
Like them.
Cain. But there are spirits loftier still—
The archangels.
Lucifer. And still loftier than the
 archangels.
Adah. Ay—but not blessed.
Lucifer. If the blessedness
Consists in slavery—no.
Adah. I have heard it said,
The seraphs *love most*—cherubim *know most*—
And this should be a cherub—since he loves
 not.
Lucifer. And if the higher knowledge
 quenches love,
What must *he be* you cannot love when
 known?
Since the all-knowing cherubim love least,
The seraphs' love can be but ignorance:
That they are not compatible, the doom

Of thy fond parents, for their daring, proves.
Choose betwixt love and knowledge—since
 there is
No other choice: your sire hath chosen
 already:
His worship is but fear.
 Adah. Oh, Cain! choose love.
 Cain. For thee, my Adah, I choose not—
 it was
Born with me—but I love nought else.
 Adah. Our parents?
 Cain. Did they love us when they snatch'd
 from the tree
That which hath driven us all from Paradise?
 Adah. We were not born then—and if we
 had been,
Should we not love them and our children,
 Cain?
 Cain. My little Enoch! and his lisping
 sister!
Could I but deem them happy, I would half
Forget——but it can never be forgotten
Through thrice a thousand generations!
 never
Shall men love the remembrance of the man
Who sow'd the seed of evil and mankind
In the same hour! They pluck'd the tree of
 science
And sin—and, not content with their own
 sorrow,
Begot *me*—*thee*—and all the few that are,
And all the unnumber'd and innumerable
Multitudes, millions, myriads, which may be,
To inherit agonies accumulated
By ages!—and *I* must be sire of such things!
Thy beauty and thy love—my love and joy,
The rapturous moment and the placid hour,
All we love in our children and each other,
But lead them and ourselves through many
 years
Of sin and pain—or few, but still of sorrow,
Intercheck'd with an instant of brief pleasure,
To Death—the unknown! Methinks the tree
 of knowledge
Hath not fulfill'd its promise:—if they sinn'd,
At least they ought to have known all things
 that are
Of knowledge—and the mystery of death.
What do they know?—that they are miserable.
What need of snakes and fruits to teach us
 that?
 Adah. I am not wretched, Cain, and if
 thou
Wert happy——
 Cain. Be thou happy, then, alone—
I will have nought to do with happiness,
Which humbles me and mine.
 Adah. Alone I could not,
Nor *would* be happy; but with those around
 us

I think I could be so, despite of death,
Which, as I know it not, I dread not, though
It seems an awful shadow—if I may
Judge from what I have heard.
 Lucifer. And thou couldst not
Alone, thou say'st, be happy?
 Adah. Alone! Oh, my God!
Who could be happy and alone, or good?
To me my solitude seems sin; unless
When I think how soon I shall see my
 brother,
His brother, and our children, and our
 parents.
 Lucifer. Yet thy God is alone; and is he
 happy,
Lonely, and good?
 Adah. He is not so; he hath
The angels and the mortals to make happy,
And thus becomes so in diffusing joy.
What else can joy be, but the spreading joy?
 Lucifer. Ask of your sire, the exile fresh
 from Eden;
Or of his first-born son: ask your own heart;
It is not tranquil.
 Adah. Alas! no! and you—
Are you of heaven?
 Lucifer. If I am not, inquire
The cause of this all-spreading happiness
(Which you proclaim) of the all-great and
 good
Maker of life and living things; it is
His secret, and he keeps it. *We* must bear,
And some of us resist, and both in vain,
His seraphs say: but it is worth the trial,
Since better may not be without: there is
A wisdom in the spirit, which directs
To right, as in the dim blue air the eye
Of you, young mortals, lights at once upon
The star which watches, welcoming the
 morn.
 Adah. It is a beautiful star; I love it for
Its beauty.
 Lucifer. And why not adore?
 Adah. Our father
Adores the Invisible only.
 Lucifer. But the symbols
Of the Invisible are the loveliest
Of what is visible; and yon bright star
Is leader of the host of heaven.
 Adah. Our father
Saith that he has beheld the God himself
Who made him and our mother.
 Lucifer. Hast *thou* seen him?
 Adah. Yes—in his works.
 Lucifer. But in his being?
 Adah. No—
Save in my father, who is God's own image;
Or in his angels, who are like to thee—
And brighter, yet less beautiful and powerful
In seeming: as the silent sunny noon,

All light, they look upon us; but thou
 seem'st
Like an ethereal night, where long white
 clouds
Streak the deep purple, and unnumber'd
 stars
Spangle the wonderful mysterious vault
With things that look as if they would be
 suns;
So beautiful, unnumber'd, and endearing,
Not dazzling, and yet drawing us to them,
They fill my eyes with tears, and so dost
 thou.
Thou seem'st unhappy: do not make us so,
And I will weep for thee.

Lucifer. Alas! those tears!
Couldst thou but know what oceans will be
 shed—

Adah. By me?

Lucifer. By all.

Adah. What all?

Lucifer. The million millions—
The myriad myriads—the all-peopled earth—
The unpeopled earth—and the o'er-peopled
 hell,
Of which thy bosom is the germ.

Adah. O Cain!
This spirit curseth us.

Cain. Let him say on;
Him will I follow.

Adah. Whither?

Lucifer. To a place
Whence he shall come back to thee in an
 hour;
But in that hour see things of many days.

Adah. How can that be?

Lucifer. Did not your Maker make
Out of old worlds this new one in few days?
And cannot I, who aided in this work,
Show in an hour what he hath made in
 many,
Or hath destroy'd in few?

Cain. Lead on.

Adah. · Will he,
In sooth, return within an hour?

Lucifer. He shall.
With us acts are exempt from time, and we
Can crowd eternity into an hour,
Or stretch an hour into eternity:
We breathe not by a mortal measurement—
But that's a mystery. Cain, come on with
 me.

Adah. Will he return?

Lucifer. Ay, woman! he alone
Of mortals from that place (the first and last
Who shall return, save One), shall come
 back to thee,
To make that silent and expectant world
As populous as this: at present there
Are few inhabitants.

Adah. Where dwellest thou?

Lucifer. Throughout all space. Where
 should I dwell? Where are
Thy God or Gods—there am I: all things are
Divided with me: life and death—and time—
Eternity—and heaven and earth—and that
Which is not heaven nor earth, but peopled
 with
Those who once peopled or shall people
 both—
These are my realms! So that I do divide
His, and possess a kingdom which is not
His. If I were not that which I have said,
Could I stand here? His angels are within
Your vision.

Adah. So they were when the fair serpent
Spoke with our mother first.

Lucifer. Cain! thou hast heard.
If thou dost long for knowledge, I can satiate
That thirst; nor ask thee to partake of fruits
Which shall deprive thee of a single good
The conqueror has left thee. Follow me.

Cain. Spirit, I have said it.

 [*Exeunt* LUCIFER *and* CAIN.

Adah (*follows exclaiming*). Cain! my
 brother! Cain!

——◆◆——

Act II.

Scene I.—*The Abyss of Space.*

Cain. I tread on air, and sink not; yet I
 fear
To sink.

Lucifer. Have faith in me, and thou
 shalt be
Borne on the air, of which I am the prince.

Cain. Can I do so without impiety?

Lucifer. Believe—and sink not! doubt—
 and perish! thus
Would run the edict of the other God,
Who names me demon to his angels; they
Echo the sound to miserable things,
Which, knowing nought beyond their shallow
 senses,
Worship the word which strikes their ear,
 and deem
Evil or good what is proclaim'd to them
In their abasement. I will have none such.
Worship or worship not, thou shalt behold
The worlds beyond thy little world, nor be
Amerced for doubts beyond thy little life,
With torture of *my* dooming. There will
 come
An hour, when, toss'd upon some water-drops,
A man shall say to a man, "Believe in me,
And walk the waters;" and the man shall
 walk

The billows and be safe. *I* will not say,
Believe in *me*, as a conditional creed
To save thee; but fly with me o'er the gulf
Of space an equal flight, and I will show
What thou dar'st not deny,—the history
Of past, and present, and of future worlds.
 Cain. Oh, god, or demon, or whate'er
 thou art,
Is yon our earth?
 Lucifer. Dost thou not recognise
The dust which form'd your father?
 Cain. Can it be?
Yon small blue circle, swinging in far ether,
With an inferior circlet near it still,
Which looks like that which lit our earthly
 night?
Is this our Paradise? Where are its walls,
And they who guard them?
 Lucifer. Point me out the site
Of Paradise.
 Cain. How should I? As we move
Like sunbeams onward, it grows small and
 smaller,
And as it waxes little, and then less,
Gathers a halo round it, like the light
Which shone the roundest of the stars,
 when I
Beheld them from the skirts of Paradise:
Methinks they both, as we recede from them,
Appear to join the innumerable stars
Which are around us; and, as we move on,
Increase their myriads.
 Lucifer. And if there should be
Worlds greater than thine own, inhabited
By greater things, and they themselves far
 more
In number than the dust of thy dull earth,
Though multiplied to animated atoms,
All living, and all doom'd to death, and
 wretched,
What wouldst thou think?
 Cain. I should be proud of thought
Which knew such things.
 Lucifer. But if that high thought were
Link'd to a servile mass of matter, and,
Knowing such things, aspiring to such things,
And science still beyond them, were chain'd
 down
To the most gross and petty paltry wants,
All foul and fulsome, and the very best
Of thine enjoyments a sweet degradation,
A most enervating and filthy cheat
To lure thee on to the renewal of
Fresh souls and bodies, all foredoom'd to be
As frail, and few so happy——
 Cain. Spirit! I
Know nought of death, save as a dreadful
 thing
Of which I have heard my parents speak, as of
A hideous heritage I owe to them

No less than life; a heritage not happy,
If I may judge, till now. But, spirit! if
It be as thou hast said (and I within
Feel the prophetic torture of its truth),
Here let me die: for to give birth to those
Who can but suffer many years, and die,
Methinks is merely propagating death,
And multiplying murder.
 Lucifer. Thou canst not
All die—there is what must survive.
 Cain. The Other
Spake not of this unto my father, when
He shut him forth from Paradise, with death
Written upon his forehead. But at least
Let what is mortal of me perish, that
I may be in the rest as angels are.
 Lucifer. *I* am angelic: wouldst thou be
 as I am?
 Cain. I know not what thou art: I see
 thy power,
And see thou show'st me things beyond *my*
 power,
Beyond all power of my born faculties,
Although inferior still to my desires
And my conceptions.
 Lucifer. What are they which dwell
So humbly in their pride, as to sojourn
With worms in clay?
 Cain. And what art thou who dwellest
So haughtily in spirit, and canst range
Nature and immortality—and yet
Seem'st sorrowful?
 Lucifer. I seem that which I am;
And therefore do I ask of thee, if thou
Wouldst be immortal?
 Cain. Thou hast said, I must be
Immortal in despite of me. I knew not
This until lately—but since it must be,
Let me, or happy or unhappy, learn
To anticipate my immortality.
 Lucifer. Thou didst before I came upon
 thee.
 Cain. How?
 Lucifer. By suffering.
 Cain. And must torture be immortal?
 Lucifer. We and thy sons will try. But
 now, behold!
Is it not glorious?
 Cain. Oh, thou beautiful
And unimaginable ether! and
Ye multiplying masses of increased
And still increasing lights! what are ye?
 what
Is this blue wilderness of interminable
Air, where ye roll along, as I have seen
The leaves along the limpid streams of Eden?
Is your course measured for ye? Or do ye
Sweep on in your unbounded revelry
Through an aërial universe of endless
Expansion—at which my soul aches to think—

Intoxicated with eternity?
Oh God! Oh Gods! or whatso'er ye are!
How beautiful ye are! how beautiful
Your works, or accidents, or whatsoe'er
They may be! Let me die, as atoms die
(If that they die), or know ye in your might
And knowledge! My thoughts are not in this
 hour
Unworthy what I see, though my dust is;
Spirit! let me expire, or see them nearer.
 Lucifer. Art thou not nearer? look back
 to thine earth!
 Cain. Where is it? I see nothing save a
 mass
Of most innumerable lights.
 Lucifer. Look there!
 Cain. I cannot see it.
 Lucifer. Yet it sparkles still.
 Cain. That!—yonder!
 Lucifer. Yea.
 Cain. And wilt thou tell me so?
Why, I have seen the fire-flies and fire-worms
Sprinkle the dusky groves and the green
 banks
In the dim twilight, brighter than yon world
Which bears them.
 Lucifer. Thou hast seen both worms and
 worlds,
Each bright and sparkling—what dost think
 of them?
 Cain. That they are beautiful in their
 own sphere,
And that the night, which makes both
 beautiful,
The little shining fire-fly in its flight,
And the immortal star in its great course,
Must both be guided.
 Lucifer. But by whom or what?
 Cain. Show me.
 Lucifer. Dar'st thou behold?
 Cain. How know I what
I' *dare* behold? As yet, thou hast shown
 nought
I dare not gaze on further.
 Lucifer. On, then, with me.
Wouldst thou behold things mortal or im-
 mortal?
 Cain. Why, what are things?
 Lucifer. *Both* partly: but what doth
Sit next thy heart?
 Cain. The things I see.
 Lucifer. But what
Sate nearest it?
 Cain. The things I have not seen,
Nor ever shall—the mysteries of death.
 Lucifer. What, if I show to thee things
 which have died,
As I have shown thee much which cannot
 die?
 Cain. Do so.

 Lucifer. Away, then! on our mighty wings.
 Cain. Oh! how we cleave the blue! The
 stars fade from us!
The earth! where is my earth? Let me look
 on it,
For I was made of it.
 Lucifer. 'Tis now beyond thee,
Less, in the universe, than thou in it;
Yet deem not that thou canst escape it; thou
Shalt soon return to earth, and all its dust:
'Tis part of thy eternity, and mine.
 Cain. Where dost thou lead me?
 Lucifer. To what was before thee!
The phantasm of the world; of which thy
 world
Is but the wreck.
 Cain. What! is it not then new?
 Lucifer. No more than life is; and that
 was ere thou
Or *I* were, or the things which seem to us
Greater than either: many things will have
No end; and some, which would pretend to
 have
Had no beginning, have had one as mean
As thou; and mightier things have been
 extinct
To make way for much meaner than we can
Surmise; for *moments* only and the *space*
Have been and must be all *unchangeable.*
But changes make not death, except to clay;
But thou art clay—and canst but com-
 prehend
That which was clay, and such thou shalt
 behold.
 Cain. Clay, spirit! what thou wilt, I can
 survey.
 Lucifer. Away, then!
 Cain. But the lights fade from me fast,
And some till now grew larger as we
 approach'd,
And wore the look of worlds.
 Lucifer. And such they are.
 Cain. And Edens in them?
 Lucifer. It may be.
 Cain. And men?
 Lucifer. Yea, or things higher.
 Cain. Ay? and serpents too?
 Lucifer. Wouldst thou have men without
 them? must no reptiles
Breathe, save the erect ones?
 Cain. How the lights recede!
Where fly we?
 Lucifer. To the world of phantoms, which
Are beings past, and shadows still to come.
 Cain. But it grows dark, and dark—the
 stars are gone!
 Lucifer. And yet thou seest.
 Cain. 'Tis a fearful light!
No sun, no moon, no lights innumerable.
The very blue of the empurpled night

Fades to a dreary twilight, yet I see
Huge dusky masses; but unlike the worlds
We were approaching, which, begirt with
 light,
Seem'd full of life even when their atmosphere
Of light gave way, and show'd them taking
 shapes
Unequal, of deep valleys and vast mountains;
And some emitting sparks, and some dis-
 playing
Enormous liquid plains, and some begirt
With luminous belts, and floating moons,
 which took,
Like them, the features of fair earth:—
 instead,
All here seems dark and dreadful.

 Lucifer. But distinct.
Thou seekest to behold death, and dead
 things?

 Cain. I seek it not; but as I know there
 are
Such, and that my sire's sin makes him and
 me,
And all that we inherit, liable
To such, I would behold at once, what I
Must one day see perforce.

 Lucifer. Behold!
 Cain. 'Tis darkness.
 Lucifer. And so it shall be ever; but we
 will
Unfold its gates!

 Cain. Enormous vapours roll
Apart—what's this?

 Lucifer. Enter!
 Cain. Can I return?
 Lucifer. Return! be sure: how else should
 death be peopled?
Its present realm is thin to what it will be
Through thee and thine.

 Cain. The clouds still open wide
And wider, and make widening circles round
 us.

 Lucifer. Advance!
 Cain. And thou!
 Lucifer. Fear not—without me thou
Couldst not have gone beyond thy world.
 On! on!

 [*They disappear through the clouds.*

Scene II.

Hades.

Enter Lucifer *and* Cain.

 Cain. How silent and how vast are these
 dim worlds!
For they seem more than one, and yet more
 peopled
Than the huge brilliant luminous orbs which
 swung

So thickly in the upper air, that I
Had deem'd them rather the bright populace
Of some all unimaginable Heaven,
Than things to be inhabited themselves,
But that on drawing near them I beheld
Their swelling into palpable immensity
Of matter, which seem'd made for life to
 dwell on,
Rather than life itself. But here, all is
So shadowy, and so full of twilight, that
It speaks of a day past.

 Lucifer. It is the realm
Of death.—Wouldst have it present?

 Cain. Till I know
That which it really is, I cannot answer.
But if it be as I have heard my father
Deal out in his long homilies, 'tis a thing—
Oh God! I dare not think on't! Cursed be
He who invented life that leads to death!
Or the dull mass of life, that, being life,
Could not retain, but needs must forfeit it—
Even for the innocent!

 Lucifer. Dost thou curse thy father?
 Cain. Cursed he not me in giving me my
 birth?
Cursed he not me before my birth, in daring
To pluck the fruit forbidden?

 Lucifer. Thou say'st well:
The curse is mutual 'twixt thy sire and thee—
But for thy sons and brother?

 Cain. Let them share it
With me, their sire and brother! What else is
Bequeath'd to me? I leave them my inherit-
 ance.
Oh, ye interminable gloomy realms
Of swimming shadows and enormous shapes,
Some fully shown, some indistinct, and all
Mighty and melancholy—what are ye?
Live ye, or have ye lived?

 Lucifer. Somewhat of both.
 Cain. Then what is death?
 Lucifer. What! Hath not he who made ye
Said 'tis another life?

 Cain. Till now he hath
Said nothing, save that all shall die.

 Lucifer. Perhaps
He one day will unfold that further secret.

 Cain. Happy the day!
 Lucifer. Yes; happy! when unfolded,
Through agonies unspeakable, and clogg'd
With agonies eternal, to innumerable
Yet unborn myriads of unconscious atoms,
All to be animated for this only!

 Cain. What are these mighty phantoms
 which I see
Floating around me?—They wear not the
 form
Of the intelligences I have seen
Round our regretted and unenter'd Eden,
Nor wear the form of man as I have view'd it

In Adam's and in Abel's, and in mine,
Nor in my sister-bride's, nor in my children's:
And yet they have an aspect, which, though not
Of men nor angels, looks like something which,
If not the last, rose higher than the first,
Haughty, and high, and beautiful, and full
Of seeming strength, but of inexplicable
Shape; for I never saw such. They bear not
The wing of seraph, nor the face of man,
Nor form of mightiest brute, nor aught that is
Now breathing; mighty yet and beautiful
As the most beautiful and mighty which
Live, and yet so unlike them, that I scarce
Can call them living.

Lucifer.　　　　　Yet they lived.

Cain.　　　　　　　　Where?

Lucifer.　　　　　　　Where
Thou livest.

Cain.　　　When?

Lucifer.　　On what thou callest earth
They did inhabit.

Cain.　　Adam is the first.

Lucifer. Of thine, I grant thee—but too
　　　mean to be
The last of these.

Cain.　　　And what are they?

Lucifer.　　　　　　　That which
Thou shalt be.

Cain.　　　But what *were* they?

Lucifer.　　　Living, high,
Intelligent, good, great, and glorious things,
As much superior unto all thy sire,
Adam, could e'er have been in Eden, as
The sixty-thousandth generation shall be,
In its dull damp degeneracy, to
Thee and thy son;—and how weak they are,
　　　judge
By thy own flesh.

Cain.　　　Ah me! and did *they* perish?

Lucifer. Yes, from their earth, as thou
　　　wilt fade from thine.

Cain. But was *mine* theirs?

Lucifer.　　　　　It was.

Cain.　　　　　　But not as now.
It is too little and too lowly to
Sustain such creatures.

Lucifer.　　True, it was more glorious.

Cain. And wherefore did it fall?

Lucifer.　　　　　Ask him who fells.

Cain. But how?

Lucifer. By a most crushing and inexorable
Destruction and disorder of the elements,
Which struck a world to chaos, as a chaos
Subsiding has struck out a world: such things,
Though rare in time, are frequent in eternity.—
Pass on, and gaze upon the past.

Cain.　　　　　'Tis awful!

Lucifer. And true. Behold these phantoms!
　　　they were once
Material as thou art.

Cain.　　　　　And must I be
Like them?

Lucifer. Let Him who made thee answer
　　　that.
I show thee what thy predecessors are,
And what they *were* thou feelest, in degree
Inferior as thy petty feelings and
Thy pettier portion of the immortal part
Of high intelligence and earthly strength.
What ye in common have with what they
　　　had
Is life, and what ye *shall* have—death: the
　　　rest
Of your poor attributes is such as suits
Reptiles engender'd out of the subsiding
Slime of a mighty universe, crush'd into
A scarcely-yet shaped planet, peopled with
Things whose enjoyment was to be in blind-
　　　ness—
A Paradise of Ignorance, from which
Knowledge was barr'd as poison. But behold
What these superior beings are or were;
Or, if it irk thee, turn thee back and till
The earth, thy task—I'll waft thee there in
　　　safety.

Cain. No: I'll stay here.

Lucifer.　　　　How long?

Cain.　　　　　　For ever! Since
I must one day return here from the earth,
I rather would remain; I am sick of all
That dust has shown me—let me dwell in
　　　shadows.

Lucifer. It cannot be: thou now behold-
　　　est as
A vision that which is reality.
To make thyself fit for this dwelling, thou
Must pass through what the things thou see'st
　　　have pass'd—
The gates of death.

Cain.　　　By what gate have we enter'd
Even now?

Lucifer. By mine! But, plighted to return,
My spirit buoys thee up to bathe in regions
Where all is breathless save thyself. Gaze on;
But do not think to dwell here till thine hour
Is come.

Cain. And these, too; can they ne'er repass
To earth again?

Lucifer.　　*Their* earth is gone for ever—
So changed by its convulsion, they would not
Be conscious to a single present spot
Of its new scarcely harden'd surface—'t was—
Oh, what a beautiful world it *was!*

Cain.　　　　　And is.
It is not with the earth, though I must till it,
I feel at war, but that I may not profit
By what it bears of beautiful, untoiling,
Nor gratify my thousand swelling thoughts
With knowledge, nor allay my thousand fears
Of death and life.

Lucifer. What thy world is thou see'st,
But canst not comprehend the shadow of
That which it was.
 Cain. And those enormous creatures,
Phantoms inferior in intelligence
(At least so seeming) to the things we have
 pass'd,
Resembling somewhat the wild habitants
Of the deep woods of earth, the hugest which
Roar nightly in the forest, but ten-fold
In magnitude and terror; taller than
The cherub-guarded walls of Eden, with
Eyes flashing like the fiery swords which
 fence them,
And tusks projecting like the trees stripp'd of
Their bark and branches—what were they?
 Lucifer. That which
The Mammoth is in thy world;—but these
 lie
By myriads underneath its surface.
 Cain. But
None on it?
 Lucifer. No: for thy frail race to war
With them would render the curse on it
 useless—
'T would be destroy'd so early.
 Cain. But why *war?*
 Lucifer. You have forgotten the denuncia-
 tion
Which drove your race from Eden—war with
 all things,
And death to all things, and disease to most
 - things,
And pangs, and bitterness; these were the
 fruits
Of the forbidden tree.
 Cain. But animals—
Did they, too, eat of it, that they must die?
 Lucifer. Your Maker told ye, *they* were
 made for you,
As you for him.—You would not have their
 doom
Superior to your own? Had Adam not
Fallen, all had stood.
 Cain. Alas! the hopeless wretches!
They too must share my sire's fate, like his
 sons;
Like them, too, without having shared the
 apple;
Like them, too, without the so dear-bought
 knowledge!
It was a lying tree—for we *know* nothing.
At least it *promised knowledge* at the *price*
Of death—but *knowledge* still: but what *knows*
 man?
 Lucifer. It may be death leads to the
 highest knowledge;
And being of all things the sole thing certain,
At least leads to the *surest* science: therefore
The tree was true, though deadly.

 Cain. These dim realms!
I see them, but I know them not.
 Lucifer. Because
Thy hour is yet afar, and matter cannot
Comprehend spirit wholly—but 't is something
To know there are such realms.
 Cain. We knew already
That there was death.
 Lucifer. But not what was beyond it.
 Cain. Nor know I now.
 Lucifer. Thou knowest that there is
A state, and many states beyond thine own—
And this thou knewest not this morn.
 Cain. But all
Seems dim and shadowy.
 Lucifer. Be content; it will
Seem clearer to thine immortality.
 Cain. And yon immeasurable liquid space
Of glorious azure which floats on beyond us,
Which looks like water, and which I should
 deem
The river which flows out of Paradise
Past my own dwelling, but that it is bankless
And boundless, and of an ethereal hue—
What is it?
 Lucifer. There is still some such on earth,
Although inferior, and thy children shall
Dwell near it—'t is the phantasm of an ocean.
 Cain. 'T is like another world; a liquid
 sun—
And those inordinate creatures sporting o'er
Its shining surface?
 Lucifer. Are its inhabitants,
The past leviathans.
 Cain. And yon immense
Serpent, which rears his dripping mane and
 vasty
Head ten times higher than the haughtiest
 cedar
Forth from the abyss, looking as he could coil
Himself around the orbs we lately look'd
 on—
Is he not of the kind which bask'd beneath
The tree in Eden?
 Lucifer. Eve, thy mother, best
Can tell what shape of serpent tempted her.
 Cain. This seems too terrible. No doubt
 the other
Had more of beauty.
 Lucifer. Hast thou ne'er beheld him?
 Cain. Many of the same kind (at least so
 call'd),
But never that precisely which persuaded
The fatal fruit, nor even of the same aspect.
 Lucifer. Your father saw him not?
 Cain. No: 'twas my mother
Who tempted him—she tempted by the
 serpent.
 Lucifer. Good man! whene'er thy wife, or
 thy sons' wives,

Tempt thee or them to aught that's new or
 strange,
Be sure thou see'st first who hath tempted
 them.
 Cain. Thy precept comes too late: there
 is no more
For serpents to tempt woman to.
 Lucifer. But there
Are some things still which woman may
 tempt man to,
And man tempt woman:—let thy sons look
 to it!
My counsel is a kind one; for 't is even
Given chiefly at my own expense; 't is true,
'T will not be follow'd, so there's little lost.
 Cain. I understand not this.
 Lucifer. The happier thou!—
Thy world and thou are still too young!
 Thou thinkest
Thyself most wicked and unhappy: is it
Not so?
 Cain. For crime, I know not; but for pain,
I have felt much.
 Lucifer. First-born of the first man!
Thy present state of sin, and thou art evil—
Of sorrow, and thou sufferest—are both Eden
In all its innocence compared to what
Thou shortly may'st be; and that state again,
In its redoubled wretchedness, a Paradise
To what thy sons' sons' sons, accumulating
In generations like to dust (which they
In fact but add to), shall endure and do.—
Now let us back to earth!
 Cain. And wherefore didst thou
Lead me here only to inform me this?
 Lucifer. Was not thy quest for know-
 ledge?
 Cain. Yes; as being
The road to happiness.
 Lucifer. If truth be so,
Thou hast it.
 Cain. Then my father's God did well
When he prohibited the fatal tree.
 Lucifer. But had done better in not
 planting it.
But ignorance of evil doth not save
From evil; it must still roll on the same,
A part of all things.
 Cain. Not of all things. No:
I'll not believe it—for I thirst for good.
 Lucifer. And who and what doth not?
 Who covets evil
For its own bitter sake?—*None*—nothing!
 't is
The leaven of all life, and lifelessness.
 Cain. Within those glorious orbs which
 we beheld,
Distant, and dazzling, and innumerable,
Ere we came down into this phantom realm,
Ill cannot come: they are too beautiful.

 Lucifer. Thou hast seen them from afar.
 Cain. And what of that?
Distance can but diminish glory—they,
When nearer, must be more ineffable.
 Lucifer. Approach the things of earth
 most beautiful,
And judge their beauty near.
 Cain. I have done this—
The loveliest thing I know is loveliest
 nearest.
 Lucifer. Then there must be delusion.—
 What is that
Which being nearest to thine eyes is still
More beautiful than beauteous things re-
 mote?
 Cain. My sister Adah.—All the stars of
 heaven,
The deep blue noon of night, lit by an orb
Which looks a spirit, or a spirit's world—
The hues of twilight—the sun's gorgeous
 coming—
His setting indescribable, which fills
My eyes with pleasant tears as I behold
Him sink, and feel my heart float softly with
 him
Along that western paradise of clouds,
The forest shade, the green bough, the bird's
 voice—
The vesper bird's, which seems to sing of
 love,
And mingles with the song of cherubim,
As the day closes over Eden's walls:—
All these are nothing, to my eyes and heart,
Like Adah's face: I turn from earth and
 heaven
To gaze on it.
 Lucifer. 'T is fair as frail mortality,
In the first dawn and bloom of young
 creation,
And earliest embraces of earth's parents,
Can make its offspring; still it is delusion.
 Cain. You think so, being not her brother.
 Lucifer. Mortal!
My brotherhood's with those who have no
 children.
 Cain. Then thou canst have no fellowship
 with us.
 Lucifer. It may be that thine own shall
 be for me.
But if thou dost possess a beautiful
Being beyond all beauty in thine eyes,
Why art thou wretched?
 Cain. Why do I exist?
Why art *thou* wretched? why are all things
 so?
Even he who made us must be, as the maker
Of things unhappy! To produce destruction
Can surely never be the task of joy,
And yet my sire says he's omnipotent:
Then why is evil—he being good? I ask'd

This question of my father; and he said,
Because this evil only was the path
To good. Strange good, that must arise
 from out
Its deadly opposite! I lately saw
A lamb stung by a reptile: the poor suckling
Lay foaming on the earth, beneath the vain
And piteous bleating of its restless dam;
My father pluck'd some herbs, and laid them to
The wound; and by degrees the helpless
 wretch
Resumed its careless life, and rose to drain
The mother's milk, who o'er it tremulous
Stood licking its reviving limbs with joy.
Behold, my son! said Adam, how from evil
Springs good!
 Lucifer. What didst thou answer?
 Cain. Nothing; for
He is my father: but I thought, that 'twere
A better portion for the animal
Never to have been *stung at all,* than to
Purchase renewal of its little life
With agonies unutterable, though
Dispell'd by antidotes.
 Lucifer. But as thou saidst
Of all beloved things thou lovest her
Who shared thy mother's milk, and giveth
 hers
Unto thy children——
 Cain. Most assuredly:
What should I be without her?
 Lucifer. What am I?
 Cain. Dost thou love nothing?
 Lucifer. What does thy God love?
 Cain. All things, my father says; but I
 confess
I see it not in their allotment here.
 Lucifer. And, therefore, thou canst not
 see if *I* love
Or no, except some vast and general purpose,
To which particular things must melt like
 snows.
 Cain. Snows! what are they?
 Lucifer. Be happier in not knowing
What thy remoter offspring must encounter;
But bask beneath the clime which knows no
 winter.
 Cain. But dost thou not love something
 like thyself?
 Lucifer. And dost thou love *thyself?*
 Cain. Yes, but love more
What makes my feelings more endurable,
And is more than myself, because I love it.
 Lucifer. Thou lovest it, because 'tis
 beautiful,
As was the apple in thy mother's eye;
And when it ceases to be so, thy love
Will cease, like any other appetite.
 Cain. Cease to be beautiful! how can
 that be?

 Lucifer. With time.
 Cain. But time has pass'd, and hitherto
Even Adam and my mother both are fair:
Not fair like Adah and the seraphim—
But very fair.
 Lucifer. All that must pass away
In them and her.
 Cain. I'm sorry for it; but
Cannot conceive my love for her the less:
And when her beauty disappears, methinks
He who creates all beauty will lose more
Than me in seeing perish such a work.
 Lucifer. I pity thee who lovest what
 must perish.
 Cain. And I thee who lov'st nothing.
 Lucifer. And thy brother—
Sits he not near thy heart?
 Cain. Why should he not?
 Lucifer. Thy father loves him well—so
 does thy God.
 Cain. And so do I.
 Lucifer. 'Tis well and meekly done.
 Cain. Meekly!
 Lucifer. He is the second born of flesh,
And is his mother's favourite.
 Cain. Let him keep
Her favour, since the serpent was the first
To win it.
 Lucifer. And his father's?
 Cain. What is that
To me? should I not love that which all
 love?
 Lucifer. And the Jehovah—the indulgent
 Lord,
And bounteous planter of barr'd Paradise—
He, too, looks smilingly on Abel.
 Cain. I
Ne'er saw him, and I know not if he smiles.
 Lucifer. But you have seen his angels.
 Cain. Rarely.
 Lucifer. But
Sufficiently to see they love your brother:
His sacrifices are acceptable.
 Cain. So be they! wherefore speak to me
 of this?
 Lucifer. Because thou hast thought of
 this ere now.
 Cain. And if
I *have* thought, why recall a thought that—
 (he pauses, as agitated)—Spirit!
Here we are in *thy* world; speak not of *mine.*
Thou hast shown me wonders: thou hast
 shown me those
Mighty pre-Adamites who walk'd the earth
Of which ours is the wreck: thou hast
 pointed out
Myriads of starry worlds, of which our own
Is the dim and remote companion, in
Infinity of life: thou hast shown me shadows
Of that existence with the dreaded name

Which my sire brought us—Death; thou hast
 shown me much—
But not all: show me where Jehovah dwells,
In his especial Paradise—or *thine:*
Where is it?
 Lucifer. Here, and o'er all space.
 Cain. But ye
Have some allotted dwelling—as all things;
Clay has its earth, and other worlds their
 tenants;
All temporary breathing creatures their
Peculiar element; and things which have
Long ceased to breathe *our* breath, have
 theirs, thou say'st;
And the Jehovah and thyself have thine—
Ye do not dwell together?
 Lucifer. No, we reign
Together; but our dwellings are asunder.
 Cain. Would there were only one of ye!
 perchance
An unity of purpose might make union
In elements which seem now jarr'd in storms.
How came ye, being spirits, wise and infinite,
To separate? Are ye not as brethren in
Your essence, and your nature, and your
 glory?
 Lucifer. Art thou not Abel's brother?
 Cain. We are brethren,
And so we shall remain; but were it not so,
Is spirit like to flesh? can it fall out?
Infinity with Immortality?
Jarring and turning space to misery—
For what?
 Lucifer. To reign.
 Cain. Did ye not tell me that
Ye are both eternal?
 Lucifer. Yea!
 Cain. And what I have seen,
Yon blue immensity, is boundless?
 Lucifer. Ay.
 Cain. And cannot ye both *reign*, then?—
 is there not
Enough?—why should ye differ?
 Lucifer. We *both* reign.
 Cain. But one of you makes evil.
 Lucifer. Which?
 Cain. Thou! for
If thou canst do man good, why dost thou not?
 Lucifer. And why not he who made? *I*
 made ye not;
Ye are *his* creatures, and not mine.
 Cain. Then leave us
His creatures, as thou say'st we are, or show.
 me
Thy dwelling, or his dwelling.
 Lucifer. I could show thee
Both; but the time will come thou shalt see
 one
Of them for evermore.
 Cain. And why not now?

Lucifer. Thy human mind hath scarcely
 grasp to gather
The little I have shown thee into calm
And clear thought; and thou wouldst go on
 aspiring
To the great double mysteries! the *two
 Principles!*
And gaze upon them on their secret thrones!
Dust! limit thy ambition; for to see
Either of these would be for thee to perish!
 Cain. And let me perish, so I see them!
 Lucifer. There
The son of her who snatch'd the apple spake!
But thou wouldst only perish, and not see
 them;
That sight is for the other state.
 Cain. Of death?
 Lucifer. That is the prelude.
 Cain. Then I dread it less,.
Now that I know that it leads to something
 definite.
 Lucifer. And now I will convey thee to
 thy world,
Where thou shalt multiply the race of Adam,
Eat, drink, toil, tremble, laugh, weep, sleep,
 and die.
 Cain. And to what end have I beheld
 these things
Which thou hast shown me?
 Lucifer. Didst thou not require
Knowledge? And have I not, in what I
 show'd,
Taught thee to know thyself?
 Cain. Alas! I seem
Nothing.
 Lucifer. And this should be the human
 sum
Of knowledge, to know mortal nature's
 nothingness;
Bequeath that science to thy children, and
'T will spare them many tortures.
 Cain. Haughty spirit!
Thou speak'st it proudly; but thyself, though
 proud,
Hast a superior.
 Lucifer. No! by heaven, which He
Holds, and the abyss, and the immensity
Of worlds and life, which I hold with him—
 No!
I have a victor—true; but no superior.
Homage he has from all—but none from me:
I battle it against him, as I battled
In highest heaven. Through all eternity,
And the unfathomable gulfs of Hades,
And the interminable realms of space,
And the infinity of endless ages,
All, all, will I dispute! And world by world,
And star by star, and universe by universe,
Shall tremble in the balance, till the great
Conflict shall cease, if ever it shall cease

Which it ne'er shall, till he or I be quench'd !
And what can quench our immortality,
Or mutual and irrevocable hate ?
He as a conqueror will call the conquer'd
Evil ; but what will be the *good* he gives ?
Were I the victor, *his* works would be deem'd
The only evil ones. And you, ye new
And scarce born mortals, what have been his
 gifts
To you already, in your little world ?
 Cain. But few ; and some of those but
 bitter.
 Lucifer. Back
With me, then, to thine earth, and try the
 rest
Of his celestial boons to you and yours.
Evil and good are things in their own essence,
And not made good or evil by the giver ;
But if he gives you good—so call him ; if
Evil springs from *him,* do not name it *mine,*
Till ye know better its true fount ; and judge
Not by words, though of spirits, but the fruits
Of your existence, such as it must be.
One good gift has the fatal apple given—
Your *reason :*—let it not be over-sway'd
By tyrannous threats to force you into faith
'Gainst all external sense and inward feeling :
Think and endure,—and form an inner world
In your own bosom—where the outward fails ;
So shall you nearer be the spiritual
Nature, and war triumphant with your own.
 [*They disappear.*

Act III.

Scene I.—*The Earth, near Eden, as in Act I.*

Enter CAIN *and* ADAH.

Adah. Hush, tread softly, Cain.
Cain. I will ; but wherefore ?
Adah. Our little Enoch sleeps upon yon
 bed
Of leaves, beneath the cypress.
 Cain. Cypress ! 't is
A gloomy tree, which looks as if it mourn'd
O'er what it shadows ; wherefore didst thou
 choose it
For our child's canopy ?
 Adah. Because its branches
Shut out the sun like night, and therefore
 seem'd
Fitting to shadow slumber.
 Cain. Ay, the last—
And longest ; but no matter—lead me to him.
 [*They go up to the child.*
How lovely he appears ! his little cheeks,
In their pure incarnation, vying with
The rose leaves strewn beneath them.

Adah. And his lips, too,
How beautifully parted ! No ; you shall not
Kiss him, at least not now : he will awake
 soon.
His hour of mid-day rest is nearly over ;
But it were pity to disturb him till
'T is closed.
 Cain. You have said well ; I will contain
My heart till then. He smiles, and sleeps !—
 Sleep on,
And smile, thou little, young inheritor
Of a world scarce less young : sleep on, and
 smile !
Thine are the hours and days when both are
 cheering
And innocent ! *thou* hast not pluck'd the
 fruit—
Thou know'st not thou art naked ! Must the
 time
Come thou shalt be amerced for sins unknown,
Which were not thine nor mine ? But now
 sleep on !
His cheeks are reddening into deeper smiles,
And shining lids are trembling o'er his long
Lashes, dark as the cypress which waves o'er
 them ;
Half open, from beneath them the clear blue
Laughs out, although in slumber. He must
 dream—
Of what ? Of Paradise !—Ay ! dream of it,
My disinherited boy ! 'T is but a dream ;
For never more thyself, thy sons, nor fathers,
Shall walk in that forbidden place of joy !
 Adah. Dear Cain ! Nay, do not whisper
 o'er our son
Such melancholy yearnings o'er the past :
Why wilt thou always mourn for Paradise ?
Can we not make another ?
 Cain. Where ?
 Adah. Here, or
Where'er thou wilt : where'er thou art, I feel
 not
The want of this so much regretted Eden.
Have I not thee, our boy, our sire, and
 brother,
And Zillah—our sweet sister, and our Eve,
To whom we owe so much besides our birth ?
 Cain. Yes—death, too, is amongst the
 debts we owe her.
 Adah. Cain ! that proud spirit, who with-
 drew thee hence,
Hath sadden'd thine still deeper. I had hoped
The promised wonders which thou hast be-
 held,
Visions, thou say'st, of past and present
 worlds,
Would have composed thy mind into the calm
Of a contented knowledge ; but I see
Thy guide hath done thee evil : still I thank
 him,

And can forgive him all, that he so soon
Hath given thee back to us.
 Cain. So soon?
 Adah. 'T is scarcely
Two hours since ye departed: two *long* hours
To *me*, but only *hours* upon the sun.
 Cain. And yet I have approach'd that sun,
 and seen
Worlds which he once shone on, and never
 more
Shall light; and worlds he never lit: me-
 thought
Years had roll'd o'er my absence.
 Adah. Hardly hours.
 Cain. The mind then hath capacity of
 time,
And measures it by that which it beholds,
Pleasing or painful; little or almighty.
I had beheld the immemorial works
Of endless beings; skirr'd extinguish'd worlds;
And, gazing on eternity, methought
I had borrow'd more by a few drops of
 ages
From its immensity: but now I feel
My littleness again. Well said the spirit,
That I was nothing!
 Adah. Wherefore said he so?
Jehovah said not that.
 Cain. No: *he* contents him
With making us the *nothing* which we are;
And after flattering dust with glimpses of
Eden and Immortality, resolves
It back to dust again—for what?
 Adah. Thou know'st—
Even for our parents' error.
 Cain. What is that
To us? they sinn'd, then *let them* die?
 Adah. Thou hast not spoken well, nor is
 that thought
Thy own, but of the spirit who was with thee.
Would *I* could die for them, so *they* might
 live!
 Cain. Why, so say I—provided that one
 victim
Might satiate the insatiable of life,
And that our little rosy sleeper there
Might never taste of death nor human sorrow,
Nor hand it down to those who spring from
 him.
 Adah. How know we that some such
 atonement one day
May not redeem our race?
 Cain. By sacrificing
The harmless for the guilty? what atone-
 ment
Were there? why, *we* are innocent: what
 have we
Done, that we must be victims for a deed
Before our birth, or need have victims to
Atone for this mysterious, nameless sin—

If it be such a sin to seek for knowledge?
 Adah. Alas! thou sinnest now, my Cain:
 thy words
Sound impious in mine ears.
 Cain. Then leave me!
 Adah. Never,
Though thy God left thee.
 Cain. Say, what have we here?
 Adah. Two altars, which our brother
 Abel made
During thine absence, whereupon to offer
A sacrifice to God on thy return.
 Cain. And how knew *he*, that *I* would be
 so ready
With the burnt offerings, which he daily
 brings
With a meek brow, whose base humility
Shows more of fear than worship, as a bribe
To the Creator?
 Adah. Surely, 't is well done.
 Cain. One altar may suffice; *I* have no
 offering.
 Adah. The fruits of the earth, the early,
 beautiful
Blossom and bud, and bloom of flowers and
 fruits;
These are a goodly offering to the Lord,
Given with a gentle and a contrite spirit.
 Cain. I have toil'd, and till'd, and sweaten
 in the sun,
According to the curse:—must I do more?
For what should I be gentle? for a war
With all the elements ere they will yield
The bread we eat? For what must I be
 grateful?
For being dust, and grovelling in the dust,
Till I return to dust? If I am nothing—
For nothing shall I be an hypocrite,
And seem well-pleased with pain? For what
 should I
Be contrite? for my father's sin, already
Expiate with what we all have undergone,
And to be more than expiated by
The ages prophesied, upon our seed.
Little deems our young blooming sleeper,
 there,
The germs of an eternal misery
To myriads is within him! better 't were
I snatch'd him in his sleep, and dash'd him
 'gainst
The rocks, than let him live to ——
 Adah. Oh, my God!
Touch not the child—my child! *thy* child!
 Oh, Cain!
 Cain. Fear not! for all the stars, and all
 the power
Which sways them, I would not accost yon
 infant
With ruder greeting than a father's kiss.
 Adah. Then, why so awful in thy speech?

Cain. I said,
'T were better that he ceased to live, than give
Life to so much of sorrow as he must
Endure, and, harder still, bequeath; but since
That saying jars you, let us only say—
'T were better that he never had been born.
 Adah. Oh, do not say so! Where were
 then the joys,
The mother's joys of watching, nourishing,
And loving him? Soft! he awakes. Sweet
 Enoch! [*She goes to the child.*
Oh, Cain! look on him; see how full of life,
Of strength, of bloom, of beauty, and of joy,
How like to me—how like to thee, when
 gentle,
For *then* we are *all* alike; is't not so, Cain?
Mother, and sire, and son, our features are
Reflected in each other; as they are
In the clear waters, when *they* are *gentle*, and
When *thou* art *gentle*. Love us, then, my
 Cain!
And love thyself for our sakes, for we love
 thee.
Look! how he laughs and stretches out his
 arms,
And opens wide his blue eyes upon thine,
To hail his father; while his little form
Flutters as wing'd with joy. Talk not of pain!
The childless cherubs well might envy thee
The pleasures of a parent! Bless him, Cain!
As yet he hath no words to thank thee, but
His heart will, and thine own too.
 Cain. Bless thee, boy!
If that a mortal blessing may avail thee,
To save thee from the serpent's curse!
 Adah. It shall.
Surely a father's blessing may avert
A reptile's subtlety.
 Cain. Of that I doubt;
But bless him ne'er the less.
 Adah. Our brother comes.
 Cain. Thy brother Abel.

Enter ABEL.

 Abel. Welcome, Cain! My brother,
The peace of God be on thee!
 Cain. Abel, hail!
 Abel. Our sister tells me that thou hast
 been wandering,
In high communion with a spirit, far
Beyond our wonted range. Was he of those
We have seen and spoken with, like to our
 father?
 Cain. No.
 Abel. Why then commune with him? he
 may be
A foe to the Most High.
 Cain. And friend to man.
Has the Most High been so—if so you term
 him?

 Abel. Term him! your words are strange
 to-day, my brother.
My sister Adah, leave us for awhile—
We mean to sacrifice.
 Adah. Farewell, my Cain;
But first embrace thy son. May his soft
 spirit,
And Abel's pious ministry, recall thee
To peace and holiness!
 [*Exit* ADAH, *with her child.*
 Abel. Where hast thou been?
 Cain. I know not.
 Abel. Nor what thou hast seen?
 Cain. The dead,
The immortal, the unbounded, the omnipo-
 tent,
The overpowering mysteries of space—
The innumerable worlds that were and are—
A whirlwind of such overwhelming things,
Suns, moons, and earths, upon their loud-
 voiced spheres
Singing in thunder round me, as have made
 me
Unfit for mortal converse: leave me, Abel.
 Abel. Thine eyes are flashing with un-
 natural light—
Thy cheek is flush'd with an unnatural hue—
Thy words are fraught with an unnatural
 sound—
What may this mean?
 Cain. It means——I pray thee, leave
 me.
 Abel. Not till we have pray'd and sacri-
 ficed together.
 Cain. Abel, I pray thee, sacrifice alone—
Jehovah loves thee well.
 Abel. Both well, I hope.
 Cain. But thee the better: I care not for
 that;
Thou art fitter for his worship than I am;
Revere him, then—but let it be alone—
At least, without me.
 Abel. Brother, I should ill
Deserve the name of our great father's son,
If, as my elder, I revered thee not,
And in the worship of our God, call'd not
On thee to join me, and precede me in
Our priesthood—'t is thy place.
 Cain. But I have ne'er
Asserted it.
 Abel. The more my grief; I pray thee
To do so now: thy soul seems labouring in
Some strong delusion; it will calm thee.
 Cain. No;
Nothing can calm me more. *Calm!* say I?
 Never
Knew I what calm was in the soul, although
I have seen the elements still'd. My Abel,
 leave me!
Or let me leave thee to thy pious purpose.

Abel. Neither; we must perform our task
together.
Spurn me not.
 Cain. If it must be so——well, then,
What shall I do?
 Abel. Choose one of those two altars.
 Cain. Choose for me: they to me are so
much turf
And stone.
 Abel. Choose thou!
 Cain. I have chosen.
 Abel. 'Tis is the highest,
And suits thee, as the elder. Now prepare
Thine offerings.
 Cain. Where are thine?
 Abel. Behold them here—
The firstlings of the flock, and fat thereof—
A shepherd's humble offering.
 Cain. I have no flocks;
I am a tiller of the ground, and must
Yield what it yieldeth to my toil—its fruit:
 [*He gathers fruits.*
Behold them in their various bloom and ripe-
ness.
 [*They dress their altars, and kindle a
 flame upon them.*
 Abel. My brother, as the elder, offer first
Thy prayer and thanksgiving with sacrifice.
 Cain. No—I am new to this; lead thou
the way,
And I will follow—as I may.
 Abel (kneeling). Oh, God!
Who made us, and who breathed the breath
of life
Within our nostrils, who hath blessed us,
And spared, despite our father's sin, to make
His children all lost, as they might have been,
Had not thy justice been so temper'd with
The mercy which is thy delight, as to
Accord a pardon like a Paradise,
Compared with our great crimes:—Sole Lord
of light,
Of good, and glory, and eternity!
Without whom all were evil, and with whom
Nothing can err, except to some good end
Of thine omnipotent benevolence—
Inscrutable, but still to be fulfill'd—
Accept from out thy humble first of shep-
herd's
First of the first-born flocks—an offering,
In itself nothing—as what offering can be
Aught unto thee?—but yet accept it for
The thanksgiving of him who spreads it in
The face of thy high heaven, bowing his
own
Even to the dust, of which he is, in honour
Of thee, and of thy name, for evermore!
 Cain (standing erect during this speech).
Spirit! whate'er or whosoe'er thou art,
Omnipotent, it may be—and, if good,

Shown in the exemption of thy deeds from
evil;
Jehovah upon earth! and God in heaven!
And it may be with other names, because
Thine attributes seem many, as thy works:—
If thou must be propitiated with prayers,
Take them! If thou must be induced with
altars,
And soften'd with a sacrifice, receive them!
Two beings here erect them unto thee.
If thou lov'st blood, the shepherd's shrine,
which smokes
On my right hand, hath shed it for thy service
In the first of his flock, whose limbs now reek
In sanguinary incense to thy skies;
Or if the sweet and blooming fruits of earth,
And milder seasons, which the unstain'd turf
I spread them on now offers in the face
Of the broad sun which ripen'd them, may
seem
Good to thee, inasmuch as they have not
Suffer'd in limb or life, and rather form
A sample of thy works, than supplication
To look on ours! If a shrine without victim,
And altar without gore, may win thy favour,
Look on it! and for him who dresseth it,
He is—such as thou mad'st him; and seeks
nothing
Which must be won by kneeling: if he's evil,
Strike him! thou art omnipotent, and
may'st—
For what can he oppose? If he be good,
Strike him, or spare him, as thou wilt! since
all
Rests upon thee; and good and evil seem
To have no power themselves, save in thy
will;
And whether that be good or ill I know not,
Not being omnipotent, nor fit to judge
Omnipotence, but merely to endure
Its mandate; which thus far I have endured.
 [*The fire upon the altar of* ABEL *kindles into
 a column of the brightest flame, and
 ascends to heaven; while a whirlwind
 throws down the altar of* CAIN, *and scat-
 ters the fruits abroad upon the earth.*
 Abel (kneeling). Oh, brother, pray! Jeho-
vah's wroth with thee.
 Cain. Why so?
 Abel. Thy fruits are scatter'd on
the earth.
 Cain. From earth they came, to earth let
them return;
Their seed will bear fresh fruit there ere the
summer:
Thy burnt flesh-off'ring prospers better; see
How heaven licks up the flames, when thick
with blood!
 Abel. Think not upon my offering's accept-
ance,

But make another of thine own before
It is too late.
 Cain. I will build no more altars,
Nor suffer any——
 Abel (*rising*). Cain! what meanest thou?
 Cain. To cast down yon vile flatt'rer of
 the clouds,
The smoky harbinger of thy dull prayers—
Thine altar, with its blood of lambs and
 kids,
Which fed on milk, to be destroy'd in blood.
 Abel (*opposing him*). Thou shalt not:—
 add not impious works to impious
Words! let that altar stand—'tis hallow'd
 now
By the immortal pleasure of Jehovah,
In his acceptance of the victims.
 Cain. *His!*
His pleasure! what was his high pleasure in
The fumes of scorching flesh and smoking
 blood,
To the pain of the bleating mothers, which
Still yearn for their dead offspring? or the
 pangs
Of the sad ignorant victims underneath
Thy pious knife? Give way! this bloody
 record
Shall not stand in the sun, to shame creation!
 Abel. Brother, give back! thou shalt not
 touch my altar
With violence: if that thou wilt adopt it,
To try another sacrifice, 'tis thine.
 Cain. Another sacrifice! Give way, or else
That sacrifice may be——
 Abel. What mean'st thou?
 Cain. Give—
Give way!—thy God loves blood!—then look
 to it:—
Give way, ere he hath *more!*
 Abel. In *his* great name, which
I stand between thee and the shrine which
 hath
Had his acceptance.
 Cain. If thou lov'st thyself,
Stand back till I have strew'd this turf along
Its native soil:—else——
 Abel (*opposing him*). I love God far more
Than life.
 Cain (*striking him with a brand, on the
 temples, which he snatches from the altar*).
 Then take thy life unto thy God,
Since he loves lives.
 Abel (*falls*). What hast thou done, my
 brother?
 Cain. Brother!
 Abel. Oh, God! receive thy servant, and
Forgive his slayer, for he knew not what
He did—Cain, give me—give me thy hand;
 and tell
Poor Zillah—

 Cain (*after a moment's stupefaction*). My
 hand! 't is all red, and with——
What?
 [*A long pause.—Looking slowly round.*
 Where am I? alone! Where's Abel?
 where
Cain? Can it be that I am he? My brother,
Awake!—why liest thou so on the green earth?
'Tis not the hour of slumber;—why so pale?
What, hast thou!—thou wert full of life this
 morn!
Abel! I pray thee, mock me not! I smote
Too fiercely, but not fatally. Ah, why
Wouldst thou oppose me? This is mockery;
And only done to daunt me:—'twas a blow—
And but a blow. Stir—stir—nay, only stir!
Why, so—that's well!—thou breath'st!
 breathe upon me!
Oh, God! Oh, God!
 Abel (*very faintly*). What's he who speaks
 of God?
 Cain. Thy murderer.
 Abel. Then may God forgive him!
 Cain,
Comfort poor Zillah:—she has but one
 brother
Now. [*ABEL dies.*
 Cain. And I none!—Who makes me
 brotherless?
His eyes are open! then he is not dead!
Death is like sleep; and sleep shuts down
 our lids.
His lips, too, are apart; why then he
 breathes;
And yet I feel it not.—His heart!—his heart!
Let me see, doth it beat? methinks——No!
 —no!
This is a vision, else I am become
The native of another and worse world.
The earth swims round me:—what is this?—
 't is wet; [*Puts his hand to his brow,
 and then looks at it.*
And yet there are no dews! 'T is blood—my
 blood—
My brother's and my own! and shed by me!
Then what have I further to do with life,
Since I have taken life from my own flesh?
But he cannot be dead!—Is silence death?
No; he will wake; then let me watch
 by him.
Life cannot be so slight, as to be quench'd
Thus quickly!—he hath spoken to me since—
What shall I say to him?—My brother!—
 No:
He will not answer to that name; for
 brethren
Smite not each other. Yet—yet—speak to
 me.
Oh! for a word more of that gentle voice,
That I may bear to hear my own again!

Enter ZILLAH.

Zillah. I heard a heavy sound; what can
 it be?
'T is Cain; and watching by my husband.
 What
Dost thou there, brother? Doth he sleep?
 Oh, heaven!
What means this paleness, and yon stream?—
 No, no!
It is not blood; for who would shed his
 blood?
Abel! what's this?—who hath done this?
 He moves not;
He breathes not: and his hands drop down
 from mine
With stony lifelessness! Ah! cruel Cain!
Why cam'st thou not in time to save him
 from
This violence? Whatever hath assail'd him,
Thou wert the stronger, and shouldst have
 stepp'd in
Between him and aggression! Father!—
 Eve!—
Adah!—come hither! Death is in the world!
 [*Exit* ZILLAH, *calling on her
 Parents, &c.*

Cain (solus). And who hath brought him
 there?—I—who abhor
The name of Death so deeply, that the
 thought
Empoison'd all my life, before I knew
His aspect—I have led him here, and given
My brother to his cold and still embrace,
As if he would not have asserted his
Inexorable claim without my aid.
I am awake at last—a dreary dream
Had madden'd me;—but *he* shall ne'er
 awake!

Enter ADAM, EVE, ADAH, *and* ZILLAH.

Adam. A voice of woe from Zillah brings
 me here.—
What do I see?—'T is true!—My son!—my
 son!
Woman, behold the serpent's work, and
 thine! [*To* EVE.
Eve. Oh! speak not of it now: the serpent's
 fangs
Are in my heart. My best beloved, Abel!
Jehovah! this is punishment beyond
A mother's sin, to take *him* from me!
Adam. Who,
Or what hath done this deed?—speak, Cain,
 since thou
Wert present; was it some more hostile
 angel,
Who walks not with Jehovah? or some wild
Brute of the forest?

Eve. Ah! a livid light
Breaks through, as from a thunder-cloud!
 yon brand
Massy and bloody! snatch'd from off the
 altar,
And black with smoke, and red with—
Adam. Speak, my son!
Speak, and assure us, wretched as we are,
That we are not more miserable still.
Adah. Speak, Cain! and say it was not
 thou!
Eve. It was.
I see it now—he hangs his guilty head,
And covers his ferocious eye with hands
Incarnadine.
Adah. Mother, thou dost him wrong—
Cain! clear thee from this horrible accusal,
Which grief wrings from our parent.
Eve. Hear, Jehovah!
May the eternal serpent's curse be on him!
For he was fitter for his seed than ours.
May all his days be desolate! May——
Adah. Hold!
Curse him not, mother, for he is thy son—
Curse him not, mother, for he is my brother,
And my betroth'd.
Eve. He hath left thee no brother—
Zillah no husband—me *no son!* for thus
I curse him from my sight for evermore!
All bonds I break between us as he broke
That of his nature, in yon——Oh death!
 death!
Why didst thou not take *me*, who first
 incurr'd thee?
Why dost thou not so now?
Adam. Eve! let not this,
Thy natural grief, lead to impiety!
A heavy doom was long forespoken to us;
And now that it begins, let it be borne
In such sort as may show our God that we
Are faithful servants to his holy will.
Eve (pointing to Cain). His will! the will
 of yon incarnate spirit
Of death, whom I have brought upon the
 earth
To strew it with the dead. May all the
 curses
Of life be on him! and his agonies
Drive him forth o'er the wilderness, like us
From Eden, till his children do by him
As he did by his brother! May the swords
And wings of fiery cherubim pursue him
By day and night—snakes spring up in his
 path—
Earth's fruits be ashes in his mouth—the
 leaves
On which he lays his head to sleep be
 strew'd
With scorpions! May his dreams be of his
 victim!

His waking a continual dread of death!
May the clear rivers turn to blood as he
Stoops down to stain them with his raging
 lip!
May every element shun or change to him!
May he live in the pangs which others die
 with!
And death itself wax something worse than
 death
To him who first acquainted him with man!
Hence, fratricide! henceforth that word is
 Cain,
Through all the coming myriads of mankind,
Who shall abhor thee, though thou wert
 their sire!
May the grass wither from thy feet! the
 woods
Deny thee shelter! earth a home! the dust
A grave! the sun his light! and heaven her
 God! [*Exit* Eve.
 Adam. Cain! get thee forth: we dwell no
 more together.
Depart! and leave the dead to me—I am
Henceforth alone—we never must meet more.
 Adah. Oh, part not with him thus, my
 father: do not
Add thy deep curse to Eve's upon his head!
 Adam. I curse him not: his spirit be his
 curse.
Come, Zillah!
 Zillah. I must watch my husband's
 corse.
 Adam. We will return again, when he is
 gone
Who hath provided for us this dread office.
Come, Zillah!
 Zillah. Yet one kiss on yon pale clay,
And those lips once so warm—my heart! my
 heart!
 [*Exeunt* Adam *and* Zillah, *weeping.*
 Adah. Cain! thou hast heard, we must
 go forth. I am ready,
So shall our children be. I will bear Enoch,
And you his sister. Ere the sun declines
Let us depart, nor walk the wilderness
Under the cloud of night.—Nay, speak to
 me,
To *me—thine own.*
 Cain. Leave me!
 Adah. Why, all have left thee.
 Cain. And wherefore lingerest thou? Dost
 thou not fear
To dwell with one who hath done this?
 Adah. I fear
Nothing except to leave thee, much as I
Shrink from the deed which leaves thee
 brotherless.
I must not speak of this—it is between thee
And the great God.
 A Voice from within exclaims, Cain! Cain!

 Adah. Hear'st thou that voice?
 The Voice within. Cain! Cain!
 Adah. It soundeth like an angel's tone.

Enter the Angel *of the Lord.*

 Angel. Where is thy brother Abel?
 Cain. Am I then
My brother's keeper?
 Angel. Cain! what hast thou done?
The voice of thy slain brother's blood cries
 out,
Even from the ground, unto the Lord!—Now
 art thou
Cursed from the earth, which open'd late her
 mouth
To drink thy brother's blood from thy rash
 hand.
Henceforth, when thou shalt till the ground,
 it shall not
Yield thee her strength; a fugitive shalt thou
Be from this day, and vagabond on earth!
 Adah. This punishment is more than he
 can bear.
Behold, thou driv'st him from the face of
 earth,
And from the face of God shall he be hid.
A fugitive and vagabond on earth,
'Twill come to pass, that whoso findeth him
Shall slay him.
 Cain. Would they could! but who
 are they
Shall slay me? Where are these on the lone
 earth
As yet unpeopled?
 Angel. Thou hast slain thy brother,
And who shall warrant thee against thy son?
 Adah. Angel of Light! be merciful, nor
 say
That this poor aching breast now nourishes
A murderer in my boy, and of his father.
 Angel. Then he would but be what his
 father is.
Did not the milk of Eve give nutriment
To him thou now see'st so besmear'd with
 blood?
The fratricide might well engender parri-
 cides.—
But it shall not be so—the Lord thy God
And mine commandeth me to set his seal
On Cain, so that he may go forth in safety.
Who slayeth Cain, a sevenfold vengeance
 shall
Be taken on his head. Come hither!
 Cain. What
Wouldst thou with me?
 Angel. To mark upon thy brow
Exemption from such deeds as thou hast
 done.
 Cain. No, let me die!

Angel. It must not be.
[*The* ANGEL *sets the mark on* CAIN'S *brow.*
Cain. It burns
My brow, but nought to that which is with-
 in it.
Is there more? let me meet it as I may.
 Angel. Stern hast thou been and stubborn
 from the womb,
As the ground thou must henceforth till;
 but he
Thou slew'st was gentle as the flocks he
 tended.
 Cain. After the fall too soon was I be-
 gotten;
Ere yet my mother's mind subsided from
The serpent, and my sire still mourn'd for
 Eden.
That which I am, I am; I did not seek
For life, nor did I make myself; but could I
With my own death redeem him from the
 dust—
And why not so? let him return to day,
And I lie ghastly! so shall be restored
By God the life to him he loved; and taken
From me a being I ne'er loved to bear.
 Angel. Who shall heal murder? what is
 done, is done;
Go forth! fulfil thy days! and be thy deeds
Unlike the last! [*The* ANGEL *disappears.*
 Adah. He's gone, let us go forth;
I hear our little Enoch cry within
Our bower.
 Cain. Ah! little knows he what he
 weeps for!
And I who have shed blood cannot shed tears!
But the four rivers would not cleanse my soul.
Think'st thou my boy will bear to look on
 me?
 Adah. If I thought that he would not, I
 would——
 Cain (*interrupting her*). No,
No more of threats: we have had too many
 of them:
Go to our children; I will follow thee.
 Adah. I will not leave thee lonely with
 the dead;
Let us depart together.
 Cain. Oh! thou dead
And everlasting witness! whose unsinking
Blood darkens earth and heaven! what thou
 now art
I know not! but if *thou* see'st what *I* am,

I think thou wilt forgive him, whom his God
Can ne'er forgive, nor his own soul.—Fare-
 well!
I must not, dare not touch what I have made
 thee.
I, who sprung from the same womb with
 thee, drain'd
The same breast, clasp'd thee often to my
 own,
In fondness brotherly and boyish, I
Can never meet thee more, nor even dare
To do that for thee, which thou shouldst
 have done
For me—compose thy limbs into their grave—
The first grave yet dug for mortality.
But who hath dug that grave? Oh, earth!
 Oh, earth!
For all the fruits thou hast render'd to me, I
Give thee back this. Now for the wilderness.
 [ADAH *stoops down and kisses the*
 body of ABEL.
 Adah. A dreary, and an early doom, my
 brother,
Has been thy lot! Of all who mourn for
 thee,
I alone must not weep. My office is
Henceforth to dry up tears, and not to shed
 them;
But yet of all who mourn, none mourn like
 me,
Not only for thyself, but him who slew thee.
Now, Cain! I will divide thy burden with
 thee.
 Cain. Eastward from Eden will we take
 our way;
'Tis the most desolate, and suits my steps.
 Adah. Lead! thou shalt be my guide, and
 may our God
Be thine! Now let us carry forth our chil-
 dren.
 Cain. And *he* who lieth there was child-
 less. I
Have dried the fountain of a gentle race,
Which might have graced his recent marriage
 couch,
And might have temper'd this stern blood of
 mine,
Uniting with our children Abel's offspring!
O Abel!
 Adah. Peace be with him!
 Cain. But with *me!*——
 [*Exeunt.*

Heaven and Earth:

A MYSTERY.

FOUNDED ON THE FOLLOWING PASSAGE IN GENESIS, CHAP. VI.: "AND IT CAME TO PASS . . . THAT THE SONS OF GOD SAW THE DAUGHTERS OF MEN THAT THEY WERE FAIR; AND THEY TOOK THEM WIVES OF ALL WHICH THEY CHOSE."

———♦♦———

"And woman wailing for her demon lover."—COLERIDGE.

———♦♦———

Dramatis Personæ.

ANGELS.—SAMIASA.
 AZAZIEL.
 RAPHAEL, THE ARCHANGEL.
MEN.—NOAH AND HIS SONS.
 IRAD.
 JAPHET.

WOMEN.—ANAH.
 AHOLIBAMAH.

Chorus of Spirits of the Earth.—
Chorus of Mortals.

PART I.

Scene I.—*A woody and mountainous district near Mount Ararat. Time, Midnight.*

Enter ANAH and AHOLIBAMAH.

Anah. Our father sleeps: it is the hour when they
Who love us are accustom'd to descend
Through the deep clouds o'er rocky Ararat:—
How my heart beats!
Aho. Let us proceed upon
Our invocation.
Anah. But the stars are hidden.
I tremble.
Aho. So do I, but not with fear
Of aught save their delay.
Anah. My sister, though
I love Azaziel more than——oh, too much!
What was I going to say? my heart grows impious.
Aho. And where is the impiety of loving
Celestial natures?
Anah. But, Aholibamah,
I love our God less since his angel loved me:
This cannot be of good; and though I know not

That I do wrong, I feel a thousand fears
Which are not ominous of right.
Aho. Then wed thee
Unto some son of clay, and toil and spin!
There's Japhet loves thee well, hath loved thee long:
Marry, and bring forth dust!
Anah. I should have loved
Azaziel not less were he mortal; yet
I am glad he is not. I cannot outlive him.
And when I think that his immortal wings
Will one day hover o'er the sepulchre
Of the poor child of clay which so adored him,
As he adores the Highest, death becomes
Less terrible; but yet I pity him:
His grief will be of ages, or at least
Mine would be such for him, were I the seraph,
And he the perishable.
Aho. Rather say,
That he will single forth some other daughter
Of earth, and love her as he once loved Anah.
Anah. And if it should be so, and she loved him,
Better thus than that he should weep for me.
Aho. If I thought thus of Samiasa's love,
All seraph as he is, I'd spurn him from me.
But to our invocation!—'Tis the hour.

Anah. Seraph!
 From thy sphere!
Whatever star contain thy glory;
 In the eternal depths of heaven
 Albeit thou watchest with "the seven,"
Though through space infinite and hoary
 Before thy bright wings worlds be
 driven,
 Yet hear!
Oh! think of her who holds thee dear!
 And though she nothing is to thee,
Yet think that thou art all to her.
 Thou canst not tell,—and never be
 Such pangs decreed to aught save me,—
 The bitterness of tears.
 Eternity is in thine years,
Unborn, undying beauty in thine eyes;
With me thou canst not sympathise,
 Except in love, and there thou must
 Acknowledge that more loving dust
Ne'er wept beneath the skies.
Thou walk'st thy many worlds, thou see'st
 The face of him who made thee great,
As he hath made me of the least
 Of those cast out from Eden's gate;
 Yet, Seraph dear!
 Oh hear!
For thou hast loved me, and I would not
 die
 Until I know what I must die in know-
 ing,
That thou forgett'st in thine eternity
 Her whose heart death could not keep
 from o'erflowing
For thee, immortal essence as thou art!
 Great is their love who love in sin and
 fear;
And such, I feel, are waging in my heart
A war unworthy: to an Adamite
 Forgive, my Seraph! that such
 thoughts appear,
 For sorrow is our element;
 Delight
An Eden kept afar from sight,
 Though sometimes with our visions
 blent.
 The hour is near
Which tells me we are not abandon'd
 quite.—
 Appear! Appear!
 Seraph!
 My own Azaziel! be but here,
And leave the stars to their own light.
Aho. Samiasa!
 Wheresoe'er
Thou rulest in the upper air—
 Or warring with the spirits who may
 dare
 Dispute with him
Who made all empires, empire; or recalling

Some wandering star, which shoots through
 the abyss,
 Whose tenants dying, while their world is
 falling,
Share the dim destiny of clay in this;
 Or joining with the inferior cherubim,
 Thou deignest to partake their hymn—
 Samiasa!
I call thee, I await thee, and I love thee.
 Many may worship thee, that will I not:
If that thy spirit down to mine may move
 thee,
 Descend and share my lot!
 Though I be form'd of clay,
 And thou of beams
More bright than those of day
 On Eden's streams,
 Thine immortality cannot repay
 With love more warm than mine
My love. There is a ray
 In me, which, though forbidden yet to shine,
 I feel was lighted at thy God's and thine.
It may be hidden long: death and decay
 Our mother Eve bequeath'd us—but my
 heart
Defies it: though this life must pass away,
 Is *that* a cause for thee and me to part?
Thou art immortal—so am I: I feel—
 I feel my immortality o'ersweep
All pains, all tears, all time, all fears, and
 peal,
 Like the eternal thunders of the deep,
Into my ears this truth—"Thou liv'st for
 ever!"
 But if it be in joy
I know not, nor would know;
That secret rests with the Almighty giver,
 Who folds in clouds the fonts of bliss and
 woe.
 But thee and me he never can destroy;
 Change us he may, but not o'erwhelm; we
 are
Of as eternal essence, and must war
With him if he will war with us: with *thee*
 I can share all things, even immortal
 sorrow;
For thou hast ventured to share life with
 me,
 And shall *I* shrink from thine eternity?
 No! though the serpent's sting should
 pierce me thorough,
 And thou thyself wert like the serpent, coil
Around me still! and I will smile,
 And curse thee not; but hold
 Thee in as warm a fold
 As——but descend, and prove
 A mortal's love
For an immortal. If the skies contain
More joy than thou canst give and take,
 remain!

Anah. Sister! sister! I view them winging
Their bright way through the parted night.
 Aho. The clouds from off their pinions
flinging,
As though they bore to-morrow's light.
 Anah. But if our father see the sight!
 Aho. He would but deem it was the moon
Rising unto some sorcerer's tune
An hour too soon.
 Anah. They come! *he* comes!—Azaziel!
 Aho. Haste
To meet them! Oh! for wings to bear
My spirit, while they hover there,
To Samiasa's breast!
 Anah. Lo! they have kindled all the west,
Like a returning sunset;—lo!
On Ararat's late secret crest
A mild and many-colour'd bow,
The remnant of their flashing path,
Now shines! and now, behold! it hath
Return'd to night, as rippling foam,
 Which the leviathan hath lash'd
From his unfathomable home,
When sporting on the face of the calm deep,
 Subsides soon after he again hath dash'd
Down, down, to where the ocean's fountains
 sleep.
 Aho. They have touch'd earth! Samiasa!
 Anah. My Azaziel!
 [*Exeunt.*

Scene II.

Enter Irad *and* Japhet.

Irad. Despond not: wherefore wilt thou
 wander thus
To add thy silence to the silent night,
And lift thy tearful eye unto the stars?
They cannot aid thee.
 Japh. But they soothe me—now
Perhaps she looks upon them as I look.
Methinks a being that is beautiful
Becometh more so as it looks on beauty,
The eternal beauty of undying things.
Oh, Anah!
 Irad. But she loves thee not.
 Japh. · Alas!
 Irad. And proud Aholibamah spurns me
 also.
 Japh. I feel for thee too.
 Irad. Let her keep her pride,
Mine hath enabled me to bear her scorn;
It may be, time too will avenge it.
 Japh. Canst thou
Find joy in such a thought?
 Irad. Nor joy nor sorrow.
I loved her well, I would have loved her better,
Had love been met with love: as 't is, I leave
 her
To brighter destinies, if so she deems them.

 Japh. What destinies?
 Irad. I have some cause to think
She loves another.
 Japh. Anah!
 Irad. No; her sister.
 Japh. What other?
 Irad. That I know not; but her air,
If not her words, tells me she loves another.
 Japh. Ay, but not Anah: she but loves her
 God.
 Irad. Whate'er she loveth, so she loves
 thee not,
What can it profit thee?
 Japh. True, nothing; but
I love.
 Irad. And so did I.
 Japh. And now thou lov'st not,
Or think'st thou lov'st not, art thou happier?
 Irad. Yes.
 Japh. I pity thee.
 Irad. Me! why?
 Japh. For being happy,
Deprived of that which makes my misery.
 Irad. I take thy taunt as part of thy
 distemper,
And would not feel as thou dost for more
 shekels
Than all our father's herds would bring, if
 weigh'd
Against the metal of the sons of Cain—
The yellow dust they try to barter with us,
As if such useless and discolour'd trash,
The refuse of the earth, could be received
For milk, and wool, and flesh, and fruits, and
 all
Our flocks and wilderness afford.—Go, Japhet,
Sigh to the stars, as wolves howl to the moon—
I must back to my rest.
 Japh. And so would I
If I could rest.
 Irad. Thou wilt not to our tents then?
 Japh. No, Irad; I will to the cavern, whose
Mouth they say opens from the internal world
To let the inner spirits of the earth
Forth when they walk its surface.
 Irad. Wherefore so?
What wouldst thou there?
 Japh. Soothe further my sad spirit
With gloom as sad: it is a hopeless spot,
And I am hopeless.
 Irad. But 't is dangerous;
Strange sounds and sights have peopled it
 with terrors.
I must go with thee.
 Japh. Irad, no; believe me
I feel no evil thought, and fear no evil.
 Irad. But evil things will be thy foe the
 more
As not being of them: turn thy steps aside,
Or let mine be with thine.

Japh. No, neither, Irad;
I must proceed alone.

Irad. Then peace be with thee!
 [*Exit* Irad.

Japh. (*solus*). Peace! I have sought it
 where it should be found,
In love—with love, too, which perhaps
 deserved it;
And, in its stead, a heaviness of heart,
A weakness of the spirit, listless days,
And nights inexorable to sweet sleep,
Have come upon me. Peace! what peace?
 the calm
Of desolation, and the stillness of
The untrodden forest, only broken by
The sweeping tempest through its groaning
 boughs;
Such is the sullen or the fitful state
Of my mind overworn. The earth's grown
 wicked,
And many signs and portents have proclaim'd
A change at hand, and an o'erwhelming doom
To perishable beings. Oh, my Anah!
When the dread hour denounced shall open
 wide
The fountains of the deep, how mightest thou
Have lain within this bosom, folded from
The elements; this bosom, which in vain
Hath beat for thee, and then will beat more
 vainly,
While thine——Oh, God! at least remit to
 her
Thy wrath! for she is pure amidst the failing
As a star in the clouds, which cannot quench,
Although they obscure it for an hour. My
 Anah!
How would I have adored thee, but thou
 wouldst not;
And still would I redeem thee—see thee live
When ocean is earth's grave, and, unopposed
By rock or shallow, the leviathan,
Lord of the shoreless sea and watery world,
Shall wonder at his boundlessness of realm.
 [*Exit* Japhet.

Enter Noah *and* Shem.

Noah. Where is thy brother Japhet?
Shem. He went forth,
According to his wont, to meet with Irad,
He said; but, as I fear, to bend his steps
Towards Anah's tents, round which he hovers
 nightly,
Like a dove round and round its pillaged nest;
Or else he walks the wild up to the cavern
Which opens to the heart of Ararat.
Noah. What doth he there? It is an evil
 spot
Upon an earth all evil; for things worse
Than even wicked men resort there: he
Still loves this daughter of a fated race,

Although he could not wed her if she loved
 him,
And that she doth not. Oh, the unhappy
 hearts
Of men! that one of my blood, knowing well
The destiny and evil of these days,
And that the hour approacheth, should indulge
In such forbidden yearnings! Lead the way;
He must be sought for!
Shem. Go not forward, father:
I will seek Japhet.
Noah. Do not fear for me:
All evil things are powerless on the man
Selected by Jehovah.—Let us on.
Shem. To the tents of the father of the
 sisters?
Noah. No; to the cavern of the Caucasus.
 [*Exeunt* Noah *and* Shem.

Scene III.

*The mountains.—A cavern, and the rocks of
 Caucasus.*

Japh. (*solus*). Ye wilds, that look eternal;
 and thou cave,
Which seem'st unfathomable; and ye moun-
 tains,
So varied and so terrible in beauty;
Here, in your rugged majesty of rocks
And toppling trees that twine their roots with
 stone
In perpendicular places, where the foot
Of man would tremble, could he reach them
 —yes,
Ye look eternal! Yet, in a few days,
Perhaps even hours, ye will be changed, rent,
 hurl'd
Before the mass of waters; and yon cave,
Which seems to lead into a lower world,
Shall have its depths search'd by the sweep-
 ing wave,
And dolphins gambol in the lion's den!
And man—Oh, men! my fellow-beings! Who
Shall weep above your universal grave,
Save I? Who shall be left to weep? My
 kinsmen,
Alas! what am I better than ye are,
That I must live beyond ye? Where shall be
The pleasant places where I thought of Anah
While I had hope? or the more savage
 haunts,
Scarce less beloved, where I despair'd for her?
And can it be!—Shall yon exulting peak,
Whose glittering top is like a distant star,
Lie low beneath the boiling of the deep?
No more to have the morning sun break forth,
And scatter back the mists in floating folds
From its tremendous brow? no more to have
Day's broad orb drop behind its head at even,
Leaving it with a crown of many hues?

No more to be the beacon of the world,
For angels to alight on, as the spot
Nearest the stars? And can those words "*no
 more*"
Be meant for thee, for all things, save for us,
And the predestined creeping things reserved
By my sire to Jehovah's bidding? May
He preserve *them*, and *I not* have the power
To snatch the loveliest of earth's daughters
 from
A doom which even some serpent, with his
 mate,
Shall 'scape to save his kind to be prolong'd,
To hiss and sting through some emerging world,
Reeking and dank from out the slime, whose
 ooze
Shall slumber o'er the wreck of this, until
The salt morass subside into a sphere
Beneath the sun, and be the monument,
The sole and undistinguish'd sepulchre,
Of yet quick myriads of all life? How much
Breath will be still'd at once! All-beauteous
 world!
So young, so mark'd out for destruction, I
With a cleft heart look on thee day by day,
And night by night, thy number'd days and
 nights.
I cannot save thee, cannot save even her
Whose love had made me love thee more; but
 as
A portion of thy dust, I cannot think
Upon thy coming doom without a feeling
Such as—Oh God! and canst thou—
 [*He pauses.*
*A rushing sound from the cavern is heard,
 and shouts of laughter—afterwards a
 Spirit passes.*
Japh. In the name
Of the Most High, what art thou?
Spirit (*laughs*). Ha! ha! ha!
Japh. By all that earth holds holiest,
 speak!
Spirit (*laughs*). Ha! ha!
Japh. By the approaching deluge! by the
 earth
Which will be strangled by the ocean! by
The deep which will lay open all her foun-
 tains!
The heaven which will convert her clouds to
 seas,
And the Omnipotent who makes and crushes!
Thou unknown, terrible, and indistinct,
Yet awful Thing of Shadows, speak to me!
Why dost thou laugh that horrid laugh?
Spirit. Why weep'st thou?
Japh. For earth and all her children.
Spirit. Ha! ha! ha!
 [*Spirit vanishes.*
Japh. How the fiend mocks the tortures
 of a world,

The coming desolation of an orb,
On which the sun shall rise and warm no life!
How the earth sleeps! and all that in it is
Sleep too upon the very eve of death!
Why should they wake to meet it? What are
 here,
Which look like death in life, and speak like
 things
Born ere this dying world? They come like
 clouds!
 [*Various Spirits pass from the cavern.*
Spirit. Rejoice!
 The abhorred race
Which could not keep in Eden their high place,
 But listen'd to the voice
 Of knowledge without power,
 Are nigh the hour
 Of death!
Not slow, not single, not by sword, nor
 sorrow,
 Nor years, nor heart-break, nor time's
 sapping motion,
Shall they drop off. Behold their last to-
 morrow!
 Earth shall be ocean!
 And no breath,
Save of the winds, be on the unbounded wave!
 Angels shall tire their wings, but find no
 spot:
Not even a rock from out the liquid grave
 Shall lift its point to save,
Or show the place where strong Despair hath
 died,
After long looking o'er the ocean wide
 For the expected ebb which cometh not:
 All shall be void,
 Destroy'd!
Another element shall be the lord
 Of life, and the abhorr'd
Children of dust be quench'd; and of each hue
Of earth nought left but the unbroken blue;
 And of the variegated mountain
 Shall nought remain
 Unchanged, or of the level plain;
 Cedar and pine shall lift their tops in vain:
All merged within the universal fountain,
Man, earth, and fire, shall die,
 And sea and sky
Look vast and lifeless in the eternal eye.
 Upon the foam
 Who shall erect a home?
Japh. (*coming forward*). My sire!
 Earth's seed shall not expire;
 Only the evil shall be put away
 From day.
Avaunt! ye exulting demons of the waste!
 Who howl your hideous joy
When God destroys whom you dare not
 destroy;
 Hence! haste!

Back to your inner caves!
Until the waves
Shall search you in your secret place,
And drive your sullen race
Forth, to be roll'd upon the tossing winds,
In restless wretchedness along all space!
Spirit.　　Son of the saved!
When thou and thine have braved
The wide and warring element;
When the great barrier of the deep is rent,
Shall thou and thine be good or happy?—
No!
Thy new world and new race shall be of
woe—
Less goodly in their aspect, in their years
Less than the glorious giants, who
Yet walk the world in pride,
The Sons of Heaven by many a mortal bride.
Thine shall be nothing of the past, save
tears.
And art thou not ashamed
Thus to survive,
And eat, and drink, and wive?
With a base heart so far subdued and tamed,
As even to hear this wide destruction named,
Without such grief and courage, as should
rather
Bid thee await the world-dissolving wave,
Than seek a shelter with thy favour'd father,
And build thy city o'er the drown'd earth's
grave?
Who would outlive their kind,
Except the base and blind?
Mine
Hateth thine
As of a different order in the sphere,
But not our own.
There is not one who hath not left a throne
Vacant in heaven to dwell in darkness here,
Rather than see his mates endure alone.
Go, wretch! and give
A life like thine to other wretches—live!
And when the annihilating waters roar
Above what they have done,
Envy the giant patriarchs then no more,
And scorn thy sire as the surviving one!
Thyself for being his son!
Chorus of Spirits issuing from the cavern.
Rejoice!
No more the human voice
Shall vex our joys in middle air
With prayer;
No more
Shall they adore;
And we, who ne'er for ages have adored
The prayer-exacting Lord,
To whom the omission of a sacrifice
Is vice;
We, we shall view the deep's salt sources
pour'd

Until one element shall do the work
Of all in chaos; until they,
The creatures proud of their poor clay,
Shall perish, and their bleached bones shall
lurk
In caves, in dens, in clefts of mountains, where
The deep shall follow to their latest lair;
Where even the brutes, in their despair,
Shall cease to prey on man and on each
other,
And the striped tiger shall lie down to die
Beside the lamb, as though he were his
brother;
Till all things shall be as they were,
Silent and uncreated, save the sky:
While a brief truce
Is made with Death, who shall forbear
The little remnant of the past creation,
To generate new nations for his use;
This remnant, floating o'er the undulation
Of the subsiding deluge, from its slime,
When the hot sun hath baked the reeking
soil
Into a world, shall give again to Time
New beings—years, diseases, sorrow,
crime—
With all companionship of hate and toil,
Until——
Japh. (*interrupting them*). The eternal
will
Shall deign to expound this dream
Of good and evil; and redeem
Unto himself all times, all things;
And, gather'd under his almighty
wings,
Abolish hell!
And to the expiated Earth
Restore the beauty of her birth,
Her Eden in an endless paradise,
Where man no more can fall as once he
fell,
And even the very demons shall do well!
Spirits. And when shall take effect this
wondrous spell?
Japh. When the Redeemer cometh; first
in pain,
And then in glory.
Spirit. Meantime still struggle in the
mortal chain,
Till earth wax hoary:
War with yourselves, and hell, and heaven,
in vain,
Until the clouds look gory
With the blood reeking from each battle
plain;
New times, new climes, new arts, new men;
but still,
The same old tears, old crimes, and oldest
ill,

Shall be amongst your race in different forms;
 But the same moral storms
Shall oversweep the future, as the waves
In a few hours the glorious giants' graves.

Chorus of Spirits.

 Brethren, rejoice!
 Mortal, farewell!
Hark! hark! already we can hear the voice
Of growing ocean's gloomy swell;
The winds, too, plume their piercing wings;
The clouds have nearly fill'd their springs;
The fountains of the great deep shall be
 broken,
And heaven set wide her windows; while
 mankind
View, unacknowledged, each tremendous
 token—
 Still, as they were from the beginning,
 blind.
 We hear the sound they cannot hear,
 The mustering thunders of the threaten-
 ing sphere;
 Yet a few hours their coming is
 delay'd;
Their flashing banners, folded still on high,
 Yet undisplay'd,
Save to the Spirit's all-pervading eye.
Howl! howl! oh Earth!
Thy death is nearer than thy recent birth;
Tremble, ye mountains, soon to shrink below
 The ocean's overflow!
The wave shall break upon your cliffs; and
 shells,
 The little shells, of ocean's least things be
Deposed where now the eagle's offspring
 dwells—
 How shall he shriek o'er the remorseless
 sea!
And call his nestlings up with fruitless yell,
Unanswer'd, save by the encroaching swell;—
While man shall long in vain for his broad
 wings,
 The wings which could not save:—
Where could he rest them, while the whole
 space brings
 Nought to his eye beyond the deep, his
 grave?
 Brethren, rejoice!
And loudly lift each superhuman voice—
 All die,
Save the slight remnant of Seth's seed—
 The seed of Seth,
Exempt for future sorrow's sake from
 death.
 But of the sons of Cain
 None shall remain;
 And all his goodly daughters
Must lie beneath the desolating waters;

Or, floating upward, with their long hair laid
Along the wave, the cruel heaven upbraid,
 Which would not spare
 Beings even in death so fair.
 It is decreed,
 All die!
And to the universal human cry
The universal silence shall succeed!
 Fly, brethren, fly!
 But still rejoice!
 We fell!
 They fall!
 So perish all
These petty foes of Heaven who shrink from
 hell!

 [*The Spirits disappear, soaring upwards.*
Japh. (*solus*). God hath proclaim'd the
 destiny of earth;
My father's ark of safety hath announced it;
The very demons shriek it from their caves;
The scroll of Enoch prophesied it long
In silent books, which, in their silence, say
More to the mind than thunder to the ear:
And yet men listen'd not, nor listen; but
Walk darkling to their doom; which, though
 so nigh,
Shakes them no more in their dim disbelief,
Than their last cries shall shake the Almighty
 purpose,
Or deaf obedient ocean, which fulfils it.
No sign yet hangs its banner in the air;
The clouds are few, and of their wonted
 texture;
The sun will rise upon the earth's last day
As on the fourth day of creation, when
God said unto him, "Shine!" and he broke
 forth
Into the dawn, which lighted not the yet
Unform'd forefather of mankind—but roused
Before the human orison the earlier
Made and far sweeter voices of the birds,
Which in the open firmament of heaven
Have wings like angels, and like them salute
Heaven first each day before the Adamites:
Their matins now draw nigh—the east is
 kindling—
And they will sing! and day will break!
 Both near,
So near the awful close! For these must drop
Their outworn pinions on the deep; and day,
After the bright course of a few brief
 morrows,—
Ay, day will rise; but upon what?—a chaos,
Which was ere day; and which, renew'd,
 makes time
Nothing! for, without life, what are the
 hours?
No more to dust than is eternity
Unto Jehovah, who created both.
Without him, even eternity would be

A void: without man, time, as made for man,
Dies with man, and is swallow'd in that deep
Which has no fountain; as his race will be
Devour'd by that which drowns his infant
　　world.—
What have we here? Shapes of both earth
　　and air?
No—*all* of heaven, they are so beautiful.
I cannot trace their features; but their forms,
How lovelily they move along the side
Of the grey mountain, scattering its mist!
And after the swart savage spirits, whose
Infernal immortality pour'd forth
Their impious hymn of triumph, they shall be
Welcome as Eden. It may be they come
To tell me the reprieve of our young world,
For which I have so often pray'd—They
　　come!
Anah! oh, God! and with her——

Enter SAMIASA, AZAZIEL, ANAH, *and*
　　　AHOLIBAMAH.

　Anah.　　　　　　　　　　Japhet!
　Sam.　　　　　　　　　　　Lo!
A son of Adam!
　Aza.　　What doth the earth-born here,
While all his race are slumbering?
　Japh.　　　　　　　　Angel! what
Dost thou on earth when thou shouldst be on
　　high?
　Aza. Know'st thou not, or forgett'st thou,
　　that a part
Of our great function is to guard thine earth?
　Japh. But all good angels have forsaken
　　earth,
Which is condemn'd; nay, even the evil fly
The approaching chaos. Anah! Anah! my
In vain, and long, and still to be, beloved!
Why walk'st thou with this spirit, in those
　　hours
When no good spirit longer lights below?
　Anah. Japhet, I cannot answer thee; yet,
　　yet
Forgive me——
　Japh. May the Heaven, which soon no more
Will pardon, do so! for thou art greatly
　　tempted.
　Aho. Back to thy tents, insulting son of
　　Noah!
We know thee not.
　Japh.　　　The hour may come when thou
May'st know me better; and thy sister know
Me still the same which I have ever been.
　Sam. Son of the patriarch, who hath ever
　　been
Upright before his God, whate'er thy gifts,
And thy words seem of sorrow, mix'd with
　　wrath,
How have Azaziel, or myself, brought on thee
Wrong?

　Japh. Wrong! the greatest of all wrongs;
　　but thou
Say'st well; though she be dust, I did not,
　　could not,
Deserve her. Farewell, Anah! I have said
That word so often! but now say it, ne'er
To be repeated. Angel! or whate'er
Thou art, or must be soon, hast thou the
　　power
To save this beautiful—*these* beautiful
Children of Cain?
　Aza.　　　　From what?
　Japh.　　　　　　　　And is it so,
That ye too know not? Angels! angels! ye
Have shared man's sin, and, it may be, now
　　must
Partake his punishment; or, at the least,
My sorrow.
　Sam.　　Sorrow! I ne'er thought till now
To hear an Adamite speak riddles to me.
　Japh. And hath not the Most High ex-
　　pounded them?
Then ye are lost, as they are lost.
　Aho.　　　　　　　　So be it!
If they love as they are loved, they will not
　　shrink ·
More to be mortal, than I would to dare
An immortality of agonies
With Samiasa!
　Anah.　　　　Sister! sister! speak not
Thus.
　Aza. Fearest thou, my Anah?
　Anah.　　　　　　　　Yes, for thee:
I would resign the greater remnant of
This little life of mine, before one hour
Of thine eternity should know a pang.
　Japh. It is for *him*, then! for the seraph
　　thou
Hast left me! That is nothing, if thou hast not
Left thy God too! for unions like to these,
Between a mortal and an immortal, cannot
Be happy or be hallow'd. We are sent
Upon the earth to toil and die; and they
Are made to minister on high unto
The Highest: but if he can *save* thee, soon
The hour will come in which celestial aid
Alone can do so.
　Anah.　　　　Ah! he speaks of death.
　Sam. Of death to *us!* and those who are
　　with us!
But that the man seems full of sorrow, I
Could smile.
　Japh. I grieve not for myself, nor fear;
I am safe, not for my own deserts, but those
Of a well-doing sire, who hath been found
Righteous enough to save his children. Would
His power was greater of redemption! or
That by exchanging my own life for hers,
Who could alone have made mine happy,
　　she,

The last and loveliest of Cain's race, could
 share
The ark which shall receive a remnant of
The seed of Seth!
 Aho. And dost thou think that we,
With Cain's, the eldest born of Adam's, blood
Warm in our veins,—strong Cain! who was
 begotten
In Paradise,—would mingle with Seth's chil-
 dren?
Seth, the last offspring of old Adam's dotage?
No, not to save all earth, were earth in peril!
Our race hath always dwelt apart from thine
From the beginning, and shall do so ever.
 Japh. I did not speak to thee, Aholibamah!
Too much of the forefather whom thou
 vauntest
Has come down in that haughty blood which
 springs
From him who shed the first, and that a
 brother's!
But thou, my Anah! let me call thee mine,
Albeit thou art not; 't is a word I cannot
Part with, although I must from thee. My
 Anah!
Thou who dost rather make me dream that
 Abel
Had left a daughter, whose pure pious race
Survived in thee, so much unlike thou art
The rest of the stern Cainites, save in beauty,
For all of them are fairest in their favour——
 Aho. (*interrupting him*). And wouldst thou
 have her like our father's foe
In mind, in soul? If *I* partook thy thought,
And dream'd that aught of *Abel* was in *her!*—
Get thee hence, son of Noah; thou makest strife.
 Japh. Offspring of Cain, thy father did so!
 Aho. But
He slew not Seth: and what hast thou to do
With other deeds between his God and him?
 Japh. Thou speakest well: his God hath
 judged him, and
I had not named his deed, but that thyself
Didst seem to glory in him, nor to shrink
From what he had done.
 Aho. He was our fathers' father;
The eldest born of man, the strongest, bravest,
And most enduring:—Shall I blush for him
From whom we had our being? Look upon
Our race; behold their stature and their
 beauty,
Their courage, strength, and length of
 days——
 Japh. They are number'd.
 Aho. Be it so! but while yet their hours
 endure,
I glory in my brethren and our fathers.
 Japh. My sire and race but glory in their
 God,
Anah! and thou?——

 Anah. Whate'er our God decrees,
The God of Seth, as Cain, I must obey,
And will endeavour patiently to obey.
But could I dare to pray in his dread hour
Of universal vengeance (if such should be),
It would not be to live, alone exempt
Of all my house. My sister! oh, my sister!
What were the world, or other worlds, or all
The brightest future, without the sweet past—
Thy love, my father's, all the life, and all
The things which sprang up with me, like the
 stars,
Making my dim existence radiant with
Soft lights which were not mine? Aholibamah!
Oh! if there should be mercy—seek it, find it:
I abhor death, because that thou must die.
 Aho. What, hath this dreamer, with his
 father's ark,
The bugbear he hath built to scare the world,
Shaken *my* sister? Are *we* not the loved
Of seraphs? and if we were not, must we
Cling to a son of Noah for our lives?
Rather than thus——But the enthusiast
 dreams
The worst of dreams, the fantasies engender'd
By hopeless love and heated vigils. Who
Shall shake these solid mountains, this firm
 earth,
And bid those clouds and waters take a shape
Distinct from that which we and all our sires
Have seen them wear on their eternal way?
Who shall do this?
 Japh. He whose one word produced them.
 Aho. Who *heard* that word?
 Japh. The universe, which leap'd
To life before it. Ah! smilest thou still in
 scorn?
Turn to thy seraphs: if they attest it not,
They are none.
 Sam. Aholibamah, own thy God!
 Aho. I have ever hail'd our Maker, Samiasa,
As thine, and mine: a God of love, not sorrow.
 Japh. Alas! what else is love but sorrow?
 Even
He who made earth in love had soon to grieve
Above its first and best inhabitants.
 Aho. 'T is said so.
 Japh. It is even so.

 Enter NOAH *and* SHEM.

 Noah. Japhet! What
Dost thou here with these children of the
 wicked?
Dread'st thou not to partake their coming
 doom?
 Japh. Father, it cannot be a sin to seek
To save an earth-born being; and behold,
These are not of the sinful, since they have
The fellowship of angels.

Noah. These are they, then,
Who leave the throne of God, to take them
 wives
From out the race of Cain; the sons of heaven,
Who seek earth's daughters for their beauty?
 Aza. Patriarch!
Thou hast said it.
 Noah. Woe, woe, woe to such communion!
Has not God made a barrier between earth
And heaven, and limited each, kind to kind?
 Sam. Was not man made in high Jehovah's
 image?
Did God not love what he had made? And
 what
Do we but imitate and emulate
His love unto created love?
 Noah. I am'
But man, and was not made to judge mankind,
Far less the sons of God; but as our God
Has deign'd to commune with me, and reveal
His judgments, I reply, that the descent
Of seraphs from their everlasting seat
Unto a perishable and perishing,
Even on the very *eve* of *perishing,* world,
Cannot be good,
 Aza. What! though it were to save?
 Noah. Not ye in all your glory can redeem
What he who made you glorious hath con-
 demn'd.
Were your immortal mission safety, 't would
Be general, not for two, though beautiful;
And beautiful they are, but not the less
Condemn'd.
 Japh. Oh, father! say it not.
 Noah. Son! son!
If that thou wouldst avoid their doom, forget
That they exist: they soon shall cease to be,
While thou shalt be the sire of a new world,
And better.
 Japh. Let me die with *this,* and *them!*
 Noah. Thou *shouldst* for such a thought,
 but shalt not; he
Who *can,* redeems thee.
 Sam. And why him and thee,
More than what he, thy son, prefers to both?
 Noah. Ask him who made thee greater
 than myself
And mine, but not less subject to his own
Almightiness. And lo! his mildest and
Least to be tempted messenger appears!

 Enter RAPHAEL *the Archangel.*

Raph. Spirits!
 Whose seat is near the throne,
 What do ye here?
Is thus a seraph's duty to be shown
 Now that the hour is near
When earth must be alone?
 Return!
 Adore and burn.

In glorious homage with the elected "seven."
 Your place is heaven.
 Sam. Raphael!
The first and fairest of the sons of God,
 How long hath this been law,
That earth by angels must be left untrod?
 Earth! which oft saw
Jehovah's footsteps not disdain her sod!
 The world he loved, and made
 For love; and oft have we obey'd
His frequent mission with delighted pinions.
 Adoring him in his least works display'd;
Watching this youngest star of his dominions;
 And, as the latest birth of his great word,
 Eager to keep it worthy of our Lord.
 Why is thy brow severe?
And wherefore speak'st thou of destruction
 near?
 Raph. Had Samiasa and Azaziel been
In their true place, with the angelic choir,
 Written in fire
 They would have seen
 Jehovah's late decree,
And not inquired their Maker's breath of me:
 But ignorance must ever be
 A part of sin;
And even the spirits' knowledge shall grow less
 As they wax proud within;
For Blindness is the first-born of Excess.
 When all good angels left the world, ye
 stay'd,
Stung with strange passions, and debased
 By mortal feelings for a mortal maid:
But ye are pardon'd thus far, and replaced
With your pure equals. Hence! away! away!
 Or stay,
 And lose eternity by that delay!
 Aza. And thou! if earth be thus forbidden
 In the decree
 To us until this moment hidden,
 Dost thou not err as we
 In being here?
 Raph. I came to call ye back to your fit
 sphere,
 In the great name and at the word of God.
Dear, dearest in themselves, and scarce less
 dear
 That which I came to do; till now we trod
Together the eternal space; together
 Let us still walk the stars. True, earth
 must die!
Her race, return'd into her womb, must
 wither,
 And much which she inherits: but oh! why
 Cannot this earth be made, or be
 destroy'd,
 Without involving ever some vast void
In the immortal ranks? immortal still
 In their immeasurable forfeiture.
Our brother Satan fell; his burning will

Rather than longer worship dared endure!
　　But ye who still are pure!
Seraphs! less mighty than that mightiest
　　　one,
　　Think how he was undone!
And think if tempting man can compensate
　For heaven desired too late?
　　　　Long have I warr'd,
　　　　Long must I war
　　With him who deem'd it hard
　To be created, and to acknowledge him
　　Who midst the cherubim
Made him as suns to a dependent star,
Leaving the archangels at his right hand
　　　dim.
I loved him—beautiful he was: oh, heaven!
Save *his* who made, what beauty and what
　　power
Was ever like to Satan's! Would the hour
　In which he fell could ever be forgiven!
The wish is impious: but, oh ye!
Yet undestroy'd, be warn'd! Eternity
　　With him, or with his God, is in your
　　　choice:
He hath not tempted you; he cannot tempt
The angels, from his further snares exempt:
　But man hath listen'd to his voice,
And ye to woman's—beautiful she is,
The serpent's voice less subtle than her kiss.
The snake but vanquish'd dust; but she will
　　draw
A second host from heaven, to break heaven's
　　law.
　　　　Yet, yet, oh fly!
　　　　Ye cannot die;
　　　　But they
　　　　Shall pass away,
While ye shall fill with shrieks the upper sky
　For perishable clay,
Whose memory in your immortality
　Shall long outlast the sun which gave them
　　day.
Think how your essence differeth from theirs
In all but suffering! why partake
The agony to which they must be heirs—
Born to be plough'd with years, and sown
　　with cares,
　And reap'd by Death, lord of the human
　　soil?
Even had their days been left to toil their
　　path
Through time to dust, unshorten'd by God's
　　wrath,
　Still they are Evil's prey and Sorrow's
　　spoil.
　Aho.　　　Let them fly!
I hear the voice which says that all must
　　die,
Sooner than our white-bearded patriarchs
　　died;

　　　　And that on high
　　　An ocean is prepared,
　　　　While from below
The deep shall rise to meet heaven's overflow.
　　　Few shall be spared,
It seems; and, of that few, the race of Cain
Must lift their eyes to Adam's God in vain.
　　　Sister! since it is so,
　　　And the eternal Lord
　　　In vain would be implored
For the remission of one hour of woe,
Let us resign even what we have adored,
And meet the wave, as we would meet the
　　sword
If not unmoved, yet undismay'd,
And wailing less for us than those who shall
Survive in mortal or immortal thrall,
　And, when the fatal waters are allay'd,
Weep for the myriads who can weep no
　　more.
Fly, seraphs! to your own eternal shore,
Where winds nor howl nor waters roar.
　　　Our portion is to die,
　　And yours to live for ever:
　But which is best, a dead eternity,
Or living, is but known to the great Giver.
　Obey him, as we shall obey;
　I would not keep this life of mine in clay
　　An hour beyond his will;
Nor see ye lose a portion of his grace,
For all the mercy which Seth's race
　　　　Find still.
　　　　Fly!
　And as your pinions bear ye back to
　　heaven,
Think that my love still mounts with thee on
　　high,
　　　Samiasa!
And if I look up with a tearless eye,
'T is that an angel's bride disdains to weep,—
Farewell! Now rise, inexorable deep!
　Anah.　　　And must we die?
　　　　And must I lose thee too,
　　　Azaziel?
　　Oh, my heart! my heart!
　　　Thy prophecies were true!
　　And yet thou wert so happy too!
The blow, though not unlook'd for, falls as
　　new:
　　　But yet depart!
　　　　Ah! why?
Yet let me not retain thee—fly!
My pangs can be but brief; but thine would
　　be
Eternal, if repulsed from heaven for me.
　　Too much already hast thou deign'd
　　　To one of Adam's race!
Our doom is sorrow: not to us alone,
But to the spirits who have not disdain'd
To love us, cometh anguish with disgrace.

The first who taught us knowledge hath been
　　hurl'd
　　From his once archangelic throne
　　　　Into some unknown world:
　　　　　　And thou, Azaziel! No—
　　　　　　Thou shalt not suffer woe
For me. Away! nor weep!
　　Thou canst not weep; but yet
　　May'st suffer more, not weeping: then
　　　　forget
Her, whom the surges of the all-strangling
　　deep
Can bring no pang like this. Fly! fly!
Being gone, 't will be less difficult to die.
　　Japh.　　Oh, say not so!
　　Father! and thou, archangel, thou!
　　Surely celestial mercy lurks below
　　　　That pure severe serenity of brow:
　　Let them not meet this sea without a
　　　　shore,
　　Save in our ark, or let me be no more!
　　Noah.　Peace, child of passion, peace!
If not within thy heart, yet with thy tongue
　　Do God no wrong!
Live as he wills it—die, when he ordains,
A righteous death, unlike the seed of Cain's.
Cease, or be sorrowful in silence; cease
To weary Heaven's ear with thy selfish
　　plaint.
　　Wouldst thou have God commit a sin for
　　　　thee?
　　　　　　Such would it be
　　　　　　To alter his intent
For a mere mortal sorrow. Be a man!
And bear what Adam's race must bear, and
　　can.
　　Japh.　Ay, father! but when they are gone,
　　　　And we are all alone,
Floating upon the azure desert, and
The depth beneath us hides our own dear
　　land,
　　And dearer, silent friends and brethren, all
　　Buried in its immeasurable breast,
Who, who, our tears, our shrieks, shall then
　　　　command?
　　Can we in desolation's peace have rest?
　　　　Oh God! be thou a God, and spare
　　　　　　Yet while 't is time;
　　Renew not Adam's fall:
　　Mankind were then but twain,
But they are numerous now as are the waves
　　And the tremendous rain,
Whose drops shall be less thick than would
　　　　their graves,
　　Were graves permitted to the seed of Cain.
　　Noah.　Silence, vain boy! each word of
　　　　thine's a crime,
Angel! forgive this stripling's fond despair.
　　Raph.　Seraphs! these mortals speak in
　　　　passion: Ye!

Who are, or should be, passionless and pure,
May now return with me.
　　Sam.　　　　　　It may not be:
We have chosen, and will endure.
　　Raph.　Say'st thou?
　　Aza.　　He hath said it, and I say, Amen!
　　Raph.　　　　Again!
　　　　Then from this hour,
　　　　Shorn as ye are of all celestial power,
　　And aliens from your God,
　　　　　　Farewell!
　　Japh.　　Alas! where shall they dwell?
Hark, hark! Deep sounds, and deeper still,
　　Are howling from the mountain's bosom:
There 's not a breath of wind upon the hill,
　　Yet quivers every leaf, and drops each
　　　　blossom:
Earth groans as if beneath a heavy load.
　　Noah.　Hark, hark! the sea-birds cry!
　　In clouds they overspread the lurid sky,
And hover round the mountain, where before
　　Never a white wing, wetted by the wave,
　　　　Yet dared to soar,
　　Even when the waters wax'd too fierce to
　　　　brave.
　　　　Soon it shall be their only shore,
　　　　　　And then, no more!
　　Japh.　　　　The sun! the sun!
He riseth, but his better light is gone;
　　　　And a black circle, bound
　　　　His glaring disk around,
Proclaims earth's last of summer days hath
　　　　shone!
　　The clouds return into the hues of night,
Save where their brazen-colour'd edges
　　　　streak
The verge where brighter morns were wont
　　　　to break.
　　Noah.　And lo! yon flash of light,
The distant thunder's harbinger, appears!
　　It cometh! hence, away!
Leave to the elements their evil prey!
Hence to where our all-hallow'd ark uprears
　　　　Its safe and wreckless sides!
　　Japh.　　Oh, father, stay!
Leave not my Anah to the swallowing tides!
　　Noah.　Must we not leave all life to such?
　　　　Begone!
　　Japh.　　　　Not I.
　　Noah.　　　　　Then die
　　　　With them!
How darest thou look on that prophetic sky,
And seek to save what all things now
　　　　condemn,
　　　　In overwhelming unison
　　　　　　With just Jehovah's wrath!
　　Japh.　Can rage and justice join in the
　　　　same path?
　　Noah.　Blasphemer! darest thou murmur
　　　　even now?

Raph. Patriarch, be still a father! smooth
 thy brow:
Thy son, despite his folly, shall not sink:
He knows not what he says, yet shall not
 drink
 With sobs the salt foam of the swelling
 waters:
But be, when passion passeth, good as thou,
 Nor perish like heaven's children with
 man's daughters.
 Aho. The tempest cometh; heaven and
 earth unite
 For the annihilation of all life.
 Unequal is the strife
Between our strength and the Eternal Might!
 Sam. But ours is with thee; we will bear
 ye far
To some untroubled star,
Where thou and Anah shalt partake our lot:
 And if thou dost not weep for thy lost
 earth,
Our forfeit heaven shall also be forgot.
 Anah. Oh! my dear father's tents, my
 place of birth,
And mountains, land, and woods! when ye
 are not,
Who shall dry up my tears?
 Aza. Thy spirit-lord.
Fear not; though we are shut from hea-
 ven,
Yet much is ours, whence we cannot be
 driven.
 Raph. Rebel! thy words are wicked, as
 thy deeds
Shall henceforth be but weak: the flaming
 sword,
Which chased the first-born out of Paradise,
Still flashes in the angelic hands.
 Aza. It cannot slay us: threaten dust
 with death,
And talk of weapons unto that which bleeds.
What are thy swords in our immortal eyes?
 Raph. The moment cometh to approve
 thy strength;
 And learn at length
How vain to war with what thy God com-
 mands:
Thy former force was in thy faith.

Enter Mortals, flying for refuge.

Chorus of Mortals.

The heavens and earth are mingling—God!
 oh God!
What have we done? Yet spare!
Hark! even the forest beasts howl forth their
 prayer!
 The dragon crawls from out his den,
 To herd, in terror, innocent with men:

And the birds scream their agony through
 air.
Yet, yet, Jehovah! yet withdraw thy rod
Of wrath, and pity thine own world's despair!
Hear not man only but all nature plead!
 Raph. Farewell, thou earth! ye wretched
 sons of clay,
I cannot, must not, aid you. 'T is decreed!
 [*Exit* RAPHAEL.
 Japh. Some clouds sweep on as vultures
 for their prey,
While others, fix'd as rocks, await the word
At which their wrathful vials shall be pour'd.
No azure more shall robe the firmament,
 Nor spangled stars be glorious: Death
 hath risen:
In the sun's place a pale and ghastly glare
Hath wound itself around the dying air.
 Aza. Come, Anah! quit this chaos-founded
 prison,
To which the elements again repair,
To turn it into what it was: beneath
The shelter of these wings thou shalt be safe,
As was the eagle's nestling once within
Its mother's.—Let the coming chaos chafe
With all its elements! Heed not their din!
A brighter world than this, where thou shalt
 breathe
Ethereal life, will we explore:
These darken'd clouds are not the only skies.
 [AZAZIEL *and* SAMIASA *fly off and dis-*
 appear with ANAH *and* AHOLIBAMAH.
 Japh. They are gone! They have dis-
 appear'd amidst the roar
Of the forsaken world; and never more,
Whether they live, or die with all earth's
 life,
Now near its last, can aught restore
Anah unto these eyes.

Chorus of Mortals.

Oh son of Noah! mercy on thy kind!
What! wilt thou leave us all—all—*all* be-
 hind?
While safe amidst the elemental strife,
Thou sitt'st within thy guarded ark?
 A Mother (offering her infant to JAPHET).
 Oh let this child embark!
I brought him forth in woe,
 But thought it joy
To see him to my bosom clinging so.
 Why was he born?
 What hath he done—
 My unwean'd son?
To move Jehovah's wrath or scorn?
What is there in this milk of mine, that death
 Should stir all heaven and earth up to
 destroy
 My boy.

And roll the waters o'er his placid breath?
Save him, thou seed of Seth!
Or cursed be—with him who made
Thee and thy race, for which we are betray'd!
 Japh. Peace! 'tis no hour for curses, but
 for prayer!

Chorus of Mortals.

For prayer!!!
And where
Shall prayer ascend,
When the swoln clouds unto the mountains
 bend
 And burst,
And gushing oceans every barrier rend,
 Until the very deserts know no thirst?
 Accursed
Be he who made thee and thy sire!
We deem our curses vain; we must expire;
 But as we know the worst,
Why should our hymn be raised, our knees
 be bent
Before the implacable Omnipotent,
Since we must fall the same?
If he hath made earth, let it be his shame,
 To make a world for torture.—Lo! they
 come,
The loathsome waters, in their rage!
And with their roar make wholesome nature
 dumb!
The forests' trees (coeval with the houi
When Paradise upsprung,
 Ere Eve gave Adam knowledge for her
 dower,
Or Adam his first hymn of slavery sung),
 So massy, vast, yet green in their old age,
 Are overtopp'd,
Their summer blossoms by the surges lopp'd,
Which rise, and rise, and rise.
Vainly we look up to the lowering skies—
 They meet the seas,
And shut out God from our beseeching eyes.
 Fly, son of Noah, fly! and take thine ease,
In thine allotted ocean-tent;
And view, all floating o'er the element,
The corpses of the world of thy young days:
 Then to Jehovah raise
 Thy song of praise!
 A Mortal. Blessed are the dead
 Who die in the Lord!
And though the waters be o'er earth out-
 spread,
 Yet, as *his* word,
 Be the decree adored!
He gave me life—he taketh but
 The breath which is his own:
And though these eyes should be for ever shut,

Nor longer this weak voice before his
 throne
Be heard in supplicating tone,
 Still blessed be the Lord,
 For what is past,
 For that which is:
 For all are his,
 From first to last—
Time, space, eternity, life, death—
 The vast known and immeasurable un-
 known.
He made, and can unmake;
And shall *I*, for a little gasp of breath,
 Blaspheme and groan?
No; let me die, as I have lived, in faith,
Nor quiver, though the universe may quake!

Chorus of Mortals.

Where shall we fly?
Not to the mountains high;
For now their torrents rush, with double roar,
 To meet the ocean, which, advancing still,
 Already grasps each drowning hill,
Nor leaves an unsearch'd cave.

Enter a Woman.

Woman. Oh, save me, save!
Our valley is no more:
 My father and my father's tent,
My brethren and my brethren's herds,
 The pleasant trees that o'er our noonday
 bent,
And sent forth evening songs from sweetest
 birds,
The little rivulet which freshen'd all
 Our pastures green,
 No more are to be seen.
When to the mountain cliff I climb'd this
 morn,
 I turn'd to bless the spot,
And not a leaf appear'd about to fall;—
 And now they are not!
Why was I born?
 Japh. To die! in youth to die!
And happier in that doom,
Than to behold the universal tomb,
 Which I
Am thus condemn'd to weep above in vain.
Why, when all perish, why must I remain?
 [*The waters rise; Men fly in every di-
 rection; many are overtaken by the
 waves; the Chorus of Mortals disperses
 in search of safety up the mountains:
 Japhet remains upon a rock, while the
 Ark floats towards him in the distance.*

Werner; or, The Inheritance:

A TRAGEDY.

TO

THE ILLUSTRIOUS GOETHE,

BY ONE OF HIS HUMBLEST ADMIRERS, THIS TRAGEDY IS DEDICATED.

PREFACE.

THE following drama is taken entirely from the "German's Tale, Kruitzner," published many years ago in "Lee's Canterbury Tales," written (I believe) by two sisters, of whom one furnished only this story and another, both of which are considered superior to the remainder of the collection. I have adopted the characters, plan, and even the language of many parts of this story. Some of the characters are modified or altered, a few of the names changed, and one character (Ida of Stralenheim) added by myself: but in the rest the original is chiefly followed. When I was young (about fourteen, I think), I first read this tale, which made a deep impression upon me; and may, indeed, be said to contain the germ of much that I have since written. I am not sure that it ever was very popular; or, at any rate, its popularity has since been eclipsed by that of other great writers in the same department. But I have generally found that those who *had* read it, agreed with me in their estimate of the singular power of mind and conception which it developes. I should also add *conception*, rather than execution; for the story might, perhaps, have been developed with greater advantage. Amongst those whose opinions agreed with mine upon this story, I could mention some very high names: but it is not necessary, nor indeed of any use; for every one must judge according to his own feelings. I merely refer the reader to the original story, that he may see to what extent I have borrowed from it; and am not unwilling that he should find much greater pleasure in perusing it than the drama which is founded upon its contents.

I had begun a drama upon this tale so far back as 1815 (the first I ever attempted, except one at thirteen years old, called "Ulric and Ilvina," which I had sense enough to burn), and had nearly completed an act, when I was interrupted by circumstances. This is somewhere amongst my papers in England; but as it has not been found, I have re-written the first, and added the subsequent acts.

The whole is neither intended, nor in any shape adapted, for the stage.

PISA, *February*, 1822.

Dramatis Personæ.

MEN.—WERNER.	ERIC.
ULRIC.	ARNHEIM.
STRALENHEIM.	MEISTER.
IDENSTEIN.	RODOLPH.
GABOR.	LUDWIG.
FRITZ.	WOMEN.—JOSEPHINE.
HENRICK.	IDA STRALENHEIM.

Scene.—*Partly on the frontier of Silesia, and partly in Siegendorf Castle, near Prague.*

Time.—The Close of the Thirty Years' War.

Act I.

Scene I.—*The Hall of a decayed Palace near
a small Town on the Northern Frontier of
Silesia—the Night tempestuous.*

WERNER *and* JOSEPHINE, *his Wife.*

Jos. My love, be calmer!
Wer. I am calm.
Jos. To me—
Yes, but not to thyself: thy pace is hurried,
And no one walks a chamber like to ours
With steps like thine when his heart is at rest.
Were it a garden, I should deem thee happy,
And stepping with the bee from flower to
 flower;
But *here!*
Wer. 'Tis chill; the tapestry lets through
The wind to which it waves: my blood is
 frozen.
Jos. Ah, no!
Wer. (*smiling*). Why! wouldst thou have
 it so?
Jos. I would
Have it a healthful current.
Wer. Let it flow
Until 'tis spilt or check'd—how soon, I care
 not.
Jos. And am I nothing in thy heart?
Wer. All—all.
Jos. Then canst thou wish for that which
 must break mine?
Wer. (*approaching her slowly*). But for
 thee I had been—no matter what,
But much of good and evil; what I am,
Thou knowest; what I might or should have
 been,
Thou knowest not: but still I love thee, nor
Shall aught divide us.
 [WERNER *walks on abruptly, and then
 approaches* JOSEPHINE.
 The storm of the night
Perhaps affects me; I'm a thing of feelings,
And have of late been sickly, as, alas!
Thou know'st by sufferings more than mine,
 my love!
In watching me.
Jos. To see thee well is much—
To see thee happy—
Wer. Where hast thou seen such?
Let me be wretched with the rest!
Jos. But think
How many in this hour of tempest shiver
Beneath the biting wind and heavy rain,
Whose every drop bows them down nearer
 earth,
Which hath no chamber for them save be-
 neath
Her surface.

Wer. And that's not the worst: who cares
For chambers? rest is all. The wretches
 whom
Thou namest—ay, the wind howls round
 them, and
The dull and dropping rain saps in their bones
The creeping marrow. I have been a soldier,
A hunter, and a traveller, and am
A beggar, and should know the thing thou
 talk'st of.
Jos. And art thou not now shelter'd from
 them all?
Wer. Yes. And from these alone.
Jos. And that is something.
Wer. True—to a peasant.
Jos. Should the nobly born
Be thankless for that refuge which their
 habits
Of early delicacy render more
Needful than to the peasant, when the ebb
Of fortune leaves them on the shoals of life?
Wer. It is not that, thou know'st it is
 not: we
Have borne all this, I'll not say patiently,
Except in thee—but we have borne it.
Jos. Well?
Wer. Something beyond our outward suf-
 ferings (though
These were enough to gnaw into our souls)
Hath stung me oft, and, more than ever, *now*.
When, but for this untoward sickness, which
Seized me upon this desolate frontier, and
Hath wasted, not alone my strength, but
 means,
And leaves us—no! this is beyond me!—but
For this I had been happy—*thou* been happy—
The splendour of my rank sustain'd—my
 name—
My father's name—been still upheld; and,
 more
Than those——
Jos. (*abruptly*). My son—our son—our
 Ulric,
Been clasp'd again in these long-empty arms,
And all a mother's hunger satisfied.
Twelve years! he was but eight then:—beau-
 tiful
He was, and beautiful he must be now,
My Ulric! my adored!
Wer. I have been full oft
The chase of Fortune; now she hath o'ertaken
My spirit where it cannot turn at bay,—
Sick, poor, and lonely.
Jos. Lonely! my dear husband?
Wer. Or worse—involving all I love, in
 this
Far worse than solitude. *Alone*, I had died,
And all been over in a nameless grave.
Jos. And I had not outlived thee; but
 pray take

Comfort! We have struggled long; and
 they who strive
With Fortune win or weary her at last,
So that they find the goal or cease to feel
Further. Take comfort,—we shall find our boy.
 Wer. We were in sight of him, of every-
 thing
Which could bring compensation for past
 sorrow—
And to be baffled thus!
 Jos. We are not baffled.
 Wer. Are we not penniless?
 Jos. We ne'er were wealthy.
 Wer. But I was born to wealth, and rank,
 and power;
Enjoy'd them, loved them, and, alas! abused
 them,
And forfeited them by my father's wrath,
In my o'er-fervent youth: but for the abuse
Long sufferings have atoned. My father's
 death
Left the path open, yet not without snares.
This cold and creeping kinsman, who so long
Kept his eye on me, as the snake upon
The fluttering bird, hath ere this time out-
 stept me,
Become the master of my rights, and lord
Of that which lifts him up to princes in
Dominion and domain.
 Jos. Who knows? our son
May have return'd back to his grandsire, and
Even now uphold thy rights for thee?
 Wer. 'Tis hopeless.
Since his strange disappearance from my
 father's,
Entailing, as it were, my sins upon
Himself, no tidings have reveal'd his course.
I parted with him to his grandsire, on
The promise that his anger would stop short
Of the third generation; but Heaven seems
To claim her stern prerogative, and visit
Upon my boy his father's faults and follies.
 Jos. I must hope better still,—at least we
 have yet
Baffled the long pursuit of Stralenheim.
 Wer. We should have done, but for this
 fatal sickness;
More fatal than a mortal malady,
Because it takes not life, but life's sole solace:
Even now I feel my spirit girt about
By the snares of this avaricious fiend :—
How do I know he hath not track'd us here?
 Jos. He does not know thy person; and
 his spies,
Who so long watch'd thee, have been left at
 Hamburgh.
Our unexpected journey, and this change
Of name, leaves all discovery far behind :
None hold us here for aught save what we
 seem.

 Wer. Save what we seem! save what we
 are—sick beggars,
Even to our very hopes.—Ha! ha!
 Jos. Alas!
That bitter laugh!
 Wer. *Who* would read in this form
The high soul of the son of a long line?
Who, in this garb, the heir of princely lands?
Who, in this sunken, sickly eye, the pride
Of rank and ancestry? In this worn cheek
And famine-hollow'd brow, the lord of halls
Which daily feast a thousand vassals?
 Jos. You
Ponder'd not thus upon these worldly things,
My Werner! when you deign'd to choose for
 bride
The foreign daughter of a wandering exile.
 Wer. An exile's daughter with an outcast
 son,
Were a fit marriage: but I still had hopes
To lift thee to the state we both were born
 for.
Your father's house was noble, though de-
 cay'd;
And worthy by its birth to match with ours.
 Jos. Your father did not think so, though
 't was noble;
But had my birth been all my claim to match
With thee, I should have deem'd it what it is.
 Wer. And what is that in thine eyes?
 Jos. All which it
Has done in our behalf,—nothing?
 Wer. How,—nothing?
 Jos. Or worse; for it has been a canker in
Thy heart from the beginning: but for this,
We had not felt our poverty but as
Millions of myriads feel it, cheerfully;
But for these phantoms of thy feudal fathers,
Thou might'st have earn'd thy bread, as
 thousands earn it;
Or, if that seem too humble, tried by com-
 merce,
Or other civic means, to amend thy fortunes.
 Wer. (*ironically*). And been an Hanseatic
 burgher? Excellent!
 Jos. Whate'er thou might'st have been,
 to me thou art
What no state high or low can ever change,
My heart's first choice;—which chose thee,
 knowing neither
Thy birth, thy hopes, thy pride; nought, save
 thy sorrows:
While they last, let me comfort or divide
 them:
When they end, let mine end with them, or
 thee!
 Wer. My better angel! Such I have ever
 found thee;
This rashness, or this weakness of my
 temper,

Ne'er raised a thought to injure thee or
 thine.
Thou didst not mar my fortunes: my own
 nature
In youth was such as to unmake an empire,
Had such been my inheritance; but now,
Chasten'd, subdued, out-worn, and taught to
 know
Myself,—to lose this for our son and thee!
Trust me, when, in my two-and-twentieth
 spring,
My father barr'd me from my fathers' house,
The last sole scion of a thousand sires
(For I was then the last), it hurt me less
Than to behold my boy and my boy's mother
Excluded in their innocence from what
My faults deserved—exclusion; although
 then
My passions were all living serpents, and
Twined like the Gorgon's round me.
 [*A loud knocking is heard.*
 Jos. Hark!
 Wer. A knocking!
 Jos. Who can it be at this lone hour?
 We have
Few visitors.
 Wer. And poverty hath none,
Save those who come to make it poorer still.
Well, I am prepared.
 [WERNER *puts his hand into his bosom, as
 if to search for some weapon.*
 Jos. Oh! do not look so. I
Will to the door. It cannot be of import
In this lone spot of wintry desolation:—
The very desert saves man from mankind.
 [*She goes to the door.*

 Enter IDENSTEIN.

 Iden. A fair good evening to my fairer
 hostess
And worthy——What's your name, my
 friend?
 Wer. Are you
Not afraid to demand it?
 Iden. Not afraid?
Egad! I am afraid. You look as if
I ask'd for something better than your name,
By the face you put on it.
 Wer. Better, sir!
 Iden. Better or worse, like matrimony:
 what
Shall I say more? You have been a guest
 this month
Here in the prince's palace—(to be sure,
His highness had resign'd it to the ghosts
And rats these twelve years—but 'tis still a
 palace)—
I say you have been our lodger, and as yet
We do not know your name.
 Wer. My name is Werner.

 Iden. A goodly name, a very worthy
 name,
As e'er was gilt upon a trader's board:
I have a cousin in the lazaretto
Of Hamburgh, who has got a wife who bore
The same. He is an officer of trust,
Surgeon's assistant (hoping to be surgeon),
And has done miracles i' the way of business.
Perhaps you are related to my relative?
 Wer. To yours?
 Jos. Oh, yes; we are, but distantly.
 (*Aside to* WERNER). Cannot you humour
 the dull gossip till
We learn his purpose?
 Iden. Well, I'm glad of that;
I thought so all along, such natural yearn-
 ings
Play'd round my heart:—blood is not water,
 cousin;
And so let's have some wine, and drink unto
Our better acquaintance: relatives should be
 Friends.
 Wer. You appear to have drank enough
 already;
And if you have not, I've no wine to offer,
Else it were yours: but this you know, or
 should know:
You see I am poor, and sick, and will not see
That I would be alone; but to your business!
What brings you here?
 Iden. Why, what should bring me here?
 Wer. I know not, though I think that I
 could guess
That which will send you hence.
 Jos. (*aside*). Patience, dear Werner!
 Iden. You don't know what has happen'd,
 then?
 Jos. How should we?
 Iden. The river has o'erflow'd.
 Jos. Alas! we have known
That to our sorrow for these five days; since
It keeps us here.
 Iden. But what you don't know is,
That a great personage, who fain would cross
Against the stream and three postilions'
 wishes,
Is drown'd below the ford, with five post-
 horses,
A monkey, and a mastiff, and a valet.
 Jos. Poor creatures! are you sure?
 Iden. Yes, of the monkey,
And the valet, and the cattle; but as yet
We know not if his excellency's dead
Or no; your noblemen are hard to drown,
As it is fit that men in office should be;
But what is certain is, that he has swallow'd
Enough of the Oder to have burst two
 peasants;
And now a Saxon and Hungarian traveller,
Who, at their proper peril, snatch'd him from

The whirling river, have sent on to crave
A lodging, or a grave, according as
It may turn out with the live or dead body.
 Jos. And where will you receive him?
 here, I hope,
If we can be of service—say the word.
 Iden. Here? no; but in the prince's own
 apartment,
As fits a noble guest:—'t is damp, no doubt,
Not having been inhabited these twelve
 years;
But then he comes from a much damper
 place,
So scarcely will catch cold in 't, if he be
Still liable to cold—and if not, why
He'll be worse lodged to-morrow: ne'erthe-
 less,
I have order'd fire and all appliances
To be got ready for the worst—that is,
In case he should survive.
 Jos.			Poor gentleman,
I hope he will, with all my heart.
 Wer.				Intendant,
Have you not learn'd his name? My Jose-
 phine,			[*Aside to his wife.*
Retire: I'll sift this fool. [*Exit* JOSEPHINE.
 Iden.			His name? oh Lord!
Who knows if he hath now a name or no?
'T is time enough to ask it when he's able
To give an answer; or if not, to put
His heir's upon his epitaph. Methought
Just now you chid me for demanding names?
 Wer. True, true, I did so: you say well
 and wisely.

 Enter GABOR.

 Gab. If I intrude, I crave——
 Iden.			Oh, no intrusion!
This is the palace; this a stranger like
Yourself; I pray you make yourself at home:
But where's his excellency? and how fares
 he?
 Gab. Wetly and wearily, but out of peril:
He paused to change his garments in a
 cottage
(Where I doff'd mine for these, and came on
 hither),
And has almost recover'd from his drenching.
He will be here anon.
 Iden.			What ho, there! bustle!
Without there, Herman, Weilburg, Peter,
 Conrad!
 [*Gives directions to different servants
 who enter.*
A nobleman sleeps here to-night—see that
All is in order in the damask chamber—
Keep up the stove—I will myself to the
 cellar—
And Madame Idenstein (my consort, stranger)

Shall furnish forth the bed-apparel; for,
To say the truth, they are marvellous scant
 of this
Within the palace precincts, since his high-
 ness
Left it some dozen years ago. And then
His excellency will sup, doubtless?
 Gab.				Faith!
I cannot tell; but I should think the pillow
Would please him better than the table, after
His soaking in your river: but for fear
Your viands should be thrown away, I mean
To sup myself, and have a friend without
Who will do honour to your good cheer with
A traveller's appetite.
 Iden.			But are you sure
His excellency——But his name: what is it?
 Gab. I do not know.
 Iden.			And yet you saved his life.
 Gab. I help'd my friend to do so.
 Iden.			Well, that's strange,
To save a man's life whom you do not know.
 Gab. Not so; for there are some I know
 so well,
I scarce should give myself the trouble.
 Iden.						Pray,
Good friend, and who may you be?
 Gab.				By my family,
Hungarian.
 Iden.	Which is call'd?
 Gab.			It matters little.
 Iden. (*aside*). I think that all the world are
 grown anonymous,
Since no one cares to tell me what he's
 call'd!
Pray, has his excellency a large suite?
 Gab.				Sufficient.
 Iden. How many?
 Gab.			I did not count them.
We came up by mere accident, and just
In time to drag him through his carriage
 window.
 Iden. Well, what would I give to save a
 great man!
No doubt you'll have a swingeing sum as
 recompense.
 Gab. Perhaps.
 Iden. Now, how much do you reckon on?
 Gab. I have not yet put up myself to sale:
In the mean time, my best reward would be
A glass of your Hockheimer—a *green* glass,
Wreath'd with rich grapes and Bacchanal
 devices,
O'erflowing with the oldest of your vintage:
For which I promise you, in case you e'er
Run hazard of being drown'd (although I own
It seems, of all deaths, the least likely for
 you),
I'll pull you out for nothing. Quick, my
 friend,

And think, for every bumper I shall quaff,
A wave the less may roll above your head.
 Iden. (*aside*). I don't much like this
 fellow—close and dry
He seems,—two things which suit me not;
 however,
Wine he shall have; if that unlock him not,
I shall not sleep to-night for curiosity.
 [*Exit* IDENSTEIN.
 Gab. (*to* WERNER). This master of the
 ceremonies is
The intendant of the palace, I presume:
'T is a fine building, but decay'd.
 Wer. The apartment
Design'd for him you rescued will be found
In fitter order for a sickly guest.
 Gab. I wonder then you occupied it not,
For you seem delicate in health.
 Wer. (*quickly*). Sir !
 Gab. Pray
Excuse me : have I said aught to offend you?
 Wer. Nothing : but we are strangers to
 each other.
 Gab. And that's the reason I would have
 us less so :
I thought our bustling host without had said
You were a chance and passing guest, the
 counterpart
Of me and my companions.
 Wer. Very true.
 Gab. Then, as we never met before, and
 never,
It may be, may again encounter, why,
I thought to cheer up this old dungeon here
(At least to me) by asking you to share
The fare of my companions and myself.
 Wer. Pray, pardon me; my health——
 Gab. Even as you please.
I have been a soldier, and perhaps am blunt
In bearing.
 Wer. I have also served, and can
Requite a soldier's greeting.
 Gab. In what service ?
The Imperial ?
 Wer. (*quickly, and then interrupting him-
 self*). I commanded—no—I mean
I served ; but it is many years ago,
When first Bohemia raised her banner 'gainst
The Austrian.
 Gab. Well, that's over now, and peace
Has turn'd some thousand gallant hearts
 adrift
To live as they best may : and, to say truth,
Some take the shortest.
 Wer. What is that ?
 Gab. Whate'er
They lay their hands on. All Silesia and
Lusatia's woods are tenanted by bands
Of the late troops, who levy on the country
Their maintenance : the Chatelains must keep

Their castle walls—beyond them 't is but
 doubtful
Travel for your rich count or full-blown baron.
My comfort is that, wander where I may,
I've little left to lose now.
 Wer. And I—nothing.
 Gab. That's harder still. You say you
 were a soldier.
 Wer. I was.
 Gab. You look one still. All soldiers are
Or should be comrades, even though enemies.
Our swords when drawn must cross, our
 engines aim
(While levell'd) at each other's hearts; but
 when
A truce, a peace, or what you will, remits
The steel into its scabbard, and lets sleep
The spark which lights the matchlock, we are
 brethren.
You are poor and sickly—I am not rich, but
 healthy;
I want for nothing which I cannot want ;
You seem devoid of this—wilt share it ?
 [GABOR *pulls out his purse.*
 Wer. Who
Told you I was a beggar?
 Gab. You yourself,
In saying you were a soldier during peace-
 time.
 Wer. (*looking at him with suspicion*). You
 know me not ?
 Gab. I know no man, not even
Myself : how should I then know one I ne'er
Beheld till half an hour since ?
 Wer. Sir, I thank you.
Your offer's noble were it to a friend,
And not unkind as to an unknown stranger,
Though scarcely prudent; but no less I
 thank you.
I am a beggar in all save his trade ;
And when I beg of any one, it shall be
Of him who was the first to offer what
Few can obtain by asking. Pardon me.
 [*Exit* WERNER.
 Gab. (*solus*). A goodly fellow by his looks,
 though worn,
As most good fellows are, by pain or pleasure,
Which tear life out of us before our time ;
I scarce know which most quickly : but he
 seems
To have seen better days, as who has not
Who has seen yesterday?—But here ap-
 proaches
Our sage intendant, with the wine : however,
For the cup's sake I'll bear the cupbearer.

 Enter IDENSTEIN.

 Iden. 'T is here ! the supernaculum !
 twenty years
Of age, if 't is a day.

Gab. Which epoch makes
Young women and old wine; and 't is great pity,
Of two such excellent things, increase of years,
Which still improves the one, should spoil the other.
Fill full—Here 's to our hostess!—your fair wife! [*Takes the glass.*

Iden. Fair!—Well, I trust your taste in wine is equal
To that you show for beauty; but I pledge you
Nevertheless.

Gab. Is not the lovely woman
I met in the adjacent hall, who, with
An air, and port, and eye, which would have better
Beseem'd this palace in its brightest days
(Though in a garb adapted to its present
Abandonment), return'd my salutation—
Is not the same your spouse?

Iden. I would she were!
But you're mistaken:—that 's the stranger's wife.

Gab. And by her aspect she might be a prince's;
Though time hath touch'd her too, she still retains
Much beauty, and more majesty.

Iden. And that
Is more than I can say for Madame Idenstein,
At least in beauty: as for majesty,
She has some of its properties which might
Be spared—but never mind!

Gab. I don't. But who
May be this stranger? He too hath a bearing
Above his outward fortunes.

Iden. There I differ.
He's poor as Job, and not so patient; but
Who he may be, or what, or aught of him,
Except his name (and that I only learn'd
To-night), I know not.

Gab. But how came he here?

Iden. In a most miserable old caleche,
About a month since, and immediately
Fell sick, almost to death. He should have died.

Gab. Tender and true!—but why?

Iden. Why, what is life
Without a living? He has not a stiver.

Gab. In that case, I much wonder that a person
Of your apparent prudence should admit
Guests so forlorn into this noble mansion.

Iden. That 's true: but pity, as you know, *does* make
One's heart commit these follies; and besides,
They had some valuables left at that time,

Which paid their way up to the present hour;
And so I thought they might as well be lodged
Here as at the small tavern, and I gave them
The run of some of the oldest palace rooms.
They served to air them, at the least as long
As they could pay for firewood.

Gab. Poor souls!

Iden. Ay,
Exceeding poor.

Gab. And yet unused to poverty,
If I mistake not. Whither were they going?

Iden. Oh! Heaven knows where, unless to heaven itself.
Some days ago that look'd the likeliest journey
For Werner.

Gab. Werner! I have heard the name:
But it may be a feign'd one.

Iden. Like enough!
But hark! a noise of wheels and voices, and
A blaze of torches from without. As sure
As destiny, his excellency 's come.
I must be at my post; will you not join me,
To help him from his carriage, and present
Your humble duty at the door?

Gab. I dragg'd him
From out that carriage when he would have given
His barony or county to repel
The rushing river from his gurgling throat.
He has valets now enough: they stood aloof then,
Shaking their dripping ears upon the shore,
All roaring "Help!" but offering none; and as
For *duty* (as you call it)—I did mine *then*,
Now do *yours.* Hence, and bow and cringe him here!

Iden. I cringe!—but I shall lose the opportunity—
Plague take it! he 'll be *here*, and I *not there!*
[*Exit* IDENSTEIN *hastily.*

Re-enter WERNER.

Wer. (*to himself*). I heard a noise of wheels and voices. How.
All sounds now jar me!
Still here! Is he not
[*Perceiving* GABOR.
A spy of my pursuer's? His frank offer
So suddenly, and to a stranger, wore
The aspect of a secret enemy;
For friends are slow at such.

Gab. Sir, you seem rapt;
And yet the time is not akin to thought.
These old walls will be noisy soon. The baron,
Or count (or whatsoe'er this half drown'd noble
May be), for whom this desolate village and

Its lone inhabitants show more respect
Than did the elements, is come.
 Iden. (*without*). This way—
This way, your excellency:—have a care,
The staircase is a little gloomy, and
Somewhat decay'd; but if we had expected
So high a guest—Pray take my arm, my lord!

Enter STRALENHEIM, IDENSTEIN, *and Attend-*
ants,—partly his own, and partly Retainers
of the Domain of which IDENSTEIN *is In-*
tendant.

 Stral. I'll rest me here a moment.
 Iden. (*to the servants*). Ho! a chair!
Instantly, knaves! [STRALENHEIM *sits down.*
 Wer. (*aside*). 'Tis he!
 Stral. I'm better now.
Who are these strangers?
 Iden. Please you, my good lord,
One says he is no stranger.
 Wer. (*aloud and hastily*). *Who* says that?
 [*They look at him with surprise.*
 Iden. Why, no one spoke *of you*, or *to*
 you!—but
Here's one his excellency may be pleased
To recognise. [*Pointing to* GABOR.
 Gab. I seek not to disturb
His noble memory.
 Stral. I apprehend
This is one of the strangers to whose aid
I owe my rescue. Is not that the other?
 [*Pointing to* WERNER.
My state when I was succour'd must excuse
My uncertainty to whom I owe so much.
 Iden. He!—no, my lord! he rather wants
 for rescue
Than can afford it. 'Tis a poor sick man,
Travel-tired, and lately risen from a bed
From whence he never dream'd to rise.
 Stral. Methought
That there were two.
 Gab. There were, in company;
But, in the service render'd to your lordship
I needs must say but *one*, and he is absent.
The chief part of whatever aid was render'd
Was *his:* it was his fortune to be first.
My will was not inferior, but his strength
And youth outstripp'd me; therefore do not
 waste
Your thanks on me. I was but a glad second
Unto a nobler principal.
 Stral. Where is he?
 An Atten. My lord, he tarried in the
 cottage where
Your excellency rested for an hour,
And said he would be here to-morrow.
 Stral. Till
That hour arrives, I can but offer thanks.
And then——

 Gab. I seek no more, and scarce deserve
So much. My comrade may speak for him-
 self.
 Stral. (*fixing his eyes upon* WERNER: *then*
 aside).
It cannot be! and yet he must be look'd to.
'Tis twenty years since I beheld him with
These eyes; and, though my agents still have
 kept
Theirs on him, policy has held aloof
My own from his, not to alarm him into
Suspicion of my plan. Why did I leave
At Hamburgh those who would have made
 assurance
If this be he or no? I thought, ere now,
To have been lord of Siegendorf, and parted
In haste, though even the elements appear
To fight against me, and this sudden flood
May keep me prisoner here till——
 [*He pauses and looks at* WERNER; *then*
 resumes.
 This man must
Be watch'd. If it is he, he is so changed,
His father, rising from his grave again,
Would pass him by unknown. I must be wary:
An error would spoil all.
 Iden. Your lordship seems
Pensive. Will it not please you to pass on?
 Stral. 'Tis past fatigue, which gives my
 weigh'd-down spirit
An outward show of thought. I will to rest.
 Iden. The prince's chamber is prepared,
 with all
The very furniture the prince used when
Last here, in its full splendour.
 (*Aside*). Somewhat tatter'd,
And devilish damp, but fine enough by torch-
 light;
And that's enough for your right noble blood
Of twenty quarterings upon a hatchment;
So let their bearer sleep 'neath something
 like one
Now, as he one day will for ever lie.
 Stral. (*rising and turning to* GABOR). Good
 night, good people! Sir, I trust to-
 morrow
Will find me apter to requite your service.
In the mean time I crave your company
A moment in my chamber.
 Gab. I attend you.
 Stral. (*after a few steps, pauses and calls*
 WERNER). Friend!
 Wer. Sir!
 Iden. Sir! Lord—oh Lord! Why don't
 you say
His lordship, or his excellency? Pray,
My lord, excuse this poor man's want of
 breeding:
He hath not been accustom'd to admission
To such a presence.

Stral. (to IDENSTEIN). Peace, intendant!
Iden. Oh!
I am dumb.
 Stral. (to WERNER). Have you been long
here?
Wer. Long?
Stral. I sought
An answer, not an echo.
Wer. You may seek
Both from the walls. I am not used to
answer
Those whom I know not.
Stral. Indeed! Ne'ertheless,
You might reply with courtesy to what
Is ask'd in kindness.
Wer. When I know it such,
I will requite—that is, *reply*—in unison.
 Stral. The intendant said you had been
detain'd by sickness—
If I could aid you—journeying the same way?
 Wer. (quickly). I am not journeying the
same way.
Stral. How know ye
That, ere you know my route?
Wer. Because there is
But one way that the rich and poor must
tread
Together. You diverged from that dread
path
Some hours ago, and I some days: hence-
forth
Our roads must lie asunder, though they tend
All to one home.
Stral. Your language is above
Your station.
 Wer. (bitterly). Is it?
Stral. Or, at least, beyond
Your garb.
 Wer. 'T is well that it is not beneath it,
As sometimes happens to the better clad.
But, in a word, what would you with me?
 Stral. (startled). I?
 Wer. Yes—you! You know me not, and
question me,
And wonder that I answer not—not knowing
My inquisitor. Explain what you would
have,
And then I'll satisfy yourself, or me.
 Stral. I knew not that you had reasons
for reserve.
 Wer. Many have such:—Have you none?
Stral. None which can
Interest a mere stranger.
Wer. Then forgive
The same unknown and humble stranger, if
He wishes to remain so to the man
Who can have nought in common with him.
 Stral. Sir,
I will not balk your humour, though unto-
ward:

I only meant you service—but good night!
Intendant, show the way! (*To* GABOR). Sir,
you will with me?
 [*Exeunt* STRALENHEIM *and Attendants,*
 IDENSTEIN *and* GABOR.
 Wer. (solus). 'T is he! I am taken in the
toils. Before
I quitted Hamburgh, Giulio, his late steward,
Inform'd me, that he had obtain'd an order
From Brandenburg's elector, for the arrest
Of Kruitzner (such the name I then bore)
when
I came upon the frontier; the free city
Alone preserved my freedom—till I left
Its walls—fool that I was to quit them! But
I deem'd this humble garb, and route ob-
scure,
Had baffled the slow hounds in their pursuit.
What's to be done? He knows me not by
person;
Nor could aught, save the eye of appre-
hension,
Have recognised *him*, after twenty years,
We met so rarely and so coldly in
Our youth. But those about him! Now
I can
Divine the frankness of the Hungarian, who
No doubt is a mere tool and spy of Stralen-
heim's,
To sound and to secure me. Without means!
Sick, poor—begirt too with the flooding
rivers,
Impassable even to the wealthy, with
All the appliances which purchase modes
Of overpowering peril, with men's lives,—
How can I hope? An hour ago methought
My state beyond despair; and now, 'tis such,
The past seems paradise. Another day,
And I'm detected,—on the very eve
Of honours, rights, and my inheritance,
When a few drops of gold might save me
still
In favouring an escape.

Enter IDENSTEIN *and* FRITZ *in conversation.*

Fritz. Immediately.
Iden. I tell you, 'tis impossible.
Fritz. It must
Be tried, however; and if one express
Fail, you must send on others, till the answer
Arrives from Frankfort, from the command-
ant.
 Iden. I will do what I can.
Fritz. And recollect
To spare no trouble; you will be repaid
Tenfold.
 Iden. The baron is retired to rest?
 Fritz. He hath thrown himself into an
easy chair

Beside the fire, and slumbers; and has
　　order'd
He may not be disturb'd until eleven,
When he will take himself to bed.
　Iden.　　　　　　　　　　　　Before
An hour is past I'll do my best to serve him.
　Fritz. Remember!　　　　　　*[Exit* FRITZ.
　Iden.　　　The devil take these great men!
　　they
Think all things made for them. Now here
　　must I
Rouse up some half a dozen shivering vassals
From their scant pallets, and, at peril of
Their lives, despatch them o'er the river
　　towards
Frankfort. Methinks the baron's own ex-
　　perience
Some hours ago might teach him fellow-
　　feeling:
But no, "it *must*," and there's an end. How
　　now?
Are you there, Mynheer Werner?
　Wer.　　　　　　　　　　You have left
Your noble guest right quickly.
　Iden.　　　　　　　　Yes—he's dozing,
And seems to like that none should sleep
　　besides.
Here is a packet for the commandant
Of Frankfort, at all risks and all expenses;
But I must not lose time: Good night!
　　　　　　　　　　　　　　　　[Exit.
　Wer.　　　　　　　　　"To Frankfort!"
So, so, it thickens! Ay, "the commandant."
This tallies well with all the prior steps
Of this cool, calculating fiend, who walks
Between me and my father's house. No
　　doubt
He writes for a detachment to convey me
Into some secret fortress.—Sooner than
This—
　　　*[*WERNER *looks around, and snatches*
　　　　up a knife lying on a table in a
　　　　recess.
Now I am master of myself at least.
Hark,—footsteps! How do I know that
　　Stralenheim
Will wait for even the show of that autho-
　　rity
Which is to overshadow usurpation?
That he suspects me's certain. I'm alone;
He with a numerous train. I weak; he strong
In gold, in numbers, rank, authority.
I nameless, or involving in my name
Destruction, till I reach my own domain;
He full-blown with his titles, which impose
Still further on these obscure petty burghers
Than they could do elsewhere. Hark!
　　nearer still!
I'll to the secret passage which communi-
cates

With the——No! all is silent—'twas my
　　fancy!—
Still as the breathless interval between
The flash and thunder:—I must hush my
　　soul
Amidst its perils. Yet I will retire,
To see if still be unexplored the passage
I wot of: it will serve me as a den
Of secrecy for some hours, at the worst.
　　　*[*WERNER *draws a panel, and exit,*
　　　　　　　closing it after him.

　　　　　Enter GABOR *and* JOSEPHINE.

　Gab. Where is your husband?
　Jos.　　　　　*Here,* I thought: I left him
Not long since in his chamber. But these
　　rooms
Have many outlets, and he may be gone
To accompany the intendant.
　Gab.　　　　　　　　Baron Stralenheim
Put many questions to the intendant on
The subject of your lord, and, to be plain,
I have my doubts if he means well.
　Jos.　　　　　　　　　　　　Alas!
What can there be in common with the proud
And wealthy baron, and the unknown Wer-
　　ner?
　Gab. That you know best.
　Jos.　　　　Or, if it were so, how
Come you to stir yourself in his behalf,
Rather than that of him whose life you
　　saved?
　Gab. I help'd to save him, as in peril;
　　but
I did not pledge myself to serve him in
Oppression. I know well these nobles, and
Their thousand modes of trampling on the
　　poor.
I have proved them; and my spirit boils up
　　when
I find them practising against the weak :—
This is my only motive.
　Jos.　　　　　　　It would be
Not easy to persuade my consort of
Your good intentions.
　Gab.　　　　　　Is he so suspicious?
　Jos. He was not once; but time and
　　troubles have
Made him what you beheld.
　Gab.　　　　　　　I'm sorry for it.
Suspicion is a heavy armour, and
With its own weight impedes more than pro-
　　tects.
Good night! I trust to meet with him at day-
　　break.　　　　　　　　*[Exit* GABOR.

　Re-enter IDENSTEIN *and some Peasants.*
　JOSEPHINE *retires up the Hall.*

　First Peasant. But if I'm drown'd?

Iden. Why, you will be well paid for 't,
And have risk'd more than drowning for as much,
I doubt not.
 Second Peasant. But our wives and families?
 Iden. Cannot be worse off than they are, and may
Be better.
 Third Peasant. I have neither, and will venture.
 Iden. That's right. A gallant carle, and fit to be
A soldier. I'll promote you to the ranks
In the prince's body-guard—if you succeed:
And you shall have besides, in sparkling coin,
Two thalers.
 Third Peasant. No more!
 Iden. Out upon your avarice!
Can that low vice alloy so much ambition?
I tell thee, fellow, that two thalers in
Small change will subdivide into a treasure.
Do not five hundred thousand heroes daily
Risk lives and souls for the tithe of one thaler?
When had you half the sum?
 Third Peasant. Never—but ne'er
The less I must have three.
 Iden. Have you forgot
Whose vassal you were born, knave?
 Third Peasant. No—the prince's,
And not the stranger's.
 Iden. Sirrah! in the prince's
Absence, I am sovereign; and the baron is
My intimate connexion;—"Cousin Idenstein!
(Quoth he) you'll order out a dozen villains."
And so, you villains! troop—march—march,
 I say;
And if a single dog's ear of this packet
Be sprinkled by the Oder—look to it!
For every page of paper, shall a hide
Of yours be stretch'd as parchment on a drum,
Like Ziska's skin, to beat alarm to all
Refractory vassals, who cannot effect
Impossibilities.—Away, ye earth-worms!
 [*Exit, driving them out.*
 Jos. (*coming forward*). I fain would shun
 these scenes, too oft repeated,
Of feudal tyranny o'er petty victims;
I cannot aid, and will not witness such.
Even here, in this remote, unnamed, dull
 spot,
The dimmest in the district's map, exist
The insolence of wealth in poverty
O'er something poorer still—the pride of rank
In servitude, o'er something still more servile;

And vice in misery affecting still
A tatter'd splendour. What a state of being!
In Tuscany, my own dear sunny land,
Our nobles were but citizens and merchants,
Like Cosmo. We had evils, but not such
As these; and our all-ripe and gushing valleys
Made poverty more cheerful, where each herb
Was in itself a meal, and every vine
Rain'd, as it were, the beverage which makes glad
The heart of man; and the ne'er unfelt sun
(But rarely clouded, and when clouded, leaving
His warmth behind in memory of his beams)
Makes the worn mantle, and the thin robe, less
Oppressive than an emperor's jewell'd purple.
But, here! the despots of the north appear
To imitate the ice-wind of their clime,
Searching the shivering vassal through his rags,
To wring his soul—as the bleak elements
His form. And 'tis to be amongst these sovereigns
My husband pants! and such his pride of birth—
That twenty years of usage, such as no
Father born in a humble state could nerve
His soul to persecute a son withal,
Hath changed no atom of his early nature;
But I, born nobly also, from my father's
Kindness was taught a different lesson.
 Father!
May thy long-tried and now rewarded spirit
Look down on us and our so long-desired
Ulric! I love my son, as thou didst me!
What's that? Thou, Werner! can it be?
 and thus?

Enter WERNER *hastily, with the knife in his hand, by the secret panel, which he closes hurriedly after him.*

 Wer. (*not at first recognising her*). Discover'd! then I'll stab——(*recognising her.*)
 Ah! Josephine,
Why art thou not at rest?
 Jos. What rest? My God!
What doth this mean?
 Wer. (*showing a rouleau*). Here's gold—gold, Josephine,
Will rescue us from this detested dungeon.
 Jos. And how obtain'd?—that knife!
 Wer. 'T is bloodless—yet.
Away—we must to our chamber.
 Jos. But whence comest thou?
 Wer. Ask not! but let us think where we
 shall go—

This—this will make us way—(*showing the
　　gold*)—I'll fit them now.
Jos. I dare not think thee guilty of dis-
　honour.
Wer. Dishonour!
Jos.　　　　　　　I have said it.
Wer.　　　　　　　　Let us hence :
'Tis the last night, I trust, that we need pass
　here.
Jos. And not the worst, I hope.
Wer.　　　　　　Hope ! I make *sure*.
But let us to our chamber.
Jos.　　　　　　Yet one question—
What hast thou *done*?
Wer. (*fiercely*). Left one thing *undone*,
　which
Had made all well : let me not think of it !
Away !
Jos. Alas, that I should doubt of thee !
　　　　　　　　　　　　　[*Exeunt.*

———

Act II.

Scene I.—*A Hall in the same Palace.*

Enter IDENSTEIN *and Others.*

Iden. Fine doings ! goodly doings ! honest
　doings !
A baron pillaged in a prince's palace !
Where, till this hour, such a sin ne'er was
　heard of.
Fritz. It hardly could, unless the rats
　despoil'd
The mice of a few shreds of tapestry.
Iden. Oh ! that I e'er should live to see
　this day !
The honour of our city's gone for ever.
Fritz. Well, but now to discover the
　delinquent :
The baron is determined not to lose
This sum without a search.
Iden.　　　　　　And so am I.
Fritz. But whom do you suspect ?
Iden.　　　　　　Suspect ! all people
Without — within — above — below—Heaven
　help me !
Fritz. Is there no other entrance to the
　chamber ?
Iden. None whatsoever.
Fritz.　　　　　Are you sure of that ?
Iden. Certain. I have lived and served
　here since my birth,
And if there were such, must have heard of
　such,
Or seen it.
Fritz. Then it must be some one who
Had access to the antechamber.
Iden.　　　　　　Doubtless.

Fritz. The man call'd *Werner's* poor !
Iden.　　　　　　Poor as a miser.
But lodged so far off, in the other wing,
By which there's no communication with
The baron's chamber, that it can't be he.
Besides, I bade him "good night" in the hall,
Almost a mile off, and which only leads
To his own apartment, about the same time
When this burglarious, larcenous felony
Appears to have been committed.
Fritz.　　　　　　There's another,
The stranger——
Iden.　　　　The Hungarian ?
Fritz.　　　　　　He who help'd
To fish the baron from the Oder.
Iden.　　　　　　　　Not
Unlikely. But, hold—might it not have been
One of the suite ?
Fritz.　　　　How ? *We*, sir !
Iden.　　　　　　No—not *you*,
But some of the inferior knaves. You say
The baron was asleep in the great chair—
The velvet chair—in his embroider'd night-
　gown ;
His toilet spread before him, and upon it
A cabinet with letters, papers, and
Several rouleaux of gold ; of which *one* only
Has disappear'd :—the door unbolted, with
No difficult access to any.
Fritz.　　　　　　Good sir,
Be not so quick ! the honour of the corps
Which forms the baron's household's un-
　impeach'd
From steward to scullion, save in the fair
　way
Of peculation ; such as in accompts,
Weights, measures, larder, cellar, buttery,
Where all men take their prey ; as also in
Postage of letters, gathering of rents,
Purveying feasts, and understanding with
The honest trades who furnish noble masters ;
But for your petty, picking, downright thiev-
　ery,
We scorn it as we do board-wages. Then
Had one of our folks done it, he would not
Have been so poor a spirit as to hazard
His neck for *one* rouleau, but have swoop'd
　all ;
Also the cabinet, if portable.
Iden. There is some sense in that——
Fritz.　　　　　　No, sir, be sure
'T was none of our corps ; but some petty,
　trivial
Picker and stealer, without art or genius.
The only question is—Who else could have
Access, save the Hungarian and yourself ?
Iden. You don't mean me ?
Fritz.　　　　　No, sir ; I honour more
Your talents——
Iden.　　　　And my principles, I hope.

Fritz. Of course. But to the point:
What's to be done?

Iden. Nothing—but there's a good deal
to be said.

We'll offer a reward; move heaven and
earth,

And the police (though there's none nearer
than

Frankfort); post notices in manuscript
(For we've no printer); and set by my clerk
To read them (for few can, save he and I);
We'll send out villains to strip beggars, and
Search empty pockets; also to arrest
All gipsies, and ill-clothed and sallow people.
Prisoners we'll have at least, if not the
culprit;

And for the baron's gold—if 't is not found,
At least he shall have the full satisfaction
Of melting twice its substance in the raising
The ghost of this rouleau. Here's alchemy
For your Lord's losses!

Fritz. He hath found a better.

Iden. Where?

Fritz. In a most immense inheritance.
The late Count Siegendorf, his distant kins-
man,

Is dead near Prague, in his castle, and my
lord

Is on his way to take possession.

Iden. Was there
No heir?

Fritz. Oh, yes; but he has disappear'd
Long from the world's eye, and perhaps the
world.

A prodigal son, beneath his father's ban
For the last twenty years: for whom his sire
Refused to kill the fatted calf; and, therefore,
If living, he must chew the husks still. But
The baron would find means to silence him,
Were he to re-appear: he's politic,
And has much influence with a certain court.

Iden. He's fortunate.

Fritz. 'Tis true, there is a grandson,
Whom the late count reclaim'd from his son's
hands,

And educated as his heir; but then
His birth is doubtful.

Iden. How so?

Fritz. His sire made
A left-hand, love, imprudent sort of marriage,
With an Italian exile's dark-eyed daughter:
Noble, they say, too; but no match for such
A house as Siegendorf's. The grandsire ill
Could brook the alliance; and could ne'er be
brought

To see the parents, though he took the son.

Iden. If he's a lad of mettle, he may yet
Dispute your claim, and weave a web that
may

Puzzle your baron to unravel.

Fritz. Why,
For mettle, he has quite enough: they say,
He forms a happy mixture of his sire
And grandsire's qualities,—impetuous as
The former, and deep as the latter; but
The strangest is, that he too disappear'd
Some months ago.

Iden. The devil he did!

Fritz. Why, yes:
It must have been at his suggestion, at
An hour so critical as was the eve
Of the old man's death, whose heart was
broken by it.

Iden. Was there no cause assign'd?

Fritz. Plenty, no doubt,
And none perhaps the true one. Some averr'd
It was to seek his parents; some because
The old man held his spirit in so strictly
(But that could scarce be, for he doted on
him):

A third believed he wish'd to serve in war,
But peace being made soon after his de-
parture,

He might have since return'd, were that the
motive;

A fourth set charitably have surmised,
As there was something strange and mystic
in him,

That in the wild exuberance of his nature
He had join'd the black bands, who lay waste
Lusatia,

The mountains of Bohemia and Silesia,
Since the last years of war had dwindled into
A kind of general condottiero system
Of bandit warfare; each troop with its chief,
And all against mankind.

Iden. That cannot be,
A young heir, bred to wealth and luxury,
To risk his life and honours with disbanded
Soldiers and desperadoes!

Fritz. Heaven best knows!
But there are human natures so allied
Unto the savage love of enterprise,
That they will seek for peril as a pleasure.
I've heard that nothing can reclaim your
Indian,

Or tame the tiger, though their infancy
Were fed on milk and honey. After all,
Your Wallenstein, your Tilly and Gustavus,
Your Bannier, and your Torstenson and
Weimar,

Were but the same thing upon a grand scale;
And now that they are gone, and peace pro-
claim'd,

They who would follow the same pastime must
Pursue it on their own account. Here comes
The baron, and the Saxon stranger, who
Was his chief aid in yesterday's escape,
But did not leave the cottage by the Oder
Until this morning.

Enter STRALENHEIM *and* ULRIC.

Stral. Since you have refused
All compensation, gentle stranger, save
Inadequate thanks, you almost check even
 them,
Making me feel the worthlessness of words,
And blush at my own barren gratitude,
They seem so niggardly, compared with what
Your courteous courage did in my behalf——
 Ulr. I pray you press the theme no
 further.
 Stral. But
Can I not serve you? You are young, and of
That mould which throws out heroes; fair in
 favour;
Brave, I know, by my living now to say so;
And doubtlessly, with such a form and heart,
Would look into the fiery eyes of war,
As ardently for glory as you dared
An obscure death to save an unknown
 stranger,
In an as perilous, but opposite, element.
You are made for the service: I have served;
Have rank by birth and soldiership, and
 friends,
Who shall be yours. 'T is true this pause of
 peace
Favours such views at present scantily;
But 't will not last, men's spirits are too
 stirring;
And, after thirty years of conflict, peace
Is but a petty war, as the times show us
In every forest, or a mere arm'd truce.
War will reclaim his own; and, in the mean
 time,
You might obtain a post, which would insure
A higher soon, and, by my influence, fail not
To rise. I speak of Brandenburg, wherein
I stand well with the Elector; in Bohemia,
Like you, I am a stranger, and we are now
Upon its frontier.
 Ulr. You perceive my garb
Is Saxon, and of course my service due
To my own sovereign. If I must decline
Your offer, 't is with the same feeling which
Induced it.
 Stral. Why, this is mere usury!
I owe my life to you, and you refuse
The acquittance of the interest of the debt,
To heap more obligations on me, till
I bow beneath them.
 Ulr. You shall say so when
I claim the payment.
 Stral. Well, sir, since you will not—
You are nobly born?
 Ulr. I have heard my kinsmen say so.
 Stral. Your actions show it. Might I ask
 your name?
 Ulr. Ulric.

Stral. Your house's?
 Ulr. When I 'm worthy of it,
I 'll answer you.
 Stral. (aside). Most probably an Austrian,
Whom these unsettled times forbid to boast
His lineage on these wild and dangerous
 frontiers,
Where the name of his country is abhorr'd.
 [*Aloud to* FRITZ *and* IDENSTEIN.
So, sirs! how have ye sped in your re-
 searches?
 Iden. Indifferent well, your excellency.
 Stral. Then
I am to deem the plunderer is caught?
 Iden. Humph!—not exactly.
 Stral. Or at least suspected?
 Iden. Oh! for that matter, very much
 suspected.
 Stral. Who may he be?
 Iden. Why, don't *you* know, my lord?
 Stral. How should I? I was fast asleep.
 Iden. And so
Was I, and that 's the cause I know no more
Than does your excellency.
 Stral. Dolt!
 Iden. Why, if
Your lordship, being robb'd, don't recognise
The rogue; how should I, not being robb'd,
 identify
The thief among so many? In the crowd,
May it please your excellency, your thief
 looks
Exactly like the rest, or rather better:
'T is only at the bar and in the dungeon,
That wise men know your felon by his
 features;
But I 'll engage, that if seen there but once,
Whether he be found criminal or no,
His face shall be so.
 Stral. (to FRITZ*).* Prithee, Fritz, inform
 me
What hath been done to trace the fellow?
 Fritz. Faith!
My lord, not much as yet, except conjecture.
 Stral. Besides the loss (which, I must
 own, affects me
Just now materially), I needs would find
The villain out of public motives; for
So dexterous a spoiler, who could creep
Through my attendants, and so many peopled
And lighted chambers, on my rest, and snatch
The gold before my scarce-closed eyes, would
 soon
Leave bare your borough, Sir Intendant!
 Iden. True:
If there were aught to carry off, my lord.
 Ulr. What is all this?
 Stral. You join'd us but this morning,
And have not heard that I was robb'd last
 night.

Ulr. Some rumour of it reach'd me as I
 pass'd
The outer chambers of the palace, but
I know no further.
 Stral. It is a strange business;
The intendant can inform you of the facts.
 Iden. Most willingly. You see——
 Stral. (*impatiently*). Defer your tale,
Till certain of the hearer's patience.
 Iden. That
Can only be approved by proofs. You see——
 Stral. (*again interrupting him, and address-*
 ing ULRIC). In short, I was asleep
 upon a chair,
My cabinet before me, with some gold
Upon it (more than I much like to lose,
Though in part only): some ingenious person
Contrived to glide through all my own attend-
 ants,
Besides those of the place, and bore away
A hundred golden ducats, which to find
I would be fain, and there's an end. Perhaps
You (as I still am rather faint) would add
To yesterday's great obligation, this,
Though slighter, yet not slight, to aid these men
(Who seem but lukewarm) in recovering it?
 Ulr. Most willingly, and without loss of
 time—
(*To* IDENSTEIN). Come hither, mynheer!
 Iden. But so much haste bodes
Right little speed, and——
 Ulr. Standing motionless
None; so let's march; we'll talk as we go on.
 Iden. But——
 Ulr. Show the spot, and then I'll answer
 you.
 Fritz. I will, sir, with his excellency's leave.
 Stral. Do so, and take yon old ass with you.
 Fritz. Hence!
 Ulr. Come on, old oracle, expound thy
 riddle!
 [*Exit with* IDENSTEIN *and* FRITZ.
 Stral. (*solus*). A stalwart, active, soldier-
looking stripling,
Handsome as Hercules ere his first labour,
And with a brow of thought beyond his years
When in repose, till his eye kindles up
In answering yours. I wish I could engage
 him:
I have need of some such spirits near me now,
For this inheritance is worth a struggle.
And though I am not the man to yield without
 one,
Neither are they who now rise up between me
And my desire. The boy, they say, 's a bold
 one;
But he hath play'd the truant in some hour
Of freakish folly, leaving fortune to
Champion his claims. That's well. The
 father, whom

For years I've track'd, as does the bloodhound,
 never
In sight, but constantly in scent, had put me
To fault; but *here* I *have* him, and that's
 better.
It must be *he!* All circumstance proclaims it;
And careless voices, knowing not the cause
Of my inquiries, still confirm it.—Yes,
The man, his bearing, and the mystery
Of his arrival, and the time; the account, too,
The intendant gave (for I have not beheld her)
Of his wife's dignified but foreign aspect;
Besides the antipathy with which we met,
As snakes and lions shrink back from each
 other
By secret instinct that both must be foes
Deadly, without being natural prey to either;
All—all—confirm it to my mind. However,
We'll grapple, ne'ertheless. In a few hours
The order comes from Frankfort, if these
 waters
Rise not the higher (and the weather favours
Their quick abatement), and I'll have him safe
Within a dungeon, where he may avouch
His real estate and name; and there's no harm
 done,
Should he prove other than I deem. This
 robbery
(Save for the actual loss) is lucky also;
He's poor, and that's suspicious—he's un-
 known,
And that's defenceless.—True, we have no
 proofs
Of guilt,—but what hath he of innocence?
Were he a man indifferent to my prospects,
In other bearings, I should rather lay
The inculpation on the Hungarian, who
Hath something which I like not; and alone
Of all around, except the intendant, and
The prince's household and my own, had in-
 gress
Familiar to the chamber.

 Enter GABOR.

 Friend, how fare you?
 Gab. As those who fare well everywhere,
 when they
Have supp'd and slumber'd, no great matter
 how—
And you, my lord?
 Stral. Better in rest than purse:
Mine inn is like to cost me dear.
 Gab. I heard
Of your late loss; but 'tis a trifle to
One of your order.
 Stral. You would hardly think so,
Were the loss yours.
 Gab. I never had so much
(At once) in my whole life, and therefore am
 not

Fit to decide. But I came here to seek you.
Your couriers are turn'd back—I have out-
 stripp'd them,
In my return.
 Stral. You!—Why?
 Gab. I went at daybreak,
To watch for the abatement of the river,
As being anxious to resume my journey.
Your messengers were all check'd like my-
 self ;
And, seeing the case hopeless, I await
The current's pleasure.
 Stral. Would the dogs were in it !
Why did they not, at least, attempt the
 passage?
I order'd this at all risks.
 Gab. Could you order
The Oder to divide, as Moses did
The Red Sea (scarcely redder than the flood
Of the swoln stream), and be obey'd, perhaps
They might have ventured.
 Stral. I must see to it :
The knaves ! the slaves !—but they shall
 smart for this. [*Exit* STRALENHEIM.
 Gab. (*solus*). There goes my noble, feudal,
 self-will'd baron !
Epitome of what brave chivalry
The preux chevaliers of the good old times
Have left us. Yesterday he would have given
His lands (if he hath any), and, still dearer,
His sixteen quarterings, for as much fresh
 air
As would have fill'd a bladder, while he lay
Gurgling and foaming halfway through the
 window
Of his o'erset and water-logg'd conveyance ;
And now he storms at half a dozen wretches
Because they love their lives too ! Yet, he 's
 right :
'T is strange they should, when such as he
 may put them
To hazard at his pleasure. Oh, thou world !
Thou art indeed a melancholy jest !
 [*Exit* GABOR.

Scene II.

The Apartment of WERNER, *in the Palace.*

Enter JOSEPHINE *and* ULRIC.

 Jos. Stand back, and let me look on thee
 again !
My Ulric !—my beloved !—can it be—
After twelve years ?
 Ulr. My dearest mother !
 Jos. Yes !
My dream is realised—how beautiful !—
How more than all I sigh'd for ! Heaven
 receive
A mother's thanks ! a mother's tears of joy !

This is indeed thy work !—At such an hour,
 too,
He comes not only as a son, but saviour.
 Ulr. If such a joy await me, it must double
What I now feel, and lighten from my heart
A part of the long debt of duty, not
Of love (for that was ne'er withheld)—forgive
 me !
This long delay was not my fault.
 Jos. I know it,
But cannot think of sorrow now, and doubt
If I e'er felt it, 't is so dazzled from
My memory by this oblivious transport !—
My son !

Enter WERNER.

 Wer. What have we here,—more strangers?
 Jos. No !
Look upon him ! What do you see ?
 Wer. A stripling,
For the first time—
 Ulr. (*kneeling*). For twelve long years, my
 father !
 Wer. Oh, God !
 Jos. He faints !
 Wer. No—I am better now—
Ulric ! (*Embraces him*).
 Ulr. My father, Siegendorf !
 Wer. (*starting*). Hush ! boy—
The walls may hear that name !
 Ulr. What then ?
 Wer. Why, then—
But we will talk of that anon. Remember,
I must be known here but as Werner. Come !
Come to my arms again ! Why, thou look'st all
I should have been, and was not. Josephine !
Sure 't is no father's fondness dazzles me ;
But, had I seen that form amid ten thousand
Youth of the choicest, my heart would have
 chosen
This for my son !
 Ulr. And yet you knew me not !
 Wer. Alas ! I have had that upon my soul
Which makes me look on all men with an eye
That only knows the evil at first glance.
 Ulr. My memory served me far more
 fondly : I
Have not forgotten aught ; and oft-times in
The proud and princely halls of—(I 'll not
 name them,
As you say that 't is perilous)—but i' the
 pomp
Of your sire's feudal mansion, I look'd back
To the Bohemian mountains many a sunset,
And wept to see another day go down
O'er thee and me, with those huge hills
 between us.
They shall not part us more.
 Wer. I know not that.
Are you aware my father is no more ?

Ulr. Oh, heavens! I left him in a green
⠀⠀old age,
And looking like the oak, worn, but still
⠀⠀steady
Amidst the elements, whilst younger trees
Fell fast around him. 'T was scarce three
⠀⠀months since.
⠀⠀*Wer.* Why did you leave him?
⠀⠀*Jos.* (*embracing* ULRIC).⠀⠀Can you ask
⠀⠀that question?
Is he not *here?*
⠀⠀*Wer.*⠀⠀True; he hath sought his parents,
And found them; but oh! *how,* and in what
⠀⠀state!
⠀⠀*Ulr.* All shall be better'd. What we have
⠀⠀to do
Is to proceed, and to assert our rights,
Or rather yours; for I waive all, unless
Your father has disposed in such a sort
Of his broad lands as to make mine the fore-
⠀⠀most,
So that I must prefer my claim for form:
But I trust better, and that all is yours.
⠀⠀*Wer.* Have you not heard of Stralenheim?
⠀⠀*Ulr.*⠀⠀I saved
His life but yesterday; he's here.
⠀⠀*Wer.*⠀⠀You saved
The serpent who will sting us all!
⠀⠀*Ulr.*⠀⠀You speak
Riddles: what is this Stralenheim to us?
⠀⠀*Wer.* Everything! One who claims our
⠀⠀father's lands:
Our distant kinsman, and our nearest foe.
⠀⠀*Ulr.* I never heard his name till now.
⠀⠀The count,
Indeed, spoke sometimes of a kinsman, who,
If his own line should fail, might be remotely
Involved in the succession; but his titles
Were never named before me—and what then?
His right must yield to ours.
⠀⠀*Wer.*⠀⠀Ay, if at Prague;
But here he is all-powerful; and has spread
Snares for thy father, which, if hitherto
He hath escaped them, is by fortune, not
By favour.
⠀⠀*Ulr.*⠀⠀Doth he personally know you?
⠀⠀*Wer.* No; but he guesses shrewdly at my
⠀⠀person,
As he betray'd last night; and I, perhaps,
But owe my temporary liberty
To his uncertainty.
⠀⠀*Ulr.*⠀⠀I think you wrong him
(Excuse me for the phrase); but Stralenheim
Is not what you prejudge him, or, if so,
He owes me something both for past and pre-
⠀⠀sent.
I saved his life, he therefore trusts in me.
He hath been plunder'd too, since he came
⠀⠀hither:
Is sick; a stranger; and as such not now

Able to trace the villain who hath robb'd him:
I have pledged myself to do so; and the busi-
⠀⠀ness
Which brought me here was chiefly that: but I
Have found, in searching for another's dross,
My own whole treasure—you, my parents!
⠀⠀*Wer.* (*agitatedly*).⠀⠀Who
Taught you to mouth that name of " villain "?
⠀⠀*Ulr.*⠀⠀What
More noble name belongs to common thieves?
⠀⠀*Wer.* Who taught you thus to brand an
⠀⠀unknown being
With an infernal stigma?
⠀⠀*Ulr.*⠀⠀My own feelings
Taught me to name a ruffian from his deeds.
⠀⠀*Wer.* Who taught you, long-sought and
⠀⠀ill-found boy! that
It would be safe for my own son to insult
⠀⠀me?
⠀⠀*Ulr.* I named a villain. What is there in
⠀⠀common
With such a being and my father?
⠀⠀*Wer.*⠀⠀Everything!
That ruffian is thy father!
⠀⠀*Jos.*⠀⠀Oh, my son!
Believe him not—and yet!——(*her voice
⠀⠀falters*).
⠀⠀*Ulr.* (*starts, looks earnestly at* WERNER *and
⠀⠀then says slowly,*)⠀⠀And you avow it?
⠀⠀*Wer.* Ulric, before you dare despise your
⠀⠀father,
Learn to divine and judge his actions.
⠀⠀Young,
Rash, new to life, and rear'd in luxury's lap,
Is it for you to measure passion's force,
Or misery's temptation? Wait—(not long,
It cometh like the night, and quickly)—
⠀⠀Wait!—
Wait till, like me, your hopes are blighted—
⠀⠀till
Sorrow and shame are handmaids of your
⠀⠀cabin;
Famine and poverty your guests at table;
Despair your bed-fellow—then rise, but not
From sleep, and judge! Should that day e'er
⠀⠀arrive—
Should you see then the serpent, who hath
⠀⠀coil'd
Himself around all that is dear and noble
Of you and yours, lie slumbering in your
⠀⠀path,
With but *his* folds between your steps and
⠀⠀happiness,
When *he,* who lives but to tear from you
⠀⠀name,
Lands, life itself, lies at your mercy, with
Chance your conductor; midnight for your
⠀⠀mantle;
The bare knife in your hand, and earth asleep,
Even to your deadliest foe; and he as 't were

Inviting death, by looking like it, while
His death alone can save you :—Thank your
 God !
If then, like me, content with petty plunder,
You turn aside——I did so.
 Ulr. But——
 Wer. (abruptly). Hear me !
I will not brook a human voice—scarce dare
Listen to my own (if that be human still)—
Hear me ! you do not know this man—I do.
He's mean, deceitful, avaricious. You
Deem yourself safe, as young and brave ; but
 learn
None are secure from desperation, few
From subtilty. My worst foe, Stralenheim,
Housed in a prince's palace, couch'd within
A prince's chamber, lay below my knife !
An instant—a mere motion—the least im-
 pulse—
Had swept him and all fears of mine from
 earth.
He was within my power—my knife was
 raised—
Withdrawn—and I'm in his :—are you not so?
Who tells you that he knows you *not?* Who
 says
He hath not lured you here to end you? or
To plunge you, with your parents, in a
 dungeon? [*He pauses.*
 Ulr. Proceed—proceed!
 Wer. *Me* he hath ever known,
And hunted through each change of time—
 name—fortune—
And why not *you?* Are you more versed in
 men ?
He wound snares round me ? flung along my
 path
Reptiles, whom, in my youth, I would have
 spurn'd
Even from my presence; but, in spurning now,
Fill only with fresh venom. Will you be
More patient ? Ulric !—Ulric !—there are
 crimes
Made venial by the occasion, and temptations
Which nature cannot master or forbear.
 Ulr. (who looks first at him, and then at
 Josephine). My mother !
 Wer. Ah ! I thought so : you have now
Only one parent. I have lost alike
Father and son, and stand alone.
 Ulr. But stay !
 [Werner *rushes out of the chamber.*
 Jos. (to Ulric). Follow him not, until this
 storm of passion
Abates. Think'st thou, that were it well for
 him,
I had not follow'd ?
 Ulr. I obey, you mother,
Although reluctantly. My first act shall not
Be one of disobedience.

 Jos. Oh ! he is good !
Condemn him not from his own mouth, but
 trust
To me, who have borne so much with him,
 and for him,
That this is but the surface of his soul,
And that the depth is rich in better things.
 Ulr. These then are but my father's prin-
 ciples ?
My mother thinks not with him ?
 Jos. Nor doth he
Think as he speaks. Alas ! long years of
 grief
Have made him sometimes thus.
 Ulr. Explain to me
More clearly, then, these claims of Stralen-
 heim,
That, when I see the subject in its bearings,
I may prepare to face him, or at least
To extricate you from your present perils.
I pledge myself to accomplish this—but would
I had arrived a few hours sooner !
 Jos. Ay !
Hadst thou but done so !

 Enter Gabor *and* Idenstein, *with*
 Attendants.

 Gab. (to Ulric). I have sought you, com-
 rade.
So this is my reward !
 Ulr. What do you mean ?
 Gab. 'Sdeath ! have I lived to these years,
 and for this !
(*To* Idenstein). But for your age and folly,
 I would——
 Iden. Help !
Hands off ! Touch an intendant !
 Gab. Do not think
I'll honour you so much as save your throat
From the Ravenstone by choking you myself.
 Iden. I thank you for the respite : but
 there are
Those who have greater need of it than me.
 Ulr. Unriddle this vile wrangling, or——
 Gab. At once, then,
The baron has been robbed, and upon me
This worthy personage has deign'd to fix
His kind suspicions—me ! whom he ne'er saw
Till yester' evening.
 Iden. Wouldst have me suspect
My own acquaintances ? You have to learn
That I keep better company.
 Gab. You shall
Keep the best shortly, and the last for all
 men,
The worms ! you hound of malice !
 [Gabor *seizes on him.*
 Ulr. (interfering). Nay, no violence;
He's old, unarm'd—be temperate, Gabor !

Gab. (*letting go* IDENSTEIN). True:
I am a fool to lose myself because
Fools deem me knave: it is their homage.

Ulr. (*to* IDENSTEIN). How
Fare you?

Iden. Help!

Ulr. I *have* help'd you.

Iden. Kill him! then
I'll say so.

Gab. I am calm—live on!

Iden. That's more
Than you shall do, if there be judge or
 judgment
In Germany. The baron shall decide!

Gab. Does *he* abet you in your accusation?

Iden. Does he not?

Gab. Then next time let him go sink
Ere I go hang for snatching him from drown-
 ing.
But here he comes!

 Enter STRALENHEIM,

Gab. (*goes up to him*). My noble lord, I'm
 here!

Stral. Well, sir!

Gab. Have you aught with me?

Stral. What should I
Have with you?

Gab. You know best, if yesterday's
Flood has not wash'd away your memory;
But that's a trifle. I stand here accused,
In phrases not equivocal, by yon
Intendant, of the pillage of your person
Or chamber :—is the charge your own or his?

Stral. I accuse no man.

Gab. Then you acquit me, baron?

Stral. I know not whom to accuse, or to
 acquit,
Or scarcely to suspect.

Gab. But you at least
Should know whom *not* to suspect. I am
 insulted—
Oppress'd here by these menials, and I look
To you for remedy—teach them their duty!
To look for thieves at home were part of it,
If duly taught; but, in one word, if I
Have an accuser, let it be a man
Worthy to be so of a man like me.
I am your equal.

Stral. You!

Gab. Ay, sir; and, for
Aught that you know, superior; but proceed—
I do not ask for hints, and surmises,
And circumstance, and proof: I know enough
Of what I have done for you, and what you
 owe me,
To have at least waited your payment rather
Than paid myself, had I been eager of
Your gold. I also know, that were I even
The villain I am deem'd, the service render'd

So recently would not permit you to
Pursue me to the death, except through
 shame,
Such as would leave your scutcheon but a
 blank.
But this is nothing: I demand of you
Justice upon your unjust servants, and
From your own lips a disavowal of
All sanction of their insolence: thus much
You owe to the unknown, who asks no more,
And never thought to have ask'd so much.

Stral. This tone
May be of innocence.

Gab. 'Sdeath! who dare doubt it,
Except such villains as ne'er had it?

Stral. You
Are hot, sir.

Gab. Must I turn an icicle
Before the breath of menials, and their
 master?

Stral. Ulric! you know this man; I found
 him in
Your company.

Gab. We found *you* in the Oder,
Would we had left you there!

Stral. I give you thanks, sir.

Gab. I've earned them; but might have
 earn'd more from others,
Perchance, if I had left you to your fate.

Stral. Ulric! you know this man?

Gab. No more than you do,
If he avouches not my honour.

Ulr. I
Can vouch your courage, and, as far as my
Own brief connexion led me, honour.

Stral. Then
I'm satisfied.

Gab. (*ironically*). Right easily, methinks.
What is the spell in his asseveration
More than in mine?

Stral. I merely said that *I*
Was satisfied—not that you are absolved.

Gab. Again! Am I accused or no?

Stral. Go to!
You wax too insolent. If circumstance
And general suspicion be against you,
Is the fault mine? Is't not enough that I
Decline all question of your guilt or inno-
 cence?

Gab. My lord, my lord, this is mere
 cozenage,
A vile equivocation; you well know
Your doubts are certainties to all around
 you—
Your looks a voice—your frowns a sentence;
 you
Are practising your power on me—because
You have it; but beware! you know not
 whom
You strive to tread on.

Stral. Threat'st thou?
Gab. Not so much
As you accuse. You hint the basest injury,
And I retort it with an open warning.
 Stral. As you have said, 't is true I owe
 you something,
For which you seem disposed to pay yourself.
 Gab. Not with your gold.
 Stral. With bootless insolence.
 [*To his Attendants and* IDENSTEIN.
You need not further to molest this man,
But let him go his way. Ulric, good morrow!
 [*Exit* STRALENHEIM, IDENSTEIN, *and*
 Attendants.
 Gab. (*following*). I'll after him and—
 Ulr. (*stopping him*). Not a step.
 Gab. Who shall
Oppose me?
 Ulr. Your own reason, with a moment's
Thought.
 Gab. Must I bear this?
 Ulr. Pshaw! we all must bear
The arrogance of something higher than
Ourselves—the highest cannot temper Satan,
Nor the lowest his vicegerents upon earth.
I've seen you brave the elements, and bear
Things which had made this silkworm cast
 his skin—
And shrink you from a few sharp sneers and
 words?
 Gab. Must I bear to be deem'd a thief? If
 't were
A bandit of the woods, I could have borne it—
There's something daring in it:—but to steal
The moneys of a slumbering man!—
 Ulr. It seems, then,
You are *not* guilty.
 Gab. Do I hear aright?
You too!
 Ulr. I merely ask'd a simple question.
 Gab. If the judge ask'd me, I would
 answer "No"—
To you I answer *thus.* [*He draws.*
 Ulr. (*drawing*). With all my heart!
 Jos. Without there! Ho! help! help!—
 Oh, God! here's murder!
 [*Exit* JOSEPHINE, *shrieking*

GABOR *and* ULRIC *fight.* GABOR *is disarmed
just as* STRALENHEIM, JOSEPHINE, IDEN-
STEIN, *&c., re-enter.*

 Jos. Oh! glorious heaven! He's safe!
 Stral. (*to* JOSEPHINE). Who's safe?
 Jos. My——
 Ulr. (*interrupting her with a stern look, and
turning afterwards to* STRALENHEIM).
 Both!
Here's no great harm done.
 Stral. What hath caused all this?
 Ulr. You, baron, I believe; but as the effect

Is harmless, let it not disturb you.—Gabor!
There is your sword; and when you bare it
 next,
Let it not be against your *friends.*
 [ULRIC *pronounces the last words slowly
 and emphatically in a low voice to*
 GABOR.
 Gab. I thank you
Less for my life than for your counsel.
 Stral. These
Brawls must end here.
 Gab. (*taking his sword*). They *shall.* You've
 wrong'd me, Ulric,
More with your unkind thoughts than sword:
 I would
The last were in my bosom rather than
The first in yours. I could have borne yon
 noble's
Absurd insinuations—ignorance
And dull suspicion are a part of his
Entail will last him longer than his lands.—
But I may fit *him* yet:—you have vanquish'd
 me.
I was the fool of passion to conceive
That I could cope with you, whom I had seen
Already proved by greater perils than
Rest in this arm. We may meet by and by,
However—but in friendship. [*Exit* GABOR.
 Stral. I will brook
No more! This outrage following up his
 insults,
Perhaps his guilt, has cancell'd all the little
I owed him heretofore for the so-vaunted
Aid which he added to your abler succour.
Ulric, you are not hurt?—
 Ulr. Not even by a scratch.
 Stral. (*to* IDENSTEIN). Intendant! take
 your measures to secure
Yon fellow: I revoke my former lenity.
He shall be sent to Frankfort with an escort,
The instant that the waters have abated.
 Iden. Secure him! He hath got his sword
 again—
And seems to know the use on 't; 't is his
 trade,
Belike;—I'm a civilian.
 Stral. Fool! are not
Yon score of vassals dogging at your heels
Enough to seize a dozen such? Hence! after
 him!
 Ulr. Baron, I do beseech you!
 Stral. I must be
Obey'd. No words!
 Iden. Well, if it must be so—
March, vassals! I'm your leader, and will
 bring
The rear up: a wise general never should
Expose his precious life—on which all rests.
I like that article of war.
 [*Exit* IDENSTEIN *and Attendants.*

Stral. Come hither,
Ulric; what does that woman here? Oh! now
I recognise her, 'tis the stranger's wife
Whom they *name* " Werner."
 Ulr. 'T is his name.
Stral. Indeed!
Is not your husband visible, fair dame?—
Jos. Who seeks him?
Stral. No one—for the present: but
I fain would parley, Ulric, with yourself
Alone.
Ulr. I will retire with you.
Jos. Not so:
You are the latest stranger, and command
All places here.
(*Aside to* ULRIC, *as she goes out*). O Ulric!
 have a care—
Remember what depends on a rash word!
Ulr. (*to* JOSEPHINE). Fear not!—
 [*Exit* JOSEPHINE.
Stral. Ulric, I think that I may trust you;
You saved my life—and acts like these beget
Unbounded confidence.
Ulr. Say on.
Stral. Mysterious
And long-engender'd circumstances (not
To be now fully enter'd on) have made
This man obnoxious—perhaps fatal to me.
Ulr. Who? Gabor, the Hungarian?
Stral. No—this " Werner "—
With the false name and habit.
Ulr. How can this be?
He is the poorest of the poor—and yellow
Sickness sits cavern'd in his hollow eye:
The man is helpless.
Stral. He is—'tis no matter;—
But if he be the man I deem (and that
He is so, all around us here—and much
That is not here—confirm my apprehension),
He must be made secure ere twelve hours
 further.
Ulr. And what have I to do with this?
Stral. I have sent
To Frankfort, to the governor, my friend,
(I have the authority to do so by
An order of the house of Brandenburg),
For a fit escort—but this cursed flood
Bars all access, and may do for some hours.
Ulr. It is abating.
Stral. That is well.
Ulr. But how
Am I concern'd?
Stral. As one who did so much
For me, you cannot be indifferent to
That which is of more import to me than
The life you rescued.—Keep your eye on *him!*
The man avoids me, knows that I now know
 him.—
Watch him!—as you would watch the wild
 boar when

He makes against you in the hunter's gap—
Like him he must be spear'd.
 Ulr. Why so?
Stral. He stands
Between me and a brave inheritance!
Oh! could you see it! But you shall.
 Ulr. I hope so.
Stral. It is the richest of the rich Bohemia,
Unscathed by scorching war. It lies so near
The strongest city, Prague, that fire and sword
Have skimm'd it lightly: so that now, besides
Its own exuberance, it bears double value
Confronted with whole realms far and near
Made deserts.
 Ulr. You describe it faithfully.
Stral. Ay—could you see it, you would
 say so—but,
As I have said, you shall.
 Ulr. I accept the omen.
 Stral. Then claim a recompense from it
 and me,
Such as *both* may make worthy your accept-
 ance
And services to me and mine for ever.
 Ulr. And this sole, sick, and miserable
 wretch—
This way-worn stranger—stands between you
 and
This Paradise?—(As Adam did between
The devil and his)—[*Aside*].
Stral. He doth.
Ulr. Hath he no right?
Stral. Right! none. A disinherited pro-
 digal,
Who for these twenty years disgraced his
 lineage
In all his acts—but chiefly by his marriage,
And living amidst commerce-fetching burgh-
 ers,
And dabbling merchants, in a mart of Jews.
Ulr. He has a wife, then?
Stral. You'd be sorry to
Call such your mother. You have seen the
 woman
He *calls* his wife.
 Ulr. Is she not so?
Stral. No more
Than he's your father:—an Italian girl,
The daughter of a banish'd man, who lives
On love and poverty with this same Werner.
Ulr. They are childless, then?
Stral. There is or was a bastard,
Whom the old man—the grandsire (as old age
Is ever doting) took to warm his bosom,
As it went chilly downward to the grave:
But the imp stands not in my path—he has
 fled,
No one knows whither; and if he had not,
His claims alone were too contemptible
To stand.—Why do you smile?

Ulr.　　　　　At your vain fears:
A poor man almost in his grasp—a child
Of doubtful birth—can startle a grandee !
　　Stral.　All's to be fear'd, where all is to be
　　　　gain'd.
　　Ulr.　True ; and aught done to save or to
　　　　obtain it.
　　Stral.　You have harp'd the very string
　　　　next to my heart.
I may depend upon you ?
　　Ulr.　　　　　'Twere too late
To doubt it.
　　Stral.　　　Let no foolish pity shake
Your bosom (for the appearance of the man
Is pitiful)—he is a wretch, as likely
To have robb'd me as the fellow more sus-
　　　pected,
Except that circumstance is less against him ;
He being lodged far off, and in a chamber
Without approach to mine ; and, to say truth,
I think too well of blood allied to mine,
To deem he would descend to such an act :
Besides, he was a soldier, and a brave one
Once—though too rash.
　　Ulr.　　　And they, my lord, we know
By our experience, never plunder till
They knock the brains out first—which makes
　　　them heirs,
Not thieves. The dead, who feel nought, can
　　　lose nothing,
Nor e'er be robb'd : their spoils are a be-
　　　quest—
No more.
　　Stral.　Go to ! you are a wag.　But say
I may be sure you'll keep an eye on this man,
And let me know his slightest movement
　　　towards
Concealment or escape ?
　　Ulr.　　　　　You may be sure
You yourself could not watch him more than I
Will be his sentinel.
　　Stral.　　　By this you make me
Yours, and for ever.
　　Ulr.　　Such is my intention.　[*Exeunt.*

Act III.

Scene I.—A Hall in the same Palace, from
*　　whence the secret passage leads.*

Enter Werner *and* Gabor.

　　Gab.　Sir, I have told my tale : if it so
　　　please you
To give me refuge for a few hours, well—
If not, I'll try my fortune elsewhere.
　　Wer.　　　　　　How
Can I, so wretched, give to Misery
A shelter ?—wanting such myself as much
As e'er the hunted deer a covert——

　　Gab.　　　　　　Or
The wounded lion his cool cave.　Methinks
You rather look like one would turn at bay,
And rip the hunter's entrails.
　　Wer.　　　　　Ah !
　　Gab.　　　　　I care not
If it be so, being much disposed to do
The same myself.　But will you shelter me ?
I am oppress'd like you—and poor like you—
Disgraced——
　　Wer. (*abruptly*).　Who told you that I was
　　　disgraced ?
　　Gab.　No one ; nor did I say *you* were so ;
　　　with
Your poverty my likeness ended ; but
I said *I* was so—and would add, with truth,
As undeservedly as *you.*
　　Wer.　　　　　Again !
As *I*?
　　Gab.　Or any other honest man.
What the devil would you have ? You don't
　　　believe me
Guilty of this base theft ?
　　Wer.　　　　　No, no—I cannot.
　　Gab.　Why that's my heart of honour ! yon
　　　young gallant—
Your miserly intendant and dense noble—
All—all suspected me ; and why ? because
I am the worst clothed and least named
　　　amongst them ;
Although, were Momus' lattice in your
　　　breasts,
My soul might brook to open it more widely
Than theirs : but thus it is—you poor and
　　　helpless—
Both still more than myself.
　　Wer.　　　　　How knew you that ?
　　Gab.　You're right : I ask for shelter at
　　　the hand
Which I call helpless ; if you now deny it,
I were well paid.　But you, who seem to
　　　have proved
The wholesome bitterness of life, know well,
By sympathy, that all the outspread gold
Of the New World the Spaniard boasts about,
Could never tempt the man who knows its
　　　worth
Weigh'd at its proper value in the balance,
Save in such guise (and there I grant its
　　　power,
Because I feel it) as may leave no nightmare
Upon his heart o' nights.
　　Wer.　　　　　What do you mean ?
　　Gab.　Just what I say ; I thought my
　　　speech was plain ;
You are no thief—nor I—and, as true men,
Should aid each other.
　　Wer.　　　It is a damn'd world, sir.
　　Gab.　So is the nearest of the two next,
　　　as

The priests say (and no doubt they should
　　　know best),
Therefore I'll stick by this—as being loth
To suffer martyrdom, at least with such
An epitaph as larceny upon my tomb.
It is but a night's lodging which I crave
To-morrow I will try the waters, as
The dove did, trusting that they have abated.
　　Wer. Abated? Is there hope of that?
　　Gab.　　　　　　　　　　There was
At noontide.
　　Wer.　　Then we may be safe.
　　Gab.　　　　　　　　Are *you*
In peril?
　　Wer. Poverty is ever so.
　　Gab. That I know by long practice. Will
　　　you not
Promise to make mine less?
　　Wer.　　　　　　Your poverty?
　　Gab. No—you don't look a leech for that
　　　disorder;
I meant my peril only: you've a roof,
And I have none; I merely seek a covert.
　　Wer. Rightly; for how should such a
　　　wretch as I
Have gold?
　　Gab.　　Scarce honestly, to say the truth
　　　on't,
Although I almost wish you had the baron's.
　　Wer. Dare you insinuate?
　　Gab.　　　　　What?
　　Wer.　　　　　　　　Are you aware
To whom you speak?
　　Gab.　　　　　No; and I am not used
Greatly to care. (*A noise heard without.*) But
　　　hark! they come!
　　Wer.　　　　　　Who come?
　　Gab. The intendant and his man-hounds
　　　after me:
I'd face them—but it were in vain to ex-
　　　pect
Justice at hands like theirs. Where shall
　　　I go?
But show me any place. I do assure you,
If there be faith in man, I am most guiltless:
Think if it were your own case!
　　Wer. (*aside*).　　　　Oh, just God!
Thy hell is not hereafter! Am I dust still?
　　Gab. I see you're moved; and it shows
　　　well in you:
I may live to requite it.
　　Wer.　　　　　Are you not
A spy of Stralenheim's?
　　Gab.　　　　　　Not I! and if
I were, what is there to espy in you?
Although, I recollect, his frequent question
About you and your spouse might lead to some
Suspicion; but you best know—what—and
　　　why.
I am his deadliest foe.

　　Wer.　　　　You?
　　Gab.　　　　　　　After such
A treatment for the service which in part
I render'd him, I am his enemy:
If you are not his friend, you will assist me.
　　Wer. I will.
　　Gab.　　But how?
　　Wer. (*showing the panel*). There is a se-
　　　cret spring:
Remember, I discover'd it by chance,
And used it but for safety.
　　Gab.　　　　　Open it,
And I will use it for the same.
　　Wer.　　　　　　I found it,
As I have said: it leads through winding
　　　walls
(So thick as to bear paths within their ribs,
Yet lose no jot of strength or stateliness),
And hollow cells, and obscure niches, to
I know not whither; you must not advance:
Give me your word.
　　Gab.　　　It is unnecessary:
How should I make my way in darkness
　　　through
A Gothic labyrinth of unknown windings?
　　Wer. Yes, but who knows to what place
　　　it may lead?
I know not—(mark you!)—but who knows it
　　　might not
Lead even into the chamber of your foe?
So strangely were contrived these galleries
By our Teutonic fathers in old days,
When man built less against the elements
Than his next neighbour. You must not
　　　advance
Beyond the two first windings; if you do
(Albeit I never pass'd them), I'll not answer
For what you may be led to.
　　Gab.　　　　　But I will.
A thousand thanks!
　　Wer. You'll find the spring more obvious
On the other side; and, when you would
　　　return,
It yields to the least touch.
　　Gab.　　　　　I'll in—farewell!
　　　　　[GABOR *goes in by the secret panel.*
　　Wer. (*solus*). What have I done? Alas!
　　　what *had* I done
Before to make this fearful? Let it be
Still some atonement that I save the man,
Whose sacrifice had saved perhaps my own—
They come! to seek elsewhere what is before
　　　them!

Enter IDENSTEIN *and Others.*

　　Iden. Is he not here? He must have
　　　vanish'd then
Through the dim Gothic glass by pious aid
Of pictured saints upon the red and yellow

Casements, through which the sunset streams
 like sunrise
On long pearl-colour'd beards and crimson
 crosses,
And gilded crosiers, and cross'd arms, and
 cowls,
And helms, and twisted armour, and long
 swords,
All the fantastic furniture of windows
Dim with brave knights and holy hermits,
 whose
Likeness and fame alike rest in some panes
Of crystal, which each rattling wind pro-
 claims
As frail as any other life or glory.
He's gone, however.

Wer. Whom do you seek?
Iden. A villain.
Wer. Why need you come so far, then?
Iden. In the search
Of him who robb'd the baron.
Wer. Are you sure
You have divined the man?
Iden. As sure as you
Stand there: but where's he gone?
Wer. Who?
Iden. He we sought.
Wer. You see he is not here.
Iden. And yet we traced him
Up to this hall. Are you accomplices?
Or deal you in the black art?
Wer. I deal plainly,
To many men the blackest.
Iden. It may be
I have a question or two for yourself
Hereafter; but we must continue now
Our search for t'other.
Wer. You had best begin
Your inquisition now: I may not be
So patient always.
Iden. I should like to know,
In good sooth, if you really are the man
That Stralenheim's in quest of.
Wer. Insolent!
Said you not that he was not here?
Iden. Yes, *one;*
But there's another whom he tracks more
 keenly,
And soon, it may be, with authority
Both paramount to his and mine. But, come!
Bustle, my boys! we are at fault.
 [*Exit* IDENSTEIN *and Attendants.*
Wer. In what
A maze hath my dim destiny involved me!
And one base sin hath done me less ill
 than
The leaving undone one far greater. Down,
Thou busy devil, rising in my heart!
Thou art too late! I'll nought to do with
 blood.

 Enter ULRIC.

Ulr. I sought you, father.
Wer. Is't not dangerous?
Ulr. No; Stralenheim is ignorant of all
Or any of the ties between us: more—
He sends me here a spy upon your actions,
Deeming me wholly his.
Wer. I cannot think it:
'Tis but a snare he winds about us both,
To swoop the sire and son at once.
Ulr. I cannot
Pause in each petty fear, and stumble at
The doubts that rise like briers in our path,
But must break through them, as an unarm'd
 carle
Would, though with naked limbs, were the
 wolf rustling
In the same thicket where he hew'd for
 bread.
Nets are for thrushes, eagles are not caught
 so:
We'll overfly or rend them.
Wer. Show me *how?*
Ulr. Can you not guess?
Wer. I cannot.
Ulr. That is strange.
Came the thought ne'er into your mind *last
 night?*
Wer. I understand you not.
Ulr. Then we shall never
More understand each other. But to change
The topic——
Wer. You mean to *pursue* it, as
'T is of our safety.
Ulr. Right; I stand corrected.
I see the subject now more clearly, and
Our general situation in its bearings.
The waters are abating; a few hours
Will bring his summon'd myrmidons from
 Frankfort,
When you will be a prisoner, perhaps worse.
And I an outcast, bastardised by practice
Of this same baron to make way for him.
Wer. And now your remedy! I thought
 to escape
By means of this accursed gold; but now
I dare not use it, show it, scarce look on it.
Methinks it wears upon its face my guilt
For motto, not the mintage of the state;
And, for the sovereign's head, my own begirt
With hissing snakes, which curl around my
 temples,
And cry to all beholders, Lo! a villain!
Ulr. You must not use it, at least now;
 but take
This ring. [*He gives* WERNER *a jewel.*
Wer. A gem! It was my father's!
Ulr. And
As such is now your own. With this you must

Bribe the intendant for his old caleche
And horses to pursue your route at sunrise,
Together with my mother.

Wer.　　　　　　　　And leave you,
So lately found, in peril too?

Ulr.　　　　　　　　Fear nothing!
The only fear were if we fled together,
For that would make our ties beyond all
　　doubt.
The waters only lie in flood between
This burgh and Frankfort; so far's in our
　　favour.
The route on to Bohemia, though encum-
　　ber'd,
Is not impassable; and when you gain
A few hours' start, the difficulties will be
The same to your pursuers. Once beyond
The frontier, and you're safe.

Wer.　　　　　　　　My noble boy!

Ulr. Hush! hush! no transports: we'll
　　indulge in them
In Castle Siegendorf! Display no gold!
Show Idenstein the gem (I know the man,
And have look'd through him): it will answer
　　thus
A double purpose. Stralenheim lost *gold*—
No jewel; therefore it could *not* be his;
And then the man who was possest of this
Can hardly be suspected of abstracting
The baron's coin, when he could thus convert
This ring to more than Stralenheim has lost
By his last night's slumber. Be not over
　　timid
In your address, nor yet too arrogant,
And Idenstein will serve you.

Wer.　　　　　　　　I will follow
In all things your direction.

Ulr.　　　　　　　　I would have
Spared you the trouble; but had I appear'd
To take an interest in you, and still more
By dabbling with a jewel in your favour,
All had been known at once.

Wer.　　　　　　My guardian angel!
This overpays the past. But how wilt thou
Fare in our absence?

Ulr.　　　　　Stralenheim knows nothing
Of me as aught of kindred with yourself.
I will but wait a day or two with him
To lull all doubts, and then rejoin my father.

Wer. To part no more!

Ulr.　　　　　I know not that; but at
The least we'll meet again once more.

Wer.　　　　　　　　My boy!
My friend! my only child, and sole pre-
　　server!
Oh, do not hate me!

Ulr.　　　　　Hate my father!

Wer.　　　　　　　　Ay,
My father hated me. Why not my son?

Ulr. Your father knew you not as I do.

Wer.　　　　　　　　Scorpions
Are in thy words! Thou know me? in this
　　guise
Thou canst not know me, I am not myself;
Yet (hate me not) I will be soon.

Ulr.　　　　　　　　I'll *wait!*
In the mean time be sure that all a son
Can do for parents shall be done for mine.

Wer. I see it, and I feel it; yet I feel
Further—that you despise me.

Ulr.　　　　　Wherefore should I?

Wer. Must I repeat my humiliation?

Ulr.　　　　　　　　No!
I have fathom'd it and you. But let us talk
Of this no more. Or if it must be ever,
Not *now*. Your error has redoubled all
The present difficulties of our house,
At secret war with that of Stralenheim:
All we have now to think of is to baffle
HIM. I have shown *one* way.

Wer.　　　　　　　The only one,
And I embrace it, as I did my son,
Who show'd *himself* and father's *safety* in
One day.

Ulr. You *shall* be safe; let that suffice.
Would Stralenheim's appearance in Bohemia
Disturb your right, or mine, if once we were
Admitted to our lands?

Wer.　　　　　　　Assuredly,
Situate as we are now, although the first
Possessor might, as usual, prove the strongest,
Especially the next in blood.

Ulr.　　　　　　　*Blood!* 'tis
A word of many meanings; in the veins,
And out of them, it is a different thing—
And so it should be, when the same in
　　blood
(As it is call'd) are aliens to each other,
Like Theban brethren: when a part is bad,
A few spilt ounces purify the rest.

Wer. I do not apprehend you.

Ulr.　　　　　　　That may be—
And should, perhaps—and yet——but get ye
　　ready;
You and my mother must away to-night.
Here comes the intendant: sound him with
　　the gem;
'Twill sink into his venal soul like lead
Into the deep, and bring up slime and mud,
And ooze too, from the bottom, as the lead
　　doth
With its greased understratum; but no less
Will serve to warn our vessels through these
　　shoals.
The freight is rich, so heave the line in
　　time!
Farewell! I scarce have time, but yet your
　　hand,
My father!——

Wer.　　　　Let me embrace thee!

Ulr. We may be
Observed: subdue your nature to the hour!
Keep off from me as from your foe!
Wer. Accursed
Be he who is the stifling cause which smothers
The best and sweetest feeling of our hearts;
At such an hour too!
Ulr. Yes, curse—it will ease you!
Here is the intendant.

 Enter IDENSTEIN.

 Master Idenstein,
How fare you in your purpose? Have you
 caught
The rogue?
Iden. No, faith!
Ulr. Well, there are plenty more:
You may have better luck another chase.
Where is the baron?
Iden. Gone back to his chamber:
And now I think on 't, asking after you
With nobly-born impatience.
Ulr. Your great men
Must be answer'd on the instant, as the
 bound
Of the stung steed replies unto the spur:
'T is well they have horses, too; for, if they
 had not,
I fear that men must draw their chariots, as
They say kings did Sesostris.
Iden. Who was he?
Ulr. An old Bohemian—an imperial gipsy.
Iden. A gipsy or Bohemian, 't is the same,
For they pass by both names. And was he
 one?
Ulr. I've heard so; but I must take leave.
 Intendant,
Your servant!—Werner (*to* WERNER *slightly*),
 if that be your name,
Yours. [*Exit* ULRIC.
Iden. A well-spoken pretty-faced young
 man!
And prettily behaved! He knows his station,
You see, sir: how he gave to each his due
Precedence!
Wer. I perceived it, and applaud
His just discernment and your own.
Iden. That 's well—
That's very well. You also know your place,
 too;
And yet I don't know that I know your place.
Wer. (*showing the ring*). Would this as-
 sist your knowledge?
Iden. How!—What!—Eh?
A jewel.
Wer. 'Tis your own on one condition.
Iden. Mine!—Name it!
Wer. That hereafter you permit me
At thrice its value to redeem it: 'tis
A family ring.

Iden. A family!—*yours!*—a gem!
I 'm breathless!
Wer. You must also furnish me,
An hour ere daybreak, with all means to quit
This place.
Iden. But is it real? Let me look on it:
Diamond, by all that 's glorious!
Wer. Come, I'll trust you:
You have guess'd, no doubt, that I was born
 above
My present seeming.
Iden. I can't say I did,
Though this looks like it: this is the true
 breeding
Of gentle blood!
Wer. I have important reasons
For wishing to continue privily
My journey hence.
Iden. So then *you are* the man
Whom Stralenheim's in quest of?
Wer. I am not;
But being taken for him might conduct
So much embarrassment to me just now,
And to the baron's self hereafter—'tis
To spare both that I would avoid all bustle.
Iden. Be you the man or no, 't is not my
 business;
Besides, I never could obtain the half
From this proud, niggardly noble, who would
 raise
The country for some missing bits of coin,
And never offer a precise reward—
But *this!*—another look!
Wer. Gaze on it freely;
At day-dawn it is yours.
Iden. Oh, thou sweet sparkler!
Thou more than stone of the philosopher!
Thou touchstone of Philosophy herself!
Thou bright eye of the Mine! thou loadstar
 of
The Soul! the true magnetic Pole to which
All hearts point duly north, like trembling
 needles!
Thou flaming Spirit of the Earth! which,
 sitting
High on the monarch's diadem, attractest
More worship than the majesty who sweats
Beneath the crown which makes his head
 ache, like
Millions of hearts which bleed to lend it
 lustre!
Shalt thou be mine? I am, methinks, already
A little king, a lucky alchymist!—
A wise magician, who has bound the devil
Without the forfeit of his soul. But come,
Werner, or what else?
Wer. Call me Werner still;
You may yet know me by a loftier title.
Iden. I do believe in thee! thou art the
 spirit

Of whom I long have dream'd in a low garb.—
But come, I'll serve thee: thou shalt be as
 free
As air, despite the waters; let us hence:
I'll show thee I am honest—(oh, thou jewel!)
Thou shalt be furnish'd, Werner, with such
 means
Of flight, that if thou wert a snail, not birds
Should overtake thee.—Let me gaze again!
I have a foster-brother in the mart
Of Hamburgh skill'd in precious stones. How
 many
Carats may it weigh?—Come, Werner, I will
 wing thee. [*Exeunt.*

Scene II.

STRALENHEIM'S *Chamber.*

STRALENHEIM *and* FRITZ.

Fritz. All's ready, my good lord!
Stral. I am not sleepy,
And yet I must to bed; I fain would say
To rest, but something heavy on my spirit,
Too dull for wakefulness, too quick for slum-
 ber,
Sits on me as a cloud along the sky,
Which will not let the sunbeams through,
 nor yet
Descend in rain and end, but spreads itself
Twixt earth and heaven, like envy between
 man
And man, an everlasting mist:—I will
Unto my pillow.
Fritz. May you rest there well!
Stral. I feel, and fear, I shall.
Fritz. And wherefore fear?
Stral. I know not why, and therefore do
 fear more,
Because an undescribable——but 't is
All folly. Were the locks (as I desired)
Changed, to-day, of this chamber? for last
 night's
Adventure makes it needful.
Fritz. Certainly,
According to your order, and beneath
The inspection of myself and the young
 Saxon
Who saved your life. I think they call him
 "Ulric."
Stral. You *think!* you supercilious slave!
 what right
Have you to *tax your* memory, which should
 be
Quick, proud, and happy to retain the *name*
Of him who saved your master, as a litany
Whose daily repetition marks your duty?—
Get hence! "*You think,*" indeed! you, who
 stood still
Howling and dripping on the bank, whilst I

Lay dying, and the stranger dash'd aside
The roaring torrent, and restored me to
Thank him—and despise you. "*You think!*"
 and scarce
Can recollect his name! I will not waste
More words on you. Call me betimes.
Fritz. Good night!
I trust to-morrow will restore your lordship
To renovated strength and temper.
 [*The scene closes.*

Scene III.

The secret Passage.

Gab. (*solus*). Four—
Five—six hours have I counted, like the
 guard
Of outposts on the never-merry clock;
That hollow tongue of time, which, even
 when
It sounds for joy, takes something from
 enjoyment
With every clang. 'Tis a perpetual knell,
Though for a marriage feast it rings: each
 stroke
Peals for a hope the less; the funeral note
Of Love deep-buried without resurrection
In the grave of Possession; while the knoll
Of long-lived parents finds a jovial echo
To triple Time in the son's ear.
 I'm cold—
I'm dark;—I've blown my fingers—num-
 ber'd o'er
And o'er my steps—and knock'd my head
 against
Some fifty buttresses—and roused the rats
And bats in general insurrection, till
Their cursed pattering feet and whirling
 wings
Leave me scarce hearing for another sound.
A light! It is at distance (if I can
Measure in darkness distance): but it blinks
As through a crevice or a key-hole, in
The inhibited direction: I must on,
Nevertheless, from curiosity.
A distant lamp-light is an incident
In such a den as this. Pray Heaven it
 lead me
To nothing that may tempt me! Else—
 Heaven aid me
To obtain or to escape it! Shining still!
Were it the star of Lucifer himself,
Or he himself girt with its beams, I could
Contain no longer. Softly: mighty well!
That corner's turn'd—so—ah! no:—right!
 it draws
Nearer. Here is a darksome angle—so,
That's weather'd.—Let me pause.—Suppose
 it leads

Into some greater danger than that which
I have escaped—no matter, 'tis a new one;
And novel perils, like fresh mistresses,
Wear more magnetic aspects:—I will on,
And be it where it may—I have my dagger,
Which may protect me at a pinch.—Burn
 still,
Thou little light! Thou art my *ignis fatuus!*
My stationary Will-o'-the-wisp!—So! so!
He hears my invocation, and fails not.

 [*The scene closes.*

Scene IV.—*A Garden.*

Enter WERNER.

 Wer. I could not sleep—and now the
 hour's at hand;
All's ready. Idenstein has kept his word;
And station'd in the outskirts of the town,
Upon the forest's edge, the vehicle
Awaits us. Now the dwindling stars begin
To pale in heaven; and for the last time I
Look on these horrible walls. Oh! never,
 never
Shall I forget them. Here I came most
 poor,
But not dishonour'd: and I leave them with
A stain,—if not upon my name, yet in
My heart!—a never-dying canker-worm,
Which all the coming splendour of the
 lands,
And rights, and sovereignty of Siegendorf
Can scarcely lull a moment. I must find
Some means of restitution, which would
 ease
My soul in part: but how without dis-
 covery?—
It must be done, however; and I'll pause
Upon the method the first hour of safety.
The madness of my misery led to this
Base infamy; repentance must retrieve it:
I will have nought of Stralenheim's upon
My spirit, though he would grasp all of
 mine;
Lands, freedom, life,—and yet he sleeps as
 soundly,
Perhaps, as infancy, with gorgeous curtains
Spread for his canopy, o'er silken pillows,
Such as when——Hark! what noise is that?
 Again!
The branches shake; and some loose stones
 have fallen
From yonder terrace.

 [ULRIC *leaps down from the terrace.*
 Ulric! ever welcome!
Thrice welcome now! this filial——
 Ulr. Stop! Before
We approach, tell me——
 Wer. Why look you so?

 Ulr. Do I
Behold my father, or——
 Wer. What?
 Ulr. An assassin?
 Wer. Insane or insolent!
 Ulr. Reply, sir, as
You prize your life, or mine!
 Wer. To what must I
Answer?
 Ulr. Are you or are you not the assassin
Of Stralenheim?
 Wer. I never was as yet
The murderer of any man. What mean you?
 Ulr. Did not you *this* night (as the night
 before)
Retrace the secret passage? Did you not
Again revisit Stralenheim's chamber? and——
 [ULRIC *pauses.*
 Wer. Proceed.
 Ulr. *Died* he not by your hand?
 Wer. Great God!
 Ulr. You are innocent, then! my father's
 innocent!
Embrace me! Yes,—your tone—your look—
 yes, yes,—
Yet *say* so.
 Wer. If I e'er, in heart or mind,
Conceived deliberately such a thought,
But rather strove to trample back to hell
Such thoughts—if e'er they glared a moment
 through
The irritation of my oppressed spirit—
May heaven be shut for ever from my hopes,
As from mine eyes!
 Ulr. But Stralenheim is dead.
 Wer. 'Tis horrible! 'tis hideous, as 'tis
 hateful!—
But what have I to do with this?
 Ulr. No bolt
Is forced; no violence can be detected,
Save on his body. Part of his own house-
 hold
Have been alarm'd; but as the intendant is
Absent, I took upon myself the care
Of mustering the police. His chamber has,
Past doubt, been enter'd secretly. Excuse
 me,
If nature——
 Wer. Oh, my boy! what unknown woes
Of dark fatality, like clouds, are gathering
Above our house!
 Ulr. My father! I acquit you!
But will the world do so? will even the
 judge,
If——But you must away this instant.
 Wer. No!
I'll face it. Who shall dare suspect me?
 Ulr. Yet
You had *no* guests—*no* visitors—no life
Breathing around you, save my mother's?

Wer. Ah!
The Hungarian!
Ulr. He is gone! he disappear'd
Ere sunset.
Wer. No; I hid him in that very
Conceal'd and fatal gallery.
Ulr. There I'll find him.
 [ULRIC *is going.*
Wer. It is too late: he had left the palace
 ere
I quitted it. I found the secret panel
Open, and the doors which lead from that
 hall
Which masks it: I but thought he had
 snatch'd the silent
And favourable moment to escape
The myrmidons of Idenstein, who were
Dogging him yester-even.
Ulr. You reclosed
The panel?
Wer. Yes; and not without reproach
(And inner trembling for the avoided peril)
At his dull heedlessness, in leaving thus
His shelterer's asylum to the risk
Of a discovery.
Ulr. You are sure you closed it?
Wer. Certain.
Ulr. That's well; but had been better, if
You ne'er had turn'd it to a den for——
 [*He pauses.*
Wer. Thieves!
Thou wouldst say: I must bear it, and de-
 serve it;
But not——
Ulr. No, father; do not speak of this:
This is no hour to think of petty crimes,
But to prevent the consequence of great ones.
Why would you shelter this man?
Wer. Could I shun it?
A man pursued by my chief foe; disgraced
For my own crime: a victim to *my* safety,
Imploring a few hours' concealment from
The very wretch who was the cause he
 needed
Such refuge. Had he been a wolf, I could
 not
Have in such circumstances thrust him
 forth.
Ulr. And like the wolf he hath repaid
 you. But
It is too late to ponder thus:—you must
Set out ere dawn. I will remain here to
Trace the murderer, if 'tis possible.
Wer. But this my sudden flight will give
 the Moloch
Suspicion: two new victims in the lieu
Of one, if I remain. The fled Hungarian,
Who seems the culprit, and——
Ulr. Who *seems?* Who else
Can be so?

Wer. Not *I*, though just now you
 doubted—
You, my *son!*—doubted—
Ulr. And do you doubt of him
The fugitive?
Wer. Boy! since I fell into
The abyss of crime (though not of *such*
 crime), I,
Having seen the innocent oppress'd for me,
May doubt even of the guilty's guilt. Your
 heart
Is free, and quick with virtuous wrath to
 accuse
Appearances; and views a criminal
In Innocence's shadow, it may be,
Because 'tis dusky.
Ulr. And if I do so,
What will mankind, who know you not, or
 knew
But to oppress? You must not stand the
 hazard.
Away!—I'll make all easy. Idenstein
Will for his own sake and his jewel's hold
His peace—he also is a partner in
Your flight—moreover——
Wer. Fly! and leave my name
Link'd with the Hungarian's, or preferr'd as
 poorest,
To bear the brand of bloodshed?
Ulr. Pshaw! leave anything
Except our fathers' sovereignty and castles,
For which you have so long panted, and in
 vain!
What *name?* You have *no name*, since that
 you bear
Is feign'd.
Wer. Most true: but still I would not
 have it
Engraved in crimson in men's memories,
Though in this most obscure abode of
 men——
Besides, the search——
Ulr. I will provide against
Aught that can touch you. No one knows
 you here
As heir of Siegendorf: if Idenstein
Suspects, 'tis *but suspicion*, and he is
A fool: his folly shall have such employ-
 ment,
Too, that the unknown Werner shall give way
To nearer thoughts of self. The laws (if e'er
Laws reach'd this village) are all in abeyance
With the late general war of thirty years,
Or crush'd, or rising slowly from the dust,
To which the march of armies trampled
 them.
Stralenheim, although noble, is unheeded
Here, save as *such*—without lands, influence,
Save what hath perish'd with him. Few
 prolong

A week beyond their funeral rites their sway
O'er men, unless by relatives, whose interest
Is roused : such is not here the case ; he died
Alone, unknown,—a solitary grave,
Obscure as his deserts, without a scutcheon,
Is all he'll have, or wants. If *I* discover
The assassin, 'twill be well—if not, believe
 me,
None else; though all the full-fed train of
 menials
May howl above his ashes (as they did
Around him in his danger on the Oder),
Will no more stir a finger *now* than *then*.
Hence! hence! I must not hear your an-
 swer.—Look!
The stars are almost faded, and the grey
Begins to grizzle the black hair of night.
You shall not answer :—Pardon me that I
Am peremptory; 'tis your son that speaks,
Your long-lost, late-found son.—Let's call my
 mother!
Softly and swiftly step, and leave the rest
To me: I'll answer for the event as far
As regards *you*, and that is the chief point,
As my first duty, which shall be observed.
We'll meet in Castle Siegendorf—once more
Our banners shall be glorious! Think of that
Alone, and leave all other thoughts to me,
Whose youth may better battle with them—
 Hence!
And may your age be happy!—I will kiss
My mother once more, then Heaven's speed
 be with you!
 Wer. This counsel's safe—but is it ho-
 nourable?
 Ulr. To save a father is a child's chief
 honour. [*Exeunt.*

—+—

Act IV.

Scene I.—*A Gothic Hall in the Castle of
 Siegendorf, near Prague.*

Enter ERIC *and* HENRICK, *Retainers of the
 Count.*

 Eric. So, better times are come at last;
 to these
Old walls new masters and high wassail—
 both
A long desideratum.
 Hen. Yes, for *masters*,
It might be unto those who long for novelty,
Though made by a new grave: but as for
 wassail,
Methinks the old Count Siegendorf main-
 tain'd
His feudal hospitality as high
As e'er another prince of the empire.
 Eric. Why

For the mere cup and trencher, we no doubt
Fared passing well; but as for merriment
And sport, without which salt and sauces
 season
The cheer but scantily, our sizings were
Even of the narrowest.
 Hen. The old count loved not
The roar of revel; are you sure that *this*
 does?
 Eric. As yet he hath been courteous as
 he's bounteous,
And we all love him.
 Hen. His reign is as yet
Hardly a year o'erpast its honey-moon,
And the first year of sovereigns is bridal :
Anon, we shall perceive his real sway
And moods of mind.
 Eric. Pray Heaven he keep the present !
Then his brave son, Count Ulric—there's
 a knight !
Pity the wars are o'er !
 Hen. Why so?
 Eric. Look on him !
And answer that yourself.
 Hen. He's very youthful,
And strong and beautiful as a young tiger.
 Eric. That's not a faithful vassal's like-
 ness.
 Hen. But
Perhaps a true one.
 Eric. Pity, as I said,
The wars are over : in the hall, who like
Count Ulric for a well-supported pride,
Which awes, but yet offends not? in the field,
Who like him with his spear in hand, when,
 gnashing
His tusks, and ripping up from right to left
The howling hounds, the boar makes for the
 thicket ?
Who backs a horse, or bears a hawk, or wears
A sword like him ? Whose plume nods knight-
 lier?
 Hen. No one's, I grant you. Do not fear,
 if war
Be long in coming, he is of that kind
Will make it for himself, if he hath not
Already done as much.
 Eric. What do you mean ?
 Hen. You can't deny his train of followers
(But few our native fellow-vassals born
On the domain) are such a sort of knaves
As—— [*Pauses.*
 Eric. What ?
 Hen. The war (you love so much) leaves
 living.
Like other parents, she spoils her worst
 children.
 Eric. Nonsense! they are all brave iron-
 visaged fellows,
Such as old Tilly loved.

Hen. And who loved Tilly?
Ask that at Magdebourg—or for that matter
Wallenstein either;—they are gone to——
Eric. Rest!
But what beyond, 'tis not ours to pronounce.
 Hen. I wish they had left us something
 of their rest:
The country (nominally now at peace)
Is over-run with—God knows who: they fly
By night, and disappear with sunrise; but
Leave us no less desolation, nay, even more,
Than the most *open* warfare.
 Eric. But Count Ulric—
What has all this to do with him?
 Hen. With *him*!
He——might prevent it. As you say he's
 fond
Of war, why makes he it not on those ma-
 rauders?
 Eric. You'd better ask himself.
 Hen. I would as soon
Ask the lion why he laps not milk.
 Eric. And here he comes!
 Hen. The devil! you'll hold your tongue?
 Eric. Why do you turn so pale?
 Hen. 'Tis nothing—but
Be silent.
 Eric. I will, upon what you have said.
 Hen. I assure you I meant nothing,—
 a mere sport
Of words, no more; besides, had it been
 otherwise,
He is to espouse the gentle Baroness
Ida of Stralenheim, the late baron's heiress;
And she, no doubt, will soften whatsoever
Of fierceness the late long intestine wars
Have given all natures, and most unto those
Who were born in them, and bred up upon
The knees of Homicide; sprinkled, as it were,
With blood even at their baptism. Prithee,
 peace
On all that I have said!

 Enter ULRIC *and* RODOLPH.

 Good morrow, Count.
 Ulr. Good morrow, worthy Henrick. Eric,
 is
All ready for the chase?
 Eric. The dogs are order'd
Down to the forest, and the vassals out
To beat the bushes, and the day looks pro-
 mising.
Shall I call forth your excellency's suite?
What courser will you please to mount?
 Ulr. The dun,
Walstein.
 Eric. I fear he scarcely has recover'd
The toils of Monday: 'twas a noble chase:
You spear'd *four* with your own hand.

 Ulr. True, good Eric;
I had forgotten—let it be the grey, then,
Old Ziska: he has not been out this fort-
 night.
 Eric. He shall be straight caparison'd.
 How many
Of your immediate retainers shall
Escort you?
 Ulr. I leave that to Weilburgh, our
Master of the horse. [*Exit* ERIC.
 Rodolph!
 Rod. My lord!
 Ulr. The news
Is awkward from the——
 [RODOLPH *points to* HENRICK.
 How now, Henrick? why
Loiter you here?
 Hen. For your commands, my lord.
 Ulr. Go to my father, and present my
 duty,
And learn if he would aught with me before
I mount. [*Exit* HENRICK.
 Rodolph, our friends have had a check
Upon the frontiers of Franconia, and
'Tis rumour'd that the column sent against
 them
Is to be strengthen'd. I must join them
 soon.
 Rod. Best wait for further and more sure
 advices.
 Ulr. I mean it—and indeed it could not
 well
Have fallen out at a time more opposite
To all my plans.
 Rod. It will be difficult
To excuse your absence to the count your
 father.
 Ulr. Yes, but the unsettled state of our
 domain
In high Silesia will permit and cover
My journey. In the mean time, when we are
Engaged in the chase, draw off the eighty
 men
Whom Wolffe leads—keep the forests on your
 route:
You know it well?
 Rod. As well as on that night
When we——
 Ulr. We will not speak of that until
We can repeat the same with like success:
And when you have join'd, give Rosenberg
 this letter. [*Gives a letter.*
Add further, that I have sent this slight
 addition
To our force with you and Wolffe, as herald
 of
My coming, though I could but spare them
 ill
At this time, as my father loves to keep
Full numbers of retainers round the castle,

Until this marriage, and its feasts and
 fooleries,
Are rung out with its peal of nuptial non-
 sense.
 Rod. I thought you loved the lady Ida?
 Ulr. Why,
I do so—but it follows not from that
I would bind in my youth and glorious years,
So brief and burning, with a lady's zone,
Although 't were that of Venus:—but I love
 her,
As woman should be loved, fairly and solely.
 Rod. And constantly?
 Ulr. I think so; for I love
Nought else.—But I have not the time to
 pause
Upon these gewgaws of the heart. Great
 things
We have to do ere long. Speed! speed! good
 Rodolph!
 Rod. On my return, however, I shall find
The Baroness Ida lost in Countess Siegen-
 dorf?
 Ulr. Perhaps my father wishes it; and
 sooth
'T is no bad policy: this union with
The last bud of the rival branch at once
Unites the future and destroys the past.
 Rod. Adieu.
 Ulr. Yet hold—we had better keep to-
 gether
Until the chase begins; then draw thou off,
And do as I have said.
 Rod. I will. But to
Return—'t was a most kind act in the count
Your father to send up to Konigsberg
For this fair orphan of the baron, and
To hail her as his daughter.
 Ulr. Wondrous kind!
Especially as little kindness till
Then grew between them.
 Rod. The late baron died
Of a fever, did he not?
 Ulr. How should I know?
 Rod. I have heard it whisper'd there was
 something strange
About his death—and even the place of it
Is scarcely known.
 Ulr. Some obscure village on
The Saxon or Silesian frontier.
 Rod. He
Has left no testament—no farewell words?
 Ulr. I am neither confessor nor notary,
So cannot say.
 Rod. Ah! here's the lady Ida.

Enter IDA STRALENHEIM.

 Ulr. You are early, my sweet cousin!
 Ida. Not *too* early,

Dear Ulric, if I do not interrupt you.
Why do you call me "*cousin*"?
 Ulr. (*smiling*). Are we not so?
 Ida. Yes, but I do not like the name;
 methinks
It sounds so cold, as if you thought upon
Our pedigree, and only weigh'd our blood.
 Ulr. (*starting*). Blood!
 Ida. Why does yours start from your
 cheeks?
 Ulr. Ay! doth it?
 Ida. It doth—but no! it rushes like a
 torrent
Even to your brow again.
 Ulr. (*recovering himself*). And if it fled,
It only was because your presence sent it
Back to my heart, which beats for you, sweet
 cousin?
 Ida. "Cousin" again.
 Ulr. Nay, then, I'll call you sister.
 Ida. I like that name still worse.—Would
 we had ne'er
Been aught of kindred!
 Ulr. (*gloomily*). Would we never had!
 Ida. Oh, heavens! and can *you wish that!*
 Ulr. Dearest Ida!
Did I not echo your own wish?
 Ida. Yes, Ulric,
But then I wish'd it not with such a glance,
And scarce knew what I said; but let me be
Sister or cousin, what you will, so that
I still to you am something.
 Ulr. You shall be
All—all——
 Ida. And you to *me* are so already;
But I can wait.
 Ulr. Dear Ida!
 Ida. Call me Ida,
Your Ida, for I would be yours, none else's—
Indeed I have none else left, since my poor
 father— [*She pauses.*
 Ulr. You have *mine*—you have *me.*
 Ida. Dear Ulric, how I wish
My father could but view my happiness,
Which wants but this!
 Ulr. Indeed!
 Ida. You would have loved him,
He you; for the brave ever love each other:
His manner was a little cold, his spirit
Proud (as is birth's prerogative); but under
This grave exterior—Would you had known
 each other!
Had such as you been near him on his
 journey,
He had not died without a friend to soothe
His last and lonely moments.
 Ulr. Who says *that!*
 Ida. What?
 Ulr. That he *died alone.*
 Ida. The general rumour

And disappearance of his servants, who
Have ne'er return'd: that fever was most
deadly
Which swept them all away.
Ulr. If they were near him,
He could not die neglected or alone.
Ida. Alas! what is a menial to a death-
bed,
When the dim eye rolls vainly round for
what
It loves?—They say he died of a fever.
Ulr. Say!
It *was* so.
Ida. I sometimes dream otherwise.
Ulr. All dreams are false.
Ida. And yet I see him as
I see you.
Ulr. Where?
Ida. In sleep—I see him lie
Pale, bleeding, and a man with a raised
knife
Beside him.
Ulr. But you do not see his *face!*
Ida (*looking at him*). No! Oh, my God!
do *you?*
Ulr. Why do you ask?
Ida. Because you look as if you saw a
murderer!
Ulr. (*agitatedly*). Ida, this is mere child-
ishness; your weakness
Infects me, to my shame: but as all feelings
Of yours are common to me, it affects me.
Prithee, sweet child, change——
Ida. Child, indeed! I have
Full fifteen summers! [*A bugle sounds.*
Rod. Hark, my lord, the bugle!
Ida (*peevishly to* RODOLPH). Why need
you tell him that? Can he not hear it
Without your echo?
Rod. Pardon me, fair baroness!
Ida. I will not pardon you, unless you
earn it
By aiding me in my dissuasion of
Count Ulric from the chase to-day.
Rod. You will not,
Lady, need aid of mine.
Ulr. I must not now
Forego it.
Ida. But you shall!
Ulr. Shall!
Ida. Yes, or be
No true knight.—Come, dear Ulric! yield to
me
In this, for this one day: the day looks
heavy,
And you are turn'd so pale and ill.
Ulr. You jest.
Ida. Indeed I do not :—ask of Rodolph.
Rod. Truly,
My lord, within this quarter of an hour

You have changed more than e'er I saw you
change
In years.
Ulr. 'T is nothing; but if 't were, the air
Would soon restore me. I'm the true
chameleon,
And live but on the atmosphere; your feasts
In castle halls, and social banquets, nurse not
My spirit—I'm a forester and breather
Of the steep mountain-tops, where I love all
The eagle loves.
Ida. Except his prey, I hope.
Ulr. Sweet Ida, wish me a fair chase,
and I
Will bring you six boars' heads for trophies
home.
Ida. And will you not stay, then? You
shall not go!
Come! I will sing to you.
Ulr. Ida, you scarcely
Will make a soldier's wife.
Ida. I do not wish
To be so; for I trust these wars are over,
And you will live in peace on your domains.

Enter WERNER *as* COUNT SIEGENDORF.

Ulr. My father, I salute you, and it
grieves me
With such brief greeting.—You have heard
our bugle;
The vassals wait.
Sieg. So let them.—You forget
To-morrow is the appointed festival
In Prague for peace restored. You are apt
to follow
The chase with such an ardour as will scarce
Permit you to return to-day, or if
Return'd, too much fatigued to join to-
morrow
The nobles in our marshall'd ranks.
Ulr. You, count,
Will well supply the place of both—I am not
A lover of these pageantries.
Sieg. No, Ulric:
It were not well that you alone of all
Our young nobility——
Ida. And far the noblest
In aspect and demeanour.
Sieg. (*to* IDA). True, dear child,
Though somewhat frankly said for a fair
damsel.—
But, Ulric, recollect too our position,
So lately reinstated in our honours.
Believe me, 't would be mark'd in any house,
But most in *ours*, that ONE should be found
wanting
At such a time and place. Besides, the
Heaven
Which gave us back our own, in the same
moment

It spread its peace o'er all, hath double
 claims
On us for thanksgiving: first, for our
 country;
And next, that we are here to share its
 blessings.
 Ulr. (*aside*). Devout, too! Well, sir, I
 obey at once.
(*Then aloud to a Servant*). Ludwig, dismiss
 the train without! [*Exit* LUDWIG.
 Ida. And so
You yield at once to him what I for hours
Might supplicate in vain.
 Sieg. (*smiling*). You are not jealous
Of me, I trust, my pretty rebel! who
Would sanction disobedience against all
Except thyself? But fear not; thou shalt
 rule him
Hereafter with a fonder sway and firmer.
 Ida. But I should like to govern *now*.
 Sieg. You shall,
Your *harp*, which by the way awaits you with
The countess in her chamber. She complains
That you are a sad truant to your music:
She attends you.
 Ida. Then good morrow, my kind kins-
 men!
Ulric, you'll come and hear me?
 Ulr. By and by.
 Ida. Be sure I'll sound it better than
 your bugles;
Then pray you be as punctual to its notes:
I'll play you King Gustavus' march.
 Ulr. And why not
Old Tilly's?
 Ida. Not that monster's! I should think
My harp-strings rang with groans, and not
 with music,
Could aught of *his* sound on it :—but come
 quickly;
Your mother will be eager to receive you.
 [*Exit.*
 Sieg. Ulric, I wish to speak with you
 alone.
 Ulr. My time's your vassal.—
(*Aside to* RODOLPH). Rodolph, hence! and do
As I directed: and by his best speed
And readiest means let Rosenberg reply.
 Rod. Count Siegendorf, command you
 aught? I am bound
Upon a journey past the frontier.
 Sieg. (*starts*). Ah!—
Where? on *what* frontier?
 Rod. The Silesian, on—
My way—(*Aside to* ULRIC).—*Where* shall I
 say?
 Ulr. (*aside to* RODOLPH). To Hamburgh.
 (*Aside to himself*). That
Word will, I think, put a firm padlock on
His further inquisition.

 Rod. Count, to Hamburgh.
 Sieg. (*agitated*). Hamburgh! No, I have
 nought to do there, nor
Am aught connected with that city. Then
God speed you!
 Rod. Fare ye well, Count Siegendorf!
 [*Exit* RODOLPH.
 Sieg. Ulric, this man, who has just de-
 parted, is
One of those strange companions whom I
 fain
Would reason with you on.
 Ulr. My lord, he is
Noble by birth, of one of the first houses
In Saxony.
 Sieg. I talk not of his birth,
But of his bearing. Men speak lightly of
 him.
 Ulr. So they will do of most men. Even
 the monarch
Is not fenced from his chamberlain's slander,
 or
The sneer of the last courtier whom he has
 made
Great and ungrateful.
 Sieg. If I must be plain,
The world speaks more than lightly of this
 Rodolph:
They say he is leagued with the "black
 bands" who still
Ravage the frontier.
 Ulr. And will you believe
The world?
 Sieg. In this case—yes.
 Ulr. In *any* case,
I thought you knew it better than to take
An accusation for a sentence.
 Sieg. Son!
I understand you: you refer to——but
My destiny has so involved about me
Her spider web, that I can only flutter
Like the poor fly, but break it not. Take
 heed,
Ulric; you have seen to what the passions
 led me:
Twenty long years of misery and famine
Quench'd them not—twenty thousand more,
 perchance,
Hereafter (or even here in *moments* which
Might date for years, did Anguish make the
 dial)
May not obliterate or expiate
The madness and dishonour of an instant.
Ulric, be warn'd by a father!—I was not
By mine, and you behold me!
 Ulr. I behold
The prosperous and beloved Siegendorf,
Lord of a prince's appanage, and honour'd
By those he rules and those he ranks
 with.

Sieg. Ah!
Why wilt thou call me prosperous, while
 I fear
For thee? Beloved, when thou lovest me
 not!
All hearts but one may beat in kindness for
 me—
But if my son's is cold!——
 Ulr. Who *dare* say that?
 Sieg. None else but I, who see it—*feel* it
 —keener
Than would your adversary, who dared say
 so,
Your sabre in his heart! But mine survives
The wound.
 Ulr. You err. My nature is not given
To outward fondling: how should it be so,
After twelve years' divorcement from my
 parents?
 Sieg. And did not *I* too pass those twelve
 torn years
In a like absence? But 'tis vain to urge
 you—
Nature was never call'd back by remon-
 strance.
Let's change the theme. I wish you to
 consider
That these young violent nobles of high
 name,
But dark deeds (ay, the darkest, if all
 Rumour
Reports be true), with whom thou consortest,
Will lead thee——
 Ulr. (*impatiently*). I'll be *led* by no man.
 Sieg. Nor
Be leader of such, I would hope: at once
To wean thee from the perils of thy youth
And haughty spirit, I have thought it well
That thou shouldst wed the lady Ida—more
As thou appear'st to love her.
 Ulr. I have said
I will obey your orders, were they to
Unite with Hecate—can a son say more?
 Sieg. He says too much in saying this.
 It is not
The nature of thine age, nor of thy blood,
Nor of thy temperament, to talk so coolly,
Or act so carelessly, in that which is
The bloom or blight of all men's happiness,
(For Glory's pillow is but restless, if
Love lay not down his cheek there): some
 strong bias,
Some master fiend is in thy service, to
Misrule the mortal who believes him slave,
And makes his every thought subservient;
 else
Thou'dst say at once—"I love young Ida,
 and
Will wed her;" or, "I love her not, and
 all

The powers of earth shall never make me."
 —So
Would I have answer'd.
 Ulr. Sir, *you wed* for love.
 Sieg. I did, and it has been my only
 refuge
In many miseries.
 Ulr. Which miseries
Had never been but for this love-match.
 Sieg. Still
Against your age and nature! Who at twenty
E'er answer'd thus till now?
 Ulr. Did you not warn me
Against your own example?
 Sieg. Boyish sophist!
In a word, do you love, or love not, Ida?
 Ulr. What matters it, if I am ready to
Obey you in espousing her?
 Sieg. As far
As you feel, nothing, but all life for her.
She's young—all-beautiful—adores you—is
Endow'd with qualities to give happiness,
Such as rounds common life into a dream
Of something which your poets cannot paint,
And (if it were not wisdom to love virtue)
For which Philosophy might barter Wisdom;
And giving so much happiness, deserves
A little in return. I would not have her
Break her heart for a man who has none to
 break;
Or wither on her stalk like some pale rose
Deserted by the bird she thought a nightingale,
According to the Orient tale. She is——
 Ulr. The daughter of dead Stralenheim,
 your foe:
I'll wed her, ne'ertheless; though, to say truth,
Just now I am not violently transported
In favour of such unions.
 Sieg. But she loves you.
 Ulr. And I love her, and therefore would
 think *twice*.
 Sieg. Alas! Love never *did* so.
 Ulr. Then 'tis time
He should begin, and take the bandage from
His eyes, and look before he leaps; till now
He hath ta'en a jump i' the dark.
 Sieg. But you consent?
 Ulr. I did, and do.
 Sieg. Then fix the day.
 Ulr. 'Tis usual,
And certes courteous, to leave that to the lady.
 Sieg. *I* will engage for *her*.
 Ulr. So will not *I*
For any woman: and as what I fix,
I fain would see unshaken, when she gives
Her answer, I'll give mine.
 Sieg. But 'tis your office
To woo.
 Ulr. Count, 't is a marriage of your making,
So be it of your wooing; but to please you,

I will now pay my duty to my mother,
With whom, you know, the lady Ida is.—
What would you have? You have forbid my
 stirring
For manly sports beyond the castle walls,
And I obey; you bid me turn a chamberer,
To pick up gloves, and fans, and knitting-
 needles,
And list to songs and tunes, and watch for
 smiles,
And smile at pretty prattle, and look into
The eyes of feminine, as though they were
The stars receding early to our wish
Upon the dawn of a world-winning battle—
What can a son or man do more?
 [*Exit* ULRIC.
Sieg. (*solus*). Too much!—
Too much of duty, and too little love!
He pays me in the coin he owes me not:
For such hath been my wayward fate, I could
 not
Fulfil a parent's duties by his side
Till now; but love he owes me, for my
 thoughts
Ne'er left him, nor my eyes long'd without
 tears
To see my child again, and now I have found
 him!
But how—obedient, but with coldness; duteous
In my sight, but with carelessness; mys-
 terious—
Abstracted—distant—much given to long
 absence,
And where—none know—in league with the
 most riotous
Of our young nobles; though, to do him
 justice,
He never stoops down to their vulgar
 pleasures;
Yet there's some tie between them which I
 cannot
Unravel. They look up to him—consult
 him—
Throng round him as a leader: but with me
He hath no confidence! Ah! can I hope it
After—what! doth my father's curse descend
Even to my child? Or is the Hungarian near
To shed more blood? or—Oh! if it should be!
Spirit of Stralenheim, dost thou walk these
 walls
To wither him and his—who, though they slew
 not,
Unlatch'd the door of death for thee? 'T was
 not
Our fault, nor is our sin: thou wert our foe,
And yet I spared thee when my own destruc-
 tion
Slept with thee, to awake with thine awaken-
 ing!
And only took—Accursed gold! thou liest

Like poison in my hands; I dare not use
 thee,
Nor part from thee; thou camest in such a
 guise,
Methinks thou wouldst contaminate all hands
Like mine. Yet I have done, to atone for thee,
Thou villainous gold! and thy dead master's
 doom,
Though he died not by me or mine, as much
As if he were my brother! I have ta'en
His orphan Ida—cherish'd her as one
Who will be mine.

Enter an ATTENDANT.

Atten. The abbot, if it please
Your excellency, whom you sent for, waits
Upon you. [*Exit* ATTENDANT.

Enter the PRIOR ALBERT.

Prior. Peace be with these walls, and all
Within them!
Sieg. Welcome, welcome, holy father!
And may thy prayer be heard!—all men have
 need
Of such, and I——
Prior. Have the first claim to all
The prayers of our community. Our convent,
Erected by your ancestors, is still
Protected by their children.
Sieg. Yes, good father;
Continue daily orisons for us
In these dim days of heresies and blood,
Though the schismatic Swede, Gustavus, is
Gone home.
Prior. To the endless home of unbelievers,
Where there is everlasting wail and woe,
Gnashing of teeth, and tears of blood, and
 fire
Eternal, and the worm which dieth not!
Sieg. True, father: and to avert those pangs
 from one,
Who, though of our most faultless holy church,
Yet died without its last and dearest offices,
Which smooth the soul through purgatorial
 pains,
I have to offer humbly this donation
In masses for his spirit.
 [SIEGENDORF *offers the gold which he
 had taken from* STRALENHEIM.
Prior. Count, if I
Receive it, 't is because I know too well
Refusal would offend you. Be assured
The largess shall be only dealt in alms,
And every mass no less sung for the dead.
Our house needs no donations, thanks to
 yours,
Which has of old endow'd it; but from you
And yours in all meet things 't is fit we obey.
For whom shall mass be said?
Sieg. (*faltering*). For—for—the dead.

Prior. His name?

Sieg. 'T is from a soul, and not a name,
I would avert perdition.

Prior. I meant not
To pry into your secret. We will pray
For one unknown, the same as for the
proudest.

Sieg. Secret! I have none: but, father,
he who's gone
Might *have* one; or, in short, he did bequeath—
No, not bequeath—but I bestow this sum
For pious purposes.

Prior. A proper deed
In the behalf of our departed friends.

Sieg. But he who's gone was not my
friend, but foe,
The deadliest and the stanchest.

Prior. Better still!
To employ our means to obtain heaven for
the souls
Of our dead enemies is worthy those
Who can forgive them living.

Sieg. But I did not
Forgive this man. I loathed him to the last,
As he did me. I do not love him now,
But——

Prior. Best of all! for this is pure religion!
You fain would rescue him you hate from
hell—
An evangelical compassion—with
Your own gold too!

Sieg. Father, 't is not my gold.

Prior. Whose then? You said it was no
legacy.

Sieg. No matter whose—of this be sure,
that he
Who own'd it never more will need it, save
In that which it may purchase from your altars:
'Tis yours, or theirs.

Prior. Is there no blood upon it?

Sieg. No; but there's worse than blood—
eternal shame!

Prior. Did he who own'd it die in his *bed*?

Sieg. Alas!
He did.

Prior. Son! you relapse into revenge,
If you regret your enemy's bloodless death.

Sieg. His death was fathomlessly deep in
blood.

Prior. You said he died in his bed, not
battle.

Sieg. He
Died, I scarce know—but—he was stabb'd
i' the dark,
And now you have it—perish'd on his pillow
By a cut-throat!—Ay!—you may look upon
me!
I am *not* the man. I'll meet your eye on that
point,
As I can one day God's.

Prior. Nor did he die
By means, or men, or instrument of yours?

Sieg. No! by the God who sees and strikes!

Prior. Nor know you
Who slew him?

Sieg. I could only guess at *one*,
And he to me a stranger, unconnected,
As unemploy'd. Except by one day's know-
ledge,
I never saw the man who was suspected.

Prior. Then you are free from guilt.

Sieg. (*eagerly*). Oh! am I?—say!

Prior. You have said so, and know best.

Sieg. Father! I have spoken
The truth, and nought but truth, if *not* the
whole;
Yet say I am *not* guilty! for the blood
Of this man weighs on me, as if I shed it,
Though, by the Power who abhorreth human
blood,
I did not!—nay, once spared it, when I might
And *could*—ay, perhaps, *should* (if our self-
safety
Be e'er excusable in such defences
Against the attacks of over-potent foes):
But pray for him, for me, and all my house;
For, as I said, though I be innocent,
I know not why, a like remorse is on me,
As if he had fallen by me or mine. Pray for
me,
Father! I have pray'd myself in vain.

Prior. I will.
Be comforted! You are innocent, and should
Be calm as innocence.

Sieg. But calmness is not
Always the attribute of innocence.
I feel it is not.

Prior. But it will be so,
When the mind gathers up its truth within it.
Remember the great festival to-morrow,
In which you rank amidst our chiefest nobles,
As well as your brave son; and smooth your
aspect,
Nor in the general orison of thanks
For bloodshed stopt, let blood you shed not rise
A cloud upon your thoughts. This were to be
Too sensitive. Take comfort, and forget
Such things, and leave remorse unto the
guilty. [*Exeunt.*

Act V.

Scene I.—*A large and magnificent Gothic Hall
in the Castle of Siegendorf, decorated with
Trophies, Banners, and Arms of that family.*

Enter ARNHEIM *and* MEISTER, *Attendants of*
COUNT SIEGENDORF.

Arn. Be quick! the count will soon return:
the ladies

Already are at the portal. Have you sent
The messengers in search of him he seeks for?

Meis. I have, in all directions, over Prague,
As far as the man's dress and figure could
By your description track him. The devil
 take
These revels and processions! All the pleasure
(If such there be) must fall to the spectators.
I'm sure none doth to us who make the show.

Arn. Go to! my lady countess comes.

Meis. I'd rather
Ride a day's hunting on an outworn jade,
Than follow in the train of a great man,
In these dull pageantries.

Arn. Begone! and rail
Within. [*Exeunt.*

Enter the COUNTESS JOSEPHINE SIEGENDORF
 and IDA STRALENHEIM.

Jos. Well, Heaven be praised! the show
 is over.

Ida. How can you say so? Never have I
 dreamt
Of aught so beautiful. The flowers, the
 boughs,
The banners, and the nobles, and the knights,
The gems, the robes, the plumes, the happy
 faces,
The coursers, and the incense, and the sun
Streaming through the stain'd windows, even
 the *tombs,*
Which look'd so calm, and the celestial hymns,
Which seem'd as if they rather came from
 heaven
Than mounted there. The bursting organ's
 peal
Rolling on high like an harmonious thunder;
The white robes and the lifted eyes; the
 world
At peace! and all at peace with one another!
Oh, my sweet mother!
 [*Embracing* JOSEPHINE.

Jos. My beloved child!
For such, I trust, thou shalt be shortly.

Ida. Oh!
I am so already. Feel how my heart beats!

Jos. It does, my love; and never may it
 throb
With aught more bitter.

Ida. Never shall it do so!
How should it? What should make us grieve?
 I hate
To hear of sorrow: how can we be sad,
Who love each other so entirely? You,
The count, and Ulric, and your daughter Ida.

Jos. Poor child!

Ida. Do you pity me?

Jos. No: I but envy,
And that in sorrow, not in the world's sense

Of the universal vice, if one vice be
More general than another.

Ida. I'll not hear
A word against a world which still contains
You and my Ulric. Did you ever see
Aught like him? How he tower'd amongst
 them all!
How all eyes follow'd him! The flowers fell
 faster—
Rain'd from each lattice at his feet, methought,
Than before all the rest; and where he trod
I dare be sworn that they grow still, nor e'er
Will wither.

Jos. You will spoil him, little flatterer,
If he should hear you.

Ida. But he never will.
I dare not say so much to him—I fear him.

Jos. Why so? he loves you well.

Ida. But I can never
Shape my thoughts *of* him into words *to* him:
Besides, he sometimes frightens me.

Jos. How so?

Ida. A cloud comes o'er his blue eyes
 suddenly,
Yet he says nothing.

Jos. It is nothing: all men,
Especially in these dark troublous times,
Have much to think of.

Ida. But I cannot think
Of aught save him.

Jos. Yet there are other men,
In the world's eye, as goodly. There's, for
 instance,
The young Count Waldorf, who scarce once
 withdrew
His eyes from yours to-day.

Ida. I did not see him,
But Ulric. Did you not see at the moment
When all knelt, and I wept? and yet me-
 thought,
Through my fast tears, though they were
 thick and warm,
I saw him smiling on me.

Jos. I could not
See aught save heaven, to which my eyes
 were rais'd,
Together with the people's.

Ida. I thought too
Of heaven, although I look'd on Ulric.

Jos. Come,
Let us retire! they will be here anon
Expectant of the banquet. We will lay
Aside these nodding plumes and dragging
 trains.

Ida. And, above all, these stiff and heavy
 jewels,
Which make my head and heart ache, as both
 throb
Beneath their glitter o'er my brow and zone.
Dear mother, I am with you.

Enter COUNT SIEGENDORF, *in full dress, from
the solemnity, and* LUDWIG.

Sieg. Is he not found?
Lud. Strict search is making everywhere;
and if
The man be in Prague, be sure he will be
found.
Sieg. Where's Ulric?
Lud. He rode round the other way
With some young nobles; but he left them
soon;
And, if I err not, not a minute since
I heard his excellency, with his train,
Gallop o'er the west drawbridge.

Enter ULRIC, *splendidly dressed.*

Sieg. (*to* LUDWIG). See they cease not
Their quest of him I have described.
 [*Exit* LUDWIG.
 Oh, Ulric!
How have I long'd for thee!
Ulr. Your wish is granted—
Behold me!
Sieg. I have seen the murderer.
Ulr. Whom? Where?
Sieg. The Hungarian, who slew Stralen-
heim.
Ulr. You dream.
Sieg. I live! and as I live, I saw him—
Heard him! he dared to utter even my name—
Ulr. What name?
Sieg. Werner! 'twas mine.
Ulr. It must be so
No more: forget it.
Sieg. Never! never! all
My destinies were woven in that name:
It will not be engraved upon my tomb,
But it may lead me there.
Ulr. To the point——the Hungarian?
Sieg. Listen!—The church was throng'd:
the hymn was raised;
" *Te Deum* " peal'd from nations rather than
From choirs, in one great cry of "God be
praised"
For one day's peace, after thrice ten dread
years,
Each bloodier than the former: I arose,
With all the nobles, and as I look'd down
Along the lines of lifted faces,—from
Our banner'd and escutcheon'd gallery, I
Saw, like a flash of lightning (for I saw
A moment and no more), what struck me
sightless
To all else—the Hungarian's face! I grew
Sick; and when I recover'd from the mist
Which curl'd about my senses, and again
Look'd down, I saw him not. The thanks-
giving
Was over, and we march'd back in procession.

Ulr. Continue.
Sieg. When we reach'd the Mul-
dau's bridge,
The joyous crowd above, the numberless
Barks mann'd with revellers in their best
garbs,
Which shot along the glancing tide below,
The decorated street, the long array,
The clashing music, and the thundering
Of far artillery, which seem'd to bid
A long and loud farewell to its great doings,
The standards o'er me, and the tramplings
round,
The roar of rushing thousands,—all—all
could not
Chase this man from my mind, although my
senses
No longer held him palpable.
Ulr. You saw him
No more, then?
Sieg. I look'd, as a dying soldier
Looks at a draught of water, for this man;
But still I saw him not; but in his stead——
Ulr. What in his stead?
Sieg. My eye for ever fell
Upon your dancing crest; the loftiest,
As on the loftiest and the loveliest head,
It rose the highest of the stream of plumes,
Which overflow'd the glittering streets of
Prague.
Ulr. What's this to the Hungarian?
Sieg. Much; for I
Had almost then forgot him in my son;
When just as the artillery ceased, and paused
The music, and the crowd embraced in lieu
Of shouting, I heard in a deep, low voice,
Distinct and keener far upon my ear
Than the late cannon's volume, this word—
 " *Werner!* "
Ulr. Utter'd by——
Sieg. HIM! I turn'd—and saw—and fell.
Ulr. And wherefore? Were you seen?
Sieg. The officious care
Of those around me dragg'd me from the spot,
Seeing my faintness, ignorant of the cause:
You, too, were too remote in the procession
(The old nobles being divided from their
children)
To aid me.
Ulr. But I'll aid you now.
Sieg. In what?
Ulr. In searching for this man, or——
When he's found,
What shall we do with him?
Sieg. I know not that.
Ulr. Then wherefore seek?
Sieg. Because I cannot rest
Till he is found. His fate, and Stralenheim's,
And ours, seem intertwisted! nor can be
Unravell'd, till——

Enter an ATTENDANT.

Atten. A stranger to wait on
Your excellency.

Sieg. Who?

Atten. He gave no name.

Sieg. Admit him, ne'ertheless.
 [*The* ATTENDANT *introduces* GABOR,
 and afterwards exit.

Gab. 'T is then Werner!

Sieg. (*haughtily*). The same you knew,
 sir, by that name; and *you!*

Gab. (*looking round*). I recognise you both:
 father and son,
It seems. Count, I have heard that you, or
 yours,
Have lately been in search of me: I am
 here.

Sieg. I have sought you, and have found
 you: you are charged
(Your own heart may inform you why) with
 such
A crime as—— [*He pauses.*

Gab. Give it utterance, and then
I'll meet the consequences.

Sieg. You shall do so—
Unless——

Gab. First, who accuses me?

Sieg. All things,
If not all men: the universal rumour—
My own presence on the spot—the place—the
 time—
And every speck of circumstance unite
To fix the blot on you.

Gab. And on *me only?*
Pause ere you answer: is no other name
Save mine, stain'd in this business?

Sieg. Trifling villain!
Who play'st with thine own guilt! Of all
 that breathe
Thou best dost know the innocence of him
'Gainst whom thy breath would blow thy
 bloody slander.
But I will talk no further with a wretch,
Further than justice asks. Answer at once,
And without quibbling, to my charge.

Gab. 'T is false!

Sieg. Who says so?

Gab. I.

Sieg. And how disprove it?

Gab. By
The presence of the murderer.

Sieg. Name him.

Gab. He
May have more names than one. Your lord-
 ship had so
Once on a time.

Sieg. If you mean me, I dare
Your utmost.

Gab. You may do so, and in safety;
I know the assassin.

Sieg. Where is he?

Gab. (*pointing to* ULRIC). Beside you!
 [ULRIC *rushes forward to attack* GA-
 BOR; SIEGENDORF *interposes.*

Sieg. Liar and fiend! but you shall not be
 slain;
These walls are mine, and you are safe
 within them. [*He turns to* ULRIC.
Ulric, repel this calumny, as I
Will do. I avow it is a growth so monstrous,
I could not deem it earth-born: but be calm;
It will refute itself. But touch him not.
 [ULRIC *endeavours to compose himself.*

Gab. Look at *him*, count, and then *hear
 me.*

Sieg. (*first to* GABOR, *and then looking at*
 ULRIC). I hear thee.
My God! you look——

Ulr. How?

Sieg. As on that dread night,
When we met in the garden.

Ulr. (*composes himself*). It is nothing.

Gab. Count, you are bound to hear me. I
 came hither
Not seeking you, but sought. When I knelt
 down
Amidst the people in the church, I dream'd
 not
To find the beggar'd Werner in the seat
Of senators and princes; but you have call'd
 me,
And we have met.

Sieg. Go on, sir.

Gab. Ere I do so,
Allow me to inquire, who profited
By Stralenheim's death? Was 't I—as poor
 as ever;
And poorer by suspicion on my name!
The baron lost in that last outrage neither
Jewels nor gold; his life alone was sought,—
A life which stood between the claims of
 others
To honours and estates scarce less than
 princely.

Sieg. These hints, as vague as vain,
 attach no less
To me than to my son.

Gab. I can't help that.
But let the consequence alight on him
Who feels himself the guilty one among us.
I speak to you, Count Siegendorf, because
I know you innocent, and deem you just.
But ere I can proceed—*dare* you protect me?
Dare you command me?
 [SIEGENDORF *first looks at the Hungarian,
 and then at* ULRIC, *who has unbuckled
 his sabre, and is drawing lines with it
 on the floor—still in its sheath.*

Ulr. (*looks at his father, and says,*) Let the man go on!

Gab. I am unarm'd, count—bid your son lay down

His sabre.

Ulr. (*offers it to him contemptuously*). Take it.

Gab. No, sir, 'tis enough
That we are both unarm'd—I would not choose
To wear a steel which may be stain'd with more
Blood than came there in battle.

Ulr. (*casts the sabre from him in contempt*). It—or some
Such other weapon, in my hand—spared yours
Once, when disarm'd and at my mercy.

Gab. True—
I have not forgotten it: you spared me for
Your own especial purpose—to sustain
An ignominy not my own.

Ulr. Proceed.
The tale is doubtless worthy the relater.
But is it of my father to hear further?
[*To* SIEGENDORF.

Sieg. (*takes his son by the hand*). My son, I
know my own innocence, and doubt not
Of yours—but I have promised this man patience;
Let him continue.

Gab. I will not detain you,
By speaking of myself much: I began
Life early—and am what the world has made me.
At Frankfort on the Oder, where I pass'd
A winter in obscurity, it was
My chance at several places of resort
(Which I frequented sometimes, but not often)
To hear related a strange circumstance
In February last. A martial force,
Sent by the state, had, after strong re-sistance,
Secured a band of desperate men, supposed
Marauders from the hostile camp.—They proved,
However, not to be so—but banditti.
Whom either accident or enterprise
Had carried from their usual haunt—the forests
Which skirt Bohemia—even into Lusatia.
Many amongst them were reported of
High rank—and martial law slept for a time.
At last they were escorted o'er the frontiers,
And placed beneath the civil jurisdiction
Of the free town of Frankfort. Of *their* fate
I know no more.

Sieg. And what is this to Ulric?

Gab. Amongst them there was said to be one man
Of wonderful endowments:—birth and for-tune,
Youth, strength, and beauty, almost super-human,
And courage as unrivall'd, were proclaim'd
His by the public rumour; and his sway,
Not only over his associates, but
His judges, was attributed to witchcraft,
Such was his influence: I have no great faith
In any magic save that of the mine—
I therefore deem'd him wealthy.—But my soul
Was roused with various feelings to seek out
This prodigy, if only to behold him.

Sieg. And did you so?

Gab. You'll hear. Chance favour'd me:
A popular affray in the public square
Drew crowds together—it was one of those
Occasions where men's souls look out of them,
And show them as they are—even in their faces:
The moment my eye met his, I exclaim'd,
"This is the man!" though he was then, as since,
With the nobles of the city. I felt sure
I had not err'd, and watch'd him long and nearly;
I noted down his form—his gesture—fea-tures,
Stature, and bearing—and amidst them all,
'Midst every natural and acquired distinc-tion,
I could discern, methought, the assassin's eye
And gladiator's heart.

Ulr. (*smiling*). The tale sounds well.

Gab. And may sound better.—He ap-pear'd to me
One of those beings to whom Fortune bends,
As she doth to the daring—and on whom
The fates of others oft depend; besides,
An indescribable sensation drew me
Near to this man, as if my point of fortune
Was to be fix'd by him.—There I was wrong.

Sieg. And may not be right now.

Gab. I follow'd him,
Solicited his notice—and obtain'd it—
Though not his friendship:—it was his in-tention
To leave the city privately—we left it
Together—and together we arrived
In the poor town where Werner was con-ceal'd,
And Stralenheim was succour'd——Now we are on
The verge—*dare* you hear further?

Sieg. I must do so—
Or I have heard too much.
 Gab. I saw in you
A man above his station—and if not
So high, as now I find you, in my then
Conceptions, 't was that I had rarely seen
Men such as you appear'd in height of mind,
In the most high of worldly rank; you were
Poor, even to all save rags: I would have
 shared
My purse, though slender, with you—you
 refused it.
 Sieg. Doth my refusal make a debt to
 you,
That thus you urge it?
 Gab. Still you owe me something,
Though not for that; and I owed you my
 safety,
At least my seeming safety, when the slaves
Of Stralenheim pursued me on the grounds
That *I* had robb'd him.
 Sieg. *I* conceal'd you—I,
Whom and whose house you arraign, reviv-
 ing viper!
 Gab. I accuse no man—save in my defence.
You, count, have made yourself accuser—
 judge:
Your hall's my court, your heart is my
 tribunal.
Be just, and *I* 'll be merciful!
 Sieg. You merciful?—
You! Base calumniator!
 Gab. I. 'T will rest
With me at last to be so. You conceal'd
 me—
In secret passages known to yourself,
You said, and to none else. At dead of
 night,
Weary with watching in the dark, and dubi-
 ous
Of tracing back my way, I saw a glimmer,
Through distant crannies, of a twinkling
 light:
I follow'd it, and reach'd a door—a secret
Portal—which open'd to the chamber, where,
With cautious hand and slow, having first
 undone
As much as made a crevice of the fastening,
I look'd through and beheld a purple bed,
And on it Stralenheim!—
 Sieg. Asleep! And yet
You slew him!—Wretch!
 Gab. He was already slain,
And bleeding like a sacrifice. My own
Blood became ice.
 Sieg. But he was all alone!
You saw none else? You did not see the——
 He pauses from agitation.
 Gab. No,
He, whom you dare not name, nor even I

Scarce dare to recollect, was not then in
The chamber.
 Sieg. (to ULRIC). Then, my boy! thou art
 guiltless still—
Thou bad'st me say *I* was so once—Oh! now
Do thou as much!
 Gab. Be patient! I can *not*
Recede now, though it shake the very walls
Which frown above us. You remember,—or
If not, your son does,—that the locks were
 changed
Beneath *his* chief inspection on the morn
Which led to this same night: how he had
 enter'd
He best knows—but within an antechamber,
The door of which was half ajar, I saw
A man who wash'd his bloody hands, and oft
With stern and anxious glance gazed back
 upon
The bleeding body—but it moved no more.
 Sieg. Oh! God of fathers!
 Gab. I beheld his features
As I see yours—but yours they were not,
 though
Resembling them—behold them in Count
 Ulric's!
Distinct as I beheld them, though the ex-
 pression
Is not now what it then was!—but it was so
When I first charged him with the crime—
 so lately.
 Sieg. This is so——
 Gab. (*interrupting him*). Nay—but hear
 me to the end!
Now you must do so.—I conceived myself
Betray'd by you and *him* (for now I saw
There was some tie between you) into this
Pretended den of refuge, to become
The victim of your guilt; and my first
 thought
Was vengeance: but, though arm'd with a
 short poniard
(Having left my sword without), I was no
 match
For him at any time, as had been proved
That morning—either in address or force.
I turn'd and fled—i' the dark: chance rather
 than
Skill made me gain the secret door of the
 hall,
And thence the chamber where you slept:
 if I
Had found you *waking*, Heaven alone can tell
What vengeance and suspicion might have
 prompted;
But ne'er slept guilt as Werner slept that
 night.
 Sieg. And yet I had horrid dreams! and
 such brief sleep,
The stars had not gone down when I awoke.

Why didst thou spare me? I dreamt of my
 father—
And now my dream is out!
 Gab. 'T is not my fault,
If I have read it.—Well! I fled and hid me—
Chance led me here after so many moons—
And show'd me Werner in Count Siegendorf!
Werner, whom I had sought in huts in vain,
Inhabited the palace of a sovereign!
You sought me and have found me—now you
 know
My secret, and may weigh its worth.
 Sieg. (*after a pause*). Indeed!
 Gab. Is it revenge or justice which in-
 spires
Your meditation?
 Sieg. Neither—I was weighing
The value of your secret.
 Gab. You shall know it
At once:—When you were poor, and I, though
 poor,
Rich enough to relieve such poverty
As might have envied mine, I offer'd you
My purse—you would not share it:—I 'll be
 franker
With you: you are wealthy, noble, trusted by
The imperial powers—you understand me?
 Sieg. Yes.
 Gab. Not quite. You think me venal, and
 scarce true:
'T is no less true, however, that my fortunes
Have made me both at present. You shall
 aid me:
I would have aided you—and also have
Been somewhat damaged in my name to save
Yours and your son's. Weigh well what I
 have said.
 Sieg. Dare you await the event of a few
 minutes'
Deliberation?
 Gab. (*casts his eyes on* ULRIC, *who is leaning
 against a pillar*). If I should do so?
 Sieg. I pledge my life for yours. With-
 draw into
This tower. [*Opens a turret door.*
 Gab. (*hesitatingly*). This is the second
 safe asylum
You have offer'd me.
 Sieg. And was not the first so?
 Gab. I know not that even now—but will
 approve
The second. I have still a further shield.—
I did not enter Prague alone; and should I
Be put to rest with Stralenheim, there are
Some tongues without will wag in my behalf.
Be brief in your decision!
 Sieg. I will be so.—
My word is sacred and irrevocable
Within *these* walls, but it extends no further.
 Gab. I 'll take it for so much.

 Sieg. (*points to* ULRIC'S *sabre, still upon
 the ground*). Take also *that*—
I saw you eye it eagerly, and him
Distrustfully.
 Gab. (*takes up the sabre*). I will; and so
 provide
To sell my life—not cheaply.
 [GABOR *goes into the turret, which*
 SIEGENDORF *closes.*
 Sieg. (*advances to* ULRIC). Now, Count
 Ulric!
For son I dare not call thee—What say'st
 thou?
 Ulr. His tale is true.
 Sieg. True, monster!
 Ulr. Most true, father!
And you did well to listen to it: what
We know, we can provide against. He must
Be silenced.
 Sieg. Ay, with half of my domains;
And with the other half, could he and thou
Unsay this villany.
 Ulr. It is no time
For trifling or dissembling. I have said
His story's true; and he too must be
 silenced.
 Sieg. How so?
 Ulr. As Stralenheim is. Are you
 so dull
As never to have hit on this before?
When we met in the garden, what except
Discovery in the act could make me know
His death? Or had the prince's household
 been
Then summon'd, would the cry for the police
Been left to such a stranger? Or should I
Have loiter'd on the way? Or could *you*,
 Werner,
The object of the baron's hate and fears,
Have fled, unless by many an hour before
Suspicion woke? I sought and fathom'd you,
Doubting if you were false or feeble: I
Perceived you were the latter: and yet so
Confiding have I found you, that I doubted
At times your weakness.
 Sieg. Parricide! no less
Than common stabber! What deed of my
 life,
Or thought of mine, could make you deem
 me fit
For your accomplice?
 Ulr. Father, do not raise
The devil you cannot lay between us. This
Is time for union and for action, not
For family disputes. While *you* were tor-
 tured,
Could *I* be calm? Think you that I have
 heard
This fellow's tale without some feeling?—
 You

Have taught me feeling for *you* and myself;
For whom or what else did you ever
 teach it?
 Sieg. Oh! my dead father's curse! 'tis
 working now.
 Ulr. Let it work on! the grave will keep
 it down!
Ashes are feeble foes: it is more easy
To baffle such, than countermine a mole,
Which winds its blind but living path beneath
 you.
Yet hear me still!—If *you* condemn me, yet
Remember *who* hath taught me once too
 often
To listen to him! *Who* proclaim'd to me
That *there were crimes* made venial by the
 occasion?
That passion was our nature? that the goods
Of Heaven waited on the goods of fortune?
Who show'd me his humanity secured
By his *nerves* only? *Who* deprived me of
All power to vindicate myself and race
In open day? By his disgrace which stamp'd
(It might be) bastardy on me, and on
Himself—a *felon's* brand! The man who is
At once both warm and weak invites to
 deeds
He longs to do, but dare not. Is it strange
That I should *act* what you could *think?*
We have done
With right and wrong: and now must only
 ponder
Upon effects, not causes. Stralenheim,
Whose life I saved from impulse, as, *un-
 known,*
I would have saved a peasant's or a dog's,
 I slew
Known as our foe—but not from vengeance.
 He
Was a rock in our way which I cut through,
As doth the bolt, because it stood between us
And our true destination—but not idly.
As stranger I preserved him, and he *owed me*
His *life:* when due, I but resumed the debt.
He, you, and I stood o'er a gulf wherein
I have plunged our enemy. *You* kindled first
The torch—*you* show'd the path: now trace
 me that
Of safety—or let me!
 Sieg. I have done with life!
 Ulr. Let us have done with that which
 cankers life—
Familiar feuds and vain recriminations
Of things which cannot be undone. We have
No more to learn or hide: I know no fear,
And have within these very walls men who
(Although you know them not) dare venture
 all things.
You stand high with the state; what passes
 here

Will not excite her too great curiosity:
Keep your own secret, keep a steady eye,
Stir not, and speak not;—leave the rest
 to me:
We must have no *third* babblers thrust
 between us. [*Exit* ULRIC.
 Sieg. (*solus*). Am I awake? are these my
 fathers' halls?
And *yon*—my son? *My* son! *mine!* who
 have ever
Abhorr'd both mystery and blood, and yet
Am plunged into the deepest hell of both!
I must be speedy, or more will be shed—
The Hungarian's!—Ulric—he hath partisans,
It seems: I might have guess'd as much. Oh
 fool!
Wolves prowl in company. He hath the key
(As I too) of the opposite door which leads
Into the turret. Now then! or once more
To be the father of fresh crimes, no less
Than of the criminal! Ho! Gabor! Gabor!
 [*Exit into the turret, closing the
 door after him.*

Scene II.

The Interior of the Turret.

GABOR *and* SIEGENDORF.

 Gab. Who calls?
 Sieg. I—Siegendorf! Take these and
 fly!
Lose not a moment!
 [*Tears off a diamond star and other
 jewels, and thrusts them into* GABOR'S
 hand.
 Gab. What am I to do
With these?
 Sieg. Whate'er you will: sell them,
 or hoard,
And prosper; but delay not, or you are lost!
 Gab. You pledged your honour for my
 safety!
 Sieg. And
Must thus redeem it. Fly! I am not master,
It seems, of my own castle—of my own
Retainers—nay, even of these very walls,
Or I would bid them fall and crush me! Fly!
Or you will be slain by——
 Gab. Is it even so?
Farewell, then! Recollect, however, count,
You sought this fatal interview!
 Sieg. I did:
Let it not be more fatal still!—Begone!
 Gab. By the same path I enter'd?
 Sieg. Yes; that's safe still;
But loiter not in Prague;—you do not know
With whom you have to deal.

Gab. I know too well—
And knew it ere yourself, unhappy sire!
Farewell! [*Exit* GABOR.
Sieg. (*solus and listening*). He hath clear'd
 the staircase. Ah! I hear
The door sound loud behind him! He is
 safe!
Safe!—Oh, my father's spirit!—I am faint—
 [*He leans down upon a stone seat, near
 the wall of the tower, in a drooping
 posture.*

Enter ULRIC, *with others armed, and with
 weapons drawn.*

Ulr. Despatch!—he's there!
Lud. The count, my lord!
Ulr. (*recognising* SIEGENDORF). *You* here,
 sir!
Sieg. Yes; if you want another victim,
 strike!
Ulr. (*seeing him stript of his jewels*). Where
 is the ruffian who hath plunder'd you?
Vassals, despatch in search of him! You see
'T was as I said—the wretch hath stript my
 father
Of jewels which might form a prince's heir-
 loom!
Away! I 'll follow you forthwith.
 [*Exeunt all but* SIEGENDORF *and* ULRIC.
 What's this?
Where is the villain?
Sieg. There are *two*, sir: which
Are you in quest of?
Ulr. Let us hear no more
Of this: he must be found. You have not
 let him
Escape!
Sieg. He's gone.
Ulr. With your connivance?
Sieg. With
My fullest, freest aid.
Ulr. Then fare you well!
 [ULRIC *is going.*
Sieg. Stop! I command—entreat—im-
 plore! Oh, Ulric!
Will you then leave me?
Ulr. What! remain to be
Denounced—dragg'd, it may be, in chains;
 and all
By your inherent weakness, half-humanity,
Selfish remorse, and temporising pity,
That sacrifices your whole race to save
A wretch to profit by our ruin! No, count,
Henceforth you have no son!
Sieg. I never had one;

And would you ne'er had borne the useless
 name!
Where will you go? I would not send you
 forth
Without protection.
Ulr. Leave that unto me.
I am not alone; nor merely the vain heir
Of your domains; a thousand, ay, ten thou-
 sand
Swords, hearts, and hands are mine.
Sieg. The foresters!
With whom the Hungarian found you first
 at Frankfort!
Ulr. Yes—men—who are worthy of the
 name! Go tell
Your senators that they look well to Prague;
Their feast of peace was early for the times;
There are more spirits abroad than have
 been laid
With Wallenstein!

 Enter JOSEPHINE *and* IDA.

Jos. What is't we hear? My
 Siegendorf!
Thank Heaven, I see you safe!
Sieg. Safe!
Ida. Yes. dear father!
Sieg. No, no; I have no children: never
 more
Call me by that worst name of parent.
Jos. What
Means my good lord?
Sieg. That you have given birth
To a demon!
Ida (*taking* ULRIC's *hand*). Who shall
 dare say this of Ulric?
Sieg. Ida, beware! there's blood upon
 that hand.
Ida (*stooping to kiss it*). I'd kiss it off,
 though it were mine.
Sieg. It is so!
Ulr. Away! it is your father's!
 [*Exit* ULRIC.
Ida. Oh, great God!
And I have loved this man!
 [IDA *falls senseless*—JOSEPHINE *stands
 speechless with horror.*
Sieg. The wretch hath slain
Them both!—My Josephine! we are now
 alone!
Would we had ever been so!—All is over
For me!—Now open wide, my sire, thy grave;
Thy curse hath dug it deeper for thy son
In mine!—The race of Siegendorf is past!

The Deformed Transformed:

A DRAMA.

ADVERTISEMENT.

THIS production is founded partly on the story of a novel called "The Three Brothers," published many years ago, from which M. G. Lewis's "Wood Demon" was also taken; and partly on the "Faust" of the great Goethe. The present publication contains the two first Parts only, and the opening chorus of the third. The rest may perhaps appear hereafter.

Dramatis Personæ.

STRANGER, *afterwards* CÆSAR.
ARNOLD.
BOURBON.
PHILIBERT.
CELLINI.

BERTHA.
OLIMPIA.

Spirits, Soldiers, Citizens of Rome, Priests, Peasants, &c.

PART I.

Scene I.—*A Forest.*

Enter ARNOLD *and his mother* BERTHA.

Bert. Out, hunchback!
Arn. I was born so, mother!
Bert. Out,
Thou incubus! Thou nightmare! Of seven sons,
The sole abortion!
Arn. Would that I had been so,
And never seen the light!
Bert. I would so too!
But as thou *hast*—hence, hence—and do thy best!
That back of thine may bear its burthen; 'tis
More high, if not so broad as that of others.
Arn. It *bears* its burthen;—but, my heart! Will it
Sustain that which you lay upon it, mother?
I love, or, at the least, I loved you: nothing
Save you, in nature, can love aught like me.
You nursed me—do not kill me!
Bert. Yes—I nursed thee,
Because thou wert my first-born, and I knew not
If there would be another unlike thee,

That monstrous sport of nature. But get hence,
And gather wood!
Arn. I will: but when I bring it,
Speak to me kindly. Though my brothers are
So beautiful and lusty, and as free
As the free chase they follow, do not spurn me;
Our milk has been the same.
Bert. As is the hedgehog's,
Which sucks at midnight from the wholesome dam
Of the young bull, until the milkmaid finds
The nipple next day sore and udder dry.
Call not thy brothers brethren! Call me not
Mother; for if I brought thee forth, it was
As foolish hens at times hatch vipers, by
Sitting upon strange eggs. Out, urchin, out!
 [*Exit* BERTHA.
Arn. (*solus*). Oh, mother!——She is gone, and I must do
Her bidding;—wearily but willingly
I would fulfil it, could I only hope
A kind word in return. What shall I do?
 [ARNOLD *begins to cut wood: in doing this he wounds one of his hands.*
My labour for the day is over now.
Accursed be this blood that flows so fast;
For double curses will be my meed now

At home—What home? I have no home, no
 kin,
No kind—not made like other creatures, or
To share their sports or pleasures. Must I
 bleed, too,
Like them? Oh, that each drop which falls
 to earth
Would rise a snake to sting them, as they
 have stung me!
Or that the devil, to whom they liken me,
Would aid his likeness! If I must partake
His form, why not his power? Is it because
I have not his will too? For one kind word
From her who bore me would still reconcile me
Even to this hateful aspect. Let me wash
The wound.
 [ARNOLD *goes to a spring, and stoops to*
 wash his hand: he starts back.
They are right; and Nature's mirror shows me
What she hath made me. I will not look on it
Again, and scarce dare think on't. Hideous
 wretch
That I am! The very waters mock me with
My horrid shadow—like a demon placed
Deep in the fountain to scare back the cattle
From drinking therein. [*He pauses.*
 And shall I live on,
A burden to the earth, myself, and shame
Unto what brought me into life! Thou blood,
Which flow'st so freely from a scratch, let me
Try if thou wilt not in a fuller stream
Pour forth my woes for ever with thyself
On earth, to which I will restore at once
This hateful compound of her atoms, and
Resolve back to her elements, and take
The shape of any reptile save myself,
And make a world for myriads of new worms!
This knife! now let me prove if it will sever
This wither'd slip of nature's nightshade—my
Vile form—from the creation, as it hath
The green bough from the forest.
 [ARNOLD *places the knife in the ground,*
 with the point upwards.
 Now 'tis set,
And I can fall upon it. Yet one glance
On the fair day, which sees no foul thing like
Myself, and the sweet sun which warm'd me,
 but
In vain. The birds—how joyously they sing!
So let them, for I would not be lamented:
But let their merriest notes be Arnold's knell;
The fallen leaves my monument; the murmur
Of the near fountain my sole elegy.
Now, knife, stand firmly, as I fain would fall!
 [*As he rushes to throw himself upon the*
 knife, his eye is suddenly caught by the
 fountain, which seems in motion.
The fountain moves without a wind: but shall
The ripple of a spring change my resolve?
No. Yet it moves again! The waters stir,

Not as with air, but by some subterrane
And rocking power of the internal world.
What's here? A mist! No more?—
 [*A cloud comes from the fountain. He*
 stands gazing upon it: it is dispelled,
 and a tall black man comes towards him.
 Arn. What would you? Speak!
Spirit or man?
 Stran. As man is both, why not
Say both in one?
 Arn. Your form is man's, and yet
You may be devil.
 Stran. So many men are that
Which is so call'd or thought, that you may
 add me
To which you please, without much wrong
 to either.
But come: you wish to kill yourself;—pursue
Your purpose.
 Arn. You have interrupted me.
 Stran. What is that resolution which can
 e'er
Be interrupted? If it be the devil
You deem, a single moment would have
 made you
Mine, and for ever, by your suicide;
And yet my coming saves you.
 Arn. I said not
You *were* the demon, but that your approach
Was like one.
 Stran. Unless you keep company
With him (and you seem scarce used to such
 high
Society), you can't tell how he approaches;
And for his aspect, look upon the fountain,
And then on me, and judge which of us twain
Looks likest what the boors believe to be
Their cloven-footed terror.
 Arn. Do you—dare *you*
To taunt me with my born deformity?
 Stran. Were I to taunt a buffalo with this
Cloven foot of thine, or the swift dromedary
With thy sublime of humps, the animals
Would revel in the compliment. And yet
Both beings are more swift, more strong,
 more mighty
In action and endurance than thyself,
And all the fierce and fair of the same kind
With thee. Thy form is natural: 'twas only
Nature's mistaken largess to bestow
The gifts which are of others upon man.
 Arn. Give me the strength then of the
 buffalo's foot,
When he spurs high the dust, beholding his
Near enemy; or let me have the long
And patient swiftness of the desert-ship,
The helmless dromedary!—and I'll bear
Thy fiendish sarcasm with a saintly patience.
 Stran. I will.
 Arn. (*with surprise*). Thou canst?

Stran. Perhaps. Would you aught else?

Arn. Thou mockest me.

Stran. Not I. Why should I mock
What all are mocking? That's poor sport,
　　methinks.
To talk to thee in human language (for
Thou canst not yet speak mine), the forester
Hunts not the wretched coney, but the boar,
Or wolf, or lion, leaving paltry game
To petty burghers, who leave once a year
Their walls, to fill their household caldrons with
Such scullion prey. The meanest gibe at
　　thee,—
Now *I* can mock the mightiest.

Arn. 　　　　　　　Then waste not
Thy time on me: I seek thee not.

Stran. 　　　　　　　Your thoughts
Are not far from me. Do not send me back:
I'm not so easily recall'd to do
Good service.

Arn. 　　What wilt thou do for me?

Stran. 　　　　　　　Change
Shapes with you, if you will, since yours so
　　irks you;
Or form you to your wish in any shape.

Arn. Oh! then you are indeed the demon,
　　for
Nought else would wittingly wear mine.

Stran. 　　　　　　I'll show thee
The brightest which the world e'er bore, and
　　give thee
Thy choice.

Arn. 　　On what condition?

Stran. 　　　　　　There's a question!
An hour ago you would have given your soul
To look like other men, and now you pause
To wear the form of heroes.

Arn. 　　　　　　No; I will not.
I must not compromise my soul.

Stran. 　　　　　　What soul,
Worth naming so, would dwell in such a
　　carcass?

Arn. 'Tis an aspiring one, whate'er the
　　tenement
In which it is mislodged. But name your
　　compact:
Must it be sign'd in blood?

Stran. 　　　　　　Not in your own.

Arn. Whose blood then?

Stran. 　　We will talk of that hereafter.
But I'll be moderate with you, for I see
Great things within you. You shall have no
　　bond
But your own will, no contract save your deeds.
Are you content?

Arn. 　　I take thee at thy word.

Stran. Now then!

　　[*The Stranger approaches the fountain,
　　　　　　and turns to* ARNOLD.
　　　　A little of your blood.

Arn. 　　　　　　For what?

Stran. To mingle with the magic of the
　　waters,
And make the charm effective.

Arn. (*holding out his wounded arm*). Take
　　it all.

Stran. Not now. A few drops will suffice
　　for this.

　　[*The Stranger takes some of* ARNOLD'S
　　　　blood in his hand, and casts it into
　　　　the fountain.

Shadows of beauty!
　　Shadows of power!
Rise to your duty—
　　This is the hour!
Walk lovely and pliant
　　From the depth of this fountain,
As the cloud-shapen giant
　　Bestrides the Hartz Mountain.
Come as ye were,
　　That our eyes may behold
The model in air
　　Of the form I will mould,
Bright as the Iris
　　When ether is spann'd;—
Such *his* desire is, [*Pointing to* ARNOLD.
　　Such my command!
Demons heroic—
　　Demons who wore
The form of the stoic
　　Or sophist of yore—
Or the shape of each victor,
　　From Macedon's boy,
To each high Roman's picture,
　　Who breathed to destroy—
Shadows of beauty!
　　Shadows of power!
Up to your duty—
　　This is the hour!

　　[*Various phantoms arise from the wa-
　　　　ters, and pass in succession before the
　　　　Stranger and* ARNOLD.

Arn. What do I see?

Stran. 　　　The black-eyed Roman, with
The eagle's beak between those eyes which
　　ne'er
Beheld a conqueror, or look'd along
The land he made not Rome's, while Rome
　　became
His, and all theirs who heir'd his very
　　name.

Arn. The phantom's bald; my quest is
　　beauty. Could I
Inherit but his fame with his defects!

Stran. His brow was girt with laurels
　　more than hairs.
You see his aspect—choose it, or reject.
I can but promise you his form; his fame
Must be long sought and fought for.

Arn. 　　　　　　I will fight, too.

But not as a mock Cæsar. Let him pass;
His aspect may be fair, but suits me not.
 Stran. Then you are far more difficult to
 please
Than Cato's sister, or than Brutus's mother,
Or Cleopatra at sixteen—an age
When love is not less in the eye than heart.
But be it so! Shadow, pass on!
 [*The phantom of Julius Cæsar disappears.*
 Arn. And can it
Be, that the man who shook the earth is
 gone,
And left no footstep?
 Stran. There you err. His substance
Left graves enough, and woes enough, and
 fame
More than enough to track his memory;
But for his shadow, 't is no more than yours,
Except a little longer and less crook'd
I' the sun. Behold another!
 [*A second phantom passes.*
 Arn. Who is he?
 Stran. He was the fairest and the bravest
 of
Athenians. Look upon him well.
 Arn. He is
More lovely than the last. How beautiful!
 Stran. Such was the curled son of
 Clinias;—Wouldst thou
Invest thee with his form?
 Arn. Would that I had
Been born with it! But since I may choose
 further,
I will *look* further.
 [*The shade of Alcibiades disappears.*
 Stran. Lo! behold again!
 Arn. What! that low, swarthy, short-
 nosed, round-eyed satyr,
With the wide nostrils and Silenus' aspect,
The splay feet and low stature! I had better
Remain that which I am.
 Stran. And yet he was
The earth's perfection of all mental beauty,
And personification of all virtue.
But you reject him?
 Arn. If his form could bring me
That which redeem'd it—no.
 Stran. I have no power
To promise that; but you may try, and find it
Easier in such a form, or in your own.
 Arn. No. I was not born for philosophy,
Though I have that about me which has
 need on 't.
Let him fleet on.
 Stran. Be air, thou hemlock-drinker!
 [*The shadow of Socrates disappears:
 another rises.*
 Arn. What's here? whose broad brow
 and whose curly beard
And manly aspect look like Hercules,

Save that his jocund eye hath more of
 Bacchus
Than the sad purger of the infernal world,
Leaning dejected on his club of conquest,
As if he knew the worthlessness of those
For whom he had fought.
 Stran. It was the man who lost
The ancient world for love.
 Arn. I cannot blame him,
Since I have risk'd my soul because I find
 not
That which he exchanged the earth for.
 Stran. Since so far
You seem congenial, will you wear his
 features?
 Arn. No. As you leave me choice, I am
 difficult,
If but to see the heroes I should ne'er
Have seen else on this side of the dim shore
Whence they float back before us.
 Stran. Hence, triumvir,
Thy Cleopatra's waiting.
 [*The shade of Antony disappears:
 another rises.*
 Arn. Who is this?
Who truly looketh like a demigod,
Blooming and bright, with golden hair, and
 stature,
If not more high than mortal, yet immortal
In all that nameless bearing of his limbs,
Which he wears as the sun his rays—a some-
 thing
Which shines from him, and yet is but the
 flashing
Emanation of a thing more glorious still.
Was *he e'er human only?*
 Stran. Let the earth speak,
If there be atoms of him left, or even
Of the more solid gold that form'd his urn.
 Arn. Who was this glory of mankind?
 Stran. The shame
Of Greece in peace, her thunderbolt in war—
Demetrius the Macedonian, and
Taker of cities.
 Arn. Yet one shadow more.
 Stran. (*addressing the shadow*). Get thee
 to Lamia's lap!
 [*The shade of Demetrius Poliorcetes
 vanishes: another rises.*
 I'll fit you still,
Fear not, my hunchback: if the shadows of
That which existed please not your nice taste,
I'll animate the ideal marble, till
Your soul be reconciled to her new garment.
 Arn. Content! I will fix here.
 Stran. I must commend
Your choice. The god-like son of the sea-
 goddess,
The unshorn boy of Peleus, with his locks
As beautiful and clear as the amber waves

Of rich Pactolus, roll'd o'er sands of gold,
Soften'd by intervening crystal, and
Rippled like flowing waters by the wind,
All vow'd to Sperchius as they were—behold
 them!
And *him*—as he stood by Polixena,
With sanction'd and with soften'd love, before
The altar, gazing on his Trojan bride,
With some remorse within for Hector slain
And Priam weeping, mingled with deep
 passion
For the sweet downcast virgin, whose young
 hand
Trembled in *his* who slew her brother. So
He stood i' the temple! Look upon him as
Greece look'd her last upon her best, the
 instant
Ere Paris' arrow flew.
 Arn. I gaze upon him
As if I were his soul, whose form shall soon
Envelope mine.
 Stran. You have done well. The greatest
Deformity should only barter with
The extremest beauty, if the proverb's true
Of mortals, that extremes meet.
 Arn. Come! Be quick!
I am impatient.
 Stran. As a youthful beauty
Before her glass. *You both* see what is not,
But dream it is what must be.
 Arn. Must I wait?
 Stran. No; that were a pity. But a word
 or two:
His stature is twelve cubits; would you so far
Outstep these times, and be a Titan? Or
(To talk canonically) wax a son
Of Anak?
 Arn. Why not?
 Stran. Glorious ambition!
I love thee most in dwarfs! A mortal of
Philistine stature would have gladly pared
His own Goliath down to a slight David:
But thou, my manikin, wouldst soar a show
Rather than hero. Thou shalt be indulged,
If such be thy desire; and yet, by being
A little less removed from present men
In figure, thou canst sway them more; for all
Would rise against thee now, as if to hunt
A new-found mammoth: and their cursed
 engines,
Their culverins, and so forth, would find way
Through our friend's armour there, with
 greater ease
Than the adulterer's arrow through his heel,
Which Thetis had forgotten to baptize
In Styx.
 Arn. Then let it be as thou deem'st best.
 Stran. Thou shalt be beauteous as the
 thing thou seest,
And strong as what it was, and——

 Arn. I ask not
For valour, since deformity is daring.
It is its essence to o'ertake mankind
By heart and soul, and make itself the
 equal—
Ay, the superior of the rest. There is
A spur in its halt movements, to become
All that the others cannot, in such things
As still are free to both, to compensate
For stepdame Nature's avarice at first.
They woo with fearless deeds the smiles of
 fortune,
And oft, like Timour the lame Tartar, win
 them.
 Stran. Well spoken! and thou doubtless
 wilt remain
Form'd as thou art. I may dismiss the mould
Of shadow, which must turn to flesh, to
 incase
This daring soul, which could achieve no less
Without it.
 Arn. Had no power presented me
The possibility of change, I would
Have done the best which spirit may to
 make
Its way with all deformity's dull, deadly
Discouraging weight upon me, like a moun-
 tain,
In feeling, on my heart as on my shoulders—
A hateful and unsightly molehill, to
The eyes of happier men. I would have
 look'd
On beauty in that sex which is the type
Of all we know or dream of beautiful
Beyond the world they brighten, with a sigh—
Not of love, but despair; nor sought to win,
Though to a heart all love, what could not
 love me
In turn, because of this vile crooked clog,
Which makes me lonely. Nay, I could have
 borne
It all, had not my mother spurn'd me from
 her.
The she-bear licks her cubs into a sort
Of shape;—my dam beheld my shape was
 hopeless.
Had she exposed me, like the Spartan, ere
I knew the passionate part of life, I had
Been a clod of the valley,—happier nothing
Than what I am. But even thus, the lowest,
Ugliest, and meanest of mankind, what cour-
 age
And perseverance could have done, perchance
Had made me something—as it has made
 heroes
Of the same mould as mine. You lately saw
 me
Master of my own life, and quick to quit it;
And he who is so is the master of
Whatever dreads to die.

Stran. Decide between
What you have been, or will be.
 Arn. I have done so.
You have open'd brighter prospects to my
 eyes,
And sweeter to my heart. As I am now,
I might be fear'd, admired, respected, loved
Of all save those next to me, of whom I
Would be loved. As thou showest me
A choice of forms, I take the one I view.
Haste! haste!
 Stran. And what shall *I* wear?
 Arn. Surely, he
Who can command all forms will choose the
 highest,
Something superior even to that which was
Pelides now before us. Perhaps *his*
Who slew him, that of Paris: or—still
 higher—
The poet's god, clothed in such limbs as are
Themselves a poetry.
 Stran. Less will content me;
For I, too, love a change.
 Arn. Your aspect is
Dusky, but not uncomely.
 Stran. If I chose,
I might be whiter; but I have a penchant
For black—it is so honest, and besides
Can neither blush with shame nor pale with
 fear;
But I have worn it long enough of late,
And now I'll take your figure.
 Arn. Mine!
 Stran. Yes. You
Shall change with Thetis' son, and I with
 Bertha,
Your mother's offspring. People have their
 tastes:
You have yours—I mine.
 Arn. Despatch! Despatch!
 Stran. Even so.
 [*The Stranger takes some earth and
 moulds it along the turf, and then
 addresses the phantom of Achilles.*
Beautiful shadow
 Of Thetis's boy!
Who sleeps in the meadow
 Whose grass grows o'er Troy:
From the red earth, like Adam,
 Thy likeness I shape,
As the being who made him,
 Whose actions I ape.
Thou clay, be all glowing,
 Till the rose in his cheek
Be as fair as, when blowing
 It wears its first streak!
Ye violets, I scatter,
 Now turn into eyes!
And thou, sunshiny water,
 Of blood take the guise!

Let these hyacinth boughs
 Be his long flowing hair,
And wave o'er his brows
 As thou wavest in air!
Let his heart be this marble
 I tear from the rock!
But his voice as the warble
 Of birds on yon oak!
Let his flesh be the purest
 Of mould, in which grew
The lily-root surest,
 And drank the best dew!
Let his limbs be the lightest
 Which clay can compound,
And his aspect the brightest
 On earth to be found!
Elements, near me,
 Be mingled and stirr'd,
Know me, and hear me,
 And leap to my word!
Sunbeams, awaken
 This earth's animation!
'T is done! He hath taken
 His stand in creation!
 [ARNOLD *falls senseless; his soul passes
 into the shape of Achilles, which rises
 from the ground; while the phantom
 has disappeared, part by part, as the
 figure was formed from the earth.*
 Arn. (*in his new form*). I love, and I shall
 be beloved! Oh, life!
At last I feel thee! Glorious spirit!
 Stran. Stop!
What shall become of your abandon'd gar-
 ment,
Yon hump, and lump, and clod of ugliness,
Which late you wore, or were?
 Arn. Who cares? Let wolves
And vultures take it, if they will.
 Stran. And if
They do, and are not scared by it, you'll say
It must be peace-time, and no better fare
Abroad i' the fields.
 Arn. Let us but leave it there
No matter what becomes on't.
 Stran. That's ungracious,
If not ungrateful. Whatsoe'er it be,
It hath sustain'd your soul full many a day.
 Arn. Ay, as the dunghill may conceal a
 gem
Which is now set in gold, as jewels should be.
 Stran. But if I give another form, it must
 be
By fair exchange, not robbery. For they
Who make men without women's aid have
 long
Had patents for the same, and do not love
Your interlopers. The devil may take men,
Not make them,—though he reap the benefit
Of the original workmanship: and therefore

Some one must be found to assume the shape
You have quitted.
 Arn. Who would do so?
 Stran. That I know not,
And therefore I must.
 Arn. You!
 Stran. I said it ere
You inhabited your present dome of beauty.
 Arn. True. I forget all things in the new
 joy
Of this immortal change.
 Stran. In a few moments·
I will be as you were, and you shall see
Yourself for ever by you, as your shadow.
 Arn. I would be spared this.
 Stran. But it cannot be.
What! shrink already, being what you are,
From seeing what you were?
 Arn. Do as thou wilt.
 Stran. (to the late form of ARNOLD, *extended
 on the earth*).
 Clay! not dead, but soul-less!
 Though no man would choose thee,
 An immortal no less
 Deigns not to refuse thee.
 Clay thou art; and unto spirit
 All clay is of equal merit.
 Fire! *without* which nought can live;
 Fire! but *in* which nought can live,
 Save the fabled salamander,
 Or immortal souls which wander,
 Praying what doth not forgive,
 Howling for a drop of water,
 Burning in a quenchless lot.
 Fire! the only element
 Where nor fish, beast, bird, nor worm,
 Save the worm which dieth not,
 Can preserve a moment's form,
 But must with thyself be blent:
 Fire! man's safeguard and his slaughter:
 Fire! Creation's first-born daughter,
 And Destruction's threaten'd son,
 When heaven with the world hath
 done:
 Fire! assist me to renew ´
 Life in what lies in my view
 Stiff and cold!
 His resurrection rests with me and you!
 One little, marshy spark of flame—
 And he again shall seem the same;
 But I his spirit's place shall hold!
 [*An ignis-fatuus flits through the wood
 and rests on the brow of the body. The
 Stranger disappears: the body rises.*
 Arn. (in his new form). Oh! horrible!
 Stran. (in ARNOLD'S *late shape*). What!
 tremblest thou?
 Arn. Not so—
I merely shudder. Where is fled the shape
Thou lately worest?

 Stran. To the world of shadows.
But let us thread the present. Whither wilt
 thou?
 Arn. Must thou be my companion?
 Stran. Wherefore not?
Your betters keep worse company.
 Arn. *My* betters!
 Stran. Oh! you wax proud, I see, of your
 new form:
I'm glad of that. Ungrateful too! That's well;
You improve apace;—two changes in an
 instant,
And you are old in the world's ways already.
But bear with me: indeed you'll find me
 useful
Upon your pilgrimage. But come, pronounce
Where shall we now be errant?
 Arn. Where the world
Is thickest, that I may behold it in
Its workings.
 Stran. That's to say, where there is war
And woman in activity. Let's see!
Spain—Italy—the new Atlantic world—
Afric, with all its Moors. In very truth,
There is small choice: the whole race are
 just now
Tugging as usual at each other's hearts.
 Arn. I have heard great things of Rome.
 Stran. A goodly choice—
And scarce a better to be found on earth,
Since Sodom was put out. The field is wide
 too;
For now the Frank, and Hun, and Spanish
 scion
Of the old Vandals, are at play along
The sunny shores of the world's garden.
 Arn. How
Shall we proceed?
 Stran. Like gallants, on good coursers.
What, ho! my chargers! Never yet were
 better,
Since Phaeton was upset into the Po.
Our pages too!

Enter two Pages, with four coal-black horses.

 Arn. A noble sight!
 Stran. And of
A nobler breed. Match me in Barbary,
Or your Kochlini race of Araby,
With these!
 Arn. The mighty steam, which volumes
 high
From their proud nostrils, burns the very air;
And sparks of flame, like dancing fire-flies,
 wheel
Around their manes, as common insects
 swarm
Round common steeds towards sunset.
 Stran. Mount, my lord:
They and I are your servitors.

Arn. And these
Our dark-eyed pages—what may be their
names?
Stran. You shall baptize them.
Arn. What! in holy water?
Stran. Why not? The deeper sinner,
better saint.
Arn. They are beautiful, and cannot, sure,
be demons.
Stran. True; the devil's always ugly; and
your beauty
Is never diabolical.
Arn. I'll call him
Who bears the golden horn, and wears such
bright
And blooming aspect, *Huon;* for he looks
Like to the lovely boy lost in the forest,
And never found till now. And for the other
And darker, and more thoughtful, who smiles
not,
But looks as serious though serene as night,
He shall be *Memnon,* from the Ethiop king
Whose statue turns a harper once a day.
And you?
Stran. I have ten thousand names, and
twice
As many attributes: but as I wear
A human shape, will take a human name.
Arn. More human than the shape (though
it was mine once)
I trust.
Stran. Then call me Cæsar.
Arn. Why, that name
Belongs to empires, and has been but borne
By the world's lords.
Stran. And therefore fittest for
The devil in disguise—since so you deem
me,
Unless you call me pope instead.
Arn. Well, then,
Cæsar thou shalt be. For myself, my name
Shall be plain Arnold still.
Cæs. We'll add a title—
"Count Arnold:" it hath no ungracious
sound,
And will look well upon a billet-doux.
Arn. Or in an order for a battle-field.
Cæs. (*sings*). To horse! to horse! my coal-
black steed
Paws the ground, and snuffs the air!
There's not a foal of Arab's breed
More knows whom he must bear;
On the hill he will not tire,
Swifter as it waxes higher;
In the marsh he will not slacken,
On the plain be overtaken;
In the wave he will not sink,
Nor pause at the brook's side to drink;
In the race he will not pant,
In the combat he'll not faint;

On the stones he will not stumble,
Time nor toil shall make him humble;
In the stall he will not stiffen,
But be winged as a griffin,
Only flying with his feet:
And will not such a voyage be sweet?
Merrily! merrily! never unsound,
Shall our bonny black horses skim over
the ground!
From the Alps to the Caucasus, ride we, or
fly!
For we'll leave them behind in the glance of
an eye.
[*They mount their horses, and disappear.*

Scene II.

A Camp before the Walls of Rome.

ARNOLD *and* CÆSAR.

Cæs. You are well enter'd now.
Arn. Ay; but my path
Has been o'er carcasses: mine eyes are full
Of blood.
Cæs. Then wipe them, and see clearly.
Why!
Thou art a conqueror; the chosen knight
And free companion of the gallant Bourbon,
Late constable of France: and now to be
Lord of the city which hath been earth's lord
Under its emperors, and—changing sex,
Not sceptre, an hermaphrodite of empire—
Lady of the old world.
Arn. How *old*? What! are there
New worlds?
Cæs. To *you.* You'll find there are such
shortly,
By its rich harvests, new disease, and gold;
From one *half* of the world named a *whole*
new one,
Because you know no better than the dull
And dubious notice of your eyes and ears.
Arn. I'll trust them.
Cæs. Do! they will deceive you sweetly,
And that is better than the bitter truth.
Arn. Dog!
Cæs. Man!
Arn. Devil!
Cæs. Your obedient humble servant.
Arn. Say *master* rather. Thou hast lured
me on,
Through scenes of blood and lust, till I am
here.
Cæs. And where wouldst thou be?
Arn. Oh, at peace—in peace.
Cæs. And where is that which is so?
From the star
To the winding worm, all life is motion; and
In life *commotion* is the extremest point
Of life. The planet wheels till it becomes

A comet, and destroying as it sweeps
The stars, goes out. The poor worm winds
 its way,
Living upon the death of other things,
But still, like them, must live and die, the
 subject
Of something which has made it live and die.
You must obey what all obey, the rule
Of fix'd necessity: against her edict
Rebellion prospers not.

Arn. And when it prospers——
Cæs. 'Tis no rebellion.
Arn. Will it prosper now?
Cæs. The Bourbon hath given orders for
 the assault,
And by the dawn there will be work.
Arn. Alas!
And shall the city yield? I see the giant
Abode of the true God, and his true saint,
Saint Peter, rear its dome and cross into
That sky whence Christ ascended from the
 cross,
Which his blood made a badge of glory and
Of joy (as once of torture unto him),
God and God's Son, man's sole and only
 refuge).
Cæs. 'Tis there, and shall be.
Arn. What?
Cæs. The crucifix
Above, and many altar shrines below.
Also some culverins upon the walls,
And harquebusses, and what not; besides
The men who are to kindle them to death
Of other men.
Arn. And those scarce mortal arches,
Pile above pile of everlasting wall,
The theatre where emperors and their sub-
 jects
(Those subjects *Romans*) stood at gaze upon
The battles of the monarchs of the wild
And wood, the lion and his tusky rebels
Of the then untamed desert, brought to joust
In the arena (as right well they might,
When they had left no human foe uncon-
 quer'd);
Made even the forest pay its tribute of
Life to their amphitheatre, as well
As Dacia men to die the eternal death
For a sole instant's pastime, and "Pass on
To a new gladiator!"—Must it fall?
Cæs. The city, or the amphitheatre?
The church, or one, or all? for you confound
Both them and me.
Arn. To-morrow sounds the assault
With the first cock-crow.
Cæs. Which, if it end with
The evening's first nightingale, will be
Something new in the annals of great sieges;
For men must have their prey after long
 toil.

Arn. The sun goes down as calmly, and
 perhaps
More beautifully, than he did on Rome
On the day Remus leapt her wall.
Cæs. I saw him.
Arn. You!
Cæs. Yes, sir. You forget I am or was
Spirit, till I took up with your cast shape,
And a worse name. I'm Cæsar and a hunch-
 back
Now. Well! the first of Cæsars was a bald-
 head,
And loved his laurels better as a wig
(So history says) than as a glory. Thus
The world runs on, but we'll be merry still.
I saw your Romulus (simple as I am)
Slay his own twin, quick-born of the same
 womb,
Because he leapt a ditch ('twas then no wall,
Whate'er it now be); and Rome's earliest
 cement
Was brother's blood; and if its native blood
Be spilt till the choked Tiber be as red
As e'er 'twas yellow, it will never wear
The deep hue of the ocean and the earth,
Which the great robber sons of fratricide
Have made their never-ceasing scene of
 slaughter
For ages.
Arn. But what have these done, their far
Remote descendants, who have lived in peace,
The peace of heaven, and in her sunshine of
Piety?
Cæs. And what had *they* done, whom the
 old
Romans o'erswept?—Hark!
Arn. They are soldiers singing
A reckless roundelay, upon the eve
Of many deaths, it may be of their own.
Cæs. And why should they not sing as
 well as swans?
They are black ones, to be sure.
Arn. So, you are learn'd,
I see, too?
Cæs. In my grammar, certes. I
Was educated for a monk of all times,
And once I was well versed in the forgotten
Etruscan letters, and—were I so minded—
Could make their hieroglyphics plainer than
Your alphabet.
Arn. And wherefore do you not?
Cæs. It answers better to resolve the
 alphabet
Back into hieroglyphics. Like your states-
 man,
And prophet, pontiff, doctor, alchymist,
Philosopher, and what not, they have built
More Babels, without new dispersion, than
The stammering young ones of the flood's
 dull ooze,

Who fail'd and fled each other. Why? why,
 marry,
Because no man could understand his neigh-
 bour.
They are wiser now, and will not separate
For nonsense. Nay, it is their brotherhood,
Their Shibboleth, their Koran, Talmud, their
Cabala; their best brick-work, wherewithal
They build more——
 Arn. (*interrupting him*). Oh, thou ever-
 lasting sneerer!
Be silent! How the soldier's rough strain seems
Soften'd by distance to a hymn-like cadence!
Listen!
 Cæs. Yes. I have heard the angels sing.
 Arn. And demons howl.
 Cæs. And man, too. Let us listen:
I love all music.

 Song of the Soldiers within.

The black bands came over
 The Alps and their snow;
With Bourbon, the rover,
 They pass'd the broad Po.
We have beaten all foemen,
 We have captured a king,
We have turn'd back on no men,
 And so let us sing!
Here's the Bourbon for ever!
 Though penniless all,
We'll have one more endeavour
 At yonder old wall.
With the Bourbon we'll gather
 At day-dawn before
The gates, and together
 Or break or climb o'er
The wall: on the ladder
 As mounts each firm foot,
Our shout shall grow gladder,
 And death only be mute.
With the Bourbon we'll mount o'er
 The walls of old Rome,
And who then shall count o'er
 The spoils of each dome?
Up! up with the lily!
 And down with the keys!
In old Rome, the seven-hilly,
 We'll revel at ease.
Her streets shall be gory,
 Her Tiber all red,
And her temples so hoary
 Shall clang with our tread.
Oh, the Bourbon! the Bourbon!
 The Bourbon for aye!
Of our song bear the burden!
 And fire, fire away!
With Spain for the vanguard,
 Our varied host comes;
And next to the Spaniard
 Beat Germany's drums;

And Italy's lances
 Are couch'd at their mother;
But our leader from France is,
 Who warr'd with his brother.
Oh, the Bourbon! the Bourbon!
 Sans country or home,
We'll follow the Bourbon,
 To plunder old Rome.
 Cæs. An indifferent song
For those within the walls, methinks, to hear.
 Arn. Yes, if they keep to their chorus.
 But here comes
The general with his chiefs and men of trust.
A goodly rebel!

 Enter the Constable BOURBON *" cum suis,"*
 &c. &c.

 Phil. How now, noble prince,
You are not cheerful?
 Bourb. Why should I be so?
 Phil. Upon the eve of conquest, such as
 ours,
Most men would be so.
 Bourb. If I were secure!
 Phil. Doubt not our soldiers. Were the
 walls of adamant,
They'd crack them. Hunger is a sharp
 artillery.
 Bourb. That they will falter is my least of
 fears.
That they will be repulsed, with Bourbon for
Their chief, and all their kindled appetites
To marshal them on—were those hoary walls
Mountains, and those who guard them like
 the gods
Of the old fables, I would trust my Titans;—
But now——
 Phil. They are but men who war with
 mortals.
 Bourb. True: but those walls have girded
 in great ages,
And sent forth mighty spirits. The past
 earth
And present phantom of imperious Rome
Is peopled with those warriors; and methinks
They flit along the eternal city's rampart,
And stretch their glorious, gory, shadowy
 hands,
And beckon me away!
 Phil. So let them! Wilt thou
Turn back from shadowy menaces of sha-
 dows?
 Bourb. They do not menace me. I could
 have faced,
Methinks, a Sylla's menace; but they clasp,
And raise, and wring their dim and deathlike
 hands,
And with their thin aspen faces and fix'd
 eyes
Fascinate mine. Look there!

Phil. I look upon
A lofty battlement.
Bourb. And there!
Phil. Not even
A guard in sight; they wisely keep below,
Shelter'd by the grey parapet from some
Stray bullet of our lansquenets, who might
Practise in the cool twilight.
Bourb. You are blind.
Phil. If seeing nothing more than may be
 seen
Be so.
Bourb. A thousand years have mann'd the
 walls
With all their heroes,—the last Cato stands
And tears his bowels, rather than survive
The liberty of that I would enslave,
And the first Cæsar with his triumphs flits
From battlement to battlement.
Phil. Then conquer
The walls for which he conquer'd, and be
 greater!
Bourb. True: so I will, or perish.
Phil. You can *not*.
In such an enterprise to die is rather
The dawn of an eternal day, than death.
 [*Count* ARNOLD *and* CÆSAR *advance.*
Cæs. And the mere men—do they too
 sweat beneath
The noon of this same ever-scorching glory?
Bourb. Ah!
Welcome the bitter hunchback! and his
 master,
The beauty of our host, and brave as beau-
 teous,
And generous as lovely. We shall find
Work for you both ere morning.
Cæs. You will find,
So please your highness, no less for yourself.
Bourb. And if I do, there will not be a
 labourer
More forward, hunchback!
Cæs. You may well say so,
For *you* have seen that back—as general,
Placed in the rear in action—but your foes
Have never seen it.
Bourb. That's a fair retort,
For I provoked it :—but the Bourbon's
 breast
Has been, and ever shall be, far advanced
In danger's face as yours, were you the *devil*.
Cæs. And if I were, I might have saved
 myself
The toil of coming here.
Phil. Why so?
Cæs. One half
Of your brave bands of their own bold accord
Will go to him, the other half be sent,
More swiftly, not less surely.
Bourb. Arnold, your

Slight crooked friend's as snake-like in his
 words
As his deeds.
Cæs. Your highness much mistakes me.
The first snake was a flatterer—I am none;
And for my deeds, I only sting when stung.
Bourb. You are brave, and that's enough
 for me; and quick
In speech as sharp in action—and that's
 more.
I am not alone a soldier, but the soldiers'
Comrade.
Cæs. They are but bad company, your
 highness;
And worse even for their friends than foes, as
 being
More permanent acquaintance.
Phil. How now, fellow!
Thou waxest insolent, beyond the privilege
Of a buffoon.
Cæs. You mean I speak the truth.
I'll lie—it is as easy: then you'll praise me
For calling you a hero.
Bourb. Philibert!
Let him alone; he's brave, and ever has
Been first, with that swart face and moun-
 tain shoulder,
In field or storm, and patient in starvation;
And for his tongue, the camp is full of
 licence,
And the sharp stinging of a lively rogue
Is, to my mind, far preferable to
The gross, dull, heavy, gloomy execration
Of a mere famish'd, sullen, grumbling slave,
Whom nothing can convince save a full meal,
And wine, and sleep, and a few maravedis,
With which he deems him rich.
Cæs. It would be well
If the earth's princes ask'd no more.
Bourb. Be silent!
Cæs. Ay, but not idle. Work yourself
 with words.
You have few to speak.
Phil. What means the audacious prater?
Cæs. To prate, like other prophets.
Bourb. Philibert!
Why will you vex him? Have we not
 enough
To think on? Arnold! I will lead the attack
To-morrow.
Arn. I have heard as much, my lord.
Bourb. And you will follow?
Arn. Since I must not lead.
Bourb. 'Tis necessary for the further
 daring
Of our too needy army, that their chief
Plant the first foot upon the foremost ladder's
First step.
Cæs. Upon its topmost, let us hope:
So shall he have his full deserts.

Bourb. The world's
Great capital perchance is ours to-morrow.
Through every change the seven-hill'd city hath
Retain'd her sway o'er nations, and the
Cæsars
But yielded to the Alarics, the Alarics
Unto the pontiffs. Roman, Goth, or priest,
Still the world's masters! Civilized, bar-
barian,
Or saintly, still the walls of Romulus
Have been the circus of an empire. Well!
'T was *their* turn—now 'tis ours; and let us
hope
That we will fight as well, and rule much
better.
Cæs. No doubt, the camp's the school of
civic rights.
What would you make of Rome?
Bourb. That which it was.
Cæs. In Alaric's time?
Bourb. No slave! in the first Cæsar's,
Whose name you bear like other curs——
Cæs. And kings!
'Tis a great name for blood-hounds.
Bourb. There's a demon
In that fierce rattlesnake thy tongue. Wilt
never
Be serious?
Cæs. On the eve of battle, no;—
That were not soldier-like. 'Tis for the
general
To be more pensive: we adventurers
Must be more cheerful. Wherefore should
we think?
Our tutelar deity, in a leader's shape,
Takes care of us. Keep thought aloof from
hosts!
If the knaves take to thinking, you will have
To crack those walls alone.
Bourb. You may sneer, since
'Tis lucky for you that you fight no worse for't.
Cæs. I thank you for the freedom; 'tis
the only
Pay I have taken in your highness' service.
Bourb. Well, sir, to-morrow you shall pay
yourself.
Look on those towers; they hold my treasury;
But, Philibert, we'll in to council. Arnold,
We would request your presence.
Arn. Prince, my service
Is yours, as in the field.
Bourb. In both we prize it,
And yours will be a post of trust at daybreak.
Cæs. And mine?
Bourb. To follow glory with the Bourbon.
Good night!
Arn. (to CÆSAR*.)* Prepare our armour for
the assault,
And wait within my tent.
[*Exeunt* BOURBON, ARNOLD, PHILIBERT, *&c.*

Cæs. (solus). Within thy tent!
Think'st thou that I pass from thee with my
presence?
Or that this crooked coffer, which contain'd
Thy principle of life, is aught to me
Except a mask? And these are men, for-
sooth!
Heroes and chiefs, the flower of Adam's
bastards!
This is the consequence of giving matter
The power of thought. It is a stubborn
substance,
And thinks chaotically, as it acts,
Ever relapsing into its first elements.
Well! I must play with these poor puppets:
'tis
The spirit's pastime in his idler hours.
When I grow weary of it, I have business
Amongst the stars, which these poor creatures
deem
Were made for them to look at. 'T were a
jest now
To bring one down amongst them, and set fire
Unto their anthill: how the pismires then
Would scamper o'er the scalding soil, and,
ceasing
From tearing down each other's nests, pipe
forth
One universal orison! Ha! ha!
[*Exit* CÆSAR.

PART II.

Scene I.—*Before the walls of Rome.*—*The
Assault: the Army in motion, with ladders
to scale the walls;* BOURBON, *with a white
scarf over his armour, foremost.*

Chorus of Spirits in the air.

I.

'T is the morn, but dim and dark.
Whither flies the silent lark?
Whither shrinks the clouded sun?
Is the day indeed begun?
Nature's eye is melancholy
O'er the city high and holy:
But without there is a din
Should arouse the saints within,
And revive the heroic ashes
Round which yellow Tiber dashes.
Oh, ye seven hills! awaken,
Ere your very base be shaken!

II.

Hearken to the steady stamp!
Mars is in their every tramp!
Not a step is out of tune,
As the tides obey the moon!

On they march, though to self-slaughter,
Regular as rolling water,
Whose high waves o'ersweep the border
Of huge moles, but keep their order.
Breaking only rank by rank.
Hearken to the armour's clank!
Look down o'er each frowning warrior,
How he glares upon the barrier:
Look on each step of each ladder,
As the stripes that streak an adder.

III.

Look upon the bristling wall,
Mann'd without an interval!
Round and round, and tier on tier,
Cannon's black mouth, shining spear,
Lit match, bell-mouth'd musquetoon,
Gaping to be murderous soon;
All the warlike gear of old,
Mix'd with what we now behold,
In this strife 'twixt old and new,
Gather like a locusts' crew.
Shade of Remus! 'tis a time
Awful as thy brother's crime!
Christians war against Christ's shrine:—
Must its lot be like to thine?

IV.

Near—and near—and nearer still,
As the earthquake saps the hill,
First with trembling, hollow motion,
Like a scarce awaken'd ocean,
Then with stronger shock and louder,
Till the rocks are crush'd to powder,—
Onward sweeps the rolling host!
Heroes of the immortal boast!
Mighty chiefs! eternal shadows!
First flowers of the bloody meadows
Which encompass Rome, the mother
Of a people without brother!
Will you sleep when nations' quarrels
Plough the root up of your laurels?
Ye who weep o'er Carthage burning,
Weep not—strike! for Rome is mourning!

V.

Onward sweep the varied nations!
Famine long hath dealt their rations.
To the wall, with hate and hunger,
Numerous as wolves, and stronger,
On they sweep. Oh, glorious city!
Must thou be a theme for pity?
Fight, like your first sire, each Roman!
Alaric was a gentle foeman,
Match'd with Bourbon's black banditti!
Rouse thee, thou eternal city;
Rouse thee! Rather give the torch
With thine own hand to thy porch,
Than behold such hosts pollute
Your worst dwelling with their foot.

VI.

Ah! behold yon bleeding spectre!
Ilion's children find no Hector;
Priam's offspring loved their brother;
Rome's great sire forgot his mother,
When he slew his gallant twin,
With inexpiable sin.
See the giant shadow stride
O'er the ramparts high and wide!
When the first o'erleapt thy wall,
Its foundation mourn'd thy fall.
Now, though towering like a Babel,
Who to stop his steps are able?
Stalking o'er thy highest dome,
Remus claims his vengeance, Rome!

VII.

Now they reach thee in their anger:
Fire and smoke and hellish clangour
Are around thee, thou world's wonder!
Death is in thy walls and under.
Now the meeting steel first clashes,
Downward then the ladder crashes,
With its iron load all gleaming,
Lying at its foot blaspheming!
Up again! for every warrior
Slain, another climbs the barrier.
Thicker grows the strife: thy ditches
Europe's mingling gore enriches.
Rome! although thy wall may perish,
Such manure thy fields will cherish,
Making gay the harvest-home;
But thy hearths, alas! oh, Rome!—
Yet be Rome amidst thine anguish,
Fight as thou wast wont to vanquish!

VIII.

Yet once more, ye old Penates!
Let not your quench'd hearths be Até's!
Yet again, ye shadowy heroes,
Yield not to these stranger Neros!
Though the son who slew his mother
Shed Rome's blood, he was your brother;
'Twas the Roman curb'd the Roman;—
Brennus was a baffled foeman.
Yet again, ye saints and martyrs,
Rise! for yours are holier charters!
Mighty gods of temples falling,
Yet in ruin still appalling!
Mightier founders of those altars,
True and Christian,—strike the assaulters!
Tiber! Tiber! let thy torrent
Show even nature's self abhorrent.
Let each breathing heart dilated
Turn, as doth the lion baited!
Rome be crush'd to one wide tomb,
But be still the Roman's Rome!

BOURBON, ARNOLD, CÆSAR, *and others, arrive
at the foot of the wall.* ARNOLD *is about
to plant his ladder.*

Bourb. Hold, Arnold! I am first.
Arn. Not so, my lord.
Bourb. Hold, sir, I charge you! Follow!
 I am proud
Of such a follower, but will brook no leader.
 [BOURBON *plants his ladder, and
 begins to mount.*
Now, boys! On! on!
 [*A shot strikes him, and* BOURBON *falls.*
Cæs. And off!
Arn. Eternal powers!
The host will be appall'd,—but vengeance!
 vengeance!
Bourb. 'T is nothing—lend me your hand.
 [BOURBON *takes* ARNOLD *by the hand,
 and rises; but as he puts his foot on
 the step, falls again.*
 Arnold! I am sped.
Conceal my fall—all will go well—conceal it!
Fling my cloak o'er what will be dust anon;
Let not the soldiers see it.
Arn. You must be
Removed; the aid of ——
Bourb. No, my gallant boy:
Death is upon me. But what is *one* life?
The Bourbon's spirit shall command them
 still.
Keep them yet ignorant that I am but clay,
Till they are conquerors—then do as you
 may.
Cæs. Would not your highness choose to
 kiss the cross?
We have no priest here, but the hilt of sword
May serve instead:—it did the same for
 Bayard.
Bourb. Thou bitter slave! to name *him* at
 this time!
But I deserve it.
Arn. (*to* CÆSAR). Villain, hold your peace!
Cæs. What, when a Christian dies? Shall
 I not offer
A Christian " Vade in pace?'
Arn. Silence! Oh!
Those eyes are glazing which o'erlook'd the
 world,
And saw no equal.
Bourb. Arnold, shouldst thou see
France——But hark! hark! the assault
 grows warmer—Oh!
For but an hour, a minute more of life,
To die within the wall! Hence, Arnold,
 hence!
You lose time—they will conquer Rome with-
 out thee.
Arn. And without *thee.*
Bourb. Not so; I'll lead them still

In spirit. Cover up my dust, and breathe
 not
That I have ceased to breathe. Away!
 and be
Victorious.
Arn. But I must not leave thee thus.
Bourb. You must—farewell—Up! up! the
 world is winning. [BOURBON *dies.*
Cæs. (*to* ARNOLD). Come, count, to busi-
 ness.
Arn. True. I'll weep hereafter.
 [ARNOLD *covers* BOURBON'S *body with a
 mantle, mounts the ladder, crying*
The Bourbon! Bourbon! On, boys! Rome is
 ours!
Cæs. Good night, lord constable! thou
 wert a man.
 [CÆSAR *follows* ARNOLD; *they reach
 the battlement;* ARNOLD *and* CÆSAR
 are struck down.
Cæs. A precious somerset! Is your count-
 ship injured?
Arn. No. [*Remounts the ladder.*
Cæs. A rare blood-hound, when his own
 is heated!
And 't is no boy's play. Now he strikes them
 down!
His hand is on the battlement—he grasps it
As though it were an altar; now his foot
Is on it, and——What have we here?—a
 Roman? [*A man falls.*
The first bird of the covey! he has fallen
On the outside of the nest. Why, how now,
 fellow?
Wounded Man. A drop of water!
Cæs. Blood's the only liquid
Nearer than Tiber.
Wounded Man. I have died for Rome.
 [*Dies.*
Cæs. And so did Bourbon, in another
 sense.
Oh, these immortal men! and their great
 motives!
But I must after my young charge. He is
By this time i' the forum. Charge! charge!
 [CÆSAR *mounts the ladder; the scene
 closes.*

Scene II.

*The City.—Combats between the Besiegers
and Besieged in the streets. Inhabitants
flying in confusion.*

Enter CÆSAR.

Cæs. I cannot find my hero; he is mix'd
With the heroic crowd that now pursue
The fugitives, or battle with the desperate.
What have we here? A cardinal or two
That do not seem in love with martyrdom.

How the old red-shanks scamper! Could they
　　doff
Their hose as they have doff'd their hats, 't
　　would be
A blessing, as a mark the less for plunder.
But let them fly; the crimson kennels now
Will not much stain their stockings, since the
　　mire
Is of the self-same purple hue.

*Enter a party fighting—*ARNOLD *at the head
　　of the Besiegers.*

　　　　　　　　　　　　He comes,
Hand in hand with the mild twins—Gore and
　　Glory.
Holla! hold, count!
　　Arn.　　　　　　Away! they must not rally.
　　Cæs. I tell thee, be not rash; a golden
　　bridge
Is for a flying enemy. I gave thee
A form of beauty, and an
Exemption from some maladies of body,
But not of mind, which is not mine to
　　give.
But though I gave the form of Thetis' son,
I dipt thee not in Styx; and 'gainst a foe
I would not warrant thy chivalric heart
More than Pelides' heel; why, then, be
　　cautious,
And know thyself a mortal still.
　　Arn.　　　　　　　　　And who
With aught of soul would combat if he were
Invulnerable? That were pretty sport.
Think'st thou I beat for hares when lions
　　roar?　　　　　[ARNOLD *rushes into the
　　　　　　　　　　　　　　　combat.*
　　Cæs. A precious sample of humanity!
Well, his blood's up; and if a little's
　　shed,
'T will serve to curb his fever.
　　　　　[ARNOLD *engages with a Roman, who
　　　　　　　　retires towards a portico.*
　　Arn.　　　　　　Yield thee, slave!
I promise quarter.
　　Rom.　　　　　That's soon said.
　　Arn.　　　　　　　　　And done—
My word is known.
　　Rom.　　　　　　So shall be my deeds.
　　　　　[*They re-engage.* CÆSAR *comes
　　　　　　　　　　　　　　　forward.*
　　Cæs. Why, Arnold! hold thine own: thou
　　hast in hand
A famous artisan, a cunning sculptor;
Also a dealer in the sword and dagger.
Not so, my musqueteer; 't was he who
　　slew
The Bourbon from the wall.
　　Arn.　　　　　　　　Ay, did he so?
Then he hath carved his monument.

　　Rom.　　　　　　　　　　　　I yet
May live to carve your better's.
　　Cæs. Well said, my man of marble!
　　Benvenuto,
Thou hast some practice in both ways;
　　and he
Who slays Cellini will have work'd as hard
As e'er thou didst upon Carrara's blocks.
　　　　　[ARNOLD *disarms and wounds* CELLINI,
　　　　　　　　*but slightly: the latter draws a pistol,
　　　　　　　　and fires; then retires, and disappears
　　　　　　　　through the portico.*
　　Cæs. How farest thou? Thou hast a
　　taste, methinks,
Of red Bellona's banquet.
　　Arn. (*staggers*).　　　　　'T is a scratch.
Lend me thy scarf. He shall not 'scape me
　　thus.
　　Cæs. Where is it?
　　Arn.　　　　　In the shoulder, not the sword
　　arm—
And that's enough. I am thirsty: would I
　　had
A helm of water!
　　Cæs.　　　　　　That's a liquid now
In requisition, but by no means easiest
To come at.
　　Arn.　　　　And my thirst increases;—but
I'll find a way to quench it.
　　Cæs.　　　　　　　　Or be quench'd
Thyself.
　　Arn. The chance is even; we will throw
The dice thereon. But I lose time in pra-
　　ting;
Prithee be quick.　　　　[CÆSAR *binds on the
　　　　　　　　　　　　　　　　scarf.*
　　　　　　　　　And what dost thou so idly?
Why dost not strike?
　　Cæs.　　　　　　Your old philosophers
Beheld mankind, as mere spectators of
The Olympic games. When I behold a prize
Worth wrestling for, I may be found a
　　Milo.
　　Arn. Ay, 'gainst an oak.
　　Cæs.　　　　　A forest, when it suits me:
I combat with a mass, or not at all.
Meantime, pursue thy sport as I do mine;
Which is just now to gaze, since all these
　　labourers
Will reap my harvest gratis.
　　Arn.　　　　　　　　Thou art still
A fiend!
　　Cæs. And thou—a man.
　　Arn. Why, such I fain would show me.
　　Cæs.　　　　　　　True—as men are.
　　Arn. And what is that?
　　Cæs.　　　Thou feelest and thou see'st.
　　　　　[*Exit* ARNOLD, *joining in the combat,
　　　　　　　　which still continues between detached
　　　　　　　　parties. The scene closes.*

Scene III.

*St. Peter's—The Interior of the Church—
The Pope at the Altar—Priests, &c., crowd-
ing in confusion, and Citizens flying for
refuge, pursued by Soldiery.*

Enter Cæsar.

A Spanish Soldier. Down with them, com-
rades! seize upon those lamps!
Cleave yon bald-pated shaveling to the chine!
His rosary's of gold!
 Lutheran Soldier. Revenge! revenge!
Plunder hereafter, but for vengeance now—
Yonder stands Anti-Christ!
 Cæs. (*interposing*). How now, schismatic?
What wouldst thou?
 Luth. Sold. In the holy name of Christ,
Destroy proud Anti-Christ. I am a Christian.
 Cæs. Yes, a disciple that would make the
founder
Of your belief renounce it, could he see
Such proselytes. Best stint thyself to
plunder.
 Luth. Sold. I say he is the devil.
 Cæs. Hush! keep that secret,
Lest he should recognise you for his own.
 Luth. Sold. Why would you save him?
I repeat he is
The devil, or the devil's vicar upon earth.
 Cæs. And that's the reason: would you
make a quarrel
With your best friends? You had far best be
quiet;
His hour is not yet come.
 Luth. Sold. That shall be seen!
 [*The Lutheran Soldier rushes forward:
a shot strikes him from one of the Pope's
Guards, and he falls at the foot of the
Altar.*
 Cæs. (*to the Lutheran*). I told you so.
 Luth. Sold. And will you not avenge me?
 Cæs. Not I! You know that "Vengeance
is the Lord's:"
You see he loves no interlopers.
 Luth. Sold. (*dying*). Oh!
Had I but slain him, I had gone on high,
Crown'd with eternal glory! Heaven, forgive
My feebleness of arm that reach'd him not,
And take thy servant to thy mercy. 'T is
A glorious triumph still; proud Babylon's
No more; the Harlot of the Seven Hills
Hath changed her scarlet raiment for sackcloth
And ashes! [*The Lutheran dies.*
 Cæs. Yes, thine own amidst the rest.
Well done, old Babel!
 [*The Guards defend themselves desper-
ately, while the Pontiff escapes, by a
private passage, to the Vatican and the
Castle of St. Angelo.*

 Cæs. Ha! right nobly battled!
Now, priest! now, soldier! the two great pro-
fessions,
Together by the ears and hearts! I have not
Seen a more comic pantomime since Titus
Took Jewry. But the Romans had the best
then;
Now they must take their turn.
 Soldiers. He hath escaped!
Follow!
 Another Sold. They have barr'd the nar-
row passage up,
And it is clogg'd with dead even to the door.
 Cæs. I am glad he hath escaped: he may
thank me for 't
In part. I would not have his bulls
abolish'd—
'T were worth one half our empire: his
indulgences
Demand some in return,—no, no, he must
not
Fall;—and, besides, his now escape may
furnish
A future miracle, in future proof
Of his infallibility.
 [*To the Spanish Soldiery.*
 Well, cut-throats!
What do you pause for? If you make not
haste,
There will not be a link of pious gold left.
And *you*, too, catholics! Would ye return
From such a pilgrimage without a relic?
The very Lutherans have more true devotion:
See how they strip the shrines!
 Soldiers. By holy Peter!
He speaks the truth; the heretics will bear
The best away.
 Cæs. And that were shame! Go to!
Assist in their conversion. [*The Soldiers dis-
perse; many quit the Church, others enter.*
 Cæs. They are gone,
And others come: so flows the wave on
wave
Of what these creatures call eternity,
Deeming themselves the breakers of the
ocean,
While they are but its bubbles, ignorant
That foam is their foundation. So another!

*Enter Olimpia, flying from the pursuit—She
springs upon the Altar.*

 Sold. She's mine!
 Another Sold. (*opposing the former*). You
lie, I track'd her first: and were she
The Pope's niece, I'll not yield her.
 [*They fight.*
 3d Sold. (*advancing towards* Olimpia). You
may settle
Your claims; I'll make mine good.

Olimp. Infernal slave!
You touch me not alive.
3d *Sold.* Alive or dead!
Olim. (*embracing a massive crucifix*). Re-
 spect your God!
3d *Sold.* Yes, when he shines in gold.
Girl, you but grasp your dowry.
 [*As he advances,* OLIMPIA, *with a strong
 and sudden effort, casts down the cruci-
 fix ; it strikes the Soldier, who falls.*
3d *Sold.* Oh, great God !
Olimp. Ah! now you recognise him.
3d *Sold.* My brain 's crush'd !
Comrades, help, ho ! All 's darkness !
 [*He dies.*
 Other Soldiers (*coming up*). Slay her,
 although she had a thousand lives :
She hath kill'd our comrade.
Olimp. Welcome such a death !
You have no life to give, which the worst
 slave
Would take. Great God ! through thy
 redeeming Son,
And thy Son's Mother, now receive me as
I would approach thee, worthy her, and him,
 and thee !

Enter ARNOLD.

Arn. What do I see ? Accursed jackals !
 Forbear !
Cœs. (*aside and laughing*). Ha ! ha ! here 's
 equity ! The dogs
Have as much right as he. But to the issue !
Soldiers. Count, she hath slain our com-
 rade.
Arn. With what weapon ?
Sold. The cross, beneath which he is
 crush'd ; behold him
Lie there, more like a worm than man ; she
 cast it
Upon his head.
Arn. Even so ; there is a woman
Worthy a brave man's liking. Were ye
 such,
Ye would have honour'd her. But get ye
 hence,
And thank your meanness, other God you
 have none,
For your existence. Had you touch'd a hair
Of those dishevell'd locks, I would have
 thinn'd
Your ranks more than the enemy. Away !
Ye jackals ! gnaw the bones the lion leaves
But not even these till he permits.
A Sold. (*murmuring*). The lion
Might conquer for himself then.
Arn. (*cuts him down*). Mutineer !
Rebel in hell—you shall obey on earth !
 [*The Soldiers assault* ARNOLD.

Arn. Come on ! I 'm glad on 't ! I will
 show you, slaves,
How you should be commanded, and who led
 you
First o'er the wall you were so shy to
 scale,
Until I waved my banners from its height,
As you are bold within it.
 [ARNOLD *mows down the foremost ; the
 rest throw down their arms.*
Soldiers. Mercy ! mercy !
Arn. Then learn to grant it. Have I
 taught you *who*
Led you o'er Rome's eternal battlements ?
Soldiers. We saw it, and we know it ; yet
 forgive
A moment's error in the heat of conquest—
The conquest which you led to.
Arn. Get you hence !
Hence to your quarters ! you will find them
 fix'd
In the Colonna palace.
Olimp. (*aside*). In my father's
 House !
Arn. (*to the Soldiers*). Leave your arms ;
 ye have no further need
Of such : the city's render'd. And mark well
You keep your hands clean, or I 'll find out a
 stream
As red as Tiber now runs, for your baptism.
Soldiers (*deposing their arms and departing*).
 We obey !
Arn. (*to* OLIMPIA). Lady, you are safe.
Olimp. I should be so,
Had I a knife even ; but it matters not—
Death hath a thousand gates ; and on the
 marble,
Even at the altar foot, whence I look down
Upon destruction, shall my head be dash'd,
Ere thou ascend it. God forgive thee, man !
Arn. I wish to merit his forgiveness, and
Thine own, although I have not injured thee.
Olimp. No ! Thou hast only sack'd my
 native land,—
No injury !—and made my father's house
A den of thieves ! No injury !—this temple—
Slippery with Roman and with holy gore !
No injury ! And now thou wouldst preserve
 me,
To be——but that shall never be !
 [*She raises her eyes to heaven, folds her
 robe round her, and prepares to dash
 herself down on the side of the Altar
 opposite to that where* ARNOLD *stands.*
Arn. Hold ! hold !
I swear.
Olimp. Spare thine already forfeit soul
A perjury for which even hell would loathe
 thee.
I know thee.

Arn. No, thou know'st me not ; I am not
Of these men, though——
 Olimp. I judge thee by thy mates ;
It is for God to judge thee as thou art.
I see thee purple with the blood of Rome ;
Take mine, 'tis all thou e'er shalt have of
 me,
And here, upon the marble of this temple,
Where the baptismal font baptized me God's,
I offer him a blood less holy
But not less pure (pure as it left me then,
A redeem'd infant) than the holy water
The saints have sanctified !
 [OLIMPIA *waves her hand to* ARNOLD *with*
 disdain, and dashes herself on the
 pavement from the Altar.
Arn. Eternal God !
I feel thee now ! Help ! help ! She 's gone.
 Cœs. (*approaches*). I am here.
Arn. Thou ! but oh, save her !
 Cœs. (*assisting him to raise* OLIMPIA). She
 hath done it well !
The leap was serious.
 Arn. Oh ! she is lifeless !
 Cœs. If
She be so, I have nought to do with that :
The resurrection is beyond me.
 Arn. Slave !
 Cœs. Ay, slave or master, 'tis all one :
 methinks
Good words, however, are as well at times.
 Arn. Words !—Canst thou aid her ?
 Cœs. I will try. A sprinkling
Of that same holy water may be useful.
 [*He brings some in his helmet from the font.*
Arn. 'Tis mix'd with blood.
 Cœs. There is no cleaner now
In Rome.
 Arn. How pale ! how beautiful ! how life-
 less !
Alive or dead, thou essence of all beauty,
I love but thee !
 Cœs. Even so Achilles loved
Penthesilea : with his form it seems
You have his heart, and yet it was no soft one.
 Arn. She breathes ! But no, 'twas nothing,
 or the last
Faint flutter life disputes with death.
 Cœs. She breathes.
 Arn. Thou say'st it ? Then 'tis truth.
 Cœs. You do me right—
The devil speaks truth much oftener than
 he 's deem'd :
He hath an ignorant audience.
 Arn. (*without attending to him*). Yes ! her
 heart beats.
Alas ! that the first beat of the only heart
I ever wish'd to beat with mine should
 vibrate
To an assassin's pulse.

 Cœs. A sage reflection,
But somewhat late i' the day. Where shall
 we bear her ?
I say she lives.
 Arn. And will she live ?
 Cœs. As much
As dust can.
 Arn. Then she is dead !
 Cœs. Bah ! bah ! You are so,
And do not know it. She will come to life—
Such as you think so, such as you now are ;
But we must work by human means.
 Arn. We will
Convey her unto the Colonna palace,
Where I have pitch'd my banner.
 Cœs. Come then ! raise her up !
 Arn. Softly !
 Cœs. As softly as they bear the dead,
Perhaps because they cannot feel the jolting.
 Arn. But doth she live indeed ?
 Cœs. Nay, never fear !
But, if you rue it after, blame not me.
 Arn. Let her but live !
 Cœs. The spirit of her life
Is yet within her breast, and may revive.
Count ! count ! I am your servant in all
 things,
And this is a new office :—'t is not oft
I am employ'd in such ; but you perceive
How stanch a friend is what you call a
 fiend.
On earth you have often only fiends for friends ;
Now *I* desert not mine. Soft ! bear her hence,
The beautiful half-clay, and nearly spirit !
I am almost enamour'd of her, as
Of old the angels of her earliest sex.
 Arn. Thou !
 Cœs. I ! But fear not. I 'll not be your
 rival.
 Arn. Rival !
 Cœs. I could be one right formidable ;
But since I slew the seven husbands of
Tobias' future bride (and after all
Was smoked out by some incense), I have laid
Aside intrigue : 'tis rarely worth the trouble
Of gaining, or—what is more difficult—
Getting rid of your prize again ; for there's
The rub ! at least to mortals.
 Arn. Prithee, peace !
Softly ! methinks her lips move, her eyes open !
 Cœs. Like stars, no doubt ; for that 's a
 metaphor
For Lucifer and Venus.
 Arn. To the palace
Colonna, as I told you !
 Cœs. Oh ! I know
My way through Rome.
 Arn. Now onward, onward ! Gently !
 [*Exeunt, bearing* OLIMPIA. *The scene*
 closes.

PART III.

Scene I.—*A Castle in the Apennines, surrounded by a wild but smiling Country. Chorus of Peasants singing before the Gates.*

Chorus.

I.

The wars are over,
 The spring is come;
The bride and her lover
 Have sought their home:
They are happy, we rejoice;
Let their hearts have an echo in every voice!

II.

The spring is come; the violet's gone,
The first-born child of the early sun:
With us she is but a winter's flower,
The snow on the hills cannot blast her bower,
And she lifts up her dewy eye of blue
To the youngest sky of the self-same hue.

III.

And when the spring comes with her host
Of flowers, that flower beloved the most
Shrinks from the crowd that may confuse
Her heavenly odour and virgin hues.

IV.

Pluck the others, but still remember
Their herald out of dim December—
The morning star of all the flowers,
The pledge of daylight's lengthen'd hours;
Nor, midst the roses, e'er forget
The virgin, virgin violet.

Enter CÆSAR.

Cæs. (*singing*). The wars are all over,
 Our swords are all idle,
 The steed bites the bridle.
The casque's on the wall.
There's rest for the rover;
 But his armour is rusty,
 And the veteran grows crusty,

As he yawns in the hall.
He drinks—but what's drinking?
A mere pause from thinking!
No bugle awakes him with life-and-death
 call.

Chorus.

But the hound bayeth loudly,
 The boar's in the wood,
And the falcon longs proudly
 To spring from her hood:
On the wrist of the noble
 She sits like a crest,
And the air is in trouble
 With birds from their nest.

Cæs. Oh! shadow of glory!
 Dim image of war!
But the chase hath no story,
 Her hero no star,
Since Nimrod, the founder
 Of empire and chase,
Who made the woods wonder
 And quake for their race.
When the lion was young,
 In the pride of his might,
Then 't was sport for the strong
 To embrace him in fight;
To go forth, with a pine
 For a spear, 'gainst the mammoth,
Or strike through the ravine
 At the foaming behemoth;
While man was in stature
 As towers in our time,
The first-born of Nature,
 And, like her, sublime!

Chorus.

But the wars are over,
 The spring is come;
The bride and her lover
 Have sought their home;
They are happy, and we rejoice;
Let their hearts have an echo from every
 voice! [*Exeunt the Peasantry, singing.*

Beppo:

A VENETIAN STORY.

Rosalind. Farewell, Monsieur Traveller: Look you lisp, and wear strange suits: disable all the benefits of your own country; be out of love with your Nativity, and almost chide God for making you that countenance you are; or I will scarce think that you have swam in a *Gondola.—As You Like It*, Act IV., Scene i.

Annotation of the Commentators.

That is, been at *Venice*, which was much visited by the young English gentlemen of those times, and was then what *Paris* is *now*—the seat of all dissoluteness.—S.A.

I.

'T is known, at least it should be, that throughout
 All countries of the Catholic persuasion,
Some weeks before Shrove Tuesday comes about,
 The people take their fill of recreation,
And buy repentance, ere they grow devout,
 However high their rank, or low their station,
With fiddling, feasting, dancing, drinking, masking,
And other things which may be had for asking.

II.

The moment night with dusky mantle covers
 The skies (and the more duskily the better),
The time less liked by husbands than by lovers
 Begins, and prudery flings aside her fetter;
And gaiety on restless tiptoe hovers,
 Giggling with all the gallants who beset her;
And there are songs and quavers, roaring, humming,
Guitars, and every other sort of strumming.

III.

And there are dresses splendid, but fantastical,
 Masks of all times and nations, Turks and Jews,
And harlequins and clowns, with feats gymnastical,
 Greeks, Romans, Yankee-doodles, and Hindoos;
All kinds of dress, except the ecclesiastical,
 All people, as their fancies hit, may choose,
But no one in these parts may quiz the clergy,—
Therefore take heed, ye Freethinkers! I charge ye.

IV.

You'd better walk about begirt with briars,
 Instead of coat and smallclothes, than put on
A single stitch reflecting upon friars,
 Although you swore it only was in fun;
They'd haul you o'er the coals, and stir the fires
 Of Phlegethon with every mother's son,
Nor say one mass to cool the caldron's bubble
That boil'd your bones, unless you paid them double.

V.

But saving this, you may put on whate'er
 You like by way of doublet, cape, or cloak,
Such as in Monmouth-street, or in Rag Fair,
 Would rig you out in seriousness or joke;
And even in Italy such places are,
 With prettier name in softer accents spoke,
For, bating Covent Garden, I can hit on
No place that's called "Piazza" in Great Britain.

VI.

This feast is named the Carnival, which being
 Interpreted, implies "farewell to flesh:"
So call'd, because the name and thing agreeing,
 Through Lent they live on fish both salt and fresh.
But why they usher Lent with so much glee in,
 Is more than I can tell, although I guess
'Tis as we take a glass with friends at parting,
In the stage-coach or packet, just at starting.

VII.

And thus they bid farewell to carnal dishes,
 And solid meats, and highly spiced ragouts,
To live for forty days on ill-dress'd fishes,
 Because they have no sauces to their stews ;
A thing which causes many "poohs" and
 "pishes,"
 And several oaths (which would not suit
 the Muse),
From travellers accustom'd from a boy
To eat their salmon, at the least, with soy ;

VIII.

And therefore humbly I would recommend
 "The curious in fish-sauce," before they
 cross
The sea, to bid their cook, or wife, or friend,
 Walk or ride to the Strand, and buy in gross
(Or if set out beforehand, these may send
 By any means least liable to loss)
Ketchup, Soy, Chili-vinegar, and Harvey,
Or by the Lord ! a Lent will well nigh
 starve ye ;

IX.

That is to say, if your religion's Roman,
 And you at Rome would do as Romans do,
According to the proverb,—although no man,
 If foreign, is obliged to fast ; and you
If Protestant, or sickly, or a woman,
 Would rather dine in sin on a ragout—
Dine and be d—d ! I don't mean to be coarse,
But that's the penalty, to say no worse.

X.

Of all the places where the Carnival
 Was most facetious in the days of yore,
For dance, and song, and serenade, and ball,
 And masque, and mime, and mystery, and
 more
Than I have time to tell now, or at all,
 Venice the bell from every city bore,—
And at the moment when I fix my story,
That sea-born city was in all her glory.

XI.

They've pretty faces yet, those same Vene-
 tians,
 Black eyes, arch'd brows, and sweet ex-
 pressions still ;
Such as of old were copied from the Grecians,
 In ancient arts by moderns mimick'd ill ;
And like so many Venuses of Titian's
 (The best's at Florence—see it, if ye will),
They look when leaning over the balcony,
Or stepp'd from out a picture by Giorgione,

XII.

Whose tints are truth and beauty at their
 best ;
 And when you to Manfrini's palace go,
That picture (howsoever fine the rest)
 Is loveliest to my mind of all the show ;
It may perhaps be also to *your* zest,
 And that's the cause I rhyme upon it so :
'T is but a portrait of his son, and wife,
And self ; but *such* a woman ! love in life !

XIII.

Love in full life and length, not love ideal,
 No, nor ideal beauty, that fine name,
But something better still, so very real,
 That the sweet model must have been the
 same ;
A thing that you would purchase, beg, or steal,
 Were't not impossible, besides a shame :
The face recalls some face, as't were with
 pain,
You once have seen, but ne'er will see again.

XIV.

One of those forms which flit by us, when we
 Are young, and fix our eyes on every face ;
And, oh ! the loveliness at times we see
 In momentary gliding, the soft grace,
The youth, the bloom, the beauty which
 agree,
 In many a nameless being we retrace,
Whose course and home we knew not, nor
 shall know,
Like the lost Pleiad seen no more below.

XV.

I said that like a picture by Giorgione
 Venetian women were, and so they *are*,
Particularly seen from a balcony
 (For beauty's sometimes best set off afar),
And there, just like a heroine of Goldoni,
 They peep from out the blind, or o'er the
 bar ;
And truth to say, they're mostly very pretty,
And rather like to show it, more's the pity !

XVI.

For glances beget ogles, ogles sighs,
 Sighs wishes, wishes words, and words a
 letter,
Which flies on wings of light-heel'd Mercuries,
 Who do such things because they know no
 better ;
And then, God knows what mischief may arise,
 When love links two young people in one
 fetter,
Vile assignations, and adulterous beds,
Elopements, broken vows, and hearts, and
 heads.

XVII.

Shakspeare described the sex in Desdemona
 As very fair, but yet suspect in fame,
And to this day from Venice to Verona
 Such matters may be probably the same,
Except that since those times was never
 known a
 Husband whom mere suspicion could in-
 flame
To suffocate a wife no more than twenty,
Because she had a "cavalier servente."

XVIII.

Their jealousy (if they are ever jealous)
 Is of a fair complexion altogether,
Not like that sooty devil of Othello's,
 Which smothers women in a bed of
 feather,
But worthier of these much more jolly
 fellows,
 When weary of the matrimonial tether
His head for such a wife no mortal bothers,
But takes at once another, or another's.

XIX.

Didst ever see a Gondola? For fear
 You should not, I'll describe it you exactly:
'T is a long cover'd boat that's common here,
 Carved at the prow, built lightly, but com-
 pactly,
Row'd by two rowers, each call'd "Gondolier,"
 It glides along the water looking blackly.
Just like a coffin clapt in a canoe,
Where none can make out what you say
 or do.

XX.

And up and down the long canals they go,
 And under the Rialto shoot along,
By night and day, all paces, swift or slow,
 And round the theatres, a sable throng,
They wait in their dusk livery of woe,—
 But not to them do woeful things belong,
For sometimes they contain a deal of fun,
Like mourning coaches when the funeral's
 done.

XXI.

But to my story.—'T was some years ago,
 It may be thirty, forty, more or less,
The Carnival was at its height, and so
 Were all kinds of buffoonery and dress;
A certain lady went to see the show,
 Her real name I know not, nor can guess,
And so we'll call her Laura, if you please,
Because it slips into my verse with ease.

XXII.

She was not old, nor young, nor at the years
 Which certain people call a "certain age,"
Which yet the most uncertain age appears,
 Because I never heard, nor could engage
A person yet by prayers, or bribes, or tears,
 To name, define by speech, or write on page,
The period meant precisely by that word,—
Which surely is exceedingly absurd.

XXIII.

Laura was blooming still, had made the best
 Of time, and time return'd the compliment,
And treated her genteelly, so that, dress'd,
 She look'd extremely well where'er she
 went;
A pretty woman is a welcome guest,
 And Laura's brow a frown had rarely bent;
Indeed, she shone all smiles, and seem'd to
 flatter
Mankind with her black eyes for looking at her.

XXIV.

She was a married woman; 'tis convenient,
 Because in Christian countries 't is a rule
To view their little slips with eyes more leni-
 ent;
 Whereas if single ladies play the fool
(Unless within the period intervenient
 A well-timed wedding makes the scandal
 cool),
I don't know how they ever can get over it,
Except they manage never to discover it.

XXV.

Her husband sail'd upon the Adriatic,
 And made some voyages, too, in other seas,
And when he lay in quarantine for pratique
 (A forty days' precaution 'gainst disease),
His wife would mount, at times, her highest
 attic,
 For thence she could discern the ship with
 ease:
He was a merchant trading to Aleppo,
His name Giuseppe, call'd more briefly,
 Beppo.

XXVI.

He was a man as dusky as a Spaniard,
 Sunburnt with travel, yet a portly figure;
Though colour'd, as it were, within a tan-
 yard,
 He was a person both of sense and
 vigour—
A better seaman never yet did man yard;
 And she, although her manners show'd no
 rigour,
Was deem'd a woman of the strictest principle,
So much as to be thought almost invincible.

XXVII.

But several years elapsed since they had met;
 Some people thought the ship was lost,
 and some
That he had somehow blunder'd into debt,
 And did not like the thought of steering
 home;
And there were several offer'd any bet,
 Or that he would, or that he would not
 come;
For most men (till by losing render'd sager)
Will back their own opinions with a wager.

XXVIII.

'T is said that their last parting was pathetic,
 As partings often are, or ought to be,
And their presentiment was quite prophetic,
 That they should never more each other
 see,
(A sort of morbid feeling, half poetic,
 Which I have known occur in two or three,)
When kneeling on the shore upon her sad
 knee
He left this Adriatic Ariadne.

XXIX.

And Laura waited long, and wept a little,
 And thought of wearing weeds, as well she
 might;
She almost lost all appetite for victual,
 And could not sleep with ease alone at
 night;
She deem'd the window-frames and shutters
 brittle
 Against a daring housebreaker or sprite,
And so she thought it prudent to connect her
With a vice-husband, *chiefly* to *protect her*.

XXX.

She chose, (and what is there they will not
 choose,
 If only you will but oppose their choice?)
Till Beppo should return from his long
 cruise,
 And bid once more her faithful heart re-
 joice,
A man some women like, and yet abuse—
 A coxcomb was he by the public voice;
A Count of wealth, they said, as well as
 quality,
And in his pleasures of great liberality.

XXXI.

And then he was a Count, and then he knew
 Music, and dancing, fiddling, French and
 Tuscan;
The last not easy, be it known to you,
 For few Italians speak the right Etruscan.

He was a critic upon operas, too,
 And knew all niceties of the sock and
 buskin;
And no Venetian audience could endure a
Song, scene, or air, when he cried "secca-
 tura!"

XXXII.

His "bravo" was decisive, for that sound
 Hush'd "Academie" sigh'd in silent awe;
The fiddlers trembled as he look'd around,
 For fear of some false note's detected flaw;
The "prima donna's" tuneful heart would
 bound,
 Dreading the deep damnation of his "bah!"
Soprano, basso, even the contra-alto,
Wish'd him five fathom under the Rialto.

XXXIII.

He patronised the Improvisatori,
 Nay, could himself extemporise some
 stanzas,
Wrote rhymes, sang songs, could also tell a
 story,
 Sold pictures, and was skilful in the dance
 as
Italians can be, though in this their glory
 Must surely yield the palm to that which
 France has;
In short, he was a perfect cavaliero,
And to his very valet seem'd a hero.

XXXIV.

Then he was faithful too, as well as amorous;
 So that no sort of female could complain,
Although they're now and then a little
 clamorous,
 He never put the pretty souls in pain;
His heart was one of those which most
 enamour us,
 Wax to receive, and marble to retain:
He was a lover of the good old school,
Who still become more constant as they cool.

XXXV.

No wonder such accomplishments should turn
 A female head, however sage and steady—
With scarce a hope that Beppo could return,
 In law he was almost as good as dead, he
Nor sent, nor wrote, nor show'd the least
 concern,
 And she had waited several years already;
And really if a man won't let us know
That he's alive, he's *dead*, or should be so.

XXXVI.

Besides, within the Alps, to every woman,
 (Although, God knows, it is a grievous sin,)
'Tis, I may say, permitted to have *two* men;
 I can't tell who first brought the custom in,

But "Cavalier Serventes" are quite common,
 And no one notices nor cares a pin;
And we may call this (not to say the worst)
A *second* marriage which corrupts the *first*.

XXXVII.

The word was formerly a "Cicisbeo,"
 But *that* is now grown vulgar and inde-
 cent;
The Spaniards call the person a "*Cortejo*,"
 For the same mode subsists in Spain,
 though recent;
In short, it reaches from the Po to Teio,
 And may perhaps at last be o'er the sea
 sent:
But Heaven preserve Old England from such
 courses!
Or what becomes of damage and divorces?

XXXVIII.

However, I still think, with all due deference
 To the fair *single* part of the creation,
That married ladies should preserve the pre-
 ference
 In *tête-à-tête* or general conversation—
And this I say without peculiar reference
 To England, France, or any other nation—
Because they know the world, and are at ease,
And being natural, naturally please.

XXXIX.

'Tis true, your budding Miss is very charm-
 ing,
 But shy and awkward at first coming out,
So much alarm'd, that she is quite alarming,
 All Giggle, Blush; half Pertness, and half
 Pout;
And glancing at *Mamma*, for fear there's
 harm in
 What you, she, it, or they, may be about,
The nursery still lisps out in all they utter—
Besides, they always smell of bread and
 butter.

XL.

But "Cavalier Servente" is the phrase
 Used in politest circles to express
This supernumerary slave, who stays
 Close to the lady as a part of dress,
Her word the only law which he obeys.
 His is no sinecure, as you may guess;
Coach, servants, gondola, he goes to call,
And carries fan and tippet, gloves and shawl.

XLI.

With all its sinful doings, I must say,
 That Italy's a pleasant place to me,
Who love to see the Sun shine every day,
 And vines (not nail'd to walls) from tree
 to tree

Festoon'd, much like the back scene of a play,
 Or melodrame, which people flock to see,
When the first act is ended by a dance
In vineyards copied from the south of France.

XLII.

I like on Autumn evenings to ride out,
 Without being forced to bid my groom be
 sure
My cloak is round his middle strapp'd about,
 Because the skies are not the most secure;
I know too that, if stopp'd upon my route,
 Where the green alleys windingly allure,
Reeling with grapes red waggons choke the
 way,—
In England 't would be dung, dust, or a dray.

XLIII.

I also like to dine on becaficas,
 To see the Sun set, sure he'll rise to-
 morrow,
Not through a misty morning twinkling
 weak as
 A drunken man's dead eye in maudlin
 sorrow,
But with all Heaven t'himself; the day will
 break as
 Beauteous as cloudless, nor be forced to
 borrow
That sort of farthing candlelight which
 glimmers
Where reeking London's smoky caldron sim-
 mers.

XLIV.

I love the language, that soft bastard Latin,
 Which melts like kisses from a female
 mouth,
And sounds as if it should be writ on satin,
 With syllables which breathe of the sweet
 South,
And gentle liquids gliding all so pat in,
 That not a single accent seems uncouth,
Like our harsh northern whistling, grunting
 guttural,
Which we're obliged to hiss, and spit, and
 sputter all.

XLV.

I like the women too (forgive my folly),
 From the rich peasant cheek of ruddy
 bronze,
And large black eyes that flash on you a
 volley
 Of rays that say a thousand things at once,
To the high dama's brow, more melancholy,
 But clear, and with a wild and liquid glance,
Heart on her lips, and soul within her eyes,
Soft as her clime, and sunny as her skies.

XLVI.

Eve of the land which still is Paradise!
 Italian beauty! didst thou not inspire
Raphael, who died in thy embrace, and vies
 With all we know of Heaven, or can desire,
In what he hath bequeath'd us?—in what
 guise,
 Though flashing from the fervour of the
 lyre,
Would *words* describe thy past and present
 glow,
While yet Canova can create below?

XLVII.

"England! with all thy faults I love thee
 still,"
 I said at Calais, and have not forgot it;
I like to speak and lucubrate my fill;
 I like the government (but that is not it);
I like the freedom of the press and quill;
 I like the Habeas Corpus (when we've
 got it);
I like a parliamentary debate,
Particularly when 'tis not too late;

XLVIII.

I like the taxes, when they're not too many;
 I like a seacoal fire, when not too dear;
I like a beef-steak, too, as well as any;
 Have no objection to a pot of beer;
I like the weather, when it is not rainy,
 That is, I like two months of every year,
And so God save the Regent, Church, and
 King!
Which means that I like all and everything.

XLIX.

Our standing army, and disbanded seamen,
 Poor's rate, Reform, my own, the nation's
 debt,
Our little riots just to show we are free men,
 Our trifling bankruptcies in the Gazette,
Our cloudy climate, and our chilly women,
 All these I can forgive, and those forget,
And greatly venerate our recent glories,
And wish they were not owing to the Tories.

L.

But to my tale of Laura,—for I find
 Digression is a sin, that by degrees
Becomes exceeding tedious to my mind,
 And, therefore, may the reader too dis-
 please—
The gentle reader, who may wax unkind,
 And caring little for the author's ease,
Insist on knowing what he means, a hard
And hapless situation for a bard.

LI.

Oh that I had the art of easy writing
 What should be easy reading! could I scale
Parnassus, where the Muses sit inditing
 Those pretty poems never known to fail,
How quickly would I print (the world de-
 lighting)
 A Grecian, Syrian, or Assyrian tale;
And sell you, mix'd with western senti-
 mentalism,
Some samples of the finest Orientalism!

LII.

But I am but a nameless sort of person,
 (A broken Dandy lately on my travels)
And take for rhyme, to hook my rambling
 verse on,
 The first that Walker's Lexicon unravels,
And when I can't find that, I put a worse on,
 Not caring as I ought for critics' cavils;
I've half a mind to tumble down to prose,
But verse is more in fashion—so here goes.

LIII.

The Count and Laura made their new ar-
 rangement,
 Which lasted, as arrangements sometimes
 do,
For half a dozen years without estrange-
 ment;
 They had their little differences, too;
Those jealous whiffs, which never any change
 meant;
 In such affairs there probably are few
Who have not had this pouting sort of
 squabble,
From sinners of high station to the rabble.

LIV.

But, on the whole, they were a happy pair,
 As happy as unlawful love could make them;
The gentleman was fond, the lady fair,
 Their chains so slight, 'twas not worth
 while to break them;
The world beheld them with indulgent air;
 The pious only wish'd "the devil take
 them!"
He took them not; he very often waits,
And leaves old sinners to be young ones' baits.

LV.

But they were young: Oh! what without
 our youth
 Would love be! What would youth be
 without love!
Youth lends it joy, and sweetness, vigour,
 truth,
 Heart, soul, and all that seems as from
 above;

But, languishing with years, it grows un-
 couth—
 One of few things experience don't im-
 prove,
Which is, perhaps, the reason why old fellows
Are always so preposterously jealous.

LVI.

It was the Carnival, as I have said
 Some six and thirty stanzas back, and so
Laura the usual preparations made,
 Which you do when your mind's made up
 to go
To-night to Mrs. Boehm's masquerade,
 Spectator, or partaker in the show;
The only difference known between the cases
Is—here, we have six weeks of "varnish'd
 faces."

LVII.

Laura, when dress'd, was (as I sang before)
 A pretty woman as was ever seen,
Fresh as the Angel o'er a new inn door,
 Or frontispiece of a new Magazine,
With all the fashions which the last month
 wore,
 Colour'd, and silver paper leaved between
That and the title-page, for fear the press
Should soil with parts of speech the parts
 of dress.

LVIII.

They went to the Ridotto;—'tis a hall
 Where people dance, and sup, and dance
 again;
Its proper name, perhaps, were a masqued
 ball,
 But that's of no importance to my strain;
'Tis (on a smaller scale) like our Vauxhall,
 Excepting that it can't be spoilt by rain;
The company is "mix'd" (the phrase I quote
 is
As much as saying they're below your no-
 tice);

LIX.

For a "mix'd company" implies that, save
 Yourself and friends, and half a hundred
 more,
Whom you may bow to without looking grave,
 The rest are but a vulgar set, the bore
Of public places, where they basely brave
 The fashionable stare of twenty score
Of well-bred persons, call'd "*The World;*"
 but I,
Although I know them, really don't know
 why.

LX.

This is the case in England; at least was
 During the dynasty of Dandies, now
Perchance succeeded by some other class
 Of imitated imitators:—how
Irreparably soon decline, alas!
 The demagogues of fashion: all below
Is frail; how easily the world is lost
By love, or war, and now and then by frost!

LXI.

Crush'd was Napoleon by the northern Thor,
 Who knock'd his army down with icy
 hammer,
Stopp'd by the *elements*, like a whaler, or
 A blundering novice in his new French
 grammar;
Good cause had he to doubt the chance of
 war,
 And as for Fortune—but I dare not d—n
 her,
Because, were I to ponder to infinity,
The more I should believe in her divinity.

LXII.

She rules the present, past, and all to be yet,
 She gives us luck in lotteries, love, and
 marriage;
I cannot say that she's done much for me
 yet;
 Not that I mean her bounties to disparage,
We've not yet closed accounts, and we shall
 see yet
 How much she'll make amends for past
 miscarriage.
Meantime the Goddess I'll no more impor-
 tune,
Unless to thank her when she's made my
 fortune.

LXIII.

To turn,—and to return;—the devil take it!
 This story slips for ever through my
 fingers,
Because, just as the stanza likes to make it,
 It needs must be, and so it rather lingers:
This form of verse began, I can't well break it,
 But must keep time and tune like public
 singers;
But if I once get through my present measure,
I'll take another when I'm next at leisure.

LXIV.

They went to the Ridotto ('tis a place
 To which I mean to go myself to-morrow,
Just to divert my thoughts a little space,
 Because I'm rather hippish, and may
 borrow

Some spirits, guessing at what kind of face
 May lurk beneath each mask; and as my
 sorrow
Slackens its pace sometimes, I'll make, or find,
Something shall leave it half an hour behind).

LXV.

Now Laura moves along the joyous crowd,
 Smiles in her eyes, and simpers on her
 lips;
To some she whispers, others speaks aloud;
 To some she curtsies, and to some she dips,
Complains of warmth, and this complaint
 avow'd,
Her lover brings the lemonade, she sips;
She then surveys, condemns, but pities still
Her dearest friends for being dress'd so ill.

LXVI.

One has false curls, another too much paint,
 A third—where did she buy that frightful
 turban?
A fourth's so pale she fears she's going to
 faint,
 A fifth's look's vulgar, dowdyish, and subur-
 ban,
A sixth's white silk has got a yellow taint,
 A seventh's thin muslin surely will be her
 bane,
And lo! an eighth appears,—"I'll see no
 more!"
For fear, like Banquo's kings, they reach a
 score.

LXVII.

Meantime, while she was thus at others gaz-
 ing,
 Others were levelling their looks at her;
She heard the men's half-whisper'd mode of
 praising,
 And, till 'twas done, determined not to
 stir;
The women only thought it quite amazing
 That, at her time of life, so many were
Admirers still,—but men are so debased,
Those brazen creatures always suit their
 taste.

LXVIII.

For my part, now, I ne'er could understand
 Why naughty women—but I won't discuss
A thing which is a scandal to the land,
 I only don't see why it should be thus;
And if I were but in a gown and band,
 Just to entitle me to make a fuss,
I'd preach on this till Wilberforce and Ro-
 milly
Should quote in their next speeches from my
 homily.

LXIX.

While Laura thus was seen, and seeing,
 smiling,
 Talking, she knew not why, and cared not
 what,
So that her female friends, with envy broil-
 ing,
 Beheld her airs and triumph, and all that;
And well-dress'd males still kept before her
 filing,
 And passing bow'd and mingled with her
 chat;
More than the rest one person seem'd to stare
With pertinacity that's rather rare.

LXX.

He was a Turk, the colour of mahogany;
 And Laura saw him, and at first was glad,
Because the Turks so much admire philogyny,
 Although their usage of their wives is sad;
'Tis said they use no better than a dog any
 Poor woman, whom they purchase like a
 pad;
They have a number, though they ne'er ex-
 hibit 'em,
Four wives by law, and concubines "ad libi-
 tum."

LXXI.

They lock them up, and veil, and guard them
 daily,
 They scarcely can behold their male re-
 lations,
So that their moments do not pass so gaily
 As is supposed the case with northern
 nations;
Confinement, too, must make them look quite
 palely;
 And as the Turks abhor long conversations,
Their days are either pass'd in doing nothing,
Or bathing, nursing, making love, and cloth-
 ing.

LXXII.

They cannot read, and so don't lisp in criti-
 cism;
 Nor write, and so they don't affect the
 muse;
Were never caught in epigram or witticism,
 Have no romances, sermons, plays, re-
 views,—
In harams learning soon would make a pretty
 schism,
 But luckily these beauties are no "Blues;"
No bustling Botherbys have they to show 'em
"That charming passage in the last new
 poem:"

LXXIII.

No solemn, antique gentleman of rhyme,
 Who having angled all his life for fame,
And getting but a nibble at a time,
 Still fussily keeps fishing on, the same
Small "Triton of the minnows," the sublime
 Of mediocrity, the furious tame,
The echo's echo, usher of the school
Of female wits, boy bards—in short, a fool!

LXXIV.

A stalking oracle of awful phrase.
 The approving "*Good!*" (by no means
 GOOD in law,)
Humming like flies around the newest blaze,
 The bluest of bluebottles you e'er saw,
Teasing with blame, excruciating with praise,
 Gorging the little fame he gets all raw,
Translating tongues he knows not even by
 letter,
And sweating plays so middling, bad were
 better.

LXXV.

One hates an author that's *all author*, fellows
 In foolscap uniforms turn'd up with ink,
So very anxious, clever, fine, and jealous,
 One do'nt know what to say to them, or
 think,
Unless to puff them with a pair of bellows;
 Of coxcombry's worst coxcombs e'en the
 pink
Are preferable to these shreds of paper,
These unquench'd snuffings of the midnight
 taper.

LXXVI.

Of these same we see several, and of others,
 Men of the world, who know the world
 like men,
Scott, Rogers, Moore, and all the better bro-
 thers,
 Who think of something else besides the
 pen;
But for the children of the "mighty mo-
 ther's,"
 The would-be wits, and can't-be gentlemen,
I leave them to their daily "tea is ready,"
Smug coterie, and literary lady.

LXXVII.

The poor dear Mussulwomen whom I men-
 tion
 Have none of these instructive pleasant
 people,
And *one* would seem to them a new invention,
 Unknown as bells within a Turkish steeple;
I think 'twould almost be worth while to
 pension
 (Though best-sown projects very often reap
 ill)
A missionary author, just to preach
Our Christian usage of the parts of speech.

LXXVIII.

No chemistry for them unfolds her gases,
 No metaphysics are let loose in lectures,
No circulating library amasses
 Religious novels, moral tales, and strictures
Upon the living manners, as they pass us;
 No exhibition glares with annual pictures;
They stare not on the stars from out their
 attics,
Nor deal (thank God for that!) in mathe-
 matics.

LXXIX.

Why I thank God for that is no great matter,
 I have my reasons, you no doubt suppose,
And as, perhaps, they would not highly flat-
 ter,
 I'll keep them for my life (to come) in
 prose;
I fear I have a little turn for satire,
 And yet methinks the older that one grows
Inclines us more to laugh than scold, though
 laughter
Leaves us so doubly serious shortly after.

LXXX.

Oh, mirth and innocence! Oh, milk and
 water!
 Ye happy mixtures of more happy days!
In these sad centuries of sin and slaughter,
 Abominable Man no more allays
His thirst with such pure beverage. No
 matter,
 I love you both, and both shall have my
 praise:
Oh, for old Saturn's reign of sugar-candy!—
Meantime I drink to your return in brandy.

LXXXI.

Our Laura's Turk still kept his eyes upon
 her,
 Less in the Mussulman than Christian way,
Which seems to say, "Madam, I do you
 honour,
 And while I please to stare, you'll please
 to stay."
Could staring win a woman, this had won
 her,
 But Laura could not thus be led astray;
She had stood fire too long and well, to
 boggle
Even at this stranger's most outlandish ogle.

LXXXII.

The morning now was on the point of break-
 ing,
 A turn of time at which I would advise
Ladies who have been dancing, or partaking
 In any other kind of exercise,
To make their preparations for forsaking
 The ball-room ere the sun begins to rise,
Because when once the lamps and candles
 fail,
His blushes make them look a little pale.

LXXXIII.

I've seen some balls and revels in my time,
 And stay'd them over for some silly reason,
And then I look'd (I hope it was no crime)
 To see what lady best stood out the season,
And though I've seen some thousands in
 their prime,
 Lovely and pleasing, and who still may
 please on,
I never saw but one (the stars withdrawn)
Whose bloom could after dancing dare the
 dawn.

LXXXIV.

The name of this Aurora I'll not mention,
 Although I might, for she was nought to me
More than that patent work of God's inven-
 tion,
 A charming woman, whom we like to see;
But writing names would merit reprehension,
 Yet if you like to find out this fair *she*,
At the next London or Parisian ball
You still may mark her cheek out-blooming
 all.

LXXXV.

Laura, who knew it would not do at all
 To meet the daylight after seven hours'
 sitting
Among three thousand people at a ball,
 To make her curtsy thought it right and
 fitting;
The Count was at her elbow with her shawl,
 And they the room were on the point of
 quitting,
When lo! those cursed gondoliers had got
Just in the very place where they *should* not.

LXXXVI.

In this they're like our coachmen, and the
 cause
 Is much the same—the crowd, and pulling,
 hauling,
With blasphemies enough to break their
 jaws,
 They make a never intermitted bawling.

At home, our Bow-street gemmen keep the
 laws,
 And here a sentry stands within your call-
 ing;
But for all that, there is a deal of swearing,
And nauseous words past mentioning or bear-
 ing.

LXXXVII.

The Count and Laura found their boat at
 last,
 And homeward floated o'er the silent tide,
Discussing all the dances gone and past;
 The dancers and their dresses, too, beside;
Some little scandals eke; but all aghast
 (As to their palace-stairs the rowers glide)
Sate Laura by the side of her Adorer,
When lo! the Mussulman was there before
 her.

LXXXVIII.

"Sir," said the Count, with brow exceeding
 grave,
 "Your unexpected presence here will make
It necessary for myself to crave
 Its import? But perhaps 'tis a mistake;
I hope it is so; and, at once to waive
 All compliment, I hope so for *your* sake;
You understand my meaning, or you *shall*."
"Sir" (quoth the Turk), "'tis no mistake at
 all:

LXXXIX.

"That lady is *my wife!*" Much wonder
 paints
 The lady's changing cheek, as well it
 might;
But where an Englishwoman sometimes
 faints,
 Italian females don't do so outright;
They only call a little on their saints,
 And then come to themselves, almost or
 quite;
Which saves much hartshorn, salts, and
 sprinkling faces,
And cutting stays, as usual in such cases.

XC.

She said,—what could she say? Why, not
 a word:
 But the Count courteously invited in
The stranger, much appeased by what he
 heard:
 "Such things, perhaps, we'd best discuss
 within,"
Said he; "don't let us make ourselves ab-
 surd
 In public, by a scene, nor raise a din,
For then the chief and only satisfaction
Will be much quizzing on the whole trans-
 action."

XCI.

They enter'd, and for coffee call'd—it came,
 A beverage for Turks and Christians both,
Although the way they make it's not the
 same.
Now Laura, much recover'd, or less loth
To speak, cries "Beppo! what's your pagan
 name?
Bless me! your beard is of amazing growth!
And how came you to keep away so long?
Are you not sensible 'twas very wrong?

XCII.

"And are you really, truly, now a Turk?
 With any other women did you wive?
Is't true they use their fingers for a fork?
 Well, that's the prettiest shawl—as I'm
 alive!
You'll give it me? They say you eat no pork.
 And how so many years did you contrive
To—Bless me! did I ever? No, I never
Saw a man grown so yellow! How's your
 liver?

XCIII.

'Beppo! that beard of yours becomes you
 not;
 It shall be shaved before you're a day
 older:
Why do you wear it? Oh! I had forgot—
 Pray do'nt you think the weather here is
 colder?
How do I look? You shan't stir from this
 spot
 In that queer dress, for fear that some
 beholder
Should find you out, and make the story
 known.
How short your hair is! Lord! how grey
 it's grown!"

XCIV.

What answer Beppo made to these demands
 Is more than I know. He was cast away
About where Troy stood once, and nothing
 stands;
Became a slave of course, and for his pay
Had bread and bastinadoes, till some bands
Of pirates landing in a neighbouring bay,
He join'd the rogues and prosper'd, and be-
 came
A renegado of indifferent fame.

XCV.

But he grew rich, and with his riches grew
 so
Keen the desire to see his home again,
He thought himself in duty bound to do so,
 And not be always thieving on the main;

Lonely he felt, at times, as Robin Crusoe,
 And so he hired a vessel come from Spain,
Bound for Corfu: she was a fine polacca,
Mann'd with twelve hands, and laden with
 tobacco.

XCVI.

Himself, and much (Heaven knows how
 gotten!) cash,
 He then embark'd, with risk of life and limb,
And got clear off, although the attempt was
 rash;
 He said that Providence protected him—
For my part, I say nothing—lest we clash
 In our opinions:—well, the ship was trim,
Set sail, and kept her reckoning fairly on,
Except three days of calm when off Cape
 Bonn.

XCVII.

They reach'd the island, he transferr'd his
 lading
 And self and live stock to another bottom,
And pass'd for a true Turkey-merchant, trad-
 ing
 With goods of various names, but I've for-
 got'em.
However, he got off by this evading,
 Or else the people would perhaps have shot
 him;
And thus at Venice landed to reclaim
His wife, religion, house, and Christian name.

XCVIII.

His wife received, the patriarch re-baptized
 him
 (He made the church a present, by the
 way);
He then threw off the garments which dis-
 guised him,
 And borrow'd the Count's smallclothes for
 a day:
His friends the more for his long absence
 prized him,
Finding he'd wherewithal to make them gay,
With dinners, where he oft became the laugh
 of them,
For stories—but I don't believe the half of
 them.

XCIX.

Whate'er his youth had suffer'd, his old age
 With wealth and talking made him some
 amends;
Though Laura sometimes put him in a rage,
 I've heard the Count and he were always
 friends.
My pen is at the bottom of a page,
 Which being finish'd, here the story ends;
'T is to be wish'd it had been sooner done,
But stories somehow lengthen when begun.

𝖉on Juan.

—◆—

"Difficile est propriè communia dicere."—HORACE.

"Dost thou think, because thou art virtuous, there shall be no more cakes and ale? Yes, by Saint Anne, and ginger shall be hot i' the mouth, too!"—SHAKESPEARE, *Twelfth Night, or What You Will.*

—◆—

Canto the First.*

—◆—

FRAGMENT.

On the back of the Poet's MS. of Canto I.

I WOULD to heaven that I were so much clay,
 As I am blood, bone, marrow, passion,
 feeling—
Because at least the past were pass'd away—
 And for the future—(but I write this reel-
 ing,
Having got drunk exceedingly to-day,
 So that I seem to stand upon the ceiling)
I say—the future is a serious matter—
And so—for God's sake—hock and soda-
 water!

DEDICATION.

I.

BOB SOUTHEY! You 're a poet — Poet-
 laureate,
 And representative of all the race;
Although 'tis true that you turn'd out a Tory
 at
 Last,—yours has lately been a common
 case;
And now, my Epic Renegade! what are ye at?
 With all the Lakers, in and out of place?
A nest of tuneful persons, to my eye
Like "four and twenty Blackbirds in a pye;

II.

"Which pye being open'd they began to sing"
 (This old song and new simile holds good),
"A dainty dish to set before the King,"
 Or Regent, who admires such kind of
 food;—

*["Begun at Venice September 6; finished Nov. 1, 1818."—B.]

And Coleridge, too, has lately taken wing,
 But like a hawk encumber'd with his
 hood,—
Explaining metaphysics to the nation—
I wish he would explain his Explanation.

III.

You, Bob! are rather insolent, you know,
 At being disappointed in your wish
To supersede all warblers here below,
 And be the only Blackbird in the dish;
And then you overstrain yourself, or so,
 And tumble downward like the flying fish
Gasping on deck, because you soar too high,
 Bob,
And fall, for lack of moisture quite a-dry,
 Bob!

IV.

And Wordsworth, in a rather long "Excur-
 sion"
 (I think the quarto holds five hundred
 pages),
Has given a sample from the vasty version
 Of his new system to perplex the sages;
'Tis poetry—at least by his assertion,
 And may appear so when the dog-star
 rages—
And he who understands it would be able
To add a story to the Tower of Babel.

V.

You—Gentlemen! by dint of long seclusion
 From better company, have kept your own
At Keswick, and, through still continued
 fusion
 Of one another's minds, at last have grown
To deem as a most logical conclusion,
 That Poesy has wreaths for you alone:
There is a narrowness in such a notion,
Which makes me wish you 'd change your
 lakes for ocean.

VI.

I would not imitate the petty thought,
 Nor coin my self-love to so base a vice,
For all the glory your conversion brought,
 Since gold alone should not have been its
 price.
You have your salary: was 't for that you
 wrought?
 And Wordsworth has his place in the
 Excise.
You 're shabby fellows—true—but poets still,
And duly seated on the immortal hill.

VII.

Your bays may hide the baldness of your
 brows—
 Perhaps some virtuous blushes;—let them
 go—
To you I envy neither fruit nor boughs—
 And for the fame you would engross below,
The field is universal, and allows
 Scope to all such as feel the inherent glow:
Scott, Rogers, Campbell, Moore, and Crabbe,
 will try
'Gainst you the question with posterity.

VIII.

For me, who, wandering with pedestrian
 Muses,
 Contend not with you on the winged steed,
I wish your fate may yield ye, when she
 chooses,
 The fame you envy, and the skill you need;
And recollect a poet nothing loses
 In giving to his brethren their full meed
Of merit, and complaint of present days
Is not the certain path to future praise.

IX.

He that reserves his laurels for posterity
 (Who does not often claim the bright
 reversion)
Has generally no great crop to spare it, he
 Being only injured by his own assertion;
And although here and there some glorious
 rarity
 Arise like Titan from the sea's immersion,
The major part of such appellants go
To—God knows where—for no one else can
 know.

X.

If, fallen in evil days on evil tongues,
 Milton appealed to the Avenger, Time,
If Time, the Avenger, execrates his wrongs,
 And makes the word "Miltonic" mean
 "*sublime*,"

He deign'd not to belie his soul in songs,
 Nor turn his very talent to a crime;
He did not loathe the Sire to laud the Son,
But closed the tyrant-hater he begun.

XI.

Think'st thou, could he—the blind Old Man—
 arise,
 Like Samuel from the grave, to freeze once
 more
The blood of monarchs with his prophecies,
 Or be alive again—again all hoar
With time and trials, and those helpless eyes,
 And heartless daughters—worn—and pale
 —and poor;
Would *he* adore a sultan? *he* obey
The intellectual eunuch Castlereagh?

XII.

Cold-blooded, smooth-faced, placid miscreant!
 Dabbling its sleek young hands in Erin's
 gore,
And thus for wider carnage taught to pant,
 Transferr'd to gorge upon a sister shore,
The vulgarest tool that Tyranny could want,
 With just enough of talent, and no more,
To lengthen fetters by another fix'd,
And offer poison long already mix'd.

XIII.

An orator of such set trash of phrase
 Ineffably—legitimately vile,
That even its grossest flatterers dare not
 praise,
 Nor foes—all nations—condescend to smile;
Not even a sprightly blunder's spark can blaze
 From that Ixion grindstone's ceaseless toil,
That turns and turns to give the world a
 notion
Of endless torments and perpetual motion.

XIV.

A bungler even in its disgusting trade,
 And botching, patching, leaving still behind
Something of which its masters are afraid,
 States to be curb'd, and thoughts to be
 confined,
Conspiracy or Congress to be made—
 Cobbling at manacles for all mankind—
A tinkering slave-maker, who mends old
 chains,
With God and man's abhorrence for its gains.

XV.

If we may judge of matter by the mind,
 Emasculated to the marrow *It*
Hath but two objects, how to serve, and bind,
 Deeming the chain it wears even men may
 fit,

Eutropius of its many masters,—blind
　To worth as freedom, wisdom as to wit,
Fearless—because *no* feeling dwells in ice,
　Its very courage stagnates to a vice.

XVI.

Where shall I turn me not to *view* its bonds,
　For I will never *feel* them;—Italy!
Thy late reviving Roman soul desponds
　Beneath the lie this State-thing breathed
　　o'er thee—
Thy clanking chain, and Erin's yet green
　wounds,
　Have voices—tongues to cry aloud for me.
Europe has slaves, allies, kings, armies still,
And Southey lives to sing them very ill.

XVII.

Meantime, Sir Laureate, I proceed to dedicate,
　In honest simple verse, this song to you.
And, if in flattering strains I do not predi-
　cate,
　'T is that I still retain my "buff and
　　blue;"
My politics as yet are all to educate:
　Apostasy's so fashionable, too,
To keep *one* creed's a task grown quite Her-
　culean:
Is it not so, my Tory, Ultra-Julian?
　　　　　VENICE, *September* 16, 1818.

I.

I WANT a hero: an uncommon want,
　When every year and month sends forth a
　　new one,
Till, after cloying the gazettes with cant,
　The age discovers he is not the true one:
Of such as these I should not care to vaunt,
　I'll therefore take our ancient friend Don
　　Juan—
We all have seen him, in the pantomime,
Sent to the devil somewhat ere his time.

II.

Vernon, the butcher Cumberland, Wolfe,
　Hawke,
　Prince Ferdinand, Granby, Burgoyne,
　　Keppel, Howe,
Evil and good, have had their tithe of talk,
　And fill'd their sign-posts then, like Welles-
　　ley now;
Each in their turn like Banquo's monarchs
　stalk,
　Followers of fame, "nine farrow" of that
　　sow:
France, too, had Buonaparté and Dumourier
Recorded in the Moniteur and Courier.

III.

Barnave, Brissot, Condorcet, Mirabeau,
　Pétion, Clootz, Danton, Marat, La Fayette,
Were French, and famous people, as we
　　know;
And there were others, scarce forgotten yet,
Joubert, Hoche, Marceau, Lannes, Desaix,
　Moreau,
With many of the military set,
Exceedingly remarkable at times,
But not at all adapted to my rhymes.

IV.

Nelson was once Britannia's god of war,
　And still should be so, but the tide is
　　turn'd;
There's no more to be said of Trafalgar,
　'T is with our hero quietly inurn'd;
Because the army's grown more popular,
　At which the naval people are concern'd,
Besides, the prince is all for the land-service,
Forgetting Duncan, Nelson, Howe, and
　Jervis.

V.

Brave men were living before Agamemnon
　And since, exceeding valorous and sage,
A good deal like him too, though quite the
　　same none;
　But then they shone not on the poet's page,
And so have been forgotten:—I condemn
　none,
　But can't find any in the present age
Fit for my poem (that is, for my new one);
So, as I said, I'll take my friend Don Juan.

VI.

Most epic poets plunge "in medias res"
　(Horace makes this the heroic turnpike
　　road),
And then your hero tells, whene'er you
　please,
　What went before—by way of episode,
While seated after dinner at his ease,
　Beside his mistress in some soft abode,
Palace, or garden, paradise, or cavern,
Which serves the happy couple for a tavern.

VII.

That is the usual method, but not mine—
　My way is to begin with the beginning;
The regularity of my design
　Forbids all wandering as the worst of sin-
　　ning,
And therefore I shall open with a line
　(Although it cost me half an hour in spin-
　　ning)
Narrating somewhat of Don Juan's father,
And also of his mother, if you'd rather.

VIII.

In Seville was he born, a pleasant city,
　Famous for oranges and women—he
Who has not seen it will be much to pity,
　So says the proverb—and I quite agree;
Of all the Spanish towns is none more pretty,
　Cadiz, perhaps—but that you soon may
　　see:—
Don Juan's parents lived beside the river,
A noble stream, and call'd the Guadalquivir.

IX.

His father's name was Jóse—*Don*, of course,
　A true Hidalgo, free from every stain
Of Moor or Hebrew blood, he traced his
　　source
　Through the most Gothic gentlemen of
　　Spain;
A better cavalier ne'er mounted horse,
　Or, being mounted, e'er got down again,
Than Jóse, who begot our hero, who
Begot—but that's to come——Well, to re-
　new:

X.

His mother was a learned lady, famed
　For every branch of every science known—
In every Christian language ever named,
　With virtues equall'd by her wit alone:
She made the cleverest people quite ashamed,
　And even the good with inward envy
　　groan,
Finding themselves so very much exceeded
In their own way by all the things that
　she did.

XI.

Her memory was a mine: she knew by heart
　All Calderon and greater part of Lopé,
So that if any actor miss'd his part
　She could have served him for the prompt-
　　er's copy;
For her Feinagle's were an useless art,
　And he himself obliged to shut up shop—he
Could never make a memory so fine as
That which adorn'd the brain of Donna Inez.

XII.

Her favourite science was the mathematical,
　Her noblest virtue was her magnanimity;
Her wit (she sometimes tried at wit) was
　Attic all,
　Her serious sayings darken'd to sublimity;
In short, in all things she was fairly what I
　call
A prodigy—her morning dress was dimity,
　Her evening silk, or, in the summer, muslin,
And other stuffs, with which I won't stay
　puzzling.

XIII.

She knew the Latin—that is, "the Lord's
　　prayer,"
　And Greek—the alphabet—I'm nearly sure;
She read some French romances here and
　　there,
　Although her mode of speaking was not
　　pure;
For native Spanish she had no great care,
　At least her conversation was obscure;
Her thoughts were theorems, her words a
　　problem,
As if she deem'd that mystery would en-
　noble 'em.

XIV.

She liked the English and the Hebrew tongue,
　And said there was analogy between 'em;
She proved it somehow out of sacred song,
　But I must leave the proofs to those who've
　　seen 'em,
But this I heard her say, and can't be wrong,
　And all may think which way their judg-
　　ments lean 'em,
"'T is strange—the Hebrew noun which
　　means 'I am,'
The English always use to govern d—n."

XV.

Some women use their tongues—she *look'd* a
　　lecture,
　Each eye a sermon, and her brow a homily,
An all-in-all sufficient self-director,
　Like the lamented late Sir Samuel Romilly,
The Law's expounder, and the State's cor-
　rector,
　Whose suicide was almost an anomaly—
One sad example more, that "All is va-
　nity,"—
(The jury brought their verdict in "In-
　sanity.")

XVI.

In short, she was a walking calculation,
　Miss Edgeworth's novels stepping from
　　their covers,
Or Mrs. Trimmer's books on education,
　Or "Cœlebs' Wife" set out in quest of
　　lovers,
Morality's prim personification,
　In which not Envy's self a flaw discovers;
To others' share let "female errors fall,"
For she had not even one—the worst of all.

XVII.

Oh! she was perfect past all parallel—
　Of any modern female saint's comparison;
So far above the cunning powers of hell,
　Her guardian angel had given up his
　　garrison;

Even her minutest motions went as well
 As those of the best time-piece made by
 Harrison :
In virtues nothing earthly could surpass her,
Save thine "incomparable oil," Macassar !

XVIII.

Perfect she was, but as perfection is
 Insipid in this naughty world of ours,
Where our first parents never learn'd to kiss
 Till they were exiled from their earlier
 bowers,
Where all was peace, and innocence, and
 bliss
 (I wonder how they got through the twelve
 hours),
Don Jóse, like a lineal son of Eve,
Went plucking various fruit without her
 leave.

XIX.

He was a mortal of the careless kind,
 With no great love for learning, or the
 learn'd,
Who chose to go where'er he had a mind,
 And never dream'd his lady was con-
 cern'd ;
The world, as usual, wickedly inclined
 To see a kingdom or a house o'erturn'd,
Whisper'd he had a mistress, some said *two*,
But for domestic quarrels *one* will do.

XX.

Now Donna Inez had, with all her merit,
 A great opinion of her own good qualities;
Neglect, indeed, requires a saint to bear it,
 And such, indeed, she was in her moral-
 ities ;
But then she had a devil of a spirit,
 And sometimes mix'd up fancies with reali-
 ties,
And let few opportunities escape
Of getting her liege lord into a scrape.

XXI.

This was an easy matter with a man
 Oft in the wrong, and never on his guard;
And even the wisest, do the best they can,
 Have moments, hours, and days, so un-
 prepared,
That you might " brain them with their lady's
 fan;"
 And sometimes ladies hit exceeding hard,
And fans turn into falchions in fair hands,
And why and wherefore no one understands.

XXII.

'Tis pity learned virgins ever wed
 With persons of no sort of education,
Or gentlemen, who, though well born and bred,
 Grow tired of scientific conversation;

I don't choose to say much upon this head,
 I'm a plain man, and in a single station,
But—Oh ! ye lords of ladies intellectual,
Inform us truly, have they not hen-peck'd
 you all ?

XXIII.

Don Jóse and his lady quarrell'd—*why*,
 Not any of the many could divine,
Though several thousand people chose to try,
 'Twas surely no concern of theirs nor
 mine;
I loathe that low vice—curiosity;
 But if there's anything in which I shine,
'Tis in arranging all my friends' affairs,
Not having, of my own, domestic cares.

XXIV.

And so I interfered, and with the best
 Intentions, but their treatment was not
 kind;
I think the foolish people were possess'd,
 For neither of them could I ever find,
Although their porter afterwards confess'd—
 But that's no matter, and the worst's
 behind,
For little Juan o'er me threw, down stairs,
A pail of housemaid's water unawares.

XXV.

A little curly-headed, good-for-nothing,
 And mischief-making monkey from his
 birth;
His parents ne'er agreed except in doting
 Upon the most unquiet imp on earth;
Instead of quarrelling, had they been but
 both in
 Their senses, they'd have sent young
 master forth
To school, or had him soundly whipp'd at
 home,
To teach him manners for the time to come.

XXVI.

Don Jóse and the Donna Inez led .
 For some time an unhappy sort of life,
Wishing each other, not divorced, but dead;
 They lived respectably as man and wife,
Their conduct was exceedingly well-bred,
 And gave no outward signs of inward
 strife,
Until at length the smother'd fire broke out,
And put the business past all kind of doubt.

XXVII.

For Inez call'd some druggists and phy-
 sicians,
 And tried to prove her loving lord was *mad*,
But as he had some lucid intermissions,
 She next decided he was only *bad* ;

Yet when they ask'd her for her depositions,
 No sort of explanation could be had,
Save that her duty both to man and God
Required this conduct—which seem'd very
 odd.

XXVIII.

She kept a journal, where his faults were
 noted,
 And open'd certain trunks of books and
 letters,
All which might, if occasion served, be
 quoted;
 And then she had all Seville for abettors,
Besides her good old grandmother (who
 doted);
The hearers of her case became repeaters,
Then advocates, inquisitors, and judges,
Some for amusement, others for old grudges.

XXIX.

And then this best and meekest woman bore
 With such serenity her husband's woes,
Just as the Spartan ladies did of yore,
 Who saw their spouses kill'd, and nobly
 chose
Never to say a word about them more—
 Calmly she heard each calumny that rose,
And saw his agonies with such sublimity,
That all the world exclaim'd, "What mag-
 nanimity!"

XXX.

No doubt this patience, when the world is
 damning us,
 Is philosophic in our former friends;
'Tis also pleasant to be deem'd magnanimous,
 The more so in obtaining our own ends;
And what the lawyers call a "malus animus"
 Conduct like this by no means compre-
 hends:
Revenge in person's certainly no virtue,
But then 'tis not my fault, if others hurt
 you.

XXXI.

And if our quarrels should rip up old stories,
 And help them with a lie or two addi-
 tional,
I'm not to blame, as you well know—no
 more is
 Any one else—they were become tradi-
 tional;
Besides, their resurrection aids our glories
 By contrast, which is what we just were
 wishing all:
And science profits by this resurrection—
Dead scandals form good subjects for dis-
 section.

XXXII.

Their friends had tried at reconciliation,
 Then their relations, who made matters
 worse,
('Twere hard to tell upon a like occasion
 To whom it may be best to have recourse—
I can't say much for friend or yet relation):
 The lawyers did their utmost for divorce,
But scarce a fee was paid on either side
Before, unluckily, Don Jóse died.

XXXIII.

He died: and most unluckily, because,
 According to all hints I could collect
From counsel learned in those kinds of laws
 (Although their talk's obscure and cir-
 cumspect),
His death contrived to spoil a charming
 cause;
 A thousand pities also with respect
To public feeling, which on this occasion
Was manifested in a great sensation.

XXXIV.

But ah! he died; and buried with him lay
 The public feeling and the lawyers' fees:
His house was sold, his servants sent away,
 A Jew took one of his two mistresses,
A priest the other—at least so they say:
 I ask'd the doctors after his disease—
He died of the slow fever called the tertian,
And left his widow to her own aversion.

XXXV.

Yet Jóse was an honourable man,
 That I must say, who knew him very well;
Therefore his frailties I'll no further scan,
 Indeed there were not many more to tell:
And if his passions now and then outran
 Discretion, and were not so peaceable
As Numa's (who was also named Pompilius),
He had been ill brought up, and was born
 bilious.

XXXVI.

Whate'er might be his worthlessness or
 worth,
 Poor fellow! he had many things to wound
 him,
Let's own—since it can do no good on earth—
 It was a trying moment that which found
 him
Standing alone beside his desolate hearth,
 Where all his household gods lay shiver'd
 round him:
No choice was left his feelings or his pride,
Save death or Doctors' Commons—so he
 died.

XXXVII.

Dying intestate, Juan was sole heir
 To a chancery suit, and messuages and
 lands,
Which, with a long minority and care,
 Promised to turn out well in proper hands:
Inez became sole guardian, which was fair,
 And answer'd but to nature's just demands;
An only son left with an only mother
Is brought up much more wisely than
 another.

XXXVIII.

Sagest of women, even of widows, she
 Resolved that Juan should be quite a
 paragon,
And worthy of the noblest pedigree:
 (His sire was of Castile, his dam from
 Aragon).
Then for accomplishments of chivalry,
 In case our lord the king should go to war
 again,
He learn'd the arts of riding, fencing, gun-
 nery,
And how to scale a fortress—or a nunnery.

XXXIX.

But that which Donna Inez most desired,
 And saw into herself each day before all
The learned tutors whom for him she hired,
 Was, that his breeding should be strictly
 moral:
Much into all his studies she inquired,
 And so they were submitted first to her, all,
Arts, sciences, no branch was made a mystery
To Juan's eyes, excepting natural history.

XL.

The languages, especially the dead,
 The sciences, and most of all the abstruse,
The arts, at least all such as could be said
 To be the most remote from common use,
In all these he was much and deeply read:
 But not a page of anything that's loose,
Or hints continuation of the species,
Was ever suffer'd, lest he should grow
 vicious.

XLI.

His classic studies made a little puzzle,
 Because of filthy loves of gods and god-
 desses,
Who in the earlier ages raised a bustle,
 But never put on pantaloons or bodices;
His reverend tutors had at times a tussle,
 And for their Æneids, Iliads, and Odysseys,
Were forced to make an odd sort of apology,
For Donna Inez dreaded the Mythology.

XLII.

Ovid's a rake, as half his verses show him,
 Anacreon's morals are a still worse sample,
Catullus scarcely has a decent poem,
 I don't think Sappho's Ode a good example,
Although Longinus tells us there is no hymn
 Where the sublime soars forth on wings
 more ample;
But Virgil's songs are pure, except that horrid
 one
Beginning with "Formosum Pastor Corydon."

XLIII.

Lucretius' irreligion is too strong
 For early stomachs, to prove wholesome
 food;
I can't help thinking Juvenal was wrong,
 Although no doubt his real intent was good,
For speaking out so plainly in his song,
 So much indeed as to be downright rude;
And then what proper person can be partial
To all those nauseous epigrams of Martial?

XLIV.

Juan was taught from out the best edition,
 Expurgated by learned men, who place,
Judiciously, from out the schoolboy's vision,
 The grosser parts; but, fearful to deface
Too much their modest bard by this omission,
 And pitying sore this mutilated case,
They only add them all in an appendix,
Which saves, in fact, the trouble of an index;

XLV.

For there we have them all "at one fell
 swoop,"
 Instead of being scatter'd through the
 pages;
They stand forth marshall'd in a handsome
 troop,
 To meet the ingenuous youth of future ages,
Till some less rigid editor shall stoop
 To call them back into their separate cages,
Instead of standing staring all together,
Like garden gods—and not so decent either.

XLVI.

The Missal too (it was the family Missal)
 Was ornamented in a sort of way
Which ancient mass-books often are, and
 this all
 Kinds of grotesques illumined; and how
 they,
Who saw those figures on the margin kiss all,
 Could turn their optics to the text and pray,
Is more than I know—But Don Juan's mother
Kept this herself, and gave her son another.

XLVII.

Sermons he read, and lectures he endured,
 And homilies, and lives of all the saints;
To Jerome and to Chrysostom inured,
 He did not take such studies for restraints;
But how faith is acquired, and then insured,
 So well not one of the aforesaid paints
As Saint Augustine in his fine Confessions,
Which make the reader envy his trans-
 gressions.

XLVIII.

This, too, was a seal'd book to little Juan—
 I can't but say that his mamma was right,
If such an education was the true one.
 She scarcely trusted him from out her
 sight;
Her maids were old, and if she took a new
 one,
You might be sure she was a perfect fright,
She did this during even her husband's life—
I recommend as much to every wife.

XLIX.

Young Juan wax'd in godliness and grace;
 At six a charming child, and at eleven
With all the promise of as fine a face
 As e'er to man's maturer growth was given.
He studied steadily and grew apace,
 And seem'd, at least, in the right road to
 heaven,
For half his days were pass'd at church, the
 other
Between his tutors, confessor, and mother.

L.

At six, I said, he was a charming child,
 At twelve he was a fine, but quiet boy;
Although in infancy a little wild,
 They tamed him down amongst them: to
 destroy
His natural spirit not in vain they toil'd,
 At least it seem'd so; and his mother's joy
Was to declare how sage, and still, and steady,
Her young philosopher was grown already.

LI.

I had my doubts, perhaps I have them still,
 But what I say is neither here nor there:
I knew his father well, and have some skill
 In character—but it would not be fair
From sire to son to augur good or ill:
 He and his wife were an ill sorted pair—
But scandal's my aversion—I protest
Against all evil speaking, even in jest.

LII.

For my part I say nothing—nothing—but
 This I will say—my reasons are my own—
That if I had an only son to put
 To school (as God be praised that I have
 none),
'Tis not with Donna Inez I would shut
 Him up to learn his catechism alone,
No—no—I'd send him out betimes to college,
For there it was I pick'd up my own know-
 ledge.

LIII.

For there one learns—'tis not for me to boast,
 Though I acquired—but I pass over *that*,
As well as all the Greek I since have lost:
 I say that there's the place—but " *Verbum
 sat,*"
I think I pick'd up too, as well as most,
 Knowledge of matters—but no matter *what*—
I never married—but, I think, I know
That sons should not be educated so.

LIV.

Young Juan now was sixteen years of age,
 Tall, handsome, slender, but well knit: he
 seem'd
Active, though not so sprightly, as a page;
 And everybody but his mother deem'd
Him almost man; but she flew in a rage
 And bit her lips (for else she might have
 scream'd)
If any said so, for to be precocious
Was in her eyes a thing the most atrocious.

LV.

Amongst her numerous acquaintance, all
 Selected for discretion and devotion,
There was the Donna Julia, whom to call
 Pretty were but to give a feeble notion
Of many charms in her as natural
 As sweetness to the flower, or salt to ocean,
Her zone to Venus, or his bow to Cupid,
(But this last simile is trite and stupid).

LVI.

The darkness of her Oriental eye
 Accorded with her Moorish origin;
(Her blood was not all Spanish, by the by;
 In Spain, you know, this is a sort of sin).
When proud Granada fell, and, forced to fly,
 Boabdil wept, of Donna Julia's kin
Some went to Africa, some stay'd in Spain,
Her great great grandmamma chose to re-
 main.

LVII.

She married (I forget the pedigree)
 With an Hidalgo, who transmitted down
His blood less noble than such blood should
 be;
 At such alliances his sires would frown,
In that point so precise in each degree
 That they bred *in and in*, as might be
 shown,
Marrying their cousins—nay, their aunts,
 and nieces,
Which always spoils the breed, if it increases.

LVIII.

This heathenish cross restored the breed
 again,
 Ruin'd its blood, but much improved its
 flesh;
For from a root the ugliest in old Spain
 Sprung up a branch as beautiful as fresh;
The sons no more were short, the daughters
 plain:
 But there's a rumour which I fain would
 hush,
'Tis said that Donna Julia's grandmamma
Produced her Don more heirs at love than
 law.

LIX.

However this might be, the race went on
 Improving still through every generation,
Until it centred in an only son,
 Who left an only daughter: my narration
May have suggested that this single one
 Could be but Julia (whom on this occasion
I shall have much to speak about), and she
Was married, charming, chaste, and twenty-
 three.

LX.

Her eye (I'm very fond of handsome eyes)
 Was large and dark, suppressing half its
 fire
Until she spoke, then through its soft dis-
 guise
 Flash'd an expression more of pride than
 ire,
And love than either; and there would arise
 A something in them which was not desire,
But would have been, perhaps, but for the soul
Which struggled through and chasten'd down
 the whole.

LXI.

Her glossy hair was cluster'd o'er a brow
 Bright with intelligence, and fair, and
 smooth;
Her eyebrow's shape was like the aërial bow,
 Her cheek all purple with the beam of
 youth,

Mounting, at times, to a transparent glow,
 As if her veins ran lightning; she, in sooth,
Possess'd an air and grace by no means
 common:
Her stature tall—I hate a dumpy woman.

LXII.

Wedded she was some years, and to a man
 Of fifty, and such husbands are in plenty;
And yet, I think, instead of such a ONE
 'T were better to have TWO of five-and-
 twenty,
Especially in countries near the sun:
 And now I think on 't, "mi vien in mente,"
Ladies even of the most uneasy virtue
Prefer a spouse whose age is short of thirty.

LXIII.

'Tis a sad thing, I cannot choose but say,
 And all the fault of that indecent sun,
Who cannot leave alone our helpless clay,
 But will keep baking, broiling, burning on,
That howsoever people fast and pray,
 The flesh is frail, and so the soul undone:
What men call gallantry, and gods adultery,
Is much more common where the climate's
 sultry.

LXIV.

Happy the nations of the moral North!
 Where all is virtue, and the winter season
Sends sin, without a rag on, shivering forth
 ('T was snow that brought St. Anthony to
 reason);
Where juries cast up what a wife is worth,
 By laying whate'er sum, in mulct, they
 please on
The lover, who must pay a handsome price,
Because it is a marketable vice.

LXV.

Alfonso was the name of Julia's lord,
 A man well looking for his years, and who
Was neither much beloved nor yet abhorr'd:
 They lived together as most people do,
Suffering each other's foibles by accord,
 And not exactly either *one* or *two*;
Yet he was jealous, though he did not show it,
For jealousy dislikes the world to know it.

LXVI.

Julia was—yet I never could see why—
 With Donna Inez quite a favourite friend;
Between their tastes there was small sym-
 pathy,
 For not a line had Julia ever penn'd:
Some people whisper (but, no doubt, they lie,
 For malice still imputes some private end)
That Inez had, ere Don Alfonso's marriage,
Forgot with him her very prudent carriage;

LXVII.

And that still keeping up the old connexion,
 Which time had lately render'd much more
 chaste,
She took his lady also in affection,
 And certainly this course was much the best:
She flatter'd Julia with her sage protection,
 And complimented Don Alfonso's taste;
And if she could not (who can?) silence
 scandal,
At least she left it a more slender handle.

LXVIII.

I can't tell whether Julia saw the affair
 With other people's eyes, or if her own
Discoveries made, but none could be aware
 Of this, at least no symptom e'er was
 shown;
Perhaps she did not know, or did not care,
 Indifferent from the first, or callous grown:
I'm really puzzled what to think or say,
She kept her counsel in so close a way.

LXIX.

Juan she saw, and, as a pretty child,
 Caress'd him often—such a thing might be
Quite innocently done, and harmless styled,
 When she had twenty years, and thirteen
 he;
But I am not so sure I should have smiled
 When he was sixteen, Julia twenty-three;
These few short years make wondrous alter-
 ations,
Particularly amongst sun-burnt nations.

LXX.

Whate'er the cause might be, they had be-
 come
 Changed; for the dame grew distant, the
 youth shy,
Their looks cast down, their greetings almost
 dumb,
 And much embarrassment in either eye;
There surely will be little doubt with some
 That Donna Julia knew the reason why,
But as for Juan, he had no more notion
Than he who never saw the sea of ocean.

LXXI.

Yet Julia's very coldness still was kind,
 And tremulously gentle her small hand
Withdrew itself from his, but left behind
 A little pressure, thrilling, and so bland
And slight, so very slight, that to the mind
 'Twas but a doubt; but ne'er magician's
 wand
Wrought change with all Armida's fairy art
 Like what this light touch left on Juan's
 heart.

LXXII.

And if she met him, though she smiled no
 more,
 She look'd a sadness sweeter than her
 smile,
As if her heart had deeper thoughts in store
 She must not own, but cherish'd more the
 while
For that compression in its burning core;
 Even innocence itself has many a wile,
And will not dare to trust itself with truth,
And love is taught hypocrisy from youth.

LXXIII.

But passion most dissembles, yet betrays
 Even by its darkness; as the blackest sky
Foretells the heaviest tempest, it displays
 Its workings through the vainly guarded
 eye,
And in whatever aspect it arrays
 Itself, 'tis still the same hypocrisy:
Coldness or anger, even disdain or hate,
Are masks it often wears, and still too late.

LXXIV.

Then there were sighs, the deeper for sup-
 pression,
 And stolen glances, sweeter for the theft,
And burning blushes, though for no trans-
 gression,
 Tremblings when met, and restlessness
 when left;
All these are little preludes to possession,
 Of which young passion cannot be bereft,
And merely tend to show how greatly love is
Embarrass'd at first starting with a novice.

LXXV.

Poor Julia's heart was in an awkward state;
 She felt it going, and resolved to make
The noblest efforts for herself and mate,
 For honour's, pride's, religion's, virtue's
 sake.
Her resolutions were most truly great,
 And almost might have made a Tarquin
 quake:
She pray'd the Virgin Mary for her grace,
As being the best judge of a lady's case.

LXXVI.

She vow'd she never would see Juan more,
 And next day paid a visit to his mother,
And look'd extremely at the opening door,
 Which, by the Virgin's grace, let in an-
 other;
Grateful she was, and yet a little sore—
 Again it opens, it can be no other,
'Tis surely Juan now—No! I'm afraid
That night the Virgin was no further pray'd.

LXXVII.

She now determined that a virtuous woman
 Should rather face and overcome tempta-
 tion,
That flight was base and dastardly, and no
 man
 Should ever give her heart the least sen-
 sation;
That is to say, a thought beyond the common
 Preference, that we must feel upon occa-
 sion,
For people who are pleasanter than others,
But then they only seem so many brothers.

LXXVIII.

And even if by chance—and who can tell?
 The devil's so very sly—she should discover
That all within was not so very well,
 And, if still free, that such or such a lover
Might please perhaps, a virtuous wife can quell
 Such thoughts, and be the better when
 they're over;
And if the man should ask, 'tis but denial:
I recommend young ladies to make trial.

LXXIX.

And then there are such things as love divine,
 Bright and immaculate, unmix'd and pure,
Such as the angels think so very fine,
 And matrons, who would be no less secure,
Platonic, perfect, "just such love as mine:"
 Thus Julia said—and thought so, to be sure;
And so I'd have her think, were I the man
On whom her reveries celestial ran.

LXXX.

Such love is innocent, and may exist
 Between young persons without any dan-
 ger:
A hand may first, and then a lip be kist;
 For my part, to such doings I'm a stranger,
But *hear* these freedoms form the utmost list
 Of all o'er which such love may be a
 ranger:
If people go beyond, 'tis quite a crime,
But not my fault—I tell them all in time.

LXXXI.

Love, then, but love within its proper limits
 Was Julia's innocent determination
In young Don Juan's favour, and to him its
 Exertion might be useful on occasion;
And, lighted at too pure a shrine to dim its
 Ethereal lustre, with what sweet persua-
 sion
He might be taught, by love and her toge-
 ther—
I really don't know what, nor Julia either.

LXXXII.

Fraught with this fine intention, and well
 fenced
 In mail of proof—her purity of soul,
She, for the future of her strength convinced,
 And that her honour was a rock, or mole,
Exceeding sagely from that hour dispensed
 With any kind of troublesome control;
But whether Julia to the task was equal
Is that which must be mention'd in the
 sequel.

LXXXIII.

Her plan she deem'd both innocent and
 feasible,
 And, surely, with a stripling of sixteen
Not scandal's fangs could fix on much that's
 seizable,
 Or if they did so, satisfied to mean
Nothing but what was good, her breast was
 peaceable:
 A quiet conscience makes one so serene!
Christians have burnt each other, quite per-
 suaded
That all the Apostles would have done as
 they did.

LXXXIV.

And if in the mean time her husband died,
 But Heaven forbid that such a thought
 should cross
Her brain, though in a dream! (and then she
 sigh'd)
 Never could she survive that common loss;
But just suppose that moment should betide,
 I only say suppose it—*inter nos.*
(This should be *entre nous*, for Julia thought
In French, but then the rhyme would go for
 nought.)

LXXXV.

I only say, suppose this supposition:
 Juan being then grown up to man's estate
Would fully suit a widow of condition,
 Even seven years hence it would not be
 too late;
And in the interim (to pursue this vision)
 The mischief, after all, could not be great,
For he would learn the rudiments of love,
I mean the seraph way of those above.

LXXXVI.

So much for Julia. Now we'll turn to Juan.
 Poor little fellow! he had no idea
Of his own case, and never hit the true one;
 In feelings quick as Ovid's Miss Medea,

He puzzled over what he found a new one,
 But not as yet imagined it could be a
Thing quite in course, and not at all alarming,
Which, with a little patience, might grow
 charming.

LXXXVII.

Silent and pensive, idle, restless, slow,
 His home deserted for the lonely wood,
Tormented with a wound he could not know,
 His, like all deep grief, plunged in solitude:
I'm fond myself of solitude or so,
 But then, I beg it may be understood,
By solitude I mean a Sultan's, not
A hermit's, with a haram for a grot.

LXXXVIII.

"Oh Love! in such a wilderness as this,
 Where transport and security entwine,
Here is the empire of thy perfect bliss,
 And here thou art a god indeed divine."
The bard I quote from does not sing amiss,
 With the exception of the second line,
For that same twining "transport and
 security"
Are twisted to a phrase of some obscurity.

LXXXIX.

The poet meant, no doubt, and thus appeals
 To the good sense and senses of mankind,
The very thing which everybody feels,
 As all have found on trial, or may find,
That no one likes to be disturb'd at meals
 Or love.—I won't say more about "en-
 twined"
Or "transport," as we knew all that before,
But beg "Security" will bolt the door.

XC.

Young Juan wander'd by the glassy brooks,
 Thinking unutterable things; he threw
Himself at length within the leafy nooks
 Where the wild branch of the cork forest
 grew;
There poets find materials for their books,
 And every now and then we read them
 through,
So that their plan and prosody are eligible,
Unless, like Wordsworth, they prove unin-
 telligible.

XCI.

He, Juan (and not Wordsworth), so pursued
 His self-communion with his own high soul,
Until his mighty heart, in its great mood,
 Had mitigated part, though not the whole
Of its disease; he did the best he could
 With things not very subject to control,
And turn'd, without perceiving his condition,
Like Coleridge, into a metaphysician.

XCII.

He thought about himself, and the whole
 earth,
 Of man the wonderful, and of the stars,
And how the deuce they ever could have
 birth;
 And then he thought of earthquakes, and
 of wars,
How many miles the moon might have in
 girth,
 Of air-balloons, and of the many bars
To perfect knowledge of the boundless
 skies;—
And then he thought of Donna Julia's eyes.

XCIII.

In thoughts like these true wisdom may dis-
 cern
 Longings sublime, and aspirations high,
Which some are born with, but the most
 part learn
 To plague themselves withal, they know
 not why:
'Twas strange that one so young should thus
 concern
 His brain about the action of the sky;
If *you* think 'twas philosophy that this did,
I can't help thinking puberty assisted.

XCIV.

He pored upon the leaves, and on the flowers,
 And heard a voice in all the winds; and
 then
He thought of wood-nymphs and immortal
 bowers,
 And how the goddesses came down to men:
He miss'd the pathway, he forgot the hours,
 And when he look'd upon his watch again,
He found how much old Time had been a
 winner—
He also found that he had lost his dinner.

XCV.

Sometimes he turn'd to gaze upon his book,
 Boscan, or Garcilasso;—by the wind
Even as the page is rustled while we look,
 So by the poesy of his own mind
Over the mystic leaf his soul was shook,
 As if 'twere one whereon magicians bind
Their spells, and give them to the passing
 gaie
According to some good old woman's tale.

XCVI.

Thus would he while his lonely hours away
 Dissatisfied, nor knowing what he wanted;
Nor glowing reverie, nor poet's lay,
 Could yield his spirit that for which it
 panted,

A bosom whereon he his head might lay,
　And hear the heart beat with the love it
　　granted,
With——several other things, which I forget,
Or which, at least, I need not mention yet.

XCVII.

Those lonely walks, and lengthening reveries,
　Could not escape the gentle Julia's eyes;
She saw that Juan was not at his ease;
　But that which chiefly may, and must
　　surprise,
Is, that the Donna Inez did not tease
　Her only son with question or surmise;
Whether it was she did not see, or would
　not,
Or, like all very clever people, could not.

XCVIII.

This may seem strange, but yet 'tis very
　common;
　For instance—gentlemen, whose ladies take
Leave to o'erstep the written rights of woman,
　And break the——Which commandment
　　is 't they break?
(I have forgot the number, and think no man
　Should rashly quote, for fear of a mistake.)
I say, when these same gentlemen are jeal-
　ous,
They make some blunder, which their ladies
　tell us.

XCIX.

A real husband always is suspicious,
　But still no less suspects in the wrong
　　place,
Jealous of some one who had no such wishes,
　Or pandering blindly to his own disgrace,
By harbouring some dear friend extremely
　vicious;
　The last indeed's infallibly the case:
And when the spouse and friend are gone
　off wholly,
He wonders at their vice, and not his folly.

C.

Thus parents also are at times short-sighted;
　Though watchful as the lynx, they ne'er
　　discover,
The while the wicked world beholds de-
　lighted,
　Young Hopeful's mistress, or Miss Fanny's
　　lover,
Till some confounded escapade has blighted
　The plan of twenty years, and all is over;
And then the mother cries, the father swears,
And wonders why the devil he got heirs.

CI.

But Inez was so anxious, and so clear
　Of sight, that I must think, on this occa-
　　sion,
She had some other motive much more near
　For leaving Juan to this new temptation,
But what that motive was, I shan't say here;
　Perhaps to finish Juan's education,
Perhaps to open Don Alfonso's eyes,
In case he thought his wife too great a prize.

CII.

It was upon a day, a summer's day;—
　Summer's indeed a very dangerous season,
And so is spring about the end of May;
　The sun, no doubt, is the prevailing reason;
But whatsoe'er the cause is, one may say,
　And stand convicted of more truth than
　　treason,
That there are months which nature grows
　more merry in,—
March has its hares, and May must have its
　heroine.

CIII.

'Twas on a summer's day—the sixth of
　June:—
　I like to be particular in dates,
Not only of the age, and year, but moon;
　They are a sort of post-house, where the
　　Fates
Change horses, making history change its
　tune,
　Then spur away o'er empires and o'er
　　states,
Leaving at last not much besides chronology,
Excepting the post-obits of theology.

CIV.

'Twas on the sixth of June, about the hour
　Of half-past six—perhaps still nearer
　　seven—
When Julia sate within as pretty a bower
　As e'er held houri in that heathenish
　　heaven
Described by Mahomet, and Anacreon Moore,
　To whom the lyre and laurels have been
　　given,
With all the trophies of triumphant song—
He won them well, and may he wear them
　long!

CV.

She sate, but not alone; I know not well
　How this same interview had taken place,
And even if I knew, I should not tell—
　People should hold their tongues in any
　　case;

No matter how or why the thing befell,
　But there were she and Juan, face to face—
When two such faces are so, 't would be
　wise,
But very difficult, to shut their eyes.

CVI.

How beautiful she look'd! her conscious
　heart
　Glow'd in her cheek, and yet she felt no
　　wrong.
Oh Love! how perfect is thy mystic art,
　Strengthening the weak, and trampling on
　　the strong!
How self-deceitful is the sagest part
　Of mortals whom thy lure hath led
　　along!—
The precipice she stood on was immense,
So was her creed in her own innocence.

CVII.

She thought of her own strength, and Juan's
　youth,
　And of the folly of all prudish fears,
Victorious virtue, and domestic truth,
　And then of Don Alfonso's fifty years:
I wish these last had not occurr'd, in sooth,
　Because that number rarely much endears,
And through all climes, the snowy and the
　sunny,
Sounds ill in love, whate'er it may in money.

CVIII.

When people say, "I've told you *fifty* times,"
　They mean to scold, and very often do;
When poets say, "I've written *fifty* rhymes,"
　They make you dread that they'll recite
　　them too;
In gangs of *fifty*, thieves commit their crimes;
　At *fifty* love for love is rare, 't is true,
But then, no doubt, it equally as true is,
A good deal may be bought for *fifty* Louis.

CIX.

Julia had honour, virtue, truth, and love
　For Don Alfonso; and she inly swore,
By all the vows below to powers above,
　She never would disgrace the ring she
　　wore,
Nor leave a wish which wisdom might re-
　prove;
　And while she ponder'd this, besides much
　　more,
One hand on Juan's carelessly was thrown,
Quite by mistake—she thought it was her
　own;

CX.

Unconsciously she lean'd upon the other,
　Which play'd within the tangles of her
　　hair;
And to contend with thoughts she could not
　smother
　She seem'd, by the distraction of her air.
'T was surely very wrong in Juan's mother
　To leave together this imprudent pair,
She who for many years had watch'd her
　son so—
I'm very certain *mine* would not have done so.

CXI.

The hand which still held Juan's, by de-
　grees
　Gently, but palpably confirm'd its grasp,
As if it said, "Detain me, if you please;"
　Yet there's no doubt she only meant to
　　clasp
His fingers with a pure Platonic squeeze;
　She would have shrunk as from a toad,
　　or asp,
Had she imagined such a thing could rouse
A feeling dangerous to a prudent spouse.

CXII.

I cannot know what Juan thought of this,
　But what he did, is much what you would
　　do;
His young lip thank'd it with a grateful kiss,
　And then, abash'd at its own joy, withdrew
In deep despair, lest he had done amiss,—
　Love is so very timid when 't is new:
She blush'd, and frown'd not, but she strove
　to speak,
And held her tongue, her voice was grown so
　weak.

CXIII.

The sun set, and up rose the yellow moon:
　The devil's in the moon for mischief; they
Who call'd her CHASTE, methinks, began too
　soon
　Their nomenclature; there is not a day,
The longest, not the twenty-first of June,
　Sees half the business in a wicked way,
On which three single hours of moonshine
　smile—
And then she looks so modest all the while.

CXIV.

There is a dangerous silence in that hour,
　A stillness, which leaves room for the full
　　soul
To open all itself, without the power
　Of calling wholly back its self-control;

The silver light which, hallowing tree and
tower,
 Sheds beauty and deep softness o'er the
 whole,
Breathes also to the heart, and o'er it throws
A loving languor, which is not repose.

CXV.

And Julia sate with Juan, half embraced
 And half retiring from the glowing arm,
Which trembled like the bosom where 't was
 placed;
 Yet still she must have thought there was
 no harm,
Or else 't were easy to withdraw her waist;
 But then the situation had its charm,
And then——God knows what next—I can't
 go on;
I'm almost sorry that I e'er begun.

CXVI.

Oh Plato! Plato! you have paved the way,
 With your confounded fantasies, to more
Immoral conduct by the fancied sway
 Your system feigns o'er the controlless
 core
Of human hearts, than all the long array
 Of poets and romancers:—You 're a bore,
A charlatan, a coxcomb—and have been,
At best, no better than a go-between.

CXVII.

And Julia's voice was lost, except in sighs,
 Until too late for useful conversation;
The tears were gushing from her gentle eyes,
 I wish, indeed, they had not had occasion;
But who, alas! can love, and then be wise?
 Not that remorse did not oppose temptation;
A little still she strove, and much repented,
And whispering "I will ne'er consent"—
 consented.

CXVIII.

'T is said that Xerxes offer'd a reward
 To those who could invent him a new
 pleasure
Methinks the requisition 's rather hard,
 And must have cost his majesty a treasure:
For my part, I 'm a moderate-minded bard,
 Fond of a little love (which I call leisure);
I care not for new pleasures, as the old
Are quite enough for me, so they but hold.

CXIX.

Oh Pleasure! you 're indeed a pleasant thing,
 Although one must be damn'd for you, no
 doubt:
I make a resolution every spring
 Of reformation, ere the year run out,

But somehow, this my vestal vow takes
 wing,
 Yet still, I trust, it may be kept throughout:
I 'm very sorry, very much ashamed,
And mean, next winter, to be quite reclaim'd.

CXX.

Here my chaste Muse a liberty must take—
 Start not! still chaster reader—she 'll be
 nice hence-
Forward, and there is no great cause to
 quake;
This liberty is a poetic licence,
Which some irregularity may make
 In the design, and as I have a high sense
Of Aristotle and the Rules, 't is fit
To beg his pardon when I err a bit.

CXXI.

This licence is to hope the reader will
 Suppose from June the sixth (the fatal day
Without whose epoch my poetic skill
 For want of facts would all be thrown
 away),
But keeping Julia and Don Juan still
 In sight, that several months have pass'd;
 we'll say
'T was in November, but I'm not so sure
About the day—the era 's more obscure.

CXXII.

We 'll talk of that anon.—'T is sweet to hear
 At midnight on the blue and moonlit deep
The song and oar of Adria's gondolier,
 By distance mellow'd, o'er the waters
 sweep;
'T is sweet to see the evening star appear;
 'T is sweet to listen as the night-winds
 creep
From leaf to leaf; 'tis sweet to view on
 high
The rainbow, based on ocean, span the sky.

CXXIII.

'T is sweet to hear the watch-dog's honest
 bark
 Bay deep-mouth'd welcome as we draw
 near home;
'T is sweet to know there is an eye will mark
 Our coming, and look brighter when we
 come;
'T is sweet to be awaken'd by the lark,
 Or lull'd by falling waters; sweet the hum
Of bees, the voice of girls, the song of birds,
The lisp of children, and their earliest words.

CXXIV.

Sweet is the vintage, when the showering
　　grapes
　In Bacchanal profusion reel to earth,
Purple and gushing; sweet are our escapes
　From civic revelry to rural mirth;
Sweet to the miser are his glittering heaps,
　Sweet to the father is his first-born's birth,
Sweet is revenge—especially to women,
Pillage to soldiers, prize-money to seamen.

CXXV.

Sweet is a legacy, and passing sweet
　The unexpected death of some old lady
Or gentleman of seventy years complete,
　Who've made "us youth" wait too—too
　　long already
For an estate, or cash, or country seat,
　Still breaking, but with stamina so steady
That all the Israelites are fit to mob its
Next owner for their double-damn'd post-
　obits.

CXXVI.

'T is sweet to win, no matter how, one's
　　laurels,
　By blood or ink; 't is sweet to put an end
To strife; 'tis sometimes sweet to have our
　quarrels,
　Particularly with a tiresome friend:
Sweet is old wine in bottles, ale in barrels;
　Dear is the helpless creature we defend
Against the world; and dear the schoolboy
　spot
We ne'er forget, though there we are forgot.

CXXVII.

But sweeter still than this, than these,
　　than all,
　Is first and passionate love—it stands
　　alone,
Like Adam's recollection of his fall;
　The tree of knowledge has been pluck'd—
　　all's known—
And life yields nothing further to recall
　Worthy of this ambrosial sin, so shown,
No doubt in fable, as the unforgiven
Fire which Prometheus filch'd for us from
　heaven.

CXXVIII.

Man's a strange animal, and makes strange
　　use
　Of his own nature, and the various arts,
And likes particularly to produce
　Some new experiment to show his parts;

This is the age of oddities let loose,
　Where different talents find their different
　　marts;
You'd best begin with truth, and when
　you've lost your
Labour, there's a sure market for imposture.

CXXIX.

What opposite discoveries we have seen!
　(Signs of true genius, and of empty
　　pockets.)
One makes new noses, one a guillotine,
　One breaks your bones, one sets them in
　　their sockets;
But vaccination certainly has been
　A kind antithesis to Congreve's rockets,
With which the Doctor paid off an old pox,
By borrowing a new one from an ox.

CXXX.

Bread has been made (indifferent) from
　　potatoes;
　And galvanism has set some corpses grin-
　　ning,
But has not answer'd like the apparatus
　Of the Humane Society's beginning,
By which men are unsuffocated gratis:
　What wondrous new machines have late
　　been spinning!
I said the small pox has gone out of late;
Perhaps it may be follow'd by the great.

CXXXI.

'T is said the great came from America;
　Perhaps it may set out on its return,—
The population there so spreads, they say
　'T is grown high time to thin it in its
　　turn,
With war, or plague, or famine, any way,
　So that civilisation they may learn;
And which in ravage the more loathsome
　evil is—
Their real lues, or our pseudo-syphilis?

CXXXII.

This is the patent age of new inventions
　For killing bodies, and for saving souls,
All propagated with the best intentions;
　Sir Humphry Davy's lantern, by which
　　coals
Are safely mined for in the mode he men-
　　tions,
　Tombuctoo travels, voyages to the Poles,
Are ways to benefit mankind, as true,
Perhaps, as shooting them at Waterloo.

CXXXIII.

Man's a phenomenon, one knows not what,
 And wonderful beyond all wondrous mea-
 sure;
'Tis pity though, in this sublime world, that
 Pleasure's a sin, and sometimes sin's a
 pleasure;
Few mortals know what end they would
 be at,
 But whether glory, power, or love, or
 treasure,
The path is through perplexing ways, and
 when
The goal is gain'd, we die, you know—and
 then——

CXXXIV.

What then?—I do not know, no more do
 you—
 And so good night.—Return we to our
 story:
'T was in November, when fine days are few,
 And the far mountains wax a little hoary,
And clap a white cape on their mantles blue;
 And the sea dashes round the promontory,
And the loud breaker boils against the rock,
And sober suns must set at five o'clock.

CXXXV.

'T was, as the watchmen say, a cloudy night;
 No moon, no stars, the wind was low or loud
By gusts, and many a sparkling hearth was
 bright
 With the piled wood, round which the
 family crowd;
There's something cheerful in that sort of
 light,
 Even as a summer sky's without a cloud:
I'm fond of fire, and crickets, and all that,
A lobster salad, and champagne, and chat.

CXXXVI.

'T was midnight—Donna Julia was in bed,
 Sleeping, most probably,—when at her door
Arose a clatter might awake the dead,
 If they had never been awoke before,
And that they have been so we all have read,
 And are to be so, at the least, once more;—
The door was fasten'd, but with voice and fist
First knocks were heard, then "Madam—
 Madam—hist!

CXXXVII.

"For God's sake, Madam—Madam—here's
 my master,
 With more than half the city at his back—
Was ever heard of such a curst disaster!
 'Tis not my fault—I kept good watch—
 Alack!

Do pray undo the bolt a little faster—
 They're on the stair just now, and in a
 crack
Will all be here; perhaps he yet may fly—
Surely the window's not so *very* high!"

CXXXVIII.

By this time Don Alfonso was arrived,
 With torches, friends, and servants in
 great number;
The major part of them had long been wived,
 And therefore paused not to disturb the
 slumber
Of any wicked woman, who contrived
 By stealth her husband's temples to en-
 cumber:
Examples of this kind are so contagious,
Were *one* not punish'd, *all* would be out-
 rageous.

CXXXIX.

I can't tell how, or why, or what suspicion
 Could enter into Don Alfonso's head;
But for a cavalier of his condition
 It surely was exceedingly ill-bred,
Without a word of previous admonition,
 To hold a levee round his lady's bed,
And summon lackeys, arm'd with fire and
 sword,
To prove himself the thing he most abhorr'd.

CXL.

Poor Donna Julia! starting as from sleep
 (Mind—that I do not say—she had not
 slept),
Began at once to scream, and yawn, and
 weep;
 Her maid, Antonia, who was an adept,
Contrived to fling the bed-clothes in a heap,
 As if she had just now from out them
 crept:
I can't tell why she should take all this
 trouble
To prove her mistress had been sleeping
 double.

CXLI.

But Julia mistress, and Antonia maid,
 Appear'd like two poor harmless women,
 who
Of goblins, but still more of men afraid,
 Had thought one man might be deterr'd by
 two,
And therefore side by side were gently laid,
 Until the hours of absence should run
 through,
And truant husband should return, and say,
"My dear, I was the first who came away."

CXLII.

Now Julia found at length a voice, and cried,
 "In heaven's name, Don Alfonso, what
 d'ye mean?
Has madness seized you? would that I had
 died
Ere such a monster's victim I had been!
What may this midnight violence betide,
 A sudden fit of drunkenness or spleen?
Dare you suspect me, whom the thought
 would kill?
Search, then, the room!"—Alfonso said, "I
 will."

CXLIII.

He search'd, *they* search'd, and rummaged
 everywhere,
 Closet and clothes-press, chest and window-
 seat,
And found much linen, lace, and several pair
 Of stockings, slippers, brushes, combs,
 complete,
With other articles of ladies fair,
 To keep them beautiful, or leave them
 neat:
Arras they prick'd and curtains with their
 swords,
And wounded several shutters, and some
 boards.

CXLIV.

Under the bed they search'd, and there they
 found—
 No matter what—it was not that they
 sought;
They open'd windows, gazing if the ground
 Had signs or footmarks, but the earth said
 nought;
And then they stared each other's faces
 round:
 'Tis odd, not one of all these seekers
 thought,
And seems to me almost a sort of blunder,
Of looking *in* the bed as well as under.

CXLV.

During this inquisition Julia's tongue
 Was not asleep—"Yes, search and search,"
 she cried,
"Insult on insult heap, and wrong on wrong!
 It was for this that I became a bride!
For this in silence I have suffer'd long
 A husband like Alfonso at my side;
But now I'll bear no more, nor here remain,
If there be law or lawyers in all Spain.

CXLVI.

"Yes, Don Alfonso! husband now no more,
 If ever you indeed deserved the name,
Is't worthy of your years?—you have three-
 score—
 Fifty, or sixty, it is all the same—
Is't wise or fitting, causeless to explore
 For facts against a virtuous woman's fame?
Ungrateful, perjured, barbarous Don Alfonso,
How dare you think your lady would go on
 so?

CXLVII.

"Is it for this I have disdain'd to hold
 The common privileges of my sex?
That I have chosen a confessor so old
 And deaf, that any other it would vex,
And never once he has had cause to scold,
 But found my very innocence perplex
So much, he always doubted I was married—
How sorry you will be when I've miscarried!

CXLVIII.

"Was it for this that no Cortejo e'er
 I yet have chosen from out the youth of
 Seville?
Is it for this I scarce went anywhere,
 Except to bull-fights, mass, play, rout, and
 revel?
Is it for this, whate'er my suitors were,
 I favour'd none—nay, was almost uncivil?
Is it for this that General Count O'Reilly,
Who took Algiers, declares I used him vilely?

CXLIX.

"Did not the Italian Musico Cazzani
 Sing at my heart six months at least in
 vain?
Did not his countryman, Count Corniani,
 Call me the only virtuous wife in Spain?
Were there not also Russians, English, many?
 The Count Strongstroganoff I put in pain,
And Lord Mount Coffeehouse, the Irish peer,
Who kill'd himself for love (with wine) last
 year.

CL.

"Have I not had two bishops at my feet?
 The Duke of Ichar, and Don Fernan Nunez?
And is it thus a faithful wife you treat?
 I wonder in what quarter now the moon is:
I praise your vast forbearance not to beat
 Me also, since the time so opportune is—
Oh, valiant man! with sword drawn and
 cock'd trigger,
Now, tell me, don't you cut a pretty figure?

CLI.

"Was it for this you took your sudden
 journey,
 Under pretence of business indispensable,
With that sublime of rascals your attorney,
 Whom I see standing there, and looking
 sensible
Of having play'd the fool? though both I
 spurn, he
 Deserves the worst, his conduct's less
 defensible,
Because, no doubt, 't was for his dirty fee,
And not from any love to you nor me.

CLII.

"If he comes here to take a deposition,
 By all means let the gentleman proceed;
You've made the apartment in a fit con-
 dition:—
 There's pen and ink for you, sir, when you
 need—
Let everything be noted with precision,
 I would not you for nothing should be
 fee'd—
But as my maid's undrest, pray turn your
 spies out."
"Oh!" sobb'd Antonia, "I could tear their
 eyes out."

CLIII.

"There is the closet, there the toilet, there
 The antechamber—search them under, over;
There is the sofa, there the great arm-chair,
 The chimney—which would really hold a
 lover.
I wish to sleep, and beg you will take care
 And make no further noise, till you discover
The secret cavern of this lurking treasure—
And when 't is found, let me, too, have that
 pleasure.

CLIV.

"And now, Hidalgo! now that you have
 thrown
 Doubt upon me, confusion over all,
Pray have the courtesy to make it known
 Who is the man you search for? how
 d'ye call
Him? what's his lineage? let him but be
 shown—
 I hope he's young and handsome—is he
 tall?
Tell me—and be assured, that since you
 stain
Mine honour thus, it shall not be in vain.

CLV.

"At least, perhaps, he has not sixty years,
 At that age he would be too old for
 slaughter,
Or for so young a husband's jealous fears—
 (Antonia! let me have a glass of water.)
I am ashamed of having shed these tears,
 They are unworthy of my father's daugh-
 ter;
My mother dream'd not in my natal hour,
That I should fall into a monster's power.

CLVI.

"Perhaps 't is of Antonia you are jealous,
 You saw that she was sleeping by my side,
When you broke in upon us with your fel-
 lows;
 Look where you please—we've nothing
 sir, to hide;
Only another time, I trust, you'll tell us,
 Or for the sake of decency abide
A moment at the door, that we may be
Drest to receive so much good company.

CLVII.

"And now, sir, I have done, and say no
 more;
 The little I have said may serve to show
The guileless heart in silence may grieve o'er
 The wrongs to whose exposure it is slow:—
I leave you to your conscience as before,
 'T will one day ask you, *why* you used me
 so?
God grant you feel not then the bitterest
 grief!
Antonia! where's my pocket-handkerchief?"

CLVIII.

She ceased, and turn'd upon her pillow; pale
 She lay, her dark eyes flashing through
 their tears,
Like skies that rain and lighten; as a veil,
 Waved and o'ershading her wan cheek,
 appears
Her streaming hair; the black curls strive,
 but fail,
 To hide the glossy shoulder, which uprears
Its snow through all;—her soft lips lie apart,
And louder than her breathing beats her
 heart.

CLIX.

The Senhor Don Alfonso stood confused;
 Antonia bustled round the ransack'd room,
And, turning up her nose, with looks abused
 Her master, and his myrmidons, of whom

Not one, except the attorney, was amused;
　He, like Achates, faithful to the tomb,
So there were quarrels, cared not for the
　　cause,
Knowing they must be settled by the laws.

CLX.

With prying snub-nose, and small eyes, he
　　stood,
　Following Antonia's motions here and there,
With much suspicion in his attitude;
　For reputations he had little care;
So that a suit or action were made good,
　Small pity had he for the young and fair,
And ne'er believed in negatives, till these
Were proved by competent false witnesses.

CLXI.

But Don Alfonso stood with downcast looks,
　And, truth to say, he made a foolish figure;
When, after searching in five hundred nooks,
　And treating a young wife with so much
　　rigour,
He gain'd no point, except some self-rebukes,
　Added to those his lady with such vigour
Had pour'd upon him for the last half hour,
Quick, thick, and heavy—as a thunder-shower.

CLXII.

At first he tried to hammer an excuse,
　To which the sole reply was tears and sobs,
And indications of hysterics, whose
　Prologue is always certain throes, and
　　throbs,
Gasps, and whatever else the owners choose:
　Alfonso saw his wife, and thought of Job's;
He saw too, in perspective, her relations,
And then he tried to muster all his patience.

CLXIII.

He stood in act to speak, or rather stammer,
　But sage Antonia cut him short before
The anvil of his speech received the hammer,
　With "Pray, sir, leave the room, and say
　　no more,
Or madam dies."—Alfonso mutter'd, "D—n
　her."
　But nothing else, the time of words was
　　o'er;
He cast a rueful look or two, and did,
He knew not wherefore, that which he was
　bid.

CLXIV.

With him retired his "*posse comitatus*,"
　The attorney last, who linger'd near the
　　door
Reluctantly, still tarrying there as late as
　Antonia let him—not a little sore

At this most strange and unexplain'd "*hiatus*"
　In Don Alfonso's facts, which just now
　　wore
An awkward look; as he revolved the case,
The door was fasten'd in his legal face.

CLXV.

No sooner was it bolted, than—Oh shame!
　Oh sin! Oh sorrow! and Oh womankind!
How can you do such things and keep your
　　fame,
　Unless this world, and t'other too, be blind?
Nothing so dear as an unfilch'd good name!
　But to proceed—for there is more behind:
With much heartfelt reluctance be it said,
Young Juan slipp'd, half-smother'd, from the
　bed.

CLXVI.

He had been hid—I don't pretend to say
　How, nor can I indeed describe the where—
Young, slender, and pack'd easily, he lay,
　No doubt, in little compass, round or
　　square;
But pity him I neither must nor may
　His suffocation by that pretty pair;
'Twere better, sure, to die so, than be shut
With maudlin Clarence in his Malmsey butt.

CLXVII.

And, secondly, I pity not, because
　He had no business to commit a sin,
Forbid by heavenly, fined by human laws,
　At least 't was rather early to begin;
But at sixteen the conscience rarely gnaws
　So much as when we call our old debts in
At sixty years, and draw the accompts of evil,
And find a deuced balance with the devil.

CLXVIII.

Of his position I can give no notion:
　'Tis written in the Hebrew Chronicle,
How the physicians, leaving pill and potion,
　Prescribed, by way of blister, a young belle,
When old King David's blood grew dull in
　motion,
　And that the medicine answer'd very well;
Perhaps 't was in a different way applied,
For David lived, but Juan nearly died.

CLXIX.

What's to be done? Alfonso will be back
　The moment he has sent his fools away.
Antonia's skill was put upon the rack,
　But no device could be brought into play—
And how to parry the renew'd attack?
　Besides, it wanted but few hours of day:
Antonia puzzled; Julia did not speak,
But press'd her bloodless lip to Juan's cheek.

CLXX.

He turn'd his lip to hers, and with his hand
 Call'd back the tangles of her wandering
 hair;
Even then their love they could not all com-
 mand,
 And half forgot their danger and despair:
Antonia's patience now was at a stand—
 "Come, come, 'tis no time now for fooling
 there,"
She whisper'd, in great wrath—"I must
 deposit
This pretty gentleman within the closet:

CLXXI.

"Pray, keep your nonsense for some luckier
 night—
 Who can have put my master in this mood?
What will become on 't—I'm in such a fright,
 The devil's in the urchin, and no good—
Is this a time for giggling? this a plight?
 Why, don't you know that it may end in
 blood?
You'll lose your life, and I shall lose my place,
My mistress all, for that half-girlish face.

CLXXII.

"Had it but been for a stout cavalier
 Of twenty-five or thirty—(come, make
 haste)
But for a child, what piece of work is here!
 I really, madam, wonder at your taste—
(Come, sir, get in)—my master must be near:
 There, for the present, at the least, he 's
 fast,
And if we can but till the morning keep
Our counsel—Juan, mind, you must not
 sleep)."

CLXXIII.

Now, Don Alfonso entering, but alone,
 Closed the oration of the trusty maid:
She loiter'd, and he told her to be gone,
 An order somewhat sullenly obey'd;
However, present remedy was none,
 And no great good seem'd answer'd if she
 staid;
Regarding both with slow and sidelong view,
She snuff'd the candle, curtsied, and with-
 drew.

CLXXIV.

Alfonso paused a minute—then begun
 Some strange excuses for his late pro-
 ceeding:
He would not justify what he had done,
 To say the best, it was extreme ill-breeding;

But there were ample reasons for it, none
 Of which he specified in this his pleading:
His speech was a fine sample, on the whole,
Of rhetoric, which the learn'd call "*rigmarole*."

CLXXV.

Julia said nought; though all the while there
 rose
 A ready answer, which at once enables
A matron, who her husband's foible knows,
 By a few timely words to turn the tables,
Which, if it does not silence, still must pose,—
 Even if it should comprise a pack of fables;
'Tis to retort with firmness, and when he
Suspects with *one*, do you reproach with *three*.

CLXXVI.

Julia, in fact, had tolerable grounds,—
 Alfonso's loves with Inez were well known;
But whether 't was that one's own guilt con-
 founds—
 But that can't be, as has been often shown,
A lady with apologies abounds;—
 It might be that her silence sprang alone
From delicacy to Don Juan's ear,
To whom she knew his mother's fame was
 dear.

CLXXVII.

There might be one more motive, which makes
 two,
 Alfonso ne'er to Juan had alluded,—
Mentioned his jealousy, but never who
 Had been the happy lover, he concluded,
Conceal'd amongst his premises; 'tis true,
 His mind the more o'er this its mystery
 brooded
To speak of Inez now were, one may say,
Like throwing Juan in Alfonso's way.

CLXXVIII.

A hint, in tender cases, is enough;
 Silence is best: besides there is a *tact*—
(That modern phrase appears to me sad stuff,
 But it will serve to keep my verse com-
 pact)—
Which keeps, when push'd by questions rather
 rough,
 A lady always distant from the fact:
The charming creatures lie with such a grace,
There's nothing so becoming to the face.

CLXXIX.

They blush, and we believe them, at least I
 Have always done so; 'tis of no great use,
In any case, attempting a reply,
 For then their eloquence grows quite
 profuse;

And when at length they're out of breath,
 they sigh,
 And cast their languid eyes down, and let
 loose
A tear or two, and then we make it up;
And then—and then—and then—sit down and
 sup.

CLXXX.

Alfonso closed his speech, and begg'd her
 pardon,
 Which Julia half withheld, and then half
 granted,
And laid conditions, he thought very hard,
 on,
Denying several little things he wanted:
He stood like Adam lingering near his garden,
 With useless penitence perplex'd and
 haunted,
Beseeching she no further would refuse,
When, lo! he stumbled o'er a pair of shoes.

CLXXXI.

A pair of shoes!—what then? not much, if
 they
 Are such as fit with ladies' feet, but these
(No one can tell how much I grieve to say)
 Were masculine; to see them, and to seize,
Was but a moment's act.—Ah! well-a-day!
 My teeth begin to chatter, my veins freeze—
Alfonso first examined well their fashion,
And then flew out into another passion.

CLXXXII.

He left the room for his relinquish'd sword,
 And Julia instant to the closet flew.
"Fly, Juan, fly! for heaven's sake—not a
 word—
 The door is open—you may yet slip through
The passage you so often have explored—
 Here is the garden-key—Fly—fly—Adieu!
Haste—haste! I hear Alfonso's hurrying
 feet—
Day has not broke—there's no one in the
 street."

CLXXXIII.

None can say that this was not good advice,
 The only mischief was, it came too late;
Of all experience 'tis the usual price,
 A sort of income-tax laid on by fate:
Juan had reach'd the room-door in a trice,
 And might have done so by the garden-
 gate,
But met Alfonso in his dressing-gown,
Who threaten'd death—so Juan knock'd him
 down.

CLXXXIV.

Dire was the scuffle, and out went the light;
 Antonia cried out "Rape!" and Julia
 "Fire!"
But not a servant stirr'd to aid the fight.
 Alfonso, pommell'd to his heart's desire,
Swore lustily he'd be revenged this night;
 And Juan, too, blasphemed an octave
 higher;
His blood was up: though young, he was a
 Tartar,
And not at all disposed to prove a martyr.

CLXXXV.

Alfonso's sword had dropp'd ere he could
 draw it,
 And they continued battling hand to hand,
For Juan very luckily ne'er saw it;
 His temper not being under great command,
If at that moment he had chanced to claw it,
 Alfonso's days had not been in the land
Much longer.—Think of husbands', lovers'
 lives!
And how ye may be doubly widows—wives!

CLXXXVI.

Alfonso grappled to detain the foe,
 And Juan throttled him to get away,
And blood ('t was from the nose) began to flow;
 At last, as they more faintly wrestling lay,
Juan contrived to give an awkward blow,
 And then his only garment quite gave way;
He fled, like Joseph, leaving it; but there,
I doubt, all likeness ends between the pair.

CLXXXVII.

Lights came at length, and men, and maids,
 who found
 An awkward spectacle their eyes before;
Antonia in hysterics, Julia swoon'd,
 Alfonso leaning, breathless, by the door;
Some half-torn drapery scatter'd on the
 ground,
 Some blood, and several footsteps, but no
 more:
Juan the gate gain'd, turn'd the key about,
And liking not the inside, lock'd the out.

CLXXXVIII.

Here ends this canto.—Need I sing, or say,
 How Juan, naked, favour'd by the night,
Who favours what she should not, found his
 way,
 And reach'd his home in an unseemly plight?
The pleasant scandal which arose next day,
 The nine days' wonder which was brought
 to light,
And how Alfonso sued for a divorce,
Were in the English newspapers, of course.

CLXXXIX.

If you would like to see the whole proceedings,
　The depositions and the cause at full,
The names of all the witnesses, the pleadings
　Of counsel to nonsuit, or to annul,
There's more than one edition, and the
　　readings
　Are various, but they none of them are dull;
The best is that in short-hand ta'en by Gurney,
Who to Madrid on purpose made a journey.

CXC.

But Donna Inez, to divert the train
　Of one of the most circulating scandals
That had for centuries been known in Spain,
　At least since the retirement of the Vandals,
First vow'd (and never had she vow'd in vain)
　To Virgin Mary several pounds of candles;
And then, by the advice of some old ladies,
She sent her son to be shipp'd off from Cadiz.

CXCI.

She had resolved that he should travel through
　All European climes, by land or sea,
To mend his former morals, and get new,
　Especially in France and Italy
(At least this is the thing most people do).
　Julia was sent into a convent: she
Grieved, but, perhaps, her feelings may be
　　better
Shown in the following copy of her Letter :—

CXCII.

" They tell me 'tis decided you depart :
　'Tis wise—'tis well, but not the less a pain ;
I have no further claim on your young heart,
　Mine is the victim, and would be again :
To love too much has been the only art
　I used ;—I write in haste, and if a stain
Be on this sheet, 'tis not what it appears ;
My eyeballs burn and throb, but have no tears.

CXCIII.

" I loved, I love you, for this love have lost
　State, station, heaven, mankind's, my own
　　esteem,
And yet cannot regret what it hath cost,
　So dear is still the memory of that dream ;
Yet, if I name my guilt, 'tis not to boast,
　None can deem harshlier of me than I deem :
I trace this scrawl because I cannot rest—
I've nothing to reproach or to request.

CXCIV.

" Man's love is of man's life a thing apart,
　'Tis woman's whole existence ; man may
　　range
The court, camp, church, the vessel, and the
　　mart ;
　Sword, gown, gain, glory, offer in exchange·

Pride, fame, ambition, to fill up his heart,
　And few there are whom these cannot
　　estrange ;
Men have all these resources, we but one,
To love again, and be again undone.

CXCV.

" You will proceed in pleasure, and in pride,
　Beloved and loving many ; all is o'er
For me on earth, except some years to hide
　My shame and sorrow deep in my heart's
　　core :
These I could bear, but cannot cast aside
　The passion which still rages as before,—
And so farewell—forgive me, love me—No,
That word is idle now—but let it go.

CXCVI.

" My breast has been all weakness, is so yet ;
　But still I think I can collect my mind ;
My blood still rushes where my spirit's set,
　As roll the waves before the settled wind ;
My heart is feminine, nor can forget—
　To all, except one image, madly blind ;
So shakes the needle, and so stands the pole,
As vibrates my fond heart to my fix'd soul.

CXCVII.

" I have no more to say, but linger still,
　And dare not set my seal upon this sheet,
And yet I may as well the task fulfil,
　My misery can scarce be more complete :
I had not lived till now, could sorrow kill ;
　Death shuns the wretch who fain the blow
　　would meet,
And I must even survive this last adieu,
And bear with life to love and pray for
　you ! "

CXCVIII.

This note was written upon gilt-edged paper
　With a neat little crow-quill, slight and
　　new ;
Her small white hand could hardly reach the
　　taper,
　It trembled as magnetic needles do,
And yet she did not let one tear escape her ;
　The seal a sun-flower ; " *Elle vous suit
　　partout,*"
The motto, cut upon a white cornelian ;
The wax was superfine, its hue vermilion.

CXCIX.

This was Don Juan's earliest scrape ; but
　　whether
　I shall proceed with his adventures is
Dependent on the public altogether ;
　We'll see, however, what they say to this,

Their favour in an author's cap's a feather,
 And no great mischief's done by their
 caprice;
And if their approbation we experience,
Perhaps they'll have some more about a year
 hence.

CC.

My poem's epic, and is meant to be
Divided in twelve books; each book contain-
 ing,
With love, and war, a heavy gale at sea,
 A list of ships, and captains, and kings
 reigning,
New characters; the episodes are three:
 A panoramic view of hell's in training,
After the style of Virgil and of Homer,
So that my name of Epic's no misnomer.

CCI.

All these things will be specified in time,
 With strict regard to Aristotle's rules,
The *Vade Mecum* of the true sublime,
 Which makes so many poets, and some
 fools:
Prose poets like blank-verse, I'm fond of
 rhyme,
 Good workmen never quarrel with their
 tools;
I've got new mythological machinery,
And very handsome supernatural scenery.

CCII.

There's only one slight difference between
 Me and my epic brethren gone before,
And here the advantage is my own, I ween
 (Not that I have not several merits more,
But this will more peculiarly be seen):
 They so embellish, that 'tis quite a bore
Their labyrinth of fables to thread through,
Whereas this story's actually true.

CCIII.

If any person doubt it, I appeal
 To history, tradition, and to facts,
To newspapers, whose truth all know and
 feel,
 To plays in five, and operas in three acts;
All these confirm my statement a good deal,
 But that which more completely faith
 exacts
Is, that myself, and several now in Seville,
Saw Juan's last elopement with the devil.

CCIV.

If ever I should condescend to prose,
 I'll write poetical commandments, which
Shall supersede beyond all doubt all those
 That went before; in these I shall enrich

My text with many things that no one knows,
 And carry precept to the highest pitch:
I'll call the work "Longinus o'er a Bottle,
Or, Every Poet his *own* Aristotle."

CCV.

Thou shalt believe in Milton, Dryden, Pope;
 Thou shalt not set up Wordsworth, Coleridge,
 Southey;
Because the first is crazed beyond all hope,
 The second drunk, the third so quaint and
 mouthy:
With Crabbe it may be difficult to cope,
 And Campbell's Hippocrene is somewhat
 drouthy:
Thou shalt not steal from Samuel Rogers, nor
Commit—flirtation with the muse of Moore.

CCVI.

Thou shalt not covet Mr. Sotheby's Muse,
 His Pegasus, nor anything that's his;
Thou shalt not bear false witness like "the
 Blues"—
 (There's one, at least, is very fond of this);
Thou shalt not write, in short, but what I
 choose:
 This is true criticism, and you may kiss—
Exactly as you please, or not,—the rod;
But if you don't, I'll lay it on, by G—d!

CCVII.

If any person should presume to assert
 This story is not moral, first, I pray,
That they will not cry out before they're
 hurt,
 Then that they'll read it o'er again, and
 say
(But, doubtless, nobody will be so pert),
 That this is not a moral tale, though gay;
Besides, in Canto Twelfth, I mean to show
The very place where wicked people go.

CCVIII.

If, after all, there should be some so blind
 To their own good this warning to despise,
Let by some tortuosity of mind,
 Not to believe my verse and their own eyes,
And cry that they "the moral cannot find,"
 I tell him, if a clergyman, he lies;
Should captains the remark, or critics, make,
They also lie too—under a mistake.

CCIX.

The public approbation I expect,
 And beg they'll take my word about the
 moral,
Which I with their amusement will connect
 (So children cutting teeth receive a coral);

Meantime they'll doubtless please to recol-
 lect
 My epical pretensions to the laurel:
For fear some prudish readers should grow
 skittish,
I've bribed my grandmother's review—the
 British.

CCX.

I sent it in a letter to the Editor,
 Who thank'd me duly by return of post—
I'm for a handsome article his creditor;
 Yet, if my gentle Muse he please to roast,
And break a promise after having made it
 her,
 Denying the receipt of what it cost,
And smear his page with gall instead of
 honey,
All I can say is—that he had the money.

CCXI.

I think that with this holy new alliance
 I may ensure the public, and defy
All other magazines of art or science,
 Daily, or monthly, or three monthly; I
Have not essay'd to multiply their clients,
 Because they tell me 'twere in vain to try,
And that the Edinburgh Review and Quar-
 terly
Treat a dissenting author very martyrly.

CCXII.

" *Non ego hoc ferrem calidâ juventâ*
 Consule Planco," Horace said, and so
Say I; by which quotation there is meant a
 Hint that some six or seven good years ago
(Long ere I dreamt of dating from the Brenta)
 I was most ready to return a blow,
And would not brook at all this sort of thing
In my hot youth—when George the Third
 was King.

CCXIII.

But now at thirty years my hair is gray—
 (I wonder what it will be like at forty?
I thought of a peruke the other day—)
 My heart is not much greener; and, in
 short, I
Have squander'd my whole summer while
 'twas May,
 And feel no more the spirit to retort; I
Have spent my life, both interest and prin-
 cipal,
And deem not, what I deem'd, my soul in-
 vincible.

CCXIV.

No more—no more—Oh! never more on me
 The freshness of the heart can fall like dew,
Which out of all the lovely things we see
 Extracts emotions beautiful and new;

Hived in our bosoms like the bag o' the bee.
 Think'st thou the honey with those objects
 grew?
Alas! 'twas not in them, but in thy power
To double even the sweetness of a flower.

CCXV.

No more—no more—Oh! never more, my
 heart,
 Canst thou be my sole world, my universe!
Once all in all, but now a thing apart,
 Thou canst not be my blessing or my curse:
The illusion's gone for ever, and thou art
 Insensible, I trust, but none the worse,
And in thy stead I've got a deal of judgment,
Though heaven knows how it ever found a
 lodgment.

CCXVI.

My days of love are over; me no more
 The charms of maid, wife, and still less of
 widow,
Can make the fool of which they made be-
 fore,—
 In short, I must not lead the life I did do;
The credulous hope of mutual minds is o'er,
 The copious use of claret is forbid too,
So for a good old-gentlemanly vice,
I think I must take up with avarice.

CCXVII.

Ambition was my idol, which was broken
 Before the shrines of Sorrow, and of Plea-
 sure;
And the two last have left me many a token
 O'er which reflection may be made at lei-
 sure;
Now, like Friar Bacon's brazen head, I've
 spoken,
 "Time is, Time was, Time's past:"—a
 chymic treasure
Is glittering youth, which I have spent be-
 times—
My heart in passion, and my head on rhymes.

CCXVIII.

What is the end of fame? 'tis but to fill
 A certain portion of uncertain paper:
Some liken it to climbing up a hill,
 Whose summit, like all hills, is lost in
 vapour;
For this men write, speak, preach, and heroes
 kill,
 And bards burn what they call their "mid-
 night taper,"
To have, when the original is dust,
A name, a wretched picture, and worse bust.

CCXIX.

What are the hopes of man? Old Egypt's
　　King
Cheops erected the first pyramid
And largest, thinking it was just the thing
　　To keep his memory whole, and mummy
　　　hid:
But somebody or other rummaging,
　　Burglariously broke his coffin's lid
Let not a monument give you or me hopes,
Since not a pinch of dust remains of Cheops.

CCXX.

But I, being fond of true philosophy,
　　Say very often to myself, "Alas!
All things that have been born were born to
　　die,
　　And flesh (which Death mows down to hay)
　　　is grass;
You've pass'd your youth not so unpleasantly,
　　And if you had it o'er again—'t would
　　　pass—
So thank your stars that matters are no
　　worse,
And read your Bible, sir, and mind your
　　purse."

CCXXI.

But for the present, gentle reader! and
　　Still gentler purchaser! the bard—that's
　　　I—
Must, with permission, shake you by the
　　hand,
　　And so your humble servant, and good-
　　　bye!
We meet again, if we should understand
　　Each other; and if not, I shall not try
Your patience further than by this short
　　sample—
'Twere well if others follow'd my example.

CCXXII.

"Go, little book, from this my solitude!
　　I cast thee on the waters—go thy ways!
And if, as I believe, thy vein be good,
　　The world will find thee after many
　　　days."
When Southey's read, and Wordsworth un-
　　derstood,
　　I can't help putting in my claim to praise—
The four first rhymes are Southey's, every
　　line:
For God's sake, reader! take them not for
　　mine!

Canto the Second.*

I.

Oh ye! who teach the ingenuous youth of
　　nations,
　　Holland, France, England, Germany, or
　　　Spain,
I pray ye flog them upon all occasions,
　　It mends their morals, never mind the
　　　pain:
The best of mothers and of educations
　　In Juan's case were but employ'd in vain,
Since, in a way that's rather of the oddest, he
Became divested of his native modesty.

II.

Had he but been placed at a public school,
　　In the third form, or even in the fourth,
His daily task had kept his fancy cool,
　　At least, had he been nurtured in the north
Spain may prove an exception to the rule,
　　But then exceptions always prove its worth—
A lad of sixteen causing a divorce
Puzzled his tutors very much, of course.

III.

I can't say that it puzzles me at all,
　　If all things be consider'd; first, there was
His lady-mother, mathematical,
　　A —— never mind;—his tutor, an old ass;
A pretty woman—(that's quite natural,
　　Or else the thing had hardly come to pass)
A husband rather old, not much in unity
With his young wife—a time, and opportu-
　　nity.

IV.

Well—well; the world must turn upon its
　　axis,
　　And all mankind turn with it, heads or
　　　tails,
And live and die, make love and pay our
　　taxes,
　　And as the veering wind shifts, shift our
　　　sails;
The king commands us, and the doctor
　　quacks us,
　　The priest instructs, and so our life exhales,
A little breath, love, wine, ambition, fame,
Fighting, devotion, dust,—perhaps a name.

V.

I said, that Juan had been sent to Cadiz—
　　A pretty town; I recollect it well—
'Tis there the mart of the colonial trade is,
　　(Or was, before Peru learn'd to rebel,)

* ["Begun at Venice, December 13, 1818,—finished
January 20, 1819."—B.]

And such sweet girls—I mean, such graceful
　　ladies,
　　Their very walk would make your bosom
　　　swell;
I can't describe it, though so much it strike,
Nor liken it—I never saw the like:

VI.

An Arab horse, a stately stag, a barb
　　New broke, a cameleopard, a gazelle,
No—none of these will do;—and then their
　　garb,
　　Their veil and petticoat—Alas! to dwell
Upon such things would very near absorb
　　A canto—then their feet and ankles,—well,
Thank Heaven I've got no metaphor quite
　　ready,
(And so, my sober Muse—come, let's be
　　steady—

VII.

Chaste Muse!—well, if you must, you must)
　　—the veil
　　Thrown back a moment with the glancing
　　　hand,
While the o'erpowering eye, that turns you
　　pale,
　　Flashes into the heart:—All sunny land
Of love! when I forget you, may I fail
　　To——say my prayers—but never was there
　　　plann'd
A dress through which the eyes give such a
　　volley,
Excepting the Venetian Fazzioli.

VIII.

But to our tale: the Donna Inez sent
　　Her son to Cadiz only to embark;
To stay there had not answer'd her intent,
　　But why?—we leave the reader in the
　　　dark—
'Twas for a voyage the young man was
　　meant,
　　As if a Spanish ship were Noah's ark,
To wean him from the wickedness of earth,
And send him like a dove of promise forth.

·IX.

Don Juan bade his valet pack his things
　　According to direction, then received
A lecture and some money: for four springs
　　He was to travel; and though Inez grieved
(As every kind of parting has its stings),
　　She hoped he would improve—perhaps
　　　believed:
A letter, too, she gave (he never read it)
Of good advice—and two or three of credit.

X.

In the mean time, to pass her hours away,
　　Brave Inez now set up a Sunday school
For naughty children, who would rather play
　　(Like truant rogues) the devil, or the fool;
Infants of three years old were taught that
　　day,
　　Dunces were whipt, or set upon a stool:
The great success of Juan's education
Spurr'd her to teach another generation.

XI.

Juan embark'd—the ship got under way,
　　The wind was fair, the water passing
　　　rough;
A devil of a sea rolls in·that bay,
　　As I, who've cross'd it oft, know well
　　　enough;
And, standing upon deck, the dashing spray
　　Flies in one's face, and makes it weather-
　　　tough:
And there he stood to take, and take again,
His first—perhaps his last—farewell of Spain.

XII.

I can't but say it is an awkward sight
　　To see one's native land receding through
The growing waters; it unmans one quite,
　　Especially when life is rather new:
I recollect Great Britain's coast looks white,
　　But almost every other country's blue,
When gazing on them, mystified by distance,
We enter on our nautical existence.

XIII.

So Juan stood, bewilder'd on the deck:
　　The wind sung, cordage strain'd, and sail-
　　　ors swore,
And the ship creak'd, the town became a
　　speck,
　　From which away so fair and fast they
　　　bore.
The best of remedies is a beef-steak
　　Against sea-sickness: try it, sir, before
You sneer, and I assure you this is true,
For I have found it answer—so may you.

XIV.

Don Juan stood, and, gazing from the stern,
　　Beheld his native Spain receding far:
First partings form a lesson hard to learn,
　　Even nations feel this when they go to
　　　war;
There is a sort of unexprest concern,
　　A kind of shock that sets one's heart ajar:
At leaving even the most unpleasant people
And places, one keeps looking at the steeple.

XV.

But Juan had got many things to leave,
　His mother, and a mistress, and no wife,
So that he had much better cause to grieve
　Than many persons more advanced in life;
And if we now and then a sigh must heave
　At quitting even those we quit in strife,
No doubt we weep for those the heart en-
　dears—
That is, till deeper griefs congeal our tears.

XVI.

So Juan wept, as wept the captive Jews
　By Babel's waters, still remembering Sion:
I'd weep,—but mine is not a weeping Muse,
　And such light griefs are not a thing to
　　die on;
Young men should travel, if but to amuse
　Themselves; and the next time their ser-
　　vants tie on
Behind their carriages their new portman-
　teau,
Perhaps it may be lined with this my canto.

XVII.

And Juan wept, and much he sigh'd and
　thought,
　While his salt tears dropp'd into the salt sea,
"Sweets to the sweet;" (I like so much to
　quote;
　You must excuse this extract,—'tis where
　　she,
The Queen of Denmark, for Ophelia brought
　Flowers to the grave;) and, sobbing often,
　　he
Reflected on his present situation,
And seriously resolved on reformation.

XVIII.

"Farewell, my Spain! a long farewell!" he
　cried,
　"Perhaps I may revisit thee no more,
But die, as many an exiled heart hath died,
　Of its own thirst to see again thy shore:
Farewell, where Guadalquivir's waters glide!
　Farewell, my mother! and, since all is o'er,
Farewell, too, dearest Julia!—(here he drew
　Her letter out again, and read it through.)

XIX.

'And oh! if e'er I should forget, I swear—
　But that's impossible, and cannot be—
Sooner shall this blue ocean melt to air,
　Sooner shall earth resolve itself to sea,
Than I resign thine image, oh, my fair!
　Or think of anything, excepting thee;
A mind diseased no remedy can physic—
(Here the ship gave a lurch, and he grew
　sea-sick.)

XX.

"Sooner shall heaven kiss earth—(here he
　fell sicker)
Oh, Julia! what is every other woe?—
(For God's sake let me have a glass of liquor;
　Pedro, Battista, help me down below.)
Julia, my love—(you rascal, Pedro, quicker)—
　Oh, Julia!—(this curst vessel pitches so)—
Beloved Julia, hear me still beseeching!"
(Here he grew inarticulate with retching.)

XXI.

He felt that chilling heaviness of heart,
　Or rather stomach, which, alas! attends,
Beyond the best apothecary's art,
　The loss of love, the treachery of friends,
Or death of those we dote on, when a part
　Of us dies with them as each fond hope
　　ends:
No doubt he would have been much more
　pathetic,
But the sea acted as a strong emetic.

XXII.

Love's a capricious power: I've known it
　hold
　Out through a fever caused by its own heat,
But be much puzzled by a cough and cold,
　And find a quinsy very hard to treat;
Against all noble maladies he's bold,
　But vulgar illnesses don't like to meet,
Nor that a sneeze should interrupt his sigh,
Nor inflammations redden his blind eye.

XXIII.

But worst of all is nausea, or a pain
　About the lower region of the bowels;
Love, who heroically breathes a vein,
　Shrinks from the application of hot towels,
And purgatives are dangerous to his reign,
　Sea-sickness death: his love was perfect,
　　how else
Could Juan's passion, while the billows roar,
Resist his stomach, ne'er at sea before?

XXIV.

The ship, call'd the most holy "Trinidada,"
　Was steering duly for the port Leghorn;
For there the Spanish family Moncada
　Were settled long ere Juan's sire was born:
They were relations, and for them he had a
　Letter of introduction, which the morn
Of his departure had been sent him by
His Spanish friends for those in Italy.

XXV.

His suite consisted of three servants and
　A tutor, the licentiate Pedrillo,
Who several languages did understand,
　But now lay sick and speechless on his pillow,

And, rocking in his hammock, long'd for land,
 His headache being increased by every bil-
 low;
And the waves oozing through the port-hole
 made
His berth a little damp, and him afraid.

XXVI.

'Twas not without some reason, for the wind
 Increased at night, until it blew a gale;
And though 'twas not much to a naval mind,
 Some landsmen would have look'd a little
 pale,
For sailors are, in fact, a different kind:
 At sunset they began to take in sail,
For the sky show'd it would come on to blow,
And carry away, perhaps, a mast or so.

XXVII.

At one o'clock the wind with sudden shift
 Threw the ship right into the trough of
 the sea,
Which struck her aft, and made an awkward
 rift,
 Started the stern-post, also shatter'd the
Whole of her stern-frame, and, ere she could
 lift
Herself from out her present jeopardy,
The rudder tore away: 'twas time to sound
The pumps, and there were four feet water
 found.

XXVIII.

One gang of people instantly was put
 Upon the pumps, and the remainder set
To get up part of the cargo, and what not;
 But they could not come at the leak as
 yet;
At last they did get at it really, but
 Still their salvation was an even bet:
The water rush'd through in a way quite
 puzzling,
While they thrust sheets, shirts, jackets,
 bales of muslin,

XXIX.

Into the opening; but all such ingredients
 Would have been vain, and they must
 have gone down,
Despite of all their efforts and expedients,
 But for the pumps: I'm glad to make them
 known
To all the brother tars who may have need
 hence,
For fifty tons of water were upthrown
By them per hour, and they all had been
 undone,
But for the maker, Mr. Mann, of London.

XXX.

As day advanced the weather seem'd to
 abate,
 And then the leak they reckon'd to reduce,
And keep the ship afloat, though three feet
 yet
 Kept two hand and one chain-pump still
 in use.
The wind blew fresh again: as it grew late
 A squall came on, and while some guns
 broke loose,
A gust—which all descriptive power tran-
 scends—
Laid with one blast the ship on her beam
 ends.

XXXI.

There she lay, motionless, and seem'd upset;
 The water left the hold, and wash'd the
 decks,
And made a scene men do not soon forget;
 For they remember battles, fires, and
 wrecks,
Or any other thing that brings regret,
 Or breaks their hopes, or hearts, or heads,
 or necks;
Thus drownings are much talk'd of by the
 divers,
And swimmers, who may chance to be sur-
 vivors.

XXXII.

Immediately the masts were cut away,
 Both main and mizen: first the mizen
 went,
The main-mast follow'd; but the ship still
 lay
 Like a mere log, and baffled our intent.
Foremast and bowsprit were cut down, and
 they
 Eased her at last (although we never
 meant
To part with all till every hope was blighted),
And then with violence the old ship righted.

XXXIII.

It may be easily supposed, while this
 Was going on, some people were unquiet,
That passengers would find it much amiss
 To lose their lives, as well as spoil their
 diet;
That even the able seaman, deeming his
 Days nearly o'er, might be disposed to
 riot,
As upon such occasions tars will ask
For grog, and sometimes drink rum from the
 cask.

XXXIV.

There's nought, no doubt, so much the spirit
 calms
 As rum and true religion: thus it was,
Some plunder'd, some drank spirits, some
 sung psalms,
 The high wind made the treble, and as
 bass
The hoarse harsh waves kept time; fright
 cured the qualms
 Of all the luckless landsmen's sea-sick
 maws:
Strange sounds of wailing, blasphemy, de-
 votion,
Clamour'd in chorus to the roaring ocean.

XXXV.

Perhaps more mischief had been done, but for
 Our Juan, who, with sense beyond his
 years,
Got to the spirit-room, and stood before
 It with a pair of pistols; and their fears,
As if Death were more dreadful by his door
 Of fire than water, spite of oaths and tears,
Kept still aloof the crew, who, ere they sunk,
Thought it would be becoming to die drunk.

XXXVI.

"Give us more grog," they cried, "for it
 will be
 All one an hour hence." Juan answer'd,
 "No!
'T is true that death awaits both you and me,
 But let us die like men, not sink below
Like brutes:"—and thus his dangerous post
 kept he,
 And none liked to anticipate the blow;
And even Pedrillo, his most reverend tutor,
Was for some rum a disappointed suitor.

XXXVII.

The good old gentleman was quite aghast,
 And made a loud and pious lamentation;
Repented all his sins, and made a last
 Irrevocable vow of reformation;
Nothing should tempt him more (this peril
 past)
 To quit his academic occupation,
In cloisters of the classic Salamanca,
To follow Juan's wake, like Sancho Panca.

XXXVIII.

But now there came a flash of hope once
 more;
 Day broke, and the wind lull'd: the masts
 were gone;
The leak increased; shoals round her, but no
 shore,
 The vessel swam, yet still she held her own.

They tried the pumps again, and though before
 Their desperate efforts seem'd all useless
 grown,
A glimpse of sunshine set some hands to
 bale—
The stronger pump'd, the weaker thrumm'd
 a sail.

XXXIX.

Under the vessel's keel the sail was pass'd,
 And for the moment it had some effect;
But with a leak, and not a stick of mast,
 Nor rag of canvas, what could they expect?
But still 'tis best to struggle to the last,
 'T is never too late to be wholly wreck'd:
And though 'tis true that man can only die
 once,
'T is not so pleasant in the Gulf of Lyons.

XL.

There winds and waves had hurl'd them,
 and from thence,
 Without their will, they carried them
 away;
For they were forced with steering to dis-
 pense,
 And never had as yet a quiet day
On which they might repose, or even com-
 mence
 A jurymast or rudder, or could say
The ship would swim an hour, which, by
 good luck,
Still swam—though not exactly like a duck.

XLI.

The wind, in fact, perhaps, was rather less,
 But the ship labour'd so, they scarce could
 hope
To weather out much longer; the distress
 Was also great with which they had to
 cope
For want of water, and their solid mess
 Was scant enough: in vain the telescope
Was used—nor sail nor shore appear'd in
 sight,
Nought but the heavy sea, and coming night.

XLII.

Again the weather threaten'd,—again blew
 A gale, and in the fore and after hold
Water appear'd; yet, though the people
 knew
 All this, the most were patient, and some
 bold,
Until the chains and leathers were worn
 through
 Of all our pumps:—a wreck complete she
 roll'd,
At mercy of the waves, whose mercies are
Like human beings during civil war.

XLIII.

Then came the carpenter, at last, with tears
 In his rough eyes, and told the captain, he
Could do no more: he was a man in years,
 And long had voyaged through many a
 stormy sea,
And if he wept at length, they were not fears
 That made his eyelids as a woman's be,
But he, poor fellow, had a wife and children,
Two things for dying people quite bewilder-
 ing.

XLIV.

The ship was evidently settling now
 Fast by the head; and, all distinction
 gone,
Some went to prayers again, and made a
 vow
 Of candles to their saints—but there were
 none
To pay them with; and some look'd o'er the
 bow;
 Some hoisted out the boats; and there was
 one
That begg'd Pedrillo for an absolution,
Who told him to be damn'd—in his con-
 fusion.

XLV.

Some lash'd them in their hammocks; some
 put on
 Their best clothes, as if going to a fair;
Some cursed the day on which they saw the
 sun,
 And gnash'd their teeth, and howling, tore
 their hair;
And others went on as they had begun,
 Getting the boats out, being well aware
That a tight boat will live in a rough sea,
Unless with breakers close beneath her lee.

XLVI.

The worst of all was, that in their condition,
 Having been several days in great distress,
'T was difficult to get out such provision
 As now might render their long suffering
 less:
Men, even when dying, dislike inanition;
 Their stock was damaged by the weather's
 stress:
Two casks of biscuit, and a keg of butter,
Were all that could be thrown into the cutter.

XLVII.

But in the long-boat they contrived to stow
 Some pounds of bread, though injured by
 the wet;
Water, a twenty-gallon cask or so;
 Six flasks of wine: and they contrived to
 get

A portion of their beef up from below,
 And with a piece of pork, moreover, met,
But scarce enough to serve them for a
 luncheon—
Then there was rum, eight gallons in a
 puncheon.

XLVIII.

The other boats, the yawl and pinnace, had
 Been stove in the beginning of the gale;
And the long-boat's condition was but bad,
 As there were but two blankets for a sail,
And one oar for a mast, which a young lad
 Threw in by good luck over the ship's rail;
And two boats could not hold, far less be
 stored,
To save one half the people then on board.

XLIX.

'T was twilight, and the sunless day went
 down
 Over the waste of waters; like a veil,
Which, if withdrawn, would but disclose the
 frown
 Of one whose hate is mask'd but to assail.
Thus to their hopeless eyes the night was
 shown,
 And grimly darkled o'er the faces pale,
And the dim desolate deep: twelve days had
 Fear
Been their familiar, and now Death was
 here.

L.

Some trial had been making at a raft,
 With little hope in such a rolling sea,
A sort of thing at which one would have
 laugh'd,
 If any laughter at such times could be,
Unless with people who too much have
 quaff'd,
 And have a kind of wild and horrid glee,
Half epileptical, and half hysterical:—
Their preservation would have been a mi-
 racle.

LI.

At half-past eight o'clock, booms, hencoops,
 spars,
 And all things, for a chance, had been cast
 loose
That still could keep afloat the struggling
 tars,
 For yet they strove, although of no great
 use:
There was no light in heaven but a few stars,
 The boats put off o'ercrowded with their
 crews;
She gave a heel, and then a lurch to port,
And, going down head foremost—sunk, in
 short.

LII.

Then rose from sea to sky the wild farewell—
　Then shriek'd the timid, and stood still the
　　brave—
Then some leap'd overboard with dreadful
　yell,
　As eager to anticipate their grave;
And the sea yawn'd around her like a hell,
　And down she suck'd with her the whirling
　　wave,
Like one who grapples with his enemy,
And strives to strangle him before he die.

LIII.

And first one universal shriek there rush'd,
　Louder than the loud ocean, like a crash
Of echoing thunder; and then all was
　hush'd,
　Save the wild wind and the remorseless
　　dash
Of billows; but at intervals there gush'd,
　Accompanied with a convulsive splash,
A solitary shriek, the bubbling cry
Of some strong swimmer in his agony.

LIV.

The boats, as stated, had got off before,
　And in them crowded several of the crew;
And yet their present hope was hardly more
　Than what it had been, for so strong it
　　blew
There was slight chance of reaching any
　shore;
　And then they were too many, though so
　　few—
Nine in the cutter, thirty in the boat,
Were counted in them when they got afloat.

LV.

All the rest perish'd; near two hundred
　souls
　Had left their bodies; and what's worse,
　　alas!
When over Catholics the ocean rolls,
　They must wait several weeks before a
　　mass
Takes off one peck of purgatorial coals,
　Because, till people know what's come to
　　pass,
They won't lay out their money on the
　dead—
It costs three francs for every mass that's
　said.

LVI.

Juan got into the long-boat, and there
　Contrived to help Pedrillo to a place;
It seem'd as if they had exchanged their
　care,
　For Juan wore the magisterial face

Which courage gives, while poor Pedrillo's
　pair
　Of eyes were crying for their owner's case:
Battista, though (a name call'd shortly Tita),
Was lost by getting at some aqua-vita.

LVII.

Pedro, his valet, too, he tried to save,
　But the same cause, conducive to his loss,
Left him so drunk, he jump'd into the wave,
　As o'er the cutter's edge he tried to cross,
And so he found a wine-and-watery grave;
　They could not rescue him although so
　　close,
Because the sea ran higher every minute,
And for the boat—the crew kept crowding
　in it.

LVIII.

A small old spaniel—which had been Don
　Jóse's,
　His father's, whom he loved, as ye may
　　think,
For on such things the memory reposes
　With tenderness—stood howling on the
　　brink,
Knowing, (dogs have such intellectual noses!)
　No doubt, the vessel was about to sink;
And Juan caught him up, and ere he stepp'd
Off threw him in, then after him he leap'd.

LIX.

He also stuff'd his money where he could
　About his person, and Pedrillo's too,
Who let him do, in fact, whate'er he would,
　Not knowing what himself to say, or do,
As every rising wave his dread renew'd;
　But Juan, trusting they might still get
　　through,
And deeming there were remedies for any ill,
Thus re-embark'd his tutor and his spaniel.

LX.

'T was a rough night, and blew so stiffly yet,
　That the sail was becalm'd between the
　　seas,
Though on the wave's high top too much to
　set,
　They dared not take it in for all the
　　breeze:
Each sea curl'd o'er the stern, and kept
　them wet,
　And made them bale without a moment's
　　ease,
So that themselves as well as hopes were
　damp'd,
And the poor little cutter quickly swamp'd.

LXI.

Nine souls more went in her: the long-boat still
　Kept above water, with an oar for mast,
Two blankets stitch'd together, answering ill
　Instead of sail, were to the oar made fast:
Though every wave roll'd menacing to fill,
　And present peril all before surpass'd,
They grieved for those who perish'd with the cutter,
And also for the biscuit-casks and butter.

LXII.

The sun rose red and fiery, a sure sign
　Of the continuance of the gale: to run
Before the sea until it should grow fine,
　Was all that for the present could be done:
A few tea-spoonfuls of their rum and wine
　Were served out to the people, who begun
To faint, and damaged bread wet through the bags,
And most of them had little clothes but rags.

LXIII.

They counted thirty, crowded in a space
　Which left scarce room for motion or exertion;
They did their best to modify their case,
　One half sate up, though numb'd with the immersion,
While t'other half were laid down in their place,
　At watch and watch; thus, shivering like the tertian
Ague in its cold fit, they fill'd their boat,
With nothing but the sky for a great coat.

LXIV.

'T is very certain the desire of life
　Prolongs it: this is obvious to physicians,
When patients, neither plagued with friends nor wife,
　Survive through very desperate conditions,
Because they still can hope, nor shines the knife
　Nor shears of Atropos before their visions:
Despair of all recovery spoils longevity,
And makes men's miseries of alarming brevity.

LXV.

'T is said that persons living on annuities
　Are longer lived than others,—God knows why,
Unless to plague the grantors,—yet so true it is,
　That some, I really think, do never die;

Of any creditors the worst a Jew it is,
　And that 's their mode of furnishing supply:
In my young days they lent me cash that way,
Which I found very troublesome to pay.

LXVI.

'T is thus with people in an open boat,
　They live upon the love of life, and bear
More than can be believed, or even thought,
　And stand like rocks the tempest's wear and tear;
And hardship still has been the sailor's lot,
　Since Noah's ark went cruising here and there;
She had a curious crew as well as cargo,
Like the first old Greek privateer, the Argo.

LXVII.

But man is a carnivorous production,
　And must have meals, at least one meal a day;
He cannot live, like woodcocks, upon suction,
　But, like the shark and tiger, must have prey;
Although his anatomical construction
　Bears vegetables, in a grumbling way,
Your labouring people think beyond all question
Beef, veal, and mutton, better for digestion.

LXVIII.

And thus it was with this our hapless crew;
　For on the third day there came on a calm,
And though at first their strength it might renew,
　And lying on their weariness like balm,
Lull'd them like turtles sleeping on the blue
　Of ocean, when they woke they felt a qualm,
And fell all ravenously on their provision,
Instead of hoarding it with due precision.

LXIX.

The consequence was easily foreseen—
　They ate up all they had, and drank their wine,
In spite of all remonstrances, and then
　On what, in fact, next day were they to dine?
They hoped the wind would rise, these foolish men!
　And carry them to shore; these hopes were fine,
But as they had but one oar, and that brittle,
It would have been more wise to save their victual.

LXX.

The fourth day came, but not a breath of air,
 And Ocean slumber'd like an unwean'd
 child :
The fifth day, and their boat lay floating
 there,
 The sea and sky were blue, and clear, and
 mild—
With their one oar (I wish they had had a
 pair)
 What could they do? and hunger's rage
 grew wild :
So Juan's spaniel, spite of his entreating,
Was kill'd, and portion'd out for present
 eating.

LXXI.

On the sixth day they fed upon his hide,
 And Juan, who had still refused, because
The creature was his father's dog that died,
 Now feeling all the vulture in his jaws,
With some remorse received (though first
 denied)
 As a great favour one of the fore-paws,
Which he divided with Pedrillo, who
Devour'd it, longing for the other too.

LXXII.

The seventh day, and no wind—the burning
 sun
 Blister'd and scorch'd, and, stagnant on
 the sea,
They lay like carcasses; and hope was none,
 Save in the breeze that came not : savagely
They glared upon each other—all was done,
 Water, and wine, and food,—and you
 might see
The longings of the cannibal arise
(Although they spoke not) in their wolfish eyes.

LXXIII.

At length one whisper'd his companion, who
 Whisper'd another, and thus it went round,
And then into a hoarser murmur grew,
 An ominous, and wild, and desperate sound;
And when his comrade's thought each
 sufferer knew,
 'Twas but his own, suppress'd till now, he
 found :
And out they spoke of lots for flesh and blood,
And who should die to be his fellow's food.

LXXIV.

But ere they came to this, they that day shared
 Some leathern caps, and what remain'd of
 shoes;
And then they look'd around them, and
 despair'd,
 And none to be the sacrifice would choose;

At length the lots were torn up, and pre-
 pared,
 But of materials that must shock the
 Muse—
Having no paper, for the want of better,
They took by force from Juan Julia's letter.

LXXV.

Then lots were made, and mark'd, and mix'd,
 and handed
 In silent horror, and their distribution
Lull'd even the savage hunger which de-
 manded,
 Like the Promethean vulture, this pollu-
 tion;
None in particular had sought or plann'd it,
 'Twas nature gnaw'd them to this reso-
 lution,
By which none were permitted to be neuter—
And the lot fell on Juan's luckless tutor.

LXXVI.

He but requested to be bled to death :
 The surgeon had his instruments, and bled
Pedrillo, and so gently ebb'd his breath,
 You hardly could perceive when he was
 dead.
He died as born, a Catholic in faith,
 Like most in the belief in which they're
 bred,
And first a little crucifix he kiss'd,
And then held out his jugular and wrist.

LXXVII.

The surgeon, as there was no other fee,
 Had his first choice of morsels for his
 pains;
But being thirstiest at the moment, he
 Preferr'd a draught from the fast-flowing
 veins :
Part was divided, part thrown in the sea,
 And such things as the entrails and the
 brains
Regaled two sharks, who follow'd o'er the
 billow—
The sailors ate the rest of poor Pedrillo.

LXXVIII.

The sailors ate him, all save three or four,
 Who were not quite so fond of animal food;
To these was added Juan, who, before
 Refusing his own spaniel, hardly could
Feel now his appetite increased much more;
 'Twas not to be expected that he should,
Even in extremity of their disaster,
Dine with them on his pastor and his master.

LXXIX.

'Twas better that he did not; for, in fact,
 The consequence was awful in the extreme;
For they, who were most ravenous in the
 act,
 Went raging mad—Lord! how they did
 blaspheme!
And foam, and roll, with strange convulsions
 rack'd,
 Drinking salt-water like a mountain-
 stream;
Tearing, and grinning, howling, screeching,
 swearing,
And, with hyæna-laughter, died despairing.

LXXX.

Their numbers were much thinn'd by this
 infliction,
 And all the rest were thin enough, Heaven
 knows;
And some of them had lost their recollection,
 Happier than they who still perceived their
 woes;
But others ponder'd on a new dissection,
 As if not warn'd sufficiently by those
Who had already perish'd, suffering madly,
For having used their appetites so sadly.

LXXXI.

And next they thought upon the master's
 mate,
 As fattest; but he saved himself, because,
Besides being much averse from such a fate,
 There were some other reasons: the first
 was,
He had been rather indisposed of late;
 And that which chiefly proved his saving
 clause,
Was a small present made to him at Cadiz,
By general subscription of the ladies.

LXXXII.

Of poor Pedrillo something still remain'd,
 But was used sparingly,—some were afraid,
And others still their appetites constrain'd,
 Or but at times a little supper made;
All except Juan, who throughout abstain'd,
 Chewing a piece of bamboo, and some lead:
At length they caught two boobies, and a
 noddy,
And then they left off eating the dead body.

LXXXIII.

And if Pedrillo's fate should shocking be,
 Remember Ugolino condescends
To eat the head of his arch-enemy
 The moment after he politely ends

His tale: if foes be food in hell, at sea
 'Tis surely fair to dine upon our friends,
When shipwreck's short allowance grows too
 scanty,
Without being much more horrible than Dante.

LXXXIV.

And the same night there fell a shower of
 rain,
 For which their mouths gaped, like the
 cracks of earth
When dried to summer dust; till taught by
 pain,
 Men really know not what good water's
 worth;
If you had been in Turkey or in Spain,
 Or with a famish'd boat's-crew had your
 berth,
Or in the desert heard the camel's bell,
You'd wish yourself where Truth is—in
 a well.

LXXXV.

It pour'd down torrents, but they were no
 richer,
 Until they found a ragged piece of sheet,
Which served them as a sort of spongy
 pitcher,
 And when they deem'd its moisture was
 complete,
They wrung it out, and though a thirsty
 ditcher
 Might not have thought the scanty draught
 so sweet
As a full pot of porter, to their thinking
They ne'er till now had known the joys of
 drinking.

LXXXVI.

And their baked lips, with many a bloody
 crack,
 Suck'd in the moisture, which like nectar
 stream'd;
Their throats were ovens, their swoln tongues
 were black
 As the rich man's in hell, who vainly
 scream'd
To beg the beggar, who could not rain back
 A drop of dew, when every drop had
 seem'd
To taste of heaven—If this be true, indeed,
Some Christians have a comfortable creed.

LXXXVII.

There were two fathers in this ghastly crew,
 And with them their two sons, of whom
 the one
Was more robust and hardy to the view,
 But he died early; and when he was gone,

His nearest messmate told his sire, who
 threw
 One glance at him, and said, "Heaven's
 will be done!
I can do nothing," and he saw him thrown
Into the deep without a tear or groan.

LXXXVIII.

The other father had a weaklier child,
 Of a soft cheek, and aspect delicate;
But the boy bore up long, and with a mild
 And patient spirit held aloof his fate;
Little he said, and now and then he smiled,
 As if to win a part from off the weight
He saw increasing on his father's heart,
With the deep deadly thought, that they
 must part.

LXXXIX.

And o'er him bent his sire, and never raised
 His eyes from off his face, but wiped the
 foam
From his pale lips, and ever on him gazed,
 And when the wish'd-for shower at length
 was come,
And the boy's eyes, which the dull film half
 glazed,
 Brighten'd, and for a moment seem'd to
 roam,
He squeezed from out a rag some drops of
 rain
Into his dying child's mouth—but in vain.

XC.

The boy expired—the father held the clay,
 And look'd upon it long, and when at last
Death left no doubt, and the dead burthen lay
 Stiff on his heart, and pulse and hope were
 past,
He watch'd it wistfully, until away
 'Twas borne by the rude wave wherein
 't was cast;
Then he himself sunk down all dumb and
 shivering,
And gave no sign of life, save his limbs
 quivering.

XCI.

Now overhead a rainbow, bursting through
 The scattering clouds, shone, spanning the
 dark sea,
Resting its bright base on the quivering
 blue;
 And all within its arch appear'd to be
Clearer than that without, and its wide hue
 Wax'd broad and waving, like a banner free,
Then changed like to a bow that's bent, and
 then
Forsook the dim eyes of these shipwreck'd
 men.

XCII.

It changed, of course; a heavenly chameleon,
 The airy child of vapour and the sun,
Brought forth in purple, cradled in vermilion,
 Baptized in molten gold, and swathed in
 dun,
Glittering like crescents o'er a Turk's pavilion,
 And blending every colour into one,
Just like a black eye in a recent scuffle
(For sometimes we must box without the
 muffle).

XCIII.

Our shipwreck'd seamen thought it a good
 omen—
 It is as well to think so, now and then;
'Twas an old custom of the Greek and
 Roman,
 And may become of great advantage when
Folks are discouraged; and most surely no
 men
Had greater need to nerve themselves again
Than these, and so this rainbow look'd like
 hope—
Quite a celestial kaleidoscope.

XCIV.

About this time a beautiful white bird,
 Web-footed, not unlike a dove in size
And plumage (probably it might have err'd
 Upon its course), pass'd oft before their
 eyes,
And tried to perch, although it saw and
 heard
 The men within the boat, and in this guise
It came and went, and flutter'd round them
 till
Night fell:—this seem'd a better omen still.

XCV.

But in this case I also must remark,
 'Twas well this bird of promise did not
 perch,
Because the tackle of our shatter'd bark
 Was not so safe for roosting as a church;
And had it been the dove from Noah's ark,
 Returning there from her successful search,
Which in their way that moment chanced to
 fall,
They would have eat her, olive-branch and all.

XCVI.

With twilight it again came on to blow,
 But not with violence; the stars shone out,
The boat made way; yet now they were so
 low,
 They knew not where nor what they were
 about;

Some fancied they saw land, and some said
 "No!"
 The frequent fog-banks gave them cause to
 doubt—
Some swore that they heard breakers, others
 guns,
And all mistook about the latter once.

XCVII.

As morning broke, the light wind died away,
 When he who had the watch sung out and
 swore,
If 't was not land that rose with the sun's ray,
 He wish'd that land he never might see
 more:
And the rest rubb'd their eyes, and saw
 a bay,
 Or thought they saw, and shaped their
 course for shore;
For shore it was, and gradually grew
Distinct, and high, and palpable to view.

XCVIII.

And then of these some part burst into tears,
 And others, looking with a stupid stare,
Could not yet separate their hopes from fears,
 And seem'd as if they had no further care;
While a few pray'd—(the first time for some
 years)—
 And at the bottom of the boat three were
Asleep: they shook them by the hand and
 head,
And tried to awaken them, but found them
 dead.

XCIX.

The day before, fast sleeping on the water,
 They found a turtle of the hawk's-bill kind,
And by good fortune, gliding softly, caught
 her,
 Which yielded a day's life, and to their
 mind
Proved even still a more nutritious matter,
 Because it left encouragement behind:
They thought that in such perils, more than
 chance
Had sent them this for their deliverance.

C.

The land appear'd a high and rocky coast,
 And higher grew the mountains as they
 drew,
Set by a current, toward it: they were lost
 In various conjectures, for none knew
To what part of the earth they had been tost,
 So changeable had been the winds that
 blew;
Some thought it was Mount Ætna, some the
 highlands
Of Candia, Cyprus, Rhodes, or other islands.

CI.

Meantime the current, with a rising gale,
 Still set them onwards to the welcome
 shore,
Like Charon's bark of spectres, dull and
 pale:
 Their living freight was now reduced to
 four,
And three dead, whom their strength could
 not avail
 To heave into the deep with those before,
Though the two sharks still follow'd them,
 and dash'd
The spray into their faces as they splash'd.

CII.

Famine, despair, cold, thirst, and heat, had
 done
 Their work on them by turns, and thinn'd
 them to
Such things a mother had not known her son
 Amidst the skeletons of that gaunt crew;
By night chill'd, by day scorch'd, thus one by
 one
 They perish'd, until wither'd to these few,
But chiefly by a species of self-slaughter,
In washing down Pedrillo with salt water.

CIII.

As they drew nigh the land, which now was
 seen
 Unequal in its aspect here and there,
They felt the freshness of its growing green,
 That waved in forest-tops, and smooth'd
 the air,
And fell upon their glazed eyes like a screen
 From glistening waves, and skies so hot
 and bare—
Lovely seem'd any object that should sweep
Away the vast, salt, dread, eternal deep.

CIV.

The shore look'd wild, without a trace of
 man,
 And girt by formidable waves; but they
Were mad for land, and thus their course
 they ran,
 Though right ahead the roaring breakers
 lay:
A reef between them also now began
 To show its boiling surf and bounding
 spray,
But finding no place for their landing better,
They ran the boat for shore,—and overset
 her.

CV.

But in his native stream, the Guadalquivir,
 Juan to lave his youthful limbs was wont;
And having learnt to swim in that sweet
 river,
 Had often turn'd the art to some account:
A better swimmer you could scarce see ever,
 He could, perhaps, have pass'd the Helles-
 pont,
As once (a feat on which ourselves we prided)
Leander, Mr. Ekenhead, and I did.

CVI.

So here, though faint, emaciated, and stark,
 He buoy'd his boyish limbs, and strove to
 ply
With the quick wave, and gain, ere it was
 dark,
 The beach which lay before him, high and
 dry:
The greatest danger here was from a shark,
 That carried off his neighbour by the
 thigh;
As for the other two, they could not swim,
So nobody arrived on shore but him.

CVII.

Nor yet had he arrived but for the oar,
 Which, providentially for him, was wash'd
Just as his feeble arms could strike no more,
 And the hard wave o'erwhelm'd him as
 't was dash'd
Within his grasp; he clung to it, and sore
 The waters beat while he thereto was
 lash'd;
At last, with swimming, wading, scrambling,
 he
Roll'd on the beach, half senseless, from the
 sea:

CVIII.

There, breathless, with his digging nails he
 clung
 Fast to the sand, lest the returning wave,
From whose reluctant roar his life he wrung,
 Should suck him back to her insatiate
 grave:
And there he lay, full length, where he was
 flung,
 Before the entrance of a cliff-worn cave,
With just enough of life to feel its pain,
And deem that it was saved, perhaps in vain.

CIX.

With slow and staggering effort he arose,
 But sunk again upon his bleeding knee
And quivering hand; and then he look'd for
 those
 Who long had been his mates upon the sea;

But none of them appear'd to share his woes,
 Save one, a corpse, from out the famish'd
 three,
Who died two days before, and now had
 found
An unknown barren beach for burial-ground.

CX.

And as he gazed, his dizzy brain spun fast,
 And down he sunk; and as he sunk, the
 sand
Swam round and round, and all his senses
 pass'd:
 He fell upon his side, and his stretch'd
 hand
Droop'd dripping on the oar (their jury-
 mast),
 And, like a wither'd lily, on the land
His slender frame and pallid aspect lay,
As fair a thing as e'er was form'd of clay.

CXI.

How long in his damp trance young Juan lay
 He knew not, for the earth was gone for
 him,
And time had nothing more of night nor day
 For his congealing blood, and senses dim;
And how this heavy faintness pass'd away
 He knew not, till each painful pulse and
 limb,
And tingling vein, seem'd throbbing back to
 life,
For Death, though vanquish'd, still retired
 with strife.

CXII.

His eyes he open'd, shut, again unclosed,
 For all was doubt and dizziness; he thought
He still was in the boat, and had but dozed,
 And felt again with his despair o'erwrought,
And wish'd it death in which he had reposed,
 And then once more his feelings back were
 brought,
And slowly by his swimming eyes was seen
A lovely female face of seventeen.

CXIII.

'Twas bending close o'er his, and the small
 mouth
 Seem'd almost prying into his for breath;
And chafing him, the soft warm hand of youth
 Recall'd his answering spirits back from
 death;
And, bathing his chill temples, tried to soothe
 Each pulse to animation, till beneath
Its gentle touch and trembling care, a sigh
To these kind efforts made a low reply.

CXIV.

Then was the cordial pour'd, and mantle flung
 Around his scarce-clad limbs; and the fair
 arm
Raised higher the faint head which o'er it
 hung;
 And her transparent cheek, all pure and
 warm,
Pillow'd his death-like forehead; then she
 wrung
 His dewy curls, long drench'd by every
 storm;
And watch'd with eagerness each throb that
 drew
A sigh from his heaved bosom—and hers, too.

CXV.

And lifting him with care into the cave,
 The gentle girl, and her attendant,—one
Young, yet her elder, and of brow less
 grave,
 And more robust of figure—then begun
To kindle fire, and as the new flames gave
 Light to the rocks that roof'd them, which
 the sun
Had never seen, the maid, or whatsoe'er
She was, appear'd distinct, and tall, and fair.

CXVI.

Her brow was overhung with coins of gold,
 That sparkled o'er the auburn of her hair,
Her clustering hair, whose longer locks were
 roll'd
 In braids behind; and though her stature
 were
Even of the highest for a female mould,
 They nearly reach'd her heel; and in her
 air
There was a something which bespoke com-
 mand,
As one who was a lady in the land.

CXVII.

Her hair, I said, was auburn; but her eyes
 Were black as death, their lashes the same
 hue,
Of downcast length, in whose silk shadow
 lies
 Deepest attraction; for when to the view
Forth from its raven fringe the full glance
 flies,
 Ne'er with such force the swiftest arrow
 flew;
'T is as the snake late coil'd, who pours his
 length,
And hurls at once his venom and his strength.

CXVIII.

Her brow was white and low, her cheek's pure
 dye
 Like twilight rosy still with the set sun;
Short upper lip—sweet lips! that make us
 sigh
 Ever to have seen such; for she was one
Fit for the model of a statuary
 (A race of mere impostors, when all 's done—
I' ve seen much finer women, ripe and real,
Than all the nonsense of their stone ideal).

CXIX.

I 'll tell you why I say so, for 't is just
 One should not rail without a decent cause:
There was an Irish lady, to whose bust
 I ne'er saw justice done, and yet she was
A frequent model; and if e'er she must
 Yield to stern Time and Nature's wrinkling
 laws,
They will destroy a face which mortal thought
Ne'er compass'd, nor less mortal chisel
 wrought.

CXX.

And such was she, the lady of the cave:
 Her dress was very different from the
 Spanish,
Simpler, and yet of colours not so grave;
 For, as you know, the Spanish women
 banish
Bright hues when out of doors, and yet, while
 wave
 Around them (what I hope will never vanish)
The basquina and the mantilla, they
Seem at the same time mystical and gay.

CXXI.

But with our damsel this was not the case:
 Her dress was many-colour'd, finely spun;
Her locks curl'd negligently round her face,
 But through them gold and gems profusely
 shone:
Her girdle sparkled, and the richest lace
 Flow'd in her veil, and many a precious stone
Flash'd on her little hand; but, what was
 shocking,
Her small snow feet had slippers, but no
 stocking.

CXXII.

The other female's dress was not unlike,
 But of inferior materials: she
Had not so many ornaments to strike,
 Her hair had silver only, bound to be
Her dowry; and her veil, in form alike,
 Was coarser; and her air, though firm, less
 free;
Her hair was thicker, but less long; her eyes
As black, but quicker, and of smaller size.

CXXIII.

And these two tended him, and cheer'd him
 both
 With food and raiment, and those soft
 attentions,
Which are—(as I must own)—of female
 growth,
 And have ten thousand delicate inventions :
They made a most superior mess of broth,
 A thing which poesy but seldom mentions,
But the best dish that e'er was cook'd since
 Homer's
Achilles order'd dinner for new comers.

CXXIV.

I 'll tell you who they were, this female pair,
 Lest they should seem princesses in disguise ;
Besides, I hate all mystery, and that air
 Of clap-trap, which your recent poets prize ;
And so, in short, the girls they really were
 They shall appear before your curious eyes,
Mistress and maid ; the first was only daughter
Of an old man, who lived upon the water.

CXXV.

A fisherman he had been in his youth,
 And still a sort of fisherman was he ;
But other speculations were, in sooth,
 Added to his connexion with the sea,
Perhaps not so respectable, in truth :
 A little smuggling, and some piracy,
Left him, at last, the sole of many masters
Of an ill-gotten million of piastres.

CXXVI.

A fisher, therefore, was he,—though of men,
 Like Peter the Apostle,—and he fish'd
For wandering merchant vessels, now and
 then,
 And sometimes caught as many as he
 wish'd ;
The cargoes he confiscated, and gain
 He sought in the slave-market too, and
 dish'd
Full many a morsel for that Turkish trade,
By which, no doubt, a good deal may be made.

CXXVII.

He was a Greek, and on his isle had built
 (One of the wild and smaller Cyclades)
A very handsome house from out his guilt,
 And there he lived exceedingly at ease :
Heaven knows what cash he got, or blood he
 spilt,
 A sad old fellow was he, if you please ;
But this I know, it was a spacious building,
Full of barbaric carving, paint, and gilding.

CXXVIII.

He had an only daughter, call'd Haidée,
 The greatest heiress of the Eastern Isles ;
Besides, so very beautiful was she,
 Her dowry was as nothing to her smiles :
Still in her teens, and like a lovely tree
 She grew to womanhood, and between
 whiles
Rejected several suitors, just to learn
How to accept a better in his turn.

CXXIX.

And walking out upon the beach, below
 The cliff,—towards sunset, on that day she
 found,
Insensible,—not dead, but nearly so,—
 Don Juan, almost famish'd, and half
 drown'd ;
But being naked, she was shock'd, you know,
 Yet deem'd herself in common pity bound,
As far as in her lay, "to take him in,
A stranger" dying, with so white a skin.

CXXX.

But taking him into her father's house
 Was not exactly the best way to save,
But like conveying to the cat the mouse,
 Or people in a trance into their grave ;
Because the good old man had so much
 "*vous*,"
 Unlike the honest Arab thieves so brave,
He would have hospitably cured the stranger
And sold him instantly when out of danger.

CXXXI.

And therefore, with her maid, she thought it
 best
 (A virgin always on her maid relies)
To place him in the cave for present rest :
 And when, at last, he open'd his black eyes,
Their charity increased about their guest ;
 And their compassion grew to such a size,
It open'd half the turnpike gates to heaven—
(St. Paul says, 'tis the toll which must be
 given).

CXXXII.

They made a fire,—but such a fire as they
 Upon the moment could contrive with such
Materials as were cast up round the bay,—
 Some broken planks, and oars, that to the
 touch
Were nearly tinder, since so long they lay
 A mast was almost crumbled to a crutch ;
But, by God's grace, here wrecks were in such
 plenty,
That there was fuel to have furnish'd twenty.

CXXXIII.

He had a bed of furs, and a pelisse,
 For Haidée stripp'd her sables off to make
His couch; and, that he might be more at ease,
 And warm, in case by chance he should
 awake,
They also gave a petticoat apiece,
 She and her maid,—and promised by day-
 break
To pay him a fresh visit, with a dish
For breakfast, of eggs, coffee, bread, and fish.

CXXXIV.

And thus they left him to his lone repose:
 Juan slept like a top, or like the dead,
Who sleep at last, perhaps (God only knows),
 Just for the present; and in his lull'd head
Not even a vision of his former woes
 Throbb'd in accursed dreams, which some-
 times spread
Unwelcome visions of our former years,
Till the eye, cheated, opens thick with tears.

CXXXV.

Young Juan slept all dreamless:—but the
 maid,
 Who smooth'd his pillow, as she left the
 den
Look'd back upon him, and a moment staid,
 And turn'd, believing that he call'd again.
He slumber'd; yet she thought, at least she
 said
 (The heart will slip, even as the tongue and
 pen),
He had pronounced her name—but she forgot
That at this moment Juan knew it not.

CXXXVI.

And pensive to her father's house she went,
 Enjoining silence strict to Zoe, who
Better than her knew what, in fact, she meant,
 She being wiser by a year or two:
A year or two's an age when rightly spent,
 And Zoe spent hers, as most women do,
In gaining all that useful sort of knowledge
Which is acquired in Nature's good old college.

CXXXVII.

The morn broke, and found Juan slumbering
 still
 Fast in his cave, and nothing clash'd upon
His rest: the rushing of the neighbouring rill,
 And the young beams of the excluded sun,
Troubled him not, and he might sleep his fill;
 And need he had of slumber yet, for none
Had suffer'd more—his hardships were com-
 parative
To those related in my grand-dad's "Narra-
 tive."

CXXXVIII.

Not so Haidée: she sadly toss'd and tumbled,
 And started from her sleep, and, turning o'er,
Dream'd of a thousand wrecks, o'er which she
 stumbled,
 And handsome corpses strew'd upon the
 shore;
And woke her maid so early that she grumbled,
 And call'd her father's old slaves up, who
 swore
In several oaths—Armenian, Turk, and
 Greek—
They knew not what to think of such a freak.

CXXXIX.

But up she got, and up she made them get,
 With some pretence about the sun, that
 makes
Sweet skies just when he rises, or is set;
 And 'tis, no doubt, a sight to see when
 breaks
Bright Phœbus, while the mountains still are
 wet
 With mist, and every bird with him awakes,
And night is flung off like a mourning suit
Worn for a husband,—or some other brute.

CXL.

I say, the sun is a most glorious sight:
 I've seen him rise full oft, indeed of late
I have sat up on purpose all the night,
 Which hastens, as physicians say, one's
 fate;
And so all ye, who would be in the right
 In health and purse, begin your day to date
From daybreak, and when coffin'd at four-
 score
Engrave upon the plate, you rose at four.

CXLI.

And Haidée met the morning face to face;
 Her own was freshest, though a feverish
 flush
Had dyed it with the headlong blood, whose
 race
 From heart to cheek is curb'd into a blush,
Like to a torrent which a mountain's base,
 That overpowers some Alpine river's rush,
Checks to a lake, whose waves in circles
 spread;
Or the Red Sea—but the sea is not red.

CXLII.

And down the cliff the island virgin came,
 And near the cave her quick light footsteps
 drew,
While the sun smiled on her with his first
 flame,
 And young Aurora kiss'd her lips with dew,

Taking her for a sister; just the same
 Mistake you would have made on seeing
 the two,
Although the mortal, quite as fresh and fair,
Had all the advantage, too, of not being air.

CXLIII.

And when into the cavern Haidée stepp'd
 All timidly, yet rapidly, she saw
That like an infant Juan sweetly slept;
 And then she stopp'd, and stood as if in awe
(For sleep is awful), and on tiptoe crept
 And wrapt him closer, lest the air, too raw,
Should reach his blood, then o'er him still as
 death
Bent, with hush'd lips, that drank his scarce-
 drawn breath.

CXLIV.

And thus like to an angel o'er the dying
 Who die in righteousness, she lean'd; and
 there
All tranquilly the shipwreck'd boy was lying,
 As o'er him lay the calm and stirless air:
But Zoe the meantime some eggs was frying,
 Since, after all, no doubt the youthful pair
Must breakfast, and betimes—lest they should
 ask it,
She drew out her provision from the basket.

CXLV.

She knew that the best feelings must have
 victual,
 And that a shipwreck'd youth would hungry
 be;
Besides, being less in love, she yawn'd a
 little,
 And felt her veins chill'd by the neigh-
 bouring sea;
And so, she cook'd their breakfast to a tittle;
 I can't say that she gave them any tea,
But there were eggs, fruit, coffee, bread, fish,
 honey,
With Scio wine,—and all for love, not money.

CXLVI.

And Zoe, when the eggs were ready, and
 The coffee made, would have fain waken'd
 Juan;
But Haidée stopp'd her with her quick small
 hand,
 And without word, a sign her finger drew on
Her lip, which Zoe needs must understand;
 And, the first breakfast spoilt, prepared a
 new one,
Because her mistress would not let her break
That sleep which seem'd as it would ne'er
 awake.

CXLVII.

For still he lay, and on his thin worn cheek
 A purple hectic play'd like dying day
On the snow-tops of distant hills; the streak
 Of sufferance yet upon his forehead lay,
Where the blue veins look'd shadowy, shrunk,
 and weak;
 And his black curls were dewy with the
 spray,
Which weigh'd upon them yet, all damp and
 salt,
Mix'd with the stony vapours of the vault.

CXLVIII.

And she bent o'er him, and he lay beneath,
 Hush'd as the babe upon its mother's breast,
Droop'd as the willow when no winds can
 breathe,
 Lull'd like the depth of ocean when at rest,
Fair as the crowning rose of the whole wreath,
 Soft as the callow cygnet in its nest;
In short, he was a very pretty fellow,
Although his woes had turn'd him rather
 yellow.

CXLIX.

He woke and gazed, and would have slept
 again,
 But the fair face which met his eyes forbade
Those eyes to close, though weariness and
 pain
 Had further sleep a further pleasure made;
For woman's face was never form'd in vain
 For Juan, so that even when he pray'd
He turn'd from grisly saints, and martyrs
 hairy,
To the sweet portraits of the Virgin Mary.

CL.

And thus upon his elbow he arose,
 And look'd upon the lady, in whose cheek
The pale contended with the purple rose,
 As with an effort she began to speak;
Her eyes were eloquent, her words would
 pose,
 Although she told him, in good modern
 Greek,
With an Ionian accent, low and sweet,
That he was faint, and must not talk, but eat.

CLI.

Now Juan could not understand a word,
 Being no Grecian; but he had an ear,
And her voice was the warble of a bird,
 So soft, so sweet, so delicately clear,
That finer, simpler music ne'er was heard;
 The sort of sound we echo with a tear,
Without knowing why—an overpowering tone,
Whence melody descends as from a throne.

CLII.

And Juan gazed as one who is awoke
 By a distant organ, doubting if he be
Not yet a dreamer, till the spell is broke
 By the watchman, or some such reality,
Or by one's early valet's cursed knock;
 At least it is a heavy sound to me,
Who like a morning slumber—for the night
Shows stars and women in a better light.

CLIII.

And Juan, too, was help'd out from his dream,
 Or sleep, or whatsoe'er it was, by feeling
A most prodigious appetite; the steam
 Of Zoe's cookery no doubt was stealing
Upon his senses, and the kindling beam
 Of the new fire, which Zoe kept up, kneeling,
To stir her viands, made him quite awake
And long for food, but chiefly a beef-steak.

CLIV.

But beef is rare within these oxless isles;
 Goat's flesh there is, no doubt, and kid, and
 mutton,
And, when a holiday upon them smiles,
 A joint upon their barbarous spits they
 put on:
But this occurs but seldom, between whiles,
 For some of these are rocks with scarce a
 hut on;
Others are fair and fertile, among which
This, though not large, was one of the most
 rich.

CLV.

I say that beef is rare, and can't help thinking
 That the old fable of the Minotaur—
From which our modern morals, rightly
 shrinking,
 Condemn the royal lady's taste who wore
A cow's shape for a mask—was only (sinking
 The allegory) a mere type, no more,
That Pasiphae promoted breeding cattle,
To make the Cretans bloodier in battle.

CLVI.

For we all know that English people are
 Fed upon beef—I won't say much of beer,
Because 'tis liquor only, and being far
 From this my subject, has no business here;
We know, too, they are very fond of war,
 A pleasure—like all pleasures—rather dear;
So were the Cretans—from which I infer
That beef and battles both were owing to her.

CLVII.

But to resume. The languid Juan raised
 His head upon his elbow, and he saw
A sight on which he had not lately gazed,
 As all his latter meals had been quite raw,

Three or four things, for which the Lord he
 praised,
 And, feeling still the famish'd vulture gnaw,
He fell upon whate'er was offer'd, like
A priest, a shark, an alderman, or pike.

CLVIII.

He ate, and he was well supplied; and she,
 Who watch'd him like a mother, would have
 fed
Him past all bounds, because she smiled to see
 Such appetite in one she had deem'd dead:
But Zoe, being older than Haidée,
 Knew (by tradition, for she ne'er had read)
That famish'd people must be slowly nurst,
And fed by spoonfuls, else they always burst.

CLIX.

And so she took the liberty to state,
 Rather by deeds than words, because the
 case
Was urgent, that the gentleman, whose fate
 Had made her mistress quit her bed to trace
The sea-shore at this hour, must leave his plate,
 Unless he wish'd to die upon the place—
She snatch'd it, and refused another morsel,
Saying, he had gorged enough to make a
 horse ill.

CLX.

Next they—he being naked, save a tatter'd
 Pair of scarce decent trowsers—went to
 work,
And in the fire his recent rags they scatter'd,
 And dress'd him, for the present, like a Turk,
Or Greek—that is, although it not much
 matter'd,
 Omitting turban, slippers, pistols, dirk,—
They furnish'd him, entire, except some
 stitches,
With a clean shirt, and very spacious breeches.

CLXI.

And then fair Haidée tried her tongue at
 speaking,
 But not a word could Juan comprehend,
Although he listen'd so that the young Greek in
 Her earnestness would ne'er have made an
 end;
And, as he interrupted not, went eking
 Her speech out to her protégé and friend,
Till pausing at the last her breath to take,
She saw he did not understand Romaic.

CLXII.

And then she had recourse to nods, and signs,
 And smiles, and sparkles of the speaking
 eye,
And read (the only book she could) the lines
 Of his fair face, and found, by sympathy,

The answer eloquent, where the soul shines
　And darts in one quick glance a long reply;
And thus in every look she saw exprest
A world of words, and things at which she
　　guess'd.

CLXIII.

And now, by dint of fingers and of eyes,
　And words repeated after her, he took
A lesson in her tongue; but by surmise,
　No doubt, less of her language than her
　　look:
As he who studies fervently the skies
　Turns oftener to the stars than to his book,
Thus Juan learn'd his alpha beta better
From Haidée's glance than any graven letter.

CLXIV.

'T is pleasing to be school'd in a strange
　　tongue
By female lips and eyes—that is, I mean,
When both the teacher and the taught are
　　young,
　As was the case, at least, where I have been;
They smile so when one 's right, and when
　　one 's wrong
　They smile still more, and then there inter-
　　vene
Pressure of hands, perhaps even a chaste
　　kiss;—
I learn'd the little that I know by this:

CLXV.

That is, some words of Spanish, Turk, and
　　Greek,
　Italian not at all, having no teachers;
Much English I cannot pretend to speak,
　Learning that language chiefly from its
　　preachers,
Barrow, South, Tillotson, whom every week
　I study, also Blair, the highest reachers
Of eloquence in piety and prose—
I hate your poets, so read none of those.

CLXVI.

As for the ladies, I have nought to say,
　A wanderer from the British world of
　　fashion,
Where I, like other "dogs, have had my day,"
　Like other men, too, may have had my
　　passion—
But that, like other things, has pass'd away,
　And all her fools whom I *could* lay the lash
　　on:
Foes, friends, men, women, now are nought
　　to me
But dreams of what has been, no more to be.

CLXVII.

Return we to Don Juan. He begun
　To hear new words, and to repeat them;
　　but
Some feelings, universal as the sun,
　Were such as could not in his breast be
　　shut
More than within the bosom of a nun:
　He was in love,—as you would be, no
　　doubt,
With a young benefactress,—so was she,
Just in the way we very often see.

CLXVIII.

And every day by daybreak—rather early
　For Juan, who was somewhat fond of rest—
She came into the cave, but it was merely
　To see her bird reposing in his nest;
And she would softly stir his locks so curly,
　Without disturbing her yet slumbering
　　guest,
Breathing all gently o'er his cheek and mouth,
As o'er a bed of roses the sweet south.

CLXIX.

And every morn his colour freshlier came,
　And every day help'd on his convalescence;
'T was well, because health in the human
　　frame
　Is pleasant, besides being true love's
　　essence,
For health and idleness to passion's flame
　Are oil and gunpowder; and some good
　　lessons
Are also learnt from Ceres and from Bacchus,
Without whom Venus will not long attack us.

CLXX.

While Venus fills the heart (without heart
　　really
　Love, though good always, is not quite so
　　good),
Ceres presents a plate of vermicelli,—
　For love must be sustain'd like flesh and
　　blood,
While Bacchus pours out wine, or hands a
　　jelly:
　Eggs, oysters, too, are amatory food;
But who is their purveyor from above
Heaven knows,—it may be Neptune, Pan, or
　　Jove.

CLXXI.

When Juan woke he found some good things
　　ready,
　A bath, a breakfast, and the finest eyes
That ever made a youthful heart less steady,
　Besides her maid's, as pretty for their size;

But I have spoken of all this already—
　And repetition's tiresome and unwise,—
Well—Juan, after bathing in the sea,
Came always back to coffee and Haidée.

CLXXII.

Both were so young, and one so innocent,
　That bathing pass'd for nothing; Juan
　　seem'd
To her, as 't were, the kind of being sent,
　Of whom these two years she had nightly
　　dream'd,
A something to be loved, a creature meant
　To be her happiness, and whom she
　　deem'd
To render happy: all who joy would win
Must share it,—Happiness was born a twin.

CLXXIII.

It was such pleasure to behold him, such
　Enlargement of existence to partake
Nature with him, to thrill beneath his touch,
　To watch him slumbering, and to see him
　　wake;
To live with him for ever were too much;
　But then the thought of parting made her
　　quake:
He was her own, her ocean-treasure, cast
Like a rich wreck—her first love, and her last.

CLXXIV.

And thus a moon roll'd on, and fair Haidée
　Paid daily visits to her boy, and took
Such plentiful precautions, that still he
　Remain'd unknown within his craggy nook;
At last her father's prows put out to sea,
　For certain merchantmen upon the look,
Not as of yore to carry off an Io,
But three Ragusan vessels bound for Scio.

CLXXV.

Then came her freedom, for she had no
　mother,
So that, her father being at sea, she was
Free as a married woman, or such other
　Female, as where she likes may freely pass,
Without even the encumbrance of a brother,
　The freest she that ever gazed on glass:
I speak of Christian lands in this comparison,
Where wives, at least, are seldom kept in
　garrison.

CLXXVI.

Now she prolong'd her visits and her talk
　(For they must talk), and he had learnt to
　　say
So much as to propose to take a walk,—
　For little had he wander'd since the day

On which, like a young flower snapp'd from
　the stalk,
　Drooping and dewy on the beach he lay,—
And thus they walk'd out in the afternoon,
And saw the sun set opposite the moon.

CLXXVII.

It was a wild and breaker-beaten coast,
　With cliffs above, and a broad sandy shore,
Guarded by shoals and rocks as by an host,
　With here and there a creek, whose aspect
　　wore
A better welcome to the tempest-tost;
　And rarely ceased the haughty billow's roar,
Save on the dead long summer days, which
　make
The outstretch'd ocean glitter like a lake.

CLXXVIII.

And the small ripple spilt upon the beach
　Scarcely o'erpass'd the cream of your
　　champagne,
When o'er the brim the sparkling bumpers
　reach,
　That spring-dew of the spirit! the heart's
　　rain!
Few things surpass old wine; and they may
　preach
　Who please,—the more because they preach
　　in vain,—
Let us have wine and women, mirth and
　laughter,
Sermons and soda-water the day after.

CLXXIX

Man, being reasonable, must get drunk;
　The best of life is but intoxication:
Glory, the grape, love, gold, in these are sunk
　The hopes of all men, and of every nation;
Without their sap, how branchless were the
　trunk
　Of life's strange tree, so fruitful on occasion!
But to return,—Get very drunk; and when
You wake with headache, you shall see what
　then.

CLXXX.

Ring for your valet—bid him quickly bring
　Some hock and soda-water, then you'll
　　know
A pleasure worthy Xerxes the great king;
　For not the blest sherbet, sublimed with
　　snow,
Nor the first sparkle of the desert spring,
　Nor Burgundy in all its sunset glow,
After long travel, ennui, love, or slaughter,
Vie with that draught of hock and soda-water.

CLXXXI.

The coast—I think it was the coast that I
 Was just describing—Yes, it *was* the coast—
Lay at this period quiet as the sky,
 The sands untumbled, the blue waves untost,
And all was stillness, save the sea-bird's cry,
 And dolphin's leap, and little billow crost
By some low rock or shelve, that made it fret
Against the boundary it scarcely wet.

CLXXXII.

And forth they wander'd, her sire being gone,
 As I have said, upon an expedition ;
And mother, brother, guardian, she had none,
 Save Zoe, who, although with due precision
She waited on her lady with the sun,
 Thought daily service was her only mission,
Bringing warm water, wreathing her long
 tresses,
And asking now and then for cast-off dresses.

CLXXXIII.

It was the cooling hour, just when the rounded
 Red sun sinks down behind the azure hill,
Which then seems as if the whole earth it
 bounded,
 Circling all nature, hush'd, and dim, and still,
With the far mountain-crescent half sur-
 rounded
On one side, and the deep sea calm and chill,
Upon the other, and the rosy sky,
With one star sparkling through it like an eye.

CLXXXIV.

And thus they wander'd forth, and hand in
 hand,
 Over the shining pebbles and the shells,
Glided along the smooth and harden'd sand,
 And in the worn and wild receptacles
Work'd by the storms, yet work'd as it were
 plann'd,
 In hollow halls, with sparry roofs and cells,
They turn'd to rest ; and, each clasp'd by an
 arm,
Yielded to the deep twilight's purple charm.

CLXXXV.

They look'd up to the sky, whose floating glow
 Spread like a rosy ocean, vast and bright ;
They gazed upon the glittering sea below,
 Whence the broad moon rose circling into
 sight ;
They heard the waves splash, and the wind
 so low,
 And saw each other's dark eyes darting light
Into each other—and, beholding this,
Their lips drew near, and clung into a kiss ;

CLXXXVI.

A long, long kiss, a kiss of youth, and love,
 And beauty, all concentrating like rays
Into one focus, kindled from above ;
 Such kisses as belong to early days,
Where heart, and soul, and sense, in concert
 move,
 And the blood's lava, and the pulse
 a blaze,
Each kiss a heart-quake,—for a kiss's strength,
I think it must be reckon'd by its length.

CLXXXVII.

By length I mean duration ; theirs endured
 Heaven knows how long—no doubt they
 never reckon'd ;
And if they had, they could not have secured
 The sum of their sensations to a second :
They had not spoken ; but they felt allured,
 As if their souls and lips each other beckon'd,
Which, being join'd, like swarming bees they
 clung—
Their hearts the flowers from whence the
 honey sprung.

CLXXXVIII.

They were alone, but not alone as they
 Who shut in chambers think it loneliness ;
The silent ocean, and the starlight bay,
 The twilight glow, which momently grew
 less,
The voiceless sands, and dropping caves, that
 lay
 Around them, made them to each other
 press,
As if there were no life beneath the sky
Save theirs, and that their life could never
 die.

CLXXXIX.

They fear'd no eyes nor ears on that lone
 beach,
 They felt no terrors from the night ; they
 were
All in all to each other ; though their speech
 Was broken words, they *thought* a language
 there,—
And all the burning tongues the passions teach
 Found in one sigh the best interpreter
Of nature's oracle—first love,—that all
Which Eve has left her daughters since her
 fall.

CXC.

Haidée spoke not of scruples, ask'd no vows,
 Nor offer'd any ; she had never heard
Of plight and promises to be a spouse,
 Or perils by a loving maid incurr'd ;

She was all which pure ignorance allows,
　　And flew to her young mate like a young
　　　bird,
And never having dreamt of falsehood, she
Had not one word to say of constancy.

CXCI.

She loved, and was beloved—she adored,
　　And she was worshipp'd; after nature's
　　　fashion,
Their intense souls, into each other pour'd,
　　If souls could die, had perish'd in that
　　　passion,—
But by degrees their senses were restored,
　　Again to be o'ercome, again to dash on;
And, beating 'gainst *his* bosom, Haidée's
　　heart
Felt as if never more to beat apart.

CXCII.

Alas! they were so young, so beautiful,
　　So lonely, loving, helpless, and the hour
Was that in which the heart is always full,
　　And, having o'er itself no further power,
Prompts deeds eternity cannot annul,
　　But pays off moments in an endless shower
Of hell-fire—all prepared for people giving
Pleasure or pain to one another living.

CXCIII.

Alas! for Juan and Haidée! they were
　　So loving and so lovely—till then never,
Excepting our first parents, such a pair
　　Had run the risk of being damn'd for ever;
And Haidée, being devout as well as fair,
　　Had, doubtless, heard about the Stygian
　　　river,
And hell and purgatory— but forgot
Just in the very crisis she should not.

CXCIV.

They look upon each other, and their eyes
　　Gleam in the moonlight; and her white
　　　arm clasps
Round Juan's head, and his around her lies
　　Half buried in the tresses which it grasps;
She sits upon his knee, and drinks his sighs,
　　He hers, until they end in broken gasps;
And thus they form a group that's quite
　　antique,
Half naked, loving, natural, and Greek.

CXCV.

And when those deep and burning moments
　　pass'd,
　　And Juan sunk to sleep within her arms,
She slept not, but all tenderly, though fast,
　　Sustain'd his head upon her bosom's
　　　charms;

And now and then her eye to heaven is cast,
　　And then on the pale cheek her breast now
　　　warms,
Pillow'd on her o'erflowing heart, which
　　pants
With all it granted, and with all it grants.

CXCVI.

An infant when it gazes on a light,
　　A child the moment when it drains the
　　　breast,
A devotee when soars the Host in sight,
　　An Arab with a stranger for a guest,
A sailor when the prize has struck in fight,
　　A miser filling his most hoarded chest,
Feel rapture; but not such true joy are
　　reaping
As they who watch o'er what they love while
　　sleeping.

CXCVII.

For there it lies so tranquil, so beloved,
　　All that it hath of life with us is living;
So gentle, stirless, helpless, and unmoved,
　　And all unconscious of the joy 't is giving;
All it hath felt, inflicted, pass'd, and proved,
　　Hush'd into depths beyond the watcher's
　　　diving;
There lies the thing we love with all its
　　errors
And all its charms, like death without its
　　terrors.

CXCVIII.

The lady watch'd her lover—and that hour
　　Of Love's, and Night's, and Ocean's
　　　solitude,
O'erflow'd her soul with their united power;
　　Amidst the barren sand and rocks so rude
She and her wave-worn love had made their
　　bower,
　　Where nought upon their passion could
　　　intrude,
And all the stars that crowded the blue
　　space
Saw nothing happier than her glowing face.

CXCIX.

Alas! the love of women! it is known
　　To be a lovely and a fearful thing;
For all of theirs upon that die is thrown,
　　And if 't is lost, life hath no more to bring
To them but mockeries of the past alone,
　　And their revenge is as the tiger's spring,
Deadly, and quick, and crushing; yet, as
　　real
Torture is theirs, what they inflict they feel.

CC.

They are right; for man, to man so oft
 unjust,
 Is always so to women; one sole bond
Awaits them, treachery is all their trust;
 Taught to conceal, their bursting hearts
 despond
Over their idol, till some wealthier lust
 Buys them in marriage—and what rests
 beyond?
A thankless husband, next a faithless lover,
Then dressing, nursing, praying, and all's
 over.

CCI.

Some take a lover, some take drams or
 prayers,
 Some mind their household, others dissi-
 pation,
Some run away, and but exchange their
 cares,
 Losing the advantage of a virtuous station;
Few changes e'er can better their affairs,
 Theirs being an unnatural situation,
From the dull palace to the dirty hovel:
Some play the devil, and then write a novel.

CCII.

Haidée was Nature's bride, and knew not
 this:
 Haidée was Passion's child, born where
 the sun
Showers triple light, and scorches even the
 kiss
 Of his gazelle-eyed daughters; she was
 one
Made but to love, to feel that she was his
 Who was her chosen: what was said or
 done
Elsewhere was nothing. She had nonght to
 fear,
Hope, care, nor love beyond,—her heart beat
 here.

CCIII.

And oh! that quickening of the heart, that
 beat!
 How much it costs us! yet each rising
 throb
Is in its cause as its effect so sweet,
 That Wisdom, ever on the watch to rob
Joy of its alchemy, and to repeat
 Fine truths; even Conscience, too, has
 a tough job
To make us understand each good old maxim,
So good—I wonder Castlereagh don't tax
 'em.

CCIV.

And now 'twas done—on the lone shore
 were plighted
 Their hearts; the stars, their nuptial
 torches, shed
Beauty upon the beautiful they lighted:
 Ocean their witness, and the cave their bed,
By their own feelings hallow'd and united,
 Their priest was Solitude, and they were wed:
And they were happy, for to their young eyes
Each was an angel, and earth paradise.

CCV.

Oh, Love! of whom great Cæsar was the
 suitor,
 Titus the master, Antony the slave,
Horace, Catullus, scholars, Ovid tutor,
 Sappho the sage blue-stocking, in whose
 grave
All those may leap who rather would be
 neuter—
 (Leucadia's rock still overlooks the wave)—
Oh, Love! thou art the very god of evil,
For, after all, we cannot call thee devil.

CCVI.

Thou mak'st the chaste connubial state
 precarious,
 And jestest with the brows of mightiest
 men:
Cæsar and Pompey, Mahomet, Belisarius,
 Have much employ'd the muse of history's
 pen:
Their lives and fortunes were extremely
 various,
 Such worthies Time will never see again;
Yet to these four in three things the same
 luck holds,
They all were heroes, conquerors, and
 cuckolds.

CCVII.

Thou mak'st philosophers; there's Epicurus
 And Aristippus, a material crew!
Who to immoral courses would allure us
 By theories quite practicable too;
If only from the devil they would insure us,
 How pleasant were the maxim (not quite
 new),
"Eat, drink, and love; what can the rest
 avail us?"
So said the royal sage Sardanapalus.

CCVIII.

But Juan! had he quite forgotten Julia?
 And should he have forgotten her so soon?
I can't but say it seems to me most truly a
 Perplexing question; but, no doubt, the
 moon

Does these things for us, and whenever
 newly a
 Strong palpitation rises, 't is her boon,
Else how the devil is it that fresh features
Have such a charm for us poor human
 creatures?

CCIX.

I hate inconstancy—I loathe, detest,
 Abhor, condemn, abjure the mortal made
Of such quicksilver clay that in his breast
 No permanent foundation can be laid;
Love, constant love, has been my constant
 guest,
 And yet last night, being at a masquerade,
I saw the prettiest creature, fresh from Milan,
Which gave me some sensations like a
 villain.

CCX.

But soon Philosophy came to my aid,
 And whisper'd, "Think of every sacred
 tie!"
" I will, my dear Philosophy!" I said,
 "But then her teeth, and then, oh, Heaven!
 her eye!
I 'll just inquire if she be wife or maid,
 Or neither—out of curiosity."
" Stop!" cried Philosophy, with air so
 Grecian
(Though she was masqued then as a fair
 Venetian);

CCXI.

" Stop!" so I stopp'd.—But to return: that
 which
Men call inconstancy is nothing more
Than admiration due where nature's rich
 Profusion with young beauty covers o'er
Some favour'd object; and as in the niche
 A lovely statue we almost adore,
This sort of adoration of the real
Is but a heightening of the "beau ideal."

CCXII.

'T is the perception of the beautiful,
 A fine extension of the faculties,
Platonic, universal, wonderful,
 Drawn from the stars, and filter'd through
 the skies,
Without which life would be extremely dull;
 In short, it is the use of our own eyes,
With one or two small senses added, just
To hint that flesh is form'd of fiery dust.

CCXIII.

Yet 't is a painful feeling, and unwilling,
 For surely if we always could perceive
In the same object graces quite as killing
 As when she rose upon us like an Eve,

'T would save us many a heart-ache, many
 a shilling
 (For we must get them anyhow, or grieve),
Whereas, if one sole lady pleased for ever,
How pleasant for the heart, as well as liver!

CCXIV.

The heart is like the sky, a part of heaven,
 But changes night and day, too, like the
 sky;
Now o'er it clouds and thunder must be
 driven,
 And darkness and destruction as on high:
But when it hath been scorch'd, and pierced,
 and riven,
 Its storms expire in water-drops; the eye
Pours forth at last the heart's blood turn'd
 to tears,—
Which make the English climate of our
 years.

CCXV.

The liver is the lazaret of bile,
 But very rarely executes its function,
For the first passion stays there such a while,
 That all the rest creep in and form a
 junction,
Like knots of vipers on a dunghill's soil,
 Rage, fear, hate, jealousy, revenge, com-
 punction,
So that all mischiefs spring up from this
 entrail,
Like earthquakes from the hidden fire call'd
 "central."

CCXVI.

In the mean time, without proceeding more
 In this anatomy, I 've finish'd now
Two hundred and odd stanzas as before,
 That being about the number I 'll allow
Each canto of the twelve, or twenty-four;
 And, laying down my pen, I make my bow,
Leaving Don Juan and Haidée to plead
For them and theirs with all who deign to
 read.

Canto the Third.

I.

Hail, Muse! *et cætera.*—We left Juan
 sleeping,
 Pillow'd upon a fair and happy breast,
And watch'd by eyes that never yet knew
 weeping,
 And loved by a young heart, too deeply
 blest

To feel the poison through her spirit
 creeping,
Or know who rested there, a foe to rest,
Had soil'd the current of her sinless years,
And turn'd her pure heart's purest blood to
 tears !

II.

Oh, Love ! what is it in this world of ours
 Which makes it fatal to be loved ? Ah why
With cypress branches hast thou wreathed
 thy bowers,
 And made thy best interpreter a sigh ?
As those who dote on odours pluck the
 flowers,
 And place them on their breast—but place
 to die—
Thus the frail beings we would fondly cherish
Are laid within our bosoms but to perish.

III.

In her first passion woman loves her lover,
 In all the others all she loves is love,
Which grows a habit she can ne'er get over
 And fits her loosely—like an easy glove,
As you may find, whene'er you like to prove
 her :
 One man alone at first her heart can
 move ;
She then prefers him in the plural number,
Not finding that the additions much en-
 cumber.

IV.

I know not if the fault be men's or theirs ;
 But one thing's pretty sure ; a woman
 planted
(Unless at once she plunge for life in
 prayers)—
After a decent time must be gallanted ;
Although, no doubt, her first of love affairs
 Is that to which her heart is wholly
 granted ;
Yet there are some, they say, who have had
 none,
But those who have ne'er end with only *one*.

V.

'Tis melancholy, and a fearful sign
 Of human frailty, folly, also crime,
That love and marriage rarely can combine,
 Although they both are born in the same
 clime ;
Marriage from love, like vinegar from wine—
 A sad, sour, sober beverage—by time
Is sharpen'd from its high celestial flavour,
Down to a very homely household savour.

VI.

There's something of antipathy, as 'twere,
 Between their present and their future
 state ;
A kind of flattery that's hardly fair
 Is used until the truth arrives too late—
Yet what can people do, except despair ?
 The same things change their names at
 such a rate ;
For instance—passion in a lover's glorious,
But in a husband is pronounced uxorious.

VII.

Men grow ashamed of being so very fond ;
 They sometimes also get a little tired
(But that, of course, is rare), and then de-
 spond :
 The same things cannot always be admired,
Yet 'tis "so nominated in the bond,"
 That both are tied till one shall have ex-
 pired.
Sad thought ! to lose the spouse that was
 adorning
Our days, and put one's servants into mourn-
 ing.

VIII.

There's doubtless something in domestic
 doings
 Which forms, in fact, true love's antithe-
 sis ;
Romances paint at full length people's woo-
 ings,
 But only give a bust of marriages ;
For no one cares for matrimonial cooings,
 There's nothing wrong in a connubial kiss :
Think you, if Laura had been Petrarch's wife,
He would have written sonnets all his life ?

IX.

All tragedies are finish'd by a death,
 All comedies are ended by a marriage ;
The future states of both are left to faith,
 For authors fear description might dis-
 parage
The worlds to come of both, or fall beneath,
 And then both worlds would punish their
 miscarriage ;
So leaving each their priest and prayer-book
 ready,
They say no more of Death or of the Lady.

X.

The only two that in my recollection
 Have sung of heaven and hell, or marriage,
 are
Dante and Milton, and of both the affection
 Was hapless in their nuptials, for some bar

Of fault or temper ruin'd the connexion
 (Such things, in fact, it don't ask much to
 mar);
But Dante's Beatrice and Milton's Eve
Were not drawn from their spouses, you con-
 ceive.

XI.

Some persons say that Dante meant theology
 By Beatrice, and not a mistress—I,
Although my opinion may require apology,
 Deem this a commentator's phantasy,
Unless indeed it was from his own knowledge
 he
 Decided thus, and show'd good reason
 why;
I think that Dante's more abstruse ecstatics
Meant to personify the mathematics.

XII.

Haidée and Juan were not married, but
 The fault was theirs, not mine: it is not
 fair,
Chaste reader, then, in any way to put
 The blame on me, unless you wish they
 were;
Then if you'd have them wedded, please to
 shut
 The book which treats of this erroneous
 pair,
Before the consequences grow too awful;
'Tis dangerous to read of loves unlawful.

XIII.

Yet they were happy,—happy in the illicit
 Indulgence of their innocent desires;
But more imprudent grown with every visit,
 Haidée forgot the island was her sire's:
When we have what we like, 'tis hard to
 miss it,
 At least in the beginning, ere one tires;
Thus she came often, not a moment losing,
Whilst her piratical papa was cruising.

XIV.

Let not his mode of raising cash seem
 strange,
 Although he fleeced the flags of every na-
 tion,
For into a prime minister but change
 His title, and 't is nothing but taxation;
But he, more modest, took an humbler range
 Of life, and in an honester vocation
Pursued o'er the high seas his watery jour-
 ney,
And merely practised as a sea-attorney.

XV.

The good old gentleman had been detain'd
 By winds and waves, and some important
 captures;
And, in the hope of more, at sea remain'd,
 Although a squall or two had damp'd his
 raptures,
By swamping one of the prizes; he had
 chain'd
 His prisoners, dividing them like chapters
In number'd lots; they all had cuffs and col-
 lars,
And averaged each from ten to a hundred
 dollars.

XVI.

Some he disposed of off Cape Matapan,
 Among his friends the Mainots; some he
 sold
To his Tunis correspondents, save one man
 Toss'd overboard unsaleable (being old):
The rest—save here and there some richer
 one,
 Reserved for future ransom—in the hold,
Were link'd alike, as for the common people
 he
Had a large order from the Dey of Tripoli.

XVII.

The merchandise was served in the same way,
 Pieced out for different marts in the Le-
 vant,
Except some certain portions of the prey,
 Light classic articles of female want,
French stuffs, lace, tweezers, toothpicks, tea-
 pot, tray,
 Guitars and castanets from Alicant,
All which selected from the spoil he gathers,
Robb'd for his daughter by the best of fathers.

XVIII.

A monkey, a Dutch mastiff, a mackaw,
 Two parrots, with a Persian cat and kittens,
He chose from several animals he saw—
 A terrier, too, which once had been a Bri-
 ton's,
Who dying on the coast of Ithaca,
 The peasants gave the poor dumb thing a
 pittance.
These to secure in this strong blowing wea-
 ther,
He caged in one huge hamper all together.

XIX.

Then having settled his marine affairs,
 Despatching single cruisers here and there,
His vessel having need of some repairs,
 He shaped his course to where his daugh-
 ter fair

Continued still her hospitable cares;
　But that part of the coast being shoal and
　　bare,
And rough with reefs which ran out many
　　a mile,
His port lay on the other side o' the isle.

XX.

And there he went ashore without delay,
　Having no custom-house nor quarantine
To ask him awkward questions on the way,
　About the time and place where he had
　　been:
He left his ship to be hove down next day,
　With orders to the people to careen;
So that all hands were busy beyond measure,
In getting out goods, ballast, guns, and trea-
　　sure.

XXI.

Arriving at the summit of a hill
　Which overlook'd the white walls of his
　　home,
He stopp'd.—What singular emotions fill
　Their bosoms who have been induced to
　　roam!
With fluttering doubts if all be well or ill—
　With love for many, and with fears for
　　some;
All feelings which o'erleap the years long
　　lost,
And bring our hearts back to their starting-
　　post.

XXII.

The approach of home to husbands and to
　　sires,
　After long travelling by land or water,
Most naturally some small doubt inspires—
　A female family's a serious matter;
(None trusts the sex more, or so much ad-
　　mires—
　But they hate flattery, so I never flatter;)
Wives in their husbands' absences grow sub-
　　tler,
And daughters sometimes run off with the
　　butler.

XXIII.

An honest gentleman at his return
　May not have the good fortune of Ulysses;
Not all lone matrons for their husbands
　　mourn,
　Or show the same dislike to suitors' kisses;
The odds are that he finds a handsome urn
　To his memory—and two or three young
　　misses
Born to some friend, who holds his wife and
　　riches;—
And that *his* Argus bites him by—the
　　breeches.

XXIV.

If single, probably his plighted fair
　Has in his absence wedded some rich
　　miser;
But all the better, for the happy pair
　May quarrel, and the lady growing wiser,
He may resume his amatory care
　As cavalier servente, or despise her;
And that his sorrow may not be a dumb one,
Write odes on the Inconstancy of Woman.

XXV.

And oh! ye gentlemen who have already
　Some chaste *liaison* of the kind—I mean
An honest friendship with a married lady—
　The only thing of this sort ever seen
To last—of all connexions the most steady,
　And the true Hymen, (the first's but a
　　screen)—
Yet for all that keep not too long away;
I've known the absent wrong'd four times a
　　day.

XXVI.

Lambro, our sea-solicitor, who had
　Much less experience of dry land than
　　ocean,
On seeing his own chimney-smoke, felt glad;
　But not knowing metaphysics, had no no-
　　tion
Of the true reason of his not being sad,
　Or that of any other strong emotion;
He loved his child, and would have wept the
　　loss of her,
But knew the cause no more than a philo-
　　sopher.

XXVII.

He saw his white walls shining in the sun,
　His garden trees all shadowy and green;
He heard his rivulet's light bubbling run,
　The distant dog-bark; and perceived be-
　　tween
The umbrage of the wood so cool and dun,
　The moving figures, and the sparkling
　　sheen
Of arms (in the East all arm)—and various
　　dyes
Of colour'd garbs, as bright as butterflies.

XXVIII.

And as the spot where they appear he nears,
　Surprised at these unwonted signs of
　　idling,
He hears—alas! no music of the spheres,
　But an unhallow'd, earthly sound of
　　fiddling!

A melody which made him doubt his ears,
 The cause being past his guessing or un-
 riddling;
A pipe, too, and a drum, and shortly after,
A most unoriental roar of laughter.

XXIX.

And still more nearly to the place advancing,
 Descending rather quickly the declivity,
Through the waved branches, o'er the green-
 sward glancing,
 'Midst other indications of festivity,
Seeing a troop of his domestics dancing
 Like dervises, who turn as on a pivot, he
Perceived it was the Pyrrhic dance so mar-
 tial,
To which the Levantines are very partial.

XXX.

And further on a group of Grecian girls,
 The first and tallest her white kerchief
 waving,
Were strung together like a row of pearls,
 Link'd hand in hand, and dancing: each
 too having
Down her white neck long floating auburn
 curls—
 (The least of which would set ten poets
 raving);
Their leader sang—and bounded to her song,
With choral step and voice, the virgin throng.

XXXI.

And here, assembled cross-legg'd round their
 trays,
 Small social parties just begun to dine;
Pilaus and meats of all sorts met the gaze,
 And flasks of Samian and of Chian wine,
And sherbet cooling in the porous vase;
 Above them their dessert grew on its
 vine,
The orange and pomegranate nodding o'er
Dropp'd in their laps, scarce pluck'd, their
 mellow store.

XXXII.

A band of children, round a snow-white ram,
 There wreathe his venerable horns with
 flowers;
While peaceful as if still an unwean'd lamb,
 The patriarch of the flock all gently cowers
His sober head, majestically tame,
 Or eats from out the palm, or playful
 lowers
His brow, as if in act to butt, and then
Yielding to their small hands, draws back
 again.

XXXIII.

Their classical profiles, and glittering dresses,
 Their large black eyes, and soft seraphic
 cheeks,
Crimson as cleft pomegranates, their long
 tresses,
 The gesture which enchants, the eye that
 speaks,
The innocence which happy childhood blesses,
 Made quite a picture of these little Greeks;
So that the philosophical beholder
Sigh'd for their sakes—that they should e'er
 grow older.

XXXIV.

Afar, a dwarf buffoon stood telling tales
 To a sedate grey circle of old smokers,
Of secret treasures found in hidden vales,
 Of wonderful replies from Arab jokers,
Of charms to make good gold and cure bad
 ails,
 Of rocks bewitch'd that open to the
 knockers,
Of magic ladies who, by one sole act,
Transform'd their lords to beasts (but that's
 a fact).

XXXV.

Here was no lack of innocent diversion
 For the imagination or the senses,
Song, dance, wine, music, stories from the
 Persian,
 All pretty pastimes in which no offence is;
But Lambro saw all these things with aver-
 sion,
 Perceiving in his absence such expenses,
Dreading that climax of all human ills
The inflammation of his weekly bills.

XXXVI.

Ah! what is man? what perils still environ
 The happiest mortals even after dinner!
A day of gold from out an age of iron
 Is all that life allows the luckiest sinner;
Pleasure (whene'er she sings, at least) 's a
 siren,
 That lures, to flay alive, the young be-
 ginner;
Lambro's reception at his people's banquet
Was such as fire accords to a wet blanket.

XXXVII.

He—being a man who seldom used a word
 Too much, and wishing gladly to surprise
(In general he surprised men with the sword)
 His daughter—had not sent before to
 advise

Of his arrival, so that no one stirr'd;
 And long he paused to reässure his eyes,
In fact much more astonish'd than delighted,
To find so much good company invited.

XXXVIII.

He did not know (alas! how men will lie!)
 That a report (especially the Greeks)
Avouch'd his death (such people never die),
 And put his house in mourning several
 weeks,—
But now their eyes and also lips were dry;
 The bloom, too, had return'd to Haidée's
 cheeks.
Her tears, too, being return'd into their fount,
She now kept house upon her own account.

XXXIX.

Hence all this rice, meat, dancing, wine, and
 fiddling,
 Which turn'd the isle into a place of plea-
 sure;
The servants all were getting drunk or idling,
 A life which made them happy beyond
 measure.
Her father's hospitality seem'd middling,
 Compared with what Haidée did with his
 treasure;
'T was wonderful how things went on im-
 proving,
While she had not one hour to spare from
 loving.

XL.

Perhaps you think, in stumbling on this
 feast,
 He flew into a passion, and in fact
There was no mighty reason to be pleased;
 Perhaps you prophesy some sudden act,
The whip, the rack, or dungeon at the least,
 To teach his people to be more exact,
And that, proceeding at a very high rate,
He show'd the royal *penchants* of a pirate.

XLI.

You're wrong.—He was the mildest manner'd
 man
 That ever scuttled ship or cut a throat,
With such true breeding of a gentleman,
 You never could divine his real thought,
No courtier could, and scarcely woman can
 Gird more deceit within a petticoat;
Pity he loved adventurous life's variety,
He was so great a loss to good society.

XLII.

Advancing to the nearest dinner tray,
 Tapping the shoulder of the nighest guest,
With a peculiar smile, which, by the way,
 Boded no good, whatever it express'd,

He asked the meaning of this holiday;
 The vinous Greek to whom he had ad-
 dress'd
His question, much too merry to divine
The questioner, fill'd up a glass of wine,

XLIII.

And without turning his facetious head,
 Over his shoulder, with a Bacchant air,
Presented the o'erflowing cup, and said,
 "Talking's dry work, I have no time to
 spare."
A second hiccup'd, "Our old master's dead,
 You'd better ask our mistress who's his
 heir."
"Our mistress!" quoth a third: "Our mis-
 tress!—pooh—
You mean our master—not the old, but new."

XLIV.

These rascals, being new comers, knew not
 whom
 They thus address'd—and Lambro's visage
 fell—
And o'er his eye a momentary gloom
 Pass'd, but he strove quite courteously to
 quell
The expression, and endeavouring to resume
 His smile, requested one of them to tell
The name and quality of his new patron,
Who seem'd to have turn'd Haidée into a
 matron.

XLV.

"I know not," quoth the fellow, "who or
 what
 He is, nor whence he came—and little
 care;
But this I know, that this roast capon's fat,
 And that good wine ne'er wash'd down
 better fare;
And if you are not satisfied with that,
 Direct your questions to my neighbour
 there;
He'll answer all for better or for worse,
For none likes more to hear himself con-
 verse."

XLVI.

I said that Lambro was a man of patience,
 And certainly he show'd the best of
 breeding,
Which scarce even France, the paragon of
 nations,
 E'er saw her most polite of sons exceeding;
He bore these sneers against his near re-
 lations,
 His own anxiety, his heart, too, bleeding,
The insults, too, of every servile glutton,
Who all the time was eating up his mutton.

XLVII.

Now in a person used to much command—
　To bid men come, and go, and come
　　again—
To see his orders done, too, out of hand—
　Whether the word was death, or but the
　　chain—
It may seem strange to find his manners
　bland;
　Yet such things are, which I cannot ex-
　　plain,
Though doubtless he who can command
　himself
Is good to govern—almost as a Guelf.

XLVIII.

Not that he was not sometimes rash or so,
　But never in his real and serious mood;
Then calm, concentrated, and still, and slow,
　He lay coil'd like the boa in the wood;
With him it never was a word and blow,
　His angry word once o'er, he shed no blood,
But in his silence there was much to rue,
And his *one* blow left little work for *two*.

XLIX.

He ask'd no further questions, and proceeded
　On to the house, but by a private way,
So that the few who met him hardly heeded,
　So little they expected him that day;
If love paternal in his bosom pleaded
　For Haidée's sake, is more than I can say,
But certainly to one deem'd dead returning,
This revel seem'd a curious mode of mourn-
　ing.

L.

If all the dead could now return to life,
　(Which God forbid!) or some, or a great
　　many,
For instance, if a husband or his wife
　(Nuptial examples are as good as any),
No doubt whate'er might be their former
　strife,
　The present weather would be much more
　　rainy—
Tears shed into the grave of the connexion
Would share most probably its resurrection.

LI.

He enter'd in the house no more his home,
　A thing to human feelings the most trying,
And harder for the heart to overcome,
　Perhaps, than even the mental pangs of
　　dying;
To find our hearthstone turn'd into a tomb,
　And round its once warm precincts palely
　　lying
The ashes of our hopes, is a deep grief,
Beyond a single gentleman's belief.

LII.

He enter'd in the house—his home no more,
　For without hearts there is no home;—and
　　felt
The solitude of passing his own door
　Without a welcome: *there* he long had
　　dwelt,
There his few peaceful days Time had swept
　o'er,
　There his warm bosom and keen eye would
　　melt
Over the innocence of that sweet child,
His only shrine of feelings undefiled.

LIII.

He was a man of a strange temperament,
　Of mild demeanour though of savage mood,
Moderate in all his habits, and content
　With temperance in pleasure, as in food,
Quick to perceive, and strong to bear, and
　meant
　For something better, if not wholly good;
His country's wrongs and his despair to
　save her
Had stung him from a slave to an enslaver.

LIV.

The love of power, and rapid gain of gold,
　The hardness by long habitude produced,
The dangerous life in which he had grown old,
　The mercy he had granted oft abused,
The sights he was accustom'd to behold,
　The wild seas, and wild men with whom
　　he cruised,
Had cost his enemies a long repentance,
And made him a good friend, but bad ac-
　quaintance.

LV.

But something of the spirit of old Greece
　Flash'd o'er his soul a few heroic rays,
Such as lit onward to the Golden Fleece
　His predecessors in the Colchian days;
'T is true he had no ardent love for peace—
　Alas! his country show'd no path to
　　praise:
Hate to the world and war with every na-
　tion
He waged, in vengeance of her degradation.

LVI.

Still o'er his mind the influence of the clime
　Shed its Ionian elegance, which show'd
Its power unconsciously full many a time,—
　A taste seen in the choice of his abode,
A love of music and of scenes sublime,
　A pleasure in the gentle stream that flow'd
Past him in crystal, and a joy in flowers,
Bedew'd his spirit in his calmer hours.

LVII.

But whatsoe'er he had of love reposed
 On that beloved daughter; she had been
The only thing which kept his heart un-
 closed
 Amidst the savage deeds he had done and
 seen,
A lonely pure affection unopposed:
 There wanted but the loss of this to wean
His feelings from all milk of human kind-
 ness,
And turn him like the Cyclops mad with
 blindness.

LVIII.

The cubless tigress in her jungle raging
 Is dreadful to the shepherd and the flock;
The ocean when its yeasty war is waging
 Is awful to the vessel near the rock;
But violent things will sooner bear as-
 suaging,
 Their fury being spent by its own shock,
Than the stern, single, deep, and wordless ire
Of a strong human heart, and in a sire.

LIX.

It is a hard although a common case
 To find our children running restive—they
In whom our brightest days we would re-
 trace,
 Our little selves re-formed in finer clay,
Just as old age is creeping on apace,
 And clouds come o'er the sunset of our
 day,
They kindly leave us, though not quite
 alone,
But in good company—the gout or stone.

LX.

Yet a fine family is a fine thing
 (Provided they don't come in after dinner);
'T is beautiful to see a matron bring
 Her children up (if nursing them don't
 thin her);
Like cherubs round an altar-piece they cling
 To the fire-side (a sight to touch a sinner).
A lady with her daughters or her nieces
Shine like a guinea and seven-shilling pieces.

LXI.

Old Lambro pass'd unseen a private gate,
 And stood within his hall at eventide;
Meantime the lady and her lover sate
 At wassail in their beauty and their pride:
An ivory inlaid table spread with state
 Before them, and fair slaves on every side;
Gems, gold, and silver, form'd the service
 mostly,
Mother of pearl and coral the less costly.

LXII.

The dinner made about a hundred dishes;
 Lamb and pistachio nuts—in short, all
 meats,
And saffron soups, and sweetbreads; and the
 fishes
 Were of the finest that e'er flounced in nets.
Drest to a Sybarite's most pamper'd wishes;
 The beverage was various sherbets
Of raisin, orange, and pomegranate juice,
Squeezed through the rind, which makes it
 best for use.

LXIII.

These were ranged round, each in its crystal
 ewer,
 And fruits, and date-bread loaves closed
 the repast,
And Mocha's berry, from Arabia pure,
 In small fine China cups, came in at last;
Gold cups of filigree made to secure
 The hand from burning underneath them
 placed,
Cloves, cinnamon, and saffron too were boil'd
Up with the coffee, which (I think) they
 spoil'd.

LXIV.

The hangings of the room were tapestry, made
 Of velvet panels, each of different hue,
And thick with damask flowers of silk inlaid;
 And round them ran a yellow border too;
The upper border, richly wrought, display'd,
 Embroider'd delicately o'er with blue,
Soft Persian sentences, in lilac letters,
From poets, or the moralists their betters.

LXV.

These Oriental writings on the wall,
 Quite common in those countries, are a
 kind
Of monitors adapted to recall,
 Like skulls at Memphian banquets, to the
 mind
The words which shook Belshazzar in his
 hall,
 And took his kingdom from him: You will
 find,
Though sages may pour out their wisdom's
 treasure,
There is no sterner moralist than Pleasure.

LXVI.

A beauty at the season's close grown hectic,
 A genius who has drunk himself to death,
A rake turn'd methodistic, or Eclectic—
 (For that's the name they like to pray
 beneath)—

But most, an alderman struck apoplectic,
 Are things that really take away the
 breath,—
And show that late hours, wine, and love are
 able
To do not much less damage than the table.

LXVII.

Haidée and Juan carpeted their feet
 On crimson satin, border'd with pale blue;
Their sofa occupied three parts complete
 Of the apartment—and appear'd quite new;
The velvet cushions (for a throne more meet)
 Were scarlet, from whose glowing centre
 grew
A sun emboss'd in gold, whose rays of tissue,
Meridian-like, were seen all light to issue.

LXVIII.

Crystal and marble, plate and porcelain,
 Had done their work of splendour; Indian
 mats
And Persian carpets, which the heart bled to
 stain,
 Over the floors were spread; gazelles and
 cats,
And dwarfs and blacks, and such like things
 that gain
 Their bread as ministers and favourites—
 (that's
To say, by degradation)—mingled there
As plentiful as in a court or fair.

LXIX.

There was no want of lofty mirrors, and
 The tables, most of ebony inlaid
With mother of pearl or ivory, stood at hand,
 Or were of tortoise-shell or rare woods
 made,
Fretted with gold or silver :—by command,
 The greater part of these were ready spread
With viands and sherbets in ice—and wine—
Kept for all comers at all hours to dine.

LXX.

Of all the dresses I select Haidée's :
 She wore two jelicks—one was of pale
 yellow;
Of azure, pink, and white was her chemise—
 'Neath which her breast heaved like a little
 billow,
With buttons form'd of pearls as large as peas,
 All gold and crimson shone her jelick's
 fellow,
And the striped white gauze baracan that
 bound her,
Like fleecy clouds about the moon, flow'd
 round her.

LXXI.

One large gold bracelet clasp'd each lovely
 arm,
 Lockless—so pliable from the pure gold
That the hand stretch'd and shut it without
 harm,
 The limb which it adorn'd its only mould;
So beautiful—its very shape would charm,
 And clinging as if loath to lose its hold;
The purest ore enclosed the whitest skin
That e'er by precious metal was held in.

LXXII.

Around, as princess of her father's land,
 A like gold bar above her instep roll'd
Announced her rank; twelve rings were on
 her hand;
 Her hair was starr'd with gems; her veil's
 fine fold
Below her breast was fasten'd with a band
 Of lavish pearls, whose worth could scarce
 be told;
Her orange silk full Turkish trousers furl'd
About the prettiest ankle in the world.

LXXIII.

Her hair's long auburn waves down to her heel
 Flow'd like an Alpine torrent which the sun
Dyes with his morning light,—and would
 conceal
 Her person if allow'd at large to run;
And still they seem'd resentfully to feel
 The silken fillet's curb, and sought to shun
Their bonds whene'er some Zephyr caught
 began
To offer his young pinion as her fan.

LXXIV.

Round her she made an atmosphere of life,
 The very air seem'd lighter from her eyes,
They were so soft and beautiful, and rife
 With all we can imagine of the skies,
And pure as Psyche ere she grew a wife—
 Too pure even for the purest human ties;
Her overpowering presence made you feel
It would not be idolatry to kneel.

LXXV.

Her eyelashes, though dark as night, were
 tinged
 (It is the country's custom), but in vain;
For those large black eyes were so blackly
 fringed,
 The glossy rebels mock'd the jetty stain,
And in their native beauty stood avenged:
 Her nails were touch'd with henna; but
 again
The power of art was turn'd to nothing, for
They could not look more rosy than before.

LXXVI.

The henna should be deeply dyed to make
 The skin relieved appear more fairly fair;
She had no need of this, day ne'er will break
 On mountain-tops more heavenly white
 than her:
The eye might doubt if it were well awake,
 She was so like a vision; I might err,
But Shakspeare also says, 'tis very silly
"To gild refined gold, or paint the lily."

LXXVII.

Juan had on a shawl of black and gold,
 But a white baracan, and so transparent
The sparkling gems beneath you might behold,
 Like small stars through the milky way
 apparent;
His turban furl'd in many a graceful fold,
 An emerald aigrette with Haidée's hair in 't
Surmounted, as its clasp, a glowing crescent,
Whose rays shone ever trembling, but in-
 cessant.

LXXVIII.

And now they were diverted by their suite,
 Dwarfs, dancing-girls, black eunuchs, and
 a poet,
Which made their new establishment com-
 plete;
 The last was of great fame, and liked to
 show it;
His verses rarely wanted their due feet—
 And for his theme—he seldom sung below it,
He being paid to satirise or flatter,
As the psalm says, "inditing a good matter."

LXXIX.

He praised the present, and abused the past,
 Reversing the good custom of old days,
An Eastern anti-jacobin at last
 He turn'd, preferring pudding to *no* praise—
For some few years his lot had been o'ercast
 By his seeming independent in his lays,
But now he sung the Sultan and the Pacha
With truth like Southey, and with verse like
 Crashaw.

LXXX.

He was a man who had seen many changes,
 And always changed as true as any needle;
His polar star being one which rather ranges,
 And not the fix'd—he knew the way to
 wheedle;
So vile he 'scaped the doom which oft avenges;
 And being fluent (save indeed when fee'd
 ill),
He lied with such a fervour of intention—
There was no doubt he earn'd his laureate
 pension.

LXXXI.

But he had genius,—when a turncoat has it,
 The "Vates irritabilis" takes care
That without notice few full moons shall
 pass it;
 Even good men like to make the public
 stare:—
But to my subject—let me see—what was
 it?—
Oh!—the third canto—and the pretty pair—
Their loves, and feasts, and house, and dress,
 and mode
Of living in their insular abode.

LXXXII.

Their poet, a sad trimmer, but no less
 In company a very pleasant fellow,
Had been the favourite of full many a mess
 Of men, and made them speeches when
 half mellow;
And though his meaning they could rarely
 guess,
 Yet still they deign'd to hiccup or to bellow
The glorious meed of popular applause,
Of which the first ne'er knows the second
 cause.

LXXXIII.

But now being lifted into high society,
 And having pick'd up several odds and ends
Of free thoughts in his travels, for variety,
 He deem'd, being in a lone isle, among
 friends,
That without any danger of a riot, he
 Might for long lying make himself amends;
And singing as he sung in his warm youth,
Agree to a short armistice with truth.

LXXXIV.

He had travell'd 'mongst the Arabs, Turks,
 and Franks,
 And knew the self-loves of the different
 nations;
And having lived with people of all ranks,
 Had something ready upon most occasions—
Which got him a few presents and some
 thanks.
 He varied with some skill his adulations;
To "do at Rome as Romans do," a piece
Of conduct was which he observed in Greece.

LXXXV.

Thus, usually, when he was asked to sing,
 He gave the different nations something
 national;
'Twas all the same to him—"God save the
 king,"
Or "*Ça ira*," according to the fashion all:

His muse made increment of anything,
 From the high lyric down to the low
 rational:
If Pindar sang horse-races, what should
 hinder
Himself from being as pliable as Pindar?

LXXXVI.

In France, for instance, he would write a
 chanson;
In England a six canto quarto tale;
In Spain he'd make a ballad or romance on
 The last war—much the same in Portugal;
In Germany, the Pegasus he'd prance on
 Would be old Goethe's—(see what says De
 Staël);
In Italy he'd ape the "Trecentisti;"
In Greece, he'd sing some sort of hymn like
 this t' ye:

1.

The isles of Greece, the isles of Greece!
 Where burning Sappho loved and sung,
Where grew the arts of war and peace,
 Where Delos rose, and Phœbus sprung!
Eternal summer gilds them yet,
But all, except their sun, is set.

2.

The Scian and the Teian muse,
 The hero's harp, the lover's lute,
Have found the fame your shores refuse:
 Their place of birth alone is mute
To sounds which echo further west
Than your sires' "Islands of the Blest."

3.

The mountains look on Marathon—
 And Marathon looks on the sea;
And musing there an hour alone,
 I dream'd that Greece might still be free;
For standing on the Persians' grave,
I could not deem myself a slave.

4.

A king sate on the rocky brow
 Which looks o'er sea-born Salamis;
And ships, by thousands, lay below,
 And men in nations;—all were his!
He counted them at break of day—
And when the sun set where were they?

5.

And where are they? and where art thou,
 My country? On thy voiceless shore
The heroic lay is tuneless now—
 The heroic bosom beats no more!
And must thy lyre, so long divine,
Degenerate into hands like mine?

6.

'Tis something, in the dearth of fame,
 Though link'd among a fetter'd race,
To feel at least a patriot's shame,
 Even as I sing, suffuse my face;
For what is left the poet here?
For Greeks a blush—for Greece a tear.

7.

Must *we* but weep o'er days more blest?
 Must *we* but blush?—Our fathers bled.
Earth! render back from out thy breast
 A remnant of our Spartan dead!
Of the three hundred grant but three,
To make a new Thermopylæ!

8.

What, silent still? and silent all?
 Ah! no;—the voices of the dead
Sound like a distant torrent's fall,
 And answer, "Let one living head,
But one arise,—we come, we come!"
'Tis but the living who are dumb.

9.

In vain—in vain: strike other chords;
 Fill high the cup with Samian wine!
Leave battles to the Turkish hordes,
 And shed the blood of Scio's vine!
Hark! rising to the ignoble call—
How answers each bold Bacchanal!

10.

You have the Pyrrhic dance as yet;
 Where is the Pyrrhic phalanx gone?
Of two such lessons, why forget
 The nobler and the manlier one?
You have the letters Cadmus gave—
Think ye he meant them for a slave?

11.

Fill high the bowl with Samian wine!
 We will not think of themes like these!
It made Anacreon's song divine:
 He served—but served Polycrates—
A tyrant; but our masters then
Were still, at least, our countrymen.

12.

The tyrant of the Chersonese
 Was freedom's best and bravest friend;
That tyrant was Miltiades!
 Oh! that the present hour would lend
Another despot of the kind!
Such chains as his were sure to bind.

13.

Fill high the bowl with Samian wine!
 On Suli's rock, and Parga's shore,
Exists the remnant of a line
 Such as the Doric mothers bore;
And there, perhaps, some seed is sown,
The Heracleidan blood might own.

14.

Trust not for freedom to the Franks—
 They have a king who buys and sells;
In native swords, and native ranks,
 The only hope of courage dwells:
But Turkish force, and Latin fraud,
Would break your shield, however broad.

15.

Fill high the bowl with Samian wine!
 Our virgins dance beneath the shade—
I see their glorious black eyes shine;
 But gazing on each glowing maid,
My own the burning tear-drop laves,
To think such breasts must suckle slaves.

16.

Place me on Sunium's marbled steep,
 Where nothing, save the waves and I,
May hear our mutual murmurs sweep;
 There, swan-like, let me sing and die:
A land of slaves shall ne'er be mine—
Dash down yon cup of Samian wine!

LXXXVII.

Thus sung, or would, or could, or should
 have sung,
 The modern Greek, in tolerable verse;
If not like Orpheus quite, when Greece was
 young,
 Yet in these times he might have done
 much worse:
His strain display'd some feeling—right or
 wrong;
 And feeling, in a poet, is the source
Of others' feeling; but they are such liars,
And take all colours—like the hands of dyers.

LXXXVIII.

But words are things, and a small drop of ink,
 Falling like dew, upon a thought, produces
That which makes thousands, perhaps mil-
 lions, think;
 'Tis strange, the shortest letter which
 man uses
Instead of speech, may form a lasting link
 Of ages; to what straits old Time reduces
Frail man, when paper—even a rag like this,
Survives himself, his tomb, and all that's his!

LXXXIX.

And when his bones are dust, his grave a
 blank,
 His station, generation, even his nation,
Become a thing, or nothing, save to rank
 In chronological commemoration,
Some dull MS. oblivion long has sank,
 Or graven stone found in a barrack's
 station
In digging the foundation of a closet,
May turn his name up, as a rare deposit.

XC.

And glory long has made the sages smile;
 'Tis something, nothing, words, illusion,
 wind—
Depending more upon the historian's style
 Than on the name a person leaves behind:
Troy owes to Homer what whist owes to
 Hoyle:
 The present century was growing blind
To the great Marlborough's skill in giving
 knocks,
Until his late Life by Archdeacon Coxe.

XCI.

Milton's the prince of poets—so we say;
 A little heavy, but no less divine:
An independent being in his day—
 Learn'd, pious, temperate in love and wine;
But his life falling into Johnson's way,
 We're told this great high priest of all the
 Nine
Was whipt at college—a harsh sire—odd
 spouse,
For the first Mrs. Milton left his house.

XCII.

All these are, *certes*, entertaining facts,
 Like Shakspeare's stealing deer, Lord
 Bacon's bribes;
Like Titus' youth, and Cæsar's earliest acts;
 Like Burns (whom Doctor Currie well
 describes);
Like Cromwell's pranks;—but although truth
 exacts
 These amiable descriptions from the scribes,
As most essential to their hero's story,
They do not much contribute to his glory.

XCIII.

All are not moralists, like Southey, when
 He prated to the world of "Pantisocrasy;"
Or Wordsworth unexcised, unhired, who then
 Season'd his pedlar poems with democracy;
Or Coleridge, long before his flighty pen
 Let to the Morning Post its aristocracy;
When he and Southey, following the same path,
Espoused two partners (milliners of Bath).

XCIV.

Such names at present cut a convict figure,
 The very Botany Bay in moral geography;
Their loyal treason, renegado rigour,
 Are good manure for their more bare
 biography,
Wordsworth's last quarto, by the way, is
 bigger
Than any since the birthday of typography;
A drowsy frowzy poem, call'd the "Excur-
 sion,"
Writ in a manner which is my aversion.

XCV.

He there builds up a formidable dyke
 Between his own and others' intellect:
But Wordsworth's poem, and his followers,
 like
Joanna Southcote's Shiloh, and her sect,
Are things which in this century do n't strike
 The public mind,—so few are the elect;
And the new births of both their stale
 virginities
Have proved but dropsies, taken for divi-
 nities.

XCVI.

But let me to my story: I must own,
 If I have any fault, it is digression,
Leaving my people to proceed alone,
 While I soliloquize beyond expression:
But these are my addresses from the throne,
 Which put off business to the ensuing
 session:
Forgetting each omission is a loss to
The world, not quite so great as Ariosto.

XCVII.

I know that what our neighbours call
 "*longueurs*,"
 (We've not so good a *word*, but have the
 thing,
In that complete perfection which insures
 An epic from Bob Southey every Spring—)
Form not the true temptation which allures
 The reader; but 't would not be hard to
 bring
Some fine examples of the *epopée*,
To prove its grand ingredient is *ennui*.

XCVIII.

We learn from Horace, "Homer sometimes
 sleeps;"
 We feel without him, Wordsworth some-
 times wakes,—
To show with what complacency he creeps,
 With his dear "*Waggoners*," around his
 lakes.

He wishes for "a boat" to sail the deeps—
 Of ocean?—No, of air; and then he makes
Another outcry for "a little boat,"
And drivels seas to set it well afloat.

XCIX.

If he must fain sweep o'er the ethereal plain,
 And Pegasus runs restive in his "Waggon,"
Could he not beg the loan of Charles's Wain?
 Or pray Medea for a single dragon?
Or if, too classic for his vulgar brain,
 He fear'd his neck to venture such a nag on,
And he must needs mount nearer to the moon,
Could not the blockhead ask for a balloon?

C.

"Pedlars," and "Boats," and "Waggons!"
 Oh! ye shades
 Of Pope and Dryden, are we come to this?
That trash of such sort not alone evades
 Contempt, but from the bathos' vast abyss
Floats scumlike uppermost, and these Jack
 Cades
 Of sense and song above your graves may
 hiss—
The "little boatman" and his "Peter Bell"
Can sneer at him who drew "Achitophel!"

CI.

T' our tale.—The feast was over, the slaves
 gone,
 The dwarfs and dancing girls had all
 retired;
The Arab lore and poet's song were done,
 And every sound of revelry expired;
The lady and her lover, left alone,
 The rosy flood of twilight's sky admired;—
Ave Maria! o'er the earth and sea,
That heavenliest hour of Heaven is worthiest
 thee!

CII.

Ave Maria! blessed be the hour!
 The time, the clime, the spot, where I so
 oft
Have felt that moment in its fullest power
 Sink o'er the earth so beautiful and soft,
While swung the deep bell in the distant
 tower,
 Or the faint dying day-hymn stole aloft,
And not a breath crept through the rosy air,
And yet the forest leaves seem'd stirr'd with
 prayer.

CIII.

Ave Maria! 'tis the hour of prayer!
 Ave Maria! 'tis the hour of love!
Ave Maria! may our spirits dare
 Look up to thine and to thy Son's above!

Ave Maria! oh that face so fair!
 Those downcast eyes beneath the Almighty
 dove—
What though 'tis but a pictured image strike,
That painting is no idol,—'tis too like.

CIV.

Some kinder casuists are pleased to say,
 In nameless print—that I have no devo-
 tion;
But set those persons down with me to pray,
 And you shall see who has the properest
 notion
Of getting into heaven the shortest way;
 My altars are the mountains and the ocean,
Earth, air, stars,—all that springs from the
 great Whole,
Who hath produced, and will receive the
 soul.

CV.

Sweet hour of twilight!—in the solitude
 Of the pine forest, and the silent shore
Which bounds Ravenna's immemorial wood,
 Rooted where once the Adrian wave flow'd
 o'er,
To where the last Cæsarean fortress stood,
 Evergreen forest! which Boccaccio's lore
And Dryden's lay made haunted ground to
 me,
How have I loved the twilight hour and thee!

CVI.

The shrill cicalas, people of the pine,
 Making their summer lives one ceaseless
 song,
Were the sole echoes, save my steed's and
 mine,
 And vesper bell's that rose the boughs
 along;
The spectre huntsman of Onesti's line,
 His hell-dogs, and their chase, and the fair
 throng
Which learn'd from this example not to fly
From a true lover,—shadow'd my mind's eye.

CVII.

Oh, Hesperus! thou bringest all good things—
 Home to the weary, to the hungry cheer,
To the young bird the parent's brooding
 wings,
 The welcome stall to the o'erlabour'd steer;
What e'er of peace about our hearthstone clings,
 Whate'er our household gods protect of
 dear,
Are gather'd round us by thy look of rest;
Thou bring'st the child, too, to the mother's
 breast.

CVIII.

Soft hour! which wakes the wish and melts
 the heart
Of those who sail the seas, on the first day
When they from their sweet friends are torn
 apart;
Or fills with love the pilgrim on his way
As the far bell of vesper makes him start,
 Seeming to weep the dying day's decay;
Is this a fancy which our reason scorns?
Ah! surely nothing dies but something
 mourns!

CIX.

When Nero perish'd by the justest doom
 Which ever the destroyer yet destroy'd,
Amidst the roar of liberated Rome,
 Of nations freed, and the world overjoy'd,
Some hands unseen strew'd flowers upon his
 tomb:
Perhaps the weakness of a heart not void
Of feeling for some kindness done, when
 power
Had left the wretch an uncorrupted hour.

CX.

But I'm digressing; what on earth has Nero,
 Or any such like sovereign buffoons,
To do with the transactions of my hero,
 More than such madmen's fellow man—
 the moon's?
Sure my invention must be down at zero,
 And I grown one of many "wooden spoons"
Of verse (the name with which we Cantabs
 please
To dub the last of honours in degrees).

CXI.

I feel this tediousness will never do—
 'T is being *too* epic, and I must cut down
(In copying) this long canto into two;
 They'll never find it out, unless I own
The fact, excepting some experienced few;
 And then as an improvement 't will be
 shown:
I'll prove that such the opinion of the critic
 is
From Aristotle *passim*.— See Ποιητικής.

Canto the Fourth.

I.

NOTHING so difficult as a beginning
 In poesy, unless perhaps the end;
For oftentimes when Pegasus seems winning
 The race, he sprains a wing, and down we
 tend,

Like Lucifer when hurl'd from heaven for
 sinning;
 Our sin the same, and hard as his to mend,
Being pride, which leads the mind to soar
 too far,
Till our own weakness shows us what we are.

II.

But time, which brings all beings to their
 level,
 And sharp Adversity, will teach at last
Man,—and, as we would hope,—perhaps the
 devil,
 That neither of their intellects are vast:
While youth's hot wishes in our red veins
 revel,
 We know not this—the blood flows on too
 fast:
But as the torrent widens towards the ocean,
We ponder deeply on each past emotion.

III.

As boy, I thought myself a clever fellow,
 And wish'd that others held the same
 opinion;
They took it up when my days grew more
 mellow,
 And other minds acknowledged my domi-
 nion:
Now my sere fancy "falls into the yellow
Leaf," and Imagination droops her pinion,
And the sad truth which hovers o'er my desk
Turns what was once romantic to burlesque.

IV.

And if I laugh at any mortal thing,
 'Tis that I may not weep; and if I weep,
'Tis that our nature cannot always bring
 Itself to apathy, for we must steep
Our hearts first in the depths of Lethe's
 spring,
 Ere what we least wish to behold will sleep:
Thetis baptized her mortal son in Styx;
A mortal mother would on Lethe fix.

V.

Some have accused me of a strange design
 Against the creed and morals of the land,
And trace it in this poem every line;
 I don't pretend that I quite understand
My own meaning when I would be *very* fine;
 But the fact is that I have nothing plann'd,
Unless it were to be a moment merry,
A novel word in my vocabulary.

VI.

To the kind reader of our sober clime
 This way of writing will appear exotic;
Pulci was sire of the half-serious rhyme,
 Who sang when chivalry was more Quixotic,

And revell'd in the fancies of the time,
 True knights, chaste dames, huge giant
 kings despotic:
But all these, save the last, being obsolete,
I chose a modern subject as more meet.

VII.

How I have treated it, I do not know;
 Perhaps no better than they have treated
 me,
Who have imputed such designs as show
 Not what they saw, but what they wish'd
 to see:
But if it gives them pleasure, be it so,
 This is a liberal age, and thoughts are
 free:
Meantime Apollo plucks me by the ear,
And tells me to resume my story here.

VIII.

Young Juan and his lady-love were left
 To their own hearts' most sweet society;
Even Time the pitiless in sorrow cleft
 With his rude scythe such gentle bosoms;
 he
Sigh'd to behold them of their hours bereft,
 Though foe to love; and yet they could
 not be
Meant to grow old, but die in happy spring,
Before one charm or hope had taken wing.

IX.

Their faces were not made for wrinkles, their
 Pure blood to stagnate, their great hearts
 to fail;
The blank grey was not made to blast their
 hair,
 But like the climes that know nor snow
 nor hail,
They were all summer; lightning might
 assail
 And shiver them to ashes, but to trail
A long and snake-like life of dull decay
Was not for them—they had too little clay.

X.

They were alone once more; for them to be
 Thus was another Eden; they were never
Weary, unless when separate: the tree
 Cut from its forest root of years—the river
Damm'd from its fountain—the child from
 the knee
 And breast maternal wean'd at once for
 ever,—
Would wither less than these two torn apart;
Alas! there is no instinct like the heart—

XI.

The heart—which may be broken: happy
 they!'
 Thrice fortunate! who of that fragile
 mould,
The precious porcelain of human clay,
 Break with the first fall: they can ne'er
 behold
The long year link'd with heavy day on day,
 And all which must be borne, and never
 told;
While life's strange principle will often lie
Deepest in those who long the most to die.

XII.

"Whom the gods love die young" was said
 of yore,
 And many deaths do they escape by this:
The death of friends, and that which slays
 even more—
 The death of friendship, love, youth, all
 that is,
Except mere breath; and since the silent
 shore
 Awaits at last even those who longest miss
The old archer's shafts, perhaps the early
 grave
Which men weep over may be meant to save.

XIII.

Haidée and Juan thought not of the dead.
 The heavens, and earth, and air, seem'd
 made for them:
They found no fault with Time, save that he
 fled;
 They saw not in themselves aught to con-
 demn;
Each was the other's mirror, and but read
 Joy sparkling in their dark eyes like a gem,
And knew such brightness was but the re-
 flection
Of their exchanging glances of affection.

XIV.

The gentle pressure, and the thrilling touch,
 The least glance better understood than
 words,
Which still said all, and ne'er could say too
 much;
 A language, too, but like to that of birds,
Known but to them, at least appearing such
 As but to lovers a true sense affords;
Sweet playful phrases, which would seem
 absurd
To those who have ceased to hear such, or
 ne'er heard.

XV.

All these were theirs, for they were children
 still,
 And children still they should have ever
 been;
They were not made in the real world to fill
 A busy character in the dull scene,
But like two beings born from out a rill,
 A nymph and her beloved, all unseen
To pass their lives in fountains and on
 flowers,
And never know the weight of human hours.

XVI.

Moons changing had roll'd on, and change-
 less found
 Those their bright rise had lighted to such
 joys
As rarely they beheld throughout their round;
 And these were not of the vain kind which
 cloys,
For theirs were buoyant spirits, never bound
 By the mere senses; and that which destroys
Most love, possession, unto them appear'd
A thing which each endearment more en-
 dear'd.

XVII.

Oh beautiful! and rare as beautiful!
 But theirs was love in which the mind
 delights
To lose itself, when the old world grows dull,
 And we are sick of its hack sounds and
 sights,
Intrigues, adventures of the common school,
 Its petty passions, marriages, and flights;
Where Hymen's torch but brands one strum-
 pet more,
Whose husband only knows her not a wh—re.

XVIII.

Hard words; harsh truth; a truth which
 many know.
 Enough.—The faithful and the fairy pair,
Who never found a single hour too slow,
 What was it made them thus exempt from
 care?
Young innate feelings all have felt below,
 Which perish in the rest, but in them were
Inherent; what we mortals call romantic,
And always envy, though we deem it frantic.

XIX.

This is in others a factitious state,
 An opium dream of too much youth and
 reading,
But was in them their nature or their fate:
 No novels e'er had set their young hearts
 bleeding,

For Haidée's knowledge was by no means
 great,
 And Juan was a boy of saintly breeding;
So that there was no reason for their loves
More than for those of nightingales or doves.

XX.

They gazed upon the sunset; 'tis an hour
 Dear unto all, but dearest to *their* eyes,
For it had made them what they were: the
 power
 Of love had first o'erwhelm'd them from
 such skies,
When happiness had been their only dower,
 And twilight saw them link'd in passion's
 ties;
Charm'd with each other, all things charm'd
 that brought
The past still welcome as the present thought.

XXI.

I know not why, but in that hour to-night,
 Even as they gazed, a sudden tremor came,
And swept, as 'twere, across their hearts'
 delight,
 Like the wind o'er a harp-string, or a flame,
When one is shook in sound, and one in
 sight:
 And thus some boding flash'd through either
 frame,
And call'd from Juan's breast a faint low sigh,
While one new tear arose in Haidée's eye.

XXII.

That large black prophet eye seem'd to dilate
 And follow far the disappearing sun,
As if their last day of a happy date
 With his broad, bright, and dropping orb
 were gone.
Juan gazed on her as to ask his fate—
 He felt a grief, but knowing cause for none,
His glance inquired of hers for some excuse
For feelings causeless, or at least abstruse.

XXIII.

She turn'd to him, and smiled, but in that sort
 Which makes not others smile; then turn'd
 aside:
Whatever feeling shook her, it seem'd short,
 And master'd by her wisdom or her pride;
When Juan spoke, too—it might be in sport—
 Of this their mutual feeling, she replied—
"If it should be so,—but—it cannot be—
Or I at least shall not survive to see."

XXIV.

Juan would question further, but she press'd
 His lips to hers, and silenced him with this,
And then dismiss'd the omen from her breast,
 Defying augury with that fond kiss;

And no doubt of all methods 'tis the best:
 Some people prefer wine—'tis not amiss;
I have tried both; so those who would a part
 take
May choose between the headache and the
 heartache.

XXV.

One of the two according to your choice,
 Woman or wine, you'll have to undergo;
Both maladies are taxes on our joys:
 But which to choose, I really hardly know;
And if I had to give a casting voice,
 For both sides I could many reasons show,
And then decide, without great wrong to
 either,
It were much better to have both than neither.

XXVI.

Juan and Haidée gazed upon each other
 With swimming looks of speechless tender-
 ness,
Which mix'd all feelings, friend, child, lover,
 brother;
 All that the best can mingle and express
When two pure hearts are pour'd in one
 another,
 And love too much, and yet cannot love
 less;
But almost sanctify the sweet excess
By the immortal wish and power to bless.

XXVII.

Mix'd in each other's arms, and heart in
 heart,
 Why did they not then die?—they had
 lived too long
Should an hour come to bid them breathe
 apart;
 Years could but bring them cruel things or
 wrong;
The world was not for them, nor the world's
 art
 For beings passionate as Sappho's song;
Love was born *with* them, *in* them, so intense,
It was their very spirit—not a sense.

XXVIII.

They should have lived together deep in woods,
 Unseen as sings the nightingale; they were
Unfit to mix in these thick solitudes
 Call'd social, haunts of Hate, and Vice, and
 Care;
How lonely every freeborn creature broods!
 The sweetest song-birds nestle in a pair;
The eagle soars alone; the gull and crow
Flock o'er their carrion, just like men below.

XXIX.

Now pillow'd cheek to cheek, in loving sleep,
 Haidée and Juan their siesta took,
A gentle slumber, but it was not deep,
 For ever and anon a something shook
Juan, and shuddering o'er his frame would
 creep;
 And Haidée's sweet lips murmur'd like a
 brook
A wordless music, and her face so fair
Stirr'd with her dream, as rose-leaves with
 the air;

XXX.

Or as the stirring of a deep clear stream
 Within an Alpine hollow, when the wind
Walks o'er it, was she shaken by the dream,
 The mystical usurper of the mind—
Oer'powering us to be whate'er may seem
 Good to the soul which we no more can bind:
Strange state of being! (for 'tis still to be),
Senseless to feel, and with seal'd eyes to see.

XXXI.

She dream'd of being alone on the sea-shore,
 Chain'd to a rock; she knew not how, but
 stir
She could not from the spot, and the loud
 roar
 Grew, and each wave rose roughly, threat-
 ening her;
And o'er her upper lip they seem'd to pour,
 Until she sobb'd for breath, and soon they
 were
Foaming o'er her lone head, so fierce and
 high—
Each broke to drown her, yet she could not
 die.

XXXII.

Anon—she was released, and then she stray'd
 O'er the sharp shingles with her bleeding
 feet,
And stumbled almost every step she made;
 And something roll'd before her in a sheet,
Which she must still pursue howe'er afraid:
 'Twas white and indistinct, nor stopp'd to
 meet
Her glance nor grasp, for still she gazed and
 grasp'd,
And ran, but it escaped her as she clasp'd.

XXXIII.

The dream changed:—in a cave she stood, its
 walls
 Were hung with marble icicles; the work
Of ages on its water-fretted halls,
 Where waves might wash, and seals might
 breed and lurk;

Her hair was dripping, and the very balls
 Of her black eyes seem'd turn'd to tears, and
 mirk
The sharp rocks look'd below each drop they
 caught,
Which froze to marble as it fell,—she thought.

XXXIV.

And wet, and cold, and lifeless at her feet,
 Pale as the foam that froth'd on his dead
 brow,
Which she essay'd in vain to clear, (how
 sweet
 Were once her cares, how idle seem'd they
 now!)
Lay Juan, nor could aught renew the beat
 Of his quench'd heart; and the sea dirges
 low
Rang in her sad ears like a mermaid's song,
And that brief dream appear'd a life too long.

XXXV.

And gazing on the dead, she thought his face
 Faded, or alter'd into something new—
Like to her father's features, till each trace
 More like and like to Lambro's aspect
 grew—
With all his keen worn look and Grecian
 grace;
 And starting, she awoke, and what to view?
Oh! Powers of Heaven! what dark eye meets
 she there?
'Tis—'tis her father's—fix'd upon the pair!

XXXVI.

Then shrieking, she arose, and shrieking fell,
 With joy and sorrow, hope and fear, to see
Him whom she deem'd a habitant where dwell
 The ocean-buried, risen from death, to be
Perchance the death of one she loved too
 well:
 Dear as her father had been to Haidée,
It was a moment of that awful kind——
I have seen such—but must not call to mind.

XXXVII.

Up Juan sprang to Haidée's bitter shriek,
 And caught her falling, and from off the
 wall
Snatch'd down his sabre, in hot haste to
 wreak
 Vengeance on him who was the cause of
 all:
Then Lambro, who till now forebore to speak,
 Smiled scornfully, and said, "Within my
 call,
A thousand scimitars await the word;
Put up, young man, put up your silly sword.'

XXXVIII.

And Haidée clung around him; "Juan, 'tis—
'Tis Lambro—'tis my father! Kneel with
 me—
He will forgive us—yes—it must be—yes.
 Oh! dearest father, in this agony
Of pleasure and of pain—even while I kiss
 Thy garment's hem with transport, can it
 be
That doubt should mingle with my filial joy?
Deal with me as thou wilt, but spare this
 boy."

XXXIX.

High and inscrutable the old man stood,
 Calm in his voice, and calm within his
 eye—
Not always signs with him of calmest mood:
 He look'd upon her, but gave no reply;
Then turn'd to Juan, in whose cheek the
 blood
 Oft came and went, as there resolved to
 die;
In arms, at least, he stood, in act to spring
On the first foe whom Lambro's call might
 bring.

XL.

"Young man, your sword;" so Lambro once
 more said:
 Juan replied, "Not while this arm is free."
The old man's cheek grew pale, but not with
 dread,
 And drawing from his belt a pistol, he
Replied, "Your blood be then on your own
 head."
 Then look'd close at the flint, as if to see
'Twas fresh—for he had lately used the
 lock—
And next proceeded quietly to cock.

XLI.

It has a strange quick jar upon the ear,
 That cocking of a pistol, when you know
A moment more will bring the sight to bear
 Upon your person, twelve yards off, or so;
A gentlemanly distance, not too near,
 If you have got a former friend for foe;
But after being fired at once or twice,
The ear becomes more Irish, and less nice.

XLII.

Lambro presented, and one instant more
 Had stopp'd this Canto, and Don Juan's
 breath,
When Haidée threw herself her boy before;
 Stern as her sire: "On me," she cried, "let
 death

Descend—the fault is mine; this fatal shore
 He found—but sought not. I have pledged
 my faith;
I love him—I will die with him: I knew
Your nature's firmness—know your daugh-
 ter's too."

XLIII.

A minute past, and she had been all tears,
 And tenderness, and infancy; but now
She stood as one who champion'd human
 fears—
 Pale, statue-like, and stern, she woo'd the
 blow;
And tall beyond her sex, and their com-
 peers,
 She drew up to her height, as if to show
A fairer mark; and with a fix'd eye scann'd
Her father's face—but never stopp'd his
 hand.

XLIV.

He gazed on her, and she on him; 'twas
 strange
 How like they look'd! the expression was
 the same;
Serenely savage, with a little change
 In the large dark eye's mutual-darted flame;
For she, too, was as one who could avenge,
 If cause should be—a lioness, though tame;
Her father's blood before her father's face
Boil'd up, and proved her truly of his race.

XLV.

I said they were alike, their features and
 Their stature, differing but in sex and
 years:
Even to the delicacy of their hand
 There was resemblance, such as true blood
 wears;
And now to see them, thus divided, stand
 In fix'd ferocity, when joyous tears,
And sweet sensations, should have welcomed
 both,
Show what the passions are in their full
 growth.

XLVI.

The father paused a moment, then withdrew
 His weapon, and replaced it; but stood
 still,
And looking on her, as to look her through,
 "Not *I*," he said, "have sought this
 stranger's ill;
Not *I* have made this desolation: few
 Would bear such outrage, and forbear to
 kill;
But I must do my duty—how thou hast
Done thine, the present vouches for the past.

XLVII.

"Let him disarm; or, by my father's head,
 His own shall roll before you like a ball!"
He raised his whistle as the word he said,
 And blew; another answer'd to the call,
And rushing in disorderly, though led,
 And arm'd from boot to turban, one and all,
Some twenty of his train came, rank on rank;
He gave the word, "Arrest or slay the
 Frank."

XLVIII.

Then, with a sudden movement, he withdrew
 His daughter; while compress'd within his
 clasp,
'Twixt her and Juan interposed the crew;
 In vain she struggled in her father's grasp—
His arms were like a serpent's coil: then flew
 Upon their prey, as darts an angry asp,
The file of pirates: save the foremost, who
Had fallen, with his right shoulder half cut
 through.

XLIX.

The second had his cheek laid open; but
 The third, a wary, cool old sworder, took
The blows upon his cutlass, and then put
 His own well in; so well, ere you could
 look,
His man was floor'd, and helpless at his foot,
 With the blood running like a little brook
From two smart sabre gashes, deep and red—
One on the arm, the other on the head.

L.

And then they bound him where he fell, and
 bore
Juan from the apartment: with a sign
Old Lambro bade them take him to the shore,
 Where lay some ships which were to sail
 at nine.
They laid him in a boat, and plied the oar
 Until they reach'd some galliots, placed in
 line;
On board of one of these, and under hatches,
They stow'd him, with strict orders to the
 watches.

LI.

The world is full of strange vicissitudes,
 And here was one exceedingly unpleasant:
A gentleman so rich in the world's goods,
 Handsome and young, enjoying all the
 present,
Just at the very time when he least broods
 On such a thing, is suddenly to sea sent,
Wounded and chain'd, so that he cannot
 move,
And all because a lady fell in love.

LII.

Here I must leave him, for I grow pathetic,
 Moved by the Chinese nymph of tears,
 green tea!
Than whom Cassandra was not more pro-
 phetic;
 For if my pure libations exceed three,
I feel my heart become so sympathetic,
 That I must have recourse to black Bohea:
'Tis pity wine should be so deleterious,
For tea and coffee leave us much more serious,

LIII.

Unless when qualified with thee, Cogniac!
 Sweet Naïad of the Phlegethontic rill!
Ah! why the liver wilt thou thus attack,
 And make, like other nymphs, thy lovers ill?
I would take refuge in weak punch, but *rack*
 (In each sense of the word), whene'er I fill
My mild and midnight beakers to the brim,
Wakes me next morning with its synonym.

LIV.

I leave Don Juan for the present, safe—
 Not sound, poor fellow, but severely wound-
 ed;
Yet could his corporal pangs amount to half
 Of those with which his Haidée's bosom
 bounded!
She was not one to weep, and rave, and chafe,
 And then give way, subdued because sur-
 rounded;
Her mother was a Moorish maid from Fez,
Where all is Eden, or a wilderness.

LV.

There the large olive rains its amber store
 In marble fonts; there grain, and flour,
 and fruit,
Gush from the earth until the land runs o'er;
 But there, too, many a poison-tree has root,
And midnight listens to the lion's roar,
 And long, long deserts scorch the camel's
 foot,
Or heaving whelm the helpless caravan;
And as the soil is, so the heart of man.

LVI.

Afric is all the sun's, and as her earth
 Her human clay is kindled; full of power
For good or evil, burning from its birth,
 The Moorish blood partakes the planet's
 hour,
And like the soil beneath it will bring forth:
 Beauty and love were Haidée's mother's
 dower;
But her large dark eye show'd deep Passion's
 force,
Though sleeping like a lion near a source.

LVII.

Her daughter, temper'd with a milder ray,
　Like summer clouds all silvery, smooth,
　　and fair,
Till slowly charged with thunder they display
　Terror to earth, and tempest to the air,
Had held till now her soft and milky way;
　But overwrought with passion and despair,
The fire burst forth from her Numidian veins,
Even as the Simoom sweeps the blasted plains.

LVIII.

The last sight which she saw was Juan's
　　gore,
　And he himself o'ermaster'd and cut down;
His blood was running on the very floor
　Where late he trod, her beautiful, her own;
Thus much she view'd an instant and no
　　more,—
　Her struggles ceased with one convulsive
　　groan;
On her sire's arm, which until now scarce
　　held
Her writhing, fell she like a cedar fell'd.

LIX.

A vein had burst, and her sweet lips' pure
　　dyes
　Were dabbled with the deep blood which
　　ran o'er;
And her head droop'd, as when the lily lies
　O'ercharged with rain: her summon'd
　　handmaids bore
Their lady to her couch with gushing eyes;
　Of herbs and cordials they produced their
　　store,
But she defied all means they could employ,
Like one life could not hold, nor death de-
　stroy.

LX.

Days lay she in that state unchanged, though
　　chill—
　With nothing livid, still her lips were red;
She had no pulse, but death seem'd absent
　　still;
　No hideous sign proclaim'd her surely dead;
Corruption came not in each mind to kill
　All hope; to look upon her sweet face bred
New thoughts of life, for it seem'd full of
　　soul—
She had so much, earth could not claim the
　　whole.

LXI.

The ruling passion, such as marble shows
　When exquisitely chisell'd, still lay there,
But fix'd as marble's unchanged aspect throws
　O'er the fair Venus, but for ever fair;

O'er the Laocoön's all eternal throes,
　And ever-dying Gladiator's air,
Their energy like life forms all their fame,
Yet looks not life, for they are still the same.

LXII.

She woke at length, but not as sleepers wake,
　Rather the dead, for life seem'd something
　　new,
A strange sensation which she must partake
　Perforce, since whatsoever met her view
Struck not on memory, though a heavy ache
　Lay at her heart, whose earliest beat still
　　true
Brought back the sense of pain without the
　　cause,
For, for a while, the furies made a pause.

LXIII.

She look'd on many a face with vacant eye,
　On many a token without knowing what;
She saw them watch her without asking
　　why,
　And reck'd not who around her pillow
　　sat;
Not speechless, though she spoke not; not a
　　sigh
　Relieved her thoughts; dull silence and
　　quick chat
Were tried in vain by those who served; she
　　gave
No sign, save breath, of having left the grave.

LXIV.

Her handmaids tended, but she heeded not;
　Her father watch'd, she turn'd her eyes
　　away;
She recognised no being, and no spot,
　However dear or cherish'd in their day;
They changed from room to room, but all
　　forgot,
　Gentle, but without memory she lay;
At length those eyes, which they would fain
　　be weaning
Back to old thoughts, wax'd full of fearful
　　meaning.

LXV.

And then a slave bethought her of a harp;
　The harper came, and tuned his instru-
　　ment;
At the first notes, irregular and sharp,
　On him her flashing eyes a moment bent,
Then to the wall she turn'd as if to warp
　Her thoughts from sorrow through her
　　heart re-sent;
And he began a long low island song
Of ancient days, ere tyranny grew strong.

LXVI.

Anon her thin wan fingers beat the wall
　In time to his old tune; he changed the
　　theme,
And sung of love; the fierce name struck
　　through all
Her recollection; on her flash'd the dream
Of what she was, and is, if ye could call
　To be so being; in a gushing stream
The tears rush'd forth from her o'erclouded
　　brain,
Like mountain mists at length dissolved in
　　rain.

LXVII.

Short solace, vain relief!—thought came too
　　quick,
　And whirl'd her brain to madness; she
　　arose
As one who ne'er had dwelt among the sick,
　And flew at all she met, as on her foes;
But no one ever heard her speak or shriek,
　Although her paroxysm drew towards its
　　close;—
Hers was a phrensy which disdain'd to rave,
Even when they smote her, in the hope to
　　save.

LXVIII.

Yet she betray'd at times a gleam of sense;
　Nothing could make her meet her father's
　　face,
Though on all other things with looks intense
　She gazed, but none she ever could retrace;
Food she refused, and raiment; no pre-
　　tence
　Avail'd for either; neither change of place,
Nor time, nor skill, nor remedy, could give
　　her
Senses to sleep—the power seem'd gone for
　　ever.

LXIX.

Twelve days and nights she wither'd thus;
　　at last,
　Without a groan, or sigh, or glance, to show
A parting pang, the spirit from her passed:
　And they who watch'd her nearest could
　　not know
The very instant, till the change that cast
　Her sweet face into shadow, dull and slow,
Glazed o'er her eyes—the beautiful, the
　　black—
Oh! to possess such lustre—and then lack!

LXX.

She died, but not alone; she held within
　A second principle of life, which might
Have dawn'd a fair and sinless child of sin;
　But closed its little being without light,

And went down to the grave unborn, wherein
　Blossom and bough lie wither'd with one
　　blight;
In vain the dews of Heaven descend above
The bleeding flower and blasted fruit of love.

LXXI.

Thus lived—thus died she; never more on
　　her
　Shall sorrow light, or shame. She was not
　　made
Through years or moons the inner weight to
　　bear,
　Which colder hearts endure till they are laid
By age in earth: her days and pleasures were
　Brief, but delightful—such as had not staid
Long with her destiny; but she sleeps well
By the sea-shore, whereon she loved to dwell.

LXXII.

That isle is now all desolate and bare,
　Its dwellings down, its tenants pass'd
　　away;
None but her own and father's grave is there,
　And nothing outward tells of human clay;
Ye could not know where lies a thing so fair,
　No stone is there to show, no tongue to say,
What was; no dirge, except the hollow sea's,
Mourns o'er the beauty of the Cyclades.

LXXIII.

But many a Greek maid in a loving song
　Sighs o'er her name; and many an islander
With her sire's story makes the night less
　　long;
　Valour was his, and beauty dwelt with her;
If she loved rashly, her life paid for wrong—
　A heavy price must all pay who thus err,
In some shape; let none think to fly the
　　danger,
For soon or late Love is his own avenger.

LXXIV.

But let me change this theme, which grows
　　too sad,
　And lay this sheet of sorrows on the shelf;
I don't much like describing people mad,
　For fear of seeming rather touch'd myself—
Besides, I've no more on this head to add;
　And as my Muse is a capricious elf,
We'll put about, and try another tack
With Juan, left half-kill'd some stanzas back.

LXXV.

Wounded and fetter'd, "cabin'd, cribb'd, con-
　　fined,"
　Some days and nights elapsed before
　　that he
Could altogether call the past to mind;
　And when he did, he found himself at sea,

Sailing six knots an hour before the wind;
 The shores of Ilion lay beneath their lee—
Another time he might have liked to see 'em,
 But now was not much pleased with Cape
 Sigæum.

LXXVI.

There, on the green and village-cotted hill, is
 (Flank'd by the Hellespont, and by the sea)
Entomb'd the bravest of the brave, Achilles;
 They say so—(Bryant says the contrary):
And further downward, tall and towering
 still, is
 The tumulus—of whom? Heaven knows;
 't may be
Patroclus, Ajax, or Protesilaus;
All heroes, who if living still would slay us.

LXXVII.

High barrows, without marble, or a name,
 A vast, untill'd, and mountain-skirted
 plain,
And Ida in the distance, still the same,
 And old Scamander (if 't is he), remain;
The situation seems still form'd for fame—
 A hundred thousand men might fight
 again,
With ease; but where I sought for Ilion's
 walls,
The quiet sheep feeds, and the tortoise
 crawls;

LXXVIII.

Troops of untended horses; here and there,
 Some little hamlets, with new names un-
 couth;
Some shepherds (unlike Paris), led to stare
 A moment at the European youth
Whom to the spot their school-boy feelings
 bear;
 A Turk, with beads in hand, and pipe in
 mouth,
Extremely taken with his own religion,
Are what I found there—but the devil a
 Phrygian.

LXXIX.

Don Juan, here permitted to emerge
 From his dull cabin, found himself a
 slave;
Forlorn, and gazing on the deep blue surge,
 O'ershadow'd there by many a hero's
 grave;
Weak still with loss of blood, he scarce could
 urge
 A few brief questions; and the answers
 gave
No very satisfactory information
About his past or present situation.

LXXX.

He saw some fellow-captives, who appear'd
 To be Italians, as they were in fact;
From them, at least, *their* destiny he heard,
 Which was an odd one; a troop going
 to act
In Sicily—all singers, duly rear'd
 In their vocation; had not been attack'd
In sailing from Livorno by the pirate,
But sold by the impresario at no high rate.

LXXXI.

By one of these, the buffo of the party,
 Juan was told about their curious case;
For although destined to the Turkish mart, he
 Still kept his spirits up—at least his face;
The little fellow really look'd quite hearty,
 And bore him with some gaiety and grace,
Showing a much more reconciled demeanour,
Than did the prima-donna and the tenor.

LXXXII.

In a few words he told their hapless story,
 Saying, "Our Machiavelian impresario,
Making a signal off some promontory,
 Hail'd a strange brig; Corpo di Caio
 Mario!
We were transferr'd on board her in a hurry,
 Without a single scudo of salario;
But if the Sultan has a taste for song,
We will revive our fortunes before long.

LXXXIII.

" The prima-donna, though a little old,
 And haggard with a dissipated life,
And subject, when the house is thin, to cold,
 Has some good notes; and then the tenor's
 wife,
With no great voice, is pleasing to behold;
 Last carnival she made a deal of strife,
By carrying off Count Cesare Cicogna
From an old Roman princess at Bologna.

LXXXIV.

"And then there are the dancers; there 's
 the Nini,
 With more than one profession gains
 by all;
Then there 's that laughing slut the Pele-
 grini,
 She, too, was fortunate last carnival,
And made at least five hundred good zec-
 chini,
 But spends so fast, she has not now a
 paul;
And then there 's the Grotesca—such a
 dancer!
Where men have souls or bodies she must
 answer.

LXXXV.

" As for the figuranti, they are like
 The rest of all that tribe;. with here and
 there
A pretty person, which perhaps may strike,
 The rest are hardly fitted for a fair;
There's one, though tall and stiffer than a
 pike,
 Yet has a sentimental kind of air
Which might go far, but she do n't dance with
 vigour;
The more's the pity, with her face and
 figure.

LXXXVI.

" As for the men, they are a middling set;
 The musico is but a crack'd old basin,
But being qualified in one way yet,
 May the seraglio do to set his face in,
And as a servant some preferment get;
 His singing I no further trust can place in:
From all the Pope makes yearly 't would
 perplex
To find three perfect pipes of the *third* sex.

LXXXVII.

" The tenor's voice is spoilt by affectation,
 And for the bass, the beast can only
 bellow;.
In fact, he had no singing education,
 An ignorant, noteless, timeless, tuneless
 fellow;
But being the prima-donna's near relation,
 Who swore his voice was very rich and
 mellow,
They hired him, though to hear him you'd
 believe
An ass was practising recitative.

LXXXVIII.

" 'T would not become myself to dwell upon
 My own merits, and though young—I see,
 sir—you
Have got a travell'd air, which speaks you
 one
 To whom the opera is by no means new:.
You've heard of Raucocanti?—I'm the man:
 The time may come when you may hear
 me too;
You was not last year at the fair of Lugo,
But next, when I'm engaged to sing there—
 do go.

LXXXIX.

" Our baritone I almost had forgot,
 A pretty lad, but bursting with conceit;
With graceful action, science not a jot,
 A voice of no great compass, and not
 sweet,

He always is complaining of his lot,
 Forsooth, scarce fit for ballads in the
 street;
In lovers' parts his passion more to breathe,
Having no heart to show, he shows his
 teeth."

XC.

Here Raucocanti's eloquent recital
 Was interrupted by the pirate crew,
Who came at stated moments to invite all
 The captives back to their sad berths; each
 threw
A rueful glance upon the waves; (which bright
 all
 From the blue skies derived a double blue,
Dancing all free and happy in the sun,)
And then went down the hatchway one by one.

XCI.

They heard next day—that in the Dardanelles,
 Waiting for his Sublimity's firman,
The most imperative of sovereign spells,
 Which everybody does without who can,
More to secure them in their naval cells,
 Lady to lady, well as man to man,
Were to be chain'd and lotted out per couple,
For the slave-market of Constantinople.

XCII.

It seems when this allotment was made out,
 There chanced to be an odd male, and odd
 female,
Who (after some discussion and some doubt,
 If the soprano might be deem'd to be male,
They placed him o'er the woman as a scout)
 Were link'd together, and it happen'd the
 male
Was Juan, who,—an awkward thing at his age,
Pair'd off with a Bacchante blooming visage.

XCIII.

With Raucocanti lucklessly was chain'd.
 The tenor; these two hated with a hate
Found only on the stage, and each more pain'd
 With this his tuneful neighbour than his
 fate;
Sad strife arose, for they were so cross-grain'd,
 Instead of bearing up without debate,
That each pull'd different ways with many
 an oath,
" Arcades ambo," *id est*—blackguards both.

XCIV.

Juan's companion was a Romagnole,
 But bred within the March of old Ancona,
With eyes that look'd into the very soul
 (And other chief points of a " bella donna"),

Bright—and as black and burning as a coal;
　And through her clear brunette complexion
　　shone a
Great wish to please—a most attractive
　　dower,
Especially when added to the power.

XCV.

But all that power was wasted upon him,
　For sorrow o'er each sense held stern
　　command;
Her eye might flash on his, but found it dim:
　And though thus chain'd, as natural her hand
Touch'd his, nor that—nor any handsome limb
　(And she had some not easy to withstand)
Could stir his pulse, or make his faith feel
　　brittle;
Perhaps his recent wounds might help a little.

XCVI.

No matter; we should ne'er too much inquire,
　But facts are facts: no knight could be
　　more true,
And firmer faith no ladye-love desire;
　We will omit the proofs, save one or two:
'Tis said no one in hand "can hold a fire
　By thought of frosty Caucasus;" but few,
I really think; yet Juan's then ordeal
Was more triumphant, and not much less real.

XCVII.

Here I might enter on a chaste description,
　Having withstood temptation in my youth,
But hear that several people take exception
　At the first two books having too much
　　truth;
Therefore I'll make Don Juan leave the ship
　　soon,
Because the publisher declares, in sooth,
Through needles' eyes it easier for the camel is
To pass, than those two cantos into families.

XCVIII.

'Tis all the same to me; I'm fond of yielding,
　And therefore leave them to the purer page
Of Smollett, Prior, Ariosto, Fielding,
　Who say strange things for so correct an
　　age;
I once had great alacrity in wielding
　My pen, and liked poetic war to wage,
And recollect the time when all this cant
Would have provoked remarks which now it
　shan't.

XCIX.

As boys love rows, my boyhood liked a
　　squabble;
　But at this hour I wish to part in peace,
Leaving such to the literary rabble,
　Whether my verse's fame be doom'd to cease

While the right hand which wrote it still is
　　able,
　Or of some centuries to take a lease;
The grass upon my grave will grow as long,
And sigh to midnight winds, but not to song.

C.

Of poets who come down to us through
　　distance
　Of time and tongues, the foster-babes of
　　Fame,
Life seems the smallest portion of existence;
　Where twenty ages gather o'er a name,
'Tis as a snow-ball which derives assistance
　From every flake, and yet rolls on the
　　same,
Even till an iceberg it may chance to grow;
But, after all, 'tis nothing but cold snow.

CI.

And so great names are nothing more than
　　nominal,
　And love of glory's but an airy lust,
Too often in its fury overcoming all
　Who would as 'twere identify their dust
From out the wide destruction, which, en-
　　tombing all,
　Leaves nothing till "the coming of the
　　just"—
Save change: I've stood upon Achilles' tomb,
And heard Troy doubted; time will doubt of
　Rome.

CII.

The very generations of the dead
　Are swept away, and tomb inherits tomb,
Until the memory of an age is fled,
　And, buried, sinks beneath its offspring's
　　doom:
Where are the epitaphs our fathers read?
　Save a few glean'd from the sepulchral
　　gloom
Which once-named myriads nameless lie
　beneath,
And lose their own in universal death.

CIII.

I canter by the spot each afternoon
　Where perish'd in his fame the hero-boy,
Who lived too long for men, but died too
　　soon
　For human vanity, the young De Foix!
A broken pillar, not uncouthly hewn,
　But which neglect is hastening to destroy,
Records Ravenna's carnage on its face,
While weeds and ordure rankle round the
　base.

CIV.

I pass each day where Dante's bones are laid:
 A little cupola, more neat than solemn,
Protects his dust, but reverence here is paid
 To the bard's tomb, and not the warrior's column:
The time must come, when both alike decay'd,
 The chieftain's trophy, and the poet's volume,
Will sink where lie the songs and wars of earth,
Before Pelides' death, or Homer's birth.

CV.

With human blood that column was cemented,
 With human filth that column is defiled,
As if the peasant's coarse contempt were vented
 To show his loathing of the spot he soil'd:
Thus is the trophy used, and thus lamented
 Should ever be those blood-hounds, from whose wild
Instinct of gore and glory earth has known
Those sufferings Dante saw in hell alone.

CVI.

Yet there will still be bards: though fame is smoke,
 Its fumes are frankincense to human thought;
And the unquiet feelings, which first woke
 Song in the world, will seek what then they sought:
As on the beach the waves at last are broke,
 Thus to their extreme verge the passions brought
Dash into poetry, which is but passion,
Or at least was so ere it grew a fashion.

CVII.

If in the course of such a life as was
 At once adventurous and contemplative,
Men who partake all passions as they pass,
 Acquire the deep and bitter power to give
Their images again as in a glass,
 And in such colours that they seem to live;
You may do right forbidding them to show 'em,
But spoil (I think) a very pretty poem.

CVIII.

Oh! ye, who make the fortunes of all books!
 Benign Ceruleans of the second sex!
Who advertise new poems by your looks,
 Your "imprimatur" will ye not annex?

What! must I go to the oblivious cooks,
 Those Cornish plunderers of Parnassian wrecks?
Ah! must I then the only minstrel be,
Proscribed from tasting your Castalian tea?

CIX.

What! can I prove "a lion" then no more?
 A ball-room bard, a foolscap, hot-press darling?
To bear the compliments of many a bore,
 And sigh, "I can't get out," like Yorick's starling;
Why then I'll swear, as poet Wordy swore
 (Because the world won't read him, always snarling),
That taste is gone, that fame is but a lottery,
Drawn by the blue-coat misses of a coterie.

CX.

Oh! "darkly, deeply, beautifully blue,"
 As some one somewhere sings about the sky,
And I, ye learned ladies, say of you;
 They say your stockings are so—(Heaven knows why,
I have examined few pair of that hue);
 Blue as the garters which serenely lie
Round the patrician left-legs, which adorn
The festal midnight, and the levée morn.

CXI.

Yet some of you are most seraphic creatures—
 But times are alter'd since, a rhyming lover,
You read my stanzas, and I read your features:
 And—but no matter, all those things are over;
Still I have no dislike to learned natures,
 For sometimes such a world of virtues cover;
I knew one woman of that purple school,
The loveliest, chastest, best, but—quite a fool.

CXII.

Humboldt, "the first of travellers," but not
 The last, if late accounts be accurate,
Invented, by some name I have forgot,
 As well as the sublime discovery's date,
An airy instrument, with which he sought
 To ascertain the atmospheric state,
By measuring "the *intensity of blue*:"
Oh, Lady Daphne! let me measure you!

CXIII.

But to the narrative:—The vessel bound
 With slaves to sell off in the capital,
After the usual process, might be found
 At anchor under the seraglio wall;

Her cargo, from the plague being safe and
 sound,
Were landed in the market, one and all,
And there with Georgians, Russians, and
 Circassians,
Bought up for different purposes and pas-
 sions.

CXIV.

Some went off dearly; fifteen hundred dollars
 For one Circassian, a sweet girl, were
 given,
Warranted virgin; beauty's brightest colours
 Had deck'd her out in all the hues of
 heaven:
Her sale sent home some disappointed
 bawlers,
 Who bade on till the hundreds reached
 eleven;
But when the offer went beyond, they knew
'T was for the Sultan, and at once withdrew.

CXV.

Twelve negresses from Nubia brought a price
 Which the West Indian market scarce
 could bring,
Though Wilberforce, at last, has made it
 twice
 What 't was ere Abolition; and the thing
Need not seem very wonderful, for vice
 Is always much more splendid than a king:
The virtues, even the most exalted, Charity,
Are saving—vice spares nothing for a rarity.

CXVI.

But for the destiny of this young troop,
 How some were bought by pachas, some
 by Jews,
How some to burdens were obliged to stoop,
 And others rose to the command of crews
As renegadoes; while in hapless group,
 Hoping no very old vizier might choose,
The females stood, as one by one they
 pick'd 'em,
To make a mistress, or fourth wife, or
 victim:

CXVII.

All this must be reserved for further song;
 Also our hero's lot, howe'er unpleasant
(Because this Canto has become too long),
 Must be postponed discreetly for the
 present;
I'm sensible redundancy is wrong,
 But could not for the muse of me put less
 in't:
And now delay the progress of Don Juan,
Till what is call'd in Ossian the fifth Duan.

Canto the Fifth.

I.

WHEN amatory poets sing their loves
 In liquid lines mellifluously bland,
And pair their rhymes as Venus yokes her
 doves,
 They little think what mischief is in hand;
The greater their success the worse it proves,
 As Ovid's verse may give to understand;
Even Petrarch's self, if judged with due
 severity,
Is the Platonic pimp of all posterity.

II.

I therefore do denounce all amorous writing,
 Except in such a way as not to attract;
Plain—simple—short, and by no means
 inviting,
 But with a moral to each error tack'd,
Form'd rather for instructing than delighting,
 And with all passions in their turn attack'd;
Now, if my Pegasus should not be shod ill,
This poem will become a moral model.

III.

The European with the Asian shore
 Sprinkled with palaces; the Ocean stream
Here and there studded with a seventy-four;
 Sophia's cupola with golden gleam;
The cypress groves; Olympus high and hoar;
 The twelve isles, and the more than I could
 dream,
Far less describe, present the very view
Which charm'd the charming Mary Montagu.

IV.

I have a passion for the name of "Mary,"
 For once it was a magic sound to me;
And still it half calls up the realms of fairy,
 Where I beheld what never was to be;
All feelings changed, but this was last to
 vary,
 A spell from which even yet I am not
 quite free:
But I grow sad—and let a tale grow cold,
Which must not be pathetically told.

V.

The wind swept down the Euxine, and the
 wave
 Broke foaming o'er the blue Symplegades;
'T is a grand sight from off "the Giant's Grave"
 To watch the progress of those rolling seas
Between the Bosphorus, as they lash and lave
 Europe and Asia, you being quite at ease:
There's not a sea the passenger e'er pukes in,
Turns up more dangerous breakers than the
 Euxine.

VI.

'T was a raw day of Autumn's bleak begin-
ning,
When nights are equal, but not so the
days :
The Parcæ then cut short the further
spinning
Of seamen's fates, and the loud tempests
raise
The waters, and repentance for past sinning
In all, who o'er the great deep take their
ways :
They vow to amend their lives, and yet they
don't ;
Because if drown'd, they can't—if spared,
they won't.

VII.

A crowd of shivering slaves of every nation,
And age, and sex, were in the market
ranged ;
Each bevy with the merchant in his station :
Poor creatures ! their good looks were
sadly changed.
All save the blacks seem'd jaded with
vexation,
From friends, and home, and freedom far
estranged ;
The negroes more philosophy display'd,—
Used to it, no doubt, as eels are to be flay'd.

VIII.

Juan was juvenile, and thus was full,
As most at his age are, of hope, and
health ;
Yet I must own, he look'd a little dull,
And now and then a tear stole down by
stealth ;
Perhaps his recent loss of blood might pull
His spirit down ; and then the loss of
wealth,
A mistress, and such comfortable quarters,
To be put up for auction amongst Tartars,

IX.

Were things to shake a stoic ; ne'ertheless,
Upon the whole his carriage was serene :
His figure, and the splendour of his dress,
Of which some gilded remnants still were
seen,
Drew all eyes on him, giving them to guess
He was above the vulgar by his mien ;
And then, though pale, he was so very
handsome ;
And then—they calculated on his ransom.

X.

Like a backgammon board the place was
dotted
With whites and blacks, in groups on show
for sale,
Though rather more irregularly spotted :
Some bought the jet, while others chose
the pale.
It chanced amongst the other people lotted,
A man of thirty, rather stout and hale,
With resolution in his dark grey eye,
Next Juan stood, till some might choose to
buy.

XI.

He had an English look ; that is, was square
In make, of a complexion white and ruddy,
Good teeth, with curling rather dark brown
hair,
And, it might be from thought, or toil, or
study,
An open brow a little mark'd with care :
One arm had on a bandage rather bloody ;
And there he stood with such *sang froid*,
that greater
Could scarce be shown even by a mere
spectator.

XII.

But seeing at his elbow a mere lad,
Of a high spirit evidently, though
At present weigh'd down by a doom which
had
O'erthrown even men, he soon began to
show
A kind of blunt compassion for the sad
Lot of so young a partner in the woe,
Which for himself he seem'd to deem no worse
Than any other scrape, a thing of course.

XIII.

" My boy ! "—said he, " amidst this motley
crew
Of Georgians, Russians, Nubians, and
what not,
All ragamuffins differing but in hue,
With whom it is our luck to cast our lot,
The only gentlemen seem I and you ;
So let us be acquainted, as we ought :
If I could yield you any consolation,
'T would give me pleasure.—Pray, what is
your nation ? "

XIV.

When Juan answer'd—" Spanish ! " he re-
plied,
" I thought, in fact, you could not be a
Greek ;
Those servile dogs are not so proudly eyed :
Fortune has play'd you here a pretty freak,

But that's her way with all men, till they're
tried;
 But never mind,—she'll turn, perhaps,
next week;
She has served me also much the same as
you,
 Except that I have found it nothing new."

XV.

"Pray, sir," said Juan, "if I may presume,
 What brought you here?"—"Oh! nothing
very rare—
Six Tartars and a drag-chain——"—"To this
doom
 But what conducted, if the question's fair,
Is that which I would learn."—"I served for
some
 Months with the Russian army here and
there;
And taking lately, by Suwarrow's bidding,
A town, was ta'en myself instead of Widdin."

XVI.

"Have you no friends?"—"I had—but, by
God's blessing,
 Have not been troubled with them lately.
Now
I have answer'd all your questions without
pressing,
 And you an equal courtesy should show."
"Alas!" said Juan, "'t were a tale dis-
tressing,
 And long besides."—"Oh! if 'tis really so,
You're right on both accounts to hold your
tongue;
A sad tale saddens doubly when 'tis long.

XVII.

"But droop not: Fortune at your time of life,
 Although a female moderately fickle,
Will hardly leave you (as she's not your wife)
 For any length of days in such a pickle.
To strive, too, with our fate were such a strife
 As if the corn-sheaf should oppose the
sickle:
Men are the sport of circumstances, when
The circumstances seem the sport of men."

XVIII.

"'Tis not," said Juan, "for my present doom
 I mourn, but for the past;—I loved a
maid:"—
He paused, and his dark eye grew full of
gloom;
 A single tear upon his eyelash staid
A moment, and then dropp'd; "but to re-
sume,
 'Tis not my present lot, as I have said,
Which I deplore so much; for I have borne
Hardships which have the hardiest overworn,

XIX.

"On the rough deep. But this last blow—"
 and here
He stopp'd again, and turn'd away his face.
"Ay," quoth his friend, "I thought it would
appear
 That there had been a lady in the case;
And these are things which ask a tender tear,
 Such as I, too, would shed if in your place:
I cried upon my first wife's dying day,
And also when my second ran away:

XX.

"My third——"—"Your third!" quoth Juan,
turning round;
 "You scarcely can be thirty: have you
three?"
"No—only two at present above ground:
 Surely, 'tis nothing wonderful to see
One person thrice in holy wedlock bound!"
 "Well, then, your third," said Juan; "what
did she?
She did not run away, too,—did she, sir?"
"No, faith."—"What then?"—"I ran away
from her."

XXI.

"You take things coolly, sir," said Juan.
 "Why,"
Replied the other, "what can a man do?
There still are many rainbows in your sky,
 But mine have vanish'd. All, when life is
new,
Commence with feelings warm, and prospects
high;
 But time strips our illusions of their hue,
And one by one in turn, some grand mistake
Casts off its bright skin yearly like the snake.

XXII.

"'Tis true, it gets another bright and fresh,
 Or fresher, brighter; but the year gone
through,
This skin must go the way, too, of all flesh,
 Or sometimes only wear a week or two;—
Love's the first net which spreads its deadly
mesh;
 Ambition, Avarice, Vengeance, Glory, glue
The glittering lime-twigs of our latter days,
Where still we flutter on for pence or praise."

XXIII.

"All this is very fine, and may be true;"
 Said Juan, "but I really don't see how
It betters present times with me or you."
 "No?" quoth the other; "yet you will
allow

By setting things in their right point of view,
 Knowledge, at least, is gain'd; for instance, now,
We know what slavery is, and our disasters
May teach us better to behave when masters.'

XXIV.

"Would we were masters now, if but to try
 Their present lessons on our Pagan friends
 here,"
Said Juan—swallowing a heart-burning sigh:
 "Heaven help the scholar, whom his fortune sends here!"
"Perhaps we shall be one day, by and by,"
 Rejoin'd the other, "when our bad luck
 mends here;
Meantime (yon old black eunuch seems to
 eye us)
I wish to G—d that somebody would buy us!

XXV.

"But after all, what *is* our present state?
 'Tis bad, and may be better—all men's lot:
Most men are slaves, none more so than the
 great,
 To their own whims and passions, and
 what not;
Society itself, which should create
 Kindness, destroys what little we had got:
To feel for none is the true social art
Of the world's stoics—men without a heart."

XXVI.

Just now a black old neutral personage
 Of the third sex stept up, and peering over
The captives, seem'd to mark their looks and
 age,
 And capabilities, as to discover
If they were fitted for the purposed cage:
 No lady e'er is ogled by a lover,
Horse by a blackleg, broadcloth by a tailor,
Fee by a counsel, felon by a jailor,

XXVII.

As is a slave by his intended bidder.
 'Tis pleasant purchasing our fellow-creatures;
And all are to be sold, if you consider
 Their passions, and are dext'rous; some
 by features
Are bought up, others by a warlike leader,
 Some by a place—as tend their years or
 natures;
The most by ready cash—but all have prices,
From crowns to kicks, according to their
 vices.

XXVIII.

The eunuch, having eyed them o'er with
 care,
 Turn'd to the merchant, and began to bid
First but for one, and after for the pair;
 They haggled, wrangled, swore, too—so
 they did!
As though they were in a mere Christian fair,
 Cheapening an ox, an ass, a lamb, or kid;
So that their bargain sounded like a battle
For this superior yoke of human cattle.

XXIX.

At last they settled into simple grumbling,
 And pulling out reluctant purses, and
Turning each piece of silver o'er, and tumbling
 Some down, and weighing others in their
 hand,
And by mistake sequins with paras jumbling,
 Until the sum was accurately scann'd,
And then the merchant giving change, and
 signing
Receipts in full, began to think of dining.

XXX.

I wonder if his appetite was good?
 Or, if it were, if also his digestion?
Methinks at meals some odd thoughts might
 intrude,
 And conscience ask a curious sort of question,
About the right divine how far we should
 Sell flesh and blood. When dinner has
 opprest one,
I think it is perhaps the gloomiest hour
Which turns up out of the sad twenty-four.

XXXI.

Voltaire says "No;" he tells you that
 Candide
 Found life most tolerable after meals;
He's wrong—unless man were a pig, indeed,
 Repletion rather adds to what he feels,
Unless he's drunk, and then no doubt he's
 freed
 From his own brain's oppression while it
 reels.
Of food I think with Philip's son, or rather
Ammon's (ill pleased with one world and one
 father);

XXXII.

I think with Alexander, that the act
 Of eating, with another act or two,
Makes us feel our mortality in fact
 Redoubled; when a roast and a ragout,

And fish, and soup, by some side dishes
 back'd,
Can give us either pain or pleasure, who
Would pique himself on intellects, whose use
Depends so much upon the gastric juice?

XXXIII.

The other evening ('t was on Friday last)—
 This is a fact, and no poetic fable—
Just as my great coat was about me cast,
 My hat and gloves still lying on the table,
I heard a shot—'t was eight o'clock scarce
 past—
And, running out as fast as I was able,
I found the military commandant
Stretch'd in the street, and able scarce to
 pant.

XXXIV.

Poor fellow! for some reason, surely bad,
 They had slain him with five slugs; and
 left him there
To perish on the pavement: so I had
 Him borne into the house and up the stair,
And stripp'd, and look'd to,—But why should
 I add
 More circumstances? vain was every care;
The man was gone: in some Italian quarrel
Kill'd by five bullets from an old gun-barrel.

XXXV.

I gazed upon him, for I knew him well;
 And though I have seen many corpses,
 never
Saw one, whom such an accident befell,
 So calm; though pierced through stomach,
 heart, and liver,
He seem'd to sleep,—for you could scarcely
 tell
 (As he bled inwardly, no hideous river
Of gore divulged the cause) that he was dead:
So as I gazed on him, I thought or said—

XXXVI.

"Can this be death? then what is life or
 death?
 Speak!" but he spoke not: "wake!" but
 still he slept:—
"But yesterday, and who had mightier
 breath?
A thousand warriors by his word were kept
In awe: he said, as the centurion saith,
 'Go,' and he goeth; 'come,' and forth he
 stepp'd.
The trump and bugle till he spake were
 dumb—
And now nought left him but the muffled
 drum."

XXXVII.

And they who waited once and worshipp'd—
 they
 With their rough faces throng'd about the
 bed
To gaze once more on the commanding clay
 Which for the last, though not the first,
 time bled;
And such an end! that he who many a day
 Had faced Napoleon's foes until they
 fled,—
The foremost in the charge or in the sally,
Should now be butcher'd in a civic alley.

XXXVIII.

The scars of his old wounds were near his
 new,
 Those honourable scars which brought him
 fame;
And horrid was the contrast to the view——
 But let me quit the theme; as such things
 claim
Perhaps even more attention than is due
 From me: I gazed (as oft I have gazed the
 same)
To try if I could wrench aught out of death
Which should confirm, or shake, or make a
 faith;

XXXIX.

But it was all a mystery. Here we are,
 And there we go:—but *where?* five bits of
 lead,
Or three, or two, or one, send very far!
 And is this blood, then, form'd but to be
 shed?
Can every element our elements mar?
 And air—earth—water—fire live—and we
 dead?
We, whose minds comprehend all things.
 No more;
But let us to the story as before.

XL.

The purchaser of Juan and acquaintance
 Bore off his bargains to a gilded boat,
Embark'd himself and them, and off they
 went thence
 As fast as oars could pull and water float;
They look'd like persons being led to sen-
 tence,
 Wond'ring what next, till the caïque was
 brought
Up in a little creek below a wall
O'ertopp'd with cypresses, dark-green and
 tall.

XLI.

Here their conductor tapping at the wicket
 Of a small iron door, 'twas open'd, and
He led them onward, first through a low
 thicket
 Flank'd by large groves, which tower'd on
 either hand:
They almost lost their way, and had to pick
 it—
 For night was closing ere they came to
 land.
The eunuch made a sign to those on board,
Who row'd off, leaving them without a word.

XLII.

As they were plodding on their winding way
 Through orange bowers, and jasmine, and
 so forth:
(Of which I might have a good deal to say,
 There being no such profusion in the North
Of oriental plants, "et cetera,"
 But that of late your scribblers think it worth
Their while to rear whole hotbeds in *their*
 works,
Because one poet travell'd 'mongst the Turks:)

XLIII.

As they were threading on their way, there
 came
Into Don Juan's head a thought, which he
 Whisper'd to his companion :—'twas the same
 Which might have then occurr'd to you or
 me.
"Methinks,"—said he,—"it would be no
 great shame
 If we should strike a stroke to set us free;
Let's knock that old black fellow on the head,
And march away—'twere easier done than
 said."

XLIV.

"Yes," said the other, "and when done,
 what then?
 How get out? how the devil got we in?
And when we once were fairly out, and when
 From Saint Bartholomew we have saved
 our skin,
To-morrow'd see us in some other den,
 And worse off than we hitherto have been;
Besides, I'm hungry, and just now would
 take,
Like Esau, for my birthright a beef-steak.

XLV.

"We must be near some place of man's
 abode;—
 For the old negro's confidence in creeping,
With his two captives, by so queer a road,
 Shows that he thinks his friends have not
 been sleeping;

A single cry would bring them all abroad:
 'Tis better therefore looking before leap-
 ing—
And there, you see, this turn has brought us
 through,
By Jove, a noble palace!—lighted too."

XLVI.

It was indeed a wide extensive building
 Which open'd on their view, and o'er the
 front
There seem'd to be besprent a deal of gilding
 And various hues, as is the Turkish wont,—
A gaudy taste, for they are little skill'd in
 The arts of which these lands were once
 the font:
Each villa on the Bosphorus looks a screen
New painted, or a pretty opera-scene.

XLVII.

And nearer as they came, a genial savour
 Of certain stews, and roast-meats, and
 pilaus,
Things which in hungry mortals' eyes find
 favour,
Made Juan in his harsh intentions pause,
 And put himself upon his good behaviour:
 His friend, too, adding a new saving clause,
Said, "In Heaven's name let's get some
 supper now,
And then I'm with you, if you're for a row."

XLVIII.

Some talk of an appeal unto some passion,
 Some to men's feelings, others to their
 reason;
The last of these was never much the fashion,
 For reason thinks all reasoning out of
 season:
Some speakers whine, and others lay the
 lash on,
 But more or less continue still to tease on,
With arguments according to their "forte;"
But no one ever dreams of being short.—

XLIX.

But I digress: of all appeals,—although
 I grant the power of pathos, and of gold,
Of beauty, flattery, threats, a shilling,—no
 Method's more sure at moments to take
 hold
Of the best feelings of mankind, which grow
 More tender, as we every day behold,
Than that all-softening, overpowering knell,
The tocsin of the soul—the dinner-bell.

L.

Turkey contains no bells, and yet men dine;
 And Juan and his friend, albeit they heard
No Christian knoll to table, saw no line
 Of lackeys usher to the feast prepared,

Yet smelt roast-meat, beheld a huge fire
 shine,
 And cooks in motion with their clean arms
 bared,
And gazed around them to the left and right,
 With the prophetic eye of appetite.

LI.

And giving up all notions of resistance,
 They follow'd close behind their sable guide,
Who little thought that his own crack'd exis-
 tence
 Was on the point of being set aside:
He motion'd them to stop at some small dis-
 tance,
 And knocking at the gate, 'twas open'd
 wide,
And a magnificent large hall display'd
The Asian pomp of Ottoman parade.

LII.

I won't describe; description is my forte,
 But every fool describes in these bright
 days
His wondrous journey to some foreign court,
 And spawns his quarto, and demands your
 praise—
Death to his publisher, to him 'tis sport;
 While Nature, tortured twenty thousand
 ways,
Resigns herself with exemplary patience
To guide-books, rhymes, tours, sketches, illus-
 trations.

LIII.

Along this hall, and up and down, some,
 squatted
 Upon their hams, were occupied at chess;
Others in monosyllable talk chatted,
 And some seem'd much in love with their
 own dress;
And divers smoked superb pipes, decorated
 With amber mouths of greater price or
 less;
And several strutted, others slept, and some
Prepared for supper with a glass of rum.

LIV.

As the black eunuch enter'd with his brace
 Of purchased Infidels, some raised their eyes
A moment, without slackening from their
 pace;
 But those who sate, ne'er stirr'd in any
 wise:
One or two stared the captives in the face,
 Just as one views a horse to guess his
 price;
Some nodded to the negro from their station,
But no one troubled him with conversation.

LV.

He leads them through the hall, and, without
 stopping,
 On through a farther range of goodly
 rooms,
Splendid but silent, save in *one*, where, drop-
 ping,
 A marble fountain echoes through the
 glooms
Of night, which robe the chamber, or where
 popping
 Some female head most curiously presumes
To thrust its black eyes through the door or
 lattice,
As wondering what the devil noise that is.

LVI.

Some faint lamps gleaming from the lofty walls
 Gave light enough to hint their farther way,
But not enough to show the imperial halls
 In all the flashing of their full array;
Perhaps there's nothing—I'll not say appals,
 But saddens more by night as well as day,
Than an enormous room without a soul
To break the lifeless splendour of the whole.

LVII.

Two or three seem so little, *one* seems no-
 thing:
 In deserts, forests, crowds, or by the shore,
There solitude, we know, has her full growth
 in
 The spots which were her realms for ever-
 more;
But in a mighty hall or gallery, both in
 More modern buildings and those built of
 yore,
A kind of death comes o'er us all alone,
Seeing what's meant for many with but one.

LVIII.

A neat, snug study on a winter's night,
 A book, friend, single lady, or a glass
Of claret, sandwich, and an appetite,
 Are things which make an English evening
 pass;
Though *certes* by no means so grand a sight
 As is a theatre lit up by gas.
I pass my evenings in long galleries solely,
And that's the reason I'm so melancholy.

LIX.

Alas! man makes that great which makes
 him little:
 I grant you in a church 'tis very well:
What speaks of heaven should by no means
 be brittle,
 But strong and lasting, till no tongue can
 tell

Their names who rear'd it; but huge houses
 fit ill—
 And huge tombs worse—mankind, since
 Adam fell:
Methinks the story of the tower of Babel
Might teach them this much better than I'm
 able.

LX.

Babel was Nimrod's hunting-box, and then
 A town of gardens, walls, and wealth a-
 mazing,
Where Nebuchadonosor, king of men,
 Reign'd, till one summer's day he took to
 grazing,
And Daniel tamed the lions in their den,
 The people's awe and admiration raising:
'Twas famous, too, for Thisbe and for Pyra-
 mus,
And the calumniated queen Semiramis.—

LXI.

That injured Queen, by chroniclers so coarse,
 Has been accused (I doubt not by conspi-
 racy)
Of an improper friendship for her horse
 (Love, like religion, sometimes runs to
 heresy):
This monstrous tale had probably its source
 (For such exaggerations here and there I
 see)
In writing "Courser" by mistake for "Cou-
 rier;"
I wish the case would come before a jury
 here.

LXII.

But to resume,—should there be (what may
 not
 Be in these days?) some infidels, who don't,
Because they can't, find out the very spot
 Of that same Babel, or because they won't
(Though Claudius Rich, Esquire, some bricks
 has got,
 And written lately two memoirs upon 't,)
Believe the Jews, those unbelievers, who
Must be believed, though they believe not
 you,

LXIII.

Yet let them think that Horace has exprest
 Shortly and sweetly the masonic folly
Of those, forgetting the great place of rest,
 Who give themselves to architecture wholly;
We know where things and men must end
 at best:
 A moral (like all morals) melancholy,
And "Et sepulchri immemor struis domos"
Shows that we build when we should but
 entomb us.

LXIV.

At last they reach'd a quarter most retired,
 Where echo woke as if from a long slum-
 ber;
Though full of all things which could be
 desired,
 One wonder'd what to do with such a
 number
Of articles which nobody required;
 Here wealth had done its utmost to en-
 cumber
With furniture an exquisite apartment,
Which puzzled Nature much to know what
 Art meant.

LXV.

It seem'd, however, but to open on
 A range or suite of further chambers, which
Might lead to heaven knows where; but in
 this one
 The moveables were prodigally rich:
Sofas 'twas half a sin to sit upon,
 So costly were they; carpets every stitch
Of workmanship so rare, they made you wish
You could glide o'er them like a golden fish.

LXVI.

The black, however, without hardly deigning
 A glance at that which wrapt the slaves
 in wonder,
Trampled what they scarce trod for fear of
 staining,
 As if the milky way their feet was under
With all its stars; and with a stretch attain-
 ing
 A certain press or cupboard niched in yon-
 der,
In that remote recess which you may see—
Or if you don't the fault is not in me,—

LXVII.

I wish to be perspicuous; and the black,
 I say, unlocking the recess, pull'd forth
A quantity of clothes fit for the back
 Of any Mussulman, whate'er his worth;
And of variety there was no lack—
 And yet, though I have said there was no
 dearth,—
He chose himself to point out what he
 thought
Most proper for the Christians he had bought.

LXVIII.

The suit he thought most suitable to each
 Was, for the elder and the stouter, first
A Candiote cloak, which to the knee might
 reach,
 And trousers not so tight that they would
 burst,

But such as fit an Asiatic breech;
 A shawl, whose folds in Cashmire had been
 nurst,
Slippers of saffron, dagger rich and handy;
 In short, all things which form a Turkish
 dandy.

LXIX.

While he was dressing, Baba, their black
 friend,
 Hinted the vast advantages which they
Might probably obtain both in the end,
 If they would but pursue the proper way
Which Fortune plainly seem'd to recommend;
 And then he added, that he needs must say,
"'Twould greatly tend to better their con-
 dition,
If they would condescend to circumcision.

LXX.

"For his own part, he really should rejoice
 To see them true believers, but no less
Would leave his proposition to their choice."
 The other, thanking him for this excess
Of goodness, in thus leaving them a voice
 In such a trifle, scarcely could express
"Sufficiently" (he said) "his approbation
Of all the customs of this polish'd nation.

LXXI.

"For his own share—he saw but small ob-
 jection
 To so respectable an ancient rite;
And, after swallowing down a slight refection,
 For which he own'd a present appetite,
He doubted not a few hours of reflection
 Would reconcile him to the business quite."
"Will it?" said Juan, sharply: "Strike me
 dead,
But they as soon shall circumcise my head!

LXXII.

"Cut off a thousand heads, before——"—
 "Now, pray,"
Replied the other, "do not interrupt:
You put me out in what I had to say.
 Sir!—as I said, as soon as I can supt,
I shall perpend if your proposal may
 Be such as I can properly accept;
Provided always your great goodness still
Remits the matter to our own free-will."

LXXIII.

Baba eyed Juan, and said, "Be so good
 As dress yourself—" and pointed out a suit
In which a Princess with great pleasure would
 Array her limbs; but Juan standing mute,

As not being in a masquerading mood,
 Gave it a slight kick with his Christian
 foot;
And when the old negro told him to "Get
 ready,"
Replied, "Old gentleman, I'm not a lady."

LXXIV.

"What you may be, I neither know nor
 care,"
 Said Baba; "but pray do as I desire:
I have no more time nor many words to
 spare."
 "At least," said Juan, "sure I may inquire
The cause of this odd travesty?"—"For-
 bear,"
Said Baba, "to be curious; 't will transpire,
No doubt, in proper place, and time, and
 season:
I have no authority to tell the reason."

LXXV.

"Then if I do," said Juan, "I'll be——"—
 "Hold!"
 Rejoin'd the negro, "pray be not pro-
 voking;
This spirit's well, but it may wax too bold,
 And you will find us not too fond of joking."
"What, sir," said Juan, "shall it e'er be told
 That I unsex'd my dress?" But Baba,
 stroking
The things down, said, "Incense me, and I
 call
Those who will leave you of no sex at all.

LXXVI.

"I offer you a handsome suit of clothes:
 A woman's, true; but then there is a cause
Why you should wear them."—"What,
 though my soul loathes
The effeminate garb?"—thus, after a short
 pause,
Sigh'd Juan, muttering also some slight oaths,
 "What the devil shall I do with all this
 gauze?"
Thus he profanely term'd the finest lace
Which e'er set off a marriage-morning face.

LXXVII.

And then he swore; and, sighing, on he
 slipp'd
 A pair of trousers of flesh-colour'd silk;
Next with a virgin zone he was equipp'd,
 Which girt a slight chemise as white as
 milk;
But tugging on his petticoat, he tripp'd,
 Which—as we say—or as the Scotch say,
 whilk,
(The rhyme obliges me to this; sometimes
Monarchs are less imperative than rhymes)—

LXXVIII.

Whilk, which (or what you please), was
 owing to
His garment's novelty, and his being awk-
 ward:
And yet at last he managed to get through
 His toilet, though no doubt a little back-
 ward:
The negro Baba help'd a little too,
 When some untoward part of raiment
 stuck hard;
And, wrestling both his arms into a gown,
He paused, and took a survey up and down.

LXXIX.

One difficulty still remain'd—his hair
 Was hardly long enough; but Baba found
So many false long tresses all to spare,
 That soon his head was most completely
 crown'd,
After the manner then in fashion there;
 And this addition with such gems was bound
As suited the *ensemble* of his toilet,
While Baba made him comb his head and
 oil it.

LXXX.

And now being femininely all array'd,
 With some small aid from scissors, paint,
 and tweezers,
He look'd in almost all respects a maid,
 And Baba smilingly exclaim'd, "You see,
 sirs,
A perfect transformation here display'd;
 And now, then, you must come along with
 me, sirs,
That is—the Lady:" clapping his hands
 twice,
Four blacks were at his elbow in a trice.

LXXXI.

"You, sir," said Baba, nodding to the one,
 "Will please to accompany those gentle-
 men
To supper; but you, worthy Christian nun,
 Will follow me: no trifling, sir; for when
I say a thing, it must at once be done.
 What fear you? think you this a lion's
 den?
Why, 'tis a palace; where the truly wise
Anticipate the Prophet's paradise.

LXXXII.

"You fool! I tell you no one means you
 harm."
 "So much the better," Juan said, "for
 them;
Else they shall feel the weight of this my arm,
 Which is not quite so light as you may deem.

I yield thus far; but soon will break the
 charm,
 If any take me for that which I seem:
So that I trust for everybody's sake,
That this disguise may lead to no mistake."

LXXXIII.

"Blockhead! come on, and see," quoth
 Baba; while
Don Juan, turning to his comrade, who
Though somewhat grieved, could scarce for-
 bear a smile
Upon the metamorphosis in view,—
"Farewell!" they mutually exclaim'd: "this
 soil
 Seems fertile in adventures strange and
 new;
One's turn'd half Mussulman, and one a
 maid,
By this old black enchanter's unsought aid."

LXXXIV.

"Farewell!" said Juan: "should we meet
 no more,
 I wish you a good appetite."—"Farewell!"
Replied the other; "though it grieves me sore:
 When we next meet, we'll have a tale to
 tell:
We needs must follow when Fate puts from
 shore.
 Keep your good name; though Eve herself
 once fell."
"Nay," quoth the maid, "the Sultan's self
 shan't carry me,
Unless his highness promises to marry me."

LXXXV.

And thus they parted, each by separate doors;
 Baba led Juan onward room by room
Through glittering galleries, and o'er marble
 floors,
 Till a gigantic portal through the gloom,
Haughty and huge, along the distance lowers;
 And wafted far arose a rich perfume:
It seem'd as though they came upon a
 shrine,
For all was vast, still, fragrant, and divine.

LXXXVI.

The giant door was broad, and bright, and
 high,
 Of gilded bronze, and carved in curious
 guise;
Warriors thereon were battling furiously;
 Here stalks the victor, there the vanquish'd
 lies;
There captives led in triumph droop the eye,
 And in perspective many a squadron flies:
It seems the work of times before the line
Of Rome transplanted fell with Constantine.

LXXXVII.

This massy portal stood at the wide close
Of a huge hall, and on its either side
Two little dwarfs, the least you could suppose,
Were sate, like ugly imps, as if allied
In mockery to the enormous gate which rose
O'er them in almost pyramidic pride:
The gate so splendid was in all its *features*,
You never thought about those little crea-
tures,

LXXXVIII.

Until you nearly trod on them, and then
You started back in horror to survey
The wondrous hideousness of those small
men,
Whose colour was not black, nor white,
nor grey,
But an extraneous mixture, which no pen
Can trace, although perhaps the pencil
may;
They were mis-shapen pigmies, deaf and
dumb,—
Monsters, who cost a no less monstrous sum.

LXXXIX.

Their duty was—for they were strong, and
though
They look'd so little, did strong things at
times—
To ope this door, which they could really do,
The hinges being as smooth as Rogers'
rhymes;
And now and then, with tough strings of the
bow,
As is the custom of those Eastern climes,
To give some rebel Pacha a cravat;
For mutes are generally used for that.

XC.

They spoke by signs—that is, not spoke at all;
And looking like two incubi, they glared
As Baba with his fingers made them fall
To heaving back the portal folds: it scared
Juan a moment, as this pair so small,
With shrinking serpent optics on him
stared;
It was as if their little looks could poison
Or fascinate whome'er they fix'd their eyes on.

XCI.

Before they enter'd, Baba paused to hint
To Juan some slight lessons as his guide:
"If you could just contrive," he said, "to
stint
That somewhat manly majesty of stride,

'T would be as well, and—(though there's
not much in 't),
To swing a little less from side to side,
Which has at times an aspect of the oddest:—
And also could you look a little modest,

XCII.

" 'T would be convenient; for these mutes
have eyes
Like needles, which may pierce those
petticoats;
And if they should discover your disguise,
You know how near us the deep Bosphorus
floats;
And you and I may chance, ere morning rise,
To find our way to Marmora without boats,
Stitch'd up in sacks—a mode of navigation
A good deal practised here upon occasion."

XCIII.

With this encouragement, he led the way
Into a room still nobler than the last;
A rich confusion form'd a disarray
In such sort, that the eye along it cast
Could hardly carry anything away,
Object on object flash'd so bright and fast;
A dazzling mass of gems, and gold, and
glitter,
Magnificently mingled in a litter.

XCIV.

Wealth had done wonders—taste not much;
such things
Occur in Orient palaces, and even
In the more chasten'd domes of Western
kings
(Of which I have also seen some six or
seven),
Where I can't say or gold or diamond flings
Great lustre, there is much to be forgiven;
Groups of bad statues, tables, chairs, and
pictures,
On which I cannot pause to make my
strictures.

XCV.

In this imperial hall, at distance lay
Under a canopy, and there reclined
Quite in a confidential queenly way,
A lady; Baba stopp'd, and kneeling sign'd
To Juan, who, though not much used to pray,
Knelt down by instinct, wondering in his
mind
What all this meant: while Baba bow'd and
bended
His head, until the ceremony ended.

XCVI.

The lady rising up with such an air
 As Venus rose with from the wave, on
 them
Bent like an antelope a Paphian pair
 Of eyes, which put out each surrounding
 gem;
And raising up an arm as moonlight fair,
 She sign'd to Baba, who first kiss'd the
 hem
Of her deep purple robe, and speaking low,
Pointed to Juan, who remain'd below.

XCVII.

Her presence was as lofty as her state;
 Her beauty of that overpowering kind,
Whose force description only would abate:
 I'd rather leave it much to your own mind,
Than lessen it by what I could relate
 Of forms and features; it would strike you
 blind
Could I do justice to the full detail;
So, luckily for both, my phrases fail.

XCVIII.

Thus much however I may add,—her years
 Were ripe, they might make six-and-twenty
 springs,
But there are forms which Time to touch
 forbears,
 And turns aside his scythe to vulgar
 things:
Such as was Mary's Queen of Scots; true—
 tears
 And love destroy; and sapping sorrow
 wrings
Charms from the charmer, yet some never
 grow
Ugly; for instance—Ninon de l'Enclos.

XCIX.

She spake some words to her attendants, who
 Composed a choir of girls, ten or a dozen,
And were all clad alike; like Juan, too,
 Who wore their uniform, by Baba chosen:
They form'd a very nymph-like looking crew,
 Which might have called Diana's chorus
 "cousin,"
As far as outward show may correspond;
I won't be bail for anything beyond.

C.

They bow'd obeisance and withdrew, retiring,
 But not by the same door through which
 came in
Baba and Juan, which last stood admiring,
 At some small distance, all he saw within

This strange saloon, much fitted for inspiring
 Marvel and praise; for both or none things
 win;
And I must say, I ne'er could see the very
Great happiness of the "Nil Admirari."

CI.

"Not to admire is all the art I know
 (Plain truth, dear Murray, needs few
 flowers of speech)
To make men happy, or to keep them so;
 (So take it in the very words of Creech)."
Thus Horace wrote we all know long ago;
 And thus Pope quotes the precept to re-
 teach
From his translation; but had *none admired*,
Would Pope have sung, or Horace been
 inspired?

CII.

Baba, when all the damsels were withdrawn,
 Motion'd to Juan to approach, and then
A second time desired him to kneel down,
 And kiss the lady's foot; which maxim when
He heard repeated, Juan with a frown
 Drew himself up to his full height again,
And said, "It grieved him, but he could not
 stoop
To any shoe, unless it shod the Pope."

CIII.

Baba, indignant at this ill-timed pride,
 Made fierce remonstrances, and then a
 threat
He mutter'd (but the last was given aside)
 About a bow-string—quite in vain; not yet
Would Juan bend, though 't were to Mahomet's
 bride:
 There's nothing in the world like *etiquette*
In kingly chambers or imperial halls,
As also at the race and county balls.

CIV.

He stood like Atlas, with a world of words
 About his ears, and nathless would not
 bend;
The blood of all his line's Castilian lords
 Boil'd in his veins, and rather than descend
To stain his pedigree, a thousand swords
 A thousand times of him had made an end;
At length perceiving the "*foot*" could not
 stand,
Baba proposed that he should kiss the hand.

CV.

Here was an honourable compromise,
 A half-way house of diplomatic rest,
Where they might meet in much more peace-
 ful guise;
 And Juan now his willingness exprest

To use all fit and proper courtesies,
 Adding, that this was commonest and best,
For through the South, the custom still
 commands
The gentleman to kiss the lady's hands.

CVI.

And he advanced, though with but a bad grace,
 Though on more *thorough-bred* or fairer
 fingers
No lips e'er left their transitory trace:
 On such as these the lip too fondly lingers,
And for one kiss would fain imprint a brace,
 As you will see, if she you love shall bring
 hers
In contact; and sometimes even a fair
 stranger's
An almost twelvemonth's constancy en-
 dangers.

CVII.

The lady eyed him o'er and o'er, and bade
 Baba retire, which he obey'd in style,
As if well used to the retreating trade;
 And taking hints in good part all the
 while,
He whisper'd Juan not to be afraid,
 And looking on him with a sort of smile,
Took leave, with such a face of satisfaction,
As good men wear who have done a virtuous
 action.

CVIII.

When he was gone, there was a sudden
 change:
 I know not what might be the lady's
 thought,
But o'er her bright brow flash'd a tumult
 strange,
 And into her clear cheek the blood was
 brought,
Blood-red as sunset summer clouds which
 range
 The verge of Heaven; and in her large eyes
 wrought,
A mixture of sensations might be scann'd,
Of half-voluptuousness and half-command.

CIX.

Her form had all the softness of her sex,
 Her features all the sweetness of the devil,
When he put on the cherub to perplex
 Eve, and paved (God knows how) the road
 to evil;
The sun himself was scarce more free from
 specks
 Than she from aught at which the eye
 could cavil;
Yet, somehow, there was something some-
 where wanting,
As if she rather *order'd* than was *granting.*—

CX.

Something imperial, or imperious, threw
 A chain o'er all she did; that is, a chain
Was thrown as 'twere about the neck of
 you,—
 And rapture's self will seem almost a pain
With aught which looks like despotism in
 view;
 Our souls at least are free, and 'tis in vain
We would against them make the flesh
 obey—
The spirit in the end will have its way.

CXI.

Her very smile was haughty, though so
 sweet;
 Her very nod was not an inclination:
There was a self-will even in her small feet,
 As though they were quite conscious of
 her station—
They trod as upon necks; and to complete
 Her state (it is the custom of her nation),
A poniard deck'd her girdle, as the sign
She was a sultan's bride (thank Heaven, not
 mine!)

CXII.

"To hear and to obey" had been from birth
 The law of all around her; to fulfil
All phantasies which yielded joy or mirth,
 Had been her slaves' chief pleasure, as her
 will;
Her blood was high, her beauty scarce of
 earth:
 Judge, then, if her caprices e'er stood
 still;
Had she but been a Christian, I've a notion
We should have found out the "perpetual
 motion."

CXIII.

Whate'er she saw and coveted was brought;
 Whate'er she did *not* see, if she supposed
It might be seen, with diligence was sought,
 And when 'twas found straightway the
 bargain closed:
There was no end unto the things she
 bought,
 Nor to the trouble which her fancies
 caused;
Yet even her tyranny had such a grace,
The women pardon'd all except her face.

CXIV.

Juan, the latest of her whims, had caught
 Her eye in passing on his way to sale;
She order'd him directly to be bought,
 And Baba, who had ne'er been known to
 fail

In any kind of mischief to be wrought,
 At all such auctions knew how to prevail:
She had no prudence, but he had; and this
Explains the garb which Juan took amiss.

CXV.

His youth and features favour'd the disguise,
 And should you ask how she, a sultan's
 bride,
Could risk or compass such strange
 phantasies,
 This I must leave sultanas to decide:
Emperors are only husbands in wives' eyes,
 And kings and consorts oft are mystified,
As we may ascertain with due precision,
Some by experience, others by tradition.

CXVI.

But to the main point, where we have been
 tending:—
 She now conceived all difficulties past,
And deem'd herself extremely condescending
 When, being made her property at last,
Without more preface, in her blue eyes
 blending
 Passion and power, a glance on him she
 cast,
And merely saying, "Christian, canst thou
 love?"
Conceived that phrase was quite enough to
 move.

CXVII.

And so it was, in proper time and place;
 But Juan, who had still his mind o'er-
 flowing
With Haidée's isle and soft Ionian face,
 Felt the warm blood, which in his face was
 glowing,
Rush back upon his heart, which fill'd apace,
 And left his cheeks as pale as snow-drops
 blowing:
These words went through his soul like Arab
 spears,
So that he spoke not, but burst into tears.

CXVIII.

She was a good deal shock'd; not shock'd at
 tears,
 For women shed and use them at their
 liking;
But there is something when man's eye
 appears
 Wet, still more disagreeable and striking:
A woman's tear-drop melts, a man's half
 sears,
 Like molten lead, as if you thrust a pike in
His heart to force it out, for (to be shorter)
To them 't is a relief, to us a torture.

CXIX.

And she would have consoled, but knew not
 how:
 Having no equals, nothing which had e'er
Infected her with sympathy till now,
 And never having dreamt what 't was to
 bear
Aught of a serious, sorrowing kind, although
 There might arise some pouting petty care
To cross her brow, she wonder'd how so near
Her eyes another's eye could shed a tear.

CXX.

But nature teaches more than power can
 spoil,
 And, when a *strong* although a strange
 sensation
Moves—female hearts are such a genial soil
 For kinder feelings, whatsoe'er their nation,
They naturally pour the "wine and oil,"
 Samaritans in every situation;
And thus Gulbeyaz, though she knew not
 why,
Felt an odd glistening moisture in her eye.

CXXI.

But tears must stop like all things else; and
 soon
 Juan, who for an instant had been moved
To such a sorrow by the intrusive tone
 Of one who dared to ask if "he *had*
 loved,"
Call'd back the stoic to his eyes, which shone
 Bright with the very weakness he re-
 proved;
And although sensitive to beauty, he
Felt most indignant still at not being free.

CXXII.

Gulbeyaz, for the first time in her days,
 Was much embarrass'd, never having met
In all her life with aught save prayers and
 praise;
 And as she also risk'd her life to get
Him whom she meant to tutor in love's
 ways,
 Into a comfortable tête-à-tête,
To lose the hour would make her quite a
 martyr,
And they had wasted now almost a quarter.

CXXIII.

I also would suggest the fitting time,
 To gentlemen in any such like case,
That is to say—in a meridian clime,
 With us there is more law given to the
 chase,

But here a small delay forms a great crime:
 So recollect that the extremest grace
Is just two minutes for your declaration—
A moment more would hurt your reputation.

CXXIV.

Juan's was good; and might have been still
 better,
 But he had got Haidée into his head:
However strange, he could not yet forget
 her,
 Which made him seem exceedingly ill-bred.
Gulbeyaz, who look'd on him as her debtor
 For having had him to her palace led,
Began to blush up to the eyes, and then
Grow deadly pale, and then blush back
 again.

CXXV.

At length, in an imperial way, she laid
 Her hand on his, and bending on him eyes,
Which needed not an empire to persuade,
 Look'd into his for love, where none replies:
Her brow grew black, but she would not
 upbraid,
 That being the last thing a proud woman
 tries;
She rose, and pausing one chaste moment,
 threw
Herself upon his breast, and there she grew.

CXXVI.

This was an awkward test, as Juan found,
 But he was steel'd by sorrow, wrath, and
 pride:
With gentle force her white arms he un-
 wound,
 And seated her all drooping by his side,
Then rising haughtily he glanced around,
 And looking coldly in her face, he cried,
" The prison'd eagle will not pair, nor I
Serve a sultana's sensual phantasy.

CXXVII.

" Thou ask'st, if I can love? be this the proof
 How much I *have* loved—that I love not
 thee!
In this vile garb, the distaff, web, and woof,
 Were fitter for me: Love is for the free!
I am not dazzled by this splendid roof;
 Whate'er thy power, and great it seems to
 be,
Heads bow, knees bend, eyes watch around
 a throne,
And hands obey—our hearts are still our
 own."

CXXVIII.

This was a truth to us extremely trite;
 Not so to her, who ne'er had heard such
 things:
She deem'd her least command must yield
 delight,
 Earth being only made for queens and kings.
If hearts lay on the left side or the right
 She hardly knew, to such perfection brings
Legitimacy its born votaries, when
Aware of their due royal rights o'er men.

CXXIX.

Besides, as has been said, she was so fair
 As even in a much humbler lot had made
A kingdom or confusion anywhere,
 And also, as may be presumed, she laid
Some stress on charms, which seldom are, if
 e'er,
 By their possessors thrown into the shade:
She thought hers gave a double "right di-
 vine;"
And half of that opinion's also mine.

CXXX.

Remember, or (if you cannot) imagine,
 Ye! who have kept your chastity when
 young,
While some more desperate dowager has been
 waging
 Love with you, and been in the dog-days
 stung
By your refusal, recollect her raging!
 Or recollect all that was said or sung
On such a subject; then suppose the face
Of a young downright beauty in this case.

CXXXI.

Suppose,—but you already have supposed,
 The spouse of Potiphar, the Lady Booby,
Phædra, and all which story has disclosed
 Of good examples; pity that so few by
Poets and private tutors are exposed,
 To educate—ye youth of Europe—you by!
But when you have supposed the few we
 know,
You can't suppose Gulbeyaz' angry brow.

CXXXII.

A tigress robb'd of young, a lioness,
 Or any interesting beast of prey,
Are similes at hand for the distress
 Of ladies who cannot have their own way;
But though my turn will not be served with
 less,
 These don't express one half what I should
 say:
For what is stealing young ones, few or many,
To cutting short their hopes of having any?

CXXXIII.

The love of offspring's nature's general law,
 From tigresses and cubs to ducks and
 ducklings;
There's nothing whets the beak, or arms the
 claw,
 Like an invasion of their babes and suck-
 lings;
And all who have seen a human nursery, saw
 How mothers love their children's squalls
 and chucklings:
This strong extreme effect (to tire no longer
Your patience) shows the cause must still be
 stronger.

CXXXIV.

If I said fire flash'd from Gulbeyaz' eyes,
 'Twere nothing—for her eyes flash'd al-
 ways fire;
Or said her cheeks assumed the deepest dyes,
 I should but bring disgrace upon the dyer,
So supernatural was her passion's rise;
 For ne'er till now she knew a check'd
 desire:
Even ye who know what a check'd woman is
(Enough, God knows!) would much fall short
 of this.

CXXXV.

Her rage was but a minute's, and 'twas well—
 A moment's more had slain her; but the
 while
It lasted 'twas like a short glimpse of hell:
 Nought's more sublime than energetic bile,
Though horrible to see, yet grand to tell,
 Like ocean warring 'gainst a rocky isle;
And the deep passions flashing through her
 form
Made her a beautiful embodied storm.

CXXXVI.

A vulgar tempest 'twere to a typhoon
 To match a common fury with her rage,
And yet she did not want to reach the moon,
 Like moderate Hotspur on the immortal
 page;
Her anger pitch'd into a lower tune,
 Perhaps the fault of her soft sex and age—
Her wish was but to "kill, kill, kill," like
 Lear's,
And then her thirst of blood was quench'd
 in tears.

CXXXVII.

A storm it raged, and like the storm it pass'd,
 Pass'd without words—in fact she could
 not speak;
And then her sex's shame broke in at last,
 A sentiment till then in her but weak,

But now it flow'd in natural and fast,
 As water through an unexpected leak;
For she felt humbled—and humiliation
Is sometimes good for people in her station.

CXXXVIII.

It teaches them that they are flesh and blood,
 It also gently hints to them that others,
Although of clay, are yet not quite of mud;
 That urns and pipkins are but fragile bro-
 thers,
And works of the same pottery, bad or good,
 Though not all born of the same sires and
 mothers;
It teaches—Heaven knows only what it
 teaches,
But sometimes it may mend, and often
 reaches.

CXXXIX.

Her first thought was to cut off Juan's head;
 Her second, to cut only his—acquaintance;
Her third, to ask him where he had been
 bred;
 Her fourth, to rally him into repentance;
Her fifth, to call her maids and go to bed;
 Her sixth, to stab herself; her seventh, to
 sentence
The lash to Baba:—but her grand resource
Was to sit down again, and cry of course.

CXL.

She thought to stab herself, but then she had
 The dagger close at hand, which made it
 awkward;
For Eastern stays are little made to pad,
 So that a poniard pierces if 'tis stuck hard:
She thought of killing Juan—but, poor lad!
 Though he deserved it well for being so
 backward,
The cutting off his head was not the art
Most likely to attain her aim—his heart.

CXLI.

Juan was moved: he had made up his mind
 To be impaled, or quarter'd as a dish
For dogs, or to be slain with pangs refined,
 Or thrown to lions, or made baits for fish,
 Rather than sin—except to his own wish:
But all his great preparatives for dying
Dissolved like snow before a woman crying.

CXLII.

As through his palms Bob Acres' valour
 oozed,
 So Juan's virtue ebb'd, I know not how;
And first he wonder'd why he had refused;
 And then, if matters could be made up
 now;

And next his savage virtue he accused,
 Just as a friar may accuse his vow,
Or as a dame repents her of her oath,
Which mostly ends in some small breach of
 both.

CXLIII.

So he began to stammer some excuses;
 But words are not enough in such a mat-
 ter,
Although you borrow'd all that e'er the muses
 Have sung, or even a Dandy's dandiest
 chatter,
Or all the figures Castlereagh abuses;
 Just as a languid smile began to flatter
His peace was making, but before he ven-
 tured
Further, old Baba rather briskly enter'd.

CXLIV.

"Bride of the Sun! and Sister of the Moon!"
 ('Twas thus he spake,) "and Empress of
 the Earth!
Whose frown would put the spheres all out
 of tune,
 Whose smile makes all the planets dance
 with mirth,
Your slave brings tidings—he hopes not too
 soon—
 Which your sublime attention may be
 worth:
The Sun himself has sent me like a ray,
To hint that he is coming up this way."

CXLV.

"Is it," exclaim'd Gulbeyaz, "as you say?
 I wish to heaven he would not shine till
 morning!
But bid my women form the Milky-way.
 Hence, my old comet! give the stars due
 warning—
And, Christian! mingle with them as you
 may,
 And as you'd have me pardon your past
 scorning"—
Here they were interrupted by a humming
Sound, and then by a cry, "The Sultan's
 coming!"

CXLVI.

First came her damsels, a decorous file,
 And then his Highness' eunuchs, black
 and white;
The train might reach a quarter of a mile:
 His majesty was always so polite
As to announce his visits a long while
 Before he came, especially at night;
For being the last wife of the Emperour,
She was of course the favourite of the four.

CXLVII.

His Highness was a man of solemn port,
 Shawl'd to the nose, and bearded to the
 eyes,
Snatch'd from a prison to preside at court,
 His lately bowstrung brother caused his
 rise;
He was as good a sovereign of the sort
 As any mentioned in the histories
Of Cantemir, or Knōllĕs, where few shine
Save Solyman, the glory of their line.

CXLVIII.

He went to mosque in state, and said his
 prayers
 With more than "Oriental scrupulosity;"
He left to his vizier all state affairs,
 And show'd but little royal curiosity:
I know not if he had domestic cares—
 No process proved connubial animosity;
Four wives and twice five hundred maids,
 unseen,
Were ruled as calmly as a Christian queen.

CXLIX.

If now and then there happen'd a slight slip,
 Little was heard of criminal or crime;
The story scarcely pass'd a single lip—
 The sack and sea had settled all in time,
From which the secret nobody could rip:
 The public knew no more than does this
 rhyme;
No scandals made the daily press a curse—
Morals were better, and the fish no worse.

CL.

He saw with his own eyes the moon was round,
 Was also certain that the earth was square,
Because he had journey'd fifty miles, and
 found
 No sign that it was circular anywhere:
His empire also was without a bound:
 'Tis true, a little troubled here and there,
By rebel pachas, and encroaching giaours,
But then they never came to "the Seven
 Towers;"

CLI.

Except in shape of envoys, who were sent
 To lodge there when a war broke out,
 according
To the true law of nations, which ne'er meant
 Those scoundrels, who have never had a
 sword in
Their dirty diplomatic hands, to vent
 Their spleen in making strife, and safely
 wording
Their lies, yclept despatches, without risk or
The singeing of a single inky whisker.

CLII.

He had fifty daughters and four dozen sons,
　Of whom all such as came of age were
　　stow'd,
The former in a palace, where like nuns
　They lived till some Bashaw was sent
　　abroad,
When she, whose turn it was, was wed at
　　once,
　Sometimes at six years old—though this
　　　seems odd,
'Tis true; the reason is, that the Bashaw
Must make a present to his sire in law.

CLIII.

His sons were kept in prison, till they grew
　Of years to fill a bowstring or the throne,
One or the other, but which of the two
　Could yet be known unto the fates alone;
Meantime the education they went through
　Was princely, as the proofs have always
　　shown;
So that the heir-apparent still was found
No less deserving to be hang'd than crown'd.

CLIV.

His Majesty saluted his fourth spouse
　With all the ceremonies of his rank,
Who clear'd her sparkling eyes and smooth'd
　　her brows,
　As suits a matron who has play'd a prank;
These must seem doubly mindful of their
　　vows,
　To save the credit of their breaking bank:
To no men are such cordial greetings given
As those whose wives have made them fit
　for heaven.

CLV.

His Highness cast around his great black
　　eyes,
　And looking, as he always look'd, perceived
Juan amongst the damsels in disguise,
　At which he seem'd no whit surprised nor
　　grieved,
But just remark'd with air sedate and wise,
　While still a fluttering sigh Gulbeyaz
　　heaved,
"I see you've bought another girl; 'tis pity
That a mere Christian should be half so
　pretty."

CLVI.

This compliment, which drew all eyes upon
　The new-bought virgin, made her blush
　　and shake.
Her comrades, also, thought themselves un-
　　done:
　Oh! Mahomet! that his Majesty should
　　take

Such notice of a giaour, while scarce to one
　Of them his lips imperial ever spake!
There was a general whisper, toss, and
　　wriggle,
But etiquette forbade them all to giggle.

CLVII.

The Turks do well to shut—at least, some-
　　times—
　The women up—because, in sad reality,
Their chastity in these unhappy climes
　Is not a thing of that astringent quality
Which in the north prevents precocious
　　crimes,
　And makes our snow less pure than our
　　morality;
The sun, which yearly melts the polar ice,
Has quite the contrary effect on vice.

CLVIII.

Thus in the East they are extremely strict,
　And wedlock and a padlock mean the same:
Excepting only when the former's pick'd
　It ne'er can be replaced in proper frame;
Spoilt, as a pipe of claret is when prick'd:
　But then their own polygamy's to blame;
Why don't they knead two virtuous souls
　for life
Into that moral centaur, man and wife?

CLIX.

Thus far our chronicle; and now we pause,
　Though not for want of matter; but 'tis
　　time,
According to the ancient epic laws,
　To slacken sail, and anchor with our
　　rhyme.
Let this fifth canto meet with due applause,
　The sixth shall have a touch of the sub-
　　lime;
Meanwhile, as Homer sometimes sleeps,
　　perhaps
You'll pardon to my Muse a few short naps.

———— ◆◆ ————

PREFACE TO
CANTOS VI. VII. AND VIII.

The details of the siege of Ismail in two of the
following cantos (*i. e.* the seventh and eighth) are
taken from a French Work, entitled "Histoire de
la Nouvelle Russie." Some of the incidents at-
tributed to Don Juan really occurred, particularly
the circumstance of his saving the infant, which
was the actual case of the late Duc de Richelieu,
then a young volunteer in the Russian service, and
afterward the founder and benefactor of Odessa,
where his name and memory can never cease to be
regarded with reverence.

In the course of these cantos, a stanza or two will be found relative to the late Marquis of Londonderry, but written some time before his decease. Had that person's oligarchy died with him, they would have been suppressed; as it is, I am aware of nothing in the manner of his death or of his life to prevent the free expression of the opinions of all whom his whole existence was consumed in endeavouring to enslave. That he was an amiable man in *private* life, may or may not be true : but with this the public have nothing to do; and as to lamenting his death, it will be time enough when Ireland has ceased to mourn for his birth. As a minister, I, for one of millions, looked upon him as the most despotic in intention, and the weakest in intellect, that ever tyrannised over a country. It is the first time indeed since the Normans that England has been insulted by a *minister* (at least) who could not speak English, and that parliament permitted itself to be dictated to in the language of Mrs. Malaprop.

Of the manner of his death little need be said, except that if a poor radical, such as Waddington or Watson, had cut his throat, he would have been buried in a cross-road, with the usual appurtenances of the stake and mallet. But the minister was an elegant lunatic—a sentimental suicide—he merely cut the "carotid artery," (blessings on their learning!) and lo! the pageant, and the Abbey! and "the syllables of dolour yelled forth" by the newspapers—and the harangue of the Coroner in a eulogy over the bleeding body of the deceased—(an Anthony worthy of such a Cæsar)—and the nauseous and atrocious cant of a degraded crew of conspirators against all that is sincere and honourable. In his death he was necessarily one of two things by the *law**—a felon or a madman—and in either case no great subject for panegyric. In his life he was—what all the world knows, and half of it will feel for years to come, unless his death prove a "moral lesson" to the surviving† Sejani of Europe. It may at least serve as some consolation to the nations, that their oppressors are not happy, and in some instances judge so justly of their own actions as to anticipate the sentence of mankind.—Let us hear no more of this man; and let Ireland remove the ashes of her Grattan from the sanctuary of Westminster. Shall the patriot of humanity repose by the Werther of politics!!!

With regard to the objections which have been made on another score to the already published

cantos of this poem, I shall content myself with two quotations from Voltaire :—"La pudeur s'est enfuite des cœurs, et s'est refugiée sur les lèvres." "Plus les mœurs sont dépravés, plus les expressions deviennent mesurées; on croit regagner en langage ce qu'on a perdu en vertu."

This is the real fact, as applicable to the degraded and hypocritical mass which leavens the present English generation, and is the only answer they deserve. The hackneyed and lavished title of Blasphemer—which, with Radical, Liberal, Jacobin, Reformer, &c., are the changes which the hirelings are daily ringing in the ears of those who will listen—should be welcome to all who recollect on *whom* it was originally bestowed. Socrates and Jesus Christ were put to death publicly as *blasphemers*, and so have been and may be many who dare to oppose the most notorious abuses of the name of God and the mind of man. But persecution is not refutation, nor even triumph : the "wretched infidel," as he is called, is probably happier in his prison than the proudest of his assailants. With his opinions I have nothing to do—they may be right or wrong—but he has suffered for them, and that very suffering for conscience' sake will make more proselytes to deism than the example of heterodox prelates to Christianity, suicide statesmen to oppression, or overpensioned homicides to the impious alliance which insults the world with the name of "Holy!" I have no wish to trample on the dishonoured or the dead; but it would be well if the adherents to the classes from whence those persons sprung should abate a little of the *cant* which is the crying sin of this double-dealing and false-speaking time of selfish spoilers, and——but enough for the present.

PISA, *July*, 1822.

Canto the Sixth.

I.

" THERE is a tide in the affairs of men,
　　Which, taken at the flood,"—you know the rest,
And most of us have found it now and then :
　　At least we think so, though but few have guess'd
The moment, till too late to come again.
　　But no doubt everything is for the best—
Of which the surest sign is in the end :
When things are at the worst they sometimes mend.

II.

There is a tide in the affairs of women,
　　Which, taken at the flood, leads—God knows where :
Those navigators must be able seamen
　　Whose charts lay down its current to a hair,

* I say by the *law* of the *land*—the laws of humanity judge more gently; but as the legitimates have always the *law* in their mouths, let them here make the most of it.

† From this number must be excepted Canning. Canning is a genius, almost a universal one, an orator, a wit, a poet, a statesman; and no man of talent can long pursue the path of his late predecessor, Lord C. If ever man saved his country, Canning *can*; but *will* he? I, for one, hope so.

Not all the reveries of Jacob Behmen
 With its strange whirls and eddies can
 compare:
Men with their heads reflect on this and
 that—
But women with their hearts on heaven
 knows what!

III.

And yet a headlong, headstrong, downright
 she,
 Young, beautiful, and daring—who would
 risk
A throne, the world, the universe, to be
 Beloved in her own way, and rather whisk
The stars from out the sky, than not be free
 As are the billows when the breeze is
 brisk—
Though such a she's a devil (if there be one),
Yet she would make full many a Manichean.

IV.

Thrones, worlds, et cetera, are so oft upset
 By commonest ambition, that when passion
O'erthrows the same, we readily forget,
 Or at the least forgive, the loving rash one.
If Anthony be well remember'd yet,
 'Tis not his conquests keep his name in
 fashion,
But Actium, lost for Cleopatra's eyes,
Outbalances all Cæsar's victories.

V.

He died at fifty for a queen of forty;
 I wish their years had been fifteen and
 twenty,
For then wealth, kingdoms, worlds are but a
 sport—I
 Remember when, though I had no great
 plenty
Of worlds to lose, yet still, to pay my court, I
 Gave what I had—a heart; as the world
 went, I
Gave what was worth a world; for worlds
 could never
Restore me those pure feelings, gone for
 ever.

VI.

'Twas the boy's "mite," and, like the
 "widow's," may
 Perhaps be weigh'd hereafter, if not now;
But whether such things do or do not weigh,
 All who have loved, or love, will still allow
Life has nought like it. God is love, they say,
 And Love's a god, or was before the brow
Of earth was wrinkled by the sins and tears
Of—but Chronology best knows the years.

VII.

We left our hero and third heroine in
 A kind of state more awkward than un-
 common,
For gentlemen must sometimes risk their skin
 For that sad tempter, a forbidden woman:
Sultans too much abhor this sort of sin,
 And don't agree at all with the wise Ro-
 man,
Heroic, stoic Cato, the sententious,
Who lent his lady to his friend Hortensius.

VIII.

I know Gulbeyaz was extremely wrong;
 I own it, I deplore it, I condemn it;
But I detest all fiction even in song,
 And so must tell the truth, howe'er you
 blame it.
Her reason being weak, her passions strong,
 She thought that her lord's heart (even
 could she claim it)
Was scarce enough; for he had fifty-nine
Years, and a fifteen-hundredth concubine.

IX.

I am not, like Cassio, "an arithmetician,"
 But by the "bookish theoric" it appears,
If 'tis summ'd up with feminine precision,
 That, adding to the account his Highness'
 years,
The fair Sultana erred from inanition;
 For, were the Sultan just to all his dears,
She could but claim the fifteen-hundredth
 part
Of what should be monopoly—the heart.

X.

It is observed that ladies are litigious
 Upon all legal objects of possession,
And not the least so when they are religious,
 Which doubles what they think of the
 transgression:
With suits and prosecutions they besiege us,
 As the tribunals show through many a
 session,
When they suspect that any one goes shares
In that to which the law makes them sole
 heirs.

XI.

Now, if this holds good in a Christian land,
 The heathen also, though with lesser
 latitude,
Are apt to carry things with a high hand,
 And take, what kings call "an imposing
 attitude;"

And for their rights connubial make a stand,
 When their liege husbands treat them with
 ingratitude;
And as four wives must have quadruple
 claims,
The Tigris hath its jealousies like Thames.

XII.

Gulbeyaz was the fourth, and (as I said)
 The favourite; but what's favour amongst
 four?
Polygamy may well be held in dread,
 Not only as a sin, but as a *bore:*
Most wise men with *one* moderate woman
 wed,
 Will scarcely find philosophy for more;
And all (except Mahometans) forbear
To make the nuptial couch a "Bed of Ware."

XIII.

His Highness, the sublimest of mankind,—
 So styled according to the usual forms
Of every monarch, till they are consign'd
 To those sad hungry Jacobins the worms,
Who on the very loftiest kings have dined,—
 His Highness gazed upon Gulbeyaz' charms,
Expecting all the welcome of a lover
(A "Highland welcome" all the wide world
 over).

XIV.

Now here we should distinguish; for howe'er
 Kisses, sweet words, embraces, and all that,
May look like what is—neither here nor there,
 They are put on as easily as a hat,
Or rather bonnet, which the fair sex wear,
 Trimm'd either heads or hearts to decorate,
Which form an ornament, but no more part
Of heads, than their caresses of the heart.

XV.

A slight blush, a soft tremor, a calm kind
 Of gentle feminine delight, and shown
More in the eyelids than the eyes, resign'd
 Rather to hide what pleases most unknown,
Are the best tokens (to a modest mind)
 Of love, when seated on his loveliest throne,
A sincere woman's breast,—for over-*warm*
Or over-*cold* annihilates the charm.

XVI.

For over-warmth, if false, is worse than truth;
 If true, 'tis no great lease of its own fire;
For no one, save in very early youth,
 Would like (I think) to trust all to desire,
Which is but a precarious bond, in sooth,
 And apt to be transferr'd to the first buyer
At a sad discount: while your over-chilly
Women, on t' other hand, seem somewhat
 silly.

XVII.

That is, we cannot pardon their bad taste,
 For so it seems to lovers swift or slow,
Who fain would have a mutual flame con-
 fess'd,
 And see a sentimental passion glow,
Even were St. Francis' paramour their guest,
 In his monastic concubine of snow;—
In short, the maxim for the amorous tribe is
Horatian, "Medio tu tutissimus ibis."

XVIII.

The "tu"'s *too* much,—but let it stand,—the
 verse
 Requires it, that's to say, the English
 rhyme,
And not the pink of old hexameters;
 But, after all, there's neither tune nor
 time
In the last line, which cannot well be worse,
 And was thrust in to close the octave's
 chime:
I own no prosody can ever rate it
As a rule, but *truth* may, if you translate it.

XIX.

If fair Gulbeyaz overdid her part,
 I know not—it succeeded, and success
Is much in most things, not less in the heart
 Than other articles of female dress.
Self-love in man, too, beats all female art;
 They lie, we lie, all lie, but love no less:
And no one virtue yet, except starvation,
Could stop that worst of vices—propagation

XX.

We leave this royal couple to repose:
 A bed is not a throne, and they may sleep,
Whate'er their dreams be, if of joys or woes:
 Yet disappointed joys are woes as deep
As any man's clay mixture undergoes.
 Our least of sorrows are such as we weep;
'Tis the vile daily drop on drop which wears
The soul out (like the stone) with petty cares.

XXI.

A scolding wife, a sullen son, a bill
 To pay, unpaid, protested or discounted
At a per-centage; a child cross, dog ill,
 A favourite horse fallen lame just as he's
 mounted,
A bad old woman making a worse will,
 Which leaves you minus of the cash you
 counted
As certain;—these are paltry things, and yet
I've rarely seen the man they did not fret.

XXII.

I'm a philosopher; confound them all!
 Bills, beasts, and men, and—no! *not*
 womankind!
With one good hearty curse I vent my gall,
 And then my stoicism leaves nought behind
Which it can either pain or evil call,
 And I can give my whole soul up to mind;
Though what *is* soul, or mind, their birth or
 growth,
Is more than I know—the deuce take them
 both!

XXIII.

So now all things are d—n'd one feels at ease,
 As after reading Athanasius' curse,
Which doth your true believer so much
 please:
I doubt if any now could make it worse
O'er his worst enemy when at his knees,
 'Tis so sententious, positive, and terse,
And decorates the book of Common Prayer,
As doth a rainbow the just clearing air.

XXIV.

Gulbeyaz and her lord were sleeping, or
 At least one of them!—Oh, the heavy night,
When wicked wives, who love some bachelor,
 Lie down in dudgeon to sigh for the light
Of the grey morning, and look vainly for
 Its twinkle through the lattice dusky
 quite—
To toss, to tumble, doze, revive, and quake
Lest their too lawful bed-fellow should wake!

XXV.

These are beneath the canopy of heaven,
 Also beneath the canopy of beds
Four-posted and silk-curtain'd, which are
 given
 For rich men and their brides to lay their
 heads
Upon, in sheets white as what bards call
 "driven
Snow." Well! 'tis all hap-hazard when
 one weds.
Gulbeyaz was an empress, but had been
Perhaps as wretched if a *peasant's quean.*

XXVI.

Don Juan in his feminine disguise,
 With all the damsels in their long array,
Had bow'd themselves before th' imperial
 eyes,
 And at the usual signal ta'en their way
Back to their chambers, those long galleries
 In the seraglio, where the ladies lay
Their delicate limbs; a thousand bosoms there
Beating for love, as the caged bird's for air.

XXVII.

I love the sex, and sometimes would reverse
 The tyrant's wish, "that mankind only had
One neck, which he with one fell stroke
 might pierce:"
My wish is quite as wide, but not so bad,
 And much more tender on the whole than
 fierce;
It being (not *now*, but only while a lad)
That womankind had but one rosy mouth,
To kiss them all at once from North to South.

XXVIII.

Oh, enviable Briareus! with thy hands
 And heads, if thou hadst all things multi-
 plied
In such proportion!—But my Muse with-
 stands
 The giant thought of being a Titan's bride,
Or travelling in Patagonian lands;
 So let us back to Lilliput, and guide
Our hero through the labyrinth of love
In which we left him several lines above.

XXIX.

He went forth with the lovely Odalisques,
 At the given signal join'd to their array:
And though he certainly ran many risks,
 Yet he could not at times keep, by the way,
(Although the consequences of such frisks
 Are worse than the worst damages men pay
In moral England, where the thing's a tax,)
From ogling all their charms from breasts
 to backs.

XXX.

Still he forgot not his disguise:—along
 The galleries from room to room they
 walk'd,
A virgin-like and edifying throng,
 By eunuchs flank'd; while at their head
 there stalk'd
A dame who kept up discipline among
 The female ranks, so that none stirr'd or
 talk'd,
Without her sanction on their she-parades:
Her title was "the Mother of the Maids."

XXXI.

Whether she was a "mother," I know not,
 Or whether they were "maids" who call'd
 her mother;
But this is her seraglio title, got
 I know not how, but good as any other;
So Cantemir can tell you, or De Tott:
 Her office was to keep aloof or smother
All bad propensities in fifteen hundred
Young women, and correct them when they
 blunder'd.

XXXII.

A goodly sinecure, no doubt! but made
 More easy by the absence of all men—
Except his majesty,—who, with her aid,
 And guards, and bolts, and walls, and now
 and then,
A slight example, just to cast a shade
 Along the rest, contrived to keep this den
Of beauties cool as an Italian convent,
Where all the passions have, alas! but one
 vent.

XXXIII.

And what is that? Devotion, doubtless—how
 Could you ask such a question?—but we
 will
Continue. As I said, this goodly row
 Of ladies of all countries at the will
Of one good man, with stately march and
 slow,
 Like water-lilies floating down a rill—
Or rather lake—for *rills* do *not* run *slowly*,—
Paced on most maiden-like and melancholy.

XXXIV.

But when they reach'd their own apartments,
 there,
 Like birds, or boys, or bedlamites broke
 loose,
Waves at spring-tide, or women anywhere
 When freed from bonds (which are of no
 great use
After all), or like Irish at a fair,
 Their guards being gone, and as it were a
 truce
Establish'd between them and bondage, they
Began to sing, dance, chatter, smile, and play.

XXXV.

Their talk, of course, ran most on the new
 comer;
 Her shape, her hair, her air, her every-
 thing:
Some thought her dress did not so much be-
 come her,
 Or wonder'd at her ears without a ring;
Some said her years were getting nigh their
 summer,
 Others contended they were but in spring;
Some thought her rather masculine in height,
While others wish'd that she had been so
 quite.

XXXVI.

But no one doubted on the whole, that she
 Was what her dress bespoke, a damsel fair,
And fresh, and "beautiful exceedingly,"
 Who with the brightest Georgians might
 compare:

XXXVII.

They wonder'd how Gulbeyaz, too, could be
 So silly as to buy slaves who might share
(If that his Highness wearied of his bride)
 Her throne and power, and everything be-
 side.

XXXVII.

But what was strangest in this virgin crew,
 Although her beauty was enough to vex,
After the first investigating view,
 They all found out as few, or fewer, specks
In the fair form of their companion new,
 Than is the custom of the gentle sex,
When they survey, with Christian eyes or
 Heathen,
In a new face "the ugliest creature breath-
 ing."

XXXVIII.

And yet they had their little jealousies,
 Like all the rest; but upon this occasion,
Whether there are such things as sympathies
 Without our knowledge or our approbation,
Although they could not see through his
 disguise,
 All felt a soft kind of concatenation,
Like magnetism, or devilism, or what
You please—we will not quarrel about that:

XXXIX.

But certain 'tis they all felt for their new
 Companion something newer still, as 'twere
A sentimental friendship through and through,
 Extremely pure, which made them all con-
 cur
In wishing her their sister, save a few
 Who wish'd they had a brother just like
 her,
Whom, if they were at home in sweet Cir-
 cassia,
They would prefer to Padisha or Pacha.

XL.

Of those who had most genius for this sort
 Of sentimental friendship, there were three,
Lolah, Katinka, and Dudù; in short
 (To save description), fair as fair can be
Were they, according to the best report,
 Though differing in stature and degree,
And clime and time, and country and com-
 plexion;
They all alike admired their new connexion.

XLI.

Lolah was dusk as India and as warm;
 Katinka was a Georgian, white and red,
With great blue eyes, a lovely hand and arm,
 And feet so small they scarce seem'd made
 to tread,

But rather skim the earth; while Dudù's
form
　　Look'd more adapted to be put to bed,
Being somewhat large, and languishing, and
lazy,
　　Yet of a beauty that would drive you crazy.

XLII.

A kind of sleepy Venus seem'd Dudù,
　　Yet very fit to "murder sleep" in those
Who gazed upon her cheek's transcendent
hue,
　　Her Attic forehead, and her Phidian nose:
Few angles were there in her form, 'tis
true,
　　Thinner she might have been, and yet
scarce lose:
Yet, after all, 'twould puzzle to say where
It would not spoil some separate charm to
pare.

XLIII.

She was not violently lively, but
　　Stole on your spirit like a May-day break-
ing;
Her eyes were not too sparkling, yet, half-
shut,
　　They put beholders in a tender taking;
She look'd (this simile's quite new) just cut
　　From marble, like Pygmalion's statue wak-
ing,
The mortal and the marble still at strife,
And timidly expanding into life.

XLIV.

Lolah demanded the new damsel's name—
　　"Juanna,"—Well, a pretty name enough.
Katinka ask'd her also whence she came—
　　"From Spain."—"But where *is* Spain?"—
"Don't ask such stuff,
Nor show your Georgian ignorance—for
shame!"
　　Said Lolah, with an accent rather rough,
To poor Katinka: "Spain's an island near
Morocco, betwixt Egypt and Tangier."

XLV.

Dudù said nothing, but sat down beside
　　Juanna, playing with her veil or hair;
And looking at her stedfastly, she sigh'd,
　　As if she pitied her for being there,
A pretty stranger, without friend or guide,
　　And all abash'd, too, at the general stare
Which welcomes hapless strangers in all
places,
With kind remarks upon their mien and
faces.

XLVI.

But here the Mother of the Maids drew near,
　　With "Ladies, it is time to go to rest:
I'm puzzled what to do with you, my dear,"
　　She added to Juanna, their new guest:
"Your coming has been unexpected here,
　　And every couch is occupied; you had best
Partake of mine; but by to-morrow early
We will have all things settled for you fairly."

XLVII.

Here Lolah interposed—"Mamma, you know
　　You don't sleep soundly, and I cannot bear
That anybody should disturb you so;
　　I'll take Juanna; we're a slenderer pair
Than you would make the half of;—don't
say no;
　　And I of your young charge will take due
care."
But here Katinka interfered, and said,
"She also had compassion and a bed."

XLVIII.

"Besides, I hate to sleep alone," quoth she.
　　The matron frown'd: "Why so?"—"For
fear of ghosts,"
Replied Katinka; "I am sure I see
　　A phantom upon each of the four posts;
And then I have the worst dreams that can be,
　　Of Guebres, Giaours, and Ginns, and Gouls
in hosts."
The dame replied, "Between your dreams
and you,
I fear Juanna's dreams would be but few.

XLIX.

"You, Lolah, must continue still to lie
　　Alone, for reasons which don't matter; you
The same, Katinka, until by and by:
　　And I shall place Juanna with Dudù,
Who's quiet, inoffensive, silent, shy,
　　And will not toss and chatter the night
through.
What say you, child?"—Dudù said nothing,
as
Her talents were of the more silent class;

L.

But she rose up, and kiss'd the matron's brow
　　Between the eyes, and Lolah on both cheeks,
Katinka too; and with a gentle bow
　　(Curt'sies are neither used by Turks nor
Greeks)
She took Juanna by the hand to show
　　Their place of rest, and left to both their
piques,
The others pouting at the matron's preference
Of Dudù, though they held their tongues
from deference.

LI.

It was a spacious chamber (Oda is
　The Turkish title), and ranged round the
　　wall
Were couches, toilets—and much more than
　　this
I might describe, as I have seen it all,
But it suffices—little was amiss;
　'Twas on the whole a nobly furnish'd hall,
With all things ladies want, save one or two,
And even those were nearer than they knew.

LII.

Dudù, as has been said, was a sweet creature,
　Not very dashing, but extremely winning,
With the most regulated charms of feature,
　Which painters cannot catch like faces sin-
　　ning
Against proportion—the wild strokes of na-
　　ture
Which they hit off at once in the beginning,
Full of expression, right or wrong, that strike,
And pleasing, or unpleasing, still are like.

LIII.

But she was a soft landscape of mild earth,
　Where all was harmony, and calm, and
　　quiet,
Luxuriant, budding; cheerful without mirth,
　Which, if not happiness, is much more
　　nigh it
Than are your mighty passions and so forth,
　Which some call "the sublime:" I wish
　　they'd try it:
I've seen your stormy seas and stormy
　　women,
And pity lovers rather more than seamen.

LIV.

But she was pensive more than melancholy,
　And serious more than pensive, and serene,
It may be, more than either—not unholy
　Her thoughts, at least till now, appear to
　　have been.
The strangest thing was, beauteous, she was
　　wholly
　Unconscious, albeit turn'd of quick seven-
　　teen,
That she was fair, or dark, or short, or tall;
She never thought about herself at all.

LV.

And therefore was she kind and gentle as
　The Age of Gold (when gold was yet un-
　　known),
By which its nomenclature came to pass;
　Thus most appropriately has been shown

"Lucus à non lucendo," not what was,
　But what was not; a sort of style that's
　　grown
Extremely common in this age, whose metal
The devil may decompose, but never settle:

LVI.

I think it may be of "Corinthian Brass,"
　Which was a mixture of all metals, but
The brazen uppermost). Kind reader! pass
　This long parenthesis: I could not shut
It sooner for the soul of me, and class
　My faults even with your own! which
　　meaneth, Put
A kind construction upon them and me:
But that you won't—then don't—I am not
　less free.

LVII.

'Tis time we should return to plain nar-
　　ration,
　And thus my narrative proceeds:—Dudù,
With every kindness short of ostentation,
　Show'd Juan, or Juanna, through and
　　through
This labyrinth of females, and each station
　Described—what's strange—in words ex-
　　tremely few:
I have but one simile, and that's a blunder,
For wordless woman, which is silent thunder.

LVIII.

And next she gave her (I say her, because
　The gender still was epicene, at least
In outward show, which is a saving clause)
　An outline of the customs of the East,
With all their chaste integrity of laws,
　By which the more a harem is increased,
The stricter doubtless grow the vestal duties
Of any supernumerary beauties.

LIX.

And then she gave Juanna a chaste kiss:
　Dudù was fond of kissing—which I'm sure
That nobody can ever take amiss,
　Because 'tis pleasant, so that it be pure,
And between females means no more than
　　this—
　That they have nothing better near, or
　　newer.
"Kiss" rhymes to "bliss" in fact as well as
　　verse—
I wish it never led to something worse.

LX.

In perfect innocence she then unmade
　Her toilet, which cost little, for she was
A child of Nature carelessly array'd:
　If fond of a chance ogle at her glass,

'T was like the fawn, which, in the lake dis-
　　play'd,
　Beholds her own shy, shadowy image pass,
When first she starts, and then returns to
　　peep,
　Admiring this new native of the deep.

LXI.

And one by one her articles of dress
　Were laid aside; but not before she offer'd
Her aid to fair Juanna, whose excess
　Of modesty declined the assistance prof-
　　fer'd:
Which pass'd well off—as she could do no
　　less;
　Though by this politesse she rather suffer'd,
Pricking her fingers with those cursed pins,
Which surely were invented for our sins,—

LXII.

Making a woman like a porcupine,
　Not to be rashly touch'd. But still more
　　dread,
Oh, ye! whose fate it is, as once 'twas
　　mine,
　In early youth, to turn a lady's maid;—
I did my very boyish best to shine
　In tricking her out for a masquerade:
The pins were placed sufficiently, but not
Stuck all exactly in the proper spot.

LXIII.

But these are foolish things to all the wise,
　And I love wisdom more than she loves
　　me;
My tendency is to philosophise
　On most things, from a tyrant to a tree;
But still the spouseless virgin *Knowledge*
　　flies.
　What are we? and whence came we? what
　　shall be
Our *ultimate* existence? what's our present?
Are questions answerless, and yet incessant.

LXIV.

There was deep silence in the chamber: dim
　And distant from each other burn'd the
　　lights,
And slumber hover'd o'er each lovely limb
　Of the fair occupants: if there be sprites,
They should have walk'd there in their
　　sprightliest trim,
　By way of change from their sepulchral
　　sites,
And shown themselves as ghosts of better
　　taste
Than haunting some old ruin or wild waste.

LXV.

Many and beautiful lay those around,
　Like flowers of different hue, and clime,
　　and root,
In some exotic garden sometimes found,
　With cost, and care, and warmth, induced
　　to shoot.
One with her auburn tresses lightly bound,
　And fair brows gently drooping, as the
　　fruit
Nods from the tree, was slumbering with
　　soft breath,
And lips apart, which show'd the pearls
　　beneath.

LXVI.

One with her flush'd cheek laid on her white
　　arm,
　And raven ringlets gather'd in dark crowd
Above her brow, lay dreaming soft and
　　warm;
　And smiling through her dream, as through
　　a cloud
The moon breaks, half unveil'd each further
　　charm,
　As, slightly stirring in her snowy shroud,
Her beauties seized the unconscious hour of
　　night
All bashfully to struggle into light.

LXVII.

This is no bull, although it sounds so; for
　'T was night, but there were lamps, as
　　hath been said.
A third's all pallid aspect offer'd more
　The traits of sleeping sorrow, and betray'd
Through the heaved breast the dream of
　　some far shore
　Beloved and deplored; while slowly stray'd
(As night-dew, on a cypress glittering, tinges
The black bough) tear-drops through her
　　eyes' dark fringes.

LXVIII.

A fourth as marble, statue-like and still,
　Lay in a breathless, hush'd, and stony
　　sleep;
White, cold, and pure, as looks a frozen
　　rill,
　Or the snow minaret on an Alpine steep,
Or Lot's wife done in salt,—or what you
　　will;—
　My similes are gather'd in a heap,
So pick and choose—perhaps you'll be
　　content
With a carved lady on a monument.

LXIX.

And lo! a fifth appears;—and what is she?
 A lady of a "certain age," which means
Certainly aged—what her years might be
 I know not, never counting past their
 teens;
But there she slept, not quite so fair to see,
 As ere that awful period intervenes
Which lays both men and women on the shelf,
To meditate upon their sins and self.

LXX.

But all this time how slept, or dream'd,
 Dudù?
 With strict inquiry I could ne'er discover,
And scorn to add a syllable untrue;
 But ere the middle watch was hardly over,
Just when the fading lamps waned dim and
 blue,
 And phantoms hover'd, or might seem to
 hover,
To those who like their company, about
The apartment, on a sudden she scream'd
 out:

LXXI.

And that so loudly, that upstarted all
 The Oda, in a general commotion:
Matron and maids, and those whom you may
 call
 Neither, came crowding like the waves of
 ocean,
One on the other, throughout the whole hall,
 All trembling, wondering, without the least
 notion
More than I have myself of what could make
The calm Dudù so turbulently wake.

LXXII.

But wide awake she was, and round her bed,
 With floating draperies and with flying
 hair,
With eager eyes, and light but hurried tread,
 And bosoms, arms, and ankles glancing
 bare,
And bright as any meteor ever bred'
 By the North Pole,—they sought her cause
 of care,
For she seem'd agitated, flush'd, and fright-
 en'd,
Her eye dilated, and her colour heighten'd.

LXXIII.

But what is strange—and a strong proof how
 great
 A blessing is sound sleep—Juanna lay
As fast as ever husband by his mate
 In holy matrimony snores away.

Not all the clamour broke her happy state
 Of slumber, ere they shook her,—so they
 say
At least,—and then she, too, unclosed her
 eyes,
And yawned a good deal with discreet
 surprise.

LXXIV.

And now commenced a strict investigation,
 Which, as all spoke at once, and more
 than once
Conjecturing, wondering, asking a narration,
 Alike might puzzle either wit or dunce
To answer in a very clear oration.
 Dudù had never pass'd for wanting sense,
But being "no orator as Brutus is,"
Could not at first expound what was amiss.

LXXV.

At length she said, that in a slumber sound
 She dream'd a dream, of walking in a
 wood—
A "wood obscure," like that where Dante
 found
 Himself in at the age when all grow good;
Life's half-way house, where dames with
 virtue crown'd
 Run much less risk of lovers turning rude;
And that this wood was full of pleasant
 fruits,
And trees of goodly growth and spreading
 roots;

LXXVI.

And in the midst a golden apple grew,—
 A most prodigious pippin—but it hung
Rather too high and distant; that she threw
 Her glances on it, and then, longing, flung
Stones and whatever she could pick up, to
 Bring down the fruit, which still perversely
 clung
To its own bough, and dangled yet in sight,
But always at a most provoking height;—

LXXVII.

That on a sudden, when she least had hope,
 It fell down of its own accord before
Her feet; that her first movement was to stoop
 And pick it up, and bite it to the core;
That just as her young lip began to ope
 Upon the golden fruit the vision bore,
A bee flew out, and stung her to the heart,
And so—she woke with a great scream and
 start.

LXXVIII.

All this she told with some confusion and
 Dismay, the usual consequence of dreams
Of the unpleasant kind, with none at hand
 To expound their vain and visionary
 gleams.

I've known some odd ones which seem'd
 really plann'd
Prophetically, or that which one deems
A "strange coincidence," to use a phrase
By which such things are settled now-a-days.

LXXIX.

The damsels, who had thoughts of some
 great harm,
 Began, as is the consequence of fear,
To scold a little at the false alarm
 That broke for nothing on their sleeping ear.
The matron, too, was wroth to leave her
 warm
 Bed for the dream she had been obliged to
 hear,
And chafed at poor Dudù, who only sigh'd,
And said, that she was sorry she had cried.

LXXX.

"I've heard of stories of a cock and bull;
 But visions of an apple and a bee,
To take us from our natural rest, and pull
 The whole Oda from their beds at half-past
 three,
Would make us think the moon is at its full.
 You surely are unwell, child! we must see,
To-morrow, what his Highness's physician
Will say to this hysteric of a vision.

LXXXI.

"And poor Juanna, too, the child's first
 night
 Within these walls, to be broke in upon
With such a clamour—I had thought it right
 That the young stranger should not lie
 alone,
And, as the quietest of all, she might
 With you, Dudù, a good night's rest have
 known:
But now I must transfer her to the charge
Of Lolah—though her couch is not so large."

LXXXII.

Lolah's eyes sparkled at the proposition;
 But poor Dudù, with large drops in her own,
Resulting from the scolding or the vision,
 Implored that present pardon might be
 shown
For this first fault, and that on no condition
 (She added in a soft and piteous tone)
Juanna should be taken from her, and
Her future dreams should be all kept in hand.

LXXXIII.

She promised never more to have a dream,
 At least to dream so loudly as just now;
She wonder'd at herself how she could
 scream—
 'T was foolish, nervous, as she must allow,

A fond hallucination, and a theme
 For laughter—but she felt her spirits low,
And begg'd they would excuse her; she'd get
 over
This weakness in a few hours, and recover.

LXXXIV.

And here Juanna kindly interposed,
 And said she felt herself extremely well
Where she then was, as her sound sleep
 disclosed,
 When all around rang like a tocsin bell;
She did not find herself the least disposed
 To quit her gentle partner, and to dwell
Apart from one who had no sin to show,
Save that of dreaming once "mal à-propos."

LXXXV.

As thus Juanna spoke, Dudù turn'd round
 And hid her face within Juanna's breast:
Her neck alone was seen, but that was found
 The colour of a budding rose's crest.
I can't tell why she blush'd, nor can expound
 The mystery of this rupture of their rest;
All that I know is, that the facts I state
Are true as truth has ever been of late.

LXXXVI.

And so good night to them—or, if you will,
 Good morrow—for the cock had crown,
 and light
Began to clothe each Asiatic hill,
 And the mosque crescent struggled into
 sight
Of the long caravan, which in the chill
 Of dewy dawn wound slowly round each
 height
That stretches to the stony belt, which girds
Asia, where Kaff looks down upon the Kurds.

LXXXVII.

With the first ray, or rather grey of morn,
 Gulbeyaz rose from restlessness; and pale
As Passion rises, with its bosom worn,
 Array'd herself with mantle, gem, and veil.
The nightingale that sings with the deep
 thorn,
 Which fable places in her breast of wail,
Is lighter far of heart and voice than those
Whose headlong passions form their proper
 woes.

LXXXVIII.

And that's the moral of this composition,
 If people would but see its real drift;—
But *that* they will not do without suspicion,
 Because all gentle readers have the gift

Of closing 'gainst the light their orbs of
　　vision
While gentle writers also love to lift
Their voices 'gainst each other, which is
　　natural,
The numbers are too great for them to
　　flatter all.

LXXXIX.

Rose the sultana from a bed of splendour,
　　Softer than the soft Sybarite's, who cried
Aloud because his feelings were too tender
　　To brook a ruffled rose-leaf by his side,—
So beautiful that art could little mend her,
　　Though pale with conflicts between love
　　　and pride;
So agitated was she with her error,
She did not even look into the mirror.

XC.

Also arose about the self-same time,
　　Perhaps a little later, her great lord,
Master of thirty kingdoms so sublime,
　　And of a wife by whom he was abhorr'd;
A thing of much less import in that clime—
　　At least to those of incomes which afford
The filling up their whole connubial cargo—
Than where two wives are under an embargo.

XCI.

He did not think much on the matter, nor
　　Indeed on any other: as a man
He liked to have a handsome paramour
　　At hand, as one may like to have a fan,
And therefore of Circassians had good store,
　　As an amusement after the Divan;
Though an unusual fit of love, or duty,
Had made him lately bask in his bride's
　　beauty.

XCII.

And now he rose; and after due ablutions
　　Exacted by the customs of the East,
And prayers and other pious evolutions,
　　He drank six cups of coffee at the least,
And then withdrew to hear about the
　　Russians,
　　Whose victories had recently increased
In Catherine's reign, whom glory still adores,
As greatest of all sovereigns and w——s.

XCIII.

But oh, thou grand legitimate Alexander!
　　Her son's son, let not this last phrase
　　　offend
Thine ear, if it should reach—and now
　　rhymes wander
　　Almost as far as Petersburgh, and lend

A dreadful impulse to each loud meander
　　Of murmuring Liberty's wide waves, which
　　　blend
Their roar even with the Baltic's—so you be
Your father's son, 't is quite enough for me.

XCIV.

To call men love-begotten, or proclaim
　　Their mothers as the antipodes of Timon,
That hater of mankind, would be a shame,
　　A libel, or whate'er you please to rhyme on:
But people's ancestors are history's game;
　　And if one lady's slip could leave a crime
　　　on
All generations, I should like to know
What pedigree the best would have to show?

XCV.

Had Catherine and the sultan understood
　　Their own true interests, which kings
　　　rarely know,
Until 't is taught by lessons rather rude,
　　There was a way to end their strife,
　　　although
Perhaps precarious, had they but thought
　　good,
　　Without the aid of prince or plenipo:
She to dismiss her guards and he his harem,
And for their other matters, meet and
　　share 'em.

XCVI.

But as it was, his Highness had to hold
　　His daily council upon ways and means
How to encounter with this martial scold,
　　This modern Amazon and queen of queans;
And the perplexity could not be told
　　Of all the pillars of the state, which leans
Sometimes a little heavy on the backs
Of those who cannot lay on a new tax.

XCVII.

Meantime Gulbeyaz, when her king was
　　gone,
　　Retired into her boudoir, a sweet place
For love or breakfast; private, pleasing, lone,
　　And rich with all contrivances which grace
Those gay recesses:—many a precious stone
　　Sparkled along its roof, and many a vase
Of porcelain held in the fetter'd flowers
Those captive soothers of a captive's hours.

XCVIII.

Mother of pearl, and porphyry, and marble,
　　Vied with each other on this costly spot;
And singing birds without were heard to
　　warble;
　　And the stain'd glass which lighted this
　　　fair grot

Varied each ray;—but all descriptions garble
 The true effect, and so we had better not
Be too minute; an outline is the best,—
 A lively reader's fancy does the rest.

XCIX.

And here she summon'd Baba, and required
 Don Juan at his hands, and information
Of what had pass'd since all the slaves re-
tired,
 And whether he had occupied their station:
If matters had been managed as desired,
 And his disguise with due consideration
Kept up; and above all, the where and how
He had pass'd the night, was what she
 wish'd to know.

C.

Baba, with some embarrassment, replied
 To this long catechism of questions, ask'd
More easily than answer'd,—that he had
 tried
 His best to obey in what he had been
 task'd;
But there seem'd something that he wish'd
 to hide,
 Which hesitation more betray'd than
 mask'd;
He scratch'd his ear, the infallible resource
To which embarrass'd people have recourse.

CI.

Gulbeyaz was no model of true patience,
 Nor much disposed to wait in word or
 deed;
She liked quick answers in all conversations;
 And when she saw him stumbling like a
 steed
In his replies, she puzzled him for fresh
 ones;
 And as his speech grew still more broken-
 kneed,
Her cheek began to flush, her eyes to sparkle,
And her proud brow's blue veins to swell
 and darkle.

CII.

When Baba saw these symptoms, which he
 knew
 To bode him no great good, he deprecated
Her anger, and beseech'd she'd hear him
 through—
 He could not help the thing which he re-
 lated:
Then out it came at length, that to Dudù
 Juan was given in charge, as hath been
 stated;
But not by Baba's fault, he said, and swore
 on
The holy camel's hump, besides the Koran.

CIII.

The chief dame of the Oda, upon whom
 The discipline of the whole harem bore,
As soon as they reënter'd their own room,
 For Baba's function stopt short at the
 door,
Had settled all; nor could he then presume
 (The aforesaid Baba) just then to do more,
Without exciting such suspicion as
Might make the matter still worse than it
 was.

CIV.

He hoped, indeed he thought, he could be
 sure,
 Juan had not betray'd himself; in fact
'T was certain that his conduct had been
 pure,
 Because a foolish or imprudent act
Would not alone have made him insecure,
 But ended in his being found out and
 sack'd,
And thrown into the sea.—Thus Baba spoke
Of all save Dudù's dream, which was no joke.

CV.

This he discreetly kept in the back ground,
 And talk'd away—and might have talk'd
 till now,
For any further answer that he found,
 So deep an anguish wrung Gulbeyaz'
 brow:
Her cheek turn'd ashes, ears rung, brain
 whirl'd round,
 As if she had received a sudden blow,
And the heart's dew of pain sprang fast and
 chilly
O'er her fair front, like Morning's on a lily.

CVI.

Although she was not of the fainting sort,
 Baba thought she would faint, but there he
 err'd—
It was but a convulsion, which though short
 Can never be described; we all have
 heard,
And some of us have felt thus "*all amort,*"
 When things beyond the common have
 occurr'd;—
Gulbeyaz proved in that brief agony
What she could ne'er express—then how
 should I?

CVII.

She stood a moment as a Pythoness
 Stands on her tripod, agonised, and full
Of inspiration gather'd from distress,
 When all the heart-strings like wild horses
 pull

The heart asunder;—then, as more or less
　　Their speed abated or their strength grew
　　　dull,
She sunk down on her seat by slow degrees,
And bow'd her throbbing head o'er trembling
　　knees.

CVIII.

Her face declined and was unseen; her hair
　　Fell in long tresses like the weeping willow,
Sweeping the marble underneath her chair,
　　Or rather sofa (for it was all pillow,
A low, soft ottoman), and black despair
　　Stirr'd up and down her bosom like a
　　　billow,
Which rushes to some shore whose shingles
　　check
Its farther course, but must receive its wreck.

CIX.

Her head hung down, and her long hair in
　　stooping
　　Conceal'd her features better than a veil;
And one hand o'er the ottoman lay drooping,
　　White, waxen, and as alabaster pale:
Would that I were a painter! to be grouping
　　All that a poet drags into detail!
Oh that my words were colours! but their
　　tints
May serve perhaps as outlines or slight hints.

CX.

Baba, who knew by experience when to talk
　　And when to hold his tongue, now held it
　　　till
This passion might blow o'er, nor dared to
　　balk
　　Gulbeyaz' taciturn or speaking will.
At length she rose up, and began to walk
　　Slowly along the room, but silent still,
And her brow clear'd, but not her troubled
　　eye;
The wind was down but still the sea ran
　　high.

CXI.

She stopp'd, and raised her head to speak—
　　but paused,
　　And then moved on again with rapid pace;
Then slacken'd it, which is the march most
　　caused
　　By deep emotion:—you may sometimes
　　　trace
A feeling in each footstep, as disclosed
By Sallust in his Catiline, who, chased
By all the demons of all passions, show'd
Their work even by the way in which he
　　trode.

CXII.

Gulbeyaz stopp'd and beckon'd Baba:—
　　"Slave!
　　Bring the two slaves!" she said in a low
　　　tone,
But one which Baba did not like to brave,
　　And yet he shudder'd, and seem'd rather
　　　prone
To prove reluctant, and begg'd leave to crave
　　(Though he well knew the meaning) to be
　　　shown
What slaves her highness wish'd to indicate,
For fear of any error, like the late.

CXIII.

"The Georgian and her paramour," replied
　　The imperial bride—and added, "Let the
　　　boat
Be ready by the secret portal's side:
　　You know the rest." The words stuck in
　　　her throat,
Despite her injured love and fiery pride;
　　And of this Baba willingly took note,
And begg'd by every hair of Mahomet's beard,
She would revoke the order he had heard.

CXIV.

"To hear is to obey," he said; "but still,
　　Sultana, think upon the consequence:
It is not that I shall not all fulfil
　　Your orders, even in their severest sense;
But such precipitation may end ill,
　　Even at your own imperative expense:
I do not mean destruction and exposure,
In case of any premature disclosure;

CXV.

"But your own feelings. Even should all
　　the rest
　　Be hidden by the rolling waves, which hide
Already many a once love-beaten breast
　　Deep in the caverns of the deadly tide—
You love this boyish, new, seraglio guest,
　　And if this violent remedy be tried—
Excuse my freedom, when I here assure you,
That killing him is not the way to cure you."

CXVI.

"What dost thou know of love or feeling!—
　　Wretch!
　　Begone!" she cried, with kindling eyes—
　　　"and do
My bidding!" Baba vanish'd, for to stretch
　　His own remonstrance further he well knew
Might end in acting as his own "Jack Ketch;"
　　And though he wish'd extremely to get
　　　through
This awkward business without harm to
　　others,
He still preferr'd his own neck to another's.

CXVII.

Away he went then upon his commission,
 Growling and grumbling in good Turkish
 phrase
Against all women of whate'er condition,
 Especially sultanas and their ways;
Their obstinacy, pride, and indecision,
 Their never knowing their own mind two
 days,
The trouble that they gave, their immorality,
Which made him daily bless his own neu-
 trality.

CXVIII.

And then he call'd his brethren to his aid,
 And sent one on a summons to the pair,
That they must instantly be well array'd,
 And above all be comb'd even to a hair,
And brought before the empress, who had
 made
Inquiries after them with kindest care :
At which Dudù look'd strange, and Juan
 silly;
But go they must at once, and will I—nill I.

CXIX.

And here I leave them at their preparation
 For the imperial presence, wherein whether
Gulbeyaz show'd them both commiseration,
 Or got rid of the parties altogether,
Like other angry ladies of her nation,—
 Are things the turning of a hair or feather
May settle; but far be 't from me to antici-
 pate
In what way feminine caprice may dissipate.

CXX.

I leave them for the present with good
 wishes,
 Though doubts of their well doing, to
 arrange
Another part of history ; for the dishes
 Of this our banquet we must sometimes
 change;
And trusting Juan may escape the fishes,
 Although his situation now seems strange,
And scarce secure, as such digressions *are*
 fair,
The Muse will take a little touch at warfare.

Canto the Seventh.

I.

O Love ! O Glory ! what are you who fly
 Around us ever, rarely to alight?
There's not a meteor in the Polar sky
 Of such transcendent and more fleeting
 flight.

Chill, and chain'd to cold earth, we lift on
 high
 Our eyes in search of either lovely light;
A thousand and a thousand colours they
Assume, then leave us on our freezing way.

II.

And such as they are, such my present
 tale is,
 A nondescript and ever-varying rhyme,
A versified Aurora Borealis,
 Which flashes o'er a waste and icy clime.
When we know what all are, we must
 bewail us,
 But ne'ertheless I hope it is no crime
To laugh at *all* things—for I wish to know
What, after *all*, are *all* things—but a *show* ?

III.

They accuse me—*Me*—the present writer of
 The present poem—of—I know not what—
A tendency to under-rate and scoff
 At human power and virtue, and all that;
And this they say in language rather rough.
 Good God! I wonder what they would
 be at!
I say no more than hath been said in Dante's
Verse, and by Solomon and by Cervantes;

IV.

By Swift, by Machiavel, by Rochefoucault,
 By Fénélon, by Luther, and by Plato;
By Tillotson, and Wesley, and Rousseau,
 Who knew this life was not worth a potato.
'T is not their fault, nor mine, if this be so,—
 For my part, I pretend not to be Cato,
Nor even Diogenes.—We live and die,
But which is best, you know no more than I.

V.

Socrates said, our only knowledge was
 "To know that nothing could be known;"
 a pleasant
Science enough, which levels to an ass
 Each man of wisdom, future, past, or
 present.
Newton (that proverb of the mind), alas !
 Declared, with all his grand discoveries
 recent,
That he himself felt only "like a youth
Picking up shells by the great ocean—Truth."

VI.

Ecclesiastes said, "that all is vanity"—
 Most modern preachers say the same, or
 show it
By their examples of true Christianity:
 In short, all know, or very soon may know
 it;

And in this scene of all-confess'd inanity,
 By saint, by sage, by preacher, and by
 poet,
Must I restrain me, through the fear of
 strife,
From holding up the nothingness of life ?

VII.

Dogs, or men !—for I flatter you in saying
 That ye are dogs—your betters far—ye
 may
Read, or read not, what I am now essaying
 To show ye what ye are in every way.
As little as the moon stops for the baying
 Of wolves, will the bright Muse withdraw
 one ray
From out her skies—then howl your idle
 wrath !
While she still silvers o'er your gloomy path.

VIII.

"Fierce loves and faithless wars"—I am not
 sure
 If this be the right reading—'t is no
 matter ;
The fact's about the same, I am secure ;
 I sing them both, and am about to batter
A town which did a famous siege endure,
 And beleaguer'd both by land and
 water
By Souvaroff, or Anglicè Suwarrow,
Who loved blood as an alderman loves
 marrow.

IX.

The fortress is call'd Ismail, and is placed
 Upon the Danube's left branch and left
 bank,
With buildings in the Oriental taste,
 But still a fortress of the foremost rank,
Or was at least, unless 't is since defaced,
 Which with your conquerors is a common
 prank :
It stands some eighty versts from the high
 sea,
And measures round of toises thousands
 three.

X.

Within the extent of this fortification
 A borough is comprised along the height
Upon the left, which from its loftier station
 Commands the city, and upon its site
A Greek had raised around this elevation
 A quantity of palisades *upright*,
So placed as to *impede* the fire of those
Who held the place, and to *assist* the foe's.

XI.

This circumstance may serve to give a notion
 Of the high talents of this new Vauban :
But the town ditch below was deep as ocean,
 The rampart higher than you'd wish to
 hang :
But then there was a great want of pre-
 caution
 (Prithee, excuse this engineering slang),
Nor work advanced, nor cover'd way was
 there,
To hint at least "Here is no thoroughfare."

XII.

But a stone bastion, with a narrow gorge,
 And walls as thick as most skulls born as
 yet ;
Two batteries, cap-à-pie, as our St. George,
 Casemated one, and t' other "à barbette,"
Of Danube's bank took formidable charge ;
 While two-and-twenty cannon duly set
Rose over the town's right side, in bristling
 tier,
Forty feet high, upon a cavalier.

XIII.

But from the river the town's open quite,
 Because the Turks could never be per-
 suaded
A Russian vessel e'er would heave in sight ;
 And such their creed was till they were
 invaded,
When it grew rather late to set things right :
 But as the Danube could not well be
 waded,
They look'd upon the Muscovite flotilla,
And only shouted, "Allah !" and "Bis
 Millah !"

XIV.

The Russians now were ready to attack ;
 But oh, ye goddesses of war and glory !
How shall I spell the name of each Cossacque
 Who were immortal, could one tell their
 story ?
Alas ! what to their memory can lack ?
 Achilles' self was not more grim and gory
Than thousands of this new and polish'd
 nation,
Whose names want nothing but—pronunci-
 ation.

XV.

Still I'll record a few, if but to increase
 Our euphony : there was Strongenoff, and
 Strokonoff,
Meknop, Serge Low, Arsniew of modern
 Greece,
 And Tschitsshakoff, and Roguenoff, and
 Chokenoff,

And others of twelve consonants apiece;
 And more might be found out, if I could
 poke enough
Into gazettes; but Fame (capricious strum-
 pet),
It seems, has got an ear as well as trumpet,

XVI.

And cannot tune those discords of narration,
 Which may be names at Moscow, into
 rhyme;
Yet there were several worth commemora-
 tion,
 As e'er was virgin of a nuptial chime;
Soft words, too, fitted for the peroration
 Of Londonderry drawling against time,
Ending in "ischskin," "ousckin," "iffskchy,"
 "ouski,"
Of whom we can insert but Rousamouski,

XVII.

Scherematoff and Chrematoff, Koklophti,
 Koclobski, Kourakin, and Mouskin Pouskin,
All proper men of weapons, as e'er scoff'd
 high
 Against a foe, or ran a sabre through skin:
Little cared they for Mahomet or Mufti,
 Unless to make their kettle-drums a new
 skin
Out of their hides, if parchment had grown
 dear,
And no more handy substitute been near.

XVIII.

Then there were foreigners of much renown,
 Of various nations, and all volunteers;
Not fighting for their country or its crown,
 But wishing to be one day brigadiers;
Also to have the sacking of a town;
 A pleasant thing to young men at their
 years.
'Mongst them were several Englishmen of
 pith,
Sixteen call'd Thomson, and nineteen named
 Smith.

XIX.

Jack Thomson and Bill Thomson;—all the
 rest
 Had been call'd " *Jemmy*," after the great
 bard;
I don't know whether they had arms or crest,
 But such a godfather's as good a card.
Three of the Smiths were Peters; but the
 best
 Amongst them all, hard blows to inflict or
 ward,
Was *he*, since so renown'd "in country
 quarters
At Halifax;" but now he served the Tartars.

XX.

The rest were Jacks and Gills and Wills and
 Bills,
 But when I've added that the elder Jack
 Smith
Was born in Cumberland among the hills,
 And that his father was an honest black-
 smith,
I've said all *I* know of a name that fills
 Three lines of the despatch in taking
 " Schmacksmith,"
A village of Moldavia's waste, wherein
He fell, immortal in a bulletin.

XXI.

I wonder (although Mars no doubt's a god I
 Praise) if a man's name in a *bulletin*
May make up for a *bullet in* his body?
 I hope this little question is no sin,
Because, though I am but a simple noddy,
 I think one Shakspeare puts the same
 thought in
The mouth of some one in his plays so doting,
Which many people pass for wits by quoting.

XXII.

Then there were Frenchmen, gallant, young,
 and gay;
 But I'm too great a patriot to record
Their Gallic names upon a glorious day;
 I'd rather tell ten lies than say a word
Of truth;—such truths are treason; they
 betray
 Their country; and as traitors are ab-
 horr'd,
Who name the French in English, save to
 show
How Peace should make John Bull the
 Frenchman's foe.

XXIII.

The Russians, having built two batteries on
 An isle near Ismail, had two ends in view;
The first was to bombard it, and knock down
 The public buildings and the private too,
No matter what poor souls might be undone.
 The city's shape suggested this, 'tis true;
Form'd like an amphitheatre, each dwelling
Presented a fine mark to throw a shell in.

XXIV.

The second object was to profit by
 The moment of the general consternation,
To attack the Turk's flotilla, which lay nigh,
 Extremely tranquil, anchor'd at its station:
But a third motive was as probably
 To frighten them into capitulation;
A phantasy which sometimes seizes warriors,
Unless they are game as bull-dogs and fox-
 terriers.

XXV.

A habit rather blameable, which is
 That of despising those we combat with,
Common in many cases, was in this
 The cause of killing Tchitchitzkoff and
 Smith;
One of the valorous " Smiths " whom we
 shall miss
 Out of those nineteen who late rhymed to
 " pith ; "
But 't is a name so spread o'er " Sir " and
 " Madam,"
That one would think the first who bore it
 " Adam."

XXVI.

The Russian batteries were incomplete,
 Because they were constructed in a hurry ;
Thus the same cause which makes a verse
 want feet,
 And. throws a cloud o'er Longman and
 John Murray,
When the sale of new books is not so fleet
 As they who print them think is necessary,
May likewise put off for a time what story
Sometimes calls " murder," and at others
 " glory."

XXVII.

Whether it was their engineer's stupidity,
 Their haste, or waste, I neither know nor
 care,
Or some contractor's personal cupidity,
 Saving his soul by cheating in the ware
Of homicide, but there was no solidity
 In the new batteries erected there ;
They either miss'd, or they were never miss'd,
And added greatly to the missing list.

XXVIII.

A sad miscalculation about distance
 Made all their naval matters incorrect ;
Three fireships lost their amiable existence
 Before they reach'd a spot to take effect ;
The match was lit too soon, and no assistance
 Could remedy this lubberly defect ;
They blew up in the middle of the river,
While, though 't was dawn, the Turks slept
 fast as ever.

XXIX.

At seven they rose, however, and survey'd
 The Russ flotilla getting under way ;
'T was nine, when still advancing undismay'd,
 Within a cable's length their vessels lay
Off Ismail, and commenced a cannonade,
 Which was return'd with interest, I may
 say,
And by a fire of musketry and grape,
And shells and shot of every size and shape.

XXX.

For six hours bore they without intermission
 The Turkish fire, and, aided by their own
Land batteries, work'd their guns with great
 precision ;
 At length they found mere cannonade alone
By no means would produce the town's sub-
 mission,
 And made a signal to retreat at one.
One bark blew up, a second near the works
Running aground, was taken by the Turks.

XXXI.

The Moslem, too, had lost both ships and
 men ;
 But when they saw the enemy retire,
Their Delhis mann'd some boats, and sail'd
 again,
 And gall'd the Russians with a heavy fire,
And tried to make a landing on the main ;
 But here the effect fell short of their desire:
Count Damas drove them back into the water
Pell-mell, and with a whole gazette of
 slaughter.

XXXII.

" If " (says the historian here) " I could re-
 port
 All that the Russians did upon this day,
I think that several volumes would fall
 short,
 And I should still have many things to
 say ; "
And so he says no more—but pays his court
 To some distinguish'd strangers in that
 fray ;
The Prince de Ligne, and Langeron, and
 Damas,
Names great as any that the roll of Fame has.

XXXIII.

This being the case, may show us what
 Fame *is :*
 For out of these three *" preux Chevaliers,"*
 how
Many of common readers give a guess
 That such existed ? (and they may live
 now
For aught we know.) Renown's all hit or
 miss ;
 There's fortune even in fame, we must
 allow.
'T is true, the Memoirs of the Prince de
 Ligne
Have half withdrawn from *him* oblivion's
 screen.

XXXIV.

But here are men who fought in gallant
　　actions
　　As gallantly as ever heroes fought,
But buried in the heap of such transactions
　　Their names are rarely found, nor often
　　　sought.
Thus even good fame may suffer sad con-
　　tractions,
　　And is extinguish'd sooner than she ought:
Of all our modern battles, I will bet
You can't repeat nine names from each
　　Gazette.

XXXV.

In short, this last attack, though rich in glory,
　　Show'd that *somewhere, somehow*, there was
　　　a fault,
And Admiral Ribas (known in Russian story)
　　Most strongly recommended an assault;
In which he was opposed by young and
　　hoary,
　　Which made a long debate; but I must
　　　halt,
For if I wrote down every warrior's speech,
I doubt few readers e'er would mount the
　　breach.

XXXVI.

There was a man, if that he was a man,
　　Not that his manhood could be call'd in
　　　question,
For had he not been Hercules, his span
　　Had been as short in youth as indigestion
Made his last illness, when, all worn and wan,
　　He died beneath a tree, as much unblest on
The soil of the green province he had wasted,
As e'er was locust on the land it blasted.

XXXVII.

This was Potemkin—a great thing in days
　　When homicide and harlotry made great;
If stars and titles could entail long praise,
　　His glory might half equal his estate.
This fellow, being six foot high, could raise
　　A kind of phantasy proportionate
In the then sovereign of the Russian people,
Who measured men as you would do a steeple.

XXXVIII.

While things were in abeyance, Ribas sent
　　A courier to the prince, and he succeeded
In ordering matters after his own bent;
　　I cannot tell the way in which he pleaded,
But shortly he had cause to be content.
　　In the mean time the batteries proceeded,
And fourscore cannon on the Danube's border
Were briskly fired and answer'd in due order.

XXXIX.

But on the thirteenth, when already part
　　Of the troops were embark'd, the siege to
　　　raise,
A courier on the spur inspired new heart
　　Into all panters for newspaper praise,
As well as dilettanti in war's art,
　　By his despatches couch'd in pithy phrase;
Announcing the appointment of that lover of
Battles to the command, Field-Marshal Sou-
　　varoff.

XL.

The letter of the prince to the same marshal
　　Was worthy of a Spartan, had the cause
Been one to which a good heart could be
　　partial—
　　Defence of freedom, country, or of laws;
But as it was mere lust of power to o'er-arch
　　all
　　With its proud brow, it merits slight
　　　applause,
Save for its style, which said, all in a trice,
"You will take Ismail at whatever price."

XLI.

"Let there be light!" said God, "and there
　　was light!"
　　"Let there be blood!" says man, and
　　　there's a sea!
The fiat of this spoil'd child of the Night
　　(For Day ne'er saw his merits) could decree
More evil in an hour, than thirty bright
　　Summers could renovate, though they
　　　should be
Lovely as those which ripen'd Eden's fruit;
For war cuts up not only branch, but root.

XLII.

Our friends, the Turks, who with loud "Al-
　　lahs" now
Began to signalise the Russ retreat,
Were damnably mistaken; few are slow
　　In thinking that their enemy is beat,
(Or *beaten*, if you insist on grammar, though
　　I never think about it in a heat,)
But here I say the Turks were much mis-
　　taken,
Who hating hogs, yet wish'd to save their
　　bacon.

XLIII.

For, on the sixteenth, at full gallop, drew
　　In sight two horsemen, who were deem'd
　　　Cossacques
For some time, till they came in nearer
　　view.
　　They had but little baggage at their backs,

For there were but three shirts between the
two;
 But on they rode upon two Ukraine hacks,
Till, in approaching, were at length descried
In this plain pair, Suwarrow and his guide.

XLIV.

"Great joy to London now!" says some
great fool,
 When London had a grand illumination,
Which to that bottle-conjuror, John Bull,
 Is of all dreams the first hallucination;
So that the streets of colour'd lamps are full,
 That sage (*said* John) surrenders at dis-
cretion
His purse, his soul, his sense, and even his
nonsense,
To gratify, like a huge moth, this *one* sense.

XLV.

'T is strange that he should further "Damn
his eyes,"
 For they are damn'd; that once all-famous
oath
Is to the devil now no further prize,
 Since John has lately lost the use of both.
Debt he calls wealth, and taxes Paradise;
 And Famine, with her gaunt and bony
growth,
Which stare him in the face, he won't
examine,
Or swears that Ceres hath begotten Famine.

XLVI.

But to the tale;—great joy unto the camp!
 To Russian, Tartar, English, French, Cos-
sacque,
O'er whom Suwarrow shone like a gas lamp,
 Presaging a most luminous attack;
Or like a wisp along the marsh so damp,
 Which leads beholders on a boggy walk,
He flitted to and fro a dancing light,
Which all who saw it follow'd, wrong or
right.

XLVII.

But certes matters took a different face;
 There was enthusiasm and much applause,
The fleet and camp saluted with great grace,
 And all presaged good fortune to their
cause.
Within a cannon-shot length of the place
 They drew, constructed ladders, repair'd
flaws
In former works, made new, prepared fascines,
And all kinds of benevolent machines.

XLVIII.

'T is thus the spirit of a single mind
 Makes that of multitudes take one direction,
As roll the waters to the breathing wind,
 Or roams the herd beneath the bull's pro-
tection;
Or as a little dog will lead the blind,
 Or a bell-wether form the flock's connexion
By tinkling sounds, when they go forth to
victual;
Such is the sway of your great men o'er little.

XLIX.

The whole camp rung with joy; you would
have thought
 That they were going to a marriage feast
(This metaphor, I think, holds good as aught,
 Since there is discord after both at least):
There was not now a luggage boy but sought
 Danger and spoil with ardour much in-
creased;
And why? because a little—odd—old man,
Stript to his shirt, was come to lead the van.

L.

But so it was; and every preparation
 Was made with all alacrity: the first
Detachment of three columns took its station,
 And waited but the signal's voice to burst
Upon the foe: the second's ordination
 Was also in three columns, with a thirst
For glory gaping o'er a sea of slaughter:
The third, in columns two, attack'd by water.

LI.

New batteries were erected, and was held
 A general council, in which unanimity,
That stranger to most councils, here prevail'd,
 As sometimes happens in a great extremity;
And every difficulty being dispell'd,
 Glory began to dawn with due sublimity,
While Souvaroff, determined to obtain it,
Was teaching his recruits to use the bayonet.

LII.

It is an actual fact, that he, commander
 In chief, in proper person deign'd to drill
The awkward squad, and could afford to
squander
 His time, a corporal's duty to fulfil;
Just as you'd break a sucking salamander
 To swallow flame, and never take it ill:
He show'd them how to mount a ladder
(which
Was not like Jacob's) or to cross a ditch.

LIII.

Also he dress'd up, for the nonce, fascines
　Like men with turbans, scimitars, and
　　dirks,
And made them charge with bayonet these
　　machines,
　By way of lesson against actual Turks;
And when well practised in these mimic
　　scenes,
　He judged them proper to assail the works;
At which your wise men sneer'd in phrases
　　witty:
He made no answer; but he took the city.

LIV.

Most things were in this posture on the eve
　Of the assault, and all the camp was in
A stern repose; which you would scarce
　　conceive;
　Yet men resolved to dash through thick
　　and thin
Are very silent when they once believe
　That all is settled:—there was little din,
For some were thinking of their home and
　　friends,
And others of themselves and latter ends.

LV.

Suwarrow chiefly was on the alert,
　Surveying, drilling, ordering, jesting, pon-
　　dering,
For the man was, we safely may assert,
　A thing to wonder at beyond most won-
　　dering;
Hero, buffoon, half-demon, and half-dirt,
　Praying, instructing, desolating, plunder-
　　ing;
Now Mars, now Momus; and when bent to
　　storm
A fortress, Harlequin in uniform.

LVI.

The day before the assault, while upon drill—
　For this great conqueror play'd the cor-
　　poral—
Some Cossacques, hovering like hawks round
　　a hill,
　Had met a party towards the twilight's
　　fall,
One of whom spoke their tongue—or well
　　or ill,
　'Twas much that he was understood at all;
But whether from his voice, or speech, or
　　manner,
They found that he had fought beneath their
　　banner.

LVII.

Whereon immediately at his request
　They brought him and his comrades to
　　head-quarters;
Their dress was Moslem, but you might have
　　guess'd
　That these were merely masquerading
　　Tartars,
And that beneath each Turkish-fashion'd vest
　Lurk'd Christianity; which sometimes
　　barters
Her inward grace for outward show, and makes
It difficult to shun some strange mistakes.

LVIII.

Suwarrow, who was standing in his shirt
　Before a company of Calmucks, drilling,
Exclaiming, fooling, swearing at the inert,
　And lecturing on the noble art of killing,—
For deeming human clay but common dirt,
　This great philosopher was thus instilling
His maxims, which to martial comprehension
Proved death in battle equal to a pension;—

LIX.

Suwarrow, when he saw this company
　Of Cossacques and their prey, turn'd round
　　and cast
Upon them his slow brow and piercing eye:—
　"Whence come ye?"—"From Constanti-
　　nople last,
Captives just now escaped," was the reply.
　"What are ye?"—"What you see us."
　　Briefly pass'd
This dialogue; for he who answer'd knew
To whom he spoke, and made his words but few.

LX.

"Your names?"—"Mine's Johnson, and my
　　comrade's Juan;
　The other two are women, and the third
Is neither man nor woman." The chief
　　threw on
　The party a slight glance, then said, "I
　　have heard
Your name before, the second is a new one:
　To bring the other three here was absurd:
But let that pass:—I think I have heard your
　　name
In the Nikolaiew regiment?"—"The same."

LXI.

"You served at Widdin?"—"Yes."—"You
　　led the attack?"
　"I did."—"What next?"—"I really hardly
　　know."
"You were the first i'the breach?"—"I was
　　not slack
　At least to follow those who might be so."

"What follow'd?"—"A shot laid me on my
　　back,
　And I became a prisoner to the foe."
"You shall have vengeance, for the town
　　surrounded
Is twice as strong as that where you were
　　wounded.

LXII.

"Where will you serve?"—"Where'er you
　　please."—"I know
You like to be the hope of the forlorn,
And doubtless would be foremost on the foe
　After the hardships you've already borne.
And this young fellow—say what can he do?
　He with the beardless chin and garments
　　torn?"
"Why, general, if he hath no greater fault
In war than love, he had better lead the
　　assault."

LXIII.

"He shall if that he dare."　Here Juan
　　bow'd
　Low as the compliment deserved.　Su-
　　warrow
Continued: "Your old regiment's allow'd,
　By special providence, to lead to-morrow,
Or it may be to-night, the assault: I have
　　vow'd
　To several saints, that shortly plough or
　　harrow
Shall pass o'er what was Ismail, and its tusk
Be unimpeded by the proudest mosque.

LXIV.

"So now, my lads, for glory!"—Here he
　　turn'd
　And drill'd away in the most classic Rus-
　　sian,
Until each high, heroic bosom burn'd
　For cash and conquest, as if from a cushion
A preacher had held forth (who nobly spurn'd
　All earthly goods save tithes) and bade
　　them push on
To slay the Pagans who resisted, battering
The armies of the Christian Empress Cathe-
　　rine.

LXV.

Johnson, who knew by this long colloquy
　Himself a favourite, ventured to address
Suwarrow, though engaged with accents high
　In his resumed amusement.　"I confess
My debt in being thus allow'd to die
　Among the foremost; but if you'd express
Explicitly our several posts, my friend
And self would know what duty to attend."

LXVI.

"Right! I was busy, and forgot.　Why, you
　Will join your former regiment, which
　　should be
Now under arms.　Ho! Katskoff, take him
　　to—
　(Here he call'd up a Polish orderly)
His post, I mean the regiment Nikolaiew:
　The stranger stripling may remain with
　　me;
He's a fine boy.　The women may be sent
To the other baggage, or to the sick tent."

LXVII.

But here a sort of scene began to ensue:
　The ladies,—who by no means had been
　　bred
To be disposed of in a way so new,
　Although their harem education led
Doubtless to that of doctrines the most true,
　Passive obedience,—now raised up the
　　head,
With flashing eyes and starting tears, and
　　flung,
Their arms, as hens their wings about their
　　young,

LXVIII.

O'er the promoted couple of brave men
　Who were thus honour'd by the greatest
　　chief
That ever peopled hell with heroes slain,
　Or plunged a province or a realm in grief.
Oh, foolish mortals! Always taught in vain!
　Oh, glorious laurel! since for one sole leaf
Of thine imaginary deathless tree,
Of blood and tears must flow the unebbing
　　sea.

LXIX.

Suwarrow, who had small regard for tears,
　And not much sympathy for blood, sur-
　　vey'd
The women with their hair about their ears
　And natural agonies, with a slight shade
Of feeling: for however habit sears
　Men's hearts against whole millions, when
　　their trade
Is butchery, sometimes a single sorrow
Will touch even heroes—and such was
　Suwarrow.

LXX.

He said,—and in the kindest Calmuck tone,—
　"Why, Johnson, what the devil do you
　　mean
By bringing women here? They shall be
　　shown
　All the attention possible, and seen

In safety to the waggons, where alone
 In fact they can be safe. You should have
 been
Aware this kind of baggage never thrives;
Save wed a year, I hate recruits with wives."

LXXI.

"May it please your excellency," thus re-
 plied
 Our British friend, "these are the wives of
 others,
And not our own. I am too qualified
 By service with my military brothers
To break the rules by bringing one's own
 bride
 Into a camp: I know that nought so
 bothers
The hearts of the heroic on a charge,
As leaving a small family at large.

LXXII.

"But these are but two Turkish ladies, who
 With their attendant aided our escape,
And afterwards accompanied us through
 A thousand perils in this dubious shape.
To me this kind of life is not so new;
 To them, poor things, it is an awkward
 scrape.
I therefore, if you wish me to fight freely,
Request that they may both be used gen-
 teelly."

LXXIII.

Meantime these two poor girls, with swim-
 ming eyes,
 Look'd on as if in doubt if they could trust
Their own protectors; nor was their surprise
 Less than their grief (and truly not less
 just)
To see an old man, rather wild than wise
 In aspect, plainly clad, besmear'd with
 dust,
Stript to his waistcoat, and that not too
 clean,
More fear'd than all the sultans ever seen.

LXXIV.

For everything seem'd resting on his nod,
 As they could read in all eyes. Now to
 them,
Who were accustom'd, as a sort of god,
 To see the sultan, rich in many a gem,
Like an imperial peacock stalk abroad
 (That royal bird, whose tail's a diadem,)
With all the pomp of power, it was a doubt
How power could condescend to do without.

LXXV.

John Johnson, seeing their extreme dismay,
 Though little versed in feelings oriental,
Suggested some slight comfort in his way:
 Don Juan, who was much more senti-
 mental,
Swore they should see him by the dawn of
 day,
 Or that the Russian army should repent
 all:
And, strange to say, they found some conso-
 lation
In this—for females like exaggeration.

LXXVI.

And then with tears, and sighs, and some
 slight kisses,
 They parted for the present—these to
 await,
According to the artillery's hits or misses,
 What sages call Chance, Providence, or
 Fate—
(Uncertainty is one of many blisses,
 A mortgage on Humanity's estate)—
While their beloved friends began to arm,
To burn a town which never did them harm.

LXXVII.

Suwarrow,—who but saw things in the gross,
 Being much too gross to see them in
 detail,
Who calculated life as so much dross,
 And as the wind a widow'd nation's wail,
And cared as little for his army's loss
 (So that their efforts should at length
 prevail)
As wife and friends did for the boils of Job,—
What was't to him to hear two women sob?

LXXVIII.

Nothing.—The work of glory still went on
 In preparations for a cannonade
As terrible as that of Ilion,
 If Homer had found mortars ready made;
But now, instead of slaying Priam's son,
 We only can but talk of escalade,
Bombs, drums, guns, bastions, batteries,
 bayonets, bullets;
Hard words, which stick in the soft Muses'
 gullets.

LXXIX.

Oh, thou eternal Homer! who couldst charm
 All ears, though long; all ages, though so
 short,
By merely wielding with poetic arm
 Arms to which men will never more resort,

Unless gunpowder should be found to harm
 Much less than is the hope of every court,
Which now is leagued young Freedom to
 annoy;
But they will not find Liberty a Troy:—

LXXX.

Oh, thou eternal Homer! I have now
 To paint a siege, wherein more men were
 slain,
With deadlier engines and a speedier blow,
 Than in thy Greek gazette of that cam-
 paign;
And yet, like all men else, I must allow,
 To vie with thee would be about as vain
As for a brook to cope with ocean's flood;
But still we moderns equal you in blood;

LXXXI.

If not in poetry, at least in fact;
 And fact is truth, the grand desideratum!
Of which, howe'er the Muse describes each
 act,
 There should be ne'ertheless a slight sub-
 stratum.
But now the town is going to be attack'd;
 Great deeds are doing—how shall I relate
 'em?
Souls of immortal generals! Phœbus watches
To colour up his rays from your despatches.

LXXXII.

Oh, ye great bulletins of Bonaparte!
 Oh, ye less grand long lists of kill'd and
 wounded!
Shade of Leonidas, who fought so hearty,
 When my poor Greece was once, as now,
 surrounded!
Oh, Cæsar's Commentaries! now impart, ye
 Shadows of glory! (lest I be confounded),
A portion of your fading twilight hues,
So beautiful, so fleeting, to the Muse.

LXXXIII.

When I call "fading" martial immortality,
 I mean, that every age and every year,
And almost every day, in sad reality,
 Some sucking hero is compell'd to rear,
Who, when we come to sum up the totality
 Of deeds to human happiness most dear,
Turns out to be a butcher in great business,
Afflicting young folks with a sort of dizziness.

LXXXIV.

Medals, rank, ribands, lace, embroidery,
 scarlet,
 Are things immortal to immortal man,
As purple to the Babylonian harlot:
 An uniform to boys is like a fan

To women; there is scarce a crimson varlet
 But deems himself the first in Glory's van.
But Glory's glory; and if you would find
What that is—ask the pig who sees the
 wind!

LXXXV.

At least *he feels it*, and some say he *sees*,
 Because he runs before it like a pig;
Or, if that simple sentence should displease,
 Say, that he scuds before it like a brig,
A schooner, or—but it is time to cease
 This Canto, ere my Muse perceives fatigue.
The next shall ring a peal to shake all
 people,
Like a bob-major from a village steeple.

LXXXVI.

Hark! through the silence of the cold, dull
 night,
 The hum of armies gathering rank on
 rank!
Lo! dusky masses steal in dubious sight
 Along the leaguer'd wall and bristling
 bank
Of the arm'd river, while with straggling
 light
 The stars peep through the vapours dim
 and dank,
Which curl in curious wreaths:—how soon
 the smoke
Of Hell shall pall them in a deeper cloak!

LXXXVII.

Here pause we for the present—as even then
 That awful pause, dividing life from death,
Struck for an instant on the hearts of men,
 Thousands of whom were drawing their
 last breath!
A moment—and all will be life again!
 The march! the charge! the shouts of
 either faith,
Hurrah! and Allah! and—one moment
 more—
The death-cry drowning in the battle's roar.

——•◆•——

Canto the Eighth.

I.

Oh, blood and thunder! and oh, blood and
 wounds!
 These are but vulgar oaths, as you may
 deem,
Too gentle reader! and most shocking
 sounds:
 And so they are; yet thus is Glory's dream

Unriddled, and as my true Muse expounds
 At present such things, since they are her
 theme,
So be they her inspirers! Call them Mars,
Bellona, what you will—they mean but wars.

II.

All was prepared—the fire, the sword, the
 men
 To wield them in their terrible array.
The army, like a lion from his den,
 March'd forth with nerve and sinews bent
 to slay,—
A human Hydra, issuing from its fen
 To breathe destruction on its winding way,
Whose heads were heroes, which cut off in
 vain,
Immediately in others grew again.

III.

History can only take things in the gross;
 But could we know them in detail, per-
 chance
In balancing the profit and the loss,
 War's merit it by no means might enhance,
To waste so much gold for a little dross,
 As hath been done, mere conquest to
 advance.
The drying up a single tear has more
Of honest fame, than shedding seas of gore.

IV.

And why?—because it brings self-appro-
 bation;
 Whereas the other, after all its glare,
Shouts, bridges, arches, pensions from a
 nation,
 Which (it may be) has not much left to
 spare,
A higher title, or a loftier station,
 Though they may make Corruption gape
 or stare,
Yet, in the end, except in freedom's battles,
Are nothing but a child of Murder's rattles.

V.

And such they are—and such they will be
 found:
 Not so Leonidas and Washington,
Whose every battle-field is holy ground,
 Which breathes of nations saved, not
 worlds undone.
How sweetly on the ear such echoes sound!
 While the mere victor's may appal or
 stun
The servile and the vain, such names will
 be
A watchword till the future shall be free.

VI.

The night was dark, and the thick mist
 allow'd
 Nought to be seen save the artillery's flame,
Which arch'd the horizon like a fiery cloud,
 And in the Danube's waters shone the
 same—
A mirror'd hell! the volleying roar, and loud
 Long booming of each peal on peal,
 o'ercame
The ear far more than thunder; for Heaven's
 flashes
Spare, or smite rarely—man's make millions
 ashes!

VII.

The column order'd on the assault scarce
 pass'd
 Beyond the Russian batteries a few toises,
When up the bristling Moslem rose at last,
 Answering the Christian thunders with like
 voices:
Then one vast fire, air, earth, and stream
 embraced,
 Which rock'd as 'twere beneath the mighty
 noises;
While the whole rampart blazed like Etna,
 when
The restless Titan hiccups in his den;

VIII.

And one enormous shout of "Allah!" rose
 In the same moment, loud as even the roar
Of war's most mortal engines, to their foes
 Hurling defiance: city, stream, and shore
Resounded "Allah!" and the clouds which
 close
 With thick'ning canopy the conflict o'er,
Vibrate to the Eternal name. Hark! through
All sounds it pierceth, "Allah! Allah! Hu!"

IX.

The columns were in movement one and all,
 But of the portion which attack'd by water,
Thicker than leaves the lives began to fall,
 Though led by Arseniew, that great son of
 slaughter,
As brave as ever faced both bomb and ball.
 "Carnage, (so Wordsworth tells you) is
 God's daughter:"
If *he* speak truth, she is Christ's sister, and
Just now behaved as in the Holy Land.

X.

The Prince de Ligne was wounded in the
 knee;
 Count Chapeau-Bras, too, had a ball
 between
His cap and head, which proves the head to be
 Aristocratic as was ever seen,

Because it then received no injury
 More than the cap; in fact, the ball could
 mean
No harm unto a right legitimate head;
" Ashes to ashes"—why not lead to lead?

XI.

Also the General Markow, Brigadier,
 Insisting on removal of the *prince*
Amidst some groaning thousands dying
 near,—
 All common fellows, who might writhe and
 wince,
And shriek for water into a deaf ear,—
 The General Markow, who could thus
 evince
His sympathy for rank, by the same token,
To teach him greater, had his own leg
 broken.

XII.

Three hundred cannon threw up their emetic,
 And thirty thousand muskets flung their
 pills
Like hail, to make a bloody diuretic.
 Mortality! thou hast thy monthly bills:
Thy plagues, thy famines, thy physicians, yet
 tick,
 Like the death-watch, within our ears the
 ills
Past, present, and to come;—but all may
 yield
To the true portrait of one battle-field;

XIII.

There the still varying pangs, which multiply
 Until their very number makes men hard
By the infinities of agony,
 Which meet the gaze, whate'er it may
 regard—
The groan, the roll in dust, the all-white eye
 Turn'd back within its socket,—these
 reward
Your rank and file by thousands, while the
 rest
May win perhaps a riband at the breast!

XIV.

Yet I love glory;—glory's a great thing:—
 Think what it is to be in your old age
Maintain'd at the expense of your good
 king:
 A moderate pension shakes full many a
 sage,
And heroes are but made for bards to sing,
 Which is still better; thus in verse to wage
Your wars eternally, besides enjoying
Half-pay for life, make mankind worth
 destroying.

XV.

The troops, already disembark'd, push'd on
 To take a battery on the right: the others,
Who landed lower down, their landing done,
 Had set to work as briskly as their
 brothers:
Being grenadiers, they mounted one by one,
 Cheerful as children climb the breasts of
 mothers,
O'er the intrenchment and the palisade,
Quite orderly, as if upon parade.

XVI.

And this was admirable; for so hot
 The fire was, that were red Vesuvius
 loaded,
Besides its lava, with all sorts of shot
 And shells or hells, it could not more have
 goaded,
Of officers a third fell on the spot,
 A thing which victory by no means boded
To gentlemen engaged in the assault:
Hounds, when the huntsman tumbles, are at
 fault.

XVII.

But here I leave the general concern,
 To track our hero on his path of fame:
He must his laurels separately earn;
 For fifty thousand heroes, name by name,
Though all deserving equally to turn
 A couplet, or an elegy to claim,
Would form a lengthy lexicon of glory,
And what is worse still, a much longer story:

XVIII.

And therefore we must give the greater
 number
 To the Gazette—which doubtless fairly
 dealt
By the deceased, who lie in famous slumber
 In ditches, fields, or wheresoe'er they felt
Their clay for the last time their souls en-
 cumber;—
 Thrice happy he whose name has been
 well spelt
In the despatch: I knew a man whose loss
Was printed *Grove*, although his name was
 Grose.

XIX.

Juan and Johnson join'd a certain corps,
 And fought away with might and main,
 not knowing
The way which they had never trod before,
 And still less guessing where they might
 be going;

But on they march'd, dead bodies trampling
 o'er,
 Firing, and thrusting, slashing, sweating,
 glowing,
But fighting thoughtlessly enough to win,
To their *two* selves, *one* whole bright bulletin.

XX.

Thus on they wallow'd in the bloody mire
 Of dead and dying thousands,—sometimes
 gaining
A yard or two of ground, which brought them
 nigher
 To some odd angle for which all were
 straining;
At other times, repulsed by the close fire,
 Which really pour'd as if all hell were
 raining
Instead of heaven, they stumbled backwards
 o'er
A wounded comrade, sprawling in his gore.

XXI.

Though 't was Don Juan's first of fields, and
 though
 The nightly muster and the silent march
In the chill dark, when courage does not
 glow
 So much as under a triumphal arch,
Perhaps might make him shiver, yawn, or
 throw
 A glance on the dull clouds (as thick as
 starch,
Which stiffen'd heaven) as if he wish'd for
 day;—
Yet for all this he did not run away.

XXII.

Indeed he could not. But what if he had?
 There *have been* and *are* heroes who begun
With something not much better, or as bad:
 Frederick the Great from Molwitz deign'd
 to 'run
For the first and last time; for, like a pad,
 Or hawk, or bride, most mortals after one
Warm bout are broken in to their new tricks,
And fight like fiends for pay or politics.

XXIII.

He was what Erin calls, in her sublime
 Old Erse or Irish, or it may be *Punic;*—
(The antiquarians who can settle time,
 Which settles all things, Roman, Greek, or
 Runic,
Swear that Pat's language sprung from the
 same clime
 With Hannibal, and wears the Tyrian tunic
Of Dido's alphabet; and this is rational
As any other notion, and not national;)—

XXIV.

But Juan was quite " a broth of a boy,"
 A thing of impulse and a child of song;
Now swimming in the sentiment of joy,
 Or the *sensation* (if that phrase seem wrong),
And afterward, if he must needs destroy,
 In such good company as always throng
To battles, sieges, and that kind of pleasure,
No less delighted to employ his leisure;

XXV.

But always without malice: if he warr'd
 Or loved, it was with what we call " the
 best
Intentions," which form all mankind's *trump
 card,*
 To be produced when brought up to the
 test.
The statesman, hero, harlot, lawyer—ward
 Off each attack, when people are in quest
Of their designs, by saying they *meant well;*
'T is pity " that such meaning should pave
 hell."

XXVI.

I almost lately have begun to doubt
 Whether hell's pavement—if it be so
 paved—
Must not have latterly been quite worn out,
 Not by the numbers good intent hath saved,
But by the mass who go below without
 Those ancient good intentions, which once
 shaved
And smooth'd the brimstone of that street of
 hell
Which bears the greatest likeness to Pall
 Mall.

XXVII.

Juan, by some strange chance, which oft
 divides
 Warrior from warrior in their grim career,
Like chastest wives from constant husbands'
 sides
 Just at the close of the first bridal year,
By one of those odd turns of Fortune's tides,
 Was on a sudden rather puzzled here,
When, after a good deal of heavy firing,
He found himself alone, and friends retiring.

XXVIII.

I don't know how the thing occurr'd—it
 might
 Be that the greater part were kill'd or
 wounded,
And that the rest had faced unto the right
 About; a circumstance which has con-
 founded

Cæsar himself, who, in the very sight
　Of his whole army, which so much abounded
In courage, was obliged to snatch a shield,
　And rally back his Romans to the field.

XXIX.

Juan, who had no shield to snatch, and was
　No Cæsar, but a fine young lad, who fought
He knew not why, arriving at this pass,
　Stopp'd for a minute, as perhaps he ought
For a much longer time; then, like an ass—
　(Start not, kind reader, since great Homer
　　thought
This simile enough for Ajax, Juan
Perhaps may find it better than a new
　one);—

XXX.

Then, like an ass, he went upon his way,
　And, what was stranger, never look'd be-
　　hind;
But seeing, flashing forward, like the day
　Over the hills, a fire enough to blind
Those who dislike to look upon a fray,
　He stumbled on, to try if he could find
A path, to add his own slight arm and forces
To corps, the greater part of which were
　corses.

XXXI.

Perceiving then no more the commandant
　Of his own corps, nor even the corps,
　　which had
Quite disappear'd—the gods know how! (I
　can't
Account for everything which may look bad
In history; but we at least may grant
　It was not marvellous that a mere lad,
In search of glory, should look on before,
Nor care a pinch of snuff about his corps:)—

XXXII.

Perceiving nor commander nor commanded,
　And left at large, like a young heir, to
　　make
His way to—where he knew not—single-
　　handed;
　As travellers follow over bog and brake
An "ignis fatuus;" or as sailors stranded
　Unto the nearest hut themselves betake;
So Juan, following honour and his nose,
Rush'd where the thickest fire announced
　most foes.

XXXIII.

He new not where he was, nor greatly cared,
　For he was dizzy, busy, and his veins
Fill'd as with lightning—for his spirit shared
　The hour, as is the case with lively brains;

And where the hottest fire was seen and heard,
　And the loud cannon peal'd his hoarsest
　　strains,
He rush'd, while earth and air were sadly
　　shaken
By thy humane discovery, Friar Bacon!

XXXIV.

And as he rush'd along, it came to pass he
　Fell in with what was late the second
　　column,
Under the orders of the General Lascy,
　But now reduced, as is a bulky volume
Into an elegant extract (much less massy)
　Of heroism, and took his place with solemn
Air 'midst the rest, who kept their valiant faces
And levell'd weapons still against the glacis.

XXXV.

Just at this crisis up came Johnson too,
　Who had "retreated," as the phrase is when
Men run away much rather than go through
　Destruction's jaws into the devil's den;
But Johnson was a clever fellow, who
　Knew when and how "to cut and come
　　again,"
And never ran away, except when running
Was nothing but a valorous kind of cunning.

XXXVI.

And so, when all his corps were dead or dying,
　Except Don Juan, a mere novice, whose
More virgin valour never dreamt of flying,
　From ignorance of danger, which indues
Its votaries, like innocence relying
　On its own strength, with careless nerves
　　and thews,—
Johnson retired a little, just to rally
Those who catch cold in "shadows of death's
　valley."

XXXVII.

And there, a little shelter'd from the shot,
　Which rain'd from bastion, battery, parapet,
Rampart, wall, casement, house—for there
　　was not
　In this extensive city, sore beset
By Christian soldiery, a single spot
　Which did not combat like the devil, as
　　yet,—
He found a number of Chasseurs, all scatter'd
By the resistance of the chase they batter'd.

XXXVIII.

And these he call'd on; and, what's strange,
　they came
　Unto his call, unlike "the spirits from
The vasty deep," to whom you may exclaim,
　Says Hotspur, long ere they will leave their
　　home.

Their reasons were uncertainty, or shame
　At shrinking from a bullet or a bomb,
And that odd impulse, which in wars or creeds
Makes men, like cattle, follow him who leads.

XXXIX.

By Jove! he was a noble fellow, Johnson,
　And though his name, than Ajax or Achilles,
Sounds less harmonious, underneath the sun
　　soon
　We shall not see his likeness: he could kill
　　his
Man quite as quietly as blows the monsoon
　Her steady breath (which some months the
　　same *still* is):
Seldom he varied feature, hue, or muscle,
And could be very busy without bustle;

XL.

And therefore, when he ran away, he did so
　Upon reflection, knowing that behind
He would find others who would fain be
　　rid so
Of idle apprehensions, which like wind
Trouble heroic stomachs. Though their lids so
　Oft are soon closed, all heroes are not blind,
But when they light upon immediate death,
Retire a little, merely to take breath.

XLI.

But Johnson only ran off, to return
　With many other warriors, as we said,
Unto that rather somewhat misty bourne,
　Which Hamlet tells us is a pass of dread.
To Jack, howe'er, this gave but slight con-
　　cern:
　His soul (like galvanism upon the dead)
Acted upon the living as on wire,
And led them back into the heaviest fire.

XLII.

Egad! they found the second time what they
　The first time thought quite terrible enough
To fly from, malgré all which people say
　Of glory, and all that immortal stuff
Which fills a regiment (besides their pay,
　That daily shilling which makes warriors
　　tough)—
They found on their return the self-same
　　welcome,
Which made some *think*, and others *know*, a
　hell come.

XLIII.

They fell as thick as harvests beneath hail,
　Grass before scythes, or corn below the
　　sickle,
Proving that trite old truth, that life's as frail
　As any other boon for which men stickle.

The Turkish batteries thrash'd them like a
　　flail,
　Or a good boxer, into a sad pickle
Putting the very bravest, who were knock'd
Upon the head before their guns were cock'd.

XLIV.

The Turks behind the traverses and flanks
　Of the next bastion, fired away like devils,
And swept, as gales sweep foam away, whole
　　ranks:
　However, Heaven knows how, the Fate who
　　levels
Towns, nations, worlds, in her revolving
　　pranks,
　So order'd it, amid these sulphury revels,
That Johnson, and some few who had not
　　scamper'd,
Reach'd the interior talus of the rampart.

XLV.

First one or two, then five, six, and a dozen
　Came mounting quickly up, for it was now
All neck or nothing, as, like pitch or rosin,
　Flame was shower'd forth above, as well's
　　below,
So that you scarce could say who best had
　　chosen,
　The gentlemen that were the first to show
Their martial faces on the parapet,
Or those who thought it brave to wait as yet.

XLVI.

But those who scaled found out that their
　　advance
　Was favour'd by an accident or blunder:
The Greek or Turkish Cohorn's ignorance
　Had palisado'd in a way you'd wonder
To see in forts of Netherlands or France—
　(Though these to our Gibraltar must knock
　　under)—
Right in the middle of the parapet
Just named, these palisades were primly set:

XLVII.

So that on either side some nine or ten
　Paces were left, whereon you could contrive
To march; a great convenience to our men,
　At least to all those who were left alive,
Who thus could form a line and fight again;
　And that which further aided them to strive
Was, that they could kick down the palisades,
Which scarcely rose much higher than grass
　　blades.

XLVIII.

Among the first—I will not say the *first*,
　For such precedence upon such occasions
Will oftentimes make deadly quarrels burst
　Out between friends as well as allied
　　nations:

The Briton must be bold who really durst
　　Put to such trial John Bull's partial
　　　patience,
As say that Wellington at Waterloo
Was beaten,—though the Prussians say so
　　too;—

XLIX.

And that if Blucher, Bulow, Gneisenau,
　　And God knows who besides in "au" and
　　　"ow,"
Had not come up in time to cast an awe
　　Into the hearts of those who fought till now
As tigers combat with an empty craw,
　　The Duke of Wellington had ceased to show
His orders, also to receive his pensions;
Which are the heaviest that our history men-
　　tions.

L.

But never mind;—"God save the king!" and
　　kings!
　　For if *he* don't, I doubt if *men* will longer—
I think I hear a little bird, who sings
　　The people by and by will be the stronger:
The veriest jade will wince whose harness
　　wrings
So much into the raw as quite to wrong her
Beyond the rules of posting,—and the mob
At last fall sick of imitating Job.

LI.

At first it grumbles, then it swears, and then,
　　Like David, flings smooth pebbles 'gainst
　　　a giant;
At last it takes to weapons such as men
　　Snatch when despair makes human hearts
　　　less pliant.
Then comes the "tug of war;"—'t will come
　　again,
　　I rather doubt; and I would fain say "fie
　　　on't,"
If I had not perceived that revolution
Alone can save the earth from hell's pollu-
　　tion.

LII.

But to continue:—I say not *the* first,
　　But of the first, our little friend Don Juan,
Walk'd o'er the walls of Ismail, as if nursed
　　Amidst such scenes—though this was quite
　　　a new one
To him, and I should hope to *most*. The
　　thirst
　　Of glory, which so pierces through and
　　　through one,
Pervaded him—although a generous creature,
As warm in heart as feminine in feature.

LIII.

And here he was—who upon woman's breast,
　　Even from a child, felt like a child; howe'er
The man in all the rest might be confest,
　　To him it was Elysium to be there;
And he could even withstand that awkward
　　test
　　Which Rousseau points out to the dubious
　　　fair,
"Observe your lover when he *leaves* your
　　arms;"
But Juan never left them while they had
　　charms,

LIV.

Unless compell'd by fate, or wave, or wind,
　　Or near relations, who are much the same.
But *here* he was!—where each tie that can
　　bind
　　Humanity must yield to steel and flame:
And *he* whose very body was all mind,
　　Flung here by fate or circumstance, which
　　　tame
The loftiest, hurried by the time and place,
Dash'd on like a spurr'd blood-horse in a
　　race.

LV.

So was his blood stirr'd while he found
　　resistance,
　　As is the hunter's at the five-bar gate,
Or double post and rail, where the existence
　　Of Britain's youth depends upon their
　　　weight,
The lightest being the safest: at a distance
　　He hated cruelty, as all men hate
Blood, until heated—and even then his own
At times would curdle o'er some heavy
　　groan.

LVI.

The General Lascy, who had been hard
　　press'd,
　　Seeing arrive an aid so opportune
As were some hundred youngsters all abreast,
　　Who came as if just dropp'd down from the
　　　moon,
To Juan, who was nearest him, address'd
　　His thanks, and hopes to take the city
　　　soon,
Not reckoning him to be a "base Bezonian"
(As Pistol calls it), but a young Livonian.

LVII.

Juan, to whom he spoke in German, knew
　　As much of German as of Sanscrit, and
In answer made an inclination to
　　The general who held him in command;

For seeing one with ribands, black and blue,
 Stars, medals, and a bloody sword in hand,
Addressing him in tones which seem'd to
 thank,
He recognised an officer of rank.

LVIII.

Short speeches pass between two men who
 speak
 No common language; and besides, in time
Of war and taking towns, when many a shriek
 Rings o'er the dialogue, and many a crime
Is perpetrated ere a word can break
 Upon the ear, and sounds of horror chime
In like church-bells, with sigh, howl, groan,
 yell, prayer, ·
There cannot be much conversation there.

LIX.

And therefore all we have related in
 Two long octaves, pass'd in a little minute;
But in the same small minute, every sin
 Contrived to get itself comprised within it.
The very cannon, deafen'd by the din,
 Grew dumb, for you might almost hear a
 linnet,
As soon as thunder, 'midst the general noise
Of human nature's agonising voice!

LX.

The town was enter'd. Oh eternity!—
 "God made the country, and man made
 the town,"
So Cowper says—and I begin to be
 Of his opinion, when I see cast down
Rome, Babylon, Tyre, Carthage, Nineveh,
 All walls men know, and many never
 known;
And pondering on the present and the past,
To deem the woods shall be our home at
 last:—

LXI.

Of all men, saving Sylla the man-slayer,
 Who passes for in life and death most lucky,
Of the great names which in our faces stare,
 The General Boon, back-woodsman of
 Kentucky,
Was happiest amongst mortals anywhere;
 For killing nothing but a bear or buck, he
Enjoy'd the lonely, vigorous, harmless days
Of his old age in wilds of deepest maze.

LXII.

Crime came not near him—she is not the child
 Of solitude; Health shrank not from him—
 for
Her home is in the rarely trodden wild,
 Where if men seek her not, and death be
 more

Their choice than life, forgive them, as
 beguiled
 By habit to what their own hearts abhor—
In cities caged. The present case in point I
Cite is, that Boon lived hunting up to ninety;

LXIII.

And what's still stranger, left behind a name
 For which men vainly decimate the throng,
Not only famous, but of that *good* fame
 Without which glory's but a tavern song—
Simple, serene, the antipodes of shame,
 Which hate nor envy e'er could tinge with
 wrong;
An active hermit, even in age the child
Of Nature, or the Man of Ross run wild.

LXIV.

'T is true he shrank from men even of his
 nation,
 When they built up unto his darling
 trees,—
He moved some hundred miles off, for a
 station
 Where there were fewer houses and more
 ease;
The inconvenience of civilisation
 Is, that you neither can be pleased nor
 please;
But where he met the individual man,
He show'd himself as kind as mortal can.

LXV.

He was not all alone: around him grew
 A sylvan tribe of children of the chase,
Whose young, unawaken'd world was ever
 new,
 Nor sword nor sorrow yet had left a trace
On her unwrinkled brow, nor could you view
 A frown on Nature's or on human face;
The free-born forest found and kept them
 free,
And fresh as is a torrent or a tree.

LXVI.

And tall, and strong, and swift of foot were
 they,
 Beyond the dwarfing city's pale abortions,
Because their thoughts had never been the
 prey
 Of care or gain: the green woods were
 their portions;
No sinking spirits told them they grew grey,
 No fashion made them apes of her dis-
 tortions;
Simple they were, not savage; and their
 rifles,
Though very true, were not yet used for
 trifles.

LXVII.

Motion was in their days, rest in their
 slumbers,
 And cheerfulness the handmaid of their
 toil;
Nor yet too many nor too few their numbers;
 Corruption could not make their hearts her
 soil;
The lust which stings, the splendour which
 encumbers,
 With the free foresters divide no spoil;
Serene, not sullen, were the solitudes
Of this unsighing people of the woods.

LXVIII.

So much for Nature:—by way of variety,
 Now back to thy great joys, Civilisation!
And the sweet consequence of large society,
 War, pestilence, the despot's desolation,
The kingly scourge, the lust of notoriety,
 The millions slain by soldiers for their
 ration,
The scenes like Catherine's boudoir at three-
 score,
With Ismail's storm to soften it the more.

LXIX.

The town was enter'd: first one column made
 Its sanguinary way good—then another;
The reeking bayonet and the flashing blade
 Clash'd 'gainst the scimitar, and babe and
 mother
With distant shrieks were heard Heaven to
 upbraid:—
 Still closer sulphury clouds began to
 smother
The breath of morn and man, where foot by
 foot
The madden'd Turks their city still dispute.

LXX.

Koutousow, he who afterwards beat back
 (With some assistance from the frost and
 snow)
Napoleon on his bold and bloody track,
 It happen'd was himself beat back just
 now:
He was a jolly fellow, and could crack
 His jest alike in face of friend or foe,
Though life, and death, and victory were at
 stake;
But here it seem'd his jokes had ceased to
 take:

LXXI.

For having thrown himself into a ditch,
 Follow'd in haste by various grenadiers,
Whose blood the puddle greatly did enrich,
 He climb'd to where the parapet appears;

But there his project reach'd its utmost pitch
 ('Mongst other deaths the General Ribau-
 pierre's
Was much regretted), for the Moslem men
Threw them all down into the ditch again.

LXXII.

And had it not been for some stray troops
 landing
 They knew not where, being carried by the
 stream
To some spot, where they lost their under-
 standing,
 And wander'd up and down as in a dream,
Until they reach'd, as daybreak was ex-
 panding,
 That which a portal to their eyes did
 seem,—
The great and gay Koutousow might have
 lain
Where three parts of his column yet remain.

LXXIII.

And scrambling round the rampart, these
 same troops,
 After the taking of the "Cavalier,"
Just as Koutousow's most "forlorn" of
 "hopes".
 Took, like chameleons, some slight tinge
 of fear,
Open'd the gate call'd "Kilia," to the
 groups
Of baffled heroes, who stood shyly near,
Sliding knee-deep in lately frozen mud,
Now thaw'd into a marsh of human blood.

LXXIV.

The Kozacks, or, if so you please, Cos-
 sacques—
 (I don't much pique myself upon ortho-
 graphy,
So that I do not grossly err in facts,
 Statistics, tactics, politics, and geography)—
Having been used to serve on horses' backs,
 And no great dilettanti in topography
Of fortresses, but fighting where it pleases
Their chiefs to order,—were all cut to pieces.

LXXV.

Their column, though the Turkish batteries
 thunder'd
 Upon them, ne'ertheless had reach'd the
 rampart,
And naturally thought they could have
 plunder'd
 The city, without being further hamper'd;

But as it happens to brave men, they
 blunder'd—
 The Turks at first pretended to have
 scamper'd,
Only to draw them 'twixt two bastion
 corners,
From whence they sallied on those Christian
 scorners.

LXXVI.

Then being taken by the tail—a taking
 Fatal to bishops as to soldiers—these
Cossacques were all cut off as day was
 breaking,
 And found their lives were let at a short
 lease—
But perish'd without shivering or shaking,
 Leaving as ladders their heap'd carcasses,
O'er which Lieutenant-Colonel Yesouskoi
March'd with the brave battalion of Po-
 louzki:—

LXXVII.

This valiant man kill'd all the Turks he met,
 But could not eat them, being in his turn
Slain by some Mussulmans, who would not
 yet,
 Without resistance, see their city burn.
The walls were won, but 't was an even bet
 Which of the armies would have cause to
 mourn:
'Twas blow for blow, disputing inch by inch,
For one would not retreat, nor t' other flinch.

LXXVIII.

Another column also suffer'd much:—
 And here we may remark with the his-
 torian,
You should but give few cartridges to such
 Troops as are meant to march with greatest
 glory on:
When matters must be carried by the touch
 Of the bright bayonet, and they all should
 hurry on,
They sometimes, with a hankering for exist-
 ence,
Keep merely firing at a foolish distance.

LXXIX.

A junction of the General Meknop's men
 (Without the General, who had fallen some
 time
Before, being badly seconded just then)
 Was made at length with those who dared
 to climb
The death-disgorging rampart once again;
 And though the Turks' resistance was sub-
 lime,
They took the bastion, which the Seraskier
Defended at a price extremely dear.

LXXX.

Juan and Johnson, and some volunteers
 Among the foremost, offer'd him good
 quarter,
A word which little suits with Seraskiers,
 Or at least suited not this valiant Tartar.
He died, deserving well his country's tears,
 A savage sort of military martyr.
An English naval officer, who wish'd
To make him prisoner, was also dish'd:

LXXXI.

For all the answer to his proposition
 Was from a pistol-shot that laid him dead;
On which the rest, without more intermis-
 sion,
 Began to lay about with steel and lead—
The pious metals most in requisition
 On such occasions: not a single head
Was spared;—three thousand Moslems
 perish'd here,
And sixteen bayonets pierced the Seraskier.

LXXXII.

The city's taken—only part by part—
 And death is drunk with gore: there's not
 a street
Where fights not to the last some desperate
 heart
 For those for whom it soon shall cease to
 beat.
Here War forgot his own destructive art
 In more destroying Nature; and the heat
Of carnage, like the Nile's sun-sodden slime,
Engender'd monstrous shapes of every crime.

LXXXIII.

A Russian officer, in martial tread
 Over a heap of bodies, felt his heel
Seized fast, as if 't were by the serpent's
 head
 Whose fangs Eve taught her human seed
 to feel:
In vain he kick'd, and swore, and writhed,
 and bled,
 And howl'd for help as wolves do for a
 meal—
The teeth still kept their gratifying hold,
As do the subtle snakes described of old.

LXXXIV.

A dying Moslem, who had felt the foot
 Of a foe o'er him, snatch'd at it, and bit
The very tendon which is most acute—
 (That which some ancient Muse or modern
 wit

Named after thee, Achilles) and quite
 through 't
He made the teeth meet, nor relinquish'd it
Even with his life—for (but they lie) 't is said
To the live leg still clung the sever'd head.

LXXXV.

However this may be, 't is pretty sure
 The Russian officer for life was lamed,
For the Turk's teeth stuck faster than a
 skewer,
 And left him 'midst the invalid and
 maim'd:
The regimental surgeon could not cure
 His patient, and perhaps was to be blamed
More than the head of the inveterate foe,
Which was cut off, and scarce even then let go.

LXXXVI.

But then the fact's a fact—and 't is the part
 Of a true poet to escape from fiction
Whene'er he can; for there is little art
 In leaving verse more free from the re-
 striction
Of truth than prose, unless to suit the mart
 For what is sometimes call'd poetic diction
And that outrageous appetite for lies
Which Satan angles with for souls, like flies.

LXXXVII.

The city's taken, but not render'd!—No!
 There's not a Moslem that hath yielded
 sword:
The blood may gush out, as the Danube's
 flow
Rolls by the city wall; but deed nor word
Acknowledge aught of dread of death or foe:
 In vain the yell of victory is roar'd
By the advancing Muscovite—the groan
Of the last foe is echoed by his own.

LXXXVIII.

The bayonet pierces and the sabre cleaves,
 And human lives are lavish'd everywhere,
As the year closing whirls the scarlet leaves
 When the stripp'd forest bows to the bleak
 air,
And groans; and thus the peopled city
 grieves,
 Shorn of its best and loveliest, and left bare;
But still it falls in vast and awful splinters,
As oaks blown down with all their thousand
 winters.

LXXXIX.

It is an awful topic—but 't is not
 My cue for any time to be terrific:
For checker'd as is seen our human lot
 With good, and bad, and worse, alike
 prolific

Of melancholy merriment, to quote
 Too much of one sort would be soporific;—
Without, or with, offence to friends or foes,
I sketch your world exactly as it goes.

XC.

And one good action in the midst of crimes
 Is "quite refreshing," in the affected
 phrase
Of these ambrosial, Pharisaic times,
 With all their pretty milk-and-water ways,
And may serve therefore to bedew these
 rhymes,
 A little scorch'd at present with the blaze
Of conquest and its consequences, which
Make epic poesy so rare and rich.

XCI.

Upon a taken bastion, where there lay
 Thousands of slaughter'd men, a yet warm
 group
Of murder'd women, who had found their
 way
 To this vain refuge, made the good heart
 droop
And shudder;—while, as beautiful as May,
 A female child of ten years tried to stoop
And hide her little palpitating breast
Amidst the bodies lull'd in bloody rest.

XCII.

Two villainous Cossacques pursued the child
 With flashing eyes and weapons: match'd
 with them,
The rudest brute that roams Siberia's wild
 Has feelings pure and polish'd as a gem,—
The bear is civilised, the wolf is mild:
 And whom for this at last must we con-
 demn?
Their natures? or their sovereigns, who
 employ
All arts to teach their subjects to destroy?

XCIII.

Their sabres glitter'd o'er her little head,
 Whence her fair hair rose twining with
 affright,
Her hidden face was plunged amidst the
 dead:
 When Juan caught a glimpse of this sad
 sight,
I shall not say exactly what he *said*,
 Because it might not solace "ears polite;"
But what he *did*, was to lay on their backs,
The readiest way of reasoning with Cos-
 sacques.

XCIV.

One's hip he slash'd, and split the other's
 shoulder,
 And drove them with their brutal yells to
 seek
If there might be chirurgeons who could
 solder
The wounds they richly merited, and
 shriek
Their baffled rage and pain; while waxing
 colder
As he turn'd o'er each pale and gory cheek,
Don Juan raised his little captive from
The heap a moment more had made her
 tomb.

XCV.

And she was chill as they, and on her face
 A slender streak of blood announced how
 near
Her fate had been to that of all her race;
 For the same blow which laid her mother
 here
Had scarr'd her brow, and left its crimson
 trace,
 As the last link with all she had held dear;
But else unhurt, she open'd her large eyes,
And gazed on Juan with a wild surprise.

XCVI.

Just at this instant, while their eyes were fix'd
 Upon each other, with dilated glance,
In Juan's look, pain, pleasure, hope, fear,
 mix'd
 With joy to save, and dread of some mis-
 chance
Unto his protégée; while hers, transfix'd
 With infant terrors, glared as from a trance,
A pure, transparent, pale, yet radiant face,
Like to a lighted alabaster vase;—

XCVII.

Up came John Johnson (I will not say
 "*Jack*,"
 For that were vulgar, cold, and common-
 place
On great occasions, such as an attack
 On cities, as hath been the present case):
Up Johnson came, with hundreds at his back,
 Exclaiming—"Juan! Juan! On, boy! brace
Your arm, and I'll bet Moscow to a dollar,
That you and I will win St. George's collar.

XCVIII.

"The Seraskier is knock'd upon the head,
 But the stone bastion still remains, wherein
The old Pacha sits among some hundreds
 dead,
 Smoking his pipe quite calmly 'midst the
 din
Of our artillery and his own: 't is said
 Our kill'd, already piled up to the chin,
Lie round the battery; but still it batters,
And grape in volleys, like a vineyard, scat-
 ters.

XCIX.

"Then up with me!"—But Juan answer'd,
 "Look
Upon this child—I saved her—must not
 leave
Her life to chance; but point me out some
 nook
 Of safety, where she less may shrink and
 grieve,
And I am with you."—Whereon Johnson took
 A glance around — and shrugg'd — and
 twitch'd his sleeve
And black silk neckcloth — and replied,
 "You're right;
Poor thing! what's to be done? I'm puzzled
 quite."

C.

Said Juan—"Whatsoever is to be
 Done, I'll not quit her till she seems secure
Of present life a good deal more than we."—
 Quoth Johnson—"*Neither* will I quite in-
 sure;
But at the least *you* may die gloriously."—
 Juan replied—"At least I will endure
Whate'er is to be borne—but not resign
This child, who is parentless, and therefore
 mine."

CI.

Johnson said—"Juan, we've no time to lose;
 The child's a pretty child—a very pretty—
I never saw such eyes—but hark! now
 choose
 Between your fame and feelings, pride and
 pity:—
Hark! how the roar increases!—no excuse
 Will serve when there is plunder in a
 city;
I should be loth to march without you, but,
By God! we'll be too late for the first cut."

CII.

But Juan was immovable; until
 Johnson, who really loved him in his way,
Pick'd out amongst his followers with some
 skill
 Such as he thought the least given up to
 prey;
And swearing if the infant came to ill
 That they should all be shot on the next
 day;
But if she were deliver'd safe and sound,
They should at least have fifty rubles round,

CIII.

And all allowances besides of plunder
　In fair proportion with their comrades;—
　　then
Juan consented to march on through thun-
　　der,
　Which thinn'd at every step their ranks of
　　men:
And yet the rest rush'd eagerly—no wonder,
　For they were heated by the hope of gain,
A thing which happens everywhere each
　　day—
No hero trusteth wholly to half pay.

CIV.

And such is victory, and such is man!
　At least nine-tenths of what we call so:—
　　God
May have another name for half we scan
　As human beings, or his ways are odd.
But to our subject: a brave Tartar khan—
　Or "sultan," as the author (to whose nod
In prose I bend my humble verse) doth call
This chieftain—somehow would not yield at
　　all

CV.

But flank'd by *five* brave sons, (such is poly-
　　gamy,
　That she spawns warriors by the score,
　　where none
Are prosecuted for that false crime bigamy),
　He never would believe the city won
While courage clung but to a single twig.—
　　Am I
　Describing Priam's Peleus', or Jove's son?
Neither—but a good, plain, old, temperate
　　man,
Who fought with his five children in the van.

CVI.

To *take* him was the point. The truly brave,
　When they behold the brave oppress'd
　　with odds,
Are touch'd with a desire to shield and
　　save;—
　A mixture of wild beasts and demi-gods
Are they—now furious as the sweeping wave,
　Now moved with pity; even as sometimes
　　nods
The rugged tree unto the summer wind,
Compassion breathes along the savage mind.

CVII.

But he would *not* be *taken*, and replied
　To all the propositions of surrender
By mowing Christians down on every side,
　As obstinate as Swedish Charles at Bender.

His five brave boys no less the foe defied;
　Whereon the Russian pathos grew less
　　tender,
As being a virtue, like terrestrial patience,
Apt to wear out on trifling provocations.

CVIII.

And spite of Johnson and of Juan, who
　Expended all their Eastern phraseology
In begging him, for God's sake, just to show
　So much less fight as might form an apology
For *them* in saving such a desperate foe—
　He hew'd away, like doctors of theology
When they dispute with sceptics; and with
　　curses
Struck at his friends, as babies beat their
　　nurses.

CIX.

Nay, he had wounded, though but slightly,
　　both
　Juan and Johnson; whereupon they fell,
The first with sighs, the second with an oath,
　Upon his angry sultanship, pell-mell,
And all around were grown exceeding wroth
　At such a pertinacious infidel,
And pour'd upon him and his sons like rain,
Which they resisted like a sandy plain

CX.

That drinks and still is dry. At last they
　　perish'd—
　His second son was levell'd by a shot;
His third was sabred; and the fourth, most
　　cherish'd
　Of all the five, on bayonets met his lot;
The fifth, who, by a Christian mother nou-
　　rish'd,
　Had been neglected, ill-used, and what not,
Because deform'd, yet died all game and
　　bottom,
To save a sire, who blush'd that he begot him.

CXI.

The eldest was a true and tameless Tartar,
　As great a scorner of the Nazarene
As ever Mahomet pick'd out for a martyr,
　Who only saw the black-eyed girls in green,
Who make the beds of those who won't take
　　quarter
　On earth, in Paradise; and when once seen,
Those houris, like all other pretty creatures,
Do just whate'er they please, by dint of
　　features.

CXII.

And what they pleased to do with the young
　　khan
　In heaven I know not, nor pretend to guess;
But doubtless they prefer a fine young man
　To tough old heroes, and can do no less;

And that's the cause no doubt why, if we scan
 A field of battle's ghastly wilderness,
For one rough, weather-beaten, veteran body,
 You 'll find ten thousand handsome coxcombs
 bloody.

CXIII.

Your houris also have a natural pleasure
 In lopping off your lately married men,
Before the bridal hours have danced their
 measure,
 And the sad, second moon grows dim again,
Or dull repentance hath had dreary leisure
 To wish him back a bachelor now and then:
And thus your houri (it may be) disputes
Of these brief blossoms the immediate fruits.

CXIV.

Thus the young khan, with houris in his
 sight,
 Thought not upon the charms of four young
 brides,
But bravely rush'd on his first heavenly
 night.
 In short, howe'er *our* better faith derides,
These black-eyed virgins make the Moslems
 fight,
 As though there were one heaven and none
 besides—
Whereas, if all be true we hear of heaven
And hell, there must at least be six or seven.

CXV.

So fully flash'd the phantom on his eyes,
 That when the very lance was in his heart,
He shouted " Allah ! " and saw Paradise
 With all its veil of mystery drawn apart,
And bright eternity without disguise
 On his soul, like a ceaseless sunrise, dart :—
With prophets, houris, angels, saints, descried
In one voluptuous blaze,—and then he died :

CXVI.

But with a heavenly rapture on his face,
 The good old khan, who long had ceased
 to see
Houris, or aught except his florid race
 Who grew like cedars round him glori-
 ously—
When he beheld his latest hero grace
 The earth, which he became like a fell'd
 tree,
Paused for a moment from the fight, and cast
A glance on that slain son, his first and last.

CXVII.

The soldiers, who beheld him drop his point,
 Stopp'd as if once more willing to concede
Quarter, in case he bade them not " aroynt ! "
 As he before had done.　He did not heed

Their pause nor signs : his heart was out of
 joint,
 And shook (till now unshaken) like a reed,
As he look'd down upon his children gone,
And felt—though done with life—he was
 alone.

CXVIII.

But 't was a transient tremor :—with a spring
 Upon the Russian steel his breast he flung,
As carelessly as hurls the moth her wing
 Against the light wherein she dies : he
 clung
Closer, that all the deadlier they might wring,
 Unto the bayonets which had pierced his
 young ;
And throwing back a dim look on his sons,
In one wide wound pour'd forth his soul at
 once.

CXIX.

'T is strange enough—the rough, tough soldiers
 who
 Spared neither sex nor age in their career
Of carnage, when this old man was pierced
 through,
 And lay before them with his children near,
Touch'd by the heroism of him they slew,
 Were melted for a moment ; though no tear
Flow'd from their bloodshot eyes, all red with
 strife,
They honour'd such determined scorn of life.

CXX.

But the stone bastion still kept up its fire,
 Where the chief pacha calmly held his
 post :
Some twenty times he made the Russ retire,
 And baffled the assaults of all their host ;
At length he condescended to inquire,
 If yet the city's rest were won or lost ;
And being told the latter, sent a bey
To answer Ribas' summons to give way.

CXXI.

In the mean time, cross-legg'd, with great
 sang-froid,
 Among the scorching ruins he sat smoking
Tobacco on a little carpet ;—Troy
 Saw nothing like the scene around ;—yet
 looking
With martial stoicism, nought seem'd to
 annoy
 His stern philosophy ; but gently stroking
His beard, he puff'd his pipe's ambrosial
 gales,
As if he had three lives, as well as tails.

CXXII.

The town was taken—whether he might yield
 Himself or bastion, little matter'd now:
His stubborn valour was no future shield.
 Ismail's no more! The crescent's silver bow
Sunk, and the crimson cross glared o'er the field,
 But red with no *redeeming* gore: the glow
Of burning streets, like moonlight on the water,
Was imaged back in blood, the sea of slaughter.

CXXIII.

All that the mind would shrink from of excesses;
 All that the body perpetrates of bad;
All that we read, hear, dream, of man's distresses;
 All that the devil would do if run stark mad;
All that defies the worst which pen expresses;
 All by which hell is peopled, or as sad
As hell—mere mortals who their power abuse—
Was here (as heretofore and since) let loose.

CXXIV.

If here and there some transient trait of pity
 Was shown, and some more noble heart broke through
Its bloody bond, and saved, perhaps, some pretty
 Child, or an aged, helpless man or two—
What's this in one annihilated city,
 Where thousand loves, and ties, and duties grew?
Cockneys of London! Muscadins of Paris!
Just ponder what a pious pastime war is.

CXXV.

Think how the joys of reading a Gazette
 Are purchased by all agonies and crimes:
Or if these do not move you, don't forget
 Such doom may be your own in after-times.
Meantime the Taxes, Castlereagh, and Debt,
 Are hints as good as sermons, or as rhymes.
Read your own hearts and Ireland's present story,
Then feed her famine fat with Wellesley's glory.

CXXVI.

But still there is unto a patriot nation,
 Which loves so well its country and its king,
A subject of sublimest exultation—
 Bear it, ye Muses, on your brightest wing!
Howe'er the mighty locust, Desolation
 Strip your green fields, and to your harvest cling,
Gaunt famine never shall approach the throne—
Though Ireland starve, great George weighs twenty stone.

CXXVII.

But let me put an end unto my theme:
 There was an end of Ismail—hapless town!
Far flash'd her burning towers o'er Danube's stream,
 And redly ran his blushing waters down.
The horrid war-whoop and the shriller scream
 Rose still; but fainter were the thunders grown:
Of forty thousand who had mann'd the wall,
Some hundreds breathed—the rest were silent all!

CXXVIII.

In one thing ne'ertheless 't is fit to praise
 The Russian army upon this occasion,
A virtue much in fashion now-a-days,
 And therefore worthy of commemoration:
The topic's tender, so shall be my phrase—
 Perhaps the season's chill, and their long station
In winter's depth, or want of rest and victual,
Had made them chaste;—they ravish'd very little.

CXXIX.

Much did they slay, more plunder, and no less
 Might here and there occur some violation
In the other line;—but not to such excess
 As when the French, that dissipated nation,
Take towns by storm: no causes can I guess,
 Except cold weather and commiseration;
But all the ladies, save some twenty score,
Were almost as much virgins as before.

CXXX.

Some odd mistakes, too, happen'd in the dark,
 Which show'd a want of lanterns, or of taste—
Indeed the smoke was such they scarce could mark
 Their friends from foes,—besides, such things from haste
Occur, though rarely, when there is a spark
 Of light to save the venerably chaste:
But six old damsels, each of seventy years,
Were all deflower'd by different grenadiers.

CXXXI.

But on the whole their continence was great;
 So that some disappointment there ensued
To those who had felt the inconvenient state
 Of "single blessedness," and thought it good

(Since it was not their fault, but only fate,
 To bear these crosses) for each waning
 prude
To make a Roman sort of Sabine wedding,
 Without the expense and the suspense of
 bedding.

CXXXII.

Some voices of the buxom middle-aged
 Were also heard to wonder in the din
(Widows of forty were these birds long caged)
 "Wherefore the ravishing did not begin!"
But while the thirst for gore and plunder
 raged,
 There was small leisure for superfluous sin;
But whether they escaped or no, lies hid
In darkness—I can only hope they did.

CXXXIII.

Suwarrow now was conqueror—a match
 For Timour or for Zinghis in his trade.
While mosques and streets, beneath his eyes,
 like thatch
 Blazed, and the cannon's roar was scarce
 allay'd,
With bloody hands he wrote his first despatch;
 And here exactly follows what he said:—
"Glory to *God* and to the Empress!" (*Powers
Eternal! such names mingled!*) "Ismail's
 ours."

CXXXIV.

Methinks these are the most tremendous
 words,
 Since "Mené, Mené, Tekel," and "Uphar-
 sin,"
Which hands or pens have ever traced of
 swords.
 Heaven help me! I'm but little of a parson:
What Daniel read was short-hand of the
 Lord's,
 Severe, sublime; the prophet wrote no
 farce on
The fate of nations;—but this Russ so witty
Could rhyme, like Nero, o'er a burning city.

CXXXV.

He wrote this Polar melody, and set it,
 Duly accompanied by shrieks and groans,
Which few will sing, I trust, but none
 forget it—
 For I will teach, if possible, the stones
To rise against earth's tyrants. Never let it
 Be said that we still truckle unto thrones;—
But ye—our children's children! think how
 we
Show'd *what things were* before the world
 was free!

CXXXVI.

That hour is not for us, but 'tis for you.
 And as, in the great joy of your millennium,
You hardly will believe such things were
 true
 As now occur, I thought that I would pen
 you 'em;
But may their very memory perish too!—
 Yet if perchance remember'd, still disdain
 you 'em
More than you scorn the savages of yore,
Who *painted* their *bare* limbs, but *not* with
 gore.

CXXXVII.

And when you hear historians talk of thrones,
 And those that sate upon them, let it be
As we now gaze upon the mammoth's bones,
 And wonder what old world such things
 could see,
Or hieroglyphics on Egyptian stones,
 The pleasant riddles of futurity—
Guessing at what shall happily be hid,
As the real purpose of a pyramid.

CXXXVIII.

Reader! I have kept my word,—at least so
 far
 As the first canto promised. You have
 now
Had sketches of love, tempest, travel, war,—
 All very accurate, you must allow,
And *epic*, if plain truth should prove no bar;
 For I have drawn much less with a long
 bow
Than my forerunners. Carelessly I sing,
But Phœbus lends me now and then a string,

CXXXIX.

With which I still can harp, and carp, and
 fiddle.
 What further hath befallen or may befall
The hero of this grand poetic riddle,
 I by and by may tell you, if at all:
But now I choose to break off in the middle,
 Worn out with battering Ismail's stubborn
 wall,
While Juan is sent off with the despatch,
For which all Petersburg is on the watch.

CXL.

This special honour was conferr'd, because
 He had behaved with courage and hu-
 manity—
Which *last* men like, when they have time to
 pause
From their ferocities, produced by vanity.

His little captive gain'd him some applause
 For saving her amidst the wild insanity
Of carnage,—and I think he was more glad
 in her
Safety, than his new order of St. Vladimir.

CXLI.

The Moslem orphan went with her protector,
 For she was homeless, houseless, helpless;
 all
Her friends, like the sad family of Hector,
 Had perish'd in the field or by the wall:
Her very place of birth was but a spectre
 Of what it had been; there the Muezzin's
 call
To prayer was heard no more! and Juan
 wept,
And made a vow to shield her, which he
 kept.

—————

Canto the Ninth.

I.

OH, Wellington! (or "Villainton")—for Fame
 Sounds the heroic syllables both ways;
France could not even conquer your great
 name,
 But punn'd it down to this facetious
 phrase—
Beating or beaten she will laugh the same,)
 You have obtain'd great pensions and much
 praise:
Glory like yours should any dare gainsay,
Humanity would rise, and thunder "Nay!"

II.

I don't think that you used Kinnaird quite
 well
 In Marinet's affair—in fact 't was shabby,
And like some other things won't do to tell
 Upon your tomb in Westminster's old
 abbey.
Upon the rest 't is not worth while to dwell,
 Such tales being for the tea-hours of some
 tabby;
But though your years as man tend fast to
 zero,
In fact your grace is still but a young hero.

III.

Though Britain owes (and pays you too) so
 much,
 Yet Europe doubtless owes you greatly
 more:
You have repair'd Legitimacy's crutch,
 A prop not quite so certain as before:

The Spanish, and the French, as well as
 Dutch,
 Have seen, and felt, how strongly you
 restore;
And Waterloo has made the world your
 debtor
(I wish your bards would sing it rather
 better).

IV.

You are "the best of cut-throats:"—do not
 start;
 The phrase is Shakspeare's, and not mis-
 applied:—
War's a brain-spattering, windpipe-slitting
 art,
 Unless her cause by right be sanctified.
If you have acted once a generous part,
 The world, not the world's masters, will
 decide,
And I shall be delighted to learn who,
Save you and yours, have gain'd by Water-
 loo?

V.

I am no flatterer—you've supp'd full of
 flattery:
 They say you like it too—'tis no great
 wonder.
He whose whole life has been assault and
 battery,
 At last may get a little tired of thunder;
And swallowing eulogy much more than
 satire, he
 May like being praised for every lucky
 blunder,
Call'd "Saviour of the Nations"—not yet
 saved,
And "Europe's Liberator"—still enslaved.

VI.

I've done. Now go and dine from off the
 plate
 Presented by the Prince of the Brazils,
And send the sentinel before your gate
 A slice or two from your luxurious meals:
He fought, but has not fed so well of late.
 Some hunger, too, they say the people
 feels:—
There is no doubt that you deserve your
 ration,
But pray give back a little to the nation.

VII.

I don't mean to reflect—a man so great as
 You, my lord duke! is far above reflection:
The high Roman fashion, too, of Cincinnatus,
 With modern history has but small con-
 nexion:

Though as an Irishman you love potatoes,
 You need not take them under your direc-
 tion;
And half a million for your Sabine farm
Is rather dear!—I'm sure I mean no harm.

VIII.

Great men have always scorn'd great recom-
 penses:
 Epaminondas saved his Thebes, and died,
Not leaving even his funeral expenses:
 George Washington had thanks, and nought
 beside,
Except the all-cloudless glory (which few
 men's is)
 To free his country: Pitt too had his pride,
And as a high-soul'd minister of state is
Renown'd for ruining Great Britain gratis.

IX.

Never had mortal man such opportunity,
 Except Napoleon, or abused it more:
You might have freed fallen Europe from the
 unity
 Of tyrants, and been blest from shore to
 shore:
And *now*—what *is* your fame? Shall the
 Muse tune it ye?
 Now—that the rabble's first vain shouts
 are o'er?
Go! hear it in your famish'd country's cries!
Behold the world! and curse your victories!

X.

As these new cantos touch on warlike feats,
 To *you* the unflattering Muse deigns to
 inscribe
Truths, that you will not read in the Gazettes,
 But which 't is time to teach the hireling
 tribe
Who fatten on their country's gore, and debts,
 Must be recited—and without a bribe.
You *did great* things: but not being *great* in
 mind,
Have left *undone* the *greatest*—and mankind.

XI.

Death laughs—Go ponder o'er the skeleton
 With which men image out the unknown
 thing
That hides the past world, like to a set sun
 Which still elsewhere may rouse a brighter
 spring:
Death laughs at all you weep for:—look upon
 This hourly dread of all! whose *threaten'd*
 sting
Turns life to terror, even though in its
 sheath:
Mark! how its lipless mouth grins without
 breath!

XII.

Mark! how it laughs and scorns at all you
 are!
 And yet *was* what you are; from *ear* to *ear*
It *laughs not*—there is now no fleshy bar
 So call'd; the Antic long hath ceased to
 hear,
But still he *smiles;* and whether near or far
 He strips from man that mantle (far more
 dear
Than even the tailor's), his incarnate skin,
White, black, or copper—the dead bones will
 grin.

XIII.

And thus Death laughs,—it is sad merriment,
 But still it *is* so; and with such example
Why should not Life be equally content
 With his superior, in a smile to trample
Upon the nothings which are daily spent
 Like bubbles on an ocean much less ample
Than the eternal deluge, which devours
Suns as rays—worlds like atoms—years like
 hours?

XIV.

"To be, or not to be? that is the question,"
 Says Shakspeare, who just now is much
 in fashion.
I am neither Alexander nor Hephæstion,
 Nor ever had for *abstract* fame much
 passion;
But would much rather have a sound diges-
 tion,
 Than Buonaparte's cancer:—could I dash
 on
Through fifty victories to shame or fame,
Without a stomach—what were a good
 name?

XV.

"Oh dura ilia messorum!"—"Oh
 Ye rigid guts of reapers!" I translate
For the great benefit of those who know
 What indigestion is—that inward fate
Which makes all Styx through one small
 liver flow.
 A peasant's sweat is worth his lord's estate:
Let *this* one toil for bread—*that* rack for
 rent,
He who sleeps best may be the most content.

XVI.

"To be, or not to be?"—Ere I decide,
 I should be glad to know that which *is*
 being;
'Tis true we speculate both far and wide,
 And deem, because we *see*, we are *all-*
 seeing:

For my part, I'll enlist on neither side,
 Until I see both sides for once agreeing.
For me, I sometimes think that life is death,
Rather than life a mere affair of breath.

XVII.

"Que sçais-je?" was the motto of Mon-
 taigne,
 As also of the first academicians;
That all is dubious which man may attain,
 Was one of their most favourite positions.
There's no such thing as certainty, that's
 plain
 As any of Mortality's conditions;
So little do we know what we're about in
This world, I doubt if doubt itself be doubt-
 ing.

XVIII.

It is a pleasant voyage perhaps to float,
 Like Pyrrho, on a sea of speculation;
But what if carrying sail capsize the boat?
 Your wise men don't know much of navi-
 gation;
And swimming long in the abyss of thought
Is apt to tire: a calm and shallow station
Well nigh the shore, where one stoops down
 and gathers
Some pretty shell, is best for moderate
 bathers.

XIX.

"But heaven," as Cassio says, "is above
 all—
 No more of this, then, let us pray!" We
 have
Souls to save, since Eve's slip and Adam's
 fall,
 Which tumbled all mankind into the grave,
Besides fish, beasts, and birds. "The
 sparrow's fall
 Is special providence," though how it gave
Offence, we know not; probably it perch'd
Upon the tree which Eve so fondly search'd.

XX.

Oh! ye immortal Gods! what is theogony?
 Oh! thou, too, mortal man! what is philan-
 thropy?
Oh! world, which was and is, what is cos-
 mogony?
 Some people have accused me of misan-
 thropy;
And yet I know no more than the mahogany
 That forms this desk, of what they mean;
 lykanthropy
I comprehend, for without transformation
Men become wolves on any slight occasion.

XXI.

But I, the mildest, meekest of mankind,
 Like Moses, or Melancthon, who have ne'er
Done anything exceedingly unkind,—
 And (though I could not now and then
 forbear
Following the bent of body or of mind)
 Have always had a tendency to spare,—
Why do they call me misanthrope? Because
They hate me, not I them:—and here we'll
 pause.

XXII.

'Tis time we should proceed with our good
 poem,—
 For I maintain that it is really good,
Not only in the body but the proem,
 However little both are understood
Just now,—but by and by the Truth will
 show 'em
 Herself in her sublimest attitude:
And till she doth, I fain must be content
To share her beauty and her banishment.

XXIII.

Our hero (and, I trust, kind reader! yours)
 Was left upon his way to the chief city
Of the immortal Peter's polish'd boors,
 Who still have shown themselves more
 brave than witty.
I know its mighty empire now allures
 Much flattery—even Voltaire's, and that's
 a pity.
For me, I deem an absolute autocrat
Not a barbarian, but much worse than that.

XXIV.

And I will war, at least in words (and—
 should
 My chance so happen—deeds), with all who
 war
With Thought;—and of Thought's foes by
 far most rude,
 Tyrants and sycophants have been and are.
I know not who may conquer: if I could
 Have such a prescience, it should be no bar
To this my plain, sworn, downright de-
 testation
Of every despotism in every nation.

XXV.

It is not that I adulate the people:
 Without *me*, there are demagogues enough,
And infidels, to pull down every steeple,
 And set up in their stead some proper
 stuff.

Whether they may sow scepticism to reap
 hell,
As is the Christian dogma rather rough,
I do not know;—I wish men to be free
As much from mobs as kings—from you as
 me.

XXVI.

The consequence is, being of no party,
 I shall offend all parties:—never mind!
My words, at least, are more sincere and
 hearty
Than if I sought to sail before the wind.
He who has nought to gain can have small
 art: he
Who neither wishes to be bound nor bind,
May still expatiate freely, as will I,
Nor give my voice to slavery's jackal cry.

XXVII.

That's an appropriate simile, *that jackal ;*—
 I've heard them in the Ephesian ruins
 howl
By night, as do that mercenary pack all,
 Power's base purveyors, who for pickings
 prowl,
And scent the prey their masters would
 attack all.
However, the poor jackals are less foul
(As being the brave lions' keen providers)
Than human insects, catering for spiders.

XXVIII.

Raise but an arm! 't will brush their web
 away,
 And without *that*, their poison and their
 claws
Are useless. Mind, good people! what I
 say—
 (Or rather peoples)—*go on* without pause!
The web of these tarantulas each day
 Increases, till you shall make common
 cause:
None, save the Spanish fly and Attic bee,
As yet are strongly stinging to be free.

XXIX.

Don Juan, who had shone in the late
 slaughter,
 Was left upon his way with the despatch,
Where blood was talk'd of as we would of
 water;
 And carcasses that lay as thick as thatch
O'er silenced cities, merely served to flatter
 Fair Catherine's pastime—who look'd on
 the match
Between these nations as a main of cocks,
Wherein she liked her own to stand like
 rocks.

XXX.

And there in a *kibitka* he roll'd on,
 (A cursed sort of carriage without springs,
Which on rough roads leaves scarcely a
 whole bone,)
Pondering on glory, chivalry, and kings,
And orders, and on all that he had done—
 And wishing that post-horses had the
 wings
Of Pegasus, or at the least post-chaises
Had feathers, when a traveller on deep
 ways is.

XXXI.

At every jolt—and they were many—still
 He turn'd his eyes upon his little charge,
As if he wish'd that she should fare less ill
 Than he, in these sad highways left at large
To ruts, and flints, and lovely Nature's skill,
 Who is no paviour, nor admits a barge
On *her* canals, where God takes sea and land,
Fishery and farm, both into his own hand.

XXXII.

At least he pays no rent, and has best right
 To be the first of what we used to call
"Gentlemen farmers" a race worn out quite,
 Since lately there have been no rents at all,
And "gentlemen" are in a piteous plight,
 And "farmers" can't raise Ceres from her
 fall:
She fell with Buonaparte—What strange
 thoughts
Arise, when we see emperors fall with oats!

XXXIII.

But Juan turn'd his eyes on the sweet child
 Whom he had saved from slaughter—what
 a trophy!
Oh! ye who build up monuments, defiled
 With gore, like Nadir Shah, that costive
 sophy,
Who, after leaving Hindostan a wild,
 And scarce to the Mogul a cup of coffee
To soothe his woes withal, was slain, the
 sinner!
Because he could no more digest his dinner;—

XXXIV.

Oh ye! or we! or he! or she! reflect,
 That *one* life saved, especially if young.
Or pretty, is a thing to recollect
 Far sweeter than the greenest laurels
 sprung
From the manure of human clay, though
 deck'd
 With all the praises ever said or sung:
Though hymn'd by every harp, unless within
Your heart joins chorus, Fame is but a din.

XXXV.

Oh! ye great authors luminous, voluminous!
　Ye twice ten hundred thousand daily
　　scribes!
Whose pamphlets, volumes, newspapers,
　　illumine us!
　Whether you're paid by government in
　　bribes,
To prove the public debt is not consuming
　　us—
　Or, roughly treading on the "courtier's
　　kibes"
With clownish heel, your popular circulation
Feeds you by printing half the realm's
　　starvation;—

XXXVI.

Oh, ye great authors!—"Apropos des
　bottes,"—
　I have forgotten what I meant to say,
As sometimes have been greater sages' lots;—
　'T was something calculated to allay
All wrath in barracks, palaces, or cots:
　Certes it would have been but thrown away,
And that's one comfort for my lost advice,
Although no doubt it was beyond all price.

XXXVII.

But let it go:—it will one day be found
　With other relics of "a former world,"
When this world shall be *former*, under-
　　ground,
　Thrown topsy-turvy, twisted, crisp'd, and
　　curl'd,
Baked, fried, or burnt, turn'd inside-out, or
　　drown'd,
　Like all the worlds before, which have been
　　hurl'd
First out of, and then back again to chaos,
The superstratum which will overlay us.

XXXVIII.

So Cuvier says:—and then shall come again
　Unto the new creation, rising out
From our old crash, some mystic, ancient
　　strain
　Of things destroy'd and left in airy doubt;
Like to the notions we now entertain
　Of Titans, giants, fellows of about
Some hundred feet in height, *not* to say *miles*,
And mammoths, and your winged crocodiles.

XXXIX.

Think if then George the Fourth should be
　dug up,
　How the new worldlings of the then new
　　East
Will wonder where such animals could sup!
　(For they themselves will be but of the
　　least:

Even worlds miscarry, when too oft they
　pup,
And every new creation hath decreased
In size, from overworking the material—
Men are but maggots of some huge Earth's
　burial).

XL.

How will—to these young people, just thrust
　out
　From some fresh Paradise, and set to
　　plough,
And dig, and sweat, and turn themselves
　about,
　And plant, and reap, and spin, and grind,
　　and sow,
Till all the arts at length are brought about,
　Especially of war and taxing,—how,
I say, will these great relics, when they
　see 'em,
Look like the monsters of a new museum!

XLI.

But I am apt to grow too metaphysical:
　"The time is out of joint,"—and so am I;
I quite forget this poem's merely quizzical,
　And deviate into matters rather dry.
I ne'er decide what I shall say, and this I
　call
　Much too poetical: men should know why
They write, and for what end; but, note or
　text,
I never know the word which will come next.

XLII.

So on I ramble, now and then narrating,
　Now pondering:—it is time we should
　　narrate.
I left Don Juan with his horses baiting—
　Now we'll get o'er the ground at a great
　　rate.
I shall not be particular in stating
　His journey, we've so many tours of late:
Suppose him then at Petersburgh; suppose
That pleasant capital of painted snows;

XLIII.

Suppose him in a handsome uniform;
　A scarlet coat, black facings, a long plume,
Waving, like sails new shiver'd in a storm,
　Over a cock'd hat in a crowded room,
And brilliant breeches, bright as a Cairn
　Gorme,
　Of yellow casimere we may presume,
White stockings drawn uncurdled as new
　milk
O'er limbs whose symmetry set off the silk;

XLIV.

Suppose him sword by side, and hat in hand,
 Made up by youth, fame, and an army
 tailor—
That great enchanter, at whose rod's com-
 mand
 Beauty springs forth, and Nature's self
 turns paler,
Seeing how Art can make her work more
 grand
 (When she don't pin men's limbs in like a
 gaoler),—
Behold him placed as if upon a pillar! He
Seems Love turn'd a lieutenant of artillery!

XLV.

His bandage slipp'd down into a cravat;
 His wings subdued to epaulettes; his
 quiver
Shrunk to a scabbard, with his arrows at
 His side as a small sword, but sharp as
 ever;
His bow converted into a cock'd hat;
 But still so like, that Psyche were more
 clever
Than some wives (who make blunders no less
 stupid),
If she had not mistaken him for Cupid.

XLVI.

The courtiers stared, the ladies whisper'd,
 and
 The empress smiled: the reigning favourite
 frown'd—
I quite forget which of them was in hand
 Just then; as they are rather numerous
 found,
Who took by turns that difficult command
 Since first her majesty was singly crown'd:
But they were mostly nervous six-foot fel-
 lows,
All fit to make a Patagonian jealous.

XLVII.

Juan was none of these, but slight and slim,
 Blushing and beardless; and yet ne'erthe-
 less
There was a something in his turn of limb,
 And still more in his eye, which seem'd to
 express,
That though he look'd like one of the
 seraphim,
 There lurk'd a man beneath the spirit's
 dress.
Besides, the empress sometimes liked a boy,
And had just buried the fair-faced Lanskoi.

XLVIII.

No wonder then that Yermoloff, or Momonoff,
 Or Scherbatoff, or any other *off*
Or *on*, might dread her majesty had not room
 enough
 Within her bosom (which was not too
 tough)
For a new flame; a thought to cast of gloom
 enough
 Along the aspect, whether smooth or rough,
Of him who, in the language of his station,
Then held that "high official situation."

XLIX.

Oh, gentle ladies! should you seek to know
 The import of this diplomatic phrase,
Bid Ireland's Londonderry's Marquess show
 His parts of speech; and in the strange
 displays
Of that odd string of words, all in a row,
 Which none divine, and every one obeys,
Perhaps you may pick out some queer *no*
 meaning,
Of that weak wordy harvest the sole glean-
 ing.

L.

I think I can explain myself without
 That sad inexplicable beast of prey—
That Sphinx, whose words would ever be a
 doubt,
 Did not his deeds unriddle them each day—
That monstrous hieroglyphic—that long
 spout
 Of blood and water, leaden Castlereagh!
And here I must an anecdote relate,
But luckily of no great length or weight.

LI.

An English lady ask'd of an Italian,
 What were the actual and official duties
Of the strange thing, some women set a value
 on,
 Which hovers oft about some married
 beauties,
Call'd "Cavalier servente?" a Pygmalion
 Whose statues warm (I fear, alas! too
 true 't is)
Beneath his art. The dame, press'd to dis-
 close them,
Said—"Lady, I beseech you to *suppose them.*"

LII.

And thus I supplicate your supposition,
 And mildest, matron-like interpretation,
Of the imperial favourite's condition.
 'Twas a high place, the highest in the
 nation

In fact, if not in rank! and the suspicion
 Of any one's attaining to his station
No doubt gave pain, where each new pair of
 shoulders,
If rather broad, made stocks rise and their
 holders.

LIII.

Juan, I said, was a most beauteous boy,
 And had retain'd his boyish look beyond
The usual hirsute seasons which destroy,
 With beards and whiskers, and the like,
 the fond
Parisian aspect, which upset old Troy
 And founded Doctors' Commons:—I have
 conn'd
The history of divorces, which, though
 chequer'd,
Calls Ilion's the first damages on record.

LIV.

And Catherine, who loved all things (save
 her lord,
 Who was gone to his place), and pass'd for
 much,
Admiring those (by dainty dames abhorr'd)
 Gigantic gentlemen, yet had a touch
Of sentiment: and he she most adored
 Was the lamented Lanskoi, who was such
A lover as had cost her many a tear,
And yet but made a middling grenadier.

LV.

Oh thou "teterrima causa" of all "belli"—
 Thou gate of life and death—thou nonde-
 script!
Whence is our exit and our entrance, well I
 May pause in pondering how all souls are
 dipt
In thy perennial fountain: how man *fell* I
 Know not, since knowledge saw her
 branches stript
Of her first fruit; but how he falls and rises,
Since, *thou* hast settled beyond all surmises.

LVI.

Some call thee "the worst cause of war,"
 but I
 Maintain thou art the *best*: for after all,
From thee we come, to thee we go, and
 why
 To get at thee not batter down a wall,
Or waste a world? since no one can deny
 Thou dost replenish worlds both great and
 small:
With, or without thee, all things at a stand
Are, or would be, thou sea of life's dry land!

LVII.

Catherine, who was the grand epitome
 Of that great cause of war, or peace, or
 what
You please (it causes all the things which be,
 So you may take your choice of this or
 that)—
Catherine, I say, was very glad to see
 The handsome herald, on whose plumage
 sat
Victory; and, pausing as she saw him kneel
With his despatch, forgot to break the seal.

LVIII.

Then recollecting the whole empress, nor
 Forgetting quite the woman (which com-
 posed
At least three parts of this great whole), she
 tore
 The letter open with an air which posed
The court, that watch'd each look her visage
 wore,
 Until a royal smile at length disclosed
Fair weather for the day. Though rather
 spacious,
Her face was noble, her eyes fine, mouth
 gracious.

LIX.

Great joy was hers, or rather joys: the first
 Was a ta'en city, thirty thousand slain.
Glory and triumph o'er her aspect burst,
 As an East Indian sunrise on the main.
These quench'd a moment her ambition's
 thirst—
 So Arab deserts drink in summer's rain:
In vain!—As fall the dews on quenchless sands,
Blood only serves to wash Ambition's hands!

LX.

Her next amusement was more fanciful;
 She smiled at mad Suwarrow's rhymes,
 who threw
Into a Russian couplet rather dull
 The whole gazette of thousands whom he
 slew.
Her third was feminine enough to annul
 The shudder which runs naturally through
Our veins, when things call'd sovereigns
 think it best
To kill, and generals turn it into jest.

LXI.

The two first feelings ran their course com-
 plete,
 And lighted first her eye, and then her
 mouth:
The whole court look'd immediately most
 sweet,
 Like flowers well water'd after a long
 drouth:—

But when on the lieutenant at her feet
 Her majesty, who liked to gaze on youth
Almost as much as on a new despatch,
 Glanced mildly, all the world was on the watch.

LXII.

Though somewhat large, exuberant, and
 truculent,
 When *wroth*—while *pleased*, she was as
 fine a figure
As those who like things rosy, ripe, and
 succulent,
 Would wish to look on, while they are in
 vigour.
She could repay each amatory look you lent
 With interest, and in turn was wont with
 rigour
To exact of Cupid's bills the full amount
At sight, nor would permit you to discount.

LXIII.

With her the latter, though at times con-
 venient,
 Was not so necessary; for they tell
That she was handsome, and though fierce
 look'd lenient,
 And always used her favourites too well.
If once beyond her boudoir's precincts in ye
 went,
 Your "fortune" was in a fair way "to
 swell
A man" (as Giles says); for though she
 would widow all
Nations, she liked man as an individual.

LXIV.

What a strange thing is man! and what a
 stranger
 Is woman! What a whirlwind is her head,
And what a whirlpool full of depth and
 danger
 Is all the rest about her! Whether wed,
Or widow, maid, or mother, she can change her
 Mind like the wind: whatever she has said
Or done, is light to what she'll say or do;—
The oldest thing on record, and yet new!

LXV.

Oh Catherine! (for of all interjections,
 To thee both *oh!* and *ah!* belong of right
In love and war) how odd are the connexions
 Of human thoughts, which jostle in their
 flight!
Just now *yours* were cut out in different
 sections:
 First Ismail's capture caught your fancy
 quite;
Next of new knights, the fresh and glorious
 batch;
And *thirdly* he who brought you the despatch!

LXVI.

Shakspeare talks of "the herald Mercury
 New lighted on a heaven-kissing hill:"
And some such visions cross'd her majesty,
 While her young herald knelt before her
 still.
'T is very true the hill seem'd rather high,
 For a lieutenant to climb up; but skill
Smooth'd even the Simplon's steep, and by
 God's blessing,
With youth and health all kisses are "hea-
 ven-kissing."

LXVII.

Her majesty look'd down, the youth look'd
 up—
 And so they fell in love;—she with his
 face,
His grace, his God-knows-what: for Cupid's
 cup
 With the first draught intoxicates apace,
A quintessential laudanum or "black drop,"
 Which makes one drunk at once, without
 the base
Expedient of full bumpers; for the eye
In love drinks all life's fountains (save tears)
 dry.

LXVIII.

He, on the other hand, if not in love,
 Fell into that no less imperious passion,
Self-love—which, when some sort of thing
 above
 Ourselves, a singer, dancer, much in fashion,
Or duchess, princess, empress, "deigns to
 prove"
 ('T is Pope's phrase) a great longing, though
 a rash one,
For one especial person out of many,
Makes us believe ourselves as good as any.

LXIX.

Besides, he was of that delighted age
 Which makes all female ages equal—when
We don't much care with whom we may
 engage,
 As bold as Daniel in the lions' den,
So that we can our native sun assuage
 In the next ocean, which may flow just
 then,
To make a twilight in, just as Sol's heat is
Quench'd in the lap of the salt sea, or Thetis.

LXX.

And Catherine (we must say thus much for
 Catherine),
 Though bold and bloody, was the kind of
 thing
Whose temporary passion was quite flattering,
 Because each lover look'd a sort of king,

Made up upon an amatory pattern,
 A royal husband in all save the *ring*—
Which, being the damn'dest part of matri-
 mony,
Seem'd taking out the sting to leave the honey.

LXXI.

And when you add to this, her womanhood
 In its meridian, her blue eyes or gray—
(The last, if they have soul, are quite as good,
 Or better, as the best examples say:
Napoleon's, Mary's (queen of Scotland),
 should
 Lend to that colour a transcendent ray;
And Pallas also sanctions the same hue,
Too wise to look through optics black or
 blue)—

LXXII.

Her sweet smile, and her then majestic figure,
 Her plumpness, her imperial condescen-
 sion,
Her preference of a boy to men much bigger
 (Fellows whom Messalina's self would pen-
 sion),
Her prime of life, just now in juicy vigour,
 With other *extras*, which we need not
 mention,—
All these, or any one of these, explain
Enough to make a stripling very vain.

LXXIII.

And that's enough, for love is vanity,
 Selfish in its beginning as its end,
Except where't is a mere insanity,
 A maddening spirit which would strive to
 blend
Itself with beauty's frail inanity,
 On which the passion's self seems to depend;
And hence some heathenish philosophers
Make love the main-spring of the universe.

LXXIV.

Besides Platonic love, besides the love
 Of God, the love of sentiment, the loving
Of faithful pairs—(I needs must rhyme with
 dove,
 That good old steam-boat which keeps
 verses moving
'Gainst reason—Reason ne'er was hand-and-
 glove
 With rhyme, but always leant less to im-
 proving
The sound than sense) besides all these pre-
 tences
To love, there are those things which words
 name senses;

LXXV.

Those movements, those improvements in
 our bodies
 Which make all bodies anxious to get out
Of their own sand-pits, to mix with a god-
 dess,
 For such all women are at first no doubt.
How beautiful that moment! and how odd is
 That fever which precedes the languid rout
Of our sensations! What a curious way
The whole thing is of clothing souls in clay!

LXXVI.

The noblest kind of love is love Platonical,
 To end or to begin with; the next grand
Is that which may be christen'd love ca-
 nonical,
 Because the clergy take the thing in hand;
The third sort to be noted in our chronicle
 As flourishing in every Christian land,
Is, when chaste matrons to their other ties
Add what may be call'd *marriage in disguise*.

LXXVII.

Well, we won't analyse—our story must
 Tell for itself: the sovereign was smitten,
Juan much flatter'd by her love, or lust;—
 I cannot stop to alter words once written,
And the two are so mix'd with human dust,
 That he who *names one*, both perchance
 may hit on:
But in such matters Russia's mighty em-
 press
Behaved no better than a common semp-
 stress.

LXXVIII.

The whole court melted into one wide whis-
 per,
 And all lips were applied unto all ears!
The elder ladies' wrinkles curl'd much crisper
 As they beheld; the younger cast some
 leers
On one another, and each lovely lisper
 Smiled as she talk'd the matter o'er; but
 tears
Of rivalship rose in each clouded eye
Of all the standing army who stood by.

LXXIX.

All the ambassadors of all the powers
 Inquired, Who was this very new young
 man,
Who promised to be great in some few hours?
 Which is full soon (though life is but a span.)
Already they beheld the silver showers
 Of rubles rain, as fast as specie can,
Upon his cabinet, besides the presents
Of several ribands, and some thousand
 peasants.

LXXX.

Catherine was generous,—all such ladies are:
Love—that great opener of the heart and
all
The ways that lead there, be they near or far,
Above, below, by turnpikes great or
small,—
Love—(though she had a cursed taste for war,
And was not the best wife, unless we call
Such Clytemnestra, though perhaps 't is
better
That one should die, than two drag on the
fetter)—

LXXXI.

Love had made Catherine make each lover's
fortune,
Unlike our own half-chaste Elizabeth,
Whose avarice all disbursements did impor-
tune,
If history, the grand liar, ever saith
The truth; and though grief her old age
might shorten,
Because she put a favourite to death,
Her vile, ambiguous method of flirtation,
And stinginess, disgrace her sex and station.

LXXXII.

But when the levée rose, and all was bustle
In the dissolving circle, all the nations'
Ambassadors began as 't were to hustle
Round the young man with their congratu-
lations.
Also the softer silks were heard to rustle
Of gentle dames, among whose recreations
It is to speculate on handsome faces,
Especially when such lead to high places.

LXXXIII.

Juan, who found himself, he knew not how,
A general object of attention, made
His answers with a very graceful bow,
As if born for the ministerial trade.
Though modest, on his unembarrass'd brow
Nature had written "gentleman." He said
Little, but to the purpose; and his manner
Flung hovering graces o'er him like a banner.

LXXXIV.

An order from her majesty consign'd
Our young lieutenant to the genial care
Of those in office: all the world look'd kind,
(As it will look sometimes with the first stare,
Which youth would not act ill to keep in
mind,)
As also did Miss Protasoff then there,
Named from her mystic office "l'Eprouveuse,"
A term inexplicable to the Muse.

LXXXV.

With *her* then, as in humble duty bound,
Juan retired,—and so will I, until
My Pegasus shall tire of touching ground.
We have just lit on a "heaven-kissing
hill,"
So lofty that I feel my brain turn round,
And all my fancies whirling like a mill;
Which is a signal to my nerves and brain,
To take a quiet ride in some green lane.

Canto the Tenth.

I.

When Newton saw an apple fall, he found
In that slight startle from his contem-
plation—
'T is *said* (for I 'll not answer above ground
For any sage's creed or calculation)—
A mode of proving that the earth turn'd round
In a most natural whirl, called "gravi-
tation;"
And this is the sole mortal who could
grapple,
Since Adam, with a fall, or with an apple.

II.

Man fell with apples, and with apples rose,
If this be true; for we must deem the mode
In which Sir Isaac Newton could disclose
Through the then unpaved stars the turn-
pike road,
A thing to counterbalance human woes:
For ever since immortal man hath glow'd
With all kinds of mechanics, and full soon
Steam-engines will conduct him to the moon.

III.

And wherefore this exordium?—Why, just
now,
In taking up this paltry sheet of paper,
My bosom underwent a glorious glow,
And my internal spirit cut a caper:
And though so much inferior, as I know,
To those who, by the dint of glass and
vapour,
Discover stars, and sail in the wind's eye,
I wish to do as much by poesy.

IV.

In the wind's eye I have sail'd, and sail; but
for
The stars, I own my telescope is dim;
But at the least I have shunn'd the common
shore,
And leaving land far out of sight, would
skim

The ocean of eternity: the roar
 Of breakers has not daunted my slight,
 trim,
But *still* sea-worthy skiff; and she may float
Where ships have founder'd, as doth many a
 boat.

V.

We left our hero, Juan, in the *bloom*
 Of favouritism, but not yet in the *blush* ;—
And far be it from my *Muses* to presume
 (For I have more than one Muse at a push)
To follow him beyond the drawing-room:
 It is enough that Fortune found him flush
Of youth, and vigour, beauty, and those
 things
Which for an instant clip enjoyment's wings.

VI.

But soon they grow again and leave their
 nest.
 "Oh!" saith the Psalmist, "that I had a
 dove's
Pinions to flee away, and be at rest!"
 And who that recollects young years and
 loves,—
Though hoary now, and with a withering
 breast,
 And palsied fancy, which no longer roves
Beyond its dimm'd eye's sphere,—but would
 much rather
Sigh like his son, than cough like his grand-
 father?

VII.

But sighs subside, and tears (even widows')
 shrink,
 Like Arno in the summer, to a shallow,
So narrow as to shame their wintry brink,
 Which threatens inundations deep and yel-
 low!
Such difference doth a few months make.
 You'd think
 Grief a rich field which never would lie
 fallow;
No more it doth, its ploughs but change their
 boys,
Who furrow some new soil to sow for joys.

VIII.

But coughs will come when sighs depart—
 and now
 And then before sighs cease; for oft the one
Will bring the other, ere the lake-like brow
 Is ruffled by a wrinkle, or the sun
Of life reach'd ten o'clock: and while a glow,
 Hectic and brief as summer's day nigh done,
O'erspreads the cheek which seems too pure
 for clay,
Thousands blaze, love, hope, die,—how happy
 they !—

IX.

But Juan was not meant to die so soon.
 We left him in the focus of such glory
As may be won by favour of the moon
 Or ladies' fancies—rather transitory
Perhaps; but who would scorn the month of
 June,
 Because December, with his breath so
 hoary,
Must come? Much rather should he court
 the ray,
To hoard up warmth against a wintry day.

X.

Besides, he had some qualities which fix
 Middle aged ladies even more than young:
The former know what's what; while new-
 fledged chicks
 Know little more of love than what is sung
In rhymes, or dreamt (for fancy will play
 tricks)
 In visions of those skies from whence Love
 sprung.
Some reckon women by their suns or years,
I rather think the moon should date the
 dears.

XI.

And why? because she's changeable and
 chaste.
 I know no other reason, whatsoe'er
Suspicious people, who find fault in haste,
 May choose to tax me with; which is not
 fair,
Nor flattering to "their temper or their
 taste,"
 As my friend Jeffrey writes with such an
 air:
However, I forgive him, and I trust
He will forgive himself;—if not, I must.

XII.

Old enemies who have become new friends
 Should so continue—'t is a point of honour;
And I know nothing which could make a-
 mends
 For a return to hatred: I would shun her
Like garlic, howsoever she extends
 Her hundred arms and legs, and fain
 outrun her.
Old flames, new wives, become our bitterest
 foes—
Converted foes should scorn to join with
 those.

XIII.

This were the worst desertion :—renegadoes,
 Even shuffling Southey, that incarnate lie,
Would scarcely join again the "reforma-
 does,"
 Whom he forsook to fill the laureate's sty:

And honest men from Iceland to Barbadoes,
 Whether in Caledon or Italy,
Should not veer round with every breath, nor
 seize
To pain, the moment when you cease to
 please.

XIV.

The lawyer and the critic but behold
 The baser sides of literature and life,
And nought remains unseen, but much un-
 told,
 By those who scour those double vales of
 strife.
While common men grow ignorantly old,
 The lawyer's brief is like the surgeon's
 knife,
Dissecting the whole inside of a question,
And with it all the process of digestion.

XV.

A legal broom's a moral chimney-sweeper,
 And that's the reason he himself's so
 dirty!
The endless soot bestows a tint far deeper
 Than can be hid by altering his shirt; he
Retains the sable stains of the dark creeper,
 At least some twenty-nine do out of thirty,
In all their habits;—not so *you*, I own;
As Cæsar wore his robe you wear your gown.

XVI.

And all our little feuds, at least all *mine*,
 Dear Jeffrey, once my most redoubted foe
(As far as rhyme and criticism combine
 To make such puppets of us things below),
Are over: Here's a health to "Auld Lang
 Syne!"
 I do not know you, and may never know
Your face—but you have acted on the whole
Most nobly, and I own it from my soul.

XVII.

And when I use the phrase of "Auld Lang
 Syne!"
 'T is not address'd to you—the more's the
 pity
For me, for I would rather take my wine
 With you, than aught (save Scott) in your
 proud city.
But somehow—it may seem a schoolboy's
 whine,
 And yet I seek not to be grand nor witty,
But I am half a Scot by birth, and bred
A whole one, and my heart flies to my
 head,—

XVIII.

As "Auld Lang Syne" brings Scotland, one
 and all,
 Scotch plaids, Scotch snoods, the blue hills,
 and clear streams,
The Dee, the Don, Balgounie's brig's *black
 wall*,
 All my boy feelings, all my gentler dreams
Of what I *then dreamt*, clothed in their own
 pall,
 Like Banquo's offspring:—floating past me
 seems
My childhood in this childishness of mine:
I care not—'t is a glimpse of Auld Lang
 Syne."

XIX.

And though, as you remember, in a fit
 Of wrath and rhyme, when juvenile and
 curly,
I rail'd at Scots to show my wrath and
 wit,
 Which must be own'd was sensitive and
 surly,
Yet 't is in vain such sallies to permit,
 They cannot quench young feelings fresh
 and early:
I "*scotch'd* not kill'd" the Scotchman in my
 blood,
And love the land of "mountain and of
 flood."

XX.

Don Juan, who was real, or ideal,—
 For both are much the same, since what
 men think
Exists when the once thinkers are less real
 Than what they thought, for mind can
 never sink,
And 'gainst the body makes a strong appeal;
 And yet 't is very puzzling on the brink
Of what is call'd eternity, to stare,
And know no more of what is here, than
 there;—

XXI.

Don Juan grew a very polish'd Russian—
 How we won't mention, *why* we need not
 say:
Few youthful minds can stand the strong
 concussion
 Of any slight temptation in their way;
But *his* just now were spread as is a
 cushion
 Smooth'd for a monarch's seat of honour:
 gay
Damsels, and dances, revels, ready money,
Made ice seem paradise, and winter sunny.

XXII.

The favour of the empress was agreeable;
 And though the duty wax'd a little hard,
Young people at his time of life should be
 able
 To come off handsomely in that regard.
He was now growing up like a green tree,
 able
 For love, war, or ambition, which reward
Their luckier votaries, till old age's tedium
Make some prefer the circulating medium.

XXIII.

About this time, as might have been antici-
 pated,
 Seduced by youth and dangerous examples,
Don Juan grew, I fear, a little dissipated;
 Which is a sad thing, and not only tramples
On our fresh feelings, but—as being partici-
 pated
 With all kinds of incorrigible samples
Of frail humanity—must make us selfish,
And shut our souls up in us like a shell-fish.

XXIV.

This we pass over. We will also pass
 The usual progress of intrigues between
Unequal matches, such as are, alas!
 A young lieutenant's with a *not old* queen,
But one who is not so youthful as she was
 In all the royalty of sweet seventeen.
Sovereigns may sway materials, but not
 matter,
And wrinkles, the d——d democrats, won't
 flatter.

XXV.

And death, the sovereign's sovereign, though
 the great
 Gracchus of all mortality, who levels,
With his *Agrarian* laws, the high estate
 Of him who feasts, and fights, and roars,
 and revels,
To one small grass-grown patch (which must
 await
 Corruption for its crop) with the poor
 devils
Who never had a foot of land till now,—
Death's a reformer, all men must allow.

XXVI.

He lived (not Death, but Juan) in a hurry
 Of waste, and haste, and glare, and gloss,
 and glitter,
In this gay clime of bear-skins black and
 furry—
 Which (though I hate to say a thing that's
 bitter)

Peep out sometimes, when things are in a
 flurry,
 Through all the "purple and fine linen,"
 fitter
For Babylon's than Russia's royal harlot—
And neutralise her outward show of scarlet.

XXVII.

And this same state we won't describe: we
 would
 Perhaps from hearsay, or from recollection;
But getting nigh grim Dante's "obscure
 wood,"
 That horrid equinox, that hateful section
Of human years, that half-way house, that
 rude
 Hut, whence wise travellers drive with
 circumspection
Life's sad post-horses o'er the dreary frontier
Of age, and looking back to youth, give *one*
 tear;—

XXVIII.

I won't describe,—that is, if I can help
 Description; and I won't reflect,—that is,
If I can stave off thought, which—as a whelp
 Clings to its teat—sticks to me through the
 abyss
Of this odd labyrinth; or as the kelp
 Holds by the rock; or as a lover's kiss
Drains its first draught of lips:—but, as I
 said,
I *won't* philosophise, and *will* be read.

XXIX.

Juan, instead of courting courts, was
 courted,—
 A thing which happens rarely: this he
 owed
Much to his youth, and much to his reported
 Valour; much also to the blood he show'd,
Like a race-horse; much to each dress he
 sported,
 Which set the beauty off in which he
 glow'd,
As purple clouds befringe the sun; but most
He owed to an old woman and his post.

XXX.

He wrote to Spain;—and all his near re-
 lations,
 Perceiving he was in a handsome way
Of getting on himself, and finding stations
 For cousins also, answer'd the same day.
Several prepared themselves for emigrations;
 And eating ices, were o'erheard to say,
That with the addition of a slight pelisse,
Madrid's and Moscow's climes were of a
 piece.

XXXI.

His mother, Donna Inez, finding, too,
 That in the lieu of drawing on his banker,
Where his assets were waxing rather few,
 He had brought his spending to a hand-
 some anchor,—
Replied, "that she was glad to see him
 through
 Those pleasures after which wild youth
 will hanker;
As the sole sign of man's being in his senses
Is, learning to reduce his past expenses.

XXXII.

" She also recommended him to God,
 And no less to God's Son, as well as
 Mother,
Warn'd him against Greek worship, which
 looks odd
 In Catholic eyes; but told him, too, to
 smother
Outward dislike, which don't look well
 abroad;
 Inform'd him that he had a little brother
Born in a second wedlock; and above
All, praised the empress's *maternal* love.

XXXIII.

" She could not too much give her appro-
 bation
 Unto an empress, who preferr'd young
 men
Whose age, and what was better still, whose
 nation
 And climate, stopp'd all scandal (now and
 then);—
At home it might have given her some
 vexation;
 But where thermometers sink down to ten,
Or five, or one, or zero, she could never
Believe that virtue thaw'd before the river."

XXXIV.

Oh for a *forty-parson power* to chant
 Thy praise, Hypocrisy! Oh for a hymn
Loud as the virtues thou dost loudly vaunt,
 Not practise! Oh for trump of cherubim!
Or the ear-trumpet of my good old aunt,
 Who, though her spectacles at last grew
 dim,
Drew quiet consolation through its hint,
When she no more could read the pious print.

XXXV.

She was no hypocrite at least, poor soul,
 But went to heaven in as sincere a way
As anybody on the elected roll,
 Which portions out upon the judgment day

Heaven's freeholds, in a sort of doomsday
 scroll,
Such as the conqueror William did repay
His knights with, lotting others' properties
Into some sixty thousand new knights' fees.

XXXVI.

I can't complain, whose ancestors are there,
 Erneis, Radulphus—eight-and-forty manors
(If that my memory doth not greatly err)
 Were their reward for following Billy's
 banners:
And though I can't help thinking 't was
 scarce fair
 To strip the Saxons of their *hydes*, like
 tanners;
Yet as they founded churches with the
 produce,
You'll deem, no doubt, they put it to a good
 use.

XXXVII.

The gentle Juan flourish'd, though at times
 He felt like other plants call'd sensitive,
Which shrink from touch, as monarchs do
 from rhymes,
 Save such as Southey can afford to give.
Perhaps he long'd in bitter frosts for climes
 In which the Neva's ice would cease to live
Before May-day: perhaps, despite his duty,
In royalty's vast arms he sigh'd for beauty:

XXXVIII.

Perhaps—but, sans perhaps, we need not
 seek
 For causes young or old: the canker-worm
Will feed upon the fairest, freshest cheek,
 As well as further drain the wither'd form:
Care, like a housekeeper, brings every week
 His bills in, and however we may storm,
They must be paid: though six days smoothly
 run,
The seventh will bring blue devils or a dun.

XXXIX.

I don't know how it was, but he grew sick:
 The empress was alarm'd, and her phy-
 sician
(The same who physick'd Peter) found the
 tick
 Of his fierce pulse betoken a condition
Which augur'd of the dead, however *quick*
 Itself, and show'd a feverish disposition;
At which the whole court was extremely
 troubled,
The sovereign shock'd, and all his medicines
 doubled.

XL.

Low were the whispers, manifold the ru-
　　mours,
　　Some said he had been poison'd by
　　　　Potemkin;
Others talk'd learnedly of certain tumours,
　　Exhaustion, or disorders of the same kin;
Some said 'twas a concoction of the humours,
　　Which with the blood too readily will claim
　　　　kin;
Others again were ready to maintain,
" 'Twas only the fatigue of last campaign."

XLI.

But here is one prescription out of many:
　" Sodæ sulphat. ʒvj. ʒfs. Mannæ optim.
Aq. fervent. f. ʒ ifs. ʒij. tinct. Sennæ
　　Haustus " (and here the surgeon came and
　　　　cupp'd him),
" R. Pulv. Com. gr. iij. Ipecacuanhæ "
　　(With more beside if Juan had not stopp'd
　　　　'em).
"Bolus Potassæ Sulphuret. sumendus,
Et haustus ter in die capiendus."

XLII.

This is the way physicians mend or end us,
　　Secundum artem: but although we sneer
In health—when ill, we call them to attend
　　us,
　　Without the least propensity to jeer;
While that " hiatus maxime deflendus,"
　　To be fill'd up by spade or mattock, 's near,
Instead of gliding graciously down Lethe,
We tease mild Baillie, or soft Abernethy.

XLIII.

Juan demurr'd at this first notice to
　　Quit; and though death had threaten'd an
　　　　ejection,
His youth and constitution bore him through,
　　And sent the doctors in a new direction.
But still his state was delicate: the hue
　　Of health but flicker'd with a faint re-
　　　　flection
Along his wasted cheek, and seem'd to gravel
The faculty—who said that he must travel.

XLIV.

The climate was too cold, they said, for him,
　　Meridian-born, to bloom in. This opinion
Made the chaste Catherine look a little grim,
　　Who did not like at first to lose her minion:
But when she saw his dazzling eye wax dim,
　　And drooping like an eagle's with clipt
　　　　pinion,
She then resolved to send him on a mission,
But in a style becoming his condition.

XLV.

There was just then a kind of a discussion,
　　A sort of treaty or negotiation,
Between the British cabinet and Russian,
　　Maintain'd with all the due prevarication
With which great states such things are apt
　　　　to push on;
　　Something about the Baltic's navigation,
Hides, train-oil, tallow, and the rights of
　　　　Thetis,
Which Britons deem their " uti possidetis."

XLVI.

So Catherine, who had a handsome way
　　Of fitting out her favourites, conferr'd
This secret charge on Juan, to display
　　At once her royal splendour, and reward
His services. He kiss'd hands the next day,
　　Received instructions how to play his card,
Was laden with all kinds of gifts and
　　　　honours,
Which show'd what great discernment was
　　　　the donor's.

XLVII.

But she was lucky, and luck's all. Your
　　queens
　　Are generally prosperous in reigning;
Which puzzles us to know what Fortune
　　means:
　　But to continue: though her years were
　　　　waning,
Her climacteric teased her like her teens;
　　And though her dignity brook'd no com-
　　　　plaining,
So much did Juan's setting off distress her,
She could not find at first a fit successor.

XLVIII.

But time, the comforter, will come at last;
　　And four-and-twenty hours, and twice that
　　　　number
Of candidates requesting to be placed,
　　Made Catherine taste next night a quiet
　　　　slumber:—
Not that she meant to fix again in haste,
　　Nor did she find the quantity encumber,
But always choosing with deliberation,
Kept the place open for their emulation.

XLIX.

While this high post of honour 's in abeyance,
　　For one or two days, reader, we request
You 'll mount with our young hero the con-
　　　　veyance
　　Which wafted him from Petersburgh: the
　　　　best

Barouche, which had the glory to display once
 The fair czarina's autocratic crest
When, a new Iphigene, she went to Tauris,
Was given to her favourite, and now *bore his.*

L.

A bull-dog, and a bull-finch, and an ermine,
 All private favourites of Don Juan;—for
(Let deeper sages the true cause determine)
 He had a kind of inclination, or
Weakness, for what most people deem mere
 vermin,
 Live animals: an old maid of threescore
For cats and birds more penchant ne'er dis-
 play'd,
Although he was not old, nor even a maid;—

LI.

The animals aforesaid occupied
 Their station: there were valets, secre-
 taries,
In other vehicles; but at his side
 Sat little Leila, who survived the parries
He made 'gainst Cossacque sabres in the wide
 Slaughter of Ismail. Though my wild
 Muse varies
Her note, she don't forget the infant girl
Whom he preserved, a pure and living pearl.

LII.

Poor little thing! She was as fair as docile,
 And with that gentle, serious character,
As rare in living beings as a fossile
 Man, 'midst thy mouldy mammoths, "grand
 Cuvier!"
Ill fitted was her ignorance to jostle
 With this o'erwhelming world, where all
 must err:
But she was yet but ten years old, and there-
 fore
Was tranquil, though she knew not why or
 wherefore.

LIII.

Don Juan loved her, and she loved him, as
 Nor brother, father, sister, daughter love.
I cannot tell exactly what it was;
 He was not yet quite old enough to prove
Parental feelings, and the other class,
 Call'd brotherly affection, could not move
His bosom,—for he never had a sister:
Ah! if he had, how much he would have
 miss'd her!

LIV.

And still less was it sensual; for besides
 That he was not an ancient debauchee,
(Who like sour fruit, to stir their veins' salt
 tides,
 As acids rouse a dormant alkali,)

Although ('*t will* happen as our planet guides)
 His youth was not the chastest that might
 be,
There was the purest Platonism at bottom
Of all his feelings—only he forgot 'em.

LV.

Just now there was no peril of temptation;
 He loved the infant orphan he had saved,
As patriots (now and then) may love a nation;
 His pride, too, felt that she was not en-
 slaved
Owing to him;—as also her salvation
 Through his means and the church's might
 be paved.
But one thing's odd, which here must be
 inserted,
The little Turk refused to be converted.

LVI.

'Twas strange enough she should retain the
 impression
 Through such a scene of change, and dread,
 and slaughter;
But though three bishops told her the trans-
 gression,
 She show'd a great dislike to holy water:
She also had no passion for confession;
 Perhaps she had nothing to confess:—no
 matter
Whate'er the cause, the church made little
 of it—
She still held out that Mahomet was a
 prophet.

LVII.

In fact, the only Christian she could bear
 Was Juan; whom she seem'd to have
 selected
In place of what her home and friends once
 were.
 He *naturally* loved what he protected:
And thus they form'd a rather curious pair,
 A guardian green in years, a ward con-
 nected
In neither clime, time, blood, with her de-
 fender;
And yet this want of ties made theirs more
 tender.

LVIII.

They journey'd on through Poland and
 through Warsaw,
 Famous for mines of salt and yokes of iron:
Through Courland also, which that famous
 farce saw
 Which gave her dukes the graceless name
 of "Biron."

'Tis the same landscape which the modern
 Mars saw
 Who march'd to Moscow, led by Fame, the
 siren!
To lose by one month's frost some twenty
 years
Of conquest, and his guard of grenadiers.

LIX.

Let this not seem an anti-climax:—" Oh!
 My guard! my old guard!" exclaim'd that
 god of clay.
Think of the Thunderer's falling down below
 Carotid-artery-cutting Castlereagh!
Alas! that glory should be chill'd by snow!
 But should we wish to warm us on our way
Through Poland, there is Kosciusko's name
Might scatter fire through ice, like Hecla's
 flame.

LX.

From Poland they came on through Prussia
 Proper.
 And Königsberg, the capital, whose vaunt,
Besides some veins of iron, lead, or copper,
 Has lately been the great Professor Kant.
Juan, who cared not a tobacco-stopper
 About philosophy, pursued his jaunt
To Germany, whose somewhat tardy millions
Have princes who spur more than their pos-
 tilions.

LXI.

And thence through Berlin, Dresden, and the
 like,
 Until he reach'd the castellated Rhine:—
Ye glorious Gothic scenes! how much ye
 strike
 All phantasies, not even excepting mine!
A grey wall, a green ruin, rusty pike,
 Make my soul pass the equinoctial line
Between the present and past worlds, and
 hover
Upon their airy confines, half-seas-over.

LXII.

But Juan posted on through Mannheim, Bonn,
 Which Drachenfels frowns over like a
 spectre
Of the good feudal times for ever gone,
 On which I have not time just now to
 lecture.
From thence he was drawn onwards to
 Cologne,
 A city which presents to the inspector
Eleven thousand maidenheads of bone,
The greatest number flesh hath ever known.

LXIII.

From thence to Holland's Hague and Hel-
 voetsluys,
 That water-land of Dutchmen and of
 ditches,
Where juniper expresses its best juice,
 The poor man's sparkling substitute for .
 riches.
Senates and sages have condemn'd its use—
 But to deny the mob a cordial, which is
Too often all the clothing, meat, or fuel,
Good government has left them, seems but
 cruel.

LXIV.

Here he embark'd, and with a flowing sail
 Went bounding for the island of the free,
Towards which the impatient wind blew half
 a gale;
 High dash'd the spray, the bows dipp'd in
 the sea,
And sea-sick passengers turn'd somewhat
 pale;
 But Juan, season'd, as he well might be,
By former voyages, stood to watch the skiffs,
Which pass'd, or catch the first glimpse of
 the cliffs.

LXV.

At length they rose, like a white wall along
 The blue sea's border; and Don Juan felt—
What even young strangers feel a little strong
 At the first sight of Albion's chalky belt—
A kind of pride that he should be among
 Those haughty shopkeepers, who sternly
 dealt
Their goods and edicts out from pole to pole
And made the very billows pay them toll.

LXVI.

I've no great cause to love that spot of earth,
 Which holds what *might have been* the
 noblest nation;
But though I owe it little but my birth,
 I feel a mix'd regret and veneration
For its decaying fame and former worth.
 Seven years (the usual term of transporta-
 tion)
Of absence lay one's old resentments level,
When a man's country's going to the devil.

LXVII.

Alas! could she but fully, truly know
How her great name is now throughout
 abhorr'd;
How eager all the earth is for the blow
 Which shall lay bare her bosom to the
 sword;

How all the nations deem her their worst foe,
 That worse than *worst of foes*, the once
 adored
False friend, who held out freedom to man-
 kind,
And now would chain them, to the very
 mind;—

LXVIII.

Would she be proud, or boast herself the
 free,
 Who is but first of slaves? The nations
 are
In prison,—but the gaoler, what is he?
 No less a victim to the bolt and bar.
Is the poor privilege to turn the key
 Upon the captive, freedom? He's as far
From the enjoyment of the earth and air
Who watches o'er the chain, as they who
 wear.

LXIX.

Don Juan now saw Albion's earliest beauties,
 Thy cliffs, *dear* Dover! harbour, and hotel;
Thy custom-house,with all its delicate duties;
 Thy waiters running mucks at every bell;
Thy packets, all whose passengers are booties
 To those who upon land or water dwell;
And last, not least, to strangers uninstructed,
Thy long, long bills, whence nothing is de-
 ducted.

LXX.

Juan, though careless, young, and magnifique,
 And rich in rubles, diamonds, cash, and
 credit,
Who did not limit much his bills per week,
 Yet stared at this a little, though he paid
 it—
(His Maggior Duomo, a smart, subtle Greek,
 Before him summ'd the awful scroll and
 read it):
But, doubtless, as the air, though seldom
 sunny,
Is free, the respiration's worth the money.

LXXI.

On with the horses! Off to Canterbury!
 Tramp, tramp o'er pebble, and splash, splash
 through puddle;
Hurrah! how swiftly speeds the post so merry!
 Not like slow Germany, wherein they
 muddle
Along the road, as if they went to bury
 Their fare; and also pause besides, to
 fuddle,
With " schnapps "—sad dogs! whom "Hunds-
 fot," or " Verflucter,"
Affect no more than lightning a conductor.

LXXII.

Now there is nothing gives a man such spirits,
 Leavening his blood as cayenne doth a
 curry,
As going at full speed—no matter where its
 Direction be, so 'tis but in a hurry,
And merely for the sake of its own merits;
 For the less cause there is for all this
 flurry,
The greater is the pleasure in arriving
And the great *end* of travel—which is driving.

LXXIII.

They saw at Canterbury the cathedral;
 Black Edward's helm, and Becket's bloody
 stone,
Were pointed out as usual by the bedral,
 In the same quaint, uninterested tone:—
There's glory again for you, gentle reader!
 All
Ends in a rusty casque and dubious bone,
Half-solved into these sodas or magnesias,
Which form that bitter draught, the human
 species.

LXXIV.

The effect on Juan was of course sublime:
 He breathed a thousand Cressys, as he saw
That casque, which never stoop'd except to
 Time.
 Even the bold Churchman's tomb excited
 awe,
Who died in the then great attempt to climb
 O'er kings, who *now* at least *must talk* of
 law
Before they butcher. Little Leila gazed,
And ask'd why such a structure had been
 raised;

LXXV.

And being told it was "God's house," she
 said
 He was well lodged, but only wonder'd how
He suffer'd Infidels in his homestead,
 The cruel Nazarenes, who had laid low
His holy temples in the lands which bred
 The True Believers;—and her infant brow
Was bent with grief that Mahomet should
 resign
A mosque so noble, flung like pearls to swine.

LXXVI.

On! on! through meadows, managed like a
 garden,
 A paradise of hops and high production;
For, after years of travel by a bard in
 Countries of greater heat, but lesser suction,

A green field is a sight which makes him
 pardon
 The absence of that more sublime con-
 struction
Which mixes up vines, olives, precipices,
Glaciers, volcanos, oranges, and ices.

LXXVII.

And when I think upon a pot of beer—
 But I won't weep!—and so drive on, pos-
 tilions!
As the smart boys spurr'd fast in their career,
 Juan admired these highways of free
 millions;
A country in all senses the most dear
 To foreigner or native, save some silly ones,
Who "kick against the pricks" just at this
 juncture,
And for their pains get only a fresh puncture.

LXXVIII.

What a delightful thing's a turnpike road!
 So smooth, so level, such a mode of shaving
The earth, as scarce the eagle in the broad
 Air can accomplish, with his wide wings
 waving.
Had such been cut in Phaeton's time, the
 god
 Had told his son to satisfy his craving
With the York mail;—but onward as we
 roll,
" Surgit amari aliquid "—the toll!

LXXIX.

Alas! how deeply painful is all payment!
 Take lives, take wives, take aught except
 men's purses.
As Machiavel shows those in purple raiment,
 Such is the shortest way to general curses.
They hate a murderer much less than a
 claimant
 On that sweet ore which everybody
 nurses.—
Kill a man's family, and he may brook it,
But keep your hands out of his breeches'
 pocket:

LXXX.

So said the Florentine; ye monarchs, hearken
 To your instructor. Juan now was borne,
Just as the day began to wane and darken,
 O'er the high hill, which looks with pride
 or scorn
Toward the great city.—Ye who have a
 spark in
 Your veins of Cockney spirit, smile or mourn
According as you take things well or ill;
Bold Britons, we are now on Shooter's Hill!

LXXXI.

The sun went down, the smoke rose up, as
 from
 A half-unquench'd volcano, o'er a space
Which well beseem'd the "Devil's drawing-
 room,"
 As some have qualified that wondrous place:
But Juan felt, though not approaching *home*,
 As one who, though he were not of the race,
Revered the soil, of those true sons the
 mother,
Who butcher'd half the earth, and bullied
 t'other.

LXXXII.

A mighty mass of brick, and smoke, and
 shipping,
 Dirty and dusky, but as wide as eye
Could reach, with here and there a sail just
 skipping
 In sight, then lost amidst the forestry
Of masts; a wilderness of steeples peeping
 On tiptoe through their sea-coal canopy;
A huge, dun cupola, like a foolscap crown
On a fool's head—and there is London Town

LXXXIII.

But Juan saw not this: each wreath of smoke
 Appear'd to him but as the magic vapour
Of some alchymic furnace, from whence broke
 The wealth of worlds (a wealth of tax and
 paper):
The gloomy clouds, which o'er it as a yoke
 Are bow'd, and put the sun out like a taper,
Were nothing but the natural atmosphere,
Extremely wholesome, though but rarely
 clear.

LXXXIV.

He paused—and so will I; as doth a crew
 Before they give their broadside. By and by,
My gentle countrymen, we will renew
 Our old acquaintance; and at least I'll try
To tell you truths *you* will not take as true,
 Because they are so;—a male Mrs. Fry,
With a soft besom will I sweep your halls,
And brush a web or two from off the walls.

LXXXV.

Oh Mrs. Fry! Why go to Newgate? Why
 Preach to poor rogues? And wherefore not
 begin
With Carlton, or with other houses? Try
 Your hand at harden'd and imperial sin.
To mend the people's an absurdity,
 A jargon, a mere philanthropic din,
Unless you make their betters better:—Fy!
I thought you had more religion, Mrs. Fry.

LXXXVI.

Teach them the decencies of good threescore;
 Cure them of tours, hussar and highland
 dresses;
Tell them that youth once gone returns no
 more,
 That hired huzzas redeem no land's dis-
 tresses;
Tell them Sir William Curtis is a bore,
 Too dull even for the dullest of excesses,
The witless Falstaff of a hoary Hal,
A fool whose bells have ceased to ring at all.

LXXXVII.

Tell them, though it may be perhaps too late
 On life's worn confine, jaded, bloated, sated,
To set up vain pretences of being great,
 'Tis not so to be good; and be it stated,
The worthiest kings have ever loved least
 state;
 And tell them——But you won't, and I
 have prated
Just now enough; but by and by I'll prattle
Like Roland's horn in Roncesvalles' battle.

—◆—

Canto the Eleventh.

I.

When Bishop Berkeley said "there was no
 matter,"
 And proved it—'twas no matter what he
 said:
They say his system 'tis in vain to batter,
 Too subtle for the airiest human head;
And yet who can believe it? I would shatter
 Gladly all matters down to stone or lead,
Or adamant, to find the world a spirit,
And wear my head, denying that I wear it.

II.

What a sublime discovery 'twas to make the
 Universe universal egotism,
That all's ideal—*all ourselves!* I'll stake the
 World (be it what you will) that *that's* no
 schism:
Oh Doubt!—if thou be'st Doubt, for which
 some take thee,
 But which I doubt extremely—thou sole
 prism
Of the Truth's rays, spoil not my draught of
 spirit!
Heaven's brandy, though our brain can hardly
 bear it.

III.

For ever and anon comes Indigestion
 (Not the most "dainty Ariel"), and per-
 plexes
Our soarings with another sort of question:
 And that which after all my spirit vexes,
Is, that I find no spot where man can rest
 eye on,
 Without confusion of the sorts and sexes,
Of beings, stars, and this unriddled wonder,
The world, which at the worst's a glorious
 blunder—

IV.

If it be chance; or if it be according
 To the old text, still better:—lest it should
Turn out so, we'll say nothing 'gainst the
 wording,
 As several people think such hazards rude.
They're right; our days are too brief for
 affording
 Space to dispute what *no one* ever could
Decide, and *everybody one day* will
Know very clearly—or at least lie still.

V.

And therefore will I leave off metaphysical
 Discussion, which is neither here nor there:
If I agree that what is, is; then this I call
 Being quite perspicuous and extremely fair;
The truth is, I've grown lately rather phthi-
 sical:
 I don't know what the reason is—the air
Perhaps; but as I suffer from the shocks
Of illness, I grow much more orthodox.

VI.

The first attack at once proved the Divinity
 (But *that* I never doubted, nor the Devil);
The next, the Virgin's mystical virginity;
 The third, the usual Origin of Evil;
The fourth at once establish'd the whole
 Trinity
 On so uncontrovertible a level,
That I devoutly wish'd the three were four
On purpose to believe so much the more.

VII.

To our theme.—The man who has stood on
 the Acropolis
And look'd down over Attica; or he
 Who has sail'd where picturesque Constanti-
 nople is,
Or seen Timbuctoo, or hath taken tea
 In small-eyed China's crockery-ware metro-
 polis,
Or sat amidst the bricks of Nineveh,
May not think much of London's first appear-
 ance—
But ask him what he thinks of it a year hence?

VIII.

Don Juan had got out on Shooter's Hill;
　Sunset the time, the place the same declivity
Which looks along that vale of good and ill
　Where London streets ferment in full activity;
While everything around was calm and still,
　Except the creak of wheels, which on their pivot he
Heard,—and that bee-like, bubbling, busy hum
Of cities, that boil over with their scum:—

IX.

I say, Don Juan, wrapt in contemplation,
　Walk'd on behind his carriage, o'er the summit,
And lost in wonder of so great a nation,
　Gave way to 't, since he could not overcome it.
"And here," he cried, "is Freedom's chosen station;
　Here peal's the people's voice, nor can it entomb it
Racks, prisons, inquisitions; resurrection
Awaits it, each new meeting or election.

X.

"Here are chaste wives, pure lives; here people pay
　But what they please; and if that things be dear,
'Tis only that they love to throw away
　Their cash, to show how much they have a year.
Here laws are all inviolate; none lay
　Traps for the traveller; every highway's clear;
Here"—he was interrupted by a knife,
With—"Damn your eyes! your money or your life!"—

XI.

These freeborn sounds proceeded from four pads
　In ambush laid, who had perceived him loiter
Behind his carriage; and, like handy lads,
　Had seized the lucky hour to reconnoitre,
In which the heedless gentleman who gads
　Upon the road, unless he prove a fighter,
May find himself within that isle of riches
Exposed to lose his life as well as breeches.

XII.

Juan, who did not understand a word
　Of English, save their shibboleth, "God damn!"
And even that he had so rarely heard,
　He sometimes thought 't was only their "Salám,"

Or "God be with you!"—and 'tis not absurd
　To think so: for half English as I am
(To my misfortune), never can I say
I heard them wish "God with you," save that way;—

XIII.

Juan yet quickly understood their gesture,
　And being somewhat choleric and sudden,
Drew forth a pocket-pistol from his vesture,
　And fired it into one assailant's pudding—
Who fell, as rolls an ox o'er in his pasture,
　And roar'd out, as he writhed his native mud in,
Unto his nearest follower or henchman,
"Oh Jack! I'm floor'd by that 'ere bloody Frenchman!"

XIV.

On which Jack and his train set off at speed,
　And Juan's suite, late scatter'd at a distance,
Came up, all marvelling at such a deed,
　And offering, as usual, late assistance.
Juan, who saw the moon's late minion bleed
　As if his veins would pour out his existence,
Stood calling out for bandages and lint,
And wish'd he had been less hasty with his flint.

XV.

"Perhaps," thought he, "it is the country's wont
　To welcome foreigners in this way: now
I recollect some innkeepers who don't
　Differ, except in robbing with a bow,
In lieu of a bare blade and brazen front.
　But what is to be done? I can't allow
The fellow to lie groaning on the road:
So take him up; I'll help you with the load."

XVI.

But ere they could perform this pious duty,
　The dying man cried, "Hold! I've got my gruel!
Oh! for a glass of *max!* We've miss'd our booty;
　Let me die where I am!" And as the fuel
Of life shrunk in his heart, and thick and sooty
　The drops fell from his death-wound, and he drew ill
His breath,—he from his swelling throat untied
A kerchief, crying "Give Sal that!"—and died.

XVII.

The cravat stain'd with bloody drops fell
 down
 Before Don Juan's feet: he could not tell
Exactly why it was before him thrown,
 Nor what the meaning of the man's
 farewell.
Poor Tom was once a kiddy upon town,
 A thorough varmint, and a *real* swell,
Full flash, all fancy, until fairly diddled,
His pockets first and then his body riddled.

XVIII.

Don Juan, having done the best he could
 In all the circumstances of the case,
As soon as "Crowner's quest" allow'd, pur-
 sued
 His travels to the capital apace;—
Esteeming it a little hard he should
 In twelve hours' time, and very little
 space,
Have been obliged to slay a free-born native
In self-defence: this made him meditative.

XIX.

He from the world had cut off a great man,
 Who in his time had made heroic bustle.
Who in a row like Tom could lead the van,
 Booze in the ken, or at the spellken hustle?
Who queer a flat? Who (spite of Bow-street's
 ban)
 On the high toby-spice so flash the muzzle?
Who on a lark, with black-eyed Sal (his
 blowing),
So prime, so swell, so nutty, and so knowing?

XX.

But Tom's no more—and so no more of Tom.
 Heroes must die; and by God's blessing
 't is
Not long before the most of them go home.
 Hail! Thamis, hail! Upon thy verge it is
That Juan's chariot, rolling like a drum
 In thunder, holds the way it can't well
 miss,
Through Kennington and all the other
 "tons,"
Which make us wish ourselves in town at
 once;—

XXI.

Through Groves, so call'd as being void of
 trees,
 (Like *lucus* from *no* light); through pros-
 pects named
Mount Pleasant, as containing nought to
 please,
 Nor much to climb; through little boxes
 framed

Of bricks, to let the dust in at your case,
 With "To be let," upon their doors pro-
 claim'd;
Through "Rows" most modestly call'd
 "Paradise,"
Which Eve might quit without much
 sacrifice;—

XXII.

Through coaches, drays, choked turnpikes,
 and a whirl
 Of wheels, and roar of voices, and con-
 fusion;
Here taverns wooing to a pint of "purl,"
 There mails fast flying off like a delusion;
There barbers' blocks with periwigs in curl
 In windows; here the lamplighter's in-
 fusion
Slowly distill'd into the glimmering glass
(For in those days we had not got to gas—);

XXIII.

Through this, and much, and more, is the
 approach
 Of travellers to mighty Babylon:
Whether they come by horse, or chaise, or
 coach,
 With slight exceptions, all the ways seem
 one.
I could say more, but do not choose to
 encroach
 Upon the Guide-book's privilege. The sun
Had set some time, and night was on the
 ridge
Of twilight, as the party cross'd the bridge.

XXIV.

That's rather fine, the gentle sound of
 Thamis—
 Who vindicates a moment, too, his stream—
Though hardly heard through multifarious
 "damme's."
 The lamps of Westminster's more regular
 gleam,
The breadth of pavement, and yon shrine
 where fame is
 A spectral resident—whose pallid beam
In shape of moonshine hovers o'er the pile—
Make this a sacred part of Albion's isle.

XXV.

The Druid's groves are gone—so much the
 better:
 Stone-Henge is not—but what the devil
 is it?—
But Bedlam still exists with its sage fetter,
 That madmen may not bite you on a visit;

The Bench too seats or suits full many a
debtor;
 The Mansion-House, too (though some
people quiz it),
To me appears a stiff yet grand erection;
But then the Abbey's worth the whole
 collection.

XXVI.

The line of lights, too, up to Charing Cross,
 Pall Mall, and so forth, have a coruscation
Like gold as in comparison to dross,
 Match'd with the Continent's illumination,
Whose cities Night by no means deigns to
 gloss.
 The French were not yet a lamp-lighting
 nation,
And when they grew so—on their new-found
 lantern,
Instead of wicks, they made a wicked man
 turn.

XXVII.

A row of gentlemen along the streets
 Suspended, may illuminate mankind,
As also bonfires made of country-seats;
 But the old way is best for the purblind:
The other looks like phosphorus on sheets,
 A sort of ignis fatuus to the mind,
Which, though 't is certain to perplex and
 frighten,
Must burn more mildly ere it can enlighten.

XXVIII.

But London's so well lit, that if Diogenes
 Could recommence to hunt his *honest man*,
And found him not amidst the various
 progenies
Of this enormous city's spreading spawn,
'T were not for want of lamps to aid his
 dodging his
Yet undiscover'd treasure. What *I* can,
I've done to find the same throughout life's
 journey,
But see the world is only one attorney.

XXIX.

Over the stones still rattling, up Pall Mall,
 Through crowds and carriages, but waxing
 thinner
As thunder'd knockers broke the long-seal'd
 spell
 Of doors 'gainst duns, and to an early
 dinner
Admitted a small party as night fell,—
 Don Juan, our young diplomatic sinner,
Pursued his path, and drove past some
 hotels,
St. James's Palace and St. James's "Hells."

XXX.

They reach'd the hotel: forth stream'd from
 the front door
 A tide of well-clad waiters, and around
The mob stood, and as usual several score
 Of those pedestrian Paphians who abound
In decent London when the daylight's o'er;
 Commodious but immoral, they are found
Useful, like Malthus, in promoting mar-
 riage.—
But Juan now is stepping from his carriage

XXXI.

Into one of the sweetest of hotels,
 Especially for foreigners—and mostly
For those whom favour or whom fortune
 swells,
 And cannot find a bill's small items costly.
There many an envoy either dwelt or dwells
 (The den of many a diplomatic lost lie),
Until to some conspicuous square they pass,
And blazon o'er the door their names in
 brass.

XXXII.

Juan, whose was a delicate commission,
 Private, though publicly important, bore
No title to point out with due precision
 The exact affair on which he was sent
 o'er.
'T was merely known, that on a secret
 mission
 A foreigner of rank had graced our shore,
Young, handsome, and accomplish'd, who
 was said
(In whispers) to have turn'd his sovereign's
 head.

XXXIII.

Some rumour also of some strange adven-
 tures
 Had gone before him, and his wars and
 loves;
And as romantic heads are pretty painters,
 And, above all, an Englishwoman's roves
Into the excursive, breaking the indentures
 Of sober reason, wheresoe'er it moves,
He found himself extremely in the fashion,
Which serves our thinking people for a
 passion.

XXXIV.

I don't mean that they are passionless, but
 quite
 The contrary; but then 't is in the head;
Yet as the consequences are as bright
 As if they acted with the heart instead,
What after all can signify the site
 Of ladies' lucubrations? So they lead
In safety to the place for which you start,
What matters if the road be head or heart?

XXXV.

Juan presented in the proper place,
 To proper placemen, every Russ credential,
And was received with all the due grimace
 By those who govern in the mood potential,
Who, seeing a handsome stripling with
 smooth face,
 Thought (what in state affairs is most
 essential)
That they as easily might *do* the youngster,
As hawks may pounce upon a woodland
 songster.

XXXVI.

They err'd, as aged men will do; but by
 And by we'll talk of that; and if we don't,
'T will be because our notion is not high
 Of politicians and their double front,
Who live by lies, yet dare not boldly lie:—
 Now what I love in women is, they won't
Or can't do otherwise than lie, but do it
So well, the very truth seems falsehood to it.

XXXVII.

And, after all, what is a lie? 'T is but
 The truth in masquerade; and I defy
Historians, heroes, lawyers, priests, to put
 A fact without some leaven of a lie.
The very shadow of true Truth would shut
 Up annals, revelations, poesy,
And prophecy—except it should be dated
Some years before the incidents related

XXXVIII.

Praised be all liars and all lies! Who now
 Can tax my mild Muse with misanthropy?
She rings the world's "Te Deum," and her
 brow
 Blushes for those who will not:—but to
 sigh
Is idle; let us like most others bow,
 Kiss hands, feet, any part of majesty,
After the good example of "Green Erin,"
Whose Shamrock now seems rather worse
 for wearing.

XXXIX.

Don Juan was presented, and his dress
 And mien excited general admiration—
I don't know which was more admired or
 less:
 One monstrous diamond drew much obser-
 vation,
Which Catherine in a moment of "ivresse"
 (In love or brandy's fervent fermentation)
Bestow'd upon him, as the public learn'd;
And, to say truth, it had been fairly earn'd.

XL.

Besides the ministers and underlings,
 Who must be courteous to the accredited
Diplomatists of rather wavering kings,
 Until their royal riddle's fully read,
The very clerks,—those somewhat dirty
 springs
 Of office, or the house of office, fed
By foul corruption into streams,—even they
Were hardly rude enough to earn their pay:

XLI.

And insolence no doubt is what they are
 Employ'd for, since it is their daily labour,
In the dear offices of peace or war;
 And should you doubt, pray ask of your
 next neighbour,
When for a passport, or some other bar
 To freedom, he applied (a grief and a
 bore),
If he found not in this spawn of taxborn
 riches,
Like lap-dogs, the least civil sons of b——s.

XLII.

But Juan was received with much "em-
 pressement:"—
 These phrases of refinement I must bor-
 row
From our next neighbour's land, where, like
 a chessman,
 There is a move set down for joy or
 sorrow,
Not only in mere talking, but the press. Man
 In islands is, it seems, downright and
 thorough,
More than on continents—as if the sea
(See Billingsgate) made even the tongue
 more free.

XLIII.

And yet the British "Damme"'s rather At-
 tic;
 Your continental oaths are but inconti-
 nent,
And turn on things which no aristocratic
 Spirit would name, and therefore even I
 won't anent
This subject quote; as it would be schis-
 matic
 In politesse, and have a sound affronting
 in 't;—
But "Damme"'s quite ethereal, though too
 daring—
 Platonic blasphemy, the soul of swearing.

XLIV.

For downright rudeness, ye may stay at
 home;
 For true or false politeness (and scarce
 that
Now) you may cross the blue deep and white
 foam—
 The first the emblem (rarely though) of
 what
You leave behind, the next of much you come
 To meet. However, 'tis no time to chat
On general topics: poems must confine
Themselves to unity, like this of mine.

XLV.

In the great world,—which, being interpreted,
 Meaneth the west or worst end of a city,
And about twice two thousand people bred
 By no means to be very wise or witty,
But to sit up while others lie in bed,
 And look down on the universe with pity,—
Juan, as an inveterate patrician,
Was well received by persons of condition.

XLVI.

He was a bachelor, which is a matter
 Of import both to virgin and to bride,
The former's hymeneal hopes to flatter;
 And (should she not hold fast by love or
 pride)
'T is also of some moment to the latter:
 A rib's a thorn in a wed gallant's side,
Requires decorum, and is apt to double
The horrid sin—and what's still worse, the
 trouble.

XLVII.

But Juan was a bachelor—of arts,
 And parts, and hearts: he danced and
 sung, and had
An air as sentimental as Mozart's
 Softest of melodies; and could be sad
Or cheerful, without any "flaws or starts,"
 Just at the proper time: and though a lad,
Had seen the world—which is a curious sight,
And very much unlike what people write.

XLVIII.

Fair virgins blush'd upon him; wedded
 dames
 Bloom'd also in less transitory hues;
For both commodities dwell by the Thames,
 The painting and the painted; youth, ce-
 ruse,
Against his heart preferr'd their usual claims,
 Such as no gentleman can quite refuse;
Daughters admired his dress, and pious
 mothers
Inquired his income, and if he had brothers.

XLIX.

The milliners who furnish "drapery Misses"
 Throughout the season, upon speculation
Of payment ere the honey-moon's last kisses
 Have waned into a crescent's coruscation,
Thought such an opportunity as this is,
 Of a rich foreigner's initiation,
Not to be overlook'd—and gave such credit,
That future bridegrooms swore, and sigh'd,
 and paid it.

L.

The Blues, that tender tribe, who sigh o'er
 sonnets,
 And with the pages of the last Review
Line the interior of their heads or bonnets,
 Advanced in all their azure's highest hue:
They talk'd bad French or Spanish, and
 upon its
 Late authors ask'd him for a hint or two;
And which was softest, Russian or Castilian?
And whether in his travels he saw Ilion?

LI.

Juan, who was a little superficial,
 And not in literature a great Drawcansir,
Examined by this learned and especial
 Jury of matrons, scarce knew what to
 answer:
His duties warlike, loving, or official,
 His steady application as a dancer,
Had kept him from the brink of Hippocrene,
Which now he found was blue instead of
 green.

LII.

However, he replied at hazard, with
 A modest confidence and calm assurance,
Which lent his learned lucubrations pith,
 And pass'd for arguments of good endur-
 ance.
That prodigy, Miss Araminta Smith
 (Who at sixteen translated "Hercules
 Furens"
Into as furious English), with her best look,
Set down his sayings in her common-place
 book.

LIII.

Juan knew several languages—as well
 He might—and brought them up with
 skill, in time
To save his fame with each accomplish'd
 belle,
 Who still regretted that he did not rhyme.
There wanted but this requisite to swell
 His qualities (with them) into sublime:
Lady Fitz-Frisky, and Miss Mævia Mannish,
Both long'd extremely to be sung in Spanish.

LIV.

However, he did pretty well, and was
 Admitted as an aspirant to all
The coteries, and, as in Banquo's glass,
 At great assemblies or in parties small,
He saw ten thousand living authors pass,
 That being about their average numeral;
Also the eighty "greatest living poets,"
As every paltry magazine can show *it's.*

LV.

In twice five years the "greatest living poet,"
 Like to the champion in the fisty ring,
Is call'd on to support his claim, or show it,
 Although 't is an imaginary thing.
Even I—albeit I'm sure I did not know it,
 Nor sought of foolscap subjects to be
 king,—
Was reckon'd, a considerable time,
The grand Napoleon of the realms of rhyme.

LVI.

But Juan was my Moscow, and Faliero
 My Leipsic, and my Mont Saint Jean seems
 Cain:
"La Belle Alliance" of dunces down at zero,
 Now that the Lion's fall'n, may rise again:
But I will fall at least as fell my hero;
 Nor reign at all, or as a *monarch* reign;
Or to some lonely isle of gaolers go,
With turncoat Southey for my turnkey Lowe.

LVII.

Sir Walter reign'd before me; Moore and
 Campbell
 Before and after: but now grown more
 holy,
The Muses upon Sion's hill must ramble
 With poets almost clergymen, or wholly:
And Pegasus has a psalmodic amble
 Beneath the very Reverend Rowley Pow-
 ley,
Who shoes the glorious animal with stilts,
A modern Ancient Pistol—by the hilts!

LVIII.

Still he excels that artificial hard
 Labourer in the same vineyard, though
 the vine
Yields him but vinegar for his reward,—
 That neutralised dull Dorus of the Nine;
That swarthy Sporus, neither man nor bard;
 That ox of verse, who *ploughs* for every
 line :—
Cambyses' roaring Romans beat at least
The howling Hebrews of Cybele's priest.—

LIX.

Then there's my gentle Euphues; who, they
 say,
 Sets up for being a sort of *moral me;*
He'll find it rather difficult some day
 To turn out both, or either, it may be.
Some persons think that Coleridge hath the
 sway;
 And Wordsworth has supporters, two or
 three;
And that deep-mouth'd Bœotian "Savage
 Landor"
Has taken for a swan rogue Southey's gan-
 der.

LX.

John Keats, who was kill'd off by one cri-
 tique,
 Just as he really promised something
 great,
If not intelligible, without Greek
 Contrived to talk about the Gods of late,
Much as they might have been supposed to
 speak.
 Poor fellow! His was an untoward fate;
'T is strange the mind, that fiery particle,
Should let itself be snuff'd out by an article.

LXI.

The list grows long of live and dead pre-
 tenders
 To that which none will gain—or none will
 know
The conqueror at least; who, ere Time ren-
 ders
 His last award, will have the long grass
 grow
Above his burnt-out brain, and sapless cin-
 ders.
 If I might augur, I should rate but low
Their chances;—they're too numerous, like
 the thirty
Mock tyrants, when Rome's annals wax'd
 but dirty.

LXII.

This is the literary *lower* empire,
 Where the prætorian bands take up the
 matter;—
A "dreadful trade," like his who "gathers
 samphire,"
 The insolent soldiery to soothe and flatter,
With the same feelings as you'd coax a vam-
 pire.
 Now, were I once at home, and in good
 satire,
I'd try conclusions with those Janizaries,
And show them *what* an intellectual war is.

LXIII.

I think I know a trick or two, would turn
　Their flanks;—but it is hardly worth my
　　while
With such small gear to give myself concern:
　Indeed I've not the necessary bile;
My natural temper's really aught but stern,
　And even my Muse's worst reproof's a
　　smile;
And then she drops a brief and modern curtsy,
And glides away, assured she never hurts ye.

LXIV.

My Juan, whom I left in deadly peril
　Amongst live poets and blue ladies, pass'd
With some small profit through that field so
　　sterile,
　Being tired in time, and neither least nor
　　last,
Left it before he had been treated very ill;
　And henceforth found himself more gaily
　　class'd
Amongst the higher spirits of the day,
The sun's true son, no vapour, but a ray.

LXV.

His morns he pass'd in business—which dis-
　sected,
　Was like all business, a laborious nothing
That leads to lassitude, the most infected
　And Centaur Nessus garb of mortal cloth-
　　ing,
And on our sofas makes us lie dejected,
　And talk in tender horrors of our loathing
All kinds of toil, save for our country's
　good—
Which grows no better, though 't is time it
　should.

LXVI.

His afternoons he pass'd in visits, luncheons,
　Lounging, and boxing; and the twilight hour
In riding round those vegetable puncheons
　Call'd "Parks," where there is neither
　　fruit nor flower
Enough to gratify a bee's slight munchings;
　But after all it is the only "bower"
(In Moore's phrase) where the fashionable
　fair
Can form a slight acquaintance with fresh
　air.

LXVII.

Then dress, then dinner, then awakes the
　world!
　Then glare the lamps, then whirl the wheels,
　　then roar
Through street and square fast flashing
　chariots hurl'd
　Like harness'd meteors; then along the floor

Chalk mimics painting; then festoons are
　twirl'd;
Then roll the brazen thunders of the door,
Which opens to the thousand happy few
An earthly Paradise of "Or Molu."

LXVIII.

There stands the noble hostess, nor shall
　sink
　With the three-thousandth curtsy; there
　　the waltz,
The only dance which teaches girls to think,
　Makes one in love even with its very faults.
Saloon, room, hall, o'erflow beyond their
　brink,
　And long the latest of arrivals halts,
'Midst royal dukes and dames condemn'd to
　climb,
And gain an inch of staircase at a time.

LXIX.

Thrice happy he who, after a survey
　Of the good company, can win a corner,
A door that's in or boudoir out of the way,
　Where he may fix himself like small "Jack
　　Horner,"
And let the Babel round run as it may,
　And look on as a mourner, or a scorner,
Or an approver, or a mere spectator,
Yawning a little as the night grows later.

LXX.

But this won't do, save by and by; and he
　Who, like Don Juan, takes an active share,
Must steer with care through all that glitter-
　ing sea
　Of gems and plumes and pearls and silks,
　　to where
He deems it is his proper place to be;
　Dissolving in the waltz to some soft air,
Or proudlier prancing with mercurial skill,
Where Science marshals forth her own
　quadrille.

LXXI.

Or, if he dance not, but hath higher views
　Upon an heiress or his neighbour's bride,
Let him take care that that which he pursues
　Is not at once too palpably descried.
Full many an eager gentleman oft rues
　His haste; impatience is a blundering
　　guide,
Amongst a people famous for reflection,
Who like to play the fool with circumspec-
　tion.

LXXII.

But, if you can contrive, get next at supper;
　Or if forestall'd, get opposite and ogle:—
Oh, ye ambrosial moments! always upper
　In mind, a sort of sentimental bogle,

Which sits for ever upon memory's crupper,
 The ghost of vanish'd pleasures once in
 vogue! Ill
Can tender souls relate the rise and fall
Of hopes and fears which shake a single ball.

LXXIII.

But these precautionary hints can touch
 Only the common run, who must pursue,
And watch, and ward; whose plans a word
 too much
 Or little overturns; and not the few
Or many (for the number's sometimes such)
 Whom a good mien, especially if new,
Or fame, or name, for wit, war, sense, or
 nonsense,
Permits whate'er they please, or *did* not long
 since.

LXXIV.

Our hero, as a hero, young and handsome,
 Noble, rich, celebrated, and a stranger,
Like other slaves of course must pay his
 ransom,
 Before he can escape from so much danger
As will environ a conspicuous man. Some
 Talk about poetry, and "rack and man-
 ger,"
And ugliness, disease, as toil and trouble;—
I wish they knew the life of a young noble.

LXXV.

They are young, but know not youth—it is
 anticipated;
 Handsome but wasted, rich without a son;
Their vigour in a thousand arms is dissi-
 pated;
 Their cash comes *from*, their wealth goes *to*
 a Jew;
Both senates see their nightly votes par-
 ticipated
 Between the tyrant's and the tribunes'
 crew;
And having voted, dined, drank, gamed, and
 whored,
The family vault receives another lord.

LXXVI.

"Where is the world?" cries Young, at
 eighty—"Where
 The world in which a man was born?" Alas!
Where is the world of *eight* years past?
 '*T was there*—
 I look for it—'t is gone, a globe of glass!
Crack'd, shiver'd, vanish'd, scarcely gazed
 on, ere
 A silent change dissolves the glittering
 mass.
Statesmen, chiefs, orators, queens, patriots,
 kings,
And dandies, all are gone on the wind's wings.

LXXVII.

Where is Napoleon the Grand? God knows:
 Where little Castlereagh? The devil can
 tell:
Where Grattan, Curran, Sheridan, all those
 Who bound the bar or senate in their spell?
Where is the unhappy Queen, with all her
 woes?
 And where the Daughter, whom the Isles
 loved well?
Where are those martyr'd saints the Five
 per Cents?
And where—oh, where the devil are the
 Rents?

LXXVIII.

Where's Brumel? Dish'd. Where's Long
 Pole Wellesley? Diddled.
 Where's Whitbread? Romilly? Where's
 George the Third?
Where is his will? (That's not so soon un-
 riddled.)
 And where is "Fum" the Fourth, our
 "royal bird?"
Gone down, it seems, to Scotland to be fid-
 dled
 Unto by Sawney's violin, we have heard:
"Caw me, caw thee"—for six months hath
 been hatching
This scene of royal itch and loyal scratching.

LXXIX.

Where is Lord This? And where my Lady
 That?
 The Honourable Mistresses and Misses?
Some laid aside like an old Opera hat,
 Married, unmarried, and remarried: (this is
An evolution oft performed of late).
 Where are the Dublin shouts—and London
 hisses?
Where are the Grenvilles? Turn'd as usual. Where
My friends the Whigs? Exactly where they
 were.

LXXX.

Where are the Lady Carolines and Fran-
 ceses?
 Divorced or doing thereanent. Ye annals
So brilliant, where the list of routs and
 dances is,—
 Thou Morning Post, sole record of the
 panels
Broken in carriages, and all the phantasies
 Of fashion,—say what streams now fill
 those channels?
Some die, some fly, some languish on the
 Continent,
Because the times have hardly left them *one*
 tenant.

LXXXI.

Some who once set their caps at cautious
 dukes,
 Have taken up at length with younger
 brothers:
Some heiresses have bit at sharpers' hooks:
 Some maids have been made wives, some
 merely mothers:
Others have lost their fresh and fairy looks:
 In short, the list of alterations bothers.
There's little strange in this, but something
 strange is
The unusual quickness of these common
 changes.

LXXXII.

Talk not of seventy years as age; in seven
 I have seen more changes, down from
 monarchs to
The humblest individual under heaven,
 Than might suffice a moderate century
 through.
I knew that nought was lasting, but now
 even
 Change grows too changeable, without be-
 ing new:
Nought's permanent among the human race,
Except the Whigs *not* getting into place.

LXXXIII.

I have seen Napoleon, who seem'd quite a
 Jupiter,
 Shrink to a Saturn. I have seen a Duke
(No matter which) turn politician stupider,
 If that can well be, than his wooden look;
But it is time that I should hoist my "blue
 Peter,"
 And sail for a new theme:—I have seen—
 and shook
To see it—the king hiss'd, and then carest;
But don't pretend to settle which was best.

LXXXIV.

I have seen the Landholders without a rap—
 I have seen Joanna Southcote—I have
 seen
The House of Commons turn'd to a tax-trap—
 I have seen that sad affair of the late
 Queen—
I have seen crowns worn instead of a fool's
 cap—
 I have seen a Congress doing all that's
 mean—
I have seen some nations, like o'erloaded
 asses,
Kick off their burthens—meaning the high
 classes.

LXXXV.

I have seen small poets, and great prosers,
 and
 Interminable—*not eternal*—speakers—
I have seen the funds at war with house and
 land—
 I have seen the country gentlemen turn
 squeakers—
I have seen the people ridden o'er like sand
 By slaves on horseback—I have seen malt
 liquors
Exchanged for "thin potations" by John
 Bull—
I have seen John half detect himself a fool.—

LXXXVI.

But "carpe diem," Juan, "carpe, carpe!"
 To-morrow sees another race as gay
And transient, and devour'd by the same
 harpy.
 "Life's a poor player,"—then "play out
 the play,
Ye villains!" and above all keep a sharp eye
 Much less on what you do than what you
 say:
Be hypocritical, be cautious, be
Not what you *seem*, but always what you *see*.

LXXXVII.

But how shall I relate in other cantos
 Of what befell our hero in the land,
Which 't is the common cry and lie to vaunt
 as
 A moral country? But I hold my hand—
For I disdain to write an Atalantis;
 But 't is as well at once to understand
You are *not* a moral people, and you know it
Without the aid of too sincere a poet.

LXXXVIII.

What Juan saw and underwent shall be
 My topic, with of course the due restriction
Which is required by proper courtesy;
 And recollect the work is only fiction,
And that I sing of neither mine nor me,
 Though every scribe, in some slight turn
 of diction,
Will hint allusions never *meant*. Ne'er doubt
This—when I speak, I *don't hint*, but *speak
 out*.

LXXXIX.

Whether he married with the third or fourth
 Offspring of some sage husband-hunting
 countess,
Or whether with some virgin of more worth
 (I mean in Fortune's matrimonial bounties)

He took to regularly peopling Earth,
 Of which your lawful, awful wedlock fount
 is,—
Or whether he was taken in for damages,
For being too excursive in his homages,—

XC.

Is yet within the unread events of time.
 Thus far, go forth, thou lay, which I will
 back
Against the same given quantity of rhyme,
 For being as much the subject of attack
As ever yet was any work sublime,
 By those who love to say that white is
 black.
So much the better!—I may stand alone,
But would not change my free thoughts for
 a throne.

—◆◆—

Canto the Twelfth.

I.

Of all the barbarous middle ages, that
 Which is most barbarous is the middle age
Of man! it is—I really scarce know what;
 But when we hover between fool and sage,
And don't know justly what we would be
 at—
A period something like a printed page,
Black letter upon foolscap, while our hair
Grows grizzled, and we are not what we
 were;—

II.

Too old for youth,—too young, at thirty-five,
 To herd with boys, or hoard with good
 threescore,—
I wonder people should be left alive;
 But since they are, that epoch is a bore:
Love lingers still, although 't were late to
 wive:
 And as for other love, the illusion's o'er;
And money, that most pure imagination,
Gleams only through the dawn of its crea-
 tion.

III.

O Gold! Why call we misers miserable?
 Theirs is the pleasure that can never pall;
Theirs is the best bower anchor, the chain
 cable
 Which holds fast other pleasures great and
 small.
Ye who but see the saving man at table,
 And scorn his temperate board, as none at
 all,
And wonder how the wealthy can be sparing,
Know not what visions spring from each
 cheeseparing.

IV.

Love or lust makes man sick, and wine much
 sicker;
 Ambition rends, and gaming gains a loss;
But making money, slowly first, then quicker,
 And adding still a little through each cross
(Which *will* come over things), beats love or
 liquor,
 The gamester's counter, or the statesman's
 dross.
O Gold! I still prefer thee unto paper,
Which makes bank credit like a bark of
 vapour.

V.

Who hold the balance of the world? Who
 reign
 O'er congress, whether royalist or liberal?
Who rouse the shirtless patriots of Spain?
 (That make old Europe's journals squeak
 and gibber all).
Who keep the world, both old and new, in
 pain
 Or pleasure? Who make politics run glib-
 ber all?
The shade of Buonaparte's noble daring?—
Jew Rothschild, and his fellow-Christian,
 Baring.

VI.

Those, and the truly liberal Lafitte,
 Are the true lords of Europe. Every loan
Is not a merely speculative hit,
 But seats a nation or upsets a throne.
Republics also get involved a bit;
 Columbia's stock hath holders not unknown
On 'Change, and even thy silver soil, Peru,
Must get itself discounted by a Jew.

VII.

Why call the miser miserable? as
 I said before: the frugal life is his,
Which in a saint or cynic ever was
 The theme of praise: a hermit would not
 miss
Canonization for the self-same cause,
 And wherefore blame gaunt wealth's aus-
 terities?
Because, you'll say, nought calls for such a
 trial;—
Then there's more merit in his self-denial.

VIII.

He is your only poet;—passion, pure
 And sparkling on from heap to heap, dis-
 plays,
Possess'd, the ore, of which *mere hopes* allure
 Nations athwart the deep: the golden rays

Flash up in ingots from the mine obscure:
 On him the diamond pours its brilliant blaze,
While the mild emerald's beam shades down
 the dies
Of other stones, to soothe the miser's eyes.

IX.

The lands on either side are his; the ship
 From Ceylon, Inde, or far Cathay, unloads
For him the fragrant produce of each trip;
 Beneath his cars of Ceres groan the roads,
And the vine blushes like Aurora's lip;
 His very cellars might be kings' abodes;
While he, despising every sensual call,
Commands—the intellectual lord of all.

X.

Perhaps he hath great projects in his mind,
 To build a college, or to found a race,
A hospital, a church,—and leave behind
 Some dome surmounted by his meagre face:
Perhaps he fain would liberate mankind
 Even with the very ore which makes them
 base;
Perhaps he would be wealthiest of his nation,
Or revel in the joys of calculation.

XI.

But whether all, or each, or none of these
 May be the hoarder's principle of action,
The fool will call such mania a disease:—
 What is his *own?* Go—look at each trans-
 action,
Wars, revels, loves—do these bring men more
 ease
 Than the mere plodding through each
 "vulgar fraction?"
Or do they benefit mankind? Lean miser!
Let spendthrifts' heirs inquire of yours—
 who's wiser?

XII.

How beauteous are rouleaus! how charming
 chests
 Containing ingots, bags of dollars, coins
(Not of old victors, all whose heads and crests
 Weigh not the thin ore where their visage
 shines,
But) of fine unclipt gold, where dully rests
 Some likeness, which the glittering cirque
 confines,
Of modern, reigning, sterling, stupid stamp:
Yes! ready money *is* Aladdin's lamp.

XIII.

"Love rules the camp, the court, the grove,
 —for love
 Is heaven, and heaven is love:"—so sings
 the bard;
Which it were rather difficult to prove
 (A thing with poetry in general hard).

Perhaps there may be something in "the
 grove,"
 At least it rhymes to "love:" but I'm pre-
 pared
To doubt (no less than landlords of their
 rental)
If "courts" and "camps" be quite so senti-
 mental.

XIV.

But if Love don't, *Cash* does, and Cash
 alone:
 Cash rules the grove, and fells it too be-
 side;
Without cash, camps were thin, and courts
 were none;
 Without cash, Malthus tells you—"take
 no brides."
So Cash rules Love the ruler, on his own
 High ground, as virgin Cynthia sways the
 tides:
And as for "Heaven being Love," why not
 say honey
Is wax? Heaven is not Love, 'tis Matri-
 mony.

XV.

Is not all love prohibited whatever,
 Excepting marriage? which is love, no
 doubt,
After a sort; but somehow people never
 With the same thought the two words have
 help'd out.
Love may exist *with* marriage, and *should*
 ever,
 And marriage also may exist without;
But love *sans* banns is both a sin and shame,
And ought to go by quite another name.

XVI.

Now if the "court," and "camp," and
 "grove," be not
 Recruited all with constant married men,
Who never coveted their neighbour's lot,
 I say *that* line's a lapsus of the pen;—
Strange too in my "buon camerado" Scott,
 So celebrated for his morals, when
My Jeffrey held him up as an example
To me;—of which these morals are a sample.

XVII.

Well, if I don't succeed, I *have* succeeded,
 And that's enough; succeeded in my youth,
The only time when much success is needed:
 And my success produced what I, in sooth,
Cared most about; it need not now be
 pleaded—
 Whate'er it was, 'twas mine; I've paid, in
 truth,
Of late, the penalty of such success,
But have not learn'd to wish it any less.

XVIII.

That suit in Chancery,—which some persons
　plead
　In an appeal to the unborn, whom they,
In the faith of their procreative creed,
　Baptize posterity, or future clay,—
To me seems but a dubious kind of reed
　To lean on for support in any way;
Since odds are that posterity will know
No more of them, than they of her, I trow.

XIX.

Why, I'm posterity—and so are you;
　And whom do we remember? Not a hun-
　　dred.
Were every memory written down all true,
　The tenth or twentieth name would be but
　　blundered.
Even Plutarch's Lives have but pick'd out a
　　few,
　And 'gainst those few your annalists have
　　thunder'd;
And Mitford in the nineteenth century
Gives, with Greek truth, the good old Greek
　the lie.

XX.

Good people all, of every degree,
　Ye gentle readers and ungentle writers,
In this twelfth Canto 'tis my wish to be
　As serious as if I had for inditers
Malthus and Wilberforce:—the last set free
　The Negroes, and is worth a million fight-
　　ers;
While Wellington has but enslaved the
　　Whites,
And Malthus does the thing 'gainst which he
　writes.

XXI.

I'm serious—so are all men upon paper;
　And why should I not form my speculation,
And hold up to the sun my little taper?
　Mankind just now seem wrapt in medita-
　　tion
On constitutions and steam-boats of vapour;
　While sages write against all procreation,
Unless a man can calculate his means
Of feeding brats the moment his wife weans.

XXII.

That's noble! That's romantic! For my
　part,
　I think that "Philo-genitiveness" is—
(Now here's a word quite after my own heart,
　Though there's a shorter a good deal than
　this.

If that politeness set it not apart;
　But I'm resolved to say nought that's
　　amiss)—
I say, methinks that "Philo-genitiveness"
Might meet from men a little more forgive-
　ness.

XXIII.

And now to business.—O my gentle Juan!
　Thou art in London—in that pleasant
　　place,
Where every kind of mischief's daily brew-
　ing,
　Which can await warm youth in its wild race.
'Tis true, that thy career is not a new one;
　Thou art no novice in the headlong chase
Of early life; but this is a new land,
Which foreigners can never understand.

XXIV.

What with a small diversity of climate,
　Of hot or cold, mercurial or sedate,
I could send forth my mandate like a primate
　Upon the rest of Europe's social state;
But thou art the most difficult to rhyme at,
　Great Britain, which the Muse may pene-
　　trate.
All countries have their "Lions," but in thee
There is but one superb menagerie.

XXV.

But I am sick of politics. Begin,
　"Paulo Majora." Juan, undecided
Amongst the paths of being "taken in,"
　Above the ice had like a skater glided:
When tired of play, he flirted without sin
　With some of those fair creatures who have
　　prided
Themselves on innocent tantalisation,
And hate all vice except its reputation.

XXVI.

But these are few, and in the end they make
　Some devilish escapade or stir, which shows
That even the purest people may mistake
　Their way through virtue's primrose paths
　　of snows;
And then men stare, as if a new ass spake
　To Balaam, and from tongue to ear o'er-
　　flows
Quicksilver small talk, ending (if you note it)
With the kind world's amen—"Who would
　have thought it?"

XXVII.

The little Leila, with her Orient eyes,
　And taciturn Asiatic disposition,
(Which saw all Western things with small
　　surprise,
　To the surprise of people of condition,

Who think that novelties are butterflies
 To be pursued as food for inanition,)
Her charming figure and romantic history
Became a kind of fashionable mystery.

XXVIII.

The women much divided—as is usual
 Amongst the sex in little things or great.
Think not, fair creatures, that I mean to
 abuse you all—
I have always liked you better than I state:
Since I've grown moral, still I must accuse
 you all
Of being apt to talk at a great rate;
And now there was a general sensation
Amongst you, about Leila's education.

XXIX.

In one point only were you settled—and
 You had reason; 'twas that a young child
 of grace,
As beautiful as her own native land,
 And far away, the last bud of her race,
Howe'er our friend Don Juan might com-
 mand
 Himself for five, four, three, or two years'
 space,
Would be much better taught beneath the eye
Of peeresses whose follies had run dry.

XXX.

So first there was a generous emulation,
 And then there was a general competition,
To undertake the orphan's education.
 As Juan was a person of condition,
It had been an affront on this occasion
 To talk of a subscription or petition;
But sixteen dowagers, ten unwed she sages,
Whose tale belongs to "Hallam's Middle
 Ages,"

XXXI.

And one or two sad, separate wives, without
 A fruit to bloom upon their withering
 bough—
Begg'd to bring *up* the little girl, and "*out*,"—
 For that's the phrase that settles all things
 now,
Meaning a virgin's first blush at a rout,
 And all her points as thorough-bred to
 show:
And I assure you, that like virgin honey
Tastes their first season (mostly if they have
 money).

XXXII.

How all the needy honourable misters,
 Each out-at-elbow peer, or desperate dandy,
The watchful mothers, and the careful sisters,
 (Who, by the by, when clever, are more
 handy

At making matches, where "'tis gold that
 glisters,"
 Than their *he* relatives), like flies o'er candy
Buzz round "*the* Fortune" with their busy
 battery,
To turn her head with waltzing and with
 flattery!

XXXIII.

Each aunt, each cousin, hath her speculation;
 Nay, married dames will now and then
 discover
Such pure disinterestedness of passion,
 I've known them court an heiress for their
 lover.
"Tantæne!" Such the virtues of high station,
 Even in the hopeful Isle, whose outlet's
 "Dover!"
While the poor rich wretch, object of these
 cares,
Has cause to wish her sire had had male heirs.

XXXIV.

Some are soon bagg'd, and some reject three
 dozen.
 'Tis fine to see them scattering refusals
And wild dismay o'er every angry cousin
 (Friends of the party), who begin accusals
Such as—"Unless Miss (Blank) meant to
 have chosen
 Poor Frederick, why did she accord pe-
 rusals
To his billets? *Why* waltz with him? Why
 I pray,
Look *yes* last night, and yet say *no* to-day?

XXXV.

"Why?—Why?—Besides, Fred really was
 attach'd;
 'Twas not her fortune—he has enough
 without:
The time will come she'll wish that she had
 snatch'd
 So good an opportunity, no doubt:—
But the old Marchioness some plan had
 hatch'd,
 As I'll tell Aurea at to-morrow's rout:
And after all poor Frederick may do better—
Pray did you see her answer to his letter?"

XXXVI.

Smart uniforms and sparkling coronets
 Are spurn'd in turn, until her turn arrives,
After male loss of time, and hearts, and bets
 Upon the sweepstakes for substantial wives;
And when at last the pretty creature gets
 Some gentleman, who fights, or writes, or
 drives,
It soothes the awkward squad of the rejected
To find how very badly she selected.

XXXVII.

For sometimes they accept some long pur-
　　suer,
　　Worn out with importunity; or fall
(But here perhaps the instances are fewer)
　　To the lot of him who scarce pursued at all.
A hazy widower turn'd of forty's sure
　　(If 'tis not vain examples to recall)
To draw a high prize : now, howe'er he got
　　her, I
See nought more strange in this than t'other
　　lottery.

XXXVIII.

I, for my part—(one "modern instance"
　　more,
　　"True, 'tis a pity—pity 'tis, 'tis true ")—
Was chosen from out an amatory score,
　　Albeit my years were less discreet than few;
But though I also had reform'd before
　　Those became one who soon were to be
　　two,
I'll not gainsay the generous public's voice,
That the young lady made a monstrous choice.

XXXIX.

Oh, pardon my digression—or at least
　　Peruse ! 'Tis always with a moral end
That I dissert, like grace before a feast :
　　For like an aged aunt, or tiresome friend,
A rigid guardian, or a zealous priest,
　　My Muse by exhortation means to mend
All people, at all times, and in most places,
Which puts my Pegasus to these grave paces.

XL.

But now I'm going to be immoral; now
　　I mean to show things really as they are,
Not as they ought to be: for I avow,
　　That till we see what's what in fact, we're
　　far
From much improvement with that virtuous
　　plough
　　Which skims the surface, leaving scarce
　　a scar
Upon the black loam long manured by Vice,
Only to keep its corn at the old price.

XLI.

But first of little Leila we'll dispose ;
　　For like a day-dawn she was young and
　　pure,
Or like the old comparison of snows,
　　Which are more pure than pleasant to be
　　sure.
Like many people everybody knows,
　　Don Juan was delighted to secure
A goodly guardian for his infant charge,
Who might not profit much by being at large.

XLII.

Besides, he had found out he was no tutor
　　(I wish that others would find out the same),
And rather wish'd in such things to stand
　　neuter,
　　For silly wards will bring their guardians
　　blame:
So when he saw each ancient dame a suitor
　　To make his little wild Asiatic tame,
Consulting " the Society for Vice
Suppression," Lady Pinchbeck was his choice.

XLIII.

Olden she was—but had been very young :
　　Virtuous she was—and had been, I believe;
Although the world has such an evil tongue
　　That——but my chaster ear will not receive
An echo of a syllable that's wrong;
　　In fact, there's nothing makes me so much
　　grieve,
As that abominable tittle-tattle,
Which is the cud eschew'd by human cattle.

XLIV.

Moreover I've remark'd (and I was once
　　A slight observer in a modest way),
And so may every one except a dunce,
　　That ladies in their youth a little gay,
Besides their knowledge of the world, and sense
　　Of the sad consequence of going astray,
Are wiser in their warnings 'gainst the woe
Which the mere passionless can never know.

XLV.

While the harsh prude indemnifies her virtue
　　By railing at the unknown and envied
　　passion,
Seeking far less to save you than to hurt you,
　　Or, what's still worse, to put you out of
　　fashion,—
The kinder veteran with calm words will
　　court you,
　　Entreating you to pause before you dash on;
Expounding and illustrating the riddle
Of epic Love's beginning, end, and middle.

XLVI.

Now whether it be thus, or that they are
　　stricter,
　　As better knowing why they should be so,
I think you'll find from many a family picture,
　　That daughters of such mothers as may
　　know
The world by experience rather than by
　　lecture,
　　Turn out much better for the Smithfield
　　Show
Of vestals brought into the marriage mart,
Than those bred up by prudes without a heart.

XLVII.

I said that Lady Pinchbeck had been talk'd
 about—
 As who has not, if female, young, and
 pretty?
But now no more the ghost of Scandal stalk'd
 about;
 She merely was deem'd amiable and witty,
And several of her best bon-mots were hawk'd
 about:
 Then she was given to charity and pity,
And pass'd (at least the latter years of life)
For being a most exemplary wife.

XLVIII.

High in high circles, gentle in her own,
 She was the mild reprover of the young,
Whenever—which means every day—they'd
 shown
 An awkward inclination to go wrong.
The quantity of good she did's unknown,
 Or at the least would lengthen out my song:
In brief, the little orphan of the East
Had raised an interest in her, which increased.

XLIX.

Juan, too, was a sort of favourite with her,
 Because she thought him a good heart at
 bottom,
A little spoil'd, but not so altogether;
 Which was a wonder, if you think who got
 him,
And how he had been toss'd, he scarce knew
 whither:
 Though this might ruin others, it did *not*
 him,
At least entirely—for he had seen too many
Changes in youth, to be surprised at any.

L.

And these vicissitudes tell best in youth;
 For when they happen at a riper age,
People are apt to blame the Fates, forsooth,
 And wonder Providence is not more sage.
Adversity is the first path to truth:
 He who hath proved war, storm, or woman's
 rage,
Whether his winters be eighteen or eighty,
Hath won the experience which is deem'd so
 weighty.

LI.

How far it profits is another matter.—
 Our hero gladly saw his little charge
Safe with a lady, whose last grown-up
 daughter
 Being long married, and thus set at large,
Had left all the accomplishments she taught
 her
 To be transmitted, like the Lord Mayor's
 barge,
To the next comer; or—as it will tell
More Muse-like—like to Cytherea's shell.

LII.

I call such things transmission; for there is
 A floating balance of accomplishment,
Which forms a pedigree from Miss to Miss,
 According as their minds or backs are bent.
Some waltz; some draw; some fathom the
 abyss
 Of metaphysics; others are content
With music; the most moderate shine as wits;
While others have a genius turn'd for fits.

LIII.

But whether fits, or wits, or harpsichords,
 Theology, fine arts, or finer stays,
May be the baits for gentlemen or lords
 With regular descent, in these our days,
The last year to the new transfers its hoards;
 New vestals claim men's eyes with the
 same praise
Of "elegant" *et cætera*, in fresh batches—
All matchless creatures, and yet bent on
 matches.

LIV.

But now I will begin my poem. 'T is
 Perhaps a little strange, if not quite new,
That from the first of Cantos up to this
 I've not begun what we have to go through.
These first twelve books are merely flourishes,
 Preludios, trying just a string or two
Upon my lyre, or making the pegs sure;
And when so, you shall have the overture.

LV.

My Muses do not care a pinch of rosin
 About what's call'd success, or not suc-
 ceeding:
Such thoughts are quite below the strain
 they have chosen;
 'Tis a "great moral lesson" they are
 reading.
I thought, at setting off, about two dozen
 Cantos would do; but at Apollo's pleading,
If that my Pegasus should not be founder'd,
I think to canter gently through a hundred.

LVI.

Don Juan saw that microcosm on stilts,
 Yclept the Great World; for it is the least,
Although the highest: but as swords have
 hilts
 By which their power of mischief is in-
 creased,

When man in battle or in quarrel tilts,
 Thus the low world, north, south, or west,
 or east,
Must still obey the high—which is their
 handle,
Their moon, their sun, their gas, their farthing
 candle.

LVII.

He had many friends who had many wives,
 and was
Well look'd upon by both, to that extent
Of friendship which you may accept or pass,
 It does nor good, nor harm: being merely
 meant
To keep the wheels going of the higher class,
 And draw them nightly when a ticket's
 sent;
And what with masquerades, and fêtes, and
 balls,
For the first season such a life scarce palls.

LVIII.

A young unmarried man, with a good name
 And fortune, has an awkward part to play;
For good society is but a game,
 "The royal game of Goose," as I may say,
Where everybody has some separate aim,
 An end to answer, or a plan to lay—
The single ladies wishing to be double,
The married ones to save the virgins trouble.

LIX.

I don't mean this as general, but particular
 Examples may be found of such pursuits:
Though several also keep their perpendicular
 Like poplars, with good principles for roots;
Yet many have a method more *reticular*—
 "Fishers for men," like sirens with soft
 lutes:
For talk six times with the same single
 lady,
And you may get the wedding dresses ready.

LX.

Perhaps you'll have a letter from the mother,
 To say her daughter's feelings are tre-
 pann'd;
Perhaps you'll have a visit from the bro-
 ther,
 All strut, and stays, and whiskers, to de-
 mand
What "your intentions are?"—One way or
 other
 It seems the virgin's heart expects your
 hand:
And between pity for her case and yours,
You'll add to Matrimony's list of cures.

LXI.

I've known a dozen weddings made even
 thus,
 And some of them high names: I have also
 known
Young men who—though they hated to
 discuss
 Pretensions which they never dream'd to
 have shown—
Yet neither frighten'd by a female fuss,
 Nor by mustachios moved, were let alone,
And lived, as did the broken-hearted fair,
In happier plight than if they form'd a pair.

LXII.

There's also nightly, to the uninitiated,
 A peril—not indeed like love or marriage,
But not the less for this to be depreciated:
 It is—I meant and mean not to disparage
The show of virtue even in the vitiated—
 It adds an outward grace unto their
 carriage—
But to denounce the amphibious sort of
 harlot,
"Couleur de rose," who's neither white nor
 scarlet.

LXIII.

Such is your cold coquette, who can't say
 "No,"
 And won't say "Yes," and keeps you on
 and off-ing
On a lee-shore, till it begins to blow—
 Then sees your heart wreck'd with an
 inward scoffing.
This works a world of sentimental woe,
 And sends new Werters yearly to their
 coffin;
But yet is merely innocent flirtation,
Not quite adultery, but adulteration.

LXIV.

"Ye gods, I grow a talker!" Let us prate.
 The next of perils, though I place it
 *stern*est,
Is when, without regard to "church or
 state,"
 A wife makes or takes love in upright
 earnest.
Abroad, such things decide few women's
 fate—
 (Such, early traveller! is the truth thou
 learnest)—
But in old England, when a young bride errs,
Poor thing! Eve's was a trifling case to
 hers.

LXV.

For 't is a low, newspaper, humdrum, lawsuit
　　Country, where a young couple of the same
　　　ages
Can't form a friendship, but the world o'er-
　　awes it.
　　Then there's the vulgar trick of those
　　　d——d damages!
A verdict—grievous foe to those who cause
　　it!—
　　Forms a sad climax to romantic homages;
Besides those soothing speeches of the
　　pleaders,
And evidences which regale all readers.

LXVI.

But they who blunder thus are raw be-
　　ginners;
　　A little genial sprinkling of hypocrisy
Has saved the fame of thousand splendid
　　sinners,
　　The loveliest oligarchs of our gynocracy;
You may see such at all the balls and
　　dinners,
　　Among the proudest of our aristocracy,
So gentle, charming, charitable, chaste—
And all by having *tact* as well as taste.

LXVII.

Juan, who did not stand in the predicament
　　Of a mere novice, had one safeguard more;
For he was sick—no, 't was not the word
　　sick I meant—
　　But he had seen so much good love before,
That he was not in heart so very weak;—
　　I meant
　　But thus much, and no sneer against the
　　　shore
Of white cliffs, white necks, blue eyes, bluer
　　stockings,
Tithes, taxes, duns, and doors with double
　　knockings.

LXVIII.

But coming young from lands and scenes
　　romantic,
　　Where lives, not lawsuits, must be risk'd
　　　for Passion,
And Passion's self must have a spice of
　　frantic,
　　Into a country where 't is half a fashion,
Seem'd to him half commercial, half pedantic,
　　Howe'er he might esteem this moral
　　　nation:
Besides (alas! his taste—forgive and pity!)
At first he did not think the women pretty.

LXIX.

I say at *first*—for he found out at *last*,
　　But by degrees, that they were fairer far
Than the more glowing dames whose lot is
　　cast
　　Beneath the influence of the eastern star.
A further proof we should not judge in
　　haste;
　　Yet inexperience could not be his bar
To taste:—the truth is, if men would confess,
That novelties *please* less than they *impress*.

LXX.

Though travell'd, I have never had the luck to
　　Trace up those shuffling negroes, Nile or
　　　Niger,
To that impracticable place Timbuctoo,
　　Where Geography finds no one to oblige
　　　her
With such a chart as may be safely stuck
　　to—
　　For Europe ploughs in Afric like "bos
　　　piger;"
But if I *had been* at Timbuctoo, there
No doubt I should be told that black is fair.

LXXI.

It is. I will not swear that black is white;
　　But I suspect in fact that white is black,
And the whole matter rests upon eye-sight.
　　Ask a blind man, the best judge. You'll
　　　attack
Perhaps this new position—but I'm right;
　　Or if I'm wrong, I'll not be ta'en aback:—
He hath no morn nor night, but all is dark
Within; and what seest thou? A dubious
　　spark.

LXXII.

But I'm relapsing into metaphysics,
　　That labyrinth, whose clue is of the same
Construction as your cures for hectic
　　phthisics,
　　Those bright moths fluttering round a
　　　dying flame:
And this reflection brings me to plain physics,
　　And to the beauties of a foreign dame,
Compared with those of our pure pearls of
　　price,
Those polar summers, *all* sun, and some ice.

LXXIII.

Or say they are like virtuous mermaids, whose
　　Beginnings are fair faces, ends mere
　　　fishes;—
Not that there's not a quantity of those
　　Who have a due respect for their own
　　　wishes.

Like Russians rushing from hot baths to
　　snows
　Are they, at bottom virtuous even when
　　vicious;
They warm into a scrape, but keep of course,
As a reserve, a plunge into remorse.

LXXIV.

But this has nought to do with their outsides.
　I said that Juan did not think them pretty
At the first blush; for a fair Briton hides
　Half her attractions—probably from pity—
And rather calmly into the heart glides,
　Than storms it as a foe would take a city;
But once there (if you doubt this, prithee try)
She keeps it for you like a true ally.

LXXV.

She cannot step as does an Arab barb,
　Or Andalusian girl from mass returning,
Nor wear as gracefully as Gauls her garb,
　Nor in her eye Ausonia's glance is burning;
Her voice, though sweet, is not so fit to warb-
　le those bravuras (which I still am learn-
　　ing
To like, though I have been seven years in
　　Italy,
And have, or had, an ear that served me
　　prettily;—

LXXVI.

She cannot do these things, nor one or two
　Others, in that off-hand and dashing style
Which takes so much—to give the devil his
　　due;
　Nor is she quite so ready with her smile,
Nor settles all things in one interview,
　(A thing approved as saving time and
　　toil);—
But though the soil may give you time and
　　trouble,
Well cultivated, it will render double.

LXXVII.

And if in fact she takes to a "grande passion,"
　It is a very serious thing indeed:
Nine times in ten 't is but caprice or fashion,
　Coquetry, or a wish to take the lead,
The pride of a mere child with a new sash on,
　Or wish to make a rival's bosom bleed:
But the tenth instance will be a tornado,
For there 's no saying what they will or may
　do.

LXXVIII.

The reason 's obvious: if there 's an éclat,
　They lose their caste at once, as do the
　　Parias;
And when the delicacies of the law
　Have fill'd their papers with their com-
　　ments various,

Society, that china without flaw,
　(The hypocrite!) will banish them like
　　Marius,
To sit amidst the ruins of their guilt:
For Fame 's a Carthage not so soon rebuilt.

LXXIX.

Perhaps this is as it should be;—it is
　A comment on the Gospel's "Sin no more,
And be thy sins forgiven;"—but upon this
　I leave the saints to settle their own score.
Abroad, though doubtless they do much
　　amiss,
　An erring woman finds an opener door
For her return to Virtue—as they call
That lady, who should be at home to all.

LXXX.

For me, I leave the matter where I find it,
　Knowing that such uneasy virtue leads
People some ten times less in fact to mind it,
　And care but for discoveries, and not
　　deeds.
And as for chastity, you'll never bind it
　By all the laws the strictest lawyer pleads,
But aggravate the crime you have not pre-
　　vented,
By rendering desperate those who had else
　repented.

LXXXI.

But Juan was no casuist, nor had ponder'd
　Upon the moral lessons of mankind:
Besides, he had not seen of several hundred
　A lady altogether to his mind.
A little "blasé"—'t is not to be wonder'd
　At, that his heart had got a tougher rind:
And though not vainer from his past success,
No doubt his sensibilities were less.

LXXXII.

He also had been busy seeing sights—
　The Parliament and all the other houses;
Had sat beneath the gallery at nights,
　To hear debates whose thunder *roused* (not
　　rouses)
The world to gaze upon those northern
　　lights,
　Which flash'd as far as where the musk-
　　bull browses;
He had also stood at times behind the
　　throne—
But Grey was not arrived, and Chatham
　　gone.

LXXXIII.

He saw, however, at the closing session,
　That noble sight, when *really* free the
　　nation,
A king in constitutional possession
　Of such a throne as is the proudest station,

Though despots know it not—till the pro-
 gression
Of freedom shall complete their education.
'T is not mere splendour makes the show
 august
To eye or heart—it is the people's trust.

LXXXIV.

There, too, he saw (whate'er he may be now)
 A Prince, the prince of princes at the
 time,
With fascination in his very bow,
 And full of promise, as the spring of prime.
Though royalty was written on his brow,
 He had *then* the grace. too, rare in every
 clime,
Of being, without alloy of fop or beau,
A finish'd gentleman from top to toe.

LXXXV.

And Juan was received, as hath been said,
 Into the best society; and there
Occurr'd what often happens, I'm afraid,
 However disciplined and debonnaire :—
The talent and good humour he display'd,
 Besides the mark'd distinction of his air,
Exposed him, as was natural, to temptation,
Even though himself avoided the occasion.

LXXXVI.

But what, and where, with whom, and when,
 · and why,
 Is not to be put hastily together;
And as my object is morality
 (Whatever people say), I don't know
 whether
I 'll leave a single reader's eyelid dry,
 But harrow up his feelings till they wither,
And hew out a huge monument of pathos,
As Philip's son proposed to do with Athos.

LXXXVII.

Here the twelfth Canto of our introduction
 Ends. When the body of the book's begun,
You 'll find it of a different construction
 From what some people say 't will be when
 done;
The plan at present 's simply in concoction.
 I can't oblige you, reader, to read on;
That 's your affair, not mine : a real spirit
Should neither court neglect, nor dread to
 bear it.

LXXXVIII.

And if my thunderbolt not always rattles,
 Remember, reader ! you have had before
The worst of tempests and the best of bat-
 tles,
 That e'er were brew'd from elements or
 gore,

Besides the most sublime of—Heaven knows
 what else ;
 An usurer could scarce expect much
 more—
But my best canto, save one on astronomy,
Will turn upon "political economy."

LXXXIX.

That is your present theme for popularity :
 Now that the public hedge hath scarce a
 stake,
It grows an act of patriotic charity,
 To show the people the best way to break.
My plan (but I, if but for singularity,
 Reserve it) will be very sure to take.
Meantime, read all the national-debt sinkers,
And tell me what you think of our great
 thinkers.

—◦+◦—

Canto the Thirteenth.

I.

I NOW mean to be serious;—it is time,
 Since laughter now-a-days is deem'd too
 serious ;
A jest at Vice by Virtue 's call'd a crime,
 And critically held as deleterious :
Besides, the sad 's a source of the sublime,
 Although when long a little apt to weary
 us ;
And therefore shall my lay soar high and
 solemn,
As an old temple dwindled to a column.

II.

The Lady Adeline Amundeville
 ('T is an old Norman name, and to be found
In pedigrees, by those who wander still
 Along the last fields of that Gothic ground)
Was high-born, wealthy by her father's will,
 And beauteous, even where beauties most
 abound,
In Britain—which of course true patriots
 find
The goodliest soil of body and of mind.

III.

I 'll not gainsay them; it is not my cue ;
 I 'll leave them to their taste, no doubt
 the best :
An eye 's an eye, and whether black or blue,
 Is no great matter, so 't is in request ;
'T is nonsense to dispute about a hue—
 The kindest may be taken as a test.
The fair sex should be always fair ; and no
 man
Till thirty, should perceive there 's a plain
 woman.

IV.

And after that serene and somewhat dull
 Epoch, that awkward corner turn'd for
 days
More quiet, when our moon's no more at
 full,
 We may presume to criticise or praise;
Because indifference begins to lull
 Our passions, and we walk in wisdom's
 ways;
Also because the figure and the face
Hint, that 'tis time to give the younger
 place.

V.

I know that some would fain postpone this
 era,
 Reluctant as all placemen to resign
Their post; but theirs is merely a chimera,
 For they have pass'd life's equinoctial line:
But then they have their claret and Madeira
 To irrigate the dryness of decline;
And county meetings, and the parliament,
And debt, and what not, for their solace sent.

VI.

And is there not religion, and reform,
 Peace, war, the taxes, and what's called
 the "Nation"?
The struggle to be pilots in a storm?
 The landed and the monied speculation?
The joys of mutual hate to keep them warm,
 Instead of love, that mere hallucination?
Now hatred is by far the longest pleasure;
Men love in haste, but they detest at leisure.

VII.

Rough Johnson, the great moralist, profess'd,
 Right honestly, "he liked an honest
 hater!"—
The only truth that yet has been confest
 Within these latest thousand years or later.
Perhaps the fine old fellow spoke in jest:—
 For my part, I am but a mere spectator,
And gaze where'er the palace or the hovel is,
Much in the mode of Goethe's Mephistophe-
 les;

VIII.

But neither love nor hate in much excess;
 Though 'twas not once so. If I sneer some-
 times,
It is because I cannot well do less,
 And now and then it also suits my rhymes.
I should be very willing to redress
 Men's wrongs, and rather check than
 punish crimes,
Had not Cervantes, in that too true tale
Of Quixote, shown how all such efforts fail.

IX.

Of all tales 'tis the saddest—and more sad,
 Because it makes us smile: his hero's
 right,
And still pursues the right;—to curb the bad
 His only object, and 'gainst odds to fight
His guerdon: 'tis his virtue makes him mad!
 But his adventures form a sorry sight;—
A sorrier still is the great moral taught
By that real epic unto all who have thought.

X.

Redressing injury, revenging wrong,
 To aid the damsel and destroy the caitiff;
Opposing singly the united strong,
 From foreign yoke to free the helpless na-
 tive:—
Alas! must noblest views, like an old song,
 Be for mere fancy's sport a theme creative,
A jest, a riddle, Fame through thick and thin
 sought!
And Socrates himself but Wisdom's Quixote?

XI.

Cervantes smiled Spain's chivalry away;
 A single laugh demolish'd the right arm
Of his own country;—seldom since that day
 Has Spain had heroes. While Romance
 could charm,
The world gave ground before her bright
 array;
 And therefore have his volumes done such
 harm,
That all their glory, as a composition,
Was dearly purchased by his land's perdition.

XII.

I'm "at my old lunes"—digression, and for-
 get
 The Lady Adeline Amundeville;
The fair most fatal Juan ever met,
 Although she was not evil nor meant ill;
But Destiny and Passion spread the net
 (Fate is a good excuse for our own will),
And caught them;—what do they *not* catch,
 methinks?
But I'm not Œdipus, and life's a Sphinx.

XIII.

I tell the tale as it is told, nor dare
 To venture a solution: "Davus sum!"
And now I will proceed upon the pair.
 Sweet Adeline, amidst the gay world's hum,
Was the Queen-Bee, the glass of all that's
 fair;
 Whose charms made all men speak, and
 women dumb.
The last's a miracle, and such was reckon'd,
And since that time there has not been a second.

XIV.

Chaste was she, to detraction's desperation,
 And wedded unto one she had loved well—
A man known in the councils of the nation,
 Cool, and quite English, imperturbable,
Though apt to act with fire upon occasion,
 Proud of himself and her: the world could
 tell
Nought against either, and both seem'd se-
 cure—
She in her virtue, he in his hauteur.

XV.

It chanced some diplomatical relations,
 Arising out of business, often brought
Himself and Juan in their mutual stations
 Into close contact. Though reserved, nor
 caught
By specious seeming, Juan's youth, and pa-
 tience,
 And talent, on his haughty spirit wrought,
And form'd a basis of esteem, which ends
In making men what courtesy calls friends.

XVI.

And thus Lord Henry, who was cautious as
 Reserve and pride could make him, and
 full slow
In judging men—when once his judgment
 was
 Determined, right or wrong, on friend or
 foe,
Had all the pertinacity pride has,
 Which knows no ebb to its imperious flow,
And loves or hates, disdaining to be guided,
Because its own good pleasure hath decided.

XVII.

His friendships, therefore, and no less aver-
 sions,
 Though oft well founded, which confirm'd
 but more
His prepossessions, like the laws of Persians
 And Medes, would ne'er revoke what went
 before.
His feelings had not those strange fits, like
 tertians,
 Of common likings, which make some de-
 plore
What they should laugh at—the mere ague
 still
Of men's regard, the fever or the chill.

XVIII.

"'Tis not in mortals to command success:
 But *do you more*, Sempronius—*don't* de-
 serve it,"
And take my word, you won't have any less.
 Be wary, watch the time, and always serve
 it;

Give gently way, when there's too great a
 press;
 And for your conscience only learn to nerve
 it,
For, like a racer, or a boxer training,
'T will make, if proved, vast efforts without
 paining.

XIX.

Lord Henry also liked to be superior,
 As most men do, the little or the great;
The very lowest find out an inferior,
 At least they think so, to exert their state
Upon: for there are very few things wearier
 Than solitary Pride's oppressive weight,
Which mortals generously would divide,
By bidding others carry while they ride.

XX.

In birth, in rank, in fortune likewise equal,
 O'er Juan he could no distinction claim;
In years he had the advantage of time's se-
 quel;
 And, as he thought, in country much the
 same—
Because bold Britons have a tongue and free
 quill,
 At which all modern nations vainly aim;
And the Lord Henry was a great debater,
So that few members kept the house up later.

XXI.

These were advantages: and then he
 thought—
 It was his foible, but by no means sinis-
 ter—
That few or none more than himself had
 caught
 Court mysteries, having been himself a
 minister:
He liked to teach that which he had been
 taught,
 And greatly shone whenever there had
 been a stir;
And reconciled all qualities which grace man,
Always a patriot, and sometimes a placeman.

XXII.

He liked the gentle Spaniard for his gravity;
 He almost honour'd him for his docility;
Because, though young, he acquiesced with
 suavity,
 Or contradicted but with proud humility.
He knew the world, and would not see de-
 pravity
 In faults which sometimes show the soil's
 fertility,
If that the weeds o'erlive not the first crop—
For then they are very difficult to stop.

XXIII.

And then he talk'd with him about Madrid,
　Constantinople, and such distant places;
Where people always did as they were bid,
　Or did what they should not with foreign
　　graces.
Of coursers also spake they: Henry rid
　Well, like most Englishmen, and loved the
　　races;
And Juan, like a true-born Andalusian,
Could back a horse, as despots ride a Russian.

XXIV.

And thus acquaintance grew, at noble routs,
　And diplomatic dinners, or at other—
For Juan stood well both with Ins and Outs,
　As in freemasonry a higher brother.
Upon his talent Henry had no doubts;
　His manner show'd him sprung from a high
　　mother;
And all men like to show their hospitality
To him whose breeding matches with his
　quality.

XXV.

At Blank-Blank Square;—for we will break
　no squares
　By naming streets: since men are so cen-
　　sorious,
And apt to sow an author's wheat with tares,
　Reaping allusions private and inglorious,
Where none were dreamt of, unto love's affairs,
　Which were, or are, or are to be notorious,
That therefore do I previously declare,
Lord Henry's mansion was in Blank-Blank
　Square.

XXVI.

Also there bin another pious reason
　For making squares and streets anonymous;
Which is, that there is scarce a single season
　Which doth not shake some very splendid
　　house
With some slight heart-quake of domestic
　treason—
　A topic scandal doth delight to rouse:
Such I might stumble over unawares,
Unless I knew the very chastest squares.

XXVII.

'Tis true, I might have chosen Piccadilly,
　A place where peccadillos are unknown;
But I have motives, whether wise or silly,
　For letting that pure sanctuary alone.
Therefore I name not square, street, place,
　until I
　Find one where nothing naughty can be
　　shown,
A vestal shrine of innocence of heart:
Such are—but I have lost the London Chart.

XXVIII.

At Henry's mansion then, in Blank-Blank
　Square,
　Was Juan a recherché, welcome guest,
As many other noble scions were;
　And some who had but talent for their crest;
Or wealth, which is a passport everywhere;
　Or even mere fashion, which indeed's the
　　best
Recommendation; and to be well drest
Will very often supersede the rest.

XXIX.

And since "there's safety in a multitude
　Of counsellors," as Solomon has said,
Or some one for him, in some sage, grave
　mood;—
　Indeed we see the daily proof display'd
In senates, at the bar, in wordy feud,
　Where'er collective wisdom can parade,
Which is the only cause that we can guess
Of Britain's present wealth and happiness;—

XXX.

But as "there's safety" grafted in the number
　"Of counsellors" for men,—thus for the sex
A large acquaintance lets not Virtue slumber;
　Or should it shake, the choice will more
　　perplex—
Variety itself will more encumber.
　'Midst many rocks we guard more against
　　wrecks;
And thus with women: howsoe'er it shocks
　some's
Self-love, there's safety in a crowd of cox-
　combs.

XXXI.

But Adeline had not the least occasion
　For such a shield, which leaves but little
　　merit
To virtue proper, or good education.
　Her chief resource was in her own high
　　spirit,
Which judged mankind at their due estima-
　tion;
　And for coquetry, she disdain'd to wear it:
Secure of admiration, its impression
Was faint as of an every-day possession.

XXXII.

To all she was polite without parade;
　To some she show'd attention of that kind
Which flatters, but is flattery convey'd
　In such a sort as cannot leave behind
A trace unworthy either wife or maid;—
　A gentle, genial courtesy of mind,
To those who were, or pass'd for meritorious,
Just to console sad glory for being glorious;

XXXIII.

Which is in all respects, save now and then,
 A dull and desolate appendage. Gaze
Upon the shades of those distinguish'd men
 Who were or are the puppet-shows of praise,
The praise of persecution. Gaze again
 On the most favour'd; and amidst the
 blaze
Of sunset halos o'er the laurel-brow'd,
What can ye recognise?—a gilded cloud.

XXXIV.

There also was of course in Adeline
 That calm patrician polish in the address,
Which ne'er can pass the equinoctial line
 Of anything which nature would express;
Just as a mandarin finds nothing fine,—
 At least his manner suffers not to guess,
That anything he views can greatly please.
Perhaps we have borrow'd this from the
 Chinese—

XXXV.

Perhaps from Horace: his "*Nil admirari*"
 Was what he call'd the "Art of Happiness;"
An art on which the artists greatly vary,
 And have not yet attain'd to much success.
However, 'tis expedient to be wary:
 Indifference certes don't produce distress;
And rash enthusiasm in good society
Were nothing but a moral inebriety.

XXXVI.

But Adeline was not indifferent: for
 (*Now* for a common-place!) beneath the
 snow,
As a volcano holds the lava more
 Within—*et cætera*. Shall I go on?—No
I hate to hunt down a tired metaphor,
 So let the often-used volcano go.
Poor thing! How frequently, by me and
 others,
It hath been stirr'd up till its smoke quite
 smothers!

XXXVII.

I'll have another figure in a trice:—
 What say you to a bottle of champagne?
Frozen into a very vinous ice,
 Which leaves few drops of that immortal
 rain,
Yet in the very centre, past all price,
 About a liquid glassful will remain;
And this is stronger than the strongest
 grape
Could e'er express in its expanded shape:

XXXVIII.

'Tis the whole spirit brought to a quint-
 essence;
 And thus the chilliest aspects may concentre
A hidden nectar under a cold presence.
 And such are many—though I only meant
 her
From whom I now deduce these moral lessons,
 On which the Muse has always sought to
 enter.
And your cold people are beyond all price,
 When once you've broken their confounded
 ice.

XXXIX.

But after all they are a North-West Passage
 Unto the glowing India of the soul;
And as the good ships sent upon that message
 Have not exactly ascertain'd the Pole
(Though Parry's efforts look a lucky presage),
 Thus gentlemen may run upon a shoal;
For if the Pole's not open, but all frost
(A chance still), 'tis a voyage or vessel lost.

XL.

And young beginners may as well commence
 With quiet cruising o'er the ocean woman;
While those who are not beginners should
 have sense
 Enough to make for port, ere Time shall
 summon
With his grey signal-flag; and the past tense,
 The dreary "*Fuimus*" of all things human,
Must be declined, while life's thin thread's
 spun out
Between the gaping heir and gnawing gout.

XLI.

But heaven must be diverted; its diversion
 Is sometimes truculent—but never mind;
The world upon the whole is worth the assertion
 (If but for comfort) that all things are kind:
And that same devilish doctrine of the
 Persian,
 Of the two principles, but leaves behind
As many doubts as any other doctrine
Has ever puzzled faith withal, or yoked her in.

XLII.

The English winter—ending in July,
 To recommence in August—now was done.
'Tis the postilion's paradise: wheels fly;
 On roads, east, south, north, west, there is
 a run.
But for post-horses who finds sympathy?
 Man's pity for himself, or for his son,
Always premising that said son at college
Has not contracted much more debt than
 knowledge.

XLIII.

The London winter's ended in July—
 Sometimes a little later. I don't err
In this: whatever other blunders lie
 Upon my shoulders, here I must aver
My Muse a glass of weatherology;
 For parliament is our barometer:
Let radicals its other acts attack,
Its sessions form our only almanack

XLIV.

When its quicksilver's down at zero,—lo!
 Coach, chariot, luggage, baggage, equipage!
Wheels whirl from Carlton palace to Soho,
 And happiest they who horses can engage;
The turnpikes glow with dust; and Rotten
 Row
Sleeps from the chivalry of this bright age;
 And tradesmen, with long bills and longer
 faces,
Sigh—as the postboys fasten on the traces.

XLV.

They and their bills, "Arcadians both," are
 left
 To the Greek kalends of another session.
Alas! to them of ready cash bereft,
 What hope remains? Of *hope* the full
 possession
Or generous draft, conceded as a gift,
 At a long date—till they can get a fresh
 one—
Hawk'd about at a discount, small or large;
Also the solace of an overcharge.

XLVI.

But these are trifles. Downward flies my lord,
 Nodding beside my lady in his carriage.
Away! away! "Fresh horses!" are the word,
 And changed as quickly as hearts after
 marriage;
The obsequious landlord hath the change
 restored;
 The postboys have no reason to disparage
Their fee; but ere the water'd wheels may
 hiss hence,
The ostler pleads too for a reminiscence.

XLVII.

'Tis granted; and the valet mounts the
 dickey—
 That gentleman of lords and gentlemen;
Also my lady's gentlewoman, tricky,
 Trick'd out, but modest more than poet's
 pen
Can paint,—" *Cosi viaggino i Ricchi!* "
 (Excuse a foreign slipslop now and then,
If but to show I've travell'd: and what's travel,
Unless it teaches one to quote and cavil?)

XLVIII.

The London winter and the country summer
 Were well nigh over. 'Tis perhaps a pity,
When nature wears the gown that doth
 become her.
To lose those best months in a sweaty city,
 And wait until the nightingale grows dumber,
 Listening debates not very wise or witty,
Ere patriots their true *country* can remem-
 ber;—
But there's no shooting (save grouse) till
 September.

XLIX.

I've done with my tirade. The world was
 gone;
 The twice two thousand, for whom earth
 was made,
Were vanish'd to be what they call alone—
 That is, with thirty servants for parade,
As many guests, or more; before whom groan
 As many covers, duly, daily laid.
Let none accuse old England's hospitality—
Its quantity is but condensed to quality.

L.

Lord Henry and the Lady Adeline
 Departed like the rest of their compeers,
The peerage, to a mansion very fine;
 The Gothic Babel of a thousand years.
None than themselves could boast a longer line,
 Where time through heroes and through
 beauties steers;
And oaks as olden as their pedigree
Told of their sires, a tomb in every tree.

LI.

A paragraph in every paper told
 Of their departure : such is modern fame:
'Tis pity that it takes no further hold
 Than an advertisement, or much the same;
When, ere the ink be dry, the sound grows cold.
 The Morning Post was foremost to pro-
 claim—
" Departure, for his country seat, to-day,
Lord H. Amundeville and Lady A.

LII.

" We understand the splendid host intends
 To entertain, this autumn, a select
And numerous party of his noble friends;
 'Midst whom we have heard, from sources
 quite correct,
The Duke of D—— the shooting season
 spends,
 With many more by rank and fashion
 deck'd;
Also a foreigner of high condition,
The envoy of the secret Russian mission."

LIII.

And thus we see—who doubts the Morning
			Post?
(Whose articles are like the "Thirty-nine,"
Which those most swear to who believe them
			most)—
Our gay Russ Spaniard was ordain'd to shine,
Deck'd by the rays reflected from his host,
	With those who, Pope says, "greatly daring
			dine."—
'T is odd, but true,—last war the News
			abounded
More with these dinners than the kill'd or
			wounded;—

LIV.

As thus: "On Thursday there was a grand
			dinner;
	Present, Lords A.B.C."—Earls, dukes, by
			name
Announced with no less pomp than victory's
			winner:
	Then underneath, and in the very same
Column: date, "Falmouth. There has lately
			been here
	The Slap-dash regiment, so well known to
			fame,
Whose loss in the late action we regret:
The vacancies are fill'd up—see Gazette."

LV.

To Norman Abbey whirl'd the noble pair,—
	An old, old monastery once, and now
Still older mansion,—of a rich and rare
	Mix'd Gothic, such as artists all allow
Few specimens yet left us can compare
	Withal: it lies perhaps a little low,
Because the monks preferr'd a hill behind,
To shelter their devotion from the wind.

LVI.

It stood embosom'd in a happy valley,
	Crown'd by high woodlands, where the
			Druid oak
Stood, like Caractacus, in act to rally
	His host, with broad arms 'gainst the
			thunderstroke,
And from beneath his boughs were seen to
			sally
	The dappled foresters; as day awoke,
The branching stag swept down with all his
			herd,
To quaff a brook which murmur'd like a bird.

LVII.

Before the mansion lay a lucid lake,
	Broad as transparent, deep, and freshly fed
By a river, which its soften'd way did take
	In currents through the calmer water
			spread

Around: the wildfowl nestled in the brake
	And sedges, brooding in their liquid bed:
The woods sloped downwards to its brink,
			and stood
With their green faces fix'd upon the flood.

LVIII.

Its outlet dash'd into a deep cascade,
	Sparkling with foam, until again subsiding,
Its shriller echoes—like an infant made
	Quiet—sank into softer ripples, gliding
Into a rivulet: and thus allay'd,
	Pursued its course, now gleaming, and now
			hiding
Its windings through the woods; now clear,
			now blue,
According as the skies their shadows threw.

LIX.

A glorious remnant of the Gothic pile
	(While yet the church was Rome's) stood
			half apart
In a grand arch, which once screen'd many
			an aisle.
	These last had disappear'd—a loss to art:
The first yet frown'd superbly o'er the soil,
	And kindled feelings in the roughest heart,
Which mourn'd the power of time's or tem-
			pest's march,
In gazing on that venerable arch.

LX.

Within a niche, nigh to its pinnacle,
	Twelve saints had once stood sanctified in
			stone;
But these had fallen, not when the friars fell,
	But in the war which struck Charles from
			his throne,
When each house was a fortalice—as tell
	The annals of full many a line undone,—
The gallant cavaliers, who fought in vain
For those who knew not to resign or reign.

LXI.

But in a higher niche, alone, but crown'd,
	The Virgin-Mother of the God-born Child,
With her Son in her blessed arms, look'd round;
	Spared by some chance when all beside
			was spoil'd;
She made the earth below seem holy ground.
	This may be superstition, weak or wild,
But even the faintest relics of a shrine
Of any worship wake some thoughts divine.

LXII.

A mighty window, hollow in the centre,
	Shorn of its glass of thousand colourings,
Through which the deepen'd glories once
			could enter,
	Streaming from off the sun like seraph's
			wings,

Now yawns all desolate: now loud, now
 fainter,
 The gale sweeps through its fretwork, and
 oft sings
The owl his anthem, where the silenced quire
Lie with their hallelujahs quench'd like fire.

LXIII.

But in the noontide of the moon, and when
 The wind is winged from one point of
 heaven,
There moans a strange unearthly sound,
 which then
Is musical—a dying accent driven
Through the huge arch, which soars and
 sinks again.
Some deem it but the distant echo given
Back to the night wind by the waterfall,
And harmonised by the old choral wall:

LXIV.

Others, that some original shape, or form
 Shaped by decay perchance, hath given the
 power
(Though less than that of Memnon's statue,
 warm
In Egypt's rays, to harp at a fix'd hour)
To this grey ruin, with a voice to charm
 Sad, but serene, it sweeps o'er tree or tower;
The cause I know not, nor can solve; but
 such
The fact:—I've heard it,—once perhaps too
 much.

LXV.

Amidst the court a Gothic fountain play'd,
 Symmetrical, but deck'd with carvings
 quaint—
Strange faces, like to men in masquerade,
 And here perhaps a monster, there a saint:
The spring gush'd through grim mouths of
 granite made,
 And sparkled into basins, where it spent
Its little torrent in a thousand bubbles,
Like man's vain glory, and his vainer troubles.

LXVI.

The mansion's self was vast and venerable,
 With more of the monastic than has been
Elsewhere preserved: the cloisters still were
 stable,
 The cells, too, and refectory, I ween:
An exquisite small chapel had been able,
 Still unimpair'd, to decorate the scene;
The rest had been reform'd, replaced, or
 sunk,
And spoke more of the baron than the
 monk.

LXVII.

Huge halls, long galleries, spacious chambers,
 join'd
By no quite lawful marriage of the arts,
Might shock a connoisseur; but when com-
 bined,
 Form'd a whole which, irregular in parts,
Yet left a grand impression on the mind,
 At least of those whose eyes are in their
 hearts:
We gaze upon a giant for his stature,
Nor judge at first if all be true to nature.

LXVIII.

Steel barons, molten the next generation
 To silken rows of gay and garter'd earls,
Glanced from the walls in goodly preserva-
 tion:
 And Lady Marys blooming into girls,
With fair long locks, had also kept their
 station:
 And countesses mature in robes and pearls:
Also some beauties of Sir Peter Lely,
Whose drapery hints we may admire them
 freely.

LXIX.

Judges in very formidable ermine
 Were there, with brows that did not much
 invite
The accused to think their lordships would
 determine
 His cause by leaning much from might to
 right:
Bishops, who had not left a single sermon;
 Attorneys-general, awful to the sight,
As hinting more (unless our judgments warp
 us)
Of the "Star Chamber" than of "Habeas
 Corpus."

LXX.

Generals, some all in armour, of the old
 And iron time, ere lead had ta'en the lead;
Others in wigs of Marlborough's martial fold,
 Huger than twelve of our degenerate breed:
Lordlings, with staves of white or keys of
 gold:
 Nimrods, whose canvas scarce contain'd
 the steed;
And here and there some stern high patriot
 stood,
Who could not get the place for which he
 sued.

LXXI.

But ever and anon, to soothe your vision,
 Fatigued with these hereditary glories,
There rose a Carlo Dolce or a Titian,
 Or wilder group of savage Salvatore's:

Here danced Albano's boys, and here the sea
 shone
 In Vernet's ocean lights; and there the
 stories
Of martyrs awed, as Spagnoletto tainted
His brush with all the blood of all the sainted.

LXXII.

Here sweetly spread a landscape of Lorraine;
 There Rembrandt made his darkness equal
 light,
Or gloomy Caravaggio's gloomier stain
 Bronzed o'er some lean and stoic anchor-
 ite:—
But, lo! a Teniers woos, and not in vain,
 Your eyes to revel in a livelier sight:
His bell-mouth'd goblet makes me feel quite
 Danish
Or Dutch with thirst—What, ho! a flask of
 Rhenish.

LXXIII.

O reader! if that thou canst read,—and know,
 'Tis not enough to spell, or even to read,
To constitute a reader; there must go
 Virtues of which both you and I have need.
Firstly, begin with the beginning—(though
 That clause is hard); and secondly, pro-
 ceed:
Thirdly, commence not with the end—or,
 sinning
In this sort, end at last with the beginning.

LXXIV.

But reader, thou hast patient been of late,
 While I, without remorse of rhyme, or fear,
Have built and laid out ground at such a rate,
 Dan Phœbus takes me for an auctioneer.
That poets were so from their earliest date,
 By Homer's "Catalogue of ships" is clear;
But a mere modern must be moderate—
 I spare you then the furniture and plate.

LXXV.

The mellow autumn came, and with it came
 The promised party, to enjoy its sweets.
The corn is cut, the manor full of game;
 The pointer ranges, and the sportsman beats
In russet jacket:—lynx-like is his aim;
 Full grows his bag, and wonder*ful* his feats.
Ah, nutbrown partridges! Ah, brilliant
 pheasants!
And ah, ye poachers!—'T is no sport for
 peasants.

LXXVI.

An English autumn, though it hath no vines,
 Blushing with Bacchant coronals along
The paths, o'er which the far festoon entwines
 The red grape in the sunny lands of song,
Hath yet a purchased choice of choicest
 wines;
 The claret light, and the Madeira strong;
If Britain mourn her bleakness, we can tell
 her,
The very best of vineyards is the cellar.

LXXVII.

Then, if she hath not that serene decline
 Which makes the southern autumn's day
 appear
As if 't would to a second spring resign
 The season, rather than to winter drear,—
Of in-door comforts still she hath a mine,—
 The sea-coal fires, the "earliest of the
 year;"
Without doors, too, she may compete in mel-
 low,
As what is lost in green is gain'd in yellow.

LXXVIII.

And for the effeminate *villeggiatura*—
 Rife with more horns than hounds—she
 hath the chase,
So animated that it might allure a
 Saint from his beads to join the jocund
 race;
Even Nimrod's self might leave the plains of
 Dura,
 And wear the Melton jacket for a space:
If she hath no wild boars, she hath a tame
Preserve of bores, who ought to be made
 game.

LXXIX.

The noble guests, assembled at the Abbey,
 Consisted of—we give the sex the *pas*—
The Duchess of Fitz-Fulke; the Countess
 Crabby;
 The Ladies Scilly, Busey;—Miss Eclat,
Miss Bombazeen, Miss Mackstay, Miss
 O'Tabby,
 And Mrs. Rabbi, the rich banker's squaw;
Also the honourable Mrs. Sleep,
Who look'd a white lamb, yet was a black
 sheep:

LXXX.

With other Countesses of Blank—but rank;
 At once the "lie" and the "élite" of
 crowds;
Who pass like water filter'd in a tank,
 All purged and pious from their native
 clouds;
Or paper turn'd to money by the Bank:
 No matter how or why, the passport
 shrouds
The "passée" and the past; for good society
Is no less famed for tolerance than piety,—

LXXXI.

That is, up to a certain point; which point
 Forms the most difficult in punctuation.
Appearances appear to form the joint
 On which it hinges in a higher station;
And so that no explosion cry "Aroint
 Thee, witch!" or each Medea has her
 Jason;
Or (to the point with Horace and with Pulci)
" *Omne tulit punctum*, quæ *miscuit utile
 dulci.*"

LXXXII.

I can't exactly trace their rule of right,
 Which hath a little leaning to a lottery.
I've seen a virtuous woman put down quite
 By the mere combination of a coterie;
Also a so-so matron boldly fight
 Her way back to the world by dint of plot-
 tery,
And shine the very *Siria* of the spheres,
Escaping with a few slight, scarless sneers.

LXXXIII.

I have seen more than I 'll say:—but we will
 see
 How our *villeggiatura* will get on.
The party still consist of thirty-three
 Of highest caste—the Brahmins of the ton.
I have named a few, not foremost in degree,
 But ta'en at hazard as the rhyme may run.
By way of sprinkling, scatter'd amongst
 these
There also were some Irish absentees.

LXXXIV.

There was Parolles, too, the legal bully,
 Who limits all his battles to the bar
And senate: when invited elsewhere, truly,
 He shows more appetite for words than
 war.
There was the young bard Rackrhyme, who
 had newly
 Come out and glimmer'd as a six weeks'
 star.
There was Lord Pyrrho, too, the great free-
 thinker;
And Sir John Pottledeep, the mighty drinker.

LXXXV.

There was the Duke of Dash, who was a—
 duke,
 "Ay, every inch a" duke; there were
 twelve peers
Like Charlemagne's—and all such peers in
 look
 And intellect, that neither eyes nor ears

For commoners had ever them mistook.
 There were the six Miss Rawbolds—pretty
 dears!
All song and sentiment; whose hearts were set
Less on a convent than a coronet.

LXXXVI.

There were four Honourable Misters, whose
 Honour was more before their names than
 after;
There was the preux Chevalier de la Ruse,
 Whom France and Fortune lately deign'd
 to waft here,
Whose chiefly harmless talent was to amuse;
 But the clubs found it rather serious
 laughter,
Because—such was his magic power to
 please—
The dice seem'd charm'd, too, with his re-
 partees.

LXXXVII.

There was Dick Dubious, the metaphysician,
 Who loved philosophy and a good dinner;
Angle, the soi-disant mathematician;
 Sir Henry Silvercup, the great race-winner.
There was the Reverend Rodomont Pre-
 cisian,
 Who did not hate so much the sin as sinner;
And Lord Augustus Fitz-Plantagenet,
Good at all things, but better at a bet.

LXXXVIII.

There was Jack Jargon, the gigantic guards-
 man;
 And General Fireface, famous in the field,
A great tactician, and no less a swordsman,
 Who ate, last war, more Yankees than he
 kill'd.
There was the waggish Welsh Judge, Jef-
 feries Hardsman,
 In his grave office so completely skill'd,
That when a culprit came for condemnation,
He had his judge's joke for consolation.

LXXXIX.

Good company's a chess-board—there are
 kings,
 Queens, bishops, knights, rooks, pawns;
 the world's a game;
Save that the puppets pull at their own
 strings,
 Methinks gay Punch hath something of the
 same.
My Muse, the butterfly hath but her wings,
 Not stings, and flits through ether without
 aim,
Alighting rarely:—were she but a hornet,
Perhaps there might be vices which would
 mourn it.

XC.

I had forgotten—but must not forget—
 An orator, the latest of the session,
Who had deliver'd well a very set
 Smooth speech, his first and maidenly
 transgression
Upon debate: the papers echoed yet
 With his début, which made a strong im-
 pression,
And rank'd with what is every day dis-
 play'd—
"The best first speech that ever yet was
 made."

XCI.

Proud of his "Hear hims!" proud, too, of
 his vote
 And lost virginity of oratory,
Proud of his learning (just enough to quote),
 He revell'd in his Ciceronian glory:
With memory excellent to get by rote,
 With wit to hatch a pun or tell a story,
Graced with some merit, and with more ef-
 frontery,
"His country's pride," he came down to the
 country.

XCII.

There also were two wits by acclamation,
 Longbow from Ireland, Strongbow from
 the Tweed,
Both lawyers and both men of education;
 But Strongbow's wit was of more polish'd
 breed;
Longbow was rich in an imagination
 As beautiful and bounding as a steed,
But sometimes stumbling over a potato,—
While Strongbow's best things might have
 come from Cato.

XCIII.

Strongbow was like a new-tuned harpsichord;
 But Longbow wild as an Æolian harp,
With which the winds of heaven can claim
 accord,
 And make a music, whether flat or sharp.
Of Strongbow's talk you would not change a
 word:
 At Longbow's phrases you might some-
 times carp:
Both wits—one born so, and the other bred,
This by his heart—his rival by his head.

XCIV.

If all these seem a heterogeneous mass
 To be assembled at a country seat,
Yet think, a specimen of every class
 Is better than a humdrum tête-à-tête.

The days of Comedy are gone, alas!
 When Congreve's fool could vie with Mo-
 lière's *bête:*
Society is smooth'd to that excess,
That manners hardly differ more than dress.

XCV.

Our ridicules are kept in the back ground—
 Ridiculous enough, but also dull;
Professions, too, are no more to be found
 Professional; and there is nought to cull
Of folly's fruit; for though your fools
 abound,
 They're barren, and not worth the pains
 to pull.
Society is now one polish'd horde,
Form'd of two mighty tribes, the *Bores* and
 Bored.

XCVI.

But from being farmers, we turn gleaners,
 gleaning
 The scanty but right-well thresh'd ears of
 truth;
And, gentle reader! when you gather meaning,
 You may be Boaz, and I—modest Ruth.
Further I'd quote, but Scripture intervening
 Forbids. A great impression in my youth
Was made by Mrs. Adams, where she cries
"That Scriptures out of church are blasphe-
 mies."

XCVII.

But what we can we glean in this vile age
 Of chaff, although our gleanings be not
 grist.
I must not quite omit the talking sage,
 Kit-Cat, the famous Conversationist,
Who, in his common-place book, had a page
 Prepared each morn for evenings. "List,
 oh list!"
"Alas, poor ghost!"—What unexpected woes
Await those who have studied their bons-
 mots!

XCVIII.

Firstly, they must allure the conversation
 By many windings to their clever clinch;
And secondly, must let slip no occasion,
 Nor *bate* (abate) their hearers of an *inch*,
But take an ell—and make a great sensation,
 If possible; and thirdly, never flinch
When some smart talker puts them to the test,
But seize the last word, which no doubt 's the
 best.

XCIX.

Lord Henry and his lady were the hosts;
 The party we have touch'd on were the
 guests.
Their table was a board to tempt even ghosts
 To pass the Styx for more substantial feasts.

I will not dwell upon ragoûts or roasts,
 Albeit all human history attests
That happiness for man—the hungry sin-
 ner!—
Since Eve ate apples, much depends on din-
 ner.

C.

Witness the lands which "flow'd with milk
 and honey,"
 Held out unto the hungry Israelites:
To this we have added since, the love of
 money,
 The only sort of pleasure which requites.
Youth fades, and leaves our days no longer
 sunny;
 We tire of mistresses and parasites;
But oh, ambrosial cash! Ah! who would lose
 thee?
When we no more can use, or even abuse
 thee!

CI.

The gentlemen got up betimes to shoot,
 Or hunt: the young, because they liked
 the sport—
The first thing boys like after play and fruit;
 The middle-aged, to make the day more
 short;
For *ennui* is a growth of English root,
 Though nameless in our language:—we
 retort
The fact for words, and let the French trans-
 late
That awful yawn which sleep cannot abate.

CII.

The elderly walk'd through the library,
 And tumbled books, or criticised the pic-
 tures,
Or saunter'd through the gardens piteously,
 And made upon the hot-house several stric-
 tures,
Or rode a nag which trotted not too high,
 Or on the morning papers read their lec-
 tures,
Or on the watch their longing eyes would fix,
Longing at sixty for the hour of six.

CIII.

But none were "gêné:" the great hour of
 union
 Was rung by dinner's knell; till then all
 were
Masters of their own time—or in commu-
 nion,
 Or solitary, as they chose to bear

The hours, which how to pass is but to few
 known.
 Each rose up at his own, and had to spare
What time he chose for dress, and broke his
 fast
When, where, and how he chose for that
 repast.

CIV.

The ladies—some rouged, some a little pale—
 Met the morn as they might. If fine, they
 rode,
Or walk'd; if foul, they read, or told a tale,
 Sung, or rehearsed the last dance from
 abroad;
Discuss'd the fashion which might next pre-
 vail,
 And settled bonnets by the newest code,
Or cramm'd twelve sheets into one little
 letter,
To make each correspondent a new debtor.

CV.

For some had absent lovers, all had friends.
 The earth has nothing like a she epistle,
And hardly heaven—because it never ends.
 I love the mystery of a female missal,
Which, like a creed, ne'er says all it intends,
 But full of cunning as Ulysses' whistle,
When he allured poor Dolon:—you had better
Take care what you reply to such a letter.

CVI.

Then there were billiards; cards, too, but *no*
 dice;—
 Save in the clubs no man of honour
 plays;—
Boats when 't was water, skating when 't was
 ice,
 And the hard frost destroy'd the scenting
 days:
And angling, too, that solitary vice,
 Whatever Izaak Walton sings or says:
The quaint, old, cruel coxcomb, in his gullet
Should have a hook, and a small trout to
 pull it.

CVII.

With evening came the banquet and the
 wine;
 The conversazione; the duet,
Attuned by voices more or less divine
 (My heart or head aches with the memory
 yet).
The four Miss Rawbolds in a glee would
 shine;
 But the two youngest loved more to be set
Down to the harp—because to music's
 charms
They added graceful necks, white hands and
 arms.

CVIII.

Sometimes a dance (though rarely on field days,
 For then the gentlemen were rather tired)
Display'd some sylph-like figures in its maze;
 Then there was small-talk ready when required;
Flirtation—but decorous; the mere praise
 Of charms that should or should not be admired.
The hunters fought their fox-hunt o'er again,
And then retreated soberly—at ten.

CIX.

The politicians, in a nook apart,
 Discuss'd the world, and settled all the spheres;
The wits watch'd every loophole for their art,
 To introduce a bon-mot head and ears;
Small is the rest of those who would be smart,
 A moment's good thing may have cost them years
Before they find an hour to introduce it;
And then, even *then*, some bore may make them lose it.

CX.

But all was gentle and aristocratic
 In this our party; polish'd, smooth, and cold,
As Phidian forms cut out of marble Attic.
 There now are no Squire Westerns as of old;
And our Sophias are not so emphatic,
 But fair as then, or fairer to behold.
We have no accomplish'd blackguards, like Tom Jones,
But gentlemen in stays, as stiff as stones.

CXI.

They separated at an early hour;
 That is, ere midnight—which is London's noon;
But in the country ladies seek their bower
 A little earlier than the waning moon.
Peace to the slumbers of each folded flower—
 May the rose call back its true colour soon!
Good hours of fair cheeks are the fairest tinters,
And lower the price of rouge—at least some winters.

Canto the Fourteenth.

I.

If from great nature's or our own abyss
 Of thought we could but snatch a certainty,
Perhaps mankind might find the path they miss—
 But then 't would spoil much good philosophy.

One system eats another up, and this
 Much as old Saturn ate his progeny;
For when his pious consort gave him stones
In lieu of sons, of these he made no bones.

II.

But System doth reverse the Titan's breakfast,
 And eats her parents, albeit the digestion
Is difficult. Pray tell me, can you make fast,
 After due search, your faith to any question?
Look back o'er ages, ere unto the stake fast
 You bind yourself, and call some mode the best one.
Nothing more true than *not* to trust your senses;
And yet what are your other evidences?

III.

For me, I know nought; nothing I deny,
 Admit, reject, contemn; and what know *you*,
Except perhaps that you were born to die?
 And both may after all turn out untrue.
An age may come, Font of Eternity,
 When nothing shall be either old or new.
Death, so call'd, is a thing which makes men weep,
And yet a third of life is pass'd in sleep.

IV.

A sleep without dreams, after a rough day
 Of toil, is what we covet most; and yet
How clay shrinks back from more quiescent clay!
 The very Suicide that pays his debt
At once without instalments (an old way
 Of paying debts, which creditors regret),
Lets out impatiently his rushing breath,
Less from disgust of life than dread of death.

V.

'Tis round him, near him, here, there, everywhere,
 And there 's a courage which grows out of fear,
Perhaps of all most desperate, which will dare
 The worst to *know* it:—when the mountains rear
Their peaks beneath your human foot, and there
 You look down o'er the precipice, and drear
The gulf of rock yawns,—you can't gaze a minute,
Without an awful wish to plunge within it.

VI.

'T is true, you don't—but, pale and struck
　　with terror,
　Retire: but look into your past impression!
And you will find, though shuddering at the
　　mirror
　Of your own thoughts, in all their self-
　　confession,
The lurking bias, be it truth or error,
　To the *unknown;* a secret prepossession,
To plunge with all your fears—but where?
　　You know not,
And that's the reason why you do—or do not.

VII.

But what's this to the purpose? you will say.
　Gent. reader, nothing; a mere speculation,
For which my sole excuse is—'t is my way;
　Sometimes *with* and sometimes without
　　occasion,
I write what's uppermost, without delay;
　This narrative is not meant for narration,
But a mere airy and fantastic basis,
To build up common things with common
　　places.

VIII.

You know, or don't know, that great Bacon
　　saith,
　"Fling up a straw, 't will show the way the
　　wind blows;"
And such a straw, borne on by human breath,
　Is poesy, according as the mind glows;
A paper kite which flies 'twixt life and death,
　A shadow which the onward soul behind
　　throws:
And mine's a bubble, not blown up for praise,
But just to play with, as an infant plays.

IX.

The world is all before me—or behind;
　For I have seen a portion of that same,
And quite enough for me to keep in mind;—
　Of passions, too, I have proved enough to
　　blame,
To the great pleasure of our friends, man-
　　kind,
　Who like to mix some slight alloy with
　　fame;
For I was rather famous in my time,
Until I fairly knock'd it up with rhyme.

X.

I have brought this world about my ears, and
　　eke
　The other; that's to say, the clergy—who
Upon my head have bid their thunders break
In pious libels by no means a few.

And yet I can't help scribbling once a week,
　Tiring old readers, nor discovering new.
In youth I wrote because my mind was full,
And now because I feel it growing dull.

XI.

But "why then publish?"—There are no
　　rewards,
　Of fame or profit when the world grows
　　weary.
I ask in turn,—Why do you play at cards?
　Why drink? Why read?—To make some
　　hour less dreary.
It occupies me to turn back regards
　On what I've seen or ponder'd, sad or
　　cheery;
And what I write I cast upon the stream,
To swim or sink—I have had at least my
　　dream.

XII.

I think that were I *certain* of success,
　I hardly could compose another line:
So long I've battled either more or less,
　That no defeat can drive me from the Nine.
This feeling 't is not easy to express,
　And yet 't is not affected, I opine.
In play, there are two pleasures for your
　　choosing—
The one is winning, and the other losing.

XIII.

Besides, my Muse by no means deals in
　　fiction:
　She gathers a repertory of facts,
Of course with some reserve and slight
　　restriction,
　But mostly sings of human things and
　　acts—
And that's one cause she meets with contra-
　　diction;
　For too much truth, at first sight, ne'er
　　attracts;
And were her object only what's call'd glory,
With more ease too she'd tell a different
　　story.

XIV.

Love, war, a tempest—surely there's variety:
　Also a seasoning slight of lucubration;
A bird's eye view, too, of that wild, Society;
　A slight glance thrown on men of every
　　station.
If you have nought else, here's at least
　　satiety,
　Both in performance and in preparation;
And though these lines should only line
　　portmanteaus,
Trade will be all the better for these Cantos.

XV.

The portion of this world which I at present
 Have taken up to fill the following sermon,
Is one of which there's no description recent:
 The reason why, is easy to determine:
Although it seems both prominent and pleasant,
 There is a sameness in its gems and ermine,
A dull and family likeness through all ages,
Of no great promise for poetic pages.

XVI.

With much to excite, there's little to exalt;
 Nothing that speaks to all men and all times;
A sort of varnish over every fault;
 A kind of common-place, even in their crimes;
Factitious passions, wit without much salt,
 A want of that true nature which sublimes
Whate'er it shows with truth; a smooth monotony
Of character, in those at least who have got any.

XVII.

Sometimes, indeed, like soldiers off parade,
 They break their ranks and gladly leave the drill;
But then the roll-call draws them back afraid,
 And they must be or seem what they were: still
Doubtless it is a brilliant masquerade:
 But when of the first sight you have had your fill,
It palls—at least it did so upon me,
This paradise of pleasure and ennui.

XVIII.

When we have made our love, and gamed our gaming,
 Drest, voted, shone, and, may be, something more;
With dandies dined; heard senators declaiming;
 Seen beauties brought to market by the score,
Sad rakes to sadder husbands chastely taming;
 There's little left but to be bored or bore.
Witness those "ci-devant jeunes hommes" who stem
The stream, nor leave the world which leaveth them.

XIX.

'Tis said—indeed a general complaint—
 That no one has succeeded in describing
The monde, exactly as they ought to paint:
 Some say, that authors only snatch, by bribing
The porter, some slight scandals strange and quaint,
 To furnish matter for their moral gibing;
And that their books have but one style in common—
My lady's prattle, filter'd through her woman.

XX.

But this can't well be true, just now; for writers
 Are grown of the beau monde a part potential:
I've seen them balance even the scale with fighters,
 Especially when young, for that's essential.
Why do their sketches fail them as inditers
 Of what they deem themselves most consequential,
The *real* portrait of the highest tribe?
'T is that, in fact, there's little to describe.

XXI.

"*Haud ignara loquor;*" these are *Nugœ*,
 "*quarum*
 Pars parva *fui,*" but still art and part.
Now I could much more easily sketch a harem,
 A battle, wreck, or history of the heart,
Than these things; and besides, I wish to spare 'em,
 For reasons which I choose to keep apart.
"*Vetabo Cereris sacrum qui vulgarit*"—
Which means, that vulgar people must not share it.

XXII.

And therefore what I throw off is ideal—
 Lower'd, leaven'd, like a history of freemasons;
Which bears the same relation to the real,
 As Captain Parry's voyage may do to Jason's.
The grand arcanum's not for men to see all;
 My music has some mystic diapasons;
And there is much which could not be appreciated
In any manner by the uninitiated.

XXIII.

Alas! worlds fall—and woman, since she fell'd
 The world (as, since that history, less polite
Than true, hath been a creed so strictly held),
 Has not yet given up the practice quite.

Poor thing of usages! coerced, compell'd,
　Victim when wrong, and martyr oft when
　　right,
Condemn'd to child-bed, as men for their sins
Have shaving too entail'd upon their chins,—

XXIV.

A daily plague, which in the aggregate
　May average on the whole with parturition.
But as to women, who can penetrate
　The real sufferings of their she condition?
Man's very sympathy with their estate
　Has much of selfishness, and more sus-
　　picion.
Their love, their virtue, beauty, education,
But form good housekeepers, to breed a
　nation.

XXV.

All this were very well, and can't be better;
　But even this is difficult, Heaven knows,
So many troubles from her birth beset her,
　Such small distinction between friends and
　　foes,
The gilding wears so soon from off her fetter,
　That——but ask any woman if she'd choose
(Take her at thirty, that is) to have been
Female or male? a schoolboy or a queen?

XXVI.

"Petticoat influence" is a great reproach,
　Which even those who obey would fain be
　　thought
To fly from, as from hungry pikes a roach;
　But since beneath it upon earth we are
　　brought,
By various joltings of life's hackney coach,
　I for one venerate a petticoat—
A garment of a mystical sublimity,
No matter whether russet, silk, or dimity.

XXVII.

Much I respect, and much I have adored,
　In my young days, that chaste and goodly
　　veil,
Which holds a treasure, like a miser's hoard,
　And more attracts by all it doth conceal—
A golden scabbard on a Damasque sword,
　A loving letter with a mystic seal,
A cure for grief—for what can ever rankle
Before a petticoat and peeping ankle?

XXVIII.

And when upon a silent, sullen day,
　With a sirocco, for example, blowing,
When even the sea looks dim with all its
　spray,
　And sulkily the river's ripple's flowing,

And the sky shows that very ancient gray,
　The sober, sad antithesis to glowing,—
'Tis pleasant, if *then* anything is pleasant,
To catch a glimpse even of a pretty peasant.

XXIX.

We left our heroes and our heroines
　In that fair clime which don't depend on
　　climate,
Quite independent of the Zodiac's signs,
　Though certainly more difficult to rhyme at,
Because the sun, and stars, and aught that
　shines,
　Mountains, and all we can be most sublime
　　at,
Are there oft dull and dreary as a *dun*—
Whether a sky's or tradesman's is all one.

XXX.

An in-door life is less poetical;
　And out-of-door hath showers, and mists,
　　and sleet,
With which I could not brew a pastoral.
　But be it as it may, a bard must meet
All difficulties, whether great or small,
　To spoil his undertaking, or complete,
And work away like spirit upon matter,
Embarrass'd somewhat both with fire and
　water.

XXXI.

Juan—in this respect, at least, like saints—
　Was all things unto people of all sorts,
And lived contentedly, without complaints,
　In camps, in ships, in cottages, or courts—
Born with that happy soul which seldom faints,
　And mingling modestly in toils or sports.
He likewise could be most things to all
　women,
Without the coxcombry of certain *she* men.

XXXII.

A fox-hunt to a foreigner is strange;
　'Tis also subject to the double danger
Of tumbling first, and having in exchange
　Some pleasant jesting at the awkward
　　stranger;
But Juan had been early taught to range
　The wilds, as doth an Arab turn'd avenger,
So that his horse, or charger, hunter, hack,
Knew that he had a rider on his back.

XXXIII.

And now in this new field, with some ap-
　plause,
　He clear'd hedge, ditch, and double post,
　　and rail,
And never *craned*, and made but few "*faux
　pas*,"
　And only fretted when the scent 'gan fail.

He broke, 'tis true, some statutes of the laws
　　Of hunting—for the sagest youth is frail;
Rode o'er the hounds, it may be, now and
　　then,
And once o'er several country gentlemen.

XXXIV.

But on the whole, to general admiration
　　He acquitted both himself and horse: the
　　　squires
Marvell'd at merit of another nation;
　　The boors cried "Dang it! who'd have
　　　thought it?"—Sires,
The Nestors of the sporting generation,
　　Swore praises, and recall'd their former
　　　fires;
The huntsman's self relented to a grin,
And rated him almost a whipper-in.

XXXV.

Such were his trophies—not of spear and
　　shield,
　　But leaps, and bursts, and sometimes foxes'
　　　brushes;
Yet I must own,—although in this I yield
　　To patriot sympathy a Briton's blushes,—
He thought at heart like courtly Chesterfield,
　　Who, after a long chase o'er hills, dales,
　　　bushes,
And what not, though he rode beyond all
　　price,
Ask'd next day, "If men ever hunted *twice*?"

XXXVI.

He also had a quality uncommon
　　To early risers after a long chase,
Who wake in winter ere the cock can sum-
　　mon
December's drowsy day to his dull race,—
A quality agreeable to woman,
　　When her soft, liquid words run on apace,
Who likes a listener, whether saint or sin-
　　ner,—
He did not fall asleep just after dinner;

XXXVII.

But, light and airy, stood on the alert,
　　And shone in the best part of dialogue,
By humouring always what they might assert,
　　And listening to the topics most in vogue,—
Now grave, now gay, but never dull or pert;
　　And smiling but in secret—cunning rogue!—
He ne'er presumed to make an error clearer;—
In short, there never was a better hearer.

XXXVIII.

And then he danced,—all foreigners excel
　　The serious Angles in the eloquence
Of pantomime,—he danced, I say, right well,
　　With emphasis, and also with good sense—

A thing in footing indispensable;
　　He danced without theatrical pretence,
Not like a ballet-master in the van
Of his drill'd nymphs, but like a gentleman.

XXXIX.

Chaste were his steps, each kept within due
　　bound,
　　And elegance was sprinkled o'er his figure;
Like swift Camilla, he scarce skimm'd the
　　ground,
　　And rather held in than put forth his
　　　vigour;
And then he had an ear for music's sound,
　　Which might defy a crotchet critic's rigour.
Such classic pas—sans flaws—set off our
　　hero,
He glanced like a personified Bolero;

XL.

Or, like a flying Hour before Aurora,
　　In Guido's famous fresco, which alone
Is worth a tour to Rome, although no more a
　　Remnant were there of the old world's sole
　　　throne.
The "*tout ensemble*" of his movements wore a
　　Grace of the soft ideal, seldom shown,
And ne'er to be described; for to the dolour
Of bards and prosers, words are void of
　　colour.

XLI.

No marvel then he was a favourite;
　　A full-grown Cupid, very much admired;
A little spoilt, but by no means so quite;
　　At least he kept his vanity retired.
Such was his tact, he could alike delight
　　The chaste, and those who are not so much
　　　inspired.
The Duchess of Fitz-Fulke, who loved "*tra-
　　casserie*,"
Began to treat him with some small "*aga-
　　cerie*."

XLII.

She was a fine and somewhat full-blown
　　blonde,
　　Desirable, distinguish'd, celebrated
For several winters in the grand, *grande
　　monde*.
　　I'd rather not say what might be related
Of her exploits, for this were ticklish ground;
　　Besides there might be falsehood in what's
　　　stated;
Her late performance had been a dead set
At Lord Augustus Fitz-Plantagenet.

XLIII.

This noble personage began to look
　　A little black upon this new flirtation;
But such small licences must lovers brook,
　　Mere freedoms of the female corporation.

Woe to the man who ventures a rebuke !
 'T will but precipitate a situation
Extremely disagreeable, but common
To calculators when they count on woman.

XLIV.

The circle smiled, then whisper'd, and then
 sneer'd ;
 The misses bridled, and the matrons
 frown'd ;
Some hoped things might not turn out as
 they fear'd ;
 Some would not deem such women could
 be found ;
Some ne'er believed one half of what they
 heard ;
 Some look'd perplex'd, and others look'd
 profound ;
And several pitied with sincere regret
Poor Lord Augustus Fitz-Plantagenet.

XLV.

But what is odd, none ever named the duke,
 Who, one might think, was something in
 the affair :
True, he was absent, and, 't was rumour'd,
 took
 But small concern about the when, or
 where,
Or what his consort did : if he could brook
 Her gaieties, none had a right to stare :
Theirs was that best of unions, past all doubt,
Which never meets, and therefore can't fall
 out.

XLVI.

But, oh ! that I should ever pen so sad a line !
 Fired with an abstract love of virtue, she,
My Dian of the Ephesians, Lady Adeline,
 Began to think the duchess' conduct free ;
Regretting much that she had chosen so bad
 a line,
 And waxing chiller in her courtesy,
Look'd grave and pale to see her friend's
 fragility,
For which most friends reserve their sensi-
 bility.

XLVII.

There 's nought in this bad world like sym-
 pathy ;
 'T is so becoming to the soul and face,
Sets to soft music the harmonious sigh,
 And robes sweet friendship in a Brussels
 lace.
Without a friend, what were humanity,
 To hunt our errors up with a good grace ?
Consoling us with—"Would you had thought
 twice !
Ah ! if you had but follow'd my advice !"

XLVIII.

O Job ! you had two friends : one 's quite
 enough,
 Especially when we are ill at ease ;
They are but bad pilots when the weather 's
 rough,
 Doctors less famous for their cures than
 fees.
Let no man grumble when his friends fall off,
 As they will do like leaves at the first
 breeze :
When your affairs come round, one way or
 t' other,
Go to the coffee-house, and take another.

XLIX.

But this is not my maxim : had it been,
 Some heart-aches had been spared me : yet
 I care not—
I would not be a tortoise in his screen
 Of stubborn shell, which waves and weather
 wear not ;
'Tis better on the whole to have felt and
 seen
 That which humanity may bear, or bear
 not ;
'T will teach discernment to the sensitive,
And not to pour their ocean in a sieve.

L.

Of all the horrid, hideous notes of woe,
 Sadder than owl-songs or the midnight
 blast,
Is that portentous phrase, " I told you so,"
 Utter'd by friends, those prophets of the
 past,
Who, 'stead of saying what you now should
 do,
 Own they foresaw that yóu wóuld fall at
 last,
And solace your slight lapse 'gainst " bonos
 mores,"
With a long memorandum of old stories.

LI.

The Lady Adeline's serene severity
 Was not confined to feeling for her friend,
Whose fame she rather doubted with pos-
 terity,
 Unless her habits should begin to mend :
But Juan also shared in her austerity,
 But mix'd with pity, pure as e'er was
 penn'd :
His inexperience moved her gentle ruth,
And (as her junior by six weeks) his youth.

LII.

These forty days' advantage of her years—
　And hers were those which can face cal-
　　culation,
Boldly referring to the list of peers
　And noble births, nor dread the enumera-
　　tion—
Gave her a right to have maternal fears
　For a young gentleman's fit education,
Though she was far from that leap year,
　　whose leap,
In female dates, strikes Time all of a heap.

LIII.

This may be fix'd at somewhere before
　　thirty—
　Say seven-and-twenty; for I never knew
The strictest in chronology and virtue
　Advance beyond, while they could pass for
　　new.
O Time! why dost not pause? Thy scythe,
　　so dirty
　With rust, should surely cease to hack and
　　hew.
Reset it: shave more smoothly, also slower,
If but to keep thy credit as a mower.

LIV.

But Adeline was far from that ripe age,
　Whose ripeness is but bitter at the best:
'Twas rather her experience made her sage,
　For she had seen the world and stood its
　　test,
As I have said in—I forget what page;
　My Muse despises reference, as you have
　　guess'd
By this time;—but strike six from seven-
　　and-twenty,
And you will find her sum of years in plenty.

LV.

At sixteen she came out; presented, vaunted,
　She put all coronets into commotion:
At seventeen, too, the world was still en-
　　chanted
　With the new Venus of their brilliant
　　ocean:
At eighteen, though below her feet still
　　panted
　A hecatomb of suitors with devotion,
She had consented to create again
That Adam, call'd "the happiest of men."

LVI.

Since then she had sparkled through three
　　glowing winters,
　Admired, adored; but also so correct,
That she had puzzled all the acutest hinters,
　Without the apparel of being circumspect:

They could not even glean the slightest
　　splinters
　From off the marble, which had no defect.
She had also snatch'd a moment since her
　　marriage
To bear a son and heir—and one miscar-
　　riage.

LVII.

Fondly the wheeling fire-flies flew around
　　her,
　Those little glitterers of the London night;
But none of these possess'd a sting to wound
　　her—
　She was a pitch beyond a coxcomb's flight.
Perhaps she wish'd an aspirant profounder;
　But whatsoe'er she wish'd, she acted right;
And whether coldness, pride, or virtue,
　　dignify
A woman, so she's good, what does it
　　signify?

LVIII.

I hate a motive, like a lingering bottle
　Which with the landlord makes too long a
　　stand,
Leaving all claretless the unmoisten'd throttle,
　Especially with politics on hand;
I hate it, as I hate a drove of cattle,
　Who whirl the dust as simooms whirl the
　　sand;
I hate it, as I hate an argument,
A laureate's ode, or servile peer's "content."

LIX.

'Tis sad to hack into the roots of things,
　They are so much intertwisted with the
　　earth;
So that the branch a goodly verdure flings,
　I reck not if an acorn gave it birth.
To trace all actions to their secret springs
　Would make indeed some melancholy
　　mirth;
But this is not at present my concern,
And I refer you to wise Oxenstiern.

LX.

With the kind view of saving an éclat,
　Both to the duchess and diplomatist,
The Lady Adeline, as soon 's she saw
　That Juan was unlikely to resist—
(For foreigners don't know that a *faux
　　pas*
　In England ranks quite on a different list
From those of other lands unblest with
　　juries,
Whose verdict for such sin a certain cure
　　is;—)

LXI.

The Lady Adeline resolved to take
　Such measures as she thought might best
　　impede
The further progress of this sad mistake.
　She thought with some simplicity indeed;
But innocence is bold even at the stake,
　And simple in the world, and doth not need
Nor use those palisades by dames erected,
Whose virtue lies in never being detected.

LXII.

It was not that she fear'd the very worst:
　His Grace was an enduring, married man,
And was not likely all at once to burst
　Into a scene, and swell the clients' clan
Of Doctors' Commons: but she dreaded first
　The magic of her Grace's talisman,
And next a quarrel (as he seem'd to fret)
With Lord Augustus Fitz-Plantagenet.

LXIII.

Her Grace, too, pass'd for being an intri-
　gante,
　And somewhat *méchante* in her amorous
　　sphere:
One of those pretty, precious plagues, which
　haunt
A lover with caprices soft and dear,
That like to *make* a quarrel, when they can't
　Find one, each day of the delightful year;
Bewitching, torturing, as they freeze or
　glow,
And—what is worst of all—won't let you go;

LXIV.

The sort of thing to turn a young man's
　head,
　Or make a Werter of him in the end.
No wonder then a purer soul should dread
　This sort of chaste *liaison* for a friend;
It were much better to be wed or dead,
　Than wear a heart a woman loves to rend.
'T is best to pause, and think, ere you rush
　on,
If that a "*bonne fortune*" be really "*bonne*."

LXV.

And first, in the o'erflowing of her heart,
　Which really knew or thought it knew no
　　guile,
She call'd her husband now and then apart,
　And bade him counsel Juan.　With a
　　smile
Lord Henry heard her plans of artless art
　To wean Don Juan from the siren's wile;
And answer'd, like a statesman or a prophet,
In such guise that she could make nothing
　of it.

LXVI.

Firstly, he said, "he never interfered
　In anybody's business but the king's:"
Next, that "he never judged from what
　appear'd,
　Without strong reason, of those sort of
　　things:"
Thirdly, that "Juan had more brain than
　beard,
　And was not to be held in leading strings;"
And fourthly, what need hardly be said
　twice,
"That good but rarely came from good ad-
　vice."

LXVII.

And, therefore, doubtless to approve the
　truth
　Of the last axiom, he advised his spouse
To leave the parties to themselves, for-
　sooth—
　At least as far as *bienséance* allows:
That time would temper Juan's faults of
　youth;
　That young men rarely made monastic
　　vows;
That opposition only more attaches——
But here a messenger brought in despatches:

LXVIII.

And being of the council call'd "the Privy,"
　Lord Henry walk'd into his cabinet,
To furnish matter for some future Livy
　To tell how he reduced the nation's debt;
And if their full contents I do not give ye,
　It is because I do not know them yet;
But I shall add them in a brief appendix,
To come between mine epic and its index.

LXIX.

But ere he went, he added a slight hint,
　Another gentle common-place or two,
Such as are coin'd in conversation's mint,
　And pass, for want of better, though not
　　new:
Then broke his packet, to see what was in 't,
　And having casually glanced it through,
Retired: and, as he went out, calmly kiss'd
　her,
Less like a young wife than an aged sister.

LXX.

He was a cold, good, honourable man,
　Proud of his birth, and proud of every-
　　thing;
A goodly spirit for a state divan,
　A figure fit to walk before a king;

Tall, stately, form'd to lead the courtly van
 On birthdays, glorious with a star and
 string;
The very model of a chamberlain—
And such I mean to make him when I reign.

LXXI.

But there was something wanting on the
 whole—
 I don't know what, and therefore cannot
 tell—
Which pretty women—the sweet souls !—
 call *soul.*
Certes it was not body; he was well
Proportion'd, as a poplar or a pole,
 A handsome man, that human miracle;
And in each circumstance of love or war
Had still preserved his perpendicular.

LXXII.

Still there was something wanting, as I've
 said—
 That undefinable " *Je ne sçais quoi,*"
Which, for what I know, may of yore have
 led
To Homer's Iliad, since it drew to Troy
 The Greek Eve, Helen, from the Spartan's
 bed;
 Though on the whole, no doubt, the Dardan
 boy
Was much inferior to King Menelaüs :—
But thus it is some women will betray us.

LXXIII.

There is an awkward thing which much per-
 plexes,
 Unless like wise Tiresias we had proved
By turns the difference of the several sexes;
 Neither can show quite *how* they would be
 loved.
The sensual for a short time but connects
 us—
 The sentimental boasts to be unmoved;
But both together form a kind of centaur,
Upon whose back 't is better not to venture.

LXXIV.

A something all-sufficient for the *heart*
 Is that for which the sex are always
 seeking :
But how to fill up that same vacant part?
 There lies the rub—and this they are but
 weak in.
Frail mariners afloat without a chart,
 They run before the wind through high
 seas breaking;
And when they have made the shore through
 every shock,
'T is odd, or odds, it may turn out a rock.

LXXV.

There is a flower call'd "Love in Idleness,"
 For which see Shakespeare's ever-blooming
 garden;—
I will not make his great description less,
 And beg his British godship's humble
 pardon,
If, in my extremity of rhyme's distress,
 I touch a single leaf where he is warden ;—
But though the flower is different, with the
 French
Or Swiss Rousseau, cry " *Voilà la Per-*
 venche ! "

LXXVI.

Eureka ! I have found it ! What I mean
 To say is, not that love is idleness,
But that in love such idleness has been
 An accessory, as I have cause to guess.
Hard labour 's an indifferent go-between ;
 Your men of business are not apt to express
Much passion, since the merchant-ship, the
 Argo,
Convey'd Medea as her supercargo.

LXXVII.

" *Beatus ille procul !*" from " *negotiis,*"
 Saith Horace : the great little poet's
 wrong;
His other maxim, " *Noscitur à sociis,*"
 Is much more to the purpose of his song ;
Though even that were sometimes too
 ferocious,
 Unless good company be kept too long ;
But, in his teeth, whate'er their state or
 station,
Thrice happy they who *have* an occupation !

LXXVIII.

Adam exchanged his Paradise for ploughing,
 Eve made up millinery with fig leaves—
The earliest knowledge from the tree so
 knowing,
 As far as I know, that the church re-
 ceives :
And since that time it need not cost much
 showing,
 That many of the ills o'er which man
 grieves,
And still more women, spring from not em-
 ploying
Some hours to make the remnant worth
 enjoying.

LXXIX.

And hence high life is oft a dreary void,
 A rack of pleasures, where we must invent
A something wherewithal to be annoy'd.
 Bards may sing what they please about
 Content ;

Contented, when translated, means but
　　cloy'd ;
And hence arise the woes of sentiment,
Blue-devils, and blue-stockings, and romances
Reduced to practice, and perform'd like
　　dances.

LXXX.

I do declare, upon an affidavit,
　　Romances I ne'er read like those I have
　　　　seen ;
Nor, if unto the world I ever gave it,
　　Would some believe that such a tale had
　　　　been :
But such intent I never had, nor have it ;
　　Some truths are better kept behind a
　　　　screen,
Especially when they would look like lies,
I therefore deal in generalities.

LXXXI.

"An oyster may be cross'd in love,"—and
　　why ?
Because he mopeth idly in his shell,
And heaves a lonely subterraqueous sigh,
　　Much as a monk may do within his cell :
And *à-propos* of monks, their piety
　　With sloth hath found it difficult to dwell ;
Those vegetables of the Catholic creed
Are apt exceedingly to run to seed.

LXXXII.

O Wilberforce ! thou man of black renown,
　　Whose merit none enough can sing or say,
Thou hast struck one immense Colossus down,
　　Thou moral Washington of Africa !
But there 's another little thing, I own,
　　Which you should perpetrate some sum-
　　　　mer's day,
And set the other half of earth to rights ;
　　You have freed the *blacks*—now pray shut up
　　　　the whites.

LXXXIII.

Shut up the bald-coot bully Alexander !
　　Ship off the Holy Three to Senegal ;
Teach them that " sauce for goose is sauce
　　　　for gander,"
　　And ask them how *they* like to be in thrall ?
Shut up each high heroic salamander,
　　Who eats fire gratis (since the pay 's but
　　　　small);
Shut up—no, *not* the King, but the Pavilion,
Or else 't will cost us all another million.

LXXXIV.

Shut up the world at large, let Bedlam out ;
　　And you will be perhaps surprised to find
All things pursue exactly the same route,
　　As now with those of *soi-disant* sound mind.

This I could prove beyond a single doubt,
　　Were there a jot of sense among mankind ;
But till that *point d'appui* is found, alas !
Like Archimedes, I leave earth as 't was.

LXXXV.

Our gentle Adeline had one defect—
　　Her heart was vacant, though a splendid
　　　　mansion ;
Her conduct had been perfectly correct,
　　As she had seen nought claiming its ex-
　　　　pansion.
A wavering spirit may be easier wreck'd,
　　Because 't is frailer, doubtless, than a stanch
　　　　one ;
But when the latter works its own undoing,
Its inner crash is like an earthquake's ruin.

LXXXVI.

She loved her lord, or thought so ; but *that*
　　love
　　Cost her an effort, which is a sad toil,
The stone of Sysiphus, if once we move
　　Our feelings 'gainst the nature of the soil.
She had nothing to complain of, or reprove,
　　No bickerings, no connubial turmoil :
Their union was a model to behold,
Serene and noble,—conjugal, but cold.

LXXXVII.

There was no great disparity of years,
　　Though much in temper ; but they never
　　　　clash'd :
They moved like stars united in their
　　　　spheres,
　　Or like the Rhone by Leman's waters
　　　　wash'd,
Where mingled and yet separate appears
　　The river from the lake, all bluely dash'd
Through the serene and placid glassy deep,
Which fain would lull its river-child to sleep.

LXXXVIII.

Now when she once had ta'en an interest
　　In anything, however she might flatter
Herself that her intentions were the best,
　　Intense intentions are a dangerous matter :
Impressions were much stronger than she
　　　　guess'd,
　　And gather'd as they run like growing
　　　　water
Upon her mind : the more so, as her breast
Was not at first too readily impress'd.

LXXXIX.

But when it was, she had that lurking demon
　　Of double nature, and thus doubly named—
Firmness yclept in heroes, kings, and seamen,
　　That is, when they succeed ; but greatly
　　　　blamed

As *obstinacy*, both in men and women,
　Whene'er their triumph pales, or star is
　　tamed :—
And 'twill perplex the casuist in morality
To fix the due bounds of this dangerous
　quality.

XC.

Had Buonaparte won at Waterloo,
　It had been firmness ; now 'tis pertinacity :
Must the event decide between the two ?
　I leave it to your people of sagacity
To draw the line between the false and true,
　If such can e'er be drawn by man's capacity :
My business is with Lady Adeline,
Who in her way too was a heroine.

XCI.

She knew not her own heart ; then how
　　should I ?
　I think not she was *then* in love with Juan :
If so, she would have had the strength to fly
　The wild sensation, unto her a new one :
She merely felt a common sympathy
　(I will not say it was a false or true one)
In him, because she thought he was in dan-
　ger,—
Her husband's friend, her own, young, and
　a stranger.

XCII.

She was, or thought she was, his friend—
　　and this
　Without the farce of friendship, or ro-
　　mance
Of platonism, which leads so oft amiss
　Ladies who have studied friendship but in
　　France,
Or Germany, where people *purely* kiss.
　To thus much Adeline would not advance ;
But of such friendship as man's may to man
　be
She was as capable as woman can be.

XCIII.

No doubt the secret influence of the sex
　Will there, as also in the ties of blood,
An innocent predominance annex,
　And tune the concord to a finer mood.
If free from passion, which all friendship
　checks,
　And your true feelings fully understood,
No friend like to a woman earth discovers,
So that you have not been nor will be lovers.

XCIV.

Love bears within its breast the very germ
　Of change ; and how should this be other-
　　wise ?
That violent things more quickly find a term
　Is shown through nature's whole analogies ;

And how should the most fierce of all be
　firm ?
　Would you have endless lightning in the
　· skies ?
Methinks Love's very title says enough :
How should "the *tender* passion" e'er be
　tough ?

XCV.

Alas ! by all experience, seldom yet
　(I merely quote what I have heard from
　　many)
Had lovers not some reason to regret
　The passion which made Solomon a zany.
I've also seen some wives (not to forget
　The marriage state, the best or worst of
　　any)
Who were the very paragons of wives,
Yet made the misery of at least two lives.

XCVI.

I've also seen some female *friends* ('tis odd,
　But true—as, if expedient, I could prove)
That faithful were through thick and thin,
　　abroad,
　At home, far more than ever yet was
　　Love—
Who did not quit me when Oppression trod
　Upon me ; whom no scandal could remove ;
Who fought, and fight, in absence, too, my
　battles,
Despite the snake Society's loud rattles.

XCVII.

Whether Don Juan and chaste Adeline
　Grew friends in this or any other sense,
Will be discuss'd hereafter, I opine :
　At present I am glad of a pretence
To leave them hovering, as the effect is fine,
　And keeps the atrocious reader in *suspense* :
The surest way for ladies and for books
To bait their tender or their tenter hooks.

XCVIII.

Whether they rode, or walk'd, or studied
　Spanish,
　To read Don Quixote in the original,
A pleasure before which all others vanish ;
　Whether their talk was of the kind call'd
　　"small,"
Or serious, are the topics I must banish
　To the next Canto ; where perhaps I shall
Say something to the purpose, and display
Considerable talent in my way.

XCIX.

Above all, I beg all men to forbear
　Anticipating aught about the matter :
They'll only make mistakes about the fair,
　And Juan too, especially the latter.

And I shall take a much more serious air
　Than I have yet done, in this epic satire.
It is not clear that Adeline and Juan
Will fall; but if they do,'t will be their ruin.

C.

But great things spring from little :—Would
　　you think,
　That in our youth, as dangerous a passion
As e'er brought man and woman to the brink
Of ruin, rose from such a slight occasion,
As few would ever dream could form the link
　Of such a sentimental situation?
You 'll never guess, I'll bet you millions,
　　milliards—
It all sprung from a harmless game at bil-
　　liards.

CI.

'T is strange,—but true; for truth is always
　　strange;
　Stranger than fiction: if it could be told,
How much would novels gain by the ex-
　　change !
　How differently the world would men be-
　　hold !
How oft would vice and virtue places change!
　The new world would be nothing to the
　　old,
If some Columbus of the moral seas
Would show mankind their souls' antipodes.

CII.

What "antres vast and deserts idle" then
　Would be discover'd in the human soul !
What icebergs in the hearts of mighty men,
　With self-love in the centre as their pole !
What Anthropophagi are nine or ten
　Of those who hold the kingdoms in control !
Were things but only 'call'd by their right
　　name,
Cæsar himself would be ashamed of fame.

———◆———

Canto the Fifteenth.

I.

Ah !—What should follow slips from my re-
　　flection ;
　Whatever follows ne'ertheless may be
As à-propos of hope or retrospection,
　As though the lurking thought had fol-
　　low'd free.
All present life is but an interjection,
　An "Oh !" or "Ah !" of joy or misery,
Or a "Ha ! ha !" or "Bah !"—a yawn, or
　　"Pooh !"
Of which perhaps the latter is most true.

II.

But, more or less, the whole 's a syncopé
　Or a singultus—emblems of emotion,
That grand antithesis to great ennui,
　Wherewith we break our bubbles on the
　　ocean,
That watery outline of eternity,
　Or miniature at least, as is my notion,
Which ministers unto the soul's delight,
In seeing matters which are out of sight.

III.

But all are better than the sigh supprest,
　Corroding in the cavern of the heart,
Making the countenance a masque of rest,
　And turning human nature to an art.
Few men dare show their thoughts of worst
　　or best;
　Dissimulation always sets apart
A corner for herself ; and therefore fiction
Is that which passes with least contradiction.

IV.

Ah ! who can tell ? Or rather, who cannot
　Remember, without telling, passion's er-
　　rors?
The drainer of oblivion, even the sot,
　Hath got blue devils for his morning mir-
　　rors:
What though on Lethe's stream he seem to
　　float,
　He cannot sink his tremours or his ter-
　　rors;
The ruby glass that shakes within his hand
Leaves a sad sediment of Time's worst sand.

V.

And as for love—O love!—We will proceed.
　The Lady Adeline Amundeville,
A pretty name as one would wish to read,
　Must perch harmonious on my tuneful
　　quill.
There 's music in the sighing of a reed ;
　There 's music in the gushing of a rill;
There 's music in all things, if men had ears :
Their earth is but an echo of the spheres.

VI.

The Lady Adeline, right honourable,
　And honour'd, ran a risk of growing less
　　so;
For few of the soft sex are very stable
　In their resolves—alas ! that I should say
　　so;
They differ as wine differs from its label,
　When once decanted ;—I presume to guess
　　so,
But will not swear : yet both upon occasion,
Till old, may undergo adulteration.

VII.

But Adeline was of the purest vintage,
 The unmingled essence of the grape ; and
 yet
Bright as a new Napoleon from its mintage,
 Or glorious as a diamond richly set ;
A page where Time should hesitate to print
 age,
 And for which Nature might forego her
 debt—
Sole creditor whose process doth involve in't
The luck of finding everybody solvent.

VIII.

O Death ! thou dunnest of all duns ! thou
 daily
 Knockest at doors, at first with modest tap,
Like a meek tradesman when, approaching
 palely,
 Some splendid debtor he would take by
 sap :
But oft denied, as patience 'gins to fail, he
 Advances with exasperated rap,
And (if let in) insists, in terms unhandsome,
On ready money, or " a draft on Ransom."

IX.

Whate'er thou takest, spare awhile poor
 Beauty !
 She is so rare, and thou hast so much prey.
What though she now and then may slip
 from duty,
 The more 's the reason why you ought to
 stay ;
Gaunt Gourmand ! with whole nations for
 your booty,
 You should be civil in a modest way :
Suppress, then, some slight feminine diseases,
And take as many heroes as Heaven pleases.

X.

Fair Adeline, the more ingenuous
 Where she was interested (as was said),
Because she was not apt, like some of us,
 To like too readily, or too high bred
To show it—(points we need not now dis-
 cuss)—
 Would give up artlessly both heart and
 head
Unto such feelings as seem'd innocent,
For objects worthy of the sentiment.

XI.

Some parts of Juan's history, which Rumour,
 That live gazette, had scatter'd to dis-
 figure,
She had heard ; but women hear with more
 good humour
 Such aberrations than we men of rigour :

Besides, his conduct, since in England, grew
 more
 Strict, and his mind assumed a manlier
 vigour ;
Because he had, like Alcibiades,
 The art of living in all climes with ease.

XII.

His manner was perhaps the more seductive,
 Because he ne'er seem'd anxious to seduce ;
Nothing affected, studied, or constructive
 Of coxcombry or conquest: no abuse
Of his attractions marr'd the fair perspective,
 To indicate a Cupidon broke loose,
And seem to say, " Resist us if you can "—
Which makes a dandy while it spoils a man.

XIII.

They are wrong—that 's not the way to set
 about it ;
 As, if they told the truth, could well be
 shown.
But, right or wrong, Don Juan was with-
 out it ;
 In fact, his manner was his own alone :
Sincere he was—at least you could not
 doubt it,
 In listening merely to his voice's tone.
The devil hath not in all his quiver's choice
An arrow for the heart like a sweet voice.

XIV.

By nature soft, his whole address held off
 Suspicion ; though not timid, his regard
Was such as rather seem'd to keep aloof,
 To shield himself than put you on your
 guard :
Perhaps 'twas hardly quite assured enough,
 But modesty 's at times its own reward,
Like virtue ; and the absence of pretension
Will go much farther than there 's need to
 mention.

XV.

Serene, accomplish'd, cheerful but not loud ;
 Insinuating without insinuation ;
Observant of the foibles of the crowd,
 Yet ne'er betraying this in conversation ;
Proud with the proud, yet courteously proud,
 So as to make them feel he knew his
 station
And theirs :—without a struggle for priority,
He neither brook'd nor claim'd superiority—

XVI.

That is, with men : with women he was what
 They pleased to make or take him for ; and
 their
Imagination 's quite enough for that :
 So that the outline 's tolerably fair,

They fill the canvas up—and "verbum sat."
 If once their phantasies be brought to bear
Upon an object, whether sad or playful,
They can transfigure brighter than a Raphael.

XVII.

Adeline, no deep judge of character,
 Was apt to add a colouring from her own:
'Tis thus the good will amiably err,
 And eke the wise, as has been often shown.
Experience is the chief philosopher,
 But saddest when his science is well
 known;
And persecuted sages teach the schools
Their folly in forgetting there are fools.

XVIII.

Was it not so, great Locke? and greater
 Bacon?
 Great Socrates? And thou, Diviner still,
Whose lot it is by man to be mistaken,
 And thy pure creed made sanction of all
 ill?
Redeeming worlds to be by bigots shaken,
 How was thy toil rewarded? We might fill
Volumes with similar sad illustrations,
But leave them to the conscience of the
 nations.

XIX.

I perch upon an humbler promontory,
 Amidst life's infinite variety:
With no great care for what is nicknamed
 glory,
 But speculating as I cast mine eye
On what may suit or may not suit my story,
 And never straining hard to versify,
I rattle on exactly as I'd talk
With anybody in a ride or walk.

XX.

I don't know that there may be much
 ability
 Shown in this sort of desultory rhyme;
But there's a conversational facility,
 Which may round off an hour upon a
 time.
Of this I'm sure at least, there's no ser-
 vility
 In mine irregularity of chime,
Which rings what's uppermost of new or
 hoary,
Just as I feel the "Improvvisatore."

XXI.

"Omnia vult belle Matho dicere—dic ali-
 quando
 Et bene, dic neutrum, dic aliquando male."
The first is rather more than mortal can do;
 The second may be sadly done or gaily;

The third is still more difficult to stand to;
 The fourth we hear, and see, and say too,
 daily:
The whole together is what I could wish
To serve in this conundrum of a dish.

XXII.

A modest hope—but modesty's my forte,
 And pride my feeble:—let us ramble on.
I meant to make this poem very short,
 But now I can't tell where it may not run.
No doubt, if I had wish'd to pay my court
 To critics, or to hail the setting sun
Of tyranny of all kinds, my concision
Were more;—but I was born for opposition.

XXIII.

But then 't is mostly on the weaker side;
 So that I verily believe if they
Who now are basking in their full-blown
 pride
 Were shaken down and "dogs had had
 their day,"
Though at the first I might perchance deride
 Their tumble, I should turn the other way,
And wax an ultra-royalist in loyalty,
Because I hate even democratic royalty.

XXIV.

I think I should have made a decent spouse,
 If I had never proved the soft condition;
I think I should have made monastic vows,
 But for my own peculiar superstition:
'Gainst rhyme I never should have knock'd
 my brows,
 Nor broken my own head, nor that of
 Priscian,
Nor worn the motley mantle of a poet,
If some one had not told me to forego it.

XXV.

But "laissez aller"—knights and dames I
 sing,
 Such as the times may furnish. 'Tis a
 flight
Which seems at first to need no lofty wing,
 Plumed by Longinus or the Stagyrite:
The difficulty lies in colouring
 (Keeping the due proportions still in sight)
With nature manners which are artificial,
And rend'ring general that which is especial.

XXVI.

The difference is, that in the days of old
 Men made the manners; manners now
 make men—
Pinn'd like a flock, and fleeced too in their
 fold,
 At least nine, and a ninth beside of ten.

Now this at all events must render cold
　　Your writers, who must either draw again
Days better drawn before, or else assume
The present, with their common-place cos-
　　tume.

XXVII.

We 'll do our best to make the best on 't :—
　　March !
　　March, my Muse ! If you cannot fly, yet
　　　　flutter ;
And when you may not be sublime, be arch,
　　Or starch, as are the edicts statesmen
　　　　utter.
We surely may find something worth re-
　　search :
　　Columbus found a new world in a cutter,
Or brigantine, or pink, of no great tonnage,
While yet America was in her non-age.

XXVIII.

When Adeline, in all her growing sense
　　Of Juan's merits and his situation,
Felt on the whole an interest intense,—
　　Partly perhaps because a fresh sensation,
Or that he had an air of innocence,
　　Which is for innocence a sad temptation—
As women hate half measures, on the whole,
She 'gan to ponder how to save his soul.

XXIX.

She had a good opinion of advice,
　　Like all who give and eke receive it gratis,
For which small thanks are still the market
　　price,
　　Even where the article at highest rate is :
She thought upon the subject twice or thrice,
　　And morally decided, the best state is
For morals, marriage ; and this question
　　carried,
She seriously advised him to get married.

XXX.

Juan replied, with all becoming deference,
　　He had a predilection for that tie ;
But that, at present, with immediate refer-
　　ence
　　To his own circumstances, there might lie
Some difficulties, as in his own preference,
　　Or that of her to whom he might apply :
That still he 'd wed with such or such a
　　lady,
If that they were not married all already.

XXXI.

Next to the making matches for herself,
　　And daughters, brothers, sisters, kith or
　　　　kin,
Arranging them like books on the same shelf,
　　There 's nothing women love to dabble in

More (like a stock-holder in growing pelf)
　　Than match-making in general : 'tis no
　　　　sin
Certes, but a preventative, and therefore
That is, no doubt, the only reason wherefore.

XXXII.

But never yet (except of course a miss
　　Unwed, or mistress never to be wed,
Or wed already, who object to this)
　　Was there chaste dame who had not in her
　　　　head
Some drama of the marriage unities,
　　Observed as strictly both at board and bed
As those of Aristotle, though sometimes
They turn out melodrames or pantomimes.

XXXIII.

They generally have some only son
　　Some heir to a large property, some friend
Of an old family, some gay Sir John,
　　Or grave Lord George, with whom perhaps
　　　　might end
A line, and leave posterity undone,
　　Unless a marriage was applied to mend
The prospect and their morals : and besides,
They have at hand a blooming glut of brides.

XXXIV.

From these they will be careful to select,
　　For this an heiress, and for that a beauty ;
For one a songstress who hath no defect,
　　For 't other one who promises much duty ;
For this a lady no one can reject,
　　Whose sole accomplishments were quite a
　　　　booty ;
A second for her excellent connexions ;
A third, because there can be no objections.

XXXV.

When Rapp the Harmonist embargo'd
　　　　marriage
　　In his harmonious settlement—(which
　　　　flourishes
Strangely enough as yet without miscarriage,
　　Because it breeds no more mouths than it
　　　　nourishes,
Without those sad expenses which disparage
　　What Nature naturally most encourages)—
Why call'd he the "Harmony" a state sans
　　wedlock ?
Now here I have got the preacher at a dead
　　lock.

XXXVI.

Because he either meant to sneer at harmony
　　Or marriage, by divorcing them thus oddly.
But whether reverend Rapp learn'd this in
　　Germany
　　Or no, 't is said his sect is rich and godly,

Pious and pure, beyond what I can term any
 Of ours, although they propagate more
 broadly.
My objection's to his title, not his ritual,
Although I wonder how it grew habitual.

XXXVII.

But Rapp is the reverse of zealous matrons,
 Who favour, malgré Malthus, generation—
Professors of that genial art, and patrons
 Of all the modest part of propagation;
Which after all at such a desperate rate
 runs,
That half its produce tends to emigration,
That sad result of passions and potatoes—
Two weeds which pose our economic Catos.

XXXVIII.

Had Adeline read Malthus? I can't tell;
 I wish she had: his book's the eleventh
 commandment,
Which says, "Thou shalt not marry," unless
 well:
 This he (as far as I can understand)
 meant.
'T is not my purpose on his views to dwell,
 Nor canvass what "so eminent a hand"
 meant;
But certes it conducts to lives ascetic,
Or turning marriage into arithmetic.

XXXIX.

But Adeline, who probably presumed
 That Juan had enough of maintenance,
Or *separate* maintenance, in case 't was
 doom'd—
 As on the whole it is an even chance
That bridegrooms, after they are fairly
 groom'd,
 May retrograde a little in the dance
Of marriage—(which might form a painter's
 fame,
Like Holbein's "Dance of Death"—but 't is
 the same);—

XL.

But Adeline determined Juan's wedding
 In her own mind, and that's enough for
 woman:
But then, with whom? There was the sage
 Miss Reading,
 Miss Raw, Miss Flaw, Miss Showman, and
 Miss Knowman,
And the two fair co-heiresses Giltbedding.
 She deem'd his merits something more
 than common:
All these were unobjectionable matches,
And might go on, if well wound up, like
 watches.

XLI.

There was Miss Millpond, smooth as summer's
 sea,
 That usual paragon, an only daughter,
Who seem'd the cream of equanimity,
 Till skimm'd—and then there was some
 milk and water,
With a slight shade of blue too, it might be
 Beneath the surface; but what did it
 matter?
Love's riotous, but marriage should have
 quiet,
And being consumptive, live on a milk diet.

XLII.

And then there was the Miss Audacia
 Shoestring,
 A dashing demoiselle of good estate,
Whose heart was fix'd upon a star or blue
 string;
 But whether English dukes grew rare of
 late,
Or that she had not harp'd upon the true
 string,
 By which such sirens can attract our
 great,
She took up with some foreign younger
 brother,
A Russ or Turk—the one's as good as
 t' other.

XLIII.

And then there was—but why should I go
 on,
 Unless the ladies should go off?—there was
Indeed a certain fair and fairy one,
 Of the best class, and better than her
 class,—
Aurora Raby, a young star who shone
 O'er life, too sweet an image for such
 glass,
A lovely being, scarcely form'd or moulded,
A rose with all its sweetest leaves yet folded;

XLIV.

Rich, noble, but an orphan; left an only
 Child to the care of guardians good and
 kind;
But still her aspect had an air so lonely!
 Blood is not water; and where shall we
 find
Feelings of youth like those which over-
 thrown lie
By death, when we are left, alas! behind,
To feel, in friendless palaces, a home
Is wanting, and our best ties in the tomb?

XLV.

Early in years, and yet more infantine
 In figure, she had something of sublime
In eyes which sadly shone, as seraphs' shine.
 All youth—but with an aspect beyond
 time;
Radiant and grave—as pitying man's decline;
 Mournful—but mournful of another's crime,
She look'd as if she sat by Eden's door,
And grieved for those who could return no
 more.

XLVI.

She was a Catholic, too, sincere, austere,
 As far as her own gentle heart allow'd,
And deem'd that fallen worship far more
 dear
 Perhaps because 't was fallen: her sires
 were proud
Of deeds and days when they had fill'd the
 ear
 Of nations, and had never bent or bow'd
To novel power; and as she was the last,
She held their old faith and old feelings
 fast.

XLVII.

She gazed upon a world she scarcely knew,
 As seeking not to know it; silent, lone,
As grows a flower, thus quietly she grew,
 And kept her heart serene within its zone.
There was awe in the homage which she
 drew;
 Her spirit seem'd as seated on a throne
Apart from the surrounding world, and strong
In its own strength—most strange in one so
 young !

XLVIII.

Now it so happen'd, in the catalogue
 Of Adeline, Aurora was omitted,
Although her birth and wealth had given her
 vogue,
 Beyond the charmers we have already
 cited;
Her beauty also seem'd to form no clog
 Against her being mention'd as well fitted,
By many virtues, to be worth the trouble
Of single gentlemen who would be double.

XLIX.

And this omission, like that of the bust
 Of Brutus at the pageant of Tiberius,
Made Juan wonder, as no doubt he must.
 This he express'd half smiling and half
 serious;
When Adeline replied with some disgust,
 And with an air, to say the least, imperious,
She marvell'd " what he saw in such a baby
As that prim, silent, cold Aurora Raby ? "

L.

Juan rejoin'd—" She was a Catholic,
 And therefore fittest, as of his persuasion ;
Since he was sure his mother would fall
 sick,
 And the Pope thunder excommunication,
If —— " But here Adeline, who seem'd to
 pique
 Herself extremely on the inoculation
Of others with her own opinions, stated—
As usual—the same reason which she late
 did.

LI.

And wherefore not ? A reasonable reason,
 If good, is none the worse for repetition ;
If bad, the best way's certainly to tease on,
 And amplify : you lose much by concision,
Whereas insisting in or out of season
 Convinces all men, even a politician ;
Or—what is just the same—it wearies out.
So the end's gain'd, what signifies the route ?

LII.

Why Adeline had this slight prejudice—
 For prejudice it was—against a creature
As pure as sanctity itself from vice,
 With all the added charm of form and
 feature,
For me appears a question far too nice,
 Since Adeline was liberal by nature;
But nature's nature, and has more caprices
Than I have time, or will, to take to pieces.

LIII.

Perhaps she did not like the quiet way
 With which Aurora on those baubles
 look'd,
Which charm most people in their earlier
 day :
 For there are few things by mankind less
 brook'd,
And womankind too, if we so may say,
 Than finding thus their genius stand
 rebuked,
Like " Anthony's by Cæsar," by the few
Who look upon them as they ought to do.

LIV.

It was not envy—Adeline had none ;
 Her place was far beyond it, and her
 mind.
It was not scorn—which could not light on
 one
 Whose greatest *fault* was leaving few to
 find.
It was not jealousy, I think : but shun
 Following the " ignes fatui " of mankind.
It was not —— but 't is easier far, alas !
To say what it was not than what it was.

LV.

Little Aurora deem'd she was the theme
 Of such discussion. She was there a
 guest;
A beauteous ripple of the brilliant stream
 Of rank and youth, though purer than the
 rest,
Which flow'd on for a moment in the beam
 Time sheds a moment o'er each sparkling
 crest.
Had she known this, she would have calmly
 smiled—
She had so much, or little, of the child.

LVI.

The dashing and proud air of Adeline
 Imposed not upon her: she saw her blaze
Much as she would have seen a glow-worm
 shine,
 Then turn'd unto the stars for loftier rays.
Juan was something she could not divine,
 Being no sibyl in the new world's ways;
Yet she was nothing dazzled by the meteor,
Because she did not pin her faith on feature.

LVII.

His fame too,—for he had that kind of fame
 Which sometimes plays the deuce with
 womankind,
A heterogeneous mass of glorious blame,
 Half virtues and whole vices being com-
 bined;
Faults which attract because they are not
 tame;
 Follies trick'd out so brightly that they
 blind:—
These seals upon her wax made no im-
 pression,
Such was her coldness or her self-possession.

LVIII.

Juan knew nought of such a character—
 High, yet resembling not his lost Haidée;
Yet each was radiant in her proper sphere:
 The island girl, bred up by the lone sea,
More warm, as lovely, and not less sincere,
 Was Nature's all: Aurora could not be,
Nor would be thus:—the difference in them
Was such as lies between a flower and gem.

LIX.

Having wound up with this sublime com-
 parison,
 Methinks we may proceed upon our
 narrative,
And, as my friend Scott says, "I sound my
 warison;"
 Scott, the superlative of my comparative—
Scott, who can paint your Christian knight
 or Saracen,
 Serf, lord, man, with such skill as none
 would share it, if
There had not been one Shakspeare and
 Voltaire,
Of one or both of whom he seems the heir.

LX.

I say, in my slight way I may proceed
 To play upon the surface of humanity.
I write the world, nor care if the world read,
 At least for this I cannot spare its vanity.
My Muse hath bred, and still perhaps may
 breed
 More foes by this same scroll: when I
 began it, I
Thought that it might turn out so—*now*
 I *know* it,
But still I am, or was, a pretty poet.

LXI.

The conference or congress (for it ended
 As congresses of late do) of the Lady
Adeline and Don Juan rather blended
 Some acids with the sweets—for she was
 heady;
But, ere the matter could be marr'd or
 mended,
 The silvery bell rang, not for "dinner
 ready,"
But for that hour, call'd *half-hour*, given to
 dress,
Though ladies' robes seem scant enough for
 less.

LXII.

Great things were now to be achieved at
 table,
 With massy plate for armour, knives and
 forks
For weapons; but what Muse since Homer's
 able
 (His feasts are not the worst part of his
 works)
To draw up in array a single day-bill
 Of modern dinners? where more mystery
 lurks,
In soups or sauces, or a sole ragoût,
Than witches, b—ches, or physicians, brew.

LXIII.

There was a goodly "soupe à la *bonne
 femme*,"
 Though God knows whence it came from;
 there was, too,
A turbot for relief of those who cram,
 Relieved with "dindon à la Parigeux:"

There also was——the sinner that I am!
 How shall I get this gourmand stanza
 through?—
"Soupe à la Beauveau," whose relief was
 dory,
Relieved itself by pork, for greater glory.

LXIV.

But I must crowd all into one grand mess,
 Or mass; for should I stretch into detail,
My Muse would run much more into excess,
 Than when some squeamish people deem
 her frail;
But though a "bonne vivante," I must
 confess
 Her stomach's not her peccant part; this
 tale
However doth require some slight refection,
Just to relieve her spirits from dejection.

LXV.

Fowls "à la Condé," slices eke of salmon,
 With "sauces Génévoises," and haunch of
 venison:
Wines, too, which might again have slain
 young Ammon—
 A man like whom I hope we sha'n't see
 many soon;
They also set a glazed Westphalian ham
 on,
 Whereon Apicius would bestow his benison;
And then there was champagne with foaming
 whirls,
As white as Cleopatra's melted pearls.

LXVI.

Then there was God knows what "à l'Alle-
 mande,"
 "A l'Espagnole," "timballe," and "sal-
 picon"—
With things I can't withstand or understand,
 Though swallow'd with much zest upon the
 whole;
And "entremets" to piddle with at hand,
 Gently to lull down the subsiding soul;
While great Lucullus' *Rome triumphal* muf-
 fles—
(*There's fame*)—young partridge fillets, deck'd
 with truffles.

LXVII.

What are the *fillets* on the victor's brow
 To these? They are rags or dust. Where
 is the arch
Which nodded to the nation's spoils below?
 Where the triumphal chariots' haughty
 march?

Gone to where victories must like dinners go.
 Farther I shall not follow the research:
But oh! ye modern heroes with your car-
 tridges,
When will your names lend lustre e'en to
 partridges?

LXVIII.

Those truffles too are no bad accessaries,
 Follow'd by "petits puits d'amour"—a
 dish
Of which perhaps the cookery rather varies,
 So every one may dress it to his wish,
According to the best of dictionaries,
 Which encyclopedise both flesh and fish;
But even sans "confitures," it no less true is,
There's pretty picking in those "petits
 puits."

LXIX.

The mind is lost in mighty contemplation
 Of intellect expanded on two courses;
And indigestion's grand multiplication
 Requires arithmetic beyond my forces.
Who would suppose, from Adam's simple
 ration,
 That cookery could have call'd forth such
 resources,
As form a science and a nomenclature
From out the commonest demands of nature?

LXX.

The glasses jingled, and the palates tingled;
 The diners of celebrity dined well;
The ladies with more moderation mingled
 In the feast, pecking less than I can tell;
Also the younger men too: for a springald
 Can't, like ripe age, in gormandise excel,
But thinks less of good eating than the
 whisper
(When seated next him) of some pretty lisper.

LXXI.

Alas! I must leave undescribed the gibier,
 The salmi, the consommé, the purée,
All which I use to make my rhymes run
 glibber
 Than could roast beef in our rough John
 Bull way:
I must not introduce even a spare rib here,
 "Bubble and squeak" would spoil my
 liquid lay,
But I have dined, and must forego, alas!
The chaste description even of a "bécasse;"

LXXII.

And fruits, and ice, and all that art refines
 From nature for the service of the goût—
Taste or the *gout*,—pronounce it as inclines
 Your stomach? Ere you dine, the French
 will do;

But *after*, there are sometimes certain signs
　Which prove plain English truer of the two.
Hast ever *had* the *gout?* I have not had it—
But I may have, and you too, reader, dread it.

LXXIII.

The simple olives, best allies of wine,
　Must I pass over in my bill of fare?
I must, although a favourite "plat" of mine
　In Spain, and Lucca, Athens, everywhere:
On them and bread 't was oft my luck to dine,
　The grass my table-cloth, in open air,
On Sunium or Hymettus, like Diogenes,
Of whom half my philosophy the progeny is.

LXXIV.

Amidst this tumult of fish, flesh, and fowl,
　And vegetables, all in masquerade,
The guests were placed according to their roll,
　But various as the various meats display'd:
Don Juan sat next an "à l'Espagnole"—
　No damsel, but a dish, as hath been said:
But so far like a lady, that 't was drest
Superbly, and contain'd a world of zest.

LXXV.

By some odd chance too, he was placed
　　between
Aurora and the Lady Adeline—
A situation difficult, I ween,
　For man therein, with eyes and heart, to
　　dine.
Also the conference which we have seen
　Was not such as to encourage him to shine,
For Adeline, addressing few words to him,
With two transcendent eyes seem'd to look
　　through him.

LXXVI.

I sometimes almost think that eyes have
　　ears:
　This much is sure, that, out of earshot,
　　things
Are somehow echoed to the pretty dears,
　Of which I can't tell whence their know-
　　ledge springs,
Like that same mystic music of the spheres,
　Which no one hears, so loudly though it
　　rings,
'T is wonderful how oft the sex have heard
Long dialogues—which pass'd without a
　　word!

LXXVII.

Aurora sat with that indifference
　Which piques a preux chevalier—as it
　　ought:
Of all offences that 's the worst offence,
　Which seems to hint you are not worth a
　　thought.

Now Juan, though no coxcomb in pretence,
　Was not exactly pleased to be so caught;
Like a good ship entangled among ice,
And after so much excellent advice.

LXXVIII.

To his gay nothings, nothing was replied,
　Or something which was nothing, as ur-
　　banity
Required. Aurora scarcely look'd aside,
　Nor even smiled enough for any vanity.
The devil was in the girl! Could it be pride?
　Or modesty, or absence, or inanity?
Heaven knows! But Adeline's malicious eyes
Sparkled with her successful prophecies,

LXXIX.

And look'd as much as if to say, "I said it;"
　A kind of triumph I'll not recommend,
Because it sometimes, as I have seen or
　　read it,
　Both in the case of lover and of friend,
Will pique a gentleman, for his own credit,
　To bring what was a jest to a serious end:
For all men prophesy what *is* or *was*,
And hate those who won't let them come to
　　pass.

LXXX.

Juan was drawn thus into some attentions,
　Slight but select, and just enough to
　　express,
To females of perspicuous comprehensions,
　That he would rather make them more
　　than less.
Aurora at the last (so history mentions,
　Though probably much less a fact than
　　guess)
So far relax'd her thoughts from their sweet
　　prison,
As once or twice to smile, if not to listen.

LXXXI.

From answering she began to question: this
　With her was rare; and Adeline, who as yet
Thought her predictions went not much
　　amiss,
　Began to dread she'd thaw to a coquette—
So very difficult, they say, it is
　To keep extremes from meeting, when
　　once set
In motion; but she here too much refined—
Aurora's spirit was not of that kind.

LXXXII.

But Juan had a sort of winning way,
　A proud humility, if such there be,
Which show'd such deference to what females
　　say,
　As if each charming word were a decree.

His tact, too, temper'd him from grave to
gay,
 And taught him when to be reserved or
 free :
He had the art of drawing people out,
Without their seeing what he was about.

LXXXIII.

Aurora, who in her indifference
 Confounded him in common with the
 crowd
Of flatterers, though she deem'd he had more
 sense
 Than whispering foplings, or than witlings
 loud—
Commenced (from such slight things will
 great commence)
 To feel that flattery which attracts the
 proud
Rather by deference than compliment,
And wins even by a delicate dissent.

LXXXIV.

And then he had good looks;—that point was
 carried
 Nem. con. amongst the women, which I
 grieve
To say leads oft to *crim. con.* with the
 married—
 A case which to the juries we may leave,
Since with digressions we too long have
 tarried.
 Now though we know of old that looks
 deceive,
And always have done, somehow these good
 looks
Make more impression than the best of books.

LXXXV.

Aurora, who look'd more on books than faces,
 Was very young, although so very sage,
Admiring more Minerva than the Graces,
 Especially upon a printed page.
But Virtue's self, with all her tightest laces,
 Has not the natural stays of strict old age;
And Socrates, that model of all duty,
Own'd to a penchant, though discreet, for
 beauty.

LXXXVI.

And girls of sixteen are thus far Socratic,
 But innocently so, as Socrates ;
And really, if the sage sublime and Attic
 At seventy years had phantasies like these,
Which Plato in his dialogues dramatic
 Has shown, I know not why they should
 displease
In virgins—always in a modest way,
Observe ; for that with me's a "sine quâ."

LXXXVII.

Also observe, that, like the great Lord Coke
 (See Littleton), whene'er I have express'd
Opinions two, which at first sight may look
 Twin opposites, the second is the best.
Perhaps I have a third too, in a nook,
 Or none at all—which seems a sorry jest :
But if a writer should be quite consistent,
How could he possibly show things existent ?

LXXXVIII.

If people contradict themselves, can I
 Help contradicting them, and everybody,
Even my veracious self ?—But that's a lie :
 I never did so, never will—how should I ?
He who doubts all things nothing can deny :
 Truth's fountains may be clear—her streams
 are muddy,
And cut through such canals of contradiction,
That she must often navigate o'er fiction.

LXXXIX.

Apologue, fable, poesy, and parable,
 Are false, but may be render'd also true,
By those who sow them in a land that's
 arable.
 'T is wonderful what fable will not do !
'T is said it makes reality more bearable :
 But what's reality ? Who has its clue ?
Philosophy ? No ; she too much rejects.
Religion ? *Yes ;* but which of all her sects ?

XC.

Some millions must be wrong, that's pretty
 clear ;
 Perhaps it may turn out that all were
 right.
God help us ! Since we have need on our
 career
 To keep our holy beacons always bright,
'T is time that some new prophet should
 appear,
 Or old indulge man with a second sight.
Opinions wear out in some thousand years,
Without a small refreshment from the
 spheres.

XCI.

But here again, why will I thus entangle
 Myself with metaphysics ? None can hate
So much as I do any kind of wrangle ;
 And yet, such is my folly, or my fate,
I always knock my head against some angle
 About the present, past, or future state :
Yet I wish well to Trojan and to Tyrian,
For I was bred a moderate Presbyterian.

XCII.

But though I am a temperate theologian,
 And also meek as a metaphysician,
Impartial between Tyrian and Trojan
 As Eldon on a lunatic commission,
In politics my duty is to show John
 Bull something of the lower world's con-
 dition.
It makes my blood boil like the springs of
 Hecla,
To see men let these scoundrel sovereigns
 break law.

XCIII.

But politics, and policy, and piety,
 Are topics which I sometimes introduce,
Not only for the sake of their variety,
 But as subservient to a moral use;
Because my business is to *dress* society,
 And stuff with *sage* that very verdant goose.
And now, that we may furnish with some
 matter all
Tastes, we are going to try the supernatural.

XCIV.

And now I will give up all argument;
 And positively henceforth no temptation
Shall "fool me to the top up of my bent;"—
 Yes, I'll begin a thorough reformation.
Indeed, I never knew what people meant
 By deeming that my Muse's conversation
Was dangerous;—I think she is as harmless
As some who labour more and yet may charm
 less.

XCV.

Grim reader! did you ever see a ghost?
 No; but you have heard—I understand—
 be dumb!
And don't regret the time you may have lost,
 For you have got that pleasure still to come:
And do not think I mean to sneer at most
 Of these things, or by ridicule benumb
That source of the sublime and the mys-
 terious:—
For certain reasons my belief is serious.

XCVI.

Serious? You laugh;—you may: that will
 I not;
 My smiles must be sincere or not at all.
I say I do believe a haunted spot
 Exists—and where? That shall I not re-
 call,
Because I'd rather it should be forgot,
 "Shadows the soul of Richard" may appal.
In short, upon that subject I've some qualms
 very
Like those of the philosopher of Malmsbury.

XCVII.

The night—(I sing by night—sometimes an
 owl,
 And now and then a nightingale)—is dim,
And the loud shriek of sage Minerva's fowl
 Rattles around me her discordant hymn:
Old portraits from old walls upon me scowl—
 I wish to heaven they would not look so
 grim;
The dying embers dwindle in the grate—
I think too that I have sat up too late:

XCVIII.

And therefore, though 'tis by no means my
 way
 To rhyme at noon—when I have other
 things
To think of, if I ever think—I say
 I feel some chilly midnight shudderings,
And prudently postpone, until mid-day,
 Treating a topic which, alas! but brings
Shadows;—but you must be in my condition
Before you learn to call this superstition.

XCIX.

Between two worlds life hovers like a star,
 'Twixt night and morn, upon the horizon's
 verge.
How little do we know that which we are!
 How less what we may be! The eternal
 surge
Of time and tide rolls on, and bears afar
 Our bubbles; as the old burst, new emerge,
Lash'd from the foam of ages; while the
 graves
Of empires heave but like some passing
 waves.

Canto the Sixteenth.

I.

THE antique Persians taught three useful
 things,
 To draw the bow, to ride, and speak the
 truth.
This was the mode of Cyrus, best of kings—
 A mode adopted since by modern youth.
Bows have they, generally with two strings,
 Horses they ride without remorse or ruth;
At speaking truth perhaps they are less
 clever,
But draw the long bow better now than
 ever.

II.

The cause of this effect, or this defect,—
 "For this effect defective comes by
 cause,"—
Is what I have not leisure to inspect;
 But this I must say in my own applause,
Of all the Muses that I recollect,
 Whate'er may be her follies or her flaws,
In some things, mine's beyond all contradic-
 tion
The most sincere that ever dealt in fiction.

III.

And as she treats all things, and ne'er re-
 treats
 From anything, this epic will contain
A wilderness of the most rare conceits,
 Which you might elsewhere hope to find
 in vain.
'Tis true there be some bitters with the
 sweets,
 Yet mix'd so slightly, that you can't com-
 plain,
But wonder they so few are, since my tale is
"De rebus cunctis et quibusdam aliis."

IV.

But of all truths which she has told, the
 most
 True is that which she is about to tell.
I said it was a story of a ghost—
 What then? I only know it so befell.
Have you explored the limits of the coast,
 Where all the dwellers of the earth must
 dwell?
'Tis time to strike such puny doubters dumb
 as
The sceptics who would not believe Columbus.

V.

Some people would impose now with au-
 thority,
 Turpin's or Monmouth Geoffry's Chronicle;
Men whose historical superiority
 Is always greatest at a miracle.
But Saint Augustine has the great priority,
 Who bids all men believe the impossible,
Because 'tis so. Who nibble, scribble, quib-
 ble, he
Quiets at once with "quia impossibile."

VI.

And therefore, mortals, cavil not at all;
 Believe:—if 'tis improbable, you must,
And if it is impossible, you shall:—
 'Tis always best to take things upon trust.

I do not speak profanely, to recall
 Those holier mysteries which the wise and
 just
Receive as gospel, and which grow more
 rooted,
As all truths must, the more they are dis-
 puted:

VII.

I merely mean to say what Johnson said,
 That in the course of some six thousand
 years,
All nations have believed that from the dead
 A visitant at intervals appears;
And what is strangest upon this strange
 head,
 Is, that whatever bar the reason rears
'Gainst such belief, there's something stronger
 still
In its behalf, let those deny who will.

VIII.

The dinner and the soirée too were done,
 The supper too discuss'd, the dames ad-
 mired,
The banqueteers had dropp'd off one by one—
 The song was silent, and the dance ex-
 pired:
The last thin petticoats were vanish'd, gone
 Like fleecy clouds into the sky retired,
And nothing brighter gleam'd through the
 saloon
Than dying tapers—and the peeping moon.

IX.

The evaporation of a joyous day
 Is like the last glass of champagne, without
The foam which made its virgin bumper gay;
 Or like a system coupled with a doubt;
Or like a soda bottle when its spray
 Has sparkled and let half its spirit out;
Or like a billow left by storms behind,
Without the animation of the wind;

X.

Or like an opiate, which brings troubled rest,
 Or none; or like—like nothing that I know
Except itself;—such is the human breast;
 A thing, of which similitudes can show
No real likeness,—like the old Tyrian vest
 Dyed purple, none at present can tell how,
If from a shell-fish or from cochineal.
So perish every tyrant's robe piece-meal!

XI.

But next to dressing for a rout or ball,
 Undressing is a woe; our robe de chambre
May sit like that of Nessus, and recall
 Thoughts quite as yellow, but less clear
 than amber.

Titus exclaim'd, "I've lost a day!" Of all
 The nights and days most people can re-
 member,
(I have had of both, some not to be dis-
 dain'd,)
I wish they'd state how many they have
 gain'd.

XII.

And Juan, on retiring for the night,
 Felt restless, and perplex'd, and compro-
 mised:
He thought Aurora Raby's eyes more bright
 Than Adeline (such is advice) advised;
If he had known exactly his own plight,
 He probably would have philosophised;
A great resource to all, and ne'er denied
Till wanted; therefore Juan only sigh'd.

XIII.

He sigh'd;—the next resource is the full
 moon,
 Where all sighs are deposited; and now
It happen'd luckily, the chaste orb shone
 As clear as such a climate will allow;
And Juan's mind was in the proper tone
 To hail her with the apostrophe—"O
 thou!"
Of amatory egotism the *Tuism*,
Which further to explain would be a truism.

XIV.

But lover, poet, or astronomer,
 Shepherd, or swain, whoever may behold,
Feel some abstraction when they gaze on her;
 Great thoughts we catch from thence (be-
 sides a cold
Sometimes, unless my feelings rather err);
 Deep secrets to her rolling light are told;
The ocean's tides and mortals' brains she
 sways,
And also hearts, if there be truth in lays.

XV.

Juan felt somewhat pensive, and disposed
 For contemplation rather than his pillow:
The Gothic chamber, where he was enclosed,
 Let in the rippling sound of the lake's
 billow,
With all the mystery by midnight caused
 Below his window waved (of course) a
 willow;
And he stood gazing out on the cascade
That flash'd and after darken'd in the shade.

XVI.

Upon his table or his toilet,—*which*
 Of these is not exactly ascertain'd,—
(I state this, for I am cautious to a pitch
 Of nicety, where a fact is to be gain'd,)
A lamp burn'd high, while he leant from a
 niche,
 Where many a Gothic ornament remain'd,
In chisell'd stone and painted glass, and all
That time has left our fathers of their hall.

XVII.

Then, as the night was clear though cold, he
 threw
 His chamber door wide open—and went
 forth
Into a gallery, of a sombre hue,
 Long, furnish'd with old pictures of great
 worth,
Of knights and dames heroic and chaste too,
 As doubtless should be people of high birth.
But by dim lights the portraits of the dead
Have something ghastly, desolate, and dread.

XVIII.

The forms of the grim knight and pictured
 saint
 Look living in the moon; and as you turn
Backward and forward to the echoes faint
 Of your own footsteps—voices from the urn
Appear to wake, and shadows wild and quaint
 Start from the frames which fence their
 aspects stern,
As if to ask how you can dare to keep
A vigil there, where all but death should
 sleep.

XIX.

And the pale smile of beauties in the grave,
 The charms of other days, in starlight
 gleams,
Glimmer on high; their buried locks still
 wave
 Along the canvas; their eyes glance like
 dreams
On ours, or spars within some dusky cave,
 But death is imaged in their shadowy
 beams.
A picture is the past; even ere its frame
Be gilt, who sate hath ceased to be the same.

XX.

As Juan mused on mutability,
 Or on his mistress—terms synonymous—
No sound except the echo of his sigh
 Or step ran sadly through that antique
 house;
When suddenly he heard, or thought so,
 nigh,
 A supernatural agent—or a mouse,
Whose little nibbling rustle will embarrass
Most people as it plays along the arras.

XXI.

It was no mouse, but lo! a monk, array'd
 In cowl and beads, and dusky garb, appear'd,
Now in the moonlight, and now lapsed in
 shade,
 With steps that trod as heavy, yet unheard;
His garments only a slight murmur made;
 He moved as shadowy as the sisters weird,
But slowly; and as he passed Juan by,
Glanced, without pausing, on him a bright
 eye.

XXII.

Juan was petrified; he had heard a hint
 Of such a spirit in these halls of old,
But thought, like most men, there was nothing in 't
 Beyond the rumour which such spots unfold,
Coin'd from surviving superstition's mint,
 Which passes ghosts in currency like gold,
But rarely seen, like gold compared with
 paper.
And did he see this? or was it a vapour?

XXIII.

Once, twice, thrice pass'd, repass'd — the
 thing of air,
 Or earth beneath, or heaven, or t' other
 place;
And Juan gazed upon it with a stare,
 Yet could not speak or move; but, on its
 base
As stands a statue, stood: he felt his hair
 Twine like a knot of snakes around his
 face;
He tax'd his tongue for words, which were
 not granted,
To ask the reverend person what he wanted.

XXIV.

The third time, after a still longer pause,
 The shadow pass'd away—but where? the
 hall
Was long, and thus far there was no great
 cause
 To think his vanishing unnatural:
Doors there were many, through which, by
 the laws
 Of physics, bodies whether short or tall
Might come or go; but Juan could not
 state
Through which the spectre seem'd to evaporate.

XXV.

He stood—how long he knew not, but it
 seem'd
 An age—expectant, powerless, with his
 eyes
Strain'd on the spot where first the figure
 gleam'd,
 Then by degrees recall'd his energies,
And would have pass'd the whole off as a
 dream,
 But could not wake; he was, he did surmise,
Waking already, and return'd at length
Back to his chamber, shorn of half his
 strength.

XXVI.

All there was as he left it: still his taper
 Burnt, and not *blue*, as modest tapers use,
Receiving sprites with sympathetic vapour;
 He rubb'd his eyes, and they did not refuse
Their office; he took up an old newspaper;
 The paper was right easy to peruse;
He read an article the king attacking,
And a long eulogy of "patent blacking."

XXVII.

This savour'd of this world; but his hand
 shook:
 He shut his door, and after having read
A paragraph, I think about Horne Tooke,
 Undrest, and rather slowly went to bed.
There, couch'd all snugly on his pillow's
 nook,
 With what he had seen his phantasy he
 fed;
And though it was no opiate, slumber crept
Upon him by degrees, and so he slept.

XXVIII.

He woke betimes; and, as may be supposed,
 Ponder'd upon his visitant or vision,
And whether it ought not to be disclosed,
 At risk of being quizz'd for superstition.
The more he thought, the more his mind was
 posed;
 In the mean time, his valet, whose precision
Was great, because his master brook'd no
 less,
Knock'd to inform him it was time to dress.

XXIX.

He dress'd; and like young people he was
 wont
 To take some trouble with his toilet, but
This morning rather spent less time upon 't;
 Aside his very mirror soon was put;

His curls fell negligently o'er his front,
 His clothes were not curb'd to their usual
 cut,
His very neckcloth's Gordian knot was tied
Almost an hair's breadth too much on one
 side.

XXX.

And when he walk'd down into the saloon,
 He sate him pensive o'er a dish of tea,
Which he perhaps had not discover'd soon,
 Had it not happen'd scalding hot to be,
Which made him have recourse unto his
 spoon;
 So much distrait he was, that all could see
That something was the matter—Adeline
The first—but *what* she could not well di-
 vine.

XXXI.

She look'd, and saw him pale, and turn'd as
 pale
 Herself; then hastily look'd down, and
 mutter'd
Something, but what's not stated in my tale.
 Lord Henry said, his muffin was ill-but-
 ter'd;
The Duchess of Fitz-Fulke play'd with her
 veil,
 And look'd at Juan hard, but nothing utter'd.
Aurora Raby with her large dark eyes
Survey'd him with a kind of calm surprise.

XXXII.

But seeing him all cold and silent still,
 And everybody wondering more or less,
Fair Adeline inquired "If he were ill?"
 He started, and said, "Yes—no—rather—
 yes."
The family physician had great skill,
 And being present, now began to express
His readiness to feel his pulse and tell
The cause, but Juan said, "He was quite
 well."

XXXIII.

"Quite well; yes,—no."—These answers
 were mysterious,
 And yet his looks appear'd to sanction
 both,
However they might savour of delirious;
 Something like illness of a sudden growth
Weigh'd on his spirit, though by no means
 serious:
 But for the rest, as he himself seem'd loth
To state the case, it might be ta'en for
 granted
It was not the physician that he wanted.

XXXIV.

Lord Henry, who had now discuss'd his
 chocolate,
 Also the muffin whereof he complain'd,
Said, Juan had not got his usual look elate,
 At which he marvell'd, since it had not
 rain'd;
Then ask'd her Grace what news were of the
 duke of late?
 Her Grace replied, *his* Grace was rather
 pain'd
With some slight, light, hereditary twinges
Of gout, which rusts aristocratic hinges.

XXXV.

Then Henry turn'd to Juan, and address'd
 A few words of condolence on his state:
"You look," quoth he, "as if you had had
 your rest
 Broke in upon by the Black Friar of late."
"What Friar?" said Juan; and he did his
 best
 To put the question with an air sedate,
Or careless; but the effort was not valid
To hinder him from growing still more pallid.

XXXVI.

"Oh! have you never heard of the Black
 Friar?
 The spirit of these walls?"—"In truth
 not I."
"Why Fame—but Fame you know's some-
 times a liar—
 Tells an odd story, of which by and by:
Whether with time the spectre has grown
 shyer,
 Or that our sires had a more gifted eye
For such sights, though the tale is half
 . believed,
The Friar of late has not been oft per-
 ceived.

XXXVII.

"The last time was——"—" I pray," said
 Adeline—
 (Who watch'd the changes of Don Juan's
 brow,
And from its context thought she could
 divine
 Connexions stronger than he chose to avow
With this same legend)—" if you but design
 To jest, you'll choose some other theme
 just now,
Because the present tale has oft been told,
And is not much improved by growing old."

XXXVIII.

"Jest!" quoth Milor; "why, Adeline, you know
 That we ourselves—'t was in the honey-moon—
Saw——"—"Well, no matter, 't was so long ago;
 But, come, I 'll set your story to a tune."
Graceful as Dian when she draws her bow,
 She seiz'd her harp, whose strings were kindled soon
As touch'd, and plaintively began to play
The air of " 'T was a Friar of Orders Gray."

XXXIX.

"But add the words," cried Henry, " which you made;
 For Adeline is half a poetess,"
Turning round to the rest, he smiling said.
 Of course the others could not but express
In courtesy their wish to see display'd
 By one *three* talents, for there were no less—
The voice, the words, the harper's skill, at once,
Could hardly be united by a dunce.

XL.

After some fascinating hesitation,—
 The charming of these charmers, who seem bound,
I can't tell why, to this dissimulation,—
 Fair Adeline, with eyes fix'd on the ground
At first, then kindling into animation,
 Added her sweet voice to the lyric sound,
And sang with much simplicity,—a merit
Not the less precious, that we seldom hear it.

1.

Beware! beware! of the Black Friar,
 Who sitteth by Norman stone,
For he mutters his prayer in the midnight air,
 And his mass of the days that are gone.
When the Lord of the Hill, Amundeville,
 Made Norman Church his prey,
And expell'd the friars, one friar still
 Would not be driven away.

2.

Though he came in his might, with King Henry's right,
 To turn church lands to lay,
With sword in hand, and torch to light
 Their walls, if they said nay;
A monk remain'd, unchased, unchain'd,
 And he did not seem form'd of clay,
For he 's seen in the porch, and he 's seen in the church,
 Though he is not seen by day.

3.

And whether for good, or whether for ill,
 It is not mine to say;
But still with the house of Amundeville
 He abideth night and day.
By the marriage-bed of their lords, 't is said,
 He flits on the bridal eve;
And 't is held as faith, to their bed of death
 He comes—but not to grieve.

4.

When an heir is born, he 's heard to mourn,
 And when aught is to befall
That ancient line, in the pale moonshine
 He walks from hall to hall.
His form you may trace, but not his face,
 'T is shadow'd by his cowl;
But his eyes may be seen from the folds between,
 And they seem of a parted soul.

5.

But beware! beware! of the Black Friar,
 He still retains his sway,
For he is yet the church's heir,
 Whoever may be the lay.
Amundeville is lord by day,
 But the monk is lord by night;
Nor wine nor wassail could raise a vassal
 To question that friar's right.

6.

Say nought to him as he walks the hall,
 And he 'll say nought to you;
He sweeps along in his dusky pall,
 As o'er the grass the dew.
Then grammercy! for the Black Friar;
 Heaven sain him! fair or foul,
And whatsoe'er may be his prayer,
 Let ours be for his soul.

XLI.

The lady's voice ceased, and the thrilling wires
 Died from the touch that kindled them to sound;
And the pause follow'd, which when song expires
 Pervades a moment those who listen round;
And then of course the circle much admires,
 Nor less applauds, as in politeness bound,
The tones, the feeling, and the execution,
To the performer's diffident confusion.

XLII.

Fair Adeline, though in a careless way,
 As if she rated such accomplishment
As the mere pastime of an idle day,
 Pursued an instant for her own content,

Would now and then, as 't were *without* display,
　Yet *with* display in fact, at times relent
To such performances with haughty smile,
　To show she *could*, if it were worth her while.

XLIII.

Now this (but we will whisper it aside)
　Was—pardon the pedantic illustration—
Trampling on Plato's pride with greater pride,
　As did the Cynic on some like occasion:
Deeming the sage would be much mortified,
　Or thrown into a philosophic passion,
For a spoilt carpet—but the "Attic bee"
Was much consoled by his own repartee.

XLIV.

Thus Adeline would throw into the shade
　(By doing easily, whene'er she chose,
What dilettanti do with vast parade)
　Their sort of *half profession;* for it grows
To something like this when too oft display'd;
　And that it is so, everybody knows,
Who have heard Miss That or This, or Lady
　　T'other,
Show off—to please their company or mother.

XLV.

Oh ! the long evenings of duets and trios !
　The admirations and the speculations;
The "Mamma Mia's !" and the "Amor
　　Mio's !"
　The "Tanti palpiti's" on such occasions:
The "Lasciami's," and quavering "Addio's !"
　Amongst our own most musical of nations;
With "Tu mi chamas's" from Portingale,
To soothe our ears, lest Italy should fail.

XLVI.

In Babylon's bravuras—as the home
　Heart-ballads of Green Erin or Gray High-
　　lands,
That bring Lochaber back to eyes that roam
　O'er far Atlantic continents or islands,
The calentures of music which o'ercome
　All mountaineers with dreams that they
　　are nigh lands,
No more to be beheld but in such visions—
Was Adeline well versed, as compositions.

XLVII.

She also had a twilight tinge of "*Blue*,"
　Could write rhymes, and compose more
　　than she wrote,
Made epigrams occasionally too
　Upon her friends, as everybody ought.
But still from that sublimer azure hue,
　So much the present dye, she was remote;
Was weak enough to deem Pope a great poet,
And what was worse, was not ashamed to
　show it.

XLVIII.

Aurora—since we are touching upon taste,
　Which now-a-days is the thermometer
By whose degrees all characters are class'd—
　Was more Shakspearian, if I do not err.
The worlds beyond this world's perplexing
　　waste
　Had more of her existence, for in her
There was a depth of feeling to embrace
Thoughts, boundless, deep, but silent too as
　　Space.

XLIX.

Not so her gracious, graceful, graceless Grace,
　The full-grown Hebe of Fitz-Fulke, whose
　　mind,
If she had any, was upon her face,
　And that was of a fascinating kind.
A little turn for mischief you might trace
　Also thereon,—but that's not much; we
　　find
Few females without some such gentle leaven,
For fear we should suppose us quite in heaven.

L.

I have not heard she was at all poetic,
　Though once she was seen reading the
　　"Bath Guide,"
And "Hayley's Triumphs," which she deem'd
　　pathetic,
　Because she said *her temper* had been tried
So much, the bard had really been prophetic
　Of what she had gone through with—since
　　a bride.
But of all verse, what most insured her praise
Were sonnets to herself, or "bouts rimés."

LI.

'T were difficult to say what was the object
　Of Adeline, in bringing this same lay
To bear on what appear'd to her the subject
　Of Juan's nervous feelings on that day.
Perhaps she merely had the simple project
　To laugh him out of his supposed dismay;
Perhaps she might wish to confirm him in it,
Though why I cannot say—at least this
　　minute.

LII.

But so far the immediate effect
　Was to restore him to his self-propriety,
A thing quite necessary to the elect,
　Who wish to take the tone of their society:
In which you cannot be too circumspect,
　Whether the mode be persiflage or piety,
But wear the newest mantle of hypocrisy,
On pain of much displeasing the gynocracy.

LIII.

And therefore Juan now began to rally
　His spirits, and without more explanation
To jest upon such themes in many a sally.
　Her Grace, too, also seized the same occasion,
With various similar remarks to tally,
　But wish'd for a still more detail'd narration
Of this same mystic friar's curious doings,
About the present family's deaths and wooings.

LIV.

Of these few could say more than has been said;
　They pass'd as such things do, for superstition
With some, while others, who had more in dread
　The theme, half credited the strange tradition;
And much was talk'd on all sides on that head:
　But Juan, when cross-question'd on the vision,
Which some supposed (though he had not avow'd it)
Had stirr'd him, answer'd in a way to cloud it.

LV.

And then, the mid-day having worn to one,
　The company prepared to separate;
Some to their several pastimes, or to none,
　Some wondering 'twas so early, some so late.
There was a goodly match too, to be run
　Between some greyhounds on my lord's estate,
And a young race-horse of old pedigree,
Match'd for the spring, whom several went to see.

LVI.

There was a picture-dealer who had brought
　A special Titian, warranted original,
So precious that it was not to be bought,
　Though princes the possessor were besieging all.
The king himself had cheapen'd it, but thought
　The civil list he deigns to accept (obliging all
His subjects by his gracious acceptation)—
Too scanty, in these times of low taxation.

LVII.

But as Lord Henry was a connoisseur,—
　The friend of artists, if not arts,—the owner,
With motives the most classical and pure,
　So that he would have been the very donor,

Rather than seller, had his wants been fewer,
　So much he deem'd his patronage an honour,
Had brought the capo d'opera, not for sale,
But for his judgment—never known to fail.

LVIII.

There was a modern Goth, I mean a Gothic
　Bricklayer of Babel, call'd an architect,
Brought to survey these grey walls, which though
　so thick,
Might have from time acquired some slight defect;
Who, after rummaging the Abbey through thick
　And thin, produced a plan whereby to erect
New buildings of correctest conformation,
And throw down old, which he call'd *restoration*.

LIX.

The cost would be a trifle—an "old song,"
　Set to some thousands ('t is the usual burden
Of that same tune, when people hum it long)—
　The price would speedily repay its worth in
An edifice no less sublime than strong,
　By which Lord Henry's good taste would go forth in
Its glory, through all ages shining sunny,
For Gothic daring shown in English money.

LX.

There were two lawyers busy on a mortgage
　Lord Henry wish'd to raise for a new purchase;
Also a lawsuit upon tenures burgage,
　And one on tithes, which sure are Discord's torches,
Kindling Religion till she throws down *her* gage,
　"Untying" squires "to fight against the churches;"
There was a prize ox, a prize pig, and ploughman,
For Henry was a sort of Sabine showman.

LXI.

There were two poachers caught in a steel trap,
　Ready for gaol, their place of convalescence;
There was a country girl in a close cap
　And scarlet cloak (I hate the sight to see, since—
Since—since—in youth, I had the sad mishap—
　But luckily I have paid few parish fees since):
That scarlet cloak, alas! unclosed with rigour,
Presents the problem of a double figure.

LXII.

A reel within a bottle is a mystery,
 One can't tell how it e'er got in or out;
Therefore the present piece of natural history
 I leave to those who are fond of solving
 doubt;
And merely state, though not for the con-
 sistory,
Lord Henry was a justice, and that Scout
The constable, beneath a warrant's banner,
Had bagg'd this poacher upon Nature's
 manor.

LXIII.

Now justices of peace must judge all pieces
 Of mischief of all kinds, and keep the game
And morals of the country from caprices
 Of those who have not a licence for the
 same;
And of all things, excepting tithes and leases,
 Perhaps these are most difficult to tame:
Preserving partridges and pretty wenches
Are puzzles to the most precautious benches.

LXIV.

The present culprit was extremely pale,
 Pale as if painted so; her cheek being red
By nature, as in higher dames less hale
 'Tis white, at least when they just rise
 from bed.
Perhaps she was ashamed of seeming frail,
 Poor soul! for she was country born and
 bred,
And knew no better in her immorality
Than to wax white—for blushes are for
 quality.

LXV.

Her black, bright, downcast, yet espiègle eye,
 Had gather'd a large tear into its corner,
Which the poor thing at times essay'd to dry,
 For she was not a sentimental mourner
Parading all her sensibility,
 Nor insolent enough to scorn the scorner,
But stood in trembling, patient tribulation,
To be call'd up for her examination.

LXVI.

Of course these groups were scatter'd here
 and there,
 Not nigh the gay saloon of ladies gent.
The lawyers in the study; and in air
 The prize pig, ploughman, poachers; the
 men sent
From town, viz. architect and dealer, were
 Both busy (as a general in his tent
Writing despatches) in their several stations,
Exulting in their brilliant lucubrations.

LXVII.

But this poor girl was left in the great hall,
 While Scout, the parish guardian of the
 frail,
Discuss'd (he hated beer yclept the "small")
 A mighty mug of *moral* double ale.
She waited until Justice could recall
 Its kind attentions to their proper pale,
To name a thing in nomenclature rather
Perplexing for most virgins—a child's father.

LXVIII.

You see here was enough of occupation
 For the Lord Henry, link'd with dogs and
 horses.
There was much bustle too, and preparation
 Below stairs on the score of second courses;
Because, as suits their rank and situation,
 Those who in counties have great land
 resources
Have "public days," when all men may
 carouse,
Though not exactly what's call'd "open
 house."

LXIX.

But once a week or fortnight, *uninvited*
 (Thus we translate a *general invitation*),
All country gentlemen, esquired or knighted,
 May drop in without cards, and take their
 station
At the full board, and sit alike delighted
 With fashionable wines and conversation;
And, as the isthmus of the grand connexion,
Talk o'er themselves the past and next
 election.

LXX.

Lord Henry was a great electioneerer,
 Burrowing for boroughs like a rat or rabbit.
But county contests cost him rather dearer,
 Because the neighbouring Scotch Earl of
 Giftgabbit
Had English influence, in the self-same
 sphere here;
 His son, the Honourable Dick Dicedrabbit,
Was member for the "other interest" (mean-
 ing
The same self-interest, with a different
 leaning).

LXXI.

Courteous and cautious therefore in his
 county,
 He was all things to all men, and dispensed
To some civility, to others bounty,
 And promises to all—which last com-
 menced

To gather to a somewhat large amount, he
 Not calculating how much they condensed;
But what with keeping some, and breaking
 others,
His word had the same value as another's.

LXXII.

A friend to freedom and freeholders—yet
 No less a friend to government—he held,
That he exactly the just medium hit
 'Twixt place and patriotism—albeit com-
 pell'd,
Such was his sovereign's pleasure, (though
 unfit,
 He added modestly, when rebels rail'd,)
To hold some sinecures he wish'd abolish'd,
But that with them all law would be de-
 molish'd.

LXXIII.

He was "free to confess"—(whence comes
 this phrase?
 Is't English? No— tis only parliamentary)
That innovation's spirit now-a-days
 Had made more progress than for the last
 century.
He would not tread a factious path to praise,
 Though for the public weal disposed to
 venture high;
As for his place, he could but say this of it,
That the fatigue was greater than the profit.

LXXIV.

Heaven, and his friends, knew that a private
 life
 Had ever been his sole and whole ambi-
 tion;
But could he quit his king in times of strife,
 Which threaten'd the whole country with
 perdition?
When demagogues would with a butcher's
 knife
 Cut through and through (oh! damnable
 incision!)
The Gordian or the Geordi-an knot, whose
 strings
Have tied together commons, lords, and
 kings.

LXXV.

Sooner "come place into the civil list
 And champion him to the utmost—" he
 would keep it,
Till duly disappointed or dismiss'd:
 Profit he cared not for, let others reap it;
But should the day come when place ceased
 to exist,
 The country would have far more cause to
 weep it:
For how could it go on? Explain who can!
He gloried in the name of Englishman.

LXXVI.

He was as independent—ay, much more—
 Than those who were not paid for inde-
 pendence,
As common soldiers, or a common——shore,
 Have in their several arts or parts as-
 cendance
O'er the irregulars in lust or gore,
 Who do not give professional attendance.
Thus on the mob all statesmen are as eager
To prove their pride, as footmen to a beggar.

LXXVII.

All this (save the last stanza) Henry said,
 And thought. I say no more—I've said
 too much;
For all of us have either heard or read—
 Off—or *upon* the hustings—some slight
 such
Hints from the independent heart or head
 Of the official candidate. I'll touch
No more on this—the dinner-bell hath rung,
And grace is said; the grace I *should* have
 sung—

LXXVIII.

But I'm too late, and therefore must make
 play.
 'Twas a great banquet, such as Albion old
Was wont to boast—as if a glutton's tray
 Were something very glorious to behold.
But 'twas a public feast and public day,—
 Quite full, right dull, guests hot, and dishes
 cold,
Great plenty, much formality, small cheer,
And everybody out of their own sphere.

LXXIX.

The squires familiarly formal, and
 My lords and ladies proudly condescend-
 ing;
The very servants puzzling how to hand
 Their plates—without it might be too much
 bending
From their high places by the sideboard's
 stand—
 Yet, like their master's, fearful of offend-
 ing.
For any deviation from the graces
Might cost both man and master too—their
 places.

LXXX.

There were some hunters bold, and coursers
 keen,
 Whose hounds ne'er err'd, nor greyhounds
 deign'd to lurch;
Some deadly shots too, Septembrizers, seen
 Earliest to rise, and last to quit the search

Of the poor partridge through his stubble
 screen.
 There were some massy members of the
 church,
Takers of tithes, and makers of good matches,
And several who sung fewer psalms than
 catches.

LXXXI.

There were some country wags too—and,
 alas!
 Some exiles from the town, who had been
 driven
To gaze, instead of pavement, upon grass,
 And rise at nine in lieu of long eleven.
And lo! upon that day it came to pass,
 I sate next that o'erwhelming son of hea-
 ven,
The very powerful parson, Peter Pith,
The loudest wit I e'er was deafen'd with.

LXXXII.

I knew him in his livelier London days,
 A brilliant diner out, though but a curate;
And not a joke he cut but earn'd its praise,
 Until preferment, coming at a sure rate,
(O Providence! how wondrous are thy ways!
 Who would suppose thy gifts sometimes
 obdurate?)
Gave him, to lay the devil who looks o'er
 Lincoln,
A fat fen vicarage, and nought to think on.

LXXXIII.

His jokes were sermons, and his sermons
 jokes;
 But both were thrown away amongst the
 fens;
For wit hath no great friend in aguish folks.
 No longer ready ears and short-hand pens
Imbibed the gay bon-mot, or happy hoax:
 The poor priest was reduced to common
 sense,
Or to coarse efforts very loud and long,
To hammer a hoarse laugh from the thick
 throng.

LXXXIV.

There *is* a difference, says the song, "be-
 tween
A beggar and a queen," or *was* (of late
The latter worse used of the two we've
 seen—
 But we'll say nothing of affairs of state);
A difference " 'twixt a bishop and a dean,"
 A difference between crockery ware and
 plate,
As between English beef and Spartan broth—
And yet great heroes have been bred by both.

LXXXV.

But of all nature's discrepancies, none
 Upon the whole is greater than the differ-
 ence
Beheld between the country and the town,
 Of which the latter merits every preference
From those who have few resources of their
 own,
 And only think, or act, or feel, with re-
 ference
To some small plan of interest or ambition—
Both which are limited to no condition.

LXXXVI.

But "en avant!" The light loves languish
 o'er
 Long banquets and too many guests, al-
 though
A slight repast makes people love much more,
 Bacchus and Ceres being, as we know,
Even from our grammar upwards, friends of
 yore
 With vivifying Venus, who doth owe
To these the invention of champagne and
 truffles:
Temperance delights her, but long fasting
 ruffles.

LXXXVII.

Dully pass'd o'er the dinner of the day;
 And Juan took his place, he knew not
 where,
Confused, in the confusion, and distrait,
 And sitting as if nail'd upon his chair:
Though knives and forks clang'd round as in
 a fray,
 He seem'd unconscious of all passing there,
Till some one, with a groan, exprest a wish
(Unheeded twice) to have a fin of fish.

LXXXVIII.

On which, at the *third* asking of the banns,
 He started; and perceiving smiles around
Broadening to grins, he colour'd more than
 once,
 And hastily—as nothing can confound
A wise man more than laughter from a
 dunce—
Inflicted on the dish a deadly wound,
And with such hurry, that, ere he could
 curb it,
He had paid his neighbour's prayer with
 half a turbot.

LXXXIX.

This was no bad mistake, as it occurr'd,
 The supplicator being an amateur;
But others, who were left with scarce a third,
 Were angry—as they well might, to be sure.

They wonder'd how a young man so absurd
　　Lord Henry at his table should endure;
And this, and his not knowing how much
　　oats
Had fall'n last market, cost his host three
　　votes.

XC.

They little knew, or might have sympathised,
　　That he the night before had seen a ghost,
A prologue which but slightly harmonised
　　With the substantial company engross'd
By matter, and so much materialised,
　　That one scarce knew at what to marvel
　　most
Of two things—how (the question rather
　　odd is)
Such bodies could have souls, or souls such
　　bodies.

XCI.

But what confused him more than smile or
　　stare,
　　From all the 'squires and 'squiresses a-
　　round,
Who wonder'd at the abstraction of his air,
　　Especially as he had been renown'd
For some vivacity among the fair,
　　Even in the country circle's narrow bound—
(For little things upon my lord's estate
Were good small talk for others still less
　　great)—

XCII.

Was, that he caught Aurora's eye on his,
　　And something like a smile upon her cheek.
Now this he really rather took amiss;
　　In those who rarely smile, their smile
　　bespeaks
A strong external motive; and in this
　　Smile of Aurora's there was nought to
　　pique,
Or hope, or love, with any of the wiles
Which some pretend to trace in ladies'
　　smiles.

XCIII.

'Twas a mere quiet smile of contemplation,
　　Indicative of some surprise and pity;
And Juan grew carnation with vexation,
　　Which was not very wise, and still less
　　witty,
Since he had gain'd at least her observation,
　　A most important outwork of the city—
As Juan should have known, had not his
　　senses
By last night's ghost been driven from their
　　defences.

XCIV.

But what was bad, she did not blush in turn,
　　Nor seem embarrass'd—quite the contrary;
Her aspect was as usual, still—*not* stern—
　　And she withdrew, but cast not down, her
　　eye,
Yet grew a little pale—with what? concern?
　　I know not; but her colour ne'er was
　　high—
Though sometimes faintly flush'd—and al-
　　ways clear,
As deep seas in a sunny atmosphere.

XCV.

But Adeline was occupied by fame
　　This day; and watching, witching, con-
　　descending
To the consumers of fish, fowl, and game,
　　And dignity with courtesy so blending,
As all must blend whose part it is to aim
　　(Especially as the sixth year is ending)
At their lord's, son's, or similar connexion's
Safe conduct through the rocks of reëlections.

XCVI.

Though this was most expedient on the
　　whole,
　　And usual—Juan, when he cast a glance
On Adeline while playing her grand rôle,
　　Which she went through as though it were
　　a dance,
Betraying only now and then her soul
　　By a look scarce perceptibly askance
(Of weariness or scorn), began to feel
Some doubt how much of Adeline was *real;*

XCVII.

So well she acted all and every part
　　By turns—with that vivacious versatility,
Which many people take for want of heart.
　　They err—'tis merely what is call'd mo-
　　bility,
A thing of temperament and not of art,
　　Though seeming so, from its supposed
　　facility;
And false—though true; for surely they're
　　sincerest
Who are strongly acted on by what is nearest.

XCVIII.

This makes your actors, artists, and ro-
　　mancers,
　　Heroes sometimes, though seldom—sages
　　never:
But speakers, bards, diplomatists, and dan-
　　cers,
　　Little that's great, but much of what is
　　clever;

Most orators, but very few financiers,
 Though all Exchequer chancellors endea-
 vour,
Of late years, to dispense with Cocker's
 rigours,
And grow quite figurative with their figures.

XCIX.

The poets of arithmetic are they
 Who, though they prove not two and two
 to be
Five, as they might do in a modest way,
 Have plainly made it out that four are
 three,
Judging by what they take, and what they
 pay.
The Sinking Fund's unfathomable sea,
That most unliquidating liquid, leaves
The debt unsunk, yet sinks all it receives.

C.

While Adeline dispensed her airs and graces,
 The fair Fitz-Fulke seem'd very much at
 ease;
Though too well bred to quiz men to their
 faces,
 Her laughing blue eyes with a glance could
 seize
The ridicules of people in all places—
 That honey of your fashionable bees—
And store it up for mischievous enjoyment;
And this at present was *her* kind employ-
 ment.

CI.

However, the day closed, as days must close;
 The evening also waned—and coffee came.
Each carriage was announced, and ladies
 rose,
 And curtsying off, as curtsies country
 dame,
Retired: with most unfashionable bows
 Their docile esquires also did the same,
Delighted with their dinner and their host,
But with the Lady Adeline the most.

CII.

Some praised her beauty: others her great
 grace;
 The warmth of her politeness, whose
 sincerity
Was obvious in each feature of her face,
 Whose traits were radiant with the rays of
 verity.
Yes: *she* was truly worthy *her* high place!
 No one could envy her deserved prosperity.
And then her dress—what beautiful sim-
 plicity
Draperied her form with curious felicity!

CIII.

Meanwhile sweet Adeline deserved their
 praises,
 By an impartial indemnification
For all her past exertion and soft phrases,
 In a most edifying conversation,
Which turn'd upon their late guests' miens
 and faces,
 And families, even to the last relation;
Their hideous wives, their horrid selves and
 dresses,
And truculent distortion of their tresses.

CIV.

True, *she* said little—'t was the rest that broke
 Forth into universal epigram;
But then 't was to the purpose what she spoke:
 Like Addison's "faint praise," so wont to
 damn,
Her own but served to set off every joke,
 As music chimes in with a melodrame.
How sweet the task to shield an absent
 friend!
I ask but this of mine, to——*not* defend.

CV.

There were but two exceptions to this keen
 Skirmish of wits o'er the departed; one
Aurora, with her pure and placid mien;
 And Juan, too, in general behind none
In gay remark on what he had heard or seen,
 Sate silent now, his usual spirits gone:
In vain he heard the others rail or rally,
He would not join them in a single sally.

CVI.

'Tis true he saw Aurora look as though
 She approved his silence; she perhaps mis-
 took
Its motive for that charity we owe
 But seldom pay the absent, nor would look
Farther; it might or it might not be so.
 But Juan, sitting silent in his nook,
Observing little in his reverie,
Yet saw this much, which he was glad to see.

CVII.

The ghost at least had done him this much
 good,
 In making him as silent as a ghost,
If in the circumstances which ensued
 He gain'd esteem where it was worth the
 most;
And certainly Aurora had renew'd
 In him some feelings he had lately lost,
Or harden'd; feelings which, perhaps ideal,
Are so divine, that I must deem them real:—

CVIII.

The love of higher things and better days;
　The unbounded hope, and heavenly ignor-
　　ance
Of what is call'd the world, and the world's
　　ways;
　The moments when we gather from a
　　glance
More joy than from all future pride or praise,
　Which kindle manhood, but can ne'er
　　entrance
The heart in an existence of its own,
Of which another's bosom is the zone.

CIX.

Who would not sigh Αἰαῖ τὰν Κυθέρειαν
　That *hath* a memory, or that *had* a heart?
Alas! *her* star must fade like that of Dian:
　Ray fades on ray, as years on years depart.
Anacreon only had the soul to tie an
　Unwithering myrtle round the unblunted
　　dart
Of Eros: but though thou hast play'd us
　　many tricks,
Still we respect thee, "Alma Venus Gene-
　trix!"

CX.

And full of sentiments, sublime as billows
　Heaving between this world and worlds
　　beyond,
Don Juan, when the midnight hour of pillows
　Arrived, retired to his; but to despond
Rather than rest. Instead of poppies, willows
　Waved o'er his couch; he meditated, fond
Of those sweet bitter thoughts which banish
　　sleep,
And make the worldling sneer, the youngling
　　weep.

CXI.

The night was as before: he was undrest,
　Saving his night-gown, which is an un-
　　dress;
Completely "sans culotte," and without vest;
　In short, he hardly could be clothed with
　　less:
But apprehensive of his spectral guest,
　He sate with feelings awkward to express
(By those who have not had such visitations),
Expectant of the ghost's fresh operations.

CXII.

And not in vain he listen'd;—Hush! what's
　　that?
　I see—I see—Ah, no!—'t is not—yet 't is—
Ye powers! it is the—the—the—Pooh! the
　　cat!
　The devil may take that stealthy pace of
　　his!

So like a spiritual pit-a-pat,
　Or tiptoe of an amatory Miss,
Gliding the first time to a rendezvous,
And dreading the chaste echoes of her shoe.

CXIII.

Again—what is't? The wind? No, no,—
　　this time
　It is the sable Friar as before,
With awful footsteps regular as rhyme,
　Or (as rhymes may be in these days) much
　　more.
Again through shadows of the night sublime,
　When deep sleep fell on men, and the
　　world wore
The starry darkness round her like a girdle
Spangled with gems—the monk made his
　blood curdle.

CXIV.

A noise like to wet fingers drawn on glass,
　Which sets the teeth on edge; and a slight
　　clatter
Like showers which on the midnight gusts
　　will pass,
　Sounding like very supernatural water,
Came over Juan's ear, which throbb'd, alas!
　For immaterialism's a serious matter;
So that even those whose faith is the most
　　great
In souls immortal, shun them tête-à-tête.

CXV.

Were his eyes open?—Yes! and his mouth
　　too.
　Surprise has this effect—to make one
　　dumb,
Yet leave the gate which eloquence slips
　　through
　As wide, as if a long speech were to come.
Nigh and more nigh the awful echoes drew,
　Tremendous to a mortal tympanum:
His eyes were open, and (as was before
Stated) his mouth. What open'd next?—the
　door.

CXVI.

It open'd with a most infernal creak,
　Like that of hell. "Lasciate ogni speranza
Voi ch' entrate!" The hinge seem'd to
　speak,
　Dreadful as Dante's rhima, or this stanza;
Or—but all words upon such themes are
　weak:
　A single shade's sufficient to entrance a
Hero—for what is substance to a spirit?
Or how is't *matter* trembles to come near it?

CXVII.

The door flew wide, not swiftly,—but, as fly
　The sea-gulls, with a steady, sober flight—
And then swung back; nor close—but stood
　awry,
Half letting in long shadows on the light,
Which still in Juan's candlesticks burn'd
　high,
For he had two, both tolerably bright,
And in the doorway, darkening darkness,
　stood
The sable Friar in his solemn hood.

CXVIII.

Don Juan shook, as erst he had been shaken
　The night before; but being sick of shaking,
He first inclined to think he had been mis-
　taken;
And then to be ashamed of such mistaking;
His own internal ghost began to awaken
　Within him, and to quell his corporal quak-
　ing—
Hinting that soul and body on the whole
Were odds against a disembodied soul.

CXIX.

And then his dread grew wrath, and his
　wrath fierce,
　And he arose, advanced—the shade re-
　treated;
But Juan, eager now the truth to pierce,
　Followed, his veins no longer cold, but
　heated,
Resolved to thrust the mystery carte and
　tierce,
　At whatsoever risk of being defeated:
The ghost stopp'd, menaced, then retired,
　until
He reach'd the ancient wall, then stood stone
　still.

CXX.

Juan put forth one arm—Eternal powers!
　It touch'd no soul, nor body, but the wall,
On which the moonbeams fell in silvery
　showers,
　Chequer'd with all the tracery of the hall;

He shudder'd, as no doubt the bravest cowers
　When he can't tell what 'tis that doth
　appal.
How odd, a single hobgoblin's nonentity
Should cause more fear than a whole host's
　identity!

CXXI.

But still the shade remain'd: the blue eyes
　glared,
　And rather variably for stony death;
Yet one thing rather good the grave had
　spared,
　The ghost had a remarkably sweet breath:
A straggling curl show'd he had been fair-
　hair'd;
　A red lip, with two rows of pearls beneath,
Gleam'd forth, as through the casement's ivy
　shroud
The moon peep'd, just escaped from a grey
　cloud.

CXXII.

And Juan, puzzled, but still curious, thrust
　His other arm forth—Wonder upon won-
　der!
It press'd upon a hard but glowing bust,
　Which beat as if there was a warm heart
　under.
He found, as people on most trials must,
　That he had made at first a silly blunder,
And that in his confusion he had caught
Only the wall, instead of what he sought.

CXXIII.

The ghost, if ghost it were, seem'd a sweet
　soul
　As ever lurk'd beneath a holy hood:
A dimpled chin, a neck of ivory, stole
　Forth into something much like flesh and
　blood;
Back fell the sable frock and dreary cowl,
　And they reveal'd—alas! that e'er they
　should!
In full, voluptuous, but *not o'er*grown bulk,
The phantom of her frolic Grace—Fitz-Fulke!

Index.

The titles of the principal pieces are printed in SMALL CAPITALS, and the first line of every distinct piece, and of every canto, in *italics*.

A.

A spirit pass'd before me, 82.
A year ago, you swore, fond she! 87.
Abencerrage, 168. "Granada's flower," 98.
Aberdeen, George Hamilton Gordon, fourth Earl of; "The travell'd Thane," 117, 848. "Aberdeen and Elgin," 123.
Aberdeen, "the auld toun" of, 899.
Abernethy, John, the eminent surgeon, 769.
Absent or present, still to thee, 65.
Absent friend. See Friend.
Abydos. See Bride of Abydos.
"Acarnania's forest wide," 198.
Acheron, 196.
"Acherusia's lake," 196; its present name, 861.
Achilles, "him who felt the Dardan's arrow," 263. Alexander's race round his tomb, 878. "The unshorn boy of Peleus," 598. Place of his sepulture, 695, 697.
Achitophel. See Dryden.
Acroceraunian mountains, 230.
Acropolis, the, Minerva's Temple, 190, 858.
Actium, 195, 861. "Lost for Cleopatra's eyes," 718.
"Ada, sole daughter of my house and heart," 203, 219.
Adam, his costume, 160; his fall, 640. "Exchanged his Paradise for ploughing," 813.
Adams, John, the drunken carrier, epitaph on, 51.
Addison, Joseph, illustrative quotations from; his Cato, 855.
ADIEU, The; written under the impression that the author would soon die, 47.
Adieu, adieu! my native shore, 178.
Adieu, thou Hill! where early joy, 47.
Adieu, ye joys of La Valette! 61.
Admiration. See Nil Admirari.
ADRIAN'S ADDRESS TO HIS SOUL, 4. His reason for wearing a beard, 856.
Adriatic, "the spouseless," and the "annual marriage," 222.
Adversity, 687; "first path to truth," 789.
Advice, good, 646; "good rarely comes from," 812; "small thanks" its "market price," 819.
Ægle, beauty and poet, has two little crimes, 65.
Æschylus, translation from the "Prometheus Vinctus" of, 6. Quotation from his "Persians," 896.
"Afric is all the sun's," 692.
Agamemnon, "Brave men lived before," 627.

AGE OF BRONZE, The, 165.
Age of Gold, 723.
Agrarian Laws, simile drawn from the, 767. Tiberius Gracchus's demand for their execution, 900.
Ah, gentle, fleeting, wav'ring sprite, 4.
Ah! heedless girl! why thus disclose, 48.
Ah! Love was never yet without, 68.
Ah!—What should follow slips from my reflection, 816.
Ajax, 859.
Albania, 194, 860.
Albanians, 195, 196, 860. Characteristics of the, 861–2; sample of their popular chants, 862.
"Albano's boys," 801.
Albano's scarce divided waves, 242.
Albion, lot of Venice shameful to, 223; "lost Albion," 140; "sees her son depart," 59. "Earth's chief dictatress," 123. Her "chalky belt," 771. Her "earliest beauties," 772.
"Albuera! glorious field of grief!" 182.
Alcæus. See Montgomery.
Alcibiades, "fairest and bravest of Athenians," 598. His "art of living," 817.
Alexander the Great and his "madman's wish," 165. His run round the tomb of Achilles, 263, 878. His characteristic reply to Parmenio, 897.
Alexander I. of Russia, "the coxcomb Czar," 170. "The Czar's look," 75. His tutor, 170. "Oh thou grand legitimate," 727. "Bald-coot bully," 814.
Alfieri, Vittorio, quotation from, 220. His last resting-place and tomb, 227. His "Tramelogedia," 511.
Alfonso, king, 164.
Alhama, ballad on the conquest of, 97.
Ali Pacha of Yanina, "Albania's chief," 196, 197, 861.
"All is vanity," 79, 730.
"Alla Hu!" explanation of, 252, 876.
Almachius. See Telemachus.
Almogava. See Boscan.
Alpinula. See Julia Alpinula.
Alps, description of the, 212.
Al Sirat, "the Bridge of Breath," 250, 875.
"Ambition's honour'd fools," 182; "steel'd thee" [Napoleon] "on too far," 208. "Vile ambition," 232; "forsook his crown to follow woman," 58. "Ambition in his humbled hour," 331. "Glorious ambition," 599. "Ambition was my idol," 649. "Blood only serves to wash Ambition's hands," 761.